Operations
Management Seventh Edition

Operations Management Seventh Edition

William J. Stevenson
Rochester Institute of Technology

Boston   Burr Ridge, IL   Dubuque, IA   Madison, WI   New York   San Francisco   St. Louis
Bangkok   Bogotá   Caracas   Kuala Lumpur   Lisbon   London   Madrid   Mexico City
Milan   Montreal   New Delhi   Santiago   Seoul   Singapore   Sydney   Taipei   Toronto

This Book Is Dedicated to You

McGraw-Hill Higher Education
A Division of The McGraw-Hill Companies

OPERATIONS MANAGEMENT
Earlier editions titled *Production/Operations Management*

Published by McGraw-Hill/Irwin, an imprint of The McGraw-Hill Companies, Inc. 1221 Avenue of the Americas, New York, NY, 10020. Copyright ©2002, 1998, 1995, 1992, 1988, 1985, by The McGraw-Hill Companies, Inc. All rights reserved. No part of this publication may be reproduced or distributed in any form or by any means, or stored in a database or retrieval system, without the prior written consent of The McGraw-Hill Companies, Inc., including, but not limited to, in any network or other electronic storage or transmission, or broadcast for distance learning.

Some ancillaries, including electronic and print components, may not be available to customers outside the United States.

This book is printed on acid-free paper.

domestic   3 4 5 6 7 8 9 0 FGR/FGR 0 9 8 7 6 5 4 3 2
international   2 3 4 5 6 7 8 9 0 FGR/FGR 0 9 8 7 6 5 4 3 2

ISBN 0-07-244390-1

Publisher: *Brent Gordon*
Executive editor: *Richard T. Hercher, Jr.*
Senior developmental editor: *Wanda J. Zeman*
Marketing manager: *Zina Craft*
Senior project manager: *Jean Lou Hess*
Production supervisor: *Debra Sylvester*
Coordinator freelance design: *Gino Cieslik*
Photo research coordinator: *Ira Roberts*
Photo researcher: *Connie Gardner*
Supplement coordinator: *Cathy Tepper*
Media technology producer: *Greg Bates*
Cover photos: *© PhotoDisc*
Interior design: *Ellen Pettengell Design*
Compositor: *GAC / Indianapolis*
Typeface: *10.5/12 Goudy*
Printer: *Quebecor World Fairfield, Inc*

Library of Congress Card Catalog number: 2001091412

INTERNATIONAL EDITION ISBN 0-07-112129-3
Copyright ©2002. Exclusive rights by The McGraw-Hill Companies, Inc. for manufacture and export. This book cannot be re-exported from the country to which it is sold by McGraw-Hill. The International Edition is not available in North America.

www.mhhe.com

The McGraw-Hill/Irwin Series Operations and Decision Sciences

OPERATIONS MANAGEMENT

Bowersox, Closs, and Cooper
Supply Chain Logistics Management
First Edition

Chase, Aquilano, and Jacobs
Operations Management for Competitive
Advantage
Ninth Edition

Chu, Hottenstein, and Greenlaw
PROSIM for Windows
Third Edition

Cohen and Apte
Manufacturing Automation
First Edition

Davis, Aquilano, and Chase
Fundamentals of Operations Management
Third Edition

Dobler and Burt
Purchasing and Supply Management
Sixth Edition

Flaherty
Global Operations Management
First Edition

Fitzsimmons and Fitzsimmons
Service Management: Operations, Strategy,
Information Technology
Third Edition

Gray and Larson
Project Management: The Managerial Process
First Edition

Hill
Manufacturing Strategy: Text & Cases
Third Edition

Hopp and Spearman
Factory Physics
Second Edition

Jacobs and Whybark
Why ERP: A Primer on SAP Implementation
First Edition

Knod and Schonberger
Operations Management: Meeting Customers'
Demands
Seventh Edition

Lambert and Stock
Strategic Logistics Management
Third Edition

Leenders and Fearon
Purchasing and Supply Chain Management
Eleventh Edition

Moses, Seshadri, and Yakir
HOM Operations Management Software for
Windows
First Edition

Nahmias
Production and Operations Analysis
Fourth Edition

Nicholas
Competitive Manufacturing Management
First Edition

Olson
Introduction to Information Systems
Project Management
First Edition

Pinedo and Chao
Operations Scheduling
First Edition

Sanderson and Uzumeri
Managing Product Families
First Edition

Schroeder
Operations Management: Contemporary
Concepts and Cases
First Edition

Simchi-Levi, Kaminsky, and Simchi-Levi
Designing and Managing the Supply Chain:
Concepts, Strategies, and Case Studies
First Edition

Sterman
Business Dynamics: Systems Thinking and
Modeling for a Complex World
First Edition

Stevenson
Operations Management
Seventh Edition

Vollmann, Berry, and Whybark
Manufacturing Planning and Control Systems
Fourth Edition

Zipkin
Foundations of Inventory Management
First Edition

QUANTITATIVE METHODS AND MANAGEMENT SCIENCE

Alwan
Statistical Process Analysis
First Edition

Bodily, Carraway, Frey, Pfeifer
Quantitative Business Analysis: Casebook
First Edition

Bodily, Carraway, Frey, Pfeifer
Quantitative Business Analysis:
Text and Cases
First Edition

Bonini, Hausman, and Bierman
Quantitative Analysis for Business Decisions
Ninth Edition

Hesse
Managerial Spreadsheet Modeling and
Analysis
First Edition

Hillier, Hillier, Lieberman
Introduction to Management Science: A
Modeling and Case Studies Approach with
Spreadsheets
First Edition

Preface

The material in this book is intended as an introduction to the field of operations management. It is suitable for both undergraduate and graduate students. The field of operations management is dynamic, and very much a part of many of the good things that are happening in business organizations. The book is intended to be interesting and informative. Much of what you learn will have practical application.

The subject matter represents a blend of concepts from industrial engineering, cost accounting, general management, quantitative methods, and statistics. Operations activities, such as forecasting, choosing a location for an office or plant, allocating resources, designing products and services, scheduling activities, and assuring and improving quality are core activities and often strategic issues in business organizations. Some of you are or will be employed directly in these areas, while others will have jobs that are indirectly related to this area. So whether this is your field of study or not, knowledge of this field will certainly benefit you and the organization you work for.

The text contains more material than one could normally hope to cover in a one-semester course. Rather than rely on the author's personal bias, each instructor can choose those topics most suited to his or her own proclivities. Those who prefer an analytic quantitative emphasis, for example, will be quite comfortable with the abundance of examples and student problems. Those who prefer a more qualitative approach will welcome the fact that some of the more quantitative material is placed in chapter supplements and that there are memo exercises, operations tours, and cases for assignment. Obviously, there are many possibilities between these two extremes.

ACKNOWLEDGMENTS

I would like to thank the reviewers of this edition who contributed significantly to the final product. They are: Kwasi Amoako-Gyampah, University of North Carolina-Greensboro; Mehmet Barut, Wichita State University; William J. Cosgrove, California Polytechnic University-Pomona; Anne Davey, Northeastern State University; Jose H. Dula, University of Mississippi; Kamvar Farahbod, California State University-San Bernardino; Richard A. Fentriss, University of South Florida; Dan Heiser, DePaul University; Timothy C. Ireland, Oklahoma State University; Thomas E. Johnson, Jr., University of South Florida; Yunus Kathawala, Eastern Illinois University; Peter Kelle, Louisiana State University; Wieslaw Kubiak, Memorial University of Newfoundland; Terry Nels Lee, Brigham Young University; Mark McKay, University of Washington; Ajay K. Mishra, SUNY Binghamton; Zubair M. Mohamed, Western Kentucky University; Sharma Pillutla, Towson University; Karen Papke- Shields, Salisbury State University; Charles Petersen, Northern Illinois University; Patrick Philipoom, University of South Carolina; Michael F. Pohlen, University of Delaware; Zinovy Radovilsky, California State-Hayward; Robert Russell, University of Tulsa; William R. Sherrard, San Diego State University; Marius M. Solomon, Northeastern University; Ulrich A. W. Tetzlaff, George Mason University; Geoff Willis, University of Central Oklahoma.

I would also like to thank all of the reviewers of previous editions for their valuable contributions to the success of this book.

Many students and instructors offered valuable suggestions, and I want to thank them as well. And, Ceyhun Ozgur and Phil F. Musa did a great job of accuracy checking.

I would also like to thank the authors of the various CD-ROM supplements and stand-alone supplements that are designed to accompany the textbook. Lee Tangedahl developed the spreadsheet templates; Mehdi Kaighobadi put together the data files; Ceyhun Ozgur updated the Instructor's Manual; Ralph Butler developed Powerpoint presentations; Seung Lae Kim updated the Test Bank and the computerized test bank; and Paul Van Ness coauthored the Study Guide.

Finally, I want to extend my thanks to all of the people at McGraw-Hill/Irwin for their efforts and support. It is always a pleasure to work with such a competent and professional group of people. Special thank yous go to Dick Hercher, Wanda Zeman, Jean Lou Hess, and Cathy Tepper.

William J. Stevenson

Note to the Student

The material in this text is part of the core knowledge in your education. Consequently, you will derive considerable benefit from your study of operations management, *regardless of your major.* Practically speaking, operations is a course in *management.*

This book describes principles and concepts of operations management. You should be aware that many of these principles and concepts are applicable to other aspects of your professional and personal life. Consequently, you should expect the benefits of your study of operations management to serve you in those other areas as well.

Some students approach this course with apprehension, and perhaps even some negative feelings. It may be that they have heard that the course contains a certain amount of quantitative material which they may feel uncomfortable with, or that the subject matter is dreary, or that the course is about "factory management." This is unfortunate, because the subject matter of this book is interesting and vital for all business students. While it is true that some of the material is quantitative, numerous examples, solved problems, and answers at the back of the book will help you with the quantitative material. As for "factory management," there is material on manufacturing as well as on services. Manufacturing is important, and something that you should know about for a number of reasons. Look around you. Most of the "things" you see were manufactured: cars, trucks, planes, clothing, shoes, computers, books, pens and pencils, desks, and cell phones. And these are just the tip of the iceberg. So it makes sense to know something about how these sorts of things are produced. Beyond all that is the fact that manufacturing is largely responsible for the high standard of living people have in industrialized countries.

After reading each chapter or supplement in the text, attending related classroom lectures, and completing assigned questions and problems, you should be able to do each of the following:

1. *Identify the key features* of that material.
2. *Define and use terminology.*
3. *Solve typical problems.*
4. *Recognize applications* of the concepts and techniques covered.
5. *Discuss the subject matter* in some depth, including its relevance, managerial considerations, and advantages and limitations.

You will encounter a number of chapter supplements. Check with your instructor to determine whether or not to study them.

This book places an emphasis on problem solving. There are many examples throughout the text illustrating solutions. In addition, at the end of most chapters and supplements you will find a group of solved problems. The examples within the chapter itself serve to illustrate concepts and techniques. Too much detail at those points would be counterproductive. Yet, later on, when you begin to solve the end-of-chapter problems, you will find the solved problems quite helpful. Moreover, those solved problems usually illustrate more and different details than the problems within the chapter.

I suggest the following approach to increase your chances of getting an "A" in this course:

1. Look over the chapter outline and learning objectives.
2. Read the chapter summary, and then skim the chapter.
3. Read the chapter and take notes using the study questions on the CD-ROM.
4. Look over and try to answer the discussion and review questions.

5. Solve the problems, referring to the solved problems and chapter examples as needed.

6. Take the quizzes on the CD.

Note that the answers to many problems are given at the end of the book. Try to solve each problem before turning to the answer. Remember—tests don't come with answers.

A study guide is also available. It includes a list of key ideas, study tips, glossaries, sample quizzes with answers, and problems with solutions. If your bookstore does not stock it, you can ask them to order it for you.

Enjoy!

W.J.S.

Brief Contents

PART ONE

Introduction

1 Introduction to Operations Management   3
2 Competitiveness, Strategy, and Productivity   37

PART TWO

Forecasting

3 Forecasting   69

PART THREE

System Design

4 Product and Service Design   127
Supplement to Chapter 4 Reliability   158
5 Capacity Planning   173
Supplement to Chapter 5 Decision Theory   196
6 Process Selection and Facility Layout   217
Supplement to Chapter 6 Linear Programming   274
7 Design of Work Systems   307
Supplement to Chapter 7 Learning Curves   342
8 Location Planning and Analysis   355
Supplement to Chapter 8 The Transportation Model   385

PART FOUR

Quality

9 Introduction to Quality   393

10 Quality Control   417
Supplement to Chapter 10 Acceptance Sampling   457
11 TQM and Quality Tools   469

PART FIVE

Supply Chain Management

12 Supply Chain Management   503
Supplement to Chapter 12 Purchasing and Supplier Management   527
13 Inventory Management   541
14 Aggregate Planning   603
15 MRP and ERP   639
16 Just-in-Time Systems   683
Supplement to Chapter 16 Maintenance   719
17 Scheduling   728

PART SIX

Project Management

18 Project Management   765

PART SEVEN

Waiting Lines and Simulation

19 Waiting Lines   817
Supplement to Chapter 19 Simulation   853

Contents

PART ONE

Introduction

CHAPTER ONE

Introduction to Operations Management 3

Introduction 4

Why Study Operations Management? 5

Functions within Business Organizations 6

The Scope of Operations Management 12

Differentiating Features of Operations Systems 13

The Operations Manager and the Management Process 16

Operations Managers and Decision Making 17

The Historical Evolution of Operations Management 21

Trends in Business 24

    Reading: Agile Manufacturing 27

    Cases: Hazel 30

        Total Recall 31

    Operations Tour: Wegmans Food Markets 31

CHAPTER TWO

Competitiveness, Strategy, and Productivity 37

Introduction 38

Competitiveness 38

Strategy 40

    Reading: Time-Based Information 49

Productivity 51

    Reading: Productivity Gains at Whirlpool 60

    Cases: An American Tragedy: How a Good Company Died 60

        Home-Style Cookies 61

        Hazel Revisited 63

    Reading: Economic Vitality 63

    Operations Tour: The US Postal Service 65

PART TWO

Forecasting

CHAPTER THREE

Forecasting 69

Introduction 70

Features Common to All Forecasts 71

Elements of a Good Forecast 72

Steps in the Forecasting Process 72

Approaches to Forecasting 73

Forecasts Based on Judgment and Opinion 73

Forecasts Based on Time Series Data 75

Associative Forecasting Techniques 91

Accuracy and Control of Forecasts 96

Choosing a Forecasting Technique 103

Using Forecast Information 104

Computers in Forecasting 104

Operations Strategy 104

    Newsclip: A Strong Channel Hub 105

    Case: M & L Manufacturing 123

PART THREE

System Design

CHAPTER FOUR

Product and Service Design   127
Introduction   128
Sources of Ideas for New or Redesigned Products and Services   130
   Readings: Managers' Journal: When Customer Research Is a Lousy Idea   132
        Vlasic on a Roll with Huge Pickle Slices   133
Legal, Ethical, and Environmental Issues   134
Other Issues in Product and Service Design   135
Designing for Manufacturing   141
   Reading: Making It (Almost) New Again   145
Designing for Services   147
Quality Function Deployment   150
Operations Strategy   154

SUPPLEMENT TO CHAPTER 4

Reliability   158
Introduction   159
Quantifying Reliability   159
Availability   165

CHAPTER FIVE

Capacity Planning   173
Introduction   174
Importance of Capacity Decisions   174
Defining and Measuring Capacity   175
Determinants of Effective Capacity   177
Determining Capacity Requirements   178
Developing Capacity Alternatives   180
Planning Service Capacity   183
Evaluating Alternatives   184
Operations Strategy   189
   Operations Tour: High Acres Landfill   194

SUPPLEMENT TO CHAPTER 5

Decision Theory   196
Introduction   197
Causes of Poor Decisions   197
Decision Environments   198

Decision Making under Certainty   198
Decision Making under Uncertainty   199
Decision Making under Risk   200
Decision Trees   201
Expected Value of Perfect Information   203
Sensitivity Analysis   204

CHAPTER SIX

Process Selection and Facility Layout   217
Introduction   218
Process Selection   219
   Readings: Tour de Force   225
        Electric Car Drives Factory Innovations   229
Layout   232
   Reading: Designing Supermarkets   241
Designing Product Layouts: Line Balancing   242
   Newsclip: Toyota Mixes and Matches   251
Designing Process Layouts   251
   Reading: Would You Like That Rare, Medium or Vacuum-Packed?   270
   Operations Tour: Morton Salt   271

SUPPLEMENT TO CHAPTER SIX

Linear Programming   274
Introduction   275
Linear Programming Models   275
Graphical Linear Programming   278
The Simplex Method   290
Computer Solutions   291
Sensitivity Analysis   293
   Case: Son, Ltd.   304

CHAPTER SEVEN

Design of Work Systems   307
Introduction   308
Operations Strategy   308
Job Design   308
   Readings: Workplace Upheavals Seem to Be Eroding Employees' Trust   311
        What Works to Cut CTD Risk, Improve Job Productivity?   322
Work Measurement   323
Compensation   333
   Reading: Making Hotplates   340

SUPPLEMENT TO CHAPTER SEVEN

Learning Curves 342
The Concept of Learning Curves   343
Applications of Learning Curves   347
Operations Strategy   349
Cautions and Criticisms   349
  Case: Product Recall   353

CHAPTER EIGHT

Location Planning and Analysis   355
The Need for Location Decisions   356
The Nature of Location Decisions   356
General Procedure for Making Location Decisions   357
Factors That Affect Location Decisions   358
  Newsclip: Innovative MCI Unit Finds Culture Shock
    in Colorado Springs   358
  Readings: Not-So-Clear Choices: Should You
        Export, or Manufacture
        Overseas?   362
      New U.S. Factory Jobs Aren't in the
        Factory   366
  Newsclip: Vying for Patients, Hospitals Think
    Location, Location   370
Global Locations   370
  Reading: Global Strategy: GM Is Building Plants in
    Developing Nations to Woo New Markets   372
Evaluating Location Alternatives   373

SUPPLEMENT TO CHAPTER EIGHT

The Transportation Model   385
Introduction   386
Location Decisions   386
Other Applications   387
Computer Solutions   388

PART FOUR

Quality

CHAPTER NINE

Introduction to Quality   393
Introduction   394
The Evolution of Quality Management   394
Quality: The Basics   395
Quality Gurus   402
Quality Awards   406
  Reading: Baldrige Core Values and Concepts   407
Quality Certification   409
  Reading: Aesop on Quality Systems   410

CHAPTER TEN

Quality Control   417
Introduction   418
Inspection   418
  Newsclip: Oops!   420
Statistical Process Control   421
Process Capability   438
Operations Strategy   442
  Cases: Toys, Inc.   453
      Tiger Tools   453
  Operations Tour: In the Chips at Jays   454

SUPPLEMENT TO CHAPTER TEN

Acceptance Sampling   457
Introduction   458
Sampling Plans   458
Operating Characteristic Curve   459
Average Quality of Inspected Lots   463

CHAPTER ELEVEN

TQM and Quality Tools   469
Introduction   470
Obstacles to Implementing TQM   473
Criticisms of TQM   473
  Reading: CalComp: Disaster Becomes Success   474
Problem Solving   475
Process Improvement   477
Tools   478
  Readings: Continuous Improvement on the Free-
        Throw Line   484
      Benchmarking Corporate Websites of
        Fortune 500 Companies   490
Operations Strategy   490
  Cases: Chick-n-Gravy Dinner Line   494
      Tip Top Markets   494
  Readings: Making Quality Pay: Return on
        Quality   496
      Quality Programs Don't Guarantee
        Results   498
      Swimming Upstream   499

PART FIVE

Supply Chain Management

CHAPTER TWELVE

Supply Chain Management   503
Introduction   504
The Need for Supply Chain Management   506

Benefits of Effective Supply Chain Management   506
Managing the Supply Chain   507
Logistics   509
   Reading: Delivering the Goods   509
   Newsclip: Efficient Consumer Response   514
E-Commerce   515
   Newsclip: Desperately Seeking E-Fulfillment   516
Creating an Effective Supply Chain   517
   Reading: Using Information to Speed
      Execution   520
   Newsclip: Supply Chain Optimization at Internet
      Speed   521
Operations Strategy   523

SUPPLEMENT TO CHAPTER TWELVE

Purchasing and Supplier Management   527

Purchasing   528
Supplier Management   533
   Reading: E-Procurement at IBM   538

CHAPTER THIRTEEN

Inventory Management   541

Introduction   542
   Newsclip: $$$ 542
The Nature and Importance of Inventories   542
Requirements for Effective Inventory
Management   545
   Reading: RFID   547
   Newsclip: Ford Triples Its Billion-Dollar Cost-
      Cutting Goal   548
How Much to Order: Economic Order Quantity
Models   551
When to Reorder with EOQ Ordering   564
How Much to Order: Fixed-Order-Interval
Model   571
The Single-Period Model   574
Operations Strategy   578
   Cases: UPD Manufacturing   593
      Harvey Industries   594
      The Dewey Stapler Company   595
   Operations Tours: Bruegger's Bagel Bakery   597
      PSC, Inc.   598

CHAPTER FOURTEEN

Aggregate Planning   603

Introduction   604
The Purpose and Scope of Aggregate Planning   607

Basic Strategies for Meeting Uneven Demand   610
Techniques for Aggregate Planning   613
Aggregate Planning in Services   622
Disaggregating the Aggregate Plan   623
Master Scheduling   624
   Case: Eight Glasses a Day   635

CHAPTER FIFTEEN

MRP and ERP   639

MRP   640
An Overview of MRP   640
MRP Inputs   642
MRP Processing   646
MRP Outputs   654
Other Considerations   654
Capacity Requirements Planning   657
MRP in Services   660
Benefits and Requirements of MRP   660
MRP II   661
   Newsclip: SAP R/3 Leads Pack of Enterprise
      Resource Planning Software Packages   663
ERP   664
   Readings: The ABCs of ERP   664
         Wireless ERP   668
   Case: DMD Enterprises   678
   Operations Tour: Stickley Furniture   679

CHAPTER SIXTEEN

Just-in-Time Systems   683

Introduction   684
   Readings: The Nuts and Bolts of Japan's
         Factories   685
         Romantic JIT and Pragmatic JIT   687
JIT Goals   687
Building Blocks   688
   Reading: Pedal Pushers   694
   Newsclip: "People" Firms Boost Profits, Study
      Shows   696
   Reading: Developing the JIT Philosophy   702
Converting to a JIT System   705
   Reading: JIT and Quality: A Perfect Fit   708
JIT in Services   709
   Reading: Box Maker Keeps Lid on Lead
      Times   709
JIT Purchasing   711
JIT II   711
Operations Strategy   711

Reading: JIT II 711
Case: Level Operations 716
Operations Tour: Boeing 716

SUPPLEMENT TO CHAPTER SIXTEEN

Maintenance 719

Introduction 720
Preventive Maintenance 721
Breakdown Programs 723
Replacement 724

CHAPTER SEVENTEEN

Scheduling 728

Scheduling Operations 728
Scheduling in Low-Volume Systems 731
Additional Service Considerations 749
Reading: Servicing Passenger Planes 751
Operations Strategy 752

PART SIX

Project Management

CHAPTER EIGHTEEN

Project Management 765

Reading: The International Space Station Project
(ISS) 766
Introduction 767
Behavioral Aspects of Project Management 768
Readings: Project Managers Have Never Been More
Critical 770
Five Ways to PUMP UP Your Champion 771
Project Life Cycle 772
Risk Management 773
Work Breakdown Structure 774
Planning and Scheduling with Gantt Charts 774
PERT and CPM 775
Deterministic Time Estimates 778
A Computing Algorithm 780
Probabilistic Time Estimates 786
Determining Path Probabilities 789
Technology 792
Simulation 793
Time–Cost Trade-Offs: Crashing 793
Advantages of Using PERT and Potential Sources of
Error 797

Strategy 797
Cases: The Case of the Mexican Crazy Quilt 812
Time, Please 813
Reading: Managing Projects with a New View 813

PART SEVEN

Waiting Lines and Simulation

CHAPTER NINETEEN

Waiting Lines 817

Reading: Waiting—A New Popular Pastime: Miss
Manners 818
Why Is There Waiting? 819
Managerial Implications of Waiting Lines 819
Goal of Waiting-Line Analysis 819
System Characteristics 821
Measures of System Performance 825
Queuing Models: Infinite-Source 825
Queuing Model: Finite-Source 833
Newsclip: Hotels Exploring Easier Customer
Check-ins 844
Other Approaches 845
Reading: Stopped at a Light? Why Not Read This,
You May Have Time 851

SUPPLEMENT TO CHAPTER NINETEEN

Simulation 853

Introduction 854
Steps in the Simulation Process 854
Monte Carlo Simulation 856
Computer Simulation 864
Advantages and Limitations of Using Simulations 865
Case: Coquille Refinery Corporation 872

APPENDIX A
Answers to Selected Problems 873

APPENDIX B
Tables 887
Photo Credits 895
Index 897

PART ONE

Introduction

Chapter 1 introduces you to the field of operations management. It describes the nature and scope of operations management, and how operations management relates to other parts of the organization. Among the important topics it covers are the different types of operations systems, a comparison of manufacturing and service operations, a brief history of operations management, and a list of trends in business that relate to operations. After you have read this chapter, you will have a good understanding of what the operations function of a business organization encompasses.

Chapter 2 discusses operations management in a broader context, and presents the issues of competition, strategy, and productivity. After you have read Chapter 2, you will understand the importance of the operations function relative to the goals of a business organization. This chapter also describes time-based strategies, which many organizations are now adopting as they seek to become more competitive and to better serve their customers.

Introduction to operations management includes two chapters:

1 Introduction to operations management, Chapter 1
2 Competitiveness, strategy, and productivity, Chapter 2

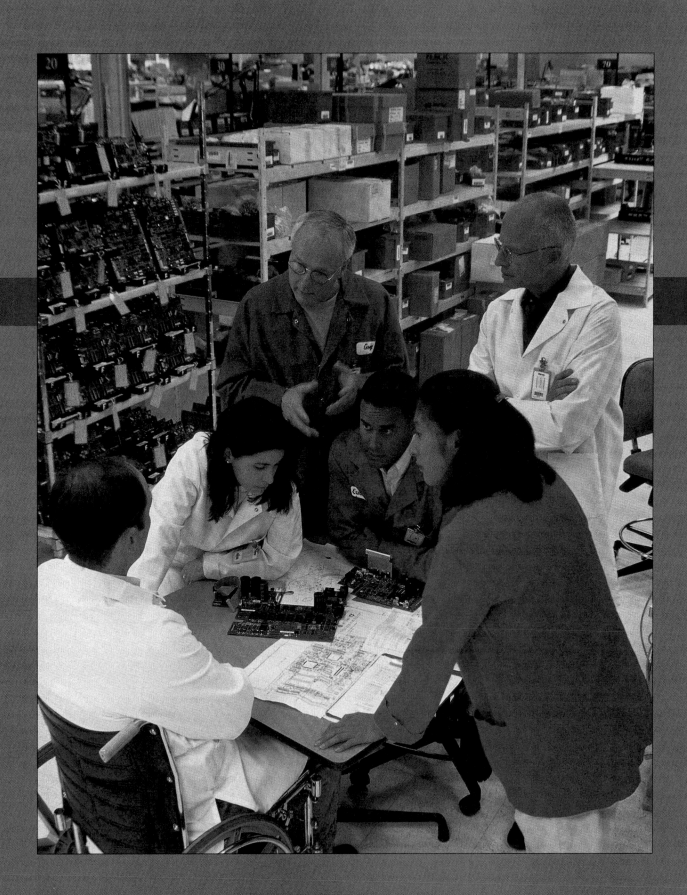

CHAPTER ONE

Introduction to Operations Management

CHAPTER OUTLINE

Introduction, 4

Why Study Operations
Management? 5
Careers in Operations
Management, 6

Functions within Business
Organizations, 6
Operations, 7
Finance, 9
Marketing, 10
Other Functions, 11

The Scope of Operations
Management, 12

Differentiating Features of
Operations Systems, 13
Degree of Standardization, 13
Type of Operation, 14
Production of Goods versus Service
Operations, 14

The Operations Manager and the
Management Process, 16

Operations Managers and Decision
Making, 17
Models, 17
Quantitative Approaches, 18
Analysis of Trade-Offs, 19
A Systems Approach, 19

Establishing Priorities, 19
Ethics, 20

The Historical Evolution of
Operations Management, 21
The Industrial Revolution, 21
Scientific Management, 21
The Human Relations Movement, 22
Decision Models and Management
Science, 23
The Influence of Japanese
Manufacturers, 23

Trends in Business, 24
Recent Trends, 24
Continuing Trends, 25

Reading: Agile Manufacturing, 27

Summary, 27

Key Terms, 28

Discussion and Review
Questions, 28

Memo Writing Exercises, 29

Cases: Hazel, 30
Total Recall, 31

Operations Tour: Wegmans Food
Markets, 31

Selected Bibliography and Further
Reading, 34

LEARNING OBJECTIVES

*After completing this chapter, you
should be able to:*

1 Define the term *operations
management.*

2 Identify the three major
functional areas of organizations
and describe how they interrelate.

3 Describe the operations function
and the nature of the operations
manager's job.

4 Differentiate between design and
operation of production systems.

5 Provide a general description of
the different types of operations.

6 Compare and contrast service and
manufacturing operations.

7 Briefly describe the historical
evolution of operations
management.

8 Describe the key aspects of
operations management decision
making.

9 Identify some of the current
trends in business that impact
operations management.

In the late 1970s, Wal-Mart was a niche marketer, with about 200 stores, mostly in the South. At the time, Sears, JC Penney, and Kmart dominated the retail market. Over the years, Wal-Mart gained market share at the expense of the previous market leaders, and it has now become the largest and most profitable retailer in the world!

In the 1990s, the Boeing Company ran into trouble when it could not meet production deadlines. As a result, Boeing lost some orders, which had a negative impact on earnings and its stock price.

Why do some companies thrive while others struggle or fail? There are a variety of reasons, to be sure. However, an important key in a company's success or failure is its *operations management*. This is the subject of this book.

This book is about operations management. The subject matter is fascinating and timely: productivity, quality, e-business, global competition, and customer service are very much in the news. All are part of operations management. This first chapter presents an introduction and overview of operations management. Among the issues it addresses are: What is operations management? Why is it important? What do operations managers do?

The chapter also provides a brief description of the historical evolution of operations management and a discussion of the trends that impact operations management.

Introduction

operations management The management of systems or processes that *create goods and/or provide services.*

Operations management is the management of processes or systems that create goods and/or provide services. It encompasses forecasting, capacity planning, scheduling, managing inventories, assuring quality, motivating employees, deciding where to locate facilities, and more.

We can use an airline company to illustrate an operations system. The system consists of the airplanes, airport facilities, and maintenance facilities, sometimes spread out over a wide territory. Most of the activities performed by management and employees fall into the realm of operations management:

Forecasting such things as weather and landing conditions, seat demand for flights, and the growth in air travel.

Capacity planning, essential for the airline to maintain the cash flow and make a reasonable profit. (Too few or too many planes, or even the right number of planes but in the wrong places, will hurt profits.)

The Pipian Bike factory in Havana employs nearly 700 people and produces 15,000 bicycles annually. Parts for the bikes come from all over the world, including Russia, India, China, and Spain.

Scheduling of planes for flights and for routine maintenance; scheduling of pilots and flight attendants; and scheduling of ground crews, counter staff, and baggage handlers.

Managing inventories of such items as foods and beverages, first-aid equipment, in-flight magazines, pillows and blankets, and life preservers.

Assuring quality, essential in flying and maintenance operations, where the emphasis is on safety. Also important in dealing with customers at ticket counters, check-in, telephone and electronic reservations, and curb service, where the emphasis is on efficiency and courtesy.

Employee motivation and training in all phases of operations.

Location of facilities according to managers' decisions on which cities to provide service for, where to locate maintenance facilities, and where to locate major and minor hubs.

Now consider a bicycle factory. This might be primarily an *assembly* operation: buying components such as frames, tires, wheels, gears, and other items from suppliers, and then assembling bicycles. The factory might also do some of the *fabrication* work itself, forming frames, making the gears and chains, and buy mainly raw materials and a few parts and materials such as paint, nuts and bolts, and tires. Among the key management tasks in either case are scheduling production, deciding which components to make and which to buy, ordering parts and materials, deciding on the style of bicycle to produce and how many, purchasing new equipment to replace old or worn out equipment, maintaining equipment, motivating workers, and ensuring that quality standards are met.

Obviously, an airline company and a bicycle factory are completely different types of operations. One is primarily a service operation, the other a producer of goods. Nonetheless, these two operations have much in common. Both involve scheduling of activities, motivating employees, ordering and managing supplies, selecting and maintaining equipment, satisfying quality standards, and—above all—satisfying customers. And in both businesses, the success of the business depends on short- and long-term planning.

Why Study Operations Management?

You may be wondering why you need to study operations management. Actually, there are a number of very good reasons. One is that operations management activities are at the core of *all* business organizations, regardless of what business they are in. Second, 50 percent or more of all jobs are in operations management-related areas—such areas as customer service, quality assurance, production planning and control, scheduling, job design, inventory management, and many more. Third, activities in all of the other areas of business organizations, such as finance, accounting, human resources, logistics, management information systems (MIS), marketing, purchasing, as well as others are all interrelated with operations management activities. So it is essential for people who work in these areas to have a basic understanding of operations management.

Business processes involve systems that extend across functional boundaries. For example, accountants need to know about inventory management, work measurement and labor standards, and processing systems in order to estimate costs, conduct audits, and prepare financial reports. Those working in finance also need to understand inventory management, but they must also be able to forecast financial needs and cash flow and understand the rationale for make-or-buy decisions, the need for funds for updating equipment, investing in new technology, investing in upgrading employee skills, and providing funds for expansion or relocation. Marketing and operations are closely linked. Included in those areas are product planning and forecasting. Moreover, in most service operations, production and marketing occur concurrently, so there is considerable overlap between marketing and operations. Those working in MIS need to understand operations management because much of their work will directly or indirectly involve operations. And, of course, those who have or want to have their own businesses will need to have a thorough knowledge of operations management.

Beyond all of this is the reality that operations management is about *management,* and *all managers* need to possess the knowledge and skills in the content areas you will learn about here. Among them are productivity, strategy, forecasting, quality, inventory control, and scheduling. Also, you will learn how to use a range of quantitative tools that enhance managerial decision making.

CAREERS IN OPERATIONS MANAGEMENT

If you are thinking of a career in operations management, you can benefit by joining one or more of the professional societies.

www.apics.com

American Production and Inventory Control Society (APICS)
500 West Annandale Road, Falls Church, Virginia 22046-4274

American Society for Quality (ASQ)
230 West Wells Street, Milwaukee, Wisconsin 53203

www.napm.org

National Association of Purchasing Management (NAPM)
2055 East Centennial Circle, Tempe, Arizona 85284

www.infoanalytic.com/asm/

Association for Systems Management
P.O. Box 38370, Cleveland, Ohio 44130-0307

www.informs.org

Institute for Operations Research and the Management Sciences (INFORMS)
901 Elkridge Landing Road, Linthicum, Maryland 21090-2909

www.poms.org

The Production and Operations Management Society (POMS)
College of Engineering, Florida International University, EAS 2460,
10555 West Flagle Street, Miami, Florida 33174

www.pmi.org

The Project Management Institute (PMI)
4 Campus Boulevard, Newtown Square, Pennsylvania 19073-3299

APICS and NAPM both offer a practitioner certification examination that can enhance your qualifications. Information about job opportunities can be obtained from all of these societies as well as from other sources, such as the Decision Sciences Institute (University Plaza, Atlanta, Georgia, 30303) and the Institute of Industrial Engineers (25 Technology Park, Norcross, Georgia, 30092).

Functions within Business Organizations

Organizations are formed to pursue goals that are achieved more efficiently by the concerted efforts of a group of people than by individuals working alone. Business organizations are devoted to producing goods and/or providing services. They may be for-profit or nonprofit organizations. Their goals, products, and services may be similar or quite different. Nonetheless, their functions and the way they operate are similar.

FIGURE 1-1

The three basic functions of business organizations

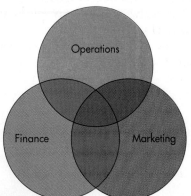

FIGURE 1-2

The three major functions of business organizations overlap

Type of Operations	Examples
Goods producing	Farming, mining, construction, manufacturing, power generation
Storage/transportation	Warehousing, trucking, mail service, moving, taxis, buses, hotels, airlines
Exchange	Retailing, wholesaling, banking, renting or leasing, library loans
Entertainment	Films, radio and television, plays, concerts, recording
Communication	Newspapers, radio and TV newscasts, telephone, satellites, the Internet

TABLE 1-1

Examples of types of operations

A typical business organization has three basic functions: finance, marketing, and operations (see Figure 1–1). These three functions, and other supporting functions, perform different but *related* activities necessary for the operation of the organization. The interdependency of the major functions is depicted by overlapping circles in Figure 1–2. The functions must interact to achieve the goals and objectives of the organization, and each makes an important contribution. Often the success of an organization depends not only on how well each area performs but also on how well the areas *interface* with each other. For instance, unless operations and marketing work together, marketing may promote goods or services that operations cannot profitably deliver, or operations may turn out goods or services for which there is no demand. Similarly, unless finance and operations people work closely, funds for expansion or new equipment may not be available when needed.

Let's take a closer look at these functions.

OPERATIONS

The operations function consists of all activities *directly* related to producing goods or providing services. Hence, it exists both in manufacturing and assembly operations, which are *goods-oriented,* and in areas such as health care, transportation, food handling, and retailing, which are primarily *service-oriented.* Table 1–1 provides illustrations of the diversity of operations management settings.

The operations function is the core of most business organizations; it is responsible for the creation of an organization's goods or services. Inputs are used to obtain finished goods or services using one or more *transformation processes* (e.g., storing, transporting, cutting). To ensure that the desired outputs are obtained, measurements are taken at various points in the transformation process (*feedback*) and then compared with previously established standards to determine whether corrective action is needed (*control*). Figure 1–3 shows the conversion process.

Table 1–2 provides some examples of inputs, transformation processes, and outputs. Although goods and services are listed separately in Table 1–2, it is important to note that goods and services often occur jointly. For example, having the oil changed in your car is a service, but the oil that is delivered is a good. Similarly, house painting is a service, but the paint is a good. The goods–service package is a continuum. It can range from primarily goods, with little service, to primarily service, with few goods. Figure 1–4 illustrates this continuum.

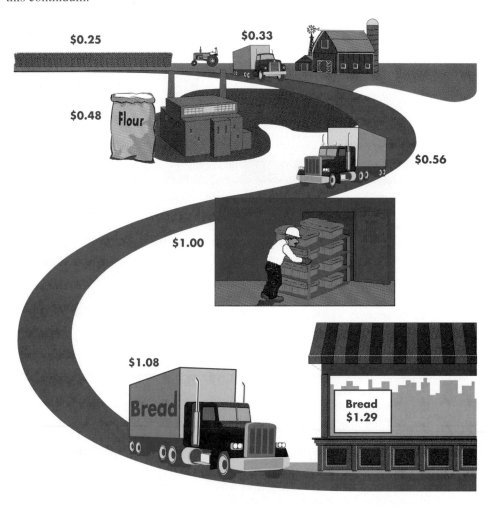

value-added The difference between the cost of inputs and the value or price of outputs.

The essence of the operations function is to *add value* during the transformation process: **Value-added** is the term used to describe the difference between the cost of inputs and the value or price of outputs. In nonprofit organizations, the value of outputs (e.g., highway construction, police and fire protection) is their value to society; the greater the value added, the greater the effectiveness of these operations. In for-profit organizations, the value of outputs is measured by the prices that customers are willing to pay for those goods or services. Firms use the money generated by value-added for research and development, investment in new facilities and equipment, paying workers, and *profits.* Consequently, the greater the value-added, the greater the amount of funds available for these purposes.

FIGURE 1-3

The operations function involves the conversion of inputs into outputs

Inputs	Transformation	Outputs
Land	Processes	Goods
Human	Cutting, drilling	Houses
Physical	Transporting	Automobiles
Intellectual	Teaching	Clothing
Raw materials	Farming	Computers
Energy	Mixing	Machines
Water	Packing	Televisions
Chemicals	Canning	Food products
Metals	Consulting	Textbooks
Wood	Copying, faxing	Magazines
Equipment		Shoes
Machines		CD players
Computers		Services
Trucks		Health care
Tools		Entertainment
Facilities		Car repair
Hospitals		Delivery
Factories		Gift wrapping
Offices		Legal
Retail stores		Banking
Other		Communication
Information		
Time		

TABLE 1-2

Examples of inputs, transformation, and outputs

One way that businesses attempt to become more productive is to examine critically whether the operations performed by their workers add value. Businesses consider those that do not add value wasteful. Eliminating or improving such operations decreases the cost of inputs or processing, thereby increasing the value-added. For instance, a firm may discover it is producing an item much earlier than the scheduled delivery date to a customer, thus requiring the storage of the item in a warehouse until delivery. In effect, additional costs are incurred by storing the item without adding to the value of the item. Reducing storage time would reduce the transformation cost and, hence, increase the value-added.

Table 1–3 provides some specific illustrations of the transformation process.

FINANCE

The finance function comprises activities related to securing resources at favorable prices and allocating those resources throughout the organization. Finance and operations management personnel cooperate by exchanging information and expertise in such activities as:

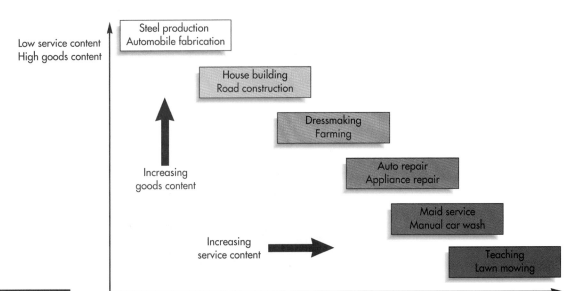

FIGURE 1-4

The goods–service continuum

TABLE 1-3

Illustrations of the transformation process

Food Processor	Inputs	Processing	Output
	Raw vegetables	Cleaning	Canned vegetables
	Metal sheets	Making cans	
	Water	Cutting	
	Energy	Cooking	
	Labor	Packing	
	Building	Labeling	
	Equipment		

Hospital	Inputs	Processing	Output
	Doctors, nurses	Examination	Healthy patients
	Hospital	Surgery	
	Medical supplies	Monitoring	
	Equipment	Medication	
	Laboratories	Therapy	

1. *Budgeting.* Budgets must be periodically prepared to plan financial requirements. Budgets must sometimes be adjusted, and performance relative to a budget must be evaluated.

2. *Economic analysis of investment proposals.* Evaluation of alternative investments in plant and equipment requires inputs from both operations and finance people.

3. *Provision of funds.* The necessary funding of operations and the amount and timing of funding can be important and even critical when funds are tight. Careful planning can help avoid cash-flow problems. Most for-profit firms obtain the majority of their funds through the revenues generated by sales of goods and services.

MARKETING

Marketing's focus is on selling and/or promoting the goods or services of an organization. Marketing is also responsible for assessing customer wants and needs, and for communicating those to operations people (short term) and to design people (long term). That is, operations needs information about demand over the short to intermediate term so that it can

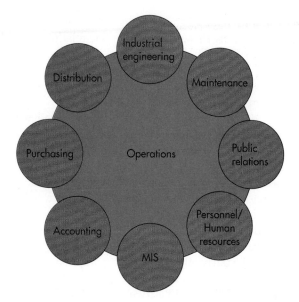

FIGURE 1-5

Operations interfaces with a number of supporting functions

plan accordingly (e.g., purchase materials or schedule work), while design people need information that relates to improving current products and services and designing new ones. Marketing, design, and production must work closely together to successfully implement design changes and to develop and produce new products. Marketing can provide valuable insight on what competitors are doing. Marketing can also supply information on consumer preferences so that design will know the kinds of products and features needed; operations can supply information about capacities and judge the *manufacturability* of designs. Operations will also have advance warning if new equipment or skills will be needed for new products or services. Finance people should be included in these exchanges in order to provide information on what funds might be available (short term) and to learn what funds might be needed for new products or services (intermediate to long term). One important piece of information marketing needs from operations is the manufacturing or service **lead time** in order to give customers realistic estimates of how long it will take to fill their orders.

lead time The time between ordering a good or service and receiving it.

Thus, marketing, operations, and finance must interface on product and process design, forecasting, setting realistic schedules, quality and quantity decisions, and keeping each other informed on the other's strengths and weaknesses.

OTHER FUNCTIONS

There are a host of other supporting functions that interface with operations. Among them are accounting and purchasing. Also, depending on the nature of the organization, they may include personnel or human resources, product design and development, industrial engineering, and maintenance (see Figure 1–5).

Accounting supplies information to management on costs of labor, materials, and overhead, and may provide reports on items such as scrap, downtime, and inventories.

Management information systems (MIS) is concerned with providing management with the information it needs to effectively manage. This occurs mainly through designing systems to capture relevant information and designing reports.

Purchasing has responsibility for procurement of materials, supplies, and equipment. Close contact with operations is necessary to ensure correct quantities and timing of purchases. The purchasing department is often called on to evaluate vendors for quality, reliability, service, price, and ability to adjust to changing demand. Purchasing is also involved in receiving and inspecting the purchased goods.

The *personnel* or *human resources* department is concerned with recruitment and training of personnel, labor relations, contract negotiations, wage and salary administration, assisting in manpower projections, and ensuring the health and safety of employees.

Public relations has responsibility for building and maintaining a positive public image of the organization. Good public relations provides many potential benefits. An obvious one is in the marketplace. Other potential benefits include public awareness of the organization as a good place to work (labor supply), improved chances of approval of zoning change requests, community acceptance of expansion plans, and instilling a positive attitude among employees.

Industrial engineering is often concerned with scheduling, performance standards, work methods, quality control, and material handling.

Distribution involves the shipping of goods to warehouses, retail outlets, or final customers.

Maintenance is responsible for general upkeep and repair of equipment, buildings and grounds, heating and air-conditioning; removing toxic wastes; parking; and perhaps security.

Many of these interfaces are elaborated on in later chapters.

The importance of operations management, both for organizations and for society, should be fairly obvious: The consumption of goods and services is an integral part of our society. Operations management is responsible for creating those goods and services. Organizations exist primarily to provide services or create goods. Hence, operations is the *core function* of an organization. Without this core, there would be no need for any of the other functions—the organization would have no purpose. Given the central nature of its function, it is not surprising that more than half of all employed people in this country have jobs in operations. Furthermore, the operations function is responsible for a major portion of the assets in most business organizations.

The Scope of Operations Management

We have already noted that the operations manager is responsible for the creation of goods and services. This encompasses acquisition of resources and the conversion of those inputs into outputs using one or more transformation processes. That involves planning, coordinating, and controlling the elements that make up the process, including workers, equipment, facilities, allocation of resources, and work methods. It also includes product and/or service design, a vital, ongoing process that most organizations must do. Operations performs this activity in conjunction with marketing. Marketing people can be a source of ideas concerning new products and services, and improvements to existing ones. Operations people can also be a source of new ideas for improvements in the processes that provide the goods or services. From a practical standpoint, product and service design and the processes that provide them are the lifeblood of a competitive organization.

A primary function of an operations manager is to guide the system by decision making. Certain decisions affect the *design* of the system, and others affect the *operation* of the system.

System design involves decisions that relate to system capacity, the geographic location of facilities, arrangement of departments and placement of equipment within physical structures, product and service planning, and acquisition of equipment. These decisions usually, but not always, require long-term commitments. *System operation* involves management of personnel, inventory planning and control, scheduling, project management, and quality assurance. In many instances, the operations manager is more involved in day-to-day operating decisions than with decisions relating to system design. However, the operations manager has a vital stake in system design because *system design essentially determines many of the parameters of system operation*. For example, costs, space, capacities, and quality are directly affected by design decisions. Even though the operations manager is not responsible for making all design decisions, he or she can provide those decision makers with a wide range of information that will have a bearing on their decisions. Table 1–4 provides additional details on the nature and scope of operations management.

Decision Area	Basic Questions	Chapter
Forecasting	What will demand be?	3
Design		
Product and service design	What do customers want? How can products and services be improved?	4
Capacity (long range)	How much capacity will be needed? How can the organization best meet capacity requirements?	5
Process selection	What processes should the organization use?	6
Layout	What is the best arrangement for departments, equipment, work flow, and storage in terms of cost, productivity?	6
Design of work systems	What is the best way to motivate employees? How can productivity be improved? How to measure work? How to improve work methods?	7
Location	What is a satisfactory location for a facility (factory, store, etc.)?	8
Operation		
Quality	How is quality defined?	9
Quality control	Are processes performing adequately? What standards should be used? Are standards being met?	10
Total quality management	How are quality goods and services achieved and improved?	11
Aggregate planning	How much capacity will be needed over the intermediate range? How can capacity needs best be met?	14
Inventory management	How much to order? When to reorder? Which items should get the most attention?	13, 15
Materials requirements planning	What materials, parts, and subassemblies will be needed, and when?	15
Scheduling	How can jobs best be scheduled? Who will do which job? Which equipment to use?	17
Project management	Which activities are the most critical to the success of a project? What are the goals of a project? What resources will be needed, and when will they be needed?	18
Waiting lines	What service capacity is appropriate?	19

TABLE 1–4

Design and operating decisions

Differentiating Features of Operations Systems

A number of features differentiate operations systems. A brief discussion of some of these features will help you to develop a better understanding of the nature and scope of operations management. The three described are degree of standardization, type of operation, and production of goods versus service operations.

DEGREE OF STANDARDIZATION

The output of production systems can range from highly standardized to highly customized. *Standardized output* means that there is a high degree of uniformity in goods or services. Standardized goods include radios, televisions, computers, newspapers, canned foods, automobile tires, pens, and pencils. Standardized services include automatic car washes, televised newscasts, taped lectures, and commercial airline service. *Customized output* means that the product or service is designed for a specific case or individual. Customized goods include eyeglasses, custom-fitted clothing, window glass (cut to order), and customized draperies. Customized services include tailoring, taxi rides, and surgery.

Systems with standardized output can generally take advantage of standardized methods, less-skilled workers, materials, and mechanization, all of which contribute to higher volumes and lower unit costs. In custom systems, on the other hand, each job is sufficiently different so that workers must be more skilled, the work moves slower, and the work is less susceptible to mechanization.

TYPE OF OPERATION

The degree of standardization and the volume of output of a product or service influence the way a firm organizes production. On one end of the scale is a single, large-scale product or service such as the launching of a space shuttle (service) or the construction of a skyscraper (product). On the other end is a continuous process, such as oil refining. Between these extremes are customized individual units of output, such as custom-made furniture, special-purpose machines, and auto repair; batches, such as paint and food products; and mass production, such as automobiles, personal computers, and appliances.

You will learn more about these different types of operations in later chapters.

PRODUCTION OF GOODS VERSUS SERVICE OPERATIONS

Production of goods results in a *tangible output,* such as an automobile, a clock radio, a golf ball, a refrigerator—anything that we can see or touch. It may take place in a factory, but can occur elsewhere. Service, on the other hand, generally implies an *act.* A physician's examination, TV and auto repair, lawn care, and projecting a film in a theater are examples of services. The majority of service jobs fall into these categories:

Government (federal, state, local).

Wholesale/retail (clothing, food, appliances, stationery, toys, etc.).

Financial services (banking, stock brokerages, insurance, etc.).

Health care (doctors, dentists, hospitals, etc.).

Personal services (laundry, dry cleaning, hair/beauty, gardening, etc.).

Business services (data processing, e-business, delivery, employment agencies, etc.).

Education (schools, colleges, etc.).

Manufacturing and service are often similar in terms of *what* is done but different in terms of *how* it is done. For example, both involve design and operating decisions. Manufacturers must decide what size factory is needed. Service organizations (e.g., hospitals) must decide what size building is needed. Both must make decisions on location, schedule and control operations, and allocation of scarce resources.

Manufacturing and service organizations differ chiefly because manufacturing is goods-oriented and service is act-oriented. The differences involve the following:

1. Customer contact
2. Uniformity of input
3. Labor content of jobs
4. Uniformity of output
5. Measurement of productivity
6. Simultaneous production and delivery
7. Quality assurance

Let us consider each of these differences.

1. Often, by its nature, service involves a much higher degree of customer contact than manufacturing. The performance of a service often occurs at the point of consumption. For example, repairing a leaky roof must take place where the roof is, and surgery requires the presence of the surgeon and the patient. On the other hand, manufacturing allows a separation between production and consumption, so that manufacturing may occur away from the consumer. This permits a fair degree of latitude in selecting work methods, assigning jobs, scheduling work, and exercising control over operations. Service operations, because of their contact with customers, can be much more limited in their range of options. Moreover, customers are sometimes a part of the system (e.g., self-service operations such as gas stations, shopping), so tight control is impossible. In addition, product-oriented operations can build up inventories of finished goods (e.g., cars, refrigerators),

enabling them to absorb some of the shocks caused by varying demand. Service operations, however, cannot build up inventories of *time* and are much more sensitive to demand variability—banks and supermarkets alternate between lines of customers waiting for service and idle tellers or cashiers waiting for customers.

2. Service operations are subject to greater variability of inputs than typical manufacturing operations. Each patient, each lawn, and each auto repair presents a specific problem that often must be diagnosed before it can be remedied. Manufacturing operations often have the ability to carefully control the amount of variability of inputs and thus achieve low variability in outputs. Consequently, job requirements for manufacturing are generally more uniform than those for services.

3. Services often require a higher labor content whereas manufacturing, with exceptions, can be more capital-intensive (i.e., mechanized).

4. Because high mechanization generates products with low variability, manufacturing tends to be smooth and efficient; service activities sometimes appear to be slow and awkward, and output is more variable. Automated services are an exception to this.

5. Measurement of productivity is more straightforward in manufacturing due to the high degree of uniformity of most manufactured items. In service operations, variations in demand intensity and in requirements from job to job make productivity measurement considerably more difficult. For example, compare the productivity of two doctors. One may have a large number of routine cases while the other does not, so their productivity appears to differ unless a very careful analysis is made.

6. In many instances customers receive the service as it is performed (e.g., haircut, dental care).

7. Quality assurance is more challenging in services when production and consumption occur at the same time. Moreover, the higher variability of input creates additional opportunity for the quality of output to suffer unless quality assurance is actively managed. Quality at the point of creation is typically more evident for services than for manufacturing, where errors can be corrected before the customer receives the output.

Service jobs are sometimes categorized as professional or nonprofessional. Wholesale/retail and personal services generally fall into the nonprofessional category. Often these jobs tend to be on the low end of the pay scale, whereas professional services (e.g., surgery, consulting) tend to be on the high end of the pay scale. Manufacturing jobs, on the other hand, don't show this bimodal tendency, and few salaries fall in either the high or low range.

Table 1–5 gives an overview of the differences between production of goods and service operations.

Although it is convenient to think in terms of systems devoted exclusively to goods or services, most real systems are a blend of both. For instance, maintenance and repair of equipment are services performed by virtually every manufacturing firm. Similarly, most service organizations typically sell goods that complement their services. Thus, a lawn care firm usually sells goods such as weed killers, fertilizers, and grass seed. Hospitals

Characteristic	Goods	Services
Output	Tangible	Intangible
Uniformity of output	High	Low
Uniformity of input	High	Low
Labor content	Low	High
Measurement of productivity	Easy	Difficult
Customer contact	Low	High
Opportunity to correct quality problems before delivery to customer	High	Low
Evaluation	Easier	More difficult
Patentable	Usually	Not usually

TABLE 1–5

Typical differences between goods and services

dispense medical and surgical supplies along with health services. Restaurants sell food. Movie theaters sell popcorn, candy, and beverages.

The service sector and the manufacturing sector are both important to the economy. The service sector now accounts for more than 70 percent of jobs in the United States. Moreover, the number of people working in services is increasing, while the number of people working in manufacturing is not. (See Figure 1–6.) More and more the U.S. economy is becoming a service economy.

The Operations Manager and the Management Process

The operations manager is the key figure in the system: he or she has the ultimate responsibility for the creation of goods or provision of services.

The kinds of jobs that operations managers oversee vary tremendously from organization to organization largely because of the different products or services involved. Thus, managing a banking operation obviously requires a different kind of expertise than managing a steelmaking operation. However, in a very important respect, the jobs are the same: They are both essentially *managerial.* The same thing can be said for the job of any operations manager regardless of the kinds of goods or services being created. In every case, the operations manager must coordinate the use of resources through the management process of planning, organizing, staffing, directing, and controlling.

Examples of the responsibilities of operations managers according to these classifications are given in Table 1–6.

FIGURE 1–6

U.S. manufacturing versus service employment, 1940–2000

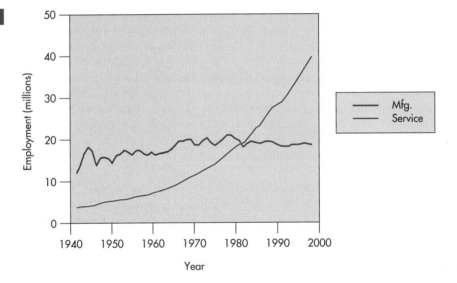

TABLE 1–6

Responsibilities of operations managers

Planning	Organizing
Capacity	Degree of centralization
Location	Subcontracting
Products and services	Staffing
Make or buy	Hiring/laying off
Layout	Use of overtime
Projects	Directing
Scheduling	Incentive plans
Controlling	Issuance of work orders
Inventory control	Job assignments
Quality control	

Operations Managers and Decision Making

The chief role of an operations manager is that of planner and decision maker. In this capacity, the operations manager exerts considerable influence over the degree to which the goals and objectives of the organization are realized.

Throughout this book, you will encounter the broad range of decisions that operations managers must make, and you will be introduced to the tools necessary to handle those decisions. This section describes general approaches to decision making, including the use of models, quantitative methods, analysis of trade-offs, and the systems approach.

MODELS

A **model** is an abstraction of reality, a simplified version of something. For example, a child's toy car is a model of a real automobile. It has many of the same visual features (shape, relative proportions, wheels) that make it suitable for the child's learning and playing. But the toy does not have a real engine, it cannot transport people, and it does not weigh 2,000 pounds.

model An abstraction of reality; a simplified representation of something.

Other examples of models include automobile test tracks and crash tests, formulas, graphs and charts, balance sheets and income statements, and financial ratios. Common statistical models include descriptive statistics such as the mean, median, mode, range, and standard deviation, as well as random sampling, the normal distribution, and regression equations.

Models are sometimes classified as physical, schematic, or mathematical:

Physical models look like their real-life counterparts. Examples include miniature cars, trucks, airplanes, toy animals and trains, and scale-model buildings. The advantage of these models is their visual correspondence with reality.

Schematic models are more abstract than their physical counterparts; that is, they have less resemblance to the physical reality. Examples include graphs and charts, blueprints, pictures, and drawings. The advantage of schematic models is that they are often relatively simple to construct and change. Moreover, they have some degree of visual correspondence.

Mathematical models are the most abstract: they do not look at all like their real-life counterparts. Examples include numbers, formulas, and symbols. These models are usually the easiest to manipulate, and they are important forms of inputs for computers and calculators.

The variety of models in use is enormous, ranging from the simple to the exotic; some are very crude, others extremely elegant. Nonetheless, all have certain common features: They are all decision-making aids and simplifications of more complex real-life phenomena. Real life involves an overwhelming amount of detail, much of which is irrelevant for any particular problem. Models ignore the unimportant details so that attention can be concentrated on the most important aspects of a situation, thus increasing the opportunity to understand a problem and its solution.

Because models play a significant role in operations management decision making, they are heavily integrated into the material of this text. For each model, try to learn (1) its purpose, (2) how it is used to generate results, (3) how these results are interpreted and used, and (4) what assumptions and limitations apply.

The last point is particularly important because virtually every model has an associated set of requirements that indicate the conditions under which the model is valid. Failure to satisfy all of the assumptions (i.e., to use a model where it isn't meant to be used) will make the results suspect. Attempts to apply the results to a problem under such circumstances can lead to disastrous consequences. Hence, it is extremely important to be aware of the assumptions and limitations of each model.

Managers use models in a variety of ways and for a variety of reasons. Models are beneficial because they:

1. Are generally easy to use and less expensive than dealing directly with the actual situation.
2. Require users to organize and sometimes quantify information and, in the process, often indicate areas where additional information is needed.
3. Provide a systematic approach to problem solving.
4. Increase understanding of the problem.
5. Enable managers to analyze "what if?" questions.
6. Require users to be specific about objectives.
7. Serve as a consistent tool for evaluation.
8. Enable users to bring the power of mathematics to bear on a problem.
9. Provide a standardized format for analyzing a problem.

This impressive list of benefits notwithstanding, models have certain limitations of which you should be aware. Two of the more important limitations are:

1. Quantitative information may be emphasized at the expense of qualitative information.
2. Models may be incorrectly applied and the results misinterpreted. The widespread use of computerized models adds to this risk because highly sophisticated models may be placed in the hands of users who are not sufficiently grounded in mathematics to appreciate the subtleties of a particular model; thus, they are unable to fully comprehend the circumstances under which the model can be successfully employed.

QUANTITATIVE APPROACHES

Quantitative approaches to problem solving often embody an attempt to obtain mathematically optimum solutions to managerial problems. Although quantitative techniques have traditionally been associated with production and operations management, it was not until World War II that major efforts were made to develop these techniques. In order to handle complex military logistics problems, interdisciplinary teams were assembled (e.g., psychologists, mathematicians, economists) to combine efforts in search of workable solutions. These efforts continued and expanded after the war, and many of the resulting techniques were applied to operations management. *Linear programming* and related mathematical techniques are widely used for optimum allocation of scarce resources. *Queuing techniques,* which originated around 1920 in the telephone industry but remained dormant until the 1950s and 1960s, are useful for analyzing situations in which waiting lines form. *Inventory models,* also popular after some early work, went through a long period of low interest but are now widely used to control inventories. *Project models* such as PERT (program evaluation and review technique) and CPM (critical path method) are useful for planning, coordinating, and controlling large-scale projects. *Forecasting techniques* are widely used in planning and scheduling. *Statistical models* are currently used in many areas of decision making.

In large measure, quantitative approaches to decision making in operations management (and in other areas of decision making) have been accepted because of the introduction of calculators and the availability of high-speed computers capable of handling the required calculations. Computers have had an enormous influence on the practice of operations management, particularly in scheduling and inventory control. Because they are capable of rapid, error-free computations and keeping track of thousands of bits of information with instantaneous retrieval, computers have had a major impact on operations management. Moreover, the growing availability of software packages covering virtually every quantitative technique has greatly increased management's use of the computer. Many heretofore impractical techniques, such as multiple regression analysis and linear programming, can now be handled with ease.

Because of the emphasis on quantitative approaches in operations management decision making, it is important not to lose sight of the fact that managers typically use a combination of qualitative and quantitative approaches, and many important decisions are based on qualitative approaches.

ANALYSIS OF TRADE-OFFS

Operations managers encounter decisions that can be described as *trade-off* decisions. For example, in deciding on the amount of inventory to stock, the manager must take into account the trade-off between the increased level of customer service that the additional inventory would yield and the increased costs required to stock that inventory. In selecting a piece of equipment, a manager must evaluate the merits of extra features relative to the cost of those extra features. And in the scheduling of overtime to increase output, the manager must weigh the value of the increased output against the higher costs of overtime (e.g., higher labor costs, lower productivity, lower quality, and greater risk of accidents).

Throughout this book you will be presented with decision models that reflect these kinds of trade-offs. Managers sometimes deal with these decisions by listing the advantages and disadvantages—the pros and cons—of a course of action to better understand the consequences of the decisions they must make. In some instances, managers add weights to the items on their list that reflect the relative importance of various factors. This can help them "net out" the potential impacts of the trade-offs on their decision. An example of this is the factor-rating approach described in the chapter on facilities location.

A SYSTEMS APPROACH

A systems viewpoint is almost always beneficial in decision making. A **system** can be defined as a set of interrelated parts that must work together. In a business organization, the organization can be thought of as a system composed of subsystems (e.g., marketing subsystem, operations subsystem, finance subsystems), which in turn are composed of lower subsystems. The systems approach emphasizes interrelationships among subsystems, but its main theme is that *the whole is greater than the sum of its individual parts.* Hence, from a systems viewpoint, the output and objectives of the organization as a whole take precedence over those of any one subsystem. An alternative approach is to concentrate on efficiency within subsystems and thereby achieve overall efficiency. But that approach overlooks the fact that organizations must operate in an environment of scarce resources and that subsystems are often in direct competition for those scarce resources, so that an orderly approach to the allocation of resources is called for.

system A set of interrelated parts that must work together.

One undesirable result of the use of quantitative techniques is that many of the techniques tend to produce solutions that are optimal in a narrow sense but may not be optimal in a broader sense (e.g., in terms of a department, plant, division, or overall organization). Consequently, managers must evaluate "optimal" solutions produced by quantitative techniques in terms of the larger framework, and perhaps modify decisions accordingly.

A systems approach is essential whenever something is being designed, redesigned, implemented, improved, or otherwise changed. It is important to take into account the impact on all parts of the system. For example, if the upcoming model of an automobile will add antilock brakes, a designer must take into account how customers will view the change, instructions for using the brakes, chances for misuse, the cost of producing the new brakes, installation procedures, recycling worn-out brakes, and repair procedures. In addition, workers will need training to make and/or assemble the brakes, production scheduling may change, inventory procedures may have to change, quality standards will have to be established, advertising must be informed of the new features, and parts suppliers must be selected.

ESTABLISHING PRIORITIES

In virtually every situation, managers discover that certain elements are more important than others. Recognizing this fact of life enables the managers to direct their efforts to where they will do the most good and to avoid wasting time and energy on insignificant elements.

Consider owning and operating an automobile. It has many parts and systems that can malfunction. Some of these are critical to the operation of the automobile: It would not function or would be dangerous to operate without them. Critical items include the engine and drive train, steering, brakes, tires, electrical system, and cooling system. In terms of maintaining and repairing the car, these items should receive the highest priority if the goal is to have safe, reliable transportation.

There are other items that are of much less importance, such as scratches in the paint, minor dents, a missing piece of chrome, and worn seatcovers. In terms of transportation, these should receive attention only after other, more important items have been attended to.

Between these two extremes lies a range of items of intermediate priority. These should be given attention corresponding to their importance to the overall goal. The list might include soft tires, weak battery, wheel alignment, noisy muffler, body rust, inoperative radio, and headlights out of adjustment.

Obviously, certain parts of an automobile are more critical to its operation than others. The same concept applies to management. By recognizing this and setting priorities, a manager will be in a position to deal more effectively with problems as they arise and to prevent many others from arising at all.

Pareto phenomenon A few factors account for a high percentage of the occurrence of some event(s).

It is axiomatic that a relatively few factors are often most important, so that dealing with those factors will generally have a disproportionately large impact on the results achieved. This is referred to as the **Pareto phenomenon,** which means that all things are not equal; some things (a few) will be very important for achieving an objective or solving a problem, and other things (many) will not. The implication is that a manager should examine each situation, searching for the few factors that will have the greatest impact, and give them the highest priority. This is one of the most important and pervasive concepts in operations management. In fact, this concept can be applied at all levels of management and to every aspect of decision making, both professional and personal.

ETHICS

Operations managers, like all managers, have the responsibility to make ethical decisions. Ethical issues arise in many aspects of operations management, including:

- worker safety: providing adequate training, maintaining equipment in good working condition, maintaining a safe working environment;
- product safety: providing products that minimize the risk of injury to users or damage to property or the environment;
- quality: honoring warranties, avoiding hidden defects;
- the environment: not doing things that will harm the environment;
- the community: being a good neighbor;
- hiring and firing workers: don't hire under false pretenses (e.g., promising a long-term job when that is not what is intended);
- closing facilities: taking into account the impact on a community, and honoring commitments that have been made;
- workers' rights: respecting workers' rights, dealing with worker problems quickly and fairly.

In making decisions, managers must consider how their decisions will affect shareholders, management, employees, customers, the community at large, and the environment. Finding solutions that will be in the best interests of all of these stakeholders is not always easy, but it is a goal that all managers should strive to achieve. Furthermore, even managers with the best intentions will sometimes make mistakes. If mistakes do occur, managers should act responsibly to correct those mistakes as quickly as possible, and to address any negative consequences.

The Historical Evolution of Operations Management

Systems for production have existed since ancient times. The Great Wall of China, the Egyptian pyramids, the ships of the Roman and Spanish empires, and the roads and aqueducts of the Romans provide examples of the human ability to organize for production. Even so, most of these examples could be classified as "public works" projects. The production of goods for sale, at least in the modern sense, and the modern factory system had their roots in the Industrial Revolution.

THE INDUSTRIAL REVOLUTION

The Industrial Revolution began in the 1770s in England and spread to the rest of Europe and to the United States during the nineteenth century. Prior to that time, goods were produced in small shops by craftsmen and their apprentices. Under that system, it was common for one person to be responsible for making a product, such as a horse-drawn wagon or a piece of furniture, from start to finish. Only simple tools were available; the machines that we use today had not been invented.

Then, a number of innovations changed the face of production forever by substituting machine power for human power. Perhaps the most significant of these was the steam engine, made practical by James Watt around 1764, because it provided a source of power to operate machines in factories. James Hargreaves' spinning jenny (1770) and Edmund Cartwright's power loom (1785) revolutionized the textile industry. Ample supplies of coal and iron ore provided materials for generating power and making machinery. The new machines, made of iron, were much stronger and more durable than the simple wooden machines they replaced.

In the earliest days of manufacturing, goods were produced using **craft production:** highly skilled workers using simple, flexible tools produced goods according to customer specifications.

craft production System in which highly skilled workers use simple, flexible tools to produce small quantities of customized goods.

Craft production had major shortcomings. Because products were made by skilled craftsmen who custom fitted parts, production was slow and costly. And when parts failed, the replacements also had to be custom made, which was also slow and costly. Another shortcoming was that production costs did not decrease as volume increased; there were no *economies of scale,* which would have provided a major incentive for companies to expand. Instead, many small companies emerged, each with its own set of standards.

A major change occurred that gave the industrial revolution a boost: the development of standard gauging systems. This greatly reduced the need for custom-made goods. Factories began to spring up and grow rapidly, providing jobs for countless people who were attracted in large numbers from rural areas.

Despite the major changes that were taking place, management theory and practice had not progressed much from early days. What was needed was an enlightened and more systematic approach to management.

SCIENTIFIC MANAGEMENT

The scientific-management era brought widespread changes to the management of factories. The movement was spearheaded by the efficiency engineer and inventor Frederick Winslow Taylor, who is often referred to as the father of scientific management. Taylor believed in a "science of management" based on observation, measurement, analysis and improvement of work methods, and economic incentives. He studied work methods in great detail to identify the best method for doing each job. Taylor also believed that management should be responsible for planning, carefully selecting and training workers, finding the best way to perform each job, achieving cooperation between management and workers, and separating management activities from work activities.

Taylor's methods emphasized maximizing output. They were not always popular with workers, who sometimes thought the methods were used to unfairly increase output without a corresponding increase in compensation. Certainly some companies did abuse workers in their quest for efficiency. Eventually, the public outcry reached the halls of Congress, and hearings were held on the matter. Taylor himself was called to testify in 1911, the same year in which his classic book, *The Principles of Scientific Management,* was published. The publicity from those hearings actually helped scientific management principles to achieve wide acceptance in industry.

A number of other pioneers also contributed heavily to this movement, including the following:

Frank Gilbreth was an industrial engineer who is often referred to as the father of motion study. He developed principles of motion economy that could be applied to incredibly small portions of a task.

Henry Gantt recognized the value of nonmonetary rewards to motivate workers, and developed a widely used system for scheduling, called Gantt charts.

Harrington Emerson applied Taylor's ideas to organization structure and encouraged the use of experts to improve organizational efficiency. He testified in a congressional hearing that railroads could save a million dollars a day by applying principles of scientific management.

Henry Ford, the great industrialist, employed scientific management techniques in his factories.

www.ford.com

During the early part of the twentieth century, automobiles were just coming into vogue in the United States. Ford's Model T was such a success that the company had trouble keeping up with orders for the cars. In an effort to improve the efficiency of operations, Ford adopted the scientific management principles espoused by Frederick Winslow Taylor. He also introduced the *moving assembly line.*

mass production System in which lower-skilled workers use specialized machinery to produce high volumes of standardized goods.

Among Ford's many contributions was the introduction of **mass production** to the automotive industry, a system of production in which large volumes of standardized goods are produced by low-skilled or semiskilled workers using highly specialized, and often costly, equipment. Ford was able to do this by taking advantage of a number of important concepts. Perhaps the key concept that launched mass production was **interchangeable parts,** sometimes attributed to Eli Whitney, an American inventor who applied the concept to assembling muskets in the late 1700s. The basis for interchangeable parts is to standardize parts so that any part in a batch of parts would fit any automobile coming down the assembly line. This meant that parts did not have to be custom fitted, as they were in craft production. The standardized parts could also be used for replacement parts. The result was a tremendous decrease in assembly time and cost. Ford accomplished this by standardizing the gauges used to measure parts during production and by using newly developed processes to produce uniform parts.

interchangeable parts Parts of a product made to such precision that they do not have to be custom fitted.

division of labor Breaking up a production process into small tasks, so that each worker performs a small portion of the overall job.

A second concept used by Ford was the **division of labor,** which Adam Smith wrote about in *The Wealth of Nations* (1776). Division of labor means that an operation, such as assembling an automobile, is divided up into a series of many small tasks, and individual workers are assigned to one of those tasks. Unlike craft production, where each worker was responsible for doing many tasks, and thus required skill, with division of labor the tasks were so narrow that virtually no skill was required.

Together, these concepts enabled Ford to tremendously increase the production rate at his factories using readily available inexpensive labor. Both Taylor and Ford were despised by many workers, because they held workers in such low regard, expecting them to perform like robots. This paved the way for the human relations movement.

THE HUMAN RELATIONS MOVEMENT

Whereas the scientific-management movement heavily emphasized the technical aspects of work design, the human relations movement emphasized the importance of the human element in job design. Lillian Gilbreth, a psychologist and the wife of Frank Gilbreth, worked with her husband, focusing on the human factor in work. (The Gilbreths were the subject of a classic 1950s film, *Cheaper by the Dozen.*) Many of her studies in the 1920s dealt with worker fatigue. In the following decades, there was much emphasis on motivation. During the 1930s, Elton Mayo conducted studies at the Hawthorne division of Western Electric. His studies revealed that in addition to the physical and technical aspects of work, worker motivation is critical for improving productivity. During the 1940s, Abraham Maslow developed motivational theories, which Frederick Hertzberg refined in the 1950s. Douglas McGregor added Theory X and Theory Y in the 1960s. These theories represented the two ends of the spectrum of how employees view work. Theory X, on the negative end, assumed that workers do not like to work, and have to be controlled—rewarded and punished—to get them to do good work. This attitude was quite common in the automobile industry and in some other industries, until the threat of global competition forced them to rethink that approach. Theory Y, on the other end of the spectrum, assumed that workers enjoy the physical and mental aspects of work and become committed to work. The Theory X approach resulted in an adversarial environment, whereas the Theory Y approach resulted in empowered workers and a more cooperative spirit. In the 1970s, William Ouchi added Theory Z, which combined the Japanese approach, with such features as lifetime employment, employee problem solving, and consensus building, and the traditional Western approach that features short-term employment, specialists, and individual decision making and responsibility.

DECISION MODELS AND MANAGEMENT SCIENCE

The factory movement was accompanied by the development of several quantitative techniques. F. W. Harris developed one of the first models in 1915: a mathematical model for inventory management. In the 1930s, three coworkers at Bell Telephone Labs, H. F. Dodge, H. G. Romig, and W. Shewhart, developed statistical procedures for sampling and quality control. In 1935, L. H. C. Tippett conducted studies that provided the groundwork for statistical-sampling theory.

At first, these quantitative models were not widely used in industry. However, the onset of World War II changed that. The war generated tremendous pressures on manufacturing output, and specialists from many disciplines combined efforts to achieve advancements in the military and in manufacturing. After the war, efforts to develop and refine quantitative tools for decision making continued, resulting in decision models for forecasting, inventory management, project management, and other areas of operations management.

During the 1960s and 1970s, management science techniques were highly regarded; in the 1980s, they lost some favor. However, the widespread use of personal computers and user-friendly software in the workplace is causing a resurgence in the popularity of these techniques.

THE INFLUENCE OF JAPANESE MANUFACTURERS

A number of Japanese manufacturers developed or refined management practices that increased the productivity of their operations and the quality of their products. This made them very competitive, sparking interest in their approaches by companies outside Japan. Their approaches emphasized quality and continual improvement, worker teams and empowerment, and achieving customer satisfaction. The Japanese can be credited with spawning the "quality revolution" that occurred in industrialized countries, and with generating widespread interest in time-based management (just-in-time production).

The influence of the Japanese on U.S. manufacturing and service companies has been enormous and promises to continue for the foreseeable future. Because of that influence, this book will provide considerable information about Japanese methods and successes.

Table 1–7 provides a chronological summary of some of the key developments in the evolution of operations management.

TABLE 1-7

*Historical summary of
operations management*

Approximate Date	Contribution/Concept	Originator
1776	Division of labor	Adam Smith
1790	Interchangeable parts	Eli Whitney
1911	Principles of scientific management	Frederick W. Taylor
1911	Motion study; use of industrial psychology	Frank and Lillian Gilbreth
1912	Chart for scheduling activities	Henry Gantt
1913	Moving assembly line	Henry Ford
1915	Mathematical model for inventory management	F. W. Harris
1930	Hawthorne studies on worker motivation	Elton Mayo
1935	Statistical procedures for sampling and quality control	H. F. Dodge, H. G. Romig, W. Shewhart, L. H. C. Tippett
1940	Operations research applications in warfare	Operations research groups
1947	Linear programming	George Dantzig
1951	Commercial digital computers	Sperry Univac
1950s	Automation	Numerous
1960s	Extensive development of quantitative tools	Numerous
1975	Emphasis an manufacturing strategy	W. Skinner
1980s	Emphasis on quality, flexibility, time-based competition, lean production	Japanese manufacturers, especially Toyota, and Taiichi Ohno
1990s	Internet, supply chains	Numerous

Trends in Business

Businesses must constantly monitor new trends and take them into account in their strategies and operations management. In this section we touch on some of the key trends that are occurring in businesses around the world.

RECENT TRENDS

Two fairly recent trends are having tremendous impact on business operations:

1. The Internet and e-business.
2. Supply chain management.

e-business Use of the Internet to transact business.

Electronic business, or **e-business**, involves the use of the Internet to transact business. E-business is changing the way business organizations interact with their customers and their suppliers. Most familiar to the general public are consumer–business transactions such as buying online or requesting information. However, business-to-business transactions, such as e-procurement, represent an increasing share of e-business. E-business is receiving increased attention from business owners and managers in developing strategies, planning, and decision making.

supply chain A sequence of activities and organizations involved in producing and delivering a good or service.

A **supply chain** is the sequence of organizations—their facilities, functions, and activities—that are involved in producing and delivering a product or service. The sequence begins with basic suppliers of raw materials and extends all the way to the final customer, as seen in Figure 1–7. Facilities might include warehouses, factories, processing centers, offices, distribution centers, and retail outlets. Functions and activities include forecasting, purchasing, inventory management, information management, quality assurance, scheduling, production, distribution, delivery, and customer service.

These trends are having a major influence on business (including accounting, finance, international business, marketing, and MIS), as well as on operations management. Their impact on operations management is discussed throughout the book, as well as in a chapter on supply chain management.

FIGURE 1-7

A simple product supply chain

CONTINUING TRENDS

A number of continuing trends influence business and operations management:

1. *Quality and process improvement.* Given a boost by the "quality revolution" of the 1980s and 1990s, quality is now ingrained in business. Where once quality was a criterion for being an "order winner," it has now become a criterion for being an "order qualifier." Some businesses use the term *total quality management (TQM)* to describe their quality efforts. A quality focus emphasizes *customer satisfaction* and often involves *teamwork.* Process improvement can result in improved quality, cost reduction, and *time reduction.* Time relates to costs and to competitive advantage, and businesses seek ways to reduce the time to bring new products and services to the marketplace, replenish supplies, and fill orders to gain a competitive edge. If two companies can provide the same product at the same price and quality, but one can deliver it four weeks earlier than the other, the quicker company will invariably get the sale. Time reductions are being achieved in processing, information retrieval, product design, and the response to customer complaints. Kodak was able to cut in half the time needed to bring a new camera to market; Union Carbide was able to cut $400 million of fixed expenses; and Bell Atlantic was able to cut the time needed to hook up long-distance carriers from 15 days to less than 1 day, at a savings of $82 million.

2. *Technology.* Technological advances have led to a vast array of new products and processes. Undoubtedly the computer has had—and will continue to have—the greatest impact on business organizations. It has revolutionized the way companies operate. Applications include product design, product features, processing technology, information processing, and communication. Technological advances in new materials, new methods, and new equipment have also made their mark on operations. Technological changes in products and processes can have major implications for production systems, affecting competitiveness and quality, but unless technology is carefully integrated into an existing system, it can do more harm than good by raising costs, reducing flexibility, and even reducing productivity. Advancements in *information technology* are having an impact on operations management. These advances began in the early 1960s using mainframe computers. Among the applications were planning and scheduling or resources. In the late 1970s, personal computers made computing power more accessible to workers and were easier to use. Applications included word processing and spreadsheet analysis. In the middle to late 1980s, network computing began to increase, with applications such as electronic data interchange (EDI) and the ability to instantaneously receive point-of-sale data. In the mid-1990s, the Internet began to play a major role in business operations.

3. *Globalization.* Global competition, global markets, global supply chains, and international operations are having a growing impact on the strategies and operations of businesses large and small around the world. The General Agreement on Tariffs and Trade (GATT) of 1994 reduced tariffs and subsidies in many countries, expanding world trade.

4. *Operations strategy.* During the 1970s and 1980s, many companies neglected to include operations strategy in their corporate strategy. Some of them paid dearly for that neglect. Now more and more companies are recognizing the importance of operations strategy on the overall success of their business as well as the necessity for relating it to their overall business strategy.

5. *Environmental issues.* Pollution control and waste disposal are key issues managers must contend with. There is increasing emphasis on reducing waste, using less toxic chemicals (e.g., lawncare services shifting to environmentally friendly approaches), recycling, making it easier for consumers to recycle products (e.g., including a shipping container for returning used laser printer cartridges), and designing products and parts that can be reused (remanufacturing products such as copying machines). The term *environmentally*

Headquartered in Battle Creek, Michigan, Kellogg Company is one of the world's leading producers of ready-to-eat cereals and grain-based convenience foods. This display of a popular Kellogg cereal is in a grocery store in Tokyo, Japan.

responsible manufacturing is sometimes used to describe these policies. Regulations are increasing in number and complexity, and penalties for pollution and inadequate control of wastes can be severe. While this has placed an added burden on some industries, society should reap tremendous benefits in cleaner air and water, and less damage to the environment in general. Some of the consequences of *not* paying attention to environmental issues can be seen in the industrialized cities of the former Soviet Union and its East European satellites, where years of neglect have resulted in catastrophic damage to the environment, which will require many years and enormous amounts of money before recovery. Waste disposal regulation has led to the creation of opportunity for businesses that specialize in waste management and recycling.

6. *Corporate downsizing.* Squeezed by competition, lagging productivity, and stockholders calling for improved profits and share prices, many corporations have responded by reducing their labor forces. This has meant that operations managers often have to find ways to produce more with fewer workers.

7. *Lean production.* This new approach to production emerged in the 1990s. It incorporates a number of the recent trends listed here, with an emphasis on quality, flexibility, time reduction, and teamwork. This has led to a *flattening* of the organizational structure, with fewer levels of management.

lean production   System that uses minimal amounts of resources to produce a high volume of high-quality goods with some variety.

Lean production systems are so named because they use much less of certain resources than mass production systems use—less space, less inventory, and fewer workers—to produce a comparable amount of output. Lean production systems use a highly skilled work force and flexible equipment. In effect, they incorporate advantages of both mass production (high volume, low unit cost) and craft production (variety and flexibility). And quality is higher than in mass production.

The skilled workers in lean production systems are more involved in maintaining and improving the system than their mass production counterparts. They are taught to stop production if they discover a defect, and to work with other employees to find and correct the cause of the defect so that it won't recur. This results in an increasing level of quality over time, and eliminates the need to inspect and rework at the end of the line.

Because lean production systems operate with lower amounts of inventory, additional emphasis is placed on anticipating when problems might occur *before* they arise, and avoiding those problems through careful planning. Even so, problems still occur at times, and quick resolution is important. Workers participate in both the planning and correction stages. Technical experts are still used, but more as consultants rather than substitutes for workers. The focus is on designing a system (products and process) so that workers will be able to achieve high levels of quality and quantity.

Compared to workers in traditional systems, much more is expected of workers in lean production systems. They must be able to function in teams, playing active roles in operating and improving the system. Individual creativity is much less important than team success. Responsibilities also are much greater, which can lead to pressure and anxiety not present in traditional systems. Moreover, a flatter organizational structure means career paths are not as steep in lean production organizations. Workers tend to become generalists rather than specialists, another contrast to more traditional organizations.

Unions often oppose conversion from a traditional system to a lean system because they view the added responsibility and multiple tasks as an expansion of job requirements without comparable increases in pay. In addition, workers sometimes complain that the company is the primary beneficiary of employee-generated improvements.

Table 1–8 provides a comparison of craft production, mass production, and lean production. Keep in mind that all three of these modes of production are in existence today.

	Craft Production	Mass Production	Lean Production
Description	High variety, customized output, with one or a few skilled workers responsible for an entire unit of output.	High volume of standardized output, emphasis on volume. Capitalizes on division of labor, specialized equipment, and interchangeable parts.	Moderate to high volume of output, with more variety than mass production. Fewer mass production buffers such as extra workers, inventory, or time. Emphasis on quality. Employee involvement and teamwork important.
Examples of Goods and Services	Home remodeling and landscaping, tailoring, portrait painting, diagnosis and treatment of injuries, surgery.	Automobiles, computers, calculators, sewing machines, compact discs, mail sorting, check clearing.	Similar to mass production.
Advantages	Wide range of choice, output tailored to customer needs.	Low cost per unit, requires mostly low-skilled workers.	Flexibility, variety, high quality of goods.
Disadvantages	Slow, requires skilled workers, few economies of scale, high cost, and low standardization.	Rigid system, difficult to accommodate changes in output volume, product design, or process design. Volume may be emphasized at the expense of quality.	No safety nets to offset any system breakdowns, fewer opportunities for employee advancement, more worker stress, requires higher-skilled workers than mass production.

TABLE 1–8

A comparison of craft, mass, and lean production

Summary

Operations management is that part of a business organization responsible for planning and coordinating the use of the organization's resources to convert inputs into outputs. The operations function is one of three primary functions of business organizations; the other two are marketing and finance.

The operations function is present in both service-oriented and product-oriented organizations. Operations decisions involve design decisions and operating decisions. Design decisions relate to capacity planning, product design, process design, layout of facilities, and selecting locations for facilities. Operating decisions relate to quality assurance, scheduling, inventory management, and project management.

The chapter provides a brief discussion of the historical evolution of operations management and recent trends in the field. Among those trends are e-business and supply chain management; global competition; increasing emphasis on quality; integrating technology into production systems; increasing worker involvement in problem solving and decision making, particularly through the use of teams; increasing emphasis on flexibility and time reduction; increasing attention to environmental issues; and lean production.

READING

Agile Manufacturing

John Holusha

www.ford.com

Agile manufacturers emphasize flexibility of operations and speed to gain a competitive edge. An example of agile manufacturing can be found in Ford Motor Company's electronic components plant in Landsdale, Pennsylvania. The plant produces about 124,000 engine controllers, antilock brake sensors, and speed control units a day. And because each product has between 400 and 500 parts, this means that there are more than 5 million individual parts to keep track of daily. Nonetheless, according to the plant manager, when an order to change a product is received, the changed units can usually be shipped within 24 hours! The plant is able to respond to change orders quickly because it has highly flexible automated equipment, computer software that has been designed to accommodate changes, and lean inventories that don't have to be worked off before changed units can be shipped.

This agile philosophy of being able to switch quickly—and economically—from one design to another, with little disruption, is being implemented throughout the Ford Motor Com-

pany. It is also being implemented in many other companies, both large and small, as they shift away from more traditional mass production methods that have heavy emphasis on volume and cost reduction into production methods that emphasize speed and flexibility. This dramatic shift in the way things are made reflects a growing trend as American companies strive to compete with foreign companies.

Perhaps central to the process of agile manufacturing is the rapid collection and processing of information. For instance, extensive use of bar codes provides information on the status of each product for Ford managers at the plant in Landsdale. Moreover, if defects are discovered, there is an electronic audit trail to trace the defect back to the exact spot in the process where it occurred, enabling management to focus efforts on correcting the cause of the problem.

Questions

1. What is an agile manufacturer?
2. What is the value of being an agile manufacturer?
3. How could the managers at the plant keep track of the five million parts each day?
4. What are the keys to being an agile manufacturer?

Source: Adapted from "Agile Manufacturers Put Premium on Speed, Flexibility" by John Holusha, the New York Times Company, 1994.

Key Terms

craft production, 21
division of labor, 22
e-business, 24
interchangeable parts, 22
lead time, 11
lean production, 26
mass production, 22

model, 17
operations management, 4
Pareto phenomenon, 20
supply chain, 24
system, 19
value-added, 8

Discussion and Review Questions

1. Briefly describe the term *operations management.*
2. Identify the three major functional areas of business organizations and briefly describe how they interrelate.
3. Describe the operations function and the nature of the operations manager's job.
4. List five important differences between goods production and service operations.
5. Briefly discuss each of these terms related to the historical evolution of operations management:
    a. Industrial Revolution
    b. Scientific management
    c. Interchangeable parts
    d. Division of labor
6. Why are services important? Why is manufacturing important?
7. What are models and why are they important?
8. Can you think of a business that doesn't have operations management?
9. List the trade-offs you would consider for each of these decisions:
    a. Driving your own car versus public transportation.
    b. Buying a computer now versus waiting for an improved model.
    c. Buying a new car versus buying a used car.
    d. Speaking up in class versus waiting to get called on by the instructor.

10. Describe each of these systems: craft production, mass production, and lean production.

11. Why might some workers prefer not to work in a lean production environment? Why might some managers resist a change from a more traditional mode of production to lean production?

12. How has technological change affected you? Are there any downsides to technological change? Explain.

13. Identify some of the current trends in operations management and relate them to recent news items or to personal experience.

14. Why do people do things that are unethical?

Memo writing exercises are intended to help you strengthen your written communication skills while applying what you have learned to issues of managerial concern. The following memo provides information on writing good memos. Use it as a guide.

Memo Writing Exercises

MEMORANDUM

To: Students using this book

From: W. Stevenson

Date: April 4, 2001

Subject: Memo writing exercises

The purpose of this memo is to introduce you to an important mode of business communication, and to provide you with information on how to write a memo.

Memos are often used to convey information within an organization, but they are also used to communicate with people outside the organization, such as suppliers, distributors, and sometimes, customers.

Memos tend to be less formal than letters. Memos should communicate business information in an organized, concise format. Even so, their length and degree of formality depend in part on the purpose of the memo, the amount of information to convey, and the intended audience. Thus, a memo reporting financial information to the chief executive officer would be more formal and probably longer than a memo to employees about the company picnic.

A variety of memo styles can be used. One style is illustrated by this memo, which is informational.

1. Use the first paragraph to state the purpose of the memo.
2. Use the second paragraph to provide major details of a proposal or major reasons for a decision or suggestion, or to indicate why you agree or disagree with a proposal or idea.
3. Use the third paragraph for minor details.
4. In a long memo, you may want to end by again stating your position on the subject.

1. Suppose that your boss, Tony Roman, who is the operations manager of your company, sends you a memo asking for your input on holding joint planning sessions with people from marketing and finance. A portion of that memo follows:

   Gail in Marketing and Jim in Finance have been bugging me lately about holding joint meetings. They're real gung-ho on this. But I'm a little concerned about agreeing to it. I don't want them to get the impression that they can come in here and tell us what to do. They don't really understand what it is we do or the kinds of problems we have. I'm sure they think we aren't doing as well as we could, but that's not any of their concern. I don't know why they just don't concentrate on what they do, and leave operations to us.

   Write a one-page memo that summarizes the potential benefits of holding joint planning meetings with Marketing and Finance.

2. Assume the role of a mid-level manager of a small company. The CEO, Rachael Barker, wants your views on a new computer network she is considering. The current network is adequate, but

the new one will provide much greater capabilities for managing files, word processing, and accessing the database.

Write a one-page memo in which you list (1) the key factors that you believe must be taken into account in making the decision, and (2) the trade-offs that must be considered.

3. Write a brief memo, responding to this one:

MEMORANDUM

To: (*Your name*), V.P. of Manufacturing

From: Deiter Smith, Production Supervisor, second shift

Date: Monday

Re: Accidental spill

We recently experienced an accidental discharge of mildly toxic chemicals into the creek that runs past one of our plants. Although there have been a few complaints of contamination from downstream property owners, I don't think that the spill can be traced back to our plant. Besides, other nearby companies have been getting away with more serious abuses for years, so let them take the heat.

I am confident that this is a one-time occurrence, so let's not blow the whole thing out of proportion. If we were to have to pay for a cleanup, this would have a big impact on quarterly profits, and our stockholders wouldn't like that one bit. Furthermore, in light of our recent efforts to promote an image of an environmental-friendly company, I say we should definitely keep quiet about this and let things die down.

What do you think?

4. Using your computer, load and then open the CD-ROM for this book. Click on "What's on this CD-ROM?" Write a half-page memo to your instructor on which of the items on the list you feel will be most helpful to you in this course.

CASE

Hazel

Hazel had worked for the same Fortune 500 company for almost 15 years. Although the company had gone through some tough times, things were starting to turn around. Customer orders were up, and quality and productivity had improved dramatically from what they had been only a few years earlier due to a companywide quality improvement program. So it came as a real shock to Hazel and about 400 of her coworkers when they were suddenly terminated following the new CEO's decision to downsize the company.

After recovering from the initial shock, Hazel tried to find employment elsewhere. Despite her efforts, after eight months of searching she was no closer to finding a job than the day she started. Her funds were being depleted and she was getting more discouraged. There was one bright spot, though: She was able to bring in a little money by mowing lawns for her neighbors. She got involved quite by chance when she heard one neighbor remark that now that his children were on their own, nobody was around to cut the grass. Almost jokingly,

Hazel asked him how much he'd be willing to pay. Soon Hazel was mowing the lawns of five neighbors. Other neighbors wanted her to work on their lawns, but she didn't feel that she could spare any more time from her job search.

However, as the rejection letters began to pile up, Hazel knew she had to make an important decision in her life. On a rainy Tuesday morning, she decided to go into business for herself—taking care of neighborhood lawns. She was relieved to give up the stress of job hunting, and she was excited about the prospect of being her own boss. But she was also fearful of being completely on her own. Nevertheless, Hazel was determined to make a go of it.

At first, business was a little slow, but once people realized Hazel was available, many asked her to take care of their lawns. Some people were simply glad to turn the work over to her; others switched from professional lawn care services. By the end of her first year in business, Hazel knew she could earn a living this way. She also performed other services such as fertilizing lawns, weeding gardens, and trimming shrubbery. Business became so good that Hazel hired two part-time workers to assist her and, even then, she believed she could expand further if she wanted to.

Questions

1. In what ways are Hazel's customers most likely to judge the quality of her lawn care services?

2. Hazel is the operations manager of her business. Among her responsibilities are forecasting, inventory management, scheduling, quality assurance, and maintenance.

   a. What kinds of things would likely require forecasts?

   b. What inventory items does Hazel probably have? Name one inventory decision she has to make periodically.

   c. What scheduling must she do? What things might occur to disrupt schedules and cause Hazel to reschedule?

   d. How important is quality assurance to Hazel's business? Explain.

   e. What kinds of maintenance must be performed?

3. What are some of the trade-offs that Hazel probably considered relative to:

   a. Working for a company instead of for herself?

   b. Expanding the business?

   c. Launching a website?

4. The town is considering an ordinance that would prohibit putting grass clippings at the curb for pickup because local landfills cannot handle the volume. What options might Hazel consider if the ordinance is passed? Name two advantages and two drawbacks of each option.

5. Hazel decided to offer the students who worked for her a bonus of $25 for ideas on how to improve the business, and they provided several good ideas. One idea that she initially rejected now appears to hold great promise. The student who proposed the idea has left, and is currently working for a competitor. Should Hazel send that student a check for the idea?

CASE

Total Recall

In mid-2000, the Firestone Tire Company issued a recall of some of its tires—those mounted on certain sport utility vehicles (SUVs) of the Ford Motor Company. This was done in response to reports that tire treads on some SUVs separated in use, causing accidents, some of which involved fatal injuries as vehicles rolled over.

At first, Firestone denied there was a problem with its tires, but it issued the recall under pressure from consumer groups and various government agencies. All of the tires in question were produced at the same tire plant, and there were calls to shut down that facility. Firestone suggested that Ford incorrectly matched the wrong tires with its SUVs. There was also the suggestion that the shock absorbers of the SUVs were rubbing against the tires, causing or aggravating the problem.

Both Ford and Firestone denied that this had been an ongoing problem. However, there was a public outcry when it was learned that Firestone had previously issued recalls of these tires in South America, but had not informed officials in other countries. Moreover, both companies had settled at least one lawsuit involving an accident caused by tread separation several years earlier.

This case raises a number of issues, some related to possible causes, as well as ethical issues.

Discuss each of these factors and their actual or potential relevance to what happened:

1. Product design.

2. Quality control.

3. Ethics.

OPERATIONS TOUR

Wegmans Food Markets

www.wegmans.com

Wegmans Food Markets, Inc., is one of the premier grocery chains in the United States. Headquartered in Rochester, New York, Wegmans operates over 70 stores, mainly in Rochester, Buffalo, and Syracuse. There are also a handful of stores elsewhere in New York State, New Jersey, and Pennsylvania. The company employs over 28,000 people, and has annual sales of over $2.0 billion. In addition to supermarkets, the company operates Chase-Pitkin Home and Garden Centers and an egg farm.

Wegmans has a strong reputation for offering its customers high product quality and excellent service. Through a combination of market research, trial and error, and listening to its customers, Wegmans has evolved into a very successful organization. In fact, Wegmans is so good at what it does that

Each supermarket has an in-store bakery.

grocery chains all over the country send representatives to Wegmans for a firsthand look at operations.

Superstores

Many of the company's stores are giant 100,000 square foot superstores, double or triple the size of average supermarkets. You can get an idea about the size of these stores from this: they usually have between 25 and 35 checkout lanes, and during busy periods, all of the checkouts are in operation. A superstore typically employs from 500 to 600 people.

Individual stores differ somewhat in terms of actual size and some special features. Aside from the features normally found in supermarkets, they generally have a full-service deli (typically a 40-foot display case), a 500 square foot fisherman's wharf that has perhaps 10 different fresh fish offerings most days, a large bakery section (each store bakes its own bread, rolls, cakes, pies, and pastries), and extra large produce sections. They also offer film processing, a complete pharmacy, a card shop, video rentals, and an Olde World Cheese™ section. In-store floral shops range in size up to 800 square feet of floor space and offer a wide variety of fresh-cut flowers, flower arrangements, vases, and plants. In-store card shops cover over 1,000 square feet of floor space. The bulk foods department provides customers with the opportunity to select the quantities they desire from a vast array of foodstuffs and some nonfood items such as birdseed and pet food.

Each store is a little different. Among the special features in some stores are a dry cleaning department, a wokery, and a salad bar. Some stores feature a Market Cafe™ that has different food stations, each devoted to preparing and serving a

certain type of food. For example, one station will have pizza and other Italian specialties, and another oriental food, and still another chicken or fish. There will also be a sandwich bar, a salad bar, and a dessert station. Customers often wander among stations as they decide what to order. In some Market Cafes, diners can have wine with their meals and have brunch on Sundays. In several affluent locations, customers can stop in on their way home from work and choose from a selection of freshly prepared dinner entrees such as medallions of beef with herb butter, chicken Marsala, stuffed flank steak with mushrooms, grilled salmon, Cajun tuna, and crab cakes, and accompaniments such as roasted red potatoes, grilled vegetables, and Caesar salad. Many Wegmans stores offer ready-made sandwiches as well as made-to-order sandwiches during the lunch hour. Some stores have a coffee shop section with tables and chairs where shoppers can enjoy regular or specialty coffees and a variety of tempting pastries.

Produce Department

The company prides itself on fresh produce. Produce is replenished as often as 12 times a day. The larger stores have produce sections that are four to five times the size of a produce section in an average supermarket. Wegmans offers locally grown produce in season. Wegmans uses a "farm to market" system whereby some local growers deliver their produce directly to individual stores, bypassing the main warehouse. That reduces the company's inventory holding costs and gets the produce into the stores as quickly as possible. Growers may use specially designed containers that go right onto the store floor instead of large bins. This avoids the bruising that often occurs

Wegmans' Market Café™

Wegmans' "farm to market" allows local growers to deliver produce directly to stores.

when fruits and vegetables are transferred from bins to display shelves and the need to devote labor to transfer the produce to shelves.

Meat Department

In addition to large display cases of both fresh and frozen meat products, many stores have a full-service butcher shop that offers a variety of fresh meat products and where butchers are available to provide customized cuts of meat for customers.

Ordering

Each department handles its own ordering. Although sales records are available from records of items scanned at the checkouts, they are not used directly for replenishing stock. Other factors, such as pricing, special promotions, local circumstances (e.g., festivals, weather conditions) must all be taken into account. However, for seasonal periods, such as holidays, managers often check scanner records to learn what past demand was during a comparable period.

The superstores typically receive one truckload of goods per day from the main warehouse. During peak periods, a store may receive two truckloads from the main warehouse. The short lead time greatly reduces the length of time an item might be out of stock, unless the main warehouse is also out of stock.

The company exercises strict control over suppliers, insisting on product quality and on-time deliveries.

Inventory Management

Wegmans uses a companywide system to keep track of inventory. Departments take a monthly inventory count to verify the

amount shown in the companywide system. Each department is responsible for ordering product. Departments receive a periodic report indicating how many days of inventory the department has on hand. Having an appropriate amount on hand is important to department managers: If they have too much inventory on hand, that will add to their department's costs, whereas having too little inventory will be reflected in low profits for the department.

Employees

The company recognizes the value of good employees. It typically invests an average of $7,000 to train each new employee. In addition to learning about store operations, new employees learn the importance of good customer service and how to provide it. The employees are helpful, cheerfully answering customer questions or handling complaints. Employees are motivated through a combination of compensation, profit sharing, and benefits. In a *Fortune* survey of employees on the best companies to work for in the United States, Wegmans ranked #16.

(Fortune, January 12, 1998, p. 85.)

Quality

Quality and customer satisfaction are utmost in the minds of Wegmans management and its employees. Private label food items as well as name brands are regularly evaluated in test kitchens, along with potential new products. Managers are responsible for checking and maintaining product and service quality in their department. Moreover, employees are encouraged to report problems to their managers.

If a customer is dissatisfied with an item, and returns it, or even a portion of the item, the customer is offered a choice of a replacement or a refund. If the item is a Wegmans brand food item, it is then sent to the test kitchen to determine the cause of the problem. If the cause can be determined, corrective action is taken.

Questions:

1. How do customers judge the quality of a supermarket?

2. Indicate how and why each of these factors is important to the successful operation of a supermarket:

   a. Customer satisfaction.

   b. Forecasting.

   c. Capacity planning.

   d. Location.

   e. Inventory management.

   f. Layout of the store.

   g. Scheduling.

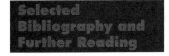

Bounds, Gregory, H. Dobbins, and Oscar S. Fowler. *Management: A Total Quality Perspective.* Cincinnati: South-Western Publishing, 1995.

Colvin, Geoffrey. "Managing in the Info Era." *Fortune,* March 6, 2000, pp. F6–F9.

Crainer, Stuart. *The Management Century.* New York: Jossey-Bass, 2000.

Hammer, Michael, and James Campy. *Reengineering the Corporation.* New York: Harper Business, 1993.

Hopp, William J., and Mark Spearman. *Factory Physics: Foundations of Manufacturing Management.* 2nd ed. Burr Ridge, IL: Irwin, 2001.

Owens, James. *Business Ethics.* Arlington, VA: Executive Publications, 1989.

Pfeiffer, Raymond S. *Ethics on the Job: Cases and Strategies.* Belmont, CA: Wadsworth Publishing Co., 1999.

Womack, James P., Daniel Jones, and Daniel Roos. *The Machine that Changed the World.* New York: Harper Perennial, 1991.

CHAPTER TWO

Competitiveness, Strategy, and Productivity

CHAPTER OUTLINE

Introduction, 38

Competitiveness, 38

Strategy, 40

   Mission, 40

   Operations Strategy, 43

   Strategy Formulation, 44

   Quality and Time Strategies, 48

Reading: Time-Based Innovation, 49

Productivity, 51

   Computing Productivity, 52

   Productivity in the Service Sector, 55

   Factors that Affect Productivity, 55

   Improving Productivity, 56

Summary, 57

Key Terms, 57

Solved Problems, 57

Discussion and Review
   Questions, 58

Memo Writing Exercises, 58

Problems, 59

Reading: Productivity Gains at
   Whirlpool, 60

Cases: An American Tragedy: How
   a Good Company Died, 60

Home-Style Cookies, 61

Hazel Revisited, 63

Reading: Economic Vitality, 63

Operations Tour: The US Postal
   Service, 65

Selected Bibliography and Further
   Reading, 66

LEARNING OBJECTIVES

After completing this chapter, you should be able to:

1 List and briefly discuss the primary ways that business organizations compete.

2 List five reasons for the poor competitiveness of some companies.

3 Define the term *strategy* and explain why strategy is important for competitiveness.

4 Contrast *strategy* and *tactics.*

5 Discuss and compare organization strategy and operations strategy, and explain why it is important to link them.

6 Describe and give examples of *time-based* strategies.

7 Define the term *productivity* and explain why it is important to organizations and to countries.

8 List some of the reasons for poor productivity and some ways of improving it.

The Cold Hard Facts

The name of the game is competition. Those who understand how to play the game will succeed; those who don't are doomed to failure. And don't think the game is just companies competing with each other. In companies that have multiple factories or divisions producing the same item or service, factories or divisions sometimes find themselves competing with each other. When a competitor—another company or a sister factory or division in the same company can turn out products better, cheaper, and faster, that spells real trouble for the factory or division that is performing at a lower level. The trouble can be layoffs or even a shutdown if the managers can't turn things around. The bottom line? Better quality, higher productivity, lower costs, and the ability to quickly respond to customer needs are more important than ever, and the bar is getting higher. Business organizations need to develop solid strategies for dealing with these issues.

This chapter discusses competitiveness, strategy, and productivity: three separate but related topics that are vitally important to business organizations. *Competitiveness* relates to how effective an organization is in the marketplace compared with other organizations that offer similar products or services; *strategy* relates to the plans that determine the direction an organization takes in pursuing its goals; and *productivity* relates to effective use of resources.

Slumping productivity gains in the late 1980s and the impressive successes of foreign competition in the U.S. marketplace caused many U.S. companies to rethink their strategies and to place increased emphasis on *operations strategy*.

Introduction

In this chapter you will learn about the different ways companies compete and why some firms do a very good job of competing. You will learn how effective strategies can lead to competitive organizations, and you will learn what productivity is, why it is important, and what organizations can do to improve it.

Competitiveness

competitiveness How effectively an organization meets the needs of customers relative to others that offer similar goods or services.

Companies must be **competitive** to sell their goods and services in the marketplace. Competitiveness is an important factor in determining whether a company prospers, barely gets by, or fails. Business organizations compete with one another in a variety of ways. These include price, quality, product or service differentiation, flexibility, time to perform certain activities, service, and managers and workers.

1. *Price* is the amount a customer must pay for the product or service. If all other factors are equal, customers will choose the product or service that has the lowest price. Organizations that compete on price may settle for lower profit margins, but most focus on lowering costs of goods or services.

2. *Quality* refers to materials and workmanship as well as design. Usually, it relates to a buyer's perceptions of how well the product or service will serve its intended purpose.

3. *Product* or *service differentiation* refers to any special features (e.g., design, cost, quality, ease of use, convenient location, warranty) that cause a product or service to be perceived by the buyer as more suitable than a competitor's product or service.

4. *Flexibility* is the ability to respond to changes. The better a company or department is at responding to changes, the greater its competitive advantage over another company that is not as responsive. The changes might relate to increases or decreases in volume demanded, or to changes in the design of goods or services.

5. *Time* refers to a number of different aspects of an organization's operations. One is how quickly a product or service is delivered to a customer. This can be facilitated by faster movement of information backward through the supply chain. Another is how

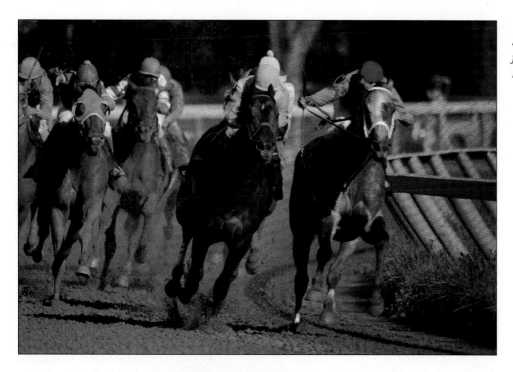

"Competitiveness" at Saratoga Springs: Thoroughbreds at the finish line in a New York Racing Association contest.

At Hertz, there is no paperwork and no waiting line once the customer is enrolled in their 'Gold' services. Car keys to a pre-selected vehicle are provided, along with a copy of the rental agreement, as soon as the driver's license is shown.

quickly new products or services are developed and brought to the market. Still another is the rate at which improvements in products or processes are made.

6. *Service* might involve after-sale activities that are perceived by customers as value-added, such as delivery, setup, warranty work, technical support, or extra attention while work is in progress, such as courtesy, keeping the customer informed, and attention to little details.

7. *Managers* and *workers* are the people at the heart and soul of an organization, and if they are competent and motivated, they can provide a distinct competitive edge by their skills and the ideas they create. One skill that is often overlooked is answering the telephone. How complaint calls or requests for information are handled can be a positive or a negative. For example, if automated answering is used, that can turn off some callers. If the person answering the call is rude, not helpful, or cuts off the call, that can produce a negative image. Conversely, if calls are handled promptly and cheerfully, that can produce a positive image and, potentially, a competitive advantage.

Some of these dimensions overlap. For example, several of the items on the list may come under the heading of *quality*.

Another issue that can be overlooked in the drive to be more competitive is the importance of *ethical behavior;* it is something that all managers should adhere to and stress to their subordinates.

Also, in the past, business organizations tended to focus inward as they sought to become more competitive by positively affecting one or more of the above-mentioned items. More recently, however, business organizations have broadened their focus to include their *supply chains,* recognizing that other organizations in their supply chains also impact all or most of the items on the preceding list.

Organizations fail, or perform poorly, for a variety of reasons. Being aware of those reasons can help managers avoid making similar mistakes. Among the chief reasons are the following:

1. Putting too much emphasis on short-term financial performance at the expense of research and development.
2. Failing to take advantage of strengths and opportunities, and/or failing to recognize competitive threats.
3. Neglecting operations strategy.
4. Placing too much emphasis on product and service design and not enough on process design and improvement.
5. Neglecting investments in capital and human resources.
6. Failing to establish good internal communications and cooperation among different functional areas.
7. Failing to consider customer wants and needs.

The key to successfully competing is to determine what customers want and then directing efforts toward meeting (or even exceeding) customer expectations. There are two basic issues that must be addressed. First: What do the customers want? Which items on the preceding list of the ways business organizations compete are important to customers? Second: What is the best way to satisfy those wants?

Operations must work with marketing to obtain information on the relative importance of the various items to each major customer or target market.

Understanding competitive issues can help managers develop successful strategies.

Strategy

strategy A plan for achieving organizational goals.

Strategies are plans for achieving goals. An organization's strategy has a long-term impact on the nature and characteristics of the organization. In large measure, strategies affect the ability of an organization to compete or, in the case of a nonprofit organization, the ability to serve its intended purpose.

In this section, you will learn about both organization strategies and operations strategies, and how they influence an organization. The nature of an organization's strategies depends on its mission.

MISSION

mission The reason for existence of an organization.

mission statement A statement of purpose that serves as a guide for strategy and decision making.

An organization's **mission** is the basis of the organization—the reason for its existence. Missions vary from organization to organization, depending on the nature of their business. Table 2–1 provides some sample mission statements.

It is important that an organization have a clear and simple **mission statement,** one which answers the question, "What business are we in?" The mission statement should serve to guide formulation of strategies for the organization as well as decision making at all levels. Not all organizations have mission statements; perhaps their leaders lack an awareness of how important such a statement is, or perhaps they are unclear about what the mission should be. Without a clear mission, an organization is unlikely to achieve its true potential, because there is little direction for formulating strategies.

Globe Metallurgical	To provide products and services that lead the silicon metal and ferroalloy industries in the highest quality at the lowest manufacturing costs. To maintain our lead, we must continually improve our products and services. We will meet our customers' needs with products, services, and technologies that represent true value. This will ensure long-term profits for growth, job security for our employees, and give our owners and shareholders sustained, high investment returns. Reprinted by permission of Globe Metallurgical, Beverly, OH.	
IBM	We create, develop, and manufacture the industry's most advanced information technologies, including computer systems, software, networking systems, storage devices, and microelectronics. We have two fundamental missions: • We strive to lead in the creation, development, and manufacture of the most advanced information technologies. • We translate advanced technologies into value for our customers as the world's largest information services company. Our professionals worldwide provide expertise within specific industries, consulting services, systems integration, and solution development and technical support. Reprinted by permission of IBM, Armonk, NY.	
Skynet Worldwide Courier	The Skynet Worldwide Courier Network sets the standard for international delivery and distribution services by consistently exceeding customer expectations. Skynet delivers customer satisfaction by: • Integrating all aspects of the transportation process. • Personalizing service worldwide. • Investing in quality people and technology. • Innovating and adapting to meet customers' unique and changing requirements. Reprinted by permission of Skynet Worldwide Courier, Miami, FL.	
Union Carbide	To grow the value of the Corporation by successfully pursuing strategies that capitalize on our business strengths in chemicals and polymers; To successfully execute wealth creation strategies that consistently deliver value to all stakeholders over the course of the business cycle. Corporate Values • Safety and environmental excellence • Customer focus • Technology leadership • People excellence • Simplicity and focus Reprinted by permission of Union Carbide, Danbury, CT.	

TABLE 2-1

Selected company mission statements

www.ibm.com

www.unioncarbide.com

Strategies and Tactics. A mission statement provides a general direction for an organization and gives rise to organizational *goals*, which provide substance to the overall mission. For example, one goal of an organization may be to capture a certain percentage of market share for a product; another goal may be to achieve a certain level of profitability. Taken together, the goals and the mission establish a destination for the organization.

s it a strategic, tactical, or operational issue? Sometimes the same issue may apply to all three levels. However, a key difference is the time frame. From a strategic perspective, long-term implications are most relevant. From tactical and operational perspectives, the time frames are much shorter. In fact, the operational time frame is often measured in days.

FIGURE 2-1

*Planning and decision
making is hierarchical in
organizations.*

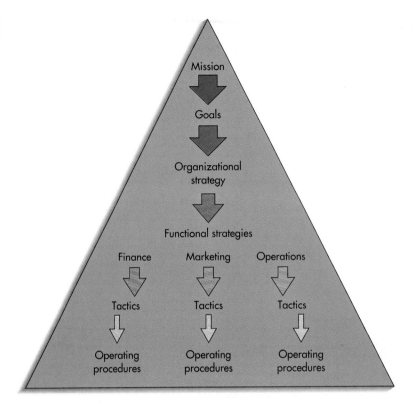

If you think of goals as destinations, then strategies are the roadmaps for reaching the destinations. Strategies provide *focus* for decision making. Generally speaking, organizations have overall strategies called *organization strategies,* which relate to the entire organization, and they also have *functional strategies,* which relate to each of the functional areas of the organization. The functional strategies should support the overall strategies of the organization, just as the organizational strategies should support the goals and mission of the organization.

tactics The methods and actions taken to accomplish strategies.

Tactics are the methods and actions used to accomplish strategies. They are more specific in nature than strategies, and they provide guidance and direction for carrying out actual *operations,* which need the most specific and detailed plans and decision making in an organization. You might think of tactics as the "how to" part of the process (e.g., how to reach the destination, following the strategy roadmap) and operations as the actual "doing" part of the process.

It should be apparent that the overall relationship that exists from the mission down to actual operations is *hierarchical* in nature. This is illustrated in Figure 2–1.

A simple example may help to put this hierarchy into perspective.

Example 1

Rita is a high school student in Southern California. She would like to have a career in business, have a good job, and earn enough income to live comfortably.

A possible scenario for achieving her goals might look something like this:

Mission: Live a good life.

Goal: Successful career, good income.

Strategy: Obtain a college education.

Tactics: Select a college and a major; decide how to finance college.

Operations: Register, buy books, take courses, study.

		Management Level	Time Horizon	Scope	Level of Detail	Relates to
The Overall Organization	Mission	Top	Long	Broad	Low	Survival, profitability
	Strategy	Senior	Long	Broad	Low	Growth rate, market share
Production/ Operations	Strategic	Senior	Moderate to long	Broad	Low	Product design, choice of location, choice of technology, new facilities
	Tactical	Middle	Moderate	Moderate	Moderate	Employment levels, output levels, equipment selection, facility layout
	Operational	Low	Short	Narrow	High	Scheduling personnel, adjusting output rates, inventory management, purchasing

TABLE 2–2

Comparison of mission, organization strategy, and operations strategy

OPERATIONS STRATEGY

The organization strategy provides the overall direction for the organization. It is broad in scope, covering the entire organization. **Operations strategy** is narrower in scope, dealing primarily with the operations aspect of the organization. Operations strategy relates to products, processes, methods, operating resources, quality, costs, lead times, and scheduling. Table 2–2 provides a comparison of an organization's mission, its overall strategy, and its operations strategy, tactics, and operations.

In order for operations strategy to be truly effective, it is important to link it to organization strategy; that is, the two should not be formulated independently. Rather, formulation of organization strategy should take into account the realities of operations' strengths and weaknesses, capitalizing on strengths and dealing with weaknesses. Similarly, operations strategy must be consistent with the overall strategy of the organization, and formulated to support the goals of the organization. This requires that senior managers work with functional units to formulate strategies that will support, rather than conflict with, each other and the overall strategy of the organization. As obvious as this may seem, it doesn't always happen in practice. Instead, we may find power struggles between various functional units. These struggles are detrimental to the organization because they pit functional units against each other rather than focusing their energy on making the organization more competitive and better able to serve the customer. Some of the latest approaches in organizations, involving teams of managers and workers, may reflect a growing awareness of the synergistic effects of working together rather than competing internally.

Operations strategy can have a major influence on the competitiveness of an organization. If it is well designed and well executed, there is a good chance that the organization will be successful; if it is not well designed or executed, the chances are much less that the organization will be successful.

In the 1970s and early 80s, operations strategy was often neglected in favor of marketing and financial strategies. That may have occurred because many chief executive officers did not come from operations backgrounds and perhaps did not fully appreciate the importance of the operations function. Mergers and acquisitions were common; leveraged buyouts were used, and conglomerates were formed that joined dissimilar operations. These did little to add value to the organization; they were purely financial in nature. Decisions were often made by individuals who were unfamiliar with the business, frequently to the detriment of that business. Meanwhile, foreign competitors began to fill the resulting vacuum with a careful focus on operations strategy.

In the late 1980s and early 90s, many companies began to realize this approach was not working. They recognized that they were less competitive than other companies. This caused them to focus attention on operations strategy. Toward that end, many firms are developing strategies that have *quality* or *time* as their central concern.

This correlates with a survey of manufacturing executives and managers who were asked to identify strategic and tactical issues that U.S. manufacturers must focus on to be

operations strategy The approach, consistent with the organization strategy, that is used to guide the operations function.

competitive on a global basis in the 1990s.[1] The top two strategic issues were quality management and manufacturing strategy. The top two tactical issues were quality control, and manufacturing planning and control systems. A key element of both organization strategy and operations strategy is strategy formulation.

STRATEGY FORMULATION

To formulate an effective strategy, senior management must take into account the *distinctive competencies* of the organizations, and they must *scan the environment.* They must determine what competitors are doing, or planning to do, and take that into account. They must critically examine other factors that could have either positive or negative effects. This is sometimes referred to as the *SWOT* approach (strengths, weaknesses, opportunities, and threats).

In formulating a successful strategy, organizations must take into account both order qualifiers and order winners. Terry Hill, in his book *Manufacturing Strategy,* describes **order qualifiers** as those characteristics that potential customers perceive as minimum standards of acceptability to be considered as a potential for purchase. However, that may not be sufficient to get a potential customer to purchase from the organization. **Order winners** are those characteristics of an organization's goods or services that cause them to be perceived as better than the competition.

Characteristics such as price, delivery reliability, delivery speed, and quality can be order qualifiers or order winners. Thus, quality may be an order winner in some situations, whereas in others, it may be an order qualifier. Over time, a characteristic that was once an order winner may become an order qualifier, and vice versa.

Obviously, it is important to determine the set of order qualifier characteristics and the set of order winner characteristics, and it is also necessary to decide on the relative importance of each characteristic so that appropriate attention can be given to the various characteristics. Marketing must make that determination and communicate it to operations.

Distinctive competencies are those special attributes or abilities possessed by an organization that give it a *competitive edge.* In effect, distinctive competencies relate to the ways that organizations compete. As noted previously, these can include price (based on some combination of low costs of resources such as labor and materials, low operating costs, and low production costs); quality (high performance or consistent quality); time (rapid delivery or on-time delivery); flexibility (variety or volume); customer service; and location. Table 2–3 lists the major distinctive competencies and examples of services and companies that exhibit those competencies.

The most effective organizations seem to use an approach that develops distinctive competencies based on customer needs as well as on what the competition is doing. Marketing and operations work closely to match customer needs with operations capabilities. Competitor competencies are important for several reasons. For example, if a competitor is able to supply high-quality products, it may be necessary to meet that high quality as a baseline. However, merely *matching* a competitor is usually not sufficient to gain market share. It may be necessary to exceed the quality level of the competitor or gain an edge by excelling in one or more other dimensions, such as rapid delivery or service after the sale.

Some of the strategies various Japanese manufacturing companies have employed since World War II are:

- *Low labor cost strategy.* Immediately after the war, exploited the (then) inexpensive labor pool.
- *Scale-based strategy.* During the 1960s, used capital-intensive methods to achieve higher labor productivity and lower unit costs.

order qualifiers Characteristics that customers perceive as minimum standards of acceptability to be considered as a potential for purchase.

order winners Characteristics of an organization's goods or services that cause it to be perceived as better than the competition.

distinctive competencies The special attributes or abilities that give an organization a competitive edge.

---

[1]Manoj K. Malhotra, Daniel C. Steele, and Varun Grover, "Important Strategic and Tactical Manufacturing Issues in the 1990s." *Decision Sciences* 25, no. 2 (March/April 1994), pp. 189–214.

	Competency	Examples of Companies or Services
Price	Low cost	U.S. first-class postage
		Motel-6, Red Roof Inns
		Mail-order computers
Quality	High-performance design and/or high quality	Sony TV
		Lexus, Cadillac
		Disneyland
		Five-star restaurants or hotels
	Consistent quality	Coca-Cola, PepsiCo
		Kodak, Xerox, Motorola
		Electrical power
Time	Rapid delivery	McDonald's restaurants
		Express Mail
		UPS
		Domino's Pizza
	On-time delivery	One-hour photo
		Federal Express
		Express Mail
Flexibility	Variety	Burger King ("Have it your way")
		Hospital emergency room
	Volume	McDonald's ("Buses welcome")
		Toyota
		Supermarkets (additional checkouts)
Service	Superior customer service	Disneyland
		Hewlett-Packard
		IBM
		Nordstroms
Location	Convenience	Supermarkets, dry cleaners
		Mall stores
		Service stations
		Banks, ATMs

TABLE 2-3

Examples of distinctive competencies

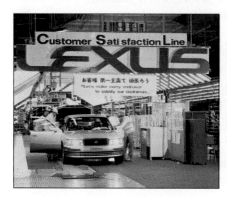

Toyota, Japan's largest automobile manufacturer, also markets the upscale, award winning Lexus line. Quality is highly valued, and workers have the authority to stop the production line if quality problems are encountered.

Automatic teller machines (ATMs) are numerous, carefully located for customer convenience, and available 24 hours. Networks have expanded to serve international customers.

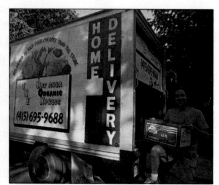

Delivering groceries and specialty food items directly to the customer is a successful new e-based business. This organic produce truck delivers perishables to a customer in San Rafael, California.

  www.lexus.com/

- *Focused factories strategy.* During the 1970s, used smaller factories that focused on narrow product lines to take advantage of specialization and achieve higher quality.
- *Flexible factories strategy.* During the 1980s, reduced the time needed to incorporate new product and process designs. Used flexible equipment that allowed volume and design changes, as well as product variety. Continued to stress quality.[2]

In the 1990s, the leading Japanese manufacturers adopted an approach that incorporates introducing new product features and practicing continuous improvement of both products and processes.

environmental scanning The considering of events and trends that present threats or opportunities for a company.

Environmental scanning is the considering of events and trends that present either threats or opportunities for the organization. Generally these include competitors' activities; changing consumer needs; legal, economic, political, and environmental issues; the potential for new markets; and the like. Depending on the nature of an organization and the locations of its customers, these issues may be global, national, regional, or local. Thus, the disintegration of the former Soviet Union in 1991–92, the reunification of Germany, and the formation of the European Union would have major input into the strategic planning of such global companies as the Ford Motor Company, General Motors, Kodak, Coca-Cola, PepsiCo, and IBM, but would have little direct impact on local businesses such as supermarkets or landscaping firms. Companies that are *local suppliers* for global companies, however, may be affected by international events.

Another key factor to consider when developing strategies is technological change, which can present real opportunities and threats to an organization. Technological changes occur in products (high-definition TV, improved computer chips, improved cellular telephone systems, and improved designs for earthquakeproof structures); in services (faster order processing, faster delivery); and in processes (robotics, automation, computer-assisted processing, point-of-sale scanners, and flexible manufacturing systems). The obvious benefit is a competitive edge; the risk is that incorrect choices, poor execution, and higher-than-expected operating costs will create competitive *disadvantages*.

Important factors may be internal or external. The key external factors are:

1. *Economic conditions.* These include the general health and direction of the economy, inflation and deflation, interest rates, tax laws, and tariffs.
2. *Political conditions.* These include favorable or unfavorable attitudes toward business, political stability or instability, and wars.
3. *Legal environment.* This includes antitrust laws, government regulations, trade restrictions, minimum wage laws, product liability laws and recent court experience, labor laws, and patents.
4. *Technology.* This can include the rate at which product innovations are occurring, current and future process technology (equipment, materials handling), and design technology.
5. *Competition.* This includes the number and strength of competitors, the basis of competition (price, quality, special features), and the ease of market entry.
6. *Markets.* This includes size, location, brand loyalties, ease of entry, potential for growth, long-term stability, and demographics.

The organization must also take into account various *internal factors* that relate to possible strengths or weaknesses. Among the key internal factors are:

1. *Human resources.* These include the skills and abilities of managers and workers; special talents (creativity, designing, problem solving); loyalty to the organization; expertise; dedication; and experience.
2. *Facilities and equipment.* Capacities, location, age, and cost to maintain or replace can have a significant impact on operations.

---

[2]George Stalk Jr. and Thomas Hout, "Competing Against Time," *Research and Technology Management* 33, no. 2 (March–April 1990), pp. 19–24.

3. *Financial resources.* Cash flow, access to additional funding, existing debt burden, and cost of capital are important considerations.

4. *Customers.* Loyalty, existing relationships, and understanding of wants and needs are important.

5. *Products and services.* These include existing products and services, and the potential for new products and services.

6. *Technology.* This includes existing technology, the ability to integrate new technology, and the probable impact of technology on current and future operations.

7. *Suppliers.* Supplier relationships, dependability of suppliers, quality, flexibility, and service are typical considerations.

8. *Other.* Other factors include patents, labor relations, company or product image, distribution channels, relationships with distributors, maintenance of facilities and equipment, access to resources, and access to markets.

After assessing internal and external factors and an organization's distinctive competence, a strategy or strategies must be formulated that will give the organization the best chance of success. Among the types of questions that may need to be addressed are the following:

What role, if any, will the Internet play?

Will the organization have a global presence?

To what extent will *outsourcing* be used?

To what extent will new products or services be introduced?

What rate of growth is desirable and *sustainable?*

What emphasis, if any, should be placed on lean production?

The organization may decide to have a single, dominant strategy (e.g., be the price leader) or to have multiple strategies. A single strategy would allow the organization to concentrate on one particular strength or market condition. On the other hand, multiple strategies may be needed to address a particular set of conditions.

Many companies are increasing their use of outsourcing to reduce overhead, gain flexibility, and take advantage of suppliers' expertise. Dell Computers provides a great example of some of the potential benefits of outsourcing as part of a business strategy.

---

www.dell.com/

In 1984, Michael Dell, then a college student, started selling personal computers from his dorm room. He didn't have the resources to make computer components, so he let others do that, choosing instead to concentrate on selling the computers. And, unlike the major computer producers, he didn't sell to dealers. Instead, he sold directly to PC buyers, eliminating some intermediaries, which allowed for lower cost and faster delivery. Although direct selling of PCs is fairly commonplace now, in those days it was a major departure from the norm.

What did Dell do that was so different from the big guys? To start, he bought components from suppliers instead of making them. That gave him tremendous leverage. He had little inventory, no R&D expenditures, and relatively few employees. And the risks associated with these were spread among his suppliers. Suppliers were willing to do this because Dell worked closely with them, and kept them informed. And because he was in direct contact with his customers, he gained tremendous insight into their expectations and needs, which he communicated to his suppliers.

Having little inventory gave Dell several advantages over his competitors. Aside from the lower costs of inventory, when new, faster computer chips became available, there was little inventory to work off, so he was able to offer the newer models much sooner than competitors with larger inventories. Also, when the prices of various components dropped, as they frequently did, he was able to take advantage of the lower prices, which kept his average costs lower than competitors'.

Today the company is worth billions, and so is Michael Dell.

By offering dependable, on-time overnight delivery, Federal Express serves customers throughout the U.S. and internationally in the delivery of urgent packages.

www.fedex.com

Growth is often a component of strategy, especially for new companies. A key aspect of this strategy is the need to seek a growth rate that is sustainable. In the 1990s, fast-food company Boston Markets dazzled investors and fast-food consumers alike. Fueled by its success, it undertook rapid expansion. By the end of the decade, the company was nearly bankrupt; it had overexpanded. In 2000, it was absorbed by fast-food giant McDonald's.

As globalization has increased, many companies realized that strategic decisions with respect to globalization must be made. One issue companies must face is that what works in one country or region will not necessarily work in another, and strategies must be carefully crafted to take these variabilities into account. Another issue is the threat of political or social upheaval. Still another issue is the difficulty of coordinating and managing far-flung operations. Indeed, "In today's global markets, you don't have to go abroad to experience international competition. Sooner or later the world comes to you."[3]

Two factors that tend to have universal strategic importance relate to quality and time. The following section discusses quality and time strategies.

QUALITY AND TIME STRATEGIES

Traditional strategies of business organizations have tended to emphasize cost minimization or product differentiation. While not abandoning those strategies, many organizations have embraced strategies based on *quality* and/or *time*. These two approaches are rapidly gaining favor throughout the business world. They are exciting and challenging, for they promise to significantly change the way business organizations operate.

quality-based strategy Strategy that focuses on quality in all phases of an organization.

Quality-based strategies focus on maintaining or improving the quality of an organization's products or services. Quality is generally a factor in both attracting and retaining customers. Quality-based strategies may be motivated by a variety of factors. They may reflect an effort to overcome an image of poor quality, a desire to catch up with the competition, a desire to maintain an existing image of high quality, or some combination of these and other factors. Quality-based strategies are the rule rather than the exception. Interestingly enough, quality-based strategies can be part of another strategy such as cost reduction or increased productivity, both of which benefit from higher quality.

time-based strategy Strategy that focuses on reduction of time needed to accomplish tasks.

Time-based strategies focus on reducing the time required to accomplish various activities (e.g., develop new products or services and market them, respond to a change in customer demand, or deliver a product or perform a service). By doing so, organizations seek to improve service to the customer and to gain a competitive advantage over rivals who take more time to accomplish the same tasks.

Time-based strategies focus on reducing the time needed to conduct the various activities in a process. The rationale is that by reducing time, costs are generally less, productivity is higher, quality tends to be higher, product innovations appear on the market sooner, and customer service is improved.

---

[3]Christopher A. Bartlett and Sumantra Ghoshal. "Going Global: Lessons from Late Movers," *Harvard Business Review,* March–April 2000, p. 139.

NEWSCLIP

A Strategy for Continuous Improvement

www.howmedica.com

I n April 1999, Stryker Howmedica set up a team to improve the running of its packaging line. A strategy based on continuous improvement was used. The team adopted an approach based on the production system of Toyota. The goal was to satisfy the customer expectations for delivery and quality, while achieving gains in productivity. After the team identified needs and set objectives, a number of improvements were implemented. A one-piece flow was established that reduced bottlenecks in the flow of devices through a clean room and the total time spent blister sealing devices was lowered. Within a short time, productivity nearly doubled from 36 devices per hour to 60 devices per hour, work-in-progress inventory fell, and a 10 percent reduction in the standard cost of product was achieved.

Source: Based on Lauraine Howley, "A Strategy for Company Improvement," *Medical Device Technology* 11, no. 2, March 2000, p. 33.

Organizations have achieved time reduction in some of the following:

Planning time: The time needed to react to a competitive threat, to develop strategies and select tactics, to approve proposed changes to facilities, to adopt new technologies, and so on.

Product/service design time: The time needed to develop and market new or redesigned products or services.

Processing time: The time needed to produce goods or provide services. This can involve scheduling, repairing equipment, wasted efforts, inventories, quality, training, and the like.

Changeover time: The time needed to change from producing one type of product or service to another. This may involve new equipment settings and attachments, different methods, equipment, schedules, or materials.

Delivery time: The time needed to fill orders.

Response time for complaints: These might be customer complaints about quality, timing of deliveries, and incorrect shipments. These might also be complaints from employees about working conditions (e.g., safety, lighting, heat or cold), equipment problems, or quality problems.

The following reading from the *Harvard Business Review* provides two examples of companies improving their competitiveness through time-based changes in the way they operate.

READING

Time-Based Innovation
George Stalk Jr.

www.mitsubishi.com

A company that can bring out new products three times faster than its competitors enjoys a huge advantage. Today, in one industry after another, Japanese manufacturers are doing just that to their Western competition:

• In projection television, Japanese producers can develop a new television in one-third the time required by U.S. manufacturers.

• In custom plastic injection molds, Japanese companies can develop the molds in one-third the time of U.S. competitors and at one-third the cost.

• In autos, Japanese companies can develop new products in half the time—and with half as many people—as the U.S. and German competition.

To accomplish their fast-paced innovations, leading Japanese manufacturers have introduced a series of organizational techniques that precisely parallel their approach to flexible manufacturing:

• In manufacturing, the Japanese stress short production runs and small lot sizes. In innovation, they favor smaller increments of improvements in new products, but introduce them more often—versus the Western approach of more significant improvements made less often.

- In the organization of product development work, the Japanese use factory cells that are cross-functional teams. Most Western new product development activity is carried out by functional centers.

- In the scheduling of work, Japanese factories stress local responsibility, just as product development scheduling is decentralized. The Western approach to both requires plodding centralized scheduling, plotting, and tracking.

The effects of this time-based advantage are devastating; quite simply, American companies are losing leadership of technology and innovation—supposedly this country's source of long-term advantage. Unless U.S. companies reduce their new product development and introduction cycles from 36–48 months to 12–18 months, Japanese manufacturers will easily out-innovate and out-perform them. Taking the initiative in innovation will require even faster cycle times.

Residential air conditioners illustrate the Japanese ability to introduce more technological innovation in smaller increments—and how in just a few years these improvements add up to remarkably superior products. The Japanese introduce innovations in air conditioners four times faster than their American competitors; in technological sophistication the Japanese products are 7 to 10 years ahead of U.S. products.

Look at the changes in Mitsubishi Electric's three-horsepower heat pump between 1975 and 1985. From 1975 to 1979, the company did nothing to the product except change the sheet metal work, partly to improve efficiency but mostly to reduce materials cost. In 1979, the technological sophistication of the product was roughly equal to that of the U.S. competition. From this point on, the Japanese first established, and then widened the lead.

In 1980, Mitsubishi introduced its first major improvement: a new product that used integrated circuits to control the air-conditioning cycle. One year later, the company replaced the integrated circuits with microprocessors and added two important innovations to increase consumer demand. The first was "quick connect" Freon lines. On the old product (and on the U.S. product), Freon lines were made from copper tubing and cut to length, bent, soldered together, purged, and filled with Freon—an operation requiring great skill to produce a reliable air conditioner. The Japanese substituted quick-connect Freon lines—precharged hoses that simply clicked together. The second innovation was simplified wiring. On the old product (and still today on the U.S. product) the unit had six color-coded wires to connect. The advent of microprocessors made possible a two-wire connection with neutral polarity.

These two changes did not improve the energy-efficiency ratio of the product; nor were they intended to. Rather, the point was to fabricate a unit that would be simpler to install and more reliable, thereby broadening distribution and in-

creasing demand. Because of these innovations, white-goods outlets could sell the new product, and local contractors could easily install it.

In 1982, Mitsubishi introduced a new version of the air conditioner featuring technological advances related to performance. A high-efficiency rotary compressor replaced the outdated reciprocating compressor. The condensing unit had louvered fins and inner fin tubes for better heat transfer. Because the balance of the system changed, all the electronics had to change. As a result, the energy-efficiency ratio improved markedly.

In 1983, Mitsubishi added sensors to the unit and more computing power, expanding the electronic control of the cycle and again improving the energy-efficiency ratio.

In 1984, Mitsubishi came out with another version of the product, this time with an inverter that made possible an even higher energy-efficiency ratio. The inverter, which requires additional electronics for the unit, allows unparalleled control over the speed of the electric motor, dramatically boosting the appliance's efficiency.

Using time-based innovation, Mitsubishi transformed its air conditioner. The changes came incrementally and steadily. Overall they gave Mitsubishi—and other Japanese companies on the same track—the position of technological leadership in the global residential air-conditioning industry.

In 1985, a U.S. air-conditioner manufacturer was just debating whether to use integrated circuits in its residential heat pump. In view of its four-to-five-year product development cycle, it could not have introduced the innovation until 1989 or 1990—putting the American company 10 years behind the Japanese. Faced with this situation, the U.S. air conditioner company followed the example of many U.S. manufacturers that have lost the lead in technology and innovation; it decided to source its air conditioners and components from its Japanese competition.

Consider the remarkable example of Atlas Door, a 10-year-old U.S. company. It has grown at an average annual rate of 15 percent in an industry with an overall annual growth rate of less than 5 percent. In recent years, its pre-tax earnings were 20 percent of sales, about five times the industry average. Atlas is debt free. In its 10th year the company achieved the number one competitive position in its industry.

The company's product: industrial doors. It is a product with almost infinite variety, involving limitless choices of width and height and material. Because of the importance of variety, inventory is almost useless in meeting customer orders; most doors can be manufactured only after the order has been placed.

Historically, the industry had needed almost four months to respond to an order for a door that was out of stock or customized. Atlas's strategic advantage was time; it could respond in weeks to any order. It had structured its order-entry, engineering, manufacturing, and logistics systems to move information and products quickly and reliably.

First, Atlas built just-in-time factories. These are fairly simple in concept. They require extra tooling and machinery to reduce changeover times and a fabrication process organized by product and scheduled to start and complete all of the parts at the same time. But even the performance of the factory—critical to the company's overall responsiveness—still only accounted for 2½ weeks of the completed product delivery cycle.

Second, Atlas compressed time at the front end of the system, where the order first entered and was processed. Traditionally, when customers, distributors, or salespeople called a door manufacturer with a request for price and delivery, they would have to wait more than one week for a response. If the desired door was not in stock, not in the schedule, or not engineered, the supplier's organization would waste even more time, pushing the search for an answer around the system.

Recognizing the opportunity to cut deeply into the time expenditure in this part of the system, Atlas first streamlined, then automated its entire order-entry, engineering, pricing, and scheduling processes. Today Atlas can price and schedule 95 percent of its incoming orders while the callers are still on the telephone. It can quickly engineer new special orders because it has preserved on computer the design and production data of all previous special orders—which drastically reduces the amount of reengineering necessary.

Third, Atlas tightly controlled logistics so that it always shipped only fully complete orders to construction sites. Orders require many components. Gathering all of them at the factory and making sure that they are with the correct order can be a time-consuming task. It is even more time-consuming, however, to get the correct parts to the job site *after* they have missed the initial shipment. Atlas developed a system to track the parts in production and the purchased parts for each order, ensuring arrival of all necessary parts at the shipping dock in time—a just-in-time logistics operation.

When Atlas started operations, distributors were uninterested in its product. The established distributors already carried the door line of a larger competitor; they saw no reason to switch suppliers except, perhaps, for a major price concession. But as a start-up, Atlas was too small to compete on price alone. Instead, it positioned itself as the door supplier of last resort, the company people came to if the established supplier could not deliver or missed a key date.

Of course, with industry lead times of almost four months, some calls inevitably came to Atlas. And when it did get a call, Atlas commanded a higher price because of its faster delivery. Atlas not only got a higher price but its time-based processes also yielded lower costs: it thus enjoyed the best of both worlds.

In 10 short years, the company replaced the leading door suppliers in 80 percent of the distributors in the country. With its strategic advantage the company could be selective, becoming the house supplier for only the strongest distributors.

In the wake of this indirect attack, the established competitors have not responded effectively. The conventional view is that Atlas is a "garage shop operator" that cannot sustain its growth: competitors expect the company's performance to degrade to the industry average as it grows larger. But this response—or nonresponse—only reflects a fundamental lack of understanding of time as the source of competitive advantage. The extra delay in responding only adds to the insurmountable lead the indirect time-based attack has created. While the traditional companies track costs and size, the new competitor derives advantage from time, staying on the cutting edge, leaving its rivals behind.

Source: Reprinted by permission of *Harvard Business Review,* "Time—The Next Source of Competitive Advantage," by George Stalk, Jr., July–August 1988. Copyright 1988 by the President and Fellows of Harvard College.

Productivity

One of the primary responsibilities of a manager is to achieve *productive use* of an organization's resources. The term *productivity* is used to describe this. **Productivity** is an index that measures output (goods and services) relative to the input (labor, materials, energy, and other resources) used to produce them. It is usually expressed as the ratio of output to input:

productivity A measure of the effective use of resources, usually expressed as the ratio of output to input.

$$\text{Productivity} = \frac{\text{Output}}{\text{Input}} \tag{2–1}$$

A productivity ratio can be computed for a single operation, a department, an organization, or an entire country.

Productivity has important implications for business organizations and for entire nations. For nonprofit organizations, higher productivity means lower costs; for profit-based organizations, productivity is an important factor in determining how competitive a company is. For a nation, the rate of *productivity growth* is of great importance. Productivity growth is the increase in productivity from one period to the next relative to the productivity in the preceding period. Thus,

Productivity in manufacturing can be greatly enhanced through the use of robotic equipment. Here, robots are building a Fiat Punto at the Melfi, Italy plant.

$$\text{Productivity growth} = \frac{\text{Current period productivity} - \text{Previous period productivity}}{\text{Previous period productivity}} \quad (2\text{--}2)$$

For example, if productivity increased from 80 to 84, the growth rate would be

$$\frac{84 - 80}{80} = .05 \text{ or } 5\%$$

Productivity growth is a key factor in a country's rate of inflation and the standard of living of its people. Productivity increases add value to the economy while keeping inflation in check. Productivity growth was a major factor in the recent long period of sustained economic growth in the United States.

COMPUTING PRODUCTIVITY

Productivity measures can be based on a single input (partial productivity), on more than one input (multifactor productivity), or on all inputs (total productivity). Table 2–4 lists some examples of productivity measures. The choice of productivity measure depends primarily on the purpose of the measurement. If the purpose is to track improvements in labor productivity, then labor becomes the obvious input measure.

Partial measures are often of greatest use in operations management. Table 2–5 provides some examples of partial productivity measures.

The units of output used in productivity measures depend on the type of job performed. The following are examples of labor productivity:

$$\frac{\text{Yards of carpet installed}}{\text{Labor hours}} = \text{Yards of carpet installed per labor hour}$$

$$\frac{\text{Number of offices cleaned}}{\text{Number of shifts}} = \text{Number of offices cleaned per shift}$$

$$\frac{\text{Board feet of lumber cut}}{\text{Number of weeks}} = \text{Board feet of lumber cut per week}$$

Similar examples can be listed for *machine productivity* (e.g., the number of pieces per hour turned out by a machine).

TABLE 2-4

Some examples of different types of productivity measures

Partial measures	$\dfrac{\text{Output}}{\text{Labor}}$	$\dfrac{\text{Output}}{\text{Machine}}$	$\dfrac{\text{Output}}{\text{Capital}}$	$\dfrac{\text{Output}}{\text{Energy}}$
Multifactor measures	$\dfrac{\text{Output}}{\text{Labor} + \text{Machine}}$		$\dfrac{\text{Output}}{\text{Labor} + \text{Capital} + \text{Energy}}$	
Total measure	$\dfrac{\text{Goods or Services produced}}{\text{All inputs used to produce them}}$			

TABLE 2-4

Some examples of different types of productivity measures

Labor Productivity	Units of output per labor hour
	Units of output per shift
	Value-added per labor hour
	Dollar value of output per labor hour
Machine Productivity	Units of output per machine hour
	Dollar value of output per machine hour
Capital Productivity	Units of output per dollar input
	Dollar value of output per dollar input
Energy Productivity	Units of output per kilowatt-hour
	Dollar value of output per kilowatt-hour

TABLE 2-5

Some examples of partial productivity measures

Example 2

Determine the productivity for these cases:

a. Four workers installed 720 square yards of carpeting in eight hours.

b. A machine produced 68 usable pieces in two hours.

Solution

a. $\text{Productivity} = \dfrac{\text{Yards of carpet installed}}{\text{Labor hours worked}}$

$= \dfrac{720 \text{ square yards}}{4 \text{ workers} \times 8 \text{ hours/worker}}$

$= \dfrac{720 \text{ yards}}{32 \text{ hours}}$

$= 22.5 \text{ yards/hour}$

b. $\text{Productivity} = \dfrac{\text{Usable pieces}}{\text{Production time}}$

$= \dfrac{68 \text{ pieces}}{2 \text{ hours}}$

$= 34 \text{ pieces/hour}$

Calculations of multifactor productivity measure inputs and outputs using a common unit of measurement, such as cost or value. For instance, the measure might use cost of inputs and price of the output:

$$\dfrac{\text{Quantity of production at standard price}}{\text{Labor cost} + \text{Materials cost} + \text{Overhead}} \qquad (2\text{--}3)$$

Example 3

Determine the multifactor productivity for the combined input of labor and machine time using the following data:

Output: 7,040 units

Input
    Labor: $1,000
    Materials: $520
    Overhead: $2,000

Solution

$$\frac{\text{Multifactor}}{\text{Productivity}} = \frac{\text{Output}}{\text{Labor} + \text{Materials} + \text{Overhead}} = \frac{7{,}040 \text{ units}}{\$1{,}000 + \$520 + \$2{,}000} = 2 \text{ units/dollar}$$

Productivity measures are useful on a number of levels. For an individual department or organization, productivity measures can be used to track performance *over time*. This allows managers to judge performance and to decide where improvements are needed. For example, if a manager finds that productivity has slipped in a certain area, the manager can examine the factors used to compute productivity to determine what has changed and then devise a means of improving productivity in subsequent periods.

Productivity measures can also be used to judge the performance of an entire industry or the productivity of a country as a whole. These productivity measures are *aggregate* measures.

In essence, productivity measurements serve as scorecards of the effective use of resources. Business leaders are concerned with productivity as it relates to *competitiveness*: If two firms both have the same level of output but one requires less input because of higher productivity, that one will be able to charge a lower price and consequently increase its share of the market. Or that firm might elect to charge the same price, thereby reaping a greater profit. Government leaders are concerned with national productivity because of the close relationship between productivity and a nation's standard of living. High levels of productivity are largely responsible for the relatively high standards of living enjoyed by people in industrial nations. Furthermore, wage and price increases not accompanied by productivity increases tend to create inflationary pressures on a nation's economy.

Productivity growth in the United States in the 1970s and 80s lagged behind that of other leading industrial countries, most notably Japan, Korea, the U.K., and West Germany. That caused concern among government officials and business leaders. Although U.S. productivity was still among the highest in the world, it was losing ground to other nations. Moreover, a significant portion of U.S. productivity could be attributed to high *agricultural* productivity; *manufacturing* productivity tended to be lower. It slowed during the 80s, but it was strong in the mid to late 90s. (See Figure 2–2.)

FIGURE 2-2

Percentage change in U.S. productivity (output per hour), 1989–1997

PRODUCTIVITY IN THE SERVICE SECTOR

Service productivity is more problematic than manufacturing productivity. In many situations, it is more difficult to measure, and thus to manage, because it involves intellectual activities and a high degree of variability. Think about medical diagnosis, surgery, consulting, legal services, customer service, and computer repair work. This makes productivity improvements more difficult to achieve. Nonetheless, because service is becoming an increasingly large portion of our economy, the issues related to service productivity will have to be dealt with.

FACTORS THAT AFFECT PRODUCTIVITY

Numerous factors affect productivity. Generally, they are methods, capital, quality, technology, and management.

A commonly held misconception is that workers are the main determinant of productivity. According to that theory, the route to productivity gains involves getting employees to work harder. However, the fact is that many productivity gains in the past have come from *technological* improvements. Familiar examples include:

Fax machines	Computerized billing and inventories
Copying machines	Automation
Microwave ovens	Calculators
The Internet	Computers, personal computers, laptops
Answering machines, voice mail, cellular phones	E-mail
	Software

However, technology alone won't guarantee productivity gains; it must be used wisely and thoughtfully. Without careful planning, technology can actually *reduce* productivity, especially if it leads to inflexibility, high costs, or mismatched operations. Another current productivity pitfall results from employees' use of computers for non–work-related activities (playing games or checking stock prices or sports scores on the Internet). Beyond all of these is the dip in productivity that results while employees learn to use new equipment or procedures that will eventually lead to productivity gains after the learning phase ends.

Standardizing processes and procedures wherever possible can have a significant impact on both productivity and quality.

Quality differences may distort productivity measurements. One way this can happen is when comparisons are made over time, such as comparing the productivity of a factory now with one in the 1970s. Quality is now much higher than it was then, but there is no simple way to incorporate quality into productivity measurements.

Use of the Internet can lower costs of a wide range of transactions, thereby increasing productivity. It is likely that this effect will continue to increase productivity in the foreseeable future.

Computer viruses can have an immense negative impact on productivity.

Searching for lost or misplaced items wastes time, hence negatively affecting productivity.

Scrap rates have an adverse effect on productivity, implying inefficient use of resources.

New workers tend to have lower productivity than seasoned workers. Thus, growing companies may experience a productivity lag.

Safety should be addressed. Accidents can take a toll on productivity.

A shortage of information technology workers and other technical workers hampers the ability of companies to update computing resources, generate and sustain growth, and take advantage of new opportunities.

Layoffs often affect productivity. The effect can be positive and negative. Initially, productivity may increase after a layoff, because the workload remains the same but fewer

FIGURE 2–3

Bottleneck operation

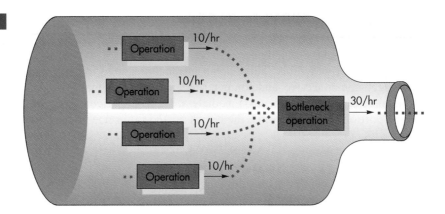

workers do the work—although they have to work harder and longer to do it. However, as time goes by, the remaining workers may experience an increased risk of burnout, and they may fear additional job cuts. The most capable workers may decide to leave.

Labor turnover has a negative effect on productivity; replacements need time to get up to speed.

Design of the workspace can impact productivity. For example, having tools and other work items within easy reach can positively impact productivity.

Incentive plans that reward productivity increases can boost productivity.

IMPROVING PRODUCTIVITY

A company or a department can take a number of key steps toward improving productivity:

1. Develop productivity measures for all operations; measurement is the first step in managing and controlling an operation.

2. Look at the system as a whole in deciding which operations are most critical; it is overall productivity that is important. This concept is illustrated in Figure 2–3, which shows several operations feeding their output into a *bottleneck* operation. The capacity of the bottleneck operation is less than the combined capacities of the operations that provide input, so units queue up waiting to be processed; hence the term bottleneck. Productivity improvements to any *non*bottleneck operation will not affect the productivity of the system. Improvements in the bottleneck operation *will* lead to increased productivity, up to the point where the output rate of the bottleneck equals the output rate of the operations feeding it.

3. Develop methods for achieving productivity improvements, such as soliciting ideas from workers (perhaps organizing teams of workers, engineers, and managers), studying how other firms have increased productivity, and reexamining the way work is done.

4. Establish reasonable goals for improvement.

5. Make it clear that management supports and encourages productivity improvement. Consider incentives to reward workers for contributions.

6. Measure improvements and publicize them.

7. Don't confuse productivity with *efficiency*. Efficiency is a narrower concept that pertains to getting the most out of a *fixed* set of resources; productivity is a broader concept that pertains to effective use of overall resources. For example, an efficiency perspective on mowing a lawn given a hand mower would focus on the best way to use the hand mower; a productivity perspective would include the possibility of using a power mower.

NEWSCLIP

Productivity Gains Curb Inflation

www.burgerking.com

Wage increases can lead to inflationary pressure—they can cause the prices consumers pay for products and services to rise. Unless, that is, they are offset by gains in productivity, which lead to an increase in profits. If that happens, a portion of the resulting profits can be used to cover the wage increases without having to raise prices.

Some Burger Kings were recently able to increase the starting pay of new workers by $1 by achieving productivity gains. The restaurants restructured the menu, combining items into meal packages such as a burger, fries, and soft drink. This enabled the counter staff to enter orders with a single key stroke instead of multiple key strokes on their point-of-sale machines, reducing the time needed to take an order. That, in turn, enabled them to take orders more quickly, increasing productivity and, consequently, reducing labor requirements, which produced higher profits.

Source: Based on "Despite Pay Increases, Gains in Productivity, Profits Curb Inflation," *The Wall Street Journal*, May 22, 1997, p. A1.

Summary

Competition is the driving force in many organizations. It may involve price, quality, special features or services, time, or other factors. To develop effective strategies for business, it is essential for organizations to determine what combinations of factors are important to customers, which factors are order qualifiers, and which are order winners.

Strategies are plans for achieving organizational goals. They provide focus for decision making. Strategies must take into account present and future customer wants, as well as the organization's strengths and weaknesses, threats and opportunities. These can run the gamut from what competitors are doing, or are likely to do, to technology, supply chain management, and e-business. Organizations generally have overall strategies that pertain to the entire organization and strategies that pertain to each of the functional areas. Functional strategies are narrower in scope and should be linked to overall strategies. Time-based strategies and quality-based strategies are among the most widely used strategies business organizations employ to serve their customers and to become more productive.

Productivity is a measure of the use of resources. There is considerable interest in productivity both from an organizational standpoint and from a national standpoint. Business organizations want higher productivity because it yields lower costs and helps them to become more competitive. Nations want higher productivity because it makes their goods and services more attractive, offsets inflationary pressures associated with higher wages, and results in a higher standard of living for their people.

Key Terms

competitiveness, 38
distinctive competencies, 44
environmental scanning, 46
mission, 40
mission statement, 40
operations strategy, 43
order qualifiers, 44

order winners, 44
productivity, 51
quality-based strategy, 48
strategy, 40
tactics, 42
time-based strategy, 48

Solved Problems

A company that processes fruits and vegetables is able to produce 400 cases of canned peaches in one-half hour with four workers. What is labor productivity?

Problem 1

Solution

$$\text{Labor productivity} = \frac{\text{Quantity produced}}{\text{Labor hours}} = \frac{400 \text{ cases}}{4 \text{ workers} \times 1/2 \text{ hour/worker}}$$

$$= 200 \text{ cases per hour}$$

Problem 2

A wrapping paper company produced 2,000 rolls of paper one day. Labor cost was $160, material cost was $50, and overhead was $320. Determine the multifactor productivity.

Solution

$$\text{Multifactor productivity} = \frac{\text{Quantity produced @ standard price}}{\text{Labor cost} + \text{Material cost} + \text{Overhead}}$$

$$= \frac{2,000 \text{ rolls}}{\$160 + \$50 + \$320}$$

$$= 3.77 \text{ rolls per dollar}$$

A variation of the multifactor productivity calculation incorporates the standard price in the numerator by multiplying the units by the standard price.

Discussion and Review Questions

1. From time to time, various groups clamor for import restrictions or tariffs on foreign-produced goods, particularly automobiles. How might these be helpful? Harmful?
2. List the key ways that organizations compete.
3. Explain the importance of identifying and differentiating order qualifiers and order winners.
4. Select two stores you shop at, and state how they compete.
5. What are distinctive competencies and how do they relate to strategy formulation?
6. Contrast the terms *strategies* and *tactics*.
7. Contrast *organization strategy* and *operations strategy*.
8. Explain the term *time-based strategies* and give three examples.
9. What is productivity and why is it important? Who is primarily responsible for productivity in an organization?
10. List some factors that can affect productivity and some ways that productivity can be improved.
11. It has been said that a typical Japanese automobile manufacturer produces more cars with fewer workers than its U.S. counterpart. What are some possible explanations for this, assuming that U.S. workers are as hardworking as Japanese workers?
12. Boeing's strategy appears to focus on its 777 mid-size plane's ability to fly into smaller, non-hub airports. Rival European Airbus' strategy appears to focus on large planes. Compare the advantages and disadvantages of these two strategies.

Memo Writing Exercises

1. Last year, your company initiated a major effort to improve productivity throughout the company. During the first few months, little improvement was made. Recently, however, major gains, exceeding 20 percent, have been made in both the packaging and equipment repair departments. You would like to commend them for their achievements, and announce to the other departments that gains are possible. You are also aware that some production employees believe that significant gains in productivity means the loss of some jobs because the company will be able to achieve the same output with fewer employees. Another local company laid off 5 percent of its workforce shortly after announcing productivity gains. Nonetheless, you believe that by achieving even modest productivity gains, your company will become more competitive and therefore be able to capture a larger share of the market. You believe that increased demand will more than offset productivity gains, and may even require hiring more employees. Naturally, you cannot guarantee this, although you are optimistic about the chances that this will occur.

   Write a one-page memo to employees that covers these points.

2. Assume the role of vice president of manufacturing of Eastern Products, Philadelphia. You are thinking about the forthcoming annual retreat of top-level managers of manufacturing, engineering, marketing, and product design to discuss strategic planning. Competitive pressures from several domestic and foreign companies give this year's meeting special significance, and you want to arrange for a truly productive session.

   In the past, some meetings haven't been as successful as you would have liked. You learned from experience that holding the meeting at corporate headquarters didn't work because the managers were too accessible to their subordinates. It's much better if the group can meet away from home territory, allowing them the opportunity to concentrate and develop camaraderie. You also found that traditional vacation spots are not conducive to achieving the best results. You want your administrative assistant to investigate agencies that specialize in business retreats.

Twelve to 14 people will attend the conference. Each will require a separate hotel room. Exercise facilities should be on the premises. Audiovisual support will be needed for video presentations, and overhead projectors and flip charts will also be needed. Light lunches should be arranged. You need to get dietary preferences from those attending.

The location for the annual retreat should not require excessive travel costs or travel time. Arrangements must be completed within two weeks.

Write a one-page memo outlining these requirements to your assistant, Armin Joseph. It is his task to investigate possible retreat locations and make all the arrangements.

Problems

1. Suppose that a company produced 300 standard bookcases last week using eight workers and it produced 240 standard bookcases this week using six workers. In which period was productivity higher? Explain.

2. The manager of a crew that installs carpeting has tracked the crew's output over the past several weeks, obtaining these figures:

Week	Crew Size	Yards Installed
1	4	960
2	3	702
3	4	968
4	2	500
5	3	696
6	2	500

Compute the labor productivity for each of the weeks. On the basis of your calculations, what can you conclude about crew size and productivity?

3. Compute the multifactor productivity measure for each of the weeks shown. What do the productivity figures suggest? Assume 40-hour weeks and an hourly wage of $12. Overhead is 1.5 times weekly labor cost. Material cost is $6 per pound. Standard price is $140 per unit.

Week	Output (units)	Workers	Material (lbs)
1	300	6	45
2	338	7	46
3	322	7	46
4	354	8	48

4. A company that makes shopping carts for supermarkets and other stores recently purchased some new equipment that reduces the labor content of the jobs needed to produce the shopping carts. Prior to buying the new equipment, the company used five workers, who produced an average of 80 carts per hour. Labor cost was $10 per hour and machine cost was $40 per hour. With the new equipment, it was possible to transfer one of the workers to another department, and equipment cost increased by $10 per hour while output increased by four carts per hour.

   a. Compute labor productivity under each system. Use carts per worker per hour as the measure of labor productivity.

   b. Compute the multifactor productivity under each system. Use carts per dollar cost (labor plus equipment) as the measure.

   c. Comment on the changes in productivity according to the two measures, and on which one you believe is the more pertinent for this situation.

5. An operation has a 10 percent scrap rate. As a result, 72 pieces per hour are produced. What is the potential increase in labor productivity that could be achieved by eliminating the scrap?

6. A manager checked production records and found that a worker produced 160 units while working 40 hours. In the previous week, the same worker produced 138 units while working 36 hours. Did the worker's productivity increase, decrease, or remain the same? Explain.

Productivity Gains at Whirlpool

www.whirlpool.com

Workers and management at Whirlpool Appliance's Benton Harbor plant in Michigan have set an example of how to achieve productivity gains, which has benefited not only the company and its stockholders, but Whirlpool customers, and the workers themselves.

Things weren't always rosy at the plant. Productivity and quality weren't good. Neither were labor–management relations. Workers hid defective parts so management wouldn't find them, and when machines broke down, workers would simply sit down until sooner or later someone came to fix it. All that changed in the late 1980s. Faced with the possibility that the plant would be shut down, management and labor worked together to find a way to keep the plant open. The way was to increase productivity—producing more without using more resources. Interestingly, the improvement in productivity didn't come by spending money on fancy machines. Rather, it was accomplished by placing more emphasis on quality. That was a shift from the old way, which emphasized volume, often at the expense of quality. To motivate workers, the company agreed to gain sharing, a plan that rewarded workers by increasing their pay for productivity increases.

The company overhauled the manufacturing process, and taught its workers how to improve quality. As quality improved, productivity went up because more of the output was good, and costs went down because of fewer defective parts that had to be scrapped or reworked. Costs of inventory also decreased, because fewer spare parts were needed to replace defective output, both at the factory and for warranty repairs. And workers have been able to see the connection between their efforts to improve quality and productivity, and their pay.

Not only was Whirlpool able to use the productivity gains to increase workers' pay, it was also able to hold the lid on price increases and to funnel some of the savings into research, which added to cost savings and quality improvement.

Questions

1. What were the two key things that Whirlpool management did to achieve productivity gains?
2. Who has benefited from the productivity gains?
3. How are productivity and quality related?
4. How can a company afford to pay its workers for productivity gains?

Source: Based on "A Whirlpool Factory Raises Productivity—And Pay of Workers," by Rick Wartzman, from *The Wall Street Journal*, 1992.

An American Tragedy: How a Good Company Died   Zachary Schiller

The Rust Belt is back. So say bullish observers as U.S. exports surge, long-moribund industries glow with new-found profits, and unemployment dips to lows not seen in a decade. But in the smokestack citadels, there's disquiet. Too many machine-tool and auto parts factories are silent; too many U.S. industries still can't hold their own.

What went wrong since the heyday of the 1960s? That's the issue Max Holland, a contributing editor of *The Nation*, takes up in his nutsy-boltsy but fascinating study, *When the Machine Stopped.**

The focus of the story is Burgmaster Corp., a Los Angeles-area machine-tool maker founded in 1944 by Czechoslovakian

*Max Holland, *When the Machine Stopped: A Contemporary Tale from Industrial America* (Boston, Mass.: Harvard Business School Press, 1988).

immigrant Fred Burg. Holland's father worked there for 29 years, and the author interviewed 22 former employees. His shop-floor view of this small company is a refreshing change from academic treatises on why America can't compete.

The discussions of spindles and numerical control can be tough going. But Holland compensates by conveying the excitement and innovation of the company's early days and the disgust and cynicism accompanying its decline. Moreover, the fate of Burgmaster and its brethren is crucial to the U.S. industrial economy: Any manufactured item is either made by a machine tool or by a machine made by a machine tool.

Producing innovative turret drills used in a wide variety of metalworking tasks, Burgmaster was a thriving enterprise by 1965, when annual sales amounted to about $8 million. The company needed backing to expand, however, so it sold out to Buffalo-based conglomerate Houdaille Industries Inc. Houdaille was in turn purchased in a 1979 leveraged buyout led by Kohlberg Kravis Roberts & Co. By 1982, when debt, competition, and a sickly machine-tool market had battered Burgmaster badly, Houdaille went to Washington with a petition to withhold the investment tax credit for certain Japanese-made machine tools.

Thanks to deft lobbying, the Senate passed a resolution supporting Houdaille's position, but President Reagan refused to go along. Houdaille's subsequent attempt to link Burgmaster up with a Japanese rival also failed, and Burgmaster was closed.

Holland uses Burgmaster's demise to explore some key issues of economic and trade policy. Houdaille's charge that a cartel led by the Japanese government had injured U.S. tool-makers, for example, became a rallying point for those who would blame a fearsome Japan Inc. for the problems of U.S. industry.

Holland describes the Washington wrangling over Houdaille in painful detail. But he does show that such government decisions are often made without much knowledge of what's going on in industry. He shows, too, that Japanese producers succeeded less because of government help than because they made better, cheaper machines.

For those who see LBOs as a symptom of what ails the U.S. economy, Holland offers plenty of ammunition. He argues persuasively that the LBO crippled Burgmaster by creating enormous pressure to generate cash. As Burgmaster pushed its products out as fast as possible, he writes, it routinely shipped defective machines. It promised customers features that engineers hadn't yet designed. And although KKR disputes the claim, Holland concludes that the LBO choked off Burgmaster's investment funds just when foreign competition made them most necessary. As for Houdaille, it was recapitalized and sold to Britain's Tube Investments Group.

But Burgmaster's problems had started even before the LBO. Holland's history of the company under Houdaille is a veritable catalog of modern management techniques that flopped. One of the most disastrous was a system for computerizing production scheduling that was too crude for complex machine-tool manufacturing. Holland gives a dramatic depiction of supply snafus that resulted in delays and cost increases.

As an independent company, "Burgmaster thrived because the Burgs knew their business," Holland writes. Their departure under Houdaille was followed by an "endless and ultimately futile search for a better formula." But, he concludes: "No formula was a substitute for management involvement on the shop floor."

In the end, however, Holland puts most of the blame for the industry's decline on government policy. He targets tax laws and macroeconomic policies that encourage LBOs and speculation instead of productive investment. He also criticizes Pentagon procurement policies for favoring exotic, custom machines over standard, low-cost models. This adds up to an industrial policy, Holland writes—a bad one.

The point is well taken, but Holland gives it excessive weight. Like their brethren in Detroit and Pittsburgh, domestic tool-makers in the 1970s were too complacent when imports seized the lower end of the product line. The conservatism that had for years served them in their cyclical industry left them ill-prepared for change. Even now some of the largest U.S. tool-makers are struggling to restructure. Blame the government, yes. But blame the industry, too.

Question

1. Write a brief report that outlines the reasons (both internal and external) for Burgmaster's demise, and whether operations management played a significant role in the demise.

Source: Reprinted from April 17, 1989, issue of *Business Week* by special permission, copyright © 1989 by The McGraw-Hill Companies.

CASE

Home-Style Cookies

The Company

The Lew-Mark Baking Company is located in a small town in western New York State. The bakery is run by two brothers, Lew and Mark, who formed the company after they purchased an Archway Cookie franchise. With exclusive rights in New York and New Jersey, it is the largest Archway franchise. The company employs fewer than 200 people, mainly blue-collar workers, and the atmosphere is informal.

The Product

The company's only product is soft cookies, of which it makes over 50 varieties. Larger companies, such as Nabisco, Sunshine, and Keebler, have traditionally produced biscuit cookies, in which most of the water has been baked out, resulting in crisp cookies. Archway cookies have no additives or preservatives. The high quality of the cookies has enabled the company to develop a strong market niche for its product.

The Customers

The cookies are sold in convenience stores and supermarkets throughout New York and New Jersey. Archway markets its cookies as "good food"—no additives or preservatives—and this appeals to a health-conscious segment of the market. Many customers are over 45 years of age, and prefer a cookie that is soft and not too sweet. Parents with young children also buy the cookies.

The Production Process

The company has two continuous band ovens that it uses to bake the cookies. The production process is called a batch processing system. It begins as soon as management gets orders from distributors. These orders are used to schedule production. At the start of each shift, a list of the cookies to be made that day is delivered to the person in charge of mixing. That person checks a master list, which indicates the ingredients needed for each type of cookie, and enters that information into the computer. The computer then determines the amount of each ingredient needed, according to the quantity of cookies ordered, and relays that information to storage silos located outside the plant where the main ingredients (flour, sugar, and cake flour) are stored. The ingredients are automatically sent to giant mixing machines where the ingredients are combined with proper amounts of eggs, water, and flavorings. After the ingredients have been mixed, the batter is poured into a cutting machine where it is cut into individual cookies. The cookies are then dropped onto a conveyor belt and transported through one of two ovens. Filled cookies, such as apple, date, and raspberry, require an additional step for filling and folding.

The nonfilled cookies are cut on a diagonal rather than round. The diagonal-cut cookies require less space than straight-cut cookies, and the result is a higher level of productivity. In addition, the company recently increased the length of each oven by 25 feet, which also increased the rate of production.

As the cookies emerge from the ovens, they are fed onto spiral cooling racks 20 feet high and 3 feet wide. As the cookies come off the cooling racks, workers place the cookies into boxes manually, removing any broken or deformed cookies in the process. The boxes are then wrapped, sealed, and labeled automatically.

Inventory

Most cookies are loaded immediately onto trucks and shipped to distributors. A small percentage are stored temporarily in the company's warehouse, but they must be shipped shortly because of their limited shelf life. Other inventory includes individual cookie boxes, shipping boxes, labels, and cellophane for wrapping. Labels are reordered frequently, in small batches, because FDA label requirements are subject to change, and the company does not want to get stuck with labels it can't use. The bulk silos are refilled two or three times a week, depending on how quickly supplies are used.

Cookies are baked in a sequence that minimizes downtime for cleaning. For instance, light-colored cookies (e.g., chocolate chip) are baked before dark-colored cookies (e.g., fudge), and oatmeal cookies are baked before oatmeal raisin cookies. This permits the company to avoid having to clean the processing equipment every time a different type of cookie is produced.

Quality

The bakery prides itself on the quality of its cookies. Cookies are sampled randomly by a quality control inspector as they come off the line to assure that their taste and consistency are satisfactory, and that they have been baked to the proper degree. Also, workers on the line are responsible for removing defective cookies when they spot them. The company has also installed an X-ray machine on the line that can detect small bits of metal filings that may have gotten into cookies during the production process. The use of automatic equipment for transporting raw materials and mixing batter has made it easier to maintain a sterile process.

Scrap

The bakery is run very efficiently and has minimal amounts of scrap. For example, if a batch is mixed improperly, it is sold for dog food. Broken cookies are used in the oatmeal cookies. These practices reduce the cost of ingredients and save on waste disposal costs. The company also uses heat reclamation: The heat that escapes from the two ovens is captured and used to boil the water that supplies the heat to the building. Also, the use of automation in the mixing process has resulted in a reduction in waste compared with the manual methods used previously.

New Products

Ideas for new products come from customers, employees, and observations of competitors' products. New ideas are first examined to determine whether the cookies can be made with existing equipment. If so, a sample run is made to determine the cost and time requirements. If the results are satisfactory, marketing tests are conducted to see if there is a demand for the product.

Potential Improvements

There are a number of areas of potential improvement at the bakery. One possibility would be to automate packing the cookies into boxes. Although labor costs are not high, automating the process might save some money and increase efficiency. So far, the owners have resisted making this change because they feel an obligation to the community to employ the 30 women who now do the boxing manually. Another possible improvement would be to use suppliers who are located closer to the plant. That would reduce delivery lead times and transportation costs, but the owners are not convinced that local suppliers could provide the same good quality. Other opportunities have been proposed in recent years, but the owners rejected them because they feared that the quality of the product might suffer.

Questions

1. Briefly describe the cookie production process.

2. What are two ways that the company has increased productivity? Why did increasing the length of the ovens result in a faster output rate?

3. Do you think that the company is making the right decision by not automating the packing of cookies? Explain your reasoning. What obligation does a company have to its employees in a situation such as this? What obligation does it have to the community? Is the size of the town a factor? Would it make a difference if the company was located in a large city? Is the size of the company a factor? What if it was a much larger company?

4. What factors cause the company to carry minimal amounts of certain inventories? What benefits result from this policy?

5. As a consumer, what things do you consider in judging the quality of cookies you buy in a supermarket?

6. What advantages and what limitations stem from the company's not using preservatives in cookies?

7. Briefly describe the company's strategy.

CASE

Hazel Revisited

(Refer to p. 30 for the Hazel Case.)

1. What competitive advantage does Hazel have over a professional lawn care service?

2. Hazel would like to increase her profits, but she doesn't believe that it would be wise to raise her prices considering the current state of the local economy. Instead, she has given some thought to increasing productivity.

   a. Explain how increased productivity could be an alternative to increased prices.

   b. What are some ways that Hazel could increase productivity?

3. Hazel is thinking about the purchase of new equipment. One would be power sidewalk edgers. She believes edgers will lead to an increase in productivity. Another would be a chain saw, which would be used for tree pruning. What trade-offs should she consider in her analysis?

4. Hazel has been fairly successful in her neighborhood, and now wants to expand to other neighborhoods, including some that are five miles away. What would be the advantages and disadvantages of doing this?

5. Hazel does not have a mission statement or a set of objectives. Take one of the following positions and defend it:

   a. Hazel doesn't need a formal mission statement and objectives. Many small businesses don't have them.

   b. She definitely needs a mission statement and a set of objectives. They would be extremely beneficial.

   c. There may be some benefit to Hazel's business, and she should consider developing one.

READING

Economic Vitality
Alan Greenspan

It is safe to say that we are witnessing this decade, in the United States, history's most compelling demonstration of the productive capacity of free peoples operating in free markets . . .

The quintessential manifestations of America's industrial might earlier this century—large steel mills, auto assembly plants, petrochemical complexes, and skyscrapers—have been replaced by a gross domestic product that has been downsized as ideas have replaced physical bulk and effort as creators of value. Today, economic value is best symbolized by exceedingly complex, miniaturized integrated circuits and the ideas—the software—that utilize them. Most of what we currently perceive as value and wealth is intellectual and impalpable.

The American economy, clearly more than most, is in the . . . continuous process by which emerging technologies push out the old. Standards of living rise when incomes created by the productive facilities employing older, increasingly obsolescent technologies are marshaled to finance the newly produced capital assets that embody cutting-edge technologies.

This is the process by which wealth is created, incremental step by incremental step. It presupposes a continuous churning of an economy as the new displaces the old. Although this process of productive obsolescence has ancient roots, it appears to have taken on a quickened pace in recent years and changed its character. The remarkable, and partly fortuitous, coming together of the technologies that make up what we label IT—information technologies—has begun to alter, fundamentally, the manner in which we do business and create economic value, often in ways that were not readily foreseeable even a decade ago.

Before the advent of what has become a veritable avalanche of information technology innovation, most twentieth-century business decision making had been hampered by dated and incomplete information about customer preferences in markets and flows of materials through a company's production systems. Relevant information was hours, days, or even weeks old. Accordingly, business managers had to double up on materials and people to protect against the inevitable misjudgments that were part and parcel of production planning. Ample inventory levels were needed to ensure output schedules, and backup teams of people and machines were required to maintain quality control and respond to unanticipated developments.

Of course, large remnants of imprecision still persist, but the remarkable surge in the availability of real-time information in recent years has sharply reduced the degree of uncertainty confronting business management. This has enabled businesses to remove large swaths of now unnecessary inventory, and dispense with much programmed worker and capital redundancies. As a consequence, growth in output per work hour has accelerated, elevating the standards of living of the average American worker.

Intermediate production and distribution processes, so essential when information and quality control were poor, are being bypassed and eventually eliminated. The proliferation of Internet websites is promising to alter significantly the way large parts of our distribution system are managed. Moreover, technological innovations have spread far beyond the factory floor and retail and wholesale distribution channels. Biotech, for example, is revolutionizing medicine and agriculture, with far reaching consequences for the quality of life not only in the United States but around the world . . .

But scientific proficiency will not be enough. Skill alone may not be sufficient to move the frontier of technology far enough to meet the many challenges that our nation will confront in the decades ahead. And technological advances alone will not buttress the democratic institutions, supported by a rule of law, which are so essential to our dynamic and vigorous American economy. Each is merely a tool, which, without the enrichment of human wisdom, is of modest value.

A crucial challenge of education is to transform skills and intelligence into wisdom—into a process of thinking capable of forming truly new insights. But learning and knowledge—and even wisdom—are not enough.

National well-being, including material prosperity, rests to a substantial extent on the personal qualities of the people who inhabit a nation. Civilization, our civilization, rests on the presumption of a productive interaction of people engaged in the division of labor, driven by a process economists label "comparative advantage." This implies mutual exchange to mutual advantage among free people.

It is decidedly not true that "nice guys finish last," as that highly original American baseball philosopher, Leo Durocher, was once alleged to have said. I do not deny that many in our society appear to have succeeded in a material way by cutting corners and manipulating associates, both in their professional and in their personal lives. But material success is possible in this world without exploiting others, and clearly, having a reputation for fair dealing is a profoundly practical virtue. We call it "goodwill" in business and add it to our balance sheets.

Trust is at the root of any economic system based on mutually beneficial exchange. In virtually all transactions, we rely on the word of those with whom we do business. Were this not the case, exchange of goods and services could not take place on any reasonable scale. Our commercial codes and contract law presume that only a tiny fraction of contracts at most need be adjudicated. If a significant number of businesspeople violated the trust upon which our interactions are based, our court system and our economy would be swamped into immobility.

In today's world, where ideas are increasingly displacing the physical in the production of economic value, competition for reputation becomes a significant driving force, propelling our economy forward. Manufactured goods often can be evaluated before the completion of a transaction. Service providers, on the other hand, usually can offer only their reputations.

The extraordinarily complex machine that we call the economy of the United States is, in the end, made up of human beings struggling to improve their lives. The individual values of those Americans and their reputations will continue to influence the structure of the institutions that support market transactions, as they have throughout our history. Without mutual trust, and market participants abiding by a rule of law, no economy can prosper. Our system works fundamentally on individual fair dealing. We need only look around today's world to realize how rare and valuable this is.

Source: Excerpted from remarks by Federal Reserve Board Chairman Alan Greenspan *Maintaining Economic Vitality* Millennium Lecture Series, sponsored by the Gerald R. Ford Foundation and Grand Valley State University, Grand Rapids, Michigan, September 8, 1999.

Questions

1. What factors have caused the output of workers per hour (productivity) to accelerate, and what has been the benefit of this?

2. What is the crucial challenge of education? What else is needed?

3. Explain the phrase "competition for reputation." What are some ways a company might do this? Does ethics play a part in this?

The US Postal Service

"Neither rain, nor snow…"

The US Postal Service is the largest postal service in the world, handling about 41% (630 million pieces a day) of the world's mail volume. The second largest is Japan, which handles only about 6% of the world's mail. The US Postal Service is huge by any standard. It employs over 760,000 workers, making it the largest civilian employer in the U.S. It has over 300,000 mail collection boxes, 38,000 post offices, 130 million mail delivery points, more than 300 processing plants to sort and ship mail, and more than 75,000 pieces of mail processing equipment. It handles over 100 billion pieces of first class mail a year, and ships about 3 billion pounds of mail on commercial airline flights, making it the airlines' largest shipper.

Processing First-Class Mail

The essence of processing the mail is sorting, which means organizing the mail into smaller and smaller subgroups to facilitate its timely delivery. Sorting involves a combination of manual and automatic operations. Much of the mail that is processed is first-class mail.

Most first-class mail is handled using automated equipment. A small portion that cannot be handled by automated equipment must be sorted by hand, just the way it was done in colonial times.

The majority of first-class mail begins at the advanced facer canceling system. This system positions each letter so that it is face up, with the stamp in the upper corner, checks to see if the address is handwritten, and pulls the hand-addressed letters off the line. It also rejects letters that have the stamp covered by tape, have no postage, third-class mail, or have meter impressions that are too light to read. The rejects are handled manually. The remaining letters are cancelled and date stamped, and then sorted to one of seven stackers.

Next the letters go to the multi-line optical character readers, which can handle both printed and pre-barcoded mail, but not hand-addressed mail. The optical reader sprays a barcode on the mail that hasn't been pre-barcoded, which represents up to an 11-digit ZIP code. For hand-addressed mail, a picture is taken of the front of the letter, and the image is displayed on a remote terminal, often in another city, where an operator views the image and provides the information that the optical readers could not determine so that a barcode can be added.

Barcode readers then sort the mail into one of 96 stackers, doing this at a rate of more than 500 a minute. The mail goes through another sort using manually-controlled mechanical equipment. At that point, the mail is separated according to whether it is local or out-of-town mail. The out-of-town mail is placed into appropriate sacks according to its destination, and moved to the outgoing send area where it will be loaded on trucks.

The local mail is moved to another machine that not only sorts the mail into local carrier delivery routes, it sorts it according to delivery walk sequence!

Small parcels, bundles of letters, and bundles of flats are sorted by a bundle-sorting machine.

Productivity

Over the years, the Postal Service has experienced an ever increasing volume of mail. Productivity has been an important factor for the Postal Service in keeping postal rates low and maintaining rapid delivery service. Two key factors in improved productivity have been the increased use of automation and the introduction of zip codes.

Mail processing underwent a major shift to mechanization during the 1950s and 1960s, which led to more rapid processing and higher productivity. In 1978, an expanded zip code was introduced. That was followed in 1983 by a four-digit expansion in zip codes. These changes required new, automated processing equipment, including the use of barcodes and optical readers. All of these changes added greatly to productivity. But even with these improvements, the Postal Service faced increasing competitive pressures.

Competition

In the late 1980s, the Postal Service experienced a slowdown in the volume of mail. Some of this was due to a slowing of the economy, but most of it was the result of increasing competition. Delivery giants FedEx and UPS, as well as other companies that offer speedy delivery and package tracking gave businesses and the general public convenient alternatives for some mail services. At the same time, there was a growing use of fax machines, electronic communications, and increased use of alternate forms of advertising such as cable TV, all of which cut into the volume of mail.

Strategies and Tactics Used to Make the Postal Service More Competitive

To meet these challenges, the Postal Service developed several strategies to become more competitive. These included reorganizing, continuing to seek ways to keep costs down, increasing productivity, and emphasizing quality and customer service. Here is an overview of the situation and the strategies and tactics used by the Postal Service.

The Postal Service began working more closely with customers to identify better ways to meet their needs and expanded customer conveniences such as stamps on consignment. With the help of business mailers, the Postal Service continued support for rates reflecting customer work-sharing features, many tied to automation, to give customers more flexibility. At the same time, the Postal Service began forming Customer Advisory Councils—groups of citizens who volunteered to work with local postal management on postal issues of interest to the community. In 1990, the Postal Service awarded two contracts to private firms to measure first-class mail service and customer satisfaction. In 1992, the Postal Service stepped up its quest to become more competitive by reducing bureaucracy and overhead in order to improve service and customer satisfaction, and to reduce the need to increase postage rates.

To help accomplish these goals, the Postal Service underwent a reorganization. Layers of management were eliminated and overhead positions were cut by about 30,000. Five regions and 73 field divisions were replaced by 10 areas, each with a manager for customer services and a manager for processing and distribution. Ten customer service areas were established, with managers for customer service and processing and distribution in each area, as well as a marketing and sales office. The new structure allowed postal managers to be focused, improved communications, and empowered employees to meet customer needs. The Postal Service also took other steps to improve service. In 1993 it implemented improvements in processing and mail delivery at major postal facilities, expanded retail hours, and developed a more user-friendly *Domestic Mail Manual.* In cooperation with business customers, the Postal Service began to develop new services to meet specific mailer needs and to overhaul and simplify its complex rate structure. It also awarded contracts for two more external tracking systems, one to measure satisfaction levels of business mailers, and the other to measure service performance of third-class mail.

The reorganization eliminated some programs, cut costs, attracted new business, and reduced the US Postal Service's projected deficit.

Questions

1. Why is it important for the Postal Service to have a high volume of mail to process?

2. What caused productivity to increase?

3. What impact did competitive pressures have on the Postal Service?

4. What measures did the Postal Service adopt to increase competitiveness?

5. What results were achieved by the Postal Service's changes?

Selected Bibliography and Further Reading

Bartlett, Christopher A. and Sumantra Ghoshal. "Going Global: Lessons from Late Movers." *Harvard Business Review,* March–April 2000, pp. 132-42.

Bernstein, Aaron. "Backlash: Behind the Anxiety of Globalization." *Business Week,* April 24, 2000, pp. 38-44.

Blackburn, Joseph D., ed. *Time-Based Competition.* Burr Ridge, IL: Business One Irwin, 1991.

Colvin, Geoffrey, "Managing in the Info Era." *Fortune,* March 6, 2000, pp. F6–F9.

Hachman, Mark. "Supply-Chain Program Boosts Productivity at Seagate Tech." *Electronic Buyers News,* January 17, 2000, p. 5.

Hill, Terry. *Manufacturing Strategy: Text and Cases,* 3rd ed. New York: McGraw-Hill, 2000.

Holstein, William J. "Are Raises Bad for America?" *U.S. News & World Report,* August 30, 1999, pp. 48–50.

Margretta, Joan. "The Power of Virtual Integration: An Interview with Dell Computer's Michael Dell." *Harvard Business Review,* March–April 1998, pp. 73–84.

Roach, Stephen. "In Search of Productivity." *Harvard Business Review,* September–October 1998, p. 153.

Ross, D. F. *Competing Through Supply Chain Management.* New York: Chapman and Hall, 1998.

Stalk, George, P. Evans, and L. E. Shulman. "Competing on Capabilities: The New Rules of Corporate Strategy." *Harvard Business Review,* March–April 1992, pp. 57–69.

PART TWO

Forecasting

This part is devoted solely to forecasting. It is presented early in the book because forecasts are the basis for a wide range of decisions that are described in the following chapters. In fact, forecasts are basic inputs for many kinds of decisions in business organizations. Consequently, it is important for *all* managers to be able to understand and use forecasts.

Although forecasts are typically developed by the marketing function, the operations function is often called on to assist in forecast development. More important, though, is the reality that operations is a major user of forecasts.

Chapter 3 provides important insights on forecasting as well as information on how to develop and monitor forecasts.

1 Forecasting, Chapter 3

Forecasting

CHAPTER OUTLINE

Introduction, 70

Features Common to All
 Forecasts, 71

Elements of a Good Forecast, 72

Steps in the Forecasting Process, 72

Approaches to Forecasting, 73
 Forecasts Based on Judgment and
  Opinion, 73
 Forecasts Based on Time Series
  (Historical) Data, 73
 Associative Forecasts, 73

Forecasts Based on Judgment and
 Opinion, 73
 Executive Opinions, 73
 Salesforce Opinions, 74
 Consumer Surveys, 74
 Other Approaches, 74

Forecasts Based on Time Series
 Data, 75
 Naive Methods, 75
 Techniques for Averaging, 76
 Techniques for Trend, 81
 Trend-Adjusted Exponential
  Smoothing, 85
 Techniques for Seasonality, 87
 Techniques for Cycles, 90

Associative Forecasting
 Techniques, 91

Simple Linear Regression, 91
Comments on the Use of Linear
 Regression Analysis, 94
Curvilinear and Multiple Regression
 Analysis, 96

Accuracy and Control of
 Forecasts, 96

Newsclip: High Forecasts Can Be
 Bad News, 97
 Summarizing Forecast Accuracy, 97
 Controlling the Forecast, 98

Choosing a Forecasting
 Technique, 103

Using Forecast Information, 104

Computers in Forecasting, 104

Operations Strategy, 104

Newsclip: A Strong Channel
 Hub, 105

Summary, 105

Key Terms, 106

Solved Problems, 108

Discussion and Review
 Questions, 114

Memo Writing Exercises, 115

Problems, 115

Case: M&L Manufacturing, 123

Selected Bibliography and Further
 Reading, 124

LEARNING OBJECTIVES

*After completing this chapter you
should be able to:*

1 List the elements of a good
 forecast.

2 Outline the steps in the
 forecasting process.

3 Describe at least three qualitative
 forecasting techniques and the
 advantages and disadvantages
 of each.

4 Compare and contrast qualitative
 and quantitative approaches to
 forecasting.

5 Briefly describe averaging
 techniques, trend and seasonal
 techniques, and regression
 analysis, and solve typical
 problems.

6 Describe two measures of
 forecast accuracy.

7 Describe two ways of evaluating
 and controlling forecasts.

8 Identify the major factors to
 consider when choosing a
 forecasting technique.

Many new car buyers have a thing or two in common. Once they make the decision to buy a new car, they want it as soon as possible. They certainly don't want to order it and then have to wait six weeks or more for delivery. If the car dealer they visit doesn't have the car they want, they'll look elsewhere. Hence, it is important for a dealer to *anticipate* buyer wants and to have those models, with the necessary options, in stock. The dealer who can correctly forecast buyer wants, and have those cars available, is going to be much more successful than a competitor who guesses instead of forecasting—and guesses wrong—and gets stuck with cars customers don't want. So how does the dealer know how many cars of each type to stock? The answer is, the dealer *doesn't* know for sure, but based on analysis of previous buying patterns, and perhaps making allowances for current conditions, the dealer can come up with a reasonable *approximation* of what buyers will want.

forecast A statement about the future.

Planning is an integral part of a manager's job. If uncertainties cloud the planning horizon, managers will find it difficult to plan effectively. Forecasts help managers by reducing some of the uncertainty, thereby enabling them to develop more meaningful plans. A **forecast** is a statement about the future.

This chapter provides a survey of business forecasting. It describes the necessary steps in preparing a forecast, basic forecasting techniques, how to monitor a forecast, and elements of good forecasts.

Introduction

People make and use forecasts all the time, both in their jobs and in everyday life. In everyday life, they forecast answers and then make decisions based on their forecasts. Typical questions they may ask are: "Can I make it across the street before that car comes?" "How much food and drink will I need for the party?" "Will I get the job?" "When should I leave to make it to class, the station, the bank, the interview, . . . , on time?" To make these forecasts, they may take into account two kinds of information. One is current factors or conditions. The other is past experience in a similar situation. Sometimes they will rely more on one than the other, depending on which approach seems more relevant at the time.

Forecasting for business purposes involves similar approaches. In business, however, more formal methods are used to make forecasts and to assess forecast accuracy. Forecasts are the basis for budgeting and planning for capacity, sales, production and inventory, personnel, purchasing, and more. Forecasts play an important role in the planning process because they enable managers to anticipate the future so they can plan accordingly.

Forecasts affect decisions and activities throughout an organization, in accounting, finance, human resources, marketing, MIS, as well as operations, and other parts of an organization. Here are some examples of uses of forecasts in business organizations:

Accounting. New product/process cost estimates, profit projections, cash management.

Finance. Equipment/equipment replacement needs, timing and amount of funding/borrowing needs.

Human resources. Hiring activities, including recruitment, interviewing, training, layoff planning, including outplacement, counseling.

Marketing. Pricing and promotion, e-business strategies, global competition strategies.

MIS. New/revised information systems; Internet services.

Operations. Schedules, work assignments and workloads, inventory planning, make-or-buy decisions, outsourcing.

Product/service design. Revision of current features, design of new products or services.

In most of these uses of forecasts, decisions in one area have consequences in other areas. Therefore, it is important for managers in different areas to coordinate decisions. For example, marketing decisions on pricing and promotion affect demand, which, in turn, will generate requirements for operations.

There are two uses for forecasts. One is to help managers *plan the system* and the other is to help them *plan the use of the system.* Planning the system generally involves long-range plans about the types of products and services to offer, what facilities and equipment to have, where to locate, and so on. Planning the use of the system refers to short-range and intermediate-range planning, which involve tasks such as planning inventory and work-force levels, planning purchasing and production, budgeting, and scheduling.

Business forecasting pertains to more than predicting demand. Forecasts are also used to predict profits, revenues, costs, productivity changes, prices and availability of energy and raw materials, interest rates, movements of key economic indicators (e.g., GNP, inflation, government borrowing), and prices of stocks and bonds. For the sake of simplicity, this chapter will focus on the forecasting of demand. Keep in mind, however, that the concepts and techniques apply equally well to the other variables.

In spite of its use of computers and sophisticated mathematical models, forecasting is not an exact science. Instead, successful forecasting often requires a skillful blending of art and science. Experience, judgment, and technical expertise all play a role in developing useful forecasts. Along with these, a certain amount of luck and a dash of humility can be helpful, because the worst forecasters occasionally produce a very good forecast, and even the best forecasters sometimes miss completely. Current forecasting techniques range from the mundane to the exotic. Some work better than others, but no single technique works all the time.

Generally speaking, the responsibility for preparing demand forecasts in business organizations lies with marketing or sales rather than operations. Nonetheless, operations people are often called on to make certain forecasts and to help others prepare forecasts. In addition, because forecasts are major inputs for many operations decisions, operations managers and staff must be knowledgeable about the kinds of forecasting techniques available, the assumptions that underlie their use, and their limitations. It is also important for managers to consider *how* forecasts affect operations. In short, forecasting is an integral part of operations management.

Features Common to All Forecasts

A wide variety of forecasting techniques are in use. In many respects, they are quite different from each other, as you shall soon discover. Nonetheless, certain features are common to all, and it is important to recognize them.

1. Forecasting techniques generally assume that the same underlying causal system that existed in the past will continue to exist in the future.

Comment. A manager cannot simply delegate forecasting to models or computers and then forget about it, because unplanned occurrences can wreak havoc with forecasts. For instance, weather-related events, tax increases or decreases, and changes in features or prices of competing products or services can have a major impact on demand. Consequently, a manager must be alert to such occurrences and be ready to override forecasts, which assume a stable causal system.

2. Forecasts are rarely perfect; actual results usually differ from predicted values. No one can predict *precisely* how an often large number of related factors will impinge upon the variable in question; this, and the presence of randomness, preclude a perfect forecast. Allowances should be made for inaccuracies.

3. Forecasts for groups of items tend to be more accurate than forecasts for individual items because forecasting errors among items in a group usually have a canceling effect. Opportunities for grouping may arise if parts or raw materials are used for multiple products or if a product or service is demanded by a number of independent sources.

4. Forecast accuracy decreases as the time period covered by the forecast—the *time horizon*—increases. Generally speaking, short-range forecasts must contend with fewer uncertainties than longer-range forecasts, so they tend to be more accurate.

An important consequence of the last point is that flexible business organizations—those that can respond quickly to changes in demand—require a shorter forecasting horizon and, hence, benefit from more accurate short-range forecasts than competitors who are less flexible and who must therefore use longer forecast horizons.

Elements of a Good Forecast

A properly prepared forecast should fulfill certain requirements:

1. The forecast should be *timely*. Usually, a certain amount of time is needed to respond to the information contained in a forecast. For example, capacity cannot be expanded overnight, nor can inventory levels be changed immediately. Hence, the forecasting horizon must cover the time necessary to implement possible changes.
2. The forecast should be *accurate* and the degree of accuracy should be stated. This will enable users to plan for possible errors and will provide a basis for comparing alternative forecasts.
3. The forecast should be *reliable*; it should work consistently. A technique that sometimes provides a good forecast and sometimes a poor one will leave users with the uneasy feeling that they may get burned every time a new forecast is issued.
4. The forecast should be expressed in *meaningful units*. Financial planners need to know how many *dollars* will be needed, production planners need to know how many *units* will be needed, and schedulers need to know what *machines* and *skills* will be required. The choice of units depends on user needs.
5. The forecast should be *in writing*. Although this will not guarantee that all concerned are using the same information, it will at least increase the likelihood of it. In addition, a written forecast will permit an objective basis for evaluating the forecast once actual results are in.
6. The forecasting technique should be *simple to understand and use*. Users often lack confidence in forecasts based on sophisticated techniques; they do not understand either the circumstances in which the techniques are appropriate or the limitations of the techniques. Misuse of techniques is an obvious consequence. Not surprisingly, fairly crude forecasting techniques enjoy widespread popularity because users are more comfortable working with them.

Steps in the Forecasting Process

There are six basic steps in the forecasting process:

1. *Determine the purpose of the forecast.* What is its purpose and when will it be needed? This will provide an indication of the level of detail required in the forecast, the amount of resources (personnel, computer time, dollars) that can be justified, and the level of accuracy necessary.
2. *Establish a time horizon.* The forecast must indicate a time limit, keeping in mind that accuracy decreases as the time horizon increases.
3. *Select a forecasting technique.*
4. *Gather and analyze relevant data.* Before a forecast can be prepared, data must be gathered and analyzed. Identify any assumptions that are made in conjunction with preparing and using the forecast.
5. *Prepare the forecast.* Use an appropriate technique.

6. *Monitor the forecast.* A forecast has to be monitored to determine whether it is performing in a satisfactory manner. If it is not, reexamine the method, assumptions, validity of data, and so on; modify as needed; and prepare a revised forecast.

Approaches to Forecasting

There are two general approaches to forecasting: qualitative and quantitative. Qualitative methods consist mainly of subjective inputs, which often defy precise numerical description. Quantitative methods involve either the extension of historical data or the development of associative models that attempt to utilize *causal (explanatory) variables* to make a forecast.

Qualitative techniques permit inclusion of *soft* information (e.g., human factors, personal opinions, hunches) in the forecasting process. Those factors are often omitted or downplayed when quantitative techniques are used because they are difficult or impossible to quantify. Quantitative techniques consist mainly of analyzing objective, or *hard,* data. They usually avoid personal biases that sometimes contaminate qualitative methods. In practice, either or both approaches might be used to develop a forecast.

FORECASTS BASED ON JUDGMENT AND OPINION

Judgmental forecasts rely on analysis of subjective inputs obtained from various sources, such as consumer surveys, the sales staff, managers and executives, and panels of experts. Quite frequently, these sources provide insights that are not otherwise available.

judgmental forecasts Forecasts that use subjective inputs such as opinions from consumer surveys, sales staff, managers, executives, and experts.

FORECASTS BASED ON TIME SERIES (HISTORICAL) DATA

Some forecasting techniques simply attempt to project past experience into the future. These techniques use historical, or time series, data with the assumption that the future will be like the past. Some models merely attempt to smooth out random variations in historical data; others attempt to identify specific patterns in the data and project or extrapolate those patterns into the future, without trying to identify causes of the patterns.

ASSOCIATIVE FORECASTS

Associative models use equations that consist of one or more *explanatory* variables that can be used to predict future demand. For example, demand for paint might be related to variables such as the price per gallon and the amount spent on advertising, as well as specific characteristics of the paint (e.g., drying time, ease of cleanup).

associative model Forecasting technique that uses explanatory variables to predict future demand.

Forecasts Based on Judgment and Opinion

In some situations, forecasters rely solely on judgment and opinion to make forecasts. If management must have a forecast quickly, there may not be enough time to gather and analyze quantitative data. At other times, especially when political and economic conditions are changing, available data may be obsolete and more up-to-date information might not yet be available. Similarly, the introduction of new products and the redesign of existing products or packaging suffer from the absence of historical data that would be useful in forecasting. In such instances, forecasts are based on executive opinions, consumer surveys, opinions of the sales staff, and opinions of experts.

EXECUTIVE OPINIONS

A small group of upper-level managers (e.g., in marketing, operations, and finance) may meet and collectively develop a forecast. This approach is often used as a part of long-range planning and new product development. It has the advantage of bringing together the considerable knowledge and talents of various managers. However, there is the risk that the view of one person will prevail, and the possibility that diffusing responsibility for the forecast over the entire group may result in less pressure to produce a good forecast.

SALESFORCE OPINIONS

The sales staff or the customer service staff is often a good source of information because of their direct contact with consumers. They are often aware of any plans the customers may be considering for the future. There are, however, several drawbacks to this approach. One is that they may be unable to distinguish between what customers would *like* to do and what they actually *will* do. Another is that these people are sometimes overly influenced by recent experiences. Thus, after several periods of low sales, their estimates may tend to become pessimistic. After several periods of good sales, they may tend to be too optimistic. In addition, if forecasts are used to establish sales quotas, there will be a conflict of interest because it is to the salesperson's advantage to provide low sales estimates.

CONSUMER SURVEYS

Because it is the consumers who ultimately determine demand, it seems natural to solicit input from them. In some instances, every customer or potential customer can be contacted. However, there are usually too many customers or there is no way to identify all potential customers. Therefore, organizations seeking consumer input usually resort to consumer surveys, which enable them to *sample* consumer opinions. The obvious advantage of consumer surveys is that they can tap information that might not be available elsewhere. On the other hand, a considerable amount of knowledge and skill is required to construct a survey, administer it, and correctly interpret the results for valid information. Surveys can be expensive and time-consuming. In addition, even under the best conditions, surveys of the general public must contend with the possibility of irrational behavior patterns. For example, much of the consumer's thoughtful information gathering before purchasing a new car is often undermined by the glitter of a new car showroom or a high-pressure sales pitch. Along the same lines, low response rates to a mail survey should—but often don't—make the results suspect.

If these and similar pitfalls can be avoided, surveys can produce useful information.

OTHER APPROACHES

A manager may solicit opinions from a number of other managers and staff people. Occasionally, outside experts are needed to help with a forecast. Advice may be needed on political or economic conditions in the United States or a foreign country, or some other aspect of importance with which an organization lacks familiarity.

Another approach is the **Delphi method.** It involves circulating a series of questionnaires among individuals who possess the knowledge and ability to contribute meaningfully. Responses are kept anonymous, which tends to encourage honest responses and reduces the risk that one person's opinion will prevail. Each new questionnaire is developed using the information extracted from the previous one, thus enlarging the scope of information on which participants can base their judgments. The goal is to achieve a consensus forecast.

The Delphi method originated in the Rand Corporation in 1948. Since that time, it has been applied to a variety of situations, not all of which involve forecasting. The discussion here is limited to its use as a forecasting tool.

As a forecasting tool, the Delphi method is useful for *technological* forecasting; that is, the technique is a method for assessing changes in technology and their impact on an organization. Often the goal is to predict *when* a certain event will occur. For instance, the goal of a Delphi forecast might be to predict when video telephones might be installed in at least 50 percent of residential homes or when a vaccine for a disease might be developed and ready for mass distribution. For the most part, these are long-term, single-time forecasts, which usually have very little hard information to go by or data that are costly

Delphi method Managers and staff complete a series of questionnaires, each developed from the previous one, to achieve a consensus forecast.

to obtain, so the problem does not lend itself to analytical techniques. Rather, judgments of experts or others who possess sufficient knowledge to make predictions are used.

Forecasts Based on Time Series Data

A **time series** is a time-ordered sequence of observations taken at regular intervals over a period of time (e.g., hourly, daily, weekly, monthly, quarterly, annually). The data may be measurements of demand, earnings, profits, shipments, accidents, output, precipitation, productivity, and the consumer price index. Forecasting techniques based on time series data are made on the assumption that future values of the series can be estimated from past values. Although no attempt is made to identify variables that influence the series, these methods are widely used, often with quite satisfactory results.

Analysis of time series data requires the analyst to identify the underlying behavior of the series. This can often be accomplished by merely *plotting* the data and visually examining the plot. One or more patterns might appear: trends, seasonal variations, cycles, and variations around an average. In addition, there can be random or irregular variations. These behaviors can be described as follows:

1. **Trend** refers to a long-term upward or downward movement in the data. Population shifts, changing incomes, and cultural changes often account for such movements.
2. **Seasonality** refers to short-term, fairly regular variations generally related to factors such as the calendar or time of day. Restaurants, supermarkets, and theaters experience weekly and even daily "seasonal" variations.
3. **Cycles** are wavelike variations of more than one year's duration. These are often related to a variety of economic, political, and even agricultural conditions.
4. **Irregular variations** are due to unusual circumstances such as severe weather conditions, strikes, or a major change in a product or service. They do not reflect typical behavior, and inclusion in the series can distort the overall picture. Whenever possible, these should be identified and removed from the data.
5. **Random variations** are residual variations that remain after all other behaviors have been accounted for.

These behaviors are illustrated in Figure 3–1 on pg. 76. The small "bumps" in the plots represent random variability.

The remainder of this section has descriptions of the various approaches to the analysis of time series data. Before turning to those discussions, one point should be emphasized: A demand forecast should be based on a time series of past *demand* rather than sales. Sales would not truly reflect demand if one or more *stockouts* occurred.

NAIVE METHODS

A simple, but widely used approach to forecasting is the naive approach. A **naive forecast** uses a single previous value of a time series as the basis of a forecast. The naive approach can be used with a stable series (variations around an average), with seasonal variations, or with trend. With a stable series, the last data point becomes the forecast for the next period. Thus, if demand for a product last week was 20 cases, the forecast for this week is 20 cases. With seasonal variations, the forecast for this "season" is equal to the value of the series last "season." For example, the forecast for demand for turkeys this Thanksgiving season is equal to demand for turkeys last Thanksgiving; the forecast of the number of checks cashed at a bank on the first day of the month next month is equal to the number of checks cashed on the first day of this month; and the forecast for highway traffic volume this Friday is equal to the highway traffic volume last Friday. For data with trend, the forecast is equal to the last value of the series plus or minus the difference between the last two values of the series. For example, suppose the last two values were 50 and 53:

time series A time-ordered sequence of observations taken at regular intervals over time.

trend A long-term upward or downward movement in data.

seasonality Short-term regular variations related to the calendar or time of day.

cycle Wavelike variation lasting more than one year.

irregular variation Caused by unusual circumstances, not reflective of typical behavior.

random variations Residual variations after all other behaviors are accounted for.

naive forecast The forecast for any period equals the previous period's actual value.

FIGURE 3–1

Trend, seasonal, cyclical, random, and irregular variations

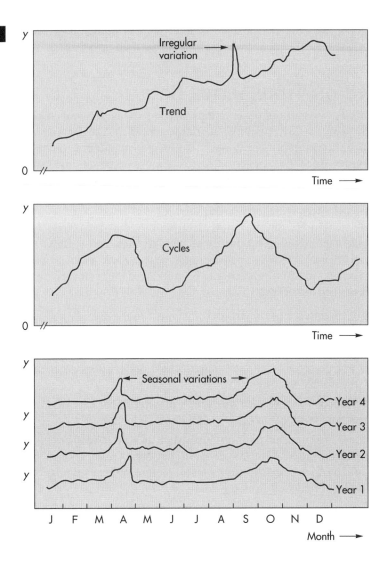

Period	Actual	Change from Previous Value	Forecast
$t-1$	50		
t	53	+3	
$t+1$			$53 + +3 = 56$

Although at first glance the naive approach may appear *too* simplistic, it is nonetheless a legitimate forecasting tool. Consider the advantages: It has virtually no cost, it is quick and easy to prepare because data analysis is nonexistent, and it is easily understandable. The main objection to this method is its inability to provide highly accurate forecasts. However, if resulting accuracy is acceptable, this approach deserves serious consideration. Moreover, even if other forecasting techniques offer better accuracy, they will almost always involve a greater cost. The accuracy of a naive forecast can serve as a standard of comparison against which to judge the cost and accuracy of other techniques. Thus, managers must answer the question: Is the increased accuracy of another method worth the additional resources required to achieve that accuracy?

TECHNIQUES FOR AVERAGING

Historical data typically contain a certain amount of random variation, or *noise,* that tends to obscure systematic movements in the data. This randomness arises from the combined

Data	NWWW
Forecast	‐ ‐ ‐ ‐

Ideal   Step change   Gradual change

FIGURE 3-2

Averaging applied to three possible patterns

influence of many—perhaps a great many—relatively unimportant factors, and it cannot be reliably predicted. Averaging techniques smooth variations in the data. Ideally, it would be desirable to completely remove any randomness from the data and leave only "real" variations, such as changes in the demand. As a practical matter, however, it is usually impossible to distinguish between these two kinds of variations, so the best one can hope for is that the small variations are random and the large variations are "real."

Averaging techniques smooth fluctuations in a time series because the individual highs and lows in the data offset each other when they are combined into an average. A forecast based on an average thus tends to exhibit less variability than the original data (see Figure 3–2). This can be advantageous because many of these movements merely reflect random variability rather than a true change in level, or trend, in the series. Moreover, because responding to changes in expected demand often entails considerable cost (e.g., changes in production rate, changes in the size of a workforce, inventory changes), it is desirable to avoid reacting to minor variations. Thus, minor variations are treated as random variations, whereas larger variations are viewed as more likely to reflect "real" changes, although these, too, are smoothed to a certain degree.

Averaging techniques generate forecasts that reflect recent values of a time series (e.g., the average value over the last several periods). These techniques work best when a series tends to vary around an average, although they can also handle step changes or gradual changes in the level of the series. Three techniques for averaging are described in this section:

1. Moving average
2. Weighted moving average
3. Exponential smoothing

Moving Average. One weakness of the naive method is that the forecast just *traces* the actual data, with a lag of one period; it does not smooth at all. But by expanding the amount of historical data a forecast is based on, this difficulty can be overcome. A **moving average** forecast uses a *number* of the most recent actual data values in generating a forecast. The moving average forecast can be computed using the following equation:

moving average Technique that averages a number of recent actual values, updated as new values become available.

$$F_t = MA_n = \frac{\sum_{i=1}^{n} A_i}{n} \tag{3–1}$$

where

i = An index that corresponds to periods

n = Number of periods (data points) in the moving average

A_i = Actual value in period i

MA = Moving average

F_t = Forecast for time period t

For example, MA_3 would refer to a three-period moving average forecast, and MA_5 would refer to a five-period moving average forecast.

Compute a three-period moving average forecast given demand for shopping carts for the last five periods.

Example 1

Period	Age	Demand	
1	5	42	
2	4	40	
3	3	43	
4	2	40	} the 3 most recent demands
5	1	41	

Solution

$$F_6 = \frac{43 + 40 + 41}{3} = 41.33$$

If actual demand in period 6 turns out to be 39, the moving average forecast for period 7 would be

$$F_7 = \frac{40 + 41 + 39}{3} = 40.00$$

Note that in a moving average, as each new actual value becomes available, the forecast is updated by adding the newest value and dropping the oldest and then recomputing the average. Consequently, the forecast "moves" by reflecting only the most recent values.

In computing a moving average, including a *moving total* column—which gives the sum of the *n* most current values from which the average will be computed—would aid computations. It is relatively simple to update the moving total: Subtract the oldest value from the newest value, and add that amount to the moving total for each update.

Figure 3–3 illustrates a three-period moving average forecast plotted against actual demand over 31 periods. Note how the moving average forecast *lags* the actual values and how smooth the forecasted values are compared with the actual values.

The moving average can incorporate as many data points as desired. In selecting the number of periods to include, the decision maker must take into account that the number of data points in the average determines its sensitivity to each new data point: The fewer the data points in an average, the more sensitive (responsive) the average tends to be. (See Figure 3–4.) If responsiveness is important, a moving average with relatively few data points should be used. This will permit quick adjustment to, say, a step change in the data, but it will also cause the forecast to be somewhat responsive even to random variations. Conversely, moving averages based on more data points will smooth more but be less responsive to "real" changes. Hence, the decision maker must weigh the cost of responding more slowly to changes in the data against the cost of responding to what might simply be random variations. A review of forecast errors can help in this decision.

The advantages of a moving average forecast are that it is easy to compute and easy to understand. A possible disadvantage is that all values in the average are weighted equally. For instance, in a 10-period moving average, each value has a weight of 1/10. Hence, the oldest value has the *same weight* as the most recent value. If a change occurs in the series, a moving average forecast can be slow to react, especially if there are a large number of values in the average. Decreasing the number of values in the average increases the weight of more recent values, but it does so at the expense of losing potential information from less recent values.

weighted average More recent values in a series are given more weight in computing a forecast.

Weighted Moving Average. A **weighted average** is similar to a moving average, except that it assigns more weight to the most recent values in a time series. For instance, the most recent value might be assigned a weight of .40, the next most recent value a weight of .30, the next after that a weight of .20, and the next after that a weight of .10. Note that the weights sum to 1.00, and that the heaviest weights are assigned to the most recent values.

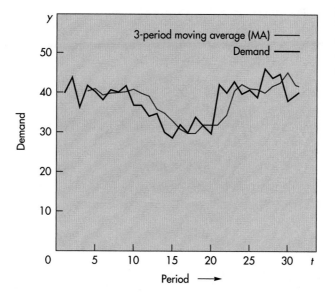

FIGURE 3–3

A moving average forecast tends to smooth and lag changes in the data

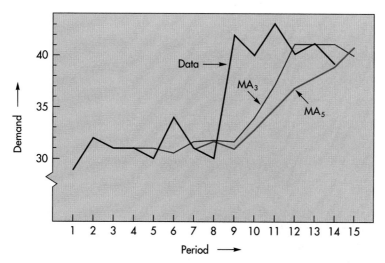

FIGURE 3–4

The more periods in a moving average, the greater the forecast will lag changes in the data

Given the following demand data,

Example 2

a. Compute a weighted average forecast using a weight of .40 for the most recent period, .30 for the next most recent, .20 for the next, and .10 for the next.

b. If the actual demand for period 6 is 39, forecast demand for period 7 using the same weights as in part *a.*

Period	Demand
1	42
2	40
3	43
4	40
5	41

a. $F_6 = .40(41) + .30(40) + .20(43) + .10(40) = 41.0$

Solution

b. $F_7 = .40(39) + .30(41) + .20(40) + .10(43) = 40.2$

Note that if four weights are used, only the *four most recent* demands are used to prepare the forecast.

The advantage of a weighted average over a simple moving average is that the weighted average is more reflective of the most recent occurrences. However, the choice of weights is somewhat arbitrary and generally involves the use of trial and error to find a suitable weighting scheme.

exponential smoothing
Weighted averaging method based on previous forecast plus a percentage of the forecast error.

Exponential Smoothing. **Exponential smoothing** is a sophisticated weighted averaging method that is still relatively easy to use and understand. Each new forecast is based on the previous forecast plus a percentage of the difference between that forecast and the actual value of the series at that point. That is:

Next forecast = Previous forecast + α(Actual − Previous forecast)

where (Actual − Previous forecast) represents the forecast error and α is a percentage of the error. More concisely,

$$F_t = F_{t-1} + \alpha(A_{t-1} - F_{t-1}) \tag{3–2a}$$

where

F_t = Forecast for period t

F_{t-1} = Forecast for the previous period

α = Smoothing constant

A_{t-1} = Actual demand or sales for the previous period

The smoothing constant α represents a percentage of the forecast error. Each new forecast is equal to the previous forecast plus a percentage of the previous error. For example, suppose the previous forecast was 42 units, actual demand was 40 units, and α = .10. The new forecast would be computed as follows:

$$F_t = 42 + .10(40 - 42) = 41.8$$

Then, if the actual demand turns out to be 43, the next forecast would be:

$$F_t = 41.8 + .10(43 - 41.8) = 41.92$$

An alternate form of formula 3–2a reveals the weighting of the previous forecast and the latest actual demand:

$$F_t = (1 - \alpha)F_{t-1} + \alpha A_{t-1} \tag{3–2b}$$

For example, if α = .10, this would be

$$F_t = .90F_{t-1} + .10 A_{t-1}$$

The quickness of forecast adjustment to error is determined by the smoothing constant, α. The closer its value is to zero, the slower the forecast will be to adjust to forecast errors (i.e., the greater the smoothing). Conversely, the closer the value of α is to 1.00, the greater the responsiveness and the less the smoothing. This is illustrated in Example 3.

Example 3

The following table illustrates two series of forecasts for a data set, and the resulting (Actual − Forecast) = Error, for each period. One forecast uses α = .10 and one uses α = .40. The following figure plots the actual data and both sets of forecasts.

Period (t)	Actual Demand	$\alpha = .10$ Forecast	$\alpha = .10$ Error	$\alpha = .40$ Forecast	$\alpha = .40$ Error
1	42	—	—	—	—
2	40	42	−2	42	−2
3	43	41.8	1.2	41.2	1.8
4	40	41.92	−1.92	41.92	−1.92
5	41	41.73	−0.73	41.15	−0.15

6	39	41.66	−2.66	41.09	−2.09
7	46	41.39	4.61	40.25	5.75
8	44	41.85	2.15	42.55	1.45
9	45	42.07	2.93	43.13	1.87
10	38	42.35	−4.35	43.88	−5.88
11	40	41.92	−1.92	41.53	−1.53
12		41.73		40.92	

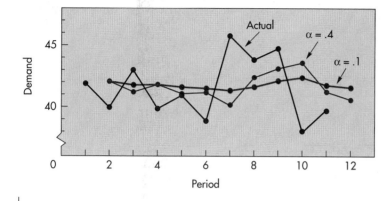

Selecting a smoothing constant is basically a matter of judgment or trial and error, using forecast errors to guide the decision. The goal is to select a smoothing constant that balances the benefits of smoothing random variations with the benefits of responding to real changes if and when they occur. Commonly used values of α range from .05 to .50. Low values of α are used when the underlying average tends to be stable; higher values are used when the underlying average is susceptible to change.

Some computer packages include a feature that permits automatic modification of the smoothing constant if the forecast errors become unacceptably large.

Exponential smoothing is one of the most widely used techniques in forecasting, partly because of its ease of calculation, and partly because of the ease with which the weighting scheme can be altered—simply by changing the value of α.

Note. A number of different approaches can be used to obtain a *starting forecast,* such as the average of the first several periods, a subjective estimate, or the first actual value as the forecast for period 2 (i.e., the naive approach). For simplicity, the naive approach is used in this book. In practice, using an average of, say, the first three values as a forecast for period 4 would provide a better starting forecast because that would tend to be more representative.

TECHNIQUES FOR TREND

Analysis of trend involves developing an equation that will suitably describe trend (assuming that trend is present in the data). The trend component may be linear, or it may not. Some commonly encountered nonlinear trend types are illustrated in Figure 3–5. A simple plot of the data can often reveal the existence and nature of a trend. The discussion here focuses exclusively on *linear* trends because these are fairly common.

There are two important techniques that can be used to develop forecasts when trend is present. One involves use of a trend equation; the other is an extension of exponential smoothing.

Trend Equation. A **linear trend equation** has the form

$$y_t = a + bt \tag{3–3}$$

linear trend equation $y_t = a + bt$, used to develop forecasts when trend is present.

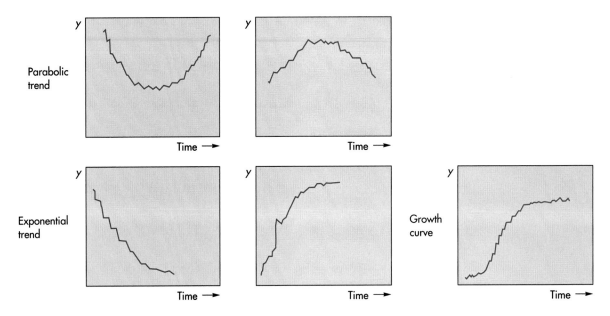

FIGURE 3–5

Graphs of some nonlinear trends

where

t = Specified number of time periods from $t = 0$

y_t = Forecast for period t

a = Value of y_t at $t = 0$

b = Slope of the line

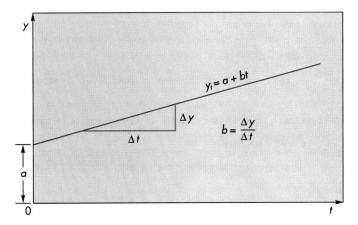

The line intersects the *y* axis where *y = a*. The slope of the line = *b*.

For example, consider the trend equation $y_t = 45 + 5t$. The value of y_t when $t = 0$ is 45, and the slope of the line is 5, which means that, on the average, the value of y_t will increase by five units for each time period. If $t = 10$, the forecast, y_t, is $45 + 5(10) = 95$ units. The equation can be plotted by finding two points on the line. One can be found by substituting some value of t into the equation (e.g., $t = 10$) and then solving for y_t. The other point is a (i.e., y_t at $t = 0$). Plotting those two points and drawing a line through them yields a graph of the linear trend line.

The coefficients of the line, *a* and *b,* can be computed from historical data using these two equations:

n	Σt	Σt²
1 ...	1	1
2 ...	3	5
3 ...	6	14
4 ...	10	30
5 ...	15	55
6 ...	21	91
7 ...	28	140
8 ...	36	204
9 ...	45	285
10 ...	55	385
11 ...	66	506
12 ...	78	650
13 ...	91	819
14 ...	105	1,015
15 ...	120	1,240
16 ...	136	1,496
17 ...	153	1,785
18 ...	171	2,109
19 ...	190	2,470
20 ...	210	2,870

TABLE 3–1

Values of Σt and Σt²

$$b = \frac{n\sum ty - \sum t \sum y}{n\sum t^2 - (\sum t)^2}$$ (3–4)

$$a = \frac{\sum y - b\sum t}{n} \text{ or } \bar{y} - b\bar{t}$$ (3–5)

where

    n = Number of periods

    y = Value of the time series

Note that these three equations are identical to those used for computing a linear regression line, except that t replaces x in the equations. Manual computation of the coefficients of a trend line can be simplified by use of Table 3–1, which lists values of $\sum t$ and $\sum t^2$ for up to 20 periods ($n = 20$).

Cell phone sales for a California-based firm over the last 10 weeks are shown in the following table. Plot the data, and visually check to see if a linear trend line would be appropriate. Then determine the equation of the trend line, and predict sales for weeks 11 and 12.

Example 4

Week	Unit Sales
1	700
2	724
3	720
4	728
5	740
6	742
7	758
8	750
9	770
10	775

Solution

a. A plot suggests that a linear trend line would be appropriate:

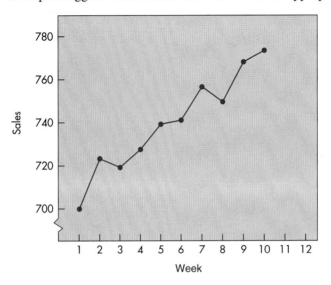

b.

Week (t)	y	ty
1	700	700
2	724	1,448
3	720	2,160
4	728	2,912
5	740	3,700
6	742	4,452
7	758	5,306
8	750	6,000
9	770	6,930
10	775	7,750
	7,407	41,358

From Table 3–1, for $n = 10$, $\Sigma t = 55$ and $\Sigma t^2 = 385$. Using Formulas 3–4 and 3–5, you can compute the coefficients of the trend line:

$$b = \frac{10(41,358) - 55(7,407)}{10(385) - 55(55)} = \frac{6,195}{825} = 7.51$$

$$a = \frac{7,407 - 7.51(55)}{10} = 699.40$$

Thus, the trend line is $y_t = 699.40 + 7.51t$, where $t = 0$ for period 0.

c. Substituting values of t into this equation, the forecasts for the next two periods (i.e., $t = 11$ and $t = 12$) are:

$$y_{11} = 699.40 + 7.51(11) = 782.01$$
$$y_{12} = 699.40 + 7.51(12) = 789.52$$

d. For purposes of illustration, the original data, the trend line, and the two projections (forecasts) are shown on the following graph:

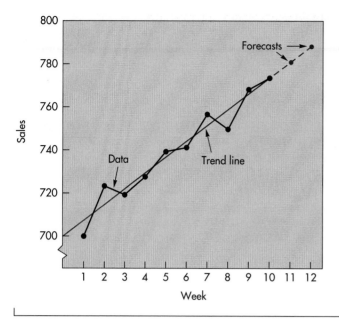

TREND-ADJUSTED EXPONENTIAL SMOOTHING

A variation of simple exponential smoothing can be used when a time series exhibits trend. It is called **trend-adjusted exponential smoothing** or, sometimes, *double smoothing,* to differentiate it from simple exponential smoothing, which is appropriate only when data vary around an average or have step or gradual changes. If a series exhibits trend, and simple smoothing is used on it, the forecasts will all lag the trend: if the data are increasing, each forecast will be too low; if decreasing, each forecast will be too high. Again, plotting the data can indicate when trend-adjusted smoothing would be preferable to simple smoothing.

trend-adjusted exponential smoothing Variation of exponential smoothing used when a time series exhibits trend.

The trend-adjusted forecast (TAF) is composed of two elements: a smoothed error and a trend factor.

$$\text{TAF}_{t+1} = S_t + T_t \tag{3–6}$$

where

S_t = Smoothed forecast

T_t = Current trend estimate

and

$$S_t = \text{TAF}_t + \alpha(A_t - \text{TAF}_t) \tag{3–7}$$
$$T_t = T_{t-1} + \beta(\text{TAF}_t - \text{TAF}_{t-1} - T_{t-1})$$

where α and β are smoothing constants. In order to use this method, one must select values of α and β (usually through trial and error) and make a starting forecast and an estimate of trend.

Example 5

Using the cell phone data from the previous example (where it was concluded that the data exhibited a linear trend), use trend-adjusted exponential smoothing to prepare forecasts for periods 5 through 11, with $\alpha_1 = .4$ and $\alpha_2 = .3$.

Solution

The initial estimate of trend is based on the net change of 28 for the *three* changes from period 1 to period 4, for an average of 9.30. The data and calculations are shown in

	t (Period)	A_t (Actual)					
Model development	1	700	$\text{Trend estimate} = \dfrac{728 - 700}{3} = \dfrac{28}{3} = 9.33$				
	2	724					
	3	720	$\text{Starting forecast} = 728 + 9.33 = 737.33$				
	4	728					

			F_t	$TAF_t + \alpha(A_t - TAF_t) = S_t$		$T_{t-1} + \beta(TAF_t - TAF_{t-1} - T_{t-1}) = T_t$	
Model test	5	740	737.33	737.33 + .4(740 − 737.33) = 738.40		9.33 + .3(0)	= 9.33
	6	742	747.73	747.73 + .4(742 − 747.73) = 745.44		9.33 + .3(747.73 − 737.33 − 9.33)	= 9.65
	7	758	755.09	755.09 + .4(758 − 755.09) = 756.25		9.65 + .3(755.09 − 747.73 − 9.65)	= 8.96
	8	750	765.22	765.22 + .4(750 − 765.22) = 759.13		8.96 + .3(765.22 − 755.09 − 8.96)	= 9.31
	9	770	768.45	768.45 + .4(770 − 768.45) = 769.07		9.31 + .3(768.45 − 765.22 − 9.31)	= 7.49
	10	775	776.56	776.56 + .4(775 − 776.56) = 775.94		7.49 + .3(776.56 − 768.45 − 7.49)	= 7.68
Forecast	11		783.61	[=	775.94	+	7.68]

Note: Some numbers don't add exactly due to rounding.

TABLE 3–2

Examples of trend-adjusted forecast calculations

Table 3–2. Notice that an initial estimate of trend is estimated from the first four values, and that the starting forecast (period 5) is developed using the previous (period 4) value of 728 plus the initial trend estimate:

Starting forecast = 728 + 9.30 = 737.33

Although manual computations are somewhat more involved for trend-adjusted smoothing than for a linear trend line, trend-adjusted smoothing has the ability to adjust to *changes* in trend. Of course, trend projections are much simpler with a trend line than with trend-adjusted forecasts, so a manager must decide which benefits are most important when choosing between these two techniques for trend.

Table 3–3 illustrates the solution obtained using the Excel template for trend-adjusted smoothing.

A plot of the actual data and predicted values is shown below.

TABLE 3-3

Using the Excel template for trend-adjusted smoothing

TECHNIQUES FOR SEASONALITY

Seasonal variations in time series data are regularly repeating upward or downward movements in series values that can be tied to recurring events. *Seasonality* may refer to regular annual variations. Familiar examples of seasonality are weather variations (e.g., sales of winter and summer sports equipment) and vacations or holidays (e.g., airline travel, greeting card sales, visitors at tourist and resort centers). The term *seasonal variation* is also applied to daily, weekly, monthly, and other regularly recurring patterns in data. For example, rush hour traffic occurs twice a day—incoming in the morning and outgoing in the late afternoon. Theaters and restaurants often experience weekly demand patterns, with demand higher later in the week. Banks may experience daily seasonal variations (heavier traffic during the noon hour and just before closing), weekly variations (heavier toward the end of the week), and monthly variations (heaviest around the beginning of the month because of social security, payroll, and welfare checks being cashed or deposited). Mail volume; sales of toys, beer, automobiles, and turkeys; highway usage; hotel registrations; and gardening also exhibit seasonal variations.

Seasonality in a time series is expressed in terms of the amount that actual values deviate from the *average* value of a series. If the series tends to vary around an average value, then seasonality is expressed in terms of that average (or a moving average); if trend is present, seasonality is expressed in terms of the trend value.

There are two different models of seasonality: additive and multiplicative. In the *additive* model, seasonality is expressed as a *quantity* (e.g., 20 units), which is added or subtracted from the series average in order to incorporate seasonality. In the *multiplicative*

seasonal variations Regularly repeating movements in series values that can be tied to recurring events.

Demand for products such as lawnmowers and snow throwers is subject to large seasonal fluctuations. Toro matches these fluctuations by reallocating its manufacturing capacity between products.

www.toro.com

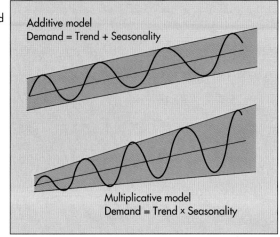

model, seasonality is expressed as a *percentage* of the average (or trend) amount (e.g., 1.10), which is then used to multiply the value of a series to incorporate seasonality. Figure 3–6 illustrates the two models for a linear trend line. In practice, businesses use the multiplicative model much more widely than the additive model, so we shall focus exclusively on the multiplicative model.

seasonal relative Percentage of average or trend.

The seasonal percentages in the multiplicative model are referred to as **seasonal relatives** or *seasonal indexes.* Suppose that the seasonal relative for the quantity of toys sold in May at a store is 1.20. This indicates that toy sales for that month are 20 percent above the monthly average. A seasonal relative of .90 for July indicates that July sales are 90 percent of the monthly average.

Knowledge of seasonal variations is an important factor in retail planning and scheduling. Moreover, seasonality can be an important factor in capacity planning for systems that must be designed to handle peak loads (e.g., public transportation, electric power plants, highways, and bridges). Knowledge of the extent of seasonality in a time series can enable one to *remove* seasonality from the data (i.e., to seasonally adjust data) in order to discern other patterns or the lack of patterns in the series. Thus, one frequently reads or hears about "seasonally adjusted unemployment" and "seasonally adjusted personal income."

The next section briefly describes how seasonal relatives are used, and the following section describes how seasonal relatives are computed.

Using Seasonal Relatives. Seasonal relatives are used in two different ways in forecasting. One way is to *deseasonalize* data; the other way is to *incorporate seasonality* in a forecast.

To deseasonalize data is to remove the seasonal component from the data in order to get a clearer picture of the nonseasonal (e.g., trend) components. Deseasonalizing data is accomplished by *dividing* each data point by its corresponding seasonal relative (e.g., divide November demand by the November relative, divide December demand by the December relative, and so on).

Incorporating seasonality in a forecast is useful when demand has both trend (or average) and seasonal components. Incorporating seasonality can be accomplished in this way:

1. Obtain trend estimates for desired periods using a trend equation.
2. Add seasonality to the trend estimates by *multiplying* (assuming a multiplicative model is appropriate) these trend estimates by the corresponding seasonal relative (e.g., multiply the November trend estimate by the November seasonal relative, multiply the December trend estimate by the December seasonal relative, and so on).

Example 6 illustrates incorporating seasonality in a forecast.

A furniture manufacturer wants to predict quarterly demand for a certain loveseat for periods 15 and 16, which happen to be the second and third quarters of a particular year. The series consists of both trend and seasonality. The trend portion of demand is projected using the equation $y_t = 124 + 7.5t$. Quarter relatives are $Q_1 = 1.20$, $Q_2 = 1.10$, $Q_3 = 0.75$, and $Q_4 = 0.95$. Use this information to predict demand for periods 15 and 16.

Example 6

The trend values at $t = 15$ and $t = 16$ are:

$$y_{15} = 124 + 7.5(15) = 236.5$$
$$y_{16} = 124 + 7.5(16) = 244.0$$

Multiplying the trend value by the appropriate quarter relative yields a forecast that includes both trend and seasonality. Given that $t = 15$ is a second quarter and $t = 16$ is a third quarter, the forecasts are:

Period 15: $236.5(1.10) = 260.15$
Period 16: $244.0(0.75) = 183.00$

Computing Seasonal Relatives. A commonly used method for representing the trend portion of a time series involves a **centered moving average.** Computations and the resulting values are the same as those for a moving average forecast. However, the values are not projected as in a forecast; instead, they are *positioned in the middle* of the periods used to compute the moving average. The implication is that the average is most representative of that point in the series. For example, assume the following time series data:

centered moving average A moving average positioned at the center of the data that were used to compute it.

Period	Demand	Three-Period Centered Average	
1	40		
2	46	42.67	Average $= \dfrac{40 + 46 + 42}{3} = 42.67$
3	42		

The three-period average is 42.67. As a centered average, it is positioned at period 2; the average is most representative of the series at that point.

The ratio of demand at period 2 to this centered average at period 2 is an estimate of the seasonal relative at that point. Because the ratio is $46/42.67 = 1.08$, the series is about 8 percent above average at that point. To achieve a reasonable estimate of seasonality for any season (e.g., Friday attendance at a theater), it is usually necessary to compute seasonal ratios for a number of seasons and then average these ratios. In the case of theater attendance, average the ratios of five or six Fridays for the Friday relative, average five or six Saturdays for the Saturday relative, and so on.

The manager of a parking lot has computed daily relatives for the number of cars per day in the lot. The computations are repeated here (about three weeks are shown for illustration). A seven-period centered moving average is used because there are seven days (seasons) per week.

Example 7

Day	Volume	Moving Total	Centered MA$_7$	Volume/MA
Tues	67			
Wed	75			
Thur	82			
Fri	98		71.86	$98/71.86 = 1.36$ (Friday)
Sat	90		70.86	$90/70.86 = 1.27$
Sun	36		70.57	$36/70.57 = 0.51$
Mon	55	$503 \div 7 =$	71.00	$55/71.00 = 0.77$
Tues	60	$496 \div 7 =$	71.14	$60/71.14 = 0.84$ (Tuesday)

Wed	73	494 etc.	70.57	73/70.57 = 1.03
Thur	85	497	71.14	85/71.14 = 1.19
Fri	99	498	70.71	99/70.71 = 1.40 (Friday)
Sat	86	494	71.29	86/71.29 = 1.21
Sun	40	498	71.71	40/71.71 = 0.56
Mon	52	495	72.00	52/72.00 = 0.72
Tues	64	499	71.57	64/71.57 = 0.89 (Tuesday)
Wed	76	502	71.86	76/71.86 = 1.06
Thur	87	504	72.43	87/72.43 = 1.20
Fri	96	501	72.14	96/72.14 = 1.33 (Friday)
Sat	88	503		
Sun	44	507		
Mon	50	505		

The estimated Friday relative is (1.36 + 1.40 + 133)/3 = 1.36. Relatives for other days can be computed in a similar manner. For example, the estimated Tuesday relative is (0.84 + 0.89)/2 = 0.87.

The number of periods needed in a centered moving average is equal to the number of "seasons" involved. For example, with monthly data, a 12-period moving average is needed. When the number of periods is even, one additional step is needed because the middle of an even set falls between two periods. The additional step requires taking a centered two-period moving average of the even-numbered centered moving average, which results in averages that "line up" with data points and, hence, permit determination of seasonal ratios. (See Solved Problem 4 at the end of this chapter for an example.)

A centered moving average is used to obtain representative values because by virtue of its centered position—it "looks forward" and "looks backward"—it is able to closely follow data movements whether they involve trends, cycles, or random variability alone. Figure 3–7 illustrates how a three-period centered moving average closely tracks the data originally shown in Figure 3–3.

TECHNIQUES FOR CYCLES

Cycles are up and down movements similar to seasonal variations but of longer duration—say, two to six years between peaks. When cycles occur in time series data, their frequent irregularity makes it difficult or impossible to project them from past data because turning points are difficult to identify. A short moving average or a naive approach

FIGURE 3-7

A centered moving average closely tracks the data

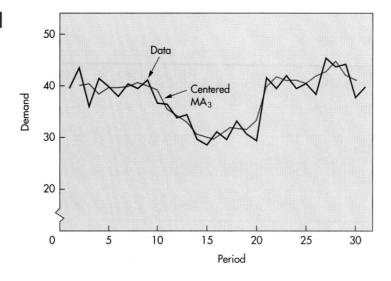

may be of some value, although both will produce forecasts that lag cyclical movements by one or several periods.

The most commonly used approach is explanatory: Search for another variable that relates to, and *leads,* the variable of interest. For example, the number of housing starts (i.e., permits to build houses) in a given month often is an indicator of demand a few months later for products and services directly tied to construction of new homes (landscaping; sales of washers and dryers, carpeting, and furniture; new demands for shopping, transportation, schools). Thus, if an organization is able to establish a high correlation with such a *leading variable* (i.e., changes in the variable precede changes in the variable of interest), it can develop an equation that describes the relationship, enabling forecasts to be made. It is important that a persistent relationship exists between the two variables. Moreover, the higher the correlation, the better the chances that the forecast will be on target.

Associative Forecasting Techniques

Associative techniques rely on identification of related variables that can be used to predict values of the variable of interest. For example, sales of beef may be related to the price per pound charged for beef and the prices of substitutes such as chicken, pork, and lamb; real estate prices are usually related to property location; and crop yields are related to soil conditions and the amounts and timing of water and fertilizer applications.

predictor variables Variables that can be used to predict values of the variable of interest.

The essence of associative techniques is the development of an equation that summarizes the effects of **predictor variables**. The primary method of analysis is known as **regression**. A brief overview of regression should suffice to place this approach into perspective relative to the other forecasting approaches described in this chapter.

regression Technique for fitting a line to a set of points.

SIMPLE LINEAR REGRESSION

The simplest and most widely used form of regression involves a linear relationship between two variables. A plot of the values might appear like that in Figure 3–8. The object in linear regression is to obtain an equation of a straight line that minimizes the sum of squared vertical deviations of data points from the line. This **least squares line** has the equation

least squares line Minimizes the sum of the squared deviations around the line.

$$y_c = a + bx \tag{3–8}$$

where

y_c = Predicted (dependent) variable

x = Predictor (independent) variable

b = Slope of the line

a = Value of y_c when $x = 0$ (i.e., the height of the line at the y intercept)

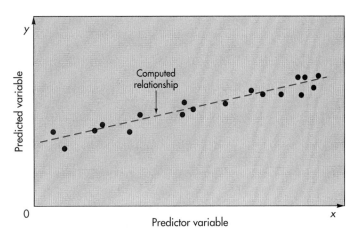

FIGURE 3–8

A straight line is fitted to a set of sample points

FIGURE 3–9

Equation of a straight line

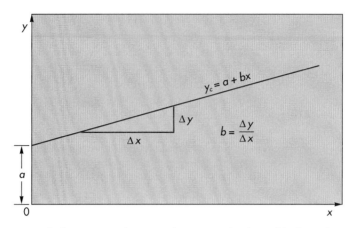

The line intersects the y axis where y = a. The slope of the line = b.

(Note: It is conventional to represent values of the predicted variable on the *y* axis and values of the predictor variable on the *x* axis.) Figure 3–9 is a graph of a linear regression line.

The coefficients *a* and *b* of the line are computed using these two equations:

$$b = \frac{n(\sum xy) - (\sum x)(\sum y)}{n(\sum x^2) - (\sum x)^2}$$ (3–9)

$$a = \frac{\sum y - b\sum x}{n} \text{ or } \bar{y} - b\bar{x}$$ (3–10)

where

   n = Number of paired observations

Example 8

Healthy Hamburgers has a chain of 12 stores in northern Illinois. Sales figures and profits for the stores are given in the following table. Obtain a regression line for the data, and predict profit for a store assuming sales of $10 million.

Sales, x	Profits, y
(in millions of dollars)	
$ 7	$0.15
2	0.10
6	0.13
4	0.15
14	0.25
15	0.27
16	0.24
12	0.20
14	0.27
20	0.44
15	0.34
7	0.17

Solution

First, plot the data and decide if a linear model is reasonable (i.e., do the points seem to scatter around a straight line? Figure 3–10 suggests they do). Next, compute the quantities $\sum x$, $\sum y$, $\sum xy$ and $\sum x^2$). Calculations are shown for these quantities in Table 3–4. One additional calculation, $\sum y^2$, is included for later use.

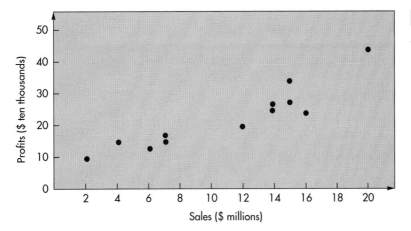

FIGURE 3-10

A linear model seems reasonable

x	y	xy	x²	y²
7	0.15	1.05	49	0.0225
2	0.10	0.20	4	0.0100
6	0.13	0.78	36	0.0169
4	0.15	0.60	16	0.0225
14	0.25	3.50	196	0.0625
15	0.27	4.05	225	0.0729
16	0.24	3.84	256	0.0576
12	0.20	2.40	144	0.0400
14	0.27	3.78	196	0.0729
20	0.44	8.80	400	0.1936
15	0.34	5.10	225	0.1156
7	0.17	1.19	49	0.0289
132	2.71	35.29	1,796	0.7159

TABLE 3-4

Calculations for regression coefficients for Healthy Hamburgers

Substituting into the equation, you find:

$$b = \frac{n(\sum xy) - (\sum x)(\sum y)}{n(\sum x^2) - (\sum x)^2} = \frac{12(35.29) - 132(2.71)}{12(1,796) - 132(132)} = 0.01593$$

$$a = \frac{\sum y - b(\sum x)}{n} = \frac{2.71 - 0.01593(132)}{12} = 0.0506$$

Thus, the regression equation is: $y_c = 0.0506 + 0.01593x$. For sales of $x = 10$ (i.e., $10 million), estimated profit is: $y_c = 0.0506 + 0.01593(10) = 0.2099$, or $209,900. (It may appear strange that substituting $x = 0$ into the equation produces a predicted profit of $50,600 because it seems to suggest that amount of profit will occur with no sales. However, the value of $x = 0$ is *outside the range of observed values.* The regression line should be used only for the range of values from which it was developed; the relationship may be nonlinear outside that range. The purpose of the *a* value is simply to establish the height of the line where it crosses the *y* axis.)

One application of regression in forecasting relates to the use of indicators. These are uncontrollable variables that tend to lead or precede changes in a variable of interest. For example, changes in the Federal Reserve Board's discount rate may influence certain business activities. Similarly, an increase in energy costs can lead to price increases for a wide range of products and services. Careful identification and analysis of indicators may yield insight into possible future demand in some situations. There are numerous published indexes and websites from which to choose.[1] These include:

Net change in inventories on hand and on order.

Interest rates for commercial loans.

Industrial output.

Consumer price index (CPI).

The wholesale price index.

Stock market prices.

Other potential indicators are population shifts, local political climates, and activities of other firms (e.g., the opening of a shopping center may result in increased sales for nearby businesses). Three conditions are required for an indicator to be valid:

1. The relationship between movements of an indicator and movements of the variable should have a logical explanation.

2. Movements of the indicator must precede movements of the dependent variable by enough time so that the forecast isn't outdated before it can be acted upon.

3. A fairly high correlation should exist between the two variables.

correlation A measure of the strength and direction of relationship between two variables.

Correlation measures the strength and direction of relationship between two variables. Correlation can range from -1.00 to $+1.00$. A correlation of $+1.00$ indicates that changes in one variable are always matched by changes in the other; a correlation of -1.00 indicates that increases in one variable are matched by decreases in the other; and a correlation close to zero indicates little *linear* relationship between two variables. The correlation between two variables can be computed using the equation

$$r = \frac{n(\sum xy) - (\sum x)(\sum y)}{\sqrt{n(\sum x^2) - (\sum x)^2} \cdot \sqrt{n(\sum y^2) - (\sum y)^2}} \tag{3–11}$$

The square of the correlation coefficient, r^2, provides a measure of the percentage of variability in the values of y that is "explained" by the independent variable. The possible values of r^2 range from 0 to 1.00. The closer r^2 is to 1.00, the greater the percentage of explained variation. A high value of r^2, say .80 or more, would indicate that the independent variable is a good predictor of values of the dependent variable. A low value, say .25 or less, would indicate a poor predictor, and a value between .25 and .80 would indicate a moderate predictor.

COMMENTS ON THE USE OF LINEAR REGRESSION ANALYSIS

Use of simple regression analysis implies that certain assumptions have been satisfied. Basically, these are:

1. Variations around the line are random. If they are random, no patterns such as cycles or trends should be apparent when the line and data are plotted.

2. Deviations around the line should be normally distributed. A concentration of values close to the line with a small proportion of larger deviations supports the assumption of normality.

3. Predictions are being made only within the range of observed values.

If the assumptions are satisfied, regression analysis can be a powerful tool. To obtain the best results, observe the following:

1. Always plot the data to verify that a linear relationship is appropriate.

---

[1]See, for example, *The National Bureau of Economic Research, The Survey of Current Business, The Monthly Labor Review,* and *Business Conditions Digest.*

2. The data may be time-dependent. Check this by plotting the dependent variable versus time; if patterns appear, use analysis of time series instead of regression, or use time as an independent variable as part of a *multiple regression analysis.*

3. A small correlation may imply that other variables are important.

In addition, note these weaknesses of regression:

1. Simple linear regression applies only to linear relationships with *one* independent variable.

2. One needs a considerable amount of data to establish the relationship—in practice, 20 or more observations.

3. All observations are weighted equally.

Example 9

Sales of 19-inch color television sets and three-month lagged unemployment are shown in the following table. Determine if unemployment levels can be used to predict demand for 19-inch color TVs and, if so, derive a predictive equation.

Period	1	2	3	4	5	6	7	8	9	10	11
Units sold	20	41	17	35	25	31	38	50	15	19	14
Unemployment % (three-month lag)	7.2	4.0	7.3	5.5	6.8	6.0	5.4	3.6	8.4	7.0	9.0

Solution

1. Plot the data to see if a linear model seems reasonable. In this case, a linear model seems appropriate *for the range of the data.*

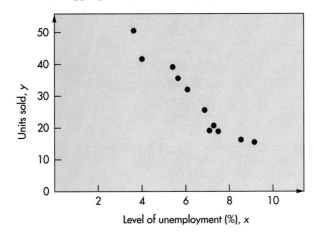

2. Compute the correlation coefficient to confirm that it is not close to zero.

x	y	xy	x^2	y^2
7.2	20	144.0	51.8	400
4.0	41	164.0	16.0	1,681
7.3	17	124.1	53.3	289
5.5	35	192.5	30.3	1,225
6.8	25	170.0	46.2	625
6.0	31	186.0	36.0	961
5.4	38	205.2	29.2	1,444
3.6	50	180.0	13.0	2,500
8.4	15	126.0	70.6	225
7.0	19	133.0	49.0	361
9.0	14	126.0	81.0	196
70.2	305	1,750.8	476.4	9,907

$$r = \frac{11(1,750.8) - 70.2(305)}{\sqrt{11(476.4) - (70.2)^2} \cdot \sqrt{11(9,907) - (305)^2}} = -.966$$

This is a fairly high negative correlation.

3. Compute the regression line:

$$b = \frac{11(1,750.8) - 70.2(305)}{11(476.4) - 70.2(70.2)} = -6.91$$

$$a = \frac{305 - (-6.9145)(70.2)}{11} = 71.85$$

$$y = 71.85 - 6.89x$$

Note that the equation pertains only to unemployment levels in the range 3.6 to 9.0, because sample observations covered only that range.

CURVILINEAR AND MULTIPLE REGRESSION ANALYSIS

Simple linear regression may prove inadequate to handle certain problems because a linear model is inappropriate or because more than one predictor variable is involved. When nonlinear relationships are present, you should employ curvilinear regression; models that involve more than one predictor require the use of multiple regression analysis. While these analyses are beyond the scope of this text, you should be aware that they are often used. The computations lend themselves more to computers than to hand calculation. Multiple regression forecasting substantially increases data requirements. In each case, it is necessary to weigh the additional cost and effort against potential improvements in accuracy of predictions.

Accuracy and Control of Forecasts

Accuracy and control of forecasts is a vital aspect of forecasting. The complex nature of most real-world variables makes it almost impossible to correctly predict future values of those variables on a regular basis. Consequently, it is important to include an indication of the extent to which the forecast might deviate from the value of the variable that actually occurs. This will provide the forecast user with a better perspective on how far off a forecast might be.

Moreover, decision makers will want to include accuracy as a factor when choosing among different techniques, along with cost. How important are good forecasts? In some instances, they can be *extremely* important. For example, IBM lost an opportunity to dominate the PC market when it severely underestimated demand for what was then a new product, while PC maker Compaq Computers and software producer Microsoft were able to capitalize on PC demand.

Accurate forecasts are necessary for the success of daily activities of every business organization. Forecasts are the basis for an organization's schedules, and unless the forecasts are accurate, schedules will be generated that may provide for too few or too many resources, too little or too much output, the wrong output, or the wrong timing of output, all of which can lead to additional costs, dissatisfied customers, and headaches for managers.

Some forecasting applications involve a series of forecasts (e.g., weekly revenues), whereas others involve a single forecast that will be used for a one-time decision (e.g., the size of a power plant). When making periodic forecasts, it is important to monitor forecast errors to determine if the errors are within reasonable bounds. If they are not, it will be necessary to take corrective action.

error Difference between the actual value and the value that was predicted for a given period.

Forecast **error** is the difference between the value that occurs and the value that was predicted for a given time period. Hence, Error = Actual − Forecast:

$$e_t = A_t - F_t \tag{3–12}$$

Positive errors result when the forecast is too low, negative errors when the forecast is too high. For example, if actual demand for a week is 100 units and forecast demand was 90 units, the forecast was too low; the error is $100 - 90 = +10$.

Forecast errors influence decisions in two somewhat different ways. One is in making a choice between various forecasting alternatives, and the other is in evaluating the success or failure of a technique in use. We shall begin by examining ways to summarize forecast error over time, and see how that information can be applied to compare forecasting alternatives. Then we shall consider methods for controlling forecasts.

NEWSCLIP

High Forecasts Can Be Bad News

Overly optimistic forecasts by retail store buyers can easily lead retailers to overorder, resulting in bloated inventories. When that happens, there is pressure on stores to cut prices in order to move the excess merchandise. Although customers delight in these markdowns, retailer profits generally suffer. Furthermore, retailers will naturally cut back on new orders while they work off their inventories, creating a ripple effect that hits the entire supply chain, from shippers, to producers, to suppliers of raw materials. The message is clear: Overly optimistic forecasts can be bad news.

Source: Based on "Bloated Inventories at Retailers May Mean Trouble for Investors" by Susan Pulliam, *The Wall Street Journal*, May 22, 1997, p. C1.

SUMMARIZING FORECAST ACCURACY

Forecast accuracy is a significant factor when deciding among forecasting alternatives. Accuracy is based on the historical error performance of a forecast.

Two commonly used measures for summarizing historical errors are the **mean absolute deviation (MAD)** and the **mean squared error (MSE)**. MAD is the average absolute error, and MSE is the average of squared errors. The formulas used to compute MAD[2] and MSE are:

mean absolute deviation (MAD) The average absolute forecast error.

mean squared error (MSE) The average of squared forecast errors.

$$\text{MAD} = \frac{\sum |\text{Actual} - \text{Forecast}|}{n} \tag{3–13}$$

$$\text{MSE} = \frac{\sum (\text{Actual} - \text{Forecast})^2}{n - 1} \tag{3–14}$$

Example 10 illustrates the computation of MAD and MSE.

Compute MAD and MSE for the following data.

Example 10

Period	Actual	Forecast	(A – F) Error	|Error|	Error²
1	217	215	2	2	4
2	213	216	−3	3	9
3	216	215	1	1	1
4	210	214	−4	4	16
5	213	211	2	2	4
6	219	214	5	5	25
7	216	217	−1	1	1
8	212	216	−4	4	16
			−2	22	76

[2] The absolute value, represented by the two vertical lines in formula 3–13, ignores minus signs; all data are treated as positive values. For example, −2 becomes +2.

Solution

Using the figures shown in the table,

$$\text{MAD} = \frac{\Sigma|e|}{n} = \frac{22}{8} = 2.75$$

$$\text{MSE} = \frac{\Sigma e^2}{n-1} = \frac{76}{8-1} = 10.86$$

From a computational standpoint, the difference between these two measures is that MAD weights all errors evenly, while MSE weights errors according to their *squared* values.

One use for these measures is to compare the accuracy of alternative forecasting methods. For instance, using either MAD or MSE, a manager could compare the results of exponential smoothing with values of .1, .2, and .3, to determine one which yields the *lowest* MAD or MSE for a given set of data.

In some instances, historical error performance is secondary to the ability of a forecast to respond to changes in data patterns. Choice among alternative methods would then focus on the cost of not responding quickly to a change relative to the cost of responding to changes that are not really there (i.e., random fluctuations).

Overall, the operations manager must settle on the relative importance of historical performance versus responsiveness and whether to use MAD or MSE to measure historical performance.

CONTROLLING THE FORECAST

It is necessary to monitor forecast errors to ensure that the forecast is performing adequately. This is accomplished by comparing forecast errors to predetermined values, or *action limits,* as illustrated in Figure 3–11. Errors that fall within the limits are judged acceptable, and errors outside of either limit signal that corrective action is needed.

There are a variety of possible sources of forecast errors, including the following:

1. The model may be inadequate due to (*a*) the omission of an important variable, (*b*) a change or shift in the variable that the model cannot deal with (e.g., sudden appearance of a trend or cycle), or (*c*) the appearance of a new variable (e.g., new competitor).
2. Irregular variations may occur due to severe weather or other natural phenomena, temporary shortages or breakdowns, catastrophes, or similar events.
3. The forecasting technique may be used incorrectly or the results misinterpreted.
4. There are always random variations in the data. Randomness is the inherent variation that remains in the data after all causes of variation have been accounted for.

A forecast is generally deemed to perform adequately when the errors exhibit only random variations. Hence, the key to judging when to reexamine the validity of a particular forecasting technique is whether forecast errors are random. If they are not random, investigate to determine which of the other sources is present and how to correct the problem.

tracking signal The ratio of cumulative forecast error to the corresponding value of MAD, used to monitor a forecast.

Forecasts can be monitored using either *tracking signals* or *control charts*. A **tracking signal** focuses on the ratio of *cumulative* forecast error to the corresponding value of MAD:

$$\text{Tracking signal} = \frac{\Sigma(\text{Actual} - \text{Forecast})}{\text{MAD}} \qquad (3\text{–}15)$$

bias Persistent tendency for forecasts to be greater or less than the actual values of a time series.

The cumulative forecast error reflects the **bias** in forecasts, which is the persistent tendency for forecasts to be greater or less than the actual values of a time series.

Tracking signal values are compared to predetermined limits based on judgment and experience. They often range from ±3 to ±8; for the most part, we shall use limits of ±4,

FIGURE 3-11

Monitoring forecast errors

FIGURE 3-12

Conceptual representation of a control chart

which are roughly comparable to three standard deviation limits. Values within the limits suggest—but do not guarantee—that the forecast is performing adequately. After an initial value of MAD has been computed, MAD can be updated using exponential smoothing:

$$\text{MAD}_t = \text{MAD}_{t-1} + \alpha(|\text{Actual} - \text{Forecast}|_t - \text{MAD}_{t-1}) \qquad (3-16)$$

The **control chart** approach involves setting upper and lower limits for *individual* forecast errors (instead of cumulative errors, as is the case with a tracking signal). The limits are multiples of the square root of MSE. This method assumes the following:

1. Forecast errors are randomly distributed around a mean of zero.

2. The distribution of errors is normal. See Figure 3–12.

The square root of MSE is used in practice as an estimate of the standard deviation of the distribution of errors.[3] That is,

$$s = \sqrt{\text{MSE}} \qquad (3-17)$$

Recall that for a normal distribution, approximately 95 percent of the values (errors in this case) can be expected to fall within limits of $0 \pm 2s$ (i.e., 0 ± 2 standard deviations), and approximately 99.7 percent of the values can be expected to fall within $\pm 3s$ of zero. Hence, if the forecast is "in control," 99.7 percent or 95 percent of the errors should fall within the limits, depending on whether $3s$ or $2s$ limits are used. Points that fall outside these limits should be regarded as evidence that corrective action is needed (i.e., the forecast is not performing adequately).

control chart Monitoring approach that sets limits for individual forecast errors; the limits are multiples of the square root of MSE.

Monthly sales of leather jackets at the Lucky Leather Shoppe for the past 24 months, and forecasts and errors for those months, are shown in the following table. Determine if the forecast is working using these approaches:

Example 11

---

[3] The actual value could be computed as $s = \dfrac{\Sigma(e - \bar{e})^2}{\sqrt{n - 1}}$.

1. A tracking signal, beginning with month 10, updating MAD with exponential smoothing. Use limits of ± 4 and $\alpha = .2$.

2. A control chart with $2s$ limits. Use data from the first eight months to develop the control chart, then evaluate the remaining data with the control chart.

Month	A (Sales)	F (Forecast)	A – F (Error)	|e|	Cumulative |e|
1	47	43	4	4	4
2	51	44	7	7	11
3	54	50	4	4	15
4	55	51	4	4	19
5	49	54	−5	5	24
6	46	48	−2	2	26
7	38	46	−8	8	34
8	32	44	−12	12	46
9	25	35	−10	10	56
10	24	26	−2	2	58
11	30	25	5	5	
12	35	32	3	3	
13	44	34	10	10	
14	57	50	7	7	
15	60	51	9	9	
16	55	54	1	1	
17	51	55	−4	4	
18	48	51	−3	3	
19	42	50	−8	8	
20	30	43	−13	13	
21	28	38	−10	10	
22	25	27	−2	2	
23	35	27	8	8	
24	38	32	6	6	
			−11		

Solution

a. The sum of absolute errors through the 10th month is 58. Hence, the initial MAD is $58/10 = 5.8$. The subsequent MADs are updated using the formula $MAD_{new} = MAD_{old} + \alpha(|e| - MAD_{old})$. The results are shown in the following table.

The tracking signal for any month is:

Cumulative error at that month

Update MAD at that month

t (Month)	|e|	$MAD_t = MAD_{t-1} + .2(|e| - MAD_{t-1})$	Cumulative Error	Tracking Signal = Cumulative Error, ÷ MAD_t
10			−20	−20/5.800 = −3.45
11	5	5.640 = 5.8 + .2(5 − 5.8)	−15	−15/5.640 = −2.66
12	3	5.112 = 5.640 + .2(3 − 5.64)	−12	−12/5.112 = −2.35
13	10	6.090 = 5.112 + .2(10 − 5.112)	−2	−2/6.090 = −0.33
14	7	6.272 = 6.090 + .2(7 − 6.090)	5	5/6.272 = 0.80
15	9	6.818 = 6.272 + .2(9 − 6.272)	14	14/6.818 = 2.05
16	1	5.654 = 6.818 + .2(1 − 6.818)	15	15/5.654 = 2.65
17	4	5.323 = 5.654 + .2(4 − 5.654)	11	11/5.323 = 2.07
18	3	4.858 = 5.323 + .2(3 − 5.323)	8	8/4.858 = 1.65
19	8	5.486 = 4.858 + .2(8 − 4.858)	0	0/5.486 = 0.00
20	13	6.989 = 5.486 + .2(13 − 5.486)	−13	−13/6.989 = −1.86

21 . . . . 10 $7.591 = 6.989 + .2(10 - 6.989)$ -23 $-23/7.591 = -3.03$
22 . . . . 2 $6.473 = 7.591 + .2(2 - 7.591)$ -25 $-25/6.473 = -3.86$
23 . . . . 8 $6.778 = 6.473 + .2(8 - 6.473)$ -17 $-17/6.778 = -2.51$
24 . . . . 6 $6.622 = 6.778 + .2(6 - 6.778)$ -11 $-11/6.622 = -1.66$

Because the tracking signal is within ± 4 every month, there is no evidence of a problem.

b. (1) Make sure that the average error is approximately zero, because a large average would suggest a biased forecast.

$$\text{Average error} = \frac{\sum \text{errors}}{n} = \frac{-11}{24} = -0.46[\text{OK}]$$

(2) Compute the standard deviation:

$$s = \sqrt{\text{MSE}} = \frac{\sum e^2}{\sqrt{n-1}}$$

$$= \frac{4^2 + 7^2 + 4^2 + 4^2 + (-5)^2 + (-2)^2 + (-8)^2 + (-12)^2}{\sqrt{8-1}} = 6.91$$

(3) Determine $2s$ control limits:

$$0 \pm 2s = 0 \pm 2(6.91) = -13.82 \text{ to } +13.82$$

(4)   i. Check that all errors are within the limits. (They are.)

    ii. Plot the data (see the following graph), and check for nonrandom patterns. Note the strings of positive and negative errors. This suggests nonrandomness (and that an improved forecast is possible). The tracking signal did not reveal this.

Plotting the errors with the help of a control chart can be very informative. A plot helps you to visualize the process and enables you to check for possible patterns *within the limits* that suggest an improved forecast is possible.[4]

Like the tracking signal, a control chart focuses attention on deviations that lie outside predetermined limits. With either approach, however, it is desirable to check for possible patterns in the errors, even if all errors are within the limits. Figure 3–13 illustrates some of the most common patterns. Checking is usually done by visual inspection although statistical tests are sometimes used. If there is a pattern, this means that errors are *predictable* and, thus, nonrandom. The implication is that the forecast can be improved. For example, trend in the errors means the errors are getting progressively worse. In a forecast based on time series data, adding or modifying a trend component may be needed. In an explanatory model, recomputing the slope or some other adjustment may be called for.

---

[4]The theory and application of control charts and the various methods for detecting patterns in the data are covered in more detail in Chapter 10, on quality control.

FIGURE 3-13

Examples of possible patterns

Time

Bias (too many observations on
one side of the zero line)

Time

Cycling (periodic upward and
downward movement)

Time

Trend (a persistent upward or
downward movement)

FIGURE 3-14

*Removal of a pattern usually
results in less variability, and
hence, narrower control limits*

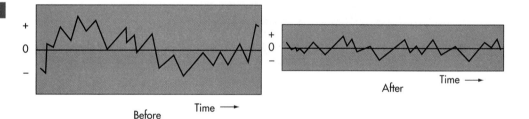

Before   Time ⟶

After   Time ⟶

Incorporating the needed changes in the forecasting model will result in less variability in forecast errors, and thus, in narrower control limits. (Revised control limits must be computed using the resulting forecast errors.) Figure 3–14 illustrates the impact on control limits due to decreased error variability.

Comment. The control chart approach is generally superior to the tracking signal approach. A major weakness of the tracking signal approach is its use of cumulative errors: Individual errors can be obscured so that large positive and negative values cancel each other. Conversely, with control charts, every error is judged individually. Thus, it can be misleading to rely on a tracking signal approach to monitor errors. In fact, the historical roots of the tracking signal approach date from before the first use of computers in business. At that time, it was much more difficult to compute standard deviations than to compute average deviations; for that reason, the concept of a tracking signal was developed. Now computers and calculators can easily provide standard deviations. Nonetheless, the use of tracking signals has persisted, probably because users are unaware of the superiority of the control chart approach.

Forecasting Method	Amount of Historical Data	Data Pattern	Forecast Horizon	Preparation Time	Personnel Background
Simple exponential smoothing	5 to 10 observations	Data should be stationary	Short	Short	Little sophistication
Trend-adjusted exponential smoothing	At least 4 or 5 observations per season	Trend	Short to medium	Short	Moderate sophistication
Trend models	10 to 20; for seasonality at least 5 per season	Trend	Short to medium	Short	Moderate sophistication
Seasonal	Enough to see 2 peaks and troughs	Handles cyclical and seasonal patterns	Short to medium	Short to moderate	Little sophistication
Causal regression models	10 observations per independent variable	Can handle complex patterns	Short, medium, or long	Long development time, short time for implementation	Considerable sophistication

Source: Adapted from J. Holton Wilson and Deborah Allison-Koerber, "Combining Subjective and Objective Forecasts Improves Results," *The Journal of Business Forecasting,* Fall 1992, p. 4.

TABLE 3–5

A guide to selecting an appropriate forecasting method

Choosing a Forecasting Technique

Many different kinds of forecasting techniques are available, and no single technique works best in every situation. When selecting a technique for a given situation, the manager or analyst must take a number of factors into consideration.

The two most important factors are *cost* and *accuracy.* How much money is budgeted for generating the forecast? What are the possible costs of errors, and what are the benefits that might accrue from an accurate forecast? Generally speaking, the higher the accuracy, the higher the cost, so it is important to weigh cost–accuracy trade-offs carefully. The best forecast is not necessarily the most accurate or the least costly; rather, it is some combination of accuracy and cost deemed best by management.

Other factors to consider in selecting a forecasting technique include the availability of historical data; the availability of computers; the ability of decision makers to utilize certain techniques; the time needed to gather and analyze data and to prepare the forecast; and any prior experience with a technique. The forecast horizon is important because some techniques are more suited to long-range forecasts while others work best for the short range. For example, moving averages and exponential smoothing are essentially short-range techniques, since they produce forecasts for the *next* period. Trend equations can be used to project over much longer time periods. When using time series data, *plotting the data* can be very helpful in choosing an appropriate method. Several of the qualitative techniques are well suited to long-range forecasts because they do not require historical data. The Delphi method and executive opinion methods are often used for long-range planning. New products and services lack historical data, so forecasts for them must be based on subjective estimates. In many cases, experience with similar items is relevant. Table 3–5 provides a guide for selecting a forecasting method. Table 3–6 (on pg. 104) provides additional perspectives on forecasts in terms of the time horizon.

In some instances, a manager might use more than one forecasting technique to obtain independent forecasts. If the different techniques produced approximately the same predictions, that would give increased confidence in the results; disagreement among the forecasts would indicate that additional analysis may be needed.

TABLE 3-6

Forecast factors, by range of forecast

Factor	Short Range	Intermediate Range	Long Range
1. Frequency	Often	Occasional	Infrequent
2. Level of aggregation	Item	Product family	Total output Type of product/ service
3. Type of model	Smoothing Projection Regression	Projection Seasonal Regression	Managerial Judgment
4. Degree of management involvement	Low	Moderate	High
5. Cost per forecast	Low	Moderate	High

Using Forecast Information

A manager can take a *reactive* or a *proactive* approach to a forecast. A reactive approach views forecasts as probable descriptions of future demand, and a manager reacts to meet that demand (e.g., adjusts production rates, inventories, the workforce). Conversely, a proactive approach seeks to actively influence demand (e.g., by means of advertising, pricing, or product/service changes).

Generally speaking, a proactive approach requires either an explanatory model (e.g., regression) or a subjective assessment of the influence on demand. It is possible that a manager might use two forecasts: one to predict what will happen under the status quo and a second one based on a "what if" approach, if the results of the status quo forecast are unacceptable.

Computers in Forecasting

Computers play an important role in preparing forecasts based on quantitative data. Their use allows managers to develop and revise forecasts quickly, and without the burden of manual computations. There is a wide range of software packages available for forecasting. The Excel® templates on your CD-ROM are an example of a spreadsheet approach. There are templates for moving averages, exponential smoothing, linear trend equation, trend-adjusted exponential smoothing, and simple linear regression. Some templates are illustrated in the Solved Problems section at the end of the chapter.

Operations Strategy

Forecasts are the basis for many decisions. Clearly, the more accurate an organization's forecasts, the better prepared it will be to take advantage of future opportunities and to reduce potential risks. Maintaining accurate, up-to-date information on prices, demand, and other variables can have a significant impact on forecast accuracy.

An organization also can do other things to improve forecasts. These do not involve searching for improved techniques but relate to the inverse relation of accuracy to the forecast horizon: Forecasts that cover shorter time frames tend to be more accurate than longer-term forecasts. Recognizing this, management might choose to devote efforts to *shortening the time horizon that forecasts must cover.* Essentially, this means shortening the *lead time* needed to respond to a forecast. This might involve building *flexibility* into operations to permit rapid response to changing demands for products and services, or to changing volumes in quantities demanded; shortening the lead time required to obtain supplies, equipment, and raw materials or the time needed to train or retrain employees; or shortening the time needed to *develop* new products and services.

Sharing forecasts or demand data throughout the supply chain can improve forecast quality in the supply chain, resulting in lower costs and shorter lead times. For example, both Hewlett-Packard and IBM require resellers to include such information in their contracts. The following Newsclip stresses the value of doing this.

NEWSCLIP

A Strong Channel Hub
Bill Roberts

www.ingrammicro.com

Big electronics companies, such as Compaq and Dell, are spending hundreds of millions of dollars on Internet-based supply chain management. And small outfits, such as resellers (often called value-added resellers, or VARs), that can't afford that kind of price tag are getting help from large electronics distributors, which are eager to connect them into vast electronic commerce networks to streamline the distribution channel.

Resellers design systems for their clients and then resell hardware and software they buy from distributors, which in turn have obtained them directly from the manufacturers. When proposing systems for clients, resellers must know how much they're going to pay for each element of the system before they make a quote—and, even more important, they have to know that the elements are available for them to purchase through distributors in a timely manner.

Take McMillan Consulting, a computer systems reseller in Fresno, Calif. Matt Furrer, a veteran sales representative for McMillan, is ecstatic that giant Ingram Micro Inc. and other electronics and computer distributors are fashioning themselves as hubs in vast Internet-based supply chains that connect everything from the smallest reseller to the largest original equipment manufacturers (OEMs).

Using Ingram's Web site, Furrer says, "I write a price quote twice as fast as I used to. I can easily write twice as many in a day. From five years ago I guarantee my business has gained, and using the Web is a factor."

Ingram has a point-to-point connection with about 30 OEMs, and can offer up the catalogs of more than 1,500, which enable it to provide McMillan and 200,000 other resellers with up-to-the minute pricing and availability information. And by having so much useful real-time information, Ingram is enhancing its role in the supply chain. "Ingram is the intermediary; they touch every transaction," says Keyur Patel, a former partner at KPMG, a consulting firm working with Ingram on its supply chain management processes. "They have a wealth of data that is captured up and down the supply chain."

Patel, who left KPMG recently to co-found wireless and broadband startup Brience Inc., believes it is only a matter of time before distributors in other industries will adopt the same model as Ingram is using for electronics. "The Internet will force companies to start sharing information," he says. "Companies in the middle of a supply chain need to become the infomediaries." Patel is referring specifically to the sharing of forecasts, which most companies keep very close to the vest. Patel and other experts say Internet-based supply chain management will only reach its ultimate efficiency when all the partners along the chain share forecasts and other information that today is most often proprietary.

Source: Excerpted from *Internet World,* June 1, 2000.

Summary

Forecasts are vital inputs for the design and the operation of the productive systems because they help managers to anticipate the future.

Forecasting techniques can be classified as qualitative or quantitative. Qualitative techniques rely on judgment, experience, and expertise to formulate forecasts; quantitative techniques rely on the use of historical data or associations among variables to develop forecasts. Some of the techniques are simple and others are complex. Some work better than others, but no technique works all the time. Moreover, all forecasts include a certain degree of inaccuracy, and allowance should be made for this. All techniques assume that the same underlying causal system that existed in the past will continue to exist in the future.

The qualitative techniques described in this chapter include consumer surveys, salesforce estimates, executive opinions, and manager and staff opinions. Two major quantitative approaches are described: analysis of time series data and associative techniques. The time series techniques rely strictly on the examination of historical data; predictions are made by projecting past movements of a variable into the future without considering specific factors that might influence the variable. Associative techniques attempt to explicitly identify influencing factors and to incorporate that information into equations that can be used for predictive purposes.

TABLE 3-7		Approaches	Brief Description
Forecasting approaches	**Judgment/opinion:**	Consumer surveys	Questioning consumers on future plans
		Direct-contact composites	Joint estimates obtained from salespeople or customer service people
		Executive opinion	Finance, marketing, and manufacturing managers join to prepare forecast
		Delphi technique	Series of questionnaires answered anonymously by knowledgeable people; successive questionnaires are based on information obtained from previous surveys
		Outside opinion	Consultants or other outside experts prepare the forecast
	Statistical:	Time series:	
		Naive	Next value in a series will equal the previous value in a comparable period
		Moving averages	Forecast is based on an average of recent values
		Exponential smoothing	Sophisticated form of weighted moving average
		Associative models:	
		Simple regression	Values of one variable are used to predict values of another variable
		Multiple regression	Two or more variables are used to predict values of another variable

All forecasts tend to be inaccurate; therefore, it is important to provide a measure of accuracy. It is possible to compute several measures of forecast accuracy that help managers to evaluate the performance of a given technique and to choose among alternative forecasting techniques. Control of forecasts involves deciding whether a forecast is performing adequately, using either a control chart or a tracking signal.

When selecting a forecasting technique, a manager must choose a technique that will serve the intended purpose at an acceptable level of cost and accuracy.

The various forecasting techniques are summarized in Table 3–7 (on page 106). Table 3–8 (on page 107) lists the formulas used in the forecasting techniques and in the methods of measuring their accuracy.

Key Terms

associative model, 73
bias, 98
centered moving average, 89
control chart, 99
correlation, 94
cycle, 75
Delphi method, 74
error, 96
exponential smoothing, 80
forecast, 70
irregular variation, 75
judgmental forecasts, 73
least squares line, 91
linear trend equation, 81
mean absolute deviation (MAD), 97

mean squared error (MSE), 97
moving average, 77
naive forecast, 75
predictor variables, 91
random variations, 75
regression, 91
seasonal variations, 87
seasonality, 75
seasonal relative, 88
time series, 75
tracking signal, 98
trend, 75
trend-adjusted exponential smoothing, 85
weighted average, 78

TABLE 3-8

Summary of formulas

Technique	Formula	Definitions
Naive forecast for stable data	$F_t = A_{t-1}$	F = Forecast A = Actual data t = Current period
Moving average forecast	$F = \dfrac{\sum\limits_{i=1}^{n} A_i}{n}$	n = Number of periods
Exponential smoothing forecast	$F_t = F_{t-1} + \alpha(A_{t-1} - F_{t-1})$	α = Smoothing factor
Linear trend forecast	$y_t = a + bt$ where $b = \dfrac{n\sum ty - \sum t \sum y}{n\sum t^2 - (\sum t)^2}$ $a = \dfrac{\sum y - b\sum t}{n}$ or $\bar{y} - bt$	a = y intercept b = Slope
Trend-adjusted forecast	$TAF_{t+1} = S_t + T_t$ where $S_t = TAF_t + \alpha(A_t - TAF_t)$ $T_t = T_{t-1} + \beta(TAF_t - TAF_{t-1} - T_{t-1})$	t = Current period TAF_{t+1} = Trend-adjusted forecast for next period S = Smoothed forecast T = Trend component
Linear regression forecast	$y_c = a + bx$ where $b = \dfrac{n(\sum xy) - (\sum x)(\sum y)}{n(\sum x^2) - (\sum x)^2}$ $a = \dfrac{\sum y - b\sum x}{n}$ or $\bar{y} - b\bar{x}$	y_c = Predicted (dependent) variable x = Predictor (independent) variable b = Slope of the line a = Value of y_c when $x = 0$
MAD	$MAD = \dfrac{\sum\limits^{n} \lvert e \rvert}{n}$	MAD = Mean absolute deviation e = Error, $A - F$
MSE	$MSE = \dfrac{\sum\limits^{n} e^2}{n-1}$	MSE = Mean squared error
Tracking signal	$TS = \dfrac{\sum\limits^{n} e}{MAD}$	
Control limits	$UCL = 0 + z\sqrt{MSE}$ $LCL = 0 - z\sqrt{MSE}$	$\sqrt{MSE}$ = standard deviation z = Number of standard deviations; 2 and 3 are typical values.

Problem 1

Forecasts based on averages. Given the following data:

Period	Number of Complaints
1	60
2	65
3	55
4	58
5	64

Prepare a forecast using each of these approaches:

a. The appropriate naive approach.

b. A three-period moving average.

c. A weighted average using weights of .50 (most recent), .30, and .20.

d. Exponential smoothing with a smoothing constant of .40.

Solution

a. The values are stable. Therefore, the most recent value of the series becomes the next forecast: 64.

b. $MA_3 = \dfrac{55 + 58 + 64}{3} = 59$

c. $F = .50(64) + .30(58) + .20(55) = 60.4$

d.

Period	Number of Complaints	Forecast	Calculations
1	60		[The previous value of series is used
2	65	60	as the starting forecast.]
3	55	62	$60 + .40(65 - 60) = 62$
4	58	59.2	$62 + .40(55 - 62) = 59.2$
5	64	58.72	$59.2 + .40(58 - 59.2) = 58.72$
6		60.83	$59.72 + .40(64 - 58.72) = 60.83$

You can also obtain the forecasts and a plot using an Excel template, as shown:

Problem 2

Time series analysis. Apple's Citrus Fruit Farm ships boxed fruit anywhere in the continental United States. Using the following information, forecast shipments for the first four months of next year.

Month	Seasonal Relative	Month	Seasonal Relative
Jan.	1.2	Jul.	0.8
Feb.	1.3	Aug.	0.6
Mar.	1.3	Sep.	0.7
Apr.	1.1	Oct.	1.0
May	0.8	Nov.	1.1
Jun.	0.7	Dec.	1.4

The monthly forecast equation being used is:

$$y_t = 402 + 3t$$

where

t_0 = January of *last* year
y_t = Number of shipments

Solution

a. Determine trend amounts for the first four months of *next* year: January, $t = 24$; February, $t = 25$; etc. Thus,

$Y_{Jan} = 402 + 3(24) = 474$
$Y_{Feb} = 402 + 3(25) = 477$
$Y_{Mar} = 402 + 3(26) = 480$
$Y_{Apr} = 402 + 3(27) = 483$

b. Multiply each monthly trend by the corresponding seasonal relative for that month.

Month	Seasonal Relative	Forecast
Jan.	1.2	474(1.2) = 568.8
Feb.	1.3	477(1.3) = 620.1
Mar.	1.3	480(1.3) = 624.0
Apr.	1.1	483(1.1) = 531.3

Linear trend line. Plot the data on a graph, and verify visually that a linear trend line is appropriate. Develop a line trend equation for the following data. Then use the equation to predict the next two values of the series.

Problem 3

Solution

Period	Demand
1	44
2	52
3	50
4	54
5	55
6	55
7	60
8	56
9	62

A plot of the data indicates that a linear trend line is appropriate:

Period, t	Demand, y	ty
1	44	44
2	52	104
3	50	150
4	54	216
5	55	275
6	55	330
7	60	420
8	56	448
9	62	558
	488	2,545

From Table 3–1, with $n = 9$,

$\Sigma t = 45$ and $\Sigma t^2 = 285$

$$b = \frac{n\Sigma ty - \Sigma t\Sigma y}{n\Sigma t^2 - (\Sigma t)^2} = \frac{9(2,545) - 45(488)}{9(285) - 45(45)} = 1.75$$

$$a = \frac{\Sigma y - b\Sigma t}{n} = \frac{488 - 1.75(45)}{9} = 45.47$$

Thus, the trend equation is $y_t = 45.47 + 1.75t$. The next two forecasts are:

$$y_{10} = 45.47 + 1.75(10) = 62.97$$
$$y_{11} = 45.47 + 1.75(11) = 64.72$$

You can also use an Excel template to obtain the coefficients and a plot. Simply replace the existing data in the template with your data.

Problem 4

Seasonal relatives. Obtain estimates of quarter relatives for these data:

Year:	1				2				3				4
Quarter:	1	2	3	4	1	2	3	4	1	2	3	4	1
Demand:	14	18	35	46	28	36	60	71	45	54	84	88	58

Solution

Note that each season has an *even* number of data points. When an even-numbered moving average is used (in this case, a four-period moving average), the "centered value" will not correspond to an actual data point; the center of 4 is *between* the second and third data points. To correct for this, a *second* set of moving averages must be computed using the MA$_4$ values. The MA$_2$ values are centered between the MA$_4$ and "line up" with actual data points. For example, the first MA$_4$ value is 28.25. It is centered between 18 and 35 (i.e., between quarter 2 and quarter 3). When the average of the first two MA_4 values is taken (i.e., MA_2) and centered, it lines up with the 35 and, hence, with quarter 3.

So, whenever an even-numbered moving average is used as a centered moving average (e.g., MA_4, MA_{12}), a second moving average, a two-period moving average, is used to achieve correspondence with periods. This procedure is not needed when the number of periods in the centered moving average is odd. See Example 7 in this chapter for an example with an odd number of periods.

Year	Quarter	Demand	MA_4	MA_2	Demand/MA_2
1	1	14			
	2	18			
	3	35	28.25	30.00	1.17
	4	46	31.75	34.00	1.35
2	1	28	36.25	39.38	0.71
	2	36	42.50	45.63	0.79
	3	60	48.75	50.88	1.18
	4	71	53.00	55.25	1.29
3	1	45	57.50	60.50	0.74
	2	54	63.50	65.63	0.82
	3	84	67.75	69.38	1.21
	4	88	71.00		
4	1	58			

	QUARTER			
	1	**2**	**3**	**4**
	0.71	0.79	1.17	1.35
	0.74	0.82	1.18	1.29
	1.45	1.61	1.21	2.64
			3.56	
Average for the quarter:	0.725	0.805	1.187	1.320

The sum of these relatives is 4.037. Multiplying each by 4.00/4.037 will standardize the relatives, making their total equal 4.00. The resulting relatives are: quarter 1, 0.718; quarter 2, 0.798; quarter 3, 1.176; quarter 4, 1.308.

Regression analysis. A large midwestern retailer has developed a graph that summarizes the effect of advertising expenditures on sales volume. Using the graph, determine an equation of the form $y = a + bx$ that describes this relationship.

Problem 5

Solution

The linear equation has the form $y = a + bx$, where a is the value of y when $x = 0$ (i.e., where the line intersects the y axis) and b is the slope of the line (the amount by which y changes for a one-unit change in x).

Accordingly, $a = 1$ and $b = (3 - 1)/(10 - 0) = 0.2$, so $y = a + bx$ becomes $y = 1 + 0.2x$. [*Note:* $(3 - 1)$ is the change in y, and $(10 - 0)$ is the change in x.]

Problem 6

Regression analysis. The owner of a small hardware store has noted a sales pattern for window locks that seems to parallel the number of break-ins reported each week in the newspaper. The data are:

Sales:	46	18	20	22	27	34	14	37	30
Break-ins:	9	3	3	5	4	7	2	6	4

a. Plot the data to determine which type of equation, linear or nonlinear, is appropriate.

b. Obtain a regression equation for the data.

c. Estimate sales when the number of break-ins is five.

Solution

a.

The graph supports a linear relationship.

b. The computations for a straight line are:

x	y	xy	x²	y²
9	46	414	81	2,116
3	18	54	9	324
3	20	60	9	400
5	22	110	25	484
4	27	108	16	729
7	34	238	49	1,156
2	14	28	4	196
6	37	222	36	1,369
4	30	120	16	900
43	248	1,354	245	7,674

$$b = \frac{n(\Sigma xy) - (\Sigma x)(\Sigma y)}{n(\Sigma x^2) - (\Sigma x)^2} = \frac{9(1,354) - 43(248)}{9(245) - 43(43)} = 4.275$$

$$a = \frac{\Sigma y - b(\Sigma x)}{n} = \frac{248 - 4.275(43)}{9} = 7.129$$

Hence, the equation is: $y_c = 7.129 + 4.275x$.

You can obtain the regression coefficients using the appropriate Excel template. Simply replace the existing data for x and y with your data. Note: be careful to enter the values for the variable you want to predict as y values. In this problem, the objective is to predict sales, so the sales values are entered in the y column.

c. For $x = 5$, $y_c = 7.129 + 4.275(5) = 28.50$.

Accuracy and control of forecasts. The manager of a large manufacturer of industrial pumps must choose between two alternative forecasting techniques. Both techniques have been used to prepare forecasts for a six-month period. Using MAD as a criterion, which technique has the better performance record?

Problem 7

		FORECAST	
Month	**Demand**	**Technique 1**	**Technique 2**
1	492	488	495
2	470	484	482
3	485	480	478
4	493	490	488
5	498	497	492
6	492	493	493

Check that each forecast has an average error of approximately zero. (See computations that follow.)

Solution

Month	**Demand**	**Technique 1**	e	$|e|$	**Technique 2**	e	$|e|$
1	492	488	4	4	495	−3	3
2	470	484	−14	14	482	−12	12
3	485	480	5	5	478	7	7
4	493	490	3	3	488	5	5
5	498	497	1	1	492	6	6
6	492	493	−1	1	493	−1	1
			−2	28		+2	34

$$\text{MAD}_1 = \frac{\Sigma|e|}{n} = \frac{28}{6} = 4.67$$

$$\text{MAD}_2 = \frac{\Sigma|e|}{n} = \frac{34}{6} = 5.67$$

Technique 1 is superior in this comparison because its MAD is smaller, although six observations would generally be too few on which to base a realistic comparison.

Problem 8

Control chart. Given the demand data that follow, prepare a naive forecast for periods 2 through 10. Then determine each forecast error, and use those values to obtain $2s$ control limits. If demand in the next two periods turns out to be 125 and 130, can you conclude that the forecasts are in control?

Period:	1	2	3	4	5	6	7	8	9	10
Demand:	118	117	120	119	126	122	117	123	121	124

Solution

For a naive forecast, each period's demand becomes the forecast for the next period. Hence, the forecasts and errors are:

Period	Demand	Forecast	Error	Error^2
1	118	—	—	—
2	117	118	−1	1
3	120	117	3	9
4	119	120	−1	1
5	126	119	7	49
6	122	126	−4	16
7	117	122	−5	25
8	123	117	6	36
9	121	123	−2	4
10	124	121	3	9
			+6	150

$$s = \frac{\Sigma \text{error}^2}{\sqrt{n-1}} = \frac{150}{\sqrt{9-1}} = 4.33 \qquad (n = \text{Number of errors})$$

The control limits are $2(4.33) = \pm 8.66$

The forecast for period 11 was 124. Demand turned out to be 125, for an error of $125 - 124 = +1$. This is within the limits of ± 8.66. If the next demand is 130 and the naive forecast is 125 (based on the period 11 demand of 125), the error is $+5$. Again, this is within the limits, so you cannot conclude the forecast is not working properly. With more values—at least five or six—you could plot the errors to see whether you could detect any patterns suggesting the presence of nonrandomness.

Discussion and Review Questions

1. What are the main advantages that quantitative techniques for forecasting have over qualitative techniques? What limitations do quantitative techniques have?
2. What are some of the consequences of poor forecasts? Explain.
3. List the specific weaknesses of each of these approaches to developing a forecast:
   a. Consumer surveys
   b. Salesforce composite
   c. Committee of managers or executives
4. Briefly describe the Delphi technique. What are its main benefits and weaknesses?
5. What is the purpose of establishing control limits for forecast errors?
6. What factors would you consider in deciding whether to use wide or narrow control limits for a forecast?
7. Contrast the use of MAD and MSE in evaluating forecasts.
8. What advantages as a forecasting tool does exponential smoothing have over moving averages?
9. How does the number of periods in a moving average affect the responsiveness of the forecast?
10. What factors enter into the choice of a value for the smoothing constant in exponential smoothing?
11. How accurate is your local five-day weather forecast? Support your answer with actual data.

12. Explain how using a centered moving average with a length equal to the length of a season eliminates seasonality from a time series.

13. Contrast the terms *sales* and *demand.*

14. Contrast the reactive and proactive approaches to forecasting. Give several examples of types of organizations or situations in which each type is used.

15. Explain how flexibility in production systems relates to the forecast horizon and forecast accuracy.

16. How is forecasting in the context of a supply chain different from forecasting for just a single organization? List possible supply chain benefits and discuss potential difficulties in doing supply chain forecasting.

17. It has been said that forecasting using exponential smoothing is like driving a car by looking in the rear-view mirror. What are the conditions that would have to exist for driving a car that are analogous to the assumptions made when using exponential smoothing?

18. Suppose a software producer is about to release a new version of its popular software. What information do you think it would take into account in forecasting initial sales?

Memo Writing Exercises

1. You have received a call from the manager of a firm where you helped set up a forecasting system. The manager, Jill Rodgers, expressed concern that forecast errors, although within the control limits, were too large, and wondered if there was anything else that could be done, or whether they would "just have to live with it." What would you suggest? Write a memo to Jill.

2. Write a short memo to your boss, Jim Oliver, outlining the merits of using a control chart to monitor forecasts rather than a tracking signal.

Problems

1. A commercial bakery has recorded sales (in dozens) for three products, as shown below:

Day	Blueberry Muffins	Cinnamon Buns	Cupcakes
1	30	18	45
2	34	17	26
3	32	19	27
4	34	19	23
5	35	22	22
6	30	23	48
7	34	23	29
8	36	25	20
9	29	24	14
10	31	26	18
11	35	27	47
12	31	28	26
13	37	29	27
14	34	31	24
15	33	33	22

   a. Predict orders for the following day for each of the products using an appropriate naive method.

   b. What should the use of *sales* data instead of *demand* imply.

2. National Mixer, Inc., sells can openers. Monthly sales for a seven-month period were as follows:

Month	Sales (000 units)
Feb.	19
Mar.	18
Apr.	15
May	20

Jun.   18
Jul.   22
Aug.   20

a. Plot the monthly data on a sheet of graph paper.

b. Forecast September sales volume using each of the following:

(1) A linear trend equation.

(2) A five-month moving average.

(3) Exponential smoothing with a smoothing constant equal to .20, assuming a March forecast of 19(000).

(4) The naive approach.

(5) A weighted average using .60 for August, .30 for July, and .10 for June.

c. Which method seems least appropriate? Why?

d. What does use of the term *sales* rather than *demand* presume?

3. A dry cleaner uses exponential smoothing to forecast equipment usage at its main plant. August usage was forecast to be 88 percent of capacity; actual usage was 89.6 percent of capacity. A smoothing constant of .1 is used.

a. Prepare a forecast for September.

b. Assuming actual September usage of 92 percent, prepare a forecast for October usage.

4. An electrical contractor's records during the last five weeks indicate the number of job requests:

Week:	1	2	3	4	5
Requests:	20	22	18	21	22

Predict the number of requests for week 6 using each of these methods:

a. Naive.

b. A four-period moving average.

c. Exponential smoothing with $\alpha = .30$.

5. A cosmetics manufacturer's marketing department has developed a linear trend equation that can be used to predict annual sales of its popular Hand & Foot Cream.

$$y_t = 80 + 15t$$

where

y_t = Annual sales (000 bottles)

t = 0 corresponds to 1990

a. Are annual sales increasing or decreasing? By how much?

b. Predict annual sales for the year 2003 using the equation.

6. From the following graph, determine the linear equation of the trend line using 1991 as the base year for Glib Sales, Inc.

Annual Sales, Glib Sales, Inc.

7. Freight car loadings over a 12-year period at a busy port are:

Week	Number	Week	Number	Week	Number
1	220	7	350	13	460
2	245	8	360	14	475
3	280	9	400	15	500
4	275	10	380	16	510
5	300	11	420	17	525
6	310	12	450	18	541

   a. Compute a linear trend line for freight car loadings.

   b. Use the trend equation to predict loadings for weeks 20 and 21.

   c. The manager intends to install new equipment when the volume reaches 800 loadings per week. Assuming the current trend continues, the loading volume will reach that level in approximately what week?

8. *a.* Develop a linear trend equation for the following data on bread deliveries, and use it to predict deliveries for periods 16 through 19.

Period	Dozen Deliveries	Period	Dozen Deliveries	Period	Dozen Deliveries
1	200	6	232	11	281
2	214	7	248	12	275
3	211	8	250	13	280
4	228	9	253	14	288
5	235	10	267	15	310

   b. Use trend-adjusted smoothing with $\alpha = .3$ and $\beta = .2$ to smooth the bread delivery data in part *a*. What is the forecast for Period 16?

9. After plotting demand for four periods, a manager has concluded that a trend-adjusted exponential smoothing model is appropriate to predict future demand. The initial estimate of trend is based on the net change of 30 for the *three* periods from 1 to 4, for an average of +10 units. Use $\alpha = .5$ and $\beta = .4$, and TAF of 250 for period 5. Develop forecasts for periods 6 through 10.

t Period	A, Actual
1	210
2	224
3	229
4	240
5	255
6	265
7	272
8	285
9	294
10	

10. A manager of a store that sells and installs hot tubs wants to prepare a forecast for January, February, and March of next year. Her forecasts are a combination of trend and seasonality. She uses the following equation to estimate the trend component of monthly demand: $y_t = 70 + 5t$, where $t = 0$ in June of last year. Seasonal relatives are 1.10 for January, 1.02 for February, and .95 for March. What demands should she predict?

11. The following equation summarizes the trend portion of quarterly sales of automatic dishwashers over a long cycle. Sales also exhibit seasonal variations. Using the information given, prepare a forecast of sales for each quarter of 2004, and the first quarter of 2005.

$$y_t = 40 - 6.5t + 2t^2$$

where

   y_t = Unit sales

   $t = 0$ at the fourth quarter of 2001

Quarter	Relative
1	1.1
2	1.0
3	.6
4	1.3

12. A gift shop in a tourist center is open on weekends (Friday, Saturday, and Sunday). The owner-manager hopes to improve scheduling of part-time employees by determining seasonal relatives for each of these days. Data on recent activity at the store (sales transactions per day) have been tabulated and are shown in the table below.

			WEEK			
	1	**2**	**3**	**4**	**5**	**6**
Friday	149	154	152	150	159	163
Saturday	250	255	260	268	273	276
Sunday	166	162	171	173	176	183

  a. Develop seasonal relatives for the shop.

  b. Use a naive trend approach to predict sales transactions for the gift shop in the previous problem for the following week.

13. The manager of a fashionable restaurant open Wednesday through Saturday says that the restaurant does about 35 percent of its business on Friday night, 30 percent on Saturday night, and 20 percent on Thursday night. What seasonal relatives would describe this situation?

14. Coal shipments from Mountain Coal Company's no. 4 mine for the past 18 weeks are:

Week	Tons Shipped	Week	Tons Shipped	Week	Tons Shipped
1	405	8	433	15	466
2	410	9	438	16	474
3	420	10	440	17	476
4	415	11	446	18	482
5	412	12	451		
6	420	13	455		
7	424	14	464		

  a. Explain why an averaging technique would not be appropriate for forecasting.

  b. Use an appropriate technique to develop a forecast for the next three weeks.

15. Obtain estimates of daily relatives for the number of customers at a restaurant for the evening meal, given the following data. (*Hint:* Use a seven-day moving average.)

Day	Number Served	Day	Number Served
1	80	15	84
2	75	16	77
3	78	17	83
4	95	18	96
5	130	19	135
6	136	20	140
7	40	21	37
8	82	22	87
9	77	23	82
10	80	24	98
11	94	25	103
12	125	26	144
13	135	27	144
14	42	28	48

16. A pharmacist has been monitoring sales of a certain over-the-counter pain reliever. Daily sales during the last 15 days were:

Day:	1	2	3	4	5	6	7	8	9
Number sold:	36	38	42	44	48	49	50	49	52
Day:	10	11	12	13	14	15			
Number sold:	48	52	55	54	56	57			

 a. Without doing any calculations, which method would you suggest using to predict future sales—a linear trend equation or trend-adjusted exponential smoothing? Why?

 b. If you learn that on some days the store ran out of the specific pain reliever, would that knowledge cause you any concern? Explain.

 c. Assume that the data refer to demand rather than sales. Using trend-adjusted smoothing with an initial forecast of 50 for week 8, an initial trend estimate of 2, and $\alpha = \beta = .3$, develop forecasts for days 9 through 16. What is the MSE for the eight forecasts for which there are actual data?

17. New car sales for a dealer in Cook County, Illinois, for the past year are shown in the following table, along with monthly (seasonal) relatives, which are supplied to the dealer by the regional distributor.

Month	Units Sold	Index	Month	Units Sold	Index
Jan.	640	0.80	Jul.	765	0.90
Feb.	648	0.80	Aug.	805	1.15
Mar.	630	0.70	Sept.	840	1.20
Apr.	761	0.94	Oct.	828	1.20
May	735	0.89	Nov.	840	1.25
Jun.	850	1.00	Dec.	800	1.25

 a. Plot the data. Does there seem to be a trend?

 b. Deseasonalize car sales.

 c. Plot the deseasonalized data on the same graph as the original data. Comment on the two graphs.

18. The following table shows a tool and die company's quarterly sales for the current year. What sales would you predict for the first quarter of next year? Quarter relatives are $Q_1 = 1.10$, $Q_2 = .99$, $Q_3 = .90$, and $Q_4 = 1.01$.

Quarter	1	2	3	4
Sales	88	99	108	141.4

19. A farming cooperative manager wants to estimate quarterly relatives for grain shipments, based on the data shown (quantities are in metric tons):

	QUARTER			
Year	1	2	3	4
1	200	250	210	340
2	210	252	212	360
3	215	260	220	358
4	225	272	233	372
5	232	284	240	381

 Determine quarter relatives. (*Hint:* Use a centered four-period moving average initially, and then use a centered two-period moving average of the four-period moving average.)

20. Long-Life Insurance has developed a linear model that it uses to determine the amount of term life insurance a family of four should have, based on the current age of the head of the household. The equation is:

 $y = 150 - .1x$

 where

y = Insurance needed ($000)

x = Current age of head of household

   a. Plot the relationship on a graph.

   b. Use the equation to determine the amount of term life insurance to recommend for a family of four if the head of the household is 30 years old.

21. Timely Transport provides local delivery service for a number of downtown and suburban businesses. Delivery charges are based on distance and weight involved for each delivery: 10 cents per pound and 15 cents per mile. Also, there is a $10 handling fee per parcel.

   a. Develop an expression that summarizes delivery charges.

   b. Determine the delivery charge for transporting a 40-pound parcel 26 miles.

22. The manager of a seafood restaurant was asked to establish a pricing policy on lobster dinners. Experimenting with prices produced the following data:

Average Number Sold per Day, y	Price, x	Average Number Sold per Day, y	Price, x
200	$6.00	155	$8.25
190	6.50	156	8.50
188	6.75	148	8.75
180	7.00	140	9.00
170	7.25	133	9.25
162	7.50		
160	8.00		

   a. Plot the data and a regression line on the same graph.

   b. Determine the correlation coefficient and interpret it.

23. The following data were collected during a study of consumer buying patterns.

Observation	x	y	Observation	x	y
1	15	74	8	18	78
2	25	80	9	14	70
3	40	84	10	15	72
4	32	81	11	22	85
5	51	96	12	24	88
6	47	95	13	33	90
7	30	83			

   a. Plot the data.

   b. Obtain a linear regression line for the data.

   c. What percentage of the variation is explained by the regression line?

   d. Use the equation determined in part *b* to predict the value of *y* for *x* = 41.

24. Lovely Lawns, Inc., intends to use sales of lawn fertilizer to predict lawn mower sales. The store manager estimates a probable six-week lag between fertilizer sales and mower sales. The pertinent data are:

Period	Fertilizer Sales (tons)	Number of Mowers Sold (six-week lag)	Period	Fertilizer Sales (tons)	Number of Mowers Sold (six-week lag)
1	1.6	10	8	1.3	7
2	1.3	8	9	1.7	10
3	1.8	11	10	1.2	6
4	2.0	12	11	1.9	11
5	2.2	12	12	1.4	8
6	1.6	9	13	1.7	10
7	1.5	8	14	1.6	9

a. Determine the correlation between the two variables. Does it appear that a relationship between these variables will yield good predictions? Explain.

b. Obtain a linear regression line for the data.

c. Predict lawn mower sales for the first week in August, given fertilizer sales six weeks earlier of 2 tons.

25. An analyst must decide between two different forecasting techniques for weekly sales of roller blades: a linear trend equation and the naive approach. The linear trend equation is $y_t = 124 + 2t$, and it was developed using data from periods 1 through 10. Based on data for periods 11 through 20 as shown in the table, which of these two methods has the greater accuracy?

t	Units Sold	t	Units Sold
11	147	16	152
12	148	17	155
13	151	18	157
14	145	19	160
15	155	20	165

26. Two different forecasting techniques (F1 and F2) were used to forecast demand for cases of bottled water. Actual demand and the two sets of forecasts are as follows:

		PREDICTED DEMAND	
Period	Demand	F1	F2
1	68	66	66
2	75	68	68
3	70	72	70
4	74	71	72
5	69	72	74
6	72	70	76
7	80	71	78
8	78	74	80

a. Compute MAD for each set of forecasts. Given your results, which forecast appears to be the most accurate? Explain.

b. Compute the MSE for each set of forecasts. Given your results, which forecast appears to be the most accurate?

c. In practice, *either* MAD *or* MSE would be employed to compute forecast errors. What factors might lead a manager to choose one rather than the other?

27. The manager of a travel agency has been using a seasonally adjusted forecast to predict demand for packaged tours. The actual and predicted values are:

Period	Demand	Predicted
1	129	124
2	194	200
3	156	150
4	91	94
5	85	80
6	132	140
7	126	128
8	126	124
9	95	100
10	149	150
11	98	94
12	85	80
13	137	140
14	134	128

a. Compute MAD for the fifth period, then update it period by period using exponential smoothing with $\alpha = .3$.

b. Compute a tracking signal for periods 5 through 14 using the initial and updated MADs. If limits of ± 3 are used, what can you conclude?

28. Two independent methods of forecasting based on judgment and experience have been prepared each month for the past 10 months. The forecasts and actual sales are as follows.

Month	Sales	Forecast 1	Forecast 2
1	770	771	769
2	789	785	787
3	794	790	792
4	780	784	798
5	768	770	774
6	772	768	770
7	760	761	759
8	775	771	775
9	786	784	788
10	790	788	788

a. Compute the MSE and MAD for each forecast. Does either method seem superior? Explain.

b. Compute a tracking signal for the 10th month for each forecast. What does it show? (Use action limits of ± 4.)

c. Compute $2s$ control limits for each forecast.

d. Prepare a naive forecast for periods 2 through 11 using the given sales data. Compute each of the following; (1) MSE, (2) MAD, (3) tracking signal at month 10, and (4) $2s$ control limits. How do the naive results compare with the other two forecasts?

29. The classified department of a monthly magazine has used a combination of quantitative and qualitative methods to forecast sales of advertising space. Results over a 20-month period are as follows:

Month	Error	Month	Error
1	−8	11	1
2	−2	12	6
3	4	13	8
4	7	14	4
5	9	15	1
6	5	16	−2
7	0	17	−4
8	−3	18	−8
9	−9	19	−5
10	−4	20	−1

a. Compute a tracking signal for months 11 through 20. Compute an initial value of MAD for month 11, and then update it for each month using exponential smoothing with $\alpha = .1$. What can you conclude? Assume limits of ± 4.

b. Using the first half of the data, construct a control chart with $2s$ limits. What can you conclude?

c. Plot the last 10 errors on the control chart. Are the errors random? What is the implication of this?

30. A textbook publishing company has compiled data on total annual sales of its business texts for the preceding nine years:

Year:	1	2	3	4	5	6	7	8	9
Sales (000):	40.2	44.5	48.0	52.3	55.8	57.1	62.4	69.0	73.7

a. Using an appropriate model, forecast textbook sales for each of the next five years.

b. Prepare a control chart for the forecast using the original data. Use 2*s* limits.

c. Suppose actual sales for the next five years turn out as follows:

Year:	10	11	12	13	14
Sales (000):	77.2	82.1	87.8	90.6	98.9

Is the forecast performing adequately? Explain.

31. A manager has just received an evaluation from an analyst on two potential forecasting alter-natives. The analyst is indifferent between the two alternatives, saying that they should be equally effective.

Period:	1	2	3	4	5	6	7	8	9	10
Data:	37	39	37	39	45	49	47	49	51	54
Alt. 1:	36	38	40	42	46	46	46	48	52	55
Alt. 2:	36	37	38	38	41	52	47	48	52	53

a. What would cause the analyst to reach this conclusion?

b. What information can you add to enhance the analysis?

32. A manager uses this equation to predict demand: $y_t = 10 + 5t$. Over the past eight periods, de-mand has been as follows.

Period, *t*:	1	2	3	4	5	6	7	8
Demand:	15	21	23	30	32	38	42	47

Is the forecast performing adequately? Explain.

33. A manager uses a trend equation plus quarterly relatives to predict demand. Quarter relatives are $Q_1 = .90$, $Q_2 = .95$, $Q_3 = 1.05$, and $Q_4 = 1.10$. The trend equation is: $y_t = 10 + 5t$. Over the past nine quarters, demand has been as follows.

Period, *t*:	1	2	3	4	5	6	7	8	9
Demand:	14	20	24	31	31	37	43	48	52

Is the forecast performing adequately? Explain.

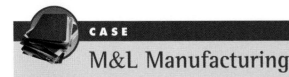

CASE

M&L Manufacturing

M&L Manufacturing makes various components for printers and copiers. In addition to supplying these items to a major manufacturer of printers and copiers, the com-pany distributes these and similar items to office supply stores and computer stores as replacement parts for printers and desk-top copiers. In all, the company makes about 20 different items. The two markets (the major manufacturer and the replacement market) require somewhat different handling. For example, re-placement products must be packaged individually whereas products are shipped in bulk to the major manufacturer.

The company does not use forecasts for production plan-ning. Instead, the operations manager decides which items to produce, and the batch size, based partly on orders, and the amounts in inventory. The products that have the fewest amounts in inventory get the highest priority. Demand is un-even, and the company has experienced being overstocked on

some items and out of others. Being understocked has occa-sionally created tensions with the managers of retail outlets. Another problem is that prices of raw materials have been creeping up, although the operations manager thinks that this might be a temporary condition.

Because of competitive pressures and falling profits, the manager has decided to undertake a number of changes. One change is to introduce more formal forecasting proce-dures in order to improve production planning and inventory management.

With that in mind, the manager wants to begin forecasting for two products. These products are important for several rea-sons. First, they account for a disproportionately large share of the company's profits. Second, the manager believes that one of these products will become increasingly important to future growth plans; and third, the other product has experienced pe-riodic out-of-stock instances.

The manager has compiled data on product demand for the two products from order records for the previous 14 weeks. These are shown in the following table.

Week	Product 1	Product 2
1	50	40
2	54	38
3	57	41
4	60	46
5	64	42
6	67	41
7	90*	41
8	76	47
9	79	42
10	82	43
11	85	42
12	87	49
13	92	43
14	96	44

*Unusual order due to flooding of customer's warehouse.

Questions

1. What are some of the potential benefits of a more formalized approach to forecasting?

2. Prepare a weekly forecast for the next four weeks for each product. Briefly explain why you chose the methods you used. (*Hint:* For product 2, a simple approach, possibly some sort of naive/intuitive approach, would be preferable to a technical approach in view of the manager's disdain of more technical methods.)

Delurgio, Stephen. *Forecasting Principles and Applications.* Burr Ridge, IL.: Irwin/McGraw-Hill, 1998.

Georgoff, D. M., and R. G. Murdick. "Manager's Guide to Forecasting." *Harvard Business Review,* January–February 1986, pp. 110–120.

Hopp, Wallace J., and Mark L. Spearman. *Factory Physics.* 2nd ed. Burr Ridge, IL.: Irwin/McGraw-Hill, 2001.

"The Impact of Forecasting on Return of Shareholder Value." *Journal of Business Forecasting,* Fall 1999, pp. 00.

Rowe, G., and G. Wright. "The Delphi Technique as a Forecasting Tool: Issues and Analysis." *International Journal of Forecasting* 15, issue 4 (October 1999). See also in the same issue: several commentaries on this article.

"Selecting the Appropriate Forecasting Method." *Journal of Business Forecasting,* Fall 1997.

Wilson, J. Holton, and Barry Keating. *Business Forecasting.* New York: McGraw-Hill, 1998.

PART THREE

System Design

Satisfying the customer begins with product and service design. Moreover, decisions made in this area impact on operations and on the organization's overall success.

Similarly, process selection and capacity planning impact on the ability of the production system to perform and to satisfy customers. Flexibility, production time, and cost are key considerations in process design.

Process selection and layout are closely related. Layout decisions involve the arrangement of the workplace, which affects the flow of work through a system and impacts productivity, cost, and flexibility. Layout decisions are influenced by decisions made in product and service design.

Capacity and location decisions influence operating costs and the ability to respond to customer demand. Location decisions also impact transportation costs, labor availability, material costs, and access to markets.

Work design focuses on the human element in production systems. Increasingly, managers are realizing that workers are a valuable asset and can contribute greatly to the organization's success. Strategic planning is beginning to incorporate employee participation to help improve production systems.

Design decisions have strategic significance for business organizations. Many of these decisions are not made by the operations manager. Nonetheless, because of the important links between operations and each strategic area, it is essential to the success of the organization to involve all of the functional areas of the organization in design decisions.

System design encompasses decisions involving:

1 Product and service design, Chapter 4
2 Capacity planning, Chapter 5
3 Process selection and facility layout, Chapter 6
4 Design of work systems, Chapter 7
5 Location planning and analysis, Chapter 8

CHAPTER FOUR

Product and Service Design

CHAPTER OUTLINE

Introduction, 128
   What Does Product and Service
      Design Do? 128
   Reasons for Product or Service
      Design or Redesign, 128
   Objectives of Product and Service
      Design, 130

Sources of Ideas for New or
   Redesigned Products and
   Services, 130
   Research and Development, 131

Reading: Manager's Journal: When
   Customer Research Is a Lousy
   Idea, 132

Reading: Vlasic on a Roll with Huge
   Pickle Slices, 133

Legal, Ethical, and Environmental
   Issues, 134

Other Issues in Product and Service
   Design, 135
   Life Cycles, 136
   Standardization, 137
   Designing for Mass
      Customization, 138
   Reliability, 139
   Robust Design, 140

Designing for Manufacturing, 141
   Concurrent Engineering, 141

Computer-Aided Design (CAD), 142
Production Requirements, 143
Recycling, 143

Newsclip: More Cars Come with a
   Shade of Green—Recycled
   Materials, 144
   Remanufacturing, 144

Reading: Making It (Almost) New
   Again, 145
   Component Commonality, 147

Designing for Services, 147
   Differences between Service Design
      and Product Design, 148
   Overview of Service Design, 149
   Design Guidelines, 149

Quality Function Deployment, 150

Newsclip: A QFD Snapshot, 152

The Kano Model, 153

Operations Strategy, 154

Summary, 155

Key Terms, 155

Discussion and Review
   Questions, 155

Memo Writing Exercises, 156

Problems, 156

Selected Bibliography and Further
   Reading, 157

Supplement: Reliability, 158

LEARNING OBJECTIVES

*After completing this chapter, you
should be able to:*

1 Explain the importance of product
   and service design.

2 List some key reasons for new or
   revised designs.

3 Name some sources of ideas for
   new or revised designs.

4 Discuss key issues in product and
   service design.

5 Explain the difference between
   recycling and remanufacturing.

6 Explain the importance of
   manufacturability.

7 Name the advantages and
   disadvantages of standardization
   in product and service design.

8 Discuss mass customization.

9 Discuss special considerations for
   service design.

As more and more women join the workforce and more families rely on two incomes, the spending and eating habits of Americans are changing. Quick meals have replaced leisurely meals. There is an increased awareness of healthy foods. And spicy foods have replaced plain foods. Fast-food chains, food companies, and supermarkets are scrambling to meet the challenge.

Spice giant McCormick is finding that sales of traditional spices are down. To compensate, the company is promoting seasoning mixes which are designed to save time. Salsa is becoming very popular, and Mexican restaurants are springing up all over. Supermarkets are offering a wide array of already prepared foods (see the Wegmans Tour in Chapter 1) as well as recipes for quick meals in their stores and on their web pages.

For these and other companies, from high tech to no tech, product and service design plays an important role in their profitability and their very survival.

The essence of any organization is the products or services it offers. There is an obvious link between the *design* of those products or services and the *success* of the organization. Organizations that have well-designed products or services are more likely to realize their goals than those with poorly designed products or services. Hence, organizations have a vital stake in achieving good product and service design.

In this chapter you will find many interesting insights into product and service design. Among the topics covered are the need for product and service design or redesign, sources of ideas for design or redesign, legal, environmental, and ethical issues, and design elements for both manufacturing and service.

Product and service design—or redesign—should be closely tied to an organization's strategy. It is a major factor in cost, quality, time to market, customer satisfaction, and competitive advantage.

Introduction

In this section you will learn what product and service designers do, the reasons for design (or redesign), and the objectives of design.

WHAT DOES PRODUCT AND SERVICE DESIGN DO?

A range of activities fall under the heading of product and service design. The activities and responsibilities of product and service design include the following (functional interactions are shown in parentheses):

1. Translate customer wants and needs into product and service requirements. (marketing)

2. Refine existing products and services. (marketing)

3. Develop new products and/or services. (marketing, operations)

4. Formulate quality goals. (quality assurance, operations)

5. Formulate cost target. (accounting)

6. Construct and test prototypes. (marketing, operations)

7. Document specifications.

Product and service design involves or affects nearly every functional area of an organization. However, marketing and operations have major involvement.

Figure 4–1 offers a humorous look at some of the ways various departments in the design process might interpret a "design." The point is that sufficient information must be obtained to clearly determine what the customer wants, and this must be communicated to those responsible for designing, producing, and marketing a particular product or service.

REASONS FOR PRODUCT OR SERVICE DESIGN OR REDESIGN

Organizations become involved in product or service design for a variety of reasons. An obvious one is to be competitive by offering new products or services. Another one is to

As proposed by the marketing department.

As specified in the product request.

As designed by the senior designer.

As produced by manufacturing.

As used by the customer.

What the customer wanted.

FIGURE 4-1

Differing views of design created through lack of information
Source: *Educational Center Newsletter,* Minneapolis, Minnesota.

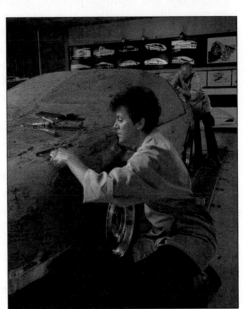

At the General Motors Tech Center in Warren, Michigan, designers carve a clay model of their new model styling.

www.gm.com

make the business grow and increase profits. Furthermore, the best organizations try to develop new products or services as an alternative to downsizing. When productivity gains result in the need for fewer workers, developing new products or services can mean adding jobs and retaining people instead of letting them go.

Sometimes product or service design is actually *redesign*. This, too, occurs for a number of reasons such as customer complaints, accidents or injuries, excessive warranty claims, or low demand. The desire to achieve cost reductions in labor or materials can also be a motivating factor.

OBJECTIVES OF PRODUCT AND SERVICE DESIGN

The objectives of product design and service design differ somewhat, but not as much as you might imagine. The overall objective for both is to satisfy the customer while making a reasonable profit.

It is important to note that although profit is generally the overall measure of design effectiveness, because the time interval between the design phase and profit realization is often considerable, more immediate measures come into play. These typically include development time and cost, the product or service cost, and the resulting product or service quality.

Quality, of course, is typically high on the list of priorities in product and service design. At one time, having high quality was enough for a product or service to stand out; now it is the norm, and those that fall below this norm are the ones that stand out.

design for operations Taking into account the capabilities of the organization in designing goods and services.

Last, but certainly not least, it is *crucial* for designers to take into account the capabilities of the organization to produce or deliver a given product or service. This is sometimes referred to as **design for operations.** When the operations involve manufacturing, the term often used is **manufacturability:** the ease with which design features can be achieved by manufacturing. Failure to take this into consideration can result in reduced productivity, reduced quality, and increased costs. For these reasons, it is wise for design to solicit input from manufacturing people throughout the design process. Likewise, in the design of services, it is important to involve service people in the design process to reduce the risk of achieving a design that looks good on paper, but doesn't work in the real world.

manufacturability The ease of fabrication and/or assembly.

Sources of Ideas for New or Redesigned Products and Services

Ideas for new and improved products or services can come from a wide range of sources, both from within the organization and from outside it.

Employees—including those who make products or deliver services to customers, salespeople, and purchasing agents, can be a rich source of ideas, if they are motivated to offer suggestions. In addition to these are two more primary sources of ideas: marketing and research. Along with assessing current needs of customers, marketing people typically are aware of problems with products or services. Marketing people are often sources of ideas based on their studies of markets, buying patterns, and familiarity with demographics. Also, marketing can help craft a vision of what customers are likely to want in the future. Some organizations have research and development departments, another source of ideas.

reverse engineering Dismantling and inspecting a competitor's product to discover product improvements.

External sources of ideas include customers, competitors, and suppliers. Customers may submit suggestions for improvements or new products, or they may be queried through the use of surveys or focus groups. One such approach is *quality function deployment,* which seeks to incorporate the "voice of the customer" into product and service design. It is described later in the chapter. Customer complaints can provide valuable insight into areas that need improvement. Similarly, product failures and warranty claims indicate where improvements are needed. One of the strongest motivators for new and improved products or services is competitors' products and services. By studying a competitor's products or services and how the competitor operates (pricing policies, return policies, warranties, location strategies, etc.), an organization can glean many ideas. Beyond that, some companies purchase a competitor's product and then carefully dismantle and inspect it, searching for ways to improve their own product. This is called **reverse engineering.** The Ford Motor Company used this tactic in developing its highly successful Taurus model: It examined competitors' automobiles, searching for best-in-class components (e.g., best hood release, best dashboard display, best door handle). Sometimes reverse engineering can enable a company to "leapfrog" the competition by developing an even better product. Suppliers are still another source of ideas, and with increased emphasis on supply chains and supplier partnerships, suppliers are becoming an important source of ideas.

Chrysler's 1.3 mile automated durability track simulates bad roads and is used to test the integrity of automobiles and trucks. Chrysler vehicles are "guided" by computer-controlled robots.

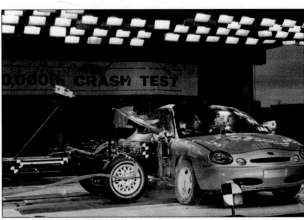

A milestone crash test performed at Ford Motor Corporation is used to plan for new side-impact head and chest air bags.

In general, design, production or operations, and marketing must work closely together, keeping each other informed and taking into account the wants and needs of the customer. In addition, legal, environmental, and ethical considerations can influence the design function.

The next section describes research and development, followed by a section on legal, ethical, and environmental issues.

RESEARCH AND DEVELOPMENT

Research and development (R&D) refers to organized efforts that are directed toward increasing scientific knowledge and product or process innovation. Most of the advances in semiconductors, medicine, communications, and space technology can be attributed to R&D efforts at colleges and universities, research foundations, government agencies, and private enterprises.

R&D efforts may involve *basic research, applied research,* or *development.*

Basic research has the objective of advancing the state of knowledge about a subject, without any near-term expectation of commercial applications.

Applied research has the objective of achieving commercial applications.

Development converts the results of applied research into useful commercial applications.

Basic research, because it does not lead to near-term commercial applications, is generally underwritten by the government and large corporations. Conversely, applied research and development, because of the potential for commercial applications, appeals to a wide spectrum of business organizations.

The benefits of successful R&D can be tremendous. Some research leads to patents, with the potential of licensing and royalties. However, many discoveries are not patentable, or companies don't wish to divulge details of their ideas so they avoid the patent route. Even so, the first organization to bring a new product or service to the market generally stands to profit from it before the others can catch up. Early products may be priced higher because a temporary monopoly exists until competitors bring their versions out.

The costs of R&D can be high. Kodak, for example, has spent more than $1 million *a day* on R&D. Large companies in the automotive, computer, communications, and pharmaceutical industries spend even more. Even so, critics say that many U.S. companies spend too little on R&D, a factor often cited in the loss of competitive advantage.

It is interesting to note that some companies are now shifting from a focus primarily on *products* to a more balanced approach that explores both product and *process* R&D. One

research and development (R&D) Organized efforts to increase scientific knowledge or product innovation.

www.kodak.com

reason is that in too many instances, product innovations (e.g., for televisions, VCRs, and microwave ovens) made by U.S. companies have ended up being produced more competitively by foreign companies with better processes.

In certain instances, research may not be the best approach, as explained in the following reading. The second reading illustrates a research success.

READING

Manager's Journal: When Customer Research Is a Lousy Idea Willard I. Zangwill

www.sony.com

Customer research is often touted as a necessary precursor to product introduction. The problem—especially for innovative products—is that it often proves wrong. For example, hair styling mousse is now a massive hit. Yet in its initial market tests in the U.S., it flopped. "Goopy and gunky" was what people said about it, and they did not like its feel when it "mooshed" through their hair.

Similarly, when the telephone answering machine was consumer tested, it faced an almost universally negative reaction. Back then, most individuals felt that using a mechanical device to answer a phone was rude and disrespectful. Today, of course, many people regard their answering machines as indispensable, and consider scheduling their daily activities without them as impossible. In the same vein, the computer mouse in its initial testing flunked, being evaluated by potential customers as awkward and unnecessary.

Because of these difficulties, some companies have gone so far as to eliminate customer research for their innovative products. According to Sony executive Kozo Ohsone, "When you introduce products that have never been invented before, what good is market research?" The Walkman was launched without the standard customer research, as is typical at Sony.

With customer research not only costly, but often in error, how can a manager determine the innovations customers want? The solution may be design-for-purpose, a new approach in which a firm uses speed and flexibility to gain customer information instead of, or in addition to, standard customer research.

To illustrate, Sony obtains information from the actual sales of various Walkman models and then quickly adjusts its product mix to conform to those sales patterns. Specifically, the process design of each Walkman model is based on a core platform containing the essential technology. But the platform is designed to be flexible, which allows a wide range of models

to be easily built on it, such as a beach model, a child's model, one that attaches to the arm, and so on.

Depending upon which models sell, the models or features are changed, but the platform remains the same. If pink is a hot selling color, they make more pink models. If beach models sell well, they make more of the existing models and also expand the line. This technique is far more accurate than deciding what to make using traditional customer research.

Similarly, without customer research, every season Seiko "throws" into the market several hundred new models of its watches. Those that customers buy, it makes more of; the others, it drops. Capitalizing on the design-for-response strategy, Seiko has a highly flexible design and production process that lets it quickly and inexpensively introduce products. Do they worry if a high percentage of the watches they introduce fail, rejected by the customers? No (unless the failure rate is extremely high), because their fast, flexible product design process has slashed the cost of failure.

When creating a new magazine, Hearst Magazines also follows this approach. Hearst learned that it was almost impossible to customer test the magazine ideas, and that it was better to launch the magazine and see what happens. To do this, Hearst has created a special group of editors with the talent and flexibility to launch almost any new magazine. Based upon the initial sales of the new magazine, they will either revise the content and format or drop the publication. Any new magazine that proves successful is spun off to run independently.

Crucial to this approach, however, is reducing the cost of the failures by keeping expenses down. Hearst accomplishes this by initially hiring one overall editor on a short-time basis, using stringers as writers, and borrowing advertising people. Also, with experience it has discovered the tricks of launching new magazine products inexpensively. For example, it has learned how to test different cover designs efficiently, and how to test sales in different markets, such as newsstands or subscribers.

Many other firms also follow the strategy of using customer research data less and fast-flexible response more, with the food industry in the lead. One of the problems with customer research into foods is that a person's desire for food is powerfully influenced by the ambiance, the dining companions and what foods were eaten recently, all of which confound and confuse the results of the customer research. Even more erratic are the results with children's food, say a new cereal or snack. The responses of kids are strongly swayed by how well they like the people doing the test and the playthings available. Worse, kids quickly change their minds, and in a taste test of several foods a child can judge one food the best but one hour later proclaim the same food as "icky."

Arthur D. Little & Co. discovered that of all new cereals introduced to the market, 92 percent had failed. Since using the full array of customer research techniques produces a success rate of only 8 percent, more and more companies are revising their thinking about doing customer research as usual. Innovative firms such as Keebler and the leading cereal makers are reducing their expenditure for customer research and instead are vigorously cutting the cost of launching new products, including making their manufacturing processes more flexible.

Design-for-response enables firms not only to employ customer research when beneficial but also to respond quickly to what the customers really want, keeping the firm on top of market shifts and surprises.

NOTE: Mr. Zangwill is a professor at the Graduate School of Business, University of Chicago, and author of *Lightning Strategies for Innovation* (Lexington, 1992).

(See related letter: "Letters to the Editor: Testing the Waters Before the Launch" *WSJ*—April 1, 1993)

READING

Vlasic on a Roll with Huge Pickle Slices

Michele Darnell

www.vlasic.com

Many were skeptical of Frank Meczkowski's plan to develop a pickle so big that a single slice could cover a hamburger.

After all, whoever saw a pickle that big—except maybe in the *Guinness Book of World Records?*

Meczkowski and his team of food researchers at Vlasic Foods International were convinced the project—given the code name Frisbee—could fly.

For about four years, they labored to cultivate a jumbo cucumber with the taste, shape and crunch to be a perfect pickle.

Made only at the company's plant in Millsboro, the monster-sized slices seem to have captured the pickle lover's fancy. They've become one of Vlasic's best-selling products since their introduction in supermarkets last March. And, the better-than-anticipated sales have helped to reverse a three-year decline in consumption of Vlasic pickles.

Hamburger Stackers are about 10 times bigger than traditional pickle chips and come in dill and bread-and-butter varieties.

"They said it just couldn't be done."

Making a bigger pickle may not sound like that big of a deal. You just grow a bigger cucumber, right?

There is more to it than that. The folks at Vlasic soon learned how tough it was to deal with gigantic cucumbers as they developed the new product and as they retooled the Delaware plant.

Meczkowski came up with the idea for the mammoth pickle slices soon after Vlasic's 1994 introduction of its Sand-

The 'Hamburger Stacker' on the burger at left dwarfs a traditional pickle slice. Stackers are 'genetically designed' using cucumbers that grow to over 3 inches in diameter and weigh five pounds.

wich Stackers—regular-size pickles sliced lengthwise so they can be draped on sandwiches.

Sandwich Stackers currently account for 20 percent of all Vlasic pickle sales.

Vlasic is the No. 1 seller of pickles in the United States, with a 32 percent share of the $800 million retail pickle market, beating out brands such as Claussen, Heinz and Peter Piper's.

To develop Hamburger Stackers, Meczkowski worked with seed researchers and others to scour the globe looking for oversized varieties of cucumbers. Most weren't in commercial production.

Vlasic's team grew different varieties in greenhouses, looking for one that would get big enough yet still make a good pickle.

It had to taste like a regular cucumber, stay crisp when pickled, have a small seed cavity and be straight enough so that it could be cut mechanically.

"We wanted it to really be a cucumber," said Meczkowski, who has worked as a food researcher for 22 years and is based at Vlasic's headquarters in New Jersey.

He said Vlasic also had to decide just how big Hamburger Stackers should be. At one point, it asked consumers who were participating in focus groups to bring in their own home-made burgers so the company could determine the perfect size for its new pickles.

Eventually, Vlasic officials found what they were looking for—a now-patented cucumber that grows 3.25 inches in diameter, easily reaches 12 to 16 inches in length and weighs about five pounds.

It looks like the watermelon's skinny runt brother.

Once the company settled on a cucumber, it had to work out details of how to get Hamburger Stackers into commercial production. One challenge was to grow the cucumbers in fields, rather than in a greenhouse.

Randy Spence, Vlasic's manager of manufacturing services, said the jumbo cucumbers grew quicker than anyone expected.

"Early on, we expected the bigger ones to grow slower, but that hasn't been the case," he said.

These days, most of the gigantic cucumbers are grown in Florida, where they are handpicked because of their size. Depending on the weather, they take about 54 days from seed to harvest.

Once harvested, they're shipped to Vlasic's plant in Sussex County. The plant employs about 260 workers year-round and 300 to 400 others from April to November.

Steven McNulty, director of plant operations at the nearly 30-year-old Millsboro facility, said the size of the new cucumbers meant they couldn't be handled in the same manner as the smaller versions used to make pickle spears and sweet gherkins.

That became obvious when Vlasic tried to process its first batch of the somewhat fragile, jumbo-sized cucumbers.

Officials didn't end up with the Hamburger Stackers they envisioned. Instead, they ended up with a batch of broken big cucumbers.

"On the first run, we broke every one," Spence said.

But it taught the company a lot about some of the retooling they'd have to do to the plant in Millsboro.

Officials at the plant began making months worth of adjustments so one of the facility's four production lines could handle the jumbo cucumbers.

"We've learned a lot," McNulty said. "And we're still learning."

Making Hamburger Stackers requires a mix of automation and the human touch. The process starts when the big cucumbers arrive by truck and are rushed into a cold-storage facility to preserve their flavor.

Once cooled, the cucumbers can be loaded onto the production line and checked for bad spots and other flaws.

They're washed by machine a couple times and sliced.

Then they're sized. Jiggling along a conveyor belt, slices that are too small are weeded out by a worker and a machine. Those that are too big also are sorted out.

Too big?

Yes, the monster-sized cucumbers can get a little too big to fit in the jar.

The cucumber slices that make the cut are mechanically stacked into jars and then topped off by hand.

Ella Mae Wilkerson, who has worked at the Vlasic plant in Millsboro for 17 years, said it takes some fast hands to make certain that outgoing jars have enough pickles packed in.

"The bigger the jar, the harder it is," she said as containers of sweet gherkins being jarred on another production line zipped by on a conveyor belt.

After being packed with pickle slices, the jars of Hamburger Stackers are filled with a combination of water, vinegar, salt and other flavorings and colorings. They are capped, vacuum-sealed and pasteurized before being labeled and packed for global distribution.

Some details of how Hamburger Stackers are made are kept secret. McNulty said that is because the company is certain its rivals would love to figure out how to make their own Hamburger Stackers.

Vlasic is the only pickle-making company with such a product on the market. "We think the competition loves the idea," McNulty said.

Apparently, so does the pickle-eating public.

About $13 million worth of Hamburger Stackers were sold in the first five months after they were introduced.

The company is optimistic that the product will continue to grow in popularity with U.S. consumers who eat about 3.5 billion hamburgers at home annually.

Source: *Rochester Democrat and Chronicle*, December 13, 1999, p. 1F.

Legal, Ethical, and Environmental Issues

Designers must be careful to take into account a wide array of legal and ethical considerations. Moreover, if there is a potential to harm the environment, then those issues also become important. Most organizations have numerous government agencies that regulate them. Among the more familiar federal agencies are the Food and Drug Administration, the

Occupational Health and Safety Administration, the Environmental Protection Agency, and various state and local agencies. Bans on cyclamates, red food dye, phosphates, and asbestos have sent designers scurrying back to their drawing boards to find alternative designs that were acceptable to both government regulators and customers. Similarly, automobile pollution standards and safety features, such as seat belts, air bags, safety glass, and energy-absorbing bumpers and frames, have had a substantial impact on automotive design. Much attention also has been directed toward toy design to remove sharp edges, small pieces that can cause choking, and toxic materials. In construction, government regulations require the use of lead-free paint, safety glass in entranceways, access to public buildings for handicapped persons, and standards for insulation, electrical wiring, and plumbing.

Product liability can be a strong incentive for design improvements. **Product liability** means that a manufacturer is liable for any injuries or damages caused by a faulty product because of poor workmanship or design. Many business firms have faced lawsuits related to their products, including Firestone Tire & Rubber, Ford and General Motors, and toy manufacturers. Manufacturers also are faced with the implied warranties created by state laws under the **Uniform Commercial Code,** which says that products carry an implication of *merchantability* and *fitness*; that is, a product must be usable for its intended purposes.

> **product liability** A manufacturer is liable for any injuries or damages caused by a faulty product.
>
> **Uniform Commercial Code** Products carry an implication of merchantability and fitness.

The suits and potential suits have led to increased legal and insurance costs, expensive settlements with injured parties, and costly recalls. Moreover, increasing customer awareness of product safety can adversely affect product image and subsequent demand for a product.

Thus, it is extremely important to design products that are reasonably free of hazards. When hazards do exist, it is necessary to install safety guards or other devices for reducing accident potential, and to provide adequate warning notices of risks. Consumer groups, business firms, and various government agencies often work together to develop industrywide standards that help avoid some of the hazards.

Ethical issues often arise in the design of products and services; it is important for managers to be aware of these issues and for designers to adhere to ethical standards. Designers are often under pressure to speed up the design process and to cut costs. These pressures often require them to make trade-off decisions, many of which involve ethical considerations. One example of what can happen is "vaporware," when a software company doesn't issue a release of software as scheduled as it struggles with production problems or bugs in the software. The company faces the dilemma of releasing the software right away or waiting until most of the bugs have been removed—knowing that the longer it waits, the longer it will be before it receives revenues and the greater the risk of damage to its reputation.

Organizations generally want designers to adhere to guidelines such as the following:

Produce designs that are consistent with the goals of the organization. For instance, if the company has a goal of high quality, don't cut corners to save cost, even in areas where it won't be apparent to customer.

Give customers the value they expect.

Make health and safety a primary concern. At risk are employees who will produce goods or deliver services, workers who will transport the products, customers who will use the products or receive the services, and the general public, which might be endangered by the products or services.

Don't design something that has the potential to harm the environment.

Other Issues in Product and Service Design

Aside from legal, environmental, and ethical issues, designers must also take into account product or service life cycles, how much standardization to incorporate, product or service reliability, and the range of operating conditions under which a product or service must function. These topics are discussed in this section. We begin with life cycles.

Among the winners of the 2000 Industrial Design Excellence Award sponsored by Business Week: Orangex Ojex Manual Juicer was produced with employees' ideas for efficiency, low cost and great tasting juice; ASF paper shredder for home use is designed to shred high volumes of paper at one time; Steelcase Leap chair has independently adjustable upper and lower back supports.

LIFE CYCLES

life cycle Incubation, growth, maturity, saturation, and decline.

Many new products and services go through a **life cycle** in terms of demand. When an item is introduced, it may be treated as a curiosity. Demand is generally low because potential buyers are not yet familiar with the item. Many potential buyers recognize that all of the bugs have probably not been worked out and that the price may drop after the introductory period. Production methods are designed for low volume. With the passage of time, design improvements usually create a more reliable and less costly product. Demand then grows for these reasons and because of increasing awareness of the product or service. Higher production volume will involve different methods and contribute to lower costs. At the next stage in the life cycle, the product or service reaches maturity: there are few, if any, design changes, and demand levels off. Eventually, the market becomes saturated, which leads to a decline in demand. In the last stage of a life cycle, some firms adopt a defensive research posture whereby they attempt to prolong the useful life of a product or service by improving its reliability, reducing costs of producing it (and, hence, the price), redesigning it, or changing the packaging. These stages are illustrated in Figure 4–2.

Consider the products in various stages of the life cycle in the music industry: Digital audio tapes are in the introductory stage, compact discs are in the growth stage, cassettes are moving from the maturity-saturation stage into the decline stage.

Some products do not exhibit life cycles: wooden pencils, paper clips, nails, knives, forks and spoons, drinking glasses, and similar items. However, most new products do.

Services, too, experience life cycles. Often these are related to the life cycles of products. For example, as older products are phased out, services such as installation and repair of the older products also phase out.

Wide variations exist in the amount of time a particular product or service takes to pass through a given phase of its life cycle: some pass through various stages in a relatively short period; others take considerably longer. Often it is a matter of the basic *need* for the item and the *rate of technological change*. Some toys, novelty items, and style items have a life cycle of less than one year, whereas other, more useful items, such as clothes washers and dryers, may last for many years before yielding to technological change.

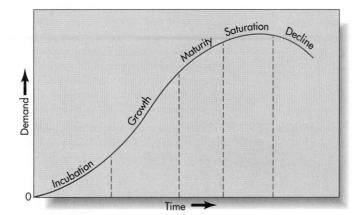

FIGURE 4-2

Products or services may exhibit life cycles over time

STANDARDIZATION

An important issue that often arises in both product/service design and process design is the degree of standardization. **Standardization** refers to the extent to which there is absence of variety in a product, service, or process. Standardized products are made in large quantities of identical items; calculators, computers, and 2 percent milk are examples. Standardized service implies that every customer or item processed receives essentially the same service. An automatic car wash is a good example; each car, regardless of how clean or dirty it is, receives the same service. Standardized processes deliver standardized service or produce standardized goods.

Standardization carries a number of important benefits as well as certain disadvantages. Standardized products mean *interchangeable parts,* which greatly lower the cost of production while increasing productivity and making replacement or repair relatively easy compared with that of customized parts. Design costs are generally lower. For example, General Motors recently has attempted to standardize key components of its automobiles across product lines; components such as brakes, electrical systems, and other "under-the-skin" parts would be the same for all GM car models. By reducing variety, GM saves time and money while increasing quality and reliability in its products.

Another benefit of standardization is reduced time and cost to train employees and reduced time to design jobs. Similarly, scheduling of work, inventory handling, and purchasing and accounting activities become much more routine.

Lack of standardization can at times lead to serious difficulties and competitive struggles, particularly when systems running under different conditions are incompatible. Consider a few examples: When VCRs were first introduced, there were two formats for tapes: VHS and Beta. Machines could play one or the other, but not both. This meant that producers needed to make two sets of tapes. High-definition television might have been introduced much earlier in the United States, but three competing—and incompatible—systems were proposed, which led to prolonged debate and study before one system could be agreed upon. The lack of standardization in computer software and operating systems (Macintosh versus IBM) has presented users with hard choices because of the difficulty in switching from one system to the other. And the use by U.S. manufacturers of the English system of measurement, while most of the rest of the world's manufacturers use the metric system, has led to problems in selling U.S. goods in foreign countries and in buying foreign machines for use in the United States. This may make it more difficult for U.S. firms to compete in the European Union. Similarly, U.S. auto manufacturers have complained for years about their inability to freely enter the Japanese market, but only recently have they begun to offer cars with steering wheels on the right side—the universal standard in Japan.

Standardization also has disadvantages. A major one relates to the reduction in variety. This can limit the range of customers to whom a product or service appeals. Customers

standardization Extent to which there is absence of variety in a product, service, or process.

www.gm.com

TABLE 4–1

Advantages and disadvantages of standardization

Advantages	1. Fewer parts to deal with in inventory and in manufacturing.
	2. Reduced training costs and time.
	3. More routine purchasing, handling, and inspection procedures.
	4. Orders fillable from inventory.
	5. Opportunities for long production runs and automation.
	6. Need for fewer parts justifies increased expenditures on perfecting designs and improving quality control procedures.
Disadvantages	1. Designs may be frozen with too many imperfections remaining.
	2. High cost of design changes increases resistance to improvements.
	3. Decreased variety results in less consumer appeal.

may reluctantly accept a product only because nothing else suits their needs. But that creates a risk that a competitor will introduce a better product or greater variety (a feature of lean production), and realize a competitive advantage. Another disadvantage is that a manufacturer may freeze (standardize) a design prematurely and, once frozen, it may find compelling reasons to resist modification. A familiar example of this is the keyboard arrangement of typewriters and computer keyboards. Studies have demonstrated that another arrangement of keys would be more efficient, but the cost of replacing all of the equipment in existence and retraining millions of typists and word processors would not be worth the benefit.

Obviously, designers must consider important issues related to standardization when making choices. The major advantages and disadvantages of standardization are summarized in Table 4–1.

DESIGNING FOR MASS CUSTOMIZATION

Companies like standardization because it enables them to produce high volumes of relatively low-cost products, albeit products with little variety. Customers, on the other hand, typically prefer more variety, although they like the low cost. The question for producers is how to resolve these issues without (1) losing the benefits of standardization and (2) incurring a host of problems that are often linked to variety. These include increasing the resources needed to achieve design variety; increasing variety in the production process, which would add to the skills necessary to produce products, causing a decrease in productivity; creating an additional inventory burden during and after production, by having to carry replacement parts for the increased variety of parts; and adding to the difficulty of diagnosing and repairing failed products. The answer, at least for some companies, is **mass customization,** a strategy of producing standardized goods or services, but incorporating some degree of customization in the final product or service. Several tactics make this possible. One is *delayed differentiation,* and another is *modular design.*

Delayed differentiation is a *postponement* tactic: the process of producing, but not quite completing, a product or service, postponing completion until customer preferences or specifications are known. There are a number of variations of this. In the case of goods, almost-finished units might be held in inventory until customer orders are received, at which time customized features are incorporated, according to customer requests. For example, furniture makers can produce dining room sets, but not apply stain, allowing customers a choice of stains. Once the choice is made, the stain can be applied in a relatively short time, thus eliminating a long wait for customers, giving the seller a competitive advantage. Similarly, various e-mail or Internet services can be delivered to customers as standardized packages, which can then be modified according to the customer's preferences. The result of delayed differentiation is a product or service with customized features that can be quickly produced, appealing to the customers' desire for variety and speed of delivery, and yet one that for the most part is standardized, enabling the producer to realize the benefits of standardized production. This technique is not new. Manufacturers of

mass customization Producing basically standardized goods, but incorporating some degree of customization.

delayed differentiation Producing, but not quite completing, a product or service until customer preferences are known.

men's clothing, for example, produce suits with pants that have legs that are unfinished, allowing customers to tailor choices as to the exact length and whether to have cuffs or no cuffs. What is new is the extent to which business organizations are finding ways to incorporate this concept into a broad range of products and services.

Modular design is a form of standardization. Modules represent groupings of component parts into subassemblies, usually to the point where the individual parts lose their separate identity. One familiar example of modular design is computers which have modular parts that can be replaced if they become defective. By arranging modules in different configurations, different computer capabilities can be obtained. For mass customization, modular design enables producers to quickly assemble modules to achieve a customized configuration for an individual customer, avoiding the long customer wait that would occur if individual parts had to be assembled. Modular design is also found in the construction industry. One firm in Rochester, New York, makes prefabricated motel rooms complete with wiring, plumbing, and even room decorations in its factory and then moves the complete rooms by rail to the construction site where they are integrated into the structure.

One advantage of modular design of equipment compared with nonmodular design is that failures are often easier to diagnose and remedy because there are fewer pieces to investigate. Similar advantages are found in ease of repair and replacement; the faulty module is conveniently removed and replaced with a good one. The manufacture and assembly of modules generally involves simplifications: fewer parts are involved, so purchasing and inventory control become more routine, fabrication and assembly operations become more standardized, and training costs often are relatively low.

The main disadvantages of modular design stem from the decrease in variety: the number of possible configurations of modules is much less than the number of possible configurations based on individual components. Another disadvantage that is sometimes encountered is the inability to disassemble a module in order to replace a faulty part; the entire module must be scrapped—usually at a higher cost.

modular design A form of standardization in which component parts are grouped into modules that are easily replaced or interchanged.

RELIABILITY

Reliability is a measure of the ability of a product, a part, a service, or an entire system to perform its intended function under a prescribed set of conditions. The importance of reliability is underscored by its use by prospective buyers in comparing alternatives and by sellers as one determinant of price. Reliability also can have an impact on repeat sales, reflect on the product's image, and, if it is too low, create legal implications.

The term **failure** is used to describe a situation in which an item does not perform as intended. This includes not only instances in which the item does not function at all, but also instances in which the item's performance is substandard or it functions in a way not intended. For example, a smoke alarm might fail to respond to the presence of smoke (not operate at all), it might sound an alarm that is too faint to provide an adequate warning (substandard performance), or it might sound an alarm even though no smoke is present (unintended response).

Reliabilities are always specified with respect to certain conditions, called **normal operating conditions.** These can include load, temperature, and humidity ranges as well as operating procedures and maintenance schedules. Failure of users to heed these conditions often results in premature failure of parts or complete systems. For example, using a passenger car to tow heavy loads will cause excess wear and tear on the drive train; driving over potholes or curbs often results in untimely tire failure; and using a calculator to drive nails might have a marked impact on its usefulness for performing mathematical operations.

reliability The ability of a product, part, or system to perform its intended function under a prescribed set of conditions.

failure Situation in which a product, part, or system does not perform as intended.

normal operating conditions The set of conditions under which an item's reliability is specified.

Improving Reliability. Reliability can be improved in a number of ways, some of which are listed in Table 4–2.

Because overall system reliability is a function of the reliability of individual components, improvements in their reliability can increase system reliability. Unfortunately, inadequate production or assembly procedures can negate even the best of designs, and this

TABLE 4-2

Potential ways to improve reliability

1. Improve component design.
2. Improve production and/or assembly techniques.
3. Improve testing.
4. Use backups.
5. Improve preventive maintenance procedures.
6. Improve user education.
7. Improve system design.

is often a source of failures. System reliability can be increased by the use of backup components. Failures in actual use can often be reduced by upgrading user education and refining maintenance recommendations or procedures. Finally, it may be possible to increase the overall reliability of the system by simplifying the system (thereby reducing the number of components that could cause the system to fail) or altering component relationships (e.g., increasing the reliability of interfaces).

A fundamental question concerning improving reliability is: How much reliability is needed? Obviously, the reliability that is needed for a light bulb isn't in the same category as the reliability that is needed for an airplane. So the answer to the question depends on the potential benefits of improvements and on the cost of those improvements. Generally speaking, reliability improvements become increasingly costly. Thus, although benefits initially may increase at a much faster rate than costs, the opposite eventually becomes true. The optimal level of reliability is the point where the incremental benefit received equals the incremental cost of obtaining it. In the short term, this trade-off is made in the context of relatively fixed parameters (e.g., costs). However, in the longer term, efforts to improve reliability and reduce costs will lead to higher optimal levels of reliability.

ROBUST DESIGN

Some products or services will function as designed only within a narrow range of conditions, while others will perform as designed over a much broader range of conditions. The latter have **robust design.** Consider a pair of fine leather boots—obviously not made for trekking through mud or snow. Now consider a pair of heavy rubber boots—just the thing for mud or snow. The rubber boots have a design that is more *robust* than the fine leather boots.

The more robust a product or service, the less likely it will fail due to a change in the environment in which it is used or in which it is performed. Hence, the more designers can build robustness into the product or service, the better it should hold up, resulting in a higher level of customer satisfaction.

A similar argument can be made for robust design as it pertains to the production process. Environmental factors can have a negative effect on the quality of a product or service. The more resistant a design is to those influences, the less likely is a negative effect. For example, many products go through a heating process: food products, ceramics, steel, petroleum products, and pharmaceutical products. Furnaces often do not heat uniformly; heat may vary either by position in an oven or over an extended period of production. One approach to this problem might be to develop a superior oven; another might be to design a system that moves the product during heating to achieve uniformity. A robust-design approach would develop a product that is unaffected by minor variations in temperature during processing.

Taguchi's Approach. Japanese engineer Genichi Taguchi's approach is based on the robust design. His premise is that it is often easier to design a product that is insensitive to environmental factors, either in manufacturing or in use, than to control the environmental factors.

The central feature of Taguchi's approach—and the feature used most often by U.S. companies—is *parameter design.* This involves determining the specification settings for

robust design Design that results in products or services that can function over a broad range of conditions.

both the product and the process that will result in robust design in terms of manufacturing variations, product deterioration, and conditions during use.

The Taguchi approach modifies the conventional statistical methods of experimental design. Consider this example. Suppose a company will use 12 chemicals in a new product it intends to produce. There are two suppliers for these chemicals, but the chemical concentrations vary slightly between the two suppliers. Classical design of experiments would require $2^{12} = 4,096$ test runs to determine which combination of chemicals would be optimum. Taguchi's approach would involve only testing a portion of the possible combinations. Relying on experts to identify the variables that would be most likely to affect important performance, the number of combinations would be dramatically reduced, perhaps to, say, 32. Identifying the best combination in the smaller sample might be a near-optimal combination instead of the optimal combination. The value of this approach is its ability to achieve major advances in product or process design fairly quickly, using a relatively small number of experiments.

Critics charge that Taguchi's methods are inefficient and incorrect, and often lead to nonoptimal solutions. Nonetheless, his methods are widely used and have been credited with helping to achieve major improvements in U.S. products and manufacturing processes.

Designing for Manufacturing

In this section, you will learn about design techniques that have greater applicability for the design of products than the design of services. Even so, you will see that they do have some relevance for service design. The topics include concurrent engineering, computer-assisted design, designing for assembly and disassembly, and the use of components for similar products.

CONCURRENT ENGINEERING

To achieve a smoother transition from product design to production, and to decrease product development time, many companies are using *simultaneous development,* or concurrent engineering. In its narrowest sense, **concurrent engineering** means bringing design and manufacturing engineering people together early in the design phase to simultaneously develop the product and the processes for creating the product. More recently, this concept has been enlarged to include manufacturing personnel (e.g., materials specialists) and marketing and purchasing personnel in loosely integrated, cross-functional teams. In addition, the views of suppliers and customers are frequently sought. The purpose, of course, is to achieve product designs that reflect customer wants as well as manufacturing capabilities.

concurrent engineering
Bringing engineering design and manufacturing personnel together early in the design phase.

Traditionally, designers developed a new product without any input from manufacturing, and then turned over the design to manufacturing, which would then have to develop a process for making the new product. This "over-the-wall" approach created tremendous challenges for manufacturing, generating numerous conflicts and greatly increasing the time needed to successfully produce a new product. It also contributed to an "us versus them" mentality.

For these and similar reasons, the simultaneous development approach has great appeal. Among the key advantages of this approach are the following:

1. Manufacturing personnel are able to identify production capabilities and capacities. Very often, they have some latitude in design in terms of selecting suitable materials and processes. Knowledge of production capabilities can help in the selection process. In addition, cost and quality considerations can be greatly influenced by design, and conflicts during production can be greatly reduced.

2. Early opportunities for design or procurement of critical tooling, some of which might have long lead times. This can result in a major shortening of the product development process, which could be a key competitive advantage.

3. Early consideration of the technical feasibility of a particular design or a portion of a design. Again, this can avoid serious problems during production.

4. The emphasis can be on *problem* resolution instead of *conflict* resolution.

However, a number of potential difficulties exist in this codevelopment approach. Two key ones are the following:

1. Longstanding existing boundaries between design and manufacturing can be difficult to overcome. Simply bringing a group of people together and thinking that they will be able to work together effectively is probably naive.

2. There must be extra communication and flexibility if the process is to work, and these can be difficult to achieve.

Hence, managers should plan to devote special attention if this approach is to work.

COMPUTER-AIDED DESIGN (CAD)

computer-aided design (CAD) Product design using computer graphics.

Computers are increasingly used for product design. **Computer-aided design (CAD)** uses computer graphics for product design. The designer can modify an existing design or create a new one on a CRT by means of a light pen, a keyboard, a joystick, or a similar device. Once the design is entered into the computer, the designer can maneuver it on the screen: It can be rotated to provide the designer with different perspectives, it can be split apart to give the designer a view of the inside, and a portion of it can be enlarged for

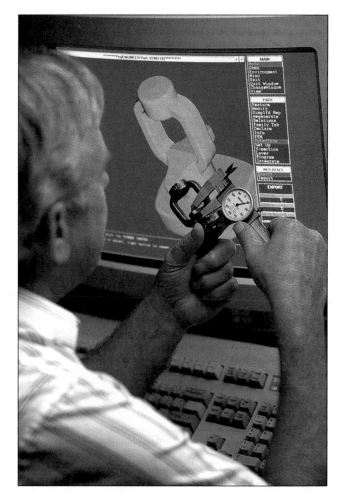

Computer-aided design (CAD) is used to design components and products to exact measurement and detail. This firehead sprinkler was designed to exact specifications and then manufactured at the Thompson Factory in Atlanta, Georgia.

closer examination. The designer can obtain a printed version of the completed design and file it electronically, making it accessible to people in the firm who need this information (e.g., marketing).

A growing number of products are being designed in this way, including transformers, automobile parts, aircraft parts, integrated circuits, and electric motors.

A major benefit of CAD is the increased productivity of designers. No longer is it necessary to laboriously prepare mechanical drawings of products or parts and revise them repeatedly to correct errors or incorporate revisions. A rough estimate is that CAD increases the productivity of designers from 3 to 10 times. A second major benefit of CAD is the creation of a database for manufacturing that can supply needed information on product geometry and dimensions, tolerances, material specifications, and so on. It should be noted, however, that CAD needs this database to function and that this entails a considerable amount of effort.

Some CAD systems allow the designer to perform engineering and cost analyses on proposed designs. For instance, the computer can determine the weight and volume of a part and do stress analysis as well. When there are a number of alternative designs, the computer can quickly go through the possibilities and identify the best one, given the designer's criteria.

PRODUCTION REQUIREMENTS

As noted earlier in the chapter, designers must take into account *production capabilities*. Design needs to clearly understand the capabilities of production (e.g., equipment, skills, types of materials, schedules, technologies, special abilities). This will help in choosing designs that match capabilities. When opportunities and capabilities do not match, management must consider the potential for expanding or changing capabilities to take advantage of those opportunities.

Forecasts of future demand can be very useful, supplying information on the timing and volume of demand, and information on demands for new products and services.

Manufacturability is a key concern for manufactured goods: Ease of fabrication and/or assembly is important for cost, productivity, and quality. With services, ease of providing the service, cost, productivity, and quality are of great concern.

The term **design for manufacturing (DFM)** is used to indicate the designing of products that are compatible with an organization's capabilities. A related concept in manufacturing is **design for assembly (DFA).** A good design must take into account not only how a product will be fabricated, but also how it will be assembled. Design for assembly focuses on reducing the number of parts in an assembly, as well as on the assembly methods and sequence that will be employed.

design for manufacturing (DFM) Designers take into account the organization's capabilities when designing a product.

design for assembly (DFA) Design focuses on reducing the number of parts in a product and on assembly methods and sequence.

RECYCLING

Recycling is sometimes an important consideration for designers. **Recycling** means recovering materials for future use. This applies not only to manufactured parts, but also to materials used during production, such as lubricants and solvents. Reclaimed metal or plastic parts may be melted down and used to make different products.

recycling Recovering materials for future use.

Companies recycle for a variety of reasons, including:

1. Cost savings.
2. Environment concerns.
3. Environmental regulations.

An interesting note: Companies that want to do business in the European Economic Community must show that a specified proportion of their products are recyclable.

The pressure to recycle has given rise to the term **design for recycling (DFR),** referring to product design that takes into account the ability to disassemble a used product to recover the recyclable parts.

design for recycling (DFR) Design facilitates the recovery of materials and components in used products for reuse.

More Cars Come with a Shade of Green— Recycled Materials

www.ford.com
www.gm.com
www.chryslercorp.com

Detroit's Big Three automakers, doing their best to build cars that don't fall apart, have a new goal: building cars that are easy to take apart.

The reason: Easy-to-remove parts are easy to recycle.

Car companies are putting the ability to recycle parts on the same level as safety, fuel economy, and costs when they design new vehicles.

For example, the Oldsmobile Aurora . . . uses scrap metal in its radiator mounting, and the bumper beams contain recycled copper and aluminum. Chrysler Corp. uses recycled tires for the splash guards on its midsize sedans.

Car parts have been recycled for years. But the auto industry only recently began to build cars with the idea of using recycled material. About 75 percent of new cars contain recycled material, mostly iron or steel used in the body.

Auto dismantlers usually buy a vehicle and remove all the parts that still work, such as seats, engines and headlights. The vehicle then goes to a shredder where it is reduced to small fragments and a huge magnet separates out the metal parts.

The challenge for auto companies is to find ways to separate the more than 20,000 different grades of plastic found in cars. About 24 percent of shredded material, known as "fluff," contains plastic, fluids, rubber, glass and other material. Most "fluff" can't be recycled.

Ford, GM and Chrysler have jointly formed the Vehicle Recycling Partnership in hopes of improving the technology to recover plastics and other material found in "fluff." Suppliers of material and the recycling industry are included in the partnership.

Manufacturers aren't suddenly becoming Friends of the Earth. "All of the recycling programs undertaken by Ford have been cost-effective," says Susan Day, vehicle recycling coordinator.

Source: *Rochester Democrat and Chronicle,* February 20, 1994, p. 11.

---

remanufacturing Refurbishing used products by replacing wornout or defective components.

www.cadillac.com

REMANUFACTURING

An emerging concept in manufacturing is the remanufacturing of products. **Remanufacturing** refers to refurbishing used products by replacing worn-out or defective components, and reselling the products. This can be done by the original manufacturer, or another company. Among the products that have remanufactured components are automobiles, printers, copiers, cameras, computers, and telephones.

By redesigning the Seville's rear bumper, Cadillac cut the number of parts, thus reducing assembly time and labor costs. The new design also led to high quality as there were few parts and steps that might be defective.

There are a number of important reasons for doing this. One is that a remanufactured product can be sold for about 50 percent of the cost of a new product. Another is that the process requires mostly unskilled and semiskilled workers. And in the global market, European lawmakers are increasingly requiring manufacturers to take back used products, because this means fewer products end up in landfills and there is less depletion of natural resources such as raw materials and fuel.

Designing products so that they can be more easily taken apart has given rise to yet another design consideration: **Design for disassembly (DFD)** includes using fewer parts and less material, and using snap-fits where possible instead of screws or nuts and bolts.

The reading "Making It (Almost) New Again" gives examples of what some companies are doing.

design for disassembly (DFD) Design so that used products can be easily taken apart.

READING

Making It (Almost) New Again Phil Ebersole

www.kodak.com

Tired: *Landfills.*
Wired: *Recycling.*
Inspired: *Remanufacturing.*

The symbol of 20th century industry was the assembly line. The symbol of 21st century industry may be the disassembly line.

Xerox Corp. and Eastman Kodak Co. design products to make them not only easy to put together, but easy to take apart.

That's because so many parts and components from their old products are refurbished and put into new ones.

Xerox and Kodak, along with Caterpillar Inc., are the leaders in a movement called remanufacturing, said Robert T. Lund, a professor of manufacturing engineering at Boston University and author of a 1996 study of the subject.

"The driving force behind remanufacturing is thrift," Lund said. "A remanufactured product can be sold for 45 to 60 percent of the cost of a new one. You have something enormously more valuable than if you ground it up as raw material."

But in a few years, remanufacturing may be more than just a good idea. European countries are developing rules to make manufacturers take back their products instead of allowing them to wind up in landfills. Europe's rules could set the standard for the world, just as California auto emissions laws set the standard for the U.S. auto industry.

The 15-nation European Union is considering a rule that would require 85 percent of a car by weight to be recycled or remanufactured by the year 2002. This would increase to 95 percent by 2015.

This goes beyond what's done now. Currently about 75 percent of the average U.S. car is recycled or remanufactured. About all the metal in a car is reused, but little plastic and other materials.

Fixing up used equipment for resale is nothing new, but Xerox and Kodak take remanufacturing to the point of breaking down the distinction between new and used.

Almost all their new copiers and single-use cameras contain remanufactured parts. Virgin and remanufactured components go through the same production lines and meet the same tests.

If you could find an all-virgin product, they say, you couldn't tell the difference between it and one that was 95 percent remanufactured.

It's a process that goes beyond recycling, because companies conserve not only raw materials, but the energy, labor and ingenuity that went into making the components.

Lund said there are 73,000 companies in 61 industries, ranging from computer chips to locomotives, who do remanufacturing. They have 480,000 employees and do $53 billion worth of business.

Rochester Institute of Technology is a leader in this movement. It operates a remanufacturing laboratory at its Center for Integrated Manufacturing Studies and publishes a quarterly called *Remanufacturing Today.*

Remanufacturing isn't easy:

- Although companies ultimately may save money, the initial costs are higher. Remanufacturing is labor-intensive. Each remanufactured component is different, so the process can't be automated.

- Remanufacturers have to overcome a reputation for low quality. "People think remanufacturing is like repair, but it isn't," said Nabil Nasr, an RIT professor of manufacturing engineering.

- Designing products for remanufacturing makes it easier for other companies to refurbish your used products and sell them in competition with you.

For example, Kodak, along with Fuji Photo Film Co. and Konica Corp., battles "reloaders"—companies that sell poorly remade cameras under their own names with cheap Chinese film and used lenses and batteries, said David M. Snook, manager of worldwide recycling for Kodak single-use cameras.

The better Kodak designs its cameras for remanufacturing, the easier Kodak makes it for reloaders.

Remanufacturing is mainly carried on by small and mid-sized companies. Few large U.S. producers remanufacture their own products to the degree Xerox and Kodak do.

Some big companies still try to discourage remanufacturing, Lund said. They regard remanufactured products as competition for their virgin products. Others, like the Big 3 automakers, sanction or subcontract remanufacturing, but do little themselves.

Richard O. Carville, manager of design and manufacturing engineering for Xerox's print cartridge business unit, said he encountered skepticism in 1990 when he proposed remanufacturing print cartridges, the part of the copier that registers and prints the xerographic image.

After the first six months, the unit made a profit. It was able to cut prices as a result of the cost savings it had achieved.

One big challenge has been persuading customers to return the print cartridges, Carville said.

The first leaflets on cartridge return were ineffective. Now, when a customer opens the print engine package, the first thing he or she sees is a prepaid United Parcel Service or Canada Post mailer, shaped like an airplane.

"Environmental partnership" cartridges are sold at a discount if the customer promises to return them. "It's not a rebate," Carville said. "It's a prebate."

Xerox has a 60 percent return rate for cartridges. For comparison, Kodak has a 74 percent return rate for its Fun Saver cameras, which, Snook says, compares favorably to recycled aluminum cans.

The print cartridges are sent, at Xerox's expense, to centers in Nogales, Ariz., and Utica, NY, where the cartridges are dismantled, cleaned and inspected. Rejected parts are ground up

NOT A THROWAWAY

Kodak's Fun Saver shows remanufacturing in action.

Step 1
Buy Kodak Fun Saver Camera loaded with Kodak Gold Film. Take pictures and drop off the entire camera to a photofinisher.

Step 2
Photofinisher ships the used camera back to Kodak's sites at Elmgrove, Guadalajara, Mexico and Chalon, France. Kodak gives incentives and premiums to encourage returns.

Step 4
New Kodak Fun Saver cameras are made from virgin and refurbished parts, with new lenses and fresh film.

Step 3
Kodak and its subcontractors take the camera apart and inspect the parts. Worn out parts are ground up and used as raw material. Usable parts are refurbished for use in new cameras. 86 percent of the cameras by weight are recycled or refurbished.

as raw material. The rest are refurbished and shipped to Webster, NY, for remanufacturing.

All plastics in Xerox copiers are impregnated with a flame-retardant material. Carville's unit worked with Underwriters Laboratories in 1992 and 1993 to get an approval process for remanufactured plastic materials. Currently Xerox plastic is approved for up to five reuses.

Carville said his unit doesn't want to franchise remanufacturers. Xerox wants to control the process so as to guarantee quality.

But from the standpoint of the customer, you can get a remanufactured product quicker and cheaper from an outside company, said James D. Condon, president of Photikon Corp. of Fairport.

His company, originally a broker in copier or printer parts, started making photoreceptor belts in 1989 and now remanufactures entire printer cartridges.

Unlike Xerox, Photikon is a true remanufacturer. Its products are completely remade, not a blend of remade and virgin parts like Xerox's. For this reason, Photikon's products can be made cheaper than Xerox's, Condon said.

Photikon has worked on products remade up to 25 times, although not by Photikon every time.

The demand for remanufactured products is booming, Condon said. Photikon's 19 employees have been working overtime for the past three months, and he expects to hire 10 more in the next year.

Xerox remanufactures about 1 million parts and 150,000 office machines each year. Kodak collects 50 million single-use cameras each year from 20 countries for remanufacturing, as well as reworking products ranging from microfilm machines to photographic film base.

Both companies use subcontractors extensively. Snook said that during the peak season, Outsource Enterprises of Rochester gets as many as 6 million single-use cameras in a week to be inspected, disassembled and sorted.

The most logical company to remanufacture a product is the original manufacturer, said Gordon H. McNeil, president of Magnetic Technologies Corp. of Pittsford, NY, which makes subsystems for Xerox and other companies. And looking at the used parts provides useful information in making new parts, he said.

He said about 35 percent of Magnetic Tech's output is remanufactured products, and this could grow to more than half in a few years.

Source: "Making It New Again and Again." Phil Ebersole, *Rochester Democrat and Chronicle,* July 14, 1997, p. E1. Used with permission.

COMPONENT COMMONALITY

Companies often have multiple products or services to offer customers. Typically, these products or services have a high degree of similarity of features and components. This is particularly true of *product families,* but it is also true of many services. Companies can realize significant benefits when a part can be used in multiple products. For example, car manufacturers employ this tactic by using internal components such as water pumps, engines, and transmissions on several automobile nameplates. In addition to the savings in design time, companies reap benefits through standard training for assembly and installation, increased opportunities for savings by buying in bulk from suppliers, and commonality of parts for repair, which reduces the inventory dealers and auto parts stores must carry. Similar benefits accrue in services. For example, in automobile repair, component commonality means less training is needed because the variety of jobs is reduced. The same applies to appliance repair, where commonality and *substitutability* of parts are typical. Multiple-use forms in financial and medical services is another example. Computer software often comprises a number of modules that are commonly used for similar applications, thereby saving the time and cost to write the code for major portions of the software.

Designing for Services

As noted, some of the discussion on product design also applies to service design.

In certain cases, product design and service design go hand in hand. This stems from the fact that goods and services often exist in combination. For example, getting an oil change for your car involves a service (draining the old oil and putting in new oil) and a good (the new oil). Likewise, having new carpeting installed involves a service (the installation) and a good (the carpet). In some cases, what a customer receives is essentially a *pure* service, as in getting a haircut or your lawn mowed. However, the vast majority of cases involve some combination of goods and services. The proportion of service might be relatively low, as is the case in manufacturing, where the emphasis is on the production of goods. But even in manufacturing, there are services such as machine repair, employee training, safety inspections, and so on. Because goods and services are so intertwined, managers must be knowledgeable about both in order to be able to manage effectively. However, there are some key differences between manufacturing and service that warrant special consideration for service design. This section outlines these key differences, gives an overview of product design, and provides a brief list of guidelines for service design.

ENGINE COMPONENTS
All internally lubricated components and: Balance Shaft and Belt, Piston, Crankshaft, Camshaft, Timing Belt, Timing Cover, Timing Chain, Timing Gears, Engine Mounts, Flexplate, Exhaust Manifolds, Intake Manifold, Turbo Intercooler, Turbo Assembly, Turbo Wastegate, Crankshaft Pulley, Oil Pan, Flywheel, Oil Pump, Engine Oil Reservoir, Engine Oil Reservoir Pump, Seals and Gaskets, Cylinder Heads, Supercharger Assembly, Valve Covers, Supercharger Intercooler, Equipment Drive Shaft; Engine Block (but only if damaged as a direct result of a mechanical failure of a covered engine component). Rotary engine components including: Rotor, Bearings, Apex Seal, Eccentric Shaft.

MANUAL TRANSMISSION
Transfer Case Components: All internally lubricated components and: Transmission Mounts, Seals and Gaskets, Clutch Master Cylinder, Clutch Release Cylinder, Gears and Shaft, Hydraulic Clutch Lines, Shift Linkage; Case (but only if damaged as a direct result of a mechanical failure of a covered manual transmission/transfer case component).

AXLE ASSEMBLY COMPONENTS
(Front, Rear, Four Wheel and All Wheel Drive): all internally lubricated components and: Propeller Shaft, Universal Joints, Thrust Washers, Seals and Gaskets, Axles and Bearings, Locking Hubs, Constant Velocity Joints and Boots, Center Support Bearing, Viscous Coupling, Drive Axle Housing (but only if damaged as a direct result of a mechanical failure of a covered drive axle assembly component).

AUTOMATIC TRANSMISSION
Transfer Case Components: All internally lubricated components and: Torque Converter, Shift Linkage, Vacuum Modulator, Seals and Gaskets, Solenoids, Transmission Mounts; Case (but only if damaged as a direct result of a mechanical failure of a covered automatic transmission/transfer case component).

SUSPENSION COMPONENTS
(Front and Rear): Upper and Lower Control Arms, Control Arm Shafts, Radius Arm, Spindle Support, Spindle, Bearings and Bushings, Tie Rod Assemblies, Upper Ball Joints, Lower Ball Joints, Steering Knuckle, Electronic Modulated Suspension Actuator.

STEERING COMPONENTS
Gear Box internal components and: Rack and Pinion, Seals and Gaskets, Power Steering Pump, Idler Arm, Relay Rod, Tie Rod, Pitman Arm, Steering Column Shaft, Steering Column Coupling, Steering Dampener, Steering Column Assembly, Steering Gear Box and Pump Housings, (but only if damaged as a direct result of a mechanical failure of a covered steering component).

FUEL SYSTEM
Fuel Pressure Regulator, Fuel Injectors, Fuel Sensors, Air Flow Meter, Fuel Pump, Fuel Tank, Carburetor, Electronic Fuel Injection System, Throttle Body.

COOLING SYSTEM
Engine Fan Shroud, Engine Fan Clutch, Engine Fan Motor, Seals and Gaskets, Engine Fan, Radiator, Water Pump, Fan Bracket Subassembly.

BRAKE COMPONENTS
Master Cylinder, Brake Booster, Seals and Gaskets, Wheel Cylinders, Disc Brake Calipers, Parking Brake Cable, Brake Line and Tubes, Proportioning Valve, Load-Sensing Proportioning Valve, Anti-Lock Braking System (ABS) Actuator.

ELECTRICAL
Power Door Locks, Power Window Motor/Regulator, Starter Solenoid, Power Seat Motors, Power Mirror Motor, Automatic Shoulder Belt Motor and Switches, Power Antenna Motor Assembly, Alternator, Distributor, Starter Motor, Wiper Motor, Sunroof Motor, Blower Motor, Cruise Control, Power Mirror Defogger, Automatic Temperature Control Module, Cruise Control Vacuum Motor, Lamp Failure Indicator Sensor, Windshield Washer Pump, Defogger Relay, Automatic-Off Headlamp System, Headlamp Washer, Manually Operated Switches, Electric Fuel Pump Assembly, Engine Cooling Fan Motor, Retractable Headlamp Motor, Clutch Starter Interlock System, Convertible Top Motor.

COMPUTERS AND ELECTRONICS
Vehicle Security System, Tilt/Telescoping Steering Computer, Variable Induction System, Electronic Fuel Injection (EFI) Computer, Electronic Instrument Display Computer, Electronically Modulated Suspension Computer, Automatic Shoulder Belt Computer, Progressive Power Steering Computer, Power Seat Computer, Sunroof Control Computer, Cruise Control Computer, Trip Computer, Electronic Ignition Module, Intrusion Monitoring System, Anti-Lock Braking System (ABS) Computer and Sensors, Electronically Controlled Transmission/Transfer Case Computer and Sensors, Engine Control Computer.

AIR CONDITIONING/HEATING
Condenser, Condenser Fan and Motor, Evaporator, Bearings, Heater Control Valve, Receiver/Dryer, Compressor Clutch Assembly, Expansion Valve, Pressure Regulator Assembly, Blower Motor, Compressor, A/C Pressure Switches, Seals and Gaskets.

VEHICLE SERVICE AGREEMENT

Toyota's Extra Care service contract protects the vehicle owner against costly mechanical and electrical repairs. This illustration uses design blueprint information to highlight covered parts and systems.

www.toyota.com

DIFFERENCES BETWEEN SERVICE DESIGN AND PRODUCT DESIGN

1. Products are generally tangible; services are generally intangible. Consequently, service design often focuses more on intangible factors (e.g., peace of mind, ambiance) than does product design.

2. In many instances services are created and delivered at the same time (e.g., a haircut, a car wash). In such instances there is less latitude in finding and correcting errors *before* the customer has a chance to discover them. Consequently, training, process design, and customer relations are particularly important.

3. Services cannot be inventoried. This poses restrictions on flexibility and makes capacity design very important.

4. Services are highly visible to consumers and must be designed with that in mind; this adds an extra dimension to process design, one that usually is not present in product design.

5. Some services have low barriers to entry and exit. This places additional pressures on service design to be innovative and cost-effective.

6. Location is often important to service design, with convenience as a major factor. Hence, design of services and choice of location are often closely linked.

Let's consider some of these differences in more detail. One is the need to consider the degree of customer contact in service design. That can range from no contact to high contact. When there is little or no contact, service design can be very much like product design. However, the greater the degree of customer contact, the greater the difference between service and product design, and the more complex service design becomes. The element of

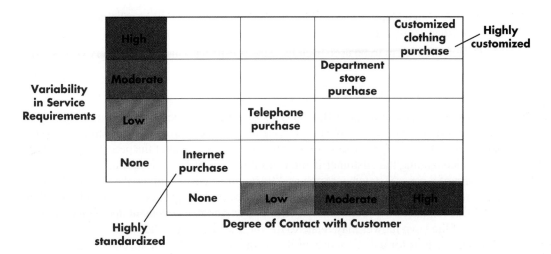

Variability in Service Requirements	**High**				**Customized clothing purchase**	**Highly customized**
	Moderate			**Department store purchase**	
	Low		**Telephone purchase**		
	None	**Internet purchase**			
		None	**Low**	**Moderate**	**High**

Highly standardized

Degree of Contact with Customer

FIGURE 4-3

Service variability and customer contact influence service design

customer contact means that service design must incorporate *process* design; when there is customer contact, the process *is* the service. Although it is desirable to consider the manufacturability of a product when designing products, the product and the process are nonetheless separate entities. The following example of service design illustrates the inseparable nature of the service/process connection when customers are a part of the system. If a refrigerator manufacturer changes the procedure it uses for assembling a refrigerator, that change will be transparent to the person who purchases the refrigerator. Conversely, if the bus company makes changes to the bus schedule, or the bus routes, those changes will not be transparent to the riders. Obviously, this service redesign could not be done realistically without considering the *process* for delivering the service.

OVERVIEW OF SERVICE DESIGN

Service design begins with the choice of a service strategy, which determines the nature and focus of the service, and the target market. This requires an assessment by top management of the potential market and profitability (or need, in the case of a nonprofit organization) of a particular service, and an assessment of the organization's ability to provide the service. Once decisions on the focus of the service and the target market have been made, the customer requirements and expectations of the target market must be determined.

Two key issues in service design are the degree of variation in service requirements, and the degree of customer contact and customer involvement in the delivery system. These have an impact on the degree to which service can be standardized or must be customized. The lower the degree of customer contact and service requirement variability, the more standardized the service can be. Service design with no contact and little or no processing variability is very much like product design. Conversely, high variability and high customer contact generally mean the service must be highly customized. These concepts are illustrated in Figure 4–3.

A related consideration in service design is the opportunity for selling: The greater the degree of customer contact, the greater the opportunities for selling.

DESIGN GUIDELINES

A number of simple but highly effective rules are often used to guide the development of service systems. The key rules are the following:

1. Have a single, unifying theme, such as convenience or speed. This will help personnel to work together rather than at cross-purposes.
2. Make sure the system has the capability to handle any expected variability in service requirements.

3. Include design features and checks to ensure that service will be reliable and will provide consistently high quality.

4. Design the system to be user-friendly. This is especially true for self-service systems.

Quality Function Deployment

quality function deployment (QFD) An approach that integrates the "voice of the customer" into the product development process.

Quality function deployment (QFD) is a structured approach for integrating the "voice of the customer" into the product or service development process. The purpose is to ensure that customer requirements are factored into every aspect of the process. Listening to and understanding the customer is the central feature of QFD. Requirements often take the form of a general statement such as, "It should be easy to adjust the cutting height of the lawn mower." Once the requirements are known, they must be translated into technical terms related to the product or service. For example, a statement about changing the height of the lawn mower may relate to the mechanism used to accomplish that, its position, instructions for use, tightness of the spring that controls the mechanism, or materials needed. For manufacturing purposes, these must be related to the materials, dimensions, and equipment used for processing.

The structure of QFD is based on a set of matrices. The main matrix relates customer requirements (what) and their corresponding technical requirements (how). This concept is illustrated in Figure 4–4.

FIGURE 4–4

An example of the house of quality. The main QFD Matrix.
Source: Ernst and Young Consulting Group, *Total Quality* (Homewood, Ill.: Dow-Jones Irwin, 1991), p. 121. Reprinted by permission.

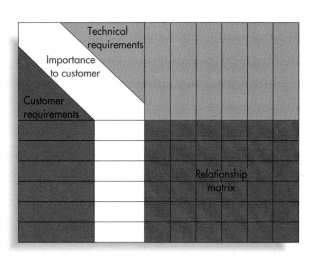

FIGURE 4–5

The house of quality

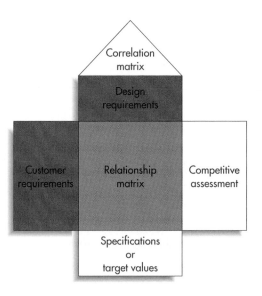

Additional features are usually added to the basic matrix to broaden the scope of analysis. Typical additional features include importance weightings and competitive evaluations. A correlational matrix is usually constructed for technical requirements; this can reveal conflicting technical requirements. With these additional features, the set of matrices has the form illustrated in Figure 4–5. It is often referred to as the *house of quality* because of its houselike appearance.

An analysis using this format is shown in Figure 4–6. The data relate to a commercial printer (customer) and the company that supplies the paper. At first glance, the display appears complex. It contains a considerable amount of information for product and process planning. Therefore, let's break it up into separate parts and consider them one at a time. To start, a key part is the list of customer requirements on the left side of the figure. Next,

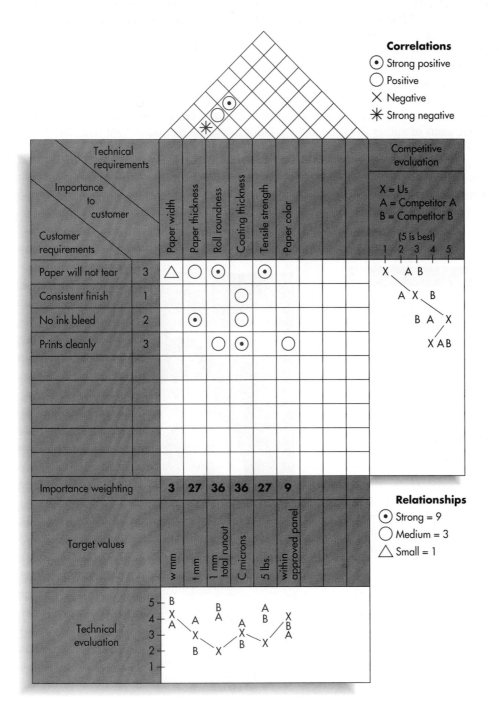

Correlations

⊙ Strong positive
◯ Positive
✕ Negative
✳ Strong negative

Relationships

⊙ Strong = 9
◯ Medium = 3
△ Small = 1

FIGURE 4–6

An example of the house of quality

note the technical requirements, listed vertically near the top. The key relationships and their degree of importance, are shown in the center of the figure. The circle with a dot inside indicates the strongest positive relationship; that is, it denotes the most important technical requirements for satisfying customer requirements. Now look at the "importance to customer" numbers that are shown next to each customer requirement (3 is the most important). Designers will take into account the importance values and the strength of correlation in determining where to focus the greatest effort.

Next, consider the correlation matrix at the top of the "house." Of special interest is the strong negative correlation between "paper thickness" and "roll roundness." Designers will have to find some way to overcome that or make a trade-off decision.

On the right side of the figure is a competitive evaluation comparing the supplier's performance on the customer requirements with each of the two key competitors (A and B). For example, the supplier (X) is worst on the first customer requirement and best on the third customer requirement. The line connects the X performances. Ideally, design will cause all of the Xs to be in the highest positions.

Across the bottom of Figure 4–6 are importance weightings, target values, and technical evaluations. The technical evaluations can be interpreted in a manner similar to that of the competitive evaluations (note the line connecting the Xs). The target values typically contain technical specifications, which we will not discuss. The importance weightings are the sums of values assigned to the relationships (see the lower right-hand key for relationship weights). The 3 in the first column is the product of the importance to the customer, 3, and the small (Δ) weight, 1. The importance weightings and target evaluations help designers focus on desired results. In this example, the first technical requirement has the lowest importance weighting, while the next four technical requirements all have relatively high importance weightings.

NEWSCLIP

A QFD Snapshot

How a pencilmaker sharpened up its product by listening to "the voice of the customer" through quality function deployment.

Devised by Japan's Professor Yoji Akao, QFD has been winning adherents since it was transplanted to the U.S. in the late 1980s. In this example of how it works, Writesharp Inc. is imaginary, but the technique in the accompanying diagram is real.

First, Writesharp's customers were surveyed to determine what they value in a pencil and how they rate the leading brands. Each wish list item was correlated with a pencil's functional characteristics (see FUNCTIONAL CHARACTERISTICS matrix). "Reverse engineering"—tearing down a competitors' product to see what makes it tick—produced the competitive benchmark measurements for the various functions.

An analysis of the plots quickly revealed that the improvement with the biggest potential was a better-quality lead (see CUSTOMER SATISFACTION/CUSTOMER DEMANDS matrix). An interdepartmental team was assigned the task of evaluating new lead formulations that would last longer and generate less dust. Another team ran tests to determine whether substituting cedar for oak in the wood casing would

Japanese Professor Akao devised the system and coined the phrase "quality function deployment." The QFD matrix combines benchmarking, customer demands, a product's characteristics, and customer satisfaction to measure and improve product quality.

improve shape quality, or hexagonality, and thus reduce the pencil's tendency to roll down slanted desktops.

| | | Functional characteristics △ Strong correlation ○ Some correlation □ Possible correlation | | | | Customer satisfaction Scale: 1 to 5 (5 = best) | | | | |
		Pencil length (inches)	Time between sharpenings (written lines)	Lead dust (particles per line)	Hexagonality	Importance rating (5 = highest)	Writesharp (now)	Competitor X (now)	Competitor Y (now)	Writesharp (target)
Customer demands	Easy to hold	○			○	3	4	3	3	4
	Does not smear		○	△		4	5	4	5	5
	Point lasts	□	△	○		5	4	5	3	5
	Does not roll	□			△	2	3	3	3	4
Benchmarks	Writesharp (now)	5	56	10	70%		Writesharp (now)	Competitor X (now)	Competitor Y (now)	Writesharp (target)
	Competitor X (now)	5	84	12	80%					
	Competitor Y (now)	4	41	10	60%					
	Writesharp (target)	5.5	100	6	80%					
	Market price						15¢	18¢	14¢	16¢
	Market share						16%	12%	32%	20%
	Profit						2¢	3¢	2¢	4¢

The lead-formulation team organized its work with a similar matrix chart, segmented to show the functional contributions of the ingredients in pencil lead. This revealed that the binder, or glue, used in forming the lead was the key variable. Tests found a polymer that dramatically reduced dusting by retaining more moisture and also wore down more slowly. While this binder was more expensive, better production controls—going slightly beyond the performance of Competitor Y—promised to reduce waste enough to trim total per-pencil manufacturing costs by 1¢.

Changing the wood, meanwhile, yielded only marginal enhancements. So the company decided to upgrade the process controls used for cutting the wood and match the quality of Competitor X (see BENCHMARKS matrix).

Source: Reprinted from October 25, 1991, issue of *Business Week* by special permission, copyright © 1991 by The McGraw-Hill Companies, Inc.

THE KANO MODEL

The *Kano model* can be an interesting way to conceptualize design characteristics in terms of customer satisfaction. It is illustrated in Figure 4–7. It describes relationships between customer needs and customer satisfaction for three categories of design characteristics: "must have" characteristics, "expected" characteristics, and "excitement" characteristics.

The "must have" characteristics are those which yield a basic level of satisfaction, but do not have the potential for increasing customer satisfaction beyond a certain level. For instance, increasing the length of refrigerator cords beyond a reasonable length will not increase customer satisfaction. Neither will making flour whiter, or producing chewing gum that keeps its flavor (while being chewed) for four weeks. In contrast, the "expected" characteristics in a design will yield a steady increase in customer satisfaction. For example, increasing the life of a tire, or the life of a roof, will yield additional customer

FIGURE 4–7

The Kano Model

FIGURE 4–7

The Kano Model

satisfaction. And the longer the life of a tire or a roof, the higher the level of customer satisfaction. However, the greatest yield comes from "excitement" characteristics, perhaps evoking a "wow" from customers. These characteristics generate a disproportionate increase in customer satisfaction.

A possible design strategy would be to identify the design characteristics in each category for a particular product or service in order to incorporate the "must have" characteristics, and then conduct a cost-benefit analysis of characteristics in the other two categories to achieve desired results. This may not be as easy as it seems, especially in the case of the "excitement" characteristics, because those are often the most difficult to identify. In fact, customers may not be able to articulate them. Consequently, it may be necessary to turn to other alternatives (e.g., trial and error) to attempt to identify them.

Operations Strategy

Product and service design is a fertile area for achieving competitive advantage and/or increasing customer satisfaction. Potential sources of such benefits include:

1. Shortening the time to market. Many Japanese companies have been able to greatly reduce the time needed to get new or improved products to the market, giving them a competitive advantage.

2. Packaging products and ancillary services to increase sales. Examples include selling PCs at a reduced cost with a two-year Internet access sign-up agreement, extended warranties on products, companies offering installation and service, and companies offering training with computer software.

3. Increasing emphasis on component commonality.

4. Using multiple-use platforms. Auto manufacturers use the same platform (basic chassis, say) for several nameplates (e.g., Jaguar S type, Lincoln LS, and Ford Thunderbird have shared the same platform). There are two basic computer platforms, PC and Mac, with many variations of computers using a particular platform.

5. Implementing tactics that will achieve the benefits of high volume while satisfying customer needs for variety, such as mass customization.

6. Continually monitoring products and services for small improvements rather than the "big bang" approach. Often the "little" things can have a positive, long-lasting effect on consumer attitudes and buying behavior.

Summary

Product and service design is a key factor in satisfying the customer. To be successful in product and service design, organizations must be continually aware of what customers want, what the competition is doing, what government regulations are, and what new technologies are available.

The design process involves motivation, ideas for improvement, organizational capabilities, and forecasting. In addition to product life cycles, legal, environmental, and ethical considerations influence design choices. What degree of standardization designers should incorporate into designs is also an important consideration. Key objectives for designers are to achieve a product or service design that will meet or exceed customer expectations, that is within cost or budget, and that takes into account the capabilities of operations. Although product design and service design are similar in some respects, a number of key differences exist between products and services that influence the way they are designed.

Successful design often incorporates many of these basic principles: Determine what customers want as a starting point; minimize the number of parts needed to manufacture an item or the number of steps to provide a service; simplify assembly or service, standardize as much as possible; and make the design robust. Trade-off decisions are common in design, and they involve such things as development time and cost, product or service cost, special features/performance, and product or service complexity.

Research and development efforts can play a significant role in product and process innovations, although these are sometimes so costly that only large companies or governments can afford to underwrite them.

Reliability of a product or service is often a key dimension in the eyes of the customer. Measuring and improving reliability are important aspects of product and service design, although other areas of the organization also have an influence on reliability.

Quality function deployment is one approach for getting customer input for product or service design.

Key Terms

computer-aided design (CAD), 142
concurrent engineering, 141
delayed differentiation, 138
design for assembly (DFA), 143
design for disassembly (DFD), 145
design for manufacturing (DFM), 143
design for operations, 130
design for recycling (DFR), 143
failure, 139
life cycle, 136
manufacturability, 130
mass customization, 138

modular design, 139
normal operating conditions, 139
product liability, 135
quality function deployment (QFD), 141
recycling, 143
reliability, 139
remanufacturing, 144
research and development (R&D), 131
reverse engineering, 130
robust design, 140
standardization, 137
Uniform Commercial Code, 135

Discussion and Review Questions

1. What are some of the factors that cause organizations to redesign their products or services?
2. Contrast applied research and basic research.
3. What is CAD? Describe some of the ways a product designer can use it.
4. Name some of the main advantages and disadvantages of standardization.
5. What is modular design? What are its main advantages and disadvantages?

6. Explain the term *design for manufacturing* and briefly explain why it is important.

7. What are some of the competitive advantages of concurrent engineering?

8. Explain the term *remanufacturing.*

9. What is meant by the term *life cycle?* Why would this be a consideration in product or service design?

10. Why is R&D a key factor in productivity improvement? Name some ways R&D contributes to productivity improvements.

11. What is *mass customization?*

12. Name two factors that could make service design much different from product design.

13. Explain the term *robust design.*

14. Explain what *quality function deployment* is and how it can be useful.

15. What is reverse engineering? Do you feel this is unethical?

Memo Writing Exercises

1. At a recent presentation, your company's CEO stated the company's intent to expand into the service sector. Currently, your company is devoted exclusively to manufacturing. Of particular interest to your supervisor, Tom Henry, were the following statements: "In all likelihood, we will use some of our own product designers for service design. They know our products and, besides, product design and service design are pretty much the same." Tom has asked you to look into this proposal. Write him a half-page memo indicating the circumstances under which this proposal might work and those under which it might not.

2. Suppose you have just received a memo questioning the merits of remanufacturing, a proposed new approach to be used by your company. The writer, Mary Barkley, a group leader in another department, is skeptical. Write a half-page memo to her on the benefits of remanufacturing.

3. Suppose you have been hired as a consultant for a supermarket chain to advise on a plan to prepare ahead of time and cook complete "package" meals to be sold as convenience items for customers. The menu will vary from day to day, but a typical menu might look like this:

✤✤✤✤✤	✤✤✤✤✤	✤✤✤✤✤
Roast leg of lamb	Filet mignon	Fried chicken
Rosemary potatoes	Pan roast potatoes	Mashed potatoes
Garden peas	Garden salad	Fruit salad
Roll, butter	French bread, butter	Biscuit, honey

Write a one-page memo to Brad Marlow, Manager of Special Services, proposing the use of delayed differentiation for this concept. Explain how it would work and outline the potential benefits as well as the potential disadvantages of your idea.

Problems

1. Prepare a table similar to Figure 4–3. Then place each of these banking transactions in the appropriate cell of the table:
   a. Make a cash withdrawal from an automatic teller machine (ATM).
   b. Make a savings deposit using a teller.
   c. Direct deposit by employer.
   d. Open a savings account.
   e. Apply for a home equity loan.

2. Prepare a table similar to Figure 4–3. Then place each of these post office transactions in the appropriate cell of the table:
   a. Buy stamps from a machine.
   b. Buy stamps from a postal clerk.
   c. Mail a package that involves checking first class and express rates.
   d. File a complaint.

3. List the steps involved in getting gasoline into your car for full service and for self service. Assume that paying cash is the only means of payment. For each list, identify the potential trouble points and indicate a likely problem.

4. Construct a list of steps for making a cash withdrawal from an automatic teller machine (ATM). Assume that the process begins at the ATM with your bank card in hand. Then identify the potential failure points (i.e., where problems might arise in the process). For each failure point, state one potential problem.

5. *a.* Refer to Figure 4–6. What two technical requirements have the highest impact on the customer requirement that the paper not tear?

   b. The following table presents technical requirements and customer requirements for the output of a laser printer. First, decide if any of the technical requirements relate to each customer requirement. Decide which technical requirement, if any, has the greatest impact on that customer requirement.

	TECHNICAL REQUIREMENTS		
Customer Requirements	**Type of Paper**	**Internal Paper Feed**	**Print Element**
Paper doesn't wrinkle			
Prints clearly			
Easy to use			

6. Prepare a table similar to that shown in Problem 5b for cookies sold in a bakery. List what you believe are the three most important customer requirements (not including cost) and the three most relevant technical requirements (not including sanitary conditions). Next, indicate by a checkmark which customer requirements and which technical requirements are related.

Selected Bibliography and Further Reading

Baldwin, Carliss C., and Kim B. Clark. "Managing in the Age of Modularity." *Harvard Business Review*, September–October 1997, pp. 84–93.

Cohen, Morris A., and Uday M. Apte. *Manufacturing Automation*. McGraw-Hill, 1997.

Duray, Rebecca, and Glenn W. Milligan. "Improving Customer Satisfaction Through Mass Customization." *Quality Progress*, August 1999, pp. 60–66.

Feitzinger, Edward, and Hau L. Lee. "Mass Customization at Hewlett-Packard: The Power of Postponement." *Harvard Business Review*, January–February 1997, pp. 116–121.

Gilmore, James, and B. Joseph Pine II. "The Four Faces of Mass Customization." *Harvard Business Review*, January–February 1997, pp. 91–101.

Gilmore, James, and B. Joseph Pine II. *Markets of One: Creating Customer-Unique Value Through Mass Customization*. Boston: Harvard Business School Press, 2000.

Gorman, Michael E. *Transforming Nature: Ethics, Invention, and Design*. Boston: Kluwer Academic Publishers, 1998.

Groover, Mikell P. *Automation, Production Systems, and Computer-Aided Manufacturing*. 2nd ed. Englewood Cliffs, NJ: Prentice Hall, 2001.

Heskett, James L., W. Earl Sasser Jr., and Leonard A. Schlesinger. *The Service Profit Chain*. New York: Free Press, 1997.

Lovelock, Christopher H. *Service Marketing: People, Technology, Strategy*. 2nd ed. Englewood Cliffs, NJ: Prentice Hall, 2001.

Prasad, Biren. *Concurrent Engineering Fundamentals: Integrated Product Development*. Englewood Cliffs, NJ: Prentice Hall PTR, 1997.

Rosenthal, Stephen R. *Effective Product Development*. Burr Ridge, IL: Irwin, 1992.

Shaw, John C. *The Service Focus*. Burr Ridge, IL: Irwin, 1990.

Ternicko, John. *Step-by-Step QFD: Customer-Driven Product Design*. 2nd ed. Boca Raton, FL: CRC Press, 1997.

Ulrich, Karl T., and Steven D. Eppinger. *Product Design and Development*. New York: McGraw-Hill, 1995.

Internet Sites

www.onlineethics.org has a long list of codes of ethics for various professional engineering and scientific societies.

SUPPLEMENT TO CHAPTER FOUR

Reliability

SUPPLEMENT OUTLINE

Introduction, 159

Quantifying Reliability, 159

Availability, 165

Key Terms, 165

Solved Problems, 165

Discussion and Review
 Questions, 168

Problems, 168

LEARNING OBJECTIVES

*After completing this supplement,
you should be able to:*

1 Define reliability.

2 Perform simple reliability
 computations.

3 Explain the purpose of
 redundancy in a system.

Introduction

Reliability is a measure of the ability of a product, service, part, or system to perform its intended function under a prescribed set of conditions. In effect, reliability is a *probability*.

Suppose that an item has a reliability of .90. This means that it has a 90 percent probability of functioning as intended. The probability it will fail is $1 - .90 = .10$, or 10 percent. Hence, it is expected that, on the average, 1 of every 10 such items will fail or, equivalently, that the item will fail, on the average, once in every 10 trials. Similarly, a reliability of .985 implies 15 failures per 1,000 parts or trials.

reliability The ability of a product, service, part, or system to perform its intended function under a prescribed set of conditions.

Quantifying Reliability

Engineers and designers have a number of techniques at their disposal for assessing the reliability. A discussion of those techniques is not within the scope of this text. Instead, let us turn to the issue of quantifying overall product or system reliability. Probability is used in two ways.

1. The probability that the product or system will function when activated.
2. The probability that the product or system will function for a given length of time.

The first of these focuses on *one point in time* and is often used when a system must operate for one time or a relatively few number of times. The second of these focuses on the *length of service*. The distinction will become more apparent as each of these approaches is described in more detail.

The probability that a system or a product will operate as planned is an important concept in system and product design. Determining that probability when the product or system consists of a number of *independent* components requires the use of the rules of probability for independent events. **Independent events** have no relation to the occurrence or nonoccurrence of each other. What follows are three examples illustrating the use of probability rules to determine whether a given system will operate successfully.

independent events Events whose occurrence or nonoccurrence do not influence each other.

Rule 1. If two or more events are independent and "success" is defined as the probability that all of the events occur, then the probability of success is equal to the product of the probabilities of the events.

Example. Suppose a room has two lamps, but to have adequate light both lamps must work (success) when turned on. One lamp has a probability of working of .90, and the other has a probability of working of .80. The probability that both will work is $.90 \times .80 = .72$. Note that the order of multiplication is unimportant: $.80 \times .90 = .72$. Also note that if the room had three lamps, three probabilities would have been multiplied.

This system can be represented by the following diagram:

Even though the individual components of a system might have high reliabilities, the system as a whole can have considerably less reliability because all components that are in series (as are the ones in the preceding example) must function. As the number of components in a series increases, the system reliability decreases. For example, a system that has eight components in a series, each with a reliability of .99, has a reliability of only $.99^8 = .923$.

Obviously, many products and systems have a large number of component parts that must all operate, and some way to increase overall reliability is needed. One approach is to use **redundancy** in the design. This involves providing backup parts for some items.

redundancy The use of backup components to increase reliability.

Rule 2. If two events are independent and "success" is defined as the probability that *at least one* of the events will occur, the probability of success is equal to the probability of either one plus 1.00 minus that probability multiplied by the other probability.

Example. There are two lamps in a room. When turned on, one has a probability of working of .90 and the other has a probability of working of .80. Only a single lamp is needed to light for success. If one fails to light when turned on, the other lamp is turned on. Hence, one of the lamps is a backup in case the other one fails. Either lamp can be treated as the backup; the probability of success will be the same. The probability of success is .90 + (1 − .90) × .80 = .98. If the .80 light is first, the computation would be .80 + (1 − .80) × .90 = .98.

This system can be represented by the following diagram.

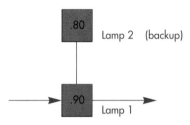

Rule 3. If three events are involved and success is defined as the probability that at least one of them occurs, the probability of success is equal to the probability of the first one (any of the events), plus the product of 1.00 minus that probability and the probability of the second event (any of the remaining events), plus the product of 1.00 minus each of the first two probabilities and the probability of the third event, and so on. This rule can be expanded to cover more than three events.

Example. Three lamps have probabilities of .90, .80, and .70 of lighting when turned on. Only one lighted lamp is needed for success; hence, two of the lamps are considered to be backups. The probability of success is:

[#1 operates]	[#1 fails	and	#2 operates]		[#1 fails	and	#2 fails	and	#3 operates]	
.90	+ (1 − .90)	×	.80	+	(1.00 − .90)	×	(1.00 − .80)	×	.70	= .994

This system can be represented by the following diagram:

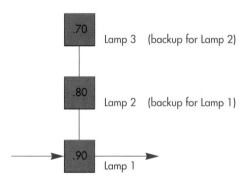

Determine the reliability of the system shown below.

The system can be reduced to a series of three components: *Solution*

| .98 | .90 + .90(1 − .90) | .95 + .92(1 − .95) |

The system reliability is, then, the product of these:

.98 × .99 × .996 = .966

The second way of looking at reliability considers the incorporation of a time dimension: Probabilities are determined relative to a specified length of time. This approach is commonly used in product warranties, which pertain to a given period of time after purchase of a product.

A typical profile of product failure rate over time is illustrated in Figure 4S−1. Because of its shape, it is sometimes referred to as a bathtub curve. Frequently, a number of products fail shortly after they are put into service, not because they wear out, but because they are defective to begin with. The rate of failures decreases rapidly once the truly defective items are weeded out. During the second phase, there are fewer failures because most of the defective items have been eliminated, and it is too soon to encounter items that fail because they have worn out. In some cases, this phase covers a relatively long period of time. In the third phase, failures occur because the products are worn out, and the failure rate increases.

Information on the distribution and length of each phase requires the collection of historical data and analysis of those data. It often turns out that the **mean time between failures (MTBF)** in the infant mortality phase can be modeled by a negative exponential distribution, such as that depicted in Figure 4S−2. Equipment failures as well as product failures may occur in this pattern. In such cases, the exponential distribution can be used

mean time between failures (MTBF) The average length of time between failures of a product or component.

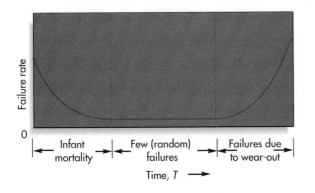

FIGURE 4S–1

Failure rate is a function of time

FIGURE 4S–2

An exponential distribution

to determine various probabilities of interest. The probability that equipment or a product put into service at time 0 will fail *before* some specified time, T, is equal to the area under the curve between 0 and T. Reliability is specified as the probability that a product will last *at least until* time T; reliability is equal to the area under the curve *beyond* T. (Note that the total area under the curve in each phase is treated as 100 percent for computational purposes.) Observe that as the specified length of service increases, the area under the curve to the right of that point (i.e., the reliability) decreases.

Determining values for the area under a curve to the right of a given point, T, becomes a relatively simple matter using a table of exponential values. An exponential distribution is completely described using a single parameter, the distribution mean, which reliability engineers often refer to as the mean time between failures. Using the symbol T to represent length of service, the probability that failure will not occur before time T (i.e., the area in the right tail) is easily determined:

$$P(\text{no failure before } T) = e^{-T/\text{MTBF}}$$

where

$$e = \text{Natural logarithm, } 2.7183 \ldots$$
$$T = \text{Length of service before failure}$$
$$\text{MTBF} = \text{Mean time between failures}$$

The probability that failure will occur before time T is 1.00 minus that amount:

$$P(\text{failure before } T) = 1 - e^{-T/\text{MTBF}}$$

Selected values of $e^{-T/\text{MTBF}}$ are listed in Table 4S–1.

TABLE 4S–1

Values of $e^{-T/\text{MTBF}}$

T/MTBF	$e^{-T/\text{MTBF}}$	T/MTBF	$e^{-T/\text{MTBF}}$	T/MTBF	$e^{-T/\text{MTBF}}$
0.10	.9048	2.60	.0743	5.10	.0061
0.20	.8187	2.70	.0672	5.20	.0055
0.30	.7408	2.80	.0608	5.30	.0050
0.40	.6703	2.90	.0550	5.40	.0045
0.50	.6065	3.00	.0498	5.50	.0041
0.60	.5488	3.10	.0450	5.60	.0037
0.70	.4966	3.20	.0408	5.70	.0033
0.80	.4493	3.30	.0369	5.80	.0030
0.90	.4066	3.40	.0334	5.90	.0027
1.00	.3679	3.50	.0302	6.00	.0025
1.10	.3329	3.60	.0273	6.10	.0022
1.20	.3012	3.70	.0247	6.20	.0020
1.30	.2725	3.80	.0224	6.30	.0018
1.40	.2466	3.90	.0202	6.40	.0017
1.50	.2231	4.00	.0183	6.50	.0015
1.60	.2019	4.10	.0166	6.60	.0014
1.70	.1827	4.20	.0150	6.70	.0012
1.80	.1653	4.30	.0136	6.80	.0011
1.90	.1496	4.40	.0123	6.90	.0010
2.00	.1353	4.50	.0111	7.00	.0009
2.10	.1255	4.60	.0101		
2.20	.1108	4.70	.0091		
2.30	.1003	4.80	.0082		
2.40	.0907	4.90	.0074		
2.50	.0821	5.00	.0067		

By means of extensive testing, a manufacturer has determined that its Super Sucker Vacuum Cleaner models have an expected life that is exponential with a mean of four years. Find the probability that one of these cleaners will have a life that ends:

a. After the initial four years of service.

b. Before four years of service are completed.

c. Not before six years of service.

MTBF = 4 years

Solution

a. $T = 4$ years:

$$T/\text{MTBF} = \frac{4 \text{ years}}{4 \text{ years}} = 1.0$$

From Table 4S−1, $e^{-1.0} = .3679$.

b. The probability of failure before $T = 4$ years is $1 - e^{-1}$, or $1 - .3679 = .6321$.

c. $T = 6$ years:

$$T/\text{MTBF} = \frac{6 \text{ years}}{4 \text{ years}} = 1.50$$

From Table 4S−1, $e^{-1.5} = .2231$.

Product failure due to wear-out can sometimes be modeled by a normal distribution. Obtaining probabilities involves the use of a table (refer to Appendix Table B). The table provides areas under a normal curve from (essentially) the left end of the curve to a specified point z, where z is a *standardized* value computed using the formula

$$z = \frac{T - \text{Mean wear-out time}}{\text{Standard deviation of wear-out time}}$$

Thus, to work with the normal distribution, it is necessary to know the mean of the distribution and its standard deviation. A normal distribution is illustrated in Figure 4S–3. Appendix Table B contains normal probabilities (i.e., the area that lies to the left of z). To obtain a probability that service life will not exceed some value T, compute z and refer to the table. To find the reliability for time T, subtract this probability from 100 percent. To obtain the value of T that will provide a given probability, locate the nearest probability under the curve *to the left* in Table B. Then use the corresponding z in the preceding formula and solve for T.

FIGURE 4S-3

A normal curve

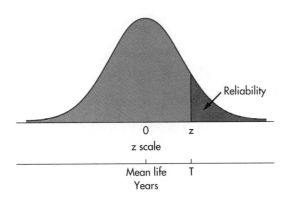

Example S-3

The mean life of a certain ball bearing can be modeled using a normal distribution with a mean of six years and a standard deviation of one year. Determine each of the following:

a. The probability that a ball bearing will wear out *before* seven years of service.

b. The probability that a ball bearing will wear out *after* seven years of service (i.e., find its reliability).

c. The service life that will provide a wear-out probability of 10 percent.

Solution

Wear-out life mean = 6 years

Wear-out life standard deviation = 1 year

Wear-out life is normally distributed

a. Compute z and use it to obtain the probability directly from Appendix Table B (see diagram).

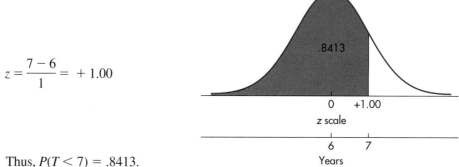

$$z = \frac{7 - 6}{1} = +1.00$$

Thus, $P(T < 7) = .8413$.

b. Subtract the probability determined in part a from 100 percent (see diagram).

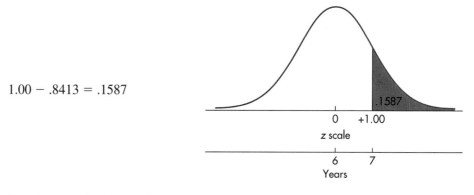

$$1.00 - .8413 = .1587$$

c. Use the normal table and find the value of z that corresponds to an area under the curve of 10% (see diagram).

$$z = -1.28 = \frac{T - 6}{1}$$

Solving for T, we find $T = 4.72$ years.

Availability

A related measure of importance to customers, and hence to designers, is **availability.** It measures the fraction of time a piece of equipment is expected to be operational (as opposed to being down for repairs). Availability can range from zero (never available) to 1.00 (always available). Companies that can offer equipment with a high availability factor have a competitive advantage over companies that offer equipment with lower availability values. Availability is a function of both the mean time between failures and the mean time to repair. The availability factor can be computed using the following formula:

$$Availability = \frac{MTBF}{MTBF + MTR}$$

where

    MTBF = Mean time between failures

    MTR = Mean time to repair

availability The fraction of time a piece of equipment is expected to be available for operation.

A copier is expected to be able to operate for 200 hours between repairs, and the mean repair time is expected to be two hours. Determine the availability of the copier.

MTBF = 200 hours, and MTR = 2 hours

$$Availability = \frac{MTBF}{MTBF + MTR} = \frac{200}{200 + 2} = .99$$

Example S-4

Solution

    Two implications for design are revealed by the availability formula. One is that availability increases as the mean time between failures increases. The other is that availability also increases as the mean repair time decreases. It would seem obvious that designers would want to design products that have a long time between failures. However, some design options enhance repairability, which can be incorporated into the product. Laser printers, for example, are designed with print cartridges that can easily be replaced.

availability, 165
independent events, 159
mean time between failures (MTBF), 161

redundancy, 159
reliability, 159

Key Terms

A product design engineer must decide if a redundant component is cost-justified in a certain system. The system in question has a critical component with a probability of .98 of operating. System failure would involve a cost of $20,000. For a cost of $100, a switch could be added that would automatically transfer the system to the backup component in the event of a failure. Should the backup be added if the backup probability is also .98?

Because no probability is given for the switch, we will assume its probability of operating when needed is 100 percent. The expected cost of failure (i.e., without the backup) is $20,000 (1 − .98) = $400.
    With the backup, the probability of *not* failing would be:

    .98 + .02(.98) = .9996

Hence, the probability of failure would be 1 − .9996 = .0004. The expected cost of failure with the backup would be the added cost of the backup plus the failure cost:

    $100 + $20,000(.0004) = $108

Because this is less than the cost without the backup, it appears that adding the backup is definitely cost justifiable.

Solved Problems

Problem 1

Solution

Problem 2

Due to the extreme cost of interrupting production, a firm has two standby machines available in case a particular machine breaks down. The machine in use has a reliability of .94, and the backups have reliabilities of .90 and .80. In the event of a failure, either backup can be pressed into service. If one fails, the other backup can be used. Compute the system reliability.

Solution

$R1 = .94$, $R2 = .90$,   and $R3 = .80$

The system can be depicted in this way:

$$R_{\text{system}} = R_1 + R_2(1 - R_1) + R_3(1 - R_2)(1 - R_1)$$
$$= .94 + .90(1 - .94) + .80(1 - .90)(1 - .94) = .9988$$

Problem 3

A hospital has three *independent* fire alarm systems, with reliabilities of .95, .97, and .99. In the event of a fire, what is the probability that a warning would be given?

Solution

A warning would *not* be given if all three alarms failed. The probability that at least one alarm would operate is $1 - P(\text{none operate})$:

$$P(\text{none operate}) = (1 - .95)(1 - .97)(1 - .99) = .000015$$
$$P(\text{warning}) = 1 - .000015 = .999985$$

Problem 4

A weather satellite has an expected life of 10 years from the time it is placed into earth orbit. Determine its probability of no wear-out before each of the following lengths of service. (Assume the exponential distribution is appropriate.)

a. 5 years.   *b.* 12 years.   *c.* 20 years.   *d.* 30 years.

Solution

MTBF = 10 years

Compute the ratio T/MTBF for $T = 5$, 12, 20, and 30, and obtain the values of $e^{-T/\text{MTBF}}$ from Table 4S–1. The solutions are summarized in the following table.

T	MTBF	T/MTBF	$e^{-T/\text{MTBF}}$
a. 5	10	0.50	.6065
b. 12	10	1.20	.3012
c. 20	10	2.00	.1353
d. 30	10	3.00	.0498

Problem 5

What is the probability that the satellite described in Solved Problem 4 will fail between 5 and 12 years after being placed into earth orbit?

Solution

$$P(5 \text{ years} < \text{failure} < 12 \text{ years}) = P \text{ (failure after 5 years)}$$
$$- P(\text{failure after 12 years})$$

Using the probabilities shown in the previous solution, you obtain:

$$P(\text{failure after 5 years}) = .6065$$
$$-P(\text{failure after 12 years}) = \frac{.3012}{.3053}$$

The corresponding area under the curve is illustrated as follows:

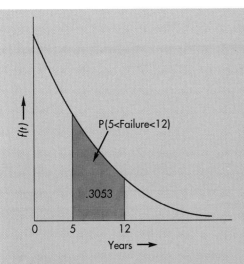

One line of radial tires produced by a large company has a wear-out life that can be modeled us-   **Problem 6**
ing a normal distribution with a mean of 25,000 miles and a standard deviation of 2,000 miles.
Determine each of the following:

a. The percentage of tires that can be expected to wear out within ± 2,000 miles of the average
   (i.e., between 23,000 miles and 27,000 miles).

b. The percentage of tires that can be expected to fail between 26,000 miles and 29,000 miles.

Notes: (1) Miles are analogous to time and are handled in exactly the same way; (2) the term   **Solution**
percentage refers to a probability.

a. The phrase "within ± 2,000 miles of the average" translates to within one standard deviation
   of the mean since the standard deviation equals 2,000 miles. Therefore the range of z is $z =$
   -1.00 to $z = +1.00$, and the area under the curve between those points is found as the difference between $P(z < +1.00)$ and $P(z < -1.00)$, using values obtained from Appendix
   Table B.

$$P(z < +1.00) = .8413$$
$$\underline{-P(z < -1.00) = .1587}$$
$$P(-1.00 < z < +1.00) = .6826$$

b. Wear-out mean = 25,000 miles
   Wear-out standard deviation = 2,000 miles

$$P(26,000 < \text{Wear-out} < 29,000) = P(z_{29,000}) - P(z < z_{26,000})$$

$$z_{29,000} = \frac{29,000 - 25,000}{2,000} = +2.00 \text{ s } .9772$$

$$z_{26,000} = \frac{26,000 - 25,000}{2,000} = +.50 \text{ s } .6915$$

The difference is .9772 − .6915 = .2857, which is the expected percent of tires that will wear out between 26,000 miles and 29,000 miles.

1. Define the term *reliability*.
2. Explain why a product or system might have an overall reliability that is low even though it is comprised of components that have fairly high reliabilities.
3. What is redundancy and how can it improve product design?

Problems

1. Consider the following system:

   Determine the probability that the system will operate under each of these conditions:
   a. The system as shown.
   b. Each system component has a backup with a probability of .90 and a switch that is 100 percent reliable.
   c. Backups with .90 probability and a switch that is 99 percent reliable.
2. A product is composed of four parts. In order for the product to function properly in a given situation, each of the parts must function. Two of the parts each have a .96 probability of functioning, and two each have a probability of .99. What is the overall probability that the product will function properly?
3. A system consists of three identical components. In order for the system to perform as intended, all of the components must perform. Each has the same probability of performance. If the system is to have a .92 probability of performing, what is the minimum probability of performing needed by each of the individual components?
4. A product engineer has developed the following equation for the cost of a system component: $C = (10P)^2$, where C is the cost in dollars and P is the probability that the component will operate as expected. The system is composed of two identical components, both of which must operate for the system to operate. The engineer can spend $173 for the two components. To the nearest two decimal places, what is the largest component probability that can be achieved?
5. The guidance system of a ship is controlled by a computer that has three major modules. In order for the computer to function properly, all three modules must function. Two of the modules have reliabilities of .97, and the other has a reliability of .99.
   a. What is the reliability of the computer?
   b. A backup computer identical to the one being used will be installed to improve overall reliability. Assuming the new computer automatically functions if the main one fails, determine the resulting reliability.
   c. If the backup computer must be activated by a switch in the event that the first computer fails, and the switch has a reliability of .98, what is the overall reliability of the system? (*Both* the switch and the backup computer must function in order for the backup to take over.)

6. One of the industrial robots designed by a leading producer of servomechanisms has four major components. Components' reliabilities are .98, .95, .94, and .90. All of the components must function in order for the robot to operate effectively.

   a. Compute the reliability of the robot.

   b. Designers want to improve the reliability by adding a backup component. Due to space limitations, only one backup can be added. The backup for any component will have the same reliability as the unit for which it is the backup. Which component should get the backup in order to achieve the highest reliability?

   c. If one backup with a reliability of .92 can be added to any one of the main components, which component should get it to obtain the highest overall reliability?

7. A production line has three machines A, B, and C, with reliabilities of .99, .96, and .93, respectively. The machines are arranged so that if one breaks down, the others must shut down. Engineers are weighing two alternative designs for increasing the line's reliability. Plan 1 involves adding an identical backup *line,* and plan 2 involves providing a backup for each *machine.* In either case, three machines (A, B, and C) would be used with reliabilities equal to the original three.

   a. Which plan will provide the higher reliability?

   b. Explain why the two reliabilities are not the same.

   c. What other factors might enter into the decision of which plan to adopt?

8. Refer to the previous problem.

   a. Assume that the single switch used in plan 1 is 98 percent reliable, while reliabilities of the machines remain the same. Recalculate the reliability of plan 1. Compare the reliability of this plan with the reliability of the plan 1 calculated in solving the original problem. How much did reliability of plan 1 decrease as a result of a 98 percent reliable switch?

   b. Assume that the three switches used in plan 2 are all 98 percent reliable, while reliabilities of the machines remain the same. Recalculate the reliability of plan 2. Compare the reliability of this plan with the reliability of the plan 2 calculated in solving the original problem. How much did reliability of plan 2 decrease?

9. A web server has five major components which must all function in order for it to operate as intended. Assuming that each component of the system has the same reliability, what is the minimum reliability each one must have in order for the overall system to have a reliability of .98?

10. Repeat Problem 9 under the condition that one of the components will have a backup with a reliability equal to that of any one of the other components.

11. Hoping to increase the chances of reaching a performance goal, the director of a research project has assigned three separate research teams the same task. The director estimates that the team probabilities are .9, .8, and .7 for successfully completing the task in the allotted time. Assuming that the teams work independently, what is the probability that the task will not be completed in time?

12. An electronic chess game has a useful life that is exponential with a mean of 30 months. Determine each of the following:

   a. The probability that any given unit will operate for at least: (1) 39 months, (2) 48 months, (3) 60 months.

   b. The probability that any given unit will fail sooner than: (1) 33 months, (2) 15 months, (3) 6 months.

   c. The length of service time after which the percentage of failed units will approximately equal: (1) 50 percent, (2) 85 percent, (3) 95 percent, (4) 99 percent.

13. A manufacturer of programmable calculators is attempting to determine a reasonable free-service period for a model it will introduce shortly. The manager of product testing has indicated that the calculators have an expected life of 30 months. Assume product life can be described by an exponential distribution.

   a. If service contracts are offered for the expected life of the calculator, what percentage of those sold would be expected to fail during the service period?

   b. What service period would result in a failure rate of approximately 10 percent?

14. Lucky Lumen light bulbs have an expected life that is exponentially distributed with a mean of 5,000 hours. Determine the probability that one of these light bulbs will last

    a. At least 6,000 hours.

    b. No longer than 1,000 hours.

    c. Between 1,000 hours and 6,000 hours.

15. Planetary Communications, Inc., intends to launch a satellite that will enhance reception of television programs in Alaska. According to its designers, the satellite will have an expected life of six years. Assume the exponential distribution applies. Determine the probability that it will function for each of the following time periods:

    a. More than 9 years.

    b. Less than 12 years.

    c. More than 9 years but less than 12 years.

    d. At least 21 years.

16. An office manager has received a report from a consultant that includes a section on equipment replacement. The report indicates that scanners have a service life that is normally distributed with a mean of 41 months and a standard deviation of 4 months. On the basis of this information, determine the percentage of scanners that can be expected to fail in the following time periods:

    a. Before 38 months of service.

    b. Between 40 and 45 months of service.

    c. Within -2 months of the mean life.

17. A major television manufacturer has determined that its 19-inch color TV picture tubes have a mean service life that can be modeled by a normal distribution with a mean of six years and a standard deviation of one-half year.

    a. What probability can you assign to service lives of at least: (1) Five years? (2) Six years? (3) Seven and one-half years?

    b. If the manufacturer offers service contracts of four years on these picture tubes, what percentage can be expected to fail from wear-out during the service period?

18. Refer to Problem 17. What service period would achieve an expected wear-out rate of:

    a. 2 percent?

    b. 5 percent?

19. Determine the availability for each of these cases:

    a. MTBF = 40 days, average repair time = 3 days.

    b. MTBF = 300 hours, average repair time = 6 hours.

20. A machine can operate for an average of 10 weeks before it needs to be overhauled, a process which takes two days. The machine is operated five days a week. Compute the availability of this machine. (Hint: all times must be in the same units.)

21. A manager must decide between two machines. The manager will take into account each machine's operating costs and initial costs, and its breakdown and repair times. Machine A has a projected average operating time of 142 hours and a projected average repair time of seven hours. Projected times for machine B are an average operating time of 65 hours and a repair time of two hours. What are the projected availabilities of each machine?

22. A designer estimates that she can (*a*) increase the average time between failures of a part by 5 percent at a cost of $450, or (*b*) reduce the average repair time by 10 percent at a cost of $200. Which option would be more cost-effective? Currently, the average time between failures is 100 hours and the average repair time is four hours.

23. Auto batteries have an average life of 2.4 years. Battery life is normally distributed with a mean of 2.7 years and a standard deviation of .3 year. The batteries are warranted to operate for a minimum of two years. If a battery fails within the warranty period, it will be replaced with a new battery at no charge. The company sells and installs the batteries. Also, the normal $5 installation charge will be waived.

    a. What percentage of batteries would you expect to fail before the warranty period expires?

    b. A competitor is offering a warranty of 30 months on its premium battery. The manager of this company is toying with the idea of using the same battery with a different exterior, labeling it as a premium battery, and offering a 30-month warranty on it. How much more would the company have to charge on its "premium" battery to offset the additional cost of replacing batteries?

    c. What other factors would you take into consideration besides the price of the battery?

Thus, compared with the effective capacity of 40 units per day, 36 units per day looks pretty good. However, compared with the design capacity of 50 units per day, 36 units per day is much less impressive although probably more meaningful.

Because effective capacity acts as a lid on actual output, the real key to improving capacity utilization is to increase effective capacity by correcting quality problems, maintaining equipment in good operating condition, fully training employees, and fully utilizing bottleneck equipment.

Hence, increasing utilization depends on being able to increase effective capacity, and this requires a knowledge of what is constraining effective capacity.

The following section explores some of the main determinants of effective capacity. It is important to recognize that the benefits of high utilization are realized only in instances where there is demand for the output. When demand is not there, focusing exclusively on utilization can be counterproductive, because the excess output not only results in additional variable costs; it also generates the costs of having to carry the output as inventory. Another disadvantage of high utilization is that operating costs may increase because of increasing waiting time due to bottleneck conditions.

Determinants of Effective Capacity

Many decisions about system design have an impact on capacity. The same is true for many operating decisions. This section briefly describes some of these factors, which are then elaborated on elsewhere in the book. The main factors relate to the following:

1. Facilities
2. Products or services
3. Processes
4. Human considerations
5. Operations
6. External forces

FACILITIES FACTORS

The design of facilities, including size and provision for expansion, is key. Locational factors, such as transportation costs, distance to market, labor supply, energy sources, and

A mass producer of large-frame computers, the Sujitsu plant in Numazu, Japan, conducts product testing. Building efficiency into product testing increases their capacity.

Artisans making rugs by hand in a carpet workshop at the Grand Bazaar in Istanbul, Turkey. Capacity is highly limited in production systems such as this, where items are specialized and produced one at a time.

room for expansion, are also important. Likewise, layout of the work area often determines how smoothly work can be performed, and environmental factors such as heating, lighting, and ventilation also play a significant role in determining whether personnel can perform effectively or whether they must struggle to overcome poor design characteristics.

PRODUCT/SERVICE FACTORS

Product or service design can have a tremendous influence on capacity. For example, when items are similar, the ability of the system to produce those items is generally much greater than when successive items differ. Thus, a restaurant that offers a limited menu can usually prepare and serve meals at a faster rate than a restaurant with an extensive menu. Generally speaking, the more uniform the output, the more opportunities there are for standardization of methods and materials, which leads to greater capacity. The particular mix of products or services rendered must also be considered since different items will have different rates of output.

PROCESS FACTORS

The quantity capability of a process is an obvious determinant of capacity. A more subtle determinant is the influence of output *quality*. For instance, if quality of output does not meet standards, the rate of output will be slowed by the need for inspection and rework activities.

HUMAN FACTORS

The tasks that make up a job, the variety of activities involved, and the training, skill, and experience required to perform a job all have an impact on the potential and actual output. In addition, employee motivation has a very basic relationship to capacity, as do absenteeism and labor turnover.

OPERATIONAL FACTORS

Scheduling problems may occur when an organization has differences in equipment capabilities among alternative pieces of equipment or differences in job requirements. Inventory stocking decisions, late deliveries, acceptability of purchased materials and parts, and quality inspection and control procedures also can have an impact on effective capacity.

Inventory shortages of even one component of an assembled item (e.g., computers, refrigerators, automobiles) can cause a temporary halt to assembly operations until new components become available. This can have a major impact on effective capacity. Thus, insufficient capacity in one area can affect overall capacity.

EXTERNAL FACTORS

Product standards, especially minimum quality and performance standards, can restrict management's options for increasing and using capacity. Thus, pollution standards on products and equipment often reduce effective capacity, as does paperwork required by government regulatory agencies by engaging employees in nonproductive activities. A similar effect occurs when a union contract limits the number of hours and type of work an employee may do.

Table 5–2 summarizes these factors. In general, *inadequate planning* is a major limiting determinant of effective capacity.

Determining Capacity Requirements

Capacity planning decisions involve both long-term and short-term considerations. Long-term considerations relate to overall *level* of capacity, such as facility size; short-term considerations relate to probable *variations* in capacity requirements created by such things as seasonal, random, and irregular fluctuations in demand. Because the time intervals

TABLE 5-2

Factors that determine effective capacity

A. Facilities
  1. Design
  2. Location
  3. Layout
  4. Environment
B. Product/Service
  1. Design
  2. Product or service mix
C. Process
  1. Quantity capabilities
  2. Quality capabilities
D. Human factors
  1. Job content
  2. Job design
  3. Training and experience
  4. Motivation

  5. Compensation
  6. Learning rates
  7. Absenteeism and labor turnover
E. Operational
  1. Scheduling
  2. Materials management
  3. Quality assurance
  4. Maintenance policies
  5. Equipment breakdowns
F. External factors
  1. Product standards
  2. Safety regulations
  3. Unions
  4. Pollution control standards

FIGURE 5-1

Common demand patterns

covered by each of these categories can vary significantly from industry to industry, it would be misleading to put times on the intervals. However, the distinction will serve as a framework within which to discuss capacity planning.

We determine *long-term* capacity needs by forecasting demand over a time horizon and then converting those forecasts into capacity requirements. Figure 5–1 illustrates some basic demand patterns that might be identified by a forecast. In addition to basic patterns there are more complex patterns, such as a combination of cycles and trends.

When trends are identified, the fundamental issues are (1) how long the trend might persist, because few things last forever, and (2) the slope of the trend. If cycles are identified, interest focuses on (1) the approximate length of the cycles, and (2) the amplitude of the cycles (i.e., deviation from average).

Short-term capacity needs are less concerned with cycles or trends than with seasonal variations and other variations from average. These deviations are particularly important because they can place a severe strain on a system's ability to satisfy demand at some times and yet result in idle capacity at other times.

An organization can identify seasonal patterns using standard forecasting techniques. Although commonly thought of as annual fluctuations, seasonal variations are also reflected

TABLE 5–3

Examples of seasonal demand patterns

Period	Items
Year	Beer sales, toy sales, airline traffic, clothing, vacations, tourism, power usage, gasoline consumption, sports and recreation, education
Month	Welfare and social security checks, bank transactions
Week	Retail sales, restaurant meals, automobile traffic, automotive rentals, hotel registrations
Day	Telephone calls, power usage, automobile traffic, public transportation, classroom utilization, retail sales, restaurant meals

in monthly, weekly, and even daily capacity requirements. Table 5–3 provides some examples of items that tend to exhibit seasonal demand patterns.

When time intervals are too short to have seasonal variations in demand, the analysis can often describe the variations by probability distributions such as a normal, uniform, or Poisson distribution. For example, we might describe the amount of coffee served during the midday meal at a luncheonette by a normal distribution with a certain mean and standard deviation. The number of customers who enter a bank branch on Monday mornings might be described by a Poisson distribution with a certain mean. It does not follow, however, that *every* instance of random variability will lend itself to description by a standard statistical distribution. Service systems in particular may experience a considerable amount of variability in capacity requirements unless requests for service can be scheduled. Manufacturing systems, because of their typical isolation from customers and the more uniform nature of production, are less likely to experience variations. Waiting-line models and simulation models can be useful when analyzing service systems. These models are described in Chapter 19.

Irregular variations are perhaps the most troublesome: They are virtually impossible to predict. They are created by such diverse forces as major equipment breakdowns, freak storms that disrupt normal routines, foreign political turmoil that causes oil shortages, discovery of health hazards (nuclear accidents, unsafe chemical dumping grounds, carcinogens in food and drink), and so on.

The link between marketing and operations is crucial to realistic determination of capacity requirements. Through customer contracts, demographic analyses, and forecasts, marketing can supply vital information to operations for ascertaining capacity needs for both the long term and the short term.

Developing Capacity Alternatives

Aside from the general considerations about the development of alternatives (i.e., conduct a reasonable search for possible alternatives, consider doing nothing, take care not to overlook nonquantitative factors), there are other things that can be done to enhance capacity management:

1. **Design flexibility into systems.** The long-term nature of many capacity decisions and the risks inherent in long-term forecasts suggest potential benefits from designing flexible systems. For example, provision for future expansion in the original design of a structure frequently can be obtained at a small price compared to what it would cost to remodel an existing structure that did not have such a provision. Hence, if future expansion of a restaurant seems likely, water lines, power hookups, and waste disposal lines can be put in place initially so that if expansion becomes a reality, modification to the existing structure can be minimized. Similarly, a new golf course may start as a nine-hole operation, but if provision is made for future expansion by obtaining options on adjacent land, it may progress to a larger (18-hole) course. Other considerations in flexible design involve layout of equipment, location, equipment selection, production planning, scheduling, and inventory policies, which will be discussed in later chapters.

2. **Differentiate between new and mature products or services.** Mature products or services tend to be more predictable in terms of capacity requirements, and they may have

limited life spans. The predictable demand pattern means less risk of choosing an incorrect capacity, but the possible limited life span of the product or service may necessitate finding an alternative use for the additional capacity at the end of the life span. New products tend to carry higher risk because of the uncertainty often associated with predicting the quantity and duration of demand. That makes flexibility appealing to managers.

3. **Take a "big picture" approach to capacity changes.** When developing capacity alternatives, it is important to consider how parts of the system interrelate. For example, when making a decision to increase the number of rooms in a motel, one should also take into account probable increased demands for parking, entertainment and food, and housekeeping. This is a "big picture" approach.

4. **Prepare to deal with capacity "chunks."** Capacity increases are often acquired in fairly large chunks rather than smooth increments, making it difficult to achieve a match between desired capacity and feasible capacity. For instance, the desired capacity of a certain operation may be 55 units per hour; but suppose that machines used for this operation are able to produce 40 units per hour each. One machine by itself would cause capacity to be 15 units per hour short of what is needed, but two machines would result in an excess capacity of 25 units per hour. The illustration becomes even more extreme if we shift the topic—to open-hearth furnaces or to the number of airplanes needed to provide a desired level of capacity.

5. **Attempt to smooth out capacity requirements.** Unevenness in capacity requirements also can create certain problems. For instance, during periods of inclement weather, public transportation ridership tends to increase substantially relative to periods of pleasant weather. Consequently, the system tends to alternate between underutilization and overutilization. Increasing the number of buses or subway cars will reduce the burden during periods of heavy demand, but this will aggravate the problem of overcapacity at other times and certainly add to the cost of operating the system.

We can trace the unevenness in demand for products and services to a variety of sources. The bus ridership problem is weather related to a certain extent, but demand could be considered to be partly random (i.e., varying because of chance factors). Still another source of varying demand is seasonality. Seasonal variations are generally easier to cope with than random variations because they are *predictable*. Consequently, management can make allowances in planning and scheduling activities and inventories. However, seasonal variations can still pose problems because of their uneven demands on the system: At certain times the system will tend to be overloaded, while at other times it will tend to be underloaded. One possible approach to this problem is to identify products or services that have complementary demand patterns, that is, patterns that tend to offset each other. For instance, demand for snow skis and demand for water skis might complement each other: Demand for water skis is greater in the spring and summer months, and demand for snow skis is greater in the fall and winter months. The same might apply to heating and air-conditioning equipment. The ideal case is one in which products or services with complementary demand patterns involve the use of the same resources but at different times, so that overall capacity requirements remain fairly stable. Figure 5–2 illustrates complementary demand patterns.

Variability in demand can pose a problem for managers. Simply adding capacity by increasing the size of the operation (e.g., increasing the size of the facility, the workforce, or the amount of processing equipment) is not always the best approach, because that reduces flexibility and adds to fixed costs. Consequently, managers often choose to respond to higher than normal demand in other ways. One way is through the use of overtime work. Another way is to subcontract some of the work. A third way is to draw down finished goods inventories during periods of high demand and replenish them during periods of slow demand. These options and others are discussed in detail in the chapter on aggregate planning.

6. **Identify the optimal operating level.** Production units typically have an ideal or optimal level of operation in terms of unit cost of output. At the ideal level, cost per unit is the lowest for that production unit; larger or smaller rates of output will result in a

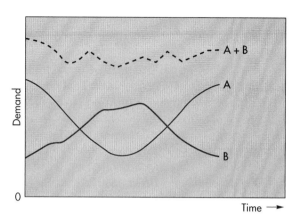

FIGURE 5-2

A and B have complementary demand patterns

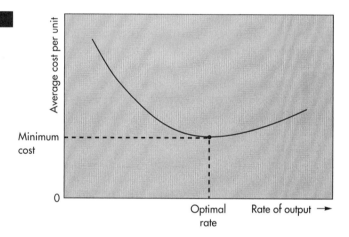

FIGURE 5-3

Production units have an optimal rate of output for minimum cost

higher unit cost. Figure 5–3 illustrates this concept. Notice how unit costs rise as the rate of output varies from the optimal level.

The explanation for the shape of the cost curve is that at low levels of output, the costs of facilities and equipment must be absorbed (paid for) by very few units. Hence, the cost per unit is high. As output is increased, there are more units to absorb the "fixed" cost of facilities and equipment, so unit costs decrease. However, beyond a certain point, unit costs will start to rise. To be sure, the fixed costs are spread over even more units, so that does not account for the increase, but other factors now become important: worker fatigue; equipment breakdowns; the loss of flexibility, which leaves less of a margin for error; and, generally, greater difficulty in coordinating operations.

Both optimal operating rate and the amount of the minimum cost tend to be a function of the general capacity of the operating unit. For example, as the general capacity of a plant increases, the optimal output rate increases and the minimum cost for the optimal rate decreases. Thus, larger plants tend to have higher optimal output rates and lower minimum costs than smaller plants. Figure 5–4 illustrates these points.

In choosing the capacity of an operating unit, management must take these relationships into account along with the availability of financial and other resources and forecasts of expected demand. To do this, it is necessary to determine enough points for each size facility to be able to make a comparison among different sizes. In some instances, facility sizes are givens, whereas in others, facility size is a continuous variable (i.e., any size can be selected). In the latter case, an ideal facility size can be selected. Usually, management must make a choice from given sizes, and none may have a minimum at the desired rate of output.

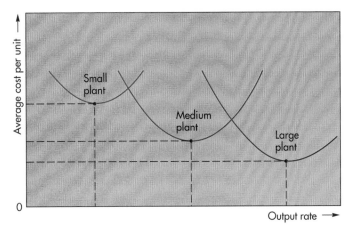

FIGURE 5-4

Minimum cost and optimal operating rate are functions of size of a production unit

Planning Service Capacity

Three very important factors in planning service capacity are (1) the need to be near customers, (2) the inability to store services, and (3) the degree of volatility of demand.

Convenience for customers is often an important aspect of service. Generally, a service must be located near customers. For example, hotel rooms must be where customers want to stay; having a vacant room in another city won't help. Thus, capacity and location are closely tied.

Capacity must also be matched with the *timing* of demand. Unlike goods, services cannot be produced in one period and stored for use in a later period. Thus, an unsold seat on an airplane, train, or bus cannot be stored for use on a later trip. Similarly, inventories of goods allow customers to immediately satisfy wants, whereas a customer who wants a service may have to wait. This can result in a variety of negatives for an organization that provides the service. Thus, speed of delivery, or customer waiting time, becomes a major concern in service capacity planning. For example, deciding on the number of police officers and fire trucks to have on duty at any given time affects the speed of response and brings into issue the *cost* of maintaining that capacity. Some of these issues are addressed in the chapter on waiting lines.

Demand volatility presents problems for capacity planners. Demand volatility tends to be higher for services than for goods, not only in timing of demand, but also in the time

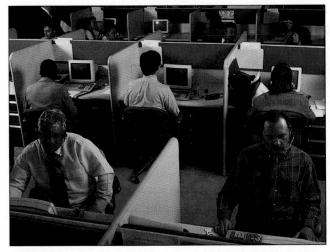

For routine service needs that come in frequently and in high volume, employees at a call center may provide customer service most efficiently.

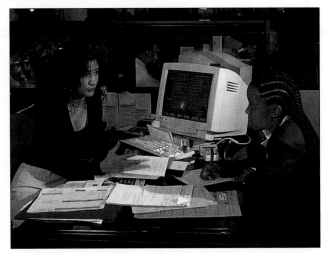

For more specialized customer service needs, individualized service may provide the best results.

required to service individual customers. For example, banks tend to experience higher volumes of demand on certain days of the week, and the number and nature of transactions tend to vary substantially for different individuals. Then, too, a wide range of social, cultural, and even weather factors can cause major peaks and valleys in demand. The fact that services can't be stored means service systems cannot turn to inventory to smooth demand requirements on the system the way goods-producing systems are able to. Instead, service planners have to devise other methods of coping with demand volatility. For example, to cope with peak demand periods, planners might consider hiring extra workers, outsourcing some or all of a service, or using pricing and promotion to shift some demand to slower periods.

In some instances, *demand management* is a strategy that can be used to offset capacity limitations. Pricing, promotions, discounts, and similar tactics can help to shift some demand away from peak periods and into slow periods, allowing organizations to achieve a closer match in supply and demand.

Evaluating Alternatives

An organization needs to examine alternatives for future capacity from a number of different perspectives. Most obvious are economic considerations: Will an alternative be economically feasible? How much will it cost? How soon can we have it? What will operating and maintenance costs be? What will its useful life be? Will it be compatible with present personnel and present operations?

Less obvious, but nonetheless important, is possible negative public opinion. For instance, the decision to build a new power plant is almost sure to stir up reaction, whether the plant is coal-fired, hydroelectric, or nuclear. Any option that could disrupt lives and property is bound to generate hostile reactions. Construction of new facilities may necessitate moving personnel to a new location. Embracing a new technology may mean retraining some people and terminating some jobs. Relocation can cause unfavorable reactions, particularly if a town is about to lose a major employer. Conversely, community pressure in a new location may arise if the presence of the company is viewed unfavorably (noise, traffic, pollution).

A number of techniques are useful for evaluating capacity alternatives from an economic standpoint. Some of the more common are cost–volume analysis, financial analysis, decision theory, and waiting-line analysis. Cost–volume analysis is described in this chapter. Financial analysis is mentioned briefly; decision analysis is described in the chapter supplement and waiting-line analysis is described in chapter 19.

CALCULATING PROCESSING REQUIREMENTS

When evaluating capacity alternatives, a necessary piece of information is the capacity requirements of products that will be processed with a given alternative. To get this information, one must have reasonably accurate demand forecasts for each product, and know the standard processing time per unit for each product on each alternative machine, the number of workdays per year, and the number of shifts that will be used.

Example 2

A department works one eight-hour shift, 250 days a year, and has these figures for usage of a machine that is currently being considered:

Product	Annual Demand	Standard Processing Time per Unit (Hr)	Processing Time Needed (Hr)
#1	400	5.0	2,000
#2	300	8.0	2,400
#3	700	2.0	1,400
			5,800

Working one eight-hour shift, 250 days a year provides an annual capacity of 8×250 = 2,000 hours per year. We can see that three of these machines would be needed to handle the required volume:

$$\frac{5,800 \text{ hours}}{2,000 \text{ hour/machine}} = 2.90 \text{ machines}$$

COST–VOLUME ANALYSIS

Cost–volume analysis focuses on relationships between cost, revenue, and volume of output. The purpose of cost–volume analysis is to estimate the income of an organization under different operating conditions. It is particularly useful as a tool for comparing capacity alternatives.

Use of the technique requires identification of all costs related to the production of a given product. These costs are then designated as fixed costs or variable costs. *Fixed costs* tend to remain constant regardless of volume of output. Examples include rental costs, property taxes, equipment costs, heating and cooling expenses, and certain administrative costs. *Variable costs* vary directly with volume of output. The major components of variable costs are generally materials and labor costs. We will assume that variable cost per unit remains the same regardless of volume of output.

Table 5–4 summarizes the symbols used in the cost–volume formulas.

The total cost associated with a given volume of output is equal to the sum of the fixed cost and the variable cost per unit times volume:

$$TC = FC + VC \tag{5–3}$$
$$VC = Q \times v \tag{5–4}$$

where v = variable cost per unit. Figure 5–5A shows the relationship between volume of output and fixed costs, total variable costs, and total (fixed plus variable) costs.

Revenue per unit, like variable cost per unit, is assumed to be the same regardless of quantity of output. Total revenue will have a linear relationship to output, as illustrated in Figure 5–5B. Assume that all output can be sold. The total revenue associated with a given quantity of output, Q, is:

$$TR = R \times Q \tag{5–5}$$

Figure 5–5C describes the relationship between profit—which is the difference between total revenue and total (i.e., fixed plus variable) cost—and volume of output. The volume at which total cost and total revenue are equal is referred to as the **break-even point (BEP).** When volume is less than the break-even point, there is a loss; when volume is greater than the break-even point, there is a profit. The greater the deviation from this point, the greater the profit or loss. Total profit can be computed using the formula:

break-even point (BEP) The volume of output at which total cost and total revenue are equal.

$$P = TR - TC = R \times Q - (FC + v \times Q)$$

TABLE 5-4

Cost–volume symbols

FC = Fixed cost
VC = Total variable cost
v = Variable cost per unit
TC = Total cost
TR = Total revenue
R = Revenue per unit
Q = Quantity or volume of output
Q_{BEP} = Break-even quantity
P = Profit

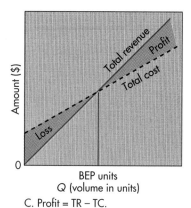

A. Fixed, variable, and total costs.

B. Total revenue increases linearly with output.

C. Profit = TR – TC.

FIGURE 5–5

Cost–volume relationships

Rearranging terms, we have

$$P = Q(R - v) - FC \qquad (5–6)$$

The required volume, Q, needed to generate a specified profit is:

$$Q = \frac{P + FC}{R - v} \qquad (5–7)$$

A special case of this is the volume of output needed for total revenue to equal total cost. This is the break-even point, computed using the formula:

$$Q_{BEP} = \frac{FC}{R - v} \qquad (5–8)$$

Example 3

The owner of Old-Fashioned Berry Pies, S. Simon, is contemplating adding a new line of pies, which will require leasing new equipment for a monthly payment of $6,000. Variable costs would be $2.00 per pie, and pies would retail for $7.00 each.

a. How many pies must be sold in order to break even?

b. What would the profit (loss) be if 1,000 pies are made and sold in a month?

c. How many pies must be sold to realize a profit of $4,000?

$$FC = \$6,000, \qquad VC = \$2 \text{ per pie}, \qquad Rev = \$7 \text{ per pie}$$

Solution

a. $Q_{BEP} = \dfrac{FC}{Rev - VC} = \dfrac{\$6,000}{\$7 - \$2} = 1,200 \text{ pies/month}$

b. For $Q = 1,000$, $P = Q(R - v) - FC = 1,000(\$7 - \$2) - \$6,000 = -\$1,000$

c. $P = \$4,000$; solve for Q using equation 5–7:

$$Q = \frac{\$4,000 + \$6,000}{\$7 - \$2} = 2,000 \text{ pies}$$

Capacity alternatives may involve *step costs,* which are costs that increase stepwise as potential volume increases. For example, a firm may have the option of purchasing one, two, or three machines, with each additional machine increasing the fixed cost, although perhaps not linearly. (See Figure 5–6A.) Then fixed costs and potential volume would

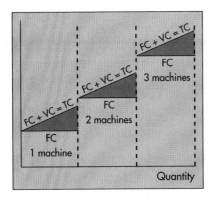

A. Step fixed costs and variable costs.

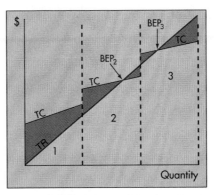

B. Multiple break-even points.

FIGURE 5-6

Break-even problem with step fixed costs

depend on the number of machines purchased. The implication is that *multiple break-even quantities* may occur, possibly one for each range. Note, however, that the total revenue line might not intersect the fixed-cost line in a particular range, meaning that there would be no break-even point in that range. This possibility is illustrated in Figure 5–6B, where there is no break-even point in the first range. In order to decide how many machines to purchase, a manager must consider projected annual demand (volume) relative to the multiple break-even points and choose the most appropriate number of machines, as Example 4 shows.

Example 4

A manager has the option of purchasing one, two, or three machines. Fixed costs and potential volumes are as follows:

Number of Machines	Total Annual Fixed Costs	Corresponding Range of Output
1	$ 9,600	0 to 300
2	15,000	301 to 600
3	$20,000	601 to 900

Variable cost is $10 per unit, and revenue is $40 per unit.

a. Determine the break-even point for each range.

b. If projected annual demand is between 580 and 660 units, how many machines should the manager purchase?

Solution

a. Compute the break-even point for each range using the formula $Q_{BEP} = FC/(R - v)$.

For one machine

$$Q_{BEP} = \frac{\$9,600}{\$40/unit - \$10/unit} = 320 \text{ units [not in range, so there is no BEP]}$$

For two machines $Q_{BEP} = \dfrac{\$15,000}{\$40/unit - \$10/unit} = 500$ units

For three machines $Q_{BEP} = \dfrac{\$20,000}{\$40/unit - \$10/unit} = 666.67$ units

b. Comparing the projected range of demand to the two ranges for which a break-even point occurs, you can see that the break-even point is 500, which is in the range 301 to 600. This means that even if demand is at the low end of the range, it would be above the break-even point and thus yield a profit. That is not true of range 601 to 900. At the top end of projected demand, the volume would still be less than the break-even point for that range, so there would be no profit. Hence, the manager should choose two machines.

Cost–volume analysis can be a valuable tool for comparing capacity alternatives if certain assumptions are satisfied:

1. One product is involved.
2. Everything produced can be sold.
3. The variable cost per unit is the same regardless of the volume.
4. Fixed costs do not change with volume changes, or they are step changes.
5. The revenue per unit is the same regardless of volume.
6. Revenue per unit exceeds variable cost per unit.

As with any quantitative tool, it is important to verify that the assumptions on which the technique is based are reasonably satisfied for a particular situation. For example, revenue per unit or variable cost per unit are not always constant. In addition, fixed costs may not be constant over the range of possible output. If demand is subject to random variations, one must take that into account in the analysis. Also, cost–volume analysis requires that fixed and variable costs can be separated, and this is sometimes exceedingly difficult to accomplish.

Cost–volume analysis works best with one product or a few products that have the same cost characteristics. Nevertheless, a notable benefit of cost–volume considerations is the conceptual framework it provides for integrating cost, revenue, and profit estimates into capacity decisions. If a proposal looks attractive using cost–volume analysis, the next step would be to develop cash flow models to see how it fares with the addition of time and more flexible cost functions.

FINANCIAL ANALYSIS

A problem that is universally encountered by managers is how to allocate scarce funds. A common approach is to use *financial analysis* to rank investment proposals.

Two important terms in financial analysis are *cash flow* and *present value:*

cash flow Difference between cash received from sales and other sources, and cash outflow for labor, material, overhead, and taxes.

Cash flow refers to the difference between the cash received from sales (of goods or services) and other sources (e.g., sale of old equipment) and the cash outflow for labor, materials, overhead, and taxes.

Present value expresses in current value the sum of all future cash flows of an investment proposal.

present value The sum, in current value, of all future cash flows of an investment proposal.

The three most commonly used methods of financial analysis are payback, present value, and internal rate of return.

Payback is a crude but widely used method that focuses on the length of time it will take for an investment to return its original cost. For example, an investment with an original cost of $6,000 and a monthly net cash flow of $1,000 has a payback period of six months. Payback ignores the *time value of money.* Its use is easier to rationalize for short-term than for long-term projects.

The *present value (PV)* method summarizes the initial cost of an investment, its estimated annual cash flows, and any expected salvage value in a single value called the *equivalent current value,* taking into account the time value of money (i.e., interest rates).

The *internal rate of return (IRR)* summarizes the initial cost, expected annual cash flows, and estimated future salvage value of an investment proposal in an *equivalent interest rate.* In other words, this method identifies the rate of return that equates the estimated future returns and the initial cost.

These techniques are appropriate when there is a high degree of *certainty* associated with estimates of future cash flows. In many instances, however, operations managers and other managers must deal with situations better described as risky or uncertain. When conditions of risk or uncertainty are present, decision theory is often applied.

DECISION THEORY

Decision theory is a helpful tool for financial comparison of alternatives under conditions of risk or uncertainty. It is suited to capacity decisions and to a wide range of other decisions managers must make. Decision theory is described in the supplement to this chapter.

WAITING-LINE ANALYSIS

Analysis of lines is often useful for designing service systems. Waiting lines have a tendency to form in a wide variety of service systems (e.g., airport ticket counters, telephone calls to a cable television company, hospital emergency rooms). The lines are symptoms of bottleneck operations. Analysis is useful in helping managers choose a capacity level that will be cost-effective through balancing the cost of having customers wait with the cost of providing additional capacity. It can aid in the determination of expected costs for various levels of service capacity.

This topic is described in Chapter 19.

Special service help when needed, such as transfers at the airport, can help keep lines moving at the ticket counter.

Operations Strategy

The strategic implications of capacity decisions can be enormous for an organization, impacting all areas of the organization. From an operations management standpoint, capacity decisions establish a set of conditions within which operations will be required to function. Hence, it is extremely important to include input from operations management people in making capacity decisions.

Flexibility can be a key issue in capacity decisions, although flexibility is not always an option, particularly in capital-intensive industries. However, where possible, flexibility allows an organization to be responsive (agile) to changes in the marketplace. Also, it reduces to a certain extent the dependence on long-range forecasts to accurately predict demand. And flexibility makes it easier for organizations to take advantage of technological and other innovations.

Bottleneck management can be a way to increase effective capacity, by scheduling non–bottleneck operations to achieve maximum utilization of bottleneck operations.

Summary

Capacity refers to a system's potential for producing goods or delivering services over a specified time interval. Capacity decisions are important because capacity is a ceiling on output and a major determinant of operating costs.

The capacity planning decision is one of the most important decisions that managers make. The capacity decision is strategic and long-term in nature, often involving a significant initial investment of capital. Capacity planning is particularly difficult in cases where returns will accrue over a lengthy period and risk is a major consideration.

A variety of factors can interfere with capacity utilization, so effective capacity is usually somewhat less than design capacity. These factors include facilities design and layout, human factors, product/service design, equipment failures, scheduling problems, and quality considerations.

Capacity planning involves long-term and short-term considerations. Long-term considerations relate to the overall level of capacity; short-term considerations relate to variations in capacity requirements due to seasonal, random, and irregular fluctuations in demand. Ideally, capacity will match demand. Thus, there is a close link between forecasting and capacity planning, particularly in the long term. In the short term, emphasis shifts to describing and coping with variations in demand.

Development of capacity alternatives is enhanced by taking a systems approach to planning, by recognizing that capacity increments are often acquired in chunks, by designing flexible systems, and by considering product/service complements as a way of dealing with various patterns of demand.

In evaluating capacity alternatives. a manager must consider both quantitative and qualitative aspects. Quantitative analysis usually reflects economic factors, and qualitative considerations include intangibles such as public opinion and personal preferences of managers. Cost–volume analysis can be useful for analyzing alternatives.

Key Terms

break-even point (BEP), 185
capacity, 174

cash flow, 188
present value, 188

Solved Problems

Problem 1

A firm's manager must decide whether to make or buy a certain item used in the production of vending machines. Cost and volume estimates are as follows:

	Make	**Buy**
Annual fixed cost	$150,000	None
Variable cost/unit	$60	$80
Annual volume (units)	12,000	12,000

a. Given these numbers, should the firm buy or make this item?

b. There is a possibility that volume could change in the future. At what volume would the manager be indifferent between making and buying?

Solution

a. Determine the annual cost of each alternative:

Total cost = Fixed cost + Volume × Variable cost

Make: $150,000 + 12,000($60) = $870,000
Buy: 0   + 12,000($80) = $960,000

Because the annual cost of making the item is less than the annual cost of buying it, the manager would reasonably choose to make the item.

b. To determine the volume at which the two choices would be equivalent, set the two total costs equal to each other, and solve for volume: $TC_{make} = TC_{buy}$. Thus, $150,000 + Q($60) = 0 + Q($80)$. Solving, $Q = 7,500$ units. Therefore, at a volume of 7,500 units a year, the manager would be indifferent between making and buying. For lower volumes, the choice would be to buy, and for higher volumes, the choice would be to make.

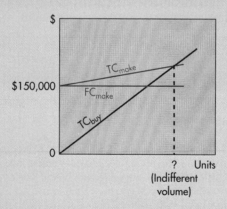

Problem 2

A small firm produces and sells novelty items in a five-state area. The firm expects to consolidate assembly of its electric turtle line at a single location. Currently, operations are in three widely scattered locations. The leading candidate for location will have a monthly fixed cost of $42,000 and variable costs of $3 per turtle. Turtles sell for $7 each. Prepare a table that shows total profits, fixed costs, variable costs, and revenues for monthly volumes of 10,000, 12,000, and 15,000 units. What is the break-even point?

Solution

Revenue = $7 per unit
Variable cost = $3 per unit

Fixed cost = $42,000 per month

Profit = $Q(R - v) - FC$

Total cost = $FC + v \times Q$

Volume	Total Revenue	Total VC	Fixed Cost	Total Cost	Total Profit
10,000	$ 70,000	$30,000	$42,000	$72,000	$(2,000)
12,000	84,000	36,000	42,000	78,000	6,000
15,000	105,000	45,000	42,000	87,000	18,000

$$Q_{BEP} = \frac{FC}{R - v} = \frac{\$42,000}{\$7 - \$3} = 10,500 \text{ units per month}$$

Refer to Problem 2. Develop an equation that can be used to compute profit for any volume. Use that equation to determine profit when volume equals 22,000 units.   **Problem 3**

Solution

Profit = $Q(R - v) - FC = Q(\$7 - \$3) - \$42,000 = \$4Q - \$42,000$

For $Q = 22,000$, profit is

$\$4(22,000) - \$42,000 = \$46,000$

A manager must decide which type of equipment to buy, Type A or Type B. Type A equipment   **Problem 4**
costs $15,000 each, and Type B costs $11,000 each. The equipment can be operated 8 hours a
day, 250 days a year.

Either machine can be used to perform two types of chemical analysis, C1 and C2. Annual
service requirements and processing times are shown in the following table. Which type of
equipment should be purchased, and how many of that type will be needed? The goal is to minimize total purchase cost.

Analysis Type	Annual Volume	PROCESSING TIME PER ANALYSIS (HR)	
		C1	C2
C1	1,200	1	2
C2	900	3	2

Total processing time (annual volume × processing time per analysis) needed by type of equip-   **Solution**
ment:

Analysis Type	A	B
C1	1,200	2,400
C2	2,700	1,800
Total	3,900	4,200

Total processing time available per piece of equipment is 8 hours/day × 250 days/year = 2,000.
Hence, one piece can handle 2,000 hours of analysis, two pieces of equipment can handle 4,000
hours, etc.

Given the total processing requirements, two of Type A would be needed, for a total cost of
2 × $15,000 = $30,000, or three of Type B, for a total cost of 3 × $11,000 = $33,000. Thus,
two pieces of Type A would have sufficient capacity to handle the load at a lower cost than three
of Type B.

1. Contrast design capacity and effective capacity.   **Discussion and**
2. List and briefly explain three factors that may inhibit capacity utilization.   **Review Questions**
3. How do long-term and short-term capacity considerations differ?
4. Give an example of a good and a service that exhibit these seasonal demand patterns:
   a. Annual
   b. Monthly

    c. Weekly

    d. Daily

5. Give some examples of building flexibility into system design.

6. Why is it important to adopt a "big picture" approach to capacity planning?

7. What is meant by "capacity in chunks," and why is that a factor in capacity planning?

8. What kinds of capacity problems do many elementary and secondary schools periodically experience? What are some alternatives to deal with those problems?

9. How can a systems approach to capacity planning be useful?

10. How do capacity decisions influence productivity?

11. Why is it important to match process capabilities with product requirements?

12. Briefly discuss how uncertainty affects capacity decisions.

13. Discuss the importance of capacity planning in deciding on the number of police officers or fire trucks to have on duty at a given time.

Memo Writing Exercises

1. Write a short memo to your boss, Al Thomas, outlining the general impact on break-even quantities of an increase in the proportion of automation in a process.

2. Write a one-page memo to Don Jones, a production supervisor. Don has questioned your practice of sometimes scheduling production that is below capacity, resulting in less than full utilization of personnel and equipment.

Problems

1. A producer of pottery is considering the addition of a new plant to absorb the backlog of demand that now exists. The primary location being considered will have fixed costs of $9,200 per month and variable costs of 70 cents per unit produced. Each item is sold to retailers at a price that averages 90 cents.

   a. What volume per month is required in order to break even?

   b. What profit would be realized on a monthly volume of 61,000 units? 87,000 units?

   c. What volume is needed to obtain a profit of $16,000 per month?

   d. What volume is needed to provide a revenue of $23,000 per month?

   e. Plot the total cost and total revenue lines.

2. A small firm intends to increase the capacity of a bottleneck operation by adding a new machine. Two alternatives, A and B, have been identified, and the associated costs and revenues have been estimated. Annual fixed costs would be $40,000 for A and $30,000 for B; variable costs per unit would be $10 for A and $12 for B; and revenue per unit would be $15 for A and $16 for B.

   a. Determine each alternative's break-even point in units.

   b. At what volume of output would the two alternatives yield the same profit?

   c. If expected annual demand is 12,000 units, which alternative would yield the higher profit?

3. A producer of felt-tip pens has received a forecast of demand of 30,000 pens for the coming month from its marketing department. Fixed costs of $25,000 per month are allocated to the felt-tip operation, and variable costs are 37 cents per pen.

   a. Find the break-even quantity if pens sell for $1 each.

   b. At what price must pens be sold to obtain a monthly profit of $15,000, assuming that estimated demand materializes?

4. A real estate agent is considering installing a cellular telephone in her car. There are three billing plans to choose from, all of which involve a weekly charge of $20. Plan A has a cost of $0.45 a minute for daytime calls and $0.20 a minute for evening calls. Plan B has a charge of $0.55 a minute for daytime calls and a charge of $0.15 a minute for evening calls. Plan C has a flat rate of $80 with 200 minutes of calls allowed per week and a cost of $0.40 per minute beyond that, day or evening.

   a. Determine the total charge under each plan for this case: 120 minutes of day calls and 40 minutes of evening calls in a week.

   b. Prepare a graph that shows total weekly cost for each plan versus daytime call minutes.

    c. If the agent will use the service for daytime calls, over what range of call minutes will each plan be optimal?

5. Refer to Problem 4. Suppose that the agent expects both daytime and evening calls. At what point (i.e., percentage of call minutes for daytime calls) would she be indifferent between plans A and B?

6. A firm plans to begin production of a new small appliance. The manager must decide whether to purchase the motors for the appliance from a vendor at $7 each or to produce them in-house. Either of two processes could be used for in-house production; one would have an annual fixed cost of $160,000 and a variable cost of $5 per unit, and the other would have an annual fixed cost of $190,000 and a variable cost of $4 per unit. Determine the range of annual volume for which each of the alternatives would be best.

7. A manager is trying to decide whether to purchase a certain part or to have it produced internally. Internal production could use either of two processes. One would entail a variable cost of $17 per unit and an annual fixed cost of $200,000; the other would entail a variable cost of $14 per unit and an annual fixed cost of $240,000. Three vendors are willing to provide the part. Vendor A has a price of $20 per unit for any volume up to 30,000 units. Vendor B has a price of $22 per unit for demand of 1,000 units or less, and $18 per unit for larger quantities. Vendor C offers a price of $21 per unit for the first 1,000 units, and $19 per unit for additional units.

    a. If the manager anticipates an annual volume of 10,000 units, which alternative would be best from a cost standpoint? For 20,000 units, which alternative would be best?

    b. Determine the range for which each alternative is best. Are there any alternatives that are never best? Which?

8. A company manufactures a product using two machine cells. Each cell has a design capacity of 250 units per day and an effective capacity of 230 units per day. At present, actual output averages 200 units per cell, but the manager estimates that productivity improvements soon will increase output to 225 units per day. Annual demand is currently 50,000 units. It is forecasted that within two years, annual demand will triple. The company could produce at the rate of 400 per day using available capacity. How many cells should the company plan to produce to satisfy predicted demand under these conditions? Assume 240 workdays per year.

9. A manager must decide which type of machine to buy, A, B, or C. Machine costs are:

Machine	Cost
A	$40,000
B	$30,000
C	$80,000

    Product forecasts and processing times on the machines are as follows:

Product	Annual Demand	PROCESSING TIME PER UNIT (MINUTES) A	B	C
1	16,000	3	4	2
2	12,000	4	4	3
3	6,000	5	6	4
4	30,000	2	2	1

    Assume that only purchasing costs are being considered. Which machine would have the lowest total cost, and how many of that machine would be needed? Machines operate 10 hours a day, 250 days a year.

10. Refer to Problem 9. Consider this additional information: The machines differ in terms of hourly operating costs: The A machines have an hourly operating cost of $10 each, B machines have an hourly operating cost of $11 each, and C machines have an hourly operating cost of $12 each. Which alternative would be selected, and how many machines, in order to minimize total cost while satisfying capacity processing requirements?

11. A manager must decide how many machines of a certain type to purchase. Each machine can process 100 customers per hour. One machine will result in a fixed cost of $2,000 per day,

while two machines will result in a fixed cost of $3,800 per day. Variable costs will be $20 per customer, and revenue will be $45 per customer.

  a. Determine the break-even point for each range.

  b. If estimated demand is 90 to 120 customers per hour, how many machines should be purchased?

12. The manager of a car wash must decide whether to have one or two wash lines. One line will mean a fixed cost of $6,000 a month, and two lines will mean a fixed cost of $10,500 a month. Each line would be able to process 15 cars an hour. Variable costs will be $3 per car, and revenue will be $5.95 per car. The manager projects an average demand of between 14 and 18 cars an hour. Would you recommend one or two lines? The car wash is open 300 hours a month.

OPERATIONS TOUR

High Acres Landfill

The High Acres Landfill is located on a 70-acre site outside Fairport, New York. Opened in 1971, it is licensed to handle residential, commercial, and industrial nonhazardous waste. The landfill has 27 employees, and it receives approximately 900 tons of waste per day.

The public often has certain preconceived notions about a landfill, chief among them that landfills are dirty and unpleasant. However, a visit to the landfill dispelled some of those misconceptions. The entrance is nicely landscaped. Most of the site is planted with grass and a few trees. Although unpleasant odors can emanate from arriving trucks or at the dump site, the remainder of the landfill is relatively free of odors.

A major portion of the landfill consists of a large hill within which the waste is buried. Initially, the landfill began not as a hill but as a large hole in the ground. After a number of years of depositing waste, the hole eventually was filled. From that point on, as additional layers were added, the landfill began to take the shape of a flattop hill. Each layer is a little narrower than the preceding one, giving the hill a slope. The sides of the

hill are planted with grass. Only the "working face" along the top remains unplanted. When the designated capacity is exhausted (this may take another 10 years), the landfill will be closed to further waste disposal. The site will be converted into a public park with hiking trails and picnic and recreation areas, and given to the town.

The construction and operation of landfills are subject to numerous state and federal regulations. For example, nonpermeable liners must be placed on the bottom and sides of the landfill to prevent leakage of liquids into the groundwater. (Independent firms monitor groundwater to determine if there is any leakage into wells placed around the perimeter of the hill.) Mindful of public opinion, every effort is made to minimize the amount of time that waste is left exposed. At the end of each day, the waste that has been deposited in the landfill is compacted and covered with six inches of soil.

The primary source of income for the landfill is the fees it charges users. The landfill also generates income from methane gas, a by-product of organic waste decomposition, that accumulates within the landfill. A collection system is in place to capture and extract the gas from the landfill, and it is then sold to the local power company. Also, the landfill has a composting operation in which leaves and other yard wastes are converted into mulch.

Part of the liner construction of a new landfill at the High Acres Landfill and Recycling Center in Fairport, New York. The hill in the background is a "closed" landfill, which has been through final cover.

Bolwijn, P. T., and T. Kumpe. "Manufacturing in the 1990's—Productivity, Flexibility, and Innovation." *Long Range Planning* 23, no. 4 (1990), pp. 44–57.

Cohen, Morris, and Uday M. Apte. *Manufacturing Automation.* Burr Ridge, IL: Richard D. Irwin, 1997.

Ettlie, John, and Henry Stoll, *Managing the Design-Manufacturing Process.* New York: McGraw-Hill, 1990.

Hill, Terry. *Manufacturing Strategy.* 2nd ed. Burr Ridge, IL: Richard D. Irwin, 1994.

Monroe, Joseph. "Strategic Use of Technology." *California Management Review,* Summer 1989, pp. 91–110.

Moore, Franklin, and Thomas E. Hendrick. *Production/Operations Management.* 9th ed. Burr Ridge, IL: Richard D. Irwin, 1985.

Upton, David. "The Management of Manufacturing Flexibility." *California Management Review* 36, no. 2, 1994, pp. 72–89.

Upton, David. "What Really Makes Factories Flexible." *Harvard Business Review,* July–August 1995, pp. 74–84.

Decision Theory

SUPPLEMENT OUTLINE

Introduction, 197

Causes of Poor Decisions, 197

Decision Environments, 198

Decision Making under
  Certainty, 198

Decision Making under
  Uncertainty, 199

Decision Making under Risk, 200

Decision Trees, 201

Expected Value of Perfect
  Information, 203

Sensitivity Analysis, 204

Summary, 206

Key Terms, 206

Solved Problems, 206

Discussion and Review
  Questions, 210

Problems, 210

Selected Bibliography and Further
  Reading, 215

LEARNING OBJECTIVES

*After completing this supplement,
you should be able to:*

1 Describe the different
  environments under which
  operations decisions are made.

2 Describe and use techniques that
  apply to decision making under
  uncertainty.

3 Describe and use the expected-
  value approach.

4 Construct a decision tree and use
  it to analyze a problem.

5 Compute the expected value of
  perfect information.

6 Conduct sensitivity analysis on a
  simple decision problem.

Introduction

Decision theory represents a general approach to decision making. It is suitable for a wide range of operations management decisions. Among them are capacity planning, product and service design, equipment selection, and location planning. Decisions that lend themselves to a decision theory approach tend to be characterized by these elements:

1. A set of possible future conditions exists that will have a bearing on the results of the decision.
2. A list of alternatives for the manager to choose from.
3. A known payoff for each alternative under each possible future condition.

To use this approach, a decision maker would employ this process:

1. Identify the possible future conditions (e.g., demand will be low, medium, or high; the number of contracts awarded will be one, two, or three; the competitor will or will not introduce a new product). These are called *states of nature.*
2. Develop a list of possible *alternatives,* one of which may be to do nothing.
3. Determine or estimate the *payoff* associated with each alternative for every possible future condition.
4. If possible, estimate the *likelihood* of each possible future condition.
5. Evaluate alternatives according to some *decision criterion* (e.g., maximize expected profit), and select the best alternative.

The information for a decision is often summarized in a **payoff table,** which shows the expected payoffs for each alternative under the various possible states of nature. These tables are helpful in choosing among alternatives because they facilitate comparison of alternatives. Consider the following payoff table, which illustrates a capacity planning problem.

payoff table Table showing the expected payoffs for each alternative in every possible state of nature.

Alternatives	POSSIBLE FUTURE DEMAND		
	Low	Moderate	High
Small facility	$10*	$10	$10
Medium facility	7	12	12
Large facility	(4)	2	16

*Present value in $ millions.

The payoffs are shown in the body of the table. In this instance, the payoffs are in terms of present values, which represent equivalent current dollar values of expected future income less costs. This is a convenient measure because it places all alternatives on a comparable basis. If a small facility is built, the payoff will be the same for all three possible states of nature. For a medium facility, low demand will have a present value of $7 million, whereas both moderate and high demand will have present values of $12 million. A large facility will have a loss of $4 million if demand is low, a present value of $2 million if demand is moderate, and a present value of $16 million if demand is high.

The problem for the decision maker is to select one of the alternatives, taking the present value into account.

Evaluation of the alternatives differs according to the degree of certainty associated with the possible future conditions.

Causes of Poor Decisions

Despite the best efforts of a manager, a decision occasionally turns out poorly due to unforeseeable circumstances. Luckily, such occurrences are not common. Often, failures can be traced to some combination of mistakes in the decision process, *bounded rationality,* or *suboptimization.*

In many cases, managers fail to appreciate the importance of each step in the decision-making process. They may skip a step or not devote enough effort to completing it before jumping to the next step. Sometimes this happens owing to a manager's style of making quick decisions or a failure to recognize the consequences of a poor decision. The manager's ego can be a factor. This sometimes happens when the manager has experienced a series of successes—important decisions that turned out right. Some managers then get the impression that they can do no wrong. But they soon run into trouble, which is usually enough to bring them back down to earth. Other managers seem oblivious to negative results and continue the process they associate with their previous successes, not recognizing that some of that success may have been due more to luck than to any special abilities of their own. A part of the problem may be the manager's unwillingness to admit a mistake. Yet other managers demonstrate an inability to make a decision; they stall long past the time when the decision should have been rendered.

Of course, not all managers fall into these traps—it seems safe to say that the majority do not. Even so, this does not necessarily mean that every decision works out as expected. Another factor with which managers must contend is **bounded rationality,** or the limits imposed on decision making by costs, human abilities, time, technology, and the availability of information. Because of these limitations, managers cannot always expect to reach decisions that are optimal in the sense of providing the best possible outcome (e.g., highest profit, least cost). Instead, they must often resort to achieving a *satisfactory* solution.

Still another cause of poor decisions is that organizations typically departmentalize decisions. Naturally, there is a great deal of justification for the use of departments in terms of overcoming span-of-control problems and human limitations. However, **suboptimization** can occur. This is a result of different departments attempting to reach a solution that is optimum for each. Unfortunately, what is optimal for one department may not be optimal for the organization as a whole.

bounded rationality The limitations on decision making caused by costs, human abilities, time, technology, and availability of information.

suboptimization The result of different departments each attempting to reach a solution that is optimum for that department.

Decision Environments

Operations management decision environments are classified according to the degree of certainty present. There are three basic categories: certainty, risk, and uncertainty.

Certainty means that relevant parameters such as costs, capacity, and demand have known values.

Risk means that certain parameters have probabilistic outcomes.

Uncertainty means that it is impossible to assess the likelihood of various possible future events.

Consider these situations:

1. Profit per unit is $5. You have an order for 200 units. How much profit will you make? (This is an example of *certainty* since unit profits and total demand are known.)
2. Profit is $5 per unit. Based on previous experience, there is a 50 percent chance of an order for 100 units and a 50 percent chance of an order for 200 units. What is expected profit? (This is an example of *risk* since demand outcomes are probabilistic.)
3. Profit is $5 per unit. The probabilities of potential demands are unknown. (This is an example of *uncertainty.*)

The importance of these different decision environments is that they require different analysis techniques. Some techniques are better suited for one category than for others. You should make note of the environments for which each technique is appropriate.

certainty Environment in which relevant parameters have known values.

risk Environment in which certain future events have probable outcomes.

uncertainty Environment in which it is impossible to assess the likelihood of various future events.

Decision Making under Certainty

When it is known for certain which of the possible future conditions will actually happen, the decision is usually relatively straightforward: Simply choose the alternative that has the best payoff under that state of nature. Example S-1 illustrates this.

Determine the best alternative in the payoff table on pg. 197 for each of the cases: It is known with certainty that demand will be: (*a*) low, (*b*) moderate, (*c*) high.

Example S-1

Solution

Choose the alternative with the highest payoff. Thus, if we know demand will be low, we would elect to build the small facility and realize a payoff of $10 million. If we know demand will be moderate, a medium factory would yield the highest payoff ($12 million versus either $10 or $2 million). For high demand, a large facility would provide the highest payoff.

Although complete certainty is rare in such situations, this kind of exercise provides some perspective on the analysis. Moreover, in some instances, there may be an opportunity to consider allocation of funds to research efforts, which may reduce or remove some of the uncertainty surrounding the states of nature.

Decision Making under Uncertainty

At the opposite extreme is complete uncertainty: no information is available on how likely the various states of nature are. Under those conditions, four possible decision criteria are *maximin, maximax, Laplace,* and *minimax regret.* These approaches can be defined as follows:

Maximin—Determine the worst possible payoff for each alternative, and choose the alternative that has the "best worst." The maximin approach is essentially a pessimistic one because it takes into account only the worst possible outcome for each alternative. The actual outcome may not be as bad as that, but this approach establishes a "guaranteed minimum."

maximin Choose the alternative with the best of the worst possible payoffs.

Maximax—Determine the best possible payoff, and choose the alternative with that payoff. The maximax approach is an optimistic, "go for it" strategy; it does not take into account any payoff other than the best.

maximax Choose the alternative with the best possible payoff.

Laplace—Determine the average payoff for each alternative, and choose the alternative with the best average. The Laplace approach treats the states of nature as equally likely.

Laplace Choose the alternative with the best average payoff of any of the alternatives.

Minimax regret—Determine the worst *regret* for each alternative, and choose the alternative with the "best worst." This approach seeks to minimize the difference between the payoff that is realized and the best payoff for each state of nature.

minimax regret Choose the alternative that has the least of the worst regrets.

The next two examples illustrate these decision criteria.

Example S-2

Referring to the payoff table on pg. 197, determine which alternative would be chosen under each of these strategies:

a. Maximin

b. Maximax

c. Laplace

Solution

a. Using maximin, the worst payoffs for the alternatives are:

Small facility:	$10 million
Medium facility:	7 million
Large facility:	−4 million

Hence, since $10 million is the best, choose to build the small facility using the maximin strategy.

b. Using maximax, the best payoffs are:

Small facility: $10 million

Medium facility: 12 million

Large facility: 16 million

The best overall payoff is the $16 million in the third row. Hence, the maximax criterion leads to building a large facility.

c. For the Laplace criterion, first find the row totals, and then divide each of those amounts by the number of states of nature (three in this case). Thus, we have:

	Row Total (in $ millions)	Row Average (in $ millions)
Small facility	$30	$10.00
Medium facility	31	10.33
Large facility	14	4.67

Because the medium facility has the highest average, it would be chosen under the Laplace criterion.

Example S–3

Solution

regret The difference between a given payoff and the best payoff for a state of nature.

Determine which alternative would be chosen using a minimax regret approach to the capacity planning program.

The first step in this approach is to prepare a table of **opportunity losses,** or **regrets.** To do this, subtract every payoff *in each column* from the best payoff in that column. For instance, in the first column, the best payoff is 10, so each of the three numbers in that column must be subtracted from 10. Going down the column, the regrets will be $10 - 10 = 0$, $10 - 7 = 3$, and $10 - (- 4) = 14$. In the second column, the best payoff is 12. Subtracting each payoff from 12 yields 2, 0, and 10. In the third column, 16 is the best payoff. The regrets are 6, 4, and 0. These results are summarized in a regret table:

	REGRETS (in $ millions)			
Alternatives	Low	Moderate	High	Worst
Small facility	$0	$2	$6	$6
Medium facility	3	0	4	4
Large facility	14	10	0	14

The second step is to identify the worst regret for each alternative. For the first alternative, the worst is 6; for the second, the worst is 4; and for the third, the worst is 14.

The best of these worst regrets would be chosen using minimax regret. The lowest regret is 4, which is for a medium facility. Hence, that alternative would be chosen.

Solved Problem 6 at the end of this supplement illustrates decision making under uncertainty when the payoffs represent costs.

The main weakness of these approaches (except for Laplace) is that they do not take into account *all* of the payoffs. Instead, they focus on the worst or best, and so they lose some information. Still, for a given set of circumstances, each has certain merits that can be helpful to a decision maker.

Decision Making under Risk

Between the two extremes of certainty and uncertainty lies the case of risk: The probability of occurrence for each state of nature is known. (Note that because the states are mutually exclusive and collectively exhaustive, these probabilities must add to 1.00.) A widely used approach under such circumstances is the *expected monetary value criterion*.

The expected value is computed for each alternative, and the one with the highest expected value is selected. The expected value is the sum of the payoffs for an alternative where each payoff is *weighted* by the probability for the relevant state of nature. Thus, the approach is:

Expected monetary value (EMV) criterion—Determine the expected payoff of each alternative, and choose the alternative that has the best expected payoff.

expected monetary value (EMV) criterion The best expected value among the alternatives.

Example S-4

Using the expected monetary value criterion, identify the best alternative for the previous payoff table for these probabilities: low = .30, moderate = .50, and high = .20.

Solution

Find the expected value of each alternative by multiplying the probability of occurrence for each state of nature by the payoff for that state of nature and summing them:

$$EV_{small} = .30(\$10) + .50(\$10) + .20(\$10) = \$10$$
$$EV_{medium} = .30(\$7) + .50(\$12) + .20(\$12) = \$10.5$$
$$EV_{large} = .30(-4) + .50(\$2) + .20(\$16) = \$3$$

Hence, choose the medium facility because it has the highest expected value.

The expected monetary value approach is most appropriate when a decision maker is neither risk averse nor risk seeking, but is risk neutral. Typically, well-established organizations with numerous decisions of this nature tend to use expected value because it provides an indication of the long-run, average payoff. That is, the expected-value amount (e.g., $10.5 million in the last example) is not an actual payoff but an expected or average amount that would be approximated if a large number of identical decisions were to be made. Hence, if a decision maker applies this criterion to a large number of similar decisions, the expected payoff for the total will approximate the sum of the individual expected payoffs.

Decision Trees

A **decision tree** is a schematic representation of the alternatives available to a decision maker and their possible consequences. The term gets its name from the treelike appearance of the diagram (see Figure 5S–1). Although tree diagrams can be used in place of a payoff table, they are particularly useful for analyzing situations that involve *sequential* decisions.

decision tree A schematic representation of the available alternatives and their possible consequences.

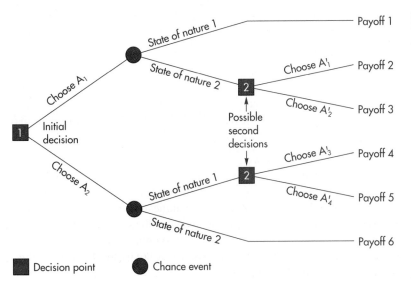

FIGURE 5S–1

Format of a decision tree

For instance, a manager may initially decide to build a small facility only to discover that demand is much higher than anticipated. In this case, the manager may then be called upon to make a subsequent decision on whether to expand or build an additional facility.

A decision tree is composed of a number of *nodes* that have *branches* emanating from them (see Figure 5S–1). Square nodes denote decision points, and circular nodes denote chance events. Read the tree from left to right. Branches leaving square nodes represent alternatives; branches leaving circular nodes represent chance events (i.e., the possible states of nature).

After the tree has been drawn, it is analyzed from *right to left*; that is, starting with the last decision that might be made. For each decision, choose the alternative that will yield the greatest return (or the lowest cost). If chance events follow a decision, choose the alternative that has the highest expected monetary value (or lowest expected cost).

Example S-5

A manager must decide on the size of a video arcade to construct. The manager has narrowed the choices to two: large or small. Information has been collected on payoffs, and a decision tree has been constructed. Analyze the decision tree and determine which initial alternative (build small or build large) should be chosen in order to maximize expected monetary value.

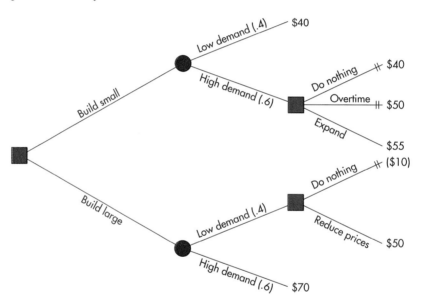

Solution

The dollar amounts at the branch ends indicate the estimated payoffs if the sequence of chance events and decisions that is traced back to the initial decision occurs. For example, if the initial decision is to build a small facility and it turns out that demand is low, the payoff will be $40 (thousand). Similarly, if a small facility is built, demand turns out high, and a later decision is made to expand, the payoff will be $55. The figures in parentheses on branches leaving the chance nodes indicate the probabilities of those states of nature. Hence, the probability of low demand is .4, and the probability of high demand is .6. Payoffs in parentheses indicate losses.

Analyze the decisions from right to left:

1. Determine which alternative would be selected for each possible second decision. For a small facility with high demand, there are three choices: *do nothing, work overtime,* and *expand.* Because *expand* has the highest payoff, you would choose it. Indicate this by placing a double slash through each of the other alternatives. Similarly, for a large facility with low demand, there are two choices: *do nothing* and *reduce prices.* You would choose *reduce prices* because it has the higher expected value, so a double slash is placed on the other branch.

2. Determine the product of the chance probabilities and their respective payoffs for the remaining branches:

Build small
Low demand	.4($40) = $16
High demand	.6($55) = 33

Build large
Low demand	.4($50) = 20
High demand	.6($70) = 42

3. Determine the expected value of each initial alternative:

Build small	$16 + $33 = $49
Build large	$20 + $42 = $62

Hence, the choice should be to build the large facility because it has a larger expected value than the small facility.

Expected Value of Perfect Information

In certain situations, it is possible to ascertain which state of nature will actually occur in the future. For instance, the choice of location for a restaurant may weigh heavily on whether a new highway will be constructed or whether a zoning permit will be issued. A decision maker may have probabilities for these states of nature; however, it may be possible to delay a decision until it is clear which state of nature will occur. This might involve taking an option to buy the land. If the state of nature is favorable, the option can be exercised; if it is unfavorable, the option can be allowed to expire. The question to consider is whether the cost of the option will be less than the expected gain due to delaying the decision (i.e., the expected payoff *above* the expected value). The expected gain is the *expected value of perfect information,* or EVPI.

Expected value of perfect information (EVPI)—the difference between the expected payoff with perfect information and the expected payoff under risk.

expected value of perfect information (EVPI) The difference between the expected payoff with perfect information and the expected payoff under risk.

Other possible ways of obtaining perfect information depend somewhat on the nature of the decision being made. Information about consumer preferences might come from market research, additional information about a product could come from product testing, or legal experts might be called on.

There are two ways to determine the EVPI. One is to compute the expected payoff under certainty and subtract the expected payoff under risk. That is,

$$\begin{array}{c}\text{Expected value of}\\\text{perfect information}\end{array} = \begin{array}{c}\text{Expected payoff}\\\text{under certainty}\end{array} - \begin{array}{c}\text{Expected payoff}\\\text{under risk}\end{array} \qquad (5S–1)$$

Example S-6

Using the information from Example S-4, determine the expected value of perfect information using Formula 5S–1.

Solution

First, compute the expected payoff under certainty. To do this, identify the best payoff under each state of nature. Then combine these by weighting each payoff by the probability of that state of nature and adding the amounts. Thus, the best payoff under low demand is $10, the best under moderate demand is $12, and the best under high demand is $16. The expected payoff under certainty is, then:

.30($10) + .50($12) + .20($16) = $12.2

The expected payoff under risk, as computed in Example 4, is $10.5. The EVPI is the difference between these:

EVPI = $12.2 − $10.5 = $1.7

This figure indicates the upper limit on the amount the decision maker should be willing to spend to obtain perfect information in this case. Thus, if the cost equals or exceeds this amount, the decision maker would be better off not spending additional money and simply going with the alternative that has the highest expected payoff.

A second approach is to use the regret table to compute the EVPI. To do this, find the expected regret for each alternative. The minimum expected regret is equal to the EVPI.

Example S–7

Determine the expected value of perfect information for the capacity-planning problem using the expected regret approach.

Solution

Using information from Examples 2, 3, and 4, we can compute the expected regret for each alternative. Thus:

Small facility	.30(0) + .50(2) + .20(6) = 2.2
Medium facility	.30(3) + .50(0) + .20(4) = 1.7 [minimum]
Large facility	.30(14) + .50(10) + .20(0) = 9.2

The lowest expected regret is 1.7, which is associated with the second alternative. Hence, the EVPI is $1.7 million, which agrees with the previous example using the other approach.

Sensitivity Analysis

Generally speaking, both the payoffs and the probabilities in this kind of a decision problem are estimated values. Consequently, it can be useful for the decision maker to have some indication of how sensitive the choice of an alternative is to changes in one or more of these values. Unfortunately, it is impossible to consider all possible combinations of every variable in a typical problem. Nevertheless, there are certain things a decision maker can do to judge the sensitivity of probability estimates.

sensitivity analysis
Determining the range of probability for which an alternative has the best expected payoff.

Sensitivity analysis provides a range of probability over which the choice of alternatives would remain the same. The approach illustrated here is useful when there are two states of nature. It involves constructing a graph and then using algebra to determine a range of probabilities for which a given solution is best. In effect, the graph provides a visual indication of the range of probability over which the various alternatives are optimal, and the algebra provides exact values of the endpoints of the ranges. Example S–8 illustrates the procedure.

Example S–8

Given the following table, determine the range of probability for state of nature #2, that is, $P(2)$, for which each alternative is optimal under the expected-value approach.

		STATE OF NATURE	
		#1	**#2**
	A	4	12
Alternative	B	16	2
	C	12	8

Solution

First, plot each alternative relative to $P(2)$. To do this, plot the #1 value on the left side of the graph and the #2 value on the right side. For instance, for alternative A, plot 4 on the left side of the graph and 12 on the right side. Then connect these two points with a straight line. The three alternatives are plotted on the graph as shown below.

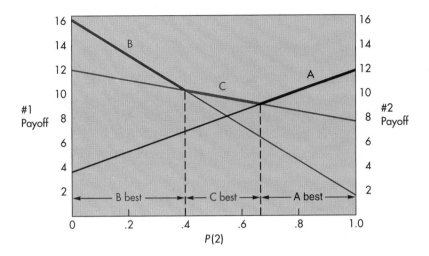

The graph shows the range of values of $P(2)$ over which each alternative is optimal. Thus, for low values of $P(2)$ [and thus high values of $P(1)$, since $P(1) + P(2) = 1.0$], alternative B will have the highest expected value; for intermediate values of $P(2)$, alternative C is best; and for higher values of $P(2)$, alternative A is best.

To find exact values of the ranges, determine where the upper parts of the lines intersect. Note that at the intersections, the two alternatives represented by the lines would be equivalent in terms of expected value. Hence, the decision maker would be indifferent between the two at that point. To determine the intersections, you must obtain the equation of each line. This is relatively simple to do. Because these are straight lines, they have the form $y = a + bx$, where a is the y-intercept value at the left axis, b is the slope of the line, and x is $P(2)$. Slope is defined as the change in y for a one-unit change in x. In this type of problem, the distance between the two vertical axes is 1.0. Consequently, the slope of each line is equal to the right-hand value minus the left-hand value. The slopes and equations are:

	#1	#2	Slope	Equation
A	4	12	$12 - 4 = +8$	$4 + 8P(2)$
B	16	2	$2 - 16 = -14$	$16 - 14P(2)$
C	12	8	$8 - 12 = -4$	$12 - 4P(2)$

From the graph, we can see that alternative B is best from $P(2) = 0$ to the point where that straight line intersects the straight line of alternative C, and that begins the region where C is better. To find that point, solve for the value of $P(2)$ at their intersection. This requires setting the two equations equal to each other and solving for $P(2)$. Thus,

$$16 - 14P(2) = 12 - 4P(2)$$

Rearranging terms yields

$$4 = 10P(2)$$

Solving yields $P(2) = .40$. Thus, alternative B is best from $P(2) = 0$ up to $P(2) = .40$. B and C are equivalent at $P(2) = .40$.

Alternative C is best from that point until its line intersects alternative A's line. To find that intersection, set those two equations equal and solve for $P(2)$. Thus,

$$4 + 8P(2) = 12 - 4P(2)$$

Rearranging terms results in

$$12P(2) = 8$$

Solving yields $P(2) = .67$. Thus, alternative C is best from $P(2) > .40$ up to $P(2) = .67$, where A and C are equivalent. For values of $P(2)$ greater than .67 up to $P(2) = 1.0$, A is best.

Note: If a problem calls for ranges with respect to $P(1)$, find the $P(2)$ ranges as above, and then subtract each $P(2)$ from 1.00 (e.g., .40 becomes .60, and .67 becomes .33).

Summary

Decision making is an integral part of operations management.

Decision theory is a general approach to decision making that is useful in many different aspects of operations management. Decision theory provides a framework for the analysis of decisions. It includes a number of techniques that can be classified according to the degree of uncertainty associated with a particular decision problem. Two visual tools useful for analyzing some decision problems are decision trees and graphical sensitivity analysis.

Key Terms

bounded rationality, 198
certainty, 198
decision tree, 201
expected monetary value (EMV) criterion, 201
expected value of perfect information (EVPI), 203
Laplace, 199
maximax, 199
maximin, 199

minimax regret, 199
opportunity losses, 200
payoff table, 197
regret, 200
risk, 198
sensitivity analysis, 204
suboptimization, 198
uncertainty, 198

Solved Problems

The following solved problems refer to this payoff table:

		New Bridge Built	No New Bridge
Alternative capacity	A	1	14
for new store	B	2	10
	C	4	6

where A = small, B = medium, and C = large.

Problem 1

Assume the payoffs represent profits. Determine the alternative that would be chosen under each of these decision criteria:

a. Maximin.

b. Maximax.

c. Laplace.

	New Bridge	No New Bridge	Maximin (worst)	Maximax (best)	Laplace (average)
A	1	14	1	14 [best]	$15 \div 2 = 7.5$ [best]
B	2	10	2	10	$12 \div 2 = 6$
C	4	6	4 [best]	6	$10 \div 2 = 5$

Solution

Thus, the alternatives chosen would be C under maximin, A under maximax, and A under Laplace.

Problem 2

Using graphical sensitivity analysis, determine the probability for no new bridge for which each alternative would be optimal.

Plot a straight line for each alternative. Do this by plotting the payoff for new bridge on the left axis and the payoff for no new bridge on the right axis and then connecting the two points. Each line represents the expected profit for an alternative for the entire range of probability of no new bridge. Because the lines represent expected profit, the line that is highest for a given value of P (no new bridge) is optimal. Thus, from the graph, you can see that for low values of this probability, alternative C is best, and for higher values, alternative A is best (B is never the highest line, so it is never optimal).

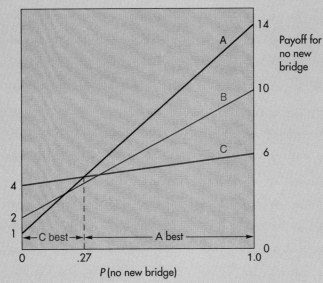

The dividing line between the ranges where C and A are optimal occurs where the two lines intersect. To find that probability, first formulate the equation for each line. To do this, let the intersection with the left axis be the y intercept; the slope equals the right-side payoff minus the left-side payoff. Thus, for C you have $4 + (6 − 4)P$, which is $4 + 2P$. For A, $1 + (14 − 1)P$, which is $1 + 13P$. Setting these two equal to each other, you can solve for P:

$$4 + 2P = 1 + 13P$$

Solving, $P = .27$. Therefore, the ranges for P(no new bridge) are:

A: $.27 < P \le 1.00$
B: never optimal
C: $0 \le P < .27$

Using the information in the payoff table, develop a table of regrets, and then:

a. Determine the alternative that would be chosen under minimax regret.

b. Determine the expected value of perfect information using the regret table, assuming that the probability of a new bridge being built is .60.

To obtain the regrets, subtract all payoffs in each column from the best payoff in the column. The regrets are:

	New Bridge	No New Bridge
A	3	0
B	2	4
C	0	8

a. Minimax regret involves finding the worst regret for each alternative and then choosing the alternative that has the "best" worst. Thus, you would choose A:

	Worst
A	3 [best]
B	4
C	8

b. Once the regret table has been developed, you can compute the EVPI as the *smallest* expected regret. Since the probability of a new bridge is given as .60, we can deduce that the probability of no new bridge is $1.00 - .60 = .40$. The expected regrets are:

A: $.60(3) + .40(0) = 1.80$

B: $.60(2) + .40(4) = 2.80$

C: $.60(0) + .40(8) = 3.20$

Hence, the EVPI is 1.80.

Problem 4

Using the probabilities of .60 for a new bridge and .40 for no new bridge, compute the expected value of each alternative in the payoff table, and identify the alternative that would be selected under the expected-value approach.

Solution

A: $.60(1) + .40(14) = 6.20$ [best]

B: $.60(2) + .40(10) = 5.20$

C: $.60(4) + .40(6) = 4.80$

Problem 5

Compute the EVPI using the information from the previous problem.

Solution

Using formula (5S–1), the EVPI is the expected payoff under certainty minus the maximum expected value. The expected payoff under certainty involves multiplying the best payoff in each column by the column probability and then summing those amounts. The best payoff in the first column is 4, and the best in the second is 14. Thus,

Expected payoff under certainty $= .60(4) + .40(14) = 8.00$

Then

EVPI $= 8.00 - 6.20 = 1.80$

(This agrees with the result obtained in Solved Problem 3*b.*)

Excel solution:

Placing the problem data in the cell positions shown, the expected monetary value (EMV) for each alternative is shown in column J.

Then, the overall EMV is obtained in column J as the maximum of the values in J5, J6, and J7.

The EVPI is obtained using the Opportunity Loss Table by summing the product of the maximum in column C4 and the probability in C4, and the product of the maximum in column D and the probability in D4.

Suppose that the values in the payoff table represent *costs* instead of profits.   **Problem 6**

a. Determine the choice that you would make under each of these strategies: maximin, *minimin*, and Laplace.*
b. Develop the regret table, and identify the alternative chosen using minimax regret. Then find the EVPI if P(new bridge) = .60.
c. Using sensitivity analysis, determine the range of P(no new bridge) for which each alternative would be optimal.
d. If P(new bridge) = .60 and P(no new bridge) = .40, find the alternative chosen to minimize expected cost.

*Note: Minimin is the reverse of maximax; for costs minimin identifies the lowest (best) cost.   **Solution**

	New Bridge	No New Bridge	Maximin (worst)	Minimin (best)	Laplace (average)
A	1	14	14	1 [best]	$15 \div 2 = 7.5$
B	2	10	10	2	$12 \div 2 = 6$
C	4	6	6 [best]	4	$10 \div 2 = 5$ [best]

b. Develop the regret table by subtracting the *lowest cost* in each column from each of the values in the column. (Note that none of the values is negative.)

	New Bridge	No New Bridge	Worst
A	0	8	8
B	1	4	4
C	3	0	3 [best]

EVPI = .60(3) + .40(0) = 1.80

c. The graph is identical to that shown in Solved Problem 2. However, the lines now represent expected *costs*, so the best alternative for a given value of P(no new bridge) is the *lowest* line. Hence, for very low values of P(no new bridge), A is best; for intermediate values, B is best; and for high values, C is best. You can set the equations of A and B, and B and C, equal to each other in order to determine the values of P(no new bridge) at their intersections. Thus,

A = B: $1 + 13P = 2 + 8P$; solving, $P = .20$
B = C: $2 + 8P = 4 + 2P$; solving, $P = .33$

Hence, the ranges are:

A best: $0 \leq P < .20$
B best: $.20 < P < .33$
C best: $.33 < P \leq 1.00$

d. Expected-value computations are the same whether the values represent costs or profits. Hence, the expected payoffs for costs are the same as the expected payoffs for profits that were computed in Solved Problem 4. However, now you want the alternative that has the *lowest* expected payoff rather than the one with the highest payoff. Consequently, alternative C is the best because its expected payoff is the lowest of the three.

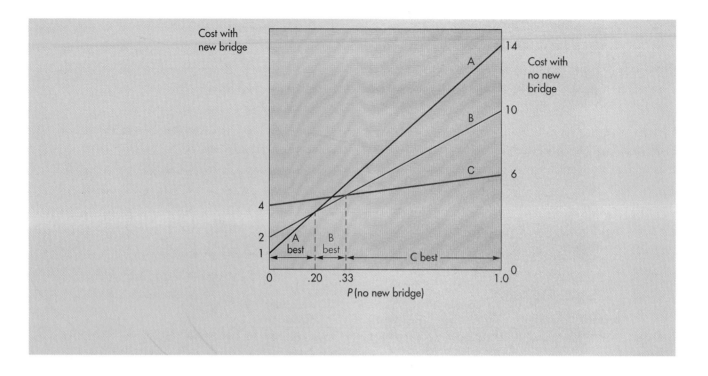

**Discussion and
Review Questions**

1. What is the chief role of the operations manager?
2. List the steps in the decision-making process.
3. Explain the term *bounded rationality.*
4. Explain the term *suboptimization.*
5. What are some of the reasons for poor decisions?
6. What information is contained in a payoff table?
7. What is sensitivity analysis, and how can it be useful to a decision maker?
8. Contrast maximax and maximin decision strategies. Under what circumstances is each appropriate?
9. Under what circumstances is expected monetary value appropriate as a decision criterion? When isn't it appropriate?
10. Explain or define each of these terms:
    a. Laplace criterion.
    b. Minimax regret.
    c. Expected value.
    d. Expected value of perfect information.
11. What information does a decision maker need in order to perform an expected-value analysis of a problem? What options are available to the decision maker if the probabilities of the states of nature are unknown? Can you think of a way you might use sensitivity analysis in such a case?
12. Suppose a manager is using maximum EMV as a basis for making a capacity decision and, in the process, obtains a result in which there is a virtual tie between two of the seven alternatives. How is the manager to make a decision?

Problems

1. A small building contractor has recently experienced two successive years in which work opportunities exceeded the firm's capacity. The contractor must now make a decision on capacity for next year. Estimated profits under each of the two possible states of nature are as shown in the table below. Which alternative should be selected if the decision criterion is:

  a. Maximax?

  b. Maximin?

  c. Laplace?

  d. Minimax regret?

	NEXT YEAR'S DEMAND	
Alternative	**Low**	**High**
Do nothing	$50*	$60
Expand	20	80
Subcontract	40	70

*Profit in $ thousands.

2. Refer to Problem 1. Suppose after a certain amount of discussion, the contractor is able to sub-jectively assess the probabilities of low and high demand: $P(\text{low}) = .3$ and $P(\text{high}) = .7$.

  a. Determine the expected profit of each alternative. Which alternative is best? Why?

  b. Analyze the problem using a decision tree. Show the expected profit of each alternative on the tree.

  c. Compute the expected value of perfect information. How could the contractor use this knowledge?

3. Refer to Problems 1 and 2. Construct a graph that will enable you to perform sensitivity analy-sis on the problem. Over what range of $P(\text{high})$ would the alternative of doing nothing be best? Expand? Subcontract?

4. A firm that plans to expand its product line must decide whether to build a small or a large fa-cility to produce the new products. If it builds a small facility and demand is low, the net pre-sent value after deducting for building costs will be $400,000. If demand is high, the firm can either maintain the small facility or expand it. Expansion would have a net present value of $450,000, and maintaining the small facility would have a net present value of $50,000.

  If a large facility is built and demand is high, the estimated net present value is $800,000. If demand turns out to be low, the net present value will be $-$10,000.

  The probability that demand will be high is estimated to be .60, and the probability of low demand is estimated to be .40.

  a. Analyze using a tree diagram.

  b. Compute the EVPI. How could this information be used?

  c. Determine the range over which each alternative would be best in terms of the value of $P(\text{demand low})$.

5. Determine the course of action that has the highest expected payoff for the decision tree on page 212.

6. The lease of Theme Park, Inc., is about to expire. Management must decide whether to renew the lease for another 10 years or to relocate near the site of a proposed motel. The town plan-ning board is currently debating the merits of granting approval to the motel. A consultant has estimated the net present value of Theme Park's two alternatives under each state of nature as shown below. What course of action would you recommend using:

  a. Maximax?

  b. Maximin?

  c. Laplace?

  d. Minimax regret?

Options	Motel Approved	Motel Rejected
Renew	$ 500,000	$4,000,000
Relocate	5,000,000	100,000

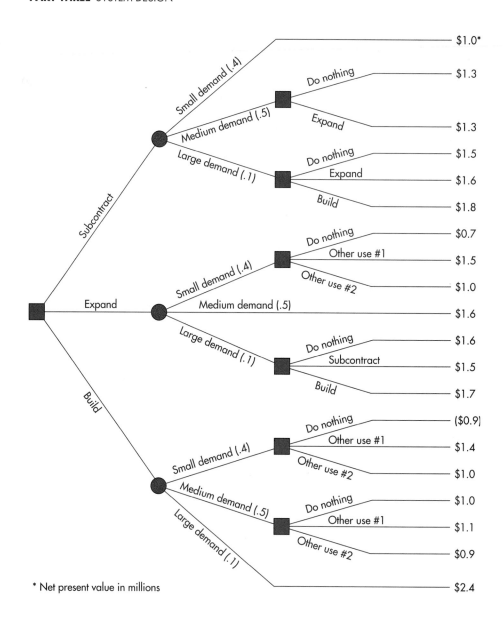

* Net present value in millions

7. Refer to Problem 6. Suppose that the management of Theme Park, Inc., has decided that there is a .35 probability that the motel's application will be approved.

   a. If management uses maximum expected monetary value as the decision criterion, which alternative should it choose?

   b. Represent this problem in the form of a decision tree.

   c. If management has been offered the option of a temporary lease while the town planning board considers the motel's application, would you advise management to sign the lease? The lease will cost $24,000.

8. Construct a graph that can be used for sensitivity analysis for the preceding problem.

   a. How sensitive is the solution to the problem in terms of the probability estimate of .35?

   b. Suppose that, after consulting with a member of the town planning board, management decides that an estimate of approval is approximately .45. How sensitive is the solution to this revised estimate? Explain.

   c. Suppose the management is confident of all the estimated payoffs except for $4 million. If the probability of approval is .35, for what range of payoff for renew/rejected will the alternative selected using maximum expected value remain the same?

9. A firm must decide whether to construct a small, medium, or large stamping plant. A consultant's report indicates a .20 probability that demand will be low and an .80 probability that demand will be high.

   If the firm builds a small facility and demand turns out to be low, the net present value will be $42 million. If demand turns out to be high, the firm can either subcontract and realize the net present value of $42 million or expand greatly for a net present value of $48 million.

   The firm could build a medium-size facility as a hedge: If demand turns out to be low, its net present value is estimated at $22 million; if demand turns out to be high, the firm could do nothing and realize a net present value of $46 million, or it could expand and realize a net present value of $50 million.

   If the firm builds a large facility and demand is low, the net present value will be −$20 million, whereas high demand will result in a net present value of $72 million.

   a. Analyze this problem using a decision tree.

   b. What is the maximin alternative?

   c. Compute the EVPI and interpret it.

   d. Perform sensitivity analysis on P(high).

10. A manager must decide how many machines of a certain type to buy. The machines will be used to manufacture a new gear for which there is increased demand. The manager has narrowed the decision to two alternatives: buy one machine or buy two. If only one machine is purchased and demand is more than it can handle, a second machine can be purchased at a later time. However, the cost per machine would be lower if the two machines were purchased at the same time.

    The estimated probability of low demand is .30, and the estimated probability of high demand is .70.

    The net present value associated with the purchase of two machines initially is $75,000 if demand is low and $130,000 if demand is high.

    The net present value for one machine and low demand is $90,000. If demand is high, there are three options. One option is to do nothing, which would have a net present value of $90,000. A second option is to subcontract; that would have a net present value of $110,000. The third option is to purchase a second machine. This option would have a net present value of $100,000.

    How many machines should the manager purchase initially? Use a decision tree to analyze this problem.

11. Determine the course of action that has the highest EMV for the accompanying tree diagram.

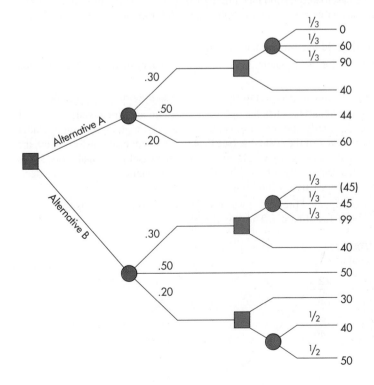

12. A firm that plans to expand its product line must decide whether to build a small or a large facility to produce the new products. If it builds a small facility and demand is low, the net present value after deducting for building costs will be $400,000. If demand is high, the firm can either maintain the small facility or expand it. Expansion would have a net present value of $450,000, and maintaining the small facility would have a net present value of $50,000.

    If a large facility is built and demand is high, the estimated net present value is $800,000. If demand turns out to be low, the net present value will be −$10,000.

    The probability that demand will be high is estimated to be .60, and the probability of low demand is estimated to be .40.

    Analyze using a tree diagram.

13. The director of social services of a county has learned that the state has mandated additional information requirements. This will place an additional burden on the agency. The director has identified three acceptable alternatives to handle the increased workload. One alternative is to reassign present staff members, the second is to hire and train two new workers, and the third is to redesign current practice so that workers can readily collect the information with little additional effort. An unknown factor is the caseload for the coming year when the new data will be collected on a trial basis. The estimated costs for various options and caseloads are shown in the following table:

	CASELOAD		
	Moderate	**High**	**Very High**
Reassign staff	$50*	60	85
New staff	60	60	60
Redesign collection	40	50	90

*Cost in $ thousands.

Assuming that past experience has shown the probabilities of various caseloads to be unreliable, what decision would be appropriate using each of the following criteria?

    a. Maximin.

    b. Maximax.

    c. Minimax regret.

    d. Laplace.

14. After contemplating the caseload question (see previous problem), the director of social services has decided that reasonable caseload probabilities are .10 for moderate, .30 for high, and .60 for very high.

    a. Which alternative will yield the minimum expected cost?

    b. Construct a decision tree for this problem. Indicate the expected costs for the three decision branches.

    c. Determine the expected value of perfect information using an opportunity loss table.

15. Suppose the director of social services has the option of hiring an additional staff member if one staff member is hired initially and the caseload turns out to be high or very high. Under that plan, the first entry in row 2 of the cost table (see Problem 13) will be 40 instead of 60, the second entry will be 75, and the last entry will be 80. Assume the caseload probabilities are as noted in Problem 14. Construct a decision tree that shows the sequential nature of this decision, and determine which alternative will minimize expected cost.

16. A manager has compiled estimated profits for various capacity alternatives but is reluctant to assign probabilities to the states of nature. The payoff table is:

		STATE OF NATURE	
		#1	**#2**
	A	$ 20*	140
Alternative	B	120	80
	C	100	40

*Cost in $ thousands.

a. Plot the expected-value lines on a graph.

b. Is there any alternative that would never be appropriate in terms of maximizing expected profit? Explain on the basis of your graph.

c. For what range of $P(2)$ would alternative A be the best choice if the goal is to maximize expected profit?

d. For what range of $P(1)$ would alternative A be the best choice if the goal is to maximize expected profit?

17. Repeat all parts of Problem 16, assuming the values in the payoff table are estimated *costs* and the goal is to minimize expected costs.

18. The research staff of a marketing agency has assembled the following payoff table of estimated profits:

		Receive Contract	Not Receive Contract
	#1	$10*	−2
Proposal	#2	8	3
	#3	5	5
	#4	0	7

*Cost in $ thousands.

Relative to the probability of not receiving the contract, determine the range of probability for which each of the proposals would maximize expected profit.

19. Given this payoff table:

		STATE OF NATURE	
		#1	#2
	A	$120*	20
Alternative	B	60	40
	C	10	110
	D	90	90

*Cost in $ thousands.

a. Determine the range of $P(1)$ for which each alternative would be best, treating the payoffs as profits.

b. Answer part *a* treating the payoffs as costs.

Bierman, Harold, Charles P. Bonini, and Warren H. Hausman. *Quantitative Analysis for Business Decisions.* 8th ed. Burr Ridge, IL: Richard D. Irwin, 1991.

Eppen, G. D., F. J. Gould, C. P. Schmidt, Jeffrey H. Moore, and Larry R. Weatherford. *Introductory Management Science.* 5th ed. Upper Saddle River, NJ: Prentice Hall, 1998.

Stevenson, William J. *Introduction to Management Science.* 3rd ed. Burr Ridge, IL: Richard D. Irwin, 1998.

Taylor, Bernard W. *Introduction to Management Science.* 6th ed. Dubuque, Iowa: William C. Brown, 1999.

Turban, Efraim, and Jack Meredith. *Fundamentals of Management Science.* New York: McGraw-Hill, 1998.

Selected Bibliography and Further Reading

CHAPTER SIX

Process Selection and Facility Layout

CHAPTER OUTLINE

Introduction, 218
  Make or Buy Decisions, 218

Process Selection, 219
  Process Types, 219
  Automation, 222

Reading: Tour de Force, 225

Reading: Electric Car Drives
  Factory Innovations, 229
  Service Process Design, 230
  Management of Technology, 230

Operations Strategy, 232

Layout, 232
  Product Layouts, 232
  Process Layouts, 235
  Fixed-Position Layouts, 237
  Combination Layouts, 238
  Cellular Layouts, 238
  Other Service Layouts, 240

Reading: Designing
  Supermarkets, 241

Designing Product Layouts: Line
  Balancing, 242
  Some Guidelines for Line
    Balancing, 247
  Other Factors, 250

Other Approaches, 250

Newsclip: Toyota Mixes and
  Matches, 251

Designing Process Layouts, 251
  Measures of Effectiveness, 253
  Information Requirements, 253
  Minimizing Transportation Costs or
    Distances, 253
  Closeness Ratings, 255
  Computer Analysis, 257

Summary, 257

Key Terms, 258

Solved Problems, 258

Discussion and Review
  Questions, 262

Memo Writing Exercises, 263

Problems, 263

Reading: Would You Like That Rare,
  Medium or Vacuum-Packed? 270

Operations Tour: Morton Salt, 271

Selected Bibliography and Further
  Reading, 273

Supplement: Linear
  Programming, 274

LEARNING OBJECTIVES

*After completing this chapter, you
should be able to:*

1 Explain the strategic importance
   of process selection.

2 Explain the influence that
   process selection has on an
   organization.

3 Describe the basic processing
   types.

4 Discuss automated approaches
   to processing.

5 Explain the need for management of technology.

6 List some reasons for redesign
   of layouts.

7 Describe the basic layout types.

8 List the main advantages and
   disadvantages of product layouts
   and process layouts.

9 Solve simple line-balancing
   problems.

10 Develop simple process layouts.

roduct and service choices, process selection, capacity planning, and choices about location and layout are among the most basic decisions managers must make because those decisions have long-term consequences for the organization.

Processes convert inputs into outputs; they are at the core of operations management. But the impact of process selection goes beyond operations management: It affects the entire organization and its ability to achieve its mission, and it affects the organization's supply chain. So process selection choices very often have strategic significance. This chapter will explain why—and how—process selection has such influence.

Process selection and facility layout (i.e., the arrangement of the workplace) are closely tied, and for that reason, these two topics are presented in a single chapter. The first part of the chapter covers the basic options for processing work. This is followed by a discussion of how processes and layout are linked. The remainder of the chapter is devoted to layout design.

Introduction

Process selection refers to the way production of goods or services is organized. It has major implications for capacity planning, layout of facilities, equipment, and design of work systems. Process selection occurs as a matter of course when new products or services are being planned. However, it also occurs periodically due to technological changes in equipment. Figure 6–1 provides an overview of where process selection fits into system design.

How an organization approaches process selection is determined by the organization's *process strategy.* Key aspects include:

- Make or buy decisions: The extent to which the organization will produce goods or provide services in-house as opposed to relying on outside organizations to produce or provide them.

- Capital intensity: The mix of equipment and labor that will be used by the organization.

- Process flexibility: The degree to which the system can be adjusted to changes in processing requirements due to such factors as changes in product or service design, changes in volume processed, and changes in technology.

Capital intensity and process flexibility are major factors if the organization chooses to make rather than buy.

MAKE OR BUY DECISIONS

outsource Obtain a good or service from an external provider.

The very first step in process planning is to consider whether to make or buy (**outsource**) some or all of a product or some or all of a service. A manufacturer might decide to purchase certain parts rather than make them; sometimes all parts are purchased, with the

FIGURE 6-1

Process selection and system design

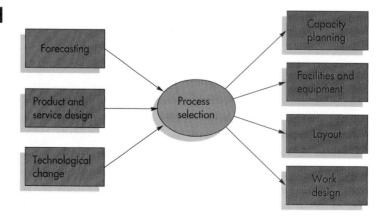

manufacturer simply performing assembly operations. Many firms contract out janitorial services, and some contract for repair services. If a decision is made to buy or contract, this lessens or eliminates the need for process selection.

In make or buy decisions, a number of factors are usually considered:

1. *Available capacity.* If an organization has available the equipment, necessary skills, and *time,* it often makes sense to produce an item or perform a service in-house. The additional costs would be relatively small compared with those required to buy items or subcontract services.

2. *Expertise.* If a firm lacks the expertise to do a job satisfactorily, buying might be a reasonable alternative.

3. *Quality considerations.* Firms that specialize can usually offer higher quality than an organization can attain itself. Conversely, unique quality requirements or the desire to closely monitor quality may cause an organization to perform a job itself.

4. *The nature of demand.* When demand for an item is high and steady, the organization is often better off doing the work itself. However, wide fluctuations in demand or small orders are usually better handled by specialists who are able to combine orders from multiple sources, which results in higher volume and tends to offset individual buyer fluctuations.

5. *Cost.* Any cost savings achieved from buying or making must be weighed against the preceding factors. Cost savings might come from the item itself or from transportation cost savings. If there are fixed costs associated with making an item that cannot be reallocated if the item is purchased, that has to be recognized in the analysis.

In some cases, a firm might choose to perform part of the work itself and let others handle the rest in order to maintain flexibility and to hedge against loss of a subcontractor. Moreover, this provides a bargaining tool in negotiations with contractors, or a head start if the firm decides later to take over the operation entirely.

If the organization decides to perform some or all of the processing, then process selection must be done.

Process Selection

Three primary questions bear on process selection:

1. How much *variety* in products or services will the system need to handle?
2. What degree of equipment *flexibility* will be needed?
3. What is the expected *volume* of output?

Answers to these questions will serve as a guide to selecting an appropriate process.

PROCESS TYPES

There are five basic process types: job shop, batch, repetitive, continuous, and project. The following four types are ongoing:

Job Shop. A job shop usually operates on a relatively small scale. It is used when a low volume of high-variety goods or services will be needed. Processing is *intermittent;* work shifts from one small job to the next, each with somewhat different processing requirements. High flexibility of equipment and skilled workers are important characteristics of a job shop. A manufacturing example of a job shop is a tool and die shop that is able to produce one-of-a-kind tools. A service example is a veterinarian's office, which is able to process a variety of animals and a variety of injuries and diseases.

Batch. Batch processing is used when a moderate volume of goods or services is desired, and it can handle a moderate variety in products or services. The equipment need not be as flexible as in a job shop, but processing is still intermittent. The skill level of workers

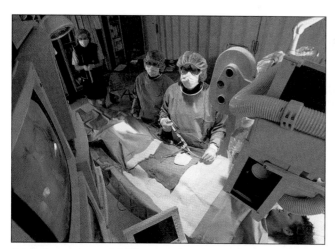

A job shop process: A Midwestern hospital medical team performs a diagnostic procedure involving a cardiac catheterization.

A batch process: Ben and Jerry's produces ice cream one flavor at a time.

www.benjerry.com
www.saturn.com
www.pepsico.com

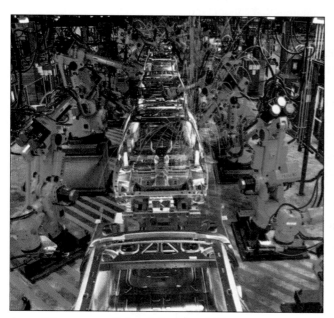

A repetitive process: Robots join and weld Saturns on an automated assembly line.

A continuous flow process: Pepsi-Cola is bottled in a flow system at GEMEX in Mexico, Pepsi's largest non-U.S. bottler.

doesn't need to be as high as in a job shop because there is less variety in the jobs being processed. Examples of batch systems include bakeries, which make bread, cakes, or cookies in batches; movie theaters, which show movies to groups (batches) of people; and airlines, which carry planeloads (batches) of people from airport to airport. Other examples of products that lend themselves to batch production are paint, ice cream, soft drinks, beer, magazines, and books. Other examples of services include plays, concerts, music videos, radio and television programs, and public address announcements.

Repetitive. When higher volumes of more standardized goods or services are needed, repetitive processing is used. The standardized output means only slight flexibility of

TABLE 6-1

Type of operation

	Job Shop	Batch	Repetitive/ Assembly	Continuous
Description	Customized goods or services	Semi-standardized goods or services	Standardized goods or services	Highly standardized goods or services
Examples of processes manufacturing service	Machine shop Beauty shop, barber shop	Bakery Classroom	Assembly line Cafeteria line	Steel mill, paper mill, etc. Central heating system
Examples of goods services	Specialty tools Hair styling	Cookies Education	Automobiles Car wash	Steel, paper, flour, sugar Heating, air conditioning
Volume	Low	Low-moderate	High	Very high
Output variety	Very high	Moderate	Low	Very low
Equipment flexibility	Very high	Moderate	Low	Very low
Advantages	Able to handle a wide variety of work	Flexibility	Low unit cost, high volume, efficient	Very efficient, very high volume
Disadvantages	Slow, high cost per unit, complex planning and scheduling	Moderate cost per unit, moderate scheduling complexity	Low flexibility, high cost of downtime	Very rigid, lack of variety, costly to change, very high cost of downtime

equipment is needed. Skill of workers is generally low. Examples of this type of system include production lines and assembly lines. In fact, this type of process is sometimes referred to as *assembly*. Familiar products made by these systems include automobiles, television sets, pencils, and computers. An example of a service system is an automatic carwash. Other examples of service include cafeteria lines and ticket collectors at sports events and concerts.

Continuous. When a very high volume of highly standardized output is desired, a continuous system is used. These systems have almost no variety in output and, hence, no need for equipment flexibility. As in assembly systems, workers are generally low skilled. Examples of products made in continuous systems include petroleum products, steel, sugar, flour, and salt. Continuous services include air monitoring, supplying electricity to homes and businesses, and the Internet.

These process types are found in a wide range of manufacturing and service settings. The ideal is to have process capabilities match product or service requirements. Failure to do so can result in inefficiencies and higher costs than are necessary, perhaps creating a competitive disadvantage.

Table 6–1 provides an overview of these processing systems.

Another consideration is that products and services often go through *life cycles* that begin with low volume, which increases as products or services become better known. When that happens, a manager must know when to shift from one type of process (e.g., job shop) to the next (e.g., batch). Of course, some operations remain at a certain level (e.g., magazine publishing), while others increase (or decrease as markets become saturated) over time. Again, it is important for a manager to assess his or her products and services and make a judgment on whether to plan for changes in processing over time.

All of these process types (job shop, batch, repetitive and continuous) are typically ongoing operations. However, there are situations that are not ongoing but instead are of limited durations. In such instances, the work is often organized as a project.

Activity/ Function	Job Shop	Batch	Repetitive	Continuous	Projects
Cost estimation	Difficult	Somewhat routine	Routine	Routine	Complex
Cost per unit	High	Moderate	Low	Low	Very high
Equipment used	General purpose	General purpose	Special purpose	Special purpose	Varied
Fixed costs	Low	Moderate	High	Very high	Varied
Variable costs	High	Moderate	Low	Very low	High
Labor skills	High	Moderate	Low	Low	Low to high
Marketing	Promote capabilities	Promote capabilities; semi-standard goods and services	Promote standardized goods/services	Promote standardized goods/services	Promote capabilities
Scheduling	Complex	Moderately complex	Routine	Routine	Complex, subject to change
Work-in-process inventory	High	High	Low	Low	Varied

TABLE 6–2

Process choice affects numerous activities/functions

project A nonrepetitive set of activities directed toward a unique goal within a limited time frame.

A **project** is used for work that is nonroutine, with a unique set of objectives to be accomplished in a limited time frame. Examples range from simple to complicated, including such things as putting on a play, consulting, making a motion picture, launching a new product or service, publishing a book, building a dam, and building a bridge. Equipment flexibility and worker skills can range from low to high.

The type of process or processes used by an organization influences a great many activities of the organization. Table 6–2 briefly describes some of those influences.

The processes discussed do not always exist in their "pure" forms. It is not unusual to find hybrid processes—processes that have elements of other process types embedded in them. For instance, companies that operate primarily in a repetitive mode, or a continuous mode, will often have repair shops (i.e., job shops) to fix or make new parts for equipment that fails. Also, if volume increases for some items, an operation that began as, say, in a job shop or batch mode may evolve into a batch or repetitive operation. This may result in having some operations in a job shop or batch mode, and others in a repetitive mode.

AUTOMATION

automation Machinery that has sensing and control devices that enable it to operate automatically.

A key question in process design is whether to automate. **Automation** is machinery that has sensing and control devices that enable it to operate automatically. If a company decides to automate, the next question is how much. Automation can range from factories that are completely automated to a single automated operation.

Automated services are also an option. Although not as plentiful as in manufacturing, automated services are becoming increasingly important. Examples range from ATM machines to automated heating and air conditioning, and include automated inspection, automated storage and retrieval systems, FedEx package sorting, mail processing, and e-mail.

Automation offers a number of advantages over human labor. It has low variability, whereas it is difficult for a human to perform a task in exactly the same way, in the same amount of time, and on a repetitive basis. In a production setting, variability is detrimental to quality and to meeting schedules. Moreover, machines do not get bored or distracted, nor do they go out on strike, ask for higher wages, or file labor grievances. Still another advantage of automation is reduction of variable costs.

Automation is frequently touted as a strategy necessary for competitiveness. For example, the Nucor Steel plant in Crawfordsville, Indiana, can produce 800,000 tons of finished strip steel a day. The plant is automated, and it produces the steel from molten metal to a hot band of finished steel in one uninterrupted process, giving this minimill a substantial productivity advantage over its foreign competitors. However, automation also has certain disadvantages and limitations compared to human labor. To begin with, it can be costly. Technology is expensive; usually it requires high volumes of output to offset high costs. In addition, automation is much less flexible than human labor. Once a process has been automated, there is substantial reason for not changing it. Moreover, workers sometimes fear automation because it might cause them to lose their jobs. That can have an adverse effect on morale and productivity.

Decision makers must carefully examine the issue of whether to automate or the degree in which to automate, so that they clearly understand all the ramifications. Also, much thought and careful planning are necessary to successfully *integrate* automation into a production system. Otherwise, it can lead to major problems. GM invested heavily in automation in the 1980s only to find its costs increasing while flexibility and productivity took a nosedive. Its market had shrunk while GM was increasing its capacity! Moreover, automation has important implications not only for cost and flexibility, but also for the fit with overall strategic priorities.

Generally speaking, there are three kinds of automation: fixed, programmable, and flexible.

Fixed automation is the most rigid of the three types. The concept was perfected by the Ford Motor Company in the early 1900s, and it has been the cornerstone of mass production in the auto industry. Sometimes referred to as Detroit-type automation, it uses high-cost, specialized equipment for a fixed sequence of operations. Low cost and high volume are its primary advantages; minimal variety and the high cost of making major changes in either product or process are its primary limitations.

Programmable automation is at the opposite end of the spectrum. It involves the use of high-cost, general-purpose equipment controlled by a computer program that provides both the sequence of operations and specific details about each operation. Changing the process is as easy (or difficult) as changing the computer program, and there is downtime while program changes are being made. This type of automation has the capability of economically producing a fairly wide variety of low-volume products in small batches. Numerically controlled (N/C) machines and some robots are applications of programmable automation.

Computer-aided manufacturing (CAM) refers to the use of computers in process control, ranging from robots to automated quality control. **Numerically controlled (N/C) machines** are programmed to follow a set of processing instructions based on mathematical relationships that tell the machine the details of the operations to be performed. The instructions are stored on a device such as a floppy disk, magnetic tape, or microprocessor. Although N/C machines have been used for many years, they are an important part of new approaches to manufacturing. Individual machines may have their own computer; this is referred to as *computerized numerical control (CNC)*. Or one computer may control a number of N/C machines, which is referred to as *direct numerical control (DNC)*.

N/C machines are best used in cases where parts are processed frequently and in small batches, where part geometry is complex, close tolerances are required, mistakes are costly, and there is the possibility of frequent changes in design. The main limitations of N/C machines are the higher skill levels needed to program the machines and their inability to detect tool wear and material variation.

The use of robots in manufacturing is sometimes an option. A **robot** consists of three parts: a mechanical arm, a power supply, and a controller. Unlike movie versions of robots, which vaguely resemble human beings, industrial robots are much less glamorous and much less mobile; most robots are stationary except for their movable arms.

Robots can handle a wide variety of tasks, including welding, assembly, loading and unloading of machines, painting, and testing. They relieve humans from heavy or dirty work and often eliminate drudgery tasks.

computer-aided manufacturing (CAM) The use of computers in process control.

numerically controlled (N/C) machines Machines that perform operations by following mathematical processing instructions.

robot A machine consisting of a mechanical arm, a power supply, and a controller.

Some uses of robots are fairly simple, others are much more complex. At the lowest level are robots that follow a fixed set of instructions. Next are programmable robots, which can repeat a set of movements after being led through the sequence. These robots "play back" a mechanical sequence much as a video recorder plays back a visual sequence. At the next level up are robots that follow instructions from a computer. At the top are robots that can recognize objects and make certain simple decisions.

"**I**f you think robots are mainly the stuff of space movies, think again. Right now, all over the world, robots are on the move. They are painting cars at Ford plants, assembling Milano cookies for Pepperidge Farms, walking into live volca-noes, driving trains in Paris, and defusing bombs in Northern Ireland. As they grow tougher, nimbler, and smarter, today's robots are doing more and more things humans can't—or don't want to—do."

Source: www.thetech.org/robotics.

Robots move in one of two ways. Point-to-point robots move to predetermined points and perform a specified operation; they then move on to the next point and perform another operation. Continuous-path robots follow a continuous (moving) path while performing an operation.

Robots can be powered pneumatically (air-driven), hydraulically (fluids under pressure), or electronically. Figures 6–2 and 6–3 illustrate robots.

Flexible automation evolved from programmable automation. It uses equipment that is more customized than that of programmable automation. A key difference between the two is that flexible automation requires significantly less changeover time. This permits almost continuous operation of equipment *and* product variety without the need to produce in batches.

In practice, flexible automation is used in several different formats.

A **manufacturing cell** consists of one or a small number of computer-controlled machines that produce a family of similar parts. The machines may be linked with automatic material handing devices.

manufacturing cell One or a few computer-controlled machines that produce a wide variety of parts.

FIGURE 6–2

Industrial robot
Source: Morris A. Cohen and Uday M. Apte, *Manufacturing Automation* (Burr Ridge, IL: Irwin/McGraw-Hill, 1997), p. 138.

www.milacron.com

Cincinnati Milacron robot system

FIGURE 6-3

Robots are used frequently and extensively in automobile plants, particularly for jobs that are repetitive, require precision, and are potentially dangerous for people. This arc welder is programmed for a specific welding task in automobile frame assembly.

READING

Tour de Force Gerald Scott

www.chryslercorp.com

A look at the goings-on inside Chrysler's plant that builds Viper and Prowler. It is the Motor City's "hottest ticket," but you can't just walk up to the front door, knock and go inside.

Rather, to tour Chrysler Corp.'s Conner Avenue Assembly Plant, you've got to be like Dorothy in "The Wizard of Oz"—persistent and resourceful.

After all, "it's not what you know but who you know" when you want to tour any auto plant. And as those things go, Chrysler's Conner Avenue plant, where the Dodge Viper and Plymouth Prowler are made on the city's east side, is easily the Motor City's equivalent of Disneyland's old "E-ticket" ride.

Public auto plant tours in Detroit are ambiguous and haphazard. The automakers say they frown on them because they distract the work force; and, with downsizing, they don't want to have to spend money on tour guides for each plant. But tours happen almost every day.

The flip side is that it's also a great way to draw attention to your product. The Chevrolet assembly plant making Corvettes in Bowling Green, Ky., for example, has hosted 40,000 people since reopening for tours in April after extensive renovations. In its one-year shutdown, attendance at the nearby National Corvette Museum dropped 25 percent.

In Detroit, the Viper-Prowler plant, as it is known, is the place to see. When comedian Jay Leno was in town to host the Auto Centennial celebrations, the Viper plant was his first stop. Ditto for Housing and Urban Development Secretary Andrew Cuomo on a whirlwind tour of the Motor City.

"We run plant tours every single day. We are the hot ticket for tours in Detroit," said John Hinckley, manager of the Conner Avenue plant.

"If you bring a group in for a tour, I'm not going to lead it. I won't have one of my management people lead it," Hinckley says. "I'll have one of the craftspersons from the floor lead it. The people who build the cars are the people who know what's going on around here."

Enhancing the Viper-Prowler plant is not your typical Detroit assembly operation. Instead of mass production techniques using robots, it's "craftsman-style" production for hand-building Vipers and Prowlers. With mass production, Chrysler can produce up to 75 cars per hour. With late shifts Chrysler's nearby Jefferson North Assembly Plant can crank out 1,114 Jeep Grand Cherokees in a 24-hour workday. By comparison, the Viper plant produces 13 Vipers a day and has a capacity for 20 Prowlers.

In Chrysler's Conner Avenue plant, the Dodge Viper and Plymouth Prowler are built individually by hand.

At 392,000 square feet, the Viper plant is a boutique compared to most massive auto plants, such as Saturn Corp.'s Spring Hill, Tenn., manufacturing complex, which is 5 million square feet. (Saturn has received so many "drop-in" visitors that it recently built a new Visitors Center.) The Jefferson North plant has 2.4 million square feet.

The Viper plant was built in 1966 as a Champion Spark Plug plant until 4-cylinder engines and 100,000-mile platinum-tipped spark plugs conspired to sharply reduce demand for replacement plugs. Chrysler acquired the vacant plant from Detroit in 1995 and moved Viper production there from a nearby plant.

"We're not the biggest plant in the area, but we've got the best work force and build the most exciting products—the Plymouth Prowler and Dodge Viper," said Hinckley, who has spent 33 years working in various Detroit auto plants for General Motors and Chrysler and is known for building and driving "kit car" racers. "We're expanding our plant, too. We also are part of the revitalization of Detroit.

"Our plant was about 380,000 square feet and we've just added another 10,000 square feet to improve our process flow and improve our quality. And it provides a little more space since we added the Prowler.

"It will allow us to do a better job of reaching the Prowler's ultimate capacity. It's about a $1 million expansion—for other large plants, that's nothing but for a facility this size it's a lot of money.

"For me it's a dream job. I've been a 'hot rodder' all my life and build race cars and racing engines, and how many hot rodders get to lead the team that runs the only hot-rod plant in the world?"

Conner Avenue is a throwback to early 20th Century, premass assembly techniques. Vipers and Prowlers are built on parallel 720-foot assembly lines, each with a dozen or so workstations, where the cars are hand-assembled. In a rarity, there are no robots in this plant.

When each workstation completes its task, the entire line advances to the next station. So in those 45-minute stops, the employees are relatively free to grab a cup of coffee or talk to tour groups, something they could never do in a plant cranking out 73 units per hour.

Plus, Viper workers love the attention—having people clamoring to see the products you're assembling can be a boost to the production team's *esprit de corps*. And the automaker's flexible labor agreement with UAW Local 212 means everybody working in the plant is a "craftsman" and

When each workstation completes its task, the entire line advances to the next station.

The Viper is built around its engine and transmission, which, according to employees, makes it a little harder to work on.

can solve any problem anywhere on the line—in most plants, job categories are sharply defined and protected.

Most large auto assembly plants still require 2,000 or more workers, while the Viper plant needs only 260.

"We do everything from tours to hi-lo [forklift] driving to mopping and sweeping, we do it all," says Andrew Stokes, a UAW craftsman who works in underbody and heavy repair.

"I'm one of the first 12 to work on the Prowler," he added. "The Prowler is a little easier to assemble but a little harder to repair. The Viper seems to be a lot more open than the Prowler is—the car seems to be built around the engine and trans and that makes it a little harder to work on. But they're two very good cars."

Thanks to such an interest from car buyers in this plant, Chrysler allows Viper customers to pick up their car as it comes out of final assembly, to meet the employees who built it and to drive it home from the plant instead of from the dealership.

Questions

1. What is different about this assembly plant compared to more typical auto assembly plants?

2. Why do you suppose there are no robots or other automation?

Source: Reprinted with permission from *Chicago Tribune.* © 1998 by The Tribune Co.

A **flexible manufacturing system (FMS)** is a group of machines that include supervisory computer control, automatic material handling, and robots or other automated processing equipment. Reprogrammable controllers enable these systems to produce a variety of *similar* products. Systems may range from three or four machines to more than a dozen. They are designed to handle intermittent processing requirements with some of the benefits of automation and some of the flexibility of individual, or stand-alone, machines (e.g., N/C machines). Flexible manufacturing systems offer reduced labor costs and more consistent quality compared with more traditional manufacturing methods, lower capital investment and higher flexibility than "hard" automation, and relatively quick changeover time. Flexible manufacturing systems appeal to managers, who hope to achieve both the flexibility of job shop processing and the productivity of repetitive processing systems.

Although these are important benefits, an FMS also has certain limitations. One is that this type of system can handle a relatively narrow range of part variety, so it must be used for a family of similar parts, which all require similar machining. Also, an FMS requires longer planning and development times than more conventional processing equipment

flexible manufacturing system (FMS) A group of machines designed to handle intermittent processing requirements and produce a variety of similar products.

A computerized control room at the North Rhine Westphalia, Germany, Thyssen manufacturing plant, which produces electrolytically galvanized sheet metal.

because of its increased complexity and cost. Furthermore, companies sometimes prefer a gradual approach to automation, and FMS represents a sizable chunk of technology.

Computer-integrated manufacturing (CIM) is a system that uses an integrating computer system to link a broad range of manufacturing activities, including engineering design, flexible manufacturing systems, and production planning and control. Not all elements are absolutely necessary. For instance, CIM might be as simple as linking two or more FMSs by a host computer. More encompassing systems can link scheduling, purchasing, inventory control, shop control, and distribution. In effect, a CIM system integrates information from other areas of an organization with manufacturing.

computer-integrated manufacturing (CIM) A system for linking a broad range of manufacturing activities through an integrating computer system.

The overall goal of using CIM is to link various parts of an organization to achieve rapid response to customer orders and/or product changes, to allow rapid production, and to reduce *indirect* labor costs.

A shining example of how process choices can lead to competitive advantages can be found at Allen-Bradley's computer-integrated manufacturing process in Milwaukee, Wisconsin. The company converted a portion of its factory to a fully automated "factory within a factory" to assemble contactors and relays for electrical motors. A handful of humans operate the factory, although once an order has been entered into the system, the machines do virtually all the work, including packaging and shipping, and quality control. Any defective items are removed from the line, and replacement parts are automatically ordered and scheduled to compensate for the defective items. The humans program the machines and monitor operations, and attend to any problems signaled by a system of warning lights.

As orders come into the plant, computers determine production requirements and schedules and order the necessary parts. Bar-coded labels that contain processing instructions are automatically placed on individual parts. As the parts approach a machine, a sensing device reads the bar code and communicates the processing instructions to the machine. The factory can produce 600 units an hour.

The company has realized substantial competitive advantages from the system. Orders can be completed and shipped within 24 hours of entry into the system, direct labor costs and inventory costs have been greatly reduced, and quality is very high.

Electric Car Drives Factory Innovations
Rebecca Blumenstein

www.gm.com

There are only about 150 of them on the road so far. Cold weather makes their batteries run down. They can go only 70 to 90 miles between rechargings, so drivers must choose their destinations carefully. Free towing is provided, however.

Even General Motors Corp. concedes that its EV1, the first electric vehicle now being mass-produced in the U.S., isn't the answer to the nation's current transportation needs. Still the teardrop-shaped vehicle may ultimately influence the way other cars are designed and built in the future. The superlight, aerodynamic car now in limited production is allowing GM to experiment with new technologies and new means of manufacturing. "We're learning from the car," says Maureen Midgley, plant manager of the Lansing Draft Centre in Lansing, Mich., where GM produces about 2,000 EV1s per year.

One big lesson has been working with new materials. Lightness is crucial to maximize the EV1's driving range, so the frame and many other parts are made of aluminum rather than steel used in most other cars. The entire frame weighs only 300 pounds, about 40 percent of a typical car frame.

That, in turn, dictates a different kind of assembly. Traditional welding doesn't work because heat disperses more rapidly through aluminum than steel and doesn't stay concentrated. Instead, GM glues the EV1's frame together with an adhesive ordinarily used by the aerospace industry and literally bakes the car in a giant oven at 375 degrees for 15 minutes.

GM says this use of light materials will likely show up in many of its future cars; removing weight to increase gas mileage is a chief goal for many auto engineers. "The EV1 allows you to put lightweight structures in all your vehicles," says Lawrence J. Oswald, a manager at GM's Alternative Propulsion Department.

The Lansing Centre itself bears little resemblance to a typical assembly plant, largely because it has taken outsourcing to the extreme. While traditional vehicle plants rely on hundreds of robots and thousands of workers along miles of assembly lines, Lansing has only 60 hourly workers who essentially build the car manually in a few stations. Suppliers deliver almost every part, premade, to the plant floor, from the 1,100-pound battery pack to the interior seats.

"Because of the technology, suppliers have had to have more involvement," says Arianna Kalian, manager of the body shop. The arrangement saves money by reducing labor and capital costs, a key hurdle the electric vehicle had to overcome to get the approval of GM's board.

Traditionally, auto workers' unions have resisted this level of outsourcing. Then again, jobs at the Lansing plant are very different from typical, high-volume plants in which workers must accomplish their assigned tasks in 60 seconds or less. The EV1 stays an average of 45 minutes at each of about a dozen stops along the line, and each worker performs dozens of tasks. The employees keep many of the functions in their head—120 to 150 times that of a regular assembly worker.

"It's like food for the brain," says Wayne Glaxner, one of the EV1 workers. Even Ms. Midgley, the plant manager and the daughter of a GM assembly-line worker, says she likes to work on the lines herself once a month to watch the car come together.

The EV1 is driving other innovations, as well. Its frame is so light that it can be wheeled into the general assembly area instead of lifted with the huge, expensive conveyors most plants use. The plant uses a lone robot to install a windshield containing an invisible electronic film that can defrost the glass without an energy-consuming blower. GM says the robot, being tested here for the first time, may some day be used in conventional assembly plants.

Once tires are mounted, the EV1 is driven to other stations. Assembly plants typically keep gas-powered cars on miles of conveyors because gasoline is too flammable to allow on a factory floor. Seats made of lightweight magnesium frames and a steering wheel are installed along with the rest of the car's futuristic-looking interior. Finally, the EV1's exterior panels—made of a lightweight composite material—are added, piece by piece, a change from traditional unit-body construction that integrates the frame with body panels made of sheets of steel.

The stations are so portable—unlike the huge monuments of automation that anchor most assembly plants—that they can be altered easily. Indeed, the entire plant can adapt quickly if new technology becomes available, and production can be expanded quickly from 2,000 cars per year to 10,000 or more if demand for electric cars warrants.

"Clearly, a manufacturer that learns either to be very flexible as a mass producer or learns to control the costs of low production is going to have a major leg up," says Mike Flynn, associate director of the University of Michigan's Office for the Study of Automotive Transportation. "This is a real significant opportunity."

To date, demand remains limited by the car's lack of range and practicality. GM is leasing the $34,000 cars for $480 to $680 per month only in Arizona and California and only through Saturn dealers, because of their reputation for friendly customer relations. Dealers need to be able to instruct drivers in the car's technical limitations, GM officials say, though they anticipate that a new nickel-metal hydride battery, available later this year, will increase the EV1's to as much as 270 miles.

Questions

1. Why is flexibility important in this instance; what advantages can it provide?

2. Name some of the major differences in the way these electric cars are produced compared to the traditional way cars are produced, and the reasons for these differences.

3. What is outsourcing, and what advantages does it provide to GM?

Source: Reprinted with permission from *The Wall Street Journal* © 1997 by Dow Jones & Company, Inc. All Rights Reserved Worldwide.

SERVICE PROCESS DESIGN

Service process design focuses on the *service delivery system* (i.e., the facilities, processes, and personnel requirements needed to provide the service). Examples of service delivery systems abound—mail service, Internet service, health care systems, transportation systems, food service, and much more. The fact that the creation of a service and the delivery of the service frequently occur at the same time is of particular concern to service designers. In part this is due to the high degree of customer contact that is required.

Service design has important implications for cost, quality, productivity, customer satisfaction, and competitive advantage. Service process design (or redesign) often begins with **service blueprinting,** which is a method for describing and analyzing a service process. A key aspect of service blueprinting is flowcharting the process. Figure 6–4 illustrates a flowchart for catalog telephone orders. Flowcharting a process helps to understand the process, and the resulting flowchart provides a visual model of the process. In Figure 6–4, potential failure points are highlighted.

service blueprint A method used in service design to describe and analyze a proposed service.

The major steps in service blueprinting are:

1. Establish boundaries for the process and decide on the level of detail that will be needed.

2. Identify the steps involved and describe them. If this is an existing process, get input from those who do it.

3. Prepare a flowchart of major process steps.

4. Identify potential failure points. Incorporate features that minimize the chances of failures.

5. Establish a time frame for service execution and an estimate of variability in processing time requirements. Time is a primary determinant of cost, so establishing a time standard for the service is important. Variability can also impact time, so an estimate of that is also important. Customers regard service time as a key concern—the shorter the service time, the better. However, there are exceptions, such as a leisurely meal at a fine restaurant and a physician who takes the time to listen to a patient rather than rush to diagnosis or treatment.

6. Analyze profitability. Determine which factors can influence profitability, positively and negatively, and determine how sensitive profitability is to these factors. For example, customer waiting time is often a key factor. Concentrate design efforts on key factors. Establish design features that protect against negative impacts and maximize positive impacts.

MANAGEMENT OF TECHNOLOGY

Technological innovations have had a widespread impact on businesses, and will continue to do so. And although technology offers numerous benefits for business organizations, it also presents numerous risks. Among the potential benefits are competitive advantages in improved quality, increased productivity, reduced costs, reduced production or service times, and increased customer satisfaction. Among the potential risks are reduced flexibility, increased fixed costs, short-term disruptions while the new technology is installed,

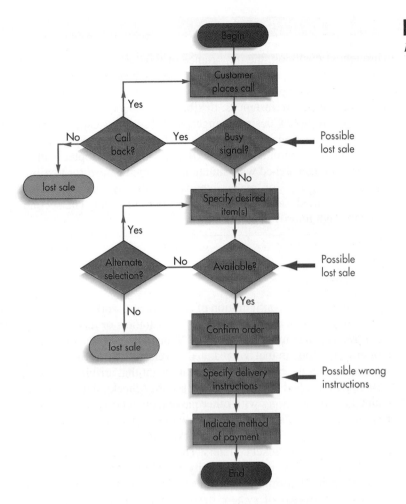

FIGURE 6-4

Flowchart of catalog call

training costs, and difficulties in integrating the new technology into the organization's systems. Still another risk is getting locked into a certain technology that may be inferior to another technology that is just over the horizon.

The implication of these potential benefits and risks is that management of technology is vitally important. Technology selection often requires engineering expertise. However, many managers charged with selecting a process may have little technical knowledge; their education and experience lie in marketing, finance, and the like. Consequently, they may tend to delegate technical decisions to engineers. Engineering white elephants are not uncommon, and neither are systems based on narrow viewpoints of problems and solutions. In the long run, the solution may be to hire and promote managers who have both managerial and technical skills and expertise. In the short run, managers must work with technical experts, asking questions and increasing their understanding of the benefits and limitations of sophisticated processing equipment and technology, and ultimately make decisions themselves.

A key consequence of the increased use of technology in business is the impact on cost structures in organizations. The proportion of total costs represented by fixed costs is becoming larger, and the proportion of variable costs is becoming smaller. This means that volume of output has a decreasing effect on total cost, a situation that can be particularly burdensome during periods of slow demand. Moreover, technology creates additional requirements for the maintenance and repair of highly specialized equipment. Managers must proceed cautiously with technology decisions, carefully weighing the benefits and risks before making what are sometimes long-term commitments.

Throughout this book, the importance of *flexibility* as a competitive strategy is stressed. However, flexibility does not always offer the best choice in processing decisions. Flexible systems or equipment is often more expensive and not as efficient as less flexible alternatives. In certain instances, flexibility is unnecessary because products are in mature stages, requiring few design changes, and there is a steady volume of output. Ordinarily, this type of situation calls for specialized processing equipment, with no need for flexibility. The implication is clear: Flexibility should be adopted with great care; its applications should be matched with situations in which a *need* for flexibility clearly exists.

In practice, decision makers choose flexible systems for either of two reasons: demands are varied, or uncertainty exists about demand. The second reason can be overcome through improved forecasting.

Layout

www.mspairport.com/

Layout refers to the configuration of departments, work centers, and equipment, with particular emphasis on movement of work (customers or materials) through the system. For example, a change in the layout at the Minneapolis-St. Paul International Airport not long ago solved a problem that had plagued travelers. In the former layout, security checkpoints were located in the boarding area. That meant that arriving passengers who were simply changing planes had to pass through a security checkpoint before being able to board their connecting flight, along with other passengers whose journeys were originating at Minneapolis-St. Paul. This created excessive waiting times for both sets of passengers. The new layout relocated the security checkpoints, moving them from the boarding area to a position close to the ticket counters. Thus, the need for passengers who were making connecting flights to pass through security was eliminated, and in the process, the waiting time for passengers departing from Minneapolis-St. Paul was considerably reduced.[1]

As in other areas of system design, layout decisions are important for three basic reasons: (1) they require substantial investments of money and effort, (2) they involve long-term commitments, which makes mistakes difficult to overcome, and (3) they have a significant impact on the cost and efficiency of operations. This section describes the main types of layout designs and the models used to evaluate design alternatives.

The need for layout planning arises both in the process of designing new facilities and in redesigning existing facilities. The most common reasons for redesign of layouts include: inefficient operations (e.g., high cost, bottlenecks), accidents or safety hazards, changes in the design of products or services, introduction of new products or services, changes in the volume of output or mix of outputs, changes in methods or equipment, changes in environmental or other legal requirements, and morale problems (e.g., lack of face-to-face contact).

The three basic types of layout are product, process, and fixed-position. *Product layouts* are most conducive to repetitive processing, *process layouts* are used for intermittent processing, and *fixed-position layouts* are used when projects require layouts. We will study the characteristics, advantages, and disadvantages of each layout type in this section. We'll also take a look at hybrid layouts, which are combinations of these pure types.

PRODUCT LAYOUTS

product layout Layout that uses standardized processing operations to achieve smooth, rapid, high-volume flow.

Product layouts are used to achieve a smooth and rapid flow of large volumes of goods or customers through a system. This is made possible by highly standardized goods or services that allow highly standardized, continual processing. The work is divided into a series of standardized tasks, permitting specialization of both labor and equipment. The large

---

[1]Based on "Airport Checkpoints Moved to Help Speed Travelers on Their Way," *Minneapolis-St. Paul Star Tribune,* January 13, 1995, p. 1B.

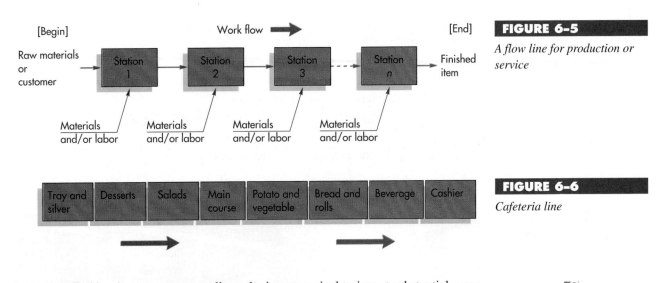

FIGURE 6–5

A flow line for production or service

FIGURE 6–6

Cafeteria line

volumes handled by these systems usually make it economical to invest substantial sums of money in equipment and job design. Because only one or a few very similar items are involved, it is feasible to arrange an entire layout to correspond to the technological processing requirements of the product or service. For instance, if a portion of a manufacturing operation required the sequence of cutting, sanding, and painting, the appropriate pieces of equipment would be arranged in that same sequence. And because each item follows the same sequence of operations, it is often possible to utilize fixed-path material-handling equipment such as conveyors to transport items between operations. The resulting arrangement forms a line like the one depicted in Figure 6–5. In manufacturing environments, the lines are referred to as **production lines** or **assembly lines,** depending on the type of activity involved. In service processes, the term *line* may or may not be used. It is common to refer to a cafeteria line as such but not a car wash, although from a conceptual standpoint the two are nearly identical. Figure 6–6 illustrates the layout of a typical cafeteria serving line. Examples of this type of layout are less plentiful in service environments because processing requirements usually exhibit too much variability to make standardization feasible. Without high standardization, many of the benefits of repetitive processing are lost. When lines are used, certain compromises may be made. For instance, an automatic car wash provides equal treatment to all cars—the same amount of soap, water, and scrubbing—even though cars may differ considerably in cleaning needs. As a result, very dirty cars may not come out completely clean, and relatively clean cars go through the same system with considerable waste of soap, water, and energy.

Product layouts achieve a high degree of labor and equipment utilization, which tends to offset their high equipment costs. Because items move quickly from operation to operation, the amount of work-in-process is often minimal. Consequently, operations are so closely tied to each other that the entire system is highly vulnerable to being shut down because of mechanical failure or high absenteeism. Maintenance procedures are geared to this. *Preventive maintenance*—periodic inspection and replacement of worn parts or those with high failure rates—reduces the probability of breakdowns during the operations. Of course, no amount of preventive activity can completely eliminate failures, so management must take measures to provide quick repair. These include maintaining an inventory of spare parts and having repair personnel available to quickly restore equipment to normal operation. These procedures are fairly expensive; because of the specialized nature of equipment, problems become more difficult to diagnose and resolve, and spare-part inventories can be extensive.

The main advantages of product layouts are:

1. A high rate of output.
2. Low unit cost due to high volume; the high cost of specialized equipment is spread over many units.

production line Standardized layout arranged according to a fixed sequence of production tasks.

assembly line Standardized layout arranged according to a fixed sequence of assembly tasks.

3. Labor specialization reduces training costs and time, and results in a wide span of supervision.

4. Low material-handling cost per unit; material handling is simplified because units follow the same sequence of operations.

5. A high utilization of labor and equipment.

6. Routing and scheduling are established in the initial design of the system; they do not require much attention once the system is operating.

7. Accounting, purchasing, and inventory control are fairly routine.

A car wash is a service assembly line with various cleaning tasks being performed in a specific order. Some facilities allow customer options such as undercarriage washing, application of a protective coating, or hand cleaning of floor mats and tires.

At the Mercedes Benz factory in Sindelfingen, Germany, sedans are turned as they proceed through assembly. The tilted assembly line allows easy access and installation of car components.

www.mercedes-benz.com

The primary disadvantages of product layouts include:

1. The intensive division of labor usually creates dull, repetitive jobs that provide little opportunity for advancement and may lead to morale problems and to repetitive stress injuries.
2. Poorly skilled workers may exhibit little interest in maintaining equipment or in the quality of output.
3. The system is fairly inflexible in response to changes in the volume of output or changes in product or process design.
4. The system is highly susceptible to shutdowns caused by equipment breakdowns or excessive absenteeism.
5. Preventive maintenance, the capacity for quick repairs, and spare-parts inventories are necessary expenses.
6. Incentive plans tied to individual output are impractical since they would cause variations among outputs of individual workers, which would adversely affect the smooth flow of work through the system.

U-Shaped Layouts. Although a straight production line may have intuitive appeal, a U-shaped line (see Figure 6–7) has a number of advantages that make it worthy of consideration. One disadvantage of a long, straight line is that it interferes with cross-travel of workers and vehicles. A U-shaped line is more compact; it often requires approximately half the length of a straight production line. In addition, a U-shaped line permits increased communication among workers on the line because workers are clustered, thus facilitating teamwork. Flexibility in work assignments is increased because workers can handle not only adjacent stations but also stations on opposite sides of the line. Moreover, if materials enter the plant at the same point that finished products leave it, a U-shaped line minimizes material handling.

Of course, not all situations lend themselves to U-shaped layouts: on highly automated lines there is less need for teamwork and communication. And entry and exit points may be on opposite sides of the building. Also, operations may need to be separated because of noise or contamination factors.

PROCESS LAYOUTS

Process layouts are designed to process items or provide services that involve a variety of processing requirements. The variety of jobs that are processed requires frequent adjustments to equipment. This causes a discontinuous work flow, which is referred to as *intermittent processing*. The layouts feature departments or other functional groupings in which similar kinds of activities are performed. A manufacturing example of a process layout is the *machine shop*, which has separate departments for milling, grinding, drilling, and so on. Items that require those operations are frequently moved in lots or batches to the departments in a sequence that varies from job to job. Consequently, variable-path material-handling equipment (forklift trucks, jeeps, tote boxes) is needed to handle the variety of routes and items. The use of *general-purpose equipment* provides the flexibility

process layouts Layouts that can handle varied processing requirements.

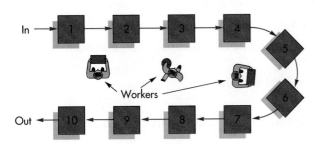

FIGURE 6–7

A U-shaped production line

FIGURE 6-8

Comparison of process and product layouts

necessary to handle a wide range of processing requirements. Workers who operate the equipment are usually skilled or semiskilled. Figure 6–8 illustrates the departmental arrangement typical of a process layout.

Process layouts are quite common in service environments. Examples include hospitals, colleges and universities, banks, auto repair shops, airlines, and public libraries. For instance, hospitals have departments or other units that specifically handle surgery, maternity, pediatrics, psychiatric, emergency, and geriatric care. And universities have separate schools or departments that concentrate on one area of study such as business, engineering, science, or math.

Because equipment in a process layout is arranged by type rather than by processing sequence, the system is much less vulnerable to shutdown caused by mechanical failure or absenteeism. In manufacturing systems especially, idle equipment is usually available to replace machines that are temporarily out of service. Moreover, because items are often processed in lots, there is considerably less interdependence between successive operations than with a product layout. Maintenance costs tend to be lower because the equipment is less specialized than that of product layouts, and the grouping of machinery permits repair personnel to become skilled in handling that type of equipment. Machine similarity reduces the necessary investment in spare parts. On the negative side, routing and scheduling must be done on a continual basis to accommodate the variety of processing demands typically imposed on these systems. Material handling is inefficient, and unit handling costs are generally much higher than in product layouts. In-process inventories can be substantial due to batch processing. Furthermore, it is not uncommon for such systems to have equipment utilization rates under 50 percent because of routing and scheduling complexities related to the variety of processing demands being handled.

In sum, process layouts have both advantages and disadvantages. The advantages of process layouts include:

1. Systems can handle a variety of processing requirements.
2. Systems are not particularly vulnerable to equipment failures.
3. General-purpose equipment is often less costly than the specialized equipment used in product layouts and is easier and less costly to maintain.
4. It is possible to use individual incentive systems.

The disadvantages of process layouts include:

1. In-process inventory costs can be high if batch processing is used in manufacturing systems.
2. Routing and scheduling pose continual challenges.
3. Equipment utilization rates are low.
4. Material handling is slow and inefficient, and more costly per unit than in product layouts.

Fixed-position layout. When a large project must remain stationary, such as building a submarine at Electric Boat, a division of General Dynamics, workers and equipment come to the site. The Seawolf weighs 9,137 tons, is 353 feet long, 40 feet in diameter, and takes more than five years to build.

5. Job complexities often reduce the span of supervision and result in higher supervisory costs than with product layouts.

6. Special attention necessary for each product or customer (e.g., routing, scheduling, machine setups) and low volumes result in higher unit costs than with product layouts.

7. Accounting, inventory control, and purchasing are much more involved than with product layouts.

FIXED-POSITION LAYOUTS

In **fixed-position layouts,** the item being worked on remains stationary, and workers, materials, and equipment are moved about as needed. This is in marked contrast to product and process layouts. Almost always, the nature of the product dictates this kind of arrangement: weight, size, bulk, or some other factor makes it undesirable or extremely difficult to move the product. Fixed-position layouts are used in large construction projects (buildings, power plants, dams), shipbuilding, and production of large aircraft and space mission rockets. In those instances, attention is focused on timing of material and equipment deliveries so as not to clog up the work site and to avoid having to relocate materials and equipment around the work site. Lack of storage space can present significant problems, for example, at construction sites in crowded urban locations. Because of the many diverse activities carried out on large projects and because of the wide range of skills required, special efforts are needed to coordinate the activities, and the span of control can be quite narrow. For these reasons, the administrative burden is often much higher than it would be under either of the other layout types. Material handling may or may not be a factor; in many cases, there is no tangible product involved (e.g., designing a computerized inventory system). When goods and materials are involved, material handling often resembles process-type, variable-path, general-purpose equipment. Projects might require use of earth-moving equipment and trucks to haul materials to, from, and around the work site, for example.

fixed-position layout Layout in which the product or project remains stationary, and workers, materials, and equipment are moved as needed.

Fixed-position layouts are widely used for farming, firefighting, road building, home building, remodeling and repair, and drilling for oil. In each case, compelling reasons bring workers, materials, and equipment to the "product's" location instead of the other way around.

COMBINATION LAYOUTS

The three basic layout types are ideal models, which may be altered to satisfy the needs of a particular situation. It is not hard to find layouts that represent some combination of these pure types. For instance, supermarket layouts are essentially process layouts, and yet we find most use fixed-path material-handling devices such as roller-type conveyors in the stockroom and belt-type conveyors at the cash registers. Hospitals also use the basic process arrangement, although frequently patient care involves more of a fixed-position approach, in which nurses, doctors, medicines, and special equipment are brought to the patient. By the same token, faulty parts made in a product layout may require off-line reworking, which involves customized processing. Moreover, conveyors are frequently observed in both farming and construction activities.

Process layouts and product layouts represent two ends of a continuum from small batches to continuous production. Process layouts are conducive to the production of a wider range of products or services than product layouts, which is desirable from a customer standpoint where customized products are often in demand. However, process layouts tend to be less efficient and have higher unit production costs than product layouts. Some manufacturers are moving away from process layouts in an effort to capture some of the benefits of product layouts. Ideally, a system is flexible and yet efficient, with low unit production costs. Cellular manufacturing, group technology, and flexible manufacturing systems represent efforts to move toward this ideal.

CELLULAR LAYOUTS

cellular manufacturing Layout in which machines are grouped into a cell that can process items that have similar processing requirements.

Cellular Manufacturing. Cellular manufacturing is a type of layout in which machines are grouped into what is referred to as a *cell.* Groupings are determined by the operations needed to perform work for a set of similar items, or *part families,* that require similar processing. The cells become, in effect, miniature versions of product layouts. The cells may have no conveyorized movement of parts between machines, or may have a flow line connected by a conveyor (automatic transfer). Figure 6–9 compares a typical functional (process) layout and a cellular manufacturing layout. Observe that in the cellular layout, machines are arranged to handle all of the operations necessary for a group (family) of similar parts. Thus, all parts follow the same route although minor variations (e.g., skipping an operation) are possible. In contrast, the functional layout involves multiple paths for parts. Moreover, there is little effort or need to identify part families; the distinction in the figure is merely for purposes of comparison.

There are numerous benefits of cellular manufacturing. These relate to the grouping of equipment and include faster processing time, less material handling, less work-in-process inventory, and reduced setup time.

group technology The grouping into part families of items with similar design or manufacturing characteristics.

Group Technology. Effective cellular manufacturing must have groups of identified items with similar processing characteristics. This strategy for product and process design is known as **group technology** and involves identifying items with similarities in either *design characteristics* or *manufacturing characteristics,* and grouping them into *part families.* Design characteristics include size, shape, and function; manufacturing or processing characteristics involve the type and sequence of operations required. In many cases, design and processing characteristics are correlated, although this is not always the case. Thus, design families may be different from processing families. Figure 6–10 illustrates a group of parts with similar processing characteristics but different design characteristics.

FIGURE 6-9

Comparison of functional and cellular manufacturing layouts
Source: Adapted from D. Fogarty and T. Hoffmann, *Production and Inventory Management* (Cincinnati: South-Western Publishing, 1983), p. 472.

FIGURE 6-10

A group of parts with similar manufacturing process requirements but different design attributes
Source: Mikell P. Groover, *Automation, Production Systems, and Computer-Aided Manufacturing* © 1980, p. 540. Reprinted by permission of Prentice Hall, Inc., Englewood Cliffs, New Jersey.

Once similar items have been identified, items can be classified according to their families, then a system can be developed that facilitates retrieval from a database for purposes of design and manufacturing. For instance, a designer can use the system to determine if there is an existing part similar or identical to one that needs to be designed. It may happen that an existing part, with some modification, is satisfactory. This greatly enhances the productivity of design. Similarly, planning the manufacturing of a new part can include matching it with one of the part families in existence, thereby alleviating much of the burden of specific processing details.

The conversion to group technology and cellular manufacturing requires a systematic analysis of parts to identify the part families. This is often a major undertaking; it is a time-consuming job that involves the analysis of a considerable amount of data. Three primary methods for accomplishing this are visual inspection, examination of design and production data, and production flow analysis.

Visual inspection is the least accurate of the three but also the least costly and the simplest to perform. Examination of design and production data is more accurate but much more time-consuming; it is perhaps the most commonly used method of analysis. Production flow analysis has a manufacturing perspective and not a design perspective, because it examines operations sequences and machine routings to uncover similarities. Moreover, the operation sequences and routings are taken as givens; in reality the existing procedures may be far from optimal.

Conversion to cellular manufacturing can involve costly realignment of equipment. Consequently, a manager must weigh the benefits of a switch from a process layout to a cellular one against the cost of moving equipment as well as the cost and time needed for grouping parts.

Flexible Manufacturing Systems. As we discussed earlier in this chapter, flexible manufacturing systems (FMSs) are more fully automated versions of cellular manufacturing: A computer controls the transfer of parts from machine to machine and the start of work at each machine. These systems are quite expensive, but they enable manufacturers to achieve some of the benefits of product layouts with small batch sizes and much greater flexibility because the system is capable of operating with little or no human intervention.

OTHER SERVICE LAYOUTS

In addition to the layouts already described, there are other layouts found in service environments, such as warehouse, retail, and office layouts.

Warehouse and Storage Layouts. The design of storage facilities presents a different set of factors than the design of factory layouts. Frequency of order is an important consideration; items that are ordered frequently should be placed near the entrance to the facility, and those ordered infrequently should be placed toward the rear of the facility. Any correlations between items are also significant (i.e., item A is usually ordered with item B), suggesting that placing those two items close together would reduce the cost and time of *picking* (retrieving) those items. Other considerations include the number and widths of aisles, the height of storage racks, rail and/or truck loading and unloading, and the need to periodically make a physical count of stored items.

Retail Layouts. The objectives that guide design of manufacturing layouts often pertain to cost minimization and product flow. However, with retail layouts such as department stores, supermarkets, and specialty stores, designers must take into account the presence of customers and the opportunity to influence sales volume and customer attitudes through carefully designed layouts. Traffic patterns and traffic flow are important factors to consider. Some large retail chains use standard layouts for all or most of their stores. This has several advantages. Most obvious is the ability to save time and money by using one layout instead of custom designing one for each store. Another advantage is to avoid confusing consumers who visit more than one store. In the case of service retail outlets, especially small ones such as dry cleaners, shoe repair, and auto service centers, layout design is much simpler.

Office Layouts. Office layouts are undergoing transformations as the flow of paperwork is replaced with the increasing use of electronic communications. That means there is less need to place office workers in a layout that optimizes the physical transfer of information or paperwork. Another trend is to create an image of openness; office walls are giving way to low-rise partitions.

READING

Designing Supermarkets
David Schardt

The produce is over here, the dairy's over there. The soft drink specials are at the end of the aisles, the candy's at the checkout. Always.

A visit to your local supermarket isn't as haphazard as it seems. It's been laid out so that you spend as much as possible on what the store wants you to buy. And that's often more than you came in for, as we learned when we spoke to supermarket industry insiders.

Here's how a typical supermarket is designed to maximize sales.

On the Edge
The more time you spend shopping along the sides and back of the supermarket, the more money the store makes. About half its profits come from perimeter items like fruits and veggies, milk and cheese, and meat, poultry, and fish. That's also where you'll find the bakery, the salad bar, and the deli. If a store wants to distinguish itself from its competitors, it's got to be here.

Space Eaters
Some foods are so profitable that they command their own aisles. Breakfast cereals bring in more dollars per foot of shelf space than any other product in the interior of the store. So most supermarkets give cereals plenty of space.

Soft drinks aren't as profitable . . . at least not on paper. But beverage manufacturers sweeten the pot with so much free merchandise and cash rebates that carbonated soft drinks end up being one of the biggest moneymakers in a typical store.

The Meating Place
Why are the meat, poultry, and seafood displays almost always along the back of the supermarket? So that you'll see them every time you emerge from an aisle. Not a bad place to put the most profitable sections of the store.

Going to the Dairy
Why are the dairy products usually as far away from the entrance as possible? Most everybody buys milk when they

shop. To reach it, they've got to walk through a good chunk of the supermarket, often along the perimeter. That's right where the store wants shoppers.

Also, stores like to "anchor" a display by putting popular items at each end. That's why milk, for example, is often at one end of the dairy case and margarine and butter at the other. You've got to run the gauntlet of cheese, yogurts, dips, etc. to get what you came for.

Paying for Space
Every year, grocery chains are offered more than 15,000 new products, nearly all of which will fail. How do stores decide which ones to stock?

Moolah, in some cases. Large supermarkets often require manufacturers to pay for shelf space. "Slotting fees," as they're called, can range from $5,000 to $25,000 per supermarket chain for each new food. The small local tofu cheese plant seldom has that kind of money to throw around.

In "Prison"
Some supermarket insiders call the aisles of the store the "prison." Once you're in one, you're stuck until you come out the other end. The "prison" is where most of the less-profitable (for the store) national and regional name brands are, so the more time you spend there, the less time you'll spend along the perimeter . . . buying higher-profit items.

Productive Produce
Think it's a coincidence that you almost always have to walk through the produce department when you enter a supermarket? The look of those shiny, neatly stacked fruits and vegetables is *the* most important influence on where people decide to shop.

It also doesn't hurt that produce is the second most profitable section (meat is first). While it occupies a little over ten percent of the typical supermarket, it brings in close to 20 percent of the store's profits.

Source: Copyright 1994, CSPI. Reprinted from *Nutrition Action Healthletter* (1875 Connecticut Avenue, N.W., Suite 300, Washington, D.C. 10009-5728).

Designing Product Layouts: Line Balancing

Assembly lines range from fairly short, with just a few operations, to long lines that have a large number of operations. Automobile assembly lines are examples of long lines. At the assembly line for Ford Mustangs in Dearborn, Michigan, a Mustang travels about nine miles from start to finish!

Figure 6–11 illustrates the major steps involved in assembling an automobile.

Many of the benefits of a product layout relate to the ability to divide required work into a series of elemental tasks (e.g., "assemble parts *C* and *D*") that can be performed quickly and routinely by low-skilled workers or specialized equipment. The durations of these elemental tasks typically range from a few seconds to 15 minutes or more. Most time requirements are so brief that it would be impractical to assign only one task to each

www.ford.com

FIGURE 6-11

Auto assembly

Source: "Computer Integrated Manufacturing," Vol. 1 in Revolution in Progress series, Chapman and Hall, London, 1990. Adapted from R. U. Ayres, Morris A. Cohen, and Uday M. Apte. *Manufacturing Automation.* Burr Ridge, IL: McGraw-Hill, 1997, p. 175.

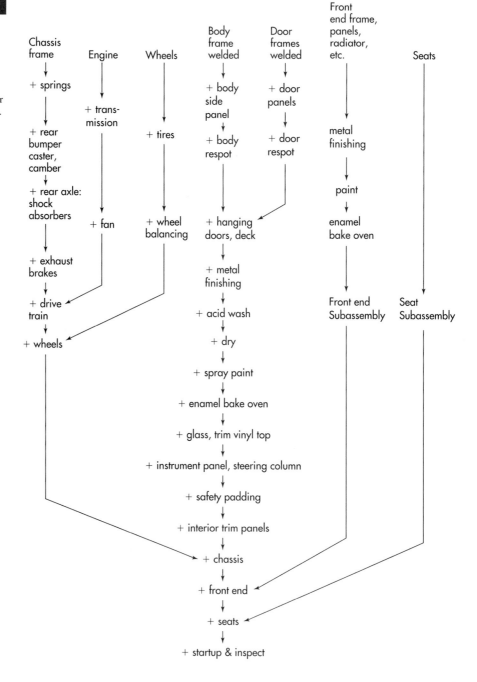

worker. For one thing, most workers would quickly become bored by the limited job scope. For another, the number of workers required to complete even a simple product or service would be enormous. Instead, tasks are usually grouped into manageable bundles and assigned to workstations staffed by one or two operators.

The process of deciding how to assign tasks to workstations is referred to as **line balancing.** The goal of line balancing is to obtain task groupings that represent approximately equal time requirements. This minimizes the idle time along the line and results in a high utilization of labor and equipment. Idle time occurs if task times are not equal among workstations; some stations are capable of producing at higher rates than others. These "fast" stations will experience periodic waits for the output from slower stations or else be forced into idleness to avoid buildups of work between stations. Unbalanced lines are undesirable in terms of inefficient utilization of labor and equipment and because they may create morale problems at the slower stations for workers who must work continuously.

Lines that are perfectly balanced will have a smooth flow of work as activities along the line are synchronized to achieve maximum utilization of labor and equipment. The major obstacle to attaining a perfectly balanced line is the difficulty of forming task bundles that have the same duration. One cause of this is that it may not be feasible to combine certain activities into the same bundle, either because of differences in equipment requirements or because the activities are not compatible (e.g., risk of contamination of paint from sanding). Another cause of difficulty is that differences among elemental task lengths cannot always be overcome by grouping tasks. A third cause of an inability to perfectly balance a line is that a required technological sequence may prohibit otherwise desirable task combinations. Consider a series of three operations that have durations of two minutes, four minutes, and two minutes, as shown in the following diagram. Ideally, the first and third operations could be combined at one workstation and have a total time equal to that of the second operation. However, it may not be possible to combine the first and third operations. In the case of an automatic car wash, scrubbing and drying operations could not realistically be combined at the same workstation due to the need to rinse cars between the two operations.

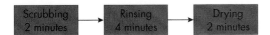

Line balancing involves assigning tasks to workstations. Usually, each workstation has one worker who handles all of the tasks at that station, although an option is to have several workers at a single workstation. For purposes of illustration, however, all of the examples and problems in this chapter have workstations with one worker. A manager could decide to use anywhere from one to five workstations to handle five tasks. With one workstation, all tasks would be done at that station; with five stations, one task would be assigned to each station. If two, three, or four workstations are used, some or all of the stations will have multiple tasks assigned to them. How does a manager decide how many stations to use?

The primary determinant is what the line's **cycle time** will be. The cycle time is the *maximum* time allowed at each workstation to perform assigned tasks before the work moves on. The cycle time also establishes the output rate of a line. For instance, if the cycle time is two minutes, units will come off the end of the line at the rate of one every two minutes.

We can gain some insight into task groupings and cycle time by considering a simple example.

Suppose that the work required to fabricate a certain product can be divided up into five elemental tasks, with the task times and precedence relationships as shown in the following diagram.

line balancing The process of assigning tasks to workstations in such a way that the workstations have approximately equal time requirements.

cycle time The maximum time allowed at each workstation to complete its set of tasks on a unit.

The task times govern the range of possible cycle times. The *minimum* cycle time is equal to the *longest* task time (1.0 minute), and the *maximum* cycle time is equal to the sum of the task times (0.1 + 0.7 + 1.0 + 0.5 + 0.2 = 2.5 minutes). The minimum cycle time would apply if there were five workstations. The maximum cycle time would apply if all tasks were performed at a single workstation. The minimum and maximum cycle times are important because they establish the potential range of output for the line, which we can compute using the following formula:

$$\text{Output capacity} = \frac{\text{OT}}{\text{CT}} \tag{6–1}$$

where

$\quad$ OT = Operating time per day

$\quad$ CT = Cycle time

Assume that the line will operate for eight hours per day (480 minutes). With a cycle time of 1.0 minute, output would be

$$\frac{480 \text{ minutes per day}}{1.0 \text{ minute per unit}} = 480 \text{ units per day}$$

With a cycle time of 2.5 minutes, the output would be

$$\frac{480 \text{ minutes per day}}{2.5 \text{ minutes per unit}} = 192 \text{ units per day}$$

Assuming that no parallel activities are to be employed (e.g., two lines), the output selected for the line must fall in the range of 192 units per day to 480 units per day.

As a general rule, the cycle time is determined by the desired output; that is, a desired output level is selected, and the cycle time is computed. If the cycle time does not fall between the maximum and minimum bounds, the desired output rate must be revised. We can compute the cycle time using this formula:

$$\text{CT} = \frac{\text{OT}}{D} \tag{6–2}$$

where

$\quad$ D = Desired output rate

For example, suppose that the desired output rate is 480 units. Using Formula 6–2, the necessary cycle time is

$$\frac{480 \text{ minutes per day}}{480 \text{ units per day}} = 1.0 \text{ minute per unit}$$

The number of workstations that will be needed is a function of both the desired output rate and our ability to combine elemental tasks into workstations. We can determine the *theoretical minimum* number of stations necessary to provide a specified rate of output as follows:

$$N_{\min} = \frac{\Sigma t}{\text{CT}} \tag{6–3}$$

where

$\quad$ $N_{\min}$ = Theoretical minimum number of stations

$\quad$ D = Desired output rate

$\quad$ Σt = Sum of task times

FIGURE 6-12

A simple precedence diagram

Suppose the desired rate of output is the maximum of 480 units per day.[2] (This will require a cycle time of 1.0 minute.) The minimum number of stations required to achieve this goal is:

$$N_{\min} = \frac{2.5 \text{ minutes per unit}}{1 \text{ minute per unit per station}} = 2.5 \text{ stations}$$

Because 2.5 stations is not feasible, it is necessary to *round up* (because 2.5 is the minimum) to three stations. Thus, the actual number of stations used will equal or exceed three, depending on how successfully the tasks can be grouped into work bundles.

A very useful tool in line balancing is a **precedence diagram.** Figure 6–12 illustrates a simple precedence diagram. It visually portrays the tasks that are to be performed along with the *sequential* requirements, that is, the *order* in which tasks must be performed. The diagram is read from left to right, so the initial task(s) are on the left and the final task is on the right. In terms of precedence requirements, we can see from the diagram, for example, that the only requirement to begin task *b* is that task *a* must be finished. However, in order to begin task *d,* tasks *b* and *c* must *both* be finished. Note that the elemental tasks are the same ones that we have been using.

precedence diagram A diagram that shows elemental tasks and their precedence requirements.

Now let's see how a line is balanced. This involves assigning tasks to workstations. Generally, no techniques are available that guarantee an optimal set of assignments. Instead, managers employ *heuristic (intuitive) rules,* which provide good and sometimes optimal sets of assignments. A number of line-balancing heuristics are in use, two of which are described here for purposes of illustration:

1. Assign tasks in order of most following tasks.
2. Assign tasks in order of greatest positional weight. Positional weight is the sum of each task's time and the times of all following tasks.

The general procedure used in line balancing is described in Table 6–3.

Example 1

Arrange the tasks shown in Figure 6–12 into three workstations. Use a cycle time of 1.0 minute. Assign tasks in order of the most number of followers.

Solution

Workstation	Time Remaining	Eligible	Assign Task	Station Idle Time
1	1.0	a, c	a	
	0.9	c	c	
	0.2	none	—	0.2
2	1.0	b	b	0.0
3	1.0	d	d	
	0.5	e	e	
	0.3	—	—	0.3
				0.5

---

[2]At first glance, it might seem that the desired output would logically be the maximum possible output. However, you will see why that is not always the best alternative.

TABLE 6–3

Line balancing procedure

1. Identify the cycle time and determine the minimum number of workstations.
2. Make assignments to workstations in order, beginning with Station 1. Tasks are assigned to workstations moving from left to right through the precedence diagram.
3. Before each assignment, use the following criteria to determine which tasks are *eligible* to be assigned to a workstation:
   a. All preceding tasks in the sequence have been assigned.
   b. The task time does not exceed the time remaining at the workstation.
   If no tasks are eligible, move on to the next workstation.
4. After each task assignment, determine the time remaining at the current workstation by subtracting the sum of times for tasks already assigned to it from the cycle time.
5. Break ties that occur using one of these rules:
   a. Assign the task with the longest task time.
   b. Assign the task with the greatest number of followers.
   If there is still a tie, choose one task arbitrarily.
6. Continue until all tasks have been assigned to workstations.
7. Compute appropriate measures (e.g., percent idle time, efficiency) for the set of assignments.

Comment: The initial "time remaining" for each workstation is equal to the cycle time. For a task to be eligible, tasks preceding it must have been assigned, and the task's time must not exceed the station's remaining time.

Example 1 was purposely simple; it was designed to illustrate the basic procedure. Later examples will illustrate tiebreaking, constructing precedence diagrams, and the positional weight method. Before considering those examples, let us first consider some measures of effectiveness that can be used for evaluating a given set of assignments.

Two widely used measures of effectiveness are:

balance delay Percentage of idle time of a line.

1. The *percentage of idle time* of the line. This is sometimes referred to as the **balance delay.** It can be computed as follows:

$$\text{Percentage of idle time} = \frac{\text{Idle time per cycle}}{N_{\text{actual}} \times \text{cycle time}} \times 100 \tag{6–4}$$

where N_{actual} = Actual number of stations.
For the preceding example, the value is:

$$\text{Percentage of idle time} = \frac{.5}{3 \times 1.0} \times 100 = 16.7\%$$

In effect, this is the average idle time divided by the cycle time, multiplied by 100. Note that cycle time refers to the actual cycle time that is achieved.

2. The *efficiency* of the line. This is computed as follows:

$$\text{Efficiency} = 100 - \text{percent idle time} \tag{6–5}$$

Here efficiency = 100% − 16.7% = 83.3%

Now let's consider the question of whether the selected level of output should equal the maximum output possible. The minimum number of workstations needed is a function of the desired output rate and, therefore, the cycle time. Thus, a lower rate of output (hence, a longer cycle time) may result in a need for fewer stations. Hence, the manager must consider whether the potential savings realized by having fewer workstations would be greater than the decrease in profit resulting from producing fewer units.

The preceding examples serve to illustrate some of the fundamental concepts of line balancing. They are rather simple; in most real-life situations, the number of branches and tasks are often much greater. Consequently, the job of line balancing can be a good deal more complex. In many instances, the number of alternatives for grouping tasks is so great that it is virtually impossible to conduct an exhaustive review of all possibilities. For this reason, many real-life problems of any magnitude are solved using heuristic approaches. The purpose of a heuristic approach is to reduce the number of alternatives that must be considered, but it does not guarantee an optimal solution.

SOME GUIDELINES FOR LINE BALANCING

In balancing an assembly line, tasks are assigned *one at a time* to the line, starting at the first workstation. At each step, the unassigned tasks are checked to determine which are eligible for assignment. Next, the eligible tasks are checked to see which of them will fit in the workstation being loaded. A heuristic is used to select one of the tasks that will fit, and the task is assigned. This process is repeated until there are no eligible tasks that will fit. Then the next workstation can be loaded. This continues until all tasks are assigned. The objective is to minimize the idle time for the line subject to technological and output constraints.

Technological constraints tell us which elemental tasks are *eligible* to be assigned at a particular position on the line. Technological constraints can result from the precedence or ordering relationships among the tasks. The precedence relationships require that certain tasks must be performed before others (and so, must be assigned to workstations before others). Thus, in a car wash, the rinsing operation must be performed before the drying operation. The drying operation is not eligible for assignment until the rinsing operation has been assigned. Technological constraints may also result from two tasks being "incompatible" (e.g., space restrictions or the nature of the operations may prevent their being placed in the same work center). For example, sanding and painting operations would not be assigned to the same work center because dust particles from the sanding operation could contaminate the paint.

Output constraints, on the other hand, determine the maximum amount of work that a manager can assign to each workstation, and this determines whether an eligible task *will fit* at a workstation. The desired output rate determines the cycle time, and the sum of the task times assigned to any workstation must not exceed the cycle time. If a task can be assigned to a workstation without exceeding the cycle time, then the task will fit.

Once it is known which tasks are *eligible* and *will fit,* the manager can select the task to be assigned (if there is more than one to choose from). This is where the heuristic rules help us decide which task to assign from among those that are eligible and will fit.

To clarify the terminology, *following tasks* are all tasks that you would encounter by following all paths from the task in question through the precedence diagram. *Preceding tasks* are all tasks you would encounter by tracing all paths *backward* from the task in question. In the precedence diagram below, tasks *b, d, e,* and *f* are followers of task *a*. Tasks *a, b,* and *c* are preceding tasks for *e*.

The *positional weight* for a task is the sum of the task times for itself and all its following tasks.

Neither of the heuristics *guarantees* the *best* solution, or even a good solution to the line-balancing problem, but they do provide guidelines for developing a solution. It may be useful to apply several different heuristics to the same problem and pick the best (least idle time) solution out of those developed.

Example 2

Using the information contained in the table shown, do each of the following:

1. Draw a precedence diagram.
2. Assuming an eight-hour workday, compute the cycle time needed to obtain an output of 400 units per day.
3. Determine the minimum number of workstations required.
4. Assign tasks to workstations using this rule: Assign tasks according to greatest number of following tasks. In case of a tie, use the tiebreaker of assigning the task with the longest processing time first.

Task	Immediate Follower	Task Time (in minutes)
a	b	0.2
b	e	0.2
c	d	0.8
d	f	0.6
e	f	0.3
f	g	1.0
g	h	0.4
h	end	0.3
		$\Sigma t = 3.8$

Solution

1. Drawing a precedence diagram is a relatively straightforward task. Begin with activities with no predecessors. We see from the list of Immediate Followers that tasks a and c do not appear. Hence, they have no immediate predecessors. We build from here.

Task b follows a, and d follows c.

Task e follows b.

Task f follows e and d.

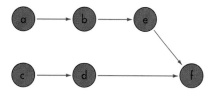

Task g follows f, and h follows g.

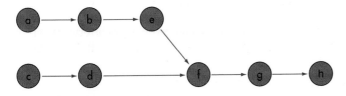

2. $CT = \dfrac{OT}{D} = \dfrac{480 \text{ minutes per day}}{400 \text{ units per day}} = 1.2 \text{ minutes per cycle}$

3. $N = \dfrac{\sum t}{CT} = \dfrac{3.8 \text{ minutes per unit}}{1.2 \text{ minutes per cycle per station}} = 3.17 \text{ stations (round to 4)}$

4. Beginning with station 1, make assignments following this procedure: Determine from the precedence diagram which tasks are eligible for assignment. Then determine which of the eligible tasks will fit the time remaining for the station. Use the tiebreaker if necessary. Once a task has been assigned, remove it from consideration. When a station cannot take any more assignments, go on to the next station. Continue until all tasks have been assigned.

Station	Time Remaining	Eligible	Will Fit	Assign (task time)	Idle
1	1.2 min.	a, c*	a, c*	a (0.2)	
	1.0 min.	c, b**	c, b**	c (0.8)	
	0.2 min.	b, d	b	b (0.2)	
	0 min.	e, d	None	—	0.0
2	1.2 min.	e, d	e, d	d (0.6)	
	0.6 min.	e	e	e (0.3)	
	0.3***	f	None	—	0.3
3	1.2 min.	f	f	f (1.0)	
	0.2 min.	g	None	—	0.2
4	1.2 min.	g	g	g (0.4)	
	0.8 min.	h	h	h (0.3)	
	0.5	—	—	—	0.5
					1.0 min.

*Neither *a* nor *c* has any predecessors, so both are eligible. Task *a* was assigned since it has more followers.

**Once *a* is assigned, *b* and *c* are now eligible. Both will fit in the time remaining of 1.0 minute. The tie cannot be broken by the "most followers" rule, so the longer task is assigned.

***Although *f* is eligible, this task will not fit, so station 2 is left with 0.3 minute of idle time per 1.2 minute cycle.

These assignments are shown in the following diagram. If you look carefully at this solution, you may discover that it can be improved upon. Thus, this solution is not necessarily optimal. One should not expect that heuristic approaches will always produce optimal solutions; they merely provide a practical way to deal with complex problems that may not lend themselves to optimizing techniques.

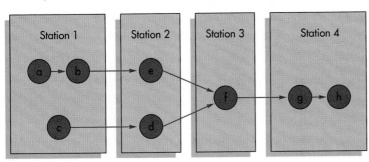

OTHER FACTORS

The preceding discussion on line balancing presents a relatively straightforward approach to approximating a balanced line. In practice, the ability to do this usually involves additional considerations, some of which are technical.

Technical considerations include skill requirements of different tasks. If skill requirements of tasks are quite different, it may not be feasible to place the tasks in the same workstation. Similarly, if the tasks themselves are incompatible (e.g., the use of fire and flammable liquids), it may not be feasible even to place them in stations that are near to each other.

Developing a workable plan for balancing a line may also require consideration of human factors as well as equipment and space limitations.

Although it is convenient to treat assembly operations as if they occur at the same rate time after time, it is more realistic to assume that whenever humans are involved, task completion times will be variable. The reasons for the variations are numerous, including fatigue, boredom, and failure to concentrate on the task at hand. Absenteeism also can affect line balance. Minor variability can be dealt with by allowing some slack along the line. However, if more variability is inherent in even a few tasks, that will severely impact the ability to achieve a balanced line.

For these reasons, lines that involve human tasks are more of an ideal than a reality. In practice, lines are rarely perfectly balanced. However, this is not entirely bad, because some unbalance means that slack exists at points along the line, which can reduce the impact of brief stoppages at some workstations. Also, workstations that have slack can be used for new workers who may not be "up to speed."

OTHER APPROACHES

There are a number of other approaches companies use to achieve a smooth flow of production. One approach is to use *parallel workstations*. These are beneficial for bottleneck operations which would otherwise disrupt the flow of product as it moves down the line. The bottlenecks may be the result of difficult or very long tasks. Parallel workstations increase the work flow and provide flexibility.

Consider this example.[3] A job has four tasks; task times are 1 minute, 1 minute, 2 minutes, and 1 minute. The cycle time for the line would be 2 minutes, and the output rate would be 30 units per hour:

$$\frac{60 \text{ minutes per hour}}{2 \text{ minutes per unit}} = 30 \text{ units per hour}$$

Using parallel stations for the third task would result in a cycle time of 1 minute because the output rate at the parallel stations would be equal to that of a single station, and allow an output rate for the line of 60 units per hour:

---

[3]Adapted from Mikell P. Groover, *Automation, Production Systems, and Computer-Aided Manufacturing,* 2nd ed. Englewood Cliffs, NJ: Prentice Hall, 1987, Chapter 6.

Another approach to achieving a balanced line is to *cross-train* workers so that they are able to perform more than one task. Then, when bottlenecks occur, the workers with temporarily increased idle time can assist other workers who are temporarily overburdened, thereby maintaining an even flow of work along the line. This is sometimes referred to as *dynamic line balancing,* and it is used most often in lean production systems.

Still another approach is to design a line to handle more than one product on the same line. This is referred to as a *mixed model line.* Naturally, the products have to be fairly similar, so that the tasks involved are pretty much the same for all products. This approach offers great flexibility in varying the amount of output of the products. The following newsclip describes one such line.

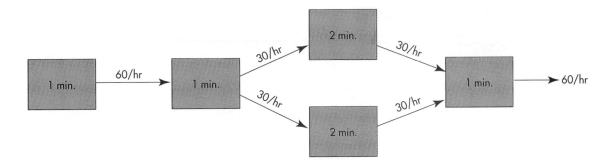

NEWSCLIP

Toyota Mixes and Matches

www.toyota.com

Toyota, long famous for producing quality cars and light trucks, decided to produce minivans in the U.S. Wanting to get into production quickly, Toyota took an ambitious step at its Georgetown, Kentucky, manufacturing plant, deciding to produce Sienna minivans at the same time—and at the same workstations—that produce Camry automobiles.

"Although Camry and Sienna are built from the same basic chassis, and share 50 percent of their parts, there are key differences. Sienna is five inches longer, three inches wider and a foot taller than Camry. Each Sienna takes up more space on the assembly line and requires more and bigger parts.

"Another automaker might shut down a plant for months to make the changes. But Toyota needed to move quickly. Delay could jeopardize booming sales of Camry.

"Out of 300 stations on the assembly line, Sienna needs different parts at 26. But only seven new production steps are needed. . . . To save time, Toyota decided not to add workstations. Instead, it selected two teams of workers, one for each shift, that are responsible for attaching Sienna-only parts. Meanwhile, engineers, working with Toyota workers, designed equipment intended to make those duties easy to perform."

As soon as a Sienna approaches one of the seven spots on the assembly line, a member of the Sienna team is there to take over. Some team members climb inside, where they scoot around on wheeled carts that look like NASA's Sojourner Mars explorer. Others attach roof racks by standing on platforms that put the van's top waist high, eliminating the need to reach.

Toyota may have shortened the time needed to start production by three years by using this innovative approach to the assembly line.

Source: Based on "Camry Assembly Line Delivers New Minivan," p. B3. Copyright 1997, *USA TODAY.* Adapted with permission.

Designing Process Layouts

The main issue in design of process layouts concerns the relative positioning of the departments involved. As illustrated in Figure 6–13, departments must be assigned to locations. The problem is to develop a reasonably good layout; some combinations will be more desirable than others. For example, some departments may benefit from adjacent locations whereas others should be separated. A lab with delicate equipment would not be

FIGURE 6-13

Work centers must be assigned to locations

Locations

A	B	C
D	E	F

Work centers to be assigned
1
2
3
4
5
6

www.mcdonalds.com

located near a department that had equipment with strong vibrations. Conversely, two departments that share some of the same equipment would benefit from being close together.

Layouts can also be influenced by external factors such as the location of entrances, loading docks, elevators, windows, and areas of reinforced flooring. Also important are noise levels, safety, and the size and locations of restrooms.

In a few instances (e.g., the layouts of supermarkets, gas stations, and fast-food chains), a sufficient number of installations having similar characteristics justify the development of standardized layouts. For example, the use of the same basic patterns in McDonald's fast-food locations facilitates construction of new structures and employee training. Food preparation, order taking, and customer service follow the same pattern throughout the chain. Installation and service of equipment are also standardized. This same concept has been successfully employed in computer software products such as Microsoft Windows® and the Macintosh® Operating System. Different applications are designed with certain basic features in common, so that a user familiar with one application can readily use other applications without having to start from scratch with each new application.

The majority of layout problems involve single rather than multiple locations, and they present unique combinations of factors that do not lend themselves to a standardized approach. Consequently, these layouts require customized designs.

A major obstacle to finding the most efficient layout of departments is the large number of possible assignments. For example, there are more than 87 billion different ways that 14 departments can be assigned to 14 locations if the locations form a single line. Different location configurations (e.g., 14 departments in a two-by-seven grid) often reduce the number of possibilities, as do special requirements (e.g., the stamping department may have to be assigned to a location with reinforced flooring). Still, the remaining number of layout possibilities is quite large. Unfortunately, no algorithms exist to identify the best layout arrangement under all circumstances. Often planners must rely on heuristic rules to guide trial-and-error efforts for a satisfactory solution to each problem.

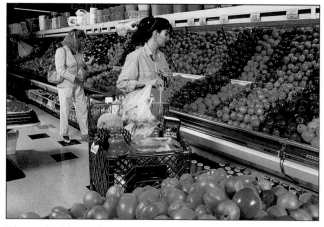

The profitable produce section of a grocery store is prominently located along the store's perimeter.

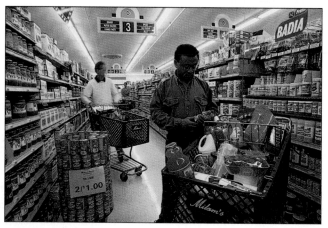

The aisle locations contain the less profitable store and name brands, including canned goods and packaged items.

MEASURES OF EFFECTIVENESS

One advantage of process layouts is their ability to satisfy a variety of processing requirements. Customers or materials in these systems require different operations and different sequences of operations, which causes them to follow different paths through the system. Material-oriented systems necessitate the use of variable-path material-handling equipment to move materials from work center to work center. In customer-oriented systems, people must travel or be transported from work center to work center. In both cases, transportation costs or time can be significant. Because of this factor, one of the major objectives in process layout is to minimize transportation cost, distance, or time. This is usually accomplished by locating departments with relatively high interdepartmental work flow as close together as possible.

Other concerns in choosing among alternative layouts include initial costs in setting up the layout, expected operating costs, the amount of effective capacity created, and the ease of modifying the system.

In situations that call for improvement of an existing layout, costs of relocating any work center must be weighed against the potential benefits of the move.

INFORMATION REQUIREMENTS

The design of process layouts requires the following information:

1. A list of departments or work centers to be arranged, their approximate dimensions, and the dimensions of the building or buildings that will house the departments.

2. A projection of future work flows between the various work centers.

3. The distance between locations and the cost per unit of distance to move loads between locations.

4. The amount of money to be invested in the layout.

5. A list of any special considerations (e.g., operations that must be close to each other or operations that must be separated).

The ideal situation is to first develop a layout and then design the physical structure around it, thus permitting maximum flexibility in design. This procedure is commonly followed when new facilities are constructed. Nonetheless, many layouts must be developed in existing structures where floor space, the dimensions of the building, location of entrances and elevators, and other similar factors must be carefully weighed in designing the layout. Note that multilevel structures pose special problems for layout planners.

MINIMIZING TRANSPORTATION COSTS OR DISTANCES

The most common goals in designing process layouts are minimization of transportation costs or distances traveled. In such cases, it can be very helpful to summarize the necessary data in *from-to charts* like those illustrated in Tables 6–4 and 6–5. Table 6–4 indicates the distance between each of the locations, and Table 6–5 indicates actual or projected work flow between each pair. For instance, the distance chart reveals that a trip from location A to location B will involve a distance of 20 meters. (Distances are often measured between department centers.) Oddly enough, the length of a trip between locations A and B may differ depending on the *direction* of the trip, due to one-way routes, elevators, or other factors. To simplify the discussion, assume a constant distance between any two locations regardless of direction. However, it is not realistic to assume that interdepartmental work flows are equal—there is no reason to suspect that department 1 will send as much work to department 2 as department 2 sends to 1. For example, several departments may send goods to packaging, but packaging may send only to the shipping department.

Transportation costs can also be summarized in from-to charts, but we shall avoid that complexity, assuming instead that costs are a direct, linear function of distance.

TABLE 6–4

Distance between locations (meters)

From \ To	LOCATION A	B	C
A	—	20	40
B	20	—	30
C	40	30	—

TABLE 6–5

Interdepartmental work flow (loads per day)

From \ To	DEPARTMENT 1	2	3
1	—	10	80
2	20	—	30
3	90	70	—

Example 3

Assign the three departments shown in Table 6–5 to locations A, B, and C, which are separated by the distances shown in Table 6–4, in such a way that transportation cost is minimized. Use this heuristic: Assign departments with the greatest interdepartmental work flow first to locations that are closest to each other.

Solution

Ranking departments according to highest work flow and locations according to highest interlocation distances helps in making assignments. If interlocation distances are independent of direction of flow, work flow between departments can be summed to achieve a clearer picture of the need for closeness. Thus:

Trip	Distance (meters)	Department Pair	Work Flow	
A–B	20	3–1	90	170
B–A	20	1–3	80	
B–C	30	3–2	70	100
C–B	30	2–3	30	
A–C	40	2–1	20	30
C–A	40	1–2	10	

From these listings, you can see that departments 1 and 3 have the highest interdepartmental work flow, and that locations A and B are the closest. Thus, it seems reasonable to consider assigning 1 and 3 to locations A and B, although it is not yet obvious which department should be assigned to which location. Further inspection of the work flow list reveals that 2 and 3 have higher work flow than 1 and 2, so 2 and 3 should probably be located more closely than 1 and 2. Hence, it would seem reasonable to place 3 between 1 and 2, or at least centralize that department with respect to the other two. The resulting assignments might appear as illustrated in Figure 6–14.

Note that work flows between departments in the diagram are the sum of the flow each way (e.g., the 170 between 1 and 3 is the combined flow of 90 loads from 3 to 1 and 80 loads from 1 to 3).

FIGURE 6–14

Interdepartmental work flows for assigned departments

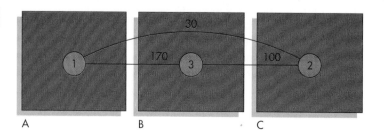

If the cost per meter to move any load is $1, you can compute the total daily transportation cost for this assignment by multiplying each department's number of loads by the trip distance, and summing those quantities:

Department	Number of Loads to:	Location	Distance to:	Loads × Distance
1	2: 10	A	C: 40	10 × 40 = 400
	3: 80		B: 20	80 × 20 = 1,600
2	1: 20	C	A: 40	20 × 40 = 800
	3: 30		B: 30	30 × 30 = 900
3	1: 90	B	A: 20	90 × 20 = 1,800
	2: 70		C: 30	70 × 30 = 2,100
				7,600

At $1 per load meter, the cost for this plan is $7,600 per day. Even though it might appear that this arrangement yields the lowest transportation cost, you cannot be absolutely positive of that without actually computing the total cost for every alternative and comparing it to this one. Although this could be done in this example, where the number of alternatives is quite small (i.e., there are 3! = 6 possible arrangements), in problems with more departments, the number is likely to be too large to even consider examining every alternative. Instead, rely on the choice of reasonable heuristic rules such as those demonstrated above to arrive at a satisfactory, if not optimal, solution.

CLOSENESS RATINGS

Although the preceding approach is widely used, it suffers from the limitation of focusing on only one objective, and many situations involve multiple criteria. Richard Muther developed a more general approach to the problem, which allows for subjective input from analysis or managers to indicate the relative importance of each combination of department pairs.[4] That information is then summarized in a grid like that shown in Figure 6–15. Read the grid in the same way as you would read a mileage chart on a road map, except that letters rather than distances appear at the intersections. The letters represent the importance of closeness for each department pair, with A being the most important and X being an undesirable pairing. Thus, in the grid it is "absolutely necessary" to locate 1 and 2 close to each other because there is an A at the intersection of those departments on the grid. On the other hand, 1 and 4 should not be close together because their intersection has an X. In practice, the letters on the grid are often accompanied by numbers that indicate the reason

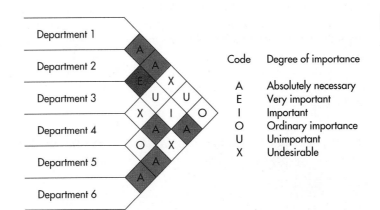

Code	Degree of importance
A	Absolutely necessary
E	Very important
I	Important
O	Ordinary importance
U	Unimportant
X	Undesirable

FIGURE 6–15

A Muther grid

[4]Richard Muther and John Wheeler, "Simplified Systematic Layout Planning," *Factory* 120, nos. 8, 9, and 10 (August, September, October, 1962) pp. 68–77, 111–19, 101–13.

for each assignment: they are omitted here to simplify the illustration. Muther suggests the following list:

1. Use same equipment or facilities.
2. Share the same personnel or records.
3. Sequence of work flow.
4. Ease of communication.
5. Unsafe or unpleasant conditions.
6. Similar work performed.

Example 4

Assign the six departments in Figure 6–14 to a 2 × 3 set of locations using the heuristic rule: Assign critical departments first.

Solution

Critical pairs of departments are those with A or X ratings. Prepare a list of those by referring to the grid:

As	Xs
1–2	1–4
1–3	3–6
2–6	3–4
3–5	
4–6	
5–6	

Next, form a cluster of A links, beginning with the department that appears most frequently in the A list (in this case, 6). For instance:

Take the remaining As in order, and add them to this main cluster where possible, rearranging the cluster as necessary. Form separate clusters for departments that do not link with the main cluster. In this case, all link with the main cluster.

Next, graphically portray the Xs:

Observe that, as it stands, the cluster of As also satisfies the X separations. It is a fairly simple exercise to fit the cluster into a 2 × 3 arrangement:

1	2	6
3	5	4

Note that the lower-level ratings have also been satisfied with this arrangement, even though no attempt was made to explicitly consider the E and I ratings. Naturally, not every problem will yield the same results, so it may be necessary to do some additional adjusting to see if improvements can be made, keeping in mind that the A and X assignments deserve the greatest consideration.

Note that departments are considered close not only when they touch side to side, but also when they touch corner to corner.

The value of this rating approach is that it permits the use of multiple objectives and subjective inputs. Its limitations relate to the use of subjective inputs in general: They are imprecise and unreliable.

COMPUTER ANALYSIS

The size and complexity of process layout problems have led to the development of a number of computerized packages. The obvious advantage of computerized analyses of layout problems is the ability to handle large problems and to consider many different layout alternatives. Even so, in some instances, the results of computer analysis require additional manual adjustments before they can be used.

Summary

Process selection choices often have strategic implications for organizations. They can affect cost, quality, productivity, customer satisfaction, and competitive advantage. Process types include job shop, batch processing, repetitive processing, continuous processing, and projects. Process type determines how work is organized, and it has implications for the entire organization and its supply chain. Process type and layout are closely related.

Layout decisions are an important aspect of the design of production systems, affecting operating costs and efficiency. Layout decisions are often closely related to process selection decisions.

Product layouts are geared to high-volume output of standardized items. Workers and equipment are arranged according to the technological sequence required by the product or service involved. Emphasis in design is on work flow through the system, and specialized processing and handling equipment is often used. Product layouts are highly vulnerable to breakdowns. Preventive maintenance reduces the occurrence of breakdowns.

Process layouts group similar activities into departments or other work centers. These systems can handle a wide range of processing requirements and are less susceptible to breakdowns. However, the variety of processing requirements necessitates continual routing and scheduling and the use of variable-path material-handling equipment. The rate of output is generally much lower than that of product layouts.

Table 6–6 summarizes product and process layouts.

Fixed-position layouts are used when size, fragility, cost, or other factors make it undesirable or impractical to move a product through a system. Instead, workers, equipment, and materials are brought to the product.

The main design efforts in product layout development focus on dividing up the work required to produce a product or service into a series of tasks that are as nearly equal as possible. The goal is to achieve a high degree of utilization of labor and equipment. In process layout, design efforts often focus on the relative positioning of departments to minimize transportation costs or to meet other requirements concerning the proximity of certain department pairs.

The large number of possible alternatives to layout problems prevents an examination of each one. Instead, heuristic rules guide discovery of alternatives. The solutions thus obtained are usually satisfactory although not necessarily optimal. Computer packages are available to reduce the effort required to obtain solutions to layout problems, but these too rely largely on heuristic methods.

TABLE 6-6

Product and process layouts compared

	Product Layout	**Process Layout**
Description	A sequential arrangement of personnel and/or equipment designed to provide standardized processing.	A functional arrangement of personnel and/or equipment designed to handle a variety of processing requirements.
Focus of layout	Balance operations to avoid bottlenecks, and attain a smooth flow of work.	Arrange equipment or departments to minimize transportation costs and/or congestion.
Processing	Repetitive or continuous.	Job shop or batch.
Examples of: goods	Automobiles, video tapes.	Furniture, baked goods.
services	Car wash, cafeteria line.	Auto repair, health care.
Product or service variety	Low.	Moderate to high.
Typical processing worker skill levels	Low, semiskilled.	Semiskilled to highly skilled.
Flexibility	Very low.	Moderate to high.
Volume	High.	Low to moderate.
Work-in-process inventory levels	Low.	High.
Material handling	Fixed path (e.g., conveyors).	Variable path (e.g., forklifts).
Primary approach to equipment maintenance	Preventive.	As needed.
Benefits	Low cost per unit, high productivity.	Can handle a variety of processing requirements.

Key Terms

assembly line, 233
automation, 222
balance delay, 246
cellular manufacturing, 238
computer-aided manufacturing (CAM), 223
computer-integrated manufacturing (CIM), 228
cycle time, 243
fixed-position layout, 237
flexible manufacturing system (FMS), 227
group technology, 238

line balancing, 243
manufacturing cell, 224
numerically controlled (N/C) machines, 223
outsource, 218
precedence diagram, 245
process layout, 235
product layout, 232
production line, 233
project, 222
robot, 223
service blueprint, 230

Solved Problems

Problem 1

The tasks shown in the following precedence diagram are to be assigned to workstations with the intent of minimizing idle time. Management has designed an output rate of 275 units per day. Assume 440 minutes are available per day.

a. Determine the appropriate cycle time.

b. What is the minimum number of stations possible?

c. Assign tasks using the "positional weight" rule: Assign tasks with highest following times (including a task's own time) first. Break ties using greatest number of following tasks.

a. $CT = \dfrac{\text{Operating time}}{\text{Desired output}} = \dfrac{440 \text{ minutes per day}}{275 \text{ units per day}} = 1.6 \text{ minutes}$

b. $N = \dfrac{\sum t}{\text{Cycle time}} = \dfrac{4.2}{1.6 \text{ minutes}} = 2.625 \text{ (round to 3)}$

c. Add positional weights (following time including task time) to the diagram:

Station	Time Remaining*	Eligible	Will Fit	Assign Task/Time	Station Idle Time
1	1.6	a, b	a, b	b/0.6	
	1.0	a, d	a	a/0.3	
	0.7	c, d	c	c/0.4	
	0.3	e, d	e	e/0.2	
	0.1	g, d	g	g/0.1	
	0	—	—	—	0
2	1.6	d	d	d/1.2	
	0.4	f	none	none	0.4
3	1.6	f	f	f/0.6	
	1.0	h	h	h/0.5	
	0.5	i	i	i/0.3	
	0.2	—	—	—	0.2
					0.6

*The initial time for each station is the cycle time computed in part *a*.

The resulting assignments are shown below.

Assign nine automobile service departments to bays in a 3 × 3 grid so that the closeness ratings in the following matrix are satisfied. (The unimportant and ordinary-importance ratings have been omitted to simplify the example.) The location of department 4 must be in the upper right-hand corner of the grid to satisfy a town ordinance.

Problem 2

Solution

Note that department 1 has many A ratings, making it a strong candidate for the center position in the grid. We can form a cluster of departments that should be close together:

Next, we can identify departmental pairings that should be avoided:

These departments should be spaced around the perimeter of the grid. After a bit of trial and error, the final grid shown below emerged. Check it against the rating matrix to see if it satisfies the ratings.

Problem 3

Five departments are to be assigned to locations B–F in the grid. (For technical reasons, department 6 must be assigned to location A.) Transportation cost is $2 per foot. The objective is to minimize total transportation cost. Information on interdepartmental work flows and distances between locations is shown in the following tables. Assign departments with the greatest interdepartmental work flow first.

DISTANCE BETWEEN LOCATIONS (FEET)

From	To	A	B	C	D	E	F
A		—	50	100	50	80	130
B			—	50	90	40	70
C				—	140	60	50
D					—	50	120
E						—	50
F							—

NUMBER OF TRIPS PER DAY BETWEEN CENTERS

From	To	1	2	3	4	5	6
1		—	90	25	23	11	18
2		35	—	8	5	10	16
3		37	2	—	1	0	7
4		41	12	1	—	4	0
5		14	16	0	9	—	3
6		32	38	13	2	2	—

A Dept. 6	B	C
D	E	F

First determine the interdepartmental work flows (e.g., for 1–2 the flow is 90 + 35 = 125). Then either rank them or arrange them from high to low. Here they have been arranged from high to low.   *Solution*

Dept.	Workflow
1–2	125
1–4	64
1–3	62
2–6	54
1–6	50
2–5	26
1–5	25
3–6	20
2–4	17
4–5	13
2–3	10
5–6	5
3–4	2
4–6	2
3–5	0

From this, we can see that departments 1 and 2 have the greatest interdepartmental work flow, so they should be close, perhaps at B and E. Next, work flows for 1–3 and 1–4 are high. Note, though, that the work flow for 3–4 is low, suggesting that they need not be close. Instead, we would place them on either side of department 1. Note also that 3–4 is only 2, 5–6 is 0, while 3–6 is 20 and 4–5 is 13. Hence, place department 3 at location D, department 4 at location F, and department 5 at location C.

A Dept. 6	B Dept. 2	C Dept. 5
D Dept. 3	E Dept. 1	F Dept. 4

Total cost:

Trip		**b** Distance	**c** Frequency	**(b × c × $2)** Cost
1–2	(B–E)	40	125	$10,000
1–3	(D–E)	50	62	6,200
1–4	(F–E)	50	64	6,400
1–5	(E–C)	60	25	3,000
1–6	(A–E)	80	50	8,000
2–3	(B–D)	90	10	1,800
2–4	(B–F)	70	17	2,380
2–5	(B–C)	50	26	2,600
2–6	(A–B)	50	54	5,400
3–4	(F–D)	120	2	480
3–5	(D–C)	140	0	0
3–6	(A–D)	50	20	2,000
4–5	(C–F)	50	13	1,300
4–6	(A–F)	130	2	520
5–6	(A–C)	100	5	1,000
				$51,080

Discussion and Review Questions

1. Explain the importance of process selection in system design.
2. Briefly describe the five process types, and indicate the kinds of situations in which each would be used.
3. Briefly discuss the advantages and disadvantages of automation.
4. Briefly describe computer-assisted approaches to production.
5. What is a flexible manufacturing system, and under what set of circumstances is it most appropriate?
6. Why is management of technology important?
7. Why might the choice of equipment that provides flexibility sometimes be viewed as a management copout?
8. What are the trade-offs that occur when a process layout is used? What are the trade-offs that occur when a product layout is used?
9. List some common reasons for redesigning layouts.
10. Briefly describe the two main layout types.
11. What are the main advantages of a product layout? The main disadvantages?
12. What are the main advantages of a process layout? The main disadvantages?
13. What is the goal of line balancing? What happens if a line is unbalanced?
14. Why are routing and scheduling continual problems in process layouts?
15. Compare equipment maintenance strategies in product and process layouts.
16. Briefly outline the impact that job sequence has on each of the layout types.
17. The City Transportation Planning Committee must decide whether to begin a long-term project to build a subway system or to upgrade the present bus service. Suppose you are an expert in fixed-path and variable-path material-handling equipment, and the committee seeks your counsel on this matter. What are the advantages and limitations of the subway and bus systems?

18. Identify the fixed-path and variable-path material-handling equipment commonly found in supermarkets.
19. What are heuristic approaches, and why are they used in designing layouts?
20. Why are product layouts atypical in service environments?
21. According to a study by the Alliance of American Insurers, it costs more than three times the original purchase price in parts and labor to replace a totally wrecked Chevrolet. Explain the reasons for this large discrepancy in terms of the processes used to assemble the original car and those required to reconstruct the wrecked car.
22. Name some ways that a layout can help or hinder productivity.
23. What is cellular manufacturing? What are its main benefits and limitations?
24. What is group technology?
25. Explain the consequences of task time variability on line balancing.

Memo Writing Exercises

1. The manager of financial services, Richard Winchester, remarked on a recent tour that a production line should be perfectly balanced, and that if done correctly, there should be little or no idle time along the line. Write a one-page memo to him, agreeing or disagreeing.
2. Write a memo to Karen Flint, plant manager, outlining the benefits of producing two products on the same assembly line, as Toyota did with its Sienna minivan and Camry automobile. Refer to the newsclip in the "Other Approaches" section of the chapter.
3. Write a one-page memo to your supervisor, Sharon Williams, relating fixed automation and flexible automation to the product-process matrix (i.e., where do they fit?). Justify your choices.

Problems

1. An assembly line with 17 tasks is to be balanced. The longest task is 2.4 minutes, and the total time for all tasks is 18 minutes. The line will operate for 450 minutes per day.
   a. What are the minimum and maximum cycle times?
   b. What range of output is theoretically possible for the line?
   c. What is the minimum number of workstations needed if the maximum output rate is to be sought?
   d. What cycle time will provide an output rate of 125 units per day?
   e. What output potential will result if the cycle time is (1) 9 minutes? (2) 15 minutes?
2. A manager wants to assign tasks to workstations as efficiently as possible, and achieve an hourly output of 33⅓ units. Assume the shop works a 60-minute hour. Assign the tasks shown in the accompanying precedence diagram (times are in minutes) to workstations using the following rules:
   a. In order of most following tasks. Tiebreaker: greatest positional weight.
   b. In order of greatest positional weight.
   c. What is the efficiency?

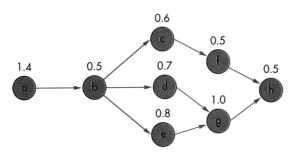

3. A manager wants to assign tasks to workstations as efficiently as possible, and achieve an hourly output of 4 units. The department uses a working time of 56 minutes per hour. Assign the tasks shown in the accompanying precedence diagram (times are in minutes) to workstations using the following rules:

    a. In order of most following tasks. Tiebreaker: greatest positional weight.

    b. In order of greatest positional weight.

    c. What is the efficiency?

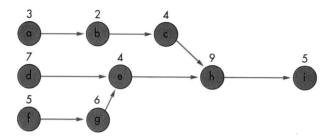

4. A large manufacturer of pencil sharpeners is planning to add a new line of sharpeners, and you have been asked to balance the process, given the following task times and precedence relationships. Assume that cycle time is to be the minimum possible.

Task	Length (minutes)	Immediate Follower
a	0.2	b
b	0.4	d
c	0.3	d
d	1.3	g
e	0.1	f
f	0.8	g
g	0.3	h
h	1.2	end

    a. Do each of the following:

        (1) Draw the precedence diagram.

        (2) Assign tasks to stations in order of greatest number of following tasks.

        (3) Determine the percentage of idle time.

        (4) Compute the rate of output that could be expected for this line assuming a 420-minute working day.

    b. Answer these questions:

        (1) What is the shortest cycle time that will permit use of only two workstations? Is this cycle time feasible? Identify the tasks you would assign to each station.

        (2) Determine the percentage of idle time that would result if two stations were used.

        (3) What is the daily output under this arrangement?

        (4) Determine the output rate that would be associated with the maximum cycle time.

5. As part of a major plant renovation project, the industrial engineering department has been asked to balance a revised assembly operation to achieve an output of 240 units per eight-hour day. Task times and precedence relationships are is follows:

Task	Duration (minutes)	Precedes Task
a	0.2	b
b	0.4	c
c	0.2	f
d	0.4	e
e	1.2	g
f	1.2	g
g	1.0	end

Do each of the following:

a. Draw the precedence diagram.

b. Determine the maximum cycle time.

c. Determine the minimum number of stations needed.

 d. Assign tasks to workstations on the basis of greatest number of following tasks. Use longest processing time as a tiebreaker. If ties still exist, assume indifference in choice.

 e. Compute the percentage of idle time for the assignment in part *d.*

6. Twelve tasks, with times and precedence requirements as shown in the following table, are to be assigned to workstations using a cycle time of 1.5 minutes. Two heuristic rules will be tried: (1) greatest positional weight, and (2) greatest number of following tasks.

  In each case, the tiebreaker will be shortest task time.

Task	Length (minutes)	Follows Task
a	0.1	—
b	0.2	a
c	0.9	b
d	0.6	c
e	0.1	—
f	0.2	d, e
g	0.4	f
h	0.1	g
i	0.2	h
j	0.7	i
k	0.3	j
l	0.2	k

 a. Draw the precedence diagram for this line.

 b. Assign tasks to stations under each of the three rules.

 c. Compute the percentage of idle time for each rule.

7. For the set of tasks given below, do the following:

 a. Develop the precedence diagram.

 b. Determine the maximum cycle time in seconds for a desired output of 500 units in a 7-hour day. Why might a manager use a cycle time of 50 seconds?

 c. Determine the minimum number of workstations for output of 500 units per day.

 d. Balance the line using the *largest positional weight* heuristic. Break ties with the *most following tasks* heuristic. Use a cycle time of 50 seconds.

 e. Calculate the percentage idle time for the line.

Task	Task Time (seconds)	Immediate Predecessors
A	45	—
B	11	A
C	9	B
D	50	—
E	26	D
F	11	E
G	12	C
H	10	C
I	9	F, G, H
J	10	I
	193	

8. A shop works a 400-minute day. The manager of the shop wants an output of 200 units per day for the assembly line that has the elemental tasks shown in the table. Do the following:

 a. Construct the precedence diagram.

 b. Assign tasks according to the *most following tasks* rule.

 c. Assign tasks according to the *greatest positional weight* rule.

 d. Compute the balance delay for each rule. Which one yields the better set of assignments in this instance?

Task	Immediately Precedes Task(s)	Task Time
a	b, c, d	0.5
b	e	1.4
c	e	1.2
d	f	0.7
e	g, j	0.5
f	i	1.0
g	h	0.4
h	k	0.3
i	j	0.5
j	k	0.8
k	m	0.9
m	end	0.3

9. Arrange six departments into a 2 × 3 grid so that these conditions are satisfied: 1 close to 2, 5 close to 2 and 6, 2 close to 5, and 3 not close to 1 or 2.

10. Using the information given in the preceding problem, develop a Muther-type grid using the letters A, O, and X. Assume that any pair of combinations not mentioned have an O rating.

11. Using the information in the following grid, determine if the department locations shown are appropriate. If not, modify the assignments so that the conditions are satisfied.

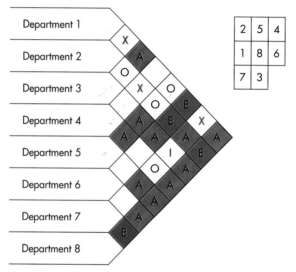

12. Arrange the eight departments shown in the accompanying Muther grid into a 2 × 4 format. *Note:* Department 1 must be in the location shown.

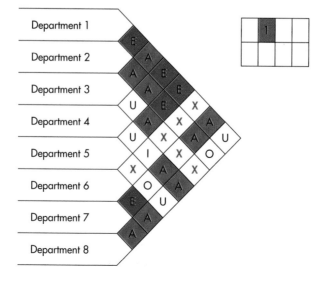

13. Arrange the departments so they satisfy the conditions shown in the following rating grid into a 3 × 3 format. Place department 5 in the lower left corner of the 3 × 3 grid.

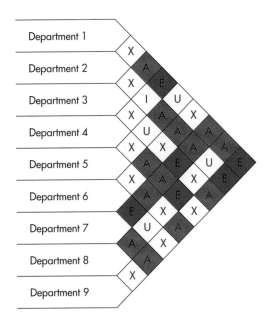

14. Determine the placement of departments for a newly designed facility that will minimize total transportation costs using the data in the following tables. Assume that reverse distances are the same. The locations are shown in the grid. Use a cost of $1 per trip yard.

Location A	Location B	Location C
	Location D	

		DISTANCE BETWEEN LOCATIONS (YARDS)		
From	**To**	**A**	**B**	**C**	**D**
A		—	40	80	70
B			—	40	50
C				—	60
D					—

		NUMBER OF TRIPS PER DAY BETWEEN DEPARTMENTS		
From	**To**	**1**	**2**	**3**	**4**
1		—	10	20	30
2			—	40	40
3				—	25
4		50	50	30	—

15. Eight work centers must be arranged in an L-shaped building. The locations of centers 1 and 3 are assigned as shown in the accompanying diagram. Assuming transportation costs are $1 per load per meter, develop a suitable layout that minimizes transportation costs using the given information. Compute the total cost. (Assume the reverse distances are the same.)

DISTANCE (METERS)

From \ To	A	B	C	D	E	F	G	H
A	—	40	40	60	120	80	100	110
B		—	60	40	60	140	120	130
C			—	45	85	40	70	90
D				—	40	50	40	45
E					—	90	50	40
F						—	40	60
G							—	40
H								—

LOADS PER DAY

From \ To	1	2	3	4	5	6	7	8
1	—	10	5	90	365	135	125	0
2	0	—	140	10	0	35	0	120
3	0	220	—	110	10	0	0	200
4	0	110	240	—	10	0	0	170
5	5	40	100	180	—	10	40	10
6	0	80	40	70	0	—	10	20
7	0	45	20	50	0	40	—	20
8	0	0	0	20	0	0	0	—

16. Develop a process layout that will minimize the total distance traveled by patients at a medical clinic, using the following information on projected departmental visits by patients and distance between locations. Assume a distance of 35 feet between the reception area and each potential location. Use the format shown.

DISTANCE BETWEEN LOCATIONS (FEET)

From \ To	A	B	C	D	E	F
A	—	40	80	100	120	160
B		—	40	60	80	120
C			—	20	40	80
D				—	20	40
E					—	40
F						—

TRIPS BETWEEN DEPARTMENTS (PER DAY)

From \ To	1	2	3	4	5	6	Reception
Reception	10	10	200	20	0	100	—
1	—	0	0	80	20	40	10
2	0	—	0	0	0	20	40
3	40	0	—	10	190	10	10
4	30	50	0	—	10	70	0
5	60	40	60	30	—	20	10
6	10	100	0	20	0	—	30

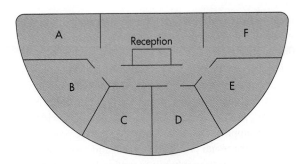

17. Ten labs will be assigned to the circular layout shown. Recalling a similar layout's congestion in the halls, the new lab manager has requested an assignment that will minimize traffic between offices. In addition, movement in the halls is restricted to a counterclockwise route. Develop a suitable layout using the following information.

NUMBER OF TRIPS PER DAY BETWEEN DEPARTMENTS

From \ To	1	2	3	4	5	6	7	8	9	10
1	—	40	1	20	20	4	0	2	6	5
2	0	—	2	15	25	10	2	12	13	6
3	50	35	—	10	13	4	0	4	7	1
4	6	1	8	—	0	14	10	20	22	11
5	3	2	7	35	—	22	5	9	19	10
6	5	5	10	0	2	—	15	0	1	20
7	20	16	50	4	9	2	—	1	3	0
8	10	6	14	2	4	44	13	—	1	25
9	5	5	18	1	2	40	30	42	—	32
10	30	30	35	20	15	5	40	10	15	—

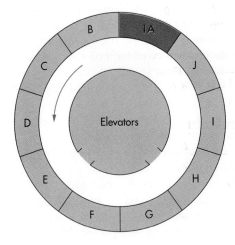

18. Rebalance the assembly line in Problem 7. This time, use the *longest operation time* heuristic. Break ties with the *most following tasks* heuristic. What is the percentage idle time for your line?

Would You Like That Rare, Medium or Vacuum-Packed?

Yumiko Ono

Let Restaurant-Goers Beware: Prix Fixe May Be Prefab; "Thaw-and-Serve" Mousse

Kirk Berkeland dabs his lips on a cloth napkin and declares himself satiated, having just polished off a plate of herb ravioli stuffed with succulently sweet bits of lobster. The New York banker considers it well worth the $14.50 he is about to be charged at Sfuzzi, an Italian restaurant in downtown Manhattan.

He should think twice, however, before complimenting the chef, for the bulk of his lunch this day actually had been shipped frozen from Denver, where Pastabilities Inc.'s food-preparation factory spits out about one machine-made, lobster-stuffed ravioli per second.

Mr. Berkeland is disheartened by the news: "I would have expected a restaurant like this to make it here."

Tons of Pasta

That is what most full-service restaurants want customers to believe, but increasingly it is no longer the case. Chefs don't advertise that they occasionally use prefabricated food, so it is hard for diners to know. But advertisements by food-processing companies in restaurant-industry magazines suggest that many eateries are serving meals just like mom used to make—when she was in a really big hurry.

"They come up with the concept, we create the item," says William Curtis, president of Pastabilities. He says the company sells tons of ravioli each week to upscale restaurants around the country.

Beany Macgregor, executive chef at Planet Hollywood International Inc., says food companies phone or send him free samples several times a day; he used to hear from them just a few times a month. "It's getting more and more prevalent," he says. He insists that he doesn't fob prefab food off on his customers. Sfuzzi Inc.'s corporate executive chef, John Diana, says lobster ravioli is one of only a few items that his chain buys premade. The herb-flavored dough has to be rolled thin, Mr. Diana explains, so it is hard to be consistent by hand.

Food-preparation companies, striving for a bigger bite of the $100 billion-a-year full-service restaurant industry, offer a diverse menu of elaborate items—from frozen Italian wedding soup to precooked marinated fajita steaks to chicken cacciatore in a vacuum-packed plastic bag.

"A Lot Easier"

Some of the companies' best customers are casual restaurants. Fuddruckers restaurants, known for grinding top-quality hamburger meat in full view of its customers, bake their cookies from the same ready-made, Otis Spunkmeyer Inc. dough that some convenience stores use to sell cheap but freshly baked cookies. The Perkins Family Restaurants chain of Memphis, Tenn., has a long shopping list: The soup comes in a boiling bag from CPC International Inc.; pork chops are butchered by Sara Lee Corp.; and the bread is baked with dough provided by two outside suppliers. A Perkins official says the premade foods help keep the menu prices reasonable and quality consistent, especially at a time when it is getting harder for the company to hire skilled kitchen help.

Even some swank eateries use premade food. Yuca, a Miami-area restaurant where dinner checks average $40 a head, sometimes uses 80%-baked, German-style dough purchased from Euro-Bake, Inc., based in Puerto Rico. "It's a hell of a lot easier," says Guillermo Veloso, Yuca's executive chef.

Mr. Veloso also recently discovered a frozen guacamole so tasty that he occasionally uses it in some recipes when fresh avocados are unavailable, rather than temporarily eighty-six some menu items. "If the quality is there, there's no reason why you can't use it," he says. "I consider our food upscale, but I'm not so close-minded as to not even try it."

Other gourmets disagree. "I still peel my garlic and my carrots," says Mark Strausman, chef at two pricey Italian restaurants in New York, Fred's and Campagna. "When I'm charging what I'm charging, I have a commitment to cook from scratch."

While food companies are happy to talk about their products, most are too discreet to reveal which restaurants they supply. Stockpot Soup Co. of Redwood, Wash., offers 52 varieties in plastic pouches, some of which end up as the soup du jour in upscale restaurants. But Gary Merritt, the company's marketing chief, clams up when asked for restaurant names. "Our product tastes like it's from scratch," he says. "If we were to come in and say it's ours . . . " he sighs, pondering the consequences. Fuddruckers agreed to use Otis Spunkmeyer's cookie dough after confirming that customers didn't have to be told they were buying the convenience-store cookies, says Richard Hendrie, a senior manager at Daka International Inc., Fuddruckers' parent company.

The number of advertisements in restaurant trade magazines indicates the premade-food business is booming. "Hours versus Ours. . . . 'Homemade' is now a matter of heat & serve," declares an ad for frozen mashed potatoes by Lamb Weston Inc., a unit of ConAgra Inc. The Yamazaki Baking Co.'s Vie de France Yamazaki subsidiary calls its "thaw-and-serve" mousse cake a "dessert of pastry-chef quality."

New products also suggest a growing market. Sara Lee late last year teamed up with a Chicago bread company to sell restaurants partially baked focaccia and panini. Land O'Lakes Inc. targets Hispanic kitchen staff with its recently created Queso Sabroso cheese-sauce concentrate for Mexican restaurants, printing the instructions (add water, heat) in English and Spanish.

Restaurants & Institutions magazine has inaugurated a new recipe column on quickie dishes that seem like they were made from scratch. Suggestions from the authors of the "Speed-Scratch" column: beef burgundy pie topped with dehydrated hash browns and bechamel sauce made from canned or frozen cream-of-chicken soup.

Restaurateurs have a powerful incentive to take advantage of such shortcuts—reducing labor costs, which equal about 30% of their revenues. Though the industry was expected to grow a healthy 4.5% in 1996, Americans are demanding more variety at cheaper prices because they are eating out much more frequently. The average check in upscale restaurants was 20% lower in 1995 than in 1985, according to inflation-adjusted figures compiled by consultants at McKinsey & Co.

There can be economic drawbacks to premade food, however. Customers at Bennigan's 200-plus restaurants were less than thrilled with some of the prefab items on its menu, in-

cluding chicken that had been breaded and frozen by a supplier, according to officials at the chain, a unit of Metromedia Co. in Dallas. So the company started having the help batter the chicken by hand. Kitchen labor costs went up 10%, but guess what? Bennigan's started selling a lot more chicken.

Questions

1. Explain the meaning of the phrase "Hours versus Ours . . . 'Homemade.'"

2. What advantages are there for restaurants to outsource?

3. What are some important disadvantages or limitations of outsourcing for restaurants?

4. Do you consider this practice to be dishonest? Unethical? Explain.

Source: Reprinted with permission of *The Wall Street Journal* © 1997 by Dow Jones & Company, Inc. All rights reserved worldwide.

OPERATIONS TOUR

Morton Salt

www.mortonintl.com

Introduction

Morton Salt is a subsidiary of Morton International, a manufacturer of specialty chemicals, air bags, and salt products. The Morton salt-processing facility in Silver Springs, New York, between Buffalo and Rochester, is one of six similar Morton salt-processing facilities in the United States. The Silver Springs plant employs about 200 people, ranging from unskilled to skilled. It produces salt products for water conditioning, grocery, industrial, and agricultural markets. The grocery business consists of 26 oz. round cans of iodized salt. Although the grocery business represents a relatively small portion of the total output (approximately 15 percent), it is the most profitable.

Salt Production

The basic raw material, salt, is obtained by injecting water into salt caverns that are located some 2,400 feet below the surface. There, the salt deposits dissolve in the water. The resulting brine is pumped to the surface where it is converted into salt crystals. The brine is boiled, and much of the liquid evaporates, leaving salt crystals and some residual moisture, which is removed in a drying process. This process is run continuously for about six weeks at a time. Initially, salt is produced at the rate of 45 tons per hour. But the rate of output decreases due to scale build up, so that by the sixth week, output is only 75 percent of the initial rate. At that point, the

process is halted to perform maintenance on the equipment and remove the scale, after which, salt production resumes.

The salt is stored in silos until it is needed for production, or it is shipped in bulk to industrial customers. Conveyors move the salt to each of the four dedicated production areas, one of which is round can production. (See diagram.) The discussion here focuses exclusively on round can production.

Round Can Production

Annual round can production averages roughly 3.8 million cans. Approximately 70 percent of the output is for the Morton label, and the rest is for private label. There are two parallel, high-speed production lines. The two lines share common processes at the beginning of the lines, and then branch out into two identical lines. Each line is capable of producing 9,600 cans per hour (160 cans per minute). The equipment is not flexible, so the production rate is fixed. The operations are completely standardized; the only variable is the brand label that is applied. One line requires 12 production workers, while both lines together can be operated by 18 workers because of the common processes. Workers on the line perform low-skilled, repetitive tasks.

The plant produces both the salt and the cans the salt is packaged in. The cans are essentially a cylinder with a top and a bottom; they are made of cardboard, except for a plastic pour spout in the top. The cylinder portion is formed from two sheets of chip board that are glued together and then rolled into a continuous tube. The glue not only binds the material, it also provides a moisture barrier. The tube is cut in a two-step process: it is first cut into long sections, and those sections are then cut into can-size pieces. The top and bottom pieces for the cans are punched from a continuous strip of cardboard.

The separate pieces move along conveyor belts to the lines where the components are assembled into cans and glued. The cans are then filled with salt and the pour spout is added. Finally, the cans are loaded onto pallets and placed into inventory, ready to be shipped to distributors.

Quality

Quality is checked at several points in the production process. Initially, the salt is checked for purity when it is obtained from the wells. Iodine and an anti-caking compound are added to the salt, and their levels are verified using chemical analysis. Crystal size is important. In order to achieve the desired size and to remove lumps, the salt is forced through a scraping screen, which can cause very fine pieces of metal to mix with the salt. However, these pieces are effectively removed by magnets that are placed at appropriate points in the process. If, for any reason, the salt is judged to be contaminated, it is diverted to a nonfood product.

Checking the quality of the cans is done primarily by visual inspection, including verifying the assembly operation is correct, checking filled cans for correct weight, inspecting cans to see that labels are properly aligned, and checking to see that metal pour spouts are correctly attached.

The equipment on the production line is sensitive to misshapen or damaged cans, and frequently jams, causing production delays. This greatly reduces the chance of a defective can getting through the process, but it reduces productivity, and the salt in the defective cans must be scrapped. The cost of quality is fairly high, owing to the amount of product that is scrapped, the large number of inspectors, and the extensive laboratory testing that is needed.

Production Planning and Inventory

The plant can sell all of the salt it produces. The job of the production scheduler is to distribute the salt that is stored in the silos to the various production areas, taking into account production capacities in each area and available inventory levels of those products. A key consideration is to make sure there is sufficient storage capacity in the silos to handle the incoming salt from brine production.

Equipment Maintenance and Repair

The equipment is 1950s vintage, and it requires a fair amount of maintenance to keep it in good working order. Even so, breakdowns occur as parts wear out. The plant has its own tool shop where skilled workers repair parts or make new parts because replacement parts are no longer available for the old equipment.

Questions

1. Briefly describe salt production, from brine production to finished round cans.

2. Briefly describe quality assurance efforts in round can production.

3. What are some of the possible reasons why the company continues to use the old processing equipment instead of buying new, more modern equipment?

4. Where would you place salt production in the product–process spectrum?

5. Determine the approximate number of tons of salt produced annually. Hints: one ton = 2,000 pounds, and one pound = 16 ounces.

6. What improvements can you suggest for the plant?

Selected Bibliography and Further Reading

Bolwijn, P. T., and T. Kumpe. "Manufacturing in the 1990's—Productivity, Flexibility, and Innovation." *Long Range Planning* 23, no. 4 (1990), pp. 44–57.

Cohen, Morris, and Uday M. Apte. *Manufacturing Automation.* Burr Ridge, IL: Richard D. Irwin, 1997.

Ettlie, John, and Henry Stoll, *Managing the Design-Manufacturing Process.* New York: McGraw-Hill, 1990.

Francis, Richard L., Leon F. McGinnis Jr., and John A. White. *Facility Layout and Location: An Analytical Approach.* 3rd ed. Englewood Cliffs, NJ: Prentice Hall, 1998.

Groover, Mikell P. *Automation, Production Systems, and Computer-Aided Manufacturing.* 2nd ed. Englewood Cliffs, NJ: Prentice Hall, 2001.

Hill, Terry. *Manufacturing Strategy.* 3rd ed. Burr Ridge, IL: Richard D. Irwin, 2001.

Kilbridge, M. D., and L. Wester. "A Heuristic Method of Assembly Line Balancing." *Journal of Industrial Engineering* 12 (July–August 1961).

Milas, Gene H. "Assembly Line Balancing . . . Let's Remove the Mystery." *Industrial Engineering,* May 1990, pp. 31–36.

Monroe, Joseph. "Strategic Use of Technology." *California Management Review,* Summer 1989, pp. 91–110.

Muther, R., and K. McPherson. "Four Approaches to Computerized Layout Planning." *Industrial Engineering* 2 (1970), pp. 39–42.

Shunk, Dan L. *Integrated Process Design and Development.* Burr Ridge, IL: Business One Irwin, 1992.

Stauffer, Robert. "Lessons Learned in Implementing New Technology." *Manufacturing Engineer,* June 1989.

Upton, David. "The Management of Manufacturing Flexibility." *California Management Review* 36, no. 2, 1994, pp. 72–89.

Upton, David. "What Really Makes Factories Flexible." *Harvard Business Review,* July–August 1995, pp. 74–84.

SUPPLEMENT TO CHAPTER 6

Linear Programming

SUPPLEMENT OUTLINE

Introduction, 275

Linear Programming Models, 275
  Model Formulation, 277

Graphical Linear Programming, 278
  Outline of Graphical Procedure, 278
  Plotting Constraints, 280
  Identifying the Feasible Solution
    Space, 283
  Plotting the Objective Function
    Line, 283
  Redundant Constraints, 287
  Solutions and Corner Points, 287
  Minimization, 288
  Slack and Surplus, 290

The Simplex Method, 290

Computer Solutions, 291

Solving LP Models Using MS
  Excel, 291

Sensitivity Analysis, 293
  Objective Function Coefficient
    Changes, 294
  Changes in the Right-Hand Side
    Value of a Constraint, 295

Key Terms, 297

Solved Problems, 297

Discussion and Review
  Questions, 299

Problems, 299

Case: Son, Ltd., 304

Selected Bibliography and Further
  Reading, 304

LEARNING OBJECTIVES

After completing this supplement, you should be able to:

1 Describe the type of problem that would lend itself to solution using linear programming.

2 Formulate a linear programming model from a description of a problem.

3 Solve simple linear programming problems using the graphical method.

4 Interpret computer solutions of linear programming problems.

5 Do sensitivity analysis on the solution of a linear programming problem.

Linear programming is a powerful quantitative tool used by operations managers and other managers to obtain optimal solutions to problems that involve restrictions or limitations, such as the available materials, budgets, and labor and machine time. These problems are referred to as *constrained optimization* problems. There are numerous examples of linear programming applications to such problems, including:

- Establishing locations for emergency equipment and personnel that will minimize response time
- Determining optimal schedules for airlines for planes, pilots, and ground personnel
- Developing financial plans
- Determining optimal blends of animal feed mixes
- Determining optimal diet plans
- Identifying the best set of worker-job assignments
- Developing optimal production schedules
- Developing shipping plans that will minimize shipping costs
- Identifying the optimal mix of products in a factory

Introduction

Linear programming (LP) techniques consist of a sequence of steps that will lead to an optimal solution to problems, in cases where an optimum exists. There are a number of different linear programming techniques; some are special-purpose (i.e., used to find solutions for specific types of problems) and others are more general in scope. This supplement covers the two general-purpose solution techniques: graphical linear programming and computer solutions. Graphical linear programming provides a visual portrayal of many of the important concepts of linear programming. However, it is limited to problems with only two variables. In practice, computers are used to obtain solutions for problems, some of which involve a large number of variables.

Linear Programming Models

Linear programming models are mathematical representations of constrained optimization problems. These models have certain characteristics in common. Knowledge of these characteristics enables us to recognize problems that can be solved using linear programming. In addition, it also can help us formulate LP models. The characteristics can be grouped into two categories: components and assumptions. First, let's consider the components.

Four components provide the structure of a linear programming model:

1. Objective.
2. Decision variables.
3. Constraints.
4. Parameters.

Linear programming algorithms require that a single goal or *objective,* such as the maximization of profits, be specified. The two general types of objectives are maximization and minimization. A maximization objective might involve profits, revenues, efficiency, or rate of return. Conversely, a minimization objective might involve cost, time, distance traveled, or scrap. The **objective function** is a mathematical expression that can be used to determine the total profit (or cost, etc., depending on the objective) for a given solution.

objective function Mathematical statement of profit (or cost, etc.) for a given solution.

Decision variables represent choices available to the decision maker in terms of amounts of either inputs or outputs. For example, some problems require choosing a combination of inputs to minimize total costs, while others require selecting a combination of outputs to maximize profits or revenues.

decision variables Amounts of either inputs or outputs.

constraints Limitations that restrict the available alternatives.

    Constraints are limitations that restrict the alternatives available to decision makers. The three types of constraints are less than or equal to ($\leq$), greater than or equal to ($\geq$), and simply equal to ($=$). A $\leq$ constraint implies an upper limit on the amount of some scarce resource (e.g., machine hours, labor hours, materials) available for use. A $\geq$ constraint specifies a minimum that must be achieved in the final solution (e.g., must contain at least 10 percent real fruit juice, must get at least 30 MPG on the highway). The $=$ constraint is more restrictive in the sense that it specifies *exactly* what a decision variable should equal (e.g., make 200 units of product A). A linear programming model can consist of one or more constraints. The constraints of a given problem define the set of all feasible combinations of decision variables; this set is referred to as the **feasible solution space.** Linear programming algorithms are designed to search the feasible solution space for the combination of decision variables that will yield an optimum in terms of the objective function.

feasible solution space The set of all feasible combinations of decision variables as defined by the constraints.

    An LP model consists of a mathematical statement of the objective and a mathematical statement of each constraint. These statements consist of symbols (e.g., x_1, x_2) that represent the decision variables and numerical values, called **parameters.** The parameters are fixed values; the model is solved *given* those values.

parameters Numerical constants.

    Example S-1 illustrates the components of an LP model.

Example S-1

$$
\text{Decision variables} \begin{cases} x_1 = \text{Quantity of product 1 to produce} \\ x_2 = \text{Quantity of product 2 to produce} \\ x_3 = \text{Quantity of product 3 to produce} \end{cases}
$$

Maximize	$5x_1 + 8x_2 + 4x_3$ (profit)	(Objective function)
Subject to		
Labor	$2x_1 + 4x_2 + 8x_3 \leq 250$ hours	
Material	$7x_1 + 6x_2 + 5x_3 \leq 100$ pounds	(Constraints)
Product 1	$x_1 \qquad\qquad \geq 10$ units	
	$x_1, x_2, x_3 \geq 0$	(Nonnegativity constraints)

    First, the model lists and defines the decision variables. These typically represent *quantities.* In this case, they are quantities of three different products that might be produced.

    Next, the model states the objective function. It includes every decision variable in the model and the contribution (profit per unit) of each decision variable. Thus, product x_1 has a profit of $5 per unit. The profit from product x_1 for a given solution will be 5 times the value of x_1 specified by the solution; the total profit from all products will be the sum of the individual product profits. Thus, if $x_1 = 10$, $x_2 = 0$, and $x_3 = 6$, the value of the objective function would be:

$$5(10) + 8(0) + 4(6) = 74$$

    The objective function is followed by a list (in no particular order) of three constraints. Each constraint has a right-side numerical value (e.g., the labor constraint has a right-side value of 250) that indicates the amount of the constraint and a relation sign that indicates whether that amount is a maximum ($\leq$), a minimum ($\geq$), or an equality ($=$). The left side of each constraint consists of the variables subject to that particular constraint and a coefficient for each variable that indicates how much of the right-side quantity *one unit* of the decision variable represents. For instance, for the labor constraint, one unit of x_1 will require two hours of labor. The sum of the values on the left side of each constraint represents the amount of that constraint used by a solution. Thus, if $x_1 = 10$, $x_2 = 0$, and $x_3 = 6$, the amount of labor used would be:

$$2(10) + 4(0) + 8(6) = 68 \text{ hours}$$

Because this amount does not exceed the quantity on the right-hand side of the constraint, it is *feasible*.

Note that the third constraint refers to only a single variable; x_1 must be at least 10 units. Its coefficient is, in effect, 1, although that is not shown.

Finally, there are the nonnegativity constraints. These are listed on a single line; they reflect the condition that no decision variable is allowed to have a negative value.

In order for linear-programming models to be used effectively, certain *assumptions* must be satisfied. These are:

1. *Linearity:* the impact of decision variables is linear in constraints and the objective function.

2. *Divisibility:* noninteger values of decision variables are acceptable.

3. *Certainty:* values of parameters are known and constant.

4. *Nonnegativity:* negative values of decision variables are unacceptable.

MODEL FORMULATION

An understanding of the components of linear programming models is necessary for model formulation. This helps provide organization to the process of assembling information about a problem into a model.

Naturally, it is important to obtain valid information on what constraints are appropriate, as well as on what values of the parameters are appropriate. If this is not done, the usefulness of the model will be questionable. Consequently, in some instances, considerable effort must be expended to obtain that information.

In formulating a model, use the format illustrated in Example 1. Begin by identifying the decision variables. Very often, decision variables are "the quantity of" something, such as $x_1 = $ the quantity of product 1. Generally, decision variables have profits, costs, times, or a similar measure of value associated with them. Knowing this can help you identify the decision variables in a problem.

Constraints are restrictions or requirements on one or more decision variables, and they refer to available amounts of resources such as labor, material, or machine time, or to minimal requirements, such as "make at least 10 units of product 1." It can be helpful to give a name to each constraint, such as "labor" or "material 1." Let's consider some of the different kinds of constraints you will encounter.

1. A constraint that refers to one or more decision variables. This is the most common kind of constraint. The constraints in Example 1 are of this type.

2. A constraint that specifies a ratio. For example, "the ratio of x_1 to x_2 must be at least 3 to 2." To formulate this, begin by setting up the ratio:

$$\frac{x_1}{x_2} \geq \frac{3}{2}$$

Then, cross multiply, obtaining

$$2x_1 \geq 3x_2$$

This is not yet in a suitable form because all variables in a constraint must be on the left side of the inequality (or equality) sign, leaving only a constant on the right side. To achieve this, we must subtract the variable amount that is on the right side from both sides. That yields:

$$2x_1 - 3x_2 \geq 0$$

[Note that the direction of the inequality remains the same.]

3. A constraint that specifies a percentage for one or more variables relative to one or more other variables. For example, "x_1 cannot be more than 20 percent of the mix." Suppose that the mix consists of variables x_1, x_2, and x_3. In mathematical terms, this would be:

$$x_1 \le .20(x_1 + x_2 + x_3)$$

As always, all variables must appear on the left side of the relationship. To accomplish that, we can expand the right side, and then subtract the result from both sides. Thus,

$$x_1 \le .20x_1 + .20x_2 + .20x_3$$

Subtracting yields

$$.80x_1 - .20x_2 - .20x_3 \le 0$$

Once you have formulated a model, the next task is to solve it. The following sections describe two approaches to problem solution: graphical solutions and computer solutions.

Graphical Linear Programming

graphical linear programming Graphical method for finding optimal solutions to two-variable problems.

Graphical linear programming is a method for finding optimal solutions to two-variable problems. This section describes that approach.

OUTLINE OF GRAPHICAL PROCEDURE

The graphical method of linear programming plots the constraints on a graph and identifies an area that satisfies all of the constraints. The area is referred to as the *feasible solution space*. Next, the objective function is plotted and used to identify the optimal point in the feasible solution space. The coordinates of the point can sometimes be read directly from the graph, although generally an algebraic determination of the coordinates of the point is necessary.

The general procedure followed in the graphical approach is:

1. Set up the objective function and the constraints in mathematical format.
2. Plot the constraints.
3. Identify the feasible solution space.
4. Plot the objective function.
5. Determine the optimum solution.

The technique can best be illustrated through solution of a typical problem. Consider the problem described in Example S-2.

Example S-2

General description: A firm that assembles computers and computer equipment is about to start production of two new types of microcomputers. Each type will require assembly time, inspection time, and storage space. The amounts of each of these resources that can be devoted to the production of the microcomputers is limited. The manager of the firm would like to determine the quantity of each microcomputer to produce in order to maximize the profit generated by sales of these microcomputers.

Additional information: In order to develop a suitable model of the problem, the manager has met with design and manufacturing personnel. As a result of those meetings, the manager has obtained the following information:

	Type 1	Type 2
Profit per unit	$60	$50
Assembly time per unit	4 hours	10 hours
Inspection time per unit	2 hours	1 hour
Storage space per unit	3 cubic feet	3 cubic feet

The manager also has acquired information on the availability of company resources. These (daily) amounts are:

Resource	Amount Available
Assembly time	100 hours
Inspection time	22 hours
Storage space	39 cubic feet

The manager met with the firm's marketing manager and learned that demand for the microcomputers was such that whatever combination of these two types of microcomputers is produced, all of the output can be sold.

In terms of meeting the assumptions, it would appear that the relationships are *linear:* The contribution to profit per unit of each type of computer and the time and storage space per unit of each type of computer is the same regardless of the quantity produced. Therefore, the total impact of each type of computer on the profit and each constraint is a linear function of the quantity of that variable. There may be a question of *divisibility* because, presumably, only whole units of computers will be sold. However, because this is a recurring process (i.e., the computers will be produced daily, a noninteger solution such as 3.5 computers per day will result in 7 computers every other day), this does not seem to pose a problem. The question of *certainty* cannot be explored here; in practice, the manager could be questioned to determine if there are any other possible constraints and whether the values shown for assembly times, and so forth, are known with certainty. For the purposes of discussion, we will assume certainty. Last, the assumption of *nonnegativity* seems justified; negative values for production quantities would not make sense.

Because we have concluded that linear programming is appropriate, let us now turn our attention to constructing a model of the microcomputer problem. First, we must define the decision variables. Based on the statement, "The manager . . . would like to determine the quantity of each microcomputer to produce," the decision variables are the quantities of each type of computer. Thus,

x_1 = quantity of type 1 to produce

x_2 = quantity of type 2 to produce

Next, we can formulate the objective function. The profit per unit of type 1 is listed as $60, and the profit per unit of type 2 is listed as $50, so the appropriate objective function is

Maximize $Z = 60x_1 + 50x_2$

where Z is the value of the objective function, given values of x_1 and x_2. Theoretically, a mathematical function requires such a variable for completeness. However, in practice, the objective function often is written without the Z, as sort of a shorthand version. That approach is underscored by the fact that computer input does not call for Z: It is understood. The output of a computerized model does include a Z, though.

Now for the constraints. There are three resources with limited availability: assembly time, inspection time, and storage space. The fact that availability is limited means that these constraints will all be $\leq$ constraints. Suppose we begin with the assembly constraint. The type 1 microcomputer requires 4 hours of assembly time per unit, whereas the type 2 microcomputer requires 10 hours of assembly time per unit. Therefore, with a limit of 100 hours available, the assembly constraint is

$4x_1 + 10x_2 \leq 100$ hours

Similarly, each unit of type 1 requires 2 hours of inspection time, and each unit of type 2 requires 1 hour of inspection time. With 22 hours available, the inspection constraint is

$2x_1 + 1x_2 \leq 22$

(Note: The coefficient of 1 for x_2 need not be shown. Thus, an alternative form for this constraint is: $2x_1 + x_2 \leq 22$.) The storage constraint is determined in a similar manner:

$$3x_1 + 3x_2 \leq 39$$

There are no other system or individual constraints. The nonnegativity constraints are

$$x_1, x_2 \geq 0$$

In summary, the mathematical model of the microcomputer problem is

x_1 = quantity of type 1 to produce
x_2 = quantity of type 2 to produce

Maximize $60x_1 + 50x_2$

Subject to
    Assembly $4x_1 + 10x_2 \leq 100$ hours
    Inspection $2x_1 + 1x_2 \leq 22$ hours
    Storage $3x_1 + 3x_2 \leq 39$ cubic feet
                    $x_1, x_2 \geq 0$

The next step is to plot the constraints.

PLOTTING CONSTRAINTS

Begin by placing the nonnegativity constraints on a graph, as in Figure 6S–1. The procedure for plotting the other constraints is simple:

1. Replace the inequality sign with an equal sign. This transforms the constraint into an *equation of a straight line.*
2. Determine where the line intersects each axis.
    a. To find where it crosses the x_2 axis, set x_1 equal to zero and solve the equation for the value of x_2.
    b. To find where it crosses the x_1 axis, set x_2 equal to zero and solve the equation for the value of x_1.
3. Mark these intersections on the axes, and connect them with a straight line. (Note: If a constraint has only one variable, it will be a vertical line on a graph if the variable is x_1, or a horizontal line if the variable is x_2.)
4. Indicate by shading (or by arrows at the ends of the constraint line) whether the inequality is greater than or less than. (A general rule to determine which side of the line satisfies the inequality is to pick the point that is not on the line, such as 0,0, and see whether it is greater than or less than the constraint amount.)
5. Repeat steps 1–4 for each constraint.

FIGURE 6S–1

Graph showing the nonnegativity constraints

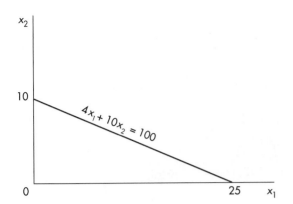

FIGURE 6S-2

Plot of the first constraint (assembly time)

Consider the assembly time constraint:

$$4x_1 + 10x_2 \leq 100$$

Removing the inequality portion of the constraint produces this straight line:

$$4x_1 + 10x_2 = 100$$

Next, identify the points where the line intersects each axis, as step 2 describes. Thus with $x_2 = 0$, we find

$$4x_1 + 10(0) = 100$$

Solving, we find that $4x_1 = 100$, so $x_1 = 25$ when $x_2 = 0$. Similarly, we can solve the equation for x_2 when $x_1 = 0$:

$$4(0) + 10x_2 = 100$$

Solving for x_2, we find $x_2 = 10$ when $x_1 = 0$.

Thus, we have two points: $x_1 = 0$, $x_2 = 10$, and $x_1 = 25$, $x_2 = 0$. We can now add this line to our graph of the nonnegativity constraints by connecting these two points (see Figure 6S–2).

Next we must determine which side of the line represents points that are less than 100. To do this, we can select a test point that is not on the line, and we can substitute the x_1 and x_2 values of that point into the left side of the equation of the line. If the result is less than 100, this tells us that all points on that side of the line are less than the value of the line (e.g., 100). Conversely, if the result is greater than 100, this indicates that the other side of the line represents the set of points that will yield values that are less than 100. A relatively simple test point to use is the origin (i.e., $x_1 = 0$, $x_2 = 0$). Substituting these values into the equation yields

$$4(0) + 10(0) = 0$$

Obviously this is less than 100. Hence, the side of the line closest to the origin represents the "less than" area (i.e., the feasible region).

The feasible region for this constraint and the nonnegativity constraints then becomes the shaded portion shown in Figure 6S–3.

For the sake of illustration, suppose we try one other point, say $x_1 = 10$, $x_2 = 10$. Substituting these values into the assembly constraint yields

$$4(10) + 10(10) = 140$$

Clearly this is greater than 100. Therefore, all points on this side of the line are greater than 100 (see Figure 6S–4).

Continuing with the problem, we can add the two remaining constraints to the graph. For the inspection constraint:

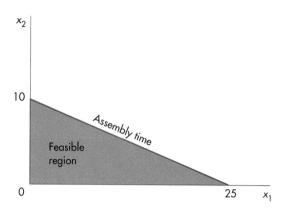

FIGURE 6S–3

The feasible region, given the first constraint and the nonnegativity constraints

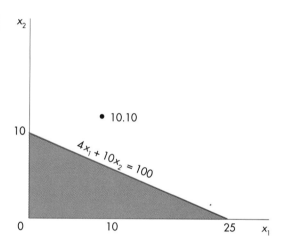

FIGURE 6S–4

The point 10, 10 is above the constraint line

1. Convert the constraint into the equation of a straight line by replacing the inequality sign with an equality sign:

   $2x_1 + 1x_2 \leq 22$ becomes $2x_1 + 1x_2 = 22$

2. Set x_1 equal to zero and solve for x_2:

   $2(0) + 1x_2 = 22$

   Solving, we find $x_2 = 22$. Thus, the line will intersect the x_2 axis at 22.

3. Next, set x_2 equal to zero and solve for x_1:

   $2x_1 + 1(0) = 22$

   Solving, we find $x_1 = 11$. Thus, the other end of the line will intersect the x_1 axis at 11.

4. Add the line to the graph (see Figure 6S–5).

Note that the area of feasibility for this constraint is below the line (Figure 6S–5). Again the area of feasibility at this point is shaded in for illustration, although when graphing problems, it is more practical to refrain from shading in the feasible region until all constraint lines have been drawn. However, because constraints are plotted one at a time, using a small arrow at the end of each constraint to indicate the direction of feasibility can be helpful.

The storage constraint is handled in the same manner:

1. Convert it into an equality:

   $3x_1 + 3x_2 = 39$

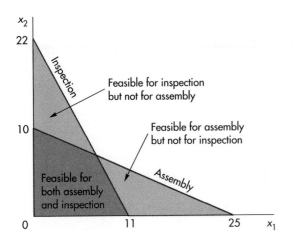

FIGURE 6S-5

Partially completed graph, showing the assembly, inspection, and nonnegativity constraints

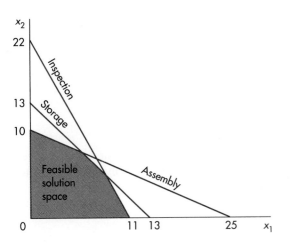

FIGURE 6S-6

Completed graph of the microcomputer problem showing all constraints and the feasible solution space

2. Set x_1 equal to zero and solve for x_2:

$$3(0) + 3x_2 = 39$$

Solving, $x_2 = 13$. Thus, $x_2 = 13$ when $x_1 = 0$.

3. Set x_2 equal to zero and solve for x_1:

$$3x_1 + 3(0) = 39$$

Solving, $x_1 = 13$. Thus, $x_1 = 13$ when $x_2 = 0$.

4. Add the line to the graph (see Figure 6S–6).

IDENTIFYING THE FEASIBLE SOLUTION SPACE

The feasible solution space is the set of all points that satisfies *all* constraints. (Recall that the x_1 and x_2 axes form nonnegativity constraints.) The heavily shaded area shown in Figure 6S–6 is the feasible solution space for our problem.

The next step is to determine which point in the feasible solution space will produce the optimal value of the objective function. This determination is made using the objective function.

PLOTTING THE OBJECTIVE FUNCTION LINE

Plotting an objective function line involves the same logic as plotting a constraint line: Determine where the line intersects each axis. Recall that the objective function for the microcomputer problem is

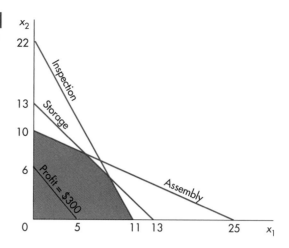

FIGURE 6S-7

Microcomputer problem with $300 profit line added

$$60x_1 + 50x_2$$

This is not an equation because it does not include an equal sign. We can get around this by simply setting it equal to some quantity. Any quantity will do, although one that is evenly divisible by both coefficients is desirable.

Suppose we decide to set the objective function equal to 300. That is,

$$60x_1 + 50x_2 = 300$$

We can now plot the line of our graph. As before, we can determine the x_1 and x_2 intercepts of the line by setting one of the two variables equal to zero, solving for the other, and then reversing the process. Thus, with $x_1 = 0$, we have

$$60(0) + 50x_2 = 300$$

Solving, we find $x_2 = 6$. Similarly, with $x_2 = 0$, we have

$$60x_1 + 50(0) = 300$$

Solving, we find $x_1 = 5$. This line is plotted in Figure 6S–7.

The profit line can be interpreted in the following way. It is an *isoprofit* line; every point on the line (i.e., every combination of x_1 and x_2 that lies on the line) will provide a profit of $300. We can see from the graph many combinations that are both on the $300 profit line and within the feasible solution space. In fact, considering noninteger as well as integer solutions, the possibilities are infinite.

Suppose we now consider another line, say the $600 line. To do this, we set the objective function equal to this amount. Thus,

$$60x_1 + 50x_2 = 600$$

Solving for the x_1 and x_2 intercepts yields these two points:

x_1 intercept x_2 intercept
$x_1 = 10$ $x_1 = 0$
$x_2 = 0$ $x_2 = 12$

This line is plotted in Figure 6S–8, along with the previous $300 line for purposes of comparison.

Two things are evident in Figure 6S–8 regarding the profit lines. One is that the $600 line is *farther* from the origin than the $300 line; the other is that the two lines are *parallel*. The lines are parallel because they both have the same slope. The slope is not affected by the right side of the equation. Rather, it is determined solely by the coefficients 60 and 50. It would be correct to conclude that regardless of the quantity we select for the value

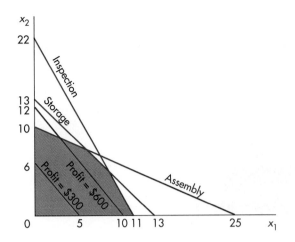

FIGURE 6S-8

Microcomputer problem with profit lines of $300 and $600

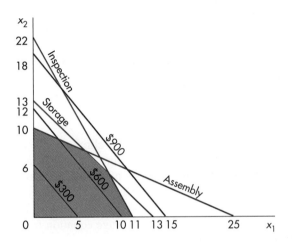

FIGURE 6S-9

Microcomputer problem with profit lines of $300, $600, and $900

of the objective function, the resulting line will be parallel to these two lines. Moreover, if the amount is greater than 600, the line will be even farther away from the origin than the $600 line. If the value is less than 300, the line will be closer to the origin than the $300 line. And if the value is between 300 and 600, the line will fall between the $300 and $600 lines. This knowledge will help in determining the optimal solution.

Consider a third line, one with the profit equal to $900. Figure 6S–9 shows that line along with the previous two profit lines. As expected, it is parallel to the other two, and even farther away from the origin. However, the line does not touch the feasible solution space at all. Consequently, there is no feasible combination of x_1 and x_2 that will yield that amount of profit. Evidently, the maximum possible profit is an amount between $600 and $900, which we can see by referring to Figure 6S–9. We could continue to select profit lines in this manner, and eventually, we could determine an amount that would yield the greatest profit. However, there is a much simpler alternative. We can plot just one line, say the $300 line. We know that all other lines will be parallel to it. Consequently, by moving this one line parallel to itself we can represent other profit lines. We also know that as we move away from the origin, the profits get larger. What we want to know is how far the line can be moved out from the origin and still be touching the feasible solution space, and the values of the decision variables at that point of greatest profit (i.e., the optimal solution). Locate this point on the graph by placing a straight edge along the $300 line (or any other convenient line) and sliding it away from the origin, being careful to keep it parallel to the line. This approach is illustrated in Figure 6S–10.

Once we have determined where the optimal solution is in the feasible solution space, we must determine the values of the decision variables at that point. Then, we can use that information to compute the profit for that combination.

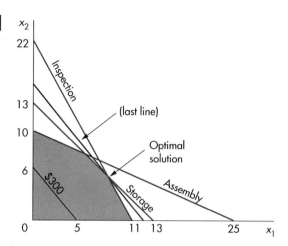

FIGURE 6S-10

Finding the optimal solution to the microcomputer problem

Note that the optimal solution is at the intersection of the inspection boundary and the storage boundary (see Figure 6S–9). In other words, the optimal combination of x_1 and x_2 must satisfy both boundary (equality) conditions. We can determine those values by solving the two equations *simultaneously*. The equations are

Inspection $2x_1 + 1x_2 = 22$

Storage $3x_1 + 3x_2 = 39$

The idea behind solving two *simultaneous equations* is to algebraically eliminate one of the unknown variables (i.e., to obtain an equation with a single unknown). This can be accomplished by multiplying the constants of one of the equations by a fixed amount and then adding (or subtracting) the modified equation from the other. (Occasionally, it is easier to multiply each equation by a fixed quantity.) For example, we can eliminate x_2 by multiplying the inspection equation by 3 and then subtracting the storage equation from the modified inspection equation. Thus,

$$3(2x_1 + 1x_2 = 22) \quad \text{becomes} \quad 6x_1 + 3x_2 = 66$$

Subtracting the storage equation from this produces

$$
\begin{array}{r}
6x_1 + 3x_2 = 66 \\
- \underline{(3x_1 + 3x_2 = 39)} \\
3x_1 + 0x_2 = 27
\end{array}
$$

Solving the resulting equation yields $x_1 = 9$. The value of x_2 can be found by substituting $x_1 = 9$ into either of the original equations or the modified inspection equation. Suppose we use the original inspection equation. We have

$$2(9) + 1x_2 = 22$$

Solving, we find $x_2 = 4$.

Hence, the optimal solution to the microcomputer problem is to produce nine type 1 computers and four type 2 computers per day. We can substitute these values into the objective function to find the optimal profit:

$$\$60(9) + \$50(4) = \$740$$

Hence, the last line—the one that would last touch the feasible solution space as we moved away from the origin parallel to the $300 profit line—would be the line where profit equaled $740.

In this problem, the optimal values for both decision variables are integers. This will not always be the case; one or both of the decision variables may turn out to be noninteger. In some situations noninteger values would be of little consequence. This would be

FIGURE 6S–11

Examples of redundant constraints

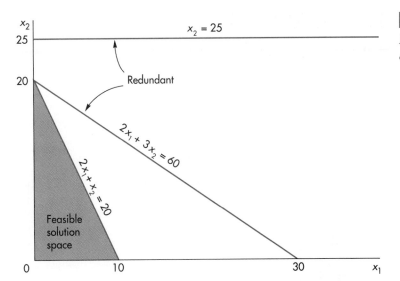

true if the decision variables were measured on a continuous scale, such as the amount of water, sand, sugar, fuel oil, time, or distance needed for optimality, or if the contribution per unit (profit, cost, etc.) were small, as with the number of nails or ball bearings to make. In some cases, the answer would simply be rounded down (maximization problems) or up (minimization problems) with very little impact on the objective function. Here, we assume that noninteger answers are acceptable as such.

Let's review the procedure for finding the optimal solution using the objective function approach:

1. Graph the constraints.

2. Identify the feasible solution space.

3. Set the objective function equal to some amount that is divisible by each of the objective function coefficients. This will yield integer values for the x_1 and x_2 intercepts and simplify plotting the line. Often, the product of the two objective function coefficients provides a satisfactory line. Ideally, the line will cross the feasible solution space close to the optimal point, and it will not be necessary to slide a straight edge because the optimal solution can be readily identified visually.

4. After identifying the optimal point, determine which two constraints intersect there. Solve their equations simultaneously to obtain the values of the decision variables at the optimum.

5. Substitute the values obtained in the previous step into the objective function to determine the value of the objective function at the optimum.

REDUNDANT CONSTRAINTS

In some cases, a constraint does not form a unique boundary of the feasible solution space. Such a constraint is called a **redundant constraint.** Two such constraints are illustrated in Figure 6S–11. Note that a constraint is redundant if it meets the following test: Its removal would not alter the feasible solution space.

When a problem has a redundant constraint, at least one of the other constraints in the problem is more restrictive than the redundant constraint.

redundant constraint A constraint that does not form a unique boundary of the feasible solution space.

SOLUTIONS AND CORNER POINTS

The feasible solution space in graphical linear programming is a polygon. Moreover, the solution to any problem will be at one of the corner points (intersections of constraints) of the polygon. It is possible to determine the coordinates of each corner point of the feasi-

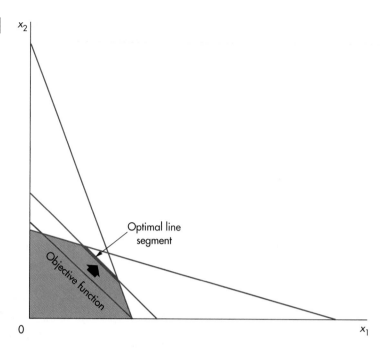

ble solution space, and use those values to compute the value of the objective function at those points. Because the solution is always at a corner point, comparing the values of the objective function at the corner points and identifying the best one (e.g., the maximum value) is another way to identify the optimal corner point. Using the graphical approach, it is much easier to plot the objective function and use that to identify the optimal corner point. However, for problems that have more than two decision variables, and the graphical method isn't appropriate, this alternate approach is used to find the optimal solution.

In some instances, the objective function will be *parallel* to one of the constraint lines that forms a *boundary of the feasible solution space*. When this happens, *every* combination of x_1 and x_2 on the segment of the constraint that touches the feasible solution space represents an optimal solution. Hence, there are multiple optimal solutions to the problem. Even in such a case, the solution will also be a corner point—in fact, the solution will be at *two* corner points: those at the ends of the segment that touches the feasible solution space. Figure 6S–12 illustrates an objective function line that is parallel to a constraint line.

MINIMIZATION

Graphical minimization problems are quite similar to maximization problems. There are, however, two important differences. One is that at least one of the constraints must be of the = or ≥ variety. This causes the feasible solution space to be away from the origin. The other difference is that the optimal point is the one closest to the origin. We find the optimal corner point by sliding the objective function (which is an *isocost* line) *toward* the origin instead of away from it.

Solve the following problem using graphical linear programming.

$$\text{Minimize} \quad Z = 8x_1 + 12x_2$$
$$\text{Subject to} \quad 5x_1 + 2x_2 \geq 20$$
$$4x_1 + 3x_2 \geq 24$$
$$x_2 \geq 2$$
$$x_1, x_2 \geq 0$$

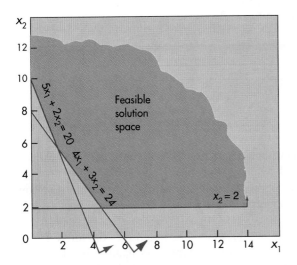

The constraints define the feasible solution space

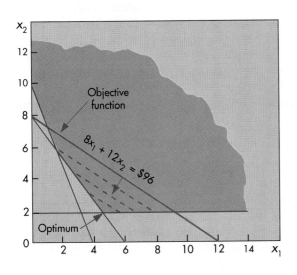

The optimum is the last point the objective function touches as it is moved toward the origin

Solution

1. Plot the constraints (shown in Figure 6S–13).

   a. Change constraints to equalities.

   b. For each constraint, set $x_1 = 0$ and solve for x_2, then set $x_2 = 0$ and solve for x_1.

   c. Graph each constraint. Note that $x_2 = 2$ is a horizontal line parallel to the x_1 axis and 2 units above it.

2. Shade the feasible solution space (see Figure 6S–13).

3. Plot the objective function.

   a. Select a value for the objective function that causes it to cross the feasible solution space. Try $8 \times 12 = 96$; $8x_1 + 12x_2 = 96$ (acceptable).

   b. Graph the line (see Figure 6S–14).

4. Slide the objective function toward the origin, being careful to keep it parallel to the original line.

5. The optimum (last feasible point) is shown in Figure 6S–14. The x_2 coordinate ($x_2 = 2$) can be determined by inspection of the graph. Note that the optimum point is at the intersection of the line $x_2 = 2$ and the line $4x_1 + 3x_2 = 24$. Substituting the value of $x_2 = 2$ into the latter equation will yield the value of x_1 at the intersection:

   $$4x_1 + 3(2) = 24 \quad x_1 = 4.5$$

Thus, the optimum is $x_1 = 4.5$ units and $x_2 = 2$.

6. Compute the minimum cost:

$$8x_1 + 12x_2 = 8(4.5) + 12(2) = 60$$

SLACK AND SURPLUS

binding constraint A constraint that forms the optimal corner point of the feasible solution space.

If a constraint forms the optimal corner point of the feasible solution space, it is called a **binding constraint.** In effect, it limits the value of the objective function; if the constraint could be relaxed (less restrictive), an improved solution would be possible. For constraints that are not binding, making them less restrictive will have no impact on the solution.

If the optimal values of the decision variables are substituted into the left side of a binding constraint, the resulting value will exactly equal the right-hand value of the constraint. However, there will be a difference with a nonbinding constraint. If the left side is greater than the right side, we say that there is **surplus;** if the left side is less than the right side, we say that there is **slack.** Slack can only occur in a $\leq$ constraint; it is the amount by which the left side is less than the right side when the optimal values of the decision variables are substituted into the left side. And surplus can only occur in a $\geq$ constraint; it is the amount by which the left side exceeds the right side of the constraint when the optimal values of the decision variables are substituted into the left side.

surplus When the values of decision variables are substituted into a $\geq$ constraint and the resulting value exceeds the right-side value.

slack When the values of decision variables are substituted into a $\leq$ constraint and the resulting value is less than the right-side value.

For example, suppose the optimal values for a problem are $x_1 = 10$ and $x_2 = 20$. If one of the constraints is

$$3x_1 + 2x_2 \leq 100$$

substituting the optimal values into the left side yields

$$3(10) + 2(20) = 70$$

Because the constraint is $\leq$, the difference between the values of 100 and 70 (i.e., 30) is slack. Suppose the optimal values had been $x_1 = 20$ and $x_2 = 20$. Substituting these values into the left side of the constraint would yield $3(20) + 2(20) = 100$. Because the left side equals the right side, this is a binding constraint; slack is equal to zero.

Now consider this constraint:

$$4x_1 + x_2 \geq 50$$

Suppose the optimal values are $x_1 = 10$ and $x_2 = 15$; substituting into the left side yields

$$4(10) + 15 = 55$$

Because this is a $\geq$ constraint, the difference between the left- and right-side values is *surplus.* If the optimal values had been $x_1 = 12$ and $x_2 = 2$, substitution would result in the left side being equal to 50. Hence, the constraint would be a binding constraint, and there would be no surplus (i.e., surplus would be zero).

The Simplex Method

simplex A linear programming algorithm that can solve problems having more than two decision variables.

The **simplex** method is a general-purpose linear programming algorithm widely used to solve large-scale problems. Although it lacks the intuitive appeal of the graphical approach, its ability to handle problems with more than two decision variables makes it extremely valuable for solving problems often encountered in operations management.

Although manual solution of linear programming problems using simplex can yield a number of insights on how solutions are derived, space limitations preclude describing it here. However, it is available on the CD that accompanies this book. The discussion here will focus on computer solutions.

Computer Solutions

The microcomputer problem will be used to illustrate computer solutions. We repeat it here for ease of reference.

Maximize $60x_1 + 50x_2$ where x_1 = the number of type 1 computers

x_2 = the number of type 2 computers

Subject to

Assembly	$4x_1 + 10x_2 \leq 100$ hours
Inspection	$2x_1 + 1x_2 \leq 22$ hours
Storage	$3x_1 + 3x_2 \leq 39$ cubic feet
	$x_1, x_2 \geq 0$

SOLVING LP MODELS USING MS EXCEL

Solutions to linear programming models can be obtained from spreadsheet software such as Microsoft's Excel. Excel has a routine called *Solver* that performs the necessary calculations.

To use Solver:

1. First, enter the problem in a worksheet, as shown in Figure 6S–15. What is not obvious from the figure is the need to enter a formula for each cell where there is a zero (Solver automatically inserts the zero after you input the formula). The formulas are for the value of the objective function and the constraints, in the appropriate cells. Before you enter the formulas, designate the cells where you want the optimal values of x_1 and x_2. Here, cells D4 and E4 are used. To enter a formula, click on the cell that the formula will pertain to, and then enter the formula, starting with an equals sign. We want the optimal value of the objective function to appear in cell G4. For G4, enter the formula

=60*D4+50*E4

The constraint formulas, using cells C7, C8, and C9, are

for C7:   =4*D4+10*E4

for C8: =2*D4+1*E4

for C9: =3*D4+3*E4

2. Now, click on <u>T</u>ools on the top of the worksheet, and in that menu, click on Sol<u>v</u>er. The Solver menu will appear as illustrated in Figure 6S–16. Begin by setting the Target Cell (i.e., indicating the cell where you want the optimal value of the objective function to appear). Note, if the activated cell is the cell designated for the value of Z when you click on the <u>T</u>ools menu, Solver will automatically set that cell as the target cell.

Highlight <u>M</u>ax if it isn't already highlighted. The Changing Cells are the cells where you want the optimal values of the decision variables to appear. Here, they are cells D4 and E4. We indicate this by the range D4:E4 (Solver will add the $ signs).

Finally, add the constraints by clicking on <u>A</u>dd . . . When that menu appears, for each constraint, enter the cell that contains the formula for the left side of the constraint, then select the appropriate inequality sign, and then enter either the right-side amount or the cell that has the right-side amount. Here, the right-side amounts are used. After you have entered each constraint, click on <u>A</u>dd, and then enter the next constraint. (Note, constraints can be entered in any order.) For the nonnegativity constraints, enter the range of cells designated for the optimal values of the decision variables. Then, click on OK rather than <u>A</u>dd, and you will return to the Sol<u>v</u>er menu. Click on <u>O</u>ptions . . . , and in the Options menu, click on Assume Linear <u>M</u>odel, and then click on OK. This will return you to the Solver Parameters menu. Click on Sol<u>v</u>e.

3. The Solver Results menu will then appear, indicating that a solution has been found, or that an error has occurred. If there has been an error, go back to the Solver Parameters menu and check to see that your constraints refer to the correct changing cells, and that the inequality directions are correct. Make the corrections and click on Solve.

Assuming everything is correct, in the Solver Results menu, in the Reports box, highlight both Answer and Sensitivity, and then click on OK.

4. Sol<u>v</u>er will incorporate the optimal values of the decision variables and the objective function in your original layout on your worksheet (see Figure 6S–17). We can see that the optimal values are type 1 = 9 units and type 2 = 4 units, and the total profit is 740. The answer report will also show the optimal values of the decision variables (upper part of Figure 6S–18), and some information on the constraints (lower part of Figure 6S–18). Of

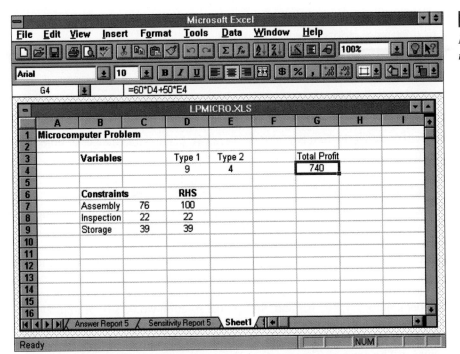

MS Excel worksheet solution to microcomputer problem

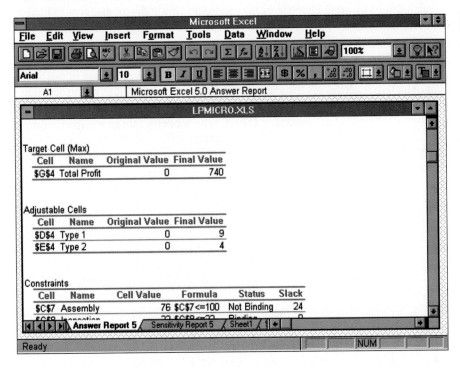

MS Excel Answer Report for microcomputer problem

particular interest here is the indication of which constraints have slack and how much slack. We can see that the constraint entered in cell C7 (assembly) has a slack of 24, and that the constraints entered in cells C8 (inspection) and C9 (storage) have slack equal to zero, indicating that they are binding constraints.

Sensitivity Analysis

Sensitivity analysis is a means of assessing the impact of potential changes to the parameters (the numerical values) of an LP model. Such changes may occur due to forces

sensitivity analysis Assessing the impact of potential changes to the numerical values of an LP model.

beyond a manager's control; or a manager may be contemplating making the changes, say, to increase profits or reduce costs.

There are three types of potential changes:

1. Objective function coefficients.
2. Right-hand values of constraints.
3. Constraint coefficients.

We will consider the first two of these here. We begin with changes to objective function coefficients.

OBJECTIVE FUNCTION COEFFICIENT CHANGES

A change in the value of an objective function coefficient can cause a change in the optimal solution of a problem. In a graphical solution, this would mean a change to another corner point of the feasible solution space. However, not every change in the value of an objective function coefficient will lead to a changed solution; generally there is a *range of values for which the optimal values of the decision variables will not change.* For example, in the microcomputer problem, if the profit on type 1 computers increased from $60 per unit to, say, $65 per unit, the optimal solution would still be to produce nine units of type 1 and four units of type 2 computers. Similarly, if the profit per unit on type 1 computers decreased from $60 to, say, $58, producing nine of type 1 and four of type 2 would still be optimal. These sorts of changes are not uncommon; they may be the result of such things as price changes in raw materials, price discounts, cost reductions in production, and so on. Obviously, when a change does occur in the value of an objective function coefficient, it can be helpful for a manager to know if that change will affect the optimal values of the decision variables. The manager can quickly determine this by referring to that coefficient's **range of optimality,** which is the range in possible values of that objective function coefficient over which the optimal values of the decision variables will not change. Before we see how to determine the range, consider the implication of the range. The range of optimality for the type 1 coefficient in the microcomputer problem is 50 to 100. That means that as long as the coefficient's value is in that range, the optimal values will be 9 units of type 1 and 4 units of type 2. Conversely, *if a change extends beyond the range of optimality, the solution will change.*

Similarly, suppose, instead, the coefficient of type 2 computers was to change. Its range of optimality is 30 to 60. As long as the value of the change doesn't take it outside of this range, nine and four will still be the optimal values. Note, however, even for changes that are *within* the range of optimality, the optimal value of the objective function *will* change. If the type 1 coefficient increased from $60 to $61, and nine units of type 1 is still optimum, profit would increase by $9: nine units times $1 per unit. Thus, for a change that is within the range of optimality, a revised value of the objective function must be determined.

Now let's see how we can determine the range of optimality using computer output.

range of optimality Range of values over which the solution quantities of all the decision variables remains the same.

Using MS Excel. There is a table for the Changing Cells (see Figure 6S–19). It shows the value of the objective function that was used in the problem for each type of computer (i.e., 60 and 50), and the allowable increase and allowable decrease for each coefficient. By subtracting the allowable decrease from the original value of the coefficient, and adding the allowable increase to the original value of the coefficient, we obtain the range of optimality for each coefficient. Thus, we find for type 1:

$$60 - 10 = 50 \quad \text{and} \quad 60 + 40 = 100$$

Hence, the range for the type 1 coefficient is 50 to 100. For type 2:

$$50 - 20 = 30 \quad \text{and} \quad 50 + 10 = 60$$

Hence the range for the type 2 coefficient is 30 to 60.

In this example, both of the decision variables are *basic* (i.e., nonzero). However, in other problems, one or more decision variables may be *nonbasic* (i.e., have an optimal value of zero). In such instances, unless the value of that variable's objective function coefficient increases by more than its reduced cost, it won't come into solution (i.e., become a basic variable). Hence, the range of optimality (sometimes referred to as the *range of insignificance*) for a nonbasic variable is from negative infinity to the sum of its current value and its reduced cost.

Now let's see how we can handle multiple changes to objective functions coefficients, that is, a change in more than one coefficient. To do this, divide each coefficient's change by the allowable change in the same direction. Thus, if the change is a decrease, divide that amount by the allowable decrease. Treat all resulting fractions as positive. Sum the fractions. If the sum does not exceed 1.00, then multiple changes are within the range of optimality and will not result in any change to the optimal values of the decision variables.

CHANGES IN THE RIGHT-HAND SIDE (RHS) VALUE OF A CONSTRAINT

In considering right-hand side changes, it is important to know if a particular constraint is binding on a solution. A constraint is binding if substituting the values of the decision variables of that solution into the left side of the constraint results in a value that is equal to the RHS value. In other words, that constraint stops the objective function from achieving a better value (e.g., a greater profit or a lower cost). Each constraint has a corresponding **shadow price,** which is a marginal value that indicates the amount by which the value of the objective function would change if there were a one-unit change in the RHS value of that constraint. If a constraint is nonbinding, its shadow price is zero, meaning that increasing or decreasing its RHS value by one unit will have no impact on the value of the objective function. Nonbinding constraints have either slack (if the constraint is ≤) or surplus (if the constraint is ≥). Suppose a constraint has 10 units of slack in the optimal solution, which means 10 units that are unused. If we were to increase or decrease the constraint's RHS value by one unit, the only effect would be to increase or decrease its slack by one unit. But there is no profit associated with slack, so the value of the objec-

shadow price Amount by which the value of the objective function would change with a one-unit change in the RHS value of a constraint.

tive function wouldn't change. On the other hand, if the change is to the RHS value of a binding constraint, then the optimal value of the objective function would change. Any change in a binding constraint will cause the optimal values of the decision variables to change, and hence, cause the value of the objective function to change. For example, in the microcomputer problem, the inspection constraint is a binding constraint, it has a shadow price of 10. That means if there was one hour less of inspection time, total profit would decrease by $10, or if there was one more hour of inspection time available, total profit would increase by $10. In general, multiplying the amount of change in the RHS value of a constraint by the constraint's shadow price will indicate the change's impact on the optimal value of the objective function. However, this is only true over a limited range called the **range of feasibility.** In this range, the value of the shadow price remains constant. Hence, as long as a change in the RHS value of a constraint is within its range of feasibility, the shadow price will remain the same, and one can readily determine the impact on the objective function.

range of feasibility Range of values for the RHS of a constraint over which the shadow price remains the same.

Let's see how to determine the range of feasibility from computer output.

Using MS Excel. In the sensitivity report there is a table labeled "Constraints" (see Figure 6S–19). The table shows the shadow price for each constraint, its RHS value and the allowable increase and allowable decrease. Adding the allowable increase to the RHS value, and subtracting the allowable decrease will produce the range of feasibility for that constraint. For example, for the inspection constraint, the range would be

$$22 + 4 = 26; \quad 22 - 4 = 18$$

Hence, the range of feasibility for Inspection is 18 to 26 hours. Similarly, for the storage constraint, the range is

$$39 - 6 = 33 \quad \text{to} \quad 39 + 4.5 = 43.5$$

The range for the assembly constraint is a little different; the assembly constraint is nonbinding (note the shadow price of 0) while the other two are binding (note their nonzero shadow prices). The assembly constraint has a slack of 24 (the difference between its RHS value of 100 and its final value of 76). With its slack of 24, its RHS value could be decreased by as much as 24 (to 76) before it would become binding. Conversely, increasing its right-hand side will only produce more slack. Thus, no amount of increase in the RHS value will make it binding, so there is no upper limit on the allowable increase. Excel indicates this by the large value (1E+30) shown for the allowable increase. So its range of feasibility has a lower limit of 76 and no upper limit.

If there are changes to more than one constraint's RHS value, analyze these in the same way as multiple changes to objective function coefficients. That is, if the change is an increase, divide that amount by that constraint's allowable increase; if the change is a decrease, divide the decrease by the allowable decrease. Treat all resulting fractions as positives. Sum the fractions. As long as the sum does not exceed 1.00, the changes are within the range of feasibility for multiple changes, and the shadow prices won't change.

Table 6S–1 summarizes the impacts of changes that fall within either the range of optimality or the range of feasibility.

Now let's consider what happens if a change goes beyond a particular range. In a situation involving the range of optimality, a change in an objective function that is beyond the range of optimality will result in a new solution. Hence, it will be necessary to recompute the solution. For a situation involving the range of feasibility, there are two cases to consider. The first case would be increasing the RHS value of a ≤ constraint to beyond the upper limit of its range of feasibility. This would produce slack equal to the amount by which the upper limit is exceeded. Hence, if the upper limit is 200, and the increase is 220, the result is that the constraint has a slack of 20. Similarly, for a ≥ constraint, going below its lower bound creates a surplus for that constraint. The second case for each of these would be exceeding the opposite limit (the lower bound for a ≤ constraint, or the upper bound for a ≥ constraint). In either instance, a new solution would have to be generated.

binding constraint, 290
constraints, 276
decision variables, 275
feasible solution space, 276
graphical linear programming, 278
objective function, 275
parameters, 276
range of feasibility, 296

range of optimality, 294
redundant constraint, 287
sensitivity analysis, 293
shadow price, 295
simplex, 290
slack, 290
surplus, 290

TABLE 6S–1

Summary of the impact of changes within their respective ranges

CHANGES TO OBJECTIVE FUNCTION COEFFICIENTS THAT ARE WITHIN THE RANGE OF OPTIMALITY

Component	Result
Values of decision variables	No change
Value of objective function	Will change

CHANGES TO RHS VALUES OF CONSTRAINTS THAT ARE WITHIN THE RANGE OF FEASIBILITY

Component	Result
Value of shadow price	No change
List of basic variables	No change
Values of basic variables	Will change
Value of objective function	Will change

Key Terms

Solved Problems

Problem 1

A small construction firm specializes in building and selling single-family homes. The firm offers two basic types of houses, model A and model B. Model A houses require 4,000 labor hours, 2 tons of stone, and 2,000 board feet of lumber. Model B houses require 10,000 labor hours, 3 tons of stone, and 2,000 board feet of lumber. Due to long lead times for ordering supplies and the scarcity of skilled and semiskilled workers in the area, the firm will be forced to rely on its present resources for the upcoming building season. It has 400,000 hours of labor, 150 tons of stone, and 200,000 board feet of lumber. What mix of model A and B houses should the firm construct if model As yield a profit of $1,000 per unit and model Bs yield $2,000 per unit? Assume that the firm will be able to sell all the units it builds.

Solution

a. Formulate the objective function and constraints:[1]

Maximize $Z = 1{,}000A + 2{,}000B$

Subject to

Labor	$4{,}000A +$	$10{,}000B$	$\leq$	400,000 labor hours
Stone	$2A +$	$3B$	$\leq$	150 tons
Lumber	$2{,}000A +$	$2{,}000B$	$\leq$	200,000 board feet
		A, B	$\geq$	0

b. Graph the constraints and objective function, and identify the optimum corner point (see graph). Note that the lumber constraint is *redundant*: It does not form a boundary of the feasible solution space.

―――――
[1]For the sake of consistency, we will assign to the horizontal axis the first decision variable mentioned in the problem. In this case, variable A will be represented on the horizontal axis and variable B on the vertical axis.

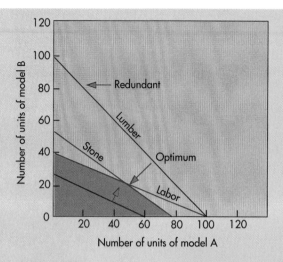

c. Determine the optimal quantities of models A and B, and compute the resulting profit. Because the optimum point is at the intersection of the stone and labor constraints, solve those two equations for their common point:

$$\text{Labor} \quad 4{,}000A + 10{,}000B = 400{,}000$$
$$\underline{-2{,}000 \times (\text{Stone } 2A + \quad 3B = \quad 150)}$$
$$4{,}000B = 100{,}000$$
$$B = \quad 25$$

Substitute $B = 25$ in one of the equations, and solve for A:

$$2A + 3(25) = 150 \qquad A = 37.5$$
$$Z = 1{,}000(37.5) + 2{,}000(25) = 87{,}500$$

Problem 2

This LP model was solved by computer:

Maximize $15x_1 + 20x_2 + 14x_3$ where x_1 = quantity of product 1
                                                                              x_2 = quantity of product 2
                                                                              x_3 = quantity of product 3

Subject to
  Labor $5x_1 + 6x_2 + 4x_3 \leq 210$ hours
  Material $10x_1 + 8x_2 + 5x_3 \leq 200$ pounds
  Machine $4x_1 + 2x_2 + 5x_3 \leq 170$ minutes
                    $x_1, x_2, x_3 \geq 0$

The following information was obtained from the output. The ranges were also computed based on the output, and they are shown as well.

```
Total profit = 548.00

Variable      Value    Reduced Cost    Range of Optimality

Product 1       0         10.6          0.00 to 25.60
Product 2       5          0            9.40 to 22.40
Product 3      32          0           12.50 to 50.00

Constraint    Slack    Shadow Price    Range of Feasibility

Labor          52          0.0         158.00 to unlimited
Material        0          2.4         170.00 to 270.91
Machine         0          0.4          50.00 to 200.00
```

a. Which decision variables are basic (i.e., in solution)?

b. By how much would the profit per unit of product 1 have to increase in order for it to have a nonzero value (i.e., for it to become a basic variable)?

c. If the profit per unit of product 2 increased by $2 to $22, would the optimal production quantities of products 2 and 3 change? Would the optimal value of the objective function change?

d. If the available amount of labor decreased by 12 hours, would that cause a change in the optimal values of the decision variables or the optimal value of the objective function? Would anything change?

e. If the available amount of material increased by 10 pounds to 210 pounds, how would that affect the optimal value of the objective function?

f. If profit per unit on product 2 increased by $1 and profit per unit on product 3 decreased by $.50, would that fall within the range of multiple changes? Would the values of the decision variables change? What would be the revised value of the objective function?

Solution

a. Products 2 and 3 are in solution (i.e., have nonzero values; the optimal value of product 2 is 5 units, and the optimal value of product 3 is 32 units.

b. The amount of increase would have to equal its *reduced cost* of $10.60.

c. No, because the change would be within its range of optimality, which has an upper limit of $22.40. The objective function value would increase by an amount equal to the quantity of product 2 and its increased unit profit. Hence, it would increase by 5($2) = $10 to $558.

d. Labor has a slack of 52 hours. Consequently, the only effect would be to decrease the slack to 40 hours.

e. Yes. The change is within the range of feasibility. The objective function value will increase by the amount of change multiplied by material's shadow price of $2.40. Hence, the objective function value would increase by 10($2.40) = $24.00. (Note: If the change had been a *decrease* of 10 pounds, which is also within the range of feasibility, the value of the objective function would have *decreased* by this amount.)

f. To determine if the changes are within the range for multiple changes, we first compute the ratio of the amount of each change to the end of the range *in the same direction.* For product 2, it is $1/$2.40 = .417; for product 3, it is −$.50/−$1.50 = .333. Next, we compute the sum of these ratios: .417 + .333 = .750. Because this does not exceed 1.00, we conclude that these changes are within the range. This means that the optimal values of the decision variables will not change. We can compute the change to the value of the objective function by multiplying each product's optimal quantity by its changed profit per unit: 5($1) + 32(−$.50) = −$11. Hence, with these changes, the value of the objective function would decrease by $11; its new value would be $548 − $11 = $537.

Discussion and Review Questions

1. For which decision environment is linear programming most suited?

2. What is meant by the term *feasible solution space*? What determines this region?

3. Explain the term *redundant constraint.*

4. What is an isocost line? An isoprofit line?

5. What does sliding an objective function line toward the origin represent? Away from the origin?

6. Briefly explain these terms:

   a. Basic variable

   b. Shadow price

   c. Range of feasibility

   d. Range of optimality

Problems

1. Solve these problems using graphical linear programming and answer the questions that follow. Use simultaneous equations to determine the optimal values of the decision variables.

   a. Maximize $Z = 4x_1 + 3x_2$

Subject to

Material $6x_1 + 4x_2 \leq 48$ lb
Labor $4x_1 + 8x_2 \leq 80$ hr
$x_1, x_2 \geq 0$

b. Maximize $Z = 2x_1 + 10x_2$

Subject to

R $10x_1 + 4x_2 \geq 40$
S $1x_1 + 6x_2 \geq 24$
T $1x_1 + 2x_2 \leq 14$
$x_1, x_2 \geq 0$

c. Maximize $Z = 6A + 3B$ (revenue)

Subject to

Material $20A + 6B \leq 600$ lb
Machinery $25A + 20B \leq 1{,}000$ hr
Labor $20A + 30B \leq 1{,}200$ hr
$A, B \geq 0$

(1) What are the optimal values of the decision variables and Z?
(2) Do any constraints have (nonzero) slack? If yes, which one(s) and how much slack does each have?
(3) Do any constraints have (nonzero) surplus? If yes, which one(s) and how much surplus does each have?
(4) Are any constraints redundant? If yes, which one(s)? Explain briefly.

2. Solve these problems using graphical linear programming and then answer the questions that follow. Use simultaneous equations to determine the optimal values of the decision variables.

a. Minimize $Z = 1.80S + 2.20T$

Subject to

Potassium $5S + 8T \geq 200$ gr
Carbohydrate $15S + 6T \geq 240$ gr
Protein $4S + 12T \geq 180$ gr
T $T \geq 10$ gr
$S, T \geq 0$

b. Minimize $Z = 2x_1 + 3x_2$

Subject to

D $4x_1 + 2x_2 \geq 20$
E $2x_1 + 6x_2 \geq 18$
F $1x_1 + 2x_2 \leq 12$
$x_1, x_2 \geq 0$

(1) What are the optimal values of the decision variables and Z?
(2) Do any constraints have (nonzero) slack? If yes, which one(s) and how much slack does each have?
(3) Do any constraints have (nonzero) surplus? If yes, which one(s) and how much surplus does each have?
(4) Are any constraints redundant? If yes, which one(s)? Explain briefly.

3. An appliance manufacturer produces two models of microwave ovens: H and W. Both models require fabrication and assembly work; each H uses four hours of fabrication and two hours of assembly, and each W uses two hours of fabrication and six hours of assembly. There are 600 fabrication hours available this week and 480 hours of assembly. Each H contributes $40 to profits, and each W contributes $30 to profits. What quantities of H and W will maximize profits?

4. A small candy shop is preparing for the holiday season. The owner must decide how many bags of deluxe mix and how many bags of standard mix of Peanut/Raisin Delite to put up. The deluxe mix has ⅔ pound raisins and ⅓ pound peanuts, and the standard mix has ½ pound raisins and ½ pound peanuts per bag. The shop has 90 pounds of raisins and 60 pounds of peanuts to work with.

Peanuts cost \$.60 per pound and raisins cost \$1.50 per pound. The deluxe mix will sell for \$2.90 per pound, and the standard mix will sell for \$2.55 per pound. The owner estimates that no more than 110 bags of one type can be sold.

a. If the goal is to maximize profits, how many bags of each type should be prepared?

b. What is the expected profit?

5. A retired couple supplement their income by making fruit pies, which they sell to a local grocery store. During the month of September, they produce apple and grape pies. The apple pies are sold for \$1.50 to the grocer, and the grape pies are sold for \$1.20. The couple is able to sell all of the pies they produce owing to their high quality. They use fresh ingredients. Flour and sugar are purchased once each month. For the month of September, they have 1,200 cups of sugar and 2,100 cups of flour. Each apple pie requires 1 ½ cups of sugar and 3 cups of flour, and each grape pie requires 2 cups of sugar and 3 cups of flour.

a. Determine the number of grape and the number of apple pies that will maximize revenues if the couple working together can make an apple pie in six minutes and a grape pie in three minutes. They plan to work no more than 60 hours.

b. Determine the amounts of sugar, flour, and time that will be unused.

6. Solve each of these problems by computer and obtain the optimal values of the decision variables and the objective function.

a. Maximize $4x_1 + 2x_2 + 5x_3$

Subject to

$$1x_1 + 2x_2 + 1x_3 \leq 25$$
$$1x_1 + 4x_2 + 2x_3 \leq 40$$
$$3x_1 + 3x_2 + 1x_3 \leq 30$$
$$x_1, x_2, x_3 \geq 0$$

b. Maximize $10x_1 + 6x_2 + 3x_3$

Subject to

$$1x_1 + 1x_2 + 2x_3 \leq 25$$
$$2x_1 + 1x_2 + 4x_3 \leq 40$$
$$1x_1 + 2x_2 + 3x_3 \leq 40$$
$$x_1, x_2, x_3 \geq 0$$

7. For Problem 6a, determine the following:

a. The range of feasibility for each constraint.

b. The range of optimality for the coefficients of the objective function.

8. For Problem 6b:

a. Find the range of feasibility for each constraint, and interpret your answers.

b. Determine the range of optimality for each coefficient of the objective function. Interpret your results.

9. A small firm makes three similar products, which all follow the same three-step process, consisting of milling, inspection, and drilling. Product A requires 12 minutes of milling, 5 minutes for inspection, and 10 minutes of drilling per unit; product B requires 10 minutes of milling, 4 minutes for inspection, and 8 minutes of drilling per unit; and product C requires 8 minutes of milling, 4 minutes for inspection, and 16 minutes of drilling. The department has 20 hours available during the next period for milling, 15 hours for inspection, and 24 hours for drilling. Product A contributes \$2.40 per unit to profit, B contributes \$2.50 per unit, and C contributes \$3.00 per unit. Determine the optimal mix of products in terms of maximizing contribution to profits for the period. Then, find the range of optimality for the profit coefficient of each variable.

10. Formulate and then solve a linear programming model of this problem, to determine how many containers of each product to produce tomorrow to maximize profits. The company makes four juice products using orange, grapefruit, and pineapple juice.

Product	Retail Price
Orange juice	\$1.00
Grapefruit juice	.90
Pineapple juice	.80
All-in-One	1.10

The All-in-One juice has equal parts of orange, grapefruit, and pineapple juice. Each product is produced in a one-quart size (there are four quarts in a gallon). On hand are 400 gallons of orange juice, 300 gallons of grapefruit juice, and 200 gallons of pineapple juice. The cost per gallon is $2.00 for orange juice, $1.60 for grapefruit juice, and $1.40 for pineapple juice.

In addition, the manager wants grapefruit juice to be used for no more than 30 percent of the number of containers produced. She wants the ratio of the number of containers of orange juice to the number of containers of pineapple juice to be at least 7 to 5.

11. A wood products firm uses leftover time at the end of each week to make goods for stock. Currently, two products on the list of items are produced for stock: a chopping board and a knife holder. Both items require three operations: cutting, gluing, and finishing. The manager of the firm has collected the following data on these products:

		TIME PER UNIT (MINUTES)		
Item	**Profit/Unit**	**Cutting**	**Gluing**	**Finishing**
Chopping board	$2	1.4	5	12
Knife holder	$6	0.8	13	3

The manager has also determined that, during each week, 56 minutes are available for cutting, 650 minutes are available for gluing, and 360 minutes are available for finishing.

a. Determine the optimal quantities of the decision variables.

b. Which resources are not completely used by your solution? How much of each resource is unused?

12. The manager of the deli section of a grocery superstore has just learned that the department has 112 pounds of mayonnaise, of which 70 pounds is approaching its expiration date and must be used. To use up the mayonnaise, the manager has decided to prepare two items: a ham spread and a deli spread. Each pan of the ham spread will require 1.4 pounds of mayonnaise, and each pan of the deli spread will require 1.0 pound. The manager has received an order for 10 pans of ham spread and 8 pans of the deli spread. In addition, the manager has decided to have at least 10 pans of each spread available for sale. Both spreads will cost $3 per pan to make, but ham spread sells for $5 per pan and deli spread sells for $7 per pan.

a. Determine the solution that will minimize cost.

b. Determine the solution that will maximize profit.

13. A manager wants to know how many units of each product to produce on a daily basis in order to achieve the highest contribution to profit. Production requirements for the products are shown in the following table.

Product	**Material 1 (pounds)**	**Material 2 (pounds)**	**Labor (hours)**
A	2	3	3.2
B	1	5	1.5
C	6	—	2.0

Material 1 costs $5 a pound, material 2 costs $4 a pound, and labor costs $10 an hour. Product A sells for $80 a unit, product B sells for $90 a unit, and product C sells for $70 a unit. Available resources each day are 200 pounds of material 1; 300 pounds of material 2; and 150 hours of labor.

The manager must satisfy certain output requirements: The output of product A should not be more than one-third of the total number of units produced; the ratio of units of product A to units of product B should be 3 to 2; and there is a standing order for 5 units of product A each day. Formulate a linear programming model for this problem, and then solve.

14. A chocolate maker has contracted to operate a small candy counter in a fashionable store. To start with, the selection of offerings will be intentionally limited. The counter will offer a regular mix of candy made up of equal parts of cashews, raisins, caramels, and chocolates, and a deluxe mix that is one-half cashews and one-half chocolates, which will be sold in one-pound boxes. In addition, the candy counter will offer individual one-pound boxes of cashews, raisins, caramels, and chocolates.

A major attraction of the candy counter is that all candies are made fresh at the counter. However, storage space for supplies and ingredients is limited. Bins are available that can hold the amounts shown in the table:

Ingredient	Capacity (pounds per day)
Cashews	120
Raisins	200
Caramels	100
Chocolates	160

In order to present a good image and to encourage purchases, the counter will make at least 20 boxes of each type of product each day. Any leftover boxes at the end of the day will be removed and given to a nearby nursing home for goodwill.

The profit per box for the various items has been determined as follows:

Item	Profit per Box
Regular	$.80
Deluxe	.90
Cashews	.70
Raisins	.60
Caramels	.50
Chocolates	.75

a. Formulate the LP model.

b. Solve for the optimal values of the decision variables and the maximum profit.

15. Given this linear programming model, solve the model and then answer the questions that follow.

Maximize $12x_1 + 18x_2 + 15x_3$ where x_1 = the quantity of product 1 to make etc.

Subject to

Machine	$5x_1 + 4x_2 + 3x_3 \leq 160$ minutes
Labor	$4x_1 + 10x_2 + 4x_3 \leq 288$ hours
Materials	$2x_1 + 2x_2 + 4x_3 \leq 200$ pounds
Product 2	$x_2 \leq 16$ units

$$x_1, x_2, x_3 \geq 0$$

a. Are any constraints binding? If so, which one(s)?

b. If the profit on product 3 was changed to $22 a unit, what would the values of the decision variables be? The objective function? Explain.

c. If the profit on product 1 was changed to $22 a unit, what would the values of the decision variables be? The objective function? Explain.

d. If 10 hours less of labor time were available, what would the values of the decision variables be? The objective function? Explain.

e. If the manager decided that as many as 20 units of product 2 could be produced (instead of 16), how much additional profit would be generated?

f. If profit per unit on each product increased by $1, would the optimal values of the decision variables change? Explain. What would the optimal value of the objective function be?

16. A garden store prepares various grades of pine bark for mulch: nuggets (x_1), mini-nuggets (x_2), and chips (x_3). The process requires pine bark, machine time, labor time, and storage space. The following model has been developed.

Maximize $9x_1 + 9x_2 + 6x_3$ (profit)

Subject to

Bark	$5x_1 + 6x_2 + 3x_3 \leq 600$ pounds
Machine	$2x_1 + 4x_2 + 5x_3 \leq 660$ minutes
Labor	$2x_1 + 4x_2 + 3x_3 \leq 480$ hours
Storage	$1x_1 + 1x_2 + 1x_3 \leq 150$ bags

$$x_1, x_2, x_3 \geq 0$$

a. What is the marginal value of a pound of pine bark? Over what range is this price value appropriate?

b. What is the maximum price the store would be justified in paying for additional pine bark?

c. What is the marginal value of labor? Over what range is this value in effect?

d. The manager obtained additional machine time through better scheduling. How much additional machine time can be effectively used for this operation? Why?

e. If the manager can obtain *either* additional pine bark or additional storage space, which one should she choose and how much (assuming additional quantities cost the same as usual)?

f. If a change in the chip operation increased the profit on chips from $6 per bag to $7 per bag, would the optimal quantities change? Would the value of the objective function change? If so, what would the new value(s) be?

g. If profits on chips increased to $7 per bag and profits on nuggets decreased by $.60, would the optimal quantities change? Would the value of the objective function change? If so, what would the new value(s) be?

h. If the amount of pine bark available decreased by 15 pounds, machine time decreased by 27 minutes, and storage capacity increased by five bags, would this fall in the range of feasibility for multiple changes? If so, what would the value of the objective function be?

CASE

Son, Ltd.

Son, Ltd., manufactures a variety of chemical products used by photoprocessors. Son was recently bought out by a conglomerate, and managers of the two organizations have been working together to improve the efficiency of Son's operations.

Managers have been asked to adhere to weekly operating budgets and to develop operating plans using quantitative methods whenever possible. The manager of one department has been given a weekly operating budget of $11,980 for production of three chemical products, which for convenience shall be referred to as Q, R, and W. The budget is intended to pay for direct labor and materials. Processing requirements for the three products, on a per unit basis, are shown in the table.

The company has a contractual obligation for 85 units of product R per week.

Material A costs $4 per pound, as does material B. Labor costs $8 an hour.

Product Q sells for $122 a unit, product R sells for $115 a unit, and product W sells for $76 a unit.

The manager is considering a number of different proposals regarding the quantity of each product to produce. The manager is primarily interested in maximizing contribution. Moreover, the manager wants to know how much labor will be needed, as well as the amount of each material to purchase.

Questions

Prepare a report that addresses the following issues:

1. The optimal quantities of products and the necessary quantities of labor and materials.

2. One proposal is to make equal amounts of the products. What amount of each will maximize contribution, and what quantities of labor and materials will be needed? How much less will total contribution be if this proposal is adopted?

3. How would you formulate the constraint for material A if it was determined that there is a 5 percent waste factor for material A and equal quantities of each product are required?

Product	Labor (hours)	Material A (pounds)	Material B (pounds)
Q	5	2	1
R	4	2	—
W	2	½	2

Selected Bibliography and Further Reading

Bierman, Harold; Charles P. Bonini; and Warren H. Hausman. *Quantitative Analysis for Business Decisions.* 9th ed. Burr Ridge, IL: Richard D. Irwin, 1997.

Gass, S. I. *An Illustrated Guide to Linear Programming.* New York: Dover, 1990.

Hillier, Frederick S.; Mark S. Hillier; and Gerald Lieberman. *Introduction to Management Science.* Burr Ridge, IL: Irwin/McGraw-Hill, 2000.

Ragsdale, Cliff T. *Spreadsheet Modeling and Decision Analysis: A Practical Introduction to Management Science.* Cambridge, MA: Course Technology, 1995.

Stevenson, W. J. *Introduction to Management Science.* 3rd ed. Burr Ridge, IL: Richard D. Irwin, 1998.

Taylor, Bernard. *Introduction to Management Science.* 6th ed. Upper Saddle River, NJ: Prentice Hall, 1999.

CHAPTER SEVEN
Design of Work Systems

CHAPTER OUTLINE

Introduction, 308

Operations Strategy, 308

Job Design, 308
   Specialization, 309
   Behavioral Approaches to Job
     Design, 310
   Motivation, 311

Reading: Workplace Upheavals
   Seem to Be Eroding Employees'
   Trust, 311
   Teams, 312
   Methods Analysis, 313
   Motion Study, 315
   Working Conditions, 318

Reading: What Works to Cut
   CTD Risk, Improve Job
   Productivity? 322

Work Measurement, 323
   Stopwatch Time Study, 324

Standard Elemental Times, 329
Predetermined Time Standards, 329
Work Sampling, 331

Compensation, 333
   Individual Incentive Plans, 334
   Group Incentive Plans, 335
   Knowledge-Based Pay Systems, 335
   Management Compensation, 335

Summary, 336

Key Terms, 337

Solved Problems, 337

Discussion and Review
   Questions, 338

Memo Writing Exercises, 338

Problems, 338

Reading: Making Hotplates, 340

Selected Bibliography and Further
   Reading, 341

Supplement: Learning Curves, 342

LEARNING OBJECTIVES

After completing this chapter, you should be able to:

1 Explain the importance of work design.

2 Briefly describe the two basic approaches to job design.

3 Discuss the advantages and disadvantages of specialization.

4 Explain the term *knowledge-based pay.*

5 Explain the purpose of methods analysis and describe how methods studies are performed.

6 Describe four commonly used techniques for motion study.

7 Discuss the impact of working conditions on job design.

8 Define a standard time.

9 Describe and compare time study methods and perform calculations.

10 Describe work sampling and perform calculations.

11 Compare stopwatch time study and work sampling.

12 Contrast time and output pay systems.

his chapter covers work design. Work design involves *job design, work measurement* and the establishment of time standards, and worker *motivation* and *compensation.*

As you read this chapter, note how decisions in other design areas have an impact on work systems, and how decisions on work design have an impact on the other areas. For example, product or service design decisions (e.g., operate a coal mine, offer computer dating service, sell sports equipment) in large measure determine the kinds of activities workers will be involved with. Similarly, layout decisions often influence work design. Process layouts tend to necessitate broader job content than product layouts. The implication of these interrelationships is that it is essential to adopt a systems approach to design; decisions in one area must be related to the overall system.

Introduction

The importance of work system design is underscored by the organization's dependence on human efforts (i.e., work) to accomplish its goals. Work design is one of the oldest aspects of operations management. In the past, it has often been deemphasized in operations management courses in favor of other topics. Recent years, however, have seen renewed interest that has come from somewhat different directions: Some of the interest has resulted from studies that reveal a general dissatisfaction felt by many workers with their jobs. And some of the interest has been sparked by increasing concerns over productivity. It is perhaps ironic that one of the oldest fields of operations management is now an important key to productivity improvement and to continuous improvement.

Operations Strategy

It is important for management to make design of work systems a key element of its operations strategy. In spite of the major advances in computers and manufacturing technology, people are still the heart of a business; they can make or break it, regardless of the technology used. Technology is important, of course, but technology alone is not enough.

The topics described in this chapter—job design, methods analysis, motion study, work standards, and compensation—all have an impact on productivity. They lack the glamour of high tech; they are closer to the back-to-the-basics fundamentals of work improvement.

Workers can be a valuable source of insight and creativity because they actually perform the jobs and are closest to the problems that arise. All too often, managers have overlooked contributions and potential contributions of employees, sometimes from ignorance and sometimes from a false sense of pride. Union–management differences are also a factor. More and more, though, companies are attempting to develop a spirit of cooperation between employees and managers, based in part on the success of Japanese companies.

In the same vein, an increasing number of companies are focusing some of their attention on improving the quality of work life and instilling pride and respect among workers. Many organizations are reaping surprising gains through worker *empowerment,* giving workers more say over their jobs.

Lean production puts added stress on workers. Managers should be aware of this, to minimize negative effects.

Job Design

job design The act of specifying the contents and methods of jobs.

Job design involves specifying the content and methods of jobs. Job designers focus on *what* will be done in a job, *who* will do the job, *how* the job will be done, and *where* the job will be done. The objectives of job design include productivity, safety, and quality of work life.

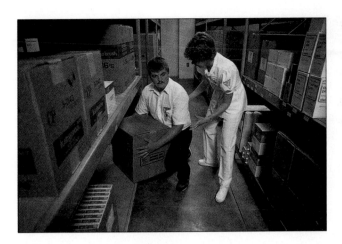

By teaching employees correct lifting techniques, organizations can head off injuries and their costs, such as absenteeism, health care and insurance costs, and reduced quality.

Ergonomics is an important part of job design. **Ergonomics** is the incorporation of human factors in the design of the workplace. It relates to design of equipment, design of work methods, and the overall design of the work environment. Among other things, ergonomics seeks to prevent common workplace injuries such as back injuries and repetitive-motion injuries by taking into account the fact that people vary in their physical dimensions and capabilities. Companies have compelling interests in reducing worker injuries. Injuries result in lower productivity, lost workdays, and increases in workers' compensation and health premiums.

ergonomics Incorporation of human factors in the design of the workplace.

The factors that affect job design and the implications of various alternatives are often so complex that a person without a good background in job design is likely to overlook important aspects of it. Workers and managers alike should be consulted in order to take advantage of their knowledge and to keep them informed. Because they are intimately involved with the work, employees can be a source of valuable ideas for job improvements. Managerial support for job design depends on the commitment and involvement of managers. It is usually easier to sell a design to these two groups if they have been included in the process. Finally, establishing a written record of the job design can serve as a basis for referral if questions arise about it.

Current practice in job design contains elements of two basic schools of thought. One might be called the *efficiency* school because it emphasizes a systematic, logical approach to job design; the other is called the *behavioral* school because it emphasizes satisfaction of wants and needs.

The efficiency approach, a refinement of Frederick Winslow Taylor's scientific management concepts, received considerable emphasis in the past. The behavioral approach emerged during the 1950s and has continued to make inroads into many aspects of job design. A main contribution of the behavioral approach is that it has reminded managers of the complexity of human beings, and that the efficiency approach may not be appropriate in every instance. It is noteworthy that specialization is a primary issue of disagreement between the efficiency and behavioral approaches.

SPECIALIZATION

The term **specialization** describes jobs that have a very narrow scope. Examples range from assembly lines to medical specialties. College professors often specialize in teaching certain courses, some auto mechanics specialize in transmission repair, and some bakers specialize in wedding cakes. The main rationale for specialization is the ability to concentrate one's efforts and thereby become proficient at that type of work.

specialization Work that concentrates on some aspect of a product or service.

Sometimes the amount of knowledge or training required of a specialist and the complexity of the work suggest that individuals who choose such work are very happy with their jobs. This seems to be especially true in the "professions" (e.g., doctors, lawyers,

TABLE 7-1

Major advantages and disadvantages of specialization in business

Advantages	
For management:	For labor:
1. Simplifies training	1. Low education and skill requirements
2. High productivity	2. Minimum responsibilities
3. Low wage costs	3. Little mental effort needed

Disadvantages	
For management:	For labor:
1. Difficult to motivate quality	1. Monotonous work
2. Worker dissatisfaction, possibly resulting in absenteeism, high turnover, disruptive tactics, poor attention to quality	2. Limited opportunities for advancement
	3. Little control over work
	4. Little opportunity for self-fulfillment

professors). At the other end of the scale are assembly line workers, who are also specialists, although much less glamorous. The advantage of these highly specialized jobs is that they yield high productivity and low unit costs, and they are largely responsible for the high standard of living that exists today in industrial nations.

Unfortunately, many of these jobs can be described as monotonous or downright boring, and they are the source of much of the dissatisfaction among industrial workers today. Even so, it would be wrong to conclude that all workers oppose this type of work. Some workers undoubtedly prefer a job with limited requirements and responsibility for making decisions. Others are not capable of handling jobs with greater scopes. Nonetheless, many workers are frustrated and this manifests itself in a number of ways. Turnover and absenteeism are often high; in the automotive industry, for example, absenteeism runs as high as 20 percent, although not every absentee is a frustrated worker on an assembly line. Workers may also take out their frustrations through disruptive tactics, deliberate slowdowns, or poor attention to product quality.

The seriousness of these problems caused job designers and others to seek ways of alleviating them. Some of those approaches are discussed in the following sections. Before we turn to them, note that the advantages and disadvantages of specialization are summarized in Table 7-1.

BEHAVIORAL APPROACHES TO JOB DESIGN

In an effort to make jobs more interesting and meaningful, job designers frequently consider job enlargement, job rotation, job enrichment, and increased use of mechanization.

job enlargement Giving a worker a larger portion of the total task, by horizontal loading.

Job enlargement means giving a worker a larger portion of the total task. This constitutes *horizontal loading*—the additional work is on the same level of skill and responsibility as the original job. The goal is to make the job more interesting by increasing the variety of skills required and by providing the worker with a more recognizable contribution to the overall output. For example, a production worker's job might be expanded so that he or she is responsible for a *sequence* of activities instead of only one activity.

job rotation Workers periodically exchange jobs.

Job rotation means having workers periodically exchange jobs. A firm can use this approach to avoid having one or a few employees stuck in monotonous jobs. It works best when workers can be transferred to more interesting jobs; there is little advantage in having workers exchange one boring job for another. Job rotation allows workers to broaden their learning experience and enables them to fill in for others in the event of sickness or absenteeism.

job enrichment Increasing responsibility for planning and coordination tasks, by vertical loading.

Job enrichment involves an increase in the level of responsibility for planning and coordination tasks. It is sometimes referred to as *vertical loading*. An example of this is to have stock clerks in supermarkets handle reordering of goods, thus increasing their responsibilities. The job enrichment approach focuses on the motivating potential of worker satisfaction.

The importance of these approaches to job design is that they have the potential to increase the motivational power of jobs by increasing worker satisfaction through improvement in the *quality of work life*. Many firms are currently involved in or seriously considering programs related to quality of work life. In addition to the aforementioned approaches, organizations are also experimenting with choice of locations (e.g., medium-sized cities or campuslike settings), flexible work hours, and teams.

MOTIVATION

Motivation is a key factor in many aspects of work life. Not only can it influence quality and productivity; it also contributes to the work environment. People work for a variety of reasons. And although compensation is often the leading reason, it is not the only reason. Other reasons include socialization, self-actualization, status, the physiological aspects of work, and a sense of purpose and accomplishment. Awareness of these factors can help management to develop a motivational framework that encourages workers to respond in a positive manner to the goals of the organization. A detailed discussion of motivation is beyond the scope of this book, but its importance to work design should be obvious.

Another factor that influences productivity and employee–management relations is *trust*. In an ideal work environment, there is a high level of trust between workers and managers. When managers trust employees, there is a greater tendency to give employees added responsibilities. When employees trust management, they are more likely to respond positively. Conversely, when they do not trust management, they are more likely to respond in less desirable ways. The following reading discusses the issue of employees distrusting managers.

READING

Workplace Upheavals Seem to Be Eroding Employees' Trust
Sue Shellenbarger

A former finance-department employee of a multinational manufacturer recalls the day his trust in his employer was shattered.

A devastating earthquake in Turkey had killed and injured thousands of people. He and his coworkers were panicked because they couldn't reach fellow employees there. At that time, he overheard his boss of three months telling the finance manager to revise sales projections for Turkey downward because they were likely to suffer—sales that accounted for only a fraction of 1% of the company's total.

"Ten thousand people, including possibly some of our own employees, were missing or dead, and she was worried about hitting sales targets," says the employee, who asked that his name not be used because he fears retaliation. "I gave my notice the following week."

Management gurus pretty much agree that trust in the workplace has been eroding since the 1980s, largely due to the layoff and acquisition binges and the accelerating pace of change. A study of 1,800 workers by Aon's Loyalty Institute, Ann Arbor, Mich., says more than one in eight, or 13%, of U.S. workers distrust their employers on the most basic level—that is, they don't feel free from fear, intimidation or harassment at work. Watson Wyatt Worldwide, Bethesda, Md., found in a study of 7,500 employees that only half trusted their senior managers.

Now that it's gone, many workplace experts are waking up to how important trust is, especially in a tight labor market. The Aon research shows that trust is such a basic requirement that without it a company's other benefits and programs won't raise employee commitment very much. Watson Wyatt also found a correlation between trust and profit. Companies where employees trusted top executives posted shareholder returns 42 percentage points higher than companies where distrust was the rule.

A common view among managers is that it's unwise, impractical or impossible to try to cultivate trust amid nonstop change and reorganizations. But that's a misfire, says the Loyalty Institute's David Stum. "The American worker knows quite well that change is never-ending. How it's handled is what can lead the worker to be secure or insecure." The basic question, Mr. Stum says, is, "Do I trust my company to be fair and honest as it goes through changes?"

The rules for building trust at work are actually pretty simple—the kinds of things we try to teach kids in elementary school. Dennis and Michelle Reina, co-authors of the 1999 book *Trust & Betrayal in the Workplace,* cite such behaviors as respecting others, sharing information, admitting mistakes, giving constructive feedback, keeping secrets, avoiding gossip and backbiting, being consistent and involving others in decision-making.

Some companies are consciously taking steps to build trust. SRA International, a Fairfax, Va., systems consultant, requires all 2,000 of its employees to take mandatory training on respect, fairness, ethics and honesty.

For employers with patience, the payoff is worth the effort. The Reinas, organizational development consultants in Stowe, Vt., tell of a manufacturing plant in a small New England town where managers had to lay off 100 of 420 employees. They held meetings to share information. They hung out on the shop floor on all three shifts to answer employees' questions and to hear their worries. They set up outplacement centers and invited other employers to the plant to meet their people.

Not surprisingly, Ms. Reina, says, when jobs opened up again at the plant, more than 80% of the layoff victims came running back.

Source: "Work and Family," *The Wall Street Journal,* June 21, 2000, p. B1. Reprinted with permission © 2000 by Dow Jones & Company, Inc. All Rights Reserved Worldwide.

TEAMS

The efforts of business organizations to become more productive, competitive, and customer-oriented have caused them to rethink how work is accomplished. Significant changes in the structure of some work environments have been the increasing use of teams and the way workers are paid, particularly in lean production systems.

In the past, nonroutine job assignments, such as dealing with customer complaints or improving a process, were typically given to one individual or to several individuals who reported to the same manager. More recently, nonroutine assignments are being given to teams who develop and implement solutions to problems. Responsibility for the assignment is shared among team members, who often decide among themselves how the work is to be accomplished.

self-directed teams Groups empowered to make certain changes in their work processes.

Self-directed teams, sometimes referred to as *self-managed teams,* are designed to achieve a higher level of teamwork and employee involvement. Although such teams are not given absolute authority to make all decisions, they are typically empowered to make changes in the work processes under their control. The underlying concept is that the

At this pit stop at the Michigan International Speedway, the Pennzoil team takes no more than 15 seconds to do a thorough maintenance check of the race car's engine, fluid levels, and tires.

www.mispeedway.com

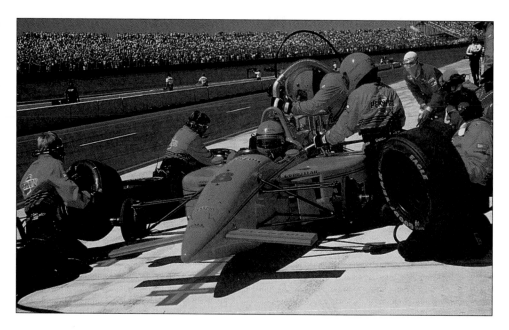

workers, who are close to the process and have the best knowledge of it, are better suited than management to make the most effective changes to improve the process. Moreover, because they have a vested interest and personal involvement in the changes, they tend to work harder to ensure that the desired results are achieved than they would if management had implemented the changes. For these teams to function properly, team members must be trained in quality, process improvement, and teamwork. Self-directed teams have a number of benefits. One is that fewer managers are necessary; very often one manager can handle several teams. Also, self-directed teams can provide improved responsiveness to problems, they have a personal stake in making the process work, and they require less time to implement improvements.

Generally, the benefits of teams include higher quality, higher productivity, and greater worker satisfaction. Moreover, higher levels of employee satisfaction can lead to less turnover and absenteeism, resulting in lower costs to train new workers and less need to fill in for absent employees. This does not mean that organizations will have no difficulties in applying the team concept. Managers, particularly middle managers, often feel threatened as teams assume more of the traditional functions of managers.

METHODS ANALYSIS

Methods analysis focuses on how a job is done. Job design often begins with a methods analysis of an overall operation. It then moves from general to specific details of the job, concentrating on arrangement of the workplace and movements of materials and/or workers. Methods analysis can be a good source of productivity improvements.

methods analysis Analyzing how a job is done.

The need for methods analysis can come from a number of different sources:

1. Changes in tools and equipment.
2. Changes in product design or introduction of new products.
3. Changes in materials or procedures.
4. Government regulations or contractual agreements.
5. Other factors (e.g., accidents, quality problems).

Methods analysis is done both for existing jobs and new jobs. Although it might seem strange to analyze methods of a new job, it is needed to establish a method for a new job. For an existing job, the procedure usually is to have the analyst observe the job as it is currently being performed and then devise improvements. For a new job, the analyst must rely on a job description and an ability to visualize the operation.

The basic procedure in methods analysis is:

1. Identify the operation to be studied, and gather all pertinent facts about tools, equipment, materials, and so on.
2. For existing jobs, discuss the job with the operator and supervisor to get their input.
3. Study and document the present method of an existing job using process charts. For new jobs, develop charts based on information about the activities involved.
4. Analyze the job.
5. Propose new methods.
6. Install the new methods.
7. Follow up installation to assure that improvements have been achieved.

Selecting an Operation to Study. Sometimes a foreman or supervisor will request that a certain operation be studied. At other times, methods analysis will be part of an overall program to increase productivity and reduce costs. Some general guidelines for selecting a job to study are to consider jobs that:

1. Have a high labor content.
2. Are done frequently.

3. Are unsafe, tiring, unpleasant, and/or noisy.

4. Are designated as problems (e.g., quality problems, scheduling bottlenecks).

Documenting the Present Method. Use charts, graphs, and verbal descriptions of the way the job is now being performed. This will provide a good understanding of the job and serve as a basis of comparison against which revisions can be judged.

Analyzing the Job and Proposing New Methods. Job analysis requires careful thought about the what, why, when, where, and who of the job. Often, simply going through these questions will clarify the review process by encouraging the analyst to take a devil's advocate attitude toward both present and proposed methods.

Analyzing and improving methods is facilitated by the use of various charts such as *flow process charts* and *worker-machine charts.*

flow process chart Chart used to examine the overall sequence of an operation by focusing on movements of the operator or flow of materials.

Flow process charts are used to review and critically examine the overall sequence of an operation by focusing on the movements of the operator or the flow of materials. These charts are helpful in identifying nonproductive parts of the process (e.g., delays, temporary storages, distances traveled). Figure 7–1 describes the symbols used in constructing a flow process chart, and Figure 7–2 illustrates a flow process chart.

The uses for flow process charts include studying the flow of material through a department, studying the sequence that documents or forms take, analyzing movement and care of surgical patients, layout of department and grocery stores, and mail handling.

Experienced analysts usually develop a checklist of questions they ask themselves to generate ideas for improvements. Some representative questions are:

1. Why is there a delay or storage at this point?

2. How can travel distances be shortened or avoided?

3. Can materials handling be reduced?

4. Would a rearrangement of the workplace result in greater efficiency?

5. Can similar activities be grouped?

6. Would the use of additional or improved equipment be helpful?

7. Does the worker have any ideas for improvements?

worker-machine chart Chart used to determine portions of a work cycle during which an operator and equipment are busy or idle.

A **worker-machine chart** is helpful in visualizing the portions of a work cycle during which an operator and equipment are busy or idle. The analyst can easily see when the operator and machine are working independently and when their work overlaps or is interdependent. One use of this type of chart is to determine how many machines or how much equipment the operator can manage. Figure 7–3 presents an example of a worker-machine chart. Among other things, the chart highlights worker and machine utilization.

Installing the Improved Method. Successful implementation of proposed method changes requires convincing management of the desirability of the new method and obtaining the cooperation of the worker. If the worker has been consulted throughout the process and has made suggestions that are incorporated in the proposed changes, this part of the task will be considerably easier than if the analyst has assumed sole responsibility for the development of the proposal.

If the proposed method constitutes a major change from the way the job has been performed in the past, workers may have to undergo a certain amount of retraining, and full implementation may take some time to achieve.

The Follow-Up. In order to ensure that changes have been made and that the proposed method is functioning as expected, the analyst should review the operation after a reasonable period and consult again with the operator.

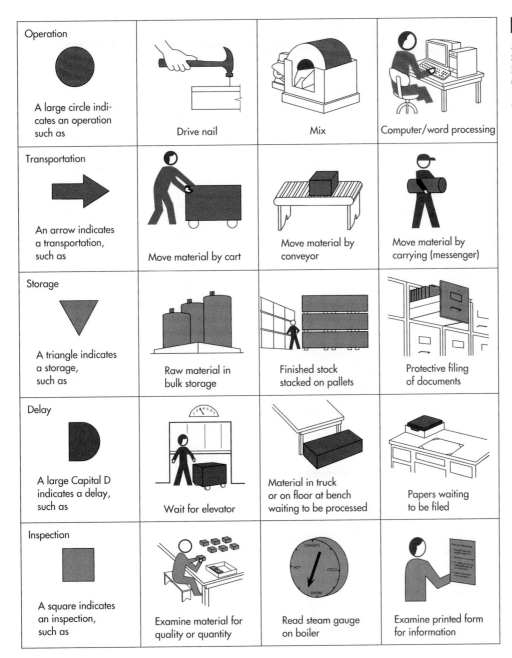

FIGURE 7–1

Process chart symbols
Source: Adapted from Benjamin W. Niebel, *Motion and Time Study,* 8th ed. (Burr Ridge, IL: Richard D. Irwin, 1988), p. 35, © 1988 by Richard D. Irwin, Inc. Reprinted by permission.

MOTION STUDY

Motion study is the systematic study of the human motions used to perform an operation. The purpose is to eliminate unnecessary motions and to identify the best sequence of motions for maximum efficiency. Hence, motion study can be an important avenue for productivity improvements. Present practice evolved from the work of Frank Gilbreth, who originated the concepts in the bricklaying trade in the early twentieth century. Through the use of motion study techniques, Gilbreth is generally credited with increasing the average number of bricks laid per hour by a factor of 3, even though he was not a bricklayer by trade. When you stop to realize that bricklaying had been carried on for centuries, Gilbreth's accomplishment is even more remarkable.

motion study Systematic study of the human motions used to perform an operation.

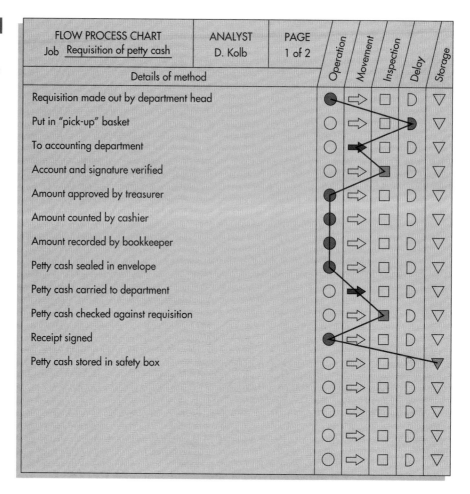

There are a number of different techniques that motion study analysts can use to develop efficient procedures. The most-used techniques are:

1. Motion study principles
2. Analysis of therbligs
3. Micromotion study
4. Charts

motion study principles
Guidelines for designing motion-efficient work procedures

Gilbreth's work laid the foundation for the development of **motion study principles,** which are guidelines for designing motion-efficient work procedures. The guidelines are divided into three categories: principles for use of the body, principles for arrangement of the workplace, and principles for the design of tools and equipment. Table 7–2 lists some examples of the principles.

In developing work methods that are motion efficient, the analyst tries to:

1. Eliminate unnecessary motions.
2. Combine activities.
3. Reduce fatigue.
4. Improve the arrangement of the workplace.
5. Improve the design of tools and equipment.

therbligs Basic elemental motions which make up a job.

Therbligs are basic elemental motions. The term *therblig* is Gilbreth spelled backwards (except for the *th*). The idea behind the development of therbligs is to break jobs

FIGURE 7-3

Worker-machine chart

Product: Bulk Food		Operator: L.W.	
Process: Weigh/price		Charted by: R.G.	

Step	Employee	Time (seconds)	Machine
1	Accepts plastic bag from customer and places on scale	0	
		1	
2	Enters price/lb	2	
3		3	Calculates and displays total price. Dispenses price sticker.
4	Obtains price sticker and removes bag	4	
		5	
5	Places price sticker on bag	6	
		7	
6	Hands bag to customer	8	

Summary

	Employee Time (seconds)	%	Machine Time (seconds)	%
Work	7	87.5	1	12.5
Idle	1	12.5	7	87.5

TABLE 7-2

Motion study principles

A. The use of the human body. Examples:
  1. Both hands should begin and end their basic divisions of accomplishment simultaneously and should not be idle at the same instant, except during rest periods.
  2. The motions made by the hands should be made symmetrically.
  3. Momentum should assist workers wherever possible and should be minimized if it must be overcome by muscular effort.
  4. Continuous curved motions are preferable to straight-line motions involving sudden and sharp changes in direction.
B. The arrangement and conditions of the workplace. Examples:
  1. Fixed locations for all tools and material should be provided to permit the best sequence and to eliminate or reduce the therbligs' search and select.
  2. Gravity bins and drop delivery should reduce reach and move times; wherever possible, ejectors should remove finished parts automatically.
  3. All materials and tools should be located within the normal working area.
C. The design of tools and equipment. Examples:
  1. Multiple cuts should be taken whenever possible by combining two or more tools in one.
  2. All levers, handles, wheels, and other control devices should be readily accessible to the operator and designed to give the best possible mechanical advantage and to utilize the strongest available muscle group.
  3. Parts should be held in position by fixtures.

Source: Adapted from Benjamin W. Niebel, *Motion and Time Study* (Burr Ridge, IL: Richard D. Irwin, Inc., 1993), pp. 206–207.

down into minute elements and base improvements on an analysis of these basic elements by eliminating, combining, or rearranging them.

Although a complete description of therbligs is outside the scope of this text, a list of some common ones will illustrate the nature of these basic elemental motions:

Mitsubishi Proton manufacturing plant in Malaysia. For interior welding, engineers and management must consider worker safety, ergonomics, time factors, and the use of technology.

www.mitsucars.com

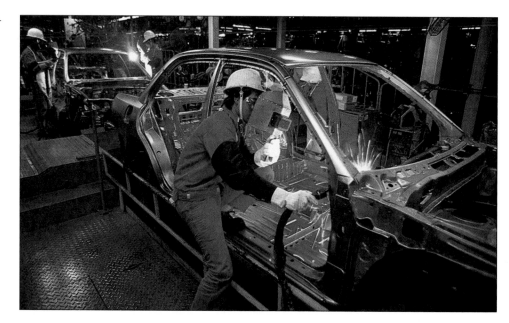

Search implies hunting for an item with the hands and/or the eyes.

Select means to choose from a group of objects.

Grasp means to take hold of an object.

Hold refers to retention of an object after it has been grasped.

Transport load means movement of an object after hold.

Release load means to deposit the object.

Some other therbligs are *inspect, position, plan, rest,* and *delay.*

Describing a job using therbligs often takes a substantial amount of work. However, for short, repetitive jobs, therbligs analysis may be justified.

Frank Gilbreth and his wife, Lillian, an industrial psychologist, were also responsible for introducing motion pictures for studying motions, called **micromotion study.** This approach is applied not only in industry but in many other areas of human endeavor, such as sports and health care. Use of the camera and slow-motion replay enables analysts to study motions that would otherwise be too rapid to see. In addition, the resulting films provide a permanent record that can be referred to, not only for training workers and analysts but also for settling job disputes involving work methods.

micromotion study Use of motion pictures and slow motion to study motions that otherwise would be too rapid to analyze.

The cost of micromotion study limits its use to repetitive activities, where even minor improvements can yield substantial savings owing to the number of times an operation is repeated, or where other considerations justify its use (e.g., surgical procedures).

Motion study analysts often use charts as tools for analyzing and recording motion studies. Activity charts and process charts such as those described earlier can be quite helpful. In addition, analysts may use a *simo chart* (see Figure 7–4) to study simultaneous motions of the hands. These charts are invaluable in studying operations such as data entry, sewing, surgical and dental procedures, and certain assembly operations.

WORKING CONDITIONS

Working conditions are an important aspect of job design. Physical factors such as temperature, humidity, ventilation, illumination, and noise can have a significant impact on worker performance in terms of productivity, quality of output, and accidents. In many instances, government regulations apply.

SIMO CHART

OPERATOR: Ken Reisch
DATE: May 21,
OPERATION: Assembly
PART: Lace Finger
METHOD: Proposed
CHART BY: Joseph Riley

FIGURE 7-4

A simultaneous motion chart
Source: Benjamin W. Niebel, *Motion and Time Study*, 8th ed. (Burr Ridge, IL: Richard D. Irwin, 1988), p. 229. © 1988 by Richard D. Irwin, Inc. Reprinted by permission.

TIME SCALE (winks)	ELEMENT TIME	LEFT-HAND DESCRIPTION	SYMBOL	MOTION CLASS	SYMBOL	RIGHT-HAND DESCRIPTION	ELEMENT TIME	TIME SCALE (winks)
4548	12	Reach for finger	RE		RE	Reach for finger	12	4548
4560	19	Grasp finger	G		G	Grasp finger	19	4560
4579	31	Move finger	M		M	Move finger	31	4579
4610	75	Position and release finger	P RL		P RL	Position and release finger	75	4610
4685	15	Reach for clamp	RE		RE	Reach for clamp	15	4685
4700	15	Grasp clamp	G		G	Grasp clamp	15	4700
4715								4715
7541	12	Grasp assembly	G		G	Grasp assembly	12	7541
	18	Move and release assembly	M RL		M RL	Move and release assembly	18	
7559								7559

SUMMARY

%	TIME	LEFT-HAND SUMMARY	SYM.	RIGHT-HAND SUMMARY	TIME	%
8.56	249	Reach	RE	Reach	245	8.4
7.49	218	Grasp	G	Grasp	221	7.6
12.16	354	Move	M	Move	413	14.2
30.47	887	Position	P	Position	1124	38.6
39.33	1145	Use	U	Use	876	30.1
1.03	30	Idle	I	Idle	0	0.0
.96	28	Release	RL	Release	32	1.1
100.0	2911	TOTALS			2911	100.0

Temperature and Humidity. Although human beings can function under a fairly wide range of temperatures, work performance tends to be adversely affected if temperatures are outside a very narrow *comfort band.* That comfort band depends on how strenuous the work is; the more strenuous the work, the lower the comfort range.

Heating and cooling are less of a problem in offices than in factories and other work environments where high ceilings allow heat to rise and where there is often a constant flow of trucks and other moving and handling equipment through large doors. These conditions make it difficult to maintain a constant temperature. Solutions range from selection of suitable clothing to space heating or cooling devices.

FIGURE 7–5

Decibel values of typical sounds (db)
Source: Benjamin W. Niebel, *Motion and Time Study,* 8th ed. (Burr Ridge, IL: Richard D. Irwin, 1988), p. 248. © 1988 by Richard D. Irwin, Inc. Reprinted by permission.

Humidity is also an important variable in maintaining a comfortable working environment.

Ventilation. Unpleasant and noxious odors can be distracting and dangerous to workers. Moreover, unless smoke and dust are periodically removed, the air can quickly become stale and unpleasant. Large fans and air-conditioning equipment are commonly used to exchange and recondition the air.

Illumination. The amount of illumination required depends largely on the type of work being performed; the more detailed the work, the higher the level of illumination needed for adequate performance. Other important considerations are the amount of glare and contrast. From a safety standpoint, good lighting in halls, stairways, and other dangerous points is important. However, because illumination is expensive, high illumination in all areas is not generally desirable.

Sometimes natural daylight can be used as a source of illumination. Not only is it free; it also provides some psychological benefits. Workers in windowless rooms may feel cut off from the outside world and experience various psychological problems. On the down side, the inability to control natural light (e.g., cloudy days) can result in dramatic changes in light intensity.

Noise and Vibrations. Noise is unwanted sound. It is caused by the vibrations of machines or equipment and by humans. Noise can be annoying or distracting, leading to errors and accidents. It can also damage or impair hearing if it is loud enough. Figure 7–5 illustrates loudness levels of some typical sounds.

Successful sound control begins with measurement of the offending sounds. In a new operation, selection and placement of equipment can eliminate or reduce many potential problems. In the case of existing equipment, it may be possible to redesign or substitute equipment. In some instances, the source of noise can be isolated from other work areas. If that isn't feasible, acoustical walls and ceilings or baffles that deflect sound waves may prove useful. Sometimes the only solution is to provide protective devices for those in the immediate vicinity (e.g., personnel who guide jet aircraft into landing gates wear protective devices over their ears).

Vibrations can be a factor in job design even without a noise component, so merely eliminating sound may not be sufficient in every case. Vibrations can come from tools, machines, vehicles, human activity, air-conditioning systems, pumps, and other sources. Corrective measures include padding, stabilizers, shock absorbers, cushioning, and rubber mountings.

Work Breaks. The frequency, length, and timing of work breaks can have a significant impact on both productivity and quality of output. One indication of the relationship between worker efficiency and work breaks is illustrated in Figure 7–6. It reveals that efficiency generally declines as the day wears on, but it also shows how breaks for lunch and rest can cause an upward shift in efficiency.

FIGURE 7-6

A typical relationship between worker efficiency and time of day
Source: Benjamin W. Niebel, *Motion and Time Study*, 8th ed. (Burr Ridge, IL: Richard D. Irwin, 1988), p. 270. © 1988 by Richard D. Irwin, Inc. Reprinted by permission.

An important variable in the rate of decline of efficiency and potential effects of work breaks is the amount of physical and/or mental requirements of the job. Steelworkers, for instance, may need rest breaks of 15 minutes per hour due to the strenuous nature of their jobs. Physical effort is not the only condition that indicates the need for work breaks. People working at CRTs also need periodic breaks; and students need study breaks.

Safety. Worker safety is one of the most basic issues in job design. This area needs constant attention from management, employees, and designers. Workers cannot be effectively motivated if they feel they are in physical danger.

From an employer standpoint, accidents are undesirable because they are expensive (insurance and compensation); they usually involve damage to equipment and/or products; they require hiring, training, and makeup work; and they generally interrupt work. From a worker standpoint, accidents mean physical suffering, mental anguish, potential loss of earnings, and disruption of the work routine.

Causes of Accidents. The two basic causes of accidents are worker *carelessness* and accident *hazards*. Under the heading of carelessness come unsafe acts. Examples include driving at high speeds, drinking and driving, failure to use protective equipment, overriding safety controls (e.g., taping control buttons down), disregarding safety procedures (e.g., running, throwing objects, cutting through, failing to observe one-way signs), improper use of tools and equipment, and failure to use reasonable caution in danger zones. Unsafe conditions include unprotected pulleys, chains, material-handling equipment, machinery, and so on. Also, poorly lit walkways, stairs, and loading docks constitute hazards. Toxic wastes, gases and vapors, and radiation hazards must be contained. In many instances, these cannot be detected without special equipment, so they would not be obvious to workers or emergency personnel. Protection against hazards involves use of proper lighting, clearly marked danger zones, use of protective equipment (hardhats, goggles, earmuffs, gloves, heavy shoes and clothing), safety devices (machine guards, dual control switches that require an operator to use both hands), emergency equipment (emergency showers, fire extinguishers, fire escapes), and thorough instruction in safety procedures and use of regular and emergency equipment. Housekeeping (clean floors, open aisles, waste removal) is another important safety factor.

An effective program of safety and accident control requires the cooperation of both workers and management. Workers must be trained in proper procedures and attitudes, and they can contribute to a reduction in hazards by pointing out hazards to management. Management must enforce safety procedures and use of safety equipment. If supervisors allow workers to ignore safety procedures or look the other way when they see violations,

Protection against hazards is necessary in operations where material or equipment may pose a danger. At Crucible Steel in Syracuse, NY, an employee wears a helmet with air mask and protective gloves as she operates a bar grinder.

workers will be less likely to take proper precautions. Some firms use contests that compare departmental safety records. However, accidents cannot be completely eliminated, and a freak accident may seriously affect worker morale and might even contribute to additional accidents. Posters can be effective, particularly if they communicate in specific terms how to avoid accidents. For example, the admonition to "be careful" is not nearly as effective as "wear hardhats," "walk, don't run," or "hold on to rail."

OSHA Occupational Safety and Health Act of 1970; Occupational Safety and Health Administration.

The enactment of the Occupational Safety and Health Act (**OSHA**) in 1970, and the creation of the Occupational Safety and Health Administration, emphasized the importance of safety considerations in systems design. The law was intended to ensure that workers in all organizations have healthy and safe working conditions. It provides specific safety regulations with inspectors to see that they are adhered to. Inspections are carried out both at random and to investigate complaints of unsafe conditions. OSHA officials are empowered to issue warnings, to impose fines, and even to invoke court-ordered shutdowns for unsafe conditions.

OSHA must be regarded as a major influence on operations management decisions in all areas relating to worker safety. OSHA has promoted the welfare and safety of workers in its role as a catalyst, spurring companies to make changes that they knew were needed but "hadn't gotten around to making."

READING

What Works to Cut CTD Risk, Improve Job Productivity?

A panel of America's leading ergonomists offers case studies that show how workplace changes can cut CTDs [cumulative trauma disorders] and boost productivity. The ideas aren't complex or expensive, and are usually developed first by plant personnel.

The new focus on "empowerment" of individual workers in America's corporations has produced some impressive results in the field of workplace ergonomics. Employees, supervisors and other in-house staff can be taught to analyze jobs and develop ideas for improvement. These individuals can be provided with training and armed with worksheets and problem-solving tools to improve their work areas. The solutions they come up with are often inexpensive or cost nothing at all.

To be sure, an ergonomist usually needs to be involved in the process: as the trainer, as a reference to help insure that the ideas are going in the right direction, to provide experience and the perspective of a trained professional and to address subtle issues or measurements which require special expertise. The effort, however, should center on the team in the workplace.

As in-house personnel become more familiar with the ergonomics process, ideas typically begin to emerge naturally without using a formal procedure. However, for the hard-to-fix problems, going through the formal process of filling out a worksheet, videotaping the job and brainstorming ideas is almost always beneficial. How effective is this team approach?

What follows are four case studies of how such groups made substantial improvements in their company's work sites:

Case Study 1: Improving the Tilt

The job: In this instance, the team focused on the operator of a bench-mounted machine. The hazards: The ergonomic problems included the operator working with a bent neck and bent wrists, in large part due to having to [compensate for] a flat work surface. The improvements: The back legs of the machine were mounted on a small block of wood, thus tilting the machine forward. Both the wrist and neck postures were simultaneously placed in an improved posture, lowering the risk of CTDs.

Cost of the improvements: None.

Case Study 2: Meat Cutting

The job: A butcher using a knife to cut meat. The hazards: The worker used highly forceful arm motions with outstretched arms and wrists bent. The improvements: For certain cuts, the front of the board was mounted on removable stops, to permit the board to be tilted at a 45-degree angle downward and away

from the butcher. Thus, the butcher could press down, rather than forward, taking advantage of gravity and larger muscle groups. The arm and wrist were also placed in a better posture.

Cost of the improvements: Less than $100.

Case Study 3: Meat Packing

The job: Removing organs with a knife. The hazards: The worker was using constant, static grasping force to hold the knife, as well as repetitive hand motions to both cut and hold the meat. The improvements: A fixture was built and mounted to the work surface to hold the knife. This appliance was innovatively designed for quick exchange of dull knives for sharpened ones, which took place five to six times a shift. (The fixture also had appropriate safety guarding.) With this knife in place, the meat could then be grasped with both hands and easily pulled through the cutting tool.

Cost of the improvements: Less than $50.

Case Study 4: Manufacturing

The job: Assembling of the final product. The hazards: The job involved repetitive lifting of the product from the main conveyor line to the workstation, then back to the conveyor. The improvements: A six-inch length of roller conveyor was added between the workstation and the main conveyor, allowing the product to be slid rather than lifted.

Cost of the improvement: Less than $50.

Source: *CTDNEWS Online* (www.ctdnews.com, n.d.).

Work Measurement

Job design determines the *content* of a job, and methods analysis determines *how* a job is to be performed. **Work measurement** is concerned with determining the *length of time* it should take to complete the job. Job times are vital inputs for manpower planning, estimating labor costs, scheduling, budgeting, and designing incentive systems. Moreover, from the workers' standpoint, time standards provide an indication of expected output. Time standards reflect the amount of time it should take an average worker to do a given job working under typical conditions. The standards include expected activity time plus allowances for probable delays.

A **standard time** is the amount of time it should take a qualified worker to complete a specified task, working at a sustainable rate, using given methods, tools and equipment, raw material inputs, and workplace arrangement. Whenever a time standard is developed for a job, it is essential to provide a complete description of the parameters of the job because the actual time to do the job is sensitive to all of these factors; changes in any one of the factors can materially affect time requirements. For instance, changes in product design or changes in job performance brought about by a methods study should trigger a new time study to update the standard time. As a practical matter, though, minor changes are occasionally made that do not justify the expense of restudying the job. Consequently, the standards for many jobs may be slightly inaccurate. Periodic time studies may be used to update the standards.

Organizations develop time standards in a number of different ways. Although some small manufacturers and service organizations rely on subjective estimates of job times, the most commonly used methods of work measurement are:

work measurement Determining how long it should take to do a job.

standard time The amount of time it should take a qualified worker to complete a specified task, working at a sustainable rate, using given methods, tools and equipment, raw materials, and workplace arrangements.

1. Stopwatch time study
2. Historical times
3. Predetermined data
4. Work sampling

The following pages describe each of these techniques in some detail.

STOPWATCH TIME STUDY

Stopwatch time study was formally introduced by Frederick Winslow Taylor in the late nineteenth century. Today it is the most widely used method of work measurement. It is especially appropriate for short, repetitive tasks.

stopwatch time study Development of a time standard based on observations of one worker taken over a number of cycles.

Stopwatch time study is used to develop a time standard based on observations of one worker taken over a number of cycles. That is then applied to the work of all others in the organization who perform the same task. The basic steps in a time study are:

1. Define the task to be studied, and inform the worker who will be studied.
2. Determine the number of cycles to observe.
3. Time the job, and rate the worker's performance.
4. Compute the standard time.

The analyst who studies the job should be thoroughly familiar with it since it is not unusual for workers to attempt to include extra motions during the study in hope of gaining a standard that allows more time per piece (i.e., the worker will be able to work at a slower pace and still meet the standard). Furthermore, the analyst will need to check that the job is being performed efficiently before setting the time standard.

In most instances, an analyst will break all but very short jobs down into basic elemental motions (e.g., reach, grasp) and obtain times for each element. There are several reasons for this: One is that some elements are not performed in every cycle, and the breakdown enables the analyst to get a better perspective on them. Another is that the worker's proficiency may not be the same for all elements of the job. A third reason is to build a file of elemental times that can be used to set times for other jobs. This use will be described later.

Workers sometimes feel uneasy about being studied and fear changes that might result. The analyst should make an attempt to discuss these things with the worker prior to studying an operation to allay such fears and to enlist the cooperation of the worker.

The number of cycles that must be timed is a function of three things: (1) the variability of observed times, (2) the desired accuracy, and (3) the desired level of confidence for the estimated job time. Very often the desired accuracy is expressed as a percentage of the mean of the observed times. For example, the goal of a time study may be to achieve an estimate that is within 10 percent of the actual mean. The sample size needed to achieve that goal can be determined using this formula:

$$n = \left(\frac{zs}{a\bar{x}}\right)^2 \tag{7–1}$$

where

     z = Number of normal standard deviations needed for desired confidence

     s = Sample standard deviation

     a = Desired accuracy percentage

     $\bar{x}$ = Sample mean

Typical values of z used in this computation are:[1]

---

[1]Theoretically, a t rather than a z value should be used because the population standard deviation is unknown. However, the use of z is simpler and provides reasonable results when the number of observations is 30 or more, as it generally is. In practice, z is used almost exclusively.

Desired Confidence (%)	z Value
90	1.65
95	1.96
95.5	2.00
98	2.33
99	2.58

Of course, the value of z for any desired confidence can be obtained from the normal table in Appendix B, Table A.

An alternate formula used when the desired accuracy is stated as an *amount* (e.g., within one minute of the true mean) instead of a percentage is:

$$n = \left(\frac{zs}{e}\right)^2 \qquad\qquad (7\text{--}2)$$

where

e = Accuracy or maximum acceptable error

To make a preliminary estimate of sample size, it is typical to take a small number of observations (i.e., 10 to 20) and compute values of $\bar{x}$ and s to use in the formula for n. Toward the end of the study, the analyst may want to recompute n using revised estimates of $\bar{x}$ and s based on the increased data available.

Note: These formulas may or may not be used in practice, depending on the person doing the time study. Often, an experienced analyst will rely on his or her judgment in deciding on the number of cycles to time.

Example 1

A time study analyst wants to estimate the time required to perform a certain job. A preliminary study yielded a mean of 6.4 minutes and a standard deviation of 2.1 minutes. The desired confidence is 95 percent. How many observations will he need (including those already taken) if the desired maximum error is:

a. ± 10 percent of the sample mean?

b. One-half minute?

Solution

a. $s = 2.1$ minutes $\qquad z = 1.96$
   $\bar{x} = 6.4$ minutes $\qquad a = 10\%$

$$n = \left(\frac{zs}{a\bar{x}}\right)^2 = \left(\frac{1.96(2.1)}{.10(6.4)}\right)^2 = 41.36 \text{ (round up to 42)}$$

b. $e = .5 \qquad n = \left(\frac{zs}{e}\right)^2 = \left(\frac{1.96(2.1)}{.5}\right)^2 = 67.77 \text{ (round up to 68)}$

Development of a time standard involves computation of three times: the *observed time* (OT), the *normal time* (NT), and the *standard time* (ST).

Observed Time. The observed time is simply the average of the recorded times. Thus,

$$OT = \frac{\sum x_i}{n} \qquad\qquad (7\text{--}3)$$

where

OT = Observed time

$\sum x_i$ = Sum of recorded times

n = Number of observations

Note: If a job element does not occur each cycle, its average time should be determined separately and that amount should be included in the observed time, OT.

Normal Time. The normal time is the observed time adjusted for worker performance. It is computed by multiplying the observed time by a *performance rating*. That is,

$$NT = OT \times PR \tag{7-4}$$

where

NT = Normal time

PR = Performance rating

This assumes that a single performance rating has been made for the entire job. If ratings are made on an element-by-element basis, the normal time is obtained by multiplying each element's average time by its performance rating and summing those values:

$$NT = \sum(\bar{x}_j \times PR_j) \tag{7-5}$$

where

$\bar{x}_j$ = Average time for element j

PR_j = Performance rating for element j

The reason for including this adjustment factor is that the worker being observed may be working at a rate different from a "normal" rate, either to deliberately slow the pace or because his or her natural abilities differ from the norm. For this reason, the observer assigns a performance rating, to adjust the observed times to an "average" pace. A normal rating is 1.00. A performance rating of .9 indicates a pace that is 90 percent of normal, whereas a rating of 1.05 indicates a pace that is slightly faster than normal. For long jobs, each element may be rated; for short jobs, a single rating may be made for an entire cycle.

When assessing performance, the analyst must compare the observed performance to his or her concept of normal. Obviously, there is room for debate about what constitutes normal performance, and performance ratings are sometimes the source of considerable conflict between labor and management. Although no one has been able to suggest a way around these subjective evaluations, sufficient training and periodic *recalibration* by analysts using training films can provide a high degree of consistency in the ratings of different analysts.

Standard Time. Normal time is the length of time a worker should take to perform a job if there are no delays or interruptions. It does not take into account such factors as personal delays (getting a drink of water or going to the restroom), unavoidable delays (machine adjustments and repairs, talking to a supervisor, waiting for materials), or rest breaks. The standard time for a job is the normal time plus an *allowance* for these delays.

The standard time is

$$ST = NT \times AF \tag{7-6}$$

where

ST = Standard time

AF = Allowance factor

Allowances can be based on either job time or time worked (e.g., a workday). If allowances are based on the *job time,* the allowance factor must be computed using the formula

$$AF_{job} = 1 + A; \qquad A = \text{Allowance percentage based on job time} \qquad (7\text{--}7)$$

This is used when different jobs have different allowances. If allowances are based on a percentage of the time worked (i.e., the *workday*), the appropriate formula is

$$AF_{day} = \frac{1}{1 - A}; \qquad A = \text{Allowance percentage based on workday} \qquad (7\text{--}8)$$

This is used when jobs are the same or similar and have the same allowance factors.

Compute the allowance factor for these two cases:

a. The allowance is 20 percent of *job* time.

b. The allowance is 20 percent of *work* time.

Example 2

$$A = .20$$

Solution

a. $AF = 1 + A = 1.20$, or 120%

b. $AF = \dfrac{1}{1 - A} = \dfrac{1}{1 - .20} = 1.25$, or 125%

Table 7–3 (on the next page) illustrates some typical allowances. In practice, allowances may be based on the judgment of the time study analyst, work sampling (described later in the chapter), or negotiations between labor and management.

Example 3 illustrates the time study process from observed times to the standard time.

A time study of an assembly operation yielded the following observed times for one element of the job, for which the analyst gave a performance rating of 1.13 Using an allowance of 20 percent of *job* time, determine the appropriate standard time for this operation.

Example 3

i Observation	Time, x (minutes)	Observation	Time (minutes)
1	1.12	6	1.18
2	1.15	7	1.14
3	1.16	8	1.14
4	1.12	9	1.19
5	1.15	Total	10.35

$$n = 9 \qquad PR = 1.13 \qquad A = .20$$

Solution

a. $OT = \dfrac{\sum x_i}{n} = \dfrac{10.35}{9} = 1.15$ minutes.

b. $NT = OT \times PR = 1.15(1.13) = 1.30$ minutes.

c. $ST = NT \times (1 + A)\ 1.30(1.20) = 1.56$ minutes.

Note: If an abnormally short time has been recorded, it typically would be assumed to be the result of observational error and thus discarded. If one of the observations in Example 3 had been .10, it would have been discarded. However, if an abnormally *long* time has been recorded, the analyst would want to investigate that observation to determine whether some irregularly occurring aspect of the task (e.g., retrieving a dropped tool or part) exists, which should legitimately be factored into the job time.

TABLE 7–3

Typical allowance percentages for working conditions

	Percent
A. Constant allowances:	
1. Personal allowance	5
2. Basic fatigue allowances	4
B. Variable allowances:	
1. Standing allowance	2
2. Abnormal position allowance:	
a. Slightly awkward	0
b. Awkward (bending)	2
c. Very awkward (lying, stretching)	7
3. Use of force or muscular energy (lifting, pulling, or pushing):	
Weight lifted (in pounds):	
5	0
10	1
15	2
20	3
25	4
30	5
35	7
40	9
45	11
50	13
60	17
70	22
4. Bad light:	
a. Slightly below recommended	0
b. Well below	2
c. Very inadequate	5
5. Atmospheric conditions (heat and humidity)—variable	0–10
6. Close attention:	
a. Fairly fine work	0
b. Fine or exacting	2
c. Very fine or very exacting	5
7. Noise level:	
a. Continuous	0
b. Intermittent—loud	2
c. Intermittent—very loud	5
d High-pitched—loud	5
8. Mental strain:	
a. Fairly complex process	1
b. Complex or wide span of attention	4
c. Very complex	8
9. Monotony:	
a. Low	0
b. Medium	1
c. High	4
10. Tediousness:	
a. Rather tedious	0
b. Tedious	2
c. Very tedious	5

Source: Benjamin W. Niebel, *Motion and Time Study,* 8th ed. (Burr Ridge, IL: Richard D. Irwin, 1988), p. 416. © 1988 by Richard D. Irwin, Inc. Reprinted by permission.

Despite the obvious benefits that can be derived from work measurement using time study, some limitations also must be mentioned. One limitation is the fact that only those jobs that can be observed can be studied. This eliminates most managerial and creative jobs, because these involve mental as well as physical aspects. Also, the cost of the study rules out its use for irregular operations and infrequently occurring jobs. Finally, it disrupts the normal work routine, and workers resent it in many cases.

STANDARD ELEMENTAL TIMES

Standard elemental times are derived from a firm's own historical time study data. Over the years, a time study department can accumulate a file of elemental times that are common to many jobs. After a certain point, many elemental times can be simply retrieved from the file, eliminating the need for analysts to go through a complete time study to obtain them.

standard elemental times
Time standards derived from a firm's historical time data.

The procedure for using standard elemental times consists of the following steps:

1. Analyze the job to identify the standard elements.
2. Check the file for elements that have historical times, and record them. Use time study to obtain others, if necessary.
3. Modify the file times if necessary (explained below).
4. Sum the elemental times to obtain the normal time, and factor in allowances to obtain the standard time.

In some cases, the file times may not pertain exactly to a specific task. For instance, standard elemental times might be on file for "move the tool 3 centimeters" and "move the tool 9 centimeters," when the task in question involves a move of 6 centimeters. However, it is often possible to interpolate between values on file to obtain the desired time estimate.

One obvious advantage of this approach is the potential savings in cost and effort created by not having to conduct a complete time study for each job. A second advantage is that there is less disruption of work, again because the analyst does not have to time the worker. A third advantage is that performance ratings do not have to be done; they are generally *averaged* in the file times. The main disadvantage of this approach is that times may not exist for enough standard elements to make it worthwhile, and the file times may be biased or inaccurate.

The method described in the following section is a variation of this approach, which helps avoid some of these problems.

PREDETERMINED TIME STANDARDS

Predetermined time standards involve the use of published data on standard elemental times. A commonly used system is *methods-time measurement* (MTM), which was developed in the late 1940s by the Methods Engineering Council. The MTM tables are based on extensive research of basic elemental motions and times. To use this approach, the analyst must divide the job into its basic elements (reach, move, turn, disengage), measure the distances involved (if applicable), rate the difficulty of the element, and then refer to the appropriate table of data to obtain the time for that element. The standard time for the job is obtained by adding the times for all of the basic elements. Times of the basic elements are measured in time measurement units (TMUs); one TMU equals .0006 minute. One minute of work may cover quite a few basic elements; a typical job may involve several hundred or more of these basic elements. The analyst needs a considerable amount of skill to adequately describe the operation and develop realistic time estimates. Table 7–4 presents a portion of the MTM tables, to give you an idea of the kind of information they provide.

predetermined time standards Published data based on extensive research to determine standard elemental times.

A high level of skill is required to generate a predetermined time standard. Analysts generally take training or certification courses to develop the necessary skills to do this kind of work.

TABLE 7-4

A portion of the MTM tables

Distance Moved (inches)	TIME (TMU)				WEIGHT ALLOWANCE			Case and Description
	A	B	C	Hand in Motion B	Weight (pounds) up to:	Dynamic Factor	Static Constant TMU	
¾ or less	2.0	2.0	2.0	1.7				
1	2.5	2.9	3.4	2.3	2.5	1.00	0	A. Move object to other hand or against stop.
2	3.6	4.6	5.2	2.9				
3	4.9	5.7	6.7	3.6	7.5	1.06	2.2	
4	6.1	6.9	8.0	4.3				
5	7.3	8.0	9.2	5.0	12.5	1.11	3.9	
6	8.1	8.9	10.3	5.7				
7	8.9	9.7	11.1	6.5	17.5	1.17	5.6	B. Move object to approximate or indefinite location.
8	9.7	10.6	11.8	7.2				
9	10.5	11.5	12.7	7.9	22.5	1.22	7.4	
10	11.3	12.2	13.5	8.6				
12	12.9	13.4	15.2	10.0	27.5	1.28	9.1	
14	14.4	14.6	16.9	11.4				
16	16.0	15.8	18.7	12.8	32.5	1.33	10.8	
18	17.6	17.0	20.4	14.2				
20	19.2	18.2	22.1	15.6	37.5	1.39	12.5	C. Move object to exact location.
22	20.8	19.4	23.8	17.0				
24	22.4	20.6	25.5	18.4	42.5	1.44	14.3	
26	24.0	21.8	27.3	19.8				
28	25.5	23.1	29.0	21.2	47.5	1.50	16.0	
30	27.1	24.3	30.7	22.7				
Additional	0.8	0.6	0.85	TMU per inch over 30 inches				

Source: MTM Association for Standards and Research. Copyrighted by the MTM Association for Standards and Research. No reprint permission without written consent from MTM Association, 16–01 Broadway, Fair Lawn, New Jersey 07410.

Among the advantages of predetermined time standards are the following:

1. They are based on large numbers of workers under controlled conditions.
2. The analyst is not required to rate performance in developing the standard.
3. There is no disruption of the operation.
4. Standards can be established even before a job is done.

Although proponents of predetermined standards claim that the approach provides much better accuracy than stopwatch studies, not everyone agrees with that claim. Some argue that many activity times are too specific to a given operation to be generalized from published data. Others argue that different analysts perceive elemental activity breakdowns in different ways, and that this adversely affects the development of times and produces varying time estimates among analysts. Still others claim that analysts differ on the degree of difficulty they assign a given task and thereby obtain different time standards.

WORK SAMPLING

Work sampling is a technique for estimating the proportion of time that a worker or machine spends on various activities and the idle time.

Unlike time study, work sampling does not require timing an activity, nor does it even involve continuous observation of the activity. Instead, an observer makes brief observations of a worker or machine at random intervals and simply notes the nature of the activity. For example, a machine may be busy or idle; a secretary may be typing, filing, talking on the telephone, and so on; and a carpenter may be carrying supplies, taking measurements, cutting wood, and so on. The resulting data are *counts* of the number of times each category of activity or nonactivity was observed.

Although work sampling is occasionally used to set time standards, its two primary uses are in (1) ratio-delay studies, which concern the percentage of a worker's time that involves unavoidable delays or the proportion of time a machine is idle, and (2) analysis of nonrepetitive jobs. In a ratio-delay study, a hospital administrator, for example, might want to estimate the percentage of time that a certain piece of X-ray equipment is not in use. In a nonrepetitive job, such as secretarial work or maintenance, it can be important to establish the percentage of time an employee spends doing various tasks.

Nonrepetitive jobs typically involve a broader range of skills than repetitive jobs, and workers in these jobs are often paid on the basis of the highest skill involved. Therefore, it is important to determine the proportion of time spent on the high-skill level. For example, a secretary may take dictation, do word processing, file, answer the telephone, schedule appointments, and do other routine office work. If the secretary spends a high percentage of time filing instead of doing word processing or taking shorthand, the compensation will be lower than for a secretary who spends a high percentage of time doing word processing and taking shorthand. Work sampling can be used to verify those percentages and can therefore be an important tool in developing the job description. In addition, work sampling can be part of a program for validation of job content that is needed for "bona fide occupational qualifications"—that is, advertised jobs requiring the skills that are specified.

Work sampling estimates include some degree of error. Hence, it is important to treat work sampling estimates as *approximations* of the actual proportion of time devoted to a given activity. The goal of work sampling is to obtain an estimate that provides a specified confidence not differing from the true value by more than a specified error. For example, a hospital administrator might request an estimate of X-ray idle time that will provide a 95 percent confidence of being within 4 percent of the actual percentage. Hence, work sampling is designed to produce a value, $\hat{p}$, which estimates the true proportion, p, within some allowable error, e: $\hat{p} \pm e$. The variability associated with sample estimates of p tends to be approximately normal for large sample sizes. The amount of maximum probable error is a function of both the sample size and the desired level of confidence.

For large samples, the maximum error e can be computed using the formula

$$e = z\sqrt{\frac{\hat{p}(1 - \hat{p})}{n}} \qquad (7\text{--}9)$$

where

z = Number of standard deviations needed to achieve desired confidence

$\hat{p}$ = Sample proportion (the number of occurrences divided by the sample size)

n = Sample size

In most instances, management will specify the desired confidence level and amount of allowable error, and the analyst will be required to determine a sample size sufficient to obtain these results. The appropriate value for n can be determined by solving formula 7–9 for n, which yields

$$n = \left(\frac{z}{e}\right)^2 \hat{p}(1 - \hat{p}) \qquad (7\text{--}10)$$

work sampling Technique for estimating the proportion of time that a worker or machine spends on various activities and the idle time.

Example 4

The manager of a small supermarket chain wants to estimate the proportion of time stock clerks spend making price changes on previously marked merchandise. The manager wants a 98 percent confidence that the resulting estimate will be within 5 percent of the true value. What sample size should she use?

Solution

$e = .05$ $z = 2.33$ (see p. 324) $\hat{p}$ is unknown

When no sample estimate of p is available, a preliminary estimate of sample size can be obtained using $\hat{p} = .50$. After 20 or so observations, a new estimate of $\hat{p}$ can be obtained from those observations and a revised value of n computed using the new $\hat{p}$. It would be prudent to recompute the value of n at two or three points during the study to obtain a better indication of the necessary sample size. Thus, the initial estimate of n is

$$n = \left(\frac{2.33}{.05}\right)^2 .50(1 - .50) = 542.89, \text{ or } 543 \text{ observations}$$

Suppose that, in the first 20 observations, stock clerks were found to be changing prices twice, making $\hat{p} = 2/20 = .10$. The revised estimate of n at that point would be

$$n = \left(\frac{2.33}{.05}\right)^2 .10(1 - .10) = 195.44, \text{ or } 196$$

Suppose a second check is made after a total of 100 observations, and $\hat{p} = .11$ at this point (including the initial 20 observations). Recomputing n yields

$$n = \left(\frac{2.33}{.05}\right)^2 .11(.89) = 212.60, \text{ or } 213$$

Perhaps the manager might make one more check to settle on a final value for n. If the computed value of n is less than the number of observations already taken, sampling would be terminated at that point.

Note: If the resulting value of n is noninteger, round *up*.

Determining the sample size is only one part of work sampling. The overall procedure consists of the following steps:

1. Clearly identify the worker(s) or machine(s) to be studied.
2. Notify the workers and supervisors of the purpose of the study to avoid arousing suspicions.
3. Compute an initial estimate of sample size using a preliminary estimate of p, if available (e.g., from analyst experience or past data). Otherwise, use $\hat{p} = .50$.
4. Develop a random observation schedule.
5. Begin taking observations. Recompute the required sample size several times during the study.
6. Determine the estimated proportion of time spent on the specified activity.

Careful problem definition can prevent mistakes such as studying the wrong worker or wrong activity. Similarly, it is important to inform related parties of the purpose and scope of the study to reduce unnecessary fears that might be generated by unannounced data collection. It is also important to obtain random observations to achieve valid results.

Observations must be spread out over a period of time so that a true indication of variability is obtained. If observations are bunched too closely in time, the behaviors observed during that time may not genuinely reflect typical performance. The degree to which observations should be spread out will depend in part on the nature of the activity studied; a decision on this is usually best left to the analyst.

TABLE 7–5

Work sampling compared with stopwatch time study

Advantages

1. Observations are spread out over a period of time, making results less susceptible to short-term fluctuations.
2. There is little or no disruption of work.
3. Workers are less resentful.
4. Studies are less costly and less time-consuming, and the skill requirements of the analyst are much less.
5. Studies can be interrupted without affecting the results.
6. Many different studies can be conducted simultaneously.
7. No timing device is required.
8. It is well suited for nonrepetitive tasks.

Disadvantages

1. There is much less detail on the elements of a job.
2. Workers may alter their work patterns when they spot the observer, thereby invalidating the results.
3. In many cases, there is no record of the method used by the worker.
4. Observers may fail to adhere to a random schedule of observations.
5. It is not well suited for short, repetitive tasks.
6. Much time may be required to move from one workplace to another and back to satisfy the randomness requirement.

Table 7–5 presents a comparison of work sampling and time study. It suggests that a work sampling approach to determining job times is less formal and less detailed, and best suited to nonrepetitive jobs.

Compensation

Compensation is a significant issue for the design of work systems. It is important for organizations to develop suitable compensation plans for their employees. If wages are too low, organizations may find it difficult to attract and hold competent workers and managers. If wages are too high, the increased costs may result in lower profits, or may force the organization to increase its prices, which might adversely affect demand for the organization's products or services.

Organizations use two basic systems for compensating employees: *time-based systems* and *output-based systems*. **Time-based systems,** also known as *hourly* and *measured daywork* systems, compensate employees for the time the employee has worked during a pay period. Salaried workers also represent a form of time-based compensation. **Output-based (incentive) systems** compensate employees according to the amount of output they produce during a pay period, thereby tying pay directly to performance.

Time-based systems are more widely used than incentive systems, particularly for office, administrative, and managerial employees, but also for blue-collar workers. One reason for this is that computation of wages is straightforward and managers can readily estimate labor costs for a given employee level. Employees often prefer time-based systems because the pay is steady and they know how much compensation they will receive for each pay period. In addition, employees may resent the pressures of an output-based system.

Another reason for using time-based systems is that many jobs do not lend themselves to the use of incentives. In some cases, it may be difficult or impossible to measure output. For example, jobs that require creative or mental work cannot be easily measured on an output basis. Other jobs may include irregular activities or have so many different forms of output that measuring output and determining pay are fairly complex. In the case of assembly lines, the use of *individual* incentives could disrupt the even flow of work;

time-based system Compensation based on time an employee has worked during a pay period.

output-based (incentive) system Compensation based on amount of output an employee produced during a pay period.

TABLE 7-6

Comparison of time-based and output-based pay systems

	Management	Worker
TIME-BASED		
Advantages	1. Stable labor costs 2. Easy to administer 3. Simple to compute pay 4. Stable output	1. Stable pay 2. Less pressure to produce than under output system
Disadvantages	1. No incentive for workers to increase output	1. Extra efforts not rewarded
OUTPUT-BASED		
Advantages	1. Lower cost per unit 2. Greater output	1. Pay related to efforts 2. Opportunity to earn more
Disadvantages	1. Wage computation more difficult 2. Need to measure output 3. Quality may suffer 4. Difficult to incorporate wage increases 5. Increased problems with scheduling	1. Pay fluctuates 2. Workers may be penalized because of factors beyond their control (e.g., machine breakdown)

however, *group* incentives are sometimes used successfully in such cases. Finally, *quality* considerations may be as important as *quantity* considerations. In health care, for example, emphasis is generally placed on both the quality of patient care and the number of patients processed.

On the other hand, situations exist where incentives are desirable. Incentives reward workers for their output, presumably causing some workers to produce more than they might under a time-based system. The advantage is that certain (fixed) costs do not vary with increases in output, so the overall cost per unit decreases if output increases. Workers may prefer incentive systems because they see a relationship between their efforts and their pay: An incentive system presents an opportunity for them to earn more money.

On the negative side, incentive systems involve a considerable amount of paperwork, computation of wages is more difficult than under time-based systems, output has to be measured and standards set, cost-of-living increases are difficult to incorporate into incentive plans, and contingency arrangements for unavoidable delays have to be developed.

Table 7–6 lists the main advantages and disadvantages of time-based and output-based plans.

In order to obtain maximum benefit from an incentive plan, the plan should be:

1. Accurate

2. Easy to apply

3. Consistent

4. Easy to understand

5. Fair

In addition, there should be an obvious relationship between effort and reward, and no limit on earnings.

Incentive systems may focus on the output of each individual or on that of a group.

INDIVIDUAL INCENTIVE PLANS

Individual incentive plans take a variety of forms. The simplest plan is *straight piecework*. Under this plan, a worker's pay is a direct linear function of his or her output. In the past, piecework plans were fairly popular. Now minimum wage legislation makes them somewhat impractical. Even so, many of the plans currently in use represent variations of the straight piecework plan. They typically incorporate a base rate that serves as a floor: Workers are guaranteed that amount as a minimum, regardless of output. The base rate is tied to an output standard; a worker who produces less than the standard will be paid at the base rate. This protects workers from pay loss due to delays, breakdowns, and similar problems. In most cases, incentives are paid for output above standard, and the pay is referred to as a *bonus.*

GROUP INCENTIVE PLANS

A variety of group incentive plans, which stress sharing of productivity gains with employees, are in use. Some focus exclusively on output, while others reward employees for output and for reductions in material and other costs. The following four plans reflect the main features of most of the plans currently in operation.

Scanlon Plan. The main feature of the plan is to encourage reductions in labor costs by allowing workers to share in the gains from any reductions achieved. The plan includes formation of worker committees to actively seek out areas for improvement.

Kaiser Plan. Like the Scanlon plan, it uses committees to suggest ways of reducing costs, with savings shared by employees. However, in addition to reductions in labor costs, it also provides for workers to share in the gains from reductions in material and supply costs.

Lincoln Plan. The Lincoln Electric Company in Cleveland, Ohio, developed this plan. It includes profit sharing, job enlargement, and participative management. Like the other plans, it uses evaluation committees to generate suggestions. The three main components of the plan are a piecework system, an annual bonus, and a stock purchase provision.

Kodak Plan. This plan uses a combination of premium wage levels and an annual bonus related to company profits instead of more traditional incentives. Workers are encouraged to help set goals and to decide on reasonable performance levels. The idea is that their involvement will make workers more apt to produce at a premium rate.

One form of group incentive is the *team approach,* which many companies are now using for problem solving and continuous improvement. The emphasis is on *team,* not *individual,* performance.

KNOWLEDGE-BASED PAY SYSTEMS

As companies shift toward lean production, a number of changes have had a direct impact on the work environment. One is that many of the buffers that previously existed are gone. Another is that fewer managers are present. Still another is increased emphasis on quality, productivity, and flexibility. Consequently, workers who can perform a variety of tasks are particularly valuable. Organizations are increasingly recognizing this, and they are setting up pay systems to reward workers who undergo training that increases their skill levels. This is sometimes referred to as **knowledge-based pay.** It is a portion of a worker's pay that is based on the knowledge and skill that the worker possesses. Knowledge-based pay has three dimensions: *Horizontal skills* reflect the variety of tasks the worker is capable of performing; *vertical skills* reflect managerial tasks the worker is capable of; and *depth skills* reflect quality and productivity results.

knowledge-based pay A pay system used by organizations to reward workers who undergo training that increases their skills.

MANAGEMENT COMPENSATION

Many organizations that traditionally rewarded managers and senior executives on the basis of *output* are now seriously reconsidering that approach. With the new emphasis on customer service and quality, reward systems are being restructured to reflect new dimensions of performance. In addition, executive pay in many companies is being more closely tied to the success of the company or division that executive is responsible for. This is quite different than the 1980s policy of increasing the compensation of top executives even as workers were being laid off and the company was losing large amounts of money!

Summary

The design of work systems involves job design, work measurement, and compensation.

Job design is concerned with the content of jobs and work methods. In the past, job design tended to focus on efficiency, but now there seems to be an increasing awareness and consideration of the behavioral aspects of work and worker satisfaction. Current concern about productivity has thrust job design into the limelight. However, the jobs usually associated with high productivity are often the same jobs that are the greatest source of worker dissatisfaction, creating somewhat of a paradox for job designers.

Analysts often use methods analysis and motion study techniques to develop the "efficiency" aspects of jobs, but these do not directly address behavioral aspects. Nonetheless, they are an important part of job design. Working conditions are also a notable aspect of job design, not only because of the behavioral and efficiency factors but also because of concern for the health and safety of workers.

Work measurement is concerned with specifying the length of time needed to complete a job. Such information is vital for personnel planning, cost estimating, budgeting, scheduling, and worker compensation. Commonly used approaches include stopwatch time study and predetermined times. A related technique is work sampling, which can also be used to obtain data on activity times. More commonly, work sampling is used to estimate the proportion of time a worker spends on a certain aspect of the job. Table 7–7 provides a summary of the formulas used in time studies and work sampling.

Organizations can choose from a variety of compensation plans. It is important to do so carefully, for compensation is key to both the worker and the organization, and, once adopted, it is usually difficult to substantially change a compensation plan.

TABLE 7-7

Summary of formulas

Time Study		Work Sampling	
A. Sample size		A. Maximum error	
$n = \left(\dfrac{zs}{a\bar{x}}\right)^2$	(7–1)	$e = z\sqrt{\dfrac{\hat{p}(1-\hat{p})}{n}}$	(7–9)
$n = \left(\dfrac{zs}{e}\right)^2$	(7–2)	B. Sample size	
B. Observed time		$n = \left(\dfrac{z}{e}\right)^2 \hat{p}(1-\hat{p})$	(7–10)
$OT = \dfrac{\sum x_i}{n}$	(7–3)		
C. Normal time		**Symbols:**	
$NT = OT \times PR$	(7–4)	a = Allowable error as percentage of average time	
$NT = \sum(\bar{x}_i \times PR_i)$	(7–5)	A = Allowance percentage	
D. Standard time		e = Maximum acceptable error	
$ST = NT \times AF$	(7–6)	n = Number of observations needed	
E. Allowance factor		NT = Normal time	
$AF_{job} = 1 + A$	(7–7)	OT = Observed, or average, time	
$AF_{day} = \dfrac{1}{1-A}$	(7–8)	PR = Performance rating	
		s = Standard deviation of observed times	
		ST = Standard time	
		x_i = Time for ith observation (i = 1, 2, 3, . . . , n)	

ergonomics, 309
flow process chart, 314
job design, 308
job enlargement, 310
job enrichment, 310
job rotation, 310
knowledge-based pay, 335
methods analysis, 313
micromotion study, 318
motion study, 315
motion study principles, 316
OSHA, 322

output-based (incentive) system, 333
predetermined time standards, 329
self-directed teams, 312
specialization, 309
standard elemental times, 329
standard time, 323
stopwatch time study, 324
therbligs, 316
time-based system, 333
work measurement, 323
work sampling, 331
worker-machine chart, 314

Key Terms

Solved Problems

A time study analyst timed an assembly operation for 30 cycles, and then computed the average time per cycle, which was 18.75 minutes. The analyst assigned a performance rating of .96, and decided that an appropriate allowance was 15 percent. Assume the allowance factor is based on the *workday*. Determine the following: the observed time (OT), the normal time (NT), and the standard time (ST).

Problem 1

Solution

OT = Average time = 18.75 minutes
NT = OT × Performance rating = 18.75 minutes × .96 = 18 minutes
$$AF = \frac{1}{1-A} = \frac{1}{1-.15} = 1.176$$
ST = NT × AF = 18 × 1.176 = 21.17 minutes

A time study analyst wants to estimate the number of observations that will be needed to achieve a specified maximum error, with a confidence of 95.5 percent. A preliminary study yielded a mean of 5.2 minutes and a standard deviation of 1.1 minutes. Determine the total number of observations needed for these two cases:

Problem 2

a. A maximum error of ±6% of the sample mean.

b. A maximum error of .40 minute.

a. $x = 5.2$ minutes $z = 2.00$ for 95.5%
   $s = 1.1$ minutes $a = .06$

Solution

$$n = \left(\frac{zs}{ax}\right)^2 = \left(\frac{2.00(1.1)}{.06(5.2)}\right)^2 = 49.72 \text{ (round to 50 observations)}$$

b. $e = .40$

$$n = \left(\frac{zs}{e}\right)^2 = \left(\frac{2.00(1.1)}{.40}\right)^2 = 30.25 \text{ (round to 31 observations)}$$

Work sampling. An analyst has been asked to prepare an estimate of the proportion of time that a turret lathe operator spends adjusting the machine, with a 90 percent confidence level. Based on previous experience, the analyst believes the proportion will be approximately 30 percent.

Problem 3

a. If the analyst uses a sample size of 400 observations, what is the maximum possible error that will be associated with the estimate?

b. What sample size would the analyst need in order to have the maximum error be no more than ±5 percent?

$\hat{p} = .30$ $z = 1.65$ (for 90 percent confidence)

Solution

a. $e = z\sqrt{\dfrac{\hat{p}(1-\hat{p})}{n}} = 1.65 \sqrt{\dfrac{.3(.7)}{400}} = .038$

b. $n = \left(\dfrac{z}{e}\right)^2 \hat{p}(1-\hat{p}) = \left(\dfrac{1.65}{.05}\right)^2 (.3)(.7) = 228.69,$ or 229

1. What is job design, and why is it important?
2. What are some of the main advantages and disadvantages of specialization from a management perspective? From a worker's perspective?
3. Contrast the meanings of the terms *job enlargement* and *job enrichment.*
4. What is the purpose of approaches such as job enlargement and job enrichment?
5. Explain the term *knowledge-based pay system.*
6. What are self-directed work teams? What are some potential benefits of using these teams?
7. Some Japanese firms have a policy of rotating their managers among different managerial jobs. In contrast, American managers are more likely to specialize in a certain area (e.g., finance or operations). Discuss the advantages and disadvantages of each of these approaches. Which do you prefer? Why?
8. What are motion study principles? How are they classified?
9. Name some reasons why methods analyses are needed. How is methods analysis linked to productivity improvements?
10. How are devices such as flow process charts and worker-machine charts useful?
11. What is a time standard? What factors must be taken into account when developing standards?
12. What are the main uses of time study information?
13. Could performance rating be avoided by studying a group of workers and averaging their times? Explain briefly.
14. If an average worker could be identified, what advantage would there be in using that person for a time study? What are some reasons why an average worker might not be studied?
15. What are the main limitations of time study?
16. Comment on the following. "At any given instant, the standard times for many jobs will not be strictly correct."
    a. Why is this so?
    b. Does this mean that those standards are useless? Explain.
17. Why do workers sometimes resent time studies?
18. What are the key advantages and disadvantages of:
    a. Time-based pay plans?
    b. Incentive plans?
19. What is work sampling? How does it differ from time study?

1. Write a one-page memo to your subordinate, Joe Brown, about self-directed work teams. Explain what self-directed teams are, and their potential benefits and risks.
2. Your supervisor, the production manager of a company that recently shifted operations from a traditional manufacturing mode to a lean production mode, has asked you to write a memo to H. Penny, the chief financial officer of the company, explaining knowledge-based pay systems. Penny is particularly interested in the rationale for adopting this pay system. In your memo, be sure to include the three categories of knowledge or skills that are covered in this system.

1. An analyst has timed a metal-cutting operation for 50 cycles. The average time per cycle was 10.40 minutes, and the standard deviation was 1.20 minutes for a worker with a performance rating of 125 percent. Assume an allowance of 16 percent of job time. Find the standard time for this operation.
2. A job was timed for 60 cycles and had an average of 1.2 minutes per piece. The performance rating was 95 percent, and workday allowances are 10 percent. Determine each of the following:
    a. Observed time
    b. Normal time
    c. Standard time

3. A time study was conducted on a job that contains four elements. The observed times and performance ratings for six cycles are shown in the following table.

Element	Performance Rating	OBSERVATIONS (MINUTES PER CYCLE)					
		1	2	3	4	5	6
1	90%	0.44	0.50	0.43	0.45	0.48	0.46
2	85	1.50	1.54	1.47	1.51	1.49	1.52
3	110	0.84	0.89	0.77	0.83	0.85	0.80
4	100	1.10	1.14	1.08	1.20	1.16	1.26

   a. Determine the average cycle time for each element.
   b. Find the normal time for each element.
   c. Assuming an allowance factor of 15 percent of job time, compute the standard time for this job.

4. Given these observed times (in minutes) for four elements of a job, determine the observed time (OT) for each element. Note: The second element only occurs every other cycle.

	CYCLE					
	1	2	3	4	5	6
Element 1	4.1	4.0	4.2	4.1	4.1	4.1
Element 2	—	1.5	—	1.6	—	1.4
Element 3	3.2	3.2	3.3	3.2	3.3	3.3
Element 4	2.7	2.8	2.7	2.8	2.8	2.8

5. Given these observed times (in minutes) for five elements of a job, determine the observed time (OT) for each element. Note: Some of the elements occur only periodically.

	CYCLE					
	1	2	3	4	5	6
Element 1	2.1	2.0	2.2	2.1	2.1	—
Element 2	—	1.1	—	1.0	—	1.2
Element 3	3.4	3.5	3.3	3.5	3.4	3.3
Element 4	4.0	—	—	4.2	—	—
Element 5	1.4	1.4	1.5	1.5	1.5	1.4

6. Using Table 7–3 (on pg. 328), develop an allowance percentage for a job element that requires the worker to lift a weight of 10 pounds while (1) standing in a slightly awkward position, (2) in light that is slightly below recommended standards, and (3) with intermittent loud noises occurring. The monotony for this element is high. Include a personal allowance of 5 percent and a basic fatigue allowance of 4 percent of job time.

7. A worker-machine operation was found to involve 3.3 minutes of machine time per cycle in the course of 40 cycles of stopwatch study. The worker's time averaged 1.9 minutes per cycle, and the worker was given a rating of 120 percent (machine rating is 100 percent). Midway through the study, the worker took a 10-minute rest break. Assuming an allowance factor of 12 percent, determine the standard time for this job.

8. A recently negotiated union contract allows workers in a shipping department 24 minutes for rest, 10 minutes for personal time, and 14 minutes for delays for each four hours worked. A time study analyst observed a job that is performed continuously and found an average time of 6.0 minutes per cycle for a worker she rated at 95 percent. What standard time is applicable for that operation?

9. The data in the table below represent time study observations for a woodworking operation.
   a. Based on the observations, determine the standard time for the operation, assuming an allowance of 15 percent.
   b. How many observations would be needed to estimate the mean time for element 2 within 1 percent of its true value with a 95.5 percent confidence?
   c. How many observations would be needed to estimate the mean time for element 2 within .01 minute of its true value with a 95.5 percent confidence?

Element	Performance Rating	OBSERVATIONS (MINUTES PER CYCLE)					
		1	**2**	**3**	**4**	**5**	**6**
1	110%	1.20	1.17	1.16	1.22	1.24	1.15
2	115	0.83	0.87	0.78	0.82	0.85	1.32*
3	105	0.58	0.53	0.52	0.59	0.60	0.54

*Unusual delay, disregard time.

10. How many observations should a time study analyst plan for in an operation that has a standard deviation of 1.5 minutes per piece if the goal is to estimate the mean time per piece to within 0.4 minute with a confidence of 95.5 percent?

11. How many work cycles should be timed to estimate the average cycle time to within 2 percent of the sample mean with a confidence of 99 percent if a pilot study yielded these times (minutes): 5.2, 5.5, 5.8, 5.3, 5.5, and 5.1?

12. In an initial survey designed to estimate the percentage of time air-express cargo loaders are idle, an analyst found that loaders were idle in 6 of the 50 observations.

   a. What is the estimated percentage of idle time?

   b. Based on the initial results, approximately how many observations would you require to estimate the actual percentage of idle time to within 5 percent with a confidence of 95 percent?

13. A job in an insurance office involves telephone conversations with policyholders. The office manager estimates that about half of the employee's time is spent on the telephone. How many observations are needed in a work sampling study to estimate that time percentage to within 6 percent and have a confidence of 98 percent?

READING

Making Hotplates
Edgar F. Huse

A group of 10 workers were responsible for assembling hotplates (instruments for heating solutions to a given temperature) for hospital and medical laboratory use. A number of different models of hotplates were being manufactured. Some had a vibrating device so that the solution could be mixed while being heated. Others heated only test tubes. Still others could heat solutions in a variety of different containers.

With the appropriate small tools, each worker assembled part of a hotplate. The partially completed hotplate was placed on a moving belt, to be carried from one assembly station to the next. When the hotplate was completed, an inspector would check it over to ensure that it was working properly. Then the last worker would place it in a specially prepared cardboard box for shipping.

The assembly line had been carefully balanced by industrial engineers, who had used a time and motion study to break the job down into subassembly tasks, each requiring about three minutes to accomplish. The amount of time calculated for each subassembly had also been "balanced" so that the task performed by each worker was supposed to take almost

exactly the same amount of time. The workers were paid a straight hourly rate.

However, there were some problems. Morale seemed to be low, and the inspector was finding a relatively high percentage of badly assembled hotplates. Controllable rejects—those "caused" by the operator rather than by faulty materials—were running about 23 percent.

After discussing the situation, management decided to try something new. The workers were called together and asked if they would like to build the hotplates individually. The workers decided they would like to try this approach, provided they could go back to the old program if the new one did not work well. After several days of training, each worker began to assemble the entire hotplate.

The change was made at about the middle of the year. Productivity climbed quickly. By the end of the year, it had leveled off at about 84 percent higher than during the first half of the year, although no other changes had been made in the department or its personnel. Controllable rejects had dropped from 23 percent to 1 percent during the same period. Absenteeism had dropped from 8 percent to less than 1 percent. The workers had responded positively to the change, and their morale was higher. As one person put it, "Now, it is *my* hotplate." Eventually, the reject rate dropped so low that all routine final inspection was done by the assembly workers themselves. The full-time inspector was transferred to another job in the organization.

Questions

1. What changes in the work situation might account for the increase in productivity and the decrease in controllable rejects?

2. What might account for the drop in absenteeism and the increase in morale?

3. What were the major changes in the situation? Which changes were under the control of the manager? Which were controlled by workers?

4. What might happen if the workers went back to the old assembly line method?

Selected Bibliography and Further Reading

Barnes, Ralph M. *Motion and Time Study: Design and Measurement of Work,* 8th ed. New York: John Wiley & Sons, 1980.

Bridger, R. S. *Introduction to Ergonomics.* New York: McGraw-Hill, 1995.

Carlisle, Brian. "Job Design Implications for Operations Managers." *International Journal of Operations and Production Management,* no. 3 (1983), pp. 40–48.

Cunningham, J. Barton, and Ted Eberle. "A Guide to Job Enrichment and Redesign." *Personnel,* February 1990, pp. 56–61.

Jorgensen, Karen. *Pay for Results: A Practical Guide to Effective Employee Compensation.* Santa Monica, CA: Merritt Publishing, 1996.

Meyers, Fred E. *Motion and Time Study for Lean Manufacturing,* 2nd ed. Englewood Cliffs, NJ: Prentice Hall, 1999.

Mundel, Marvin E., and David L. Danner. *Motion and Time Study: Improving Productivity,* 7th ed. Englewood Cliffs, NJ: Prentice Hall, 1994.

Neibel, Benjamin, and Andris Freivalds. *Methods, Standards, and Work Design,* 10th ed. New York: McGraw-Hill, 1999.

Osborn, Jack D., Linda Moran, Ed Musslewhite, and John Zenger. *Self-Directed Work Teams.* Burr Ridge, IL: Richard D. Irwin, 1990.

SUPPLEMENT TO CHAPTER SEVEN

Learning Curves

SUPPLEMENT OUTLINE

The Concept of Learning
Curves, 343

Applications of Learning
Curves, 347

Operations Strategy, 349

Cautions and Criticisms, 349

Solved Problems, 350

Discussion and Review
Questions, 350

Problems, 351

Selected Bibliography and Further
Reading, 352

Case: Product Recall, 353

LEARNING OBJECTIVES

*After completing this supplement,
you should be able to:*

1 Explain the concept of a learning
curve.

2 Make time estimates based on
learning curves.

3 List and briefly describe some of
the main applications of learning
curves.

4 Outline some of the cautions and
criticisms of learning curves.

L earning is usually occurring when humans are involved; this is a basic consideration in the design of work systems. It is important to be able to predict how learning will affect task times and costs. This supplement addresses those issues.

The Concept of Learning Curves

Human performance of activities typically shows improvement when the activities are done on a repetitive basis: The time required to perform a task decreases with increasing repetitions. *Learning curves* summarize this phenomenon. The degree of improvement and the number of tasks needed to realize the major portion of the improvement is a function of the task being done. If the task is short and somewhat routine, only a modest amount of improvement is likely to occur, and it generally occurs during the first few repetitions. If the task is fairly complex and has a longer duration, improvements will occur over a longer interval (i.e., a larger number of repetitions). Therefore, learning factors have little relevance for planning or scheduling routine activities, but they do have relevance for complex repetitive activities.

Figure 7S–1 illustrates the basic relationship between increasing repetitions and a decreasing time per repetition. It should be noted that the curve will never touch the horizontal axis; that is, the time per unit will never be zero.

The general relationship is alternatively referred to as an experience curve, a progress function, or an improvement function. Experts agree that the learning effect is the result of other factors in addition to actual worker learning. Some of the improvement can be traced to preproduction factors, such as selection of tooling and equipment, product design, methods analysis, and, in general, the amount of effort expended prior to the start of the work. Other contributing factors may involve changes after production has begun, such as changes in methods, tooling, and design. In addition, management input can be an important factor through improvements in planning, scheduling, motivation, and control.

Changes that are made once production is under way can cause a temporary *increase* in time per unit until workers adjust to the change, even though they eventually lead to an increased output rate. If a number of changes are made during production, the learning curve would be more realistically described by a series of scallops instead of a smooth curve, as illustrated in Figure 7S–2. Nonetheless, it is convenient to work with a smooth curve, which can be interpreted as the *average* effect.

From an organizational standpoint, what makes the learning effect more than an interesting curiosity is its *predictability,* which becomes readily apparent if the relationship is plotted on a log-log scale (see Figure 7S–3). The straight line that results reflects a constant learning percentage, which is the basis of learning curve estimates: Every *doubling* of repetitions results in a *constant percentage* decrease in the time per repetition. This applies both to the *average* and to the *unit* time. Typical decreases range from 10 percent to 20 percent. By convention, learning curves are referred to in terms of the *complements* of

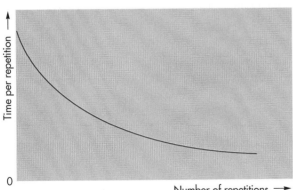

FIGURE 7S–1

The learning effect: time per repetition decreases as the number of repetitions increases

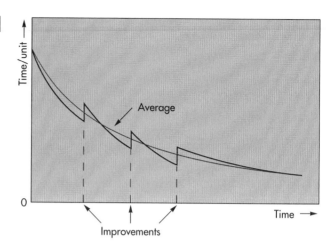

FIGURE 7S–2

*Improvements may create a
scallop effect in the curve*

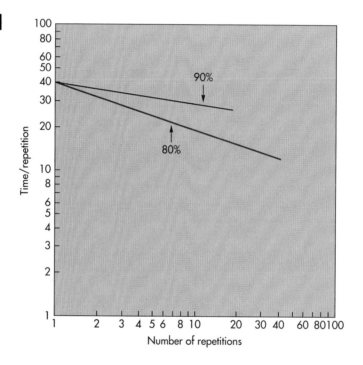

FIGURE 7S–3

*On a log-log graph, learning
curves are straight lines*

their improvement rates. For example, an 80 percent learning curve denotes a 20 percent
decrease in unit (or average) time with each doubling of repetitions, and a 90 percent
curve denotes a 10 percent improvement rate. Note that a 100 percent curve would imply
no improvement at all.

Example S–1

An activity is known to have an 80 percent learning curve. It has taken a worker 10 hours
to produce the first unit. Determine expected completion times for these units: the 2nd,
4th, 8th, and 16th (note successive doubling of units).

Solution

Each time the cumulative output doubles, the time per unit for that amount should be approximately equal to the previous time multiplied by the learning percentage (80 percent
in this case). Thus:

Unit	Unit Time (hours)		
1		=	10
2	0.8(10)	=	8
4	0.8(8)	=	6.4
8	0.8(6.4)	=	5.12
16	0.8(5.12)	=	4.096

Example S–1 illustrates an important point and also raises an interesting question. The point is that the time reduction *per unit* becomes less and less as the number of repetitions increases. For example, the second unit required two hours less time than the first, and the improvement from the 8th to the 16th unit was only slightly more than one hour. The question raised is: How are times computed for values such as three, five, six, seven, and other units that don't fall into this pattern?

There are two ways to obtain the times. One is to use a formula; the other is to use a table of values.

First, consider the formula approach. The formula is based on the existence of a linear relationship between the time per unit and the number of units when these two variables are expressed in logarithms.

The unit time (i.e., the number of direct labor hours required) for the *n*th unit can be computed using the formula

$$T_n = T_1 \times n^b \tag{7S–1}$$

where

T_n = Time for *n*th unit

T_1 = Time for first unit

b = ln learning percent ÷ ln 2; ln stands for the natural logarithm

To use the formula, you need to know the time for the first unit and the learning percentage. For example, for an 80 percent curve with $T_1 = 10$ hours, the time for the third unit would be computed as

$$T_3 = 10(3^{\ln .8/\ln 2}) = 7.02$$

The second approach is to use a "learning factor" obtained from a table such as Table 7S–1.

The table shows two things for some selected learning percentages. One is a unit value for the number of repetitions (unit number). This enables us to easily determine how long any unit will take to produce. The other is a cumulative value, which enables us to compute the total number of hours needed to complete any given number of repetitions. The computation for both is a relatively simple operation: Multiply the table value by the time required for the first unit.

To find the time for an individual unit (e.g., the 10th unit), use the formula

$$T_n = T_1 \times \text{unit time factor} \tag{7S–2}$$

Thus, for an 85 percent curve, with $T_1 = 4$ hours, the time for the 10th unit would be $4 \times .583 = 2.33$ hours. To find the time for all units up to a specified unit (e.g., the first 10 units), use the formula

$$\sum T_n = T_1 \times \text{total time factor} \tag{7S–3}$$

Thus, for an 85 percent curve, with $T_1 = 4$ hours, the total time for all 10 units (including the time for unit 1) would be $4 \times 7.116 = 28.464$ hours.

TABLE 7S–1

Learning curve coefficients

TABLE 7S–1

Learning curve coefficients

Unit Number	70% Unit Time	70% Total Time	75% Unit Time	75% Total Time	80% Unit Time	80% Total Time	85% Unit Time	85% Total Time	90% Unit Time	90% Total Time
1	1.000	1.000	1.000	1.000	1.000	1.000	1.000	1.000	1.000	1.000
2	.700	1.700	.750	1.750	.800	1.800	.850	1.850	.900	1.900
3	.568	2.268	.634	2.384	.702	2.502	.773	2.623	.846	2.746
4	.490	2.758	.562	2.946	.640	3.142	.723	3.345	.810	3.556
5	.437	3.195	.513	3.459	.596	3.738	.686	4.031	.783	4.339
6	.398	3.593	.475	3.934	.562	4.299	.657	4.688	.762	5.101
7	.367	3.960	.446	4.380	.534	4.834	.634	5.322	.744	5.845
8	.343	4.303	.422	4.802	.512	5.346	.614	5.936	.729	6.574
9	.323	4.626	.402	5.204	.493	5.839	.597	6.533	.716	7.290
10	.306	4.932	.385	5.589	.477	6.315	.583	7.116	.705	7.994
11	.291	5.223	.370	5.958	.462	6.777	.570	7.686	.695	8.689
12	.278	5.501	.357	6.315	.449	7.227	.558	8.244	.685	9.374
13	.267	5.769	.345	6.660	.438	7.665	.548	8.792	.677	10.052
14	.257	6.026	.334	6.994	.428	8.092	.539	9.331	.670	10.721
15	.248	6.274	.325	7.319	.418	8.511	.530	9.861	.663	11.384
16	.240	6.514	.316	7.635	.410	8.920	.522	10.383	.656	12.040
17	.233	6.747	.309	7.944	.402	9.322	.515	10.898	.650	12.690
18	.226	6.973	.301	8.245	.394	9.716	.508	11.405	.644	13.334
19	.220	7.192	.295	8.540	.388	10.104	.501	11.907	.639	13.974
20	.214	7.407	.288	8.828	.381	10.485	.495	12.402	.634	14.608
21	.209	7.615	.283	9.111	.375	10.860	.490	12.892	.630	15.237
22	.204	7.819	.277	9.388	.370	11.230	.484	13.376	.625	15.862
23	.199	8.018	.272	9.660	.364	11.594	.479	13.856	.621	16.483
24	.195	8.213	.267	9.928	.359	11.954	.475	14.331	.617	17.100
25	.191	8.404	.263	10.191	.355	12.309	.470	14.801	.613	17.713
26	.187	8.591	.259	10.449	.350	12.659	.466	15.267	.609	18.323
27	.183	8.774	.255	10.704	.346	13.005	.462	15.728	.606	18.929
28	.180	8.954	.251	10.955	.342	13.347	.458	16.186	.603	19.531
29	.177	9.131	.247	11.202	.338	13.685	.454	16.640	.599	20.131
30	.174	9.305	.244	11.446	.335	14.020	.450	17.091	.596	20.727

Example S–2

Production Airplanes is negotiating a contract for the production of 20 small jet aircraft. The initial jet required the equivalent of 400 days of direct labor. The learning percentage is 80 percent. Estimate the expected number of days of direct labor for:

a. The 20th jet.

b. All 20 jets.

c. The average time for 20 jets.

Solution

Using Table 7S–1 with $n = 20$ and an 80 percent learning percentage, you find these factors: Unit time = .381. Total time = 10.485.

a. Expected time for 20th jet: 400(.381) = 152.4 labor days.

b. Expected total time for all 20: 400(10.485) = 4,194 labor days.

c. Average time for 20: 4,194 ÷ 20 = 209.7 labor days.

Use of Table 7S–1 requires a time for the first unit. If for some reason the completion time of the first unit is not available, or if the manager believes the completion time for some later unit is more reliable, the table can be used to obtain an estimate of the initial time.

The manager in Example S–2 believes that some unusual problems were encountered in producing the first jet and would like to revise that estimate based on a completion time of 276 days for the third jet.

Solution

The unit value for $n = 3$ and an 80 percent curve is .702 (Table 7S–1). Divide the actual time for unit 3 by the table value to obtain the revised estimate for unit 1's time: 276 days ÷ .702 = 393.2 labor days.

Applications of Learning Curves

Learning curve theory has found useful applications in a number of areas, including:

1. Manpower planning and scheduling.
2. Negotiated purchasing.
3. Pricing new products.
4. Budgeting, purchasing, and inventory planning.
5. Capacity planning.

Knowledge of output projections in learning situations can help managers make better decisions about how many workers they will need than they could determine from decisions based on initial output rates. Of course, managers obviously recognize that improvement will occur; what the learning curve contributes is a method for quantifying expected future improvements.

Negotiated purchasing often involves contracting for specialized items that may have a high degree of complexity. Examples include aircraft, computers, and special-purpose equipment. The direct labor cost per unit of such items can be expected to decrease as the size of the order increases. Hence, negotiators first settle on the number of units and then negotiate price on that basis. The government requires learning curve data on contracts that involve large, complex items. For contracts that are terminated before delivery of all units, suppliers can use learning curve data to argue for an increase in the unit price for the smaller number of units. Conversely, the government can use that information to negotiate a lower price per unit on follow-on orders on the basis of projected additional learning gains.

Managers must establish prices for their new products and services, often on the basis of production of a few units. Generalizing from the cost of the first few units would result in a much higher price than can be expected after a greater number of units have been produced. Actually, the manager needs to use the learning curve to avoid underpricing as well as overpricing. The manager may project initial costs by using the learning progression known to represent an organization's past experience, or else do a regression analysis of the initial results.

The learning curve projections help managers to plan costs and labor, purchasing, and inventory needs. For example, initial cost per unit will be high and output will be fairly low, so purchasing and inventory decisions can reflect this. As productivity increases, purchasing and/or inventory actions must allow for increased usage of raw materials and purchased parts to keep pace with output. Because of learning effects, the usage rate will increase over time. Hence, failure to refer to a learning curve would lead to substantial *overestimates* of labor needs and *underestimates* of the rate of material usage.

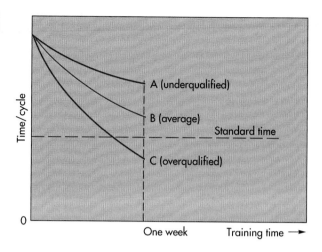

FIGURE 7S–4

Worker learning curves can help guide personnel job placement

The learning principles can sometimes be used to evaluate new workers during training periods. This is accomplished by measuring each worker's performance, graphing the results, and comparing them to an expected rate of learning. The comparison reveals which workers are underqualified, average, and overqualified for a given type of work (see Figure 7S–4). Moreover, measuring a worker's progress can help predict whether the worker will make a quota within a required period of time.

Boeing uses learning curves to estimate weight reduction in new aircraft designs. Weight is a major factor in winning contracts because it is directly related to fuel economy.

Example S–4

Use learning curve theory to predict the number of repetitions (units) that will be needed for a trainee to achieve a unit time of 6 minutes if the trainee took 10 minutes to do the first unit and a learning curve of 90 percent is operative.

a. Use the learning table.

b. Use the log formula.

Solution

a. The table approach can be used for the learning percentages that are listed across the top of the table, such as the 90 percent curve in this example. The table approach is based on formula 7S–2:

$T_n = T_1 \times$ unit table factor

Setting T_n equal to the specified time of 6 minutes and solving for the unit table factor yields

6 min = 10 min × unit table factor. Solving, unit table factor = 6 min ÷ 10 min = .600.

From Table 7S–1, under 90% in the Unit Time column, we find .599 at 29 units. Hence, approximately 29 units will be required to achieve the specified time.

b. Using the log formula,

(1) Compute the ratio of specified time to first unit time: 6 min ÷ 10 min = .600.

(2) Compute the ratio of ln learning percentage to ln 2: ln .90 ÷ ln 2 = −0.1053605 ÷ 0.6931472 = −0.1520.

(3) Find n such that $n^{-.1520} = .600$: $\sqrt[-.1520]{.600} = 28.809$. Round to 29. Hence, 29 units (repetitions) will be needed to achieve a time of 6 minutes.

Learning curves often have strategic implications for market entry, when an organization hopes to rapidly gain market share. The use of time-based strategies can contribute to this. An increase in market share creates additional volume, enabling operations to quickly move down the learning curve, thereby decreasing costs and, in the process, gaining a competitive advantage. In some instances, the volumes are sufficiently large that operations will shift from batch mode to repetitive operation, which can lead to further cost reductions.

Learning curve projections can be useful for capacity planning. Having realistic time estimates based on learning curve theory, managers can translate that information into actual capacity needs, and plan on that basis.

Cautions and Criticisms

Managers using learning curves should be aware of their limitations and pitfalls. This section briefly outlines some of the major cautions and criticisms of learning curves.

1. Learning rates may differ from organization to organization and by type of work. Therefore, it is best to base learning rates on empirical studies rather than assumed rates where possible.

2. Projections based on learning curves should be regarded as *approximations* of actual times and treated accordingly.

3. Because time estimates are based on the time for the first unit, considerable care should be taken to ensure that the time is valid. It may be desirable to revise the base time as later times become available. Since it is often necessary to estimate the time for the first unit prior to production, this caution is very important.

4. It is possible that at some point the curve might level off or even tip upward, especially near the end of a job. The potential for savings at that point is so slight that most jobs do not command the attention or interest to sustain improvements. Then, too, some of the better workers or other resources may be shifted into new jobs that are starting up.

5. Some of the improvements may be more apparent than real: Improvements in times may be caused in part by *increases* in *indirect* labor costs.

6. In mass production situations, learning curves may be of initial use in predicting how long it will take before the process stabilizes. For the most part, however, the concept does *not* apply to mass production because the decrease in time per unit is imperceptible for all practical purposes (see Figure 7S–5).

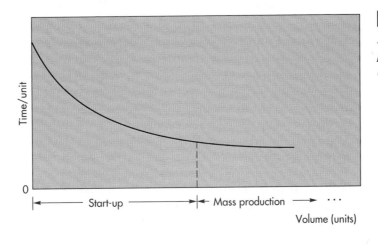

FIGURE 7S-5

Learning curves are useful for production startup, but not usually for mass production

7. Users of learning curves sometimes fail to include carryover effects; previous experience with similar activities can reduce activity times, although it should be noted that the *learning rate* remains the same.

8. Shorter product life cycles, flexible manufacturing, and cross-functional workers can affect the ways in which learning curves may be applied.

Solved Problems

Problem 1

An assembly operation has a 90 percent learning curve. The line has just begun work on a new item; the initial unit required 28 hours. Estimate the time that will be needed to complete:

a. The first five units.

b. Units 20 through 25.

Solution

Use the total time factor in the 90 percent column of Table 7S–1.

a. Table value: 4.339.

Estimated time for five units: 28(4.339) = 121.49 hours.

b. The total time for units 20 through 25 can be determined by subtraction:

	Hours
Total time for 25 units:	28(17.713) = 495.96
−Total time for 19 units:	28(13.974) = 391.27
Total time for 20 through 25	104.69

Problem 2

A manager wants to determine an appropriate learning rate for a new type of work his firm will undertake. He has obtained completion times for the initial six repetitions of a job of this type. What learning rate is appropriate?

Unit	Completion Time (hours)
1	15.9
2	12.0
3	10.1
4	9.1
5	8.4
6	7.5

Solution

According to theory, the time per unit decreases at a constant rate each time the output *doubles* (e.g., unit 1 to 2, 2 to 4, and 3 to 6). The ratios of these observed times will give us an approximate rate. Thus,

$$\frac{\text{Unit 2}}{\text{Unit 1}} = \frac{12.0}{15.9} = .755 \qquad \frac{\text{Unit 4}}{\text{Unit 2}} = \frac{9.1}{12.0} = .758 \qquad \frac{\text{Unit 6}}{\text{Unit 3}} = \frac{7.5}{10.1} = .743$$

Not surprisingly, there is some variability; the rate is usually a smoothed approximation. Even so, the ratios are fairly close—a rate of 75 percent seems reasonable in this case.

Discussion and Review Questions

1. If the learning phenomenon applies to all human activity, why isn't the effect noticeable in mass production or high-volume assembly work?

2. Under what circumstances might a manager prefer a learning rate of approximately 100 percent (i.e., no "learning")?

3. What would a learning percentage of 120 percent imply?

4. Explain how an increase in indirect labor cost can contribute to a decrease in direct labor cost per unit.

5. List the kinds of factors that create the learning effect.

6. Explain how changes in a process, once it is under way, can cause scallops in a learning curve.

7. Name some areas in which learning curves are useful.

8. What factors might cause a learning curve to tip up toward the end of a job?

9. Users of learning curves sometimes fail to include carryover effects; previous experience with similar activities can reduce initial activity times, although it should be noted that the *learning rate* remains the same. What is the implication of this item from the list of cautions and criticisms?

Problems

1. An aircraft company has an order to refurbish the interiors of 18 jet aircraft. The work has a learning curve percentage of 80. On the basis of experience with similar jobs, the industrial engineering department estimates that the first plane will require 300 hours to refurbish. Estimate the amount of time needed to complete:

   a. The fifth plane.

   b. The first five planes.

   c. All 18 planes.

2. Estimate the time it will take to complete the 4th unit of a 12-unit job involving a large assembly if the initial unit required approximately 80 hours for each of these learning percentages:

   a. 72 percent

   b. 87 percent

   c. 95 percent

3. A small contractor intends to bid on a job installing 30 in-ground swimming pools. Because this will be a new line of work for the contractor, he believes there will be a learning effect for the job. After reviewing time records from a similar type of activity, the contractor is convinced that an 85 percent curve is appropriate. He estimates that the first pool will take his crew eight days to install. How many days should the contractor budget for:

   a. The first 10 pools?

   b. The second 10 pools?

   c. The final 10 pools?

4. A job is known to have a learning percentage equal to 82. If the first unit had a completion time of 20 hours, estimate the times that will be needed to complete the third and fourth units.

5. A manager wants to determine an appropriate learning percentage for a certain activity. Toward that end, times have been recorded for completion of each of the first six repetitions. They are:

Repetition	Time (minutes)
1	46
2	39
3	35
4	33
5	32
6	30

   a. Determine the approximate learning percentage.

   b. Using your answer from part *a,* estimate the average completion time per repetition assuming a total of 30 repetitions are planned.

6. Students in an operations management class have been assigned four similar homework problems. One student noted that it took her 50 minutes to complete the first problem. Assume that the four problems are similar and that a 70 percent learning curve is appropriate. How much time can this student plan to spend solving the remaining problems?

7. A subcontractor is responsible for outfitting six satellites that will be used for solar research. Four of the six have been completed in a total of 600 hours. If the crew has a 75 percent learning curve, how long should it take them to finish the last two units?

8. The 5th unit of a 25-unit job took 14.5 hours to complete. If a 90 percent learning curve is appropriate:

    a. How long should it take to complete the last unit?

    b. How long should it take to complete the 10th unit?

    c. Estimate the average time per unit for the 25 units.

9. The labor cost to produce a certain item is $8.50 per hour. Job setup costs $50 and material costs are $20 per unit. The item can be purchased for $88.50 per unit. The learning rate is 90 percent. Overhead is charged at a rate of 50 percent of labor, materials, and setup costs.

    a. Determine the unit cost for 20 units, given that the first unit took 5 hours to complete.

    b. What is the minimum production quantity necessary to make production cost less than purchase cost?

10. A firm has a training program for a certain operation. The progress of trainees is carefully monitored. An established standard requires a trainee to be able to complete the sixth repetition of the operation in six hours or less. Those who are unable to do this are assigned to other jobs.

    Currently, three trainees have each completed two repetitions. Trainee A had times of 9 hours for the first and 8 hours for the second repetition; trainee B had times of 10 hours and 8 hours for the first and second repetitions; and trainee C had times of 12 and 9 hours.

    Which trainee(s) do you think will make the standard? Explain your reasoning.

11. The first unit of a job took 40 hours to complete. The work has a learning percentage of 88. The manager wants time estimates for units 2, 3, 4, and 5. Develop those time estimates.

12. A manager wants to estimate the remaining time that will be needed to complete a five-unit job. The initial unit of the job required 12 hours, and the work has a learning percentage of 77. Estimate the total time remaining to complete the job.

13. A job is supposed to have a learning percentage of 82. Times for the first four units were 30.5, 28.4, 27.2, and 27.0 minutes. Does a learning percentage of 82 seem reasonable? Justify your answer using appropriate calculations.

14. The 5th unit of a 10-unit job took five hours to complete. The 6th unit has been worked on for two hours, but is not yet finished. Estimate the *additional* amount of time needed to finish the 10-unit job if the work has a 75 percent learning rate.

15. Estimate the number of repetitions each of the workers listed in the following table will require to reach a time of 7 hours per unit. Time is in hours.

Trainee	T_1	T_2
Art	11	9.9
Sherry	10.5	8.4
Dave	12	10.2

16. Estimate the number of repetitions that new service worker Irene will require to achieve "standard" if the standard is 18 minutes per repetition. She took 30 minutes to do the initial repetition and 25 minutes to do the next repetition.

17. Estimate the number of repetitions each of the workers listed in the following table will require to achieve a standard time of 25 minutes per repetition. Time is in minutes.

Trainee	T_1	T_2
Beverly	36	31
Max	40	36
Antonio	37	30

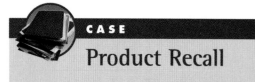

CASE

Product Recall

An automobile manufacturer is conducting a product recall after it was discovered that a possible defect in the steering mechanism could cause loss of control in certain cars. The recall covers a span of three model years. The company sent out letters to car owners promising to repair the defect at no cost at any dealership.

    The company's policy is to pay the dealer a fixed amount for each repair. The repair is somewhat complicated, and the company expected learning to be a factor. In order to set a reasonable rate for repairs, company engineers conducted a number of repairs themselves. It was then decided that a rate of $88 per repair would be appropriate, based on a flat hourly rate of $22 per hour and a 90 percent learning rate.

Shortly after dealers began making repairs, the company received word that several dealers were encountering resistance from workers who felt the flat rate was much too low and who were threatening to refuse to work on those jobs. One of the dealers collected data on job times and sent that information to the company: Three mechanics each completed two repairs. Average time for the first unit was 9.6 hours, and average time for the second unit was 7.2 hours. The dealer has suggested a rate of $110 per repair.

You have been asked to investigate the situation and to prepare a report.

Questions

1. Prepare a list of questions that you will need to have answered in order to analyze this situation.

2. Prepare a list of observations regarding the information provided in the case.

3. What preliminary thoughts do you have on solutions/partial solutions to the points you have raised?

Abernathy, W. J. "The Limits of the Learning Curve." *Harvard Business Review,* September–October 1974, pp. 109–19.

Argote, Linda, and Dennis Epple. "Learning Curves in Manufacturing." *Science* 247 (February 1990), pp. 920–24.

Belkauoi, Ahmed. *The Learning Curve.* Westport, CT: Greenwood Publishing Group, 1986.

Fabrycky, W. J., P. M. Ghare, and P. E. Torgersen. *Industrial Operations Research.* Englewood Cliffs, NJ: Prentice Hall, 1972.

Teplitz, Charles J. *The Learning Curve Deskbook.* Westport, CT: Greenwood Publishing Group, 1991.

CHAPTER EIGHT

Location Planning and Analysis

CHAPTER OUTLINE

The Need for Location
   Decisions, 356

The Nature of Location
   Decisions, 356
   Strategic Importance of Location
      Decisions, 356
   Objectives of Location
      Decisions, 357
   Location Options, 357

General Procedure for Making
   Location Decisions, 357

Factors That Affect Location
   Decisions, 358

Newsclip: Innovative MCI Unit
   Finds Culture Shock in Colorado
   Springs, 358
   Regional Factors, 359

Reading: Not-So-Clear Choices:
   Should You Export, or
   Manufacture Overseas? 362
   Community Considerations, 365
   Site-Related Factors, 366

Reading: New U.S. Factory Jobs
   Aren't in the Factory, 366
   Multiple Plant Manufacturing
      Strategies, 367
   Service and Retail Locations, 369

Newsclip: Vying for Patients,
   Hospitals Think Location,
   Location, 370

Global Locations, 370

Reading: Global Strategy: GM
   Is Building Plants in
   Developing Nations to Woo
   New Markets, 372

Evaluating Location
   Alternatives, 373
   Locational Cost-Profit-Volume
      Analysis, 373
   The Transportation Model, 375
   Factor Rating, 375
   The Center of Gravity Method, 376

Summary, 379

Key Terms, 379

Solved Problems, 379

Discussion and Review
   Questions, 381

Memo Writing Exercises, 381

Problems, 381

Selected Bibliography and Further
   Reading, 384

Supplement: The Transportation
   Model, 385

LEARNING OBJECTIVES

*After completing this chapter, you
should be able to:*

1 List some of the main reasons
   organizations need to make
   location decisions.

2 Explain why location decisions
   are important.

3 Discuss the options that are
   available for location decisions.

4 Describe some of the major
   factors that affect location
   decisions.

5 Outline the decision process for
   making these kinds of decisions.

6 Use the techniques presented to
   solve typical problems.

When a well-known real estate broker was asked what the three most important determinants of the value of a property are, he said, "That's easy. Location, location, and location."

In the residential real estate market, location is an important factor. Although the style of house, number of bedrooms and bathrooms, level of maintenance, and how modern the kitchen is undoubtedly enter into the picture, some locations are just more desirable than others.

In many respects, the choice of location for a business organization is every bit as important as it is for a house, although for different reasons.

Location decisions represent a key part of the strategic planning process of virtually every organization. And, although it might appear that location decisions are one-time problems pertaining to new organizations, existing organizations often have a bigger stake in these kinds of decisions than new organizations.

This chapter examines location analysis. It begins with a brief overview of the reasons firms must make location decisions, the nature of these decisions, and a general procedure for developing and evaluating location alternatives.

The Need for Location Decisions

Existing organizations may need to make location decisions for a variety of reasons. Firms such as banks, fast-food chains, supermarkets, and retail stores view locations as part of marketing strategy, and they look for locations that will help them to expand their markets. Basically, the location decisions in those cases reflect the *addition* of new locations to an existing system.

A similar situation occurs when an organization experiences a growth in demand for its products or services that cannot be satisfied by expansion at an existing location. The addition of a new location to complement an existing system is often a realistic alternative.

Some firms face location decisions through depletion of basic inputs. For example, fishing and logging operations are often forced to relocate due to the temporary exhaustion of fish or forests at a given location. Mining and petroleum operations face the same sort of situation, although usually with a longer time horizon.

For other firms, a shift in markets causes them to consider relocation, or the costs of doing business at a particular location reach a point where other locations begin to look more attractive.

The Nature of Location Decisions

Location decisions for many types of businesses are made infrequently, but they tend to have a significant impact on the organization. In this section we look at the importance of location decisions, the usual objectives managers have when making location choices, and some of the options that are available to them.

STRATEGIC IMPORTANCE OF LOCATION DECISIONS

There are several reasons that location decisions are a highly important part of production systems design. One is that they entail a long-term commitment, which makes mistakes difficult to overcome. A second is that location decisions often have an impact on investment requirements, operating costs and revenues, and operations. A poor choice of location might result in excessive transportation costs, a shortage of qualified labor, loss of competitive advantage, inadequate supplies of raw materials, or some similar condition that is detrimental to operations. For services, a poor location could result in lack of customers and/or high operating costs. For both manufacturing and services, location decisions can have a significant impact on competitive advantage. And a third reason for the importance of location decisions is their strategic importance to supply chains.

OBJECTIVES OF LOCATION DECISIONS

As a general rule, profit-oriented organizations base their decisions on profit potential, whereas nonprofit organizations strive to achieve a balance between cost and the level of customer service they provide. It would seem to follow that all organizations attempt to identify the "best" location available. However, this is not necessarily the case.

In many instances, no single location may be significantly better than the others. There may be numerous acceptable locations from which to choose, as shown by the wide variety of locations where successful organizations can be found. Furthermore, the number of possible locations that would have to be examined to find the best location may be too large to make an exhaustive search practical. Consequently, most organizations do not set out with the intention of identifying the *one best* location; rather, they hope to find a number of *acceptable* locations from which to choose.

Location criteria can depend on where a business is in the *supply chain*. For instance, at the retail end of a chain, site selection tends to focus more on accessibility, consumer demographics (population density, age distribution, average buyer income), traffic patterns, and local customs. Businesses at the beginning of a supply chain, if they are involved in supplying raw materials, are often located near the source of the raw materials. Businesses in the middle of the chain may locate near suppliers or near their markets, depending on a variety of circumstances. For example, businesses involved in storing and distributing goods often choose a central location to minimize distribution costs.

Web-based retail businesses are much less dependent on location decisions; they can exist just about anywhere.

LOCATION OPTIONS

Managers generally consider four options in location planning. One is to expand an existing facility. This option can be attractive if there is adequate room for expansion, especially if the location has desirable features that are not readily available elsewhere. Expansion costs are often less than those of other alternatives.

Another option is to add new locations while retaining existing ones, as is done in many retail operations. In such cases, it is essential to take into account what the impact will be on the total system. Opening a new store in a shopping mall may simply draw customers who already patronize an existing store in the same chain, rather than expand the market. On the other hand, adding locations can be a defensive strategy designed to maintain a market share or to prevent competitors from entering a market.

A third option is to shut down at one location and move to another. An organization must weigh the costs of a move and the resulting benefits against the costs and benefits of remaining in an existing location. A shift in markets, exhaustion of raw materials, and the cost of operations often cause firms to consider this option seriously.

Finally, organizations have the option of doing nothing. If a detailed analysis of potential locations fails to uncover benefits that make one of the previous three alternatives attractive, a firm may decide to maintain the status quo, at least for the time being.

General Procedure for Making Location Decisions

The way an organization approaches location decisions often depends on its size and the nature or scope of its operations. New or small organizations tend to adopt a rather informal approach to location decisions. New firms typically locate in a certain area simply because the owner lives there. Similarly, managers of small firms often want to keep operations in their backyard, so they tend to focus almost exclusively on local alternatives. Large established companies, particularly those that already operate in more than one location, tend to take a more formal approach. Moreover, they usually consider a wider range of geographic locations. The discussion here pertains mainly to a formal approach to location decisions.

The general procedure for making location decisions usually consists of the following steps:

1. Decide on the criteria to use for evaluating location alternatives, such as increased revenues or community service.
2. Identify important factors, such as location of markets or raw materials.
3. Develop location alternatives:
    a. Identify the general region for a location.
    b. Identify a small number of community alternatives.
    c. Identify site alternatives among the community alternatives.
4. Evaluate the alternatives and make a selection.

Step (1) is simply a matter of managerial preference. Steps (2) through (4) may need some elaboration.

Factors That Affect Location Decisions

Many factors influence location decisions. However, it often happens that one or a few factors are so important that they dominate the decision. For example, in manufacturing, the potentially dominating factors usually include availability of an abundant energy and water supply and proximity to raw materials. Thus, nuclear reactors require large amounts of water for cooling, heavy industries such as steel and aluminum production need large amounts of electricity, and so on. Transportation costs can be a major factor. In service organizations, possible dominating factors are market related and include traffic patterns, convenience, and competitors' locations, as well as proximity to the market. For example, car rental agencies locate near airports and midcity, where their customers are.

Once an organization has determined the most important factors, it will try to narrow the search for suitable alternatives to one geographic region. Then a small number of community-site alternatives are identified and subjected to detailed analysis. Community and site factors are often so intertwined that it makes sense to consider them jointly.

NEWSCLIP

Innovative MCI Unit Finds Culture Shock in Colorado Springs

Alex Markels

www.mci.com

Convinced this town's spectacular setting would inspire his workers, Richard Liebhaber figured "build it, and they will come."

In 1991, the chief technology officer of MCI Communications Corp. decided to relocate MCI's brain trust—the 4,000-employee Systems Engineering division that created numerous breakthrough products—from MCI's Washington, D.C., headquarters to Colorado Springs. An avid skier, he believed the mountains, low crime rate, healthy climate and rock-bottom real-estate prices would be "a magnet for the best and brightest" computer software engineers.

He rejected warnings from at least half a dozen senior executives that Colorado Springs' isolated and politically conservative setting would actually repel the eclectic, ethnically diverse engineers MCI hoped to attract. Mr. Liebhaber argued that new hires would jump at the chance to live in ski country, while veterans would stay longer, reducing MCI's more than 15% annual turnover rate in Washington. The move, he contended, would also save money by cutting MCI's facilities, labor and recruiting costs. Besides, four other high-tech companies—including Digital Equipment Corp. and Apple Computer Inc.—had recently moved there. "One of the things that gave me more comfort was the fact that these other guys had selected Colorado Springs," Mr. Liebhaber says.

He was mistaken.

While many rank-and-file MCI employees, buoyed by generous relocation packages, made the move, numerous key executives and engineers, and hundreds of the division's 51%

minority population, said no, or fled Colorado Springs soon after relocating.

Living in "Wonder Bread"

"It was like living in a loaf of Wonder Bread," says James Finucane, who is of Japanese descent and whose wife is from Argentina. A veteran senior engineer, Mr. Finucane was considered MCI's top engineer until he took a job with a competitor back east in 1994. "There's no culture, no diversity, no research university, no vitality or resiliency to the job market."

The move isolated MCI's engineers from top management and from marketing colleagues at headquarters, undermining the spontaneous collaborations that had generated some of company's most innovative products. Meanwhile, the professionals Mr. Liebhaber hoped to recruit from outside proved difficult and expensive to woo, pushing the move's total cost to about $200 million—far more than MCI officials anticipated. "Most of the savings we had hoped for never materialized," says LeRoy Pingho, a senior executive who oversaw the relocation.

As numerous companies consider relocating to smaller cities and towns, MCI's move shows the perils of transplanting urban professionals to the nation's heartland and segregating key operations. Dozens of former and current employees say Systems Engineering has lost its innovative and productive edge at a time when competition in telecommunications is fiercer than ever.

Moving Expenses

When the move was announced in March 1991, many rank-and-file workers were enthusiastic. MCI's relocation policy paid for every expense imaginable. Costing an average of $100,000 per employee, it included up to six months of temporary housing and living expenses, private-school tuition for workers' children and a full month's pay for miscellaneous expenses. And there were exceptional housing bargains. "In Alexandria, [Va.,] we had a tiny place on a 50-by-112-foot

lot," says Jerome Sabolik, a senior software engineer. "For the same money, we got a 3,000-square-foot house on 2½ acres." Thousands of workers—far more than Mr. Liebhaber expected—took advantage of the offer, undercutting his plans to recruit lower-cost employees in Colorado.

But there was far less enthusiasm among senior managers. James Zucco, Mr. Ditchfield's successor and the head of Systems Engineering, stayed behind and eventually left to join AT&T Corp. Also staying put was Gary Wiesenborn, the division's No. 2 executive, who later moved to Bell Atlantic Corp. Mr. Pingho, who oversaw the division's financial planning and budgeting, declined to move and quit in 1993.

There was also significant fallout among the division's minority population. Although MCI declines to provide specific numbers, it confirms there was a reduction. According to former employees who had access to Equal Employment Opportunity Commission data, there were roughly 1,300 African-Americans on Systems Engineering's staff and a combined 700 Asians and Hispanics before the relocation. Since the relocation, minority representation has been cut almost in half, to about 600 blacks and a combined 500 Asians and Hispanics. "It was a disaster for diversity," Mr. Ditchfield says.

But MCI officials say that despite the reduction, its Colorado division is still more ethnically diverse than other local companies. "We think that we have numbers that are significantly better than the available work force there," says William D. Wooten, a senior vice president of human resources.

Among those who opted out: Tony Martin, a vice president of operations who is Asian-American, and Rod Avery, who designed the complex billing system for MCI's successful "Friends & Family" long-distance program. One of the company's highest ranking African-Americans, Mr. Avery, moved to AT&T.

Source: Reprinted with permission from *The Wall Street Journal* © 1996 Dow Jones & Company, Inc. All Rights Reserved Worldwide.

REGIONAL FACTORS

The primary regional factors involve raw materials, markets, and labor considerations.

Location of Raw Materials. Firms locate near or at the source of raw materials for three primary reasons: necessity, perishability, and transportation costs. Mining operations, farming, forestry, and fishing fall under *necessity*. Obviously, such operations must locate close to the raw materials. Firms involved in canning or freezing of fresh fruit and vegetables, processing of dairy products, baking, and so on, must consider *perishability* when considering location. *Transportation costs* are important in industries where processing eliminates much of the bulk connected with a raw material, making it much less expensive to transport the product or material after processing. Examples include aluminum reduction, cheese making, and paper production. Where inputs come from different locations, some firms choose to locate near the geographic center of the sources. For instance, steel producers use large quantities of both coal and iron ore, and many are located

Tropicana, an orange juice producer, has processing plants in Florida and California. Locating the processing near their supply, the orange groves, provides time and cost savings in the transportation of perishable fruit.

www.tropicana.com

somewhere between the Appalachian coal fields and iron ore mines. Transportation costs are often the reason that vendors locate near their major customers. Moreover, regional warehouses are used by supermarkets and other retail operations to supply multiple outlets. Often the choice of new locations and additional warehouses reflects the locations of existing warehouses or retail outlets.

Location of Markets. Profit-oriented firms frequently locate near the markets they intend to serve as part of their competitive strategy, whereas nonprofit organizations choose locations relative to the needs of the users of their services. Other factors include distribution costs or the perishability of a finished product.

Retail sales and services are usually found near the center of the markets they serve. Examples include fast-food restaurants, service stations, dry cleaners, and supermarkets. Quite often their products and those of their competitors are so similar that they rely on convenience to attract customers. Hence, these businesses seek locations with high population densities or high traffic. The competition/convenience factor is also important in locating banks, hotels and motels, auto repair shops, drugstores, newspaper kiosks, and shopping centers. Similarly, doctors, dentists, lawyers, barbers, and beauticians typically serve clients who reside within a limited area.

Competitive pressures for retail operations can be extremely vital factors. In some cases, a market served by a particular location may be too small to justify two or more competitors (e.g., one hamburger franchise per block), so that a search for potential locations tends to concentrate on locations without competitors. The opposite also might be true; it could be desirable to locate near competitors. Large department stores often locate near each other, and small stores like to locate in shopping centers that have large department stores as anchors. The large stores attract large numbers of shoppers who become potential customers in the smaller stores or in the other large stores.

Some firms must locate close to their markets because of the perishability of their products. Examples include bakeries, flower shops, and fresh seafood stores. For other types of firms, distribution costs are the main factor in closeness to market. For example, sand and gravel dealers usually serve a limited area because of the high distribution costs associated with their products. Still other firms require close customer contact, so they too tend to locate within the area they expect to serve. Typical examples are tailor shops, home remodelers, home repair services, cabinetmakers, rug cleaners, and lawn and garden services.

Locations of many government services are near the markets they are designed to serve. Hence, post offices are typically scattered throughout large metropolitan areas. Police and emergency health care locations are frequently selected on the basis of client needs. For instance, police patrols often concentrate on high crime areas, and emergency health care facilities are usually found in central locations to provide ready access from all directions.

Many foreign manufacturing companies have located manufacturing operations in the United States, because it is a major market for their products. Chief among them are automobile manufacturers, most notably Japanese, but other nations are also represented. Another possible reason that Japanese producers decided to locate in the United States was to offset possible negative consumer sentiment related to job losses of U.S. workers. Thousands of U.S. auto workers are now employed in U.S. manufacturing plants of Japanese and other foreign companies.

Software can be helpful in location analysis. For example, a **geographical information systems (GIS)** is a computer-based tool for collecting, storing, retrieving, and displaying demographic data on maps. The data might involve age, incomes, type of employment, type of housing, or other similar data. The maps can be global, national, regional, state or province, county, city, or town. Analysts have the ability to answer a number of questions that are either impossible to answer, or very time-consuming to answer, using more traditional methods.

geographical information system (GIS) A computer-based tool for collecting, storing, retrieving, and displaying demographic data on maps.

Labor Factors. Primary labor considerations are the cost and availability of labor, wage rates in an area, labor productivity and attitudes toward work, and whether unions are a serious potential problem.

Labor costs are very important for labor-intensive organizations. The shift of the textile industry from the New England states to southern states was due partly to labor costs.

Skills of potential employees may be a factor, although some companies prefer to train new employees rather than rely solely on previous experience. Increasing specialization in many industries makes this possibility even more likely than in the past. Although most companies concentrate on the supply of blue-collar workers, some firms are more interested in scientific and technical people as potential employees, and they look for areas with high concentrations of those types of workers.

Worker attitudes toward turnover, absenteeism, and similar factors may differ among potential locations—workers in large urban centers may exhibit different attitudes than workers in small towns or rural areas. Furthermore, worker attitudes in different parts of the country or in different countries may be markedly different.

Some companies offer their current employees jobs if they move to a new location. However, in many instances, employees are reluctant to move, especially when it means leaving families and friends. Furthermore, in families with two wage earners, relocation would require that one wage earner give up a job and then attempt to find another job in the new location.

Climate and taxes. Climate and taxes sometimes play a role in location decisions. For example, a string of unusually severe winters in northern states may cause some firms to seriously consider moving to a milder climate, especially if delayed deliveries and work disruptions caused by inability of employees to get to work have been frequent. Similarly, the business and personal income taxes in some states reduce their attractiveness to companies seeking new locations. Many companies have been attracted to some Sun Belt states by ample supplies of low-cost energy or labor, the climate, and tax considerations. Also, tax and monetary incentives are major factors in attracting or keeping professional sports franchises.

Foreign Locations. The growth in multinational operations over the past several decades is evidence of the importance of foreign locations. Some firms are attracted to foreign locations because of nearby deposits of aluminum, copper, timber, oil, or other natural resources. Other firms view foreign locations as a way to expand their markets, and still others are attracted by ample supplies of labor. Some countries may offer financial incentives to companies to create jobs for their people. Developing countries may establish tariffs to protect their young industries from outside competition, which may also reduce the amount of "foreign" competition a firm must face if it locates in such a country. Until the North American Free Trade Agreement eliminated restrictions, the Fisher-Price Toy Company factory in Matamoros, Mexico, was not allowed to sell in Mexico the Muppet toys it makes. U.S. companies with factories in Mexico could import raw materials duty-free, but they were required to export all of their output.

Many developing countries offer an abundant supply of cheap labor. For example, a considerable amount of the clothes sold in the United States bear labels indicating they were made in Korea, China, or Taiwan. In some instances, it is less expensive to ship raw materials or semifinished goods to foreign countries for fabrication and assembly, and then ship them to their final destinations, than it is to produce them in the United States. However, the final cost per unit is the most important factor. In some cases, the low cost of labor in a foreign country can be negated by low productivity and shipping costs.

High production costs in Germany have contributed to a number of German companies locating some of their production facilities in lower-cost countries. Among them are industrial products giant Siemens, A.G. (a semiconductor plant in Britain), drug makers Bayer, A.G. (a plant in Texas) and Hoechst, A.G. (a plant in China), and automakers Mercedes (plants in Spain, France, and Alabama), and BMW (a plant in Spartansburg, South Carolina).

A firm contemplating a foreign location must carefully weigh the potential benefits against the potential problems. A major factor is the stability of a country's government and its attitude toward American firms. Import restrictions can pose problems with bringing in equipment and spare parts.

Some of the problems of a foreign location can be caused by language and cultural differences between the United States and the host country. U.S. firms often find it necessary to use U.S. technical personnel but find it difficult to convince workers to move to a foreign country; workers may have to leave their families behind or else subject them to substandard housing or educational systems. Companies are now exerting additional efforts to reduce these obstacles. Some provide housing allowances and have schools for U.S. children. They are also improving their efforts to see that the employees they send abroad are familiar with local customs and have a reasonable facility with the language of the host country.

One factor that has negatively impacted the bottom line of some U.S. firms operating plants in foreign countries is the level of corruption present, erasing some of the envisioned benefits of lower labor or transportation costs.

READING

Not-So-Clear Choices: Should You Export, or Manufacture Overseas?
Russ Banham

Bob Moog has a child's imagination coupled with killer business instincts. When the board-games company he created in 1985 sought growth through global expansion 2 years later, Moog faced the usual two options: export the product or manufacture it overseas for local distribution. Moog chose the latter.

"We decided for a number of reasons to manufacture our board game, '20 Questions,' in Holland for distribution throughout Europe," said Moog, president of University Games Corp. of Burlingame, CA. Moog's company started with a $20,000 loan and spent its first two years in a 20 ft. by 30 ft. room sublet from the father of Moog's former girlfriend, before blossoming into a $50 million-per-year, international company.

International sales make up 8 percent of University Games revenue. Moog predicts that international sales will rise to 35 percent in the next 3 years because of new overseas ventures. This year, the company expanded into Australia. Unlike the

European ventures, however, Moog decided that it was more economical to import its products into Australia from the US manufacturing facility.

"Our anticipated initial sales in Australia just did not warrant a manufacturing operation there at this juncture," Moog said. "If sales pick up down the line, we may then examine local manufacturing."

Moog's dual strategy is not unique. One of the toughest questions a company confronts when pondering an international sales strategy is: to export, or not to export?

While exporting is often the least risky method of selling overseas, it frequently involves significant transportation, logistics, and tax-related costs that may make it uneconomical when compared with foreign manufacturing.

On the other hand, foreign manufacturing, while potentially a more competitive way of entering an overseas market has its own bugaboos. Political instability, fluctuating market conditions, and the huge capital costs to set up an overseas manufacturing operation are daunting challenges. Determining the best way to go often involves solving a perplexing conundrum. "It boils down to a trade-off between classic cost-and-time considerations and eco-political factors," said Richard Powers, president of Insight Inc., a provider of management support systems based in Bend, OR.

With exporting, a company must evaluate the various modes of transportation that would be involved in getting the goods there, and how this relates to the cycle time of putting the product in the marketplace. Some products are time-sensitive; others are less so.

On the other hand, if a company determines that an overseas manufacturing operation best meets its needs, it must examine the eco-political factors involved, such as tariff and duty drawbacks and international tax issues. "It may be less expensive, given these factors, for a company to incur the logistics costs of exporting than to risk the eco-political costs," Powers explained.

Trade-Offs and Traps

In addition to weighing these trade-offs, there are other related factors affecting the decision to either export or locate a plant overseas. To compete in their market, for example, some countries require that some form of local infrastructure be in place.

"Sometimes you run into government contracts where the only way to distribute a product in that country is to have it made locally," said Fred Ehrsam, vice president at Bain & Co., a Boston-based strategy consulting firm. "In China, for instance, you pretty much have to build something there in order to enter that market."

Certain products also dictate the international sales strategy to be taken. "If your company makes drinking glasses, you'll want to manufacture them in whatever country you plan to sell them," observed Scott Setrakian, a director in the San Francisco office of Mercer Management Consulting. "Drinking glasses, generally speaking, are pretty cheap to make and expensive to ship."

Political instability is another guiding force in a company's decision-making process. "If you want to sell in Russia, you're facing political instability as your biggest single operating risk," noted John Koopman, a principal in Mercer's Toronto office. "In Western Europe, this is not an issue. In Asia, there's a little risk, but in Russia it's a given." Other factors include time, the distance to the market, and price. Certain products require short lead times and, thus may best be delivered via a locally manufactured plant. "This is where you get into issues like transportation costs, tariffs and duties, labor expenses, and how much it costs to build a plant," Ehrsam explained.

The maturity of a company's product affects this decision. A product expected to require design changes, for example, may not fit well with foreign manufacturing plans. "It's pretty hard to implement changes to a product when the product is fairly far removed from the product development and engineering people," Ehrsam continued. "Tactically, you want to be moving products offshore that are relatively stable."

Another factor is the skill of the labor force in the market being considered. "You have to question whether or not the labor pool—no matter how low-cost—can be trained to do the things you need," Ehrsam added.

Best Laid Plans

Perhaps the best way for many companies to enter a foreign market is to first export there, but with an eye toward building overseas in the future. "Exporting will give you a feel for the product and its market potential," Powers said. "Instead of jumping in the lake head first, exporting allows you to get your toes wet. It may cost more, but you're able to hedge your risks."

Such a strategy worked well for IPSCO, Inc. In the early 1980s, the Regina Saskatchewan-based steel producer exported its steel pipe and flat steel to the United States from Canada—despite significant transportation costs. Once the company realized there was significant US demand for its products, it decided to set up shop there.

"Fundamentally it is very expensive to transport pipe steel from Canada to the United States," explained Mario Dalla-Vicenza, IPSCO senior vice president. "Unlike flat steel, which you're able to transport up to the maximum load-bearing capability of a railcar, pipe steel—because it is hollow—fills the volume of a railcar before it fills the maximum load-bearing capability. So, there's a fundamental freight cost disadvantage." To overcome this drawback and make the company more competitive with US pipe producers, IPSCO acquired pipe mills in Camanche, IA, and in Geneva, NE.

Other companies also have found it expedient to export first. "I used to work for a company called Mexx, a Netherlands-based fashion supplier," Koopman said. "We entered Australia, South Africa, and the Eastern bloc countries via an export strategy, and when that worked, we set up local warehousing and distribution subsidiaries."

Buying an overseas plant, as opposed to starting one de novo, is a high-stakes proposition for many companies. "The culture within the walls is critical with respect to the ongoing operation of the firm," Setrakian stated. He advises a joint venture with a prospective acquisition "as a way of feeling it out before buying it."

Some companies may follow two routes in this regard: acquiring a going venture in one country but starting one from scratch in another. Mercer Management, for example, built its overseas consulting business via both strategies. "In Europe, we concluded that there were sound opportunities to build by acquisition, while in Asia we felt the best way to proceed was by opening our own offices de novo," Setrakian said.

Mercer bought consulting firms in Germany, France, and Spain, but opened its own offices in Hong Kong and Singapore. "We felt Europe was a reasonably mature market with strong and well-grounded acquisition opportunities, but that similar opportunities did not exist in Asia," Setrakian added.

Companies seeking an international presence often must choose between [their] own dedicated sales force versus third-party agents doing the work for them. Others, such as University Games, follow an international sales strategy using third-party distributors.

"We identify the foreign markets we want to penetrate, and then form a business venture with a local distributor that will give us a large degree of control," Moog said. " In Australia, we expect to run a print of 5,000 board games. These we will manufacture in the US. If we reach a run of 25,000 games, however, we would then establish a sub-contracting venture with a local manufacturer in Australia or New Zealand to print the games." Smack dab between exporting and overseas manufacturing is another alternative: foreign product assembly. "Sometimes this is a better option because the duties in a particular country may be low on components but high on finished goods," Ehrsam said. "In a market in which a company has a fairly weak presence to begin with, it may actually be able to enjoy fairly good production and manufacturing costs by getting a local vendor to do the work for you."

CPC International favors full-scale overseas manufacturing to either foreign product assembly or exporting. "We rely on exporting chiefly as a means of entering a new marketplace," said Gale Griffin, vice president at the Englewood Cliffs, NJ-based food company. "We then like to move from an exporting environment into local manufacturing."

CPC manufactures much well-known food brands as Hellmann's Mayonnaise and the Knorr's line of soups. Altogether, the company manufactures in 62 of the 110 countries in which it markets its products.

CPC uses local personnel and managers almost exclusively when operating overseas. "We look for people who understand the markets and can compete very effectively within them," Griffin said. "They help you understand local government reg-

ulations, which can be tricky. We also let our local managers do their own marketing, figuring they know their own markets and how to compete there better than Englewood Cliffs does."

Mexx also sought out qualified locals to be its eyes and ears in a foreign market. "Such an individual can help develop the link between your business and the local marketplace," Koopman said. "Without this understanding of the local market, the risk of failure is tremendous."

Local relationships give local distributors and buyers peace of mind that they're dealing with a local company, he added. "You want to make the local buyer in France think he is dealing with a French company," Koopman said. "They want to feel they're dealing with the decision-maker, not some emissary from New York in another time zone."

Finding someone qualified to fill these shoes is as easy as calling an executive search firm or accessing the Internet. "There are many qualified people looking to represent all kinds of companies on the Net," Powers noted.

Power's company, Insight, offers a computer software model that can help companies find the right overseas representatives. Called the Global Supply Chain Model, the software guides companies through the maze of decisions required to develop an international sales strategy, from how many plants [are] needed to satisfy global markets to the best means to source products. The software costs $30,000, excluding consulting services. The task of finding a local rep should not be taken lightly, especially when it concerns finding someone to manage an overseas plant. "Having a plant manager who can create a culture from the ground up with the right discipline and values to develop a solid team of people is crucial to the success of the endeavor," Ehrsam said. "I've seen the best prepared and executed strategies succeed or fall to pieces on the basis of that one individual."

On the Ground

The litany of missteps by companies overeager to enter a foreign market makes entertaining reading. General Motors, for example, still winces at its decision to sell its Chevy Nova in Spain without pausing to consider that "nova" in Spanish translates into "doesn't go."

Other hastily made international sales strategies include K-Mart's decision to open a store in Singapore. The company's traditional and successful formula in the United States is to purchase land—usually on the perimeter of a town—at inexpensive prices. "In Singapore, such a large tract was unavailable at a cheap price, and the company ended up with an expensive location," Koopman said. "The strategy was not successful."

"If you're thinking of setting up shop overseas, assume that no matter how many things you thought of, there will be five you missed," Koopman advised. "At Mexx, for example, we learned that Frenchmen like their pants unfinished—so they can put cuffs on them. In Germany, however, 95 percent of pants are sold finished. There's a real danger exporting too far away from a market without someone on the ground to guide you."

While some elements making up an international sales strategy can be predicted with a degree of certainty, others—like currency exchange values—are capricious at best. "At Mexx, we planned twice to enter the Italian market," Koopman recalled. "In both cases, one week before we were set to launch our clothing line there, the Italian lira was devalued 20 percent—meaning our prices would increase by 20 percent. Both times we were forced to cancel our plans." Another unpredictable element is regulation. "A company may decide to set up shop in, say, Malaysia, because it considers the tariffs to be too high to export there successfully," Ehrsam said. "Next thing you know, the government of Malaysia decides to lower its tariffs significantly. Suddenly, you realize it may have been cheaper to export there rather than incur the huge capital costs of a plant."

Technology obsolescence and improvements in logistics play similar, unpredictable roles. A company may spend hundreds of thousands of dollars building a foreign facility weeks before a new automated manufacturing system renders its technology a buggy in an age of automobiles.

Moreover, a new way of moving goods faster, more efficiently and less expensively may materialize, reversing the status quo and making exporting a more cost-effective means of reaching a marketplace.

Ultimately, no matter which way a company chooses to enter a foreign market, it needs a pair of fleet feet. "It's very im-portant, especially with new economies, to get in as early as possible," Griffin counseled. "You want to establish market leadership for your brand, and the fact is, the first one there often has the best chance."

CPC should know: The company entered Eastern Europe within days of the fall of the Berlin Wall. It is now the market leader in much of the region.

"In Poland, we're number one in potato products, soups, and sauces; and number two in bouillons and mayonnaise," Griffin boasted.

Certainly, that's something to chew on.

Questions

1. What advantages and disadvantages does exporting have?

2. What advantages and disadvantages does foreign manufacturing have?

3. Explain this statement: "Perhaps the best way for many companies to enter a foreign market is to first export there, but with an eye toward building overseas in the future."

4. What are the advantages of employing local personnel and managers when operating overseas?

5. What relevance do currency exchange rates have for foreign trade?

6. What other factors might be relevant?

Source: *International Business,* November/December 1997, pp. 23–25.

COMMUNITY CONSIDERATIONS

Many communities actively try to attract new businesses because they are viewed as potential sources of future tax revenues and new job opportunities. However, communities do not, as a rule, want firms that will create pollution problems or otherwise lessen the quality of life in the community. Local groups may actively seek to exclude certain companies on such grounds, and a company may have to go to great lengths to convince local officials that it will be a "responsible citizen." Furthermore, some organizations discover that even though overall community attitude is favorable, there may still be considerable opposition to specific sites from nearby residents who object to possible increased levels of noise, traffic, or pollution. Examples of this include community resistance to airport expansion, changes in zoning, construction of nuclear facilities, and highway construction.

From a company standpoint, a number of factors determine the desirability of a community as a place for its workers and managers to live. They include facilities for education, shopping, recreation, transportation, religious worship, and entertainment; the quality of police, fire, and medical services; local attitudes toward the company; and the size of the community. Community size can be particularly important if a firm will be a major employer in the community; a future decision to terminate or reduce operations in that location could have a serious impact on the economy of a small community.

Other community-related factors are the cost and availability of utilities, environmental regulations, taxes (state and local, direct and indirect), and often a laundry list of enticements offered by state or local governments that can include bond issues, tax abatements, low-cost loans, grants, and worker training.

Geographical information systems are increasingly used as a valuable location and supply chain support. With the aid of satellite signals, this tracking device for cars and trucks can pinpoint a current location and direct drivers to their destinations in real time.

SITE-RELATED FACTORS

The primary considerations related to sites are land, transportation, and zoning or other restrictions.

Evaluation of potential sites may require consulting with engineers or architects, especially in the case of heavy manufacturing or the erection of large buildings or facilities with special requirements. Soil conditions, load factors, and drainage rates can be critical and often necessitate certain kinds of expertise in evaluation.

Because of the long-term commitment usually required, land costs may be secondary to other site-related factors, such as room for future expansion, current utility and sewer capacities—and any limitations on these that could hinder future growth—and sufficient parking space for employees and customers. In addition, for many firms access roads for trucks or rail spurs are important.

Industrial parks may be worthy alternatives for firms involved in light manufacturing or assembly, warehouse operations, and customer service facilities. Typically, the land is already developed—power, water, and sewer hookups have been attended to, and zoning restrictions do not require special attention. On the negative side, industrial parks may place restrictions on the kinds of activities that a company can conduct, which can limit options for future development of a firm's products and services as well as the processes it may consider. Sometimes stringent regulations governing the size, shape, and architectural features of buildings limit managerial choice in these matters. Also, there may not be an adequate allowance for possible future expansion.

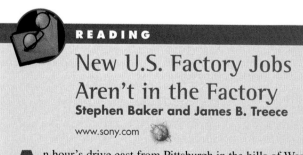

READING

New U.S. Factory Jobs Aren't in the Factory

Stephen Baker and James B. Treece

www.sony.com

An hour's drive east from Pittsburgh in the hills of Westmoreland County, Pa., stands a symbol of America's manufacturing renaissance. In 1988, the sprawling former auto assembly plant was abandoned, a Rust Belt relic, its workers scattered to other jobs or the unemployment rolls. Then two years ago, Sony Corp. arrived. Today, Westmoreland is one of the world's most advanced electronics plants, churning out thousands of big-screen television sets. And this is no border-style *maquiladora*, with Americans merely snapping together Japanese-made parts. Fully 80 percent of the components are U.S. made.

Why does Sony make televisions in Pennsylvania? The U.S. is the world's largest tv market by far, especially for big-screen versions, and the closer Sony gets to its customers, the less it has to spend on shipping.

Moreover, the U.S. has a strong industrial structure—wide roads, clean water, educated workers, and plenty of suppliers—and a superb technical base. Drawing on resources at nearby Carnegie-Mellon University helped Sony engineers build a robot that automatically fine-tunes the televisions before shipping.

Sony's plant is part of a fundamental shift in manufacturing—one that will leave the U.S. well positioned for global competition in the coming decades. Taking advantage of great economies of scale, manufacturers long built huge mass-production plants, then shipped their products to distant markets. But today, the trend is toward smaller, more flexible, less labor-intensive operations near the customers.

That's as true for steel and autos as it is for TV sets. Built close to their industrial customers the low-cost U.S. minimills run by Nucor Corp., Birmingham Steel Corp., and others are among the world's most efficient steel plants. In autos, U.S. production this year will surpass Japan's for the first time since 1979, thanks in part to more than a million Hondas, Nissans, and Toyotas pouring out of factories in Ohio, Tennessee, and Kentucky.

And it's not just currency swings and local-content concerns that lure manufacturers to the U.S. In no other market in the world do American, Asian, and European manufacturers compete so directly and freely. "If you are successful in the U.S., you are proving that you are a global player," says Helmut Werner, chairman of Mercedes-Benz. The company is setting up an assembly plant in Alabama.

Manuals in German

Don't expect the manufacturing renaissance in the U. S. to spark a boom in factory jobs, however. Just as the mechanization of agriculture a century ago all but emptied the farms, the new factory model means fewer workers are needed to put the final product together. The number of U.S. workers employed in manufacturing has fallen by 3.2 million since the peak of 21 million in 1979. Yet manufacturing output has remained stable as a percentage of gross national product. "We did not see any trends toward lower manufacturing activity," says economist Gordan Richards of the National Association of Manufacturers.

Yet as these factory jobs vanish, a new manufacturing-driven economic sector will emerge—industries such as computer software, robot making, and countless services that will add jobs to supply the leaner manufacturers. At Carnegie Group Inc. in Pittsburgh, technicians are putting together software to guide Ford Motor Co.'s engineers through circuit board design. And they devise programs that translate Caterpillar Inc.'s mountains of technical manuals into German, Russian, and other languages.

Carnegie Group is expanding from 125 to 200 workers this year alone. Says Chief Executive Dennis Yablonsky: "It's a wide universe of technology companies that service manufacturing. The jobs add up pretty quickly."

These support industries, with their high component of knowledge skills, constitute nothing less than a second tier of the manufacturing industries. "A smaller percentage of our workforce will be in production," comments Carnegie Mellon University professor Richard L. Florida. "But a much larger percentage will be supporting that."

These U.S. systems analysts, robot makers, and software engineers will increasingly be selling their wares around the globe. Indeed, 20 years after the much-ballyhooed deindustrialization of America, the U.S. keeps discovering new ways to make things.

Questions

1. What are three important reasons why foreign companies want to locate in the United States?

2. Does the addition of foreign manufacturers setting up manufacturing plants in the United States mean there will be a boom in factory jobs? Explain.

3. What kind of jobs and industries will increase due to the increase in manufacturing? What implications does this have for workers in the near future in terms of education?

Source: Baker, Stephen, and Treece, James B., "New U.S. Factory Jobs Aren't in the Factory," *Business Week*, Special 1994 Bonus Issue, p. 160. Reprinted with Permission.

For firms with executives who travel frequently, the size and proximity of the airport or train station as well as travel connections can be important, although schedules and connections are subject to change.

Table 8–1 provides a summary of the factors that affect location decisions.

MULTIPLE PLANT MANUFACTURING STRATEGIES

When companies have multiple manufacturing facilities, they can organize operations in several ways. One is to assign different product lines to different plants. Another is to assign different market areas to different plants. And a third is to assign different processes to different plants. Each strategy carries certain cost and managerial implications, as well as competitive advantages.

TABLE 8-1

Factors affecting location decisions

Level	Factors	Considerations
Regional	Location of raw materials or supplies	Proximity, modes and costs of transportation, quantity available
	Location of markets	Proximity, distribution costs, target market, trade practices/restrictions
	Labor	Availability (general and for specific skills), age distribution of workforce, work attitudes, union or nonunion, productivity, wage scales, unemployment compensation laws
Community	Quality of life	Schools, churches, shopping, housing, transportation, entertainment, recreation, cost of living
	Services	Medical, fire, and police
	Attitudes	Pro/con
	Taxes	State/local, direct and indirect
	Environmental regulations	State/local
	Utilities	Cost and availability
	Development support	Bond issues, tax abatement, low-cost loans, grants
Site	Land	Cost, degree of development required, soil characteristics and drainage, room for expansion, parking
	Transportation	Type (access roads, rail spurs, air freight)
	Environmental/legal	Zoning restrictions

Product Plant Strategy. With this strategy, entire products or product lines are produced in separate plants, and each plant usually supplies the entire domestic market. This is essentially a decentralized approach, with each plant focusing on a narrow set of requirements that entails specialization of labor, materials, and equipment along product lines. Specialization often results in economies of scale and, compared with multipurpose plants, lower operating costs. Plant locations may be widely scattered or clustered relatively close to one another.

Market Area Plant Strategy. With this strategy, plants are designed to serve a particular geographic segment of a market (e.g., the West Coast, the Northeast). Individual plants produce most if not all of a company's products and supply a limited geographical area. Although operating costs tend to be higher than those of product plants, significant savings on shipping costs for comparable products can be made. This arrangement is particularly desirable when shipping costs are high due to volume, weight, or other factors. Such arrangements have the added benefit of rapid delivery and response to local needs. This approach requires centralized coordination of decisions to add or delete plants, or to expand or downsize current plants due to changing market conditions.

Process Plant Strategy. With this strategy, different plants concentrate on different aspects of a process. Automobile manufacturers often use this approach, with different plants for engines, transmissions, body stamping, and even radiators. This approach is best suited to products that have numerous components; separating the production of components results in less confusion than if all production was carried out at the same location.

When an organization uses process plants, coordination of production throughout the system becomes a major issue and requires a highly informed, centralized administration to achieve effective operation. A key benefit is that individual plants are highly specialized and generate volumes that yield economies of scale.

Multiple plants have an additional benefit: the increase in learning opportunities that occurs when similar operations are being done in different plants. Similar problems tend

Mall of America in Minnesota is a four-level shopping mall, as well as a tourist destination. Unique features such as an amusement park, night clubs, a huge aquarium, and stock car races serve to draw customers and support anchor stores, such as Bloomingdale's, and a large variety of specialty shops.

www.mallofamerica.com

to arise, and solutions to those problems as well as improvements in general in products and processes made at one plant can be shared with other plants.

SERVICE AND RETAIL LOCATIONS

Service and retail are typically governed by somewhat different considerations than manufacturing organizations in making location decisions. For one thing, nearness to raw materials is usually not a factor, nor is concern about processing requirements. But customer access is usually a prime consideration. Manufacturers tend to be cost-focused, concerned with labor, energy, and material costs and availability, and distribution costs. Service and retail businesses tend to be revenue focused, concerned with demographics such as age, income, and education, population/drawing area, competition, traffic volume/patterns, and customer access/parking.

Retail and service organizations typically place traffic volume and convenience high on the list of important factors. Specific types of retail or service businesses may pay more attention to certain factors due to the nature of their business or their customers. If a business is unique, and has its own drawing power, nearness to competitors may not be a factor. However, generally retail businesses prefer locations that are near other retailers (although not necessarily competitors) because of the higher traffic volumes and convenience to customers. Thus, automobile dealerships often tend to locate near each other, and restaurants and specialty stores often locate in and around malls, benefiting from the high traffic.

Medical services are often located near hospitals for convenience of patients. Doctors' offices may be located near hospitals, or grouped in other, centralized areas with other doctors' offices. Available public transportation is often a consideration.

Good transportation and/or parking facilities can be vital to retail establishments. Downtown areas have a competitive disadvantage in attracting shoppers compared to malls because malls offer ample free parking and nearness to residential areas.

Customer safety and security can be key factors, particularly in urban settings, for all types of services that involve customers coming to the service location (as opposed, say, to in-home services such as home repair and rug cleaning).

Competitors' locations can be of significance. In some cases, firms will want to locate near competitors to benefit from the concentration of potential customers. Mall stores and auto dealers are good examples. In other cases, locating near similar businesses is not important because there are no competitors. And in some cases, it is important *not* to be near a competitor (e.g., another franchise operation of the same fast-food chain).

Vying for Patients, Hospitals Think Location, Location

Doreen Carvajal

The mood is as vital as the medicine at the elegant Upper East Side clinic squeezed among the fashionable addresses of Calvin Klein, Ralph Lauren and Barneys New York.

Silk magnolias bloom in the marble lobby, and abstract oil paintings dominate the pale rose corridors of Columbia-Presbyterian Medical Center's new satellite at East 60th Street and Madison Avenue.

The clinic is one of many ways for Columbia-Presbyterian to draw new patients for routine services as well as to feed its main hospital in Washington Heights for more complicated ones. A free shuttle regularly ferries the clinic's patients northwest along the Hudson River, an indirect route skirting Harlem on the way to the hospital, where the neighbors are not elegant boutiques, but the less fabled Self-Serve Laundromat and El Presidente cafeteria.

Location is becoming fiercely important to hospitals in New York's competitive medical marketplace as managed-care systems, so popular elsewhere, begin to take hold here. In the new world of fixed reimbursements, shorter hospital stays and tighter rationing of highly specialized services, hospitals must make their money from volume rather than from service fees.

The resulting battle for market share—and for new patients—is being waged not with scalpel and stethoscope, but with hammer and nails, in the neighborhoods where potential customers live.

"New York has been relatively slow to follow the rest of the country toward managed health care because it was so regulated," said Kenneth E. Raske, president of the Greater New York Hospital Association. "But they're here now. And they're going to have a profound influence on redrafting the map of New York health care."

Emerging as hospitals' most promising source of new patients are clinics like Columbia-Presbyterian Eastside, which, in health care jargon, are called "centers," lest potential patients confuse these gleaming outposts with conventional clinics that cater to the poor and uninsured. To attract middle-class patients wary of leaving their protected blocks, the city's huge hospitals are branching out to ethnic enclaves, upscale New York neighborhoods, affluent suburban communities, and even distant American expatriate communities in Eastern Europe.

Four months ago, Columbia-Presbyterian created a satellite in Moscow and more centers are planned for Warsaw, Prague, St. Petersburg, Budapest and possibly Beijing.

"Our feeling is that there will be no hospitals in the future," said Dr. William T. Speck, president of Columbia-Presbyterian. "And probably, in the next 10 or 20 years most of the activity will take place in a center or maybe even in homes."

Hospital executives contend that satellites, which typically have no beds and no provision for round-the-clock care, are cheaper to operate than highly specialized hospitals, which provide all the incidental services of a hotel. Babies, for instance, can be delivered at alternative sites for half a hospital's $9,000 fee, Dr. Speck said.

Not surprisingly, Columbia-Presbyterian is planning a birthing center just a block away from its Madison Avenue location.

Among the questions that should be considered are the following:

1. How can sales, market share, and profit be optimized for the entire set of locations? Solutions might include some combination of upgrading facilities, expanding some sites, adding new outlets, and closing or changing the locations of some outlets.

2. What are the potential sales to be realized from each potential solution?

3. Where should outlets be located to maximize market share, sales, and profits without negatively impacting other outlets? This can be a key cause of friction between the operator of a franchise store and the franchising company.

4. What probable effects would there be on market share, sales, and profits if a competitor located nearby?

Table 8–2 briefly compares service/retail site selection criteria with manufacturing criteria.

Global Locations

Recent trends in locating facilities, particularly manufacturing facilities, reflect a combination of competitive and technological factors. One trend has been that of foreign producers,

Manufacturing/Distribution	Service/Retail
Cost focus	**Revenue focus**
Transportation modes/costs	Demographics: age, income, education
Energy availability/costs	Population/drawing area
Labor cost/availability/skills	Competition
Building/leasing costs	Traffic volume/patterns
	Customer access/parking

TABLE 8–2

A comparison of service/retail considerations and manufacturing considerations

Foreign Government	a. Policies on foreign ownership of production facilities
	Local content requirements
	Import restrictions
	Currency restrictions
	Environment regulations
	Local product standards
	b. Stability issues
Cultural Differences	Living circumstances for foreign workers and their dependents
	Religious holidays/traditions
Customer Preferences	Possible "buy locally" sentiment
Labor	Level of training and education of workers
	Work practices
	Possible regulations limiting number of foreign employees
	Language differences
Resources	Availability and quality of raw materials, energy, transportation

TABLE 8–3

Factors relating to foreign locations

especially automotive firms, to locate plants in the United States. The United States represents a tremendous market for cars, trucks, and recreational vehicles. By locating in the United States, these firms can shorten delivery time and reduce delivery costs. Furthermore, they can avoid any future tariffs or quotas that might be applied to imports.

A development that affects location decisions was the passage of GATT in 1994. One of its provisions was the reduction and elimination of various tariffs. Consequently, location within the borders of a country to escape tariffs is now much less of an issue.

An ethical issue has been the use of "sweatshops," which employ workers at low wages in poor working conditions. Consumer protests have caused a number of companies to cease this practice.

Another trend is just-in-time manufacturing techniques (see Chapter 16), which encourage suppliers and customers to locate near each other to reduce supplier lead times. For this reason, some U.S. firms are reconsidering decisions to locate offshore. Moreover, in light manufacturing (e.g., electronics), low-cost labor is becoming less important than nearness to markets; users of electronics components want suppliers that are close to their manufacturing facilities. One offshoot of this is the possibility that the future will see a trend toward smaller factories located close to markets. In some industries, small, automated **microfactories** with narrow product focuses will be located near major markets to reduce response time.

It is likely that advances in information technology will enhance the ability of manufacturing firms to gather, track, and distribute information that links purchasing, marketing, and distribution with design, engineering, and manufacturing. This will reduce the need for these functions to be located close together, thereby permitting a strategy of locating production facilities near major markets.

Table 8–3 above provides a checklist of considerations pertaining to decisions on global operations.

microfactory Small factory with a narrow product focus, located near major markets.

READING

Global Strategy: GM Is Building Plants in Developing Nations to Woo New Markets

Rebecca Blumenstein

www.gm.com

ROSARIO, Argentina—On the outskirts of this city more than 6,000 miles from Detroit, bulldozers have been running around the clock moving the fertile topsoil to make way for a General Motors Corp. auto-assembly plant of tomorrow.

The state-of-the-art plant, on a remote road in what had been a remote part of the automotive world, is at the center of GM's aggressive shift away from its roots in North America to the developing world. GM is quietly building so many plants in so many corners of the world that the No. 1 automaker has decided to save money by building essentially the same plant in Argentina, Poland, China and Thailand—simultaneously.

This "four-plant strategy" is GM's biggest international expansion, costing at least $2.2 billion. The company has designed the plants to look so much alike that engineers may mistake which country they are in. And the assembly lines are being set up so that a glitch in a robot in Thailand, rather than turning into an expensive engineering problem that requires an expert for each machine at each plant, may well be solved by a quick call to Rosario or to Shanghai, China.

Expandable and Efficient

But the significance of GM's new plants extends much further. They are being built to be easily expandable as demand in developing markets grows. And they are being laid out in a giant U-shape so that suppliers can cart in an increasing array of already assembled parts to cut GM's costs, something GM can't do in the U.S. because of union resistance.

The new factories illustrate, more than anything else, how the nature of multinational corporations is changing as today's marketplace turns global. Just a few years ago, GM's South American plants were churning out Chevy Chevettes that hadn't been produced in the U.S. for years. The auto industry viewed the world largely as a dumping ground for obsolete technology and outdated models.

Now, the industry is seeking future growth by concentrating its investments in the developing world and turning it into a showcase for the latest in technology and lean manufacturing. And GM is pursuing that global strategy more vigorously than any of its rivals, though every other major auto maker sees the need to tap into emerging markets, and some have a substantial foreign presence. Nobody, however, is building plants on the scale of GM, which recently announced plans for a fifth and even more advanced new plant, in southern Brazil.

The entire Rosario plant is designed to be lean. Its total cost, at $350 million, is one of the lowest for a new GM plant; $1 billion had been the rule-of-thumb price tag for a new assembly plant of any size. Moreover, the investment here includes a high-tech stamping machine that will press metal parts more quickly than any other GM press and an engine plant that will deliver to the assembly line engines with air conditioning, transmission and belts already installed.

Workers will do many tasks, a key principle of lean manufacturing, and will be assigned to teams working autonomously. Every worker will be responsible for an entire process in the assembly operation, including even the cleaning and basic maintenance of machines. In Japan, that is a common approach, but it is inconceivable in a GM plant in the U.S. because of union work rules, which allow only specified categories of skilled workers to repair and maintain machines.

Although the four plants are designed to be as similar as possible, they do have differences, ranging from efforts to protect machines from rusting in Thailand's humid climate to China's poor transportation system. There, Mr. Stevens says, "We are going to have things delivered to our Shanghai plant by bicycle."

Questions

1. Briefly describe GM's four-plant strategy.

2. What are some signs of GM's shift in global thinking?

3. List the lean manufacturing elements of the Rosario plant.

4. What are some nonlabor local conditions that had to be taken into consideration in designing individual plants?

Two other factors are causing companies to locate manufacturing facilities in countries that contain their markets (e.g., Japanese auto companies establishing factories in the United States). One is to counter negative sentiments such as "not made in this country." Thus, Japanese factories in the United States produce cars made by U.S. workers. The second factor relates to currency fluctuations and devaluations. These changes can have a significant impact on demand and, hence, on profits. Changes in currency value alter the price of foreign goods, but not the price of goods produced within a country. For instance, if the value of a country's currency falls relative to that of other countries, prices within the country don't change, but foreign-produced goods become more expensive. If demand is elastic, then demand for those foreign goods will fall. Furthermore, currency changes may result in increased costs of parts supplied by foreign producers. By locating and selling within a country, and buying from suppliers in that country, manufacturers can avoid the impact of currency changes.

Evaluating Location Alternatives

There are a number of techniques that are helpful in evaluating location alternatives: locational cost-profit-volume analysis, factor rating, and the center of gravity method.

LOCATIONAL COST-PROFIT-VOLUME ANALYSIS

The economic comparison of location alternatives is facilitated by the use of cost-volume-profit analysis. The analysis can be done numerically or graphically. The graphical approach will be demonstrated here because it enhances understanding of the concept and indicates the ranges over which one of the alternatives is superior to the others.

The procedure for **locational cost-profit-volume analysis** involves these steps:

1. Determine the fixed and variable costs associated with each location alternative.
2. Plot the total-cost lines for all location alternatives on the same graph.
3. Determine which location will have the lowest total cost for the expected level of output. Alternatively, determine which location will have the highest profit.

This method assumes the following:

1. Fixed costs are constant for the range of probable output.
2. Variable costs are linear for the range of probable output.
3. The required level of output can be closely estimated.
4. Only one product is involved.

For a cost analysis, compute the total cost for each location:

$$\text{Total cost} = FC + v \times Q \qquad (8-1)$$

where

FC = Fixed cost
v = Variable cost per unit
Q = Quantity or volume of output

> **locational cost-profit-volume analysis** Technique for evaluating location choices in economic terms.

Fixed and variable costs for four potential plant locations are shown below:

> **Example 1**

Location	Fixed Cost per Year	Variable Cost per Unit
A	$250,000	$11
B	100,000	30
C	150,000	20
D	200,000	35

a. Plot the total-cost lines for these locations on a single graph.
b. Identify the range of output for which each alternative is superior (i.e., has the lowest total cost).
c. If expected output at the selected location is to be 8,000 units per year, which location would provide the lowest total cost?

Solution

a. To plot the total-cost lines, select an output that is approximately equal to the expected output level (e.g., 10,000 units per year). Compute the total cost for each location at that level:

	Fixed Cost	+	Variable Cost	=	Total Cost
A . . .	$250,000	+	$11(10,000)	=	$360,000
B . . .	100,000	+	30(10,000)	=	400,000
C . . .	150,000	+	20(10,000)	=	350,000
D . . .	200,000	+	35(10,000)	=	550,000

Plot each location's fixed cost (at Output = 0) and the total cost at 10,000 units; and connect the two points with a straight line. (See the accompanying graph.)

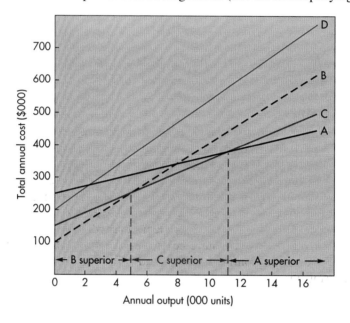

b. The *approximate* ranges for which the various alternatives will yield the lowest costs are shown on the graph. Note that location D is never superior. The *exact* ranges can be determined by finding the output level at which lines B and C and lines C and A cross. To do this, set their total cost equations equal and solve for Q, the break-even output level. Thus, for B and C:

$$\begin{matrix} (B) & & (C) \end{matrix}$$
$$\$100,000 + \$30Q = \$150,000 + \$20Q$$

Solving, you find $Q = 5,000$ units per year.

For C and A:

$$\begin{matrix} (C) & & (A) \end{matrix}$$
$$\$150,000 + \$20Q = \$250,000 + \$11Q$$

Solving, $Q = 11,111$ units per year.

c. From the graph, you can see that for 8,000 units per year, location C provides the lowest total cost.

For a profit analysis, compute the total profit for each location:

$$\text{Total profit} = Q(R - vC) - FC \tag{8–2}$$

where

R = Revenue per unit

Solved Problem 2 at the end of the chapter illustrates profit analysis.

Where the expected level of output is close to the middle of the range over which one alternative is superior, the choice is readily apparent. If the expected level of output is very close to the edge of a range, it means that the two alternatives will yield comparable annual costs, so management would be indifferent in choosing between the two *in terms of total cost*. However, it is important to recognize that, in most situations, other factors besides cost must also be considered. Later in this section, a general scheme for including a broad range of factors is described. First, let's consider another kind of cost often considered in location decisions: transportation costs.

THE TRANSPORTATION MODEL

Transportation costs sometimes play an important role in location decisions. These can stem from the movement of either raw materials or finished goods. If a facility will be the sole source or destination of shipments, the company can include the transportation costs in a locational cost-volume analysis by incorporating the transportation cost per unit being shipped into the variable cost per unit. (If raw materials are involved, the transportation cost must be converted into cost per unit of *output* in order to correspond to other variable costs.)

When a problem involves shipment of goods from multiple sending points to multiple receiving points, and a new location (sending or receiving point) is to be added to the system, the company should undertake a separate analysis of transportation. In such instances the *transportation model* of linear programming is very helpful. It is a special-purpose algorithm used to determine the minimum transportation cost that would result if a potential new location were to be added to an existing system. It can also be used if a *number* of new facilities are to be added or if an entire new system is being developed. The model is used to analyze each of the configurations considered, and it reveals the minimum costs each entails. This information can then be included in the evaluation of location alternatives. Solved Problem 1 illustrates how results of a transportation analysis can be combined with the results of a locational cost-volume analysis. See also the chapter supplement.

FACTOR RATING

A typical location decision involves both qualitative and quantitative inputs, which tend to vary from situation to situation depending on the needs of each organization. **Factor rating** is a general approach that is useful for evaluating a given alternative and comparing alternatives. The value of factor rating is that it provides a rational basis for evaluation and facilitates comparison among alternatives by establishing a *composite* value for each alternative that summarizes all related factors. Factor rating enables decision makers to incorporate their personal opinions and quantitative information in the decision process.

factor rating General approach to evaluating locations that includes quantitative and qualitative inputs.

The following procedure is used to develop a factor rating:

1. Determine which factors are relevant (e.g., location of market, water supply, parking facilities, revenue potential).

2. Assign a weight to each factor that indicates its relative importance compared with all other factors. Typically, weights sum to 1.00.

3. Decide on a common scale for all factors (e.g., 0 to 100).

4. Score each location alternative.

5. Multiply the factor weight by the score for each factor, and sum the results for each location alternative.

6. Choose the alternative that has the highest composite score.

This procedure is illustrated in the next example.

Example 2

A photo-processing company intends to open a new branch store. The table below contains information on two potential locations. Which is the better alternative?

Solution

Factor	Weight	SCORES (OUT OF 100) Alt. 1	Alt. 2	WEIGHTED SCORES Alternative 1	Alternative 2
Proximity to existing store	.10	100	60	.10(100) = 10.0	.10(60) = 6.0
Traffic volume	.05	80	80	.05(80) = 4.0	.05(80) = 4.0
Rental costs	.40	70	90	.40(70) = 28.0	.40(90) = 36.0
Size	.10	86	92	.10(86) = 8.6	.10(92) = 9.2
Layout	.20	40	70	.20(40) = 8.0	.20(70) = 14.0
Operating costs	.15	80	90	.15(80) = 12.0	.15(90) = 13.5
	1.00			70.6	82.7

Alternative 2 is better because it has the higher composite score.

In some cases, managers may prefer to establish minimum *thresholds* for composite scores. If an alternative fails to meet that minimum, they can reject it without further consideration. If none of the alternatives meets the minimum, this means that either additional alternatives must be identified and evaluated or the minimum threshold must be reevaluated.

THE CENTER OF GRAVITY METHOD

center of gravity method
Method for locating a distribution center that minimizes distribution cost.

The **center of gravity method** is a method to determine the location of a distribution center that will minimize distribution costs. It treats distribution cost as a linear function of the distance and the quantity shipped. The quantity to be shipped to each destination is assumed to be fixed (i.e., will not change over time). An acceptable variation is that quantities are allowed to change, as long as their relative amounts remain the same (e.g., seasonal variations).

The method includes the use of a map that shows the locations of destinations. The map must be accurate and drawn to scale. A coordinate system is overlaid on the map to determine relative locations. The location of the 0,0 point of the coordinate system, and its scale, is unimportant. Once the coordinate system is in place, you can determine the coordinates of each destination. (See Figure 8–1, parts a and b.)

If the quantities to be shipped to every location are *equal,* you can obtain the coordinates of the center of gravity (i.e., the location of the distribution center) by finding the average of the x coordinates and the average of the y coordinates (see Figure 8–1). These averages can be easily determined using the following formulas:

$$\bar{x} = \frac{\sum x_i}{n}$$

$$\bar{y} = \frac{\sum y_i}{n}$$

(8–3)

where

x_i = x coordinate of destination i

y_i = y coordinate of destination i

n = number of destinations

When the number of units to be shipped are not the same for all destinations (usually the case), a *weighted average* must be used to determine the center of gravity, with the weights being the *quantities* to be shipped.

a. Map showing destination.

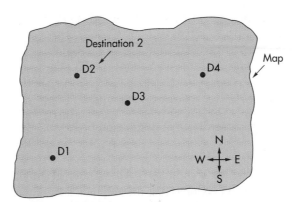

FIGURE 8-1

Center of gravity method
a. *Map showing destination.*
b. *Add a coordinate system.*
c. *Center of gravity.*

b. Add a coordinate system.

c. Center of gravity.

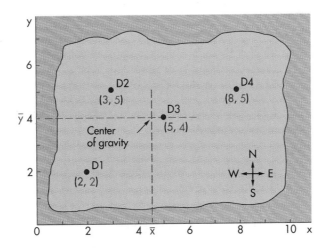

The appropriate formulas are:

$$\bar{x} = \frac{\sum x_i Q_i}{\sum Q_i} \qquad\qquad (8\text{–}4)$$

$$\bar{y} = \frac{\sum y_i Q_i}{\sum Q_i}$$

where

Q_i = Quantity to be shipped to destination i

x_i = x coordinate of destination i

y_i = y coordinate of destination i

Example 3

Determine the coordinates of the center of gravity for the problem that is depicted in Figure 8–1c. Assume that the shipments from the center of gravity to each of the four destinations will be equal quantities.

Solution

The coordinates of the destinations can be obtained from Figure 8–1b:

$$\bar{x} = \frac{\sum x_i}{n} = \frac{18}{4} \qquad \bar{y} = \frac{\sum y_i}{n} = \frac{16}{4}$$
$$= 4.5 \qquad\qquad\qquad = 4$$

Destination	x, y
D1	2, 2
D2	3, 5
D3	5, 4
D4	8, 5
	18, 16

Hence, the center of gravity is at (4.5, 4), which places it just west of destination D3 (see Figure 8–1).

Example 4

Suppose that the shipments for the problem depicted in Figure 8–1a are not all equal, but instead are the following:

Destination	x, y	Weekly Quantity
D1	2, 2	800
D2	3, 5	900
D3	5, 4	200
D4	8, 5	100
		2,000

Determine the center of gravity.

Solution

Because the quantities to be shipped differ among destinations, you must use the weighted average formulas.

$$\bar{x} = \frac{\sum x_i Q_i}{\sum Q_i} = \frac{2(800) + 3(900) + 5(200) + 8(100)}{2,000} = \frac{6,100}{2,000} = 3.05 \ [\text{round to } 3]$$

$$\bar{y} = \frac{\sum y_i Q_i}{\sum Q_i} = \frac{2(800) + 5(900) + 4(200) + 5(100)}{2,000} = \frac{7,400}{2,000} = 3.7$$

Hence, the coordinates of the center of gravity are approximately (3, 3.7). This would place it south of destination D2, which has coordinates of 3, 5). (See Figure 8–2.)

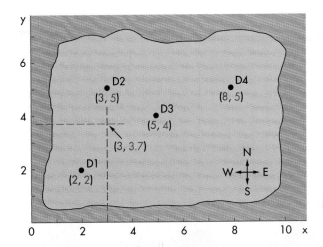

FIGURE 8-2

Center of gravity for Example 4

Summary

Location decisions confront both new and existing organizations. Growth, market shifts, depletion of raw materials, and the introduction of new products and services are among the reasons organizations are concerned with location decisions. The importance of these decisions is underscored by the long-term commitment they typically involve and by their potential impact on the operating system.

The primary location options available to existing organizations are to expand an existing location, move to a new location, maintain existing facilities while adding another facility in a new location, or do nothing.

In practice, the major influences on location decisions are location of raw materials, labor supply, market considerations, community-related factors, site-related factors, and climate. Foreign locations may be attractive in terms of labor costs, abundance of raw materials, or as potential markets for a firm's products or services. Problems organizations sometimes encounter in foreign countries include language differences, cultural differences, bias, and political instability.

A common approach to narrowing the range of location alternatives is to first identify a country or region that seems to satisfy overall needs and then identify a number of community-site alternatives for more in-depth analysis. A variety of methods are used to evaluate location alternatives. Those described in the chapter include locational cost-profit-volume analysis, factor rating, and the center of gravity method. The transportation model was mentioned briefly; the chapter supplement contains a more complete description of that subject.

There are numerous commercial software packages available for location analysis. In addition to the models described, many packages employ linear programming or mixed integer programming algorithms. In addition, some software packages use heuristic approaches to obtain reasonable solutions to location problems.

Key Terms

center of gravity method, 376
factor rating, 375
geographical information system (GIS), 361

locational cost-profit-volume analysis, 373
microfactory, 371

Solved Problems

Problem 1

Cost analysis. A farm implements dealer is seeking a fourth warehouse location to complement three existing warehouses. There are three potential locations: Charlotte, N.C.; Atlanta, Ga.; and Columbia, S.C. Charlotte would involve a fixed cost of $4,000 per month and a variable cost of $4 per unit; Atlanta would involve a fixed cost of $3,500 per month and a variable cost of $5 per unit; and Columbia would involve a fixed cost of $5,000 per month and a variable cost of $6 per unit. Use of the Charlotte location would increase system transportation costs by $19,000 per month, Atlanta by $22,000 per month, and Columbia by $18,000 per month. Which location would result in the lowest total cost to handle 800 units per month?

Solution

Given: Volume = 800 units per month

	FC per Month	Variable Cost per Unit, v	Transportation Cost per Month
Charlotte	$4,000	$4	$19,000
Atlanta	3,500	5	22,000
Columbia	5,000	6	18,000

Monthly total cost = FC + VC + Transportation cost

Charlotte: $4,000 + $4 per unit × 800 units + $19,000 = $26,200
Atlanta:　 3,500 + 5 per unit × 800 units + 22,000 = 29,500
Columbia: 5,000 + 6 per unit × 800 units + 18,000 = 27,800

Hence, Charlotte would have the lowest total cost for this monthly volume.

Problem 2

Profit analysis. A manufacturer of staplers is about to lose its lease, so it must move to another location. Two sites are currently under consideration. Fixed costs would be $8,000 per month at site A and $9,400 per month at site B. Variable costs are expected to be $5 per unit at site A and $4 per unit at site B. Monthly demand has been steady at 8,800 units for the last several years and is not expected to deviate from that amount in the foreseeable future. Assume staplers sell for $6 per unit. Determine which location would yield the higher profit under these conditions.

Solution

Profit = $Q(R - v) -$ FC

Site	Revenue	FC	v	Monthly Profit
A	$52,800	$8,000	$44,000	$ 800
B	$52,800	$9,400	$35,200	$8,200

Hence, site B is expected to yield the higher monthly profit.

Problem 3

Factor rating. Determine which location has the highest factor rating given the following information:

		LOCATION	
Factor	Weight	A	B
Labor cost	.50	20	40
Material cost	.30	10	30
Supplier base	.20	50	10
	1.00		

Solution

Combining the weights with the location scores, we can see that location B has the higher score:

		LOCATION		WEIGHTED SCORES	
Factor	Weight	A	B	A	B
Labor cost	.50	20	40	.50(20) = 10	.50(40) = 20
Material cost	.30	10	30	.30(10) = 3	.30(30) = 9
Supplier base	.20	50	10	.20(50) = 10	.20(10) = 2
	1.00			23	31

1. In what ways can the location decision have an impact on the production system?
2. Respond to this statement: "The importance of the location decision is often vastly overrated; the fact that virtually every type of business is located in every section of the country means there should be no problem in finding a suitable location."
3. What community factors influence location decisions?
4. How are manufacturing and nonmanufacturing location decisions similar? Different?
5. What are the potential benefits of locating in foreign countries? Potential drawbacks?
6. What is factor rating, and how does it work?
7. Outline the general approach for developing location alternatives.
8. What are the basic assumptions in locational cost-profit-volume analysis?
9. Discuss recent trends in location and possible future strategies.

1. You must decide which of several sites will be best for the location of a third restaurant in the company's chain in a suburb of a medium-sized city. Write a one-page memo to your employee, Jim Watson, outlining the information you will need from him before you can analyze the location alternatives.
2. You have been asked to provide a location analysis on whether your company should expand an existing manufacturing plant or close the plant and move to a larger plant recently vacated by a bankrupt firm. Write a one-page memo to your supervisor, Karen Saunders, outlining the factors you will consider in your analysis.

1. A newly formed firm must decide on a plant location. There are two alternatives under consideration: locate near the major raw materials or locate near the major customers. Locating near the raw materials will result in lower fixed and variable costs than locating near the market, but the owners believe there would be a loss in sales volume because customers tend to favor local suppliers. Revenue per unit will be $185 in either case. Using the following information, determine which location would produce the greater profit.

	Omaha	Kansas City
Annual fixed costs ($ millions)	$1.2	$1.4
Variable cost per unit	$36	$47
Expected annual demand (units)	8,000	12,000

2. The owner of Genuine Subs, Inc., hopes to expand the present operation by adding one new outlet. She has studied three locations. Each would have the same labor and materials costs (food, serving containers, napkins, etc.) of $1.76 cents per sandwich. Sandwiches sell for $2.65 each in all locations. Rent and equipment costs would be $5,000 per month for location A, $5,500 per month for location B, and $5,800 per month for location C.

   a. Determine the volume necessary at each location to realize a monthly profit of $10,000.

   b. If expected sales at A, B, and C are 21,000 per month, 22,000 per month, and 23,000 per month, respectively, which location would yield the greatest profits?

3. A small producer of machine tools wants to move to a larger building, and has identified two alternatives. Location A has annual fixed costs of $800,000 and variable costs of $14,000 per unit; location B has annual fixed costs of $920,000 and variable costs of $13,000 per unit. The finished items sell for $17,000 each.

   a. At what volume of output would the two locations have the same total cost?

   b. For what range of output would location A be superior? For what range would B be superior?

4. A company that produces pleasure boats has decided to expand one of its lines. Current facilities are insufficient to handle the increased workload, so the company is considering three alternatives, A (new location), B (subcontract), and C (expand existing facilities).

    Alternative A would involve substantial fixed costs but relatively low variable costs: fixed costs would be $250,000 per year, and variable costs would be $500 per boat. Subcontracting would involve a cost per boat of $2,500, and expansion would require an annual fixed cost of $50,000 and a variable cost of $1,000 per boat.

    a. Find the range of output for each alternative that would yield the lowest total cost.

    b. Which alternative would yield the lowest total cost for an expected annual volume of 150 boats?

    c. What other factors might be considered in choosing between expansion and subcontracting?

5. Rework Problem 4b using this additional information: Expansion would result in an increase of $70,000 per year in transportation costs, subcontracting would result in an increase of $25,000 per year, and adding a new location would result in an increase of $4,000 per year.

6. A firm that has recently experienced an enormous growth rate is seeking to lease a small plant in Memphis, Tenn., Biloxi, Miss., or Birmingham, Ala. Prepare an economic analysis of the three locations given the following information: Annual costs for building, equipment, and administration would be $40,000 for Memphis, $60,000 for Biloxi, and $100,000 for Birmingham. Labor and materials are expected to be $8 per unit in Memphis, $4 per unit in Biloxi, and $5 per unit in Birmingham. The Memphis location would increase system transportation costs by $50,000 per year, the Biloxi location by $60,000 per year, and the Birmingham location by $25,000 per year. Expected annual volume is 10,000 units.

7. A retired auto mechanic hopes to open a rustproofing shop. Customers would be local new-car dealers. Two locations are being considered, one in the center of the city and one on the outskirts. The central city location would involve fixed monthly costs of $7,000 and labor, materials, and transportation costs of $30 per car. The outside location would have fixed monthly costs of $4,700 and labor, materials, and transportation costs of $40 per car. Dealer price at either location will be $90 per car.

    a. Which location will yield the greatest profit if monthly demand is (1) 200 cars? (2) 300 cars?

    b. At what volume of output will the two sites yield the same monthly profit?

8. For each of the four types of organizations shown, rate the importance of each factor in terms of making location decisions using L = low importance, M = moderate importance, and H = high importance.

Factor	Local Bank	Steel Mill	Food Ware-house	Public School
Convenience for customers	_____	_____	_____	_____
Attractiveness of building	_____	_____	_____	_____
Nearness to raw materials	_____	_____	_____	_____
Large amounts of power	_____	_____	_____	_____
Pollution controls	_____	_____	_____	_____
Labor cost and availability	_____	_____	_____	_____
Transportation costs	_____	_____	_____	_____
Construction costs	_____	_____	_____	_____

9. Using the following factor ratings, determine which location alternative should be chosen on the basis of maximum composite score, A, B, or C.

Factor (100 points each)	Weight	LOCATION		
		A	**B**	**C**
Convenient	.15	80	70	60
Parking facilities	.20	72	76	92
Display area	.18	88	90	90
Shopper traffic	.27	94	86	80
Operating costs	.10	98	90	82
Neighborhood	.10	96	85	75
	1.00			

10. A manager has received an analysis of several cities being considered for a new office complex. The data (10 points maximum) are

Factor	LOCATION		
	A	**B**	**C**
Business services	9	5	5
Community services .	7	6	7
Real estate cost	3	8	7
Construction costs . . .	5	6	5
Cost of living	4	7	8
Taxes	5	5	4
Transportation	6	7	8

  a. If the manager weights the factors equally, how would the locations stack up?

  b. If business services and construction costs are given weights that are double the weights of the other factors, how would the locations stack up?

11. A toy manufacturer produces toys in five locations throughout the country. Raw materials (primarily barrels of powdered plastic) will be shipped from a new, centralized warehouse whose location is to be determined. The monthly quantities to be shipped to each location are the same. A coordinate system has been established, and the coordinates of each location have been determined as shown. Determine the coordinates of the centralized warehouse.

Location	(x, y)
A	3, 7
B	8, 2
C	4, 6
D	4, 1
E	6, 4

12. A clothing manufacturer produces women's clothes at four locations in Mexico. Relative locations have been determined, as shown in the table below. The location of a central shipping point for bolts of cloth must now be determined. Weekly quantities to be shipped to each location are shown below. Determine the coordinates of the location that will minimize distribution costs.

Location	(x, y)	Weekly Quantity
A	5, 7	15
B	6, 9	20
C	3, 9	25
D	9, 4	30

13. A company that handles hazardous waste wants to minimize the shipping cost for shipments to a disposal center from five receiving stations it operates. Given the locations of the receiving stations and the volumes to be shipped daily, determine the location of the disposal center.

Location of Processing Station, (x, y)	Volume, Tons per Day
10, 5	26
4, 1	9
4, 7	25
2, 6	30
8, 7	40

14. Determine the center of gravity for the destinations shown on the following map. Monthly shipments will be the quantities listed in the table.

Destination	Quantity
D1	900
D2	300
D3	700
D4	600
D5	800

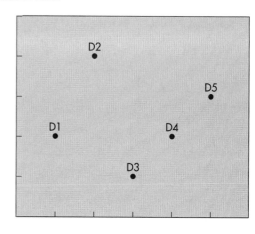

Selected Bibliography and Further Reading

Ballou, Ronald H. *Business Logistics Management,* 4th ed. Englewood Cliffs, NJ: Prentice Hall, 1999.

Francis, Richard L., Leon F. McGinnis Jr., and John A. White. *Layout and Location: An Analytical Approach,* 3rd ed. Englewood Cliffs, NJ: Prentice Hall, 1998.

Grimshaw, David J. *Bringing Geographical Information Systems into Business.* New York: John Wiley & Sons, 2000.

Lyne, Jack. "Quality-of-Life Factors Dominate Many Facility Location Decisions." *Site Selection Handbook.* August, 1988, pp. 868–70.

The Transportation Model

SUPPLEMENT OUTLINE

Introduction, 386

Location Decisions, 386

Other Applications, 387

Computer Solutions, 388

Problems, 388

Bibliography and Further
Reading, 390

LEARNING OBJECTIVES

*After completing this supplement,
you should be able to:*

1 Describe the nature of a
transportation problem.

2 Set up transportation problems in
the general linear programming
format.

3 Interpret computer solutions.

The transportation problem involves finding the lowest-cost plan for distributing stocks of goods or *supplies* from multiple origins to multiple destinations that *demand* the goods. For instance, a firm might have three factories, all of which are capable of producing identical units of the same product, and four warehouses that stock or demand those products, as depicted in Figure 8S–1. The *transportation model* can be used to determine how to allocate the supplies available from the various factories to the warehouses that stock or demand those goods, in such a way that total shipping cost is minimized. Usually, analysis of the problem will produce a shipping plan that pertains to a certain period of time (day, week), although once the plan is established, it will generally not change unless one or more of the parameters of the problem (supply, demand, unit shipping cost) changes.

Introduction

Although Figure 8S–1 illustrates the nature of the transportation problem, in real life managers must often deal with allocation problems that are considerably larger in scope. A beer maker may have four or five breweries and hundreds or even thousands of distributors, and an automobile manufacturer may have eight assembly plants scattered throughout the United States and Canada and thousands of dealers that must be supplied with those cars. In such cases, the ability to identify the optimal distribution plan makes the transportation model very important.

The shipping (supply) points can be factories, warehouses, departments, or any other place from which goods are sent. Destinations can be factories, warehouses, departments, or other points that receive goods. The information needed to use the model consists of the following:

1. A list of the origins and each one's capacity or supply quantity per period.
2. A list of the destinations and each one's demand per period.
3. The unit cost of shipping items from each origin to each destination.

This information is arranged into a *transportation table* (see Table 8S–1).

The transportation model is one of a class of linear programming models, so named because of the linear relationships among variables. In the transportation model, transportation costs are treated as a direct linear function of the number of units shipped.

Use of the transportation model implies that certain assumptions are satisfied. The major ones are:

1. The items to be shipped are homogeneous (i.e., they are the same regardless of their source or destination).
2. Shipping cost per unit is the same regardless of the number of units shipped.
3. There is only one route or mode of transportation being used between each origin and each destination.

Location Decisions

The transportation model can be used to compare location alternatives in terms of their impact on the total distribution costs for a system. The procedure involves working through a separate problem for each location being considered and then comparing the resulting total costs.

If other costs, such as production costs, differ among locations, these can easily be included in the analysis, provided they can be determined on a per-unit basis. In this regard, note that merely adding or subtracting a constant to all cost values in any row or column will not affect the optimum solution; any additional costs should only be included if they have a varying effect within a row or column.

The transportation problem involves determining a minimum-cost plan for shipping from multiple sources to multiple destinations

A transportation table

Other Applications

We have seen how the transportation model can be used to minimize the costs associated with distributing goods, and we have seen how the model can be used for comparing location alternatives. The model is also used in a number of other ways. For example, in a slight variation of the model, profits can be used in place of costs. In such cases, each of the cell profits can be subtracted from the largest profit, and the remaining values (opportunity costs) can be treated in the same manner as shipping costs.

Some of the other uses of the model include production planning and scheduling (see Chapter 14), problems involving assignment of personnel or jobs to certain departments or machines (see Chapter 17), capacity planning, and transshipment problems.[1]

The use of the transportation model for capacity planning parallels its use for location decisions. An organization can subject proposed capacity alternatives to transportation

---

[1]Transshipment relates to problems with major distribution centers that in turn redistribute to smaller market destinations. See, for example, W. J. Stevenson, *Introduction to Management Science,* 3rd ed. (Burr Ridge, IL: Richard D. Irwin, 1998).

analysis to determine which one would generate the lowest total shipping cost. For example, it is perhaps intuitively obvious that a factory or warehouse that is close to its market—or has low transportation costs for some other reason—should probably have a larger capacity than other locations. Of course, many problems are not so simple, and they require actual use of the model.

Computer Solutions

Although manual solution of transportation problems is fairly straightforward, computer solutions are generally preferred, particularly for moderate or large problems. Many software packages call for data input in the same tabular form used throughout this chapter. A more general approach is to format the problem as a standard linear programming model (i.e., specify the objective function and a set of constraints). That approach enables one to use the more general version of an LP package to solve a transportation problem. Let's consider this general approach.

The decision variables for a transportation model are the quantities to be shipped. Because each cell represents a potential transportation route, each must have a decision variable. We can use the symbol x_{1A} to represent the decision variable for cell 1-A, x_{1B} for cell 1-B, and so on. The objective function consists of the cell costs and these cell symbols:

$$\text{Minimize } 4x_{1A} + 7x_{1B} + 7x_{1C} + 1x_{1D} + 12x_{2A} + 3x_{2B} + 8x_{2C}$$
$$+ 8x_{2D} + 8x_{3A} + 10x_{3B} + 16x_{3C} + 5x_{3D}$$

Because the amounts allocated in any row or column must add to the row or column total, each row and column must have a constraint. Thus, we have

$$\text{Supply (rows) } x_{1A} + x_{1B} + x_{1C} + x_{1D} = 100$$
$$x_{2A} + x_{2B} + x_{2C} + x_{2D} = 200$$
$$x_{3A} + x_{3B} + x_{3C} + x_{3D} = 150$$

$$\text{Demand (columns) } x_{1A} + x_{2A} + x_{3A} = 80$$
$$x_{1B} + x_{2B} + x_{3B} = 90$$
$$x_{1C} + x_{2C} + x_{3C} = 120$$
$$x_{1D} + x_{2D} + x_{3D} = 160$$

We do not need a constraint for the total; the row and column constraints take care of this.

If supply and demand are not equal, add an extra (dummy) row or column with the necessary supply (demand) for equality to the table before writing the constraints.

Another approach to transportation problems is to use spreadsheet software. The Excel templates can also be used to solve transportation problems. Figure 8S–2 illustrates the Excel worksheet for the preceding problem.

Problems

1. Solve this LP problem using the transportation method. Find the optimal transportation plan and the minimum cost. Also, decide if there is an alternate solution. If there is one, identify it.

$$\text{Minimize } 8x_{11} + 2x_{12} + 5x_{13} + 2x_{21} + x_{22}$$
$$+ 3x_{23} + 7x_{31} + 2x_{32} + 6x_{33}$$

$$\text{Subject to } x_{11} + x_{12} + x_{13} = 90$$
$$x_{21} + x_{22} + x_{23} = 105$$
$$x_{31} + x_{32} + x_{33} = 105$$
$$x_{11} + x_{21} + x_{31} = 150$$
$$x_{12} + x_{22} + x_{32} = 75$$
$$x_{13} + x_{23} + x_{33} = 75$$
$$\text{All variables } \geq 0$$

FIGURE 8S-2

Excel template for Table 8S–1

2. A toy manufacturer wants to open a third warehouse that will supply three retail outlets. The new warehouse will supply 500 units of backyard playsets per week. Two locations are being studied, N1 and N2. Transportation costs for location N1 to stores A, B, and C are $6, $8, and $7, respectively; for location N2, the costs are $10, $6, and $4, respectively. The existing system is shown in the following table. Which location would result in the lower transportation costs for the system?

3. A large firm is contemplating construction of a new manufacturing facility. The two leading locations are Toledo and Cincinnati. The new factory would have a supply capacity of 160 units per week. Transportation costs from each potential location and existing locations are shown in the following table. Determine which location would provide the lower transportation costs.

From Toledo to	Cost per Unit	From Cincinnati to	Cost per Unit
A	$18	A	$ 7
B	8	B	17
C	13	C	13

	A	B	C	Supply (Units/week)
1	10	14	10	210
2	12	17	20	140
3	11	11	12	150
Demand (Units/week)	220	220	220	

4. A large retailer is planning to open a new store. Three locations in California are currently under consideration: South Coast Plaza (SCP), Fashion Island (FI), and Laguna Hills (LH). Transportation costs for the locations and costs, demands, and supplies for existing locations and warehouses (origins), are shown below. Each of the locations has a demand potential of 300 units per week. Which location would yield the lowest transportation costs for the system?

FROM WAREHOUSE	To		
	SCP	**FI**	**LH**
1	$ 4	$7	$5
2	11	6	5
3	5	5	6

	A	B	Supply (Units/week)
1	15	9	660
2	10	7	340
3	14	18	200
Demand (Units/week)	400	500	

Bierman, Harold; Charles P. Bonini; and Warren H. Hausman. *Quantitative Analysis for Business Decisions.* 8th ed. Burr Ridge, IL: Richard D. Irwin, 1991.

Stevenson, William J. *Introduction to Management Science.* 3rd ed. Burr Ridge, IL: Richard D. Irwin, 1998.

PART FOUR

Quality

The topics in this part relate to quality. There are three chapters: Chapter 9 introduces quality concepts and the thinking of quality "gurus." Chapter 10 explains quality control procedures. Chapter 11 describes total quality management (TQM) tools.

Our windows are found in the homes builders care about most. Their own.

CHAPTER NINE

Introduction to Quality

CHAPTER OUTLINE

Introduction, 394

The Evolution of Quality
Management, 394

Quality: The Basics, 395
The Dimensions of Quality, 395
The Determinants of Quality, 396
The Consequences of Poor
Quality, 398

Newsclip: Medical Mistakes Kill
Almost 98,000 a Year, 400
Benefits of Good Quality, 400
Responsibility for Quality, 400
The Costs of Quality, 401
Ethics and Quality, 402

Quality Gurus, 402
W. Edwards Deming, 402
Joseph M. Juran, 403
Armand Feigenbaum, 404
Philip Crosby, 404

Kaoru Ishikawa, 406
Genichi Taguchi, 406

Quality Awards, 406
The Baldrige Award, 406

Reading: Baldrige Core Values and
Concepts, 407
The Deming Prize, 409

Quality Certification, 409
ISO 9000, 409

Reading: Aesop on Quality
Systems, 410
ISO 14000, 412

Summary, 412

Key Terms, 413

Discussion and Review
Questions, 413

Memo Writing Exercises, 413

Selected Bibliography and Further
Reading, 413

LEARNING OBJECTIVES

*After completing this chapter, you
should be able to:*

1 Define the term *quality*.

2 Explain why quality is important
and the consequences of poor
quality.

3 Discuss the determinants of
quality.

4 List and describe the various costs
associated with quality.

5 Discuss ISO 9000 and ISO
14000.

6 Discuss the philosophies of
quality gurus.

This chapter is the first of three chapters on quality. In this chapter you will learn about the evolution of quality management, definitions of quality, the costs of quality and the consequences of poor quality, and you will learn about some quality awards and certification.

Introduction

quality The ability of a product or service to consistently meet or exceed customer expectations.

www.honda.com
www.nissandriven.com
www.toyota.com

Broadly defined, **quality** refers to the ability of a product or service to consistently meet or exceed customer expectations. Prior to the increased level of Japanese competition in the U.S. marketplace in the 1970s and 1980s, quality was not uppermost in the minds of U.S. business organizations. They tended to focus on cost and productivity rather than on quality. It wasn't that quality was *un*important, it just wasn't *very* important.

Partly because of this thinking, foreign companies, many of them Japanese, captured a significant share of the U.S. market. In the automotive sector, leading Japanese manufacturers, Honda, Nissan, and Toyota, became major players in the auto sales market in the United States. Both Honda and Toyota have built a reputation for quality and reliability in their cars.

Many U.S. companies changed their views about quality after that, and changed them drastically. Stung by the success of foreign competitors, they embraced quality in a big way. They hired consultants, sent their people (including top executives) to seminars, and initiated a vast array of quality improvement programs. These companies clearly recognized the importance of quality and that quality isn't something that is tacked on as a special feature, but an *integral part* of a product or service. In the 1990s, U.S. automakers began to close the quality gap.

The Evolution of Quality Management

Prior to the Industrial Revolution, skilled craftsmen performed all stages of production. Pride of workmanship and reputation often provided the motivation to see that a job was done right. Lengthy guild apprenticeships caused this attitude to carry over to new workers. Moreover, one person or a small group of people were responsible for an entire product.

A division of labor accompanied the Industrial Revolution; each worker was then responsible for only a small portion of each product. Pride of workmanship became less meaningful because workers could no longer identify readily with the final product. The responsibility for quality control shifted to the foremen. Inspection was either nonexistent or haphazard, although in some instances 100 percent inspection was used.

Frederick Winslow Taylor, the "Father of Scientific Management," gave new emphasis to quality by including product inspection and gauging in his list of fundamental areas of manufacturing management. G. S. Radford improved Taylor's methods. Two of his most significant contributions were the notions of involving quality considerations early in the product design stage and making connections between high quality, increased productivity, and lower costs.

In 1924, W. Shewhart of Bell Telephone Laboratories introduced statistical control charts that could be used to monitor production. Around 1930, H. F. Dodge and H. G. Romig, also of Bell Labs, introduced tables for acceptance sampling. Nevertheless, statistical quality control procedures were not widely used until World War II, when the U.S. government began to require vendors to use them.

World War II caused a dramatic increase in emphasis on quality control. The U.S. Army refined sampling techniques for dealing with large shipments of arms from many suppliers. By the end of the 1940s, the U.S. Army, Bell Labs, and major universities were training engineers in other industries in the use of statistical sampling techniques. About the same time, professional quality organizations were emerging throughout the country. One of these organizations was the American Society for Quality Control (ASQC, now known as ASQ). Over the years, the society has promoted quality with its publications, seminars and conferences, and training programs.

During the 1950s, the quality movement evolved into quality assurance. Quality guru W. Edwards Deming encouraged Japanese manufacturers to adopt statistical quality control methods, promising that this would help them to rebuild their manufacturing base and to compete in world markets.

At about the same time, another quality guru, Joseph Juran, began his "cost of quality" approach, emphasizing accurate and complete identification and measurement of the costs of quality. He stressed the desirability of lowering costs associated with prevention, and advocated using quality control techniques to accomplish this.

In the mid-1950s, Armand Feigenbaum proposed *total quality control,* which enlarged the realm of quality efforts from its primary focus on manufacturing to also include product design and incoming raw materials. One important feature of his work was greater involvement of upper management in quality.

During the 1960s, the concept of "zero defects" gained favor. Championed by quality guru Philip Crosby, this approach focused on employee motivation and awareness, and the expectation of perfection from each employee. It evolved from the success of the Martin Company in producing a "perfect" missile for the U.S. Army.

In the 1970s, quality assurance methods gained increasing emphasis in services including government operations, health care, banking, and the travel industry.

Something else happened in the 1970s that had a global impact on quality. An embargo on oil sales instituted by OPEC (the Organization of Petroleum Exporting Countries) caused an increase in energy costs, and automobile buyers became more interested in fuel-efficient, lower-cost vehicles. Japanese auto producers, who had been improving their products at the urging of Deming and Juran, were poised to take advantage of these changes, and they captured an increased share of the automobile market. The quality of their automobiles enhanced the reputation of Japanese producers, opening the door for a wide array of Japanese-produced goods.

American producers, stunned by their loss of market share, spent much of the late 1970s and the 1980s trying to improve the quality of their goods while lowering their costs.

The evolution of quality took a dramatic shift from quality assurance to a strategic approach to quality in the late 1970s. Up until that time, the main emphasis had been on finding and correcting defective products before they reached the market. It was still a reactive approach. The strategic approach is proactive, focusing on preventing mistakes from occurring altogether. Quality and profits are more closely linked. This approach also places greater emphasis on customer satisfaction, and it involves all levels of management as well as workers in a continuing effort to increase quality.

Quality: The Basics

Any serious effort to deal with quality must begin with a clear understanding of the meaning of the word *quality.*

THE DIMENSIONS OF QUALITY

The term *quality* is used in a variety of ways. Sometimes it refers to the grade of a product, such as "USDA Choice" or "grade A" eggs. At other times, it refers to materials, workmanship, or special features, such as "waterproof" or "subtle aroma." And sometimes it is related to price, as in "cheap" or "expensive."

The implication in these various connotations of quality is that customers value certain aspects of a product or service, and therefore associate those aspects with the quality that they perceive a product or service has. In fact, it may be obvious that from a customer perspective, quality does not pertain to a single aspect of a product or service, but to a number of different *dimensions* of the product or service.

Examples of some of the quality dimensions for a product and a service

Dimension	(Product) Automobile	(Service) Automobile Repair
1. Performance	Everything works, fit and finish	All work done, at agreed price
	Ride, handling, grade of materials used	Friendliness, courtesy Competency, quickness
2. Aesthetics	Interior design, soft touch	Clean work/waiting areas
3. Special features		
Convenience	Placement of gauges and controls	Location, call when ready
High tech	Cellular phone, DVD player	Computer diagnostics
4. Safety	Antilock brakes, airbags	Separate waiting area
5. Reliability	Infrequency of breakdowns	Work done correctly, ready when promised
6. Durability	Useful life in miles, resistance to rust and corrosion	Work holds up over time
7. Perceived quality	Top-rated car	Award-winning service department
8. Service after sale	Handling of complaints and/or requests for information	Handling of complaints

dimensions of quality Performance, aesthetics, special features, conformance, safety, reliability, durability, perceived quality, and service after sale.

Although they may vary somewhat from product to product, or between a product and a service, generally speaking, the **dimensions of quality** include:[1]

Performance—main characteristics of the product or service.

Aesthetics—appearance, feel, smell, taste.

Special features—extra characteristics.

Conformance—how well a product or service corresponds to design specifications, and to the customer's expectations.

Safety—risk of injury or harm.

Reliability—consistency of performance.

Durability—the useful life of the product or service.

Perceived quality—indirect evaluation of quality (e.g., reputation).

Service after sale—handling of complaints or checking on customer satisfaction.

These dimensions are further described by the examples presented in Table 9–1. When referring to a product, a customer sometimes judges the first four dimensions by its *fitness for use.*

Notice that price is *not* a dimension of quality.

THE DETERMINANTS OF QUALITY

The degree to which a product or a service successfully satisfies its intended purpose has four primary determinants. They are:

1. Design.
2. How well it conforms to the design.
3. Ease of use.
4. Service after delivery.

---

[1]Adapted from David Garvin, "What Does Quality Really Mean?" *Sloan Management Review* 26, no. 1 (1984), pp. 25–43.

Digital micrometers collect precise measurements and send the information directly into a computer database. This lightweight model, manufactured by Mitutoyo, has a display that stays on for the life of the battery, which lasts over a year.

www.mitutoyo.com

The design phase is the starting point for the level of quality eventually achieved. Design involves decisions about the specific characteristics of a product or service such as size, shape, and location. **Quality of design** refers to the intention of designers to include or exclude certain features in a product or service. For example, many different models of automobiles are on the market today. They differ in size, appearance, roominess, fuel economy, comfort, and materials used. These differences reflect choices made by designers that determine the quality of design. Design decisions must take into account customer wants, production or service capabilities, safety and liability (both during production and after delivery), costs, and other similar considerations.

Designers may determine customer wants from information provided by marketing, perhaps through the use of consumer surveys or other market research. Marketing may

quality of design Intention of designers to include or exclude features in a product or service.

organize focus groups of consumers to express their views on a product or service (what they like and don't like, and what they would like to have).

Designers must work closely with representatives of operations to ascertain that designs are manufacturable; that is, that production or service has the equipment, capacity, and skills necessary to produce or provide a particular design.

A poor design can result in difficulties in production or service. For example, materials might be difficult to obtain, specifications difficult to meet, or procedures difficult to follow. Moreover, if a design is inadequate or inappropriate for the circumstances, the best workmanship in the world may not be enough to achieve the desired quality. Also, we cannot expect a worker to achieve good results if the given tools or procedures are inadequate. Similarly, a superior design usually cannot offset poor workmanship.

quality of conformance The degree to which goods or services conform to the intent of the designers.

Quality of conformance refers to the degree to which goods and services conform to (i.e., *achieve*) the intent of the designers. This is affected by factors such as the capability of equipment used; the skills, training, and motivation of workers; the extent to which the design lends itself to production; the monitoring process to assess conformance; and the taking of corrective action (e.g., through problem solving) when necessary.

The determination of quality does not stop once the product or service has been sold or delivered. *Ease of use* and user instructions are important. They increase the chances, but do not guarantee, that a product will be used for its intended purposes and in such a way that it will continue to function properly and safely. (When faced with liability litigation, companies often argue that injuries and damages occurred because the user misused the product.) Much of the same reasoning can be applied to services. Customers, patients, clients, or other users must be clearly informed on what they should or should not do; otherwise, there is the danger that they will take some action that will adversely affect quality. Some examples include the doctor who fails to specify that a medication should be taken *before* meals and *not* with orange juice and the attorney who neglects to inform a client of a deadline for filing a claim.

Much consumer education takes the form of printed instructions and labeling. Thus, manufacturers must ensure that directions for unpacking, assembling, using, maintaining, and adjusting the product—and what to do if something goes wrong (e.g., flush eyes with water, call a physician, induce vomiting, do not induce vomiting, disconnect set immediately)—are *clearly visible* and *easily understood*.

For a variety of reasons, products do not always perform as expected, and services do not always yield the desired results. Whatever the reason, it is important from a quality standpoint to remedy the situation—through recall and repair of the product, adjustment, replacement or buyback, or reevaluation of a service—and do whatever is necessary to bring the product or service up to standard.

THE CONSEQUENCES OF POOR QUALITY

It is important for management to recognize the different ways that the quality of a firm's products or services can affect the organization and to take these into account in developing and maintaining a quality assurance program. Some of the major ways that quality affects an organization are:

1. Loss of business
2. Liability
3. Productivity
4. Costs

Poor designs or defective products or services can result in *loss of business*. Failure to devote adequate attention to quality can damage a profit-oriented organization's image and lead to a decreased share of the market, or it can lead to increased criticism and/or controls for a government agency or nonprofit organization.

A potentially . . . devastating consequence to the bottom line is the reaction of the consumer who receives a defective or otherwise unsatisfactory product or service. A recent study

As a quality control measure, wind tunnel testing is done for a crop duster to check the aerial dispersal of liquid chemicals over crops at various aircraft speeds. The aircraft have wind-driven pumps under the fuselage that push liquids through booms—mounted at the edge of the wings—for dispersal through specially designed nozzles.

showed that, while a satisfied customer will tell a few people about his or her experience, a dissatisfied person will tell an average of 19 others.

Unfortunately, the company is usually the last to know of dissatisfaction. People rarely complain directly to the provider of poor quality goods and services. In fact, studies suggest that people usually complain, if at all, to their most immediate contact (e.g., a salesperson or service manager) and that these complaints are rarely transmitted further. A more common response is simply to switch to a competing product or service. Typically, formal complaints are received from less than 5 percent of dissatisfied customers.[2]

Organizations must pay special attention to their potential *liability* due to damages or injuries resulting from either faulty design or poor workmanship. This applies to both products and services. Thus, a poorly designed steering arm on a car might cause the driver to lose control of the car, but so could improper assembly of the steering arm. However, the net result is the same. Similarly, a tree surgeon might be called to cable a tree limb. If the limb later falls and causes damage to a neighbor's car, the accident might be traced to a poorly designed procedure for cabling or to improper workmanship. Liability for poor quality has been well established in the courts. An organization's liability costs can often be substantial, especially if large numbers of items are involved, as in the automobile industry, or if potentially widespread injury or damage is involved (e.g., an accident at a nuclear power plant). Express written warranties as well as implied warranties generally guarantee the product as safe when used as intended. The courts have tended to extend this to *foreseeable* uses, even if these uses were not intended by the producer. In the health care field, medical malpractice claims and insurance costs are contributing to skyrocketing costs and have become a major issue nationwide.

Productivity and quality are often closely related. Poor quality can adversely affect productivity during the manufacturing process if parts are defective and have to be reworked or if an assembler has to try a number of parts before finding one that fits properly. Also, poor quality in tools and equipment can lead to injuries and defective output, which must be reworked or scrapped, thereby reducing the amount of usable output for a

---

[2]The Ernst & Young Quality Improvement Consulting Group, *Total Quality: An Executive's Guide for the 1990s* (Burr Ridge, IL: Irwin Professional Publishing: 1990), pp. 6–7.

Medical Mistakes Kill almost 98,000 a Year

Medical mistakes kill tens of thousands of people a year, says a new report by the National Academy of Sciences.

The report said that medical errors kill nearly 98,000 people a year. This exceeds the number of people who die annually from highway accidents (about 43,450), breast cancer (42,300) or AIDS (16,500), the study said.

The group called for a new federal agency to protect patients and said that Congress should require all health care providers to report medical mistakes that cause serious injury or death. The panel said that the United States should strive to reduce medical errors by 50 percent in five years.

Errors range from a simple miscommunication about a drug's name between a doctor and a nurse to the erroneous programming of a complex medical device. They include wrong diagnoses from mislabeled blood tubes, mistaken treatments because of poorly labeled drugs and improper dosing because of faulty calculations.

Source: *The New York Times,* November 30, 1999, p. 1A.

given amount of input. Similarly, poor service can mean having to redo the service and reduce service productivity. Conversely, improving and maintaining good quality can have a positive effect on productivity.

BENEFITS OF GOOD QUALITY

Business organizations with good or excellent quality typically benefit in a variety of ways: an enhanced reputation for quality, an increased market share, greater customer loyalty, lower liability costs, fewer production or service problems—which yields higher productivity, fewer complaints from customers, lower production costs, and higher profits. Annual studies by the National Institute of Standards indicate that winners of the Baldrige quality award, described later in the chapter, outperform the S&P 500 Index by a significant amount. [3]

RESPONSIBILITY FOR QUALITY

It is true that all members of an organization have some responsibility for quality, but certain areas of the organization are involved in activities that make them key areas of responsibility. They include top management, design, procurement, production/operations, quality assurance, packaging and shipping, marketing and sales, and customer service.

Top management. Top management has the ultimate responsibility for quality. While establishing strategies for quality, top management must institute programs to improve quality; guide, direct, and motivate managers and workers; and set an example by being involved in quality initiatives. Examples include taking training in quality, issuing periodic reports on quality, and attending meetings on quality.

Design. Quality products and services begin with design. This includes not only features of the product or service; it also includes attention to the *processes* that will be required to produce the products and/or the services that will be required to deliver the service to customers.

Procurement. The procurement department has responsibility for obtaining goods and services that will not detract from the quality of the organization's goods and services.

Production/operations. Production/operations has responsibility to ensure that processes yield products and services that conform to design specifications. Monitoring processes and finding and correcting root causes of problems are important aspects of this responsibility.

Quality assurance. Quality assurance is responsible for gathering and analyzing data on problems and working with operations to solve problems.

---

[3] " 'Baldrige Index' Outperforms S&P 500 by Almost 5 to 1." Press release available at www.quality.nist.gov/.

TABLE 9–2

Summary of quality costs

Category	Description	Examples
Internal failure costs	Costs related to defective products or services before they are delivered to customers	Rework costs, problem solving, material and product losses, scrap, and downtime
External failure costs	Costs related to delivering substandard products or services to customers	Returned goods, reworking costs, warranty costs, loss of goodwill, liability claims, and penalties
Appraisal costs	Costs related to measuring, evaluating, and auditing materials, parts, products, and services to assess conformance with quality standards	Inspection equipment, testing, labs, inspectors, and the interruption of production to take samples
Prevention costs	Costs related to reducing the potential for quality problems	Quality improvement programs, training, monitoring, data collection and analysis, and design costs

Packaging and shipping. This department must ensure that goods are not damaged in transit, that packages are clearly labeled, that instructions are included, that all parts are included, and shipping occurs in a timely manner.

Marketing and sales. This department has the responsibility to determine customer needs and to communicate them to appropriate areas of the organization. In addition, it has the responsibility to report any problems with products or services.

Customer service. Customer service is often the first department to learn of problems. It has the responsibility to communicate that information to appropriate departments, deal in a reasonable manner with customers, work to resolve problems, and follow up to confirm that the situation has been effectively remedied.

Poor quality increases certain *costs* incurred by the organization. The following section provides further detail on costs associated with quality.

THE COSTS OF QUALITY

Any serious attempt to deal with quality issues must take into account the costs associated with quality. Those costs can be classified into four categories:

Internal failure costs   *Appraisal* costs

External failure costs   *Prevention* costs

Failure costs are incurred by defective parts or products or by faulty services. **Internal failures** are those discovered during the production process; **external failures** are those discovered after delivery to the customer. Internal failures occur for a variety of reasons, including defective material from vendors, incorrect machine settings, faulty equipment, incorrect methods, incorrect processing, carelessness, and faulty or improper material handling procedures. The costs of internal failures include lost production time, scrap and rework, investigation costs, possible equipment damage, and possible employee injury. Rework costs involve the salaries of workers and the additional resources needed to perform the rework (e.g., equipment, energy, raw materials). Beyond those costs are items such as inspection of reworked parts, disruption of schedules, the added costs of parts and materials in inventory waiting for reworked parts, and the paperwork needed to keep track of the items until they can be reintegrated into the process. External failures are defective products or poor service that go undetected by the producer. Resulting costs include warranty work, handling of complaints, replacements, liability/litigation, payments to customers or discounts used to offset the inferior quality, loss of customer goodwill, and opportunity costs related to lost sales. Table 9–2 summarizes failure costs.

failure costs Costs caused by defective parts or products or by faulty services.

internal failures Failures discovered during production.

external failures Failures discovered after delivery to the customer.

appraisal costs Costs of activities designed to ensure quality or uncover defects.

prevention costs Costs of preventing defects from occurring.

Appraisal costs relate to inspection, testing, and other activities intended to uncover defective products or services, or to assure that there are none. They include the cost of inspectors, testing, test equipment, labs, quality audits, and field testing.

Prevention costs relate to attempts to prevent defects from occurring. They include costs such as planning and administration systems, working with vendors, training, quality control procedures, and extra attention in both the design and production phases to decrease the probability of defective workmanship.

Internal and external costs represent costs related to poor quality, whereas appraisal and prevention costs represent investments for achieving good quality.

ETHICS AND QUALITY

All members of an organization have an obligation to perform their duties in an ethical manner. Ethical behavior comes into play in many situations that involve quality. One major category is substandard work, including defective products and substandard service, poor designs, shoddy workmanship, and substandard parts and raw materials. Having knowledge of this and failing to correct and *report it* in a timely manner is unethical and can have a number of negative consequences. These can include increased costs for organizations in terms of decreased productivity, an increase in the accident rate among employees, inconveniences and injuries to customers, and increased liability costs.

A related issue is how an organization chooses to deal with information about quality problems in products that are already in service. For example, automakers and tire makers in recent years have been accused of withholding information about actual or potential quality problems; they failed to issue product recalls, or failed to divulge information, choosing instead to handle any complaints that arose on an individual basis.

Quality Gurus

A core of quality experts has shaped modern quality practices. Among the most famous of this core of "gurus" are Deming, Juran, Feigenbaum, Ishikawa, Taguchi, and Crosby. Together, these great thinkers have had a tremendous impact on the management and control of quality, and the way companies operate.

W. EDWARDS DEMING

Deming Prize Prize established by the Japanese and awarded annually to firms that distinguish themselves with quality management programs.

Deming was the senior guru. A statistics professor at New York University in the 1940s, he went to Japan after World War II to assist the Japanese in improving quality and productivity. The Union of Japanese Scientists, who had invited Deming, were so impressed that in 1951, after a series of lectures presented by Deming, they established the **Deming Prize,** which is awarded annually to firms that distinguish themselves with quality management programs.

Although the Japanese revered Deming, he was largely unknown to business leaders in the United States. In fact, he worked with the Japanese for almost 30 years before he gained recognition in his own country. Before his death in 1993, U.S. companies turned their attention to Deming, embraced his philosophy, and requested his assistance in setting up quality improvement programs.

Deming compiled a famous list of 14 points he believed were the prescription needed to achieve quality in an organization (see Table 9–3). His message is that the cause of inefficiency and poor quality is the *system,* not the employees. Deming felt that it was *management's responsibility* to correct the system to achieve the desired results. In addition to the 14 points, Deming stressed the need to reduce variation in output (deviation from a standard), which can be accomplished by distinguishing between *special causes* of variation (i.e., correctable) and *common causes* of variation (i.e., random).

The key elements of Deming's 14 points are constancy of purpose, continual improvement, and profound knowledge. *Profound knowledge* involves (1) an appreciation for a system, (2) a theory of variation, (3) a theory of knowledge, and (4) psychology. Dem-

TABLE 9–3

Deming's 14 points

1. Create constancy of purpose toward improvement of product and service with a plan to become competitive and to stay in business. Decide to whom top management is responsible.
2. Adopt the new philosophy. We are in a new economic age. We can no longer live with commonly accepted levels of delays, mistakes, defective materials, and defective workmanship.
3. Cease dependence on mass inspection. Require, instead, statistical evidence that quality is built in. (*Prevent* defects rather than *detect* defects.)
4. End the practice of awarding business on the basis of price tag. Instead, depend on meaningful measures of quality along with price. Eliminate suppliers that cannot qualify with statistical evidence of quality.
5. Find problems. It is management's job to work continually on the system (design, incoming materials, composition of material, maintenance, improvement of machine, training, supervision, retraining).
6. Institute modern methods of training on the job.
7. The responsibility of foremen must be changed from sheer numbers to quality . . . [which] will automatically improve productivity. Management must prepare to take immediate action on reports from foremen concerning barriers such as inherent defects, machines not maintained, poor tools, and fuzzy operational definitions.
8. Drive out fear, so that everyone may work effectively for the company.
9. Break down barriers between departments. People in research, design, sales, and production must work as a team to foresee problems of production that may be encountered with various materials and specifications.
10. Eliminate numerical goals, posters, and slogans for the work force, asking for new levels of productivity without providing methods.
11. Eliminate work standards that prescribe numerical quotas.
12. Remove barriers that stand between the hourly worker and his right to pride of workmanship.
13. Institute a vigorous program of education and retraining.
14. Create a structure in top management that will push every day on the above 13 points.

Source: W. Edwards Deming, *Quality, Productivity, and Competitive Position* (Cambridge, MA: MIT, Center for Advanced Engineering Study, 1982), pp. 16–17.

ing's concept of profound knowledge incorporates the beliefs and values about learning that guided Japan's rise to a world economic power.

Appreciation for the system is the starting point, and it refers to everyone in the organization working to achieve optimization. Toward that end, management must eliminate internal competition. Reducing *variation* is an important key to quality improvement, but it is necessary to differentiate between random variation and correctable variation, and to focus on the latter. Deming believed that *knowledge* comes from theory, and that learning cannot occur within an organization without a theory of knowledge. Deming felt that *psychology* was the most powerful element of profound knowledge. He believed that workers want to create and learn, but that management unintentionally often does things such as establishing rating systems that rob them of their internal motivation. He believed that management's greatest challenge in achieving quality was in motivating workers to contribute their collective efforts to achieve a common goal. Last, Deming felt that in order to benefit from the concept of profound knowledge, it was necessary to embrace the concept in its entirety.

JOSEPH M. JURAN

Juran, like Deming, taught Japanese manufacturers how to improve the quality of their goods, and he, too, can be regarded as a major force in Japan's success in quality. He made his first trip to Japan a few years after the publication in 1951 of his *Quality Control Handbook*. Juran's approach to quality may be the closest to Deming's of all the gurus, although his approach differs on the importance of statistical methods and what an organization must do to achieve quality. Whereas Deming's work envisioned a "transformation," Juran believes that an organization can manage for quality. He doesn't think that managing quality is as difficult as Deming thought, although he does admit that most

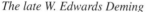

The late W. Edwards Deming   *Joseph M. Juran*   *Philip B. Crosby*

quality programs that fail do so because the companies do not realize how difficult developing new processes can be. Juran also places less emphasis on statistical methods than Deming. It is his view that quality begins by knowing what customers want.

Juran views quality as fitness-for-use. He also believes that roughly 80 percent of quality defects are management controllable; thus, management has the responsibility to correct this deficiency. He describes quality management in terms of a *trilogy* consisting of quality planning, quality control, and quality improvement. According to Juran, quality planning is necessary to establish processes that are *capable* of meeting quality standards; that quality control is necessary in order to know when corrective action is needed; and that quality improvement will help to find better ways of doing things. A key element of Juran's philosophy is the commitment of management to continual improvement.

Juran is credited as one of the first to measure the cost of quality, and he demonstrated the potential for increased profits that would result if the costs of poor quality could be reduced. Also, he made a series of videotapes entitled "Juran on Quality," which are available from the Juran Institute in Wilton, Connecticut.

Juran proposed 10 steps for quality improvement. These are shown in Table 9–4.

ARMAND FEIGENBAUM

Feigenbaum was instrumental in advancing the "cost of nonconformance" approach as a reason for management to commit to quality. At the age of 24, he was General Electric's top expert on quality. He recognized that quality was not simply a collection of tools and techniques, but a "total field." He saw that when improvements were made in a process, other areas of the company also achieved improvements. Feigenbaum's understanding of systems theory led him to create an environment in which people could learn from each other's successes, and his leadership and open work environment led to cross-functional teamwork.

In 1961, his book *Total Quality Control* was published, in which he layed out quality principles in 40 steps. Table 9–5 lists some of the key ideas that differentiate him from the other gurus.

According to Feigenbaum, it is the customer who defines quality. Deming would disagree; in his philosophy, companies should get to know their customers so well that they can anticipate their future needs.

PHILIP B. CROSBY

Crosby worked at Martin Marietta in the 1960s. While he was there, he developed the concept of *zero defects* and popularized the phrase "Do it right the first time." He stressed

TABLE 9–4

Juran's 10 steps for quality improvement

1. Build awareness for the need and opportunity for improvement.
2. Set goals for improvement.
3. Organize people to reach the goals.
4. Provide training throughout the organization.
5. Carry out projects to solve problems.
6. Report progress.
7. Give recognition.
8. Communicate results.
9. Keep score.
10. Maintain momentum by making annual improvement part of the regular systems and processes of the company.

Source: Joseph M. Juran, ed. *Quality Control Handbook* (New York: McGraw-Hill, 1951).

TABLE 9–5

Key elements of Feigenbaum's philosophy of quality control

1. Total quality control is a system for integrating quality development, maintenance, and improvement efforts in an organization that will enable engineering, marketing, production, and service to function at optimal economic levels while achieving customer satisfaction.
2. The "control" aspect of quality control should involve setting quality standards, appraising performance relative to these standards, taking corrective action when the standards are not met, and planning for improvement in the standards.
3. Factors that affect quality can be divided into two major categories: technological and human. The human factor is the more important one.
4. Operating quality costs can be divided into four categories: prevention costs, appraisal costs, internal failure costs, and external failure costs.
5. It is important to control quality at the source.

Source: Adapted from Peter Capezio and Debra Morehouse, *Taking the Mystery Out of TQM*, 2nd ed., © 1995, published by Career Press, Franklin Lakes, NJ, pp. 100–101.

prevention, and he argued against the idea that "there will always be some level of defectives." He was the corporate vice president for quality for ITT in the 1970s and was instrumental in making quality a concern of top company executives. In 1979, his book *Quality Is Free* was published. The title is based on a quote from the CEO of ITT. The book explains quality concepts in simple terms.

In accordance with the concept of zero defects, Crosby believes that any level of defects is too high, and that management must install programs that help the organization move toward that goal. Among some of his key points are the following.[4]

1. Top management must demonstrate its commitment to quality and its willingness to give support to achieve good quality.
2. Management must be persistent in efforts to achieve good quality.
3. Management must spell out clearly what it wants in terms of quality and what workers must do to achieve that.
4. Make it (or do it) right the first time.

Unlike the other gurus, Crosby maintains that achieving quality can be relatively easy. His book *Quality without Tears: The Art of Hassle-Free Management* was published in 1984. The quality-is-free concept is that the costs of poor quality are much greater than traditionally defined. According to Crosby, these costs are so great that rather than viewing quality efforts as costs, organizations should view them as a way to reduce costs, because the improvements generated by quality efforts will more than pay for themselves.

[4]Philip Crosby, *Quality without Tears: The Art of Hassle-Free Management* (New York: McGraw-Hill, 1984).

TABLE 9–6

A summary of key contributors to quality management

Contributor	Key Contributions
Deming	14 points; special versus common causes of variation
Juran	Quality is fitness-for-use; quality trilogy
Feigenbaum	Quality is a total field; the customer defines quality
Crosby	Quality is free; zero defects
Ishikawa	Cause-and-effect diagrams; quality circles
Taguchi	Taguchi loss function

KAORU ISHIKAWA

The late Japanese expert on quality was strongly influenced by both Deming and Juran, although he made significant contributions of his own to quality management. Among his key contributions were the development of the cause-and-effect diagram (also known as a fishbone diagram) for problem solving and the implementation of quality circles, which involve workers in quality improvement. He was the first quality expert to call attention to the *internal customer*—the next person in the process. He was a strong proponent of the need for companies to have a shared vision in order to unite everyone in the organization in a common goal, and he is widely recognized for his efforts to make quality control "user friendly" for workers.

GENICHI TAGUCHI

Taguchi is best known for the Taguchi loss function, which involves a formula for determining the cost of poor quality. The idea is that the deviation of a part from a standard causes a loss, and the combined effect of deviations of all parts from their standards can be large, even though each individual deviation is small. In contrast to Taguchi, Deming believed that it is impossible to determine the actual cost of the lack of quality, and Crosby believes that it would be difficult to apply the concept in most U.S. firms. Nonetheless, Taguchi's method is credited with helping the Ford Motor Company to reduce its warranty losses by achieving less variation in the output of transmissions.

Table 9–6 provides a summary of the important contributions of the gurus to modern quality management.

Quality Awards

Quality awards have been established to generate awareness and interest in quality. The Malcolm Baldrige Award and the Deming Prize are two well-known awards given annually to firms that have integrated quality management in their operations.

THE BALDRIGE AWARD

In 1987, Congress passed the Malcolm Baldrige National Quality Improvement Act. This legislation was designed to inspire increased efforts on the part of businesses located in the United States to improve the quality of their products and services. Named after the late Malcolm Baldrige, an industrialist and former secretary of commerce, the annual **Baldrige Award** is administered by the National Institute of Standards and Technology.

Baldrige Award Annual award given by the U.S. government to recognize quality achievements of U.S. companies.

The purpose of the award competition is to stimulate efforts to improve quality, to recognize quality achievements of U.S. companies, and to publicize successful programs. A maximum of two awards are given annually in each of three categories: large manufacturer, large service organization, and small business (500 or fewer employees).

Businesses that compete for the award are required to submit an application of no more than 75 pages documenting their quality systems. Those who pass an initial screening must undergo a more intense evaluation by examiners from government and industry, and consultants. The examination includes an on-site visit. Applicants are evaluated in seven main areas: leadership, information and analysis, strategic planning, human resource management, quality assurance of products and services, quality results, and customer satisfaction. A key feature of the Baldrige competition is the "Core Values and Concepts" portion (see www.quality.gov for a complete description of award criteria and scoring). The current core values (2000) are summarized in the following reading.

READING

Baldrige Core Values and Concepts

The criteria for the Baldrige Award are related to a set of core values and concepts. These serve as a foundation for integrating key business requirements within a results-oriented framework. The core values and concepts are:

Visionary Leadership

An organization's senior leaders need to set directions and create a customer focus, clear and visible values, and high expectations, balancing the needs of all stakeholders. Leaders need to ensure the creation of strategies, systems, and methods for achieving excellence, stimulation innovation, and building knowledge and capabilities.

Customer Driven

Being customer driven is a strategic concept directed toward customer retention, market share gain, and growth. It includes not only defect and error reduction, meeting specifications, and reducing complaints, but also how well the organization is able to recover from defects and mistakes.

Organizational and Personal Learning

Organizational learning refers to continuous improvement of existing approaches and processes and adaptation to change, leading to new goals and/or approaches.

Organizations invest in employee personal learning through education, training, and opportunities for continuing growth. Opportunities might include job rotation and increased pay for demonstrated knowledge and skills.

Valuing Employees and Partners

Valuing employees means committing to their satisfaction, development, and well-being. Increasingly, this involves more flexible, high performance work practices tailored to employees with diverse workplace and home life needs. Major challenges in the area of valuing employees include: (1) demonstrating your leaders' commitment to your employees; (2) providing recognition opportunities that go beyond the normal compensation system; (3) providing opportunities for development and growth within your organization; (4) sharing your organization's knowledge so your employees can better serve your customers and contribute to achieving your strategic objectives; and (5) creating an environment that encourages risk taking.

Organizations need to build internal and external partnerships to better accomplish overall goals. Internal partnerships might include labor–management cooperation, such as agreements with your unions. Partnerships with employees might entail employee development, cross-training, or new work organizations, such as high performance work teams. Internal partnerships also might involve creating network relationships among your work units to improve flexibility, responsiveness, and knowledge sharing.

External partnerships might be with customers, suppliers, and education organizations. Strategic partnerships or alliances are increasingly important kinds of external partnerships. Such partnerships might offer entry into new markets or a bias for new products or services. Also, partnerships might permit the blending of your organization's core competencies or leadership capabilities with the complementary strengths and capabilities of partners, thereby enhancing overall capability, including speed and flexibility.

Agility

Success in globally competitive markets demands creating a capacity for rapid change and flexibility. All aspects of electronic commerce require more rapid, flexible, and customized responses. Businesses face ever-shorter cycles for introductions of new or improved products and services. Faster and more flexible response to customers is now a more critical requirement. Major improvements in response time often require simplification of work units and processes and/or the ability for rapid changeover from one process to another. Cross-trained employees are vital assets in such a demanding environment.

Focus on the Future

Pursuit of sustainable growth and market leadership requires a strong future orientation and a willingness to make long-term commitments to key stakeholders . . . Major components of a future focus include developing employees and suppliers, seeking opportunities for innovation, and fulfilling public responsibilities.

Managing for Innovation

Innovation [should involve] making meaningful change to improve an organization's products, services, and processes and create new value for the organization's stakeholders. Innovation should focus on leading your organization to new dimensions of performance . . . Organizations should be structured in such a way that innovation becomes part of the culture and daily work.

Management by Fact

Data and analysis support a variety of purposes, such as planning, reviewing your overall performance, improving operations, and comparing your performance with competitors or with "best practices" benchmarks.

A major consideration in performance improvement involves the selection and use of performance measures or indicators.

Public Responsibility and Citizenship

An organization's leadership needs to stress its responsibilities to the public and needs to practice good citizenship. These responsibilities refer to basic expectations of your organization—business ethics and protection of public health, safety, and the environment. Health, safety, and the environment include your organization's operations as well as the life cycles of your products and services. Also, organizations need to emphasize resource conservation and waste reduction at the source. Planning should anticipate adverse impacts from production, distribution, transportation, use, and disposal of your products. Plans should seek to prevent problems, to provide a forthright response if problems occur, and to make available information and support needed to maintain public awareness, safety, and confidence. Organizations should not only meet all local, state, and federal laws and regulatory requirements, they should treat these and related requirements as opportunities for continuous improvement "beyond mere compliance."

Focus on Results and Creating Value

An organization's performance measurements need to focus on key results. Results should be focused on creating and balancing value for all your stakeholders—customers, employees, stockholders, suppliers and partners, the public, and the community . . . To meet the sometimes conflicting and changing aims that balancing value implies, organizational strategy needs to explicitly include all stakeholder requirements. This will help to ensure that actions and plans meet differing stakeholder needs and avoid adverse impacts on any stakeholders.

Systems Perspective

The Baldrige Criteria provide a systems perspective for managing your organization and achieving performance excellence. The core values and the seven Baldrige Categories form the building blocks of the system. However, successful management of the overall enterprise requires synthesis and alignment. Synthesis means looking at your organization as a whole and focusing on what is important to the whole enterprise. Alignment means concentrating on key organizational linkages among requirements given in the Baldrige Categories.

Criteria for Performance Excellence Framework

The Core Values and Concepts are embodied in seven categories, as follows:

1. Leadership

2. Strategic Planning

3. Customer and Market Focus

4. Information and Analysis

5. Human Resource Focus

6. Process Management

7. Business Results

Source: Adapted from Criteria 2000 at the National Institute of Standards and Technology website: www.quality.nist.gov.

Examiners check the extent to which top management incorporates quality values in daily management; whether products or services are at least as good as those of competitors; whether employees receive training in quality techniques; if the business works with suppliers to improve quality; and if customers are satisfied. All applicants receive a written summary of the strengths and weaknesses of their quality management and suggestions for improvement.

The Baldrige Award has been both praised and criticized.[5] Among the praises are: It has raised the quality-consciousness of U.S. businesses, those who compete find the process motivating, and some contenders have made giant strides in quality and competitiveness. Among the criticisms: The award process involves tremendous amounts of time and effort for both employees and top management at substantial cost (sometimes millions of dollars); applicants nominate themselves (as opposed to being nominated by satisfied customers); winning does not mean that a business has top-quality products or has solved all of its quality problems; and winning may be followed by relaxation under the belief that "we have it made." Some critics say that the number of awards (a maximum of six per year) is too few, considering the large number of organizations that are potential candidates.

---

[5]See, for example, "Is the Baldrige Overblown?" *Fortune,* July 1, 1991, pp. 61–65; and "Does the Baldrige Award Really Work?" *Harvard Business Review,* January–February 1992, pp. 126–47.

THE DEMING PRIZE

The Deming Prize, named in honor of the late W. Edwards Deming, is Japan's highly coveted award recognizing successful quality efforts. It is given annually to any company that meets the award's standards. Although typically given to Japanese firms, in 1989, Florida Power and Light became the first U.S. company to win the award.

The major focus of the judging is on statistical quality control, making it much narrower in scope than the Baldrige Award, which focuses more on customer satisfaction. Companies that win the Deming Prize tend to have quality programs that are detailed and well-communicated throughout the company. Their quality improvement programs also reflect the involvement of senior management and employees, customer satisfaction, and training.

Japan also has an additional award, the Japan Prize, fashioned roughly after the Baldrige Award.

Quality Certification

Many firms that do business internationally recognize the importance of quality certification.

ISO 9000

The purpose of the International Organization for Standardization (ISO) is to promote worldwide standards that will improve operating efficiency, improve productivity, and reduce costs. The ISO is composed of the national standards bodies of 91 countries. The U.S. representative body is the American National Standards Institute (ANSI). The work of the ISO is conducted by some 180 technical committees. ISO 9000 is the work of the Quality Management and Quality Assurance Committee.

The **ISO 9000** series is a set of international standards on quality management and quality assurance. These standards are critical for companies doing business internationally, particularly in Europe. They must go through a process that involves documenting quality procedures and on-site assessment. The process often takes 12 to 18 months. With certification comes *registration* in an ISO directory that companies seeking suppliers can refer to for a list of certified companies. They are generally given preference over unregistered companies. More than 40,000 companies are registered worldwide; three-fourths of them are located in Europe.

A key requirement for registration is that a company review, refine, and map functions such as process control, inspection, purchasing, training, packaging, and delivery. Similar to the Baldrige Award, the review process involves considerable self-appraisal, resulting in problem identification and improvement. Unlike the Baldrige Award, registered companies face an ongoing series of audits, and they must be reregistered every three years.

There are essentially seven standards associated with the ISO 9000 series. Table 9–7 outlines them.

In addition to the obvious benefits of certification for companies who want to deal with the European Union, the ISO 9000 certification and registration process is particularly helpful for companies that do not currently have a quality management system; it provides guidelines for establishing the system and making it effective.

ISO 9000 A set of international standards on quality management and quality assurance, critical to international business.

ISO 9000	Helps companies determine which standard of ISO 9001, 9002, and 9003 applies.
ISO 9001	Outlines guidelines for companies that engage in design, development, production, installation, and servicing of products or service.
ISO 9002	Similar to ISO 9001, but excludes companies engaged in design and development.
ISO 9003	Covers companies engaged in final inspection and testing.
ISO 9004	The guidelines for applying the elements of the Quality Management System.
ISO 10011	Quality system auditing guide.
ISO 10013	Quality manual development guide.

TABLE 9–7

The ISO 9000 series

Critics complain that the emphasis is on documentation and procedures rather than quality of output.

Note that major changes were introduced to the ISO 9000 standards in December 2000. These included:

The title changed to Quality Management Systems—Requirements

ISO 9002 and 9003 eliminated

Eight quality management principles formed the basis of the new standards

Documentation requirements reduced

Measuring and monitoring of customer satisfaction required

Emphasis on continual improvement

ISO 9001 and ISO 14000 linked

The quality management principles are:

1. A systems approach to management.
2. Continual improvement.
3. Factual approach to decision making.
4. Mutually beneficial supplier relationships.
5. Customer focus.
6. Leadership.
7. People involvement.
8. Process approach.

Registrars are allowed to continue assessing on the previous version until December 2003.[6]

If you'd like to learn more about ISO standards, visit the International Organization for Standardization website at www.ISO.ch/welcome.html or the American Society for Quality website at www.asq.org/.

READING

Aesop on Quality Systems   Denise E. Robitaille

What can Aesop's fable about the goat and the goatherd teach us about quality auditing?

Imagine that the master of a medium-sized goat farm is preparing for a third-party audit to be conducted on behalf of a local dairy that wishes to purchase some of his goats. He takes great care with his goats, knowing well-tended animals produce the best milk. He is also proud that his beautiful goats have won numerous prizes at town fairs.

Two days before the audit, the master's goatherd, whose evening task is to gather all the goats and return them to their pen for the night, has trouble with one recalcitrant goat, which refuses to budge. The goatherd, after much fruitless cajoling,

throws several stones at the goat to frighten her into the pen. In the process, he breaks one of her horns. The goatherd begs the goat not to tell the master. The goat replies, "I may be silent. But the broken horn will speak for itself."

When the auditor arrives, the master regales him with numerous examples of how well his goats are treated. The auditor proceeds to assess the herd and finds the goat with the broken horn. Despite all he has been told, the auditor is required to report that although the master has insisted the animals are well treated, the objective evidence is a goat with a broken horn. The data clearly indicate inconsistencies between this vendor's procedures and the actual practice.

The client, an avid proponent of ISO 9000, concludes through his vendor assessment process that the goatherd will have to implement corrective action and provide verification before he can be qualified to sell the dairy any goats.

Aesop, a fabulist who lived in the sixth century B.C., traveled through Greece and the Mediterranean area as an instruc-

---

[6]Source: The John D. Hromi Center for Quality and Applied Statistics, Rochester Institute of Technology.

tor, philosopher, and diplomat. His advice was sought on matters of state. Through his fables, he created an amusing vehicle for illustrating the foibles of human beings. Filled with object lessons that survive into our time, his tales provide insight into the breakdowns and pitfalls 20th century businesses contend with every day.

The Ant and the Grasshopper

A Grasshopper happened upon an Ant who was toiling in preparation for the long winter ahead. She asked of the Ant, "Why do you work so hard on such a pleasant day? Why not dance and sing as I do?" The Ant responded, "I need to plan and prepare myself for the cold weather to come." The Grasshopper laughed and danced away. When the first snows fell the Grasshopper perished. The Ant, snug and secure in her well-provisioned nest, survived and, indeed, prospered oblivious to the tempest outside her home.

More than two centuries ago, Aesop identified the value of good planning and the dire consequences of failing to do so. Today, that value is articulated in the second clause of the ISO 9000 standard. The first clause of the ISO 9000 standard specifically addresses the need to make available necessary resources to ensure the fulfillment of the quality objectives. And we have found that planning is the first step of W. Edwards Deming's plan-do-study-act cycle. Careful planning is an indisputable key element of any quality system.

The Wild Boar and the Fox

A Fox observed a Wild Boar sharpening his tusks. There appearing to be no imminent danger, so the Fox asked, "Why do you sharpen your teeth when your enemies are not around?" The Wild Boar responded, "I would have no time to sharpen them if my enemies were upon me."

Aesop gives us a powerful case for the ninth clause of the ISO 9000 standard, which clearly mandates equipment be maintained so it is reliable when needed. How many of us have missed an important ship date because a vital piece of equipment failed at a critical period due to lack of maintenance?

The Farmer and the Stork

A Farmer cast a net upon his fields in an attempt to capture the cranes that had been eating his seed. In with the cranes, he snared a Stork. The Stork pleaded for his life, saying, "Honorable Farmer, I am not like these others who came to steal your seed. I am a Stork." The Farmer replied, "You may very well be a stork, but from the evidence here, I can only assume that you, too, have come to eat my seeds." And with that he slew the Stork along with the cranes.

The ISO 10011 standard addresses the guidelines for auditing a quality system. An auditor's role is to report findings objectively. Documentation and records should be accurate and reflect actual practices. Evidence that contradicts the auditee will result in an auditor finding inconsistencies between procedures and practices.

Belling the Cat

Once there were a colony of mice inhabiting a large house. The mice were constantly attacked by a cunning and overzealous Cat. The mice held a council in which they discussed how to solve their problem. A clever young mouse rose and offered the following solution: "If we could hear the Cat coming, we would be able to flee in time. Therefore, I propose that we hang a bell around the Cat's neck." The mice cheered wildly over the brilliant solution until an aged mouse stepped to the podium. The elder mouse spoke. "I have only one question. Who shall bell the Cat?"

Returning to Deming's cycle and to any plans for corrective/preventive action, it is wisest to consider the stakeholders and the organization's capability to implement a plan. Many plans fail due to this failure to assess human resources and adequately address constraints. It is always easiest to come up with a plan when someone else is accountable for its implementation.

The Ass and the Mule

An Ass and a Mule were both heavily laden with wares for the monthly fair. The Ass, being smaller and less agile on steep slopes, asked the Mule to relieve him of his burden. The Mule ignored his pleas. Shortly thereafter, the Ass collapsed under his burden and died. The master skinned the dead animal and then placed both his load and the Ass's hide on the Mule's back. The Mule was obliged to carry not only his load, but that of his dead companion.

Imagine the ass is an overburdened department. The mule represents management. Failing to recognize that the department is over-taxed and in need of assistance, management actually contributes to the collapse of an essential process and is left with the need to assume the consequences of that breakdown. Had management fulfilled the mandate to provide adequate resources, the breakdown would have been avoided.

The Pig, the Sheep, and the Goat

The Pig, the Sheep, and the Goat were all penned in for the night. The Pig whined of his condition. The Sheep and the Goat, wearied by his constant complaining, finally said, "We are in the same pen with you. Yet you do not hear us whining." The Pig answered, "The master takes from you only your wool and your milk. It is a different matter with me."

This last fable reiterates the need for management's involvement in the implementation of a quality system. If managers attempt to detach themselves from accountability for the achievement of a goal, they may very well find that their staff assigns to itself the role of the pig and identifies executive managers as the sheep and goats. The fable also serves as an object lesson for Deming's tenet: "Drive out fear."

The Dying Father and His Sons

A Father on his death bed told his Sons that there was a great treasure to be found in his vineyard. After he had died the Sons raced out into the fields and overturned all the soil in search of the prize. No treasure was found, but, due to the revitalization of the soil, the vineyard yielded a bountiful harvest.

Many companies pursue registration to ISO 9000 or another quality standard under pressure from their customers or as a marketing strategy. Along the way to implementation, they discover they have so improved their procedures and processes that the benefits exceed all their expectations, and their company prospers.

The Boy Bathing and the Traveler

A Traveler happened upon a drowning Boy who had foolishly chosen to bathe in a river with a swift current. The Traveler chastised the Boy for his imprudence and then left him to drown. As he sank beneath the water the Boy thought, "How worthless it is to offer criticism without aid."

None of us would leave a drowning victim to perish. We might, however, leave a process owner to tread water by failing to provide problem-solving skills or necessary resources.

Consider the unproductive nature of a quality system that does not seamlessly integrate the audit function, corrective action, and the mandate for management to provide necessary resources. In such an instance, management only looks at a list of nonconformances and does not provide a vehicle for root-cause analysis or direction for corrective action. The auditee is left without the adequate resources to properly address his problem.

A further lesson that may be derived from all of Aesop's fables is a reminder that quality systems should reflect common sense. ISO 9000 or any quality standard should only exist as a framework that facilitates the fulfillment of the quality objectives. But, the fundamentals are not new. Good planning, accountability, objective evidence, and maintenance are concepts with validity that have long survived the test of time. Indeed, as has been illustrated, they have been around for over two millennia.

Bibliography

Aesop's Fables, translated by George F. Townsend (Garden City, NY: Doubleday & Co., 1968).

Source: Reprinted with permission from *Quality Progress,* December 1997.

ISO 14000

> **ISO 14000** A set of international standards for assessing a company's environmental performance.

The International Organization for Standardization introduced a set of environmental standards in 1996: **ISO 14000** is intended to assess a company's performance in terms of environmental responsibility. Initially, ISO 14000 began as a program of voluntary guidelines and certification. The standards for certification bear upon three major areas:

Management systems—Systems development and integration of environmental responsibilities into business planning.

Operations—Consumption of natural resources and energy.

Environmental systems—Measuring, assessing, and managing emissions, effluents, and other waste streams.

Proponents hope that the ISO 14000 will receive the same high interest that the ISO 9000 standards have in the international business community, and will result in businesses giving more attention to environmental responsibilities.

Summary

The success of foreign companies in North American markets revealed them as formidable competitors. They built reputations for quality products. Moreover, they achieved their success using management techniques quite different from those traditionally practiced in the United States. This caused American managers to reexamine their own approaches and to adopt some of those different approaches in order to improve quality and become more competitive.

Quality is defined according to various dimensions that pertain to customer satisfaction. The consequences of poor quality include loss of market share, liability claims, a decrease in productivity, and an increase in costs. Determinants of quality are design, conformance to design, ease of use, and service after delivery.

Modern quality management is directed at preventing mistakes rather than finding them after they occur. Currently, the business community shows widespread interest in improving quality and competitiveness.

The chapter includes a description of the key contributors to quality management, and it outlines the ISO 9000 international quality standards.

Two awards of distinction, the Baldrige Award and the Deming Prize, are given annually to organizations that have shown great achievement in quality management.

appraisal costs, 402
Baldrige Award, 406
Deming Prize, 402
dimensions of quality, 396
external failures, 401
failure costs, 401
internal failures, 401

ISO 9000, 409
ISO 14000, 412
prevention costs, 402
quality, 394
quality of conformance, 398
quality of design, 397

Key Terms

1. List and briefly explain the dimensions of quality.
2. Explain the terms *quality of design* and *quality of conformance.*
3. What are some possible consequences of poor quality?
4. Use the dimensions of quality to describe typical characteristics of these products and services:
   a. A television set
   b. A restaurant meal (product)
   c. A restaurant meal (service)
   d. Painting a house
5. List the determinants of quality.
6. Describe the quality–ethics connection.
7. Select one of the quality gurus and briefly describe his major contributions to quality management.
8. What is ISO 9000, and why is it important for global businesses to have ISO 9000 certification?
9. Briefly explain how a company can achieve lower production costs by improving the quality of its products or services.

Discussion and Review Questions

1. Write a one-page memo to your supervisor, Penny Lane, summarizing the benefits of doing a task right the first time.
2. Suppose that your company is considering entering the competition for a Baldrige Award. Prepare a one-page memo outlining both the pros and cons of doing so to the head of operations, Tom Cartwright.

Memo Writing Exercises

Ansari, Shahid, Janice Bell, Thomas Klammer, and Carol Lawrence. *Measuring and Managing Quality Costs.* New York: McGraw-Hill, 1997.

Besterfield, Dale H., Carol Besterfield-Micha, Glen Besterfield, and Mary Besterfield-Sacre. *Total Quality Management,* 2nd ed. Englewood Cliffs, NJ: Prentice Hall, 1999.

Block, M. R. *Implementing ISO 14001.* Milwaukee: ASQC Quality Press, 1997.

Butman, John. *Juran: A Lifetime of Influence.* New York: John Wiley & Sons, 1997.

Capezio, Peter, and Debra Morehouse. *Taking the Mystery Out of TQM: A Practical Guide to Total Quality Management,* 2nd ed. Franklin Lakes, NJ: National Press Publications, 1995.

Chakrapani, C. *How to Measure Service Quality and Customer Satisfaction: The Informal Field Guide for Tools and Techniques.* Chicago: American Marketing Association, 1998.

Cole, R. E. *Managing Quality Fads: How American Business Learned to Play the Quality Game.* New York: Oxford University Press, 1999.

Dale, Barrie G., ed. *Managing Quality,* 3rd ed. Oxford, UK: Blackwell Publishers, 1999.

Foster, Thomas A. *Managing Quality: An Integrative Approach.* Englewood Cliffs, NJ: Prentice Hall, 2001.

Garvin, David A. *Managing Quality.* New York: Free Press, 1988.

Goetsch, David L., and Stanley B. Davis. *Quality Management: Introduction to Total Quality Management for Production, Processing, and Services,* 3rd ed. Englewood Cliffs, NJ: Prentice Hall, 2000.

Gryna, Derek S., and Frank M. Gryna. "Quality in Banking Starts with Four Assessments." *Quality Progress,* August 1999, pp. 27–34.

Harrington, H. James, Erik K. C. Esseling, and Harm Van Nimwegen. *Business Process Improvement Workbook: Documentation, Analysis, Design, and Management of*

Selected Bibliography and Further Reading

Business Process Improvement. New York: McGraw-Hill, 1997.

Ireland, Samuel. "Quality and Nonprofit Organizations." *Quality Progress,* March 1999, pp. 96–99.

Jacques, March Laree. "The Call of Quality: Doing Right Things Right." *Quality Progress,* September 1999, pp. 48–54.

Juran, Joseph M. *Juran's Quality Handbook.* New York: McGraw-Hill, 1999.

La Lopa, Joseph M., and Richard F. Marecki. "The Critical Role of Quality in the Tourism Industry." *Quality Progress,* August 1999, pp. 37–41.

Milakovich, M. E. *Improving Service Quality: Achieving High Performance in the Public and Private Sectors.* Delray Beach, FL: St. Lucie Press, 1995.

Pyzdek, Thomas. "Quality Profession Must Learn to Heed Its Own Advice." *Quality Progress,* June 1999, pp. 60–64.

Ross, Joel E. *Total Quality Management: Text, Cases, and Readings,* 3rd ed. Boca Raton, FL: St. Lucie Press, 1999.

Scherkenbach, W. W. *The Deming Route to Quality and Productivity: Roadmaps and Roadblocks.* Rockville, MD: Mercury Press/Fairchild Publications, 1990.

Stamatis, D. H. *Documenting and Auditing for ISO 9000 and QS-9000: Tools for Ensuring Certification or Registration.* Burr Ridge, IL: Irwin, 1996.

Stamatis, D. H. *Total Quality Services: Principles, Practices, and Implementation.* Delray Beach, FL: St. Lucie Press, 1996.

Steeples, Marion M. "The Quality–Ethics Connection." *Quality Progress,* June 1994, pp. 73–75.

Summers, Donna. *Quality,* 2nd ed. Englewood Cliffs, NJ: Prentice Hall, 2000.

Zuckerman, A. *ISO 9000 Made Easy: A Cost-Saving Guide to Documentation and Registration.* New York: AMACOM, 1995.

Zuckerman, A. *International Standards Desk Reference: Your Passport to World Markets, ISO 9000, CE Mark, QS-9000, SSM, ISO 14000, Q 9000, American, European, and Global Standards Systems.* New York: AMACOM, 1997.

CHAPTER TEN

Quality Control

CHAPTER OUTLINE

Introduction, 418

Inspection, 418
How Much to Inspect and How
Often, 419

Newsclip: Oops! 420
Where to Inspect in the Process, 420
Centralized versus On-Site
Inspection, 421

Statistical Process Control, 421
The Control Process, 422
Variations and Control, 423
Control Charts, 424
Control Charts for Variables, 427
Control Charts for Attributes, 430
Managerial Considerations
concerning Control Charts, 434
Run Tests, 435

Process Capability, 438
Capability Analysis, 438
C_p, 440

C_{pk}, 440
Limitations of Capability
Indexes, 442

Operations Strategy, 442

Summary, 442

Key Terms, 442

Solved Problems, 443

Discussion and Review
Questions, 447

Memo Writing Exercises, 448

Problems, 448

Cases: Toys, Inc., 453
Tiger Tools, 453

Operations Tour: In the Chips at
Jays, 454

Selected Bibliography and Further
Reading, 456

Supplement: Acceptance
Sampling, 457

LEARNING OBJECTIVES

*After completing this chapter, you
should be able to:*

1 List and briefly explain the
elements of the control process.

2 Explain how control charts are
used to monitor a process, and the
concepts that underlie their use.

3 Use and interpret control charts.

4 Use run tests to check for
nonrandomness in process output.

5 Assess process capability.

quality control A process that evaluates output relative to a standard, and takes corrective action when output doesn't meet standards.

This chapter covers quality control. The purpose of quality control is to assure that processes are performing in an acceptable manner. Companies accomplish this by monitoring process output using statistical techniques. **Quality control** is a process that measures output relative to a standard, and acts when output does not meet standards. If the results are acceptable, no further action is required; unacceptable results call for corrective action.

Introduction

The best companies emphasize *designing quality into the process,* thereby greatly reducing the need for inspection or control efforts. As you might expect, different business organizations are in different stages of this evolutionary process: The least progressive rely heavily on inspection. Many occupy a middle ground that involves some inspection and a great deal of process control. The most progressive have achieved an inherent level of quality that is sufficiently high that they can avoid wholesale inspection activities and process control activities. That is the ultimate goal. Figure 10–1 illustrates these phases of quality assurance.

Quality assurance that relies primarily on inspection of previously produced items is referred to as *acceptance sampling.* It is described in the chapter supplement. Quality control efforts that occur during production are referred to as *statistical process control,* and these we examine in the following sections.

Inspection

inspection Appraisal of goods or services.

Inspection is an appraisal activity that compares goods or services to a standard. Inspection can occur at three points: before production, during production, and after production. The logic of checking conformance before production is to make sure that inputs are acceptable. The logic of checking conformance during production is to make sure that the conversion of inputs into outputs is proceeding in an acceptable manner. The logic of checking conformance of output is to make a final verification of conformance before passing goods on to customers.

Inspection before and after production often involves *acceptance sampling* procedures; monitoring during the production process is referred to as *process control.* Figure 10–2 gives an overview of where these two procedures are applied in the production process.

FIGURE 10–1

Approaches to quality assurance

Inspection before/after production	Corrective action during production	Quality built into the process
Acceptance sampling	Process control	Continuous improvement

The least progressive → The most progressive

FIGURE 10–2

Acceptance sampling and process control

Inputs → Transformation → Outputs

Acceptance sampling   Process control   Acceptance sampling

To determine whether a process is functioning as intended or to verify that a batch or lot of raw materials or final products does not contain more than a specified percentage of defective goods, it is necessary to physically examine at least some of the items in question. The purpose of inspection is to provide information on the degree to which items conform to a standard. The basic issues are:

1. How much to inspect and how often.

2. At what points in the process inspection should occur.

3. Whether to inspect in a centralized or on-site location.

4. Whether to inspect attributes (i.e., *count* the number of times something occurs) or variables (i.e., *measure* the value of a characteristic).

Consider, for example, inspection at an intermediate step in the manufacture of personal computers. Because inspection costs are often significant, questions naturally arise on whether one needs to inspect every computer or whether a small sample of computers will suffice. Moreover, although inspections could be made at numerous points in the production process, it is not generally cost-effective to make inspections at every point. Hence, the question comes up of which points should be designated for inspections. Once these points have been identified, a manager must decide whether to remove the computers from the line and take them to a lab, where specialized equipment might be available to perform certain tests, or to test them where they are being made. We will examine these points in the following sections.

HOW MUCH TO INSPECT AND HOW OFTEN

The amount of inspection can range from no inspection whatsoever to inspection of each item numerous times. Low-cost, high-volume items such as paper clips, roofing nails, and wooden pencils often require little inspection because (1) the cost associated with passing defective items is quite low and (2) the processes that produce these items are usually highly reliable, so that defects are rare. Conversely, high-cost, low-volume items that have large costs associated with passing defective products often require more intensive inspections. Thus, critical components of a manned-flight space vehicle are closely scrutinized because of the risk to human safety and the high cost of mission failure. In high-volume systems, *automated* inspection is one option that may be employed.

The majority of quality control applications lies somewhere between the two extremes. Most require some inspection, but it is neither possible nor economically feasible to critically examine every part of a product or every aspect of a service for control purposes. The cost of inspection, resulting interruptions of a process or delays caused by inspection, and the manner of testing typically outweigh the benefits of 100 percent inspection. However, the cost of letting undetected defects slip through is sufficiently high that inspection cannot be completely ignored. The amount of inspection needed is governed by the costs of inspection and the expected costs of passing defective items. As illustrated in Figure 10–3, if inspection activities increase, inspection costs increase, but the costs of undetected defects decrease. The traditional goal was to minimize the sum of these two costs. In other words, it may not pay to attempt to catch every defect, particularly if the cost of inspection exceeds the penalties associated with letting some defects get through. Current thinking is that every reduction in defective output reduces costs, although not primarily by inspection.

As a rule, operations with a high proportion of human involvement necessitate more inspection effort than mechanical operations, which tend to be more reliable.

The frequency of inspection depends largely on the rate at which a process may go out of control or the number of lots being inspected. A stable process will require only infrequent checks, whereas an unstable one or one that has recently given trouble will require more frequent checks. Likewise, many small lots will require more samples than a few large lots because it is important to obtain sample data from each lot.

FIGURE 10-3

Traditional view:
The amount of inspection is
optimal when the sum of the
costs of inspection and passing
defectives is minimized

NEWSCLIP

Oops!

The Federal Aviation Administration (FAA) has an interesting device it uses to test the strength of airplane windshields in collisions with birds. The device propels dead chickens at the windshield at typical velocities to determine if the windshield can withstand the impact without breaking.

Officials in another country asked to borrow the device to test windshields of a high-speed train that country was developing.

The results of the initial test were astounding. Not only did the windshield break, the dead chicken went through the back of the engineer's chair and lodged in the wall behind it! The inspectors reduced the velocity of the next chicken, but the results were similar, much to the dismay of both the inspectors and the designers. After additional testing, the inspectors wondered if perhaps the device was defective, or perhaps they were using it incorrectly.

When FAA officials were informed of the results, they were dumbfounded. They had never experienced similar results through numerous trials with the device. Further investigation led to a solution to the problem—and a slight addition to the instructions for future users of the machine: *Thaw chicken before using.*

Source: Based on "Inside the Beltway" by John McCaslin, *The Washington Times,* May 15, 1996.

WHERE TO INSPECT IN THE PROCESS

Many operations have numerous possible inspection points. Because each inspection adds to the cost of the product or service, it is important to restrict inspection efforts to the points where they can do the most good. In manufacturing, some of the typical inspection points are:

1. *Raw materials and purchased parts.* There is little sense in paying for goods that do not meet quality standards and in expending time and effort on material that is bad to begin with.

2. *Finished products.* Customer satisfaction and the firm's image are at stake here, and repairing or replacing products in the field is usually much more costly than doing it at the factory. Likewise, the seller is usually responsible for shipping costs on returns, and payments for goods or service may be held up pending delivery of satisfactory goods or remedial service.

3. *Before a costly operation.* The point is to not waste costly labor or machine time on items that are already defective.

4. *Before an irreversible process.* In many cases, items can be reworked up to a certain point; beyond that point they cannot. For example, pottery can be reworked prior to firing. After that, defective pottery must be discarded or sold as seconds at a lower price.

5. *Before a covering process.* Painting, plating, and assemblies often mask defects.

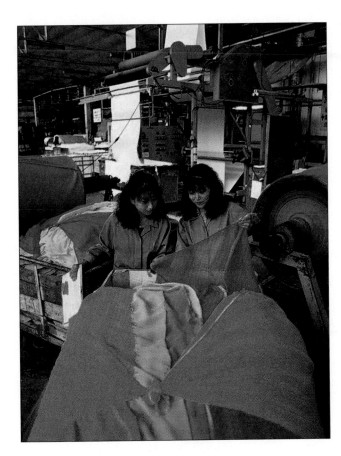

Women inspecting cloth at a textile plant in Korea. A visual inspection can often uncover obvious defects such as tears or uneven weave or color.

In the service sector, inspection points are incoming purchased materials and supplies, personnel, service interfaces (e.g., service counter), and outgoing completed work (e.g., repaired appliances). Table 10–1 illustrates a number of examples.

CENTRALIZED VERSUS ON-SITE INSPECTION

Some situations require that inspections be performed *on site*. For example, inspecting the hull of a ship for cracks requires inspectors to visit the ship. At other times, specialized tests can best be performed in a lab (e.g., medical tests, analyzing food samples, testing metals for hardness, running viscosity tests on lubricants).

The central issue in the decision concerning on-site or lab inspections is whether the advantages of specialized lab tests are worth the time and interruption needed to obtain the results. Reasons favoring on-site inspection include quicker decisions and avoidance of introduction of extraneous factors (e.g., damage or other alteration of samples during transportation to the lab). On the other hand, specialized equipment and a more favorable test environment (less noise and confusion, lack of vibrations, absence of dust, and no workers "helping" with inspections) offer strong arguments for using a lab.

Some companies rely on self-inspections by operators if errors can be traced back to specific operators. This places responsibility for errors at their source (*quality at the source*).

Statistical Process Control

Quality control is concerned with the **quality of conformance** of a process: Does the output of a process conform to the intent of design? Toward that end, managers use **statistical process control** to evaluate the output of a process to determine its acceptability. To do this, they take periodic samples from the process and compare them with a predetermined standard. If the sample results are not acceptable, they stop the process and take corrective action. If the sample results are acceptable, they allow the process to continue.

quality of conformance A product or service conforms to specifications.

statistical process control Statistical evaluation of the output of a process during production.

Type of Business	Inspection Points	Characteristics
Fast food	Cashier	Accuracy
	Counter area	Appearance, productivity
	Eating area	Cleanliness, no loitering
	Building and grounds	Appearance, safety hazards
	Kitchen	Cleanliness, purity of food, food storage, health regulations
	Parking lot	Safety, good lighting
Hotel/motel	Accounting/billing	Accuracy, timeliness
	Building and grounds	Appearance and safety
	Main desk	Appearance, waiting times, accuracy of bills
	Maid service	Completeness, productivity
	Personnel	Appearance, manners, productivity
	Reservations/occupancy	Over/underbooking, percent occupancy
	Restaurants	Kitchen, menus, meals, bills
	Room service	Waiting time, quality of food
	Supplies	Ordering, receiving, inventories
Supermarket	Cashiers	Accuracy, courtesy, productivity
	Deliveries	Quality, quantity
	Produce	Freshness, ample stock
	Aisles and stockrooms	Uncluttered layout
	Inventory control	Stock-outs
	Shelf stock	Ample supply, rotation of perishables
	Shelf displays	Appearance
	Checkouts	Waiting time
	Shopping carts	Good working condition, ample supply, theft/vandalism
	Parking lot	Safety, good lighting
	Personnel	Appearance, productivity

Two statistical tools are used for quality control: *control charts* and *run tests.* Often, they are used together. Both are used to test for *nonrandomness* in data, which implies a process is out of control.

THE CONTROL PROCESS

Sampling and corrective action are only a part of the control process. Effective control requires the following steps:

1. Define.
2. Measure.
3. Compare to a standard.
4. Evaluate.
5. Take corrective action if necessary.
6. Evaluate corrective action.

The first step means to define in sufficient detail what is to be controlled. It is not enough, for example, to simply refer to a painted surface. The paint can have a number of important characteristics such as its thickness, hardness, and resistance to fading or chipping. Different characteristics may require different approaches for control purposes.

Only those characteristics that can be counted or measured are candidates for control. Thus, it is important to consider how measurement will be accomplished.

There must be a standard of comparison that can be used to evaluate the measurements. This will relate to the level of quality being sought.

Management must establish a definition of *out of control.* Even a process that is functioning as it should will not yield output that conforms exactly to a standard, simply because

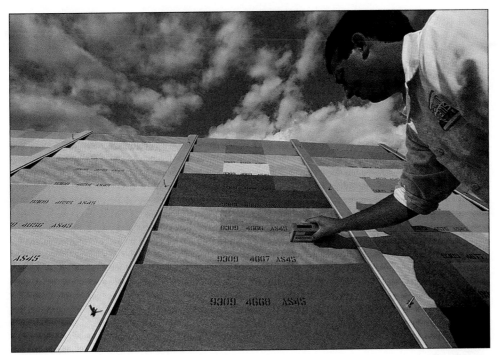

In its product testing, Sherwin-Williams, North America's largest manufacturer of paints and varnishes, tests its paints for longevity and durability. The company operates more than 2,100 paint stores in the U.S., Canada, and Puerto Rico, and is a major supplier for Sears and Wal-Mart.

www.sherwin-williams.com

of the natural (i.e., random) variations inherent in all processes, manual or mechanical—a certain amount of variation is inevitable. The main task of quality control is to distinguish random from *nonrandom* variability, because nonrandom variability means that a process is out of control.

When a process is judged out of control, corrective action must be taken. This involves uncovering the cause of nonrandom variability (e.g., worn equipment, incorrect methods, failure to follow specified procedures) and correcting it.

To ensure that corrective action is effective, the output of a process must be monitored for a sufficient period of time to verify that the problem has been eliminated.

In a nutshell, control is achieved by inspecting a portion of the goods or services, comparing the results to a predetermined standard, evaluating departures from the standard, taking corrective action when necessary, and following up to ensure that problems have been corrected.

VARIATIONS AND CONTROL

All processes that provide a good or a service exhibit a certain amount of "natural" variation in their output. The variations are created by the combined influences of countless minor factors, each one so unimportant that even if it could be identified and eliminated, the decrease in process variability would be negligible. In effect, this variability is inherent in the process. It is often referred to as *chance* or **random variation.** In Deming's terms, this is referred to as *common variability.* The amount of inherent variability differs from process to process. For instance, older machines generally exhibit a higher degree of natural variability than newer machines, partly because of worn parts and partly because new machines may incorporate design improvements that lessen the variability in their output.

A second kind of variability in process output is called **assignable variation.** In Deming's terms, this is referred to as *special variation.* Unlike natural variation, the main sources of assignable variation can usually be identified (assigned to a specific cause) and eliminated. Tool wear, equipment that needs adjustment, defective materials, human factors (carelessness, fatigue, noise and other distractions, failure to follow correct procedures, and so on) and problems with measuring devices are typical sources of assignable variation.

random variation Natural variations in the output of a process, created by countless minor factors.

assignable variation In process output, a variation whose cause can be identified.

The sampling distribution of means is normal, and it has less variability than the process

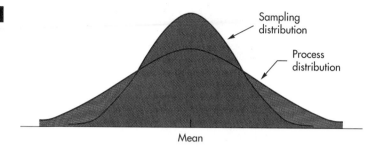

When samples of process output are taken, and sample *statistics* such as the sample mean or range are computed, they exhibit the same kind of variability; that is, there is variation in the values of sample means, and variation in the values of sample ranges. The variability of a sample statistic can be described by its *sampling distribution,* which is a theoretical distribution that describes the *random* variability of sample statistics.

The goal of sampling is to determine whether nonrandom—and thus, correctable—sources of variation are present in the output of a process. The sampling distribution provides the theoretical basis for accomplishing this. Let's see how this is done.

Suppose there is a process for filling bottles with soft drink. If the amount of soft drink in a large number of bottles is measured accurately, we would discover slight differences among the bottles. If these amounts were arranged on a graph, the frequency distribution would reflect the *process variability.* The values would be clustered close to the process average (e.g., 16 ounces), but some of the values would vary somewhat from the mean.

If we return to the process and take *samples* of 10 bottles each and compute the *mean* amount of soft drink in each sample, we would discover that these values also vary, just as the *individual* values varied. They, too, would have a distribution of values.

If the process contained *only* random variability, the distribution of process values would represent the inherent process variability, and the distribution of sample means would represent the random variability of all possible sample means.

The two distributions are illustrated in Figure 10–4. The sampling distribution exhibits much less variability (i.e., it is less spread out) than the process distribution. This reflects the *averaging* that occurs in computing the sample means: High and low values in samples tend to offset each other, resulting in less variability among sample means than among individual values. Note that both distributions have the same mean; the mean of the sampling distribution is exactly equal to the mean of the process. Finally, note that the sampling distribution is a *normal* distribution, even if the process distribution isn't normal. The *central limit theorem* provides the basis for the assumption that the sampling distribution will be normal or at least approximately normal, even if the population (i.e., the process) is not.

The normal distribution can be used to help judge whether a process is performing adequately. If the output reflects only random variability, one would conclude that the process is *stable* (i.e., in control). But if there is evidence of nonrandom variability, one would conclude that the process is unstable (i.e., out of control). To understand how the normal distribution is used, consider the following: Approximately 95.5 percent of the area under a normal curve (and, hence, 95.5 percent of the sample means) will have values that are within ±2 standard deviations of the distribution mean, and approximately 99.7 percent of the sample means will have values that are within ±3 standard deviations of the distribution mean. (See Figure 10–5.) These values are typically used for control limits.

CONTROL CHARTS

control chart A time-ordered plot of sample statistics, used to distinguish between random and nonrandom variability.

A **control chart** is a *time-ordered* plot of sample statistics. It is used to distinguish between random variability and nonrandom variability. The basis for the control chart is the sampling distribution, which essentially describes random variability. There is, however, one minor difficulty relating to the use of a normal sampling distribution. The theoretical

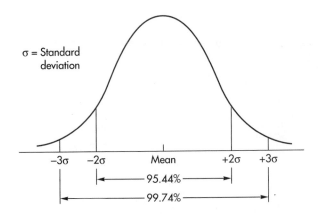

Percentage of values within given ranges in a normal distribution

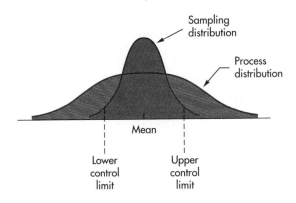

Control limits are based on the sampling distribution

distribution extends in either direction to *infinity.* Therefore, *any* value is theoretically possible, even one that is a considerable distance from the mean of the distribution. However, as a practical matter, we know that, say, 99.7 percent of the values will be within ±3 standard deviations of the mean of the distribution. Therefore, we could decide to set the limit, so to speak, at values that represent ±3 standard deviations from the mean, and conclude that any value that was farther away than these limits was a nonrandom variation. In effect, these limits are **control limits:** the dividing lines between what will be designated as random deviations from the mean of the distribution and what will be designated as nonrandom deviations from the mean of the distribution. Figure 10–6 illustrates how control limits are based on the sampling distribution.

Control charts have two limits that separate random variation and nonrandom variation. The larger value is the *upper control limit* (UCL), and the smaller value is the *lower control limit* (LCL). A sample statistic that falls between these two limits suggests (but does not prove) randomness, while a value outside or on either limit suggests (but does not prove) nonrandomness.

It is important to recognize that because any limits will leave some area in the *tails* of the distribution, there is a small probability that a value will fall outside the limits *even though only random variations are present.* For example, if ±2 sigma (standard deviation) limits are used, they would include 95.5 percent of the values. Consequently, the complement of that number (100 percent − 95.5 percent = 4.5 percent) would not be included. That percentage (or *probability*) is sometimes referred to as the probability of a **Type I error,** where the "error" is concluding that nonrandomness is present when only randomness is present. It is also referred to as an *alpha* risk, where alpha (α) is the sum of the probabilities in the two tails. Figure 10–7 illustrates this concept.

Using wider limits (e.g., ±3 sigma limits) reduces the probability of a Type I error because it decreases the area in the tails. However, wider limits make it more difficult to detect nonrandom variations *if* they are present. For example, the mean of the process might

control limits The dividing lines between random and nonrandom deviations from the mean of the distribution.

Type I error Concluding a process is not in control when it actually is.

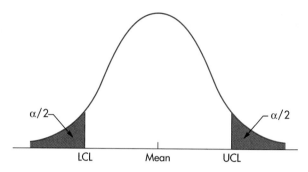

FIGURE 10-7

The probability of a Type I error

$\alpha/2$ $\alpha/2$

LCL   Mean   UCL

α = Probability of a Type I error

FIGURE 10-8

Example of a control chart

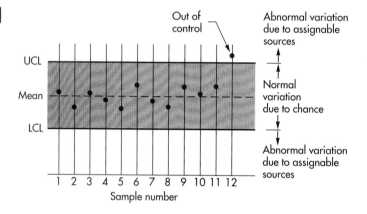

Out of control

Abnormal variation due to assignable sources

UCL

Mean

LCL

Normal variation due to chance

Abnormal variation due to assignable sources

1 2 3 4 5 6 7 8 9 10 11 12
Sample number

FIGURE 10-9

Each observation is compared to the selected limits of the sampling distribution

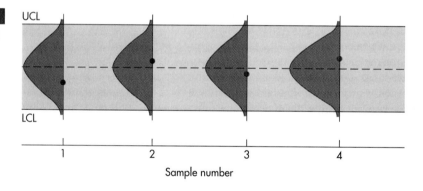

UCL

LCL

1   2   3   4

Sample number

Type II error Concluding a process is in control when it is not.

variables Generate data that are *measured.*

attributes Generate data that are *counted.*

shift (an assignable cause of variation) enough to be detected by two-sigma limits, but not enough to be readily apparent using three-sigma limits. That could lead to a second kind of error, known as a **Type II error,** which is concluding that a process is in control when it is really out of control (i.e., nonrandom variations are not present, when they are). In theory, the costs of making each error should be balanced by their probabilities. However, in practice, two-sigma limits and three-sigma limits are commonly used without specifically referring to the probability of a Type II error.

Figure 10–8 illustrates the components of a control chart. Each sample is represented by a single value (e.g., the sample mean) on the chart. Moreover, each value is compared to the extremes of the sampling distribution (the control limits) to judge if it is within the acceptable (random) range. Figure 10–9 illustrates this concept.

There are four commonly used control charts. Two are used for **variables,** and two are used for **attributes.** Attribute data are *counted* (e.g., the number of defective parts in a sample, the number of calls per day); variables data are *measured,* usually on a continuous scale (e.g., amount of time needed to complete a task, length or width of a part).

The two control charts for variables data are described in the next section, and the two control charts for attribute data are described in the section following that.

CONTROL CHARTS FOR VARIABLES

Mean and range charts are used to monitor variables. Control charts for means monitor the *central tendency* of a process, and range charts monitor the *dispersion* of a process.

Mean Charts. A **mean control chart,** sometimes referred to as an $\bar{x}$ ("x-bar") chart, can be constructed in one of two ways. The choice depends on what information is available. Although the value of the standard deviation of a process, σ, is often unknown, if a reasonable estimate is available, one can compute control limits using these formulas:

mean control chart Control chart used to monitor the central tendency of a process.

Upper control limit (UCL): $= \bar{\bar{x}} + z\sigma_{\bar{x}}$ (10–1)

Lower control limit (LCL): $= \bar{\bar{x}} - z\sigma_{\bar{x}}$

where

$\sigma_{\bar{x}} = \sigma/\sqrt{n}$

$\sigma_{\bar{x}} =$ Standard deviation of distribution of sample means

$\sigma =$ Process standard deviation

$n =$ Sample size

$z =$ Standard normal deviate

$\bar{x} =$ Average of sample means

The following example illustrates the use of these formulas.

A quality inspector took five samples, each with four observations, of the length of time to process loan applications at a credit union. The analyst computed the mean of each sample and then computed the grand mean. All values are in minutes. Use this information to obtain three-sigma (i.e., $z=3$) control limits for means of future times. It is known from previous experience that the standard deviation of the process is .02 minute.

Example 1

		Sample				
		1	**2**	**3**	**4**	**5**
	1	12.11	12.15	12.09	12.12	12.09
	2	12.10	12.12	12.09	12.10	12.14
Observation	**3**	12.11	12.10	12.11	12.08	12.13
	4	12.08	12.11	12.15	12.10	12.12
	x̄	12.10	12.12	12.11	12.10	12.12

Solution

$\bar{\bar{x}} = \dfrac{12.10 + 12.12 + 12.11 + 12.10 + 12.12}{5} = 12.11$

Using Formula 10–1, with $z = 3$, $n = 4$ observations per sample, and $\sigma = .02$, we find

UCL: $12.11 + 3\left(\dfrac{.02}{\sqrt{4}}\right) = 12.14$

LCL: $12.11 - 3\left(\dfrac{.02}{\sqrt{4}}\right) = 12.08$

Note: If one applied these control limits to these data, one would judge the process to be *in control* because all of the sample means have values that fall within the control limits. The fact that some of the *individual* measurements fall outside of the control limits (e.g., the first observation in Sample 2 and the last observation in Sample 3) is irrelevant. You can see why by referring to Figure 10–7: *individual* values are represented by the process distribution, a large portion of which lies outside of the control limits for *means.*

A second approach is to use the sample *range* as a measure of process variability. The appropriate formulas for control limits are

$$\text{UCL} = \bar{\bar{x}} + A_2\bar{R}$$ (10–2)
$$\text{LCL} = \bar{\bar{x}} - A_2\bar{R}$$

where

A_2 = A factor from Table 10–2

$\bar{R}$ = Average of sample ranges

Example 2	Twenty samples of $n = 8$ have been taken from a cleaning operation. The average sample range for the 20 samples was .016 minute, and the average mean was 3 minutes. Determine three-sigma control limits for this process.
Solution	$\bar{\bar{x}} = 3$ cm, $\bar{R} = .016$, $A_2 = .37$ for $n = 8$ (from Table 10–2)

$$\text{UCL} = \bar{\bar{x}} + A_2\bar{R} = 3 + .37(.016) = 3.006 \text{ minutes}$$
$$\text{LCL} = \bar{\bar{x}} - A_2\bar{R} = 3 + .37(.016) = 2.994 \text{ minutes}$$

Note that this approach assumes that the range is in control.

range control chart Control chart used to monitor process dispersion.

Range Charts. **Range control charts** (*R*-charts) are used to monitor process dispersion; they are sensitive to changes in process dispersion. Although the underlying sampling distribution is not normal, the concepts for use of range charts are much the same as those for use of mean charts. Control limits for range charts are found using the average sample range in conjunction with these formulas:

$$\text{UCL}_R = D_4\bar{R}$$ (10–3)
$$\text{LCL}_R = D_3\bar{R}$$

where values of D_3 and D_4 are obtained from Table 10–2.

Example 3	Twenty-five samples of $n = 10$ observations have been taken from a milling process. The average sample range was .01 centimeter. Determine upper and lower control limits for sample ranges.
Solution	$\bar{R} = .01$ cm, $n = 10$

From Table 10–2, for $n = 10$, $D_4 = 1.78$ and $D_3 = .22$.

$$\text{UCL}_R = 1.78(.01) = .0178 \text{ or } .018$$
$$\text{LCL}_R = .22(.01) = .0022 \text{ or } .002$$

In Example 3, a sample range of .018 centimeter or more would suggest that the process variability had increased. A sample range of .002 or less would imply that the

Number of Observations in Subgroup, n	Factor for $\bar{x}$ Chart, A_2	FACTORS FOR R CHARTS	
		Lower Control Limit, D_3	Upper Control Limit, D_4
2	1.88	0	3.27
3	1.02	0	2.57
4	0.73	0	2.28
5	0.58	0	2.11
6	0.48	0	2.00
7	0.42	0.08	1.92
8	0.37	0.14	1.86
9	0.34	0.18	1.82
10	0.31	0.22	1.78
11	0.29	0.26	1.74
12	0.27	0.28	1.72
13	0.25	0.31	1.69
14	0.24	0.33	1.67
15	0.22	0.35	1.65
16	0.21	0.36	1.64
17	0.20	0.38	1.62
18	0.19	0.39	1.61
19	0.19	0.40	1.60
20	0.18	0.41	1.59

TABLE 10–2

*Factors for **three-sigma** control limits for $\bar{x}$ and R charts*

Source: Adapted from Eugene Grant and Richard Leavenworth, *Statistical Quality Control*, 5th ed. (New York: McGraw-Hill, 1980).

process variability had decreased. In the former case, this means that the process was producing too much variation; we would want to investigate this in order to remove the cause of variation. In the latter case, even though decreased variability is desirable, we would want to determine what was causing it: Perhaps an improved method has been used, in which case we would want to identify it. Possibly the improved quality has come at the expense of productivity, or this was only a random occurrence. Hence, it can be beneficial to investigate points beyond the lower limit as well as points beyond the upper limit in a range chart.

Using Mean and Range Charts. Mean control charts and range control charts provide different perspectives on a process. As we have seen, mean charts are sensitive to shifts in the process mean, whereas range charts are sensitive to changes in process dispersion. Because of this difference in perspective, both types of charts might be used to monitor the same process. The logic of using both is readily apparent in Figure 10–10. In 10–10A, the mean chart picks up the shift in the process mean, but because the dispersion is not changing, the range chart fails to indicate a problem. Conversely, in 10–10B, a change in process dispersion is less apt to be detected by the mean chart than by the range chart. Thus, use of both charts provides more complete information than either chart alone. Even so, a single chart may suffice in some cases. For example, a process may be more susceptible to changes in the process mean than to changes in dispersion, so it might be unnecessary to monitor dispersion. Because of the time and cost of constructing control charts, gathering the necessary data, and evaluating the results, only those aspects of a process that tend to cause problems should be monitored.

Once control charts have been set up, they can serve as a basis for deciding when to interrupt a process and search for assignable causes of variation. To determine initial control limits, one can use the following procedure.

FIGURE 10-10

Mean and range charts used together complement each other

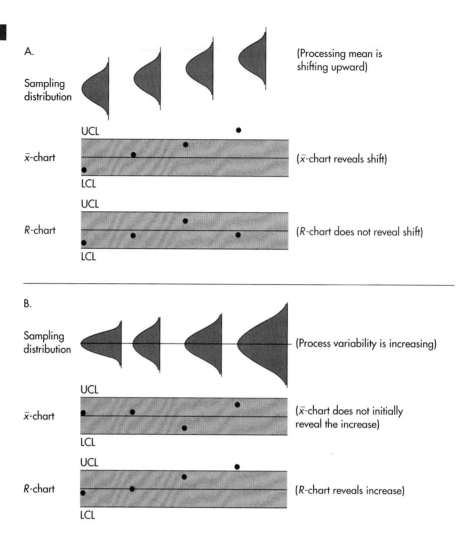

1. Obtain 20 to 25 samples. Compute the appropriate sample statistic(s) for each sample (e.g., mean).
2. Establish preliminary control limits using the formulas, and graph them.
3. Plot the sample statistics on the control chart(s), and note whether any points fall outside the control limits.
4. If you find no out-of-control signals, assume that the process is in control. If not, investigate and correct assignable causes of variation. Then resume the process and collect another set of observations upon which control limits can be based.

CONTROL CHARTS FOR ATTRIBUTES

Control charts for attributes are used when the process characteristic is *counted* rather than measured. For example, the number of defective items in a sample is counted, whereas the length of each item is measured. There are two types of attribute control charts, one for the fraction of defective items in a sample (a *p*-chart) and one for the number of defects per unit (a *c-chart*). A *p-chart* is appropriate when the data consist of two categories of items. For instance, if glass bottles are inspected for chipping and cracking, both the good bottles and the defective ones can be counted. However, one can count the

TABLE 10–3

p-chart or c-chart?

The following tips should help you select the type of control chart, a *p*-chart or a *c*-chart, that is appropriate for a particular application:

Use a *p*-chart:

1. When observations can be placed into one of *two categories*. Examples include items (observations) that can be classified as:
   a. Good or bad.
   b. Pass or fail.
   c. Operate or don't operate.
2. When the data consist of multiple samples of *n* observations each (e.g., 15 samples of *n* = 20 observations each).

Use a *c*-chart:

When only the number of occurrences per unit of measure can be counted; nonoccurrences cannot be counted. Examples of occurrences and units of measure include:

a. Scratches, chips, dents, or errors per item.
b. Cracks or faults per unit of distance (e.g., meters, miles).
c. Breaks or tears, per unit of area (e.g., square yard, square meter).
d. Bacteria or pollutants per unit of volume (e.g., gallon, cubic foot, cubic yard).
e. Calls, complaints, failures, equipment breakdowns, or crimes per unit of time (e.g., hour, day, month, year).

number of accidents that occur during a given period of time but *not* the number of accidents that did not occur. Similarly, one can count the number of scratches on a polished surface, the number of bacteria present in a water sample, and the number of crimes committed during the month of August, but one cannot count the number of nonoccurrences. In such cases, a *c-chart* is appropriate. See Table 10–3.

p-Chart. A *p*-chart is used to monitor the proportion of defective items generated by a process. The theoretical basis for a *p*-chart is the binomial distribution, although for large sample sizes, the normal distribution provides a good approximation to it. Conceptually, a *p*-chart is constructed and used in much the same way as a mean chart.

p-**chart** Control chart for attributes, used to monitor the proportion of defective items in a process.

The center line on a *p*-chart is the average fraction defective in the population, *p*. The standard deviation of the sampling distribution when *p* is known is

$$\sigma_p = \sqrt{\frac{p(1-p)}{n}}$$

Control limits are computed using the formulas

$$\text{UCL}_p = p + z\sigma_p \qquad (10\text{–}4)$$
$$\text{LCL}_p = p - z\sigma_p$$

If *p* is unknown, it can be estimated from samples. That estimate, $\bar{p}$, replaces *p* in the preceding formulas, as illustrated in Example 4.

Note: Because the formula is an approximation, it sometimes happens that the computed LCL is negative. In those instances, zero is used as the lower limit.

Example 4

An inspector counted the number of defective monthly billing statements of a company telephone in each of 20 samples. Using the following information, construct a control chart that will describe 99.74 percent of the chance variation in the process when the process is in control. Each sample contained 100 statements.

Sample	Number of Defectives	Sample	Number of Defectives
1	4	11	8
2	10	12	12
3	12	13	9
4	3	14	10
5	9	15	21
6	11	16	10
7	10	17	8
8	22	18	12
9	13	19	10
10	10	20	16
			220

Solution

z for 99.74 percent is 3.00 (from Appendix Table A).

$$\bar{p} = \frac{\text{Total number of defectives}}{\text{Total number of observations}} = \frac{220}{20(100)} = .11$$

$$\hat{\sigma}_p = \sqrt{\frac{\bar{p}(1 - \bar{p})}{n}} = \sqrt{\frac{.11(1 - .11)}{100}} = .03$$

Control limits are:

$$\text{UCL}_p = \bar{p} + z(\hat{\sigma}_p) = .11 + 3.00(.03) = .20$$

$$\text{LCL}_p = \bar{p} - z(\hat{\sigma}_p) = .11 - 3.00(.03) = .02$$

Plotting the control limits and the sample fraction defective, you can see that the process is not in control: sample 8 ($^{22}/_{100} = .22$) and sample 15 ($^{21}/_{100} = .21$) are above the upper control limit.

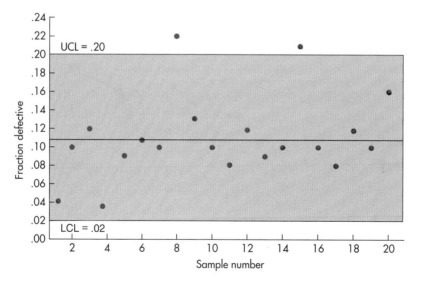

c-Chart. When the goal is to control the number of *occurrences* (e.g., defects) *per unit,* a **c-chart** is used. Units might be automobiles, hotel rooms, typed pages, or rolls of carpet. The underlying sampling distribution is the Poisson distribution. Use of the Poisson distribution assumes that defects occur over some *continuous* region and that the probability of more than one defect at any particular spot is negligible. The mean number of defects per unit is c and the standard deviation is $\sqrt{c}$. For practical reasons, the normal approximation to the Poisson is used. The control limits are

c-chart Control chart for attributes, used to monitor the number of defects per unit.

$$UCL_c = c + z\sqrt{c} \qquad (10\text{--}5)$$

$$LCL_c = c - z\sqrt{c}$$

If the value of c is unknown, as is generally the case, the sample estimate, $\bar{c}$, is used in place of c.

Example 5

Rolls of coiled wire are monitored using a c-chart. Eighteen rolls have been examined, and the number of defects per roll has been recorded in the following table. Is the process in control? Plot the values on a control chart using three standard deviation control limits.

Sample	Number of Defectives	Sample	Number of Defectives
1	3	10	1
2	2	11	3
3	4	12	4
4	5	13	2
5	1	14	4
6	2	15	2
7	4	16	1
8	1	17	3
9	2	18	1
			45

Solution

$$\bar{c} = 45/18 = 2.5$$

$$UCL_c = \bar{c} + 3\sqrt{\bar{c}} = 2.5 + 3\sqrt{2.5} = 7.24$$

$$LCL_c = c - 3\sqrt{\bar{c}} = 2.5 - 3\sqrt{2.5} = -.66 \rightarrow 0$$

If the process average is unknown, it can be estimated from sample data, using $\bar{c}$ = Number of defects ÷ Number of samples.

When the computed lower control limit is negative, the effective lower limit is zero. The calculation sometimes produces a negative lower limit due to the use of the normal distribution to approximate the Poisson distribution: The normal is symmetrical, whereas the Poisson is not symmetrical when c is close to zero.

Standardization is the key component of McDonald's strategy and all foods are prepared according to a strict reference manual. Farmers even have special guidelines to follow in growing potatoes for french fries. Here, quality assurance staff checks all aspects of french fries, from the sweetness of the ketchup to the length of the fries.

www.mcdonalds.com

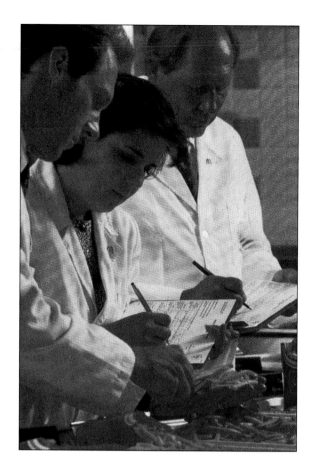

MANAGERIAL CONSIDERATIONS CONCERNING CONTROL CHARTS

Using control charts adds to the cost and time needed to obtain output. Ideally a process is so good that the desired level of quality could be achieved without the use of any control charts. The best organizations strive to reach this level, but many are not yet there, so they employ control charts at various points in their processes. In those organizations, managers must make a number of important decisions about the use of control charts:

1. At what points in the process to use control charts.
2. What size samples to take.
3. What type of control chart to use (i.e., variables or attribute).

   The decision about where to use control charts should focus on those aspects of the process that (1) have a tendency to go out of control and (2) are critical to the successful operation of the product or service.

   Sample size is important for two reasons. One is that cost and time are functions of sample size; the greater the sample size, the greater the cost to inspect those items (and the greater the lost product if destructive testing is involved) and the longer the process must be held up while waiting for the results of sampling. The second reason is that smaller samples are more likely to reveal a change in the process than larger samples because a change is more likely to take place *within* the large sample, but *between* small samples. Consequently, a sample statistic such as the sample mean in the large sample could combine both "before-change" and "after-change" observations, whereas in two smaller samples, the first could contain "before" observations and the second "after" observations, making detection of the change more likely.

In some instances, a manager can choose between using a control chart for variables (a mean chart) and a control chart for attributes (a p-chart). If the manager is monitoring the diameter of a drive shaft, either the diameter could be measured and a mean chart used for control, or the shafts could be inspected using a *go, no-go gauge*—which simply indicates whether a particular shaft is within specification without giving its exact dimensions—and a p-chart could be used. Measuring is more costly and time-consuming per unit than the yes-no inspection using a go, no-go gauge, but because measuring supplies more information than merely counting items as good or bad, one needs a much smaller sample size for a mean chart than a p-chart. Hence, a manager must weigh the time and cost of sampling against the information provided.

RUN TESTS

Analysts often supplement control charts with a **run test,** which is another kind of test for randomness. This enables an analyst to do a better job of detecting abnormalities in a process and provides insights into correcting a process that is out of control. A variety of run tests are available; this section describes two that are widely used.

run test A test for randomness.

When a process is stable or in statistical control, the output it generates will exhibit random variability over a period of time. The presence of patterns, such as trends, cycles, or bias in the output indicates that assignable, or nonrandom, causes of variation exist. Hence, a process that produces output with such patterns is not in a state of statistical control. This is true even though all points on a control chart may be within the control limits. For this reason, it is usually prudent to subject control chart data to run tests to determine whether patterns can be detected.

A **run** is defined as a sequence of observations with a certain characteristic, followed by one or more observations with a different characteristic. The characteristic can be anything that is observable. For example, in the series A A A B, there are two runs: a run of three As followed by a run of one B. Underlining each run helps in counting them. In the series A̲A̲ B̲ B̲ B̲ A̲, the underlining indicates three runs.

run Sequence of observations with a certain characteristic.

Two useful run tests involve examination of the number of runs *up and down* and runs above and below the *median.*[1] In order to count these runs, the data are transformed into a series of Us and Ds (for *up* and *down*) and into a series of As and Bs (for *above* and *below* the median). Consider the following sequence, which has a median of 36.5. The first two values are below the median, the next two are above it, the next to last is below, and the last is above. Thus, there are four runs:

25	29	42	40	35	38
B̲	B̲	A̲	A̲	B̲	A̲

In terms of up and down, there are three runs in the same data. The second value is up from the first value, the third is up from the second, the fourth is down from the third, and so on:

25	29	42	40	35	38
—	U̲	U̲	D̲	D̲	U̲

(The first value does not receive either a U or a D because nothing precedes it.)

If a plot is available, the runs can be easily counted directly from the plot, as illustrated in Figures 10–11 and 10–12.

To determine whether any patterns are present in control chart data, one must transform the data into both As and Bs and Us and Ds, and then count the number of runs in each case. These numbers must then be compared with the number of runs that would be expected in a completely random series. For both the median and the up/down run tests,

---

[1]The median and mean are approximately equal for control charts. The use of the median depends on its ease of determination; use the mean instead of the median if it is given.

FIGURE 10-11

Counting above/below median runs

Counting Above/Below Median Runs

<u>B</u>   <u>A   A</u>   <u>B</u>   <u>A</u>   <u>B   B   B</u>   <u>A   A</u>   <u>B</u>   (7 runs)

FIGURE 10-12

Counting up/down runs

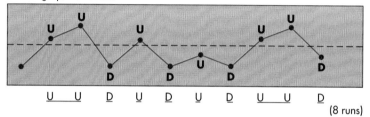

Counting Up/Down Runs

<u>U</u>   <u>U</u>   <u>D</u>   <u>U</u>   <u>D</u>   <u>U</u>   <u>D</u>   <u>U   U</u>   <u>D</u>

(8 runs)

the expected number of runs is a function of the number of observations in the series. The formulas are

$$E(r)_{med} = \frac{N}{2} + 1 \tag{10–6a}$$

$$E(r)_{u/d} = \frac{2N - 1}{3} \tag{10–7a}$$

where N is the number of observations or data points, and $E(r)$ is the expected number of runs.

The actual number of runs in any given set of observations will vary from the expected number, due to chance and any patterns that might be present. Chance variability is measured by the standard deviation of runs. The formulas are

$$\sigma_{med} = \sqrt{\frac{N - 1}{4}} \tag{10–6b}$$

$$\sigma_{u/d} = \sqrt{\frac{16N - 29}{90}} \tag{10–7b}$$

Distinguishing chance variability from patterns requires use of the sampling distributions for median runs and up/down runs. Both distributions are approximately normal. Thus, for example, 95.5 percent of the time a random process will produce an observed number of runs within two standard deviations of the expected number. If the observed number of runs falls in that range, there are probably no nonrandom patterns; for observed numbers of runs beyond such limits, we begin to suspect that patterns are present. Too few or too many runs can be an indication of nonrandomness.

In practice, it is often easiest to compute the number of standard deviations, z, by which an observed number of runs differs from the expected number. This z value would then be compared to the value ± 2 (z for 95.5 percent) or some other desired value (e.g., ± 1.96 for 95 percent, ± 2.33 for 98 percent). A test z that exceeds the desired limits indicates patterns are present. (See Figure 10–13.) The computation of z takes the form

$$z_{test} = \frac{\text{Observed number of runs} - \text{Expected number of runs}}{\text{Standard deviation of number of runs}}$$

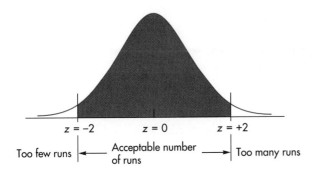

FIGURE 10-13

A sampling distribution for runs is used to distinguish chance variation from patterns

For the median and up/down tests, one can find z using these formulas:

Median:
$$z = \frac{r - [(N/2) + 1]}{\sqrt{(N-1)/4}} \qquad (10\text{--}8)$$

Up and down:
$$z = \frac{r - [(2N-1)/3]}{\sqrt{(16N - 29)/90}} \qquad (10\text{--}9)$$

where

N = Total number of observations

r = Observed number of runs of either As and Bs or Us and Ds, depending on which test is involved.

It is desirable to apply both run tests to any given set of observations because each test is different in terms of the types of patterns it can detect. Sometimes both tests will pick up a certain pattern, but sometimes only one will detect nonrandomness. If either does, the implication is that some sort of nonrandomness is present in the data.

Twenty sample means have been taken from a process. The means are shown in the following table. Use median and up/down run tests with $z = 2$ to determine if assignable causes of variation are present. Assume the median is 11.0.

Example 6

The means are marked according to above/below the median and up/down. The solid lines represent the runs.

Solution

Sample	A/B	Mean	U/D	Sample	A/B	Mean	U/D
1	B	10.0	—	11	B	10.7	D
2	B	10.4	U	12	A	11.3	U
3	B	10.2	D	13	B	10.8	D
4	A	11.5	U	14	A	11.8	U
5	B	10.8	D	15	A	11.2	D
6	A	11.6	U	16	A	11.6	U
7	A	11.1	D	17	A	11.2	D
8	A	11.2	U	18	B	10.6	D
9	B	10.6	D	19	B	10.7	U
10	B	10.9	U	20	A	11.9	U

A/B: 10 runs   U/D: 17 runs

The expected number of runs for each test is

$$E(r)_{med} = \frac{N}{2} + 1 = \frac{20}{2} + 1 = 11$$

$$E(r)_{u/d} = \frac{2N - 1}{3} = \frac{2(20) - 1}{3} = 13$$

The standard deviations are

$$\sigma_{med} = \sqrt{\frac{N-1}{4}} = \sqrt{\frac{20-1}{4}} = 2.18$$

$$\sigma_{u/d} = \sqrt{\frac{16N-29}{90}} = \sqrt{\frac{16(20)-29}{90}} = 1.80$$

The z_{test} values are

$$z_{med} = \frac{10-11}{2.18} = -.46$$

$$z_{u/d} = \frac{17-13}{1.80} = +2.22$$

Although the median test does not reveal any pattern, because its z_{test} value is within the range ± 2, the up/down test does; its value exceeds $+2$. Consequently, nonrandom variations are probably present in the data and, hence, the process is not in control.

If ties occur in either test (e.g., a value equals the median or two values in a row are the same), assign A/B or U/D in such a manner that that z_{test} is as large as possible. If z_{test} still does not exceed ± 2 (± 1.96, etc.), you can be reasonably confident that a conclusion of randomness is justified.

Process Capability

The variability of a process can significantly impact quality. Three commonly used terms refer to the variability of process output. Each term relates to a slightly different aspect of that variability, so it is important to differentiate these terms.

specifications A range of acceptable values established by engineering design or customer requirements.

Specifications or *tolerances* are established by engineering design or customer requirements. They indicate a range of values in which individual units of output must fall in order to be acceptable.

Control limits are statistical limits that reflect the extent to which *sample statistics* such as means and ranges can vary due to randomness alone.

process variability Natural or inherent variability in a process.

Process variability reflects the natural or inherent (i.e., random) variability in a process. It is measured in terms of the process standard deviation.

Control limits and process variability are directly related: control limits are based on sampling variability, and sampling variability is a function of process variability. On the other hand, there is no direct link between specifications and either control limits or process variability. They are specified in terms of a product or service, not in terms of the *process* by which the product or service is generated. Hence, in a given instance, the output of a process may or may not conform to specifications, even though the process may be statistically in control. That is why it is also necessary to take into account the *capability* of a process. The term **process capability** refers to the inherent variability of process output *relative to* the variation allowed by the design specifications. The following section describes capability analysis.

process capability The inherent variability of process output relative to the variation allowed by the design specification.

CAPABILITY ANALYSIS

Capability analysis is the determination of whether the inherent variability of the process output falls within the acceptable range of variability allowed by the design specifications for the process output. If it is within the specifications, the process is said to be "capable." If it is not, the manager must decide how to correct the situation.

A. Process variability matches specifications

B. Process variability well within specifications

C. Process variability exceeds specifications

FIGURE 10–14

Process capability and specifications may or may not match

Consider the three cases illustrated in Figure 10–14. In the first case, process capability and output specifications are well matched, so that nearly all of the process output can be expected to meet the specifications. In the second case, the process variability is much less than what is called for, so that virtually 100 percent of the output should be within tolerance. In the third case, however, the specifications are tighter than what the process is capable of, so that even when the process is functioning as it should, a sizable percentage of the output will fail to meet the specifications. In other words, the process could be in control and still generate unacceptable output. Thus, we cannot automatically assume that a process that is in control will provide desired output. Instead, we must specifically check whether a process is *capable* of meeting specifications and not simply set up a control chart to monitor it. A process should be in control and within specifications *before* production begins—in essence, "Set the toaster correctly at the start. Don't burn the toast and then scrape it!"

In instances such as case C in Figure 10–14, a manager might consider a range of possible solutions: (1) redesign the process so that it can achieve the desired output, (2) use an alternative process that can achieve the desired output, (3) retain the current process but attempt to eliminate unacceptable output using 100 percent inspection, and (4) examine the specifications to see whether they are necessary or could be relaxed without adversely affecting customer satisfaction.

Obviously, process variability is the key factor in process capability. It is measured in terms of the process standard deviation; process capability is typically deemed to be ± 3 standard deviations from the process mean. To determine whether the process is capable, compare this ± 3 standard deviations value to the specifications that are expressed as an allowance deviation from an ideal value. For example, suppose the ideal length of time to perform a service is 10 minutes, and an acceptable range of variation around this time is ± 1 minute. If the process has a standard deviation of .5 minute, it would not be capable because ± 3 standard deviations would be ± 1.5 minutes, exceeding the specification of ± 1 minute.

Example 7

A *manager* has the option of using any one of three machines for a job. The machines and their standard deviations are listed below. Determine which machines are capable if the specifications are 1.00 mm and 1.60 mm.

Machine	Standard Deviation (mm)
A	0.10
B	0.08
C	0.13

Solution

Determine the capability of each machine (i.e., 6 standard deviations) and compare that value to the specification *difference* of .60 mm.

Machine	Standard Deviation (mm)	Machine Capability
A	0.10	0.60
B	0.08	0.48
C	0.13	0.78

We can see that both machine A and machine B are capable of producing output that is within the specs, but that machine C is not, because it exceeds the specification width of .60. See Figure 10–14 for a visual portrayal of these results.

C_p

To express the capability of a machine or process, some companies use the ratio of the specification width to the process capability. It can be computed using the following formula:

$$\text{Process capability ratio, } C_p = \frac{\text{Specification width}}{\text{Process width}} \tag{10–10}$$

$$= \frac{\text{Upper specification} - \text{Lower specification}}{6\sigma}$$

Example 8

Compute the process capability index for each machine in Example 7.

Solution

The specification width in Example 7 is .60 mm. Hence, to determine the capability index for each machine, divide .60 by the process width (i.e., 6 standard deviations) of each machine. The results are shown in the following table:

Machine	Standard Deviation (mm)	Machine Capability	C_p
A	0.10	0.60	0.60/0.60 = 1.00
B	0.08	0.48	0.60/0.48 = 1.25
C	0.13	0.78	0.60/0.78 = 0.77

Using the capability ratio, you can see that for a process to be capable, it must have a capability ratio of at least 1.00. A ratio of 1.00 implies that 99.74% of the output of a process can be expected to be within the specifications. Moreover, the greater the capability ratio, the greater the probability that the output of a machine or process will fall within design specifications.

The Motorola Corporation is well known for its use of the term *six-sigma,* which refers to its goal of achieving a process variability so small that the design specifications represent six standard deviations of the process. That means a process capability ratio equal to 2.00, resulting in an extremely small probability of getting any output not within the design specifications. This is illustrated in Figure 10–15.

To get an idea of how a capability ratio of 2.00 compares to a ratio of 1.00 in terms of defective items, consider that if the U.S. Postal Service had a capability ratio of 1.00 for delivery errors of first-class mail, this would translate into about 10,000 misdelivered pieces per day; if the capability ratio was 2.00, that number would drop to about 1,000 pieces a day.

C_{pk}

If a process is not centered, a slightly different measure is used to compute its capability. This ratio is represented by the symbol C_{pk}. It is computed by finding the difference between each of the specification limits and the mean, identifying the smaller difference, and dividing that difference by three standard deviations of the process. Thus, C_{pk} is equal to the *smaller* of

$$\frac{\text{Upper specification} - \text{Process mean}}{3\sigma} \tag{10–11}$$

and

3-sigma capability

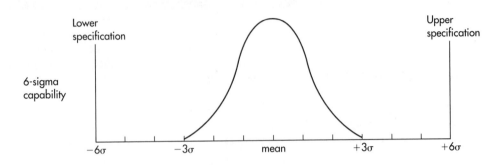

6-sigma capability

FIGURE 10-15

Three-sigma versus six-sigma capability

$$\frac{\text{Process mean} - \text{Lower specification}}{3\sigma}$$

A process has a mean of 9.20 grams and a standard deviation of .30 gram. The lower specification limit is 8.00 grams and the upper specification limit is 10.00 grams. Compute C_{pk}.

Example 9

1. Compute the ratio for the lower specification:

$$\frac{\text{Process mean} - \text{Lower specification}}{3\sigma} = \frac{9.20 - 8.00}{3(.30)} = \frac{1.20}{.90} = 1.33$$

Solution

2. Compute the ratio for the upper specification:

$$\frac{\text{Upper specification} - \text{Process mean}}{3\sigma} = \frac{10.00 - 9.20}{3(.30)} = \frac{.80}{.90} = .89$$

The smaller of the two ratios is .89, so this is the C_{pk}. Because the C_{pk} is less than 1.00, the process is *not* capable. Note that if C_p had been used, it would have given the false impression that the process was capable.

$$C_p = \frac{\text{Upper specification} - \text{Lower specification}}{6\sigma} = \frac{10.00 - 8.00}{6(.30)} = \frac{2.00}{1.80} = 1.11$$

You might be wondering why a process wouldn't be centered as a matter of course. One reason is that only a range of acceptable values, not a target value, may be specified. A better reason is that the cost of nonconformance is greater for one specification limit than it is for nonconformance for the other specification limit. In that case, it would make sense to balance the cost per nonconforming unit, multiplied by the probability of nonconformance, for the two specification limits. This would result in a non-centered process.

LIMITATIONS OF CAPABILITY INDEXES

There are several risks of using a capability index:

1. The process may not be stable, in which case a capability index is meaningless.
2. The process output may not be normally distributed, in which case inferences about the fraction of output that isn't acceptable will be incorrect.
3. The process is not centered but the C_p index is used, giving a misleading result.

Operations Strategy

It is neither necessary nor desirable to use control charts on every production process. Some processes are highly stable; other processes that previously produced unacceptable output may have been subjected to improvements that resulted in quality being *designed into* the process or product, making continual monitoring unnecessary. To use a "shotgun" approach that puts control charts on many processes would be wasteful.

Managers should use control charts on processes that tend to go out of control and, even then, only on a temporary basis until the causative problems have been permanently corrected. Similarly, when a process is changed significantly or a new process is introduced, it makes sense to monitor the output until it becomes apparent that the process is stable. After that, unless there is some compelling reason to believe that the process is likely to become unstable, there would be no reason to continue with a control chart.

Many organizations use computerized control charts. This allows for real-time feedback and, hence, a quicker response when an out-of-control situation is indicated.

Summary

This chapter describes inspection and statistical process control. Inspection means examining the output of a process to determine whether it is acceptable. Key issues in inspection include where to inspect in the process, how often to inspect, and whether to inspect on-site or in a laboratory.

Statistical process control focuses on detecting departures from randomness in a process. Two basic tools of process control are control charts and run tests. The general theory of control charts is discussed, and four types of control charts—two for variables and two for attributes—and two types of run tests are described in the chapter. The chapter ends with a discussion of process capability. Process capability studies are used to determine if the output of a process will satisfy specifications. They can provide valuable information for managers in terms of reducing costs and avoiding problems created by generating output that is not within specifications. Table 10–4 provides a summary of formulas.

Key Terms

assignable variation, 423
attributes, 426
c-chart, 432
control chart, 424
control limits, 425
inspection, 418
mean control chart, 427
p-chart, 431
process capability, 438
process variability, 438
quality control, 418

quality of conformance, 421
random variation, 423
range control chart, 428
run, 435
run test, 435
specifications, 438
statistical process control, 421
Type I error, 425
Type II error, 426
variables, 426

TABLE 10–4

Summary of formulas

CONTROL CHARTS		
Name	**Symbol**	**Control Limits**
Mean	$\bar{x}$	$\bar{\bar{x}} \pm z\dfrac{\sigma}{\sqrt{n}}$ or $\bar{\bar{x}} \pm A_2\bar{R}$
Range	R	$UCL = D_4\bar{R}$, $LCL = D_3\bar{R}$
Fraction defective	p	$\bar{p} \pm z\sqrt{\dfrac{\bar{p}(1-\bar{p})}{n}}$
Number of defects	c	$\bar{c} \pm z\sqrt{\bar{c}}$

RUN TESTS				
	NUMBER OF RUNS		**Standard Deviation**	**z**
Name	**Observed**	**Expected**		
Median	r	$\dfrac{N}{2} + 1$	$\sqrt{\dfrac{N-1}{4}}$	$\dfrac{r - [(N/2) + 1]}{\sqrt{(N-1)/4}}$
Up/down	r	$\dfrac{2N-1}{3}$	$\sqrt{\dfrac{16N-29}{90}}$	$\dfrac{r - [(2N-1)/3]}{\sqrt{(16N-29)/90}}$

PROCESS CAPABILITY		
Name	**Symbol**	**Formula**
Capability Index for a centered process	C_p	$\dfrac{\text{Specification width}}{6\sigma \text{ of process}}$
Capability Index for a noncentered process	C_{pk}	Smaller of $\begin{cases} \dfrac{\text{Mean} - \text{Lower specification}}{3\sigma} \\[2mm] \dfrac{\text{Upper specification} - \text{Mean}}{3\sigma} \end{cases}$

Solved Problems

Problem 1

Solution

Process distribution and sampling distribution. An industrial process that makes 3-foot sections of plastic pipe produces pipe with an average inside diameter of 1 inch and a standard deviation of .05 inch.

a. If you randomly select one piece of pipe, what is the probability that its inside diameter will exceed 1.02 inches, assuming the population is normal?

b. If you select a random sample of 25 pieces of pipe, what is the probability that the sample mean will exceed 1.02 inches?

$\mu = 1.00$, $\sigma = .05$

a. $z = \dfrac{x - \mu}{\sigma} = \dfrac{1.02 - 1.00}{.05} = 0.4$

Using Appendix B, Table A, $P(z > .4) = .5000 - .1554 = .3446$.

b. $z = \dfrac{\bar{x} - \cdot}{\sigma/\sqrt{n}} = \dfrac{1.02 - 1.00}{.05/\sqrt{25}} = 2.00$

Using Appendix B, Table A, P(z > 2.00) = .5000 − .4772 = .0228

Problem 2

Control charts for means and ranges. Processing new accounts at a bank is intended to average 10 minutes each. Five samples of four observations each have been taken. Use the sample data in conjunction with Table 10–2 to construct upper and lower control limits for both a mean chart and a range chart. Do the results suggest that the process is in control?

	Sample 1	Sample 2	Sample 3	Sample 4	Sample 5
	10.2	10.3	9.7	9.9	9.8
	9.9	9.8	9.9	10.3	10.2
	9.8	9.9	9.9	10.1	10.3
	10.1	10.4	10.1	10.5	9.7
Totals	40.0	40.4	39.6	40.8	40.0

Solution

a. Determine the mean and range of each sample.

$\bar{x} = \dfrac{\sum x}{n}$, Range = Largest − Smallest

Sample	Mean	Range
1	40.0/4 = 10.0	10.2 − 9.8 = 0.4
2	40.4/4 = 10.1	10.4 − 9.8 = 0.6
3	39.6/4 = 9.9	10.1 − 9.7 = 0.4
4	40.8/4 = 10.2	10.5 − 9.9 = 0.6
5	40.0/4 = 10.0	10.3 − 9.7 = 0.6

b. Compute the average mean and average range:

$\bar{x} = \dfrac{10.0 + 10.1 + 9.9 + 10.2 + 10.0}{5} = \dfrac{50.2}{5} = 10.04$

$\bar{R} = \dfrac{0.4 + 0.6 + 0.4 + 0.6 + 0.6}{5} = \dfrac{2.6}{5} = 0.52$

c. Obtain factors A_2, D_4, and D_3 from Table 10–2 for $n = 4$: $A_2 = 0.73$, $D_4 = 2.28$, $D_3 = 0$.

d. Compute upper and lower limits:

$$\text{UCL}_{\bar{x}} = \bar{\bar{x}} + A_2\bar{R} = 10.04 + 0.73(.52) = 10.42$$
$$\text{LCL}_{\bar{x}} = \bar{\bar{x}} - A_2\bar{R} = 10.04 + 0.73(.52) = 9.66$$
$$\text{UCL}_R = D_4\bar{R} = 2.28(.52) = 1.19$$
$$\text{LCL}_R = D_3\bar{R} = 0(.52) = 0$$

e. Plot sample means and ranges on their respective control charts, or otherwise verify that points are within limits.

The smallest sample mean is 9.9, and the largest is 10.2. Both are well within the control limits. Similarly, the largest sample range is .6, which is also within the control limits. Hence, the results suggest that the process is in control. Note, however, that for illustrative purposes, the number of samples is deliberately small; 20 or more samples would give a clearer indication of control limits and whether the process is in control.

Type I error (alpha risk). After several investigations of points outside control limits revealed nothing, a manager began to wonder about the probability of a Type I error for the control limits used ($z = 1.90$). **Problem 3**

a. Determine the alpha risk for this value of z.

b. What z would provide an alpha risk of about 2 percent?

a. Using Appendix B, Table A, find that the area under the curve between $z = 0$ and $z = +1.90$ is .4713. Therefore, the area (probability) of values *within* -1.90 to $+1.90$ is $2(.4713) = .9426$, and the area *beyond* these values is $1 - .9426 = .0574$. Hence, the alpha risk is 5.74%. **Solution**

b. The alpha risk (Type I error probability is always specified as an *area* in the tail(s) of a distribution. With control charts, you are involved with two-sided control limits. Consequently, half of the risk lies in each tail. Hence, the area in the right tail is 1 percent, or .0100. This means that .4900 should be the area under the curve between $z = 0$ and the value of z you are looking for. The closest value is .4901 for $z = 2.33$. Thus, control limits based on $z = \pm2.33$ provide an alpha risk of about 2 percent.

p-chart and c-chart. Using the appropriate control chart, determine two-sigma control limits for each case: **Problem 4**

a. An inspector found an average of 3.9 scratches in the exterior paint of each of the automobiles being prepared for shipment to dealers.

b. Before shipping lawnmowers to dealers, an inspector attempts to start each mower and notes any that do not start on the first try. The lot size is 100 mowers, and an average of 4 did not start (4 percent).

The choice between these two types of control charts relates to whether *two* types of results can be counted (*p*-chart) or whether *only occurrences* can be counted (*c*-chart). **Solution**

a. The inspector can only count the scratches that occurred, not the ones that did not occur. Consequently, a *c*-chart is appropriate. The sample average is 3.9 scratches per car. Two-sigma control limits are found using the formulas

$$\text{UCL} = \bar{c} + z\sqrt{\bar{c}}$$
$$\text{LCL} = \bar{c} - z\sqrt{\bar{c}}$$

where $\psi = 3.9$ and $z = 2$. Thus,

$$\text{UCL} = 3.9 + 2\sqrt{3.9} = 7.85 \text{ scratches}$$
$$\text{LCL} = 3.9 - 2\sqrt{3.9} = -.05, \text{ so the lower limit is 0 scratches}$$

(Note: Round to zero only if the computed lower limit is negative.)

b. The inspector can count both the lawnmowers that started and those that did not start. Consequently, a *p*-chart is appropriate. Two-sigma control limits can be computed using the following:

$$\text{UCL} = \bar{p} + z\sqrt{\frac{\bar{p}(1 - \bar{p})}{n}}$$

$$LCL = \bar{p} - z\sqrt{\frac{\bar{p}(1-\bar{p})}{n}}$$

where

$$\bar{p} = .04$$
$$n = 100$$
$$z = 2$$

Thus,

$$UCL = .04 + 2\sqrt{\frac{.04(96)}{100}} = .079$$

$$LCL = .04 - 2\sqrt{\frac{.04(.96)}{100}} = .001$$

Problem 5

Run tests. The number of defective items per sample for 11 samples is shown below. Determine if nonrandom patterns are present in the sequence.

	SAMPLE										
	1	**2**	**3**	**4**	**5**	**6**	**7**	**8**	**9**	**10**	**11**
Number of defectives ..	22	17	19	25	18	20	21	17	23	23	24

Solution

Since the median isn't given, it must be estimated from the sample data. To do this, array the data from low to high; the median is the middle value. (In this case, there are an odd number of values. For an even number of values, average the middle two to obtain the median.) Thus,

```
17   17   18   19   20   21   22   23   23   24   25
     (5 below)              ↑              (5 above)
                         median
```

The median is 21.

Next, code the observations using A/B and U/D:

Sample	A/B	Number of Defectives	U/D
1	|A	22	—
2	|B	17	|D
3	|B	19	|U
4	|A	25	|U
5	|B	18	|D
6	|B	20	|U
7	tie	21	|U
8	|B	17	|D
9	|A	23	|U
10	|A	23	tie
11	|A	24	|U

Note that each test has tied values. How these are resolved can affect the number of observed runs. Suppose that you adhere to this rule: Assign a letter (A or B, U or D) so that the resulting difference between the observed and expected number of runs is as large as possible. To accomplish this, it is necessary to initially ignore ties and count the runs to see whether there are too many or too few. Then return to the ties and make the assignments. The rationale for this rule is that it is a conservative method for retaining data; if you conclude that the data are random using this approach, you can be reasonably confident that the method has not "created" randomness. With this in mind, assign a B to sample 7 since the expected number of runs is

$$E(r)_{med} = N/2 + 1 = 11/2 + 1 = 6.5$$

and the difference between the resulting number of runs, 5, and 6.5 is greater than between 6.5 and 7 (which occurs if A is used instead of B). Similarly, in the up/down test, a U for sample 10 produces 6 runs, whereas a D produces 8 runs. Since the expected number of runs is

$$E(r)_{u/d} = (2N - 1) \div 3 = (22 - 1) \div 3 = 7$$

it makes no difference which one is used: both yield a difference of 1. For the sake of illustration, a D is assigned.

The computations for the two tests are summarized below. Each test has a z value that is within the range of ± 2.00. Because neither test reveals nonrandomness, you may conclude that the data are random.

	Runs Observed	$E(r)$	σ_r	z	Conclude
Median	5	6.5	1.58	−0.95	Random
Up/down	8	7.0	1.28	0.78	Random

Discussion and Review Questions

1. List the steps in the control process.
2. What are the key concepts that underlie the construction and interpretation of control charts?
3. What is the purpose of a control chart?
4. Why is order of observation important in process control?
5. Briefly explain the purpose of each of these control charts:
   a. x-bar
   b. Range
   c. p-chart
   d. c-chart
6. What is a run? How are run charts useful in process control?
7. If all observations are within control limits, does that guarantee that the process is random? Explain.
8. Why is it usually desirable to use both a median run test and an up/down run test on the same data?
9. If both run tests are used, and neither reveals nonrandomness, does that prove that the process is random? Explain.
10. Define and contrast control limits, specifications, and process variability.
11. A customer has recently tightened the specs for a part your company supplies. The specs are now much tighter than the machine being used for the job is capable of. Briefly identify alternatives you might consider to resolve this problem. (See Figure 10–14C.)
12. A new order has come into your department. The capability of the machine used for this type of work will enable virtually all of the output to be well within the specs. (See Figure 10–14B.)
   a. What benefits might be derived from this situation?
   b. What alternatives might be considered by the manager?
13. Answer these questions about inspection:
   a. What level of inspection is optimal?
   b. What factors guide the decision of how much to inspect?
   c. What are the main considerations in choosing between centralized inspection and on-site inspection?
   d. What points are potential candidates for inspection?
14. What two basic assumptions must be satisfied in order to use a process capability index?
15. How important is it for managers to maintain and promote ethical behavior in dealing with quality issues? Does your answer depend on the product or service involved?
16. Classify each of the following as either a Type I error or a Type II error:
   a. Putting an innocent person in jail.
   b. Releasing a guilty person from jail.

c. Eating (or not eating) a cookie that fell on the floor.

d. Not seeing a doctor as soon as possible after ingesting poison.

Memo Writing Exercises

1. Suppose you recently received a memo from your manager, Sid Twickenham, in which he asks for your input on the possibility of switching from the use of a *p*-chart to an *x*-bar chart to monitor a process. He wants to know the circumstances under which such a change would be acceptable, and the advantages and costs of making the switch.

   Write a memo in response.

2. You receive a complaint about defective explosion-proof fittings found coming from a process. The fittings are produced during the first and second shifts, but defective fittings occur only during the second shift. You must decide whether to proceed with continuous monitoring of the process or to use a control chart to periodically monitor the process in order to pinpoint the cause of the defective fittings.

   Write a memo to your subordinate, Arnie Green, asking him to research the complaint. Indicate to Green what information he should obtain in order for you to make your decision.

Problems

1. Specifications for a part for a DVD player state that the part should weigh between 24 and 25 ounces. The process that produces the parts yields a mean of 24.5 ounces and a standard deviation of .2 ounce. The distribution of output is normal.

   a. What percentage of parts will not meet the weight specs?

   b. Within what values will 95.44 percent of sample means of this process fall, if samples of $n = 16$ are taken and the process is in control (random)?

2. An automatic filling machine is used to fill 1-liter bottles of cola. The machine's output is approximately normal with a mean of 1.0 liter and a standard deviation of .01 liter. Output is monitored using means of samples of 25 observations.

   a. Determine upper and lower control limits that will include roughly 95.5 percent of the sample means when the process is in control.

   b. Given these sample means: 1.005, 1.001, .998, 1.002, .995, and .999, is the process in control?

3. Checkout time at a supermarket is monitored using a mean and a range chart. Six samples of $n = 20$ observations have been obtained and the sample means and ranges computed:

Sample	Mean	Range
1	3.06	0.42
2	3.15	0.50
3	3.11	0.41
4	3.13	0.46
5	3.06	0.46
6	3.09	0.45

   a. Using the factors in Table 10–2, determine upper and lower limits for mean and range charts.

   b. Is the process in control?

4. Computer upgrades have a nominal time of 80 minutes. Samples of five observations each have been taken, and the results are as listed. Using factors from Table 10–2, determine upper and lower control limits for mean and range charts, and decide if the process is in control.

			SAMPLE		
1	**2**	**3**	**4**	**5**	**6**
79.2	80.5	79.6	78.9	80.5	79.7
78.8	78.7	79.6	79.4	79.6	80.6
80.0	81.0	80.4	79.7	80.4	80.5
78.4	80.4	80.3	79.4	80.8	80.0
81.0	80.1	80.8	80.6	78.8	81.1

5. Using samples of 200 credit card statements, an auditor found the following:

Sample	1	2	3	4
Number of errors	4	2	5	9

   a. Determine the fraction defective in each sample.

   b. If the true fraction defective for this process is unknown, what is your estimate of it?

   c. What is your estimate of the mean and standard deviation of the sampling distribution of fractions defective for samples of this size?

   d. What control limits would give an alpha risk of .03 for this process?

   e. What alpha risk would control limits of .047 and .003 provide?

   f. Using control limits of .047 and .003, is the process in control?

   g. Suppose that the long-term fraction defective of the process is known to be 2 percent. What are the values of the mean and standard deviation of the sampling distribution?

   h. Construct a control chart for the process, assuming a fraction defective of 2 percent, using two-sigma control limits. Is the process in control?

6. A medical facility does MRIs for sports injuries. Occasionally a test yields inconclusive results and must be repeated. Using the following sample data and $n = 200$, construct a control chart for the fraction defective using two-sigma limits. Is the process in control? If not, eliminate any values that are outside the limits and compute revised limits.

						SAMPLE							
1	**2**	**3**	**4**	**5**	**6**	**7**	**8**	**9**	**10**	**11**	**12**	**13**
Number of retests .. 1	2	2	0	2	1	2	0	2	7	3	2	1

7. The postmaster of a small western town receives a certain number of complaints each day about mail delivery. Construct a control chart with three-sigma limits using the following data. Is the process in control?

							DAY						
1	**2**	**3**	**4**	**5**	**6**	**7**	**8**	**9**	**10**	**11**	**12**	**13**	**14**
Number of complaints .. 4	10	14	8	9	6	5	12	13	7	6	4	2	10

8. Construct a control chart with three-sigma limits for the number of defects per spool of cable, given the following data. Is the process in control?

Observation	Number of Defects	Observation	Number of Defects
1	2	8	0
2	3	9	2
3	1	10	1
4	0	11	3
5	1	12	1
6	3	13	2
7	2	14	0

9. After a number of complaints about its directory assistance, a telephone company examined samples of calls to determine the frequency of wrong numbers given to callers. Each sample consisted of 100 calls. The manager stated that the error rate is about 4 percent. Assuming that to be true, construct a control chart using 95 percent limits. Is the process in control? Is the manager's assertion about the error rate correct? Explain.

Sample	Number of Errors	Sample	Number of Errors
1	5	9	5
2	3	10	9
3	5	11	3
4	7	12	4
5	4	13	5
6	6	14	6
7	8	15	6
8	4	16	7

10. Specifications for a metal shaft are much wider than the machine used to make the shafts is capable of. Consequently, the decision has been made to allow the cutting tool to wear a certain amount before replacement. The tool wears at the rate of .004 centimeter per piece. The process has a natural variation, σ, of .01 centimeter and is normally distributed. Specifications are 15.0 to 15.2 centimeters, and $n = 1$. For three-sigma limits, how many shafts can the process turn out before tool replacement becomes necessary? (See diagram.)

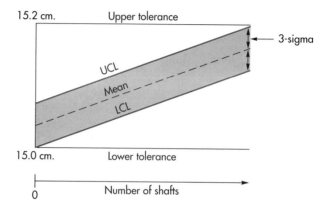

11. Specifications for the computer upgrades in Problem 4 are 78 minutes and 81 minutes. Based on the data given in the problem, are the specifications being met? Estimate the percentage of process output that can be expected to fall within the specifications.

12. The time needed for checking in at a hotel is to be investigated. Historically, the process has had a standard deviation equal to .146. The means of 39 samples of $n = 14$ are:

Sample	Mean	Sample	Mean	Sample	Mean
1	3.86	14	3.81	27	3.81
2	3.90	15	3.83	28	3.86
3	3.83	16	3.86	29	3.98
4	3.81	17	3.82	30	3.96
5	3.84	18	3.86	31	3.88
6	3.83	19	3.84	32	3.76
7	3.87	20	3.87	33	3.83
8	3.88	21	3.84	34	3.77
9	3.84	22	3.82	35	3.86
10	3.80	23	3.89	36	3.80
11	3.88	24	3.86	37	3.84
12	3.86	25	3.88	38	3.79
13	3.88	26	3.90	39	3.85

a. Construct an $\bar{x}$-chart for this process with three-sigma limits. Is the process in control?

b. Analyze the data using a median run test and an up/down run test. What can you conclude?

13. For each of the accompanying control charts, analyze the data using both median and up/down run tests with $z = \pm 1.96$ limits. Are nonrandom variations present? Assume the center line is the long-term median.

14. Analyze the data in the problems listed below using median and up/down run tests with $z = \pm 2$.

   a. Problem 8.

   b. Problem 7.

15. Use both types of run tests to analyze the daily expense voucher listed. Assume a median of $31.

Day	Amount	Day	Amount	Day	Amount
1	$27.69	21	$28.60	41	$26.76
2	28.13	22	20.02	42	30.51
3	33.02	23	26.67	43	29.35
4	30.31	24	36.40	44	24.09
5	31.59	25	32.07	45	22.45
6	33.64	26	44.10	46	25.16
7	34.73	27	41.44	47	26.11
8	35.09	28	29.62	48	29.84
9	33.39	29	30.12	49	31.75
10	32.51	30	26.39	50	29.14
11	27.98	31	40.54	51	37.78
12	31.25	32	36.31	52	34.16
13	33.98	33	27.14	53	38.28
14	25.56	34	30.38	54	29.49
15	24.46	35	31.96	55	30.81
16	29.65	36	32.03	56	30.60
17	31.08	37	34.40	57	34.46
18	33.03	38	25.67	58	35.10
19	29.10	39	35.80	59	31.76
20	25.19	40	32.23	60	34.90

16. A company has just negotiated a contract to produce a part for another firm. In the process of manufacturing the part, the inside diameter of successive parts becomes smaller and smaller as the cutting tool wears. However, the specs are so wide relative to machine capabilities that it is possible to set the diameter initially at a large value and let the process run for a while before replacing the cutting tool.

   The inside diameter decreases at an average rate of .001 cm per part, and the process has a standard deviation of .01 cm. The variability is approximately normal. Assuming three-sigma control limits, how frequently must the tool be replaced if the process specs are 3 cm and 3.5 cm, and the initial setting of the UCL is at the upper spec? Use $n = 1$.

17. (Refer to Solved Problem 2.) Suppose the process specs are 9.65 and 10.35 minutes. Based on the data given, does it appear that the specs are being met? If not, what should one look for?

18. A production process consists of a three-step operation. The scrap rate is 10 percent for the first step and 6 percent for the other two steps.

   a. If the desired daily output is 450 units, how many units must be started to allow for loss due to scrap?

   b. If the scrap rate for each step could be cut in half, how many units would this save in terms of the scrap allowance?

   c. If the scrap represents a cost of $10 per unit, how much is it costing the company per day for the original scrap rate?

19. (Refer to the data in Example 5.) Two additional observations have been taken. The first resulted in three defects, and the second had four defects. Using the set of 20 observations, perform run tests on the data. What can you conclude about the data?

20. A teller at a drive-up window at a bank had the following service times (in minutes) for 20 randomly selected customers:

SAMPLE			
1	2	3	4
4.5	4.6	4.5	4.7
4.2	4.5	4.6	4.6
4.2	4.4	4.4	4.8
4.3	4.7	4.4	4.5
4.3	4.3	4.6	4.9

a. Determine the mean of each sample.

b. If the process parameters are unknown, estimate its mean and standard deviation.

c. Estimate the mean and standard deviation of the sampling distribution.

d. What would three-sigma control limits for the process be? What alpha risk would they provide?

e. What alpha risk would control limits of 4.14 and 4.86 provide?

f. Using limits of 4.14 and 4.86, are any sample means beyond the control limits? If so, which one(s)?

g. Construct control charts for means and ranges using Table 10–2. Are any samples beyond the control limits? If so, which one(s)?

h. Explain why the control limits are different for means in parts d and g.

i. If the process has a known mean of 4.4 and a known standard deviation of .18, what would three-sigma control limits be for a mean chart? Are any sample means beyond the control limits? If so, which one(s)?

21. A process that produces computer chips has a mean of .03 defective chips and a standard deviation of .003 chips. The allowable variation is from .02 to .04 defectives.

a. Compute the capability ratio for the process.

b. Is the process capable?

22. Given the following list of machines, the standard deviation for each, and specifications for a job that may be processed on that machine, determine which machines are capable of performing the given jobs.

Machine	Standard Deviation (in.)	Job Specification (±in.)
001	0.02	0.05
002	0.04	0.07
003	0.10	0.18
004	0.05	0.15
005	0.01	0.04

23. Suppose your manager presents you with the following information about machines that could be used for a job, and wants your recommendation on which one to choose. The specification width is .48 mm. In this instance, you can narrow the set of choices, but you probably wouldn't make a recommendation without an additional piece of information. Explain the logic of the last statement.

Machine	Cost per Unit ($)	Standard Deviation (mm)
A	20	0.079
B	12	0.080
C	11	0.084
D	10	0.081

24. Each of the processes listed is noncentered with respect to the specifications for that process. Compute the appropriate capability index for each, and decide if the process is capable.

Process	Mean	Standard Deviation	Lower Spec	Upper Spec
H	15.0	0.32	14.1	16.0
K	33.0	1.00	30.0	36.5
T	18.5	0.50	16.5	20.1

25. An appliance manufacturer wants to contract with a repair shop to handle authorized repairs in Indianapolis. The company has set an acceptable range of repair time of 50 minutes to 90 minutes. Two firms have submitted bids for the work. In test trials, one firm had a mean repair time of 68 minutes with a standard deviation of 6.2 minutes and the other firm had a mean repair time of 72 minutes with a standard deviation of 5.1 minutes. Which firm would you choose? Why?

26. As part of an insurance company's training program, participants learn how to conduct an analysis of clients' insurability. The goal is to have participants achieve a time in the range of 30 to 45 minutes. Test results for three participants were: Armand, a mean of 38 minutes and a standard deviation of 3 minutes; Jerry, a mean of 37 minutes and a standard deviation of 2.5 minutes; and Melissa, a mean of 37.5 minutes and a standard deviation of 2.5 minutes.

    a. Which of the participants would you judge to be capable? Explain.

    b. Can the value of the C_{pk} exceed the value of C_p for a given participant? Explain.

CASE

Toys, Inc.

TOYS, Inc. is a 20-year-old company engaged in the manufacture and sale of toys and board games. The company has built a reputation on quality and innovation. Although the company is one of the leaders in its field, sales have leveled off in recent years. For the most recent six-month period, sales actually declined compared with the same period last year. The production manager, Ed Murphy, attributed the lack of sales growth to "the economy." He was prompted to undertake a number of belt-tightening moves that included cuts in production costs and layoffs in the design and product development departments. Although profits are still flat, he believes that within the next six months, the results of his decisions will be reflected in increased profits.

The vice president of sales, Joe Martin, has been concerned with customer complaints about the company's REALISTIC™ line of working-model factories, farms, and service stations. The moving parts on certain models have become disengaged and fail to operate or operate eratically. His assistant, Keith McNally, has proposed a trade-in program by which customers could replace malfunctioning models with new ones. McNally believes that this will demonstrate goodwill and appease dissatisfied customers. He also proposes rebuilding the trade-ins and selling them at discounted prices in the company's retail outlet store. He doesn't think that this will take away from sales of new models. Under McNally's program, no new staff would be needed. Regular workers would perform needed repairs during periods of seasonal slowdowns, thus keeping production level.

When Steve Bukowski, a production assistant, heard Keith's proposal, he said that a better option would be to increase inspection of finished models before they were shipped. "With 100 percent inspection, we can weed out any defective models and avoid the problem entirely."

Take the role of a consultant who has been called in for advice by the company president, Marybeth Corbella. What do you recommend?

CASE

Tiger Tools

Tiger Tools, a division of Drillmore Industries, was about to launch a new product. Production Manager Michelle York asked her assistant, Jim Peterson, to check the capability of the oven used in the process. Jim obtained 18 random samples of 20 pieces each. The results of those samples are shown in the following table. After he analyzed the data, he concluded that the process was not capable based on a specification width of 1.20 cm.

Michelle was quite disappointed when she heard this. She had hoped that with the introduction of the new product her operation could run close to full capacity and regain some of its lost luster. The company had a freeze on capital expenditures of more than $10,000, and a replacement oven would cost many times that amount. Jim Peterson worked with the oven crew to see if perhaps different settings could produce the desired results, but they were unable to achieve any meaningful improvements.

Sample	Mean	Range
1	45.01	.85
2	44.99	.89
3	45.02	.86
4	45.00	.91
5	45.04	.87
6	44.98	.90
7	44.91	.86
8	45.04	.89
9	45.00	.85
10	44.97	.91
11	45.11	.84
12	44.96	.87
13	45.00	.86
14	44.92	.89
15	45.06	.87
16	44.94	.86
17	45.00	.85
18	45.03	.88

Still not ready to concede, Michelle contacted one of her former professors and explained the problem. The professor suggested obtaining another set of samples, this time using a smaller sample size and taking more samples. Michelle then conferred with Jim and they agreed that he would take 27 samples of five observations each. The results are shown in the following table.

Sample	Mean	Range
1	44.96	.42
2	44.98	.39
3	44.96	.41
4	44.97	.37
5	45.02	.39
6	45.03	.40
7	45.04	.39
8	45.02	.42
9	45.08	.38
10	45.12	.40
11	45.07	.41
12	45.02	.38
13	45.01	.41
14	44.98	.40
15	45.00	.39
16	44.95	.41
17	44.94	.43
18	44.94	.40
19	44.87	.38
20	44.95	.41
21	44.93	.39
22	44.96	.41
23	44.99	.40
24	45.00	.44
25	45.03	.42
26	45.04	.38
27	45.03	.40

Consider the following questions, and then write a brief report to Michelle summarizing your findings.

1. How did Jim conclude that the process was not capable based on his first set of samples? (Hint: Estimate the process standard deviation, σ, using $A_2\bar{R} \approx 3\dfrac{\sigma}{\sqrt{n}}$).

2. Does the second set of samples show anything that the first set didn't? Explain what and why.

3. Assuming the problem can be found and corrected, what impact do you think this would have on the capability of the process? Compute the potential process capability.

4. If small samples can reveal something that large samples might not, why not just take small samples in every situation?

OPERATIONS TOUR

In the Chips at Jays
Neil Steinberg
www.jaysfoods.com

A potato chip is a delicate thing. Fragile. A pound of pressure will crush it. So when you're moving 250 tons of chips through your plant, as they do every day at Jays Foods, you need to have a system.

"You don't buy potato crumbs, you buy potato chips," said Tom Howe, CEO and co-owner of the Chicago company, at 99th and Cottage Grove. Jays makes 125 different types and brands of chips and several hundred varieties of popcorn, puffs, twists, pretzels and assorted bagged munchies.

Jays combats the tendency of potato chips to crush into flinders with a variety of conveyor belts, radial filling chutes and gently vibrating slides, where masses of chips, a yard deep, are gradually massaged forward, the outer layer of chips shearing away like the face of a glacier.

The raw material is far easier to handle. An entire semitrailer of sturdy North Dakota "chipping" potatoes can be emptied in a matter of minutes, by backing the trailer onto a hydraulic lift, tilting it 45 degrees and letting the potatoes—

grown for their thin skins and low moisture—tumble out.

About a dozen semi-trailers' worth of potatoes arrive every day. The potatoes are immediately separated into big and small sizes for a purpose both reasonable and extraordinary: Big potatoes make big chips that go into large bags; small potatoes make small chips for lunch-size bags.

"Nobody wants to open a small bag and find three big potato chips in it," Howe said.

Computers keep track of everything, shunting potatoes to 15,000-pound holding bins. Each bin feeds into a pipe containing a turning screw—a version of the ancient Archimedes screw used to pump water—that moves the pota-

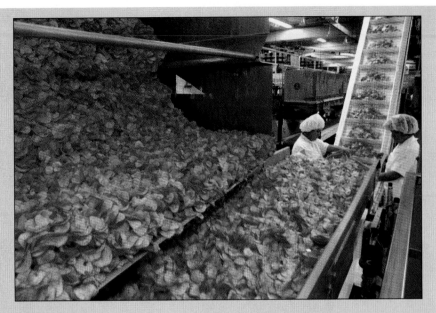

toes from the bin to conveyor belts, to where they are washed and skinned—the skin scrubbed off by metal bristle brushes.

No machine can detect if a potato is rotten inside. So a pair of human inspectors reach into the passing brown parade and give the potatoes a quick squeeze. Occasionally, they snatch one and slice it open, usually revealing black areas of rot, a skill they attribute to experience.

"I *know*," said Alicia Jimenez, asked to explain what about a potato tips her off to slice it open and find rot.

The naked potatoes are sent into high-speed chippers—spinning brass rings, each with eight blades inside, straight blades for straight chips, ripple blades for ripple chips.

The blades cut the potatoes, but the potatoes take their revenge. Every three hours the blades are dulled and the line must be stopped so the old rings can be replaced by new rings with sharpened blades.

The sheer quantity of slicing spews big foamy banks of starch from either side of the chipper, which calls to mind a washing machine gone berserk.

Potato chips account for about 55 percent of Jays' business.

The raw chips spend three minutes cooking in hot corn oil, which is constantly circulated and filtered. Then they are salted, and flavorings—barbecue, for instance, or sour cream and onion—are added.

After the chips are fried, there is another quality check, in which workers pluck burned and deformed chips out of the masses passing by. The chips are conveyed on a link grid, wide enough to let broken chips fall through.

The chips also are laser-inspected, rushing, in a single layer, over a complex device called an Opti-Sort Scanner. Chips with dark spots or holes are detected by a laser, which instructs one of 82 small tubes to fire a puff of air that knocks the substandard chip off the line, into a discard bin.

The discards—about 3 percent of production—are gathered up and used: Starch is drawn out and sold to cornstarch

makers; the rest goes to hog feed. Just as the stockyards were said to use every part of the pig but the squeal, at Jays every part of the potato is used but the rich, earthy smell.

Jays even tried to sell burnt chips to the public once, about 20 years ago. "Consumers kept telling us they liked the brown chips," said Len Japp Jr., recalling the "Brownies" variety. "It went over like a lead balloon." Japp and his father, now 93 and honorary chairman of the board, sold the company to Borden in 1986. "They almost ruined it," Howe said, citing a slump in product quality and neglect of the Jays distribution system. "They lost the connection with the consumer."

By 1994, Jays was on the rocks and the Japps, allied with Howe, bought the company back. "Not too many people have a second chance in life," said Japp, whose children are in the company.

Getting the chips in the bags is another challenge: You can't just fill up bags and seal them; the chips would be smashed. Rather, a conveyor pours chips—gently—onto the central hub of a large, wheel-like device, where the chips scatter into 15 buckets that are, basically, scales. A computer monitors the weight of each bucket and opens up the exact combination that, in this case, will fill a 14-ounce bag. The bags are packed into boxes that read: "HANDLE LIKE EGGS."

While not exactly perishable, potato chips do have a shelf life of about eight weeks, only one day of which is spent at the plant.

"Potatoes that are in this morning will be in our branches tomorrow morning, ready to hit the streets," Howe said. Jays is still a regional brand, sold in Illinois, Indiana, Michigan, Wisconsin and Missouri. But business has grown 50 percent in the past two years.

"We connect to people's lifestyle," Howe said. "People treat themselves with Jays. We're in the fun food business."

Source: Reprinted with permission of *Chicago Sun-Times,* December 26, 1997.

Selected Bibliography and Further Reading

Besterfield, Dale H., Carol Besterfield-Micha, Glen Besterfield, and Mary Besterfield-Sacre. *Total Quality Management,* 2nd ed. Englewood Cliffs, NJ: Prentice Hall, 1999.

Derman, C., and S. M. Ross. *Statistical Aspects of Quality Control.* San Diego: Academic Press, 1997.

Evans, James R., and W. M. Lindsay. *The Management and Control of Quality.* Cincinnati: South-Western College Publications, 1999.

Gitlow, Howard, Alan Oppenheim, and Rosa Oppenheim. *Quality Management: Tools and Methods for Improvement,* 2nd ed. Burr Ridge, IL: Irwin, 1995.

Goetsch, David L., and Stanley B. Davis. *Quality Management: Introduction to Total Quality Management for Production, Processing, and Services,* 3rd ed. Upper Saddle River, NJ: Prentice Hall, 2000.

Grant, Eugene L., and Richard Leavenworth. *Statistical Quality Control.* New York: McGraw-Hill, 1996.

Griffith, Gary K. *The Quality Technician's Handbook,* 4th ed. Upper Saddle River, NJ: Prentice Hall, 2000.

Gyrna, Frank, Jr. *Quality Planning and Analysis.* New York: McGraw-Hill, 2001.

Juran, Joseph M. *Juran's Quality Handbook.* New York: McGraw-Hill, 1999.

Kolarik, William J. *Creating Quality Process Design for Results.* New York: McGraw-Hill, 1999.

Mitra, Amitava. *Fundamentals of Quality Control and Improvement,* 2nd ed. Englewood Cliffs, NJ: Prentice Hall, 1998.

Montgomery, Douglas C. *Introduction to Statistical Quality Control, 4th ed.* New York: John Wiley and Sons, 2001.

Ott, Ellis, Edward G. Schilling, and Dean Neubauer. *Process Quality Control.* New York: McGraw-Hill, 2000.

Smith, Gerald, *Statistical Process Control and Process Improvement,* 3rd ed. Englewood Cliffs, NJ: Prentice Hall, 1997.

Summers, Donna. *Quality,* 2nd ed. Upper Saddle River, NJ: Prentice Hall, 2000.

Acceptance Sampling

SUPPLEMENT OUTLINE

Introduction, 458

Sampling Plans, 458
    Single-Sampling Plan, 458
    Double-Sampling Plan, 458
    Multiple-Sampling Plan, 459
    Choosing a Plan, 459

Operating Characteristic Curve, 459

Average Quality of Inspected
    Lots, 463

Key Terms, 464

Solved Problems, 465

Discussion and Review
    Questions, 466

Problems, 466

Selected Bibliography and Further
    Reading, 467

LEARNING OBJECTIVES

*After completing this supplement,
you should be able to:*

1 Explain the purpose of acceptance
sampling.

2 Contrast acceptance sampling and
process control.

3 Compare and contrast single and
multiple sampling plans.

4 Determine the average outgoing
quality of inspected lots.

Introduction

Acceptance sampling is a form of inspection that is applied to lots or batches of items either before or after a process instead of during the process. In the majority of cases, the lots represent incoming purchased items or final products awaiting shipment to warehouses or customers. The purpose of acceptance sampling is to decide whether a lot satisfies predetermined standards. Lots that satisfy these standards are *passed* or *accepted;* those that do not are *rejected.* Rejected lots may be subjected to 100 percent inspection, or purchased goods may be returned to the supplier for credit or replacement (especially if destructive testing is involved).

Acceptance sampling procedures are most useful when one or more of the following conditions exist:

1. A large number of items must be processed in a short time.
2. The cost consequences of passing defectives are low.
3. Destructive testing is required.
4. Fatigue or boredom caused by inspecting large numbers of items leads to inspection errors.

Acceptance sampling procedures can be applied to both attribute (counts) and variable (measurements) inspection. However, inspection of attributes is perhaps more widely used, so for purposes of illustration, the discussion here focuses exclusively on attribute sampling plans.

Sampling Plans

A key element of acceptance sampling is the sampling plan. **Sampling plans** specify the lot size, N; the sample size, n; the number of samples to be taken; and the acceptance/rejection criteria. A variety of sampling plans can be used. Some plans call for selection of a single sample, and others call for two or more samples, depending on the nature of the plan. The following paragraphs briefly describe some of the different kinds of plans.

SINGLE-SAMPLING PLAN

In this plan, one random sample is drawn from each lot, and every item in the sample is examined and classified as either "good" or "defective." If any sample contains more than a specified number of defectives, c, that lot is rejected.

DOUBLE-SAMPLING PLAN

A double-sampling plan allows for the opportunity to take a second sample if the results of the initial sample are inconclusive. For example, if the quality of the initial sample is high, the lot can be accepted without need for a second sample. If the quality in the initial sample is poor, sampling can also be terminated and the lot rejected. For results between those two cases, a second sample is then taken and the items inspected, after which the lot is either accepted or rejected on the basis of the evidence obtained from both samples. A double-sampling plan specifies the lot size, the size of the initial sample, accept/reject criteria for the initial sample, the size of the second sample, and a single acceptance number.

With a double-sampling plan, two values are specified for the number of defective items, a lower level, c_1, and an upper level, c_2. For instance, the lower level might be two defectives and the upper level might be five defectives. Using those values as decision rules, the first sample is taken. If the number of defective items in the first sample is less than or equal to the lower value (i.e., c_1), the lot is judged to be good and sampling is terminated. Conversely, if the number of defectives exceeds the upper value (i.e., c_2), the lot is rejected. If the number of defectives falls somewhere in between, a second sample is taken and the number of defectives in both samples is compared to a third value, c_3. For example, c_3 might be six. If the combined number of defectives does not exceed that value, the lot is accepted; otherwise, the lot is rejected.

MULTIPLE-SAMPLING PLAN

A multiple-sampling plan is similar to a double-sampling plan except that more than two samples may be required. A sampling plan will specify each sample size and two limits for each sample. The values increase with the number of samples. If, for any sample, the cumulative number of defectives found (i.e., those in the present sample plus those found in all previous samples) exceeds the upper limit specified for that sample, sampling is terminated and the lot is rejected. If the cumulative number of defectives is less than or equal to the lower limit, sampling is terminated and the lot is passed. If the number is between the two limits, another sample is taken. The process continues until the lot is either accepted or rejected.

CHOOSING A PLAN

The cost and time required for inspection often dictate the kind of sampling plan used. The two primary considerations are the number of samples needed and the total number of observations required. Single-sampling plans involve only a single sample, but the sample size is large relative to the total number of observations taken under double- or multiple-sampling plans. Where the cost to obtain a sample is relatively high compared with the cost to analyze the observations, a single-sampling plan is more desirable. For instance, if a sample of moon soil is needed, clearly the cost of returning for a second or third sample far outweighs the cost of analyzing a single large sample. Conversely, where item inspection costs are relatively high, such as destructive testing, it may be better to use double or multiple sampling because the average number of items inspected per lot will be lower. This stems from the fact that a very good or very poor lot quality will often show up initially, and sampling can be terminated.

Operating Characteristic Curve

An important feature of a sampling plan is how it discriminates between lots of high and low quality. The ability of a sampling plan to discriminate is described by its **operating characteristic (OC) curve.** A typical curve for a single-sampling plan is shown in Figure 10S–1. The curve shows the probability that a given sampling plan will result in lots with various *fractions defective* being accepted. For example, the graph shows that a lot with 3 percent of defectives (a fraction defective of .03) would have a probability of about .90 of being accepted (and a probability of $1.00 - .90 = .10$ of being rejected). Note the downward relationship: As lot quality decreases, the probability of acceptance decreases, although the relationship is not linear.

A sampling plan does not provide perfect discrimination between good and bad lots; some low-quality lots will invariably be accepted, and some lots with very good quality will invariably be rejected. Even lots containing more than 20 percent defectives still have some probability of acceptance, whereas lots with as few as 3 percent defectives have some chance of rejection.

The degree to which a sampling plan discriminates between good and bad lots is a function of the steepness of the graph's OC curve: the steeper the curve, the more discriminating the sampling plan. (See Figure 10S–2.) Note the curve for an ideal plan (i.e., one that can discriminate perfectly between good and bad lots). To achieve that, you need to inspect 100 percent of each lot. Obviously, if you are going to do that, theoretically, *all* of the defectives can be eliminated (although errors and boredom might result in a few defectives remaining). However, the point is that 100 percent inspection provides a perspective from which to view the OC curves of other sampling plans.

operating characteristic (OC) curve Probability curve that shows the probabilities of accepting lots with various fractions defective.

FIGURE 10S–1

A typical OC curve for proportions

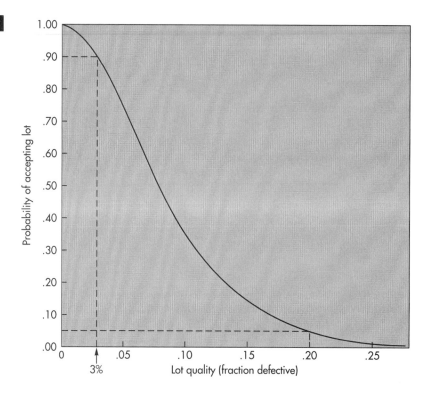

FIGURE 10S–2

The steeper the OC curve, the more discriminating the sampling plan

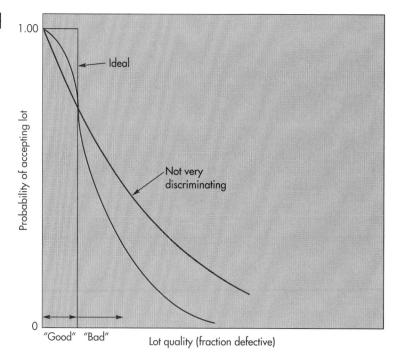

Be aware that the cost and time needed to conduct 100 percent inspection often rule out 100 percent inspection, as does destructive testing, leaving acceptance sampling as the only viable alternative.

For these reasons, buyers ("consumers") are generally willing to accept lots that contain small percentages of defective items as "good," especially if the cost related to a few defects is low. Often this percentage is in the neighborhood of 1 percent to 2 percent defective. This figure is known as the **acceptable quality level (AQL).**

acceptable quality level (AQL) The percentage level of defects at which consumers are willing to accept lots as "good."

FIGURE 10S–3

The AQL indicates good lots, and the LTPD indicates bad lots

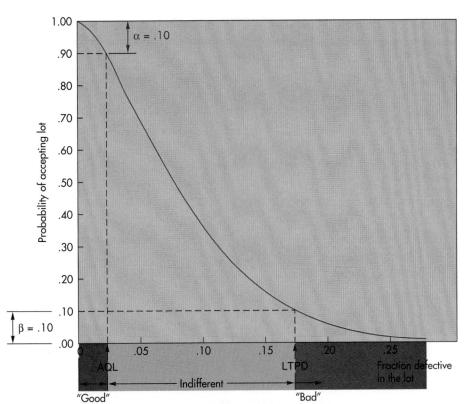

Because of the inability of random sampling to clearly identify lots that contain more than this specified percentage of defective items, consumers recognize that some lots that actually contain more will be accepted. However, there is usually an upper limit on the percentage of defective items that a consumer is willing to tolerate in accepted lots. This is known as the **lot tolerance percent defective (LTPD).** Thus, consumers want quality equal to or better than the AQL, and are willing to live with some lots with quality as poor as the LTPD, but they prefer not to accept any lots with a defective percentage that exceeds the LTPD. The probability that a lot containing defectives exceeding the LTPD will be accepted is known as the **consumer's risk,** or *beta* (β), or the probability of making a *Type II error.* The probability that a lot containing the acceptable quality level will be rejected is known as the **producer's risk,** *alpha* (α), or the probability of making a *Type I error.* Many sampling plans are designed to have a producer's risk of 5 percent and a consumer's risk of 10 percent, although other combinations are also used. It is possible by trial and error to design a plan that will provide selected values for alpha and beta given the AQL and the LTPD. However, standard references such as the government MIL-STD tables are widely used to obtain sample sizes and acceptance criteria for sampling plans. Figure 10S–3 illustrates an OC curve with the AQL, LTPD, producer's risk, and consumer's risk.

A certain amount of insight is gained by actually constructing an OC curve. Suppose you want the curve for a situation in which a sample of $n = 10$ items is drawn from lots containing $N = 2,000$ items, and a lot is accepted if no more than $c = 1$ defective is found. Because the sample size is small relative to the lot size, it is reasonable to use the binomial distribution to obtain the probabilities that a lot will be accepted for various lot qualities.[1] A portion of the cumulative binomial table found in Appendix Table D is reproduced here to facilitate the discussion.

lot tolerance percent defective (LTPD) The upper limit on the percentage of defects that a consumer is willing to accept.

consumer's risk The probability that a lot containing defects exceeding the LTPD will be accepted.

producer's risk The probability that a lot containing the acceptable quality level will be rejected.

---

[1]Since sampling is generally performed "without replacement," if the ratio n/N is 5 percent or more, the hypergeometric distribution is more appropriate since the probability of finding a defect would vary from observation to observation. We shall consider only the more general case of the binomial distribution (i.e., $n/N < 5$ percent).

FIGURE 10S–4

QC curve for n = 10, c = 1

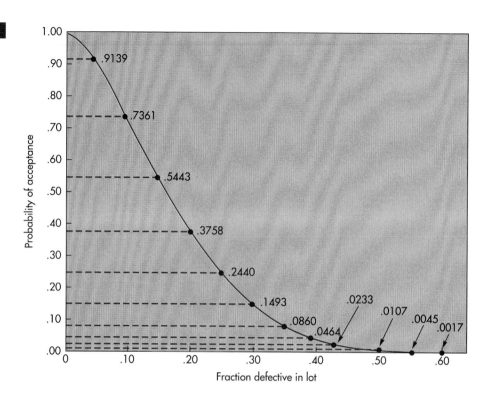

n	x	.05	.10	.15	.20	.25	.30	.35	.40	.45	.50	.55	.60
10 ...	0	.5987	.3487	.1969	.1074	.0563	.0282	.0135	.0060	.0025	.0010	.0003	.0001
$c = 1 \rightarrow$	1	.9139	.7361	.5443	.3758	.2440	.1493	.0860	.0464	.0233	.0107	.0045	.0017
	2	.9885	.9298	.8202	.6778	.5256	.3828	.2616	.1673	.0996	.0547	.0274	.0123
	3	.9990	.9872	.9500	.8791	.7759	.6496	.5138	.3823	.2660	.1719	.1020	.0548

FRACTION DEFECTIVE, p

To use the table, select various lot qualities (values of p listed across the top of the table), beginning with .05, and find the probability that a lot with that percentage of defects would be accepted (i.e., the probability of finding zero or one defect in this case). For $p = .05$, the probability of one or no defects is .9139. For a lot with 10 percent defective (i.e., a fraction defective of .10), the probability of one or fewer defects drops to .7361, and for 15 percent defective, the probability of acceptance is .5443. In effect, you simply read the probabilities across the row for $c = 1$. By plotting these points (e.g., .05 and .9139, .10 and .7361) on a graph and connecting them, you obtain the OC curve illustrated in Figure 10S–4.

When $n > 20$ and $p < .05$, the Poisson distribution is useful in constructing operating characteristic curves for proportions. In effect, the Poisson distribution is used to approximate the binomial distribution. The Poisson approximation involves treating the mean of the binomial distribution (i.e., np) as the mean of the Poisson (i.e., μ):

$$\mu = np \tag{10S–1}$$

As with the binomial distribution, you select various values of lot quality, p, and then determine the probability of accepting a lot (i.e., finding two or fewer defects) by referring to the cumulative Poisson table. Values of p in increments of .01 are often used in this regard. Example S–1 illustrates this use of the Poisson table.

Example S–1

Use the cumulative Poisson table to construct an OC curve for this sampling plan:

$$N = 5{,}000, \qquad n = 80, \qquad c = 2$$

Selected Values of p	$\mu = np$	$P_{ac}[P\,(x \le 2)$ from Appendix Table C]
.01	80(.01) = 0.8	.953
.02	80(.02) = 1.6	.783
.03	80(.03) = 2.4	.570
.04	80(.04) = 3.2	.380
.05	80(.05) = 4.0	.238
.06	80(.06) = 4.8	.143
.07	80(.07) = 5.6	.082
.08	80(.08) = 6.4	.046

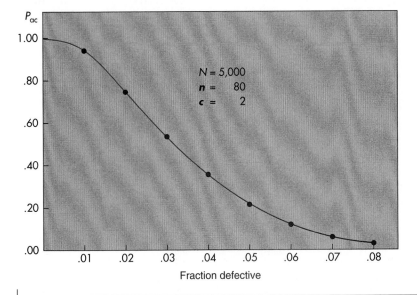

Operating characteristic curves can be constructed for variables sampling plans as well as for attributes sampling plans. To go into detail is beyond the scope of this presentation. The purpose here is merely to illustrate the concept of an OC curve and to show how its construction is based on an underlying *sampling distribution.*

Average Quality of Inspected Lots

An interesting feature of acceptance sampling is that the level of inspection automatically adjusts to the quality of lots being inspected, assuming rejected lots are subjected to 100 percent inspection. The OC curve reveals that the greater the percentage of defects in a lot, the less likely the lot is to be accepted. Generally speaking, good lots have a high probability and bad lots have a low probability of being accepted. If the lots inspected are mostly good, few will end up going through 100 percent inspection. The poorer the quality of the lots, the greater the number of lots that will come under close scrutiny. This tends to improve overall quality of lots by weeding out defects. In this way, the level of inspection is affected by lot quality.

If all lots have some given fraction defective, p, the **average outgoing quality (AOQ)** of the lots can be computed using the following formula, assuming defective items are re-placed with good items:

average outgoing quality (AOQ) Average of rejected lots (100 percent inspection) and accepted lots (a sample of items inspected).

$$\text{AOQ} = P_{ac} \times p\left(\frac{N - n}{N}\right) \qquad (10S\text{--}2)$$

where

P_{ac} = Probability of accepting the lot N = Lot size

p = Fraction defective n = Sample size

In practice, the last term is often omitted since it is usually close to 1.0 and therefore has little effect on the resulting values. The formula then becomes

$$AOQ = P_{ac} \times p \qquad\qquad\qquad (10S–3)$$

Use this formula instead of 10S–2 for computing AOQ values.

Example S–2

Construct the AOQ curve for this situation:

$$N = 500, n = 10, c = 1$$

Solution

Let values of p vary from .05 to .40 in steps of .05. You can read the probabilities of acceptance, P_{ac} from Appendix B, Table D.

$$AOQ = P_{ac} \times p$$

p	P_{ac}	AOQ
.05	.9139	.046
.10	.7361	.074
.15	.5443	.082
.20	.3758	.075
.25	.2440	.061
.30	.1493	.045
.35	.0860	.030
.40	.0464	.019

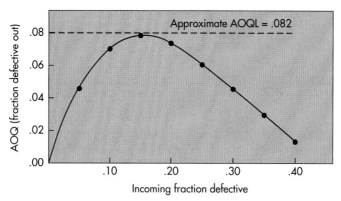

The average outgoing quality limit (AOQL) is just above 8 percent.

By allowing the percentage, p, to vary, a curve such as the one in Example S–2 can be constructed in the same way that an OC curve is constructed. The curve illustrates the point that if lots are very good or very bad, the average outgoing quality will be high. The maximum point on the curve becomes apparent in the process of calculating values for the curve.

There are several managerial implications of the graph in Example S–2. First, a manager can determine the worst possible outgoing quality. Second, the manager can determine the amount of inspection that will be needed by obtaining an estimate of the incoming quality. Moreover, the manager can use this information to establish the relationship between inspection cost and the incoming fraction defective, thereby underscoring the benefit of implementing process improvements to reduce the incoming fraction defective rather than trying to weed out bad items through inspection.

Key Terms

acceptable quality level (AQL), 460
acceptance sampling, 458
average outgoing quality (AOQ), 463
consumer's risk, 461

lot tolerance percent defective (LTPD), 461
operating characteristic (OC) curve, 459
producer's risk, 461
sampling plans, 458

Problem 1

Inspection. A process for manufacturing shock absorbers for light trucks produces 5 percent defectives. Inspection cost per shock is $0.40, and 100 percent inspection generally catches all defects, due to the nature of the inspection and the small volume produced. Any defects installed on trucks must eventually be replaced at a cost of $12 per shock. Is 100 percent inspection justified?

Solution

Five percent of the output is defective. The expected cost per shock for replacement is thus .05($12) = 60 cents. Since this is greater than the inspection cost per shock of 40 cents, 100 percent inspection is justified.

Problem 2

Acceptance sampling. Shipments of 300 boxes of glassware are received at a warehouse of a large department store. Random samples of five boxes are checked, and the lot is rejected if more than one box reveals breakage. Construct the OC curve for this plan.

Solution

When the sample size is less than 5 percent of the lot size, the binomial distribution can be used to obtain P_{ac} for various lot percentages defective. Here, $n/N = 5/300 = .017$, so the binomial can be used. A portion of the cumulative binomial table is shown below. Note that $c = 1$.

CUMULATIVE BINOMIAL PROBABILITIES

p = FRACTION DEFECTIVE

n	x	.05	.10	.15	.20	.25	.30
5	0	.7738	.5905	.4437	.3277	.2373	.1681
$c = 1 \rightarrow$	1	.9974	.9185	.8352	.7373	.6328	.5282
	2	.9988	.9914	.9734	.9421	.8965	.8369
	3	1.0000	.9995	.9978	.9933	.9844	.9692
	4	1.0000	1.0000	.9999	.9997	.9990	.9976
	5	1.0000	1.0000	1.0000	1.0000	1.0000	1.0000

.35	.40	.45	.50	.55	.60	.65	.70	.75	.80
.1160	.0778	.0503	.0313	.0185	.0102	.0053	.0024	.0010	.0003
.4284	.3370	.2562	.1875	.1312	.0870	.0540	.0308	.0156	.0067
.7648	.6826	.5931	.5000	.4069	.3174	.2352	.1631	.1035	.0579
.9460	.9130	.8688	.8125	.7438	.6630	.5716	.4718	.3672	.2627
.9947	.9898	.9815	.9688	.9497	.9222	.8840	.8319	.7627	.6723
1.0000	1.0000	1.0000	1.0000	1.0000	1.0000	1.0000	1.0000	1.0000	1.0000

The table indicates that $P_{ac} = .9974$ when lot quality is 5 percent defective, .9185 for 10 percent defective, .8352 for 15 percent, and so on. The resulting curve is:

Develop the AOQ curve for the previous problem.

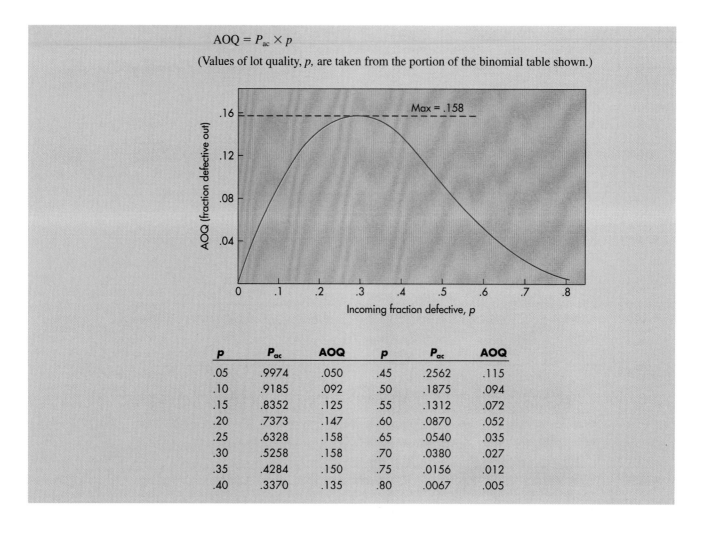

$$AOQ = P_{ac} \times p$$

(Values of lot quality, *p*, are taken from the portion of the binomial table shown.)

p	P_{ac}	AOQ	p	P_{ac}	AOQ
.05	.9974	.050	.45	.2562	.115
.10	.9185	.092	.50	.1875	.094
.15	.8352	.125	.55	.1312	.072
.20	.7373	.147	.60	.0870	.052
.25	.6328	.158	.65	.0540	.035
.30	.5258	.158	.70	.0380	.027
.35	.4284	.150	.75	.0156	.012
.40	.3370	.135	.80	.0067	.005

Discussion and Review Questions

1. What is the purpose of acceptance sampling?
2. How does acceptance sampling differ from process control?
3. What is an operating characteristic curve, and how is it useful in acceptance sampling?
4. What general factors govern the choice between single-sampling plans and multiple-sampling plans?
5. Briefly explain or define each of these terms.
   a. AOQ
   b. AOQL
   c. LTPD
   d. Producer's risk
   e. Consumer's risk

Problems

1. An assembly operation for trigger mechanisms of a semiautomatic spray gun produces a small percentage of defective mechanisms. Management must decide whether to continue the current practice of 100 percent inspection or to replace defective mechanisms after final assembly when all guns are inspected. Replacement at final assembly costs $30 each; inspection during trigger assembly costs $12 per hour for labor and overhead. The inspection rate is one trigger per minute.
   a. Would 100 percent inspection during trigger assembly be justified if there are (1) 4 percent defective? (2) 1 percent defective?

b. At what point would management be indifferent between 100 percent inspection of triggers and only final inspection?

2. Random samples of $n = 20$ circuit breakers are tested for damage caused by shipment in each lot of 4,000 received. Lots with more than one defective are pulled and subjected to 100 percent inspection.

   a. Construct the OC curve for this sampling plan.

   b. Construct the AOQ curve for this plan, assuming defectives found during 100 percent inspection are replaced with good parts. What is the approximate AOQL?

3. Auditors use a technique called *discovery sampling* in which a random sample of items is inspected. If any defects are found, the entire lot of items sampled is subjected to 100 percent inspection.

   a. Draw an OC curve for the case where a sample of 15 credit accounts will be inspected out of a total of 8,000 accounts.

   b. Draw an OC curve for the case where 150 accounts out of 8,000 accounts will be examined. (Hint: Use $p = .001, .002, .003, \ldots$)

   c. Draw the AOQ curve for the preceding case, and estimate the AOQL.

4. Random samples of lots of textbooks are inspected for defective books just prior to shipment to the warehouse. Each lot contains 3,000 books.

   a. On a single graph, construct OC curves for $n = 100$ and (1) $c = 0$, (2) $c = 1$, and (3) $c = 2$. (Hint: Use $p = .001, .002, .003, \ldots$)

   b. On a single graph, construct OC curves for $c = 2$ and (1) $n = 5$, (2) $n = 20$, and (3) n = 120.

5. A manufacturer receives shipments of several thousand parts from a supplier every week. The manufacturer has the option of conducting a 100 percent inspection before accepting the parts. The decision is based on a random sample of 15 parts. If parts are not inspected, defectives become apparent during a later assembly operation, at which time replacement cost is $6.25 per unit. Inspection cost for 100 percent inspection is $1 per unit.

   a. At what fraction defective would the manufacturer be indifferent between 100 percent inspection and leaving discovery of defectives until the later assembly operation?

   b. For the sample size used, what is the maximum number of sample defects that would cause the lot to be passed without 100 percent inspection, based on your answer to part *a*?

   c. If the shipment actually contains 5 percent defective items:
      (1) What is the correct decision?
      (2) What is the probability it would be rejected in favor of 100 percent inspection?
      (3) What is the probability that it would be accepted without 100 percent inspection?
      (4) What is the probability of a Type I error? A Type II error?

   d. Answer the questions in part *c* for a shipment that contains 20 percent defective items.

6. (Refer to Problem 5c.) Suppose there are two defects in the sample.

   a. If the acceptance number is $c = 1$, what decision should be made? What type of error is possible?

   b. If the acceptance number is $c = 3$, what decision should be made? What type of error is possible?

   c. Determine the average outgoing quality for each of these percent defective if $c = 1$.
      (1) 5 percent.
      (2) 10 percent.
      (3) 15 percent.
      (4) 20 percent.

Duncan, A. J. *Quality Control and Industrial Statistics,* 5th ed. Burr Ridge, IL: Richard D. Irwin, 1986.

Enrick, Norbert L. *Quality Reliability and Process Improvement.* 8th ed. New York: Industrial Press, 1985.

Juran, J. M., and F. M. Gryma Jr. *Quality Planning and Analysis.* 2nd ed. New York: McGraw-Hill, 1980.

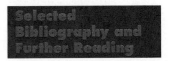
Selected Bibliography and Further Reading

CHAPTER ELEVEN

TQM and Quality Tools

CHAPTER OUTLINE

Introduction, 470

Obstacles to Implementing
   TQM, 473

Criticisms of TQM, 473

Reading: CalComp: Disaster
   Becomes Success, 474

Problem Solving, 475
   The Plan-Do-Study-Act Cycle, 475

Process Improvement, 477

Tools, 478

Reading: Continuous Improvement
   on the Free-Throw Line, 484
   Illustrations of the Use of Graphical
      Tools, 486
   Methods for Generating Ideas, 487

Reading: Benchmarking Corporate
   Websites of Fortune 500
   Companies, 490

Operations Strategy, 490

Summary, 491

Key Terms, 491

Discussion and Review
   Questions, 491

Memo Writing Exercises, 491

Problems, 492

Cases: Chick-n-Gravy Dinner
   Line, 494

   Tip Top Markets, 494

Reading: Making Quality Pay:
   Return on Quality, 496

Reading: Quality Programs Don't
   Guarantee Results, 498

Reading: Swimming Upstream, 499

Selected Bibliography and Further
   Reading, 500

LEARNING OBJECTIVES

*After completing this chapter, you
should be able to:*

1 Describe TQM.
2 Give an overview of problem
   solving.
3 Give an overview of process
   improvement.
4 Describe and use various quality
   tools.

At Motorola in Schaumburg, Illinois, new cell phones are put through the Dust Room and a variety of creative "torture" tests to ensure that they will endure the rigors of everyday use.

www.motorola.com

A primary role of management is to lead an organization in its daily operation and to maintain it as a viable entity into the future. Quality has become an important factor in both of these objectives.

Although ostensibly always an objective of business, customer satisfaction, *in customer terms,* became a specific goal in the late 1980s. Providing high quality was recognized as a key element for success. Most large corporations taking that path have documented their success. First, they survived the strong overseas competition that had set the high quality levels and now have regained some of their former markets. Smaller companies are also adopting similar goals.

Management, with a new approach, has played the critical role. The new approach is reflected in expressed changes in policy. The Ford Motor Company *operating philosophy* is a good example:

> The operating philosophy of Ford Motor Company is to meet customer needs and expectations by establishing and maintaining an environment which encourages all employees to pursue never-ending improvement in the quality and productivity of products and services throughout the corporation, its supply base, and its dealer organization.[1]

Introduction

total quality management (TQM) A philosophy that involves everyone in an organization in a continual effort to improve quality and achieve customer satisfaction.

The term **total quality management (TQM)** refers to a quest for quality in an organization. There are three key philosophies in this approach. One is a never-ending push to improve, which is referred to as *continuous improvement;* the second is the *involvement of everyone* in the organization; and the third is a goal of *customer satisfaction,* which means meeting or exceeding customer expectations. TQM expands the traditional view of quality—looking only at the quality of the final product or services—to *looking at the quality of every aspect of the process* that produces the product or service. TQM systems are intended to prevent poor quality from occurring.

We can describe the TQM approach as follows:

1. Find out what customers want. This might involve the use of surveys, focus groups, interviews, or some other technique that integrates the customer's voice in the decision-

---

[1]Reprinted from Thomas J. Cartin, *Principles and Practices of TQM* (Milwaukee: ASQC Quality Press, 1993), p. 29.

making process. Be sure to include the *internal customer* (the next person in the process) as well as the *external customer* (the final customer).

2. Design a product or service that will meet (or exceed) what customers want. Make it easy to use and easy to produce.

3. Design processes that facilitate doing the job right the first time. Determine where mistakes are likely to occur and try to prevent them. When mistakes do occur, find out why so that they are less likely to occur again. Strive to make the process "mistake-proof." This is sometimes referred to as a **fail–safing:** Elements are incorporated in product or service design which make it virtually impossible for an employee (or sometimes a customer) to do something incorrectly. The Japanese term for this is *pokayoke*. Examples include parts that fit together one way only and appliance plugs that can be inserted into a wall outlet the correct way only. Another term that is sometimes used is *foolproofing*, but use of this term may be taken to imply that employees (or customers) are fools—not a wise choice!

4. Keep track of results, and use them to guide improvement in the system. Never stop trying to improve.

5. Extend these concepts to suppliers and to distribution.

Many companies have successfully implemented TQM programs. Among them are General Electric and Motorola, both of which are known for their "six-sigma" programs, a term generally associated with extremely high process capability, but more appropriately referring to a quality program in general. In fact, competitive pressures and shorter product life cycles are leading a wide variety of companies to undertake TQM-type initiatives. General Electric puts selected employees through a high-level statistical training program. Upon completion, they are certified as "black belt" qualified. These employees then train others and also serve as consultants.

Successful TQM programs are built through the dedication and combined efforts of everyone in the organization. Top management must be committed and involved. If it isn't, TQM will become just another fad that quickly dies and fades away.

The preceding description provides a good idea of what TQM is all about, but it doesn't tell the whole story. A number of other elements of TQM are important, including:

1. *Continuous improvement.* The *philosophy* that seeks to improve all factors related to the process of converting inputs into outputs on an ongoing basis is called **continuous improvement.** It covers equipment, methods, materials, and people. Under continuous improvement, the old adage "If it ain't broke, don't fix it" gets transformed into "Just because it isn't broke doesn't mean it can't be improved."

The concept of continuous improvement was not new, but it did not receive much interest in the United States for a while, even though it originated here. However, many Japanese companies used it for years, and it became a cornerstone of the Japanese approach to production. The Japanese use the term **kaizen** to refer to continuous improvement. The successes of Japanese companies caused other companies to reexamine many of their approaches. This resulted in a strong interest in the continuous improvement approach.

2. *Competitive benchmarking.* This involves identifying other organizations that are the best at something and studying how they do it to learn how to improve your operation. The company need not be in the same line of business. For example, Xerox used the mail-order company L.L. Bean to benchmark order filling.

3. *Employee empowerment.* Giving workers the responsibility for improvements and the authority to make changes to accomplish them provides strong motivation for employees. This puts decision making into the hands of those who are closest to the job and have considerable insight into problems and solutions.

4. *Team approach.* The use of teams for problem solving and to achieve consensus takes advantage of group synergy, gets people involved, and promotes a spirit of cooperation and shared values among employees.

5. *Decisions based on facts rather than opinions.* Management gathers and analyzes data as a basis for decision making.

fail–safing Incorporating design elements that prevent incorrect procedures.

www.trekbikes.com

continuous improvement Philosophy that seeks to make never-ending improvements to the process of converting inputs into outputs.

kaizen Japanese term for continuous improvement.

6. *Knowledge of tools.* Employees and managers are trained in the use of quality tools.

7. *Supplier quality.* Suppliers must be included in quality assurance and quality improvement efforts so that their processes are capable of delivering quality parts and materials in a timely manner.

8. *Champion.* A TQM champion's job is to promote the value and importance of TQM principles throughout the company.

9. *Quality at the source.* **Quality at the source** refers to the philosophy of making each worker responsible for the quality of his or her work. This incorporates the notions of "do it right" and "if it isn't right, fix it." Workers are expected to provide goods or services that meet specifications and to find and correct mistakes that occur. In effect, each worker becomes a quality inspector for his or her work. When the work is passed on to the next operation in the process (the internal customer) or, if that step is the last in the process, to the ultimate customer, the worker is "certifying" that it meets quality standards.

This accomplishes a number of things: (1) it places direct responsibility for quality on the person(s) who directly affect it; (2) it removes the adversarial relationship that often exists between quality control inspectors and production workers; and (3) it motivates workers by giving them control over their work as well as pride in it.

quality at the source The philosophy of making each worker responsible for the quality of his or her work.

Sign on the wall of a company cafeteria

> Sometimes they can be cranky, and it may sometimes seem like they expect too much, but they do provide our paychecks and our benefits, such as sick leave, maternity leave, health insurance, and three weeks of paid vacation time each year. And what about all the new equipment we've been getting lately? They pay for that, too. And a lot more. So the next time you see them, give them a great big smile to show how much you appreciate them—our *customers!*

10. *Suppliers* are partners in the process, and long-term relationships are encouraged. This gives suppliers a vital stake in providing quality goods and services. Suppliers, too, are expected to provide quality at the source, thereby reducing or eliminating the need to inspect deliveries from suppliers.

It would be incorrect to think of TQM as merely a collection of techniques. Rather, TQM reflects a whole new attitude toward quality. It is about the *culture* of an organization. To truly reap the benefits of TQM, the culture of an organization must change.

Table 11–1 illustrates the differences between cultures of a TQM organization and a more traditional organization.

TABLE 11–1

Comparing the cultures of TQM and traditional organizations

Aspect	Traditional	TQM
Overall mission	Maximize return on investment	Meet or exceed customer satisfaction
Objectives	Emphasis on short term	Balance of long term and short term
Management	Not always open; sometimes inconsistent objectives	Open; encourages employee input; consistent objectives
Role of manager	Issue orders; enforce	Coach, remove barriers, build trust
Customer requirements	Not highest priority; may be unclear	Highest priority; important to identify and understand
Problems	Assign blame; punish	Identify and resolve
Problem solving	Not systematic; individuals	Systematic; teams
Improvement	Erratic	Continuous
Suppliers	Adversarial	Partners
Jobs	Narrow, specialized; much individual effort	Broad, more general; much team effort
Focus	Product oriented	Process oriented

Obstacles to Implementing TQM

Companies have had varying success in implementing TQM. Some have been quite successful, but others have struggled. Part of the difficulty may be with the process by which it is implemented rather than with the principles of TQM. Among the factors cited in the literature are:

1. Lack of a companywide definition of quality: Efforts aren't coordinated; people are working at cross-purposes, addressing different issues, using different measures of success.

2. Lack of a strategic plan for change: Lessens the chance of success; ignores need to address strategic implications of change.

3. Lack of a customer focus: Without this, there is a risk of customer dissatisfaction.

4. Poor interorganizational communication: The left hand doesn't know what the right hand is doing; frustration, waste, and confusion ensue.

5. Lack of employee empowerment: Gives the impression of not trusting employees to fix problems; adds "red tape" and delays solutions.

6. View of quality as a "quick fix": Needs to be a long-term, continuing effort.

7. Emphasis on short-term financial results: "Duct-tape" solutions often treat symptoms; spend a little now—a lot more later.

8. Inordinate presence of internal politics and "turf" issues: These can sap the energy of an organization and derail the best of ideas.

9. Lack of strong motivation: Managers need to make sure employees are motivated.

10. Lack of time to devote to quality initiatives: Don't add more work without adding additional resources.

11. Lack of leadership:[2] Managers need to be leaders.

This list of potential problems can serve as a guideline for organizations contemplating implementing TQM or as a checklist for those having trouble implementing it.

Criticisms of TQM

TQM programs are touted as a way for companies to improve their competitiveness, which is a very worthwhile objective. Nonetheless, TQM programs are not without criticism. Some of the major ones are:

1. Blind pursuit of TQM programs: Overzealous advocates may focus attention on quality even though other priorities may be more important (e.g., responding quickly to a competitor's advances).

2. Programs may not be linked to the strategies of the organization in a meaningful way.

3. Quality-related decisions may not be tied to market performance. For instance, customer satisfaction may be carried to the extent that its cost far exceeds any direct or indirect benefit of doing so.

4. Failure to carefully plan a program before embarking on it can lead to false starts, employee confusion, and meaningless results.

Note that there is nothing inherently wrong with TQM; the problem is how some individuals or organizations misuse it. Let's turn our attention to problem solving and process improvement.

---

[2]Gary Salegna and Farzaneh Fazel, "Obstacles to Implementing Quality," *Quality Progress,* July 2000, p. 53. *See also* Nabil Tamimi and Rose Sebastianelli, "The Barriers to Total Quality," *Quality Progress,* June 1998, pp. 57–60; and Robert Masters, "Overcoming the Barriers to TQM's Success," *Quality Progress,* May 1996, pp. 53–55.

CalComp: Disaster Becomes Success

Michelle Vranizan

www.calcomp.com

Flash back to the early 1980s. The only thing world-class about CalComp was the mess it was in.

The company that practically invented the computer plotter—a device engineers and architects use to print intricate, oversized schematics—had become arrogant, inattentive and lazy.

Every last plotter that rolled off the assembly line didn't work well enough to ship without some rejiggering. A legion of field technicians was needed to make house calls on installed machines that malfunctioned every few weeks. Competitors such as Hewlett-Packard jumped into the breach, stealing dissatisfied customers.

Flash forward to the CalComp of the 1990s, recognized as a leader in world-class manufacturing. No more mass assembly lines. No more bugs. No more field technicians.

Hewlett-Packard still sells more pen plotters. But CalComp is a strong No. 2 and has a tight grip on other segments of the plotter and digitizer business. Now bursting with confidence, the $525 million subsidiary of Lockheed Corp. is plowing into other areas of the multibillion dollar computer graphics industry.

The difference between the early 1980s and the 1990s? Quality.

Specifically, a quality program spearheaded by then CalComp President William Conlin that permeates every square inch of the company's grassy Anaheim headquarters and the attitudes of its 2,800 employees.

At CalComp, quality boils down to pleasing customers with gracefully built, innovative products that work from the start, rarely break down, are competitively priced and are upgraded faster than the other guy's.

"We built a manufacturing system that improves every day," said Bernard Masson, senior vice president of the plotter division, which accounts for about 60 percent of CalComp's revenue. "The product we build tomorrow will be better than the ones we build today."

In the early 1970s and 1980s, CalComp's manufacturing process was fractured. Product design and manufacturing weren't coordinated. The company stockpiled parts and the plotter division alone had more than 650 suppliers. A plotter was only tested for imperfections after it was made.

The system worked as long as CalComp only sold 1,000 or so plotters a year to customers who used mainframes or minicomputers, also very temperamental machines prone to breakdowns.

Then along came personal computers, which worked straight out of the box. When personal computers became the preferred tools for engineering and graphics, CalComp managers realized the old way of doing things had to go.

Conlin signed on in late 1983 and CalComp took its first steps toward world-class manufacturing soon after.

CalComp embraced the teachings of quality gurus such as W. Edwards Deming and Richard J. Schonberger, focusing first on the factory.

In the beginning, changes were simple, such as writing down the steps it took to assemble a plotter—something CalComp had never done before, Masson said.

Next, assembly workers were taught quality principles, given a say in how things were done and encouraged to catch mistakes on the line.

Other steps CalComp took:

1. When a new product is conceived, a team of more than a dozen people representing virtually every department shepherds it from development to delivery. With this kind of teamwork engineers don't end up designing parts that factory workers can't put together, said Linda Gronski, an operating unit manager in the plotter division.

2. Instead of stockpiling parts, CalComp cut inventories to the bare minimum and now takes delivery of just enough parts for the next week's work. Some suppliers even deliver parts on a daily basis.

3. CalComp put strict quality controls on suppliers and reduced its vendors in the plotter division to about 180. CalComp started a three-tier preferred-supplier program, dubbed "a mini-Malcolm Baldrige award" contest by one supplier. Parts from suppliers on the higher tier are expected to be so perfect CalComp doesn't even inspect them before building them into products.

By keeping inventories down, CalComp cut its overhead costs. It also can avoid writing off obsolete parts should demand shift suddenly and can direct energies to new products more quickly, company executives said.

Readjusting attitudes toward work was the most important part of the jump to quality, CalComp managers said.

Today, front-line workers are treated with as much respect as executives. Assembly workers are never reprimanded for stopping the line if they can't solve a problem. Gronski and other production managers wear beepers and are expected to attend to problems immediately.

Suppliers said they benefited from classes at CalComp on quality processes: They use the information to transform their businesses and attract other customers.

"When Xerox found out where we were with CalComp, they decided to send a team of people out to visit us," said Harry Esayian, owner of Zac Precision in Anaheim, which makes machine parts for dozens of CalComp products.

Draftsmen and engineers who use CalComp plotters and digitizers might be unfamiliar with the company's quality programs. But they appreciate the results.

"I'm always talking up the plotter because it's a good deal," said customer David Terry, who has a Santa Ana engineering firm that designs waste water-treatment plants. "They're low-cost and no-maintenance. We're real happy."

Questions

1. In general terms, what was wrong in the early 1980s at CalComp?

2. Specifically, what was wrong with:

   a. design and manufacturing?

   b. inventory?

   c. suppliers?

3. In general terms, what change helped to turn things around at CalComp?

4. What steps were taken to improve the situation?

5. What benefits have resulted from the changes?

Source: *The Orange County Register,* March 1, 1992.

L.L. Bean has been in business for over 80 years and prides itself on its attention to quality at a reasonable price. The company is committed to finding longer lasting materials and making improvements in manufacturing that ensure durability.

www.llbean.com

Problem Solving

Problem solving is one of the basic procedures of TQM. In order to be successful, problem-solving efforts should follow a standard approach. Table 11–2 describes the basic steps in the TQM problem-solving process.

An important aspect of problem solving in the TQM approach is *eliminating* the cause so that the problem does not recur. This is why users of the TQM approach often like to think of problems as "opportunities for improvement."

THE PLAN-DO-STUDY-ACT CYCLE

The **plan-do-study-act (PDSA) cycle,** also referred to as either the Shewhart cycle or the Deming wheel, is the conceptual basis for problem-solving activities. The cycle is illustrated in Figure 11–1. Representing the process with a circle underscores its continuing nature.

plan-do-study-act (PDSA) cycle A framework for problem solving and improvement activities.

TABLE 11-2

Basic steps in problem solving

Step 1　Define the problem and establish an improvement goal.
Give problem definition careful consideration; don't rush through this step because this will serve as the focal point of problem-solving efforts.

Step 2　Collect data.
The solution must be based on *facts*. Possible tools include check sheet, scatter diagram, histogram, run chart, and control chart.

Step 3　Analyze the problem.
Possible tools include Pareto chart, cause-and-effect diagram.

Step 4　Generate potential solutions.
Methods include brainstorming, interviewing, and surveying.

Step 5　Choose a solution.
Identify the criteria for choosing a solution. (Refer to the goal established in Step 1.) Apply criteria to potential solutions and select the best one.

Step 6　Implement the solution.
Keep everyone informed.

Step 7　Monitor the solution to see if it accomplishes the goal.
If not, modify the solution, or return to Step 1. Possible tools include control chart and run chart.

FIGURE 11-1

A. The PDSA cycle

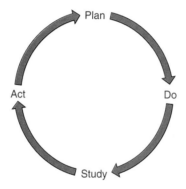

B. The PDSA cycle applied to problem solving.
Source: Reprinted by permission of Prentice-Hall, Upper Saddle River, NJ. From Donna Summers, *Quality,* 2nd ed. (Upper Saddle River, NJ: Prentice Hall, 2000), p. 67.

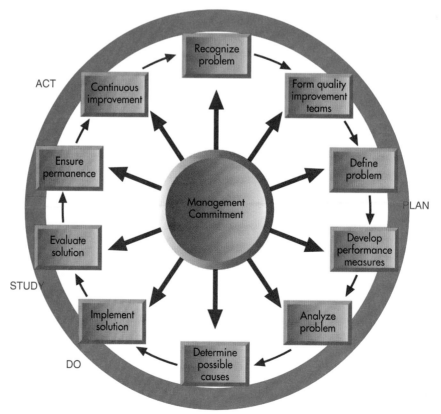

There are four basic steps in the cycle:

Plan. Begin by studying the current process. Document that process. Then collect data on the process or problem. Next, analyze the data and develop a plan for improvement. Specify measures for evaluating the plan.

Do. Implement the plan, on a small scale if possible. Document any changes made during this phase. Collect data systematically for evaluation.

Study. Evaluate the data collection during the *do* phase. Check how closely the results match the original goals of the *plan* phase.

Act. If the results are successful, *standardize* the new method and communicate the new method to all people associated with the process. Implement training for the new method. If the results are unsuccessful, revise the plan and repeat the process or cease this project.

In replicating successful results elsewhere in the organization, the cycle is repeated. Similarly, if the plan was unsuccessful and you wish to make further modifications, repeat this cycle.

Employing this sequence of steps provides a systematic approach to continuous improvement.

Process Improvement

Process improvement is a *systematic* approach to improving a process. It involves documentation, measurement, and analysis for the purpose of improving the functioning of a process. Typical goals of process improvement include increasing customer satisfaction, achieving higher quality, reducing waste, reducing cost, increasing productivity, and speeding up the process.

Table 11–3 provides an overview of process improvement, and Figure 11–2 shows its cyclical nature.

process improvement A systematic approach to improving a process.

TABLE 11–3

Overview of process improvement

A. Process mapping

1. Collect information about the process; identify each step in the process. For each step, determine:
   The inputs and outputs.
   The people involved.
   All decisions that are made.
   Document such measures as time, cost, space used, waste, employee morale and any employee turnover, accidents and/or safety hazards, working conditions, revenues and/or profits, quality, and customer satisfaction, as appropriate.
2. Prepare a flowchart that *accurately* depicts the process; note that too little detail will not allow for meaningful analysis, and too much detail will overwhelm analysts and be counterproductive. Make sure that key activities and decisions are represented.

B. Analyze the process

1. Ask these questions about the process:
   Is the flow logical?
   Are any steps or activities missing?
   Are there any duplications?
2. Ask these questions about each step:
   Is the step necessary? Could it be eliminated?
   Does the step add value?
   Does any waste occur at this step?
   Could the time be shortened?
   Could the cost to perform the step be reduced?
   Could two (or more) steps be combined?

C. Redesign the process
Using the results of the analysis, redesign the process. Document the improvements; potential measures include reductions in time, cost, space, waste, employee turnover, accidents, safety hazards, and increases/improvements in employee morale, working conditions, revenues/profits, quality, and customer satisfaction.

FIGURE 11-2

*The process improvement cycle
is another version of the plan-
do-study-act cycle*

Tools

There are a number of tools that an organization can use for problem solving and process improvement. This section describes eight of these tools. The tools aid in data collection and interpretation, and provide the basis for decision making.

The first seven tools are often referred to as the *seven basic quality tools*. Figure 11–3 provides a quick overview of the seven tools.

flowchart A diagram of the steps in process.

Flowcharts. A **flowchart** is a visual representation of a process. As a problem-solving tool, a flowchart can help investigators in identifying possible points in a process where problems occur. Figure 11–4 (on page 480) illustrates a flowchart.

The diamond shapes in the flowchart represent decision points in the process, and the rectangular shapes represent procedures. The arrows show the direction of "flow" of the steps in the process.

To construct a simple flowchart, begin by listing the steps in a process. Then classify each step as either a procedure or a decision (or check) point. Try to not make the flowchart too detailed, or it may be overwhelming, but be careful not to omit any key steps.

check sheet A tool for recording and organizing data to identify a problem.

Check Sheets. A **check sheet** is a simple tool frequently used for problem identification. Check sheets provide a format that enables users to record and organize data in a way that facilitates collection and analysis. This format might be one of simple checkmarks. Check sheets are designed on the basis of what the users are attempting to learn by collecting data.

Many different formats can be used for a check sheet and there are many different types of sheets. One frequently used form of check sheet deals with type of defect, another with location of defects. These are illustrated in Figures 11–5 and 11–6 (on pages 480 and 481).

Figure 11–5 shows tallies that denote the type of defect and the time of day each occurred. Problems with missing labels tend to occur early in the day and smeared print tends to occur late in the day, whereas offcenter labels are found throughout the day. Identifying types of defects and when they occur can help in pinpointing causes of the defects.

Figure 11–6 makes it easy to see where defects on the product are occurring. In this case, defects seem to be occurring on the tips of the thumb and first finger, in the finger valleys (especially between the thumb and first finger), and in the center of the gloves. Again, this may help determine why the defects occur and lead to a solution.

histogram A chart of an empirical frequency distribution.

Histograms. A **histogram** can be useful in getting a sense of the distribution of observed values. Among other things, one can see if the distribution is symmetrical, what the range of values is, and if there are any unusual values. Figure 11–7 (on page 481) illustrates a histogram. Note the two peaks. This suggests the possibility of *two* distributions with different centers. Possible causes might be two workers or two suppliers with different quality.

Flowchart

A diagram of the steps in a process

Check sheet

A tool for organizing and collecting data; a tally of problems or other events by category

	Day			
Defect	1	2	3	4
A	///		////	/
B	//	/	//	///
C	/	////	//	////

Histogram

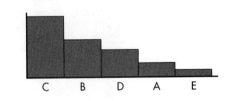

A chart that shows an empirical frequency distribution

Pareto chart

A diagram that arranges categories from highest to lowest frequency of occurrence

Scatter diagram

A graph that shows the degree and direction of relationship between two variables

Control chart

A statistical chart of time-ordered values of a sample statistic (e.g., sample means)

Cause–and–effect diagram

A diagram used to organize a search for the cause(s) of a problem; also known as a *fishbone* diagram

FIGURE 11-3

The seven basic quality tools

FIGURE 11-4

A flowchart

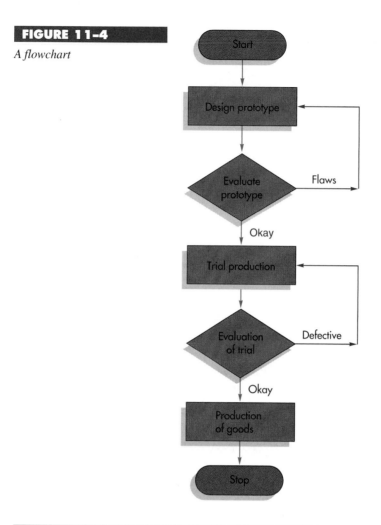

FIGURE 11-5

An example of a check sheet

Day	Time	Type of Defect					Total
		Missing label	Off-center	Smeared print	Loose or folded	Other	
M	8-9	IIII	II				6
	9-10		III				3
	10-11	I	III	I			5
	11-12		I		I	I (Torn)	3
	1-2		I				1
	2-3		II	III	I		6
	3-4		II	IIIII			8
Total		5	14	10	2	1	32

Pareto analysis Technique for classifying problem areas according to degree of importance, and focusing on the most important.

Pareto Analysis. Pareto analysis is a technique for focusing attention on the most important problem areas. The Pareto concept, named after the nineteenth-century Italian economist Vilfredo Pareto, is that a relatively few factors generally account for a large percentage of the total cases (e.g., complaints, defects, problems). The idea is to classify the cases according to degree of importance, and focus on resolving the most important, leaving the less important. Often referred to as the 80–20 rule, the Pareto concept states that approximately 80 percent of the problems come from 20 percent of the items. For instance, 80 percent of machine breakdowns come from 20 percent of the machines, and 80 percent of the product defects come from 20 percent of the causes of defects.

FIGURE 11–6

A special purpose check sheet

× = Location of a defect

FIGURE 11–7

A histogram

Frequency

Repair time (minutes)

Often, it is useful to prepare a chart that shows the number of occurrences by category, arranged in order of frequency. Figure 11–8 illustrates such a chart corresponding to the check sheet shown in Figure 11–5. The dominance of the problem with offcenter labels becomes apparent. Presumably, the manager and employees would focus on trying to resolve this problem. Once they accomplished that, they could address the remaining defects in similar fashion; "smeared print" would be the next major category to be resolved, and so on. Additional check sheets would be used to collect data to verify that the defects in these categories have been eliminated or greatly reduced. Hence, in later Pareto diagrams, categories such as "offcenter" may still appear but would be much less prominent.

Scatter Diagrams. A **scatter diagram** can be useful in deciding if there is a correlation between the values of two variables. A correlation may point to a cause of a problem. Figure 11–9 shows an example of a scatter diagram. In this particular diagram, there is a *positive* (upward sloping) relationship between the humidity and the number of errors per hour. High values of humidity correspond to high numbers of errors, and vice versa. On the other hand, a *negative* (downward sloping) relationship would mean that when values of one variable are low, values of the other variable are high, and vice versa.

The higher the correlation between the two variables, the less scatter in the points; the points will tend to line up. Conversely, if there were little or no relationship between two variables, the points would be completely scattered. In Figure 11–9, the correlation between humidity and errors seems strong, because the points appear to scatter along an imaginary line.

scatter diagram A graph that shows the degree and direction of relationship between two variables.

Control Charts. A **control chart** can be used to monitor a process to see if the process output is random. It can help detect the presence of *correctable* causes of variation. Figure 11–10 illustrates a control chart. Control charts can also indicate when a problem occurred and give insight into what caused the problem. Control charts are described in detail in Chapter 10.

control chart A statistical chart of time-ordered values of a sample statistic.

Cause-and-Effect Diagrams. A **cause-and-effect diagram** offers a structured approach to the search for the possible cause(s) of a problem. It is also known as a **fishbone**

cause-and-effect diagram Used to search for the cause(s) of a problem; also called *fishbone diagram.*

FIGURE 11-8

A Pareto diagram based on data in Figure 11–5

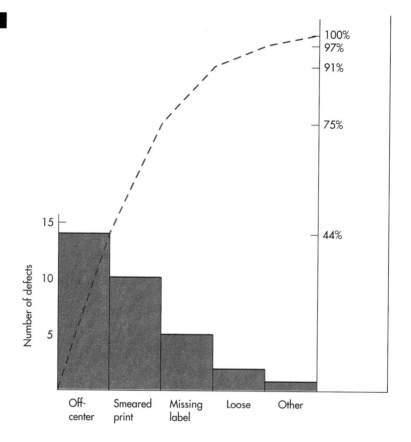

FIGURE 11-9

A scatter diagram

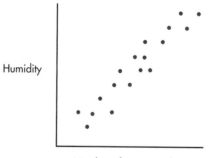

FIGURE 11-10

A control chart

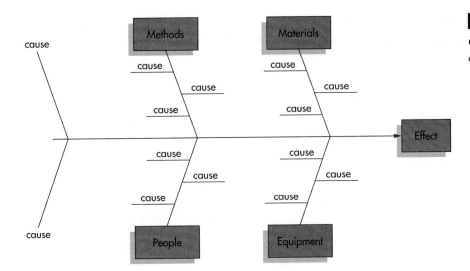

FIGURE 11-11

One format of a cause-and-effect diagram

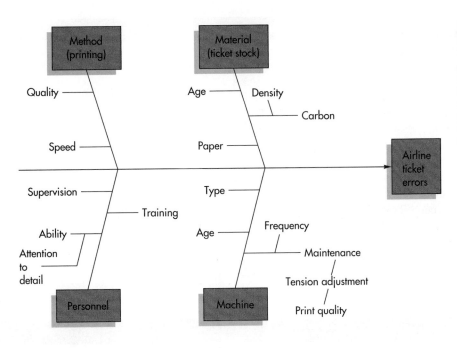

FIGURE 11-12

Cause-and-effect diagram for airline ticket errors
Source: Reprinted from Howard Git-low, Alan Oppenheim, and Rosa Op-penheim, *Quality Management: Tools and Methods for Improvement* (Burr Ridge, IL: Richard D. Irwin, 1995), p. 313, by permission.

diagram because of its shape, or an *Ishikawa diagram,* after the Japanese professor who developed the approach to aid workers overwhelmed by the number of possible sources of problems when problem solving. This tool helps to organize problem-solving efforts by identifying *categories* of factors that might be causing problems. Often this tool is used after brainstorming sessions, to organize the ideas generated. Figure 11–11 illustrates one form of a cause-and-effect diagram.

An example of an application of such a cause-and-effect diagram is shown in Figure 11–12. Each of the factors listed in the diagram is a potential source of ticket errors. Some are more likely causes than others, depending on the nature of the errors. If the cause is still not obvious at this point, additional investigation into the *root cause* may be necessary, involving a more in-depth analysis. Often, more detailed information can be obtained by asking *who, what, where, when, why,* and *how* questions about factors that appear to be the most likely sources of problems.

Continuous Improvement on the Free-Throw Line

Timothy Clark and Andrew Clark

I n 1924, Walter Shewhart developed a problem-solving method to continually improve quality by reducing variation (the difference between the ideal outcome and the actual situation). To help guide improvement efforts, Shewhart outlined a process referred to as the plan-do-study-act (PDSA) cycle. The PDSA cycle combined with the traditional concepts of decision making and problem solving are what my son and I used to continuously improve his basketball free-throw shooting.

Recognizing the Problem

Identify the facts. I had observed over a three-year period from 1991 to 1993 that in basketball games, my son Andrew's free-throw shooting percentage averaged between 45 percent and 50 percent.

Identify and define the process. Andrew's process for shooting free throws was simple: Go to the free-throw line, bounce the ball four times, aim, and shoot.

The desired outcome was a higher free-throw shooting percentage. An ideal outcome, or perfection, would be one in which 100 percent of the shots fall through the middle of the rim, land at the same spot on the floor every time, and roll straight back in the shooter's direction after landing.

Plot the points. To confirm my observations on the results of the current process, we went to the YMCA and Andrew shot five sets of 10 free throws for a total of 50 shots. His average was 42 percent. Results were recorded on a run chart (see Figure 1). I estimated the process was stable.

Decision Making

Identify the causes. Causes of variation in any process can be identified through the general categories of people, equipment, materials, methods, environment, and measurement. A cause-and-effect diagram is used to graphically illustrate the relationship between the effect—a low free-throw shooting percentage—and the principal causes (see Figure 2).

In analyzing my son's process, I noticed that he did not stand at the same place on the free-throw line every time. I believed his inconsistent shooting position affected the direction of the shot. If the shot goes left or right, there is a smaller probability that the ball will have a lucky bounce and go in. I also noticed that he didn't seem to have a consistent focal point.

Figure 1. Free-Throw Shooting Run Chart

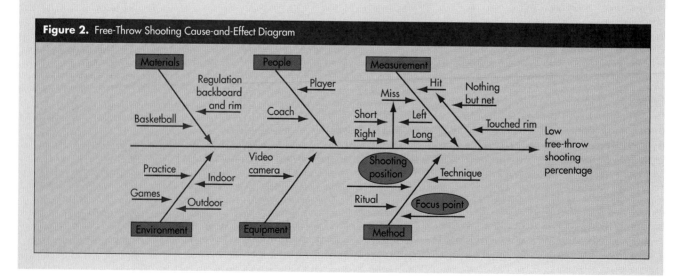

Figure 2. Free-Throw Shooting Cause-and-Effect Diagram

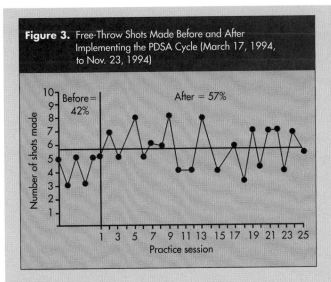

Figure 3. Free-Throw Shots Made Before and After Implementing the PDSA Cycle (March 17, 1994, to Nov. 23, 1994)

Figure 4. Determining Whether the Free-Throw Process Is Stable (March 17, 1994, to Jan. 18, 1996)

Develop, analyze, and select alternatives. The alternatives selected for Andrew, a right-handed shooter, were for him to line up his right foot on the middle of the free-throw line, focus on the middle of the front part of the rim, and visualize the perfect shot before he released the ball. The modified process is:

1. Stand at the center of the free-throw line.

2. Bounce the ball four times.

3. Focus on the middle of the front part of the rim, and visualize a perfect shot.

4. Shoot.

Develop an action plan. The course of action at this point was for Andrew to shoot five more sets of 10 free throws to test the effectiveness of the changes.

Problem Solving

Implement the selected alternative and compare actual with expected results. The new process resulted in a 36 percent improvement in Andrew's average free-throw percentage at basketball practice, which raised his average to 57 percent (see Figure 3). The new process was first implemented in games toward the end of the 1994 season, and in the last three games, Andrew hit nine of his 13 free throws for a free-throw shooting average of 69 percent.

During the 1995 season, Andrew made 37 of his 52 free throws in games for an average of 71 percent. In one extremely close game where the other team was forced to foul Andrew's team in an effort to get the ball back, Andrew hit seven of his seven shots, which helped his team win the game. In team practices, the coaches had the players shoot two free throws and then rotate. For the entire season, Andrew hit 101 of 169 of his team practice free throws for an average of 60 percent.

As we monitored Andrew's process from March 17, 1994, to Jan. 18, 1996, we plotted the total number of practice shots made out of 50, using Shewhart's number-of-affected-units control chart (see Figure 4).

In the late summer of 1995, Andrew went to a basketball camp where he was advised to change his shooting technique, which reduced his shooting percentage during the 1996 season to 50 percent. We then reinstalled his old process, and his shooting percentage returned to its former level. In one series of 50 practice free throws, he hit 35 of 50 shots for an average of 70 percent and in another set, he hit an average of 64 percent. During the remaining team practices, Andrew hit 14 of 20 for an average of 70 percent.

During the 1996 and 1997 seasons, Andrew was a point guard and had fewer opportunities to shoot free throws, but he made nine of them for an average of 75 percent.

Overall benefits. In addition to the tangible results, such as improved free-throw shooting, the intangible benefits were also significant. For example, Andrew's confidence improved, and he learned how to determine when changes to his shooting technique resulted in improvement. W. Edwards Deming referred to this type of knowledge as profound.

Continuous Improvement

Take appropriate action based on study results. In preparation for the 1998 season, Andrew's priorities for improvement are to continue to monitor his free-throw shooting to ensure it remains stable and to work on improving the shooting percentage of his two- and three-point shots.

Developing a knowledge and understanding of variation will change the way you look at the world forever and can lead to unprecedented levels of quality.

Source: © 1997 American Society for Quality. Reprinted with permission.

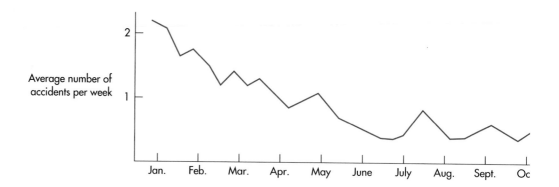

FIGURE 11–13

*A run chart shows
performance over time*

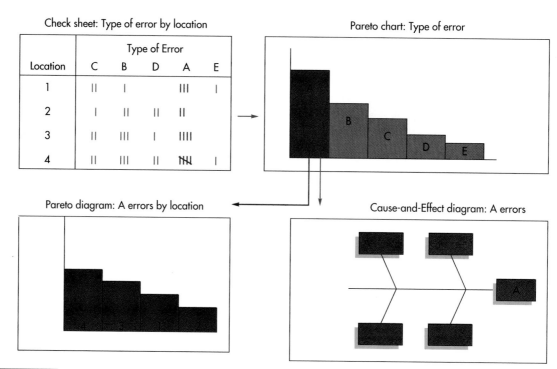

FIGURE 11–14

*Employing graphical tools in
problem solving*

run chart Tool for tracking
results over a period of time.

Run Charts. A **run chart** can be used to track the values of a variable over time. This can
aid in identifying trends or other patterns that may be occurring. Figure 11–13 provides an
example of a run chart showing a decreasing trend in accident frequency over time. Important advantages of run charts are ease of construction and ease of interpretation.

ILLUSTRATIONS OF THE USE OF GRAPHICAL TOOLS

This section presents some illustrations of the use of graphical tools in process or product
improvement. Figure 11–14 begins with a check sheet that can be used to develop a
Pareto chart of the types of errors found. That leads to a more focused Pareto diagram of
the most frequently occurring type of error, followed (moving right) by a cause-and-effect

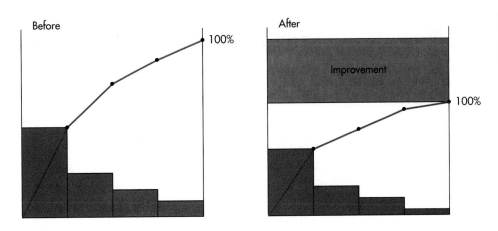

FIGURE 11-15

Comparison of before and after using Pareto charts

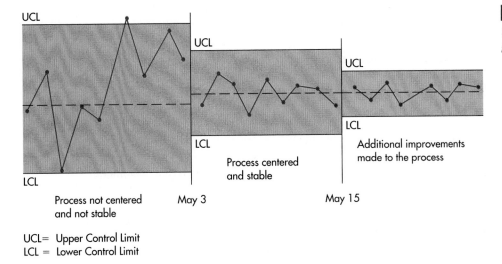

FIGURE 11-16

Using a control chart to track improvements

diagram of the second most frequently occurring error. Additional cause-and-effect diagrams, such as errors by location, might also be used.

Figure 11–15 shows how Pareto charts measure the amount of improvement achieved in a before-and-after scenario of errors.

Figure 11–16 illustrates how control charts track two phases of improvement in a process that was initially out of control.

METHODS FOR GENERATING IDEAS

Some additional tools that are useful for problem solving and/or for process improvement are brainstorming, quality circles, interviewing, and benchmarking.

Brainstorming. **Brainstorming** is a technique in which a group of people share thoughts and ideas on problems in a relaxed atmosphere that encourages unrestrained collective thinking. The goal is to generate a free flow of ideas on identifying problems, and finding causes, solutions, and ways to implement solutions. In successful brainstorming, criticism is absent, no single member is allowed to dominate sessions, and all ideas are welcomed.

brainstorming Technique for generating a free flow of ideas in a group of people.

Quality Circles. One way companies have tapped employees for ideas concerning quality improvement is through **quality circles.** The circles comprise a number of workers

quality circles Groups of workers who meet to discuss ways of improving products or processes.

who get together periodically to discuss ways of improving products and processes. Not only are quality circles a valuable source of worker input, they also can motivate workers, if handled properly, by demonstrating management interest in worker ideas. Quality circles are usually less structured and more informal than teams involved in continuous improvement, but in some organizations quality circles have evolved into continuous improvement teams. Perhaps a major distinction between quality circles and teams is the amount of authority given to the teams. Typically, quality circles have had very little authority to implement any but minor changes; continuous improvement teams are sometimes given a great deal of authority. Consequently, continuous improvement teams have the added motivation generated by *empowerment.*

The team approach works best when it reaches decisions based on consensus. This may involve one or more of the following methods:

1. *List reduction* is applied to a list of possible problems or solutions. Its purpose is to clarify items, and in the *process,* reduce the list of items by posing questions about affordability, feasibility, and likelihood of solving the problem for each item.

2. A *balance sheet* approach lists the pros and cons of each item and focuses discussion on important issues.

3. *Paired comparisons* is a process by which each item on a list is compared with every other item, two at a time. For each pair, team members select the preferred item. This approach forces a choice between items. It works best when the list of items is small: say, five or fewer.

interviewing Technique for identifying problems and collecting information.

Interviewing. Another technique a firm can use to identify problems or collect information about a problem is **interviewing.** Internal problems may require interviewing employees; external problems may require interviewing external customers.

Ideas for improvement can come from a number of sources: research and development, customers, competitors, and employees. Customer satisfaction is the ultimate goal of improvement activities, and customers can offer many valuable suggestions about products and the service process. However, they are unlikely to have suggestions for manufacturing processes.

benchmarking Process of measuring performance against the best in the same or another industry.

Benchmarking. Benchmarking is an approach that can inject new energy into improvement efforts. Summarized in Table 11–4, benchmarking is the process of measuring an organization's performance on a key customer requirement against the best in the industry, or against the best in any industry. Its purpose is to establish a standard against which performance is judged, and to identify a model for learning how to improve. A benchmark demonstrates the degree to which customers of other organizations are satisfied. Once a

Motorola's "six-sigma" quality program is now a benchmark goal in many industries. Motorola works closely with suppliers to improve the quality of parts as shown here.

benchmark has been identified, the goal is to meet or exceed that standard through improvements in appropriate processes.

The benchmarking process usually involves these steps:

1. Identify a critical process that needs improvement (e.g., order entry, distribution, service after sale).
2. Identify an organization that excels in the process, preferably the best.
3. Contact the benchmark organization, visit it, and study the benchmark activity.
4. Analyze the data.
5. Improve the critical process at your own organization.

Selecting an industry leader provides insight into what competitors are doing; but competitors may be reluctant to share this information. Several organizations are responding to this difficulty by conducting benchmarking studies and providing that information to other organizations without revealing the sources of the data.

Selecting organizations that are world leaders in different industries is another alternative. For example, the Xerox Corporation uses many benchmarks: For employee involvement, Procter & Gamble; for quality process, Florida Power and Light and Toyota; for high-volume production, Kodak and Canon; for billing collection, American Express; for research and development, AT&T and Hewlett-Packard; for distribution, L.L. Bean and Hershey Foods; and for daily scheduling, Cummins Engine.

Vol. 1, Tape 1, Seg. 1
Caterpillar, Cummins Engine

The 5W2H Approach. Asking questions about the current process can lead to important insights about why the current process isn't working as well as it could, as well as potential ways to improve it. One method is called the **5W2H** (5 "w" words and 2 "h" words) approach (see Table 11–5).

5W2H approach A method of asking questions about a process that includes what, why, where, when, who, how, and how much.

1. What organization does it the best?
2. How do they do it?
3. How do we do it now?
4. How can we change to match or exceed the best?

TABLE 11–4

The benchmarking approach

TABLE 11–5

The 5W2H approach

Category	5W2H	Typical Questions	Goal
Subject	What?	What is being done?	Identify the focus of analysis.
Purpose	Why?	Why is this necessary?	Eliminate unnecessary tasks.
Location	Where?	Where is it being done? Why is it done there? Would it be better to do it someplace else?	Improve the location.
Sequence	When?	When is it done? Would it be better to do it at another time?	Improve the sequence.
People	Who?	Who is doing it? Could someone else do it better?	Improve the sequence or output.
Method	How?	How is it being done? Is there a better way?	Simplify tasks, improve output.
Cost	How much?	How much does it cost now? What would the new cost be?	Select an improved method.

Source: Adapted from Alan Robinson, *Continuous Improvement in Operations: A Systematic Approach to Waste Reduction* (Cambridge, MA: Productivity Press, 1991), p. 246.

READING

Benchmarking Corporate Websites of Fortune 500 Companies

www.dow.com

More and more people are using the Internet. And when these people want information about a company's products or services, they often go to the company's website. In a study of the home pages of Fortune 500 companies, 13 factors were deemed critical to quality. Those factors, and the survey results, are shown below:

1. Use of meta tags (e.g., keywords used by search engines) Yes, 70%; no, 30%

2. Meaningful home page title   Yes, 97%; no, 3%

3. Unique domain name Yes, 91%; no, 9%

4. Search engine site registration 97% (average)

5. Server reliability 99% (average)

6. Average speed of loading (seconds) 28k, 19.3; 56k, 10.9; T1, 2.6 sec.

7. Average number of bad links   .40

8. Average number of spelling errors   .16

9. Visibility of contact information Yes, 74%; no, 26%

10. Indication of last update date   Yes, 17%; no, 63%

11. A privacy policy   Yes, 53%; no, 47%

12. Presence of a search engine   Yes, 59%; no, 41%

13. Translation to multiple languages   Yes, 11%; no, 89%

The corporations are doing well on most factors, but they need improvement on the last five.

The list is a handy reference other organizations can use to benchmark their existing home pages to see where improvements are needed or to develop effective home pages.

Question

Give one reason for the importance of each factor.

Source: Based on Nabil Tamimi, Murli Rajan, and Rose Sebastianelli, "Benchmarking the Home Pages of 'Fortune 500' Companies," *Quality Progress,* July 2000, pp. 47–51.

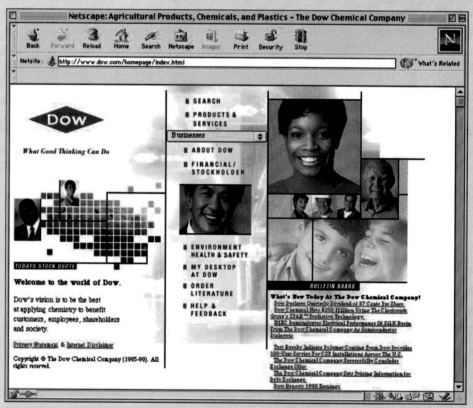

Dow Chemical Company home page provides easy access to detailed information as a service in support of its products.

Operations Strategy

In order for total quality management to be successful, it is essential that a majority of those in an organization "buy in" to the idea. Otherwise, there is a risk that a significant portion of the benefits of the approach will not be realized. Therefore, it is important to give this sufficient attention, and to confirm that concordance exists before plunging ahead. A key aspect of this is a "top-down" approach: Top management needs to be visibly involved and needs to be supportive, both financially and emotionally. Also important is education of managers and workers in the concepts, tools, and procedures of quality. Again, if education is incomplete, there is the risk that TQM will not produce the desired benefits.

Summary

Total quality management is a never-ending pursuit of quality that involves everyone in an organization. The driving force is customer satisfaction; a key philosophy is continuous improvement. Training of managers and workers in quality concepts, tools, and procedures is an important aspect of the approach. Teams are an integral part of TQM.

Two major aspects of the TQM approach are problem solving and process improvement.

Key Terms

benchmarking, 488
brainstorming, 487
cause-and-effect diagram, 481
check sheet, 478
continuous improvement, 471
control chart, 481
fail–safing, 471
fishbone diagram, 481
5W2H approach, 489
flowchart, 478
histogram, 478

interviewing, 488
kaizen, 471
Pareto analysis, 480
plan-do-study-act (PDSA) cycle, 475
process improvement, 477
quality at the source, 472
quality circles, 487
run chart, 486
scatter diagram, 481
total quality management (TQM), 470

Discussion and Review Questions

1. What are the key elements of the TQM approach? What is the driving force behind TQM?
2. Briefly describe each of the seven quality tools.
3. Briefly define or explain each of these tools:
   a. Brainstorming
   b. Benchmarking
   c. Run charts
4. Explain each of these methods:
   a. The plan-do-study-act cycle
   b. The 5W2H approach
5. List the steps of problem solving.
6. Select four tools and describe how they could be used in problem solving.
7. List the steps of process improvement.
8. Select four tools and describe how they could be used for process improvement.

Memo Writing Exercises

1. The vice president of manufacturing of your company, June Seymour, has asked you to write her a memo that lists the key elements of a total quality management approach and outlines the benefits and risks of adopting a TQM approach for the company.

   Write a one- to two-page memo to her.
2. You are an assistant to the production manager of a large company. The company wants to give worker teams in several departments additional authority and responsibility to see whether quality and productivity in those areas are increased. However, the proposal has met with resistance from both managers and worker teams.

   Write a one-page memo to Jeff Rogers, the production manager, discussing the probable causes of the resistance and potential solutions for overcoming it.
3. Select a task that you do on a regular basis, such as taking notes in class, doing a homework assignment, grocery shopping, or another task. Write a one-page, quality-at-the-source memo on the difficulties you might encounter by not doing it correctly the first time.

1. Make a check sheet and then a Pareto diagram for the following car repair shop data.

Ticket No.	Work	Ticket No.	Work
1	Tires	16	Tires
2	Lube & oil	17	Lube & oil
3	Tires	18	Brakes
4	Battery	19	Tires
5	Lube & oil	20	Brakes
6	Lube & oil	21	Lube & oil
7	Lube & oil	22	Brakes
8	Brakes	23	Transmission
9	Lube & oil	24	Brakes
10	Tires	25	Lube & oil
11	Brakes	26	Battery
12	Lube & oil	27	Lube & oil
13	Battery	28	Battery
14	Lube & oil	29	Brakes
15	Lube & oil	30	Tires

2. An air-conditioning repair department manager has compiled data on the primary reason for 41 service calls for the previous week, as shown in the table. Using the data, make a check sheet for the problem types for each customer type, and then construct a Pareto diagram for each type of customer.

Job Number	Problem/ Customer Type	Job Number	Problem/ Customer Type	Job Number	Problem/ Customer Type
301	F/R	315	F/C	329	O/C
302	O/R	316	O/C	330	N/R
303	N/C	317	W/C	331	N/R
304	N/R	318	N/R	332	W/R
305	W/C	319	O/C	333	O/R
306	N/R	320	F/R	334	O/C
307	F/R	321	F/R	335	N/R
308	N/C	322	O/R	336	W/R
309	W/R	323	F/R	337	O/C
310	N/R	324	N/C	338	O/R
311	N/R	325	F/R	339	F/R
312	F/C	326	O/R	340	N/R
313	N/R	327	W/C	341	O/C
314	W/C	328	O/C		

Key: Problem type: Customer type:
     N = Noisy   C = Commercial customer
     F = Equipment failure   R = Residential customer
     W = Runs warm
     O = Odor

3. Prepare a run chart for the occurrences of defective computer monitors based on the following data, which an analyst obtained from the process for making the monitors. Workers are given a 15-minute break at 10:15 A.M. and 3:15 P.M., and a lunch break at noon. What can you conclude?

Interval Start Time	Number of Defects	Interval Start Time	Number of Defects
8:00	1	1:00	1
8:15	0	1:15	0
8:30	0	1:30	0
8:45	1	1:45	1

9:00	0	2:00	1
9:15	1	2:15	0
9:30	1	2:30	2
9:45	2	2:45	2
10:00	3	3:00	3
10:30	1	3:30	0
10:45	0	3:45	1
11:00	0	4:00	0
11:15	0	4:15	0
11:30	1	4:30	1
11:45	3	4:45	3

4. Prepare a run diagram for this 911 call data. Use five-minute intervals (i.e., count the calls received in each five-minute interval. Use intervals of 0–4, 5–9, etc.). Note: Two or more calls may occur in the same minute; there were three operators on duty this night. What can you conclude from the run chart?

Call	Time	Call	Time
1	1:03	22	1:56
2	1:06	23	1:56
3	1:09	24	2:00
4	1:11	25	2:00
5	1:12	26	2:01
6	1:17	27	2:02
7	1:21	28	2:03
8	1:27	29	2:03
9	1:28	30	2:04
10	1:29	31	2:06
11	1:31	32	2:07
12	1:36	33	2:08
13	1:39	34	2:08
14	1:42	35	2:11
15	1:43	36	2:12
16	1:44	37	2:12
17	1:47	38	2:13
18	1:48	39	2:14
19	1:50	40	2:14
20	1:52	41	2:16
21	1:53	42	2:19

5. Suppose that a table lamp fails to light when turned on. Prepare a simple cause-and-effect diagram to analyze possible causes.

6. Prepare a cause-and-effect diagram to analyze the possible causes of late delivery of parts ordered from a supplier.

7. Prepare a cause-and-effect diagram to analyze why a machine has produced a large run of defective parts.

8. Prepare a scatter diagram for each of these data sets and then express in words the apparent relationship between the two variables. Put the first variable on the horizontal axis and the second variable on the vertical axis.

a.

Age	24	30	22	25	33	27	36	58	37	47	54	28	42	55
Absenteeism rate	6	5	7	6	4	5	4	1	3	2	2	5	3	1

b.

Temperature (F)	65	63	72	66	82	58	75	86	77	65	79
Error rate	1	2	0	0	3	3	1	5	2	1	3

9. Prepare a flowchart that describes going to the library to study for an exam. Your flowchart should include these items: finding a place at the library to study, checking to see if you have your book, paper, highlighter, etc., traveling to the library, and the possibility of moving to another location if the place you chose to study starts to get crowded.

10. College students trying to register for a course sometimes find that the course has been closed, or the section they want has been closed. Prepare a cause-and-effect diagram for this problem.

11. The county sheriff's department responded to an unusually large number of vehicular accidents along a quarter-mile stretch of highway in recent months. Prepare a cause-and-effect diagram for this problem.

CASE

Chick-n-Gravy Dinner Line

The operations manager of a firm that produces frozen dinners had received numerous complaints from supermarkets about the firm's Chick-n-Gravy dinners. The manager then asked her assistant, Ann, to investigate the matter and to report her recommendations.

Ann's first task was to determine what problems were generating the complaints. The majority of complaints centered on five defects: underfilled packages, a missing item, spills/mixed items, unacceptable taste, and improperly sealed packages.

Next, she took samples of dinners from the two production lines and examined each sample, making note of any defects that she found. A summary of those results is shown in the table.

The data resulted from inspecting approximately 800 frozen dinners. What should Ann recommend to the manager?

			DEFECT OBSERVED				
Date	Time	Line	Underfilled	Missing Item	Spill/ Mixed	Unacceptable Taste	Improperly Sealed
5/12	0900	1		√√	√	√√√	
5/12	1330	2			√√		√√
5/13	1000	2				√	√√√
5/13	1345	1	√√		√√		
5/13	1530	2		√	√√√		√
5/14	0830	1		√√√		√√√	
5/14	1100	2	√		√	√√	
5/14	1400	1			√		√
5/15	1030	1		√√√		√√√√√	
5/15	1145	2			√	√√	
5/15	1500	1	√		√		
5/16	0845	2				√√	√√
5/16	1030	1		√√√	√	√√√	
5/16	1400	1					
5/16	1545	2	√	√√√√	√	√	√√

CASE

Tip Top Markets

Tip Top Markets is a regional chain of supermarkets located in the Southeastern United States. Karen Martin, manager of one of the stores, was disturbed by the large number of complaints from customers at her store, particularly on Tuesdays, so she obtained complaint records from the store's customer service desk for the last eight Tuesdays. These are shown below.

Assume you have been asked to help analyze the data and to make recommendations for improvement. Analyze the data using a check sheet, a Pareto diagram, and run charts. Then construct a cause-and-effect diagram for the leading category on your Pareto diagram.

On July 15, changes were implemented to reduce out-of-stock complaints, improve store maintenance, and reduce checkout lines/pricing problems. Do the results of the last two weeks reflect improvement?

Based on your analysis, prepare a list of recommendations that will address customer complaints.

June 1

out of orange yogurt
bread stale
checkout lines too long
overcharged
double charged
meat smelled strange
charged for item not purchased
couldn't find the sponges
meat tasted strange
store too cold
light out in parking lot

produce not fresh
lemon yogurt past sell date
couldn't find rice
milk past sell date
stock clerk rude
cashier not friendly
out of maple walnut ice cream
something green in meat
didn't like music
checkout lines too slow

June 8

fish smelled funny
out of diet bread
dented can
out of hamburger rolls
fish not fresh
cashier helpful
meat tasted bad
ATM ate card
slippery floor
music too loud

undercharged
out of roses
meat spoiled
overcharged on two items
store too warm
out of ice
telephone out of order
overcharged
rolls stale
bread past sale date

June 15

wanted smaller size
too cold in store
out of Wheaties
out of Minute Rice
cashier rude
fish tasted fishy
ice cream thawed
double charged on hard rolls
long wait at checkout
wrong price on item
overcharged
fish didn't smell right

overcharged on special
couldn't find aspirin
undercharged
checkout lines too long
out of diet cola
meat smelled bad
overcharged on eggs
bread not fresh
didn't like music
lost wallet
overcharged on bread

June 22

milk past sales date
store too warm
foreign object in meat
store too cold
eggs cracked
couldn't find lard
out of 42 oz. Tide
fish really bad
windows dirty

couldn't find oatmeal
out of Bounty paper towels
overcharged on orange juice
lines too long at checkout
couldn't find shoelaces
out of Smucker's strawberry jam
out of Frosty Flakes cereal
out of Thomas' English Muffins

June 29

checkout line too long
out of Dove soap
out of Bisquick
eggs cracked
store not clean
store too cold
cashier too slow
out of skim milk
charged wrong price

restroom not clean
couldn't find sponges
checkout lines slow
out of 18 oz. Tide
out of Campbell's turkey soup
out of pepperoni sticks
checkout lines too long
meat not fresh
overcharged on melon

July 6

out of straws
out of bird food
overcharged on butter
out of masking tape
stockboy was helpful
lost child
meat looked bad
overcharged on butter
out of Swiss chard
too many people in store
out of bubble bath
out of Dial soap

store too warm
price not as advertised
need to open more checkouts
shopping carts hard to steer
debris in aisles
out of Drano
out of Chinese cabbage
store too warm
floors dirty and sticky
out of Diamond chopped walnuts

July 13

wrong price on spaghetti	undercharged
water on floor	out of brown rice
store looked messy	out of mushrooms
store too warm	overcharged
checkout lines too long	checkout wait too long
cashier not friendly	shopping cart broken
out of Cheese Doodles	couldn't find aspirin
triple charged	out of brown lunch bags
out of Saran Wrap	out of straws
out of Dove Bars	

July 20

out of low-salt pickles	out of large eggs
checkout lines too slow	out of cranapple juice
found keys in parking lot	out of pretzels
lost keys	out of apricot jam
wrong price on sale item	telephone out of order
overcharged on corn	out of cocktail sauce
wrong price on baby food	water on floor
out of 18 oz. Tide	out of frozen onion rings
out of green tea	out of frozen squash
checkout lines too long	out of powdered sugar
out of romaine lettuce	out of nonfat peanut butter

July 27

out of dill pickles	wanted to know who won the lottery
reported accident in parking lot	
wrong price on cranapple juice	store too warm
out of carrot juice	oatmeal spilled in bulk section
out of licorice sticks	telephone out of order
out of chocolate milk	out of Lava soap
out of Dove Bars	water on floor
windows dirty	out of glazed doughnuts
out of iceberg lettuce	out of baby carrots
like store decorations	spaghetti sauce on floor
out of St. John's wort	out of Peter Pan crunchy peanut butter
out of vanilla soy milk	

READING

Making Quality Pay: Return on Quality

Start with an effective quality program. Companies that don't have the basics, such as process and inventory controls and other building blocks, will find a healthy return on quality elusive.

Calculate the cost of current quality initiatives. Cost of warranties, problem prevention, and monitoring activities all count. Measure these against the returns for delivering a product or service to the customer.

Determine what key factors retain customers—and what drives them away. Conduct detailed surveys. Forecast market changes, especially quality and new-product initiatives of competitors.

Focus on quality efforts most likely to improve customer satisfaction at a reasonable cost. Figure the link between each dollar spent on quality and its effect on customer retention and market share.

Roll out successful programs after pilot-testing the most promising efforts and cutting the ones that don't have a big impact. Closely monitor results. Build word of mouth by publicizing success stories.

Improve programs continually. Measure results against anticipated gains. Beware of the competition's initiative and don't hesitate to revamp programs accordingly. Quality never rests.

When the "total quality" mantra swept U.S. boardrooms in the 1980s, few companies responded with the fervor and dedication of Varian Associates Inc. The scientific-equipment maker put 1,000 of its managers through a four-day course on quality. The company's Silicon Valley headquarters buzzed with quality-speak. Talk of work teams and cycle times replaced discussion of electrons and X-rays. There was even a mascot, Koala T—a manager who wore a koala costume and roamed Varian's cafeteria handing out homilies about quality.

And it wasn't just buzzwords and bear suits. Varian went about virtually reinventing the way it did business—with what seemed to be stunning results. A unit that makes vacuum systems for computer clean rooms boosted on-time delivery from 42 percent to 92 percent. The radiation-equipment service department ranked No. 1 in its industry for prompt customer visits. The semiconductor unit cut the time it took to put out new designs by 14 days. W. Edwards Deming and J. M. Juran, the famous management consultants and leading prophets of quality, would have been proud.

But while Varian thought it was playing quality by the book, the final chapter didn't feature the happy ending the company expected. Obsessed with meeting production schedules, the staff in that vacuum-equipment unit didn't return customers' phone calls and the operation ended up losing market share. Radiation-repair people were so rushed to meet deadlines that they left before explaining their work to customers. Sure, Varian could boast about quality. . . . "All of the quality-based charts went up and to the right, but everything else went down," says Richard M. Levy, executive vice-president for quality.

Levy isn't the only one who's dismayed. Countless other managers have heeded the siren song of total quality management, or TQM, only to discover that quality doesn't necessarily pay. At Johnson & Johnson, quality teams for several product lines crisscrossed the country, benchmarking against other companies, but costs skyrocketed. In 1990, Wallace Co. won the Malcolm Baldrige National Quality Award. Two years later, the oil equipment company filed for Chapter 11 as the cost of its quality programs soared and oil prices collapsed.

Rallying Cry

Of course, the quest for quality doesn't always have unhappy results. Detroit, for instance, finally caught the quality wave in the 1980s, and it's hard not to shudder at the thought of how the Big Three would be faring today if they were still turning out Chevy Citations instead of Saturns. And much of the rest of U.S. industry would be locked out of the game in today's global economy without the quality strides of the past few years.

But at too many companies, it turns out, the push for quality can be as badly misguided as it is well-intended. It can be popular with managers and their consultants, but as at Varian, it can devolve into a mechanistic exercise that proves meaningless to customers. And quality that means little to customers doesn't produce a payoff in improved sales, profits, or market share. It's wasted effort and expense.

That's why a growing number of companies and management thinkers are starting to refine the notion. Today's rallying cry: return on quality. Concepts such as better product designs and swifter manufacturing aren't being rejected, but advocates of the new theory are abandoning the narrow statistical benchmarks worshiped by some TQM acolytes. Instead, managers

are trying to make sure that the quality they offer is the quality their customers want. And they're starting to use sophisticated financial tools to ensure that quality programs have a payoff. Roland Rust, a Vanderbilt University professor of management and one of ROQ's chief apostles, says executives have to worry about only one thing: "If we're not going to make money off of it, we're not going to do it."

The ROQ revisionism is attracting a growing number of corporate devotees across a wide spectrum of industries. Banking giant NationsBank Corp., for example, now measures every improvement in service, from adding tellers to offering new mortgage products, in terms of added revenue. Telecommunications powerhouse GTE Corp. is looking for quality at reasonable costs. Even companies that were in the vanguard of the 1980s quality push are considering the benefits of ROQ. "We're trying to isolate quality improvements that just don't add any value to the service that is delivered to the customer," says Michael E. Reed, managing director of operations at Federal Express Corp.

For FedEx, a 1990 Baldrige recipient, that has meant rethinking its original quality goals. In its sorting operation, for example, FedEx stressed speed over accuracy. Workers met schedules, but the number of misdirected packages soared as they scrambled to meet deadlines. FedEx eventually fixed most errors, but redirecting each wayward package cost it some $50. Now, the Memphis-based shipper has eased the sorting crunch by investing $100 million in new equipment that routes packages to various destinations.

ROQ is more than just a new twist on an old theme. Many companies believe that applying a bottom-line discipline to quality is crucial at a time when the economy is rebounding and competition is growing. AT&T CEO Robert E. Allen, for example, receives a quarterly report from each of the company's 53 business units that spells out quality improvements and their subsequent financial impact.

Return Threshold

Everything from the installation of new technology to methods of improving billing accuracy is held up against an array of financial yardsticks, such as potential sales gains and return on capital. Based on its experience, AT&T has found that when customers perceive improved quality, it shows up in better financial results three months later. "This is the most important thing that AT&T has ever done," Allen told a meeting of top managers the day before his June board presentation.

To win approval from AT&T's top management these days, proponents of any new quality initiative must first demonstrate that the effort will yield at least a 30 percent drop in defects and a 10 percent return on investment. Ma Bell used those criteria last year to maintain its supremacy in the toll-free 800-number market. To reduce service outages—its customers' biggest complaint—AT&T mulled a vast modernization program. But it seemed unlikely that the staggering $1 billion-plus project would net enough new customers to clear the 10 percent investment-return threshold. Instead, Ma Bell invested $300 million in backup power equipment to guard against failures in its 800-number system. "It isn't the old 'Give me money and I'll fix it' stuff," says Phillip M. Scanlan, a corporate quality officer. "We're taking the cost out of making our system better."

Chasing Prizes

Of course, quality was always supposed to make bottom-line sense. In the Deming and Juran doctrines, empowered employees would make quicker and more market-based decisions. Faster and better manufacturing processes would lead to improved products and broader market share. That message was popularized by Deming in the 1950s, and it soon became the cornerstone of Japanese management theory. The quality theory emigrated to the U.S. in the 1980s as American companies tried to duplicate the Japanese miracle.

For some of them, including Motorola, Intel, Hewlett-Packard, and General Electric, excellence became the norm. But others among the legions who followed Deming came to confuse process with purpose. Quality devotees grew obsessed with methodology—cost-cutting, defect reduction, quicker cycle times, continual improvement. Before too long, customer concerns seemed to fall by the wayside.

Quality became its own reward. Standards were more important than sales. And companies appeared more interested in chasing prizes than profits. Pleasing the International Standards Organization, which sets European quality standards, became a paramount concern for some companies. Meanwhile, Baldrige wannabes often tripped and fell as they tried to complete an obstacle course of requirements that emphasizes process over proceeds. "There's been an insufficient focus on the aspect of quality improvements that will make the largest contribution to overall financial performance," admits Curt W. Reimann, director of the Baldrige Quality Award.

The new focus on the relationship between quality and financial returns does have its detractors. Critics say it's just a smokescreen behind which companies are cutting back on their quality efforts. A healthier economy and rising sales may be prompting them to slack off on the costly discipline of TQM. And some companies—Hewlett-Packard among them—argue it's a mistake to take a bean-counter's view of something as fundamental as quality. Yes, HP makes its decisions about quality based on sound business considerations. But that doesn't mean it takes out a calculator every time it launches a quality program. "Saying that this is a quality move and this is what it's worth is like saying, 'What's my left lung worth?'" says Richard LeVitt, director of corporate quality. "Quality is intrinsic to our whole business."

Ironing It Out

To its advocates, ROQ is about getting companies back to something that's equally intrinsic to everyone's business: customer focus. Instead of talking about attracting new customers with dazzling statistical displays of quality, ROQ emphasizes customer retention. After all, selling more to existing customers is a cheaper way to build market share than luring business away from competitors. "Customers are an economic asset. They're not on the balance sheet, but they should be," says Claess Fornell, a University of Michigan professor who is a leading ROQ advocate. Extensive surveying, perhaps even inviting customers into design and production processes, helps companies identify the key factors that affect customers' buying decisions.

Questions

1. According to the ROQ approach, how should a company decide which quality activities to fund?

2. What criticisms does the author level at those who don't use ROQ to guide quality efforts?

3. What risks are there in rigidly applying the ROQ approach?

Quality Programs Don't Guarantee Results

U.S. companies have poured millions of dollars into quality programs in the last few years. Unfortunately, the programs do not always achieve the results companies expect. The McKinsey Consulting Group has developed several useful guidelines for executives concerning quality programs:

Don't promote continuous improvement if dramatic results are needed. Sagging sales and profits often imply the need for something more than incremental improvement. Continuous improvement programs should be reserved for those instances where an organization has already achieved substantial quality results but still wants to improve its operations.

Link quality programs to strategic planning. Then, set goals for the program, and evaluate senior management, based on how well those goals are met. However, let lower-level employees set their own goals in order to get them involved, and to motivate their best performance.

Focus programs on market "break points." Customers may not be able to perceive a difference between an on-time delivery performance of 90 percent and one of say, 95 percent, although they would perceive a difference between 90 percent and 99 percent on-time delivery. So determine what the break points are, and don't waste resources on improving performance that does not achieve a higher break point.

Choose a single theme. It is important for everybody to be rowing in the same direction. Note, however, that a single focus does carry a risk: It may become an end in itself.

Emphasize results as well as the process. Focusing exclusively on the process carries the risk of diverting attention from results, and may also lead to excessive buildup in staff associated with the program. Instead, set specific goals in terms of *measurable* results.

Questions

1. List some of the ways a company can judge whether its quality program is working.

2. Explain the importance of measurements for quality programs.

3. For each guideline, explain the rationale.

Source: Based on "When Quality Control Gets in the Way of Quality," by Graham Sharman, *The Wall Street Journal,* ©1992.

READING

Swimming Upstream
Theodore B. Kinni

An early convert to the philosophy of *kaizen,* Richard Chang has been preaching the gospel of continuous improvement for two decades. Founder of Irvine, Calif.-based Richard Chang Associates, Inc., a diversified organizational-consulting firm and publishing house, Mr. Chang currently serves as a senior examiner for the Malcolm Baldrige National Quality Award and judge for California's Governor's Golden State Quality Award.

He is also a prolific writer, having penned 14 books himself. He is the publisher of The Practical Guide Book Series, a collection of four series including the eight-volume Quality Improvement Series—which covers process-improvement methodology, techniques, and tools. In the following interview he explains for IW readers how the spirit of kaizen is successfully infused throughout a small company.

IW: *What are the environmental prerequisites of kaizen?*

CHANG: Typically, you need to run a lean or even under-staffed operation. . . . You have to make an investment in training and must also hire people who are open to continuous improvement—they are hard to find. . . . Finally, especially in a small company, the philosophy must come from the top. The CEO can't be a reactive firefighter, but must behave in a manner consistent with continuous improvement. Also, instead of taking a punishment approach, you have to look at problems and mistakes as learning opportunities.

IW: *If we can create such an environment, what's next?*

CHANG: Oftentimes, you would then create a sense of vision and core values that includes the principles of kaizen. You must also build reinforcement into your reward systems and align corporate goals with continuous improvement. Remember, kaizen has to be the way you run your business; it can't just be an extra program you tack on to the operation.

If you think of that as Phase One, Phase Two is then about building capacity. This is when you concentrate on the skills that make you capable of continuously improving the business. People tend to skip this—they want to get right to the results.

IW: *What would a typical continuous-improvement-initiative rollout look like?*

CHANG: We use a technique called discovery meetings. We simply gather groups of employees and ask them to think about areas that need improvement. It's just some downtime to sit and think. From that we can begin to look at opportunities for improvement.

IW: *Do discovery meetings turn into giant gripe sessions?*

CHANG: In the beginning, yes, you tend to get a lot of ideas connected to dissatisfaction. The first meeting or two may be mostly discovery baggage, but you have to let the emoting happen. We suggest making some quick fixes to help build confidence that we really plan to act on the results of these meetings. Soon, with some coaching and leading, the groups get to work processes and develop worthy opportunities.

IW: *How much of the workforce is involved in these meetings?*

CHANG: At the early stages, no more than 15 percent to 25 percent. I'm not an advocate of the blanket approach.

IW: *When improvement opportunities are established, what happens?*

CHANG: Put the teams to work on the problems they identified. Now is the perfect time to start training. This gives people the opportunity to learn and apply the learning at the same time.

When the projects are complete, and before the groups disband, have the teams collect feedback and data, and then transfer ownership of the process to them. Now they take responsibility for continuously improving the process and other members of the workforce can start their training.

IW: *Don't opportunities for improvement eventually dry up?*

CHANG: There is a certain point when the process capability might max out and the benefit you get from incremental improvements is not worth the cost. When your processes top out, that's when reengineering comes in. A complete overhaul, in turn, leads to more rounds of continuous improvement. That's how continuous improvement and reengineering complement each other.

IW: *Can you tip us off to the pitfalls?*

CHANG: There are five that I like to describe in medical terms. "Widespread implementation rash" is when companies try to do too much, too fast. This is a philosophy; you don't get in and get out. Then there is "key process selection deficiency"—don't improve the petty cash process, make the work important. "Elevated doses of training" is when people train the whole workforce before they have established the environmental conditions for success. "High count of quality teams" is when we get team mania. The goal is not to implement teams; it's to improve processes. Last is "persistent process measurement cost," which occurs when organizations start improving processes before they are measured. The result is that they have no way of knowing whether they got anything worthwhile accomplished.

IW: *If you only had a moment to sum up continuous improvement, what would you tell us?*

CHANG: I usually end my speeches with some version of this thought: Implementing continuous-improvement initiatives is like swimming upstream against the downward flow of habit.

Source: Reprinted with permission from *Industry Week,* January 23, 1995. Copyright Penton Publishing, Inc., Cleveland, Ohio.

Selected Bibliography and Further Reading

Besterfield, Dale H., Carol Besterfield-Micha, Glen Besterfield, and Mary Besterfield-Sacre. *Total Quality Management.* 2nd ed. Englewood Cliffs, NJ: Prentice Hall, 1999.

Brassard, Michael, and Diane Ritter. *The Memory Jogger II: A Pocket Guide of Tools for Continuous Improvement and Effective Planning.* Methuen, MA: Goal/QPC, 1994.

Cappels, Thomas. *Financially Focused Quality: TQM in the 21st Century.* Boca Raton, FL: St. Lucie Press, 1999.

Gitlow, Howard, Alan Oppenheim, and Rosa Oppenheim. *Quality Management: Tools and Methods for Improvement.* 2nd ed. Burr Ridge, IL: Irwin, 1995.

Giffith, Gary K. *The Quality Technician's Handbook.* 4th ed. Upper Saddle River, NJ: Prentice Hall, 2000.

Harry, Mikel, and Richard Schroeder. *Six Sigma: The Breakthrough Management Strategy Revolutionizing the World's Top Corporations.* New York: Currency, 2000.

Hendricks, Kevin B., and Vinod R. Singhal. "Don't Count TQM Out." *Quality Progress,* April 1999, pp. 35–41.

Juran, Joseph M. *Juran's Quality Handbook.* New York: McGraw-Hill, 1999.

Lientz, B. P., and P. Rea. *How to Plan and Implement Business Process Improvement.* San Diego, CA: Harcourt Brace Professional Publications, 1998.

Lynch, R. L., and K. F. Cross. *Measure Up! Yardsticks for Continuous Improvement.* 2nd ed. Cambridge, MA: Blackwell, 1995.

Mears, P. *Quality Improvement Tools and Techniques.* New York: McGraw-Hill, 1995.

Mitra, Amitava. *Fundamentals of Quality Control and Improvement.* 2nd ed. Englewood Cliffs, NJ: Prentice Hall, 1998.

Oppenheim, Bohdan W., and Zbigniew H. Przasnyski. "Total Quality Requires Serious Training." *Quality Progress,* October 1999, pp. 63–73.

Salegna, Gary, and Farzaneh Fazel. "Obstacles to Implementing Quality." *Quality Progress,* July 2000, pp. 53–57.

Smith, Gerald. *Statistical Process Control and Process Improvement.* 3rd ed. Englewood Cliffs, NJ: Prentice Hall, 1997.

Stevenson, William J. "Supercharging Your Pareto Analysis." *Quality Progress,* October 2000, pp. 51–55.

Straker, D. *A Toolbook for Quality Improvement and Problem Solving.* New York: Prentice Hall, 1995.

Summers, Donna. *Quality.* 2nd ed. Upper Saddle River, NJ: Prentice Hall, 2000.

PART FIVE

Supply Chain Management

The topics in this part relate to operating and controlling the systems that produce goods and provide services. Supply chain management refers to management of all of the functions, facilities, and activities, both within and external to a business organization, that make up a value chain. Inventory management is concerned with determining how much to order and when to order. Aggregate planning involves intermediate planning to balance capacity and expected demand. MRP (materials requirements planning) involves inventory and order planning for assembled goods. ERP (enterprise resource planning) concerns integrated computerized record keeping for the purpose of better coordination of the operations of a business organization. Just-in-time is a lean production approach that strives to coordinate activities and movement of goods to achieve a balanced operating system. Scheduling is concerned with short-term planning of the timing of operations.

The chapters in this part cover the following topics:

1 Supply Chain Management, Chapter 12

2 Inventory Management, Chapter 13

3 Aggregate Planning, Chapter 14

4 MRP & ERP, Chapter 15

5 Just-in-Time Systems, Chapter 16

6 Scheduling, Chapter 17

CHAPTER TWELVE

Supply Chain Management

CHAPTER OUTLINE

Introduction, 504

Value Chains, Supply Chains, and Demand Chains, 504

The Need for Supply Chain Management, 506

Benefits of Effective Supply Chain Management, 506

Managing the Supply Chain, 507

Elements of Supply Chain Management, 507

Strategic, Tactical, and Operating Issues, 508

Performance Measures, 508

Logistics, 509

Reading: Delivering the Goods, 509

Movement within a Facility, 511

Incoming and Outgoing Shipments, 512

Evaluating Shipping Alternatives, 512

Electronic Data Interchange, 513

Newsclip: Efficient Consumer Response, 514

Distribution Requirements Planning, 514

JIT Deliveries, 514

The Global Supply Chain, 515

E-Commerce, 515

Newsclip: Desperately Seeking E-Fulfillment, 516

Creating an Effective Supply Chain, 517

Keys to Effective Supply Chains, 517

Steps in Creating an Effective Supply Chain, 519

Reading: Using Information to Speed Execution, 520

Optimizing the Supply Chain, 520

Challenges, 520

Newsclip: Supply Chain Optimization at Internet Speed, 521

Operations Strategy, 523

Summary, 524

Key Terms, 524

Solved Problem, 524

Discussion and Review Questions, 525

Memo Writing Exercises, 525

Problems, 525

Internet Sites, 526

Selected Bibliography and Further Reading, 525

Supplement: Purchasing and Supplier Management, 527

LEARNING OBJECTIVES

After completing this chapter, you should be able to:

1 Explain what a supply chain is.

2 Explain the need to manage a supply chain and potential benefits of doing so.

3 Explain the increasing importance of outsourcing.

4 State the objective of supply chain management.

5 List the elements of supply chain management.

6 Identify the strategic, tactical, and operations issues in supply chain management.

7 Describe the bullwhip effect and the reasons why it occurs.

8 Explain the value of strategic partnering.

9 Discuss the importance of supply chain management for e-commerce.

10 Discuss the critical importance of information exchange across a supply chain.

11 Outline the key steps, and potential challenges, in creating an effective supply chain.

Last year American companies spent $670 billion—a gaping 10.5 percent of GDP—to wrap, bundle, load, unload, sort, reload, and transport goods. So clogged is the gross national pipeline with unnecessary steps and redundant stockpiles that the grocery industry alone believes it can wash $30 billion, or nearly 10 percent of its annual operating costs, out of the system. A typical box of breakfast cereal spends a stunning 104 days getting from factory to supermarket, haltingly progressing through a concatenation of wholesalers, distributors, brokers, diverters, and consolidators, each of which has a warehouse. Says James Alampi, president of Van Waters & Rogers, the largest U.S. chemical distributor: "Frankly, the cost of making a product is almost irrelevant. You have far more opportunity to get cost out of the supply chain than you do out of manufacturing. There's so much duplication and inefficiency."

Think of supply-chain management as nothing less than the reengineering of the entire economy—one convoluted chain at a time. Once you start reconceptualizing your company as a collection of business processes, it becomes dauntingly clear that those processes extend beyond the portals of any one building, the boundaries of any one corporation, and the borders of any one country. Says Harold Sirkin, a vice president of the Boston Consulting Group: "As the economy changes, as competition becomes more global, it's no longer company vs. company but supply chain vs. supply chain."

Source: Excerpted from *Fortune*, November 28, 1994, ©1994 Time, Inc.

This chapter covers the basics of supply chain management. Among other things, you will learn what a supply chain is, why there is a need for supply chain management, what the key elements in managing a supply chain are, what steps are necessary in creating an effective supply chain, and what some of the challenges are in supply chain management.

Introduction

supply chain A sequence of organizations—their facilities, functions, and activities—that are involved in producing and delivering a product or service.

A **supply chain** is the sequence of organizations—their facilities, functions, and activities—that are involved in producing and delivering a product or service. The sequence begins with basic suppliers of raw materials and extends all the way to the final customer. Facilities include warehouses, factories, processing centers, distribution centers, retail outlets, and offices. Functions and activities include forecasting, purchasing, inventory management, information management, quality assurance, scheduling, production, distribution, delivery, and customer service. There are two kinds of movement in these systems: the physical movement of material, generally in the direction of the end of the chain (although not all material starts at the beginning of the chain), and exchange of information, which moves in both directions along the chain.

Every business organization is part of at least one supply chain, and many are part of multiple supply chains. The number and type of organizations in a supply chain are determined by whether the supply chain is manufacturing or service oriented. Figure 12–1 illustrates typical manufacturing and service supply chains.

VALUE CHAINS, SUPPLY CHAINS, AND DEMAND CHAINS

value chain A supply chain.

Supply chains are sometimes referred to as **value chains,** a term that reflects the concept that value is added as goods and services progress through the chain. Supply or value chains are typically comprised of separate business organizations, rather than just a single organization. Moreover, the supply or value chain has two components for each organization: a supply component and a demand component. The supply component starts at the beginning of the chain and ends with the internal operations of the organization. The demand component of the chain starts at the point where the organization's output is delivered to its immediate customer and ends with the final customer in the chain. The *demand chain* is the sales and distribution portion of the value chain. The length of each component depends on where a particular organization is in the chain; the closer the organization is to the final customer, the shorter its demand component and the longer its supply component. Figure 12–2 illustrates these concepts.

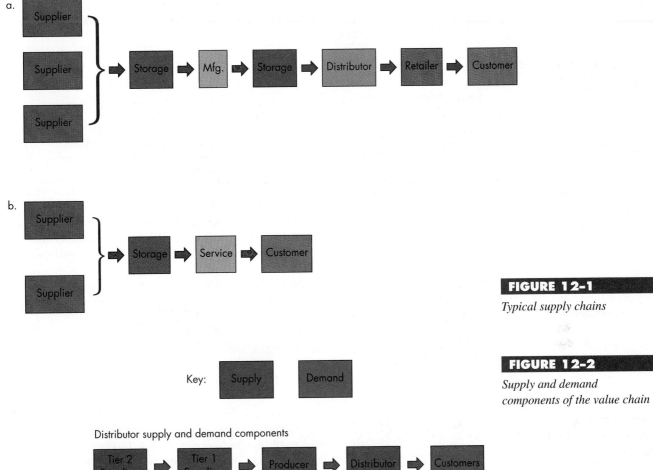

All organizations, regardless of where they are in the chain, must deal with supply and demand issues. The goal of supply chain management is to link all components of the supply chain so that market demand is met as efficiently as possible across the entire chain. This requires matching supply and demand at each stage of the chain. Note that except for the beginning supplier(s) and the final customer(s), the organizations in a supply chain are both customers and suppliers, as illustrated in Figure 12–3.

Initial Supplier	⇨	Customer / Supplier	↗	Customer / Supplier	↗	Customer / Supplier	⇨	Final Customer

FIGURE 12-3

Links in the supply chain

The Need for Supply Chain Management

In the past, most organizations did little to manage their supply chains. Instead, they tended to concentrate on their own operations and on their immediate suppliers. However, a number of factors make it desirable for business organizations to actively manage their supply chains. The major factors are:

1. *The need to improve operations.* During the last decade, many organizations adopted practices such as lean production and TQM. As a result, they were able to achieve improved quality while wringing much of the excess costs out of their systems. Although there is still room for improvement, for many organizations, the major gains have been realized. Opportunity now lies largely with procurement, distribution, and logistics—the supply chain.

outsourcing Buying goods or services instead of producing or providing them in-house.

2. *Increasing levels of outsourcing.* Organizations are increasing their levels of **outsourcing,** buying goods or services instead of producing or providing them themselves. As outsourcing increases, organizations are spending increasing amounts on supply-related activities (wrapping, packaging, moving, loading and unloading, and sorting). A significant amount of the cost and time spent on these and other related activities may be unnecessary.

3. *Increasing transportation costs.* Transportation costs are increasing, and they need to be more carefully managed.

4. *Competitive pressures.* Competitive pressures have led to an increasing number of new products, shorter product development cycles, and increased demand for customization. And in some industries, most notably consumer electronics, product life cycles are relatively short. Added to this are adoption of quick-response strategies and efforts to reduce lead times.

5. *Increasing globalization.* Increasing globalization has expanded the physical length of supply chains.

6. *Increasing importance of e-commerce.* The increasing importance of e-commerce has added new dimensions to business buying and selling and has presented new challenges.

7. *The complexity of supply chains.* Supply chains are complex; they are dynamic, and they have many inherent uncertainties that can adversely affect the supply chain, such as inaccurate forecasts, late deliveries, substandard quality, equipment breakdowns, and canceled or changed orders.

8. *The need to manage inventories.* Inventories play a major role in the success or failure of a supply chain, so it is important to coordinate inventory levels throughout a supply chain. Shortages can severely disrupt the timely flow of work and have far-reaching impacts, while excess inventories add unnecessary costs. It would not be unusual to find inventory shortages in some parts of a supply chain and excess inventories in other parts of the same supply chain.

www.apl.com

www.campbellsoups.com
www.hp.com
www.obermeyer.com
www.walmart.com

Benefits of Effective Supply Chain Management

Effective supply chain management offers numerous benefits. For example, Campbell Soup doubled its inventory turnover rate, Hewlett-Packard cut deskjet printer supply costs by 75 percent, Sport Obermeyer doubled profits and increased sales by 60 percent in two years, and National Bicycle increased its market share from 5 percent to 29 percent.[1] And

---

[1] Marshall Fisher, "What Is the Right Supply Chain for Your Product?" *Harvard Business Review,* March/April 1997, pp. 105–16.

Element	Typical Issues	Chapter(s)
Customers	Determining what products and/or services customers want.	3, 4
Forecasting	Predicting the quantity and timing of customer demand.	3
Design	Incorporating customers, wants, manufacturability, and time to market.	4
Processing	Controlling quality, scheduling work.	10, 17
Inventory	Meeting demand requirements while managing the costs of holding inventory.	13, 14, 15
Purchasing	Evaluating potential suppliers, supporting the needs of operations on purchased goods and services.	12S
Suppliers	Monitoring supplier quality, on-time delivery, and flexibility; maintaining supplier relations.	12S
Location	Determining the location of facilities.	8
Logistics	Deciding how to best move and store materials.	This chapter

TABLE 12–1

Elements of supply chain management

effective supply chain management helped Wal-Mart become the largest and most profitable retailer in the world!

Generally, benefits of effective supply chain management include lower inventories, lower costs, higher productivity, improved ability to respond to fluctuations in demand, shorter lead times, higher profits, and greater customer loyalty.

Managing the Supply Chain

Supply chain management involves coordinating activities across the supply chain. Central to this is taking customer demand and translating it into corresponding activities at each level of the supply chain. The key elements in this process are outlined in the next section.

ELEMENTS OF SUPPLY CHAIN MANAGEMENT

The key elements of supply chain management are listed in Table 12–1. The first element, customers, is the driving element. Typically, marketing is responsible for determining what customers want as well as forecasting the quantities and timing of customer demand. Product and service design must match customer wants with operations capabilities.

Processing occurs in each component of the supply chain; it is the core of each organization. The major portion of processing occurs in the organization that produces the product or service for the final customer (the organization that assembles the computer, services the car, etc.). A major aspect of this for both the internal and external portions of a supply chain is scheduling.

Inventory is a staple in most supply chains. Balance is the main objective; too little causes delays and disrupts schedules, but too much adds unnecessary costs.

Purchasing is the link between an organization and its suppliers. It is responsible for obtaining goods and/or services that will be used to produce products or provide services for the organization's customers. Purchasing selects suppliers, negotiates contracts, establishes alliances, and acts as liaison between suppliers and various internal departments. Purchasing is taking on increased importance in supply chain management. Several factors have contributed to this:

1. Increasing outsourcing, which has reached the point where materials costs are often much greater than labor costs.

2. Increasing conversion to lean production and just-in-time requirements, which has meant smaller lots, the need for precise timing of deliveries, high quality, and exact quantities.

3. Increasing globalization.

FIGURE 12–4

Processing within an organization involves its internal supply chain

The supply portion of a value chain is made up of one or more suppliers, all links in the chain, and each one capable of having an impact on the effectiveness—or the ineffectiveness—of the supply chain. Moreover, it is essential that the planning and execution be carefully coordinated between suppliers and all members of the demand portion of their chains.

Location can be a factor in a number of ways. Where suppliers are located can be important, as can location of processing facilities. Nearness to market, or nearness to sources of supply, or nearness to both may be critical. Also, delivery time and cost are usually affected by location.

Logistics involves the movement and storage of materials. The success of the supply chain depends on efficiency and timeliness. Logistics is discussed in more detail in an upcoming section.

STRATEGIC, TACTICAL, AND OPERATING ISSUES

Strategic Issues. Strategic decisions generally have long-term impact on a supply chain. The key strategic issue is the design of the supply chain. This involves determining the number, location, and capacity of facilities. It may also involve such issues as make or buy.

Strategic alliances are becoming more widespread as business organizations reduce the number of suppliers they use to move in the direction of lean production. Organizations recognize the influence that suppliers can have on cost, quality, and lead times. Moreover, such alliances enable customers to free up some resources, affording suppliers the benefit of long-term relationships, one of which is less worry about competition. And all parties can benefit from data sharing because it allows improved planning and scheduling.

Tactical Issues. Tactical issues involve policies related to such areas as inventory, procurement, processing, logistics, and quality. Guided by strategy, they in turn provide guidance for operations decisions.

Operating Issues. The important operational issues in supply chain management relate to production planning and control and to scheduling of deliveries of goods and services. It can also depend on make-or-buy decisions, some of which are made at this level.

The supply chain is comprised of an internal (in-house) portion and an external portion, as illustrated in Figure 12–4. Operating issues primarily relate to an organization's in-house activities.

Make-or-buy decisions affect the nature and scope of supply chains. An organization has more ability to control the internal portion of its supply chain than the external portion and, hence, to initiate improvements. Therefore, make-or-buy decisions should take into consideration the loss of control as one of the trade-offs of buying.

Operations planning and control includes internal activities related to scheduling, assigning due dates to orders, and movement of materials within a facility, from the receipt of deliveries from suppliers, to internal processing, to packaging and shipping of outgoing goods.

Table 12–2 summarizes typical issues at each of these levels.

PERFORMANCE MEASURES

It is important to measure and track the performance of the supply chain, particularly because multiple organizations are involved. A variety of measures can be used for this

Strategic Issues	Tactical Issues	Operating Issues
Design of the supply chain	Inventory policies	Quality control
Partnering	Purchasing policies	Production planning and control
	Production policies	
	Transportation policies	
	Quality policies	

TABLE 12-2

Supply chain issues

Perspective	Metrics
Reliability	On-time delivery
	Order fulfillment lead time
	Fill rate (fraction of demand met from stock)
	Perfect order fulfillment
Flexibility	Supply chain response time
	Upside production flexibility
Expenses	Supply chain management cost
	Warranty cost as a percentage of revenue
	Value added per employee
Assets/utilization	Total inventory days of supply
	Cash-to-cash cycle time
	Net asset turns

Source: Based on information available at www.supply-chain.org by the Supply Chain Council.

TABLE 12-3

SCOR (Supply Chain Operations Reference model) metrics

purpose. One approach is to use the Supply Chain Operations Reference (SCOR) model, a portion of which is presented in Table 12–3. The SCOR model represents an effort to standardize measurement of supply chain performance.

Logistics

Logistics refers to the movement of materials and information within a facility and to incoming and outgoing shipments of goods and materials. Materials include all of the physical items used in a production process. In addition to raw materials and work in process, there are support items such as fuels, equipment, parts, tools, lubricants, office supplies, and more.

logistics The movement of materials and information within a facility and to incoming and outgoing shipments of goods and materials.

READING

Delivering the Goods

www.compaq.com

Logistics has become a hot competitive advantage as companies struggle to get the right stuff to the right place at the right time.

It comes down to this: All your TQM and reengineering and teamwork and delighting the customers are riding on the back of a double-clutching, diesel-guzzling, steel-girded mastodon rumbling down the highway while the rest of the economy sleeps. A 23-ton rig laden with odometers and speedometers for General Motors' Saturn assembly plant in Tennessee is just one link in a supply chain that covers more than 99,000 miles every day. That's 36 million miles a year, not long enough to reach the planet that shares the name of the popular GM car, but plenty long enough to command attention.

Call it distribution or logistics or supply-chain management. By whatever name, it is the sinuous, gritty, and cumbersome process by which companies move materials, parts, and products to customers. In industry after industry, from cars and clothing to computers and chemicals, executives have plucked this once dismal discipline off the loading dock and placed it near the top of the corporate agenda. Hard-pressed to knock out competitors on quality or price, companies are trying to gain an edge through their ability to deliver the right stuff in the right amount at the right time. Says Robert Sabath,

Ryder company delivers (in trucks labeled 'Saturn') bins of speedometers and odometers to Saturn's Spring Hill, Tennessee plant. Thursday, 9 A.M.: A Ryder truck arrives at a Saturn supplier in Winchester, Virginia.

Drivers check the onboard computer, which provides destination and routing information, along with estimated travel times.

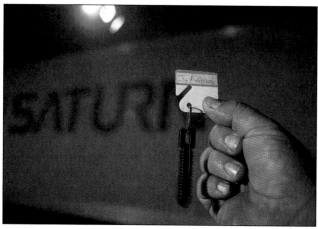

Spring Hill, Tennessee, Friday, 3 A.M.: After parking the trailer in a computer-assigned spot in Ryder's switching yard two miles from the Saturn plant, the driver downloads a key-shaped floppy disk

from the onboard computer into Ryder's mainframe, which generates performance reports for Saturn.

12:50 P.M.: The trailer approaches the Saturn plant.

12:53 P.M.: The trailer arrives at one of Saturn's 56 receiving docks just in time for Saturn workers to unload the bins and unwrap the pre-inspected instruments to ready them for the production line.

www.saturnbp.com

a vice president with Mercer Management Consulting in Chicago: "Logistics, long an unsung, operations-intensive area, has suddenly become very strategic."

Just how strategic? Compaq Computer, the world's No.1 producer of PCs, estimates it has lost $500 million to $1 billion in sales because its laptops and desktops weren't available when and where customers were ready to buy them. Says chief financial officer Daryl White: "We've done most of what we need to do to be more competitive. We've changed the way we develop products, manufacture, market, and advertise. The one piece of the puzzle we haven't addressed is logistics. It's the next source of competitive advantage. The possibilities are just astounding."

Source: Excerpted from "Delivering the Goods," *Fortune,* November 28, 1994, © 1994 Time, Inc.

MOVEMENT WITHIN A FACILITY

Movement of goods within a manufacturing facility is part of production control. Figure 12–5 shows the many steps where materials move within a manufacturing facility:

1. From incoming vehicles to receiving.
2. From receiving to storage.
3. From storage to the point of use (e.g., a work center).
4. From one work center to the next or to temporary storage.
5. From the last operation to final storage.
6. From storage to packaging/shipping.
7. From shipping to outgoing vehicles.

FIGURE 12-5

Movement within a facility

In some instances, the goods being moved are supplies; in other instances, the goods are actual products or partially completed products; and in still other instances, the goods are raw materials or purchased parts.

Movement of materials must be coordinated to arrive at the appropriate destinations at appropriate times. Workers and supervisors must take care so that items are not lost, stolen, or damaged during movement.

INCOMING AND OUTGOING SHIPMENTS

traffic management Overseeing the shipment of incoming and outgoing goods.

Overseeing the shipment of incoming and outgoing goods comes under the heading of **traffic management.** This function handles schedules and decisions on shipping method and times, taking into account costs of various alternatives, government regulations, the needs of the organization relative to quantities and timing, and external factors such as potential shipping delays or disruptions e.g., highway construction, truckers' strikes).

Computer tracking of shipments often helps to maintain knowledge of the current status of shipments as well as to provide other up-to-date information on costs and schedules.

EVALUATING SHIPPING ALTERNATIVES

A situation that often arises in some businesses is the need to make a choice between rapid (but more expensive) shipping alternatives such as overnight or second-day air and slower (but less expensive) alternatives. In some instances, an overriding factor justifies sending a shipment by the quickest means possible, so there is little or no choice involved. However, in other instances, urgency is not the primary consideration, so there is a choice. The decision in such cases often focuses on the cost savings of slower alternatives versus the incremental holding cost (here, the annual dollar amount that could be earned by the revenue from the item being shipped) that would result from using the slower alternative. An important assumption is that the seller gets paid upon receipt of the goods by the buyer (e.g., through electronic data interchange).

The incremental holding cost incurred by using the slower alternative is computed as

$$\text{Incremental holding cost} = \frac{H(d)}{365} \tag{12–1}$$

where H = annual earning potential of shipped item

d = difference (in days) between shipping alternatives

Example 1

Determine which shipping alternative, one day or three days, is best when the holding cost of an item is $1,000 per year, the one-day shipping cost is $40, and the three-day shipping cost is:
a. $35   *b.* $30

Solution

H = $1,000 per year

Time savings = 2 days using 1-day shipping

Holding cost for additional 2 days = $1,000 × (2/365) = $5.48

a. Cost savings = $5. Because the actual savings of $5 is less than the holding cost ($5.48), use the one-day alternative.

b. Cost savings = $10. Because the actual savings of $10 exceeds the savings in holding cost of $5.48, use the three-day alternative.

Increasingly, the Internet is linking customers with factories so that products can be customized by buyers. At this Volvo assembly line, cars are manufactured after being ordered on the Internet.

www.volvocars.com

ELECTRONIC DATA INTERCHANGE

Electronic data interchange (EDI) is the direct, computer-to-computer transmission of interorganizational transactions, including purchase orders, shipping notices, debit or credit memos, and more. Among the reasons companies are increasingly using EDI are:

electronic data interchange (EDI) The direct transmission of interorganizational transactions, computer-to-computer, including purchase orders, shipping notices, and debit or credit memos.

- Increased productivity.
- Reduction of paperwork.
- Lead time and inventory reduction.
- Facilitation of just-in-time (JIT) systems.
- Electronic transfer of funds.
- Improved control of operations.
- Reduction in clerical labor.
- Increased accuracy.

The use of EDI linkages with other organizations can be part of a strategy to achieve a competitive advantage by leveraging logistics performance. In addition, in some JIT environments, EDI serves as the signal for replenishment from the manufacturer to the supplier.

There are many applications of EDI in the retail industries involving electronic communication between retailers and vendors. Dubbed *quick response,* the approach is based on scanning bar codes and transmitting that information to vendors. The purpose is to create a just-in-time replenishment system that is keyed to customer buying patterns. Retailers use Universal Product Code (UPC) scanning or point-of-sale (POS) scanning at the registers which use price-look-up (PLU) to track customer buying. Efficient consumer response (ECR) is a variation of quick response used by the supermarket industry to provide supermarkets, distributors, and suppliers with key data on buying patterns so that they can make better decisions on replenishment.

Quick-response approaches have several benefits. Among them are reduced dependency on forecasts and the ability to achieve a closer match between supply and demand. In addition, there is the strong possibility of saving on inventory carrying costs.

Wal-Mart has a satellite network for electronic data interchange that allows vendors to directly access point-of-sale data in real time, enabling them to improve their forecasting and inventory management. Wal-Mart also uses the system for issuing purchase orders and receiving invoices from its vendors.

efficient consumer response (ECR) A quick response initiative using EDI and bar codes specific to the food industry.

Efficient consumer response (ECR) is a supply chain management initiative specific to the food industry. It reflects companies' efforts to achieve quick response using EDI and bar codes. The following newsclip illustrates how some supermarkets benefit from this.

NEWSCLIP

Efficient Consumer Response

www.spartanstores.com

At first glance, your average supermarket looks like a marvel of supply-chain efficiency. Think of the wide aisles, the fully stocked shelves, the wondrous variety, the endless checkout lines (OK, you can't have everything). But pull back the curtain, Toto, and the wizardry fades fast. Behind the scenes is an industry that actually rewards people for building unnecessary inventory. All along the supply chain, sellers push discounted products onto merchandise buyers, who in turn are compensated for purchasing things cheaply even though they may languish in a warehouse for months on end. So addled are the industry's practices that a whole class of characters known as diverters thrives by buying caseloads of discounted food in one state and transporting them to another where the discount isn't being offered.

But the grocery business has been locked out of its torpor by some big-footed players with very efficient distribution systems. These "alternative format" retailers, of which Wal-Mart is the largest and most menacing, have been stealing market share from supermarkets.

To parry the threat, food manufacturers, wholesalers, and retailers have allied around an industrywide initiative known as efficient consumer response (ECR). A study by consultants from Kurt Salmon Associates in Atlanta concluded that the industry could save $24 billion in operating costs and another $6 billion in interest expenses by streamlining its logistics and changing its behavior.

Spartan Stores, a Grand Rapids food distributor and a leader in the ECR movement, was recently able to shut down a 300,000-square-foot warehouse, which cost $1 million a year to operate, when it stopped stockpiling discounted products. Says Keith Wagar, vice president of procurement and inbound logistics: "We've got to eliminate all the activities that don't add value to the consumer. Our only chance is to look at the transaction from manufacturer to consumer as a single process. It's a strategy for survival, a strategy for growth."

Source: Excerpted from *Fortune,* November 28, 1994, © 1994 Time, Inc.

DISTRIBUTION REQUIREMENTS PLANNING

distribution requirements planning (DRP) A system for inventory management and distribution planning.

Distribution requirements planning (DRP) is a system for inventory management and distribution planning. It is especially useful in multiechelon warehousing systems (factory and regional warehouses). It extends the concepts of material requirements planning (MRP) to multiechelon warehouse inventories, starting with demand at the end of the channel and working back through the warehouse system to obtain time-phased replenishment schedules for moving inventories through the warehouse network. In effect, management uses DRP to plan and coordinate transportation, warehousing, workers, equipment, and financial flows.

JIT DELIVERIES

JIT systems often require frequent deliveries of small shipments. This can place a tremendous burden on the delivery system in several respects. One is the increased traffic that results. Instead of one large delivery per week, a company switching to JIT may require many smaller loads every day. Multiply that by the number of parts obtained from suppliers, and you can begin to appreciate the potential traffic nightmare, resulting delays in receiving shipments, and disruption in production. Also, there is the likely increase in transportation cost per unit. There is often a fixed cost per delivery (e.g., per truck), even if only a partial load is delivered. Smaller trucks are one possibility, but that, too, will generate a cost.

Another aspect of JIT deliveries became apparent during a strike of United Parcel Service (UPS) employees in mid-1997. The strike was a prolonged one, and many companies that used UPS for JIT deliveries were forced to scramble to find alternative means of supply. This severely taxed some of the other rapid-delivery organizations, and deliveries fell behind schedule, causing disruptions to JIT-based companies.

Because of these factors, it is necessary to carefully weigh the costs and benefits of using frequent, small deliveries, and select a lot size that *balances* all relevant costs.

Some companies are outsourcing their logistics management, turning over warehousing and distribution to companies that specialize in these areas. This is called *third-party logistics*. One possible reason for this is a desire to concentrate on one's core business, employing a company that specializes in logistics to provide certain benefits, such as a well-developed logistics information system, experienced logistics personnel, and the ability to obtain more favorable transportation rates.

THE GLOBAL SUPPLY CHAIN

As international trade barriers fall, more companies are expanding global operations. This is presenting tremendous opportunities and opening up previously untapped markets for products and services. It has also increased the number of competitors, and even companies that operate only within a single country are faced with increased foreign competition.

Managing a global supply chain that may have far flung customers and/or suppliers magnifies some of the challenges of managing a domestic supply chain. Obviously, distances and lead times become more critical as the supply chain becomes longer. So, too, does the possibility of having to deal with (perhaps many) different languages and cultures. Currency differences and monetary fluctuations are other factors that must be dealt with, and possibly additional modes of transportation.

E-Commerce

The commercial blossoming of the Internet has led to an explosion of Internet-related activities, many of which have a direct impact on organizations' supply chains, even if those organizations aren't themselves users of the Internet. **E-commerce** refers to the use of electronic technology to facilitate business transactions. E-commerce involves the interaction of different business organizations as well as the interaction of individuals with business organizations. Applications include Internet buying and selling, e-mail, order and shipment tracking, and electronic data interchange. In addition, companies use e-commerce to promote their products or services, and to provide information about them. Delivery firms have seen the demand for their services increase dramatically due to e-commerce. Among them are giants UPS and FedEx.

e-commerce The use of electronic technology to facilitate business transactions.

www.ups.com
www.fedex.com

Table 12–4 lists some of the numerous advantages of e-commerce.

There are two essential features of e-commerce businesses: the website and order fulfillment. Companies may invest considerable time and effort in front-end design (the website), but the back end (order fulfillment) is at least as important. It involves order processing, billing, inventory management, warehousing, packing, shipping, and delivery.

Many of the problems that occur with Internet selling are supply-related. The ability to order quickly creates an expectation in customers that the remainder of the process will proceed smoothly and quickly. But the same capability that enables quick ordering also enables demand fluctuations that can inject a certain amount of chaos to the system, almost guaranteeing that there won't be a smooth or quick delivery. Oftentimes the rate at which orders come in via the Internet greatly exceeds an organization's ability to fulfill them. Not too long ago, Toys "R" Us had that experience during the busy Christmas season; it ended up offering thousands of disappointed customers a $100 coupon to make up for it.

In the early days of Internet selling, many organizations thought they could avoid bearing the costs of holding inventories by acting solely as intermediaries, having their suppliers ship directly to their customers. Although this approach worked for some companies, it failed for others, usually because suppliers ran out of certain items. This led

TABLE 12-4

Advantages of e-commerce

Companies and publishers have a global presence and the customer has global choices and easy access to information.

Companies can improve competitiveness and quality of service by allowing access to their services any place, any time. Companies also have the ability to monitor customers' choices and requests electronically.

Companies can analyze the interest in various products based on the number of hits and requests for information.

Companies can collect detailed information about clients' preferences, which enables mass customization and personalized products. An example is the purchase of PCs over the web, where the buyer specifies the final configuration.

Supply chain response times are shortened. The biggest impact is on products that can be delivered directly on the web, such as forms of publishing and software distribution.

The roles of the intermediary and sometimes the traditional retailer or service provider are reduced or eliminated entirely in a process called *disintermediation*. This process reduces costs and adds alternative purchasing options.

Substantial cost savings and substantial price reductions related to the reduction of transaction costs can be realized. Companies that provide purchasing and support through the web can save significant personnel costs.

E-commerce allows the creation of virtual companies that distribute only through the web, thus reducing costs. Amazon.com and other net vendors can afford to sell for a lower price because they do not need to maintain retail stores and, in many cases, warehouse space.

The playing field is leveled for small companies which lack significant resources to invest in infrastructure and marketing.

Source: Reprinted by permission from David Simchi-Levi, Philip Kaminsky, and Edith Simchi-Levi, *Designing and Managing the Supply Chain: Concepts, Strategies, and Case Studies,* New York: Irwin/McGraw-Hill, 2000, p. 235.

www.amazon.com
www.webvan.com
www.fingerhut.com

some companies to rethink the strategy. Industry giants such as Amazon.com, barnesand-noble.com, and online grocer Webvan Group built huge warehouses around the country so they could maintain greater control over their inventories. Still others are outsourcing fulfillment, turning over that portion of their business to third-party fulfillment operators such as former catalog fulfillment company Fingerhut, now a unit of Federated Department Stores.

Using third-party fulfillment means losing control over fulfillment. It might also result in fulfillers substituting their standards for the company they are serving, and using the fulfiller's shipping price structure. On the other hand, an e-commerce company may not have the resources or infrastructure to do the job itself. Another alternative might be to form a strategic partnership with a "bricks and mortar" company. This can be a quick way to jump start an e-commerce business. In any case, somewhere in the supply chain there has to be a bricks-and-mortar facility.

NEWSCLIP

Desperately Seeking E-Fulfillment

www.fingerhut.com

Fingerhut is now a major e-commerce fulfillment player, thanks as much to its massive data warehouse of customer

information as to its four million square feet of high tech warehouse space.

In addition to handling its own business, Fingerhut handles the back end of other high-volume retailers, such as Wal-Mart and eToys. Their massive warehouse in St. Cloud, MN, can process as many as 30,000 items per hour.

Big shippers like UPS and Federal Express have also successfully branched into e-commerce fulfillment. In addition to their traditional shipping niche, they'll warehouse your inventory for you, handle all back-end tasks, and offer complete solutions including web site design, development, and hosting. Their e-commerce edge came not only from their overnight, single-order delivery infrastructure, but also from having already developed package-tracking software.

Hiring a fulfillment giant is de rigueur these days for huge "click and bricks" retailers like Wal-Mart and Pier One, who have to switch in a hurry from their old operating model of moving big pallets of goods to stores to moving single items to individuals.

Third-party fulfillers are treasured for their efficiencies and advanced technology. But some can be unresponsive and not always capable of supporting [clients'] software. There has also been some grumbling in *Barrons* that the big third-party fulfillers are doomed middlemen, a mere transitory phase for e-commerce.

Source: Excerpted from Judith Silverstein, "Desperately Seeking E-Fulfillment," *Digital Chicago,* November/December 1999, pp. 29–30.

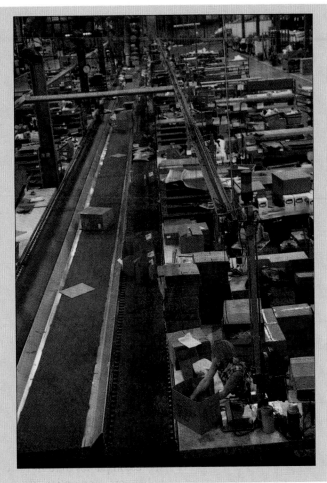

Behind the scenes of e-commerce: Order processing and fulfillment at Fingerhut.

A growing portion of e-commerce involves business-to-business (B2B) commerce rather than business-to-consumer commerce. To facilitate business-to-business commerce, B2B marketplaces are created. Figure 12–6 describes B2B marketplaces and marketplace enablers.

Creating an Effective Supply Chain

Creating an effective supply chain requires linking the market, distribution channel, processing, and suppliers. The design of a supply chain should enable all participants in the chain to achieve significant gains, hence giving them an incentive to cooperate. It should enable participants to (1) share forecasts, (2) determine the status of orders in real time, and (3) access inventory data of partners.

KEYS TO EFFECTIVE SUPPLY CHAINS

Successful supply chain management requires integration of all aspects of the supply chain: suppliers, warehouses, factories, distributors, and retail outlets. This requires cooperation among supply chain partners in planning, coordination of activities, and information sharing, which, in turn, requires partners to agree on common goals (goal sharing). This requires trust and a willingness to cooperate to achieve the common goals. Coordination and information sharing are critical to the effective operation of a supply chain.

Information exchange must be reciprocal: Partners share forecasts and sales data, as well as information on inventory quantities, impending shortages, breakdowns, delays,

B2B marketplace types

Type	Description	Examples
Buyer exchange	An industry marketplace dominated by large buyers or a group of buyers. Suppliers bid to fill contracts at lowest cost (reverse auction).	Covisint FreeMarkets
MRO-catalog hub	Marketplace that aggregates supplies used in maintenance, repair, and operations, such as oil and paperclips.	Grainger Equalfooting
Supplier exchange	Producers band together to create an online market.	ChipCenters MetalSite
BPO	Hubs and/or applications service providers (ASP) that manage non–core company functions such as HR or payroll.	Employease Cadence Network
Neutral exchange	Independent marketplace not dominated by buyers or sellers. Often set up by independent startups.	Gofish.com Altra

B2B marketplace enablers

Type	Description	Examples
Financial	Provide financial and other resources for web-enhanced commerce.	Accel Partners Internet Capital Group
Technology	Provide software, applications, and expertise necessary to create B2B marketplace.	Oracle Commerce One

FIGURE 12-6

Business-to-business marketplaces

Source: *Forbes*, July, 2000.

and other problems that could impact the timely flow of products and services through the chain. Information has a time value, and the longer it takes to disseminate information once it materializes, the lower its value. Thus, instead of each organization in a supply chain making plans based on a combination of actual orders plus forecasts of demand of its immediate customer, by sharing data on end-customer sales and partner inventory on a real-time basis, each organization in the chain can develop plans that contribute to synchronization across the chain.

STEPS IN CREATING AN EFFECTIVE SUPPLY CHAIN

Creation of an effective supply chain entails several key steps. They are:

1. Develop strategic objectives and tactics. These will guide the process.

2. Integrate and coordinate activities in the internal portion of the chain. This requires (1) overcoming barriers caused by functional thinking that lead to attempts to optimize a subset of a system rather than the system as a whole, and (2) transferring data and coordinating activities.

3. Coordinate activities with suppliers and with customers. This involves addressing supply and demand issues.

4. Coordinate planning and execution across the supply chain. This requires a system for transferring data across the supply chain and allowing access to data to those who engage in operations to which it will be useful.

5. Consider the possibilities of forming *strategic partnerships*. **Strategic partnering** occurs when two or more business organizations that have complementary products or services that would *strategically* benefit the others agree to join so that each may realize a strategic benefit. One way this occurs is when a supplier agrees to hold inventory for a customer, thereby reducing the customer's cost of holding the inventory, in exchange for the customer agreeing to a long-term commitment, thereby relieving the supplier of the costs that would be needed to continually find new customers, negotiate prices and services, and so on.

strategic partnering Two or more business organizations that have complementary products or services join so that each may realize a strategic benefit.

F(armer, talking to himself:) I have a horse, but no plow to plow my land; my neighbor has a plow, but no horse to plow his land, and all I read about these days is strategic partnering! What we need is a solution to our problems.

In many cases, organizations have accomplished much of what is required to achieve the second and third steps in the process; it is the first and last steps that will require attention. In all steps, designers must address the following performance drivers:

1. Quality
2. Cost
3. Flexibility
4. Velocity
5. Customer service

Quality, cost, and customer service are perhaps obvious. Flexibility refers to the ability to adjust to changes in order quantities but also to the ability to adjust to changes in product or service requirements. Velocity refers to the rate or speed of travel through the system. Velocity is important in two areas: materials and information. **Inventory velocity** refers to the rate at which inventory (material) goes through the system. Faster is better: The quicker materials pass through the supply chain, the lower inventory costs will be, and the quicker products and services will be delivered to the customer. **Information velocity** refers to the speed at which information is transferred within a supply chain. Again, faster is better: The quicker information (two-way flow) is available to decision makers, the better their decisions will be in planning and coordinating their parts of the supply chain.

inventory velocity The rate at which inventory (material) goes through the supply chain.

information velocity The rate at which information is communicated in a supply chain.

Using Information to Speed Execution

Kevin Rollins

www.dell.com

Most of the managerial challenges at Dell Computer have to do with what we call *velocity*—speeding the pace of every element of our business. Life cycles in our business are measured in months, not years, and if you don't move fast, you're out of the game. Managing velocity is about managing information—using a constant flow of information to drive operating practices, from the performance measures we track to how we work with our suppliers.

Performance Metrics

At Dell, we use the balance sheet and the fundamentals of the P&L on a monthly basis as tools to manage operations. From the balance sheet, we track three cash-flow measures very closely. We look at weekly updates of how many days of inventory we have, broken out by product component. We can then work closely with our suppliers so we end up with the right inventory. When it's not quite right, we can use our direct-sales model to steer customers toward comparable products that we do have. So we use inventory information to work both the front and back ends at the same time.

We also track and manage receivables and payables very tightly. This is basic blocking and tackling, but we give it a high priority. The payoff is that we have a negative cash-conversion cycle of five days—that is, we get paid before we have to pay our suppliers. Since our competitors usually have to support their resellers by offering them credit, the direct model gives us an inherent cost advantage. And the more we can shorten our cash-collection cycle, the greater our advantage.

The real-time performance measures in the P&L that we regard as the best indicators of the company's health are our margins, our average selling price, and the overhead associated with selling. We split the P&L into these core elements by customer segment, by product, and by country. These metrics can alert us instantly to problems, for example, with the mix of products being sold in any particular country.

Working with Suppliers

The greatest challenge in working with suppliers is getting them in sync with the fast pace we have to maintain. The key to making it work is information. The right information flows allow us to work with our partners in ways that enhance speed, either directly by improving logistics or indirectly by improving quality.

Take our service strategy, for example. Customers pay us for service and support, and we contract with third-party maintainers (TPMs) to make the service calls. Customers call us when they have problems, and that initial call will trigger two electronic dispatches—one to ship the needed parts directly from Dell to the customers' sites and one to dispatch the TPMs to the customers. Our role as information broker facilitates the TPMs' work by making sure the necessary parts will be on-site when they arrive.

But our role doesn't stop there. Because poor quality creates friction in the system, which slows us down, we want to capture information that can be used to fix problems so they won't happen again. So we take back the bad part to diagnose what went wrong, and we feed that information back to our suppliers so they can redesign the component. Clearly, we couldn't operate that way if we were dealing with hundreds of suppliers. So for us, working with a handful of partners is one of the keys to improving quality—and therefore speed—in our system.

Kevin Rollins is vice chairman of Dell Computer Corporation.

Source: *Harvard Business Review,* March–April 1998, p. 81.

OPTIMIZING THE SUPPLY CHAIN

Optimizing the supply chain means maximizing shareholder and customer value. This is achieved by fully integrating all members of the supply chain, collaboratively balancing resources of chain members, and optimizing the flow of goods, services, and information from source to end customer. To do this, it is necessary to maximize the velocity of information transfer and minimize response time.

CHALLENGES

Barriers to Integration of Separate Organizations. Organizations, and their functional areas, have traditionally had an inward focus. They set up buffers between them and their suppliers. Changing that attitude can be difficult. The objective of supply chain management is to be efficient across the entire supply chain.

NEWSCLIP

Supply Chain Optimization at Internet Speed
G. Berton Latamore

New supply chain optimization tools and Web-based services enable manufacturers to save money, deliver goods faster, and provide better service.

Summary

Five years ago supply chain optimization (SCO) was a tool for large, complex manufacturers making strategic, brick-and-mortar decisions; today's more agile tools can help most manufacturers make both immediate tactical and long-term strategic plans.

SCO covers a lot of ground—from Web-based collaborative order planning to shipping optimization.

Manufacturers must first understand what they need, then match those needs with tools that can best meet them. SCO also requires a higher level of trust and openness among trading partners, based on a new attitude toward suppliers and customers.

SCO requires changes in internal operating methods and a culture that embraces the opportunities that revolutionary new technology presents, rather than a continuing focus on old operating methods.

Source: Copyright 2000 by APICS—The Educational Society for Resource Management. From *APICS—The Performance Advantage,* May 2000.

One difficulty in achieving this objective is that different components of the supply chain often have conflicting objectives. For example, to reduce their inventory holding costs, some companies opt for frequent small deliveries of supplies. This can result in increased holding costs for suppliers, so the cost is merely transferred to suppliers. Similarly, within an organization, functional areas often make decisions with a narrow focus, doing things that "optimize" results under their control; in so doing, however, they may suboptimize results for the overall organization. To be effective, organizations must adopt a *systems approach* to both the internal and external portions of their supply chains, being careful to make decisions that are consistent with optimizing the supply chain.

Another difficulty is that for supply chain management to be successful, organizations in the chain must allow other organizations access to their data. There is a natural reluctance to do this in many cases. One reason can be lack of trust; another can be unwillingness to share proprietary information in general; and another can be that an organization, as a member of multiple chains, fears exposure of proprietary information to competitors.

Getting CEOs, Boards of Directors, Managers, and Employees "Onboard." CEOs and boards of directors need to be convinced of the potential payoffs from supply chain management. And because much of supply chain management involves a change in the way business has been practiced for an extended period of time, getting managers and workers to adopt new attitudes and practices that are consistent with effective supply chain operations poses a real challenge.

Dealing with Trade-offs. The article "Managing Supply Chain Inventory: Pitfalls and Opportunities" lists a number of trade-offs that must be taken into account in structuring a supply chain:[2]

1. *Lot size–inventory trade-off.* Producing or ordering large lot sizes yields benefits in terms of quantity discounts and lower annual setup costs, but it increases the amount of safety stock carried by suppliers and, hence, the carrying cost. It also can create what is known as the *bullwhip effect.*

If you were to examine the quantities of inventory at each stage of many supply chains, starting at the customer end of the chain and working back toward the initial suppliers, you would find progressively larger inventories of some items. Figure 12–7 illustrates this effect. This phenomenon is called the **bullwhip effect.** It is caused by the way inventories are

bullwhip effect Inventories are progressively larger moving backward through a supply chain.

---

[2]Hau L. Lee and C. Billington, "Managing Supply Chain Inventory: Pitfalls and Opportunities," *Sloan Management Review,* Spring 1992, pp. 65–73.

FIGURE 12-7

The Bullwhip Effect.

replenished at various points along a supply chain. For a variety of reasons, organizations tend to periodically order batches of an item from their suppliers. This creates "lumpy" demand for suppliers and, hence, high-variability demand, which causes suppliers to carry relatively large amounts of safety stock. Starting with the final customer and moving backward through the supply chain, batch sizes tend to increase, thereby increasing the level of safety stock carried. What is so striking about this phenomenon is that any demand variations that exist at the customer end of the supply chain get magnified as orders are generated back through the supply chain.

Techniques such as setup time reduction and *CONWIP* (constant work in process) systems can alleviate some of the desire to do this because they make smaller lot sizes economical.

2. Inventory–transportation cost trade-off. Suppliers prefer to ship full truckloads instead of partial loads in order to spread shipping costs over as many units as possible. This leads to higher holding costs for customers. Solutions include combining orders to realize full truckloads, downsizing truck capacity, and shipping late in the process along with *cross-docking.* **Cross-docking** is a technique whereby goods arriving at a warehouse from a supplier are unloaded from the supplier's truck and immediately loaded on one or more outbound trucks, thereby avoiding storage at the warehouse completely. Wal-Mart is among the companies that have used this technique successfully to reduce inventory holding costs and to reduce lead times.

3. Lead time–transportation cost trade-off. Suppliers usually prefer to ship in full loads, as mentioned previously. But waiting for sufficient orders and/or production to achieve a full load increases lead time. In addition to the preceding suggestions, improved forecasting information to suppliers might improve the timing of their production and orders to their suppliers.

4. Product variety–inventory trade-off. Higher product variety generally means smaller lot sizes, which results in higher setup costs, as well as higher transportation and inventory management costs. One possible means of reducing some costs is **delayed differentiation,** which means producing standard components and subassemblies, then waiting until late in the process to add differentiating features. For example, an automobile producer may produce and ship cars without radios, allowing customers to select from a range of radios which can be installed by the dealer, thereby eliminating that variety from much of the supply chain.

5. Cost–customer service trade-off. Producing and shipping in large lots reduces costs, but it increases lead times, as previously noted. One approach to reducing lead time is to ship directly from a warehouse to the customer, bypassing a retail outlet. Reducing one or more steps in a supply chain by cutting out one or more intermediaries is referred to as **disintermediation.** Although transportation costs are higher, storage costs are lower.

Small Businesses. Small businesses may be reluctant to embrace supply chain management because it can involve specialized, complicated software as well as sharing sensitive information with outside companies. Nonetheless, in order for them to survive, they may have to do so.

---

cross-docking Goods arriving at a warehouse from a supplier are unloaded from the supplier's truck and loaded onto outbound trucks, thereby avoiding warehouse storage.

delayed differentiation Production of standard components and subassemblies, which are held until late in the process to add differentiating features.

disintermediation Reducing one or more steps in a supply chain by cutting out one or more intermediaries.

Problem	Potential Improvement	Benefits	Possible Drawbacks
Large inventories	Smaller, more frequent deliveries, cross-docking	Reduced holdings costs	Traffic congestion, increased ordering costs, increased supplier costs
Long lead times	Delayed differentiation Disintermediation	Quick response Quick response	May not be feasible May need to absorb functions
Large number of parts	Modular construction	Fewer parts to keep track of, simpler ordering	Less variety
Cost, quality	Outsourcing	Reduced cost, higher quality, fewer internal problems, remaining operations more focused	Loss of control
Variability	Shorter lead times, better forecasts, reduction in product/service variety	Better able to match supply and demand	Less variety

TABLE 12–5

Benefits and possible drawbacks of potential improvements to a supply chain

Variability and Uncertainty. Variations create uncertainty, thereby causing inefficiencies in a supply chain. Variations occur in incoming shipments from suppliers, internal operations, deliveries of products or services to customers, and customer demands. Increases in product and service variety add to uncertainty, because organizations have to deal with a broader range and frequent changes in operations. Hence, when deciding to increase variety, organizations should consider this trade-off.

Although variations exist throughout most supply chains, decision makers often treat the uncertainties as if they were certainties and make decisions on that basis. In fact, systems are often designed on the basis of certainty, so they may not be able to cope with uncertainty. Unfortunately, uncertainties are detrimental to scheduling, leading to various undesirable occurrences, including inventory buildups, bottleneck delays, missed delivery dates, and frustration for employees and customers at all stages of a supply chain.

Long Lead Times. Response time is an important issue in supply chain management. Long lead times impair the ability of a supply chain to quickly respond to changing conditions, such as changes in the quantity or timing of demand, changes in product or service design, and quality or logistics problems. Therefore, it is important to work to reduce long product lead times and long collaborative lead times, and a plan should be in place to deal with problems when they arise.

Table 12–5 lists some potential solutions to supply chain problems and possible drawbacks.

Operations Strategy

Supply chain management creates value through changes in time, location, and quantity. Moreover, supply chain management holds great potential for competitive advantage. To realize that potential, management must *integrate* and *streamline* a diverse set of activities that relate to purchasing, suppliers, inventory management, logistics, and information sharing. Of course, much of this represents a significant departure from the way business has traditionally been conducted. Naturally, those attitudes and behaviors, and the systems in place to support them, are deeply ingrained. Consequently, an important task for managers at all levels is to overcome those ways of thinking and adopt new ways of thinking that are necessary to achieve effective supply chain management.

Summary

A supply chain consists of all the organizations, facilities, materials, and activities involved in producing and delivering a product or service, from the initial suppliers to the final customer. Supply chains have two major portions, a supply portion and a demand portion, and each has its own set of management issues. The length of each portion depends on where a particular organization is in the chain; the closer the organization is to the final customer, the shorter its demand portion and the longer its supply portion. The term *supply chain* usually refers to both supply and demand portions.

Supply chain management represents a shift in focus for many business organizations. Until recently, firms tended to focus mainly on their own operations as they attempted to cut costs, improve quality, and meet delivery schedules. But because effective supply chain management offers the benefits of lower operating costs, reduced inventories, product availability, and customer satisfaction, more and more firms are using supply chains to meet their objectives. Among the reasons for this shift are (1) the major internal improvements have been made; (2) outsourcing is increasing, which has led to higher transportation costs, a greater need to manage suppliers, and an increase in the importance of the purchasing function; (3) expanding global operations have increased the physical length of supply chains; and (4) the number of new products has increased, along with pressures for shorter product-development cycles, shorter lead times, and quick response.

The elements of supply chain management include customers, forecasting, product and service design, processing, inventory management, purchasing, supplier management, location decisions, and logistics.

Purchasing is the link between an organization and its suppliers. Purchasing selects suppliers, negotiates contracts, forges alliances, and serves as a liaison between the organization and its suppliers.

Logistics involves the movement of goods and materials in a supply chain. This includes incoming materials, movement within a facility, and outgoing goods. It also includes overseeing the two-way flow of information across the supply chain.

The explosion of e-commerce business activities has introduced tremendous opportunities, and it underscores the importance of effective supply chain management. Electronic data interchange is being increasingly used for purchasing, order confirmation and payment, and arranging shipment. Companies adopt electronic data interchange to improve customer service, reduce cost, improve quality, and, in the process, gain a competitive edge.

The objective of supply chain management is to be efficient across the entire supply chain. Among the difficulties in achieving this objective are barriers to integration, the need to deal with numerous trade-offs, variability of demand and lead times, and long lead times. Transactions between companies participating in supply chain management are based on mutual trust, long-term relationships, and shared information. Supply chain partners use information technology to improve scheduling of operations and inventory management.

Key Terms

bullwhip effect, 521
cross-docking, 522
delayed differentiation, 522
disintermediation, 522
distribution requirements planning (DRP), 514
e-commerce, 515
efficient consumer response (ECR), 514
electronic data interchange (EDI), 513

information velocity, 519
inventory velocity, 519
logistics, 509
outsourcing, 506
strategic partnering, 519
supply chain, 504
traffic management, 512
value chain, 504

Solved Problem

Problem

Determine which shipping alternative is best if the annual holding cost of an item is 25 percent of unit price, and a single unit with a price of $6,000 is to be shipped, either by two-day freight at a cost of $400 or five-day freight at a cost of $350.

Solution

$H = .25(\$6,000) = \$1,500$ per year
$d = 5$ days $- 2$ days $=$ additional 3 days
Cost savings $= \$400 - \$350 = \$50$

$$\text{Incremental holding cost} = H\left(\frac{d}{365}\right)$$

$$= \$1,500\left(\frac{3}{365}\right)$$

$$= \$12.33$$

The added cost to hold the item is less than the cost savings of $50. Hence, use the five-day alternative.

Discussion and Review Questions

1. What is a supply chain?
2. What is the need to manage a supply chain, and what are some potential benefits of doing so?
3. What are the elements of supply chain management?
4. What are the strategic, tactical, and operations issues in supply chain management?
5. What is the bullwhip effect, and why does it occur? How can it be overcome?
6. Explain the increasing importance of purchasing.
7. What is meant by the term *inventory velocity* and why is this important? What is *information velocity,* and why is it important?
8. Explain strategic partnering.
9. What impact has e-commerce had on supply chain management?
10. What are some of the advantages of e-commerce?
11. What are some of the trade-offs that might be factors in designing a supply chain?
12. Locate an Internet website for a railroad that offers freight transportation, and determine the kinds of products it handles.

Memo Writing Exercises

1. Go to a logistics website and find out what types of logistics services the company offers. Write a brief memo to your instructor listing typical types of services.
2. Go to the Operations Management Center (OMC) web page. Find a recent article on supply chain management and write a brief summary of it for your instructor.

Problems

1. A manager at Strateline Manufacturing must choose between two shipping alternatives: two-day freight and five-day freight. Using five-day freight would cost $135 less than using two-day freight. The primary consideration is holding cost, which is $10 per unit a year. Two thousand items are to be shipped. Which alternative would you recommend? Explain.
2. Determine which shipping alternative would be most economical to ship 80 boxes of parts when each box has a price of $200 and holding costs are 30 percent of price, given this shipping information:

Alternative	Shipping Cost
Overnight	$300
Two day	260
Six day	180

3. A manager must make a decision on shipping. There are two shippers, A and B. Both offer a two-day rate. In addition, A offers a three-day rate and a nine-day rate, and B offers a four-day rate and a seven-day rate. Annual holding costs are 35 percent of unit price. Three hundred boxes are to be shipped, and each box has a price of $140. Which shipping alternative would you recommend? Explain.

Selected Bibliography and Further Reading

Anders, George. "Virtual Reality: Web Firms Go On Warehouse Building Boom." The *Wall Street Journal,* September 8, 1999, p. B1.

Ballou, Ronald H. *Business Logistics Management,* 4th ed. Englewood Cliffs, NJ: Prentice Hall, 1999.

Bender, Paul S. "Debunking 5 Supply Chain Myths." *Supply Chain Management Review,* 4, no. 1 (March 2000), pp. 52–58.

Bender, Paul S. "How to Design an Optimum Worldwide Supply Chain." *Supply Chain Management Review,* Spring 1997.

Bhatnagar, Rohit, and S. Viswanathan "Re-engineering Global Supply Chains: Alliances between Manufacturing Firms and Global Logistics Services Providers." *International Journal of Physical Distribution and Logistics Management* 30, no. 1 (2000), pp. 13–14.

Blackwell, Roger D., and Kristina Blackwell. "The Century of the Consumer: Converting Supply Chains into Demand Chains." *Supply Chain Management,* Fall 1999.

Bovet, David, and Yossi Sheffi. "The Brave New World of Supply Chain Management." *Supply Chain Management Review,* Spring 1998, pp. 14–20.

Chopra, Sunil, and Peter Meindl. *Supply Chain Management: Strategy, Planning, and Operation.* Upper Saddle River, NJ: Prentice Hall, 2001.

Copacino, William C. *Supply Chain Management: The Basics and Beyond.* Boca Raton, FL: St. Lucie Press, 1997.

Dornier, Phillippe-Pierre, Ricardo Ernst, Michel Fender, and Panos Kouvelis. *Global Operations and Logistics: Text and Cases.* New York: Wiley, 1998.

Fisher, Marshall. "What is the Right Supply Chain for Your Product?" *Harvard Business Review,* March–April 1997.

Handfield, Robert B., and Ernest L. Nichols Jr. *Introduction to Supply Chain Management.* Englewood Cliffs, NJ: Prentice Hall, 1999.

Harvard Business Review on Managing the Value Chain. Boston: Harvard Business School Press, 2000. A collection of articles, some of which are listed separately in this section.

Hill, Terry. *Manufacturing Strategy: Text and Cases.* New York: McGraw-Hill, 2000.

Lee, Hau L., and C. Billington, "Managing Supply Chain Inventory: Pitfalls and Opportunities." *Sloan Management Review,* Spring 1992, pp. 65–73.

Lee, Hau L., V. Padmanaghan, and Seunjin Whang. "The Paralyzing Curse of the Bullwhip Effect in Supply Chains." *Sloan Management Review,* Spring 1997, pp. 93–102.

Margretta, Joan. "The Power of Virtual Integration: An Interview with Dell Computer's Michael Dell." *Harvard Business Review,* March–April 1998, pp. 73–84.

Margretta, Joan. "Fast, Global, and Entrepreneurial: Supply Chain Management, Hong Kong Style." *Harvard Business Review,* Sept.–Oct. 1998, pp. 102–14.

Martin, Justin, "Are You as Good as You Think You Are?" *Fortune,* September 30, 1996 pp. 145–46.

Metz, Peter J. "Demystifying the Supply Chain." *Supply Chain Management Review,* Winter 1998.

Ptak, Carol A., and Eli Schragenheim. *ERP: Tools, Techniques, and Applications for Integrating the Supply Chain.* Boca Raton, FL: St. Lucie Press, 1999.

Ross, D. F. *Competing through Supply Chain Management.* New York: Chapman and Hall, 1998.

Silverstein, Judith. "Desperately Seeking E-Fulfillment." *Digital Chicago,* November/December 1999, pp. 22–47.

Simchi-Levi, David, Philip Kaminsky, and Edith Simchi-Levi. *Designing and Managing the Supply Chain: Concepts, Strategies, and Case Studies.* Irwin/McGraw-Hill, 2000.

Supply Chain Linkages. An entire issue of *Decision Sciences* [29, no. 3, (Summer 1998)] with a research focus on supply chain linkages.

Walker, William T., and Karen Alber. "Understanding Supply Chain Management." *APICS—The Performance Advantage,* January 1999.

Internet Sites

www.supply-chain.org. Supply Chain Council. SCOR model.
www.supply-chainlink.com. Cahners Publishing. *Supply Chain Management Review* and other resources.
www.internetsolutions.enterprise.hp.com/supplychain/personalenrichment/index.
www.forbesbest.com.

Purchasing and Supplier Management

SUPPLEMENT OUTLINE

Purchasing, 528
  Purchasing Interfaces, 528
  The Purchasing Cycle, 530
  Value Analysis, 530
  Make or Buy, 531
  Determining Prices, 532
  Centralized versus Decentralized
    Purchasing, 533
  Ethics in Purchasing, 533

Supplier Management, 533
  Choosing Suppliers, 533
  Supplier Audits, 535

Supplier Certification, 535
Supplier Relationships, 535
Supplier Partnerships, 536

Summary, 537

Key Terms, 537

Discussion and Review
  Questions, 537

Memo Writing Exercises, 537

Problems, 537

Reading: E-Procurement at
  IBM, 538

Selected Bibliography and Further
  Reading, 539

LEARNING OBJECTIVES

*After completing this supplement,
you should be able to:*

1 Explain the importance of the
  purchasing function in business
  organizations.

2 Describe the responsibilities of
  purchasing.

3 Explain the term *value analysis*.

4 Compare the advantages of
  centralized purchasing with those
  of decentralized purchasing.

5 Identify several guidelines for
  ethical behavior in purchasing.

6 List several important factors in
  choosing suppliers.

7 Explain how supplier partnerships
  can be advantageous to an
  organization.

Purchasing is "critical to supply chain efficiency because it is the job of purchasing to select suppliers and then establish mutually beneficial relationships with them. Without good suppliers and without superior purchasing, supply chains cannot compete in today's" marketplace. Purchasing is also very involved in product design and development work. Many "manufacturers have found out that manufacturing costs can be reduced, product quality maximized, and new products brought to market at a much faster rate if purchasing brings key suppliers into the product design and development at the earliest stage of the process." And purchasing is directly involved in the implementation of e-commerce systems.

Source: Based on Kevin R. Fitzgerald, "Purchasing Occupies Key Position in Supply Chains," *Supply Chain Yearbook 2000,* New York: Cahners Business Information, 2000, p. 21.

In this supplement, you will learn about the purchasing function and supplier management as they operate in most organizations. In particular, you will learn what purchasing managers do, the importance of purchasing, the purchasing cycle, guidelines for ethical behavior in purchasing, and various aspects of supplier management, including vendor analysis, supplier audits, and strategic partnering.

Purchasing

Purchasing is responsible for obtaining the materials, parts, supplies, and services needed to produce a product or provide a service. You can get some idea of the importance of purchasing when you consider that in manufacturing upwards of 60 percent of the cost of finished goods comes from purchased parts and materials. Furthermore, the percentages for purchased inventories are even higher for retail and wholesale companies, sometimes exceeding 90 percent. Nonetheless, the importance of purchasing is more than just the cost of goods purchased; other important factors include the *quality* of goods and services and the *timing* of deliveries of goods or services, both of which can have a significant impact on operations.

The goal of purchasing is to develop and implement purchasing plans for products and services that support operations strategies. Among the duties of purchasing are identifying sources of supply, negotiating contracts, maintaining a database of suppliers, obtaining goods and services that meet or exceed operations requirements in a timely and cost-efficient manner, and managing suppliers. Thus, purchasing selects suppliers, negotiates contracts, establishes alliances, and acts as liaison between suppliers and various internal departments.

Purchasing is taking on increased importance as organizations place greater emphasis on supply chain management, quality improvement, lean production, and outsourcing. Moreover, business-to-business buying relationships are changing: Although traditional relationships currently account for the lion's share of buying relationships, they are expected to decrease substantially by the middle of the decade, while web-based auctions and managed inventory relationships are expected to grow. In addition, increasing globalization will continue to have an impact on purchasing.

PURCHASING INTERFACES

Purchasing has interfaces with a number of other functional areas, as well as with outside suppliers. Purchasing is the connecting link between the organization and its suppliers. In this capacity, it exchanges information with suppliers and functional areas. The interactions between purchasing and these other areas are briefly summarized in the following paragraphs.

Operating units constitute the main source of requests for purchased materials, and close cooperation between these units and the purchasing department is vital if quality, quantity, and delivery goals are to be met. Cancellations, changes in specifications, or changes in quantity or delivery times must be communicated immediately for purchasing to be effective.

The purchasing department may require the assistance of the *legal* department in contract negotiations, in drawing up bid specifications for nonroutine purchases, and to help interpret legislation on pricing, product liability, and contracts with suppliers.

Accounting is responsible for handling payments to suppliers and must be notified promptly when goods are received in order to take advantage of possible discounts. In many firms, *data processing* is handled by the accounting department, which keeps inventory records, checks invoices, and monitors vendor performance.

Design and *engineering* usually prepare material specifications, which must be communicated to purchasing. Because of its contacts with suppliers, purchasing is often in a position to pass information about new products and materials improvements on to design personnel. Also, design and purchasing people may work closely to determine whether changes in specifications, design, or materials can reduce the cost of purchased items (see the following section on value analysis).

Receiving checks incoming shipments of purchased items to determine whether quality, quantity, and timing objectives have been met, and it moves the goods to temporary storage. Purchasing must be notified when shipments are late; accounting must be notified when shipments are received so that payments can be made; and both purchasing and accounting must be apprised of current information on continuing vendor evaluation.

Suppliers or vendors work closely with purchasing to learn what materials will be purchased and what kinds of specifications will be required in terms of quality, quantity, and deliveries. Purchasing must rate vendors on cost, reliability, and so on (see the later section on vendor analysis). Good supplier relations can be important on rush orders and changes, and vendors provide a good source of information on product and material improvements.

Figure 12S–1 summarizes the purchasing interfaces.

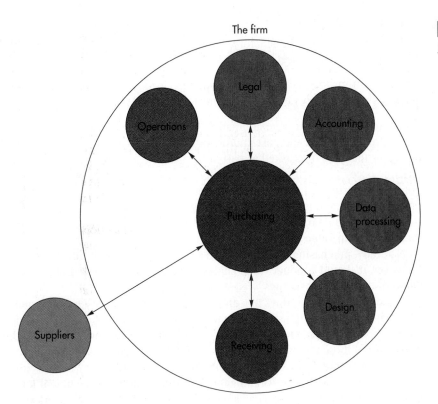

FIGURE 12S–1

Purchasing interfaces

THE PURCHASING CYCLE

purchasing cycle Series of steps that begin with a request for purchase and end with notification of shipment received in satisfactory condition.

The **purchasing cycle** begins with a request from within the organization to purchase material, equipment, supplies, or other items from outside the organization, and the cycle ends when the purchasing department is notified that a shipment has been received in satisfactory condition. The main steps in the cycle are these:

1. *Purchasing receives the requisition.* The requisition includes (*a*) a description of the item or material desired, (*b*) the quantity and quality necessary, (*c*) desired delivery dates, and (*d*) who is requesting the purchase.

2. *Purchasing selects a supplier.* The purchasing department must identify suppliers who have the capability of supplying the desired goods. If no suppliers are currently listed in the files, new ones must be sought. Vendor ratings may be referred to in choosing among vendors, or perhaps rating information can be relayed to the vendor with the thought of upgrading future performance.

3. *Purchasing places the order with a vendor.* If the order involves a large expenditure, particularly for a one-time purchase of equipment, for example, vendors will usually be asked to bid on the job, and operating and design personnel may be asked to assist in negotiations with a vendor. Large-volume, continuous-usage items may be covered by blanket purchase orders, which often involve annual negotiation of prices with deliveries subject to request throughout the year. Moderate-volume items may also have blanket purchase orders, or they may be handled on an individual basis. Small purchases may be handled directly between the operating unit requesting a purchased item and the supplier, although some control should be exercised over those purchases so they don't get out of hand.

4. *Monitoring orders.* Routine follow-up on orders, especially large orders or those with lengthy lead times, allows the purchasing department to project potential delays and relay that information to the operating units. Conversely, the purchasing department must communicate changes in quantities and delivery needs of the operating units to suppliers to allow them time to change their plans.

5. *Receiving orders.* Receiving must check incoming shipments for quality and quantity. It must notify purchasing, accounting, and the operating unit that requested the goods. If the goods are not satisfactory, they may have to be returned to the supplier or subjected to further inspection.

VALUE ANALYSIS

value analysis Examination of the function of purchased parts and materials in an effort to reduce cost and/or improve performance.

Value analysis refers to an examination of the *function* of purchased parts and materials in an effort to reduce the cost and/or improve the performance of those items. Typical questions that would be asked as part of the analysis include: Could a cheaper part or material be used? Is the function necessary? Can the function of two or more parts or components be performed by a single part for a lower cost? Can a part be simplified? Could product specifications be relaxed, and would this result in a lower price? Could standard parts be substituted for nonstandard parts? Table 12S–1 provides a checklist of questions that can guide a value analysis.

Naturally, purchasing cannot perform an investigation each time materials are ordered. However, it should conduct value analysis periodically on large dollar-volume items because of the potential savings.

Although purchasing does not ordinarily have the authority to implement changes on the basis of a value analysis, it can make suggestions to operating units, designers, and suppliers, which may lead to improved performance of purchased goods and/or reduction of the cost of those goods. Purchasing can offer a different perspective to the analysis, and purchasing people, because of their association with suppliers, possess information not known to others within the organization. If a fair amount of technical knowledge is required to review a part or service, a team can be formed with representatives from design and operations to work with purchasing to conduct the analysis.

1. Select an item that has a high annual dollar volume. This can be material, a purchased item, or a service.
2. Identify the function of the item.
3. Obtain answers to these kinds of questions:
   a. Is the item necessary; does it have value; can it be eliminated?
   b. Are there alternative sources for the item?
   c. Can the item be provided internally?
   d. What are the advantages of the present arrangement?
   e. What are the disadvantages of the present arrangement?
   f. Could another material, part, or service be used instead?
   g. Can specifications be less stringent to save cost or time?
   h. Can two or more parts be combined?
   i. Can more/less processing be done on the item to save cost or time?
   j. Do suppliers/providers have suggestions for improvements?
   k. Do employees have suggestions for improvements?
   l. Can packaging be improved or made less costly?
4. Analyze the answers obtained as well as answers to other questions that arise, and make recommendations.

TABLE 12S–1

Overview of value analysis

MAKE OR BUY

Business organizations do not typically own all of the resources, or provide all of the activities, necessary to produce a product or service. Not only would that be prohibitively expensive, but there are other organizations that focus on a particular portion of the process, thus offering greater expertise and more timely delivery.

Buying goods or services from outside sources instead of making the goods or providing the services within house is referred to as **outsourcing.** Some companies do little outsourcing, preferring to do almost everything themselves, whereas others engage in extensive outsourcing. For example, some personal computer companies buy most or all of the parts for the computers they sell from suppliers, and merely assemble the computers. Services can also be outsourced, and it is not unusual for companies to outsource data processing, payroll and benefits, maintenance, field service and repair, food services, and more.

outsourcing Buying goods or services from outside sources rather than making or providing them in-house.

Companies may outsource for a variety of reasons. Chief among them is the ability of the outside source to provide materials, parts, or services better, cheaper, or more efficiently. An outside supplier, for example, that is a large-scale producer of a certain part or service, can—because of economies of scale—provide the part or service at a lower cost than the company can achieve. Expertise and knowledge are other key reasons for outsourcing. Or a supplier may hold a patent on a necessary part. Using outsourcing gives a company added flexibility. Outsourcing often increases when companies downsize, as they narrow their focus to core activities and subcontract the other activities.

Outsourcing carries risks as well as benefits. Among the risks are loss of control, greater dependency on suppliers, and loss of the ability to perform in-house. Generally an organization takes into account the following kinds of factors in deciding whether to outsource:

1. Cost to do it in-house versus cost to buy, including start-up costs, versus cost to outsource.
2. Stability of demand and possible seasonality.
3. Quality available from suppliers compared with a firm's own quality capabilities.
4. The desire to maintain close control over operations.
5. Idle capacity available within the organization.
6. Lead times for each alternative.
7. Who has patents, expertise, and so on, if these are factors.
8. Stability of technology (if a technology is changing, it may be better to use a supplier).

9. The degree to which the necessary operations are consistent with, or in conflict with, current operations.

10. *Strategy.* Strategic considerations may outweigh other factors in some instances. Of course, not every make-or-buy decision has strategic implications, but some do, so it is essential to assign make-or-buy decisions into strategic, tactical, and operational categories and to treat them accordingly.

In some cases, a firm might choose to perform part of the work itself and let others handle the rest in order to maintain expertise in that area, maintain flexibility, and hedge against loss of a subcontractor. Moreover, this provides a bargaining tool in negotiations with subcontractors or a head start if the firm later decides to take over the operation entirely.

Obviously, there are many dimensions to make-or-buy decisions, and the intent here is to simply point out some of the key considerations. The following example illustrates how one might look at the cost dimension.

Example S-1

Analyze the following data to determine the total annual cost of making and of buying.

	Make	**Buy**
Expected annual volume	20,000 units	20,000 units
Variable cost per unit	$5.00	$6.00
Annual fixed costs	$30,000	

Solution

Total annual cost = Fixed cost + Variable cost per unit × Estimated annual volume

Make: $30,000 + \$5 \times 20,000 = \$130,000$

Buy: $\$0 + \$6 \times 20,000 = \$120,000$

In this instance, buying would save $10,000 a year. This information would be combined with information on other relevant factors to decide which alternative would be better.

DETERMINING PRICES

Organizations typically determine prices in one of three ways: published price lists, competitive bidding, and negotiation.

In many instances, organizations buy products and services that have fixed or *predetermined prices.* This is generally the case for standard items that are bought infrequently and/or in small quantities.

For large orders of standard products and services, *competitive bidding* is common. The purchasing department sends requests for bids to potential suppliers, asking vendors to quote a price for a specified quantity and quality of items or for a specified service to be performed. Government purchases of standard goods or services are usually made through competitive bidding.

Negotiated purchasing is used for special purchasing situations—when specifications are vague, when one or a few customized products or services are involved (e.g., space exploration), and when few potential sources exist. Several myths concerning negotiated purchasing should be recognized:

1. Negotiation is a win–lose confrontation.

2. The main goal is to obtain the lowest possible price.

3. Each negotiation is an isolated transaction.[1]

---

[1]Richard J. Tersine, *Production/Operations Management: Concepts, Structure, and Analysis,* 4th ed. (New York: Elsevier North-Holland Publishing, 1994).

No one likes to be taken advantage of. Furthermore, contractors and suppliers need a reasonable profit to survive. Therefore, a take-it-or-leave-it approach or one that capitalizes on the weaknesses of the other party will serve no useful purpose and may have detrimental effects that surface later. The most reasonable approach is one of give and take, with each side giving and receiving some concessions.

CENTRALIZED VERSUS DECENTRALIZED PURCHASING

Purchasing can be centralized or decentralized. Centralized purchasing means that purchasing is handled by one special department. Decentralized purchasing means that individual departments or separate locations handle their own purchasing requirements.

Centralized purchasing may be able to obtain lower prices than decentralized units if the higher volume created by combining orders enables it to take advantage of quantity discounts offered on large orders. Centralized purchasing may also be able to obtain better service and closer attention from suppliers. In addition, centralized purchasing often enables companies to assign certain categories of items to specialists, who tend to be more efficient because they are able to concentrate their efforts on relatively few items instead of spreading themselves across many items.

centralized purchasing Purchasing is handled by one special department.

Decentralized purchasing has the advantage of awareness of differing "local" needs and being better able to respond to those needs. Decentralized purchasing usually can offer quicker response than centralized purchasing. Where locations are widely scattered, decentralized purchasing may be able to save on transportation costs by buying locally, which has the added attraction of creating goodwill in the community.

decentralized purchasing Individual departments or separate locations handle their own purchasing requirements.

Some organizations manage to take advantage of both centralization and decentralization by permitting individual units to handle certain items while centralizing purchases of other items. For example, small orders and rush orders may be handled locally or by departments, while centralized purchases would be used for high-volume, high-value items for which discounts are applicable or specialists can provide better service than local buyers or departments.

ETHICS IN PURCHASING

Ethical behavior is important in all aspects of business. This is certainly true in purchasing, where the temptations for unethical behavior can be enormous. Buyers often hold great power, and salespeople are often eager to make a sale. Unless both parties act in an ethical manner, the potential for abuse is very real. Furthermore, with increased globalization, the challenges are particularly great because a behavior regarded as customary in one country might be regarded as unethical in another country.

The National Association of Purchasing Management has established a set of guidelines for ethical behavior. (See Table 12S–2.) As you read through the list, you get insight into the scope of ethics issues in purchasing.

Supplier Management

Reliable and trustworthy suppliers are a vital link in an effective supply chain. Timely deliveries of goods or services and high quality are just two of the ways that suppliers can contribute to effective operations. A purchasing manager may function as an "external operations manager," working with suppliers to coordinate supplier operations and buyer needs.

In this section, various aspects of supplier management are described, including supplier audits, supplier certification, and supplier partnering. The section starts with an aspect that can have important ramifications for the entire organization: choosing suppliers.

CHOOSING SUPPLIERS

In many respects, choosing a vendor involves taking into account many of the same factors associated with making a major purchase (e.g., a car or stereo system). A company

TABLE 12S–2

Guidelines for ethical behavior in purchasing

Principles

1. Loyalty to employer.
2. Justice to those you deal with.
3. Faith in your profession.

Standards of purchasing practice

1. Avoid appearance of unethical or compromising practice.
2. Follow the lawful instructions of your employer.
3. Refrain from private activity that might conflict with the interests of your employer.
4. Refrain from soliciting or accepting gifts, favors, or services from present or potential suppliers.
5. Handle confidential or proprietary employer or supplier information with due care.
6. Practice courtesy and impartiality in all aspects of your job.
7. Refrain from reciprocal agreements that constrain competition.
8. Know and obey the letter and spirit of laws governing purchasing.
9. Demonstrate support for small, disadvantaged, and minority-owned businesses.
10. Discourage involvement in employer-sponsored programs of nonbusiness, personal purchases.
11. Enhance the profession by maintaining current knowledge and the highest ethical standards.
12. Conduct international purchasing in accordance with the laws, customs, and practices of foreign countries, but consistent with the laws of the United States, your organization's policies, and these guidelines.

Source: Adapted from *Principles and Standards of Purchasing Practice,* National Association of Purchasing Management, adopted 1992.

TABLE 12S–3

Choosing a supplier

Factor	Typical Questions
Quality and quality assurance	What procedures does the supplier have for quality control and quality assurance? Are quality problems and corrective actions documented?
Flexibility	How flexible is the supplier in handling changes in delivery schedules, quantity, and product or service changes?
Location	Is the supplier nearby?
Price	Are prices reasonable given the entire package the supplier will provide? Is the supplier willing to negotiate prices? Is the supplier willing to cooperate to reduce costs?
Product or service changes	How much advance notification does the supplier require for product or service changes?
Reputation and financial stability	What is the reputation of the supplier? How financially stable is the supplier?
Flexibility	How flexible is the supplier in handling changes in delivery schedules, quantity, and product or service changes?
Lead times and on-time delivery	What lead times can the supplier provide? What procedures does the supplier have for assuring on-time deliveries? What procedures does the supplier have for documenting and correcting problems?
Other accounts	Is the supplier heavily dependent on other customers, causing a risk of giving priority to those needs over ours?

considers price, quality, the supplier's reputation, past experience with the supplier, and service after the sale. The main difference is that a company, because of the quantities it orders and production requirements, often provides suppliers with detailed specifications of the materials or parts it wants instead of buying items off the shelf, although most organizations buy standard items that way. The main factors a company takes into account when it selects a vendor are outlined in Table 12S–3.

Because different factors are important for different situations, purchasing must decide, with the help of operations, the importance of each factor (i.e., how much weight to give to each factor), and then rate potential vendors according to how well they can be expected to perform against this list. This process is called **vendor analysis**, and it is conducted periodically, or whenever there is a significant change in the weighting assigned to the various factors.

vendor analysis Evaluating the sources of supply in terms of price, quality, reputation, and service.

SUPPLIER AUDITS

Periodic audits of suppliers are a means of keeping current on suppliers' production (or service) capabilities, quality and delivery problems and resolutions, and suppliers' performance on other criteria. If an audit reveals problem areas, a buyer can attempt to find a solution before more serious problems develop. Among the factors typically covered by a supplier audit are management style, quality assurance, materials management, the design process used, process improvement policies, and procedures for corrective action and follow-up.

Supplier audits are also an important first step in supplier certification programs.

SUPPLIER CERTIFICATION

Supplier certification is a detailed examination of the policies and capabilities of a supplier. The certification process verifies that a supplier meets or exceeds the requirements of a buyer. This is generally important in supplier relationships, but it is particularly important when buyers are seeking to establish a long-term relationship with suppliers. Certified suppliers are sometimes referred to as *world class* suppliers. One advantage of using certified suppliers is that the buyer can eliminate much or all of the inspection and testing of delivered goods. And although problems with supplier goods or services might not be totally eliminated, there is much less risk than with noncertified suppliers.

Rather than develop their own certification program, some companies rely on standard industry certifications such as ISO 9000, perhaps the most widely used international certification.

SUPPLIER RELATIONSHIPS

Purchasing has the ultimate responsibility for establishing and maintaining good supplier relationships. The type of relationship is often related to the length of a contract between buyers and sellers. Short-term contracts involve competitive bidding. Companies post specifications and potential suppliers bid on the contracts. Suppliers are kept at arm's length, and the relationship is minimal. Business may be conducted through computerized interaction. Medium-term contracts often involve ongoing relationships. Long-term contracts often evolve into partnerships, with buyers and sellers cooperating on various issues that tend to benefit both parties. Increasingly, business organizations are establishing long-term relationships with suppliers in certain situations that are based on *strategic* considerations.

American firms have become increasingly aware of the importance of building good relations with their suppliers. In the past, too many firms regarded their suppliers as adversaries and dealt with them on that basis. One lesson learned from the Japanese is that numerous benefits derive from good supplier relations, including supplier flexibility in terms of accepting changes in delivery schedules, quality, and quantities. Moreover, suppliers can often help identify problems and offer suggestions for solving them. Thus, simply choosing and switching suppliers on the basis of price is a very shortsighted approach to handling an ongoing need.

Many Japanese firms rely on one or a few suppliers to handle their needs. In contrast, many U.S. firms deal with numerous suppliers. Perhaps they want to remain flexible, and possibly there are advantages in playing off one against the others. Although reducing the number of suppliers to one or a few, as the Japanese have done, may be too extreme, a

Aspect	Adversary	Partner
Number of suppliers	Many; play one off against the others	One or a few
Length of relationship	May be brief	Long-term
Low price	Major consideration	Moderately important
Reliability	May not be high	High
Openness	Low	High
Quality	May be unreliable; buyer inspects	At the source; vendor certified
Volume of business	May be low due to many suppliers	High
Flexibility	Relatively low	Relatively high
Location	Widely dispersed	Nearness is important for short lead times and quick service

more realistic approach for U.S. firms is to move in the direction of reducing the number of suppliers.

Keeping good relations with suppliers is increasingly recognized as an important factor in maintaining a competitive edge. Many companies are adopting a view of suppliers as partners. This viewpoint stresses a stable relationship with relatively few reliable suppliers who can provide high-quality supplies, maintain precise delivery schedules, and remain flexible relative to changes in productive specifications and delivery schedules. A comparison of the contrasting views of suppliers is provided in Table 12S–4.

SUPPLIER PARTNERSHIPS

More and more business organizations are seeking to establish partnerships with other organizations in their supply chains. This implies fewer suppliers, longer-term relationships, sharing of information (forecasts, sales data, problem alerts), and cooperation in planning. Among the possible benefits are higher quality, increased delivery speed and reliability, lower inventories, lower costs, higher profits, and, in general, improved operations. This is underscored by an article that appeared in *Purchasing*. The article identified nine areas in which potential ideas from suppliers could lead to improved operations.[2]

1. Reduce the cost of making a purchase.
2. Reduce transportation costs.
3. Reduce production costs.
4. Improve product quality.
5. Improve product design.
6. Reduce time to market.
7. Improve customer satisfaction.
8. Reduce inventory costs.
9. Introduce new products or services.

The organizations that stand the best chance of tapping into these ideas are those that have good supplier relations and are genuinely open to supplier input. Supplier partnerships work best when they lead to savings in inventories and the ability to plan and stabilize operations.

There are a number of obstacles to supplier partnerships, not the least of which is that because many of the benefits go to the buyer, suppliers may be hesitant to enter into such relationships. Suppliers may have to increase their investment in equipment, which might put a strain on cash flow. Another possibility is that the cultures of the buyer and supplier might be quite different and not lend themselves to such an arrangement.

---

[2]Jim Morgan, "Nine Ways Suppliers Can Improve Competitiveness," *Purchasing*, November 24, 1994, pp. 7–9.

Strategic partnerships are those that convey strategic benefits to one or both partners. One area where this approach has been used is the computer industry, where startup companies such as Dell Computers lacked the resources to design and build computers. Internet companies have also benefited from strategic partnering with established companies. These partnerships allow startup companies, or companies venturing into new fields, to take advantage of the resources and expertise of other companies. The other companies benefit by locking in buyers who have the potential for helping them grow their own businesses.

Summary

The purchasing function in business organizations is becoming increasingly important. Among the reasons are increased levels of outsourcing, increased use of the Internet, greater emphasis on supply chain management, globalization, and continuing efforts to reduce costs and increase quality.

Among purchasing responsibilities are obtaining the materials, parts, supplies, and services needed to produce a product or provide a service. Price, quality, and reliability and speed of delivery are important variables. Purchasing selects suppliers, negotiates contracts, establishes alliances, and acts as liaison between suppliers and various internal departments. It also is involved in value analysis, vendor analysis, make-or-buy analysis, supplier audits, and supplier certification.

In many business organizations there is a move to reduce the number of suppliers and to establish and maintain longer-term relationships with suppliers. Supplier partnerships may involve cooperation that takes the form of sharing of planning and information, and perhaps cooperation in product and process design.

An underlying consideration in purchasing, as in all areas of business, is maintaining ethical standards. The supplement provides a recommended set of ethical practices in purchasing.

Key Terms

centralized purchasing, 533
decentralized purchasing, 533
outsourcing, 531
purchasing cycle, 530
value analysis, 530
vendor analysis, 535

Discussion and Review Questions

1. Explain the importance of the purchasing function in business organizations.
2. Describe what purchasing managers do.
3. Describe how purchasing interacts with two other functional areas of an organization.
4. Describe value analysis. Why is the purchasing department a good location for this task?
5. Discuss centralization versus decentralization in purchasing. What are the advantages of each?
6. Describe vendor analysis.
7. Describe supplier certification and explain why it can be important.
8. Compare viewing suppliers as adversaries with viewing them as partners.
9. What new considerations does purchasing for JIT operations have compared to purchasing for more traditional operations?

Memo Writing Exercises

1. Write a brief memo to your instructor on how your understanding of the purchasing function has been changed by reading this supplement.
2. Write a brief memo to your instructor on why you think that outsourcing has increased in recent years and whether you think the trend will continue.
3. Write a one-page memo to your instructor outlining the advantages of strategic partnering.

Problems

1. Given the following data, determine the total annual cost of making and of buying. Estimated demand is 15,000 units a year.

	Make	Vendor A	Vendor B
Variable cost per unit	$ 8	$11	$ 10
Annual fixed costs	$20,000	$ 0	$5,000 (annual charge)

2. Given the following data, determine the total annual cost of making and of buying. Estimated demand is 10,000 units a year.

	MAKE		Buy
	Process A	Process B	
Variable cost per unit	$ 50	$ 52	$51
Annual fixed costs	$40,000	$36,000	
Transportation cost per unit			$ 2

3. For the previous problem, suppose that the operations manager has said that it would be possible to achieve a 10 percent reduction in the fixed costs of Process B and a five percent reduction in B's variable costs. Would that be enough to change your answer if the estimated annual cost to achieve those savings was $8,000? Explain.

READING

E-Procurement at IBM

www.ibm.com

■■ In 1999, IBM did what would seem to be a near impossible task. It began doing business with 12,000 suppliers over the Internet—sending purchase orders, receiving invoices and paying suppliers, all using the World Wide Web as its transaction-processing network."

Setting up 12,000 suppliers to do business on the Internet was relatively easy compared to the resistance of suppliers to link to IBM via EDI (electronic data interchange). Suppliers who didn't have large contracts with IBM balked at EDI because of the expense of special software and a VAN (value-added network) that were needed to do EDI. No such problem with using the Internet: suppliers don't need special software or a costly VAN to do business with IBM.

The Internet's simplicity reduces costs for IBM and its suppliers. IBM estimated that it saved $500 million in 1999 by moving procurement to the Web, and believes that is only the tip of the iceberg. Much of the savings came from eliminating intermediaries. IBM uses the Web to manage multiple tiers of suppliers and as a tool to work with suppliers to improve quality and reduce costs.

But cost reduction was not the only reason IBM switched to Internet procurement. Web-based procurement is a key part of its supplier management strategy: IBM sees great value in using the Internet to collaborate with suppliers and tap into their expertise much more rapidly than previously. "The Internet will also allow IBM to collaborate with suppliers over scheduling issues. If the company wants to increase production of a certain product it will be able to check with compo-

nent suppliers and determine if suppliers can support the increase. If there are schedule cutbacks, [it] will be able to notify suppliers almost instantaneously and excess inventory can be avoided."

And although supply chains are viewed as sequential, IBM doesn't necessarily want to manage them that way. Rather, it wants to use the Internet to manage multiple tiers of suppliers simultaneously. An example of this is how it deals with CMs (contracts manufacturers). The company sends forecasts and purchase orders to the CMs for the printed circuit boards they supply. It also gives all the component manufacturers the requirements and they ship parts directly to the CM. The company estimates it saved in excess of $150 million in 1999. "The savings were the difference between contract manufacturers' price for components used on the boards and IBM's price that it had negotiated with component suppliers."

Because the Internet is becoming crucial to IBM's supplier-management strategies, IBM is trying to make it easier for suppliers to do business over the Web. The company has developed a Web-based portal to provide a single entry point to IBM. As is the case with most large companies, IBM has multiple interfaces with its suppliers, including engineering, quality, as well as purchasing, and typically suppliers have to connect to separate URLs (Universal Resource Locators) in a company. IBM's portal provides a single point of entry for suppliers, making it easier for suppliers to do business with IBM and increasing the speed of the supply chain. Speed is vitally important in the electronics industry due to very short product life cycles. If products don't get to the market quickly, most of the profit opportunity is lost.

Still another benefit envisioned by IBM will be the ability to form strategic alliances with some of its suppliers. In the past, the fact that many suppliers used by IBM for its production processes were as far as 12,000 miles away made it difficult to build strategic alliances with them. IBM believes that using the Internet will strengthen relations and enable it to develop alliances.

"The Internet also will play an important role in IBM's general procurement . . . IBM was doing EDI with core production suppliers, but not with . . . other forms of general procurement. Purchasers were still faxing and phoning orders, which is timely and costly."

Additional cost savings come from small volume, one-of-a-kind special purchases, because of the speed and ease of using the Internet.

Web-based procurement will eliminate mistakes that occur during the procurement process due to having to type or enter prices and other figures on paper documents.

Questions

1. How did IBM achieve cost reductions by using the Internet for procurement?

2. What advantage did IBM's use of the Internet have for small suppliers?

3. Aside from cost reduction, what major value does IBM envision for its interaction with suppliers?

4. How does use of the Internet for procurement reduce mistakes? Indicate how using the Internet made that benefit possible.

5. How does having a web-based portal help IBM's suppliers?

Source: Based on James Carbone, "E-Procurement at IBM: POs Are Just the Beginning," *Purchasing* 128, no. 4 (March 23, 2000), p. S50.

Selected Bibliography and Further Reading

Fitzgerald, Kevin R. "Purchasing Occupies Key Position in Supply Chains." *Supply Chain Yearbook 2000,* New York: Cahners Business Information, 2000, p. 21.

Hill, Terry. *Manufacturing Strategy: Text and Cases.* New York: McGraw-Hill, 2000.

Leenders, Michael R., and Harold F. Fearon. *Purchasing and Supply Management* 11th ed. New York: Irwin/McGraw-Hill, 1997.

Pooler, Victor H., and David J. Pooler. *Purchasing and Supply Chain Management: Creating the Vision.* New York: Chapman and Hall, 1997.

Schorr, John E. *Purchasing in the 21st Century: A Guide to State-of-the-Art Techniques and Strategies.* Essex Junction, VT: Oliver Wight Companies, 1992.

CHAPTER THIRTEEN
Inventory Management

CHAPTER OUTLINE

Introduction, 542

Newsclip: $$$, 542

The Nature and Importance of
Inventories, 542
    Functions of Inventory, 543
    Objectives of Inventory Control, 544

Requirements for Effective
Inventory Management, 545
    Inventory Counting Systems, 545

Reading: RFID, 547
    Demand Forecasts and Lead-Time
        Information, 547
    Cost Information, 547

Newsclip: Ford Triples Its Billion-
Dollar Cost-Cutting Goal 548
    Classification System, 548

How Much to Order: Economic
Order Quantity Models, 551
    Basic Economic Order Quantity
        (EOQ) Model, 551
    Economic Production Quantity
        (EPQ), 556
    Quantity Discounts, 558

When to Reorder with EOQ
Ordering, 564
    Shortages and Service Levels, 568

How Much to Order: Fixed-Order-
Interval Model, 571
    Reasons to Use the Fixed-Order-
        Interval Model, 571
    Determining the Amount to
        Order, 571
    Benefits and Disadvantages, 574

The Single-Period Model, 574
    Continuous Stocking Levels, 574
    Discrete Stocking Levels, 576

Operations Strategy, 578

Summary, 578

Key Terms, 580

Solved Problems, 580

Discussion and Review
Questions, 585

Memo Writing Exercises, 585

Problems, 585

Cases: UPD Manufacturing, 593
    Harvey Industries, 594
    The Dewey Stapler Company, 595

Operations Tour: Bruegger's Bagel
Bakery, 597

Operations Tour: PSC, Inc., 598

Selected Bibliography and Further
Reading, 601

LEARNING OBJECTIVES

*After completing this chapter, you
should be able to:*

1 Define the term *inventory* and
list the major reasons for hold-
ing inventories.

2 List the main requirements for
effective inventory management.

3 Discuss periodic and perpetual
review systems.

4 Describe the A-B-C approach
and explain how it is useful.

5 Discuss the objectives of inven-
tory management.

6 Describe the basic EOQ model
and its assumptions and solve
typical problems.

7 Describe the economic produc-
tion quantity model and solve
typical problems.

8 Describe the quantity discount
model and solve typical
problems.

9 Describe reorder point models
and solve typical problems.

10 Describe situations in which the
single-period model would be
appropriate, and solve typical
problems.

Good inventory management is important for the successful operation of most businesses and their supply chains. Operations, marketing, and finance have interests in good inventory management. Poor inventory management hampers operations, diminishes customer satisfaction, and increases operating costs.

Some organizations have excellent inventory management and many have satisfactory inventory management. Too many, however, have unsatisfactory inventory management, which sometimes is a sign that management does not recognize the importance of inventories. More often than not, though, the recognition is there. What is lacking is an understanding of what needs to be done and how to do it. This chapter presents the concepts that underlie good inventory management.

This chapter also describes management of finished goods, raw materials, purchased parts, and retail items. Topics include functions of inventories, requirements for effective inventory management, objectives of inventory control, and techniques for determining *how much* to order and *when* to order. Emphasis is on inventory analysis.

Introduction

inventory A stock or store of goods.

An **inventory** is a stock or store of goods. Firms typically stock hundreds or even thousands of items in inventory, ranging from small things such as pencils, paper clips, screws, nuts, and bolts to large items such as machines, trucks, construction equipment, and airplanes. Naturally, many of the items a firm carries in inventory relate to the kind of business it engages in. Thus, manufacturing firms carry supplies of raw materials, purchased parts, partially finished items, and finished goods, as well as spare parts for machines, tools, and other supplies. Department stores carry clothing, furniture, carpeting, stationery, appliances, gifts, cards, and toys. Some also stock sporting goods, paints, and tools. Hospitals stock drugs, surgical supplies, life-monitoring equipment, sheets and pillow cases, and more. Supermarkets stock fresh and canned foods, packaged and frozen foods, household supplies, magazines, baked goods, dairy products, produce, and other items.

NEWSCLIP

$$$

We proceed as follows. First look for a five-by-five-by-three-foot bin of gears or parts that looks like it has been there awhile. Pick up a gear and ask, casually, "How much is this worth?" You then ask, "How many of these are in the bin?" followed by, "How long has this bin been here?" and, "What's your cost of money for this company?" I recall one case in a nameless South American country where the unit cost times the number of parts times the time it had been there times the interest rate resulted in a cost-per-day figure that would insure comfortable retirement for the plant manager on the bank of the Rio de la Plata at one of the better resorts to be found there. The plant manager suddenly realized that what he

was holding was not just a chunk of high-test steel, but was *real money*. He then pointed out that *he* now understood the value of the inventory but could I suggest a way to drive the point home to upper management? I suggested that he go to the accounting department and borrow enough money to be equal to the bin's value for as long as it had been sitting there, and pile it on the top of the bin. I further suggested that he do that for every bin on the production line. We rapidly figured out that by the time we had the money piled up on the bin, you would not even be able to *see* the bin. My opinion was that if the upper managers were given a tour of the line with the money piled up, they would *never* forget it.

Source: Gene Woolsey, "On Doing Good Things and Dumb Things in Production and Inventory Control," *Interfaces* 5, no. 3 (May 1975). Copyright 1975, The Institute of Management Science. Reprinted by permission.

The Nature and Importance of Inventories

Inventories are a vital part of business. Not only are they necessary for operations, but also they contribute to customer satisfaction. To get a sense of the significance of inventories, consider the following: Although the amounts and dollar values of inventories carried by different types of firms varies widely, a typical firm probably has about 30 percent of its current assets and perhaps as much as 90 percent of its working capital invested in inventory. One widely used measure of managerial performance relates to *return on investment* (ROI), which is profit after taxes divided by total assets. Because inventories may represent a significant portion of total assets, a reduction of inventories can result in a significant increase in ROI.

The major source of revenues for retail and wholesale businesses is the sale of merchandise (i.e., inventory). In fact, in terms of dollars, the inventory of goods held for sale is one of the largest assets of a merchandising business.

A typical manufacturing firm carries different kinds of inventories, including the following:

Raw materials and purchased parts.

Partially completed goods, called *work-in-process* (WIP).

Finished-goods inventories (manufacturing firms) or merchandise (retail stores).

Replacement parts, tools, and supplies.

Goods-in-transit to warehouses or customers (pipeline inventory).

Service firms do not carry these kinds of inventories, although they do carry inventories of supplies and equipment. To understand why firms have inventories at all, you need to be aware of the various functions of inventory.

FUNCTIONS OF INVENTORY

Inventories serve a number of functions. Among the most important are the following:

1. To meet anticipated demand.
2. To smooth production requirements.
3. To decouple components of the production–distribution system.
4. To protect against stockouts.
5. To take advantage of order cycles.
6. To hedge against price increases or to take advantage of quantity discounts.
7. To permit operations.

Let's take a look at each of these.

1. *To meet anticipated customer demand.* A customer can be a person who walks in off the street to buy a new stereo system, a mechanic who requests a tool at a tool crib, or a manufacturing operation. These inventories are referred to as *anticipation stocks* because they are held to satisfy expected (i.e., *average*) demand.

2. *To smooth production requirements.* Firms that experience seasonal patterns in demand often build up inventories during off-season periods to meet overly high requirements during certain seasonal periods. These inventories are aptly named *seasonal inventories.* Companies that process fresh fruits and vegetables deal with seasonal inventories. So do stores that sell greeting cards, skis, snowmobiles, or Christmas trees.

3. *To decouple operations.* Historically, manufacturing firms have used inventories as buffers between successive operations to maintain continuity of production that would otherwise be disrupted by events such as breakdowns of equipment and accidents that cause a portion of the operation to shut down temporarily. The buffers permit other operations to continue temporarily while the problem is resolved. Similarly, firms have used buffers of raw materials to insulate production from disruptions in deliveries from suppliers, and finished goods inventory to buffer sales operations from manufacturing disruptions. More recently, companies have taken a closer look at buffer inventories, recognizing the cost and space they require, and realizing that finding and eliminating sources of disruptions can greatly decrease the need for decoupling operations.

4. *To protect against stockouts.* Delayed deliveries and unexpected increases in demand increase the risk of shortages. Delays can occur because of weather conditions, supplier stockouts, deliveries of wrong materials, quality problems, and so on. The risk of shortages can be reduced by holding *safety stocks,* which are stocks in excess of average demand to compensate for *variabilities* in demand and lead time.

5. *To take advantage of order cycles.* To minimize purchasing and inventory costs, a firm often buys in quantities that exceed immediate requirements. This necessitates storing some or all of the purchased amount for later use. Similarly, it is usually economical to produce in large rather than small quantities. Again, the excess output must be stored for later use. Thus, inventory storage enables a firm to buy and produce in *economic lot sizes* without having to try to match purchases or production with demand requirements in the short run. This results in *periodic* orders, or order *cycles.* The resulting stock is known as *cycle stock.* Order cycles are not always based on economic lot sizes. In some instances, it is practical or economical to group orders and/or to order at fixed intervals.

6. *To hedge against price increases.* Occasionally a firm will suspect that a substantial price increase is about to be made and purchase larger-than-normal amounts to avoid the increase. The ability to store extra goods also allows a firm to take advantage of price discounts for larger orders.

7. *To permit operations.* The fact that production operations take a certain amount of time (i.e., they are not instantaneous) means that there will generally be some work-in-process inventory. In addition, intermediate stocking of goods—including raw materials, semifinished items, and finished goods at production sites, as well as goods stored in warehouses—leads to *pipeline* inventories throughout a production-distribution system.

OBJECTIVES OF INVENTORY CONTROL

Inadequate control of inventories can result in both under- and overstocking of items. Understocking results in missed deliveries, lost sales, dissatisfied customers, and production bottlenecks; overstocking unnecessarily ties up funds that might be more productive elsewhere. Although overstocking may appear to be the lesser of the two evils, the price tag for excessive overstocking can be staggering when inventory holding costs are high—as illustrated by the little story about the bin of gears at the beginning of the chapter—and matters can easily get out of hand. It is not unheard of for managers to discover that their firm has a 10-year supply of some item. (No doubt the firm got a good buy on it!)

Inventory management has two main concerns. One is the *level of customer service,* that is, to have the right goods, in sufficient quantities, in the right place, at the right time. The other is the *costs of ordering and carrying inventories.*

The overall objective of inventory management is to achieve satisfactory levels of customer service while keeping inventory costs within reasonable bounds. Toward this end, the decision maker tries to achieve a balance in stocking. He or she must make two fundamental decisions: the *timing* and *size* of orders (i.e., when to order and how much to order). The greater part of this chapter is devoted to models that can be applied to assist in making those decisions.

Managers have a number of measures of performance they can use to judge the effectiveness of inventory management. The most obvious, of course, is customer satisfaction, which they might measure by the number and quantity of backorders and/or customer complaints. A widely used measure is **inventory turnover**, which is the ratio of annual cost of goods sold to average inventory investment. The turnover ratio indicates how many times a year the inventory is sold. Generally, the higher the ratio, the better, because that implies more efficient use of inventories. A benefit of this measure is that it can be used to compare companies of different size in the *same* industry. Another useful measure is days of inventory on hand, a number that indicates the expected number of days of sales that can be supplied from existing inventory. Here, a balance is desirable; a high number of days might imply excess inventory, while a low number might imply a risk of running out of stock.

inventory turnover Ratio of average cost of goods sold to average inventory investment.

Requirements for Effective Inventory Management

Management has two basic functions concerning inventory. One is to establish a system of keeping track of items in inventory, and the other is to make decisions about how much and when to order. To be effective, management must have the following:

1. A system to *keep track of the inventory* on hand and on order.
2. A reliable *forecast of demand* that includes an indication of possible *forecast error.*
3. Knowledge of *lead times* and *lead time variability.*
4. Reasonable estimates of inventory *holding costs, ordering costs,* and *shortage costs.*
5. A *classification system* for inventory items.

Let's take a closer look at each of these requirements.

INVENTORY COUNTING SYSTEMS

Inventory counting systems can be periodic or perpetual. Under a **periodic system,** a physical count of items in inventory is made at periodic intervals (e.g., weekly, monthly) in order to decide how much to order of each item. Many small retailers use this approach: A manager periodically checks the shelves and stockroom to determine the quantity on hand. Then the manager estimates how much will be demanded prior to the next delivery period and bases the order quantity on that information. An advantage of this type of system is that orders for many items occur at the same time, which can result in economies in processing and shipping orders. There are also several disadvantages of periodic reviews. One is a lack of control between reviews. Another is the need to protect against shortages between review periods by carrying extra stock.

A **perpetual inventory system** (also known as a *continual* system) keeps track of removals from inventory on a continuous basis, so the system can provide information on the current level of inventory for each item. When the amount on hand reaches a predetermined minimum, a fixed quantity, Q, is ordered. An obvious advantage of this system is the control provided by the continuous monitoring of inventory withdrawals. Another advantage is the fixed-order quantity; management can determine an optimal order quantity. One disadvantage of this approach is the added cost of record keeping. Moreover, a physical count of inventories must still be performed periodically to verify records

periodic system Physical count of items in inventory made at periodic intervals (weekly, monthly).

perpetual inventory system System that keeps track of removals from inventory continuously, thus monitoring current levels of each item.

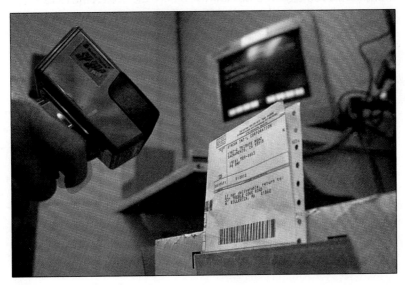

A DuPont Merck employee uses a bar code scanner to quickly and accurately record pharmaceutical supply inventory at the Billerica, Massachusetts location. This particular product will be used for diagnostic imaging of heart patients.

because of errors, pilferage, spoilage, and other factors that can reduce the effective amount of inventory. Bank transactions such as customer deposits and withdrawals are examples of continuous recording of inventory changes.

Perpetual systems range from very simple to very sophisticated. A **two-bin system,** a very elementary system, uses two containers for inventory. Items are withdrawn from the first bin until its contents are exhausted. It is then time to reorder. Sometimes an order card is placed at the bottom of the first bin. The second bin contains enough stock to satisfy expected demand until the order is filled, plus an extra cushion of stock that will reduce the chance of a stockout if the order is late or if usage is greater than expected. The advantage of this system is that there is no need to record each withdrawal from inventory; the disadvantage is that the reorder card may not be turned in for a variety of reasons (e.g., misplaced, the person responsible forgets to turn it in).

Perpetual systems can be either *batch* or *on-line*. In batch systems, inventory records are collected periodically and entered into the system. In on-line systems, the transactions are recorded immediately. The advantage of on-line systems is that they are always up-to-date. In batch systems, a sudden surge in demand could result in reducing the amount of inventory below the reorder point between the periodic read-ins. Frequent batch collections can minimize that problem.

Supermarkets, discount stores, and department stores have always been major users of periodic counting systems. Today, most have switched to computerized checkout systems using a laser scanning device that reads a **universal product code** (UPC), or *bar code,* printed on an item tag or on packaging. A typical grocery product code is illustrated here.

> **two-bin system** Two containers of inventory; reorder when the first is empty.

> **universal product code** Bar code printed on a label that has information about the item to which it is attached.

The zero on the left of the bar code identifies this as a grocery item, the first five numbers (14800) indicate the manufacturer (Mott's), and the last five numbers (23208) indicate the specific item (natural-style applesauce). Items in small packages, such as candy and gum, use a six-digit number.

UPC scanners represent a major change in the inventory systems of stores that use them. In addition to their increase in speed and accuracy, these systems give managers continuous information on inventories, reduce the need for periodic inventories and order-size determinations, and improve the level of customer service by indicating the price and quantity of each item on the customer's receipt, as illustrated below.

```
BRACO CAPELLINI           .79
BUB YUM DBL LIME          .30 T
2/LO FAT MILK H G        1.03
EUROP ROLLS               .91
HUNTS TOMATO              .55
NEWSPAPER                 .35
KR CAS BRICK CHEES       1.59
GRAPES-GREEN
  .91 LB @ .89 PER LB     .81
TAX DUE                   .02
TOTAL                    6.35

CASH                    20.00*
CHANGE                  13.65

8/07/98 18:01 21  16  23100  2570
```

Bar coding represents an important development for other sectors of business besides retailing. Manufacturing and service industries also benefit from the simplified production and inventory control it provides. In manufacturing, bar codes attached to parts, subassemblies, and finished goods greatly facilitate counting and monitoring activities. Automatic routing, scheduling, sorting, and packaging can also be done using bar codes.

READING

RFID

Radio frequency identification (RFID) is a relatively new automatic identification and data capture (AIDC) technology, first appearing in tracking and access applications during the 1980s. These wireless AIDC systems allow for non-contact reading and consequently are effective in manufacturing and other hostile environments where barcode labels could not survive. RFID has established itself in a wide range of markets including livestock identification and automated vehicle identification (AVI) systems because of its ability to track moving objects. The technology has become a primary player in automated data collection, identification, and analysis systems worldwide.

The significant advantage of all types of RFID systems is the non-contact, non–line-of-sight nature of the technology. Tags can be read through a variety of substances such as snow, fog, ice, paint, crusted grime, and other visually and environmentally challenging conditions where barcodes or other optically read technologies would be useless. RFID tags can also be read in challenging circumstances at remarkable speeds, in most cases responding in less than 100 milliseconds. The read/write capability of an active RFID system is also a significant advantage in interactive applications such as work-in-process or maintenance tracking. Though it is a costlier technology compared with barcode, RFID has become indispensable for a wide range of automated data collection and identification applications that would not be possible otherwise.

Source: http://AIMGLOBAL.org/technologies/rfid/. Aim, Inc. 634 Alpha Drive, Pittsburgh, PA 15238-2802.

DEMAND FORECASTS AND LEAD-TIME INFORMATION

Inventories are used to satisfy demand requirements, so it is essential to have reliable estimates of the amount and timing of demand. Similarly, it is essential to know how long it will take for orders to be delivered. In addition, managers need to know the extent to which demand and **lead time** (the time between submitting an order and receiving it) might vary; the greater the potential variability, the greater the need for additional stock to reduce the risk of a shortage between deliveries. Thus, there is a crucial link between forecasting and inventory management.

lead time Time interval between ordering and receiving the order.

Point-of sale (POS) systems electronically record actual sales. Knowledge of actual sales can greatly enhance forecasting and inventory management: By relaying information about actual demand in real time, these systems enable management to make any necessary changes to restocking decisions. These systems are being increasingly emphasized as an important input to effective supply chain management by making this information available to suppliers.

point-of-sale (POS) system Method for electronically tracking sales and inventory.

COST INFORMATION

Three basic costs are associated with inventories: holding, transaction (ordering), and shortage costs.

Holding or **carrying costs** relate to physically having items in storage. Costs include interest, insurance, taxes (in some states), depreciation, obsolescence, deterioration, spoilage, pilferage, breakage, and warehousing costs (heat, light, rent, security). They also include opportunity costs associated with having funds which could be used elsewhere tied up in inventory. Note that it is the *variable* portion of these costs that is pertinent.

holding (carrying) cost Cost to carry an item in inventory for a length of time, usually a year.

The significance of the various components of holding cost depends on the type of item involved, although taxes, interest, and insurance are generally based on the dollar value of an inventory. Items that are easily concealed (e.g., pocket cameras, transistor radios, calculators) or fairly expensive (cars, TVs) are prone to theft. Fresh seafood, meats and poultry, produce, and baked goods are subject to rapid deterioration and spoilage. Dairy products, salad dressings, medicines, batteries, and film also have limited shelf lives.

Holding costs are stated in either of two ways: as a percentage of unit price or as a dollar amount per unit. In any case, typical annual holding costs range from 20 percent to 40 percent of the value of an item. In other words, to hold a $100 item for one year could cost from $20 to $40.

ordering costs Costs of ordering and receiving inventory.

Ordering costs are the costs of ordering and receiving inventory. They are the costs that vary with the actual placement of an order. These include determining how much is needed, preparing invoices, shipping costs, inspecting goods upon arrival for quality and quantity, and moving the goods to temporary storage. Ordering costs are generally expressed as a fixed dollar amount per order, regardless of order size.

When a firm produces its own inventory instead of ordering it from a supplier, the costs of machine setup (e.g., preparing equipment for the job by adjusting the machine, changing cutting tools) are analogous to ordering costs; that is, they are expressed as a fixed charge per production run, regardless of the size of the run.

shortage costs Costs resulting when demand exceeds the supply of inventory on hand; often unrealized profit per unit.

Shortage costs result when demand exceeds the supply of inventory on hand. These costs can include the opportunity cost of not making a sale, loss of customer goodwill, late charges, and similar costs. Furthermore, if the shortage occurs in an item carried for internal use (e.g., to supply an assembly line), the cost of lost production or downtime is considered a shortage cost. Such costs can easily run into hundreds of dollars a minute or more. Shortage costs are sometimes difficult to measure, and they may be subjectively estimated.

NEWSCLIP

Ford Triples its Billion-Dollar Cost-Cutting Goal

www.ford.com

The Ford Motor Company exceeded its original goal of cutting out $1 billion in costs in 1997. One major chunk of savings was the result of worker suggestions; in one case teams from two assembly plants visited each others' plants and offered suggestions on ways to improve production. Another major chunk came from the use of standard parts—using the same parts in different models. Not only did this reduce design and assembly costs, it reduced the number of different parts carried in inventory, and simplified record keeping. At the same time, it increased production flexibility. Beyond that, standard parts help lessen the chance of experiencing out-of-stock incidents, which can result in costly shutdowns at assembly plants; and standard parts mean dealers don't have to carry as many different replacement parts.

Source: Based in part on "Ford Triples Its Billion-Dollar Cost-Cutting Goal," Micheline Maynard, *USA TODAY,* December 15, 1997, p. 1B.

CLASSIFICATION SYSTEM

An important aspect of inventory management is that items held in inventory are not of equal importance in terms of dollars invested, profit potential, sales or usage volume, or stockout penalties. For instance, a producer of electrical equipment might have electric generators, coils of wire, and miscellaneous nuts and bolts among the items carried in inventory. It would be unrealistic to devote equal attention to each of these items. Instead, a more reasonable approach would be to allocate control efforts according to the *relative importance* of various items in inventory.

A-B-C approach Classifying inventory according to some measure of importance, and allocating control efforts accordingly.

The **A-B-C approach** classifies inventory items according to some measure of importance, usually annual dollar usage (i.e., dollar value per unit multiplied by annual usage rate), and then allocates control efforts accordingly. Typically, three classes of items are used: A (very important), B (moderately important), and C (least important). However, the actual number of categories may vary from organization to organization, depending

A gas lineman for a public works company is processing data on a worksite in Ventura, California. Entering and processing data on-site allows for more accurate, up-to-date records of costs as well as inventory for repairs and replacement of gas lines.

on the extent to which a firm wants to differentiate control efforts. With three classes of items, A items generally account for about 15 to 20 percent of the *number* of items in inventory but about 60 to 70 percent of the *dollar usage.* At the other end of the scale, C items might account for about 60 percent of the number of items but only about 10 percent of the dollar usage of an inventory. These percentages vary from firm to firm, but in most instances a relatively small number of items will account for a large share of the value or cost associated with an inventory, and these items should receive a relatively greater share of control efforts. For instance, A items should receive close attention through frequent reviews of amounts on hand and control over withdrawals, where possible, to make sure that customer service levels are attained. The C items should receive only loose control (two-bin system, bulk orders), and the B items should have controls that lie between the two extremes.

Note that C items are not necessarily *un*important; incurring a stockout of C items such as the nuts and bolts used to assemble manufactured goods can result in a costly shutdown of an assembly line. However, due to the low annual dollar volume of C items, there may not be much additional cost incurred by ordering larger quantities of some items, or ordering them a bit earlier.

Classify the inventory items as A, B, or C based on annual dollar value, given the following information:

Example 1

Item	Annual Demand	×	Unit Cost	=	Annual Dollar Value
1	1,000		$4,300		$4,300,000
2	5,000		720		3,600,000
3	1,900		500		950,000
4	1,000		710		710,000
5	2,500		250		625,000
6	2,500		192		480,000
7	400		200		80,000
8	500		100		50,000
9	200		210		42,000
10	1,000		35		35,000
11	3,000		10		30,000
12	9,000		3		27,000

Solution

The first two items have a relatively high annual dollar value, so it seems reasonable to classify them as A items. The next four items appear to have moderate annual dollar values and should be classified as B items. The remainder are C items, based on their relatively low dollar value.

Although annual dollar volume may be the primary factor in classifying inventory items, a manager may take other factors into account in making exceptions for certain items (e.g., changing the classification of a C item to an A item). Factors may include the risk of obsolescence, the risk of a stockout, the distance of a supplier, and so on.

Figure 13–1 illustrates the A-B-C concept.

Managers use the A-B-C concept in many different settings to improve operations. One key use occurs in customer service, where a manager can focus attention on the most important aspects of customer service by categorizing different aspects as very important, important, or of only minor importance. The point is to not overemphasize minor aspects of customer service at the expense of major aspects.

Another application of the A-B-C concept is as a guide to **cycle counting,** which is a physical count of items in inventory. The purpose of cycle counting is to reduce discrepancies between the amounts indicated by inventory records and the actual quantities of inventory on hand. Accuracy is important because inaccurate records can lead to disruptions in production, poor customer service, and unnecessarily high inventory carrying costs.

cycle counting A physical count of items in inventory.

The key questions concerning cycle counting for management are:

1. How much accuracy is needed?
2. When should cycle counting be performed?
3. Who should do it?

www.apics~stlouis.com

APICS, formerly known as the American Production and Inventory Control Society, recommends the following guidelines for inventory record accuracy: ± 0.2 percent for A items, ± 1 percent for B items, and ± 5 percent for C items.

Some companies use certain events to trigger cycle counting, whereas others do it on a periodic (scheduled) basis. Events that can trigger a physical count of inventory include an out-of-stock report written on an item indicated by inventory records to be in stock, an inventory report that indicates a low or zero balance of an item, and a specified level of activity (e.g., every 2,000 units sold).

Some companies use regular stockroom personnel to do cycle counting during periods of slow activity while others contract with outside firms to do it on a periodic basis. Use of an outside firm provides an independent check on inventory and may reduce the risk of problems created by dishonest employees. Still other firms maintain full-time personnel to do cycle counting.

FIGURE 13-1

A typical A-B-C breakdown in relative annual dollar value of items and number of items by category

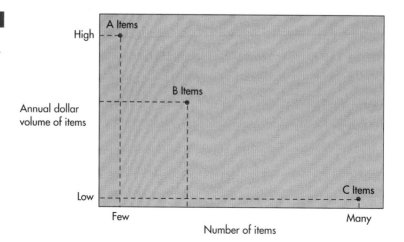

How Much to Order: Economic Order Quantity Models

The question of how much to order is frequently determined by using an **economic order quantity (EOQ)** model. EOQ models identify the optimal order quantity by minimizing the sum of certain annual costs that vary with order size. Three order size models are described here:

1. The basic economic order quantity model.
2. The economic production quantity model.
3. The quantity discount model.

BASIC ECONOMIC ORDER QUANTITY (EOQ) MODEL

The basic EOQ model is the simplest of the three models. It is used to identify the order size that will minimize the sum of the annual costs of holding inventory and ordering inventory. The unit purchase price of items in inventory is not generally included in the total cost because the unit cost is unaffected by the order size unless quantity discounts are a factor. If holding costs are specified as a percentage of unit cost, then unit cost is indirectly included in the total cost as a part of holding costs.

The basic model involves a number of assumptions. They are listed in Table 13–1.

Inventory ordering and usage occur in cycles. Figure 13–2 illustrates several inventory cycles. A cycle begins with receipt of an order of Q units, which are withdrawn at a constant rate over time. When the quantity on hand is just sufficient to satisfy demand during lead time, an order for Q units is submitted to the supplier. Because it is assumed that both the usage rate and the lead time do not vary, the order will be received at the precise instant that the inventory on hand falls to zero. Thus, orders are timed to avoid both excess stock and stockouts (i.e., running out of stock).

The optimal order quantity reflects a trade-off between carrying costs and ordering costs: As order size varies, one type of cost will increase while the other decreases. For example, if the order size is relatively small, the average inventory will be low, resulting in low carrying costs. However, a small order size will necessitate frequent orders, which will

economic order quantity (EOQ) The order size that minimizes total cost.

Finished goods inventory.

Parts inventory.

TABLE 13-1

Assumptions of the basic EOQ model

1. Only one product is involved.
2. Annual demand requirements are known.
3. Demand is spread evenly throughout the year so that the demand rate is reasonably constant.
4. Lead time does not vary.
5. Each order is received in a single delivery.
6. There are no quantity discounts.

FIGURE 13-2

The inventory cycle: profile of inventory level over time

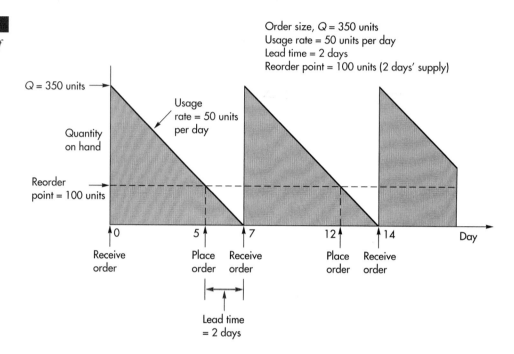

drive up annual ordering costs. Conversely, ordering large quantities at infrequent intervals can hold down annual ordering costs, but that would result in higher average inventory levels and therefore increased carrying costs. Figure 13–3 illustrates these two extremes.

Thus, the ideal solution is an order size that causes neither a few very large orders nor many small orders, but one that lies somewhere between. The exact amount to order will depend on the relative magnitudes of carrying and ordering costs.

Annual carrying cost is computed by multiplying the average amount of inventory on hand by the cost to carry one unit for one year, even though any given unit would not necessarily be held for a year. The average inventory is simply half of the order quantity: The amount on hand decreases steadily from Q units to 0, for an average of $(Q + 0)/2$, or $Q/2$. Using the symbol H to represent the average annual carrying cost per unit, the *total annual carrying cost* is

$$\text{Annual carrying cost} = \frac{Q}{2}H$$

where

Q = Order quantity in units

H = holding (carrying) cost per unit

Carrying cost is thus a linear function of Q: Carrying costs increase or decrease in direct proportion to changes in the order quantity Q, as Figure 13–4A illustrates.

On the other hand, annual ordering cost will decrease as order size increases because for a given annual demand, the larger the order size, the fewer the number of orders

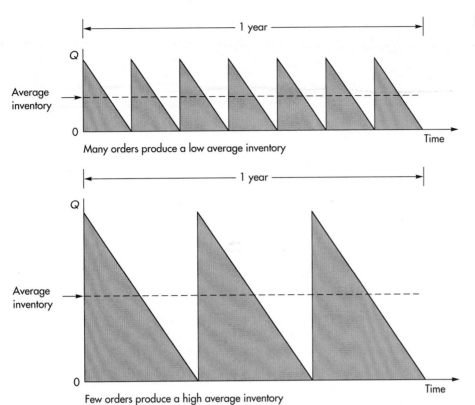

Average inventory

Many orders produce a low average inventory

Average inventory

Few orders produce a high average inventory

FIGURE 13-3

Average inventory level and number of orders per year are inversely related: as one increases, the other decreases

A. Carrying costs are linearly related to order size.

B. Ordering costs are inversely and nonlinearly related to order size.

C. The total-cost curve is U-shaped.

FIGURE 13-4

Carrying cost, ordering cost, and total cost curve

needed. For instance, if annual demand is 12,000 units and the order size is 1,000 units per order, there must be 12 orders over the year. But if $Q = 2,000$ units, only six orders will be needed; if $Q = 3,000$ units, only four orders will be needed. In general, the number of orders per year will be D/Q, where $D =$ Annual demand and $Q =$ Order size. Unlike carrying costs, ordering costs are relatively insensitive to order size; regardless of the amount of an order, certain activities must be done, such as determine how much is needed, periodically evaluate sources of supply, and prepare the invoice. Even inspection of the shipment to verify quality and quantity characteristics is not strongly influenced by order size since large shipments are sampled rather than completely inspected. Hence, there is a fixed ordering cost. *Annual ordering cost* is a function of the number of orders per year and the ordering cost per order:

$$\text{Annual ordering cost} = \frac{D}{Q} S$$

where

$D =$ Demand, usually in units per year

$S =$ Ordering cost

Because the number of orders per year, D/Q, decreases as Q increases, annual ordering cost is inversely related to order size, as Figure 13–4B illustrates.

The total annual cost associated with carrying and ordering inventory when Q units are ordered each time is

$$\text{TC} = \begin{matrix}\text{Annual}\\\text{carrying}\\\text{cost}\end{matrix} + \begin{matrix}\text{Annual}\\\text{ordering}\\\text{cost}\end{matrix} = \frac{Q}{2} H + \frac{D}{Q} S \qquad (13\text{–}1)$$

(Note that D and H must be in the same units, e.g., months, years). Figure 13–4C reveals that the total-cost curve is U-shaped (i.e., convex, with one minimum) and that *it reaches its minimum at the quantity where carrying and ordering costs are equal.* An expression for the optimal order quantity, Q_0, can be obtained using calculus.[1] The result is the formula

$$Q_0 = \sqrt{\frac{2DS}{H}} \qquad (13\text{–}2)$$

Thus, given annual demand, the ordering cost per order, and the annual carrying cost per unit, one can compute the optimal (economic) order quantity. The minimum total cost is then found by substituting Q_0 for Q in Formula 13–1.

The length of an order cycle (i.e., the time between orders) is

$$\text{Length of order cycle} = \frac{Q_0}{D} \qquad (13\text{–}3)$$

Example 2

A local distributor for a national tire company expects to sell approximately 9,600 steel-belted radial tires of a certain size and tread design next year. Annual carrying cost is $16 per tire, and ordering cost is $75. The distributor operates 288 days a year.

---

[1]We can find the minimum point of the total-cost curve by differentiating TC with respect to Q, setting the result equal to zero, and solving for Q. Thus,

1. $\dfrac{d\text{TC}}{dQ} = \dfrac{dQ}{2} H + d(D/Q)S = H/2 - DS/Q^2$

2. $0 = H/2 - DS/Q^2$, so $Q^2 = \dfrac{2DS}{H}$ and $Q = \sqrt{\dfrac{2DS}{H}}$

Note that the second derivative is positive, which indicates a minimum has been obtained.

a. What is the EOQ?

b. How many times per year does the store reorder?

c. What is the length of an order cycle?

d. What is the total annual cost if the EOQ quantity is ordered?

Solution

$D = 9,600$ tires per year

$H = \$16$ per unit per year

$S = \$75$

a. $Q_0 = \sqrt{\dfrac{2DS}{H}} = \sqrt{\dfrac{2(9,600)75}{16}} = 300$ tires

b. Number of orders per year: $D/Q_0 = \dfrac{9,600 \text{ tires}}{300 \text{ tires}} = 32.$

c. Length of order cycle: $Q_0/D = \dfrac{300 \text{ tires}}{9,600 \text{ tires/yr}} = \frac{1}{32}$ of a year, which is $\frac{1}{32} \times 288$, or nine workdays.

d. TC = Carrying cost + Ordering cost

$\quad = (Q_0/2)H + (D/Q_0)S$

$\quad = (300/2)16 + (9,600/300)75$

$\quad = \$2,400 + \$2,400$

$\quad = \$4,800.$

Note that the ordering and carrying costs are equal at the EOQ, as illustrated in Figure 13–4C.

Carrying cost is sometimes stated as a percentage of the purchase price of an item rather than as a dollar amount per unit. However, as long as the percentage is converted into a dollar amount, the EOQ formula is still appropriate.

Piddling Manufacturing assembles security monitors. It purchases 3,600 black-and-white cathode ray tubes a year at $65 each. Ordering costs are $31, and annual carrying costs are 20 percent of the purchase price. Compute the optimal quantity and the total annual cost of ordering and carrying the inventory.

Example 3

Solution

$D = 3,600$ cathode ray tubes per year

$S = \$31$

$H = .20(\$65) = \$13$

$Q_0 = \sqrt{\dfrac{2DS}{H}} = \sqrt{\dfrac{2(3,600)(31)}{13}} = 131$ cathode ray tubes

TC = Carrying costs + Ordering costs

$\quad = \quad (Q_0/2)H \quad + \quad (D/Q_0)S$

$\quad = \quad (131/2)13 \quad + \quad (3,600/131)31$

$\quad = \quad\quad \$852 \quad\quad + \quad\quad \$852 \quad\quad = \$1,704$

FIGURE 13-5

The total-cost curve is relatively flat near the EOQ

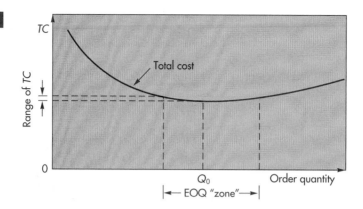

Comment. Holding and ordering costs, and annual demand, are typically estimated values rather than values that can be precisely determined, say, from accounting records. Holding costs are sometimes *designated* rather than computed by managers. Consequently, the EOQ should be regarded as an *approximate* quantity rather than an exact quantity. Thus, rounding the calculated value is perfectly acceptable; stating a value to several decimal places would tend to give an unrealistic impression of the precision involved. An obvious question is: How good is this "approximate" EOQ in terms of minimizing cost? The answer is that the EOQ is fairly robust; the total cost curve is relatively flat near the EOQ, especially to the right of the EOQ. In other words, even if the resulting EOQ differs from the actual EOQ, total costs will not increase much at all. This is particularly true for quantities larger than the real EOQ, because the total cost curve rises very slowly to the right of the EOQ. (See Figure 13–5.)

ECONOMIC PRODUCTION QUANTITY (EPQ)

The batch mode of production is widely used in production. Even in assembly operations, portions of the work are done in batches. The reason for this is that in certain instances, the capacity to produce a part exceeds the part's usage or demand rate. As long as production continues, inventory will continue to grow. In such instances, it makes sense to periodically produce such items in batches, or *lots.*

The assumptions of the EPQ model are similar to those of the EOQ model, except that instead of orders received in a single delivery, units are received incrementally during production. The assumptions are:

1. Only one item is involved.
2. Annual demand is known.
3. The usage rate is constant.
4. Usage occurs continually, but production occurs periodically.
5. The production rate is constant.
6. Lead time does not vary.
7. There are no quantity discounts.

Figure 13–6 illustrates how inventory is affected by periodically producing a batch of a particular item.

During the production phase of the cycle, inventory builds up at a rate equal to the difference between production and usage rates. For example, if the daily production rate is 20 units and the daily usage rate is 5 units, inventory will build up at the rate of 20 − 5 = 15 units per day. As long as production occurs, the inventory level will continue to build; when production ceases, the inventory level will begin to decrease. Hence, the inventory level will be maximum at the point where production ceases. When the amount of inventory on hand is exhausted, production is resumed, and the cycle repeats itself.

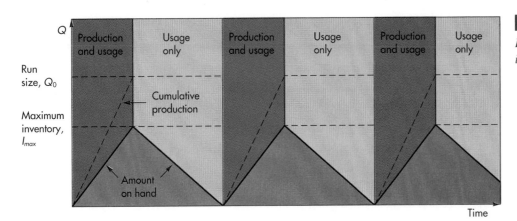

FIGURE 13-6

EOQ with incremental inventory replenishment

Because the company makes the product itself, there are no ordering costs as such. Nonetheless, with every production run (batch) there are setup costs—the costs required to prepare the equipment for the job, such as cleaning, adjusting, and changing tools and fixtures. Setup costs are analogous to ordering costs because they are independent of the lot (run) size. They are treated in the formula in exactly the same way. The larger the run size, the fewer the number of runs needed and, hence, the lower the annual setup cost. The number of runs or batches is D/Q, and the annual setup cost is equal to the number of runs per year times the setup cost per run: $(D/Q)S$.

Total cost is

$$TC_{min} = \text{Carrying cost} + \text{Setup cost} = \left(\frac{I_{max}}{2}\right)H + (D/Q_0)S \qquad (13\text{--}4)$$

where

I_{max} = Maximum inventory

The economic run quantity is

$$Q_0 = \sqrt{\frac{2DS}{H}}\sqrt{\frac{p}{p-u}} \qquad (13\text{--}5)$$

where

p = Production or delivery rate

u = Usage rate

The cycle time (the time between orders or between the beginnings of runs) for the economic run size model is a function of the run size and usage (demand) rate:

$$\text{Cycle time} = \frac{Q_0}{u} \qquad (13\text{--}6)$$

Similarly, the run time (the production phase of the cycle) is a function of the run size and the production rate:

$$\text{Run time} = \frac{Q_0}{p} \qquad (13\text{--}7)$$

The maximum and average inventory levels are

$$I_{max} = \frac{Q_0}{p}(p-u) \quad \text{and} \quad I_{average} = \frac{I_{max}}{2} \qquad (13\text{--}8)$$

Example 4

A toy manufacturer uses 48,000 rubber wheels per year for its popular dump truck series. The firm makes its own wheels, which it can produce at a rate of 800 per day. The toy trucks are assembled uniformly over the entire year. Carrying cost is $1 per wheel a year. Setup cost for a production run of wheels is $45. The firm operates 240 days per year. Determine the:

a. Optimal run size
b. Minimum total annual cost for carrying and setup
c. Cycle time for the optimal run size
d. Run time

Solution

$D = 48,000$ wheels per year

$S = \$45$

$H = \$1$ per wheel per year

$p = 800$ wheels per day

$u = 48,000$ wheels per 240 days, or 200 wheels per day

a. $Q_0 = \sqrt{\dfrac{2DS}{H}} \sqrt{\dfrac{p}{p - u}} = \sqrt{\dfrac{2(48,000)45}{1}} \sqrt{\dfrac{800}{800 - 200}} = 2,400$ wheels

b. $TC_{min} = $ Carrying cost + Setup cost $= \left(\dfrac{I_{max}}{2}\right) H + (D/Q_0)S$

Thus, you must first compute I_{max}:

$I_{max} = \dfrac{Q_0}{p}(p - u) = \dfrac{2,400}{800}(800 - 200) = 1,800$ wheels

$TC = \dfrac{1,800}{2} \times \$1 + \dfrac{48,000}{2,400} \times \$45 = \$900 + \$900 = \$1,800$

Note again the equality of cost (in this example, setup and carrying costs) at the EOQ.

c. Cycle time $= \dfrac{Q_0}{u} = \dfrac{2,400 \text{ wheels}}{200 \text{ wheels per day}} = 12$ days

Thus, a run of wheels will be made every 12 days.

d. Run time $= \dfrac{Q_0}{p} = \dfrac{2,400 \text{ wheels}}{800 \text{ wheels per day}} = 3$ days.

Thus, each run will require three days to complete.

QUANTITY DISCOUNTS

quantity discounts Price reductions for large orders.

Quantity discounts are price reductions for large orders offered to customers to induce them to buy in large quantities. For example, a Chicago surgical supply company publishes the price list shown in Table 13–2 for boxes of gauze strips. Note that the price per box decreases as order quantity increases.

If quantity discounts are offered, the buyer must weigh the potential benefits of reduced purchase price and fewer orders that will result from buying in large quantities against the increase in carrying costs caused by higher average inventories. The buyer's goal with quantity discounts is to select the order quantity that will minimize total cost, where total cost is the sum of carrying cost, ordering cost, *and* purchasing cost:

Order Quantity	Price per Box
1 to 44	$2.00
45 to 69	1.70
70 or more	1.40

TABLE 13-2

Price list for extra-wide gauze strips

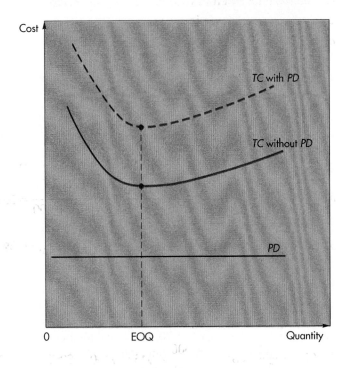

FIGURE 13-7

Adding PD doesn't change the EOQ

$$TC = \text{Carrying cost} + \text{Ordering cost} + \text{Purchasing cost} \qquad (13\text{--}9)$$

$$= \left(\frac{Q}{2}\right)H + \left(\frac{D}{Q}\right)S + PD$$

where

P = Unit price

Recall that in the basic EOQ model, determination of order size does not involve the purchasing cost. The rationale for not including unit price is that under the assumption of no quantity discounts, price per unit is the same for all order sizes. Inclusion of unit price in the total-cost computation in that case would merely increase the total cost by the amount P times D. A graph of total annual purchase cost versus quantity would be a horizontal line. Hence, including purchasing costs would merely raise the total-cost curve by the same amount (PD) at every point. That would not change the EOQ. (See Figure 13–7.)

When quantity discounts are offered, there is a separate U-shaped total-cost curve for each unit price. Again, including unit prices merely raises each curve by a constant amount. However, because the unit prices are all different, each curve is raised by a different amount: Smaller unit prices will raise a total-cost curve less than larger unit prices. Note that no one curve applies to the entire range of quantities; each curve applies to only a *portion* of the range. (See Figure 13–8.) Hence, the applicable or *feasible* total cost is initially on the curve with the highest unit price and then drops down, curve by curve, at the *price breaks,* which are the minimum quantities needed to obtain the discounts. Thus, in Table 13–2, the price breaks for gauze strips are at 45 and 70 boxes. The result is a total-cost curve with *steps* at the price breaks.

FIGURE 13-8

*The total-cost curve with
quantity discounts is composed
of a portion of the total-cost
curve for each price*

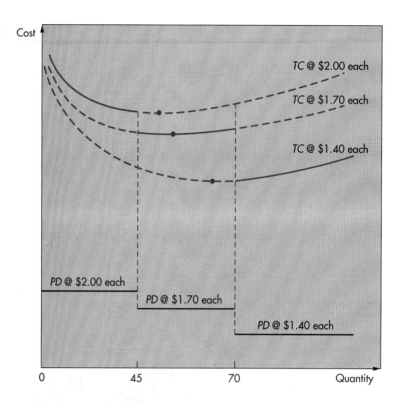

Even though each curve has a minimum, those points are not necessarily feasible. For
example, the minimum point for the $1.40 curve in Figure 13–8 appears to be about 65
units. However, the price list shown in Table 13–2 indicates that an order size of 65 boxes
will involve a unit price of $1.70. The actual total-cost curve is denoted by the solid lines;
only those price–quantity combinations are feasible. The objective of the quantity discount model is to identify an order quantity that will represent the lowest total cost for the
entire set of curves.

There are two general cases of the model. In one, carrying costs are constant (e.g., $2
per unit); in the other, carrying costs are stated as a percentage of purchase price (e.g., 20
percent of unit price). When carrying costs are constant, there will be a single minimum
point: all curves will have their minimum point at the same quantity. Consequently, the
total-cost curves line up vertically, differing only in that the lower unit prices are reflected
by lower total-cost curves as shown in Figure 13–9A. (For purposes of illustration, the
horizontal purchasing cost lines have been omitted.)

When carrying costs are specified as a percentage of unit price, each curve will have a
different minimum point. Because carrying costs are a percentage of price, lower prices
will mean lower carrying costs and larger minimum points. Thus, as price decreases, each
curve's minimum point will be to the right of the next higher curve's minimum point. (See
Figure 13–9B.)

The procedure for determining the overall EOQ differs slightly, depending on which of
these two cases is relevant. For carrying costs that are constant, the procedure is as follows:

1. Compute the common minimum point.

2. Only one of the unit prices will have the minimum point in its feasible range since the
   ranges do not overlap. Identify that range.

   a. If the feasible minimum point is on the lowest price range, that is the optimal order
      quantity.

   b. If the feasible minimum point is in any other range, compute the total cost for the
      minimum point and for the price breaks of all *lower* unit costs. Compare the total
      costs; the quantity (minimum point or price break) that yields the lowest total cost
      is the optimal order quantity.

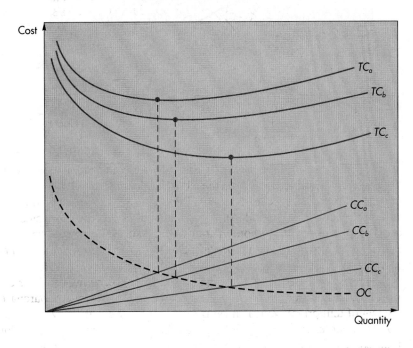

FIGURE 13-9

Comparison of TC curves for constant carrying costs and carrying costs that are a percentage of unit costs

A. *When carrying costs are constant, all curves have their minimum at the same quantity.*

B. *When carrying costs are stated as a percentage of unit price, the minimum points do not line up.*

The maintenance department of a large hospital uses about 816 cases of liquid cleanser annually. Ordering costs are $12, carrying costs are $4 per case a year, and the new price schedule indicates that orders of less than 50 cases will cost $20 per case, 50 to 79 cases will cost $18 per case, 80 to 99 cases will cost $17 per case, and larger orders will cost $16 per case. Determine the optimal order quantity and the total cost.

Example 5

See Figure 13–10:

Solution

$D = 816$ cases per year $S = \$12$ $H = \$4$ per case per year

Range	Price
1 to 49	$20
50 to 79	18
80 to 99	17
100 or more	16

1. Compute the common EOQ: $= \sqrt{\dfrac{2DS}{H}} = \sqrt{\dfrac{2(816)12}{4}} = 70$ cases

FIGURE 13-10

Total-cost curves for Example 5

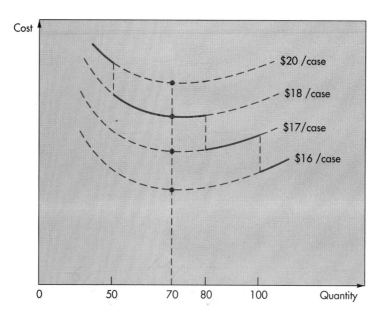

2. The 70 cases can be bought at $18 per case because 70 falls in the range of 50 to 79 cases. The total cost to purchase 816 cases a year, at the rate of 70 cases per order, will be

$$TC_{70} = \text{Carrying cost} + \text{Order cost} + \text{Purchase cost}$$
$$= (Q/2)H + (D/Q_0)S + PD$$
$$= (70/2)4 + (816/70)12 + 18(816) = \$14,968$$

Because lower cost ranges exist, each must be checked against the minimum cost generated by 70 cases at $18 each. In order to buy at $17 per case, at least 80 cases must be purchased. (Because the TC curve is rising, 80 cases will have the lowest TC for that curve's feasible region.) The total cost at 70 cases will be

$$TC_{80} = (80/2)4 + (816/80)12 + 17(816) = \$14,154$$

To obtain a cost of $16 per case, at least 100 cases per order are required, and the total cost will be

$$TC_{100} = (100/2)4 + (816/100)12 + 16(816) = \$13,354$$

Therefore, because 100 cases per order yields the lowest total cost, 100 cases is the overall optimal order quantity.

When carrying costs are expressed as a percentage of price, determine the best purchase quantity with the following procedure:

1. Beginning with the lowest unit price, compute the minimum points for each price range until you find a feasible minimum point (i.e., until a minimum point falls in the quantity range for its price).

2. If the minimum point for the lowest unit price is feasible, it is the optimal order quantity. If the minimum point is not feasible in the lowest price range, compare the total cost at the price break for all *lower* prices with the total cost of the largest feasible minimum point. The quantity that yields the lowest total cost is the optimum.

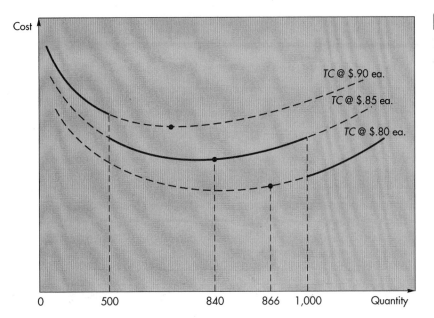

FIGURE 13-11

*Total-cost curves for
Example 6*

Example 6

Surge Electric uses 4,000 toggle switches a year. Switches are priced as follows: 1 to 499, 90 cents each; 500 to 999, 85 cents each; and 1,000 or more, 80 cents each. It costs approximately $30 to prepare an order and receive it, and carrying costs are 40 percent of purchase price per unit on an annual basis. Determine the optimal order quantity and the total annual cost.

See Figure 13–11:

$D = 4,000$ switches per year $\quad S = \$30 \quad H = .40P$

Range	Unit Price	H
1 to 499	$0.90	.40(0.90) = .36
500 to 999	$0.85	.40(0.85) = .34
1,000 or more	$0.80	.40(0.80) = .32

Find the minimum point for each price, starting with the lowest price, until you locate a feasible minimum point.

$$\text{minimum point}_{0.80} = \sqrt{\frac{2DS}{H}} = \sqrt{\frac{2(4,000)30}{.32}} = 866 \text{ switches}$$

Because an order size of 866 switches will cost $0.85 each rather than $0.80 each, 866 is not a feasible minimum point for $0.80 per switch. Next, try $0.85 per unit.

$$\text{minimum point}_{0.85} = \sqrt{\frac{2(4,000)30}{.34}} = 840 \text{ switches}$$

This is feasible; it falls in the $0.85 per switch range of 500 to 999.

Now compute the total cost for 840, and compare it to the total cost of the minimum quantity necessary to obtain a price of $0.80 per switch.

$$\text{TC} = \text{Carrying costs} + \text{Ordering costs} + \text{Purchasing costs}$$

$$= \left(\frac{Q}{2}\right)H \quad + \quad \left(\frac{D}{Q}\right)S \quad + \quad PD$$

$$\text{TC}_{840} = \frac{840}{2}(.34) \quad + \quad \frac{4,000}{840}(30) \quad + \quad 0.85(4,000) \quad = \$3,686$$

$$TC_{1,000} = \frac{1,000}{2}(.32) \quad + \quad \frac{4,000}{1,000}(30) \quad + \quad .80(4,000) \quad = \$3,480$$

Thus, the minimum-cost order size is 1,000 switches.

When to Reorder with EOQ Ordering

reorder point (ROP) When the quantity on hand of an item drops to this amount, the item is reordered.

EOQ models answer the question of how much to order, but not the question of when to order. The latter is the function of models that identify the **reorder point (ROP)** in terms of a *quantity:* The reorder point occurs when the quantity on hand drops to a predetermined amount. That amount generally includes expected demand during lead time and perhaps an extra cushion of stock, which serves to reduce the probability of experiencing a stockout during lead time. Note that in order to know when the reorder point has been reached, a *perpetual* inventory is required.

The goal in ordering is to place an order when the amount of inventory on hand is sufficient to satisfy demand during the time it takes to receive that order (i.e., lead time). There are four determinants of the reorder point quantity:

1. The rate of demand (usually based on a forecast).
2. The lead time.
3. The extent of demand and/or lead time variability.
4. The degree of stockout risk acceptable to management.

If demand and lead time are both constant, the reorder point is simply

$$ROP = d \times LT \tag{13–10}$$

where

d = Demand rate (units per day or week)

LT = Lead time in days or weeks

Note: Demand and lead time must have the same time units.

Example 7

Tingly takes Two-a-Day vitamins, which are delivered to his home by a routeman seven days after an order is called in. At what point should Tingly reorder?

Solution

Usage = 2 vitamins a day

Lead time = 7 days

ROP = Usage × Lead time

= 2 vitamins per day × 7 days = 14 vitamins

Thus, Tingly should reorder when 14 vitamin tablets are left.

safety stock Stock that is held in excess of expected demand due to variable demand rate and/or lead time.

When variability is present in demand or lead time, it creates the possibility that actual demand will exceed expected demand. Consequently, it becomes necessary to carry additional inventory, called **safety stock,** to reduce the risk of running out of inventory (a stockout) during lead time. The reorder point then increases by the amount of the safety stock:

$$ROP = \frac{\text{Expected demand}}{\text{during lead time}} + \text{Safety stock} \tag{13–11}$$

For example, if expected demand during lead time is 100 units, and the desired amount of safety stock is 10 units, the ROP would be 110 units.

FIGURE 13-12

Safety stock reduces risk of stockout during lead time

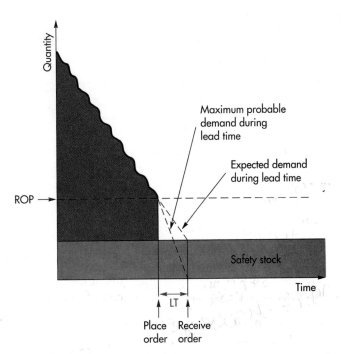

Figure 13–12 illustrates how safety stock can reduce the risk of a stockout during lead time (LT). Note that stockout protection is needed only during lead time. If there is a sudden surge at any point during the cycle, that will trigger another order. Once that order is received, the danger of an imminent stockout is negligible.

Because it costs money to hold safety stock, a manager must carefully weigh the cost of carrying safety stock against the reduction in stockout risk it provides. The customer *service level* increases as the risk of stockout decreases. Order cycle **service level** can be defined as the probability that demand will not exceed supply during lead time (i.e., that the amount of stock on hand will be sufficient to meet demand). Hence, a service level of 95 percent implies a probability of 95 percent that demand will not exceed supply during lead time. An equivalent statement that demand will be satisfied in 95 percent of such instances does *not* mean that 95 percent of demand will be satisfied. The risk of a stockout is the complement of service level; a customer service level of 95 percent implies a stockout risk of 5 percent. That is,

Service level = 100 percent – Stockout risk

Later you will see how the order cycle service level relates to the *annual* service level.

The amount of safety stock that is appropriate for a given situation depends on the following factors:

1. The average demand rate and average lead time.

2. Demand and lead time variability.

3. The desired service level.

For a given order cycle service level, the greater the variability in either demand rate or lead time, the greater the amount of safety stock that will be needed to achieve that service level. Similarly, for a given amount of variation in demand rate or lead time, achieving an increase in the service level will require increasing the amount of safety stock. Selection of a service level may reflect stockout costs (e.g., lost sales, customer dissatisfaction) or it might simply be a policy variable (e.g., the manager wants to achieve a specified service level for a certain item).

service level Probability that demand will not exceed supply during lead time.

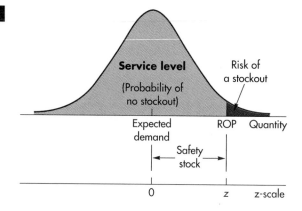

FIGURE 13–13

The ROP based on a normal distribution of lead time demand

Let us look at several models that can be used in cases when variability is present. The first model can be used if an estimate of expected demand during lead time and its standard deviation are available. The formula is

$$\text{ROP} = \frac{\text{Expected demand}}{\text{during lead time}} + z\sigma_{d\text{LT}} \qquad (13\text{–}12)$$

where

z = Number of standard deviations

$\sigma_{d\text{LT}}$ = The standard deviation of lead time demand

The models generally assume that any variability in demand rate or lead time can be adequately described by a normal distribution. However, this is not a strict requirement; the models provide approximate reorder points even where actual distributions depart from normal.

The value of z (see Figure 13–13) used in a particular instance depends on the stockout risk that the manager is willing to accept. Generally, the smaller the risk the manager is willing to accept, the greater the value of z. Use Appendix B, Table B to obtain the value of z, given a desired service level for lead time.

Example 8

Suppose that the manager of a construction supply house determined from historical records that demand for sand during lead time averages 50 tons. In addition, suppose the manager determined that demand during lead time could be described by a normal distribution that has a mean of 50 tons and a standard deviation of 5 tons. Answer these questions, assuming that the manager is willing to accept a stockout risk of no more than 3 percent:

a. What value of z is appropriate?

b. How much safety stock should be held?

c. What reorder point should be used?

Solution

Expected lead time demand = 50 tons

$\sigma_{d\text{LT}}$ = 5 tons

Risk = 3 percent

a. From Appendix B, Table B, using a service level of $1 - .03 = .9700$, you obtain a value of $z = +1.88$.

b. Safety stock = $z\sigma_{d\text{LT}} = 1.88(5) = 9.40$ tons

c. ROP = Expected lead time demand + Safety stock = $50 + 9.40 = 59.40$ tons

When data on lead time demand are not readily available, Formula 13–12 cannot be used. Nevertheless, data are generally available on daily or weekly demand, and on the length of lead time. Using those data, a manager can determine whether demand and/or lead time is variable, and if variability exists in one or both, the related standard deviation(s). For those situations, one of the following formulas can be used:

If only demand is variable, then $\sigma_{dLT} = \sqrt{LT}\sigma_d$, and the reorder point is

$$ROP = \bar{d} \times LT + z\sqrt{LT}\sigma_d \tag{13–13}$$

where

$\bar{d} = $ *Average* daily or weekly demand

$\sigma_d = $ Standard deviation of demand per day or week

$LT = $ Lead time in days or weeks

If only lead time is variable, then $\sigma_{dLT} = d\sigma_{LT}$, and the reorder point is

$$ROP = d \times \overline{LT} + zd\sigma_{LT} \tag{13–14}$$

where

$d = $ Daily or weekly demand

$\overline{LT} = $ *Average* lead time in days or weeks

$\sigma_{LT} = $ Standard deviation of lead time in days or weeks

If both demand and lead time are variable, then

$$\sigma_{dLT} = \sqrt{\overline{LT}\sigma_d^2 + \bar{d}^2\sigma_{LT}^2}$$

and the reorder point is

$$ROP = \bar{d} \times \overline{LT} + z\sqrt{\overline{LT}\sigma_d^2 + \bar{d}^2\sigma_{LT}^2} \tag{13–15}$$

Note: Each of these models assumes that demand and lead time are *independent*.

A restaurant uses an average of 50 jars of a special sauce each week. Weekly usage of sauce has a standard deviation of 3 jars. The manager is willing to accept no more than a 10 percent risk of stockout during lead time, which is two weeks. Assume the distribution of usage is normal.

Example 9

a. Which of the above formulas is appropriate for this situation? Why?

b. Determine the value of z.

c. Determine the ROP.

Solution

$\bar{d} = 50$ jars per week $LT = 2$ weeks

$\sigma_d = 3$ jars per week   Acceptable risk = 10 percent, so service level is .90

a. Because only demand is variable (i.e., has a standard deviation), Formula 13–13 is appropriate.

b. From Appendix B, Table B, using a service level of .9000, you obtain $z = +1.28$.

c. $ROP = \bar{d} \times LT + z\sqrt{LT}\sigma_d = 50 \times 2 + 1.28\sqrt{2}(3) = 100 + 5.43 = 105.43$.

Comment. The logic of the three formulas for the reorder point may not be immediately obvious. The first part of each formula is the expected demand, which is the product of daily (or weekly) demand and the number of days (or weeks) of lead time. The second part of the formula is z times the standard deviation of lead time demand. For the formula in which only demand is variable, daily (or weekly) demand is assumed to be normally

FIGURE 13-14

Lead time demand

distributed and has the same mean and standard deviation (see Figure 13–14). The standard deviation of demand for the entire lead time is found by summing the *variances* of daily (or weekly) demands, and then finding the square root of that number because, unlike variances, standard deviations are not additive. Hence, if the daily standard deviation is σ_d, the *variance* is σ_d^2, and if lead time is four days, the variance of lead time demand will equal the sum of the 4 variances, which is $4\sigma_d^2$. The standard deviation of lead time demand will be the square root of this, which is equal to $2\sigma_d$. In general, this becomes $\sqrt{LT}\sigma_d$ and, hence, the last part of Formula 13–13.

When only lead time is variable, the explanation is much simpler. The standard deviation of lead time demand is equal to the constant daily demand multiplied by the standard deviation of lead time.

When both demand and lead time are variable, the formula appears truly impressive. However, it is merely the result of squaring the standard deviations of the two previous formulas to obtain their variances, summing them, and then taking the square root.

SHORTAGES AND SERVICE LEVELS

The ROP computation does not reveal the expected *amount* of shortage for a given lead time service level. The expected number of units short can, however, be very useful to a manager. This quantity can easily be determined from the same information used to compute the ROP, with one additional piece of information (see Table 13–3). Use of the table assumes that the distribution of lead time demand can be adequately represented by a normal distribution. If it can, the expected number of units short in each order cycle is given by this formula:

$$E(n) = E(z)\sigma_{dLT} \tag{13–16}$$

where

$E(n) = $ Expected number of units short per order cycle

$E(z) = $ Standardized number of units short obtained from Table 13–3

$\sigma_{dLT} = $ Standard deviation of lead time demand

Example 10

Suppose the standard deviation of lead time demand is known to be 20 units. Lead time demand is approximately normal.

a. For a lead time service level of 90 percent, determine the expected number of units short for any order cycle.

z	Lead Time Service Level	E(z)	z	Lead Time Service Level	E(z)	z	Lead Time Service Level	E(z)	z	Lead Time Service Level	E(z)
-2.40	.0082	2.403	-0.80	.2119	0.920	0.80	.7881	0.120	2.40	.9918	0.003
-2.36	.0091	2.363	-0.76	.2236	0.889	0.84	.7995	0.112	2.44	.9927	0.002
-2.32	.0102	2.323	-0.72	.2358	0.858	0.88	.8106	0.104	2.48	.9934	0.002
-2.28	.0113	2.284	-0.68	.2483	0.828	0.92	.8212	0.097	2.52	.9941	0.002
-2.24	.0125	2.244	-0.64	.2611	0.798	0.96	.8315	0.089	2.56	.9948	0.002
-2.20	.0139	2.205	-0.60	.2743	0.769	1.00	.8413	0.083	2.60	.9953	0.001
-2.16	.0154	2.165	-0.56	.2877	0.740	1.04	.8508	0.077	2.64	.9959	0.001
-2.12	.0170	2.126	-0.52	.3015	0.712	1.08	.8599	0.071	2.68	.9963	0.001
-2.08	.0188	2.087	-0.48	.3156	0.684	1.12	.8686	0.066	2.72	.9967	0.001
-2.04	.0207	2.048	-0.44	.3300	0.657	1.16	.8770	0.061	2.76	.9971	0.001
-2.00	.0228	2.008	-0.40	.3446	0.630	1.20	.8849	0.056	2.80	.9974	0.0008
-1.96	.0250	1.969	-0.36	.3594	0.597	1.24	.8925	0.052	2.84	.9977	0.0007
-1.92	.0274	1.930	-0.32	.3745	0.576	1.28	.8997	0.048	2.88	.9980	0.0006
-1.88	.0301	1.892	-0.28	.3897	0.555	1.32	.9066	0.044	2.92	.9982	0.0005
-1.84	.0329	1.853	-0.24	.4052	0.530	1.36	.9131	0.040	2.96	.9985	0.0004
-1.80	.0359	1.814	-0.20	.4207	0.507	1.40	.9192	0.037	3.00	.9987	0.0004
-1.76	.0392	1.776	-0.16	.4364	0.484	1.44	.9251	0.034	3.04	.9988	0.0003
-1.72	.0427	1.737	-0.12	.4522	0.462	1.48	.9306	0.031	3.08	.9990	0.0003
-1.68	.0465	1.699	-0.08	.4681	0.440	1.52	.9357	0.028	3.12	.9991	0.0002
-1.64	.0505	1.661	-0.04	.4840	0.419	1.56	.9406	0.026	3.16	.9992	0.0002
-1.60	.0548	1.623	0.00	.5000	0.399	1.60	.9452	0.023	3.20	.9993	0.0002
-1.56	.0594	1.586	0.04	.5160	0.379	1.64	.9495	0.021	3.24	.9994	0.0001
-1.52	.0643	1.548	0.08	.5319	0.360	1.68	.9535	0.019	3.28	.9995	0.0001
-1.48	.0694	1.511	0.12	.5478	0.342	1.72	.9573	0.017	3.32	.9995	0.0001
-1.44	.0749	1.474	0.16	.5636	0.324	1.76	.9608	0.016	3.36	.9996	0.0001
-1.40	.0808	1.437	0.20	.5793	0.307	1.80	.9641	0.014	3.40	.9997	0.0001
-1.36	.0869	1.400	0.24	.5948	0.290	1.84	.9671	0.013			
-1.32	.0934	1.364	0.28	.6103	0.275	1.88	.9699	0.012			
-1.28	.1003	1.328	0.32	.6255	0.256	1.92	.9726	0.010			
-1.24	.1075	1.292	0.36	.6406	0.237	1.96	.9750	0.009			
-1.20	.1151	1.256	0.40	.6554	0.230	2.00	.9772	0.008			
-1.16	.1230	1.221	0.44	.6700	0.217	2.04	.9793	0.008			
-1.12	.1314	1.186	0.48	.6844	0.204	2.08	.9812	0.007			
-1.08	.1401	1.151	0.52	.6985	0.192	2.12	.9830	0.006			
-1.04	.1492	1.117	0.56	.7123	0.180	2.16	.9846	0.005			
-1.00	.1587	1.083	0.60	.7257	0.169	2.20	.9861	0.005			
-0.96	.1685	1.049	0.64	.7389	0.158	2.24	.9875	0.004			
-0.92	.1788	1.017	0.68	.7517	0.148	2.28	.9887	0.004			
-0.88	.1894	0.984	0.72	.7642	0.138	2.32	.9898	0.003			
-0.84	.2005	0.952	0.76	.7764	0.129	2.36	.9909	0.003			

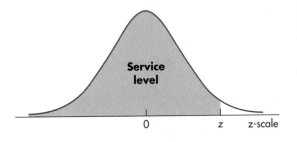

TABLE 13-3

Normal distribution service levels and unit normal loss function b. What lead time service level would an expected shortage of 2 units imply?

Solution

$\sigma_{d\text{LT}} = 20$ units

a. Lead time (cycle) service level = .90. From Table 13–3, $E(z) = 0.048$. Using Formula 13–16, $E(n) = 0.048(20 \text{ units}) = 0.96$, or about 1 unit.

b. For the case where $E(n) = 2$, you must solve for $E(z)$ and then use Table 13–3 to determine the lead time service that implies. Thus, $E(n) = E(z)\sigma_{d\text{LT}}$, so $E(z) = E(n)/\sigma_{d\text{LT}} = 2/20 = 0.100$. From Table 13–3, this implies a service level of approximately 81.5 percent (interpolating).

The expected number of units short is just that—an expected or *average* amount; the exact number of units short in any given cycle will be an amount close to that. Moreover, if discrete items are involved, the actual number of units short in any cycle will be an integer.

Having determined the expected number of units short for an order cycle, you can determine the expected number of units short per year. It is simply the expected number of units short per cycle multiplied by the number of cycles (orders) per year. Thus,

$$E(N) = E(n)\frac{D}{Q} \tag{13–17}$$

where

$E(N)$ = Expected number of units short per year

Example 11

Given the following information, determine the expected number of units short per year.

$$D = 1,000 \qquad Q = 250 \qquad E(n) = 2.5$$

Solution

Using the formula $E(N) = E(n)\dfrac{D}{Q}$,

$$E(N) = 2.5\left(\frac{1,000}{250}\right) = 10.0 \text{ units per year}$$

It is sometimes convenient to think of service level in annual terms. One definition of annual service level is the percentage of demand filled directly from inventory. This is also known as the *fill rate*. Thus, if $D = 1,000$, and 990 units were filled directly from inventory (shortages totaling 10 units over the year were recorded), the annual service level (fill rate) would be $990/1,000 = 99$ percent. The annual service level and the lead time service level can be related using the following formula:

$$\text{SL}_{\text{annual}} = 1 - \frac{E(N)}{D} \tag{13–18}$$

Using Formulas 13–17 and 13–16,

$$E(N) = E(n)D/Q = E(z)\sigma_{d\text{LT}}\,D/Q$$

Thus,

$$\text{SL}_{\text{annual}} = 1 - \frac{E(z)\sigma_{d\text{LT}}}{Q} \tag{13–19}$$

Example 12

Given a lead time service level of 90, $D = 1,000$, $Q = 250$, and $\sigma_{d\text{LT}} = 16$, determine the annual service level, and the amount of cycle safety stock that would provide an annual service level of .98. From Table 13–3, $E(z) = 0.048$ for a 90 percent lead time service level.

a. Using Formula 13–19:

$$SL_{annual} = 1 - 0.048(16)/250 = .997$$

b. Using Formula 13–19, and an annual service level of .98, solve for $E(z)$:

$$.98 = 1 - E(z)(16)/250$$

Solving, $E(z) = 0.312$. From Table 13–3, with $E(z) = 0.312$, you can see that this value of $E(z)$ is a little more than the value of 0.307. So it appears that an acceptable value of z might be 0.19. The necessary safety stock to achieve the specified annual service level is equal to $z\sigma_{dLT}$. Hence, the safety stock is $0.19(16) = 3.04$, or approximately 3 units.

Note that in the preceding example, a lead time service level of 90 percent provided an annual service level of 99.7 percent. Naturally, different values of D, Q, and σ_{dLT} will tend to produce different results for a cycle service level of 90 percent. Nonetheless, the annual service level will usually be greater than the cycle service level. In addition, since the annual service level as defined relates to the percentage of units short per year, it makes sense to base cycle service levels on a specified annual service level. This means setting the annual level, using Formula 13–19 to solve for $E(z)$, and then using that value to obtain the service level for the order cycles.

How Much to Order: Fixed–Order–Interval Model

The **fixed-order-interval (FOI) model** is used when orders must be placed at fixed time intervals (weekly, twice a month, etc.): Fixed-interval ordering is widely used by retail businesses. The question to be answered at each order point is: How much should be ordered for the next (fixed) interval? If demand is variable, the order size will tend to vary from cycle to cycle. This is quite different from an EOQ/ROP approach in which the order size generally remains fixed from cycle to cycle, while the length of the cycle varies (shorter if demand is above average, and longer if demand is below average).

fixed-order-interval (FOI) model Orders are placed at fixed time intervals.

REASONS TO USE THE FIXED-ORDER-INTERVAL MODEL

In some cases, a supplier's policy might encourage orders at fixed intervals. Even when that is not the case, grouping orders for items from the same supplier can produce savings in shipping costs. Furthermore, some situations do not readily lend themselves to continuous monitoring of inventory levels. Many retail operations (e.g., drugstores, small grocery stores) fall into this category. The alternative for them is to use fixed-interval ordering, which requires only periodic checks of inventory levels.

DETERMINING THE AMOUNT TO ORDER

If both the demand rate and lead time are constant, the fixed-interval model and the fixed-quantity model function identically. The differences in the two models become apparent only when examined under conditions of variability. Like the ROP model, the fixed-interval model can have variations in demand only, in lead time only, or in both demand and lead time. However, for the sake of simplicity and because it is perhaps the most frequently encountered situation, the discussion here will focus only on *variable demand* and *constant lead time.*

Figure 13–15 provides a comparison of the fixed-quantity and fixed-interval systems. In the fixed-quantity arrangement, orders are triggered by a *quantity* (ROP), while in the fixed-interval arrangement orders are triggered by a *time.* Therefore, the fixed-interval system must have stockout protection for lead time plus the next order cycle, but the fixed-quantity system needs protection only during lead time because additional orders

FIGURE 13-15

*Comparison of fixed-quantity
and fixed-interval ordering*

*Fixed
quantity*

*Fixed
interval*

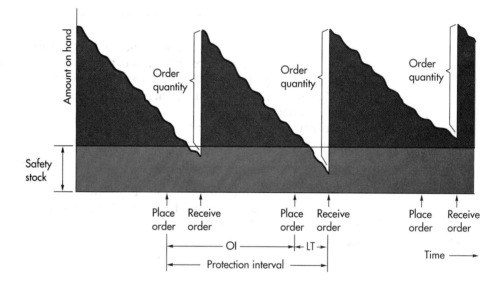

can be placed at any time and will be received shortly (lead time) thereafter. Consequently, there is a greater need for safety stock in the fixed-interval model than in the fixed-quantity model. Note, for example, the large dip into safety stock during the second order cycle with the fixed-interval model.

Both models are sensitive to demand experience just prior to reordering, but in somewhat different ways. In the fixed-quantity model, a higher-than-normal demand causes a *shorter time* between orders, whereas in the fixed-interval model, the result is a *larger order size*. Another difference is that the fixed-quantity model requires close monitoring of inventory levels in order to know *when* the amount on hand has reached the reorder point. The fixed-interval model requires only a periodic review (i.e., physical inspection) of inventory levels just prior to placing an order to determine how much is needed.

Order size in the fixed-interval model is determined by the following computation:

$$
\begin{array}{lllll}
\text{Amount} \\ \text{to order}
& = &
\begin{array}{c} \text{Expected demand} \\ \text{during protection} \\ \text{interval} \end{array}
& + &
\begin{array}{c} \text{Safety} \\ \text{stock} \end{array}
& - &
\begin{array}{c} \text{Amount on hand} \\ \text{at reorder time} \end{array}
\end{array}
\tag{13–20}
$$

$$
= \quad \bar{d}(\text{OI} + \text{LT}) \quad + z\sigma_d\sqrt{\text{OI} + \text{LT}} - \quad A
$$

where

OI = Order interval (length of time between orders)

A = Amount on hand at reorder time

As in previous models, we assume that demand during the protection interval is normally distributed.

Given the following information, determine the amount to order.

Example 13

$\bar{d}$ = 30 units per day   Desired service level = 99 percent

σ_d = 3 units per day   Amount on hand at reorder time = 71 units

LT = 2 days   OI = 7 days

z = 2.33 for 99 percent service level

Solution

$$\underset{\text{to order}}{\text{Amount}} = \bar{d}(\text{OI} + \text{LT}) + z\sigma_d\sqrt{\text{OI} + \text{LT}} - A$$

$$= 30(7 + 2) + 2.33(3)\sqrt{7 + 2} - 71 = 220 \text{ units}$$

An issue related to fixed-interval ordering is the risk of a stockout. From the perspective (i.e., the point in time) of placing an order, there are two points in the order cycle at which a stockout could occur. One is shortly after the order is placed, while waiting to receive the current order (refer to Figure 13–15). The second point is near the end of the cycle, while waiting to receive the next order.

To find the initial risk of a stockout, use the ROP formula (13–13), setting ROP equal to the quantity on hand when the order is placed, and solve for z, then obtain the service level for that value of z from Appendix B, Table B and subtract it from 1.0000 to get the risk of a stockout.

To find the risk of a stockout at the end of the order cycle, use the fixed-interval formula (13–20) and solve for z. Then obtain the service level for that value of z from Appendix B, Table B and subtract it from 1.0000 to get the risk of a stockout.

Let's look at an example.

Given the following information:

Example 14

LT = 4 days   A = 43 units

OI = 12 days   Q = 171 units

d = 10 units/day

σ_d = 2 units/day

Determine the risk of a stockout at

a. The end of the initial lead time.

b. The end of the second lead time.

a. For the risk of stockout for the first lead time, we use Formula 13–15. Substituting the given values, we get $43 = 10 \times 4 + z(2)(2)$. Solving, $z = +.75$. From Appendix B, Table B, the service level is .7734. The risk is $1 - .7734 = .2266$, which is fairly high.

Solution

b. For the risk of a stockout at the end of the second lead time, we use Formula 13–20. Substituting the given values we get $171 = 10 \times (4 + 12) + z\,4(2) - 43$. Solving, $z = +6.75$. This value is way out in the right tail of the normal distribution, making the service level virtually 100 percent, and, thus, the risk of a stockout at this point is essentially equal to zero.

Overall, we can say that the risk of a stockout initially is fairly high for the initial lead time but almost negligible for the second lead time.

BENEFITS AND DISADVANTAGES

The fixed-interval system results in the tight control needed for A items in an A-B-C classification due to the periodic reviews it requires. In addition, when two or more items come from the same supplier, grouping orders can yield savings in ordering, packing, and shipping costs. Moreover, it may be the only practical approach if inventory withdrawals cannot be closely monitored.

On the negative side, the fixed-interval system necessitates a larger amount of safety stock for a given risk of stockout because of the need to protect against shortages during an entire order interval plus lead time (instead of lead time only), and this increases the carrying cost. Also, there are the costs of the periodic reviews.

The Single-Period Model

single-period model Model for ordering of perishables and other items with limited useful lives.

The **single-period model** (sometimes referred to as the *newsboy problem*) is used to handle ordering of perishables (fresh fruits, vegetables, seafood, cut flowers) and items that have a limited useful life (newspapers, magazines, spare parts for specialized equipment). The *period* for spare parts is the life of the equipment, assuming that the parts cannot be used for other equipment. What sets unsold or unused goods apart is that they are not typically carried over from one period to the next, at least not without penalty. Day-old baked goods, for instance, are often sold at reduced prices, leftover seafood may be discarded, and out-of-date magazines may be offered to used book stores at bargain rates. There may even be some cost associated with disposal of leftover goods.

Analysis of single-period situations generally focuses on two costs: shortage and excess. Shortage cost may include a charge for loss of customer goodwill as well as the opportunity cost of lost sales. Generally, **shortage cost** is simply unrealized profit per unit. That is,

shortage cost Generally, the unrealized profit per unit.

$$C_{\text{shortage}} = C_s = \text{Revenue per unit} - \text{Cost per unit}$$

If a shortage or stockout relates to an item used in production or to a spare part for a machine, then shortage cost refers to the actual cost of lost production.

excess cost Difference between purchase cost and salvage value of items left over at the end of a period.

Excess cost pertains to items left over at the end of the period. In effect, excess cost is the difference between purchase cost and salvage value. That is,

$$C_{\text{excess}} = C_e = \text{Original cost per unit} - \text{Salvage value per unit}$$

If there is cost associated with disposing of excess items, the salvage will be negative and will therefore *increase* the excess cost per unit.

The goal of the single-period model is to identify the order quantity, or stocking level, that will minimize the long-run excess and shortage costs.

There are two general categories of problems that we will consider: those for which demand can be approximated using a continuous distribution (perhaps a theoretical one such as a uniform or normal distribution) and those for which demand can be approximated using a discrete distribution (say, historical frequencies or a theoretical distribution such as the Poisson). The kind of inventory can indicate which type of model might be appropriate. For example, demand for petroleum, liquids, and gases tends to vary over some *continuous scale,* thus lending itself to description by a continuous distribution. Demand for tractors, cars, and computers is expressed in terms of the *number of units* demanded and lends itself to description by a discrete distribution.

CONTINUOUS STOCKING LEVELS

The concept of identifying an optimal stocking level is perhaps easiest to visualize when demand is *uniform.* Choosing the stocking level is similar to balancing a seesaw, but instead of a person on each end of the seesaw, we have excess cost per unit (C_e) on one

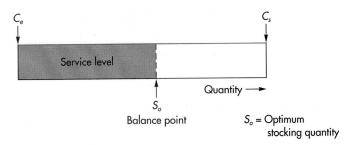

FIGURE 13–16

The optimal stocking level balances unit shortage and excess costs

end of the distribution and shortage cost per unit (C_s) on the other. The optimal stocking level is analogous to the fulcrum of the seesaw; the stocking level equalizes the cost weights, as illustrated in Figure 13–16.

The *service level* is the *probability* that demand will not exceed the stocking level, and computation of the service level is the key to determining the optimal stocking level, S_o.

$$\text{Service level} = \frac{C_s}{C_s + C_e} \qquad (13\text{--}21)$$

where

C_s = Shortage cost per unit

C_e = Excess cost per unit

If actual demand exceeds S_o, there is a shortage; hence, C_s is on the right end of the distribution. Similarly, if demand is less than S_o, there is an excess, so C_e is on the left end of the distribution. When $C_e = C_s$, the optimal stocking level is halfway between the endpoints of the distribution. If one cost is greater than the other, S_o will be closer to the larger cost.

Sweet cider is delivered weekly to Cindy's Cider Bar. Demand varies uniformly between 300 liters and 500 liters per week. Cindy pays 20 cents per liter for the cider and charges 80 cents per liter for it. Unsold cider has no salvage value and cannot be carried over into the next week due to spoilage. Find the optimal stocking level and its stockout risk for that quantity.

Example 15

C_e = Cost per unit − Salvage value per unit

   = \$0.20   − \$0

   = \$0.20 per unit

Solution

C_s = Revenue per unit − Cost per unit

   = \$0.80   − \$0.20

   = \$0.60 per unit

$$\text{SL} = \frac{C_s}{C_s + C_e} = \frac{\$0.60}{\$0.60 + \$0.20} = .75$$

Thus, the optimal stocking level must satisfy demand 75 percent of the time. For the uniform distribution, this will be at a point equal to the minimum demand plus 75 percent of the difference between maximum and minimum demands:

$$S_o = 300 + 0.75(500 - 300) = 450 \text{ liters}$$

The stockout risk is $1.00 - 0.75 = 0.25$.

A similar approach applies when demand is normally distributed.

Example 16

Cindy's Cider Bar also sells a blend of cherry juice and apple cider. Demand for the blend is approximately normal, with a mean of 200 liters per week and a standard deviation of 10 liters per week. $C_s = 60$ cents per liter, and $C_e = 20$ cents per liter. Find the optimal stocking level for the apple-cherry blend.

Solution

$$SL = \frac{C_s}{C_s + C_e} = \frac{\$0.60}{\$0.60 + \$0.20} = .75$$

This indicates that 75 percent of the area under the normal curve must be to the left of the stocking level. Appendix B, Table B shows that a value of z between $+0.67$ and $+0.68$, say, $+0.675$, will satisfy this. Thus,

$$S_o = 200 \text{ liters} + 0.675(10 \text{ liters}) = 206.75 \text{ liters}$$

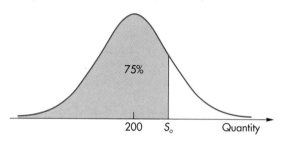

DISCRETE STOCKING LEVELS

When stocking levels are discrete rather than continuous, the service level computed using the ratio $C_s/(C_s + C_e)$ usually does not coincide with a feasible stocking level (e.g., the optimal amount may be *between* five and six units). The solution is to stock at the *next higher level* (e.g., six units). In other words, choose the stocking level so that the desired service level is equaled or *exceeded*. Figure 13–17 illustrates this concept.

The next example illustrates the use of an empirical distribution, followed by an example that illustrates the use of a Poisson distribution.

FIGURE 13-17

The service level achievement must equal or exceed the ratio $C_s/C_s + C_e$

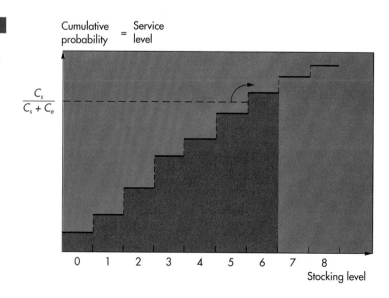

Example 17

Historical records on the use of spare parts for several large hydraulic presses are to serve as an estimate of usage for spares of a newly installed press. Stockout costs involve down-time expenses and special ordering costs. These average $4,200 per unit short. Spares cost $800 each, and unused parts have zero salvage. Determine the optimal stocking level.

Number of Spares Used	Relative Frequency	Cumulative Frequency
0	.20	.20
1	.40	.60
2	.30	.90
3	.10	1.00
4 or more	.00	
	1.00	

Solution

$$C_s = \$4,200 \qquad C_e = \$800 \qquad SL = \frac{C_s}{C_s + C_e} = \frac{\$4,200}{\$4,200 + \$800} = .84$$

The cumulative-frequency column indicates the percentage of time that demand did not exceed (was equal to or less than) some amount. For example, demand does not exceed one spare 60 percent of the time, or two spares 90 percent of the time. Thus, in order to achieve a service level of *at least* 84 percent, it will be necessary to stock two spares (i.e., to go to the next higher stocking level).

Example 18

Demand for long-stemmed red roses at a small flower shop can be approximated using a Poisson distribution that has a mean of four dozen per day. Profit on the roses is $3 per dozen. Leftover flowers are marked down and sold the next day at a loss of $2 per dozen. Assume that all marked-down flowers are sold. What is the optimal stocking level?

Solution

$$C_s = \$3 \qquad C_e = \$2 \qquad SL = \frac{C_s}{C_s + C_e} = \frac{\$3}{\$3 + \$2} = .60$$

Obtain the cumulative frequencies from the Poisson table (Appendix B, Table C) for a mean of 4.0:

Demand (dozen per day)	Cumulative Frequency
0	.018
1	.092
2	.238
3	.434
4	.629
5	.785
⋮	⋮

Compare the service level to the cumulative frequencies. In order to attain a service level of at least .60, it is necessary to stock four dozen.

One final point about discrete stocking levels: If the computed service level is *exactly* equal to the cumulative probability associated with one of the stocking levels, there are *two* equivalent stocking levels in terms of minimizing long-run cost—the one with equal probability and the next higher one. In the preceding example, if the ratio had been equal to .629, we would be indifferent between stocking four dozen and stocking five dozen roses each day.

Inventories are a necessary part of doing business, but having too much inventory is not good. One reason is that inventories tend to hide problems; they make it easier to live with problems rather than eliminate them. Another reason is that inventories are costly to maintain. Consequently, a wise operations strategy is to work toward cutting back inventories by (1) reducing lot sizes and (2) reducing safety stocks.

Ordering in bulk can have adverse effects on the *supply chain,* sometimes resulting in excessive buildups of inventories in the chain. Therefore, managers need to take into account the effect of traditional economic ordering practices on the entire system. Recall that the economic order quantity is based on the relationship

$$Q = \sqrt{\frac{2DS}{H}}$$

One possibility for reducing the economic order quantity is to work to reduce the ordering cost, *S*. This might be accomplished by standardized procedures and perhaps by using *electronic data interchange* with suppliers. Another possibility is to examine holding cost, *H*. If this is understated, using a larger value will reduce the order quantity.

Japanese manufacturers use smaller lot sizes than their Western counterparts because they have a different perspective on inventory carrying costs. In addition to the usual components (e.g., storage, handling, obsolescence), the Japanese recognize the opportunity costs of disrupting the work flow, inability to place machines and workers closer together (which encourages cooperation, socialization, and communication), and hiding problems related to product quality and equipment breakdown. When these are factored in, carrying costs become higher—perhaps much higher—than before.

Companies may be able to achieve additional reductions in inventory by reducing the amount of safety stock carried. Important factors in safety stock are lead time and lead time variability, reductions of which will result in lower safety stocks. Firms can often realize these reductions by working with suppliers, choosing suppliers located close to the buyer, and shifting to smaller lot sizes.

Sharing demand data throughout the supply chain can alleviate the unnecessary buildup of safety stock in the supply chain that occurs when information isn't shared. Manufacturers and suppliers can judge the timing of orders from customers, and customers can use information about suppliers' inventories to set reasonable lead times. Another option is to employ *vendor-managed inventory systems,* where the supplier has the responsibility for inventory replenishment.

To achieve these reductions, an A-B-C approach is very beneficial. This means that all phases of operation should be examined, and those showing the greatest potential for improvement should be attacked first. Early results will demonstrate the benefits of this strategy to both management and workers, making both parties more willing to lend their support to additional efforts.

Last, it is important to make sure that inventory records be kept *accurate* and *up-to-date.* Estimates of holding costs, ordering costs, setup costs, and lead times should be reviewed periodically and updated as necessary.

Summary

Good inventory management is often the mark of a well-run organization. Inventory levels must be planned carefully in order to balance the cost of holding inventory and the cost of providing reasonable levels of customer service. Successful inventory management requires a system to keep track of inventory transactions, accurate information about demand and lead times, realistic estimates of certain inventory-related costs, and a priority system for classifying the items in inventory and allocating control efforts.

Model	Formula	Symbols
1. Basic EOQ	$Q_0 = \sqrt{\dfrac{2DS}{H}}$ (13–2) $TC = \dfrac{Q}{2}H + \dfrac{D}{Q}S$ (13–1) Length of order cycle $= \dfrac{Q_0}{D}$ (13–3)	Q_0 = Economic order quantity D = Annual demand S = Order cost H = Annual carrying cost per unit
2. Economic production quantity	$Q_0 = \sqrt{\dfrac{2DS}{H}}\sqrt{\dfrac{p}{p-u}}$ (13–5) $TC = \dfrac{I_{max}}{2}H + \dfrac{D}{Q}S$ (13–4) Cycle time $= \dfrac{Q}{u}$ (13–6) Run time $= \dfrac{Q}{p}$ (13–7) $I_{max} = \dfrac{Q_0}{p}(p-u)$ (13–8)	Q_0 = Optimal run or order size p = Production or delivery rate u = Usage rate I_{max} = Maximum inventory level
3. Quantity discounts	$TC = \dfrac{Q}{2}H + \dfrac{D}{Q}S + PD$ (13–9)	P = Unit price
4. Reorder point under: *a.* Constant demand and lead time *b.* Variable demand rate *c.* Variable lead time *d.* Variable lead time and demand	$ROP = d(LT)$ (13–10) $ROP = \bar{d}LT + z\sqrt{LT}\,(\sigma_d)$ (13–13) $ROP = d\overline{LT} + zd(\sigma_{LT})$ (13–14) $ROP = \bar{d}LT + z\sqrt{\overline{LT}\sigma_d^2 + \bar{d}^2\sigma_{LT}^2}$ (13–15)	ROP = Quantity on hand at reorder point d = Demand rate LT = Lead time $\bar{d}$ = Average demand rate σ_d = Standard deviation of demand rate z = Standard normal deviation $\overline{LT}$ = Average lead time σ_{LT} = Standard deviation of lead time
5. ROP shortages *a.* Units short per cycle *b.* Units short per year *c.* Annual service level	$E(n) = E(z)\sigma_{dLT}$ (13–16) $E(N) = E(n)\dfrac{D}{Q}$ (13–17) $SL_{annual} = 1 - \dfrac{E(z)\sigma_{dLT}}{Q}$ (13–19)	$E(n)$ = Expected number short per cycle $E(z)$ = Standardized number short σ_{dLT} = Standard deviation of lead time demand $E(N)$ = Expected number short per year SL_{annual} = Annual service level
6. Fixed interval	$Q = \bar{d}(OI + LT) + z\sigma_d\sqrt{OI + LT} - A$ (13–20)	OI = Time between orders A = Amount on hand at order time
7. Single period	$SL = \dfrac{C_s}{C_s + C_e}$ (13–21)	SL = Service level C_s = Shortage cost per unit C_e = Excess cost per unit

TABLE 13–4

Summary of inventory formulas

Four classes of models are described: EOQ, ROP, fixed-interval, and the single-period model. The first three are appropriate if unused items can be carried over into subsequent periods. The single-period model is appropriate when items cannot be carried over. EOQ models address the question of how much to order. The ROP models address the question of when to order and are particularly helpful in dealing with situations that include variations in either demand rate or lead time. ROP models involve service level and safety stock considerations. When the time between orders is fixed, the FOI model is useful. The single-period model is used for items which have a "shelf life" of one period. The models presented in this chapter are summarized in Table 13–4 on the preceding page.

Key Terms

A-B-C approach, 548
cycle counting, 550
economic order quantity (EOQ), 551
excess cost, 574
fixed-order-interval (FOI) model, 571
holding (carrying) cost, 547
inventory, 542
inventory turnover, 544
lead time, 547
ordering costs, 548
periodic system, 545

perpetual inventory system, 545
point-of-sale (POS) system, 547
quantity discounts, 558
reorder point (ROP), 564
safety stock, 564
service level, 565
shortage costs, 548, 574
single-period model, 574
two-bin system, 546
universal product code, 546

Solved Problems

Problem 1

Basic EOQ. A toy manufacturer uses approximately 32,000 silicon chips annually. The chips are used at a steady rate during the 240 days a year that the plant operates. Annual holding cost is 60 cents per chip, and ordering cost is $24. Determine:

a. The optimal order size.

b. The number of workdays in an order cycle.

Solution

$D = 32,000$ chips per year $S = \$24$

$H = \$.60$ per unit per year

a. $Q_0 = \sqrt{\dfrac{2DS}{H}} = \sqrt{\dfrac{2(32,000)\$24}{\$.60}} = 1,600$ chips.

b. $\dfrac{Q_0}{D} = \dfrac{1,600 \text{ chips}}{32,000 \text{ chips/yr.}} = \dfrac{1}{20}$ year (i.e., $\frac{1}{20} \times 240$ days), or 12 days.

Problem 2

Economic production quantity. The Dine Corporation is both a producer and a user of brass couplings. The firm operates 220 days a year and uses the couplings at a steady rate of 50 per day. Couplings can be produced at a rate of 200 per day. Annual storage cost is $1 per coupling, and machine setup cost is $35 per run.

a. Determine the economic run size.

b. Approximately how many runs per year will there be?

c. Compute the maximum inventory level.

d. Determine the length of the *pure consumption* portion of the cycle.

Solution

$D = 50$ units per day $\times$ 220 days per year $= 11,000$ units per year

$S = \$35$

$H = \$1$ per unit per year

$p = 200$ units per day

$u = 50$ units per day

a. $Q_0 = \sqrt{\dfrac{2DS}{H}}\sqrt{\dfrac{p}{p-u}} = \sqrt{\dfrac{2(11,000)35}{1}}\sqrt{\dfrac{200}{200-50}} = 1,013$ units.

b. Number of runs per year: $D/Q_0 = 11,000/1,013 = 10.86$, or 11.

c. $I_{max} = \dfrac{Q_0}{p}(p-u) = \dfrac{1,013}{200}(200-50) = 759.75$ or 760 units.

d. Length of cycle $= \dfrac{Q_0}{u} = \dfrac{1,013 \text{ units}}{50 \text{ units per day}} = 20.26$ days

　　Length of run $= \dfrac{Q_0}{p} = \dfrac{1,013 \text{ units}}{200 \text{ units per day}} = 5.065$ days

　　Length of pure consumption portion $=$ Length of cycle $-$ Length of run

　　　　　　　$= 20.26 - 5.065 = 15.20$ days.

Quantity discounts. A small manufacturing firm uses roughly 3,400 pounds of chemical dye a year. Currently the firm purchases 300 pounds per order and pays $3 per pound. The supplier has just announced that orders of 1,000 pounds or more will be filled at a price of $2 per pound. The manufacturing firm incurs a cost of $100 each time it submits an order and assigns an annual holding cost of 17 percent of the purchase price per pound.

Problem 3

a. Determine the order size that will minimize the total cost.

b. If the supplier offered the discount at 1,500 pounds instead of 1,000 pounds, what order size would minimize total cost?

　　$D = 3,400$ pounds per year　　$S = \$100$　　$H = 0.17P$

Solution

a. Compute the EOQ for $2 per pound:

The quantity ranges are

Range	Unit Price
1 to 999	$3
1,000+	$2

　　$Q_{\$2/pound} = \sqrt{\dfrac{2DS}{H}} = \sqrt{\dfrac{2(3,400)100}{0.17(2)}} = 1,414$ pounds

Because this quantity is feasible at $2 per pound, it is the optimum.

b. When the discount is offered at 1,500 pounds, the EOQ for the $2 per pound range is no longer feasible. Consequently, it becomes necessary to compute the EOQ for $3 per pound and compare the total cost for that order size with the total cost using the price break quantity (i.e., 1,500).

　　$Q_{\$3/pound} = \sqrt{\dfrac{2DS}{H}} = \sqrt{\dfrac{2(3,400)100}{0.17(3)}} = 1,155$ pounds

　　$TC = \left(\dfrac{Q}{2}\right)H \quad + \quad \left(\dfrac{D}{Q}\right)S \quad + \quad PD$

　　$TC_{1,155} = \left(\dfrac{1,155}{2}\right)0.17(3) + \left(\dfrac{3,400}{1,155}\right)100 + 3(3,400)$

　　　　$= \quad \$294.53 \quad + \quad \$294.37 \quad + \$10,200 \; = \$10,789$

　　$TC_{1,500} = \left(\dfrac{1,500}{2}\right)0.17(2) + \left(\dfrac{3,400}{1,500}\right)100 + 2(3,400)$

　　　　$= \quad \$255 \quad\quad + \quad \$226.67 \quad + \$6,800 \; = \$7,282$

Hence, because it would result in a lower total cost, 1,500 is the optimal order size.

Problem 4

ROP for variable demand and constant lead time. The housekeeping department of a motel uses approximately 400 washcloths per day. The actual number tends to vary with the number of guests on any given night. Usage can be approximated by a normal distribution that has a mean of 400 and a standard deviation of 9 washcloths per day. A linen supply company delivers towels and washcloths with a lead time of three days. If the motel policy is to maintain a stockout risk of 2 percent, what is the minimum number of washcloths that must be on hand at reorder time, and how much of that amount can be considered safety stock?

Solution

$\bar{d} = 400$ washcloths per day $LT = 3$ days
$\sigma_d = \;\;\;9$ washcloths per day   Risk = 2 percent, so service level = 98 percent

From Appendix B, Table B, the z value that corresponds to an area under the normal curve to the left of z for 98 percent is about $+2.055$.

$$ROP = \bar{d}LT + z\sqrt{LT}\sigma_d = 400(3) + 2.055\sqrt{3}(9)$$
$$= 1,200 + 32.03, \text{ or approximately } 1,232 \text{ washcloths}$$

Safety stock is approximately 32 washcloths.

Problem 5

ROP for constant demand and variable lead time. The motel in the preceding example uses approximately 600 bars of soap each day, and this tends not to vary by more than a few bars either way. Lead time for soap delivery is normally distributed with a mean of six days and a standard deviation of two days. A service level of 90 percent is desired. Find the ROP.

Solution

$\bar{d} = 600$ bars per day
SL = 90 percent, so $z = +1.28$ (from Appendix B, Table B)
$\overline{LT} = 6$ days
$\sigma_{LT} = 2$ days
$$ROP = \bar{d}\,\overline{LT} + zd(\sigma_{LT}) = 600(6) + 1.28(600)2$$
$$= 5,136 \text{ bars of soap}$$

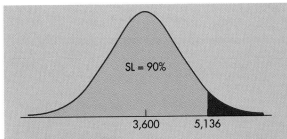

SL = 90%

3,600   5,136

Problem 6

ROP for variable demand rate and variable lead time. The motel replaces broken glasses at a rate of 25 per day. In the past, this quantity has tended to vary normally and have a standard deviation of 3 glasses per day. Glasses are ordered from a Cleveland supplier. Lead time is normally distributed with an average of 10 days and a standard deviation of 2 days. What ROP should be used to achieve a service level of 95 percent?

Solution

$\bar{d} = 25$ glasses per day $\overline{LT} = 10$ days
$\sigma_d = 3$ glasses per day $\sigma_{LT} = 2$ days
SL = 95 percent, so $z = +1.65$ (Appendix B, Table B)

$$\text{ROP} = \bar{d}\,\overline{LT} + z\sqrt{\overline{LT}\sigma_d^2 + \bar{d}\sigma_{LT}^2}$$
$$= 25(10) + 1.65\sqrt{10(3)^2 + (25)^2(2)^2} = 334 \; glasses$$

SL = 95%

250   334

Problem 7

Shortages and service levels. The manager of a store that sells office supplies has decided to set an annual service level of 96 percent for a certain model of telephone answering equipment. The store sells approximately 300 of this model a year. Holding cost is $5 per unit annually, ordering cost is $25, and $\sigma_{dLT} = 7$.

a. What average number of units short per year will be consistent with the specified annual service level?

b. What average number of units short per cycle will provide the desired annual service level?

c. What lead time service level is necessary for the 96 percent annual service level?

Solution

$SL_{annual} = 96$ percent $D = 300$ units $H = \$5$ $S = \$25$ $\sigma_{dLT} = 7$

a. $E(N) = (1 - SL_{annual})\,D = (1 - .96)(300) = 12$ units.

b. $E(N) = E(n)\dfrac{D}{Q}$. Solving for $E(n)$, you have

$$E(n) = E(N) \div \left(\dfrac{D}{Q}\right) = 12 \div \left(\dfrac{300}{Q}\right)$$

$$Q = \sqrt{\dfrac{2DS}{H}} = \sqrt{\dfrac{2(300)(35)}{5}} = 54.77 \text{ (round to 55)}$$

Then $E(n) = 12 \div \left(\dfrac{300}{55}\right) = 2.2$.

c. In order to find the lead time service level, you need the value of $E(z)$. Because the value of $E(n)$ is 2.2 and $E(n) = E(z)\sigma_{dLT}$, you have $2.2 = E(z)(7)$. Solving gives $E(z) = 2.2 \div 7 = 0.314$. Interpolating in Table 13–3 gives the approximate lead time service level. Thus,

$$\frac{0.307 - 0.314}{0.307 - 0.324} = \frac{.5793 - x}{.5793 - .5636}$$

Solving,

$$x = .5728$$

[To interpolate, find the two values between which the computed number falls in the $E(z)$ column. Then find the difference between the computed value and one end of the range, and divide by the difference between the two ends of the range. Perform the corresponding calculation on the two service levels using x for the unknown value, and solve for x. Often, simply "eyeballing" the unknown value will suffice.]

Problem 8

Fixed-order-interval model. A lab orders a number of chemicals from the same supplier every 30 days. Lead time is five days. The assistant manager of the lab must determine how much of one of these chemicals to order. A check of stock revealed that eleven 25-ml jars are on hand. Daily usage of the chemical is approximately normal with a mean of 15.2 ml per day and a standard deviation of 1.6 ml per day. The desired service level for this chemical is 95 percent.

 a. How many jars of the chemical should be ordered?
 b. What is the average amount of safety stock of the chemical?

Solution

$\bar{d} = 15.2$ ml per day, OI = 30 days, SL = 95% requires $z = 1.65$
$\sigma_d = 1.6$ ml per day, LT = 5 days, A = 11 jars $\times$ 25 ml per jar = 275 ml

 a. $\dfrac{\text{Amount}}{\text{to order}} = \bar{d}(\text{OI} + \text{LT}) + z\sigma_d\sqrt{\text{OI} + \text{LT}} - A$

$= 15.2(30 + 5) + 1.65(1.6)\sqrt{30 + 5} - 275 - 272.62$ ml

Convert this to number of jars:

$\dfrac{272.62 \text{ ml}}{25 \text{ ml per jar}} = 10.90$ or 11 jars

 b. Safety stock $= z\sigma_d\sqrt{\text{OI} + \text{LT}} = 1.65(1.6)\sqrt{30 + 5} = 15.62$ ml.

Problem 9

A firm that installs cable TV systems uses a certain piece of equipment for which it carries two spare parts. The parts cost $500 each and have no salvage value. Part failures can be modeled by a Poisson distribution with a mean of two failures during the useful life of the equipment. Holding and disposal costs are negligible. Estimate the apparent range of shortage cost.

Solution

C_s is unknown $C_e = 500

The Poisson table (Appendix B, Table C) provides these values for a mean of 2.0:

Number of Failures	Cumulative Probability
0	.135
1	.406
2	.677
3	.857
4	.947
5	.983
⋮	⋮

For the optimal stocking level, the service level must usually be rounded up to a feasible stocking level. Hence, you know that the service level must have been between .406 and .677 in order to make two units the optimal level. By setting the service level equal first to .406 and then to .677, you can establish bounds on the possible range of shortage costs.

$$\frac{C_s}{C_s + $500} = .406, \text{ so } C_s = .406($500 + C_s)$$

Solving, you find $C_s = 341.75.

Similarly,

$$\frac{C_s}{C_s + \$500} = .677, \text{ so } C_s = .677(\$500 + C_s)$$

Solving, you find $C_s = \$1,047.99$. Hence, the apparent range of shortage cost is $341.75 to $1,047.99.

Discussion and Review Questions

1. What are the primary reasons for holding inventory?
2. What are the requirements for effective inventory management?
3. Briefly describe each of the costs associated with inventory.
4. Contrast independent and dependent demand with respect to inventories.
5. Why might it be inappropriate to use inventory turnover ratios to compare inventory performance of companies that are in different industries?
6. List the major assumptions of the EOQ model.
7. How would you respond to the criticism that EOQ models tend to provide misleading results because values of D, S, and H are, at best, educated guesses?
8. Explain briefly how a higher carrying cost can result in a decrease in inventory.
9. What is safety stock, and what is its purpose?
10. Under what circumstances would the amount of safety stock held be
    a. Large?   *b.* Small?   *c.* Zero?
11. What is meant by the term *service level*? Generally speaking, how is service level related to the amount of safety stock held?
12. Describe briefly the A-B-C approach to inventory control.
13. The purchasing agent for a company that assembles and sells air-conditioning equipment in a Latin American country has noted that the cost of compressors has increased significantly each time they have reordered. The company uses an EOQ model to determine order size. What are the implications of this price escalation with respect to order size? What factors other than price must be taken into consideration?
14. Explain how a decrease in setup time can lead to a decrease in the average amount of inventory a firm holds, and why that would be beneficial.
15. What is the single-period model, and under what circumstances is it appropriate?
16. Can the optimal stocking level in the single-period model ever be less than expected demand? Explain briefly.
17. What are some ways that a company can reduce the need for inventories?

Memo Writing Exercises

1. A fellow manager has just returned from a conference with a revolutionary idea: Eliminate all inventory. Write a memo to this manager in which you outline the reasons why this is not a desirable idea.
2. In an effort to become more efficient and build better supplier relations, your manager, Jane Furman, has examined the company's current practice of using eight different suppliers for eight different items and considered switching to a single supplier who would supply all eight items. However, she discovered that the new supplier will handle orders only on a fixed-interval basis. Write a one-page memo to Furman outlining the cost factors that might increase, and those that might decrease, along with a brief explanation for each factor, under the proposed system.

Problems

1. The manager of an automobile repair shop hopes to achieve a better allocation of inventory control efforts by adopting an A-B-C approach to inventory control. Given the monthly usages in the following table, classify the items in A, B, and C categories according to dollar usage.

Item	Usage	Unit Cost
4021 ...	50	$1,400
9402 ...	300	12
4066 ...	40	700
6500 ...	150	20
9280 ...	10	1,020
4050 ...	80	140
6850 ...	2,000	15
3010 ...	400	20
4400 ...	7,000	5

2. The following table contains figures on the monthly volume and unit costs for a random sample of 16 items from a list of 2,000 inventory items at a health care facility.

Item	Unit Cost	Usage
K34	10	200
K35	25	600
K36	36	150
M10	16	25
M20	20	80
Z45	80	200
F14	20	300
F95	30	800
F99	20	60
D45	10	550
D48	12	90
D52	15	110
D57	40	120
N08	30	40
P05	16	500
P09	10	30

    a. Develop an A-B-C classification for these items.

    b. How could the manager use this information?

    c. After reviewing your classification scheme, suppose that the manager decides to place item P05 into the A category. What are some possible explanations for this decision?

3. A large bakery buys flour in 25-pound bags. The bakery uses an average of 4,860 bags a year. Preparing an order and receiving a shipment of flour involves a cost of $4 per order. Annual carrying costs are $30 per bag.

    a. Determine the economic order quantity.

    b. What is the average number of bags on hand?

    c. How many orders per year will there be?

    d. Compute the total cost of ordering and carrying flour.

    e. If annual ordering cost were to increase by $1 per order, how much would that affect the minimum total annual cost?

4. A large law firm uses an average of 40 packages of copier paper a day. The firm operates 260 days a year. Storage and handling costs for the paper are $3 a year per pack, and it costs approximately $6 to order and receive a shipment of paper.

    a. What order size would minimize total annual ordering and carrying costs?

    b. Compute the total annual cost using your order size from part *a.*

    c. Except for rounding, are annual ordering and carrying costs always equal at the EOQ?

    d. The office manager is currently using an order size of 200 packages. The partners of the firm expect the office to be managed "in a cost-efficient manner." Would you recommend that the office manager use the optimal order size instead of 200 packages? Justify your answer.

5. Garden Variety Flower Shop uses 750 clay pots a month. The pots are purchased at $2 each. Annual carrying costs are estimated to be 30 percent of cost, and ordering costs are $20 per order. The manager has been using an order size of 1,500 flower pots. The store's accounting firm estimates carrying cost to be 30 percent of purchase of price per unit. The manager continues to use an order size of 1,500 flower pots.

   a. What additional annual cost is the shop incurring by staying with this order size?

   b. Other than cost savings, what benefit would using the optimal order quantity yield?

6. A produce distributor uses 800 packing crates a month, which it purchases at a cost of $10 each. The manager has assigned an annual carrying cost of 35 percent of the purchase price per crate. Ordering costs are $28. Currently the manager orders once a month. How much could the firm save annually in ordering and carrying costs by using the EOQ?

7. A manager receives a forecast for next year. Demand is projected to be 600 units for the first half of the year and 900 units for the second half. The monthly holding cost is $2 per unit, and it costs an estimated $55 to process an order.

   a. Assuming that monthly demand will be level during each of the six-month periods covered by the forecast (e.g., 100 per month for each of the first six months), determine an order size that will minimize the sum of ordering and carrying costs that can be used for each of the six-month periods.

   b. Why is it important to be able to assume that demand will be level during each six-month period?

   c. If the vendor is willing to offer the manager a discount of $10 *per order* for ordering in multiples of 50 units (e.g., 50, 100, 150), would you advise the manager to take advantage of the offer in either period? If so, what order size would you recommend?

8. A food processor uses approximately 27,000 glass jars a month for its fruit juice product. Because of storage limitations, a lot size of 4,000 jars has been used. Monthly holding cost is 18 cents per jar, and reordering cost is $60 per order. The company operates an average of 20 days a month.

   a. What penalty is the company incurring by its present order size?

   b. The manager would prefer ordering 10 times each month but would have to justify any change in order size. One possibility is to simplify order processing to reduce the ordering cost. What ordering cost would enable the manager to justify ordering every other day?

   c. Suppose that after investigating ordering cost, the manager is able to reduce it to $50. How else could the manager justify using an order size that would be consistent with ordering every other day?

9. The Friendly Sausage Factory (FSF) can produce hot dogs at a rate of 5,000 per day. FSF supplies hot dogs to local stores and restaurants at a steady rate of 250 per day. The cost to prepare the equipment for producing hot dogs is $22. Annual holding costs are 15 cents per hot dog. The factory operates 300 days a year. Find

   a. The optimal run size.

   b. The number of runs per year.

   c. The length (in days) of a run.

10. A chemical firm produces sodium bisulfate in 100-pound bags. Demand for this product is 20 tons per day. The capacity for producing the product is 50 tons per day. Setup costs $100, and storage and handling costs are $5 per ton a year. The firm operates 200 days a year. (Note: 1 ton = 2,000 pounds.)

   a. How many bags per run are optimal?

   b. What would the average inventory be for this lot size?

   c. Determine the approximate length of a production run, in days.

   d. About how many runs per year would there be?

   e. How much could the company save annually if the setup cost could be reduced to $25 per run?

11. A company is about to begin production of a new product. The manager of the department that will produce one of the components for the product wants to know how often the machine used to produce the item will be available for other work. The machine will produce the item at a rate of 200 units a day. Eighty units will be used daily in assembling the final product. Assembly will take place five days a week, 50 weeks a year. The manager estimates that it will take

almost a full day to get the machine ready for a production run, at a cost of $60. Inventory holding costs will be $2 a year.

a. What run quantity should be used to minimize total annual costs?

b. What is the length of a production run in days?

c. During production, at what rate will inventory build up?

d. If the manager wants to run another job between runs of this item, and needs a minimum of 10 days per cycle for the other work, will there be enough time?

12. A company manufactures hair dryers. It buys some of the components, but it makes the heating element, which it can produce at the rate of 800 per day. Hair dryers are assembled daily, 250 days a year, at a rate of 300 per day. Because of the disparity between the production and usage rates, the heating elements are periodically produced in batches of 2,000 units.

a. Approximately how many *batches* of heating elements are produced annually?

b. If production on a batch begins when there is no inventory of heating elements on hand, how much inventory will be on hand *two days later?*

c. What is the average inventory of elements, assuming each production cycle begins when there are none on hand?

d. The same equipment that is used to make the heating elements could also be used to make a component for another of the firm's products. That job would require four days, including setup. Setup time for making a batch of the heating elements is a half day. Is there enough time to do this job between production of batches of heating elements? Explain.

13. A mail-order house uses 18,000 boxes a year. Carrying costs are 20 cents per box a year, and ordering costs are $32. The following price schedule applies. Determine:

a. The optimal order quantity.

b. The number of orders per year.

Number of Boxes	Price per Box
1,000 to 1,999	$1.25
2,000 to 4,999	1.20
5,000 to 9,999	1.18
10,000 or more	1.15

14. A jewelry firm buys semiprecious stones to make bracelets and rings. The supplier quotes a price of $8 per stone for quantities of 600 stones or more, $9 per stone for orders of 400 to 599 stones, and $10 per stone for lesser quantities. The jewelry firm operates 200 days per year. Usage rate is 25 stones per day, and ordering costs are $48.

a. If carrying costs are $2 per year for each stone, find the order quantity that will minimize total annual cost.

b. If annual carrying costs are 30 percent of unit cost, what is the optimal order size?

c. If lead time is six working days, at what point should the company reorder?

15. A manufacturer of exercise equipment purchases the pulley section of the equipment from a supplier who lists these prices: less than 1,000, $5 each; 1,000 to 3,999, $4.95 each; 4,000 to 5,999, $4.90 each; and 6,000 or more, $4.85 each. Ordering costs are $50, annual carrying costs are 40 percent of purchase cost, and annual usage is 4,900 pulleys. Determine an order quantity that will minimize total cost.

16. A company will begin stocking remote control devices. Expected monthly demand is 800 units. The controllers can be purchased from either supplier A or supplier B. Their price lists are as follows:

SUPPLIER A		SUPPLIER B	
Quantity	Unit Price	Quantity	Unit Price
1–199	$14.00	1–149	$14.10
200–499	13.80	150–349	13.90
500+	13.60	350+	13.70

Ordering cost is $40 and annual holding cost is 25 percent of unit price per unit. Which supplier should be used and what order quantity is optimal if the intent is to minimize total annual costs?

17. A manager just received a new price list from a supplier. It will now cost $1.00 a box for order quantities of 801 or more boxes, $1.10 a box for 200 to 800 boxes, and $1.20 a box for smaller quantities. Ordering cost is $80 per order and carrying costs are $10 per box a year. The firm uses 3,600 boxes a year. The manager has suggested a "round number" order size of 800 boxes. The manager's rationale is that with a U-shaped cost curve that is fairly flat at its minimum, the difference in total annual cost between 800 and 801 units would be small anyway. How would you reply to the manager's suggestion? What order size would you recommend?

18. A newspaper publisher uses roughly 800 feet of baling wire each day to secure bundles of newspapers while they are being distributed to carriers. The paper is published Monday through Saturday. Lead time is six workdays. What is the appropriate reorder point quantity, given that the company desires a service level of 95 percent, if that stockout risk for various levels of safety stock are as follows: 1,500 feet, 0.10; 1,800 feet, 0.05; 2,100 feet, 0.02; and 2,400 feet, 0.01?

19. Given this information:

    Expected demand during lead time = 300 units

    Standard deviation of lead time demand = 30 units

    Determine each of the following, assuming that lead time demand is distributed normally:

    a. The ROP that will provide a risk of stockout of 1 percent during lead time.

    b. The safety stock needed to attain a 1 percent risk of stockout during lead time.

    c. Would a stockout risk of 2 percent require more or less safety stock than a 1 percent risk? Explain. Would the ROP be larger, smaller, or unaffected if the acceptable risk was 2 percent instead of 1 percent? Explain.

20. Given this information:

    Lead-time demand = 600 pounds

    Standard deviation of lead-time demand = 52 pounds

    Acceptable stockout risk during lead time = 4 percent

    a. What amount of safety stock is appropriate?

    b. When should this item be reordered?

21. Demand for walnut fudge ice cream at the Sweet Cream Dairy can be approximated by a normal distribution with a mean of 21 gallons per week and a standard deviation of 3.5 gallons per week. The new manager desires a service level of 90 percent. Lead time is two days, and the dairy is open seven days a week. (Hint: Work in terms of weeks.)

    a. If an ROP model is used, what ROP would be consistent with the desired service level?

    b. If a fixed-interval model is used instead of an ROP model, what order size would be needed for the 90 percent service level with an order interval of 10 days and a supply of 8 gallons on hand at the order time? If the previous order was made 8 days ago, what is the probability of a stockout before the order arrives?

    c. Suppose the manager is using the ROP model described in part a. One day after placing an order with the supplier, the manager receives a call from the supplier that the order will be delayed because of problems at the supplier's plant. The supplier promises to have the order there in two days. After hanging up, the manager checks the supply of walnut fudge ice cream and finds that 2 gallons have been sold since the order was placed. Assuming the supplier's promise is valid, what is the probability that the dairy will run out of this flavor before the shipment arrives?

22. The injection molding department of a company uses an average of 30 gallons of special lubricant a day. The supply of the lubricant is replenished when the amount on hand is 170 gallons. It takes four days for an order to be delivered. Safety stock is 50 gallons, which provides a stockout risk of 9 percent. What amount of safety stock would be needed if the acceptable risk of a stockout is 3 percent?

23. A company uses 85 circuit boards a day in a manufacturing process. The person who orders the boards follows this rule: Order when the amount on hand drops to 625 boards. Orders are delivered approximately six days after being placed. The delivery time is normal with a mean of six days and a standard deviation of 1.10 days. What is the probability that the supply of circuit

boards will be exhausted before the order is received if boards are reordered when the amount on hand drops to 625 boards?

24. One item a computer store sells is supplied by a vendor who handles only that item. Demand for that item recently changed, and the store manager must determine when to replenish it. The manager wants a probability of at least 96 percent of not having a stockout during lead time. The manager expects demand to average a dozen units a day and have a standard deviation of 2 units a day. Lead time is variable, averaging four days with a standard deviation of one day. Assume normality and that seasonality is not a factor.

  a. When should the manager reorder to achieve the desired probability?

  b. Why might the model not be appropriate if seasonality was present?

25. The manager of a car wash received a revised price list from the vendor who supplies soap, and a promise of a shorter lead time for deliveries. Formerly the lead time was four days, but now the vendor promises a reduction of 25 percent in that time. Annual usage of soap is 4,500 gallons. The car wash is open 360 days a year. Assume that daily usage is normal, and that it has a standard deviation of 2 gallons per day. The ordering cost is $30 and annual carrying cost is $3 a gallon. The revised price list (cost per gallon) is shown in the table.

Quantity	Unit Price
1–399	$2.00
400–799	1.70
800+	1.62

  a. What order quantity is optimal?

  b. What ROP is appropriate if the acceptable risk of a stockout is 1.5 percent?

26. A small copy center uses five 500-sheet boxes of copy paper a week. Experience suggests that usage can be well approximated by a normal distribution with a mean of five boxes per week and a standard deviation of one-half box per week. Two weeks are required to fill an order for letterhead stationery. Ordering cost is $2, and annual holding cost is 20 cents per box.

  a. Determine the economic order quantity, assuming a 52-week year.

  b. If the copy center reorders when the supply on hand is 12 boxes, compute the risk of a stockout.

  c. If a fixed interval of seven weeks instead of an ROP is used for reordering, what risk does the copy center incur that it will run out of stationery before this order arrives if it orders 36 boxes when the amount on hand is 12 boxes?

27. Ned's Natural Foods sells unshelled peanuts by the pound. Historically, Ned has observed that daily demand is normally distributed with a mean of 80 pounds and a standard deviation of 10 pounds. Lead time also appears normally distributed with a mean of eight days and a standard deviation of one day.

  a. What ROP would provide stockout risk of 10 percent during lead time?

  b. What is the expected number of units (pounds) short per cycle?

28. Regional Supermarket is open 360 days per year. Daily use of cash register tape averages 10 rolls. Usage appears normally distributed with a standard deviation of 2 rolls per day. The cost of ordering tape is $1, and carrying costs are 40 cents per roll a year. Lead time is three days.

  a. What is the EOQ?

  b. What ROP will provide a lead time service level of 96 percent?

  c. What is the expected number of units short per cycle with 96 percent? Per year?

  d. What is the annual service level?

29. A service station uses 1,200 cases of oil a year. Ordering cost is $40, and annual carrying cost is $3 per case. The station owner has specified an *annual* service level of 99 percent.

  a. What level of safety stock is appropriate if lead time demand is normally distributed with a mean of 80 cases and a standard deviation of 5 cases?

  b. What is the risk of a stockout during lead time?

30. Weekly demand for diesel fuel at a department of parks depot is 250 gallons. The depot operates 52 weeks a year. Weekly usage is normal, and has a standard deviation of 14 gallons.

Holding cost for the fuel is $1 a month, and it costs $20 in administrative time to submit an order for more fuel. It takes one-half week to receive a delivery of diesel fuel. Determine the amount of safety stock that would be needed if the manager wants

a. An annual service level of 98 percent. What is the implication of negative safety stock?

b. The expected number of units short per order cycle to be no more than 5 gallons.

31. A drugstore uses fixed-order cycles for many of the items it stocks. The manager wants a service level of .98. Determine the order size that will be consistent with this service level for the items in the table for an order interval of 14 days and a lead time of 2 days:

Item	Average Daily Demand	Standard Deviation	Quantity on Hand
K033	60	5	420
K144	50	4	375
L700	8	2	160

32. A manager must set up inventory ordering systems for two new production items, P34 and P35. P34 can be ordered at any time, but P35 can only be ordered once every four weeks. The company operates 50 weeks a year, and the weekly usage rates for both items are normally distributed. The manager has gathered the following information about the items:

	Item P34	Item P35
Average weekly demand	60 units	70 units
Standard deviation	4 units per week	5 units per week
Unit cost	$15	$20
Annual holding cost	30%	30%
Ordering cost	$70	$30
Lead time	2 weeks	2 weeks
Acceptable stockout risk	2.5%	2.5%

a. When should the manager reorder each item?

b. Compute the order quantity for P34.

c. Compute the order quantity for P35 if 110 units are on hand at the time the order is placed.

33. Given the following list of items,

a. Classify the items as A, B, or C.

b. Determine the economic order quantity for each item (round to the nearest whole unit).

Item	Estimated Annual Demand	Ordering Cost	Holding Cost (%)	Unit Price
H4-010	20,000	50	20	2.50
H5-201	60,200	60	20	4.00
P6-400	9,800	80	30	28.50
P6-401	16,300	50	30	12.00
P7-100	6,250	50	30	9.00
P9-103	4,500	50	40	22.00
TS-300	21,000	40	25	45.00
TS-400	45,000	40	25	40.00
TS-041	800	40	25	20.00
V1-001	26,100	25	35	4.00

34. Demand for jelly doughnuts on Saturdays at Don's Doughnut Shoppe is shown in the following table. Determine the optimal number of doughnuts, in dozens, to stock if labor, materials, and overhead are estimated to be $3.20 per dozen, doughnuts are sold for $4.80 per dozen, and leftover doughnuts at the end of each day are sold the next day at half price. What is the *resulting* service level?

Demand (dozens)	Relative Frequency
19	.01
20	.05
21	.12
22	.18
23	.13
24	.14
25	.10
26	.11
27	.10
28	.04
29	.02

35. A public utility intends to buy a turbine as part of an expansion plan and must now decide on the number of spare parts to order. One part, no. X135, can be purchased for $100 each. Carrying and disposal costs are estimated to be 145 percent of the purchase price over the life of the turbine. A stockout would cost roughly $88,000 due to downtime, ordering, and "special purchase" factors. Historical records based on the performance of similar equipment operating under similar conditions suggest that demand for spare parts will tend to approximate a Poisson distribution with a mean of 3.2 parts for the useful life of the turbine.

    a. What is the optimal number of spares to order?

    b. Carrying no spare parts would be the best strategy for what range of shortage cost?

36. Skinner's Fish Market buys fresh Boston bluefish daily for $4.20 per pound and sells it for $5.70 per pound. At the end of each business day, any remaining bluefish is sold to a producer of cat food for $2.40 per pound. Daily demand can be approximated by a normal distribution with a mean of 80 pounds and a standard deviation of 10 pounds. What is the optimal stocking level?

37. A small grocery store sells fresh produce, which it obtains from a local farmer. During the strawberry season, demand for fresh strawberries can be reasonably approximated using a normal distribution with a mean of 40 quarts per day and a standard deviation of 6 quarts per day. Excess costs run 35 cents per quart. The grocer orders 49 quarts per day.

    a. What is the implied cost of shortage per quart?

    b. Why might this be a reasonable figure?

38. Demand for devil's food whipped-cream layer cake at a local pastry shop can be approximated using a Poisson distribution with a mean of six per day. The manager estimates it costs $9 to prepare each cake. Fresh cakes sell for $12. Day-old cakes sell for $9 each. What stocking level is appropriate if one-half of the day-old cakes are sold and the rest thrown out?

39. Burger Prince buys top-grade ground beef for $1.00 per pound. A large sign over the entrance guarantees that the meat is fresh daily. Any leftover meat is sold to the local high school cafeteria for 80 cents per pound. Four hamburgers can be prepared from each pound of meat. Burgers sell for 60 cents each. Labor, overhead, meat, buns, and condiments cost 50 cents per burger. Demand is normally distributed with a mean of 400 pounds per day and a standard deviation of 50 pounds per day. What daily order quantity is optimal? (Hint: Shortage cost must be in dollars per pound.)

40. Demand for rug-cleaning machines at Clyde's U-Rent-It is shown in the following table. Machines are rented by the day only. Profit on the rug cleaners is $10 per day. Clyde has four rug-cleaning machines.

Demand	Frequency
0	.30
1	.20
2	.20
3	.15
4	.10
5	.05
	1.00

a. Assuming that Clyde's stocking decision is optimal, what is the implied range of excess cost per machine?

b. Your answer from part a has been presented to Clyde, who protests that the amount is too low. Does this suggest an increase or a decrease in the number of rug machines he stocks? Explain.

c. Suppose now that the $10 mentioned as profit is instead the excess cost per day for each machine and that the shortage cost is unknown. Assuming that the optimal number of machines is four, what is the implied range of shortage cost per machine?

41. A manager is going to purchase new processing equipment and must decide on the number of spare parts to order with the new equipment. The spares cost $200 each, and any unused spares will have an expected salvage value of $50 each. The probability of usage can be described by this distribution:

Number	0	1	2	3
Probability	.10	.50	.25	.15

If a part fails and a spare is not available, it will take two days to obtain a replacement and install it. The cost for idle equipment is $500 per day. What quantity of spares should be ordered?

42. A Las Vegas supermarket bakery must decide how many wedding cakes to prepare for the upcoming weekend. Cakes cost $33 each to make, and they sell for $60 each. Unsold cakes are reduced to half-price on Monday, and typically one-third of those are sold. Any that remain are donated to a nearby senior center. Analysis of recent demand resulted in the following table:

Demand	0	1	2	3
Probability	.15	.35	.30	.20

How many cakes should be prepared to maximize expected profit?

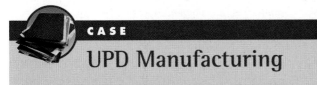

CASE

UPD Manufacturing

UPD Manufacturing produces a range of health-care appliances for hospital as well as for home use. The company has experienced a steady demand for its products, which are highly regarded in the health-care field. Recently the company has undertaken a review of its inventory ordering procedures as part of a larger effort to reduce costs.

One of the company's products is a blood pressure testing kit. UPD manufactures all of the components for the kit in-house except for the digital display unit. The display units are ordered at six-week intervals from the supplier. This ordering system began about five years ago, because the supplier insisted on it. However, that supplier was bought out by another supplier about a year ago, and the six-week ordering requirement is no longer in place. Nonetheless, UPD has continued to use the six-week ordering policy. According to purchasing manager Tom Chambers, "Unless somebody can give me a reason for changing, I'm going to stick with what we've been doing. I don't have time to reinvent the wheel."

Further discussions with Tom revealed a cost of $32 to order and receive a shipment of display units from the supplier. The company assembles 89 kits a week. Also, information from Sara James, in Accounting, indicated a weekly carrying cost of $.08 for each display unit.

The supplier has been quite reliable with deliveries; orders are received five working days after they are faxed to the supplier. Tom indicated that as far as he was concerned, lead-time variability is virtually nonexistent.

Questions

1. Would using an order interval other than every six weeks reduce costs? If so, what order interval would be best, and what order size would that involve?

2. Would you recommend changing to the optimal order interval? Explain.

CASE

Harvey Industries

Background

Harvey Industries, a Wisconsin company, specializes in the assembly of high-pressure washer systems and in the sale of repair parts for these systems. The products range from small portable high-pressure washers to large industrial installations for snow removal from vehicles stored outdoors during the winter months. Typical uses for high-pressure water cleaning include:

Automobiles

Airplanes

Building maintenance

Barns

Engines

Ice cream plants

Lift trucks

Machinery

Swimming pools

Industrial customers include General Motors, Ford, Chrysler, Delta Airlines, United Parcel Service, and Shell Oil Company.

Although the industrial applications are a significant part of its sales, Harvey Industries is primarily an assembler of equipment for coin operated self-service car wash systems. The typical car wash is of concrete block construction with an equipment room in the center, flanked on either side by a number of bays. The cars are driven into the bays where the owner can wash and wax the car, utilizing high-pressure hot water and liquid wax. A dollar bill changer is available to provide change for the use of the equipment and the purchase of various products from dispensers. The products include towels, tire cleaner, and upholstery cleaner.

In recent years Harvey Industries has been in financial difficulty. The company has lost money for three of the last four years, with the last year's loss being $17,174 on sales of $1,238,674. Inventory levels have been steadily increasing to their present levels of $124,324.

The company employs 23 people with the management team consisting of the following key employees: president, sales manager, manufacturing manager, controller, and purchasing manager. The abbreviated organization chart reflects the reporting relationship of the key employees and the three individuals who report directly to the manufacturing manager.

Current Inventory Control System

The current inventory control "system" consists of orders for stock replenishment being made by the stockroom foreman, the purchasing manager, or the manufacturing manager whenever one of them notices that the inventory is low. An order for replenishment of inventory is also placed whenever someone (either a customer or an employee in the assembly area) wants an item and it is not in stock.

Some inventory is needed for the assembly of the high-pressure equipment for the car wash and industrial applications. There are current and accurate bills of material for these assemblies. The material needs to support the assembly schedule are generally known well in advance of the build schedule.

The majority of inventory transactions are for repair parts and for supplies used by the car washes, such as paper towels, detergent, and wax concentrate. Because of the constant and rugged use of the car wash equipment, there is a steady demand for the various repair parts.

The stockroom is well organized, with parts stored in locations according to each vendor. The number of vendors is relatively limited, with each vendor generally supplying many different parts. For example, the repair parts from Allen Bradley, a manufacturer of electrical motors, are stocked in the same location. These repair parts will be used to provide service for the many electrical motors that are part of the high-pressure pump and motor assembly used by all of the car washes.

Because of the heavy sales volume of repair parts, there are generally two employees working in the stockroom—a stockroom foreman who reports to the manufacturing manager and an assistant to the foreman. One of these two employees will handle customer orders. Many customers stop by and order the parts and supplies they need. Telephone orders are also received and are shipped by United Parcel Service the same day.

The assembly area has some inventory stored on the shop floor. This inventory consists of low-value items that are used every day, such as nuts, bolts, screws, and washers. These purchased items do not amount to very much dollar volume throughout the year. Unfortunately, oftentimes the assembly area is out of one of these basic items and this causes a significant amount of downtime for the assembly lines.

Paperwork is kept to a minimum. A sales slip listing the part numbers and quantities sold to a customer is generally made out for each sale. If the assembly department needs items that are not stocked on the assembly floor, someone from that department will enter the stockroom and withdraw the necessary material. There is no paperwork made out for the items needed on the assembly floor.

There were 973 different part numbers purchased for stock last year and those purchases amounted to $314,673. An analysis of inventory records shows that $220,684 was spent on just 179 of the part numbers.

Fortunately for Harvey Industries, most of the items they purchase are stocked by either the manufacturer or by a wholesaler. When it is discovered that the company is out of stock on an item, it generally takes only two or three days to replenish the stock.

Due to the company's recent losses, its auditing firm became concerned about the company's ability to continue in business. Recently the company sold off excess vacant land adjoining its manufacturing facility to generate cash to meet its financial obligations.

New President

Because of the recent death of the owner, the trust department of a Milwaukee Bank (as trustee for the state) has taken over the company's affairs and has appointed a new company president. The new president has identified many problem areas—one of which is improper inventory control. He has retained you as a consultant to make specific recommendations concerning a revised inventory control system. What are your recommendations and their rationale?

Source: This case was prepared by Donald F. Condit of the Lawrence Technological University, Southfield, Michigan, as a basis for class discussion rather than to illustrate either effective or ineffective organizational practices. It was presented at the Midwest Case Writers Association Workshop, 1984, and accepted by referees of the Midwest Case Writers Association for international distribution. Reprinted by permission.

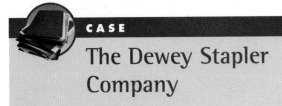

CASE

The Dewey Stapler Company

From: Martin Crane,
      Sales Manager

To: Allen Grace, President

Dear Allen:

Well, it has been a very disappointing year. We've missed our quota by 10 or 15 percent in virtually every district and this is the year I had such high hopes for. When we decided to open up four branch warehouses rather than shipping from our central location only, I was convinced that this would give us better customer service. The last of the warehouses was opened up last May, just before our peak summer season, so perhaps some of the problem is just not having enough experience with branch warehouses. But I think it goes deeper than that.

Our warehouse people are authorized to keep a one-month supply of inventory on hand. While I know you feel strongly that the substantial increase in inventory we had during the year was due to the warehouse program, I can't see why it requires any more inventory to keep a month's supply on hand in four branches and a main location than it did to keep a month's supply on hand back at the main location. A month's supply is a month's supply no matter how you look at it.

To my way of thinking, the real problem is customer service. Our salespeople are demoralized. They simply can't get the stock shipped out of the warehouses because the warehouses don't have it on hand. Forty percent of our customer orders, of course, are still being shipped out of the main location. Our warehouse people tell me that these customer orders get preference and their stock replenishment orders are pushed aside.

Allen, we've got to solve this problem. There's no sense in having a salesforce if we can't have the stock to back them up. I propose the plant location be required to ship warehouse stocking orders just the same as they ship customer orders.

They should treat the warehouses like a customer. In fact, the warehouses are their *biggest* customer and should be serviced accordingly. I propose also that the one-month inventory guideline be removed. Let the warehouse people stock whatever they think they need to support the salesforce. I would volunteer to have my district managers sit with the branch warehouse people to give them some idea of what they should really be ordering.

Allen, this branch warehouse program has been as big a disappointment to me as it has to you. I know you're concerned about the fact that inventories have been going up, but I frankly attribute that to poor management back at the plant. And, quite honestly, Allen, I don't think that people at the plant realize our problems out here in the field or are giving us the kind of support we need. Without it, we have no chance of making the sales quota. Instead of selling, I'm spending most of my time playing chaplain to a bunch of demoralized salespeople.

Sincerely,

Martin

From: Robert Ellers,
Inventory Manager

To: Allen Grace, President

Dear Mr. Grace:

You asked me what my plans were to respond to Martin Crane's letter of January 5. I don't know where to start. This warehouse program has really torn us apart.

We thought that when branch warehouses were added, we would simply have to split some of the stock we had among the warehouses. Instead, we've had to build up the inventory very substantially. We don't get any plans from the warehouses at all. All we see is orders. We have no idea what their inventory position is when we get the orders and we only get them two to three weeks before we have to ship them. Then comes the moment of truth. We have a shortage on a particular item. Here's a customer order and also a warehouse stock replenishment order. Does the warehouse really need it? We know the customer does. In practice, I must admit we wind up waiting until the warehouse screams although we know we may very well be hurting customer service at the branch warehouses.

Mr. Grace, I'm more worried about *this* year than I was about last. Some warehouses showed a disturbing tendency to keep their inventories low during the off-season so that they could boast about their inventory turnover. Then during the peak season, they expect me to turn the faucet on back at the plant. We don't have enough storage space at the plant to build up the inventory required during the off-season in order to keep people working at a steady rate. We need this inventory buildup in order to give good service during the peak season. I've been told repeatedly by plant management that we must keep people working at a steady rate.

All this squabbling about inventory levels prompts me to suggest an approach. We normally would manufacture in a lot size that would be equivalent to about a three-months' supply. When we do that, why don't I just ship a three-months' supply out to each branch warehouse, and then we won't have to bother worrying about them until the next lot is manufactured. Then they can't complain that they're not getting their fair share.

One of the disturbing elements that you may not have heard about is that Frank, our traffic manager, has now suggested that we ship to the West Coast warehouses by sea. This would mean going through the Panama Canal and would substantially increase our lead time and reduce our flexibility. He says, "Flexibility is like motherhood. I'm talking a $50,000 savings in transportation costs, and if you guys have to work a little harder to make that happen, so be it."

Mr. Grace, I really am almost at my wit's end. Perhaps one of the things we ought to consider would be a computer system for tying all of the warehouses together so we could cover a shortage at one warehouse by shipping from another warehouse. Last September, I checked on items that were out of stock in the Atlanta warehouse and I found that virtually every one of them was in adequate supply throughout the system; i.e., we either had them in Dallas, Los Angeles, Chicago, or back at the main plant. This type of computer system would be expensive, but perhaps this is the answer to our service problem.

Sincerely,

Robert Ellers

Question

The Dewey Stapler Company has some very serious problems. A number of misconceptions about inventory management in the company need to be corrected. Take the position of a consultant called in by Allen Grace, the president. You have enough information in these letters to give him some very helpful recommendations. Write a memo outlining your thoughts. Include a discussion of what will happen to service levels if total inventory investment remains constant.

Source: Reprinted by permission from Oliver W. Wright, *Production and Inventory Management in the Computer Age* (Boston: Cahners, 1974).

Bruegger's Bagel Bakery

www.brueggers.com

Bruegger's Bagel Bakery makes and sells a variety of bagels, including plain, onion, poppyseed, and cinnamon raisin, as well as assorted flavors of cream cheese. Bagels are the major source of revenue for the company.

The bagel business is a $3 billion dollar industry. Bagels are very popular with consumers. Not only are they relatively low in fat, they are filling, and they taste good! Investors like the bagel industry because it can be highly profitable: it only costs about $.10 to make a bagel, and they can be sold for $.50 each or more. Although some bagel companies have done poorly in recent years, due mainly to poor management, Bruegger's business is booming; it is number one nationally, with over 450 shops that sell bagels, coffee, and bagel sandwiches for takeout or on-premise consumption. Many stores in the Bruegger's chain generate an average of $800,000 in sales annually.

Production of bagels is done in batches, according to flavor, with each flavor being produced on a daily basis. Production of bagels at Bruegger's begins at a processing plant, where the basic ingredients of flour, water, yeast, and flavorings are combined in a special mixing machine. After the dough has been thoroughly mixed, it is transferred to another machine that shapes the dough into individual bagels. Once the bagels have been formed, they are loaded onto refrigerated trucks for shipping to individual stores. When the bagels reach a store, they are unloaded from the trucks and temporarily stored while they rise. The final two steps of processing involve boiling the bagels in a kettle of water and malt for one minute, and then baking the bagels in an oven for approximately 15 minutes.

The process is depicted in Figure 1.

Quality is an important feature of a successful business. Customers judge the quality of bagels by their appearance (size, shape, and shine), taste, and consistency. Customers are also sensitive to the service they receive when they make their purchases. Bruegger's devotes careful attention to quality at every stage of operation, from choosing suppliers of ingredients, careful monitoring of ingredients, and keeping equipment in good operating condition to monitoring output at each step in the process. At the stores, employees are instructed to watch for deformed bagels and to remove them when they find them. (Deformed bagels are returned to a processing plant where they are sliced into bagel chips, packaged, and then taken back to the stores for sale, thereby reducing the scrap rate.) Employees who work in the stores are carefully chosen and then trained so that they are competent to operate the necessary equipment in the stores and to provide the desired level of service to customers.

The company operates with minimal inventories of raw materials and inventories of partially completed bagels at the plant and very little inventory of bagels at the stores. One reason for this is to maintain a high degree of freshness in the final product by continually supplying fresh product to the stores. A second reason is to keep costs down; minimal inventories mean less space is needed for storage.

Questions

1. Bruegger's maintains relatively little inventory at either its plants or its retail stores. List the benefits and risks of this policy.

2. Quality is very important to Bruegger's.

   a. What features of bagels do customers look at to judge their quality?

   b. At what points in the production process do workers check bagel quality?

   c. List the steps in the production process, beginning with purchasing ingredients, and ending with the sale, and state how quality can be positively affected at each step.

3. Which inventory models could be used for ordering the ingredients for bagels? Which model do you think would be most appropriate for deciding how many bagels to make in a given batch?

4. Bruegger's has bagel-making machines at its plants. Another possibility would be to have a bagel-making machine at each store. What advantages does each alternative have?

Processing plant   A retail store

PSC, Inc.

www.pscnet.com

PSC designs and produces a variety of laser bar code scanning devices. The products include hand-held bar code readers, high-speed fixed position industrial scanners, and retail checkout scanners as well as a full line of accessories, software, and supplies to support its products. Headquartered in Eugene, OR, the company has manufacturing facilities in Eugene, and Paris, France, with roughly 1,200 employees worldwide.

Products

Bar code scanners are designed for a variety of situations that can involve long range scanning, reading small bar codes, and performing high-speed scans. They are used extensively in industry, business, and government to manage and control the entire supply chain, which includes suppliers, production, warehousing, distribution, retail sales, and service. Examples of bar code readers include the familiar point-of-sale scanners encountered at supermarkets and other retail stores. They come in a variety of forms, ranging from hand-held to built-in models. High-speed, unattended scanners are used for automated material handling and sorting. Typical installations include high-volume distribution centers such as JC Penney's catalog operation and airport baggage handling systems. The company also produces "reader engines" that it supplies to other companies for use in their products. These may be as small as 1.2 cubic inches. One application for an "engine product" is found in lottery ticket validation machines. Use of bar code readers has greatly increased the speed and accuracy of data collection, resulting in increased productivity, improved production and inventory tracking and control, and improved market information.

Operations

Forecasting. Forecasting is not a significant activity at PSC due to several factors. There is high standardization of scanner components, which creates stability in usage requirements. Supplier lead times are relatively short, often only a few days. Orders are typically small; seventy percent of all orders are for 10 units or less. There is a fair degree of production flexibility, particularly in terms of product customization. As a result of these factors, the company relies mainly on short-term, moving average forecasts.

Product design. PSC has adopted a "Taguchi approach" in the design of many of its products, designing them to perform effectively under a broad range of operating conditions. For example, many of its hand-held scanners can operate at temperatures ranging from $-22°$ F to $120°$ F, and can withstand drops onto concrete surfaces from heights up to six feet and still function. This has enabled the company to offer warranties ranging from 24 to 36 months, far exceeding the industry standard of 3 to 12 months.

Layout. PSC has developed an efficient production layout that consists of assembly lines and work centers. The assembly lines handle standardized production and subassemblies and the work centers handle final assembly and customization of products. Assembly lines are U-shaped to facilitate communication among workers. The work centers are designed for production flexibility; they can be reconfigured in about 4 hours. Work centers are staffed by teams of three to six cross-trained workers who are responsible for an order from start to finish.

The production process. Production involves a combination of assembly line and batch processing that provides high volume as well as flexibility to customized individual orders. Because of the high standardization among the internal components of different scanners, many of the subassemblies can be produced on assembly lines. Customization is done primarily on the external portion of various products according to customer specification.

The production process for scanner engines is depicted in the process flowchart shown in the figure. The process begins when an order is received from a customer. The order is then configured according to customer specifications. Next it is entered into the computer to obtain a bill of materials (BOM), and the order is transmitted to production control so that it can be scheduled for production. A "traveler" packet containing product specifications and the BOM is created. It will accompany the order throughout the process.

The traveler is sent to the "kitting" area where standard parts and any customized parts are obtained and placed into a bin ("kit") and then placed in a flow rack until the assigned work center is ready for the job (i.e., a pull system).

The next phase of the process transforms unprogrammed, panelized circuit boards into programmed boards. The boards first pass through a screen printer which uses a stencil to coat the boards with a solder paste. Next the boards pass through a chip mounter which enters values for the smaller, passive components of the circuit board at a rate of 25,000 parts per hour. A second mounter enters values for the larger, programmable components at a rate of 7,000 parts per hour. The slower rate for the larger components is offset by the fact that there are fewer of those components. The process ends up being balanced, and no bottlenecks occur.

The programmed boards move by conveyor to a station for visual inspection. Rejects are returned to the chip mounter area, and boards that pass are sent through an oven to solidify

PSC Inc. Scanner Engine Production Process Flow Chart

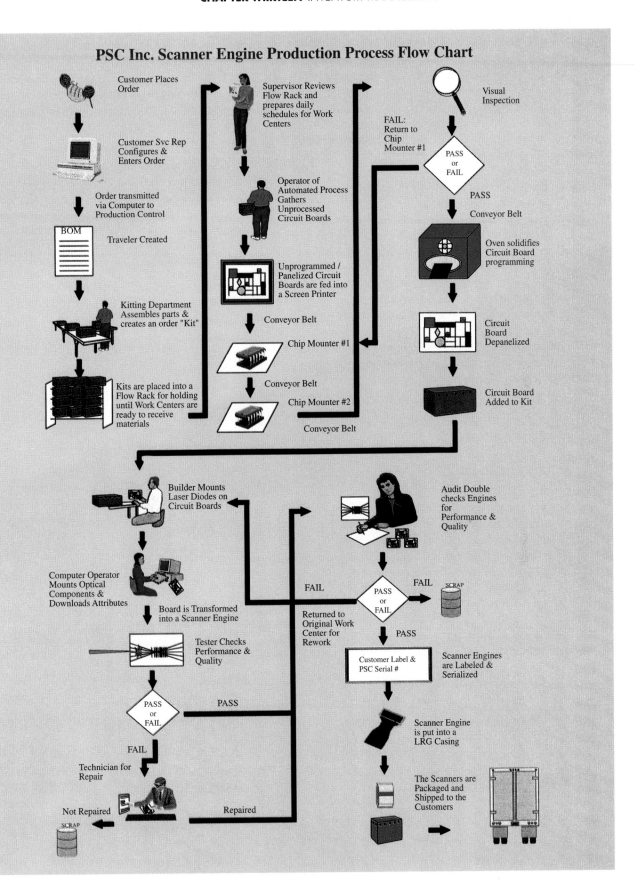

Customer Places Order

Customer Svc Rep Configures & Enters Order

Order transmitted via Computer to Production Control

BOM — Traveler Created

Kitting Department Assembles parts & creates an order "Kit"

Kits are placed into a Flow Rack for holding until Work Centers are ready to receive materials

Supervisor Reviews Flow Rack and prepares daily schedules for Work Centers

Operator of Automated Process Gathers Unprocessed Circuit Boards

Unprogrammed / Panelized Circuit Boards are fed into a Screen Printer

Conveyor Belt

Chip Mounter #1

Conveyor Belt

Chip Mounter #2

Conveyor Belt

Visual Inspection

FAIL: Return to Chip Mounter #1

PASS or FAIL

PASS

Conveyor Belt

Oven solidifies Circuit Board programming

Circuit Board Depanelized

Circuit Board Added to Kit

Builder Mounts Laser Diodes on Circuit Boards

Computer Operator Mounts Optical Components & Downloads Attributes

Board is Transformed into a Scanner Engine

Tester Checks Performance & Quality

PASS or FAIL

PASS

FAIL

Technician for Repair

Not Repaired

SCRAP

Repaired

Returned to Original Work Center for Rework

FAIL

Audit Double checks Engines for Performance & Quality

PASS or FAIL

FAIL

SCRAP

PASS

Customer Label & PSC Serial #

Scanner Engines are Labeled & Serialized

Scanner Engine is put into a LRG Casing

The Scanners are Packaged and Shipped to the Customers

the solder, making the programming permanent. The circuit boards are then removed from the panels and placed into the kit. The kits are then taken to designated work centers for customization and placement in scanner engines.

Work centers typically have builders, computer operators, and a tester. A builder mounts the laser diodes on the circuit board and passes it to a computer operator who downloads the customer specifications into the microprocessor of the scan engine. The operator also mounts the optical components and adjusts them for the design of the scanner (e.g., long range scanning). Next, the engine goes to the tester, who checks to make sure that the scanner is capable of reading bar codes and laser characteristics. Engines that fail are sent for repair and later retested. If the engine fails a second time, it is either returned for further repair or scrapped. Engines which pass are placed in an electrostatic bag which protects them from static electricity that could damage the programming.

Engines are then sent to Audit for another check for performance quality.

Engines that pass are incorporated into the final product, a serial number is added, along with a label, and the product is sent to the packing area and then shipped to the customer.

Scheduling. Scheduling is done using spreadsheets to generate material requirements plans. An updated master schedule is distributed daily to management.

Inventory. The company uses a variety of methods for inventory management, and it attempts to minimize the amount of inventory it maintains. A computer determines component requirements and generates purchase orders for the components for each order, and then appropriate orders for various components from vendors are prepared. However, the company maintains a stock of standard components which are replenished using a reorderpoint system. The company has adopted point-of-use replenishment for some areas of operations, having deliveries come directly to the production floor. Finished products are immediately shipped to the customer, which enhances the company's delivery performance and avoids finished goods inventory.

Suppliers. Approximately 40 vendors supply parts and materials to PSC, each of which has been subjected to a multiple-step supplier certification program that includes the supplier completing a self-evaluation questionnaire; an on-site visit of supplier facilities by a team from PSC made up of people from engineering, purchasing, and operations; a probation period; and rating of products using government MIL-STD 105 spec-

ifications. Vendor performance is tracked on product quality, delivery, and service.

When an item is removed from inventory, it is scanned into the computer, and then information on some components is transmitted directly to suppliers, along with purchase orders to restock the components.

Quality. Quality is strongly emphasized at PSC. Employees are trained in quality concepts and the use of quality tools. Training is incorporated on-the-job so that employees can see the practical applications of what they are learning. Employees are responsible for performing in-process quality checks (quality at the source), and to report any defects they discover to their supervisor. Defects are assigned to one of three categories for problem solving:

- Operator/training error. The supervisor notifies a trainer who then provides appropriate retraining.

- Process/equipment problem. The supervisor notifies the manufacturing engineer who is then responsible for diagnosing the cause and correcting the problem.

- Parts/material problem. The supervisor notifies quality assurance, who then notifies the vendor to correct the problem. Defective parts are either scrapped or returned to the vendor.

Lean Production

PSC strives to operate on lean production principles. In addition to emphasizing high levels of quality, production flexibility, low levels of inventories, and having some deliveries come right to the production floor, its organization structure is fairly flat, and it uses a team approach. Still another feature of lean production is that many of PSC's workers are multi-skilled. The company encourages employees to master new skills through a pay-for-skill program, and bases hourly pay rates on the number of skills a worker can perform.

Business Strategy

The company has developed what it believes is a strong strategy for success. Strategic initiatives include anticipating customer demand for miniaturization and the ability to customize products; expanding its proprietary technology; and expanding internationally into Western Europe (now accounts for about 35 percent of sales) and the Pacific rim (now accounts for about 10 percent of sales). Several plants or groups are ISO certified, which has been important for European sales. The company intends to continue to expand its product lines through acquisition of other companies.

Brooks, Roger B., and Larry W. Wilson. *Inventory Record Accuracy: Unleashing the Power of Cycle Counting.* Essex Junction, VT: Oliver Wight, 1993.

Fogarty, Donald W., John H. Blackstone, and Thomas R. Hoffmann. *Production and Inventory Management.* 2nd ed. Cincinnati, OH: South-Western Publishing Co., 1991.

Hopp, Wallace J., and Mark L. Spearman. *Factory Physics.* 2nd ed. New York: Irwin/McGraw-Hill, 2001.

Peterson, R., and E. A. Silver. *Decision Systems for Inventory Management and Production Planning.* 2nd ed. New York: John Wiley & Sons, 1998.

Tersine, Richard J. *Principles of Inventory and Materials Management.* 4th ed. New York: Elsevier North-Holland, 1994.

Vollman, Thomas E., William L. Berry, and D. Clay Whybark. *Manufacturing Planning and Control Systems.* 5th ed. Burr Ridge, IL: Richard D. Irwin, 1997.

Zipkin, Paul. *Foundations of Inventory Management.* New York: Irwin/McGraw-Hill, 2000.

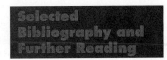
Selected Bibliography and Further Reading

CHAPTER FOURTEEN

Aggregate Planning

CHAPTER OUTLINE

Introduction, 604
  Intermediate Planning in
    Perspective, 604
  The Concept of Aggregation, 605
  An Overview of Aggregate
    Planning, 606

The Purpose and Scope of Aggregate
  Planning, 607
  Demand and Capacity, 607
  Inputs to Aggregate Planning, 607
  Demand and Capacity Options, 608

Basic Strategies for Meeting Uneven
  Demand, 610
  Choosing a Strategy, 612

Techniques for Aggregate
  Planning, 613
  Informal Techniques, 613
  Mathematical Techniques, 618

Aggregate Planning in Services, 622

Disaggregating the Aggregate
  Plan, 623

Master Scheduling, 624
  Inputs, 624
  Outputs, 624
  Stabilizing the Master Schedule, 627

Summary, 628

Key Terms, 628

Solved Problems, 629

Discussion and Review
  Questions, 631

Memo Writing Exercises, 632

Problems, 632

Case: Eight Glasses a Day, 635

Selected Bibliography and Further
  Reading, 636

LEARNING OBJECTIVES

*After completing this chapter, you
should be able to:*

1 Explain what aggregate planning
is and how it is useful.

2 Identify the variables decision
makers have to work with in
aggregate planning and some of
the possible strategies they can
use.

3 Describe some of the graphical
and quantitative techniques
planners use.

4 Prepare aggregate plans and
compute their costs.

aggregate planning Intermediate-range capacity planning,
usually covering 2 to 12
months.

he purpose of this chapter is to introduce the concept of aggregate planning, discuss
the pertinent costs and possible strategies, and illustrate some of the different approaches currently in use.

In the spectrum of production planning, **aggregate planning** is intermediate-range capacity planning that typically covers a time horizon of 2 to 12 months, although in some companies it may extend to as much as 18 months. It is particularly useful for organizations that experience seasonal or other fluctuations in demand or capacity. The goal of aggregate planning is to achieve a production plan that will effectively utilize the organization's resources to satisfy expected demand. Planners must make decisions on output rates, employment levels and changes, inventory levels and changes, back orders, and subcontracting.

Introduction

INTERMEDIATE PLANNING IN PERSPECTIVE

Organizations make capacity decisions on three levels: long term, intermediate term, and short term. Long-term decisions relate to product and service selection (i.e., determining which products or services to offer), facility size and location, equipment decisions, and layout of facilities. These long-term decisions essentially define the capacity constraints within which intermediate planning must function. Intermediate decisions, as noted above, relate to general levels of employment, output, and inventories, which in turn define the boundaries within which short-range capacity decisions must be made. Thus, short-term decisions essentially consist of deciding the best way to achieve desired results within the constraints resulting from long-term and intermediate-term decisions. Short-term decisions involve scheduling jobs, workers and equipment, and the like. The three levels of capacity decisions are depicted in Table 14–1. Long-term capacity decisions were covered in Chapter 5, and scheduling and related matters are covered in Chapter 17. This chapter covers intermediate capacity decisions.

Many business organizations develop a *business plan* that encompasses both long-term and intermediate-term planning. The business plan establishes guidelines for the organization, taking into account the organization's strategies and policies; forecasts of demand

TABLE 14–1

*Overview of planning levels
(chapter numbers are shown)*

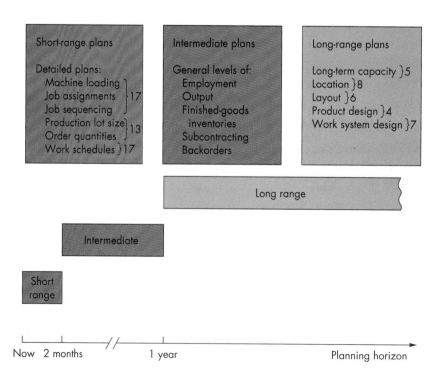

for the organization's products or services; and economic, competitive, and political conditions. A key objective in business planning is to coordinate the intermediate plans of various organization functions, such as marketing, operations, and finance. In manufacturing companies, coordination also includes engineering and materials management. Consequently, all of these functional areas must work together to formulate the aggregate plan. Aggregate planning decisions are strategic decisions that define the framework within which operating decisions will be made. They are the starting point for scheduling and production control systems. They provide input for financial plans; they involve forecasting input and demand management, and they may require changes in employment levels. And if the organization is involved in *time-based competition,* it will be important to incorporate some flexibility in the aggregate plan. Moreover, the plans must fit into the framework established by the organization's long-term goals and strategies, and the limitations established by long-term facility and capital budget decisions. In the operations function, a *production plan*—service organizations may refer to this as an *operations plan*—is developed to guide the more detailed planning that eventually leads to a *master schedule.* Figure 14–1 illustrates the planning sequence.

Aggregate planning can also serve as an important input to other strategic decisions; for example, management may decide to add capacity when aggregate planning alternatives for temporarily increasing capacity, such as working overtime and subcontracting, are too costly.

THE CONCEPT OF AGGREGATION

Aggregate planning is essentially a "big picture" approach to planning. Planners usually try to avoid focusing on individual products or services—unless of course the organization has only one major product or service. Instead, they focus on a group of similar products or services, or sometimes an entire product or service line. For example, for purposes of aggregate planning, planners in a company producing television sets would not concern themselves with 21-inch sets versus 25-inch or 27-inch sets. Instead, planners would lump all models together and deal with them as though they were a single product; hence,

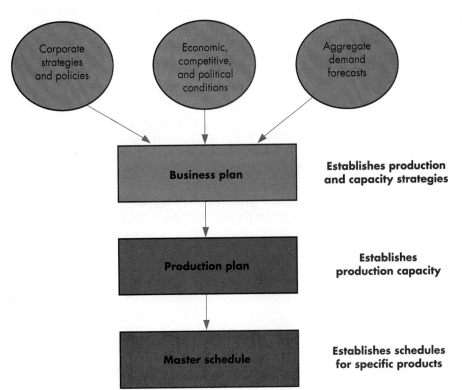

FIGURE 14-1

Planning sequence

Rubbermaid Incorporated, a multinational manufacturer and marketer of commercial and household food containers and other items, produces more than 4,000 products sold in 100 countries at retail establishments and direct to customers. At its corporate headquarters in Wooster, Ohio, planners discuss product performance.

www.rubbermaid.com

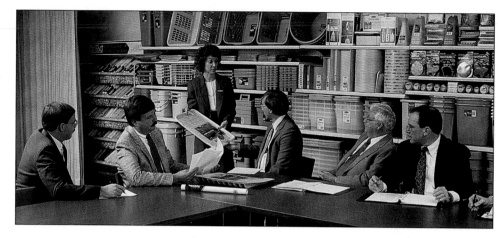

the term *aggregate* planning. For purposes of aggregate planning, a bicycle company might lump all the different sizes and styles of bikes it produced into a single category of "bikes." Similarly, when fast-food companies such as McDonalds, Burger King, or Wendy's plan employment and output levels, they don't try to determine how demand will be broken down into the various options they offer; they focus on overall demand and the overall capacity they want to provide.

Now, consider how aggregate planning might work in a large department store. Space allocation is often an aggregate decision. That is, a manager might decide to allocate 20 percent of the available space in the clothing department to women's sportswear, 30 percent to juniors, and so on, without regard for what brand names will be offered or how much of juniors will be slacks. The aggregate measure might be square feet of space or racks of clothing.

In each of these examples, an aggregate approach permits planners to make general decisions about intermediate-range capacity without having to deal with highly specific details. They can instead concern themselves with overall decisions on levels of output, employment, and inventories. They do this by lumping demand for all products into one or a few categories, and planning on that basis.

For purposes of aggregate planning, it is often convenient to think of capacity in terms of labor hours or machine hours per period, or output rates (barrels per period, units per period), without worrying about how much of a particular item will actually be involved. This approach frees planners to make general decisions about the use of resources without having to get into the complexities of individual product or service requirements. Product groupings make the problem of obtaining an acceptable unit of aggregation easier because product groupings may lend themselves to the same aggregate measures.

Why do organizations need to do aggregate planning? The answer is twofold. One part is related to *planning:* It takes time to implement plans. For instance, if plans call for increasing the size of facilities and/or hiring (and training) new workers, that will take time. The second part is strategic: *Aggregation* is important because it is not possible to predict with any degree of accuracy the timing and volume of demand for individual items. So if an organization were to "lock in" on individual items, it would lose the flexibility to respond to the market.

Finally, aggregate planning is important because it can help synchronize flow throughout the supply chain; it affects costs, equipment utilization, employment levels, and customer satisfaction.

AN OVERVIEW OF AGGREGATE PLANNING

Aggregate planning begins with a forecast of aggregate demand for the intermediate range. This is followed by a general plan to meet demand requirements by setting output,

Inputs	Outputs
Resources	Total cost of a plan
Workforce/production rates	Projected levels of
Facilities and equipment	Inventory
Demand forecast	Output
Policy statements on workforce changes	Employment
Subcontracting	Subcontracting
Overtime	Backordering
Inventory levels/changes	
Back orders	
Costs	
Inventory carrying cost	
Back orders	
Hiring/firing	
Overtime	
Inventory changes	
Subcontracting	

TABLE 14–2

Aggregate planning inputs and outputs

employment, and finished-goods inventory levels. Managers might consider a number of plans, each of which must be examined in light of feasibility and cost. If a plan is reasonably good but has minor difficulties, it may be reworked. Conversely, a poor plan should be discarded and alternative plans considered until an acceptable one is uncovered. The production plan is essentially the output of aggregate planning.

Aggregate plans are updated periodically, often monthly, to take into account updated forecasts and other changes. This results in a *rolling planning horizon* (i.e., the aggregate plan always covers the next 12–18 months).

The Purpose and Scope of Aggregate Planning

In this section, we examine the basic problem addressed by aggregate planning—the balancing of supply and demand—along with the purpose of aggregate planning, the primary decision variables available to planners, and associated costs. If supply and demand aren't in balance, there will be added costs of adjusting the system as well as opportunity costs.

DEMAND AND CAPACITY

Aggregate planners are concerned with the *quantity* and the *timing* of expected demand. If total expected demand for the planning period is much different from available capacity over that same period, the major approach of planners will be to try to achieve a balance by altering capacity, demand, or both. On the other hand, even if capacity and demand are approximately equal for the planning horizon as a whole, planners may still be faced with the problem of dealing with uneven demand *within* the planning interval. In some periods, expected demand may exceed projected capacity, in others expected demand may be less than projected capacity, and in some periods the two may be equal. The task of aggregate planners is to achieve rough equality of demand and capacity over the entire planning horizon. Moreover, planners are usually concerned with minimizing the cost of the production plan, although cost is not the only consideration.

INPUTS TO AGGREGATE PLANNING

Effective aggregate planning requires good *information*. First, the available resources over the planning period must be known. Then, a forecast of expected demand must be available. Finally, planners must take into account any policies regarding changes in employment levels (e.g., some organizations view layoffs as extremely undesirable, so they would use that only as a last resort).

Table 14–2 lists the major inputs to aggregate planning.

DEMAND AND CAPACITY OPTIONS

Management has a wide range of decision options at its disposal for purposes of aggregate planning. These include changing prices, promotion, backlogging orders, using overtime, using part-time workers, subcontracting, adding or deleting extra shifts, and stockpiling inventories. Some of these, such as pricing and promotion, represent options that are intended to alter the pattern of demand and are usually handled by marketing. Use of part-time workers, overtime, and subcontracting represent options that are intended to alter capacity or supply. We can examine these options in more detail.

Demand Options. The basic demand options are the following:

1. *Pricing.* Pricing differentials are commonly used to shift demand from peak periods to off-peak periods. Some hotels, for example, offer lower rates for weekend stays, and some airlines offer lower fares for night travel. Movie theaters may offer reduced rates for matinees, and some restaurants offer "early bird specials" in an attempt to shift some of the heavier dinner demand to an earlier time that traditionally has less traffic. Some restaurants also offer smaller portions at reduced rates, and most have smaller portions and prices for children. The smaller portions act to decrease demand. To the extent that pricing is effective, demand will be shifted so that it corresponds more closely to capacity, albeit for an *opportunity cost* that represents the lost profit stemming from capacity insufficient to meet demand during certain periods.

An important factor to consider is the *degree* of price elasticity for the product or service; the more the elasticity, the more effective pricing will be in influencing demand patterns.

2. *Promotion.* Advertising and other forms of promotion, such as displays and direct marketing, can sometimes be very effective in shifting demand so that it conforms more closely to capacity. Obviously, timing of these efforts and knowledge of response rates and response patterns will be needed to achieve the desired results. Unlike pricing policy, there is much less control over the timing of demand; there is always the risk that promotion can worsen the condition it was intended to improve.

3. *Back orders.* An organization can shift demand to other periods by allowing back orders. That is, orders are taken in one period and deliveries promised for a later period. The success of this approach depends on how willing customers are to wait for delivery. Moreover, the costs associated with back orders can be difficult to pin down since it would include lost sales, annoyed or disappointed customers, and perhaps additional paperwork.

4. *New demand.* Many organizations are faced with the problem of having to provide products or services for peak demand in situations where demand is very uneven. For instance, demand for bus transportation tends to be more intense during the morning and late afternoon rush hours but much lighter at other times. Creating new demand for buses at other times (e.g., trips by schools, clubs, and senior citizen groups) would make use of the excess capacity during those slack times. Similarly, many fast-food restaurants are open for breakfast to use their capacities more fully, and some landscaping firms in northern climates use their equipment during the winter months for snow removal. Manufacturing firms that experience seasonal demands for certain products (e.g., snowblowers) are sometimes able to develop a demand for a complementary product (e.g., lawn mowers, garden equipment) that makes use of the same production processes. They thereby achieve a more consistent use of labor, equipment, and facilities.

Capacity Options. The basic capacity options are the following:

1. *Hire and lay off workers.* The extent to which operations are labor intensive determines the impact that changes in the workforce level will have on capacity. The resource requirements of each worker can also be a factor. For instance, if a supermarket usually has 10 of 14 checkout lines operating, an additional four checkout workers could be added. Hence, the ability to add workers is constrained at some point by other resources needed to support the workers. Conversely, there may be a lower limit on the number of workers needed to maintain a viable operation (e.g., a skeleton crew).

Union contracts may restrict the amount of hiring and laying off a company can do. Moreover, because laying off can present serious problems for workers, some firms have policies that either prohibit or limit downward adjustments to a workforce. On the other hand, hiring presumes an available supply of workers. This may change from time to time and, at times of low supply, has an impact on the ability of an organization to pursue this approach.

Another consideration is the skill level of workers. Highly skilled workers are generally more difficult to find than lower-skilled workers, and recruiting them involves greater costs. So the usefulness of this option is limited by the need for highly skilled workers.

Use of hiring and laying off entails certain costs. Hiring costs include recruitment, screening, and training to bring new workers "up to speed." And quality may suffer. Some savings may occur if workers who have recently been laid off are rehired. Layoff costs include severance pay, the cost of realigning the remaining workforce, potential bad feelings toward the firm on the part of workers who have been laid off, and some loss of morale for workers who are retained (i.e., in spite of company assurances, some workers will believe that in time they too may be laid off).

An increasing number of organizations view workers as assets rather than as variable costs, and would not consider this approach. Instead, they might use slack time for other purposes.

2. *Overtime/slack time.* Use of overtime or slack time is a less severe method for changing capacity than hiring and laying off workers, and it can be used across the board or selectively as needed. It can also be implemented more quickly than hiring and laying off and allows the firm to maintain a steady base of employees. The use of overtime can be especially attractive in dealing with seasonal demand peaks by reducing the need to hire and train people who will have to be laid off during the off-season. Overtime also permits the company to maintain a skilled workforce and employees to increase earnings. Moreover, in situations with crews, it is often necessary to use a full crew rather than to hire one or two additional people. Thus, having the entire crew work overtime would be preferable to hiring extra people.

It should be noted that some union contracts allow workers to refuse overtime. In those cases, it may be difficult to muster a full crew to work overtime or to get an entire production line into operation after regular hours. Although workers often like the additional income overtime can generate, they may not appreciate having to work on short notice or the fluctuations in income that result. Still other considerations relate to the fact that overtime often results in lower productivity, poorer quality, more accidents, and increased payroll costs, whereas idle time results in less efficient use of machines and other fixed assets.

The use of slack when demand is less than capacity can be an important consideration. Some organizations use this time for training. It can also give workers time for problem solving and process improvement, while retraining skilled workers.

3. *Part-time workers.* In certain instances, the use of part-time workers is a viable option—much depends on the nature of the work, training and skills needed, and union agreements. Seasonal work requiring low-to-moderate job skills lends itself to part-time workers, who generally cost less than regular workers in hourly wages and fringe benefits. However, unions may regard such workers unfavorably because they typically do not pay union dues and may lessen the power of unions. Department stores, restaurants, and supermarkets make use of part-time workers. So do parks and recreation departments, resorts, travel agencies, hotels, and other service organizations with seasonal demands. In order to be successful, these organizations must be able to hire part-time employees when they are needed.

Some companies use contract workers, also called *independent contractors,* to fill certain needs. Although they are not regular employees, often they work alongside regular workers. In addition to having different pay scales and no benefits, they can be added or subtracted from the workforce with greater ease than regular workers, giving companies great flexibility in adjusting the size of the workforce.

4. *Inventories.* The use of finished-goods inventories allows firms to produce goods in one period and sell or ship them in another period, although this involves holding or carrying those goods as inventory until they are needed. The cost includes not only storage costs and the cost of money tied up that could be invested elsewhere, but also the cost of insurance, obsolescence, deterioration, spoilage, breakage, and so on. In essence, inventories can be built up during periods when production capacity exceeds demand and drawn down in periods when demand exceeds production capacity.

This method is more amenable to manufacturing than to service industries since manufactured goods can be stored whereas services generally cannot. However, an analogous approach used by services is to make efforts to streamline services (e.g., standard forms) or otherwise do a portion of the service during slack periods (e.g., organize the workplace). In spite of these possibilities, services tend not to make much use of inventories to alter capacity requirements.

5. *Subcontracting.* Subcontracting enables planners to acquire temporary capacity, although it affords less control over the output and may lead to higher costs and quality problems. The question of whether to make or buy (i.e., in manufacturing) or to perform a service or hire someone else to do the work generally depends on factors such as available capacity, relative expertise, quality considerations, cost, and the amount and stability of demand.

In some cases, a firm might choose to perform part of the work itself and let others handle the rest in order to maintain flexibility and as a hedge against loss of a subcontractor. Moreover, this gives the organization a bargaining tool in negotiations with contractors and a head start if it decides at a later date to take over the operation entirely. As an alternative to subcontracting, an organization might consider *outsourcing:* contracting with another organization to supply some portion of the goods or services on a regular basis.

Basic Strategies for Meeting Uneven Demand

As you see, managers have a wide range of decision options they can consider for achieving a balance of demand and capacity in aggregate planning. Since the options that are most suited to influencing demand fall more in the realm of marketing than in operations (with the exception of backlogging), we shall concentrate on the capacity options, which are in the realm of operations but include the use of back orders.

Aggregate planners might adopt a number of strategies. Some of the more prominent ones are:

1. Maintain a level workforce.

2. Maintain a steady output rate.

3. Match demand period by period.

4. Use a combination of decision variables.

While other strategies might be considered, these will suffice to give you a sense of how aggregate planning operates in a vast number of organizations. The first three strategies are "pure" strategies because each has a single focal point; the last strategy is "mixed" because it lacks the single focus. Under a **level capacity strategy,** variations in demand are met by using some combination of inventories, overtime, part-time workers, subcontracting, and back orders. Matching capacity to demand implies a **chase demand strategy;** the planned output for any period would be equal to expected demand for that period.

Many organizations regard a level workforce as very appealing. Since workforce changes through hiring and laying off can have a major impact on the lives and morale of employees and can be disruptive for managers, organizations often prefer to handle uneven demand in other ways. Moreover, changes in workforce size can be very costly, and there is always the risk that there will not be a sufficient pool of workers with the appropriate skills when needed. Aside from these considerations, such changes can involve a significant amount of paperwork. Unions tend to favor a level workforce because the freedom to hire and lay off workers diminishes union strengths.

To maintain a constant level of output and still meet demand requirements, an organization must resort to some combination of subcontracting, backlogging, and use of inventories to absorb fluctuations. Subcontracting requires an investment in evaluating sources of supply as well as possible increased costs, less control over output, and perhaps quality considerations. Backlogs can lead to lost sales, increased record keeping, and lower levels of customer service. Allowing inventories to absorb fluctuations can entail substantial costs by having money tied up in inventories, having to maintain relatively large storage facilities, and incurring other costs related to inventories. Furthermore, inventories are not usually an alternative for service-oriented organizations. However, there are certain advantages, such as minimum costs of recruitment and training, minimum overtime and idle-time costs, fewer morale problems, and stable use of equipment and facilities.

A chase demand strategy presupposes a great deal of ability and willingness on the part of managers to be flexible in adjusting to demand. A major advantage of this approach is that inventories can be kept relatively low, which can yield substantial savings for an organization. A major disadvantage is the lack of stability in operations—the atmosphere is one of dancing to demand's tune. Also, when forecast and reality differ, morale can suffer, since it quickly becomes obvious to workers and managers that efforts have been wasted. Figure 14–2 provides a comparison of the two strategies, using a varying demand pattern to highlight the differences in the two approaches. The same demand pattern is used for each approach. In the upper portion of the figure the pattern is shown. Notice that there are three situations: (1) demand and capacity are equal; (2) demand is less than capacity; and (3) demand exceeds capacity.

The middle portion of the figure illustrates what happens with a chase approach. When normal capacity would exceed demand, capacity is cut back to match demand. Then, when demand exceeds normal capacity, the chase approach is to temporarily increase capacity to match demand.

The bottom portion of the figure illustrates the level-output strategy. When demand is less than capacity, output continues at normal capacity, and the excess output is put into inventory in anticipation of the time when demand exceeds capacity. When demand exceeds capacity, inventory is used to offset the shortfall in output.

Organizations may opt for a strategy that involves some combination of the pure strategies. This allows managers greater flexibility in dealing with uneven demand and perhaps in experimenting with a wide variety of approaches. However, the absence of a clear focus may lead to an erratic approach and confusion on the part of employees.

level capacity strategy Maintaining a steady rate of regular-time output while meeting variations in demand by a combination of options.

chase demand strategy Matching capacity to demand; the planned output for a period is set at the expected demand for that period.

A possible uneven demand pattern

Chase demand strategy

Level output strategy

FIGURE 14–2

Comparison of chase and level strategies

CHOOSING A STRATEGY

Whatever strategy an organization is considering, two important factors are *company policy* and *costs*. Company policy may set constraints on the available options or the extent to which they can be used. For instance, company policy may discourage layoffs except under extreme conditions. Subcontracting may not be a viable alternative due to the desire to maintain secrecy about some aspect of the manufacturing of the product (e.g., a secret formula or blending process). Union agreements often impose restrictions. For example, a union contract may specify both minimum and maximum numbers of hours part-time workers can be used.

As a rule, aggregate planners seek to match supply and demand within the constraints imposed on them by policies or agreements and at minimum cost. They usually evaluate

IBM planners need to balance large product lines. These computers use some of the same parts, labor, and assembly facilities, so planning is necessary to avoid parts shortages and match demand. Shown here is the PC Model 300PL with G72 and P200 monitors.

www.ibm.com

alternatives in terms of their overall costs. In the next section, a number of techniques for aggregate planning are described and presented with some examples of cost evaluation of alternative plans.

Techniques for Aggregate Planning

Numerous techniques help decision makers with the task of aggregate planning. Generally, they fall into one of two categories: informal trial-and-error techniques and mathematical techniques. In practice, informal techniques are more frequently used. However, a considerable amount of research has been devoted to mathematical techniques, and even though they are not as widely used, they often serve as a basis for comparing the effectiveness of alternative techniques for aggregate planning. Thus, it will be instructive to briefly examine them as well as the informal techniques.

A general procedure for aggregate planning consists of the following steps:

1. Determine demand for each period.
2. Determine capacities (regular time, overtime, subcontracting) for each period.
3. Identify company or departmental policies that are pertinent (e.g., maintain a safety stock of 5 percent of demand, maintain a reasonably stable workforce).
4. Determine unit costs for regular time, overtime, subcontracting, holding inventories, back orders, layoffs, and other relevant costs.
5. Develop alternative plans and compute the cost for each.
6. If satisfactory plans emerge, select the one that best satisfies objectives. Otherwise, return to step 5.

It can be helpful to use a worksheet that summarizes demand, capacity, and cost for each plan, such as the one illustrated in Table 14–3. In addition, graphs can be used to guide development of alternatives.

INFORMAL TECHNIQUES

Informal approaches consist of developing simple tables or graphs that enable planners to visually compare projected demand requirements with existing capacity. Alternatives are usually evaluated in terms of their overall costs. The chief disadvantage of such techniques is that they do not necessarily result in the optimal aggregate plan.

Very often, graphs can be used to guide the development of alternatives. Some planners prefer cumulative graphs while others prefer to see a period-by-period breakdown of a plan. For instance, Figure 14–3 shows a cumulative graph for a plan with steady output

TABLE 14-3

Worksheet

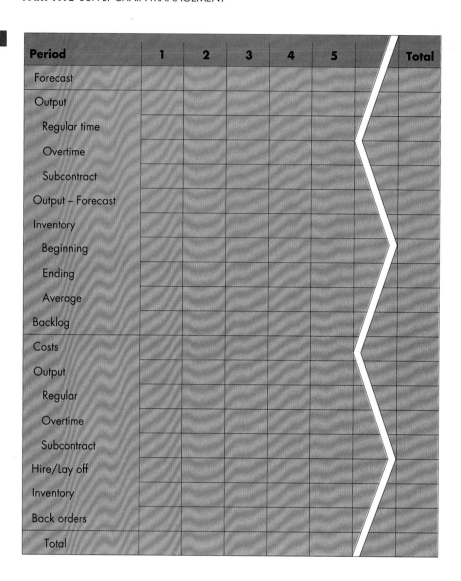

Period	1	2	3	4	5		Total
Forecast							
Output							
Regular time							
Overtime							
Subcontract							
Output – Forecast							
Inventory							
Beginning							
Ending							
Average							
Backlog							
Costs							
Output							
Regular							
Overtime							
Subcontract							
Hire/Lay off							
Inventory							
Back orders							
Total							

FIGURE 14-3

A cumulative graph

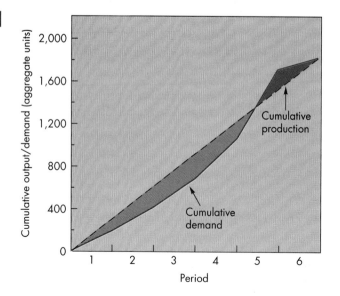

(the slope of the dashed line represents the production rate) and inventory absorption of demand variations. Figure 14–2 is an example of a period-by-period graph. The obvious advantage of a graph is that it provides a visual portrayal of a plan. The preference of the planner determines which of these two types of graphs is chosen.

Two examples illustrate the development and comparison of aggregate plans. In the first example, regular output is held steady, with inventory absorbing demand variations. In the second example, a lower rate of regular output is used, supplemented by use of overtime. In both examples, some backlogs are allowed to build up.

These examples and other examples and problems in this chapter are based on the following assumptions:

1. The regular output capacity is the same in all periods. No allowance is made for holidays, different numbers of workdays in different months, and so on. This assumption simplifies computations.

2. Cost (back order, inventory, subcontracting, etc.) is a linear function composed of unit cost and number of units. This often has a reasonable approximation to reality, although there may be only narrow ranges over which this is true. Cost is sometimes more of a step function.

3. Plans are feasible; that is, sufficient inventory capacity exists to accommodate a plan, subcontractors with appropriate quality and capacity are standing by, and changes in output can be made as needed.

4. All costs associated with a decision option can be represented by a lump sum or by unit costs that are independent of the quantity involved. Again, a step function may be more realistic; but for purposes of illustration and simplicity, this assumption is appropriate.

5. Cost figures can be reasonably estimated and are constant for the planning horizon.

6. Inventories are built up and drawn down at a uniform rate and output occurs at a uniform rate throughout each period. However, backlogs are treated as if they exist for an entire period, even though in periods where they initially appear, they would tend to build up toward the end of the period. Hence, this assumption is a bit unrealistic for some periods, but it simplifies computations.

In the examples and problems in this chapter, we use the following relationships to determine the number of workers, the amount of inventory, and the cost of a particular plan.

The number of workers available in any period is

$$\begin{array}{c}\text{Number of}\\\text{workers in}\\\text{a period}\end{array} = \begin{array}{c}\text{Number of}\\\text{workers at end of}\\\text{the previous period}\end{array} + \begin{array}{c}\text{Number of new}\\\text{workers at start of}\\\text{the period}\end{array} - \begin{array}{c}\text{Number of laid-off}\\\text{workers at start of}\\\text{the period}\end{array}$$

Note: An organization would not hire and lay off simultaneously, so at least one of the last two terms will equal zero.

The amount of inventory at the end of a given period is

$$\begin{array}{c}\text{Inventory}\\\text{at the end of}\\\text{a period}\end{array} = \begin{array}{c}\text{Inventory}\\\text{at end of the}\\\text{previous period}\end{array} + \begin{array}{c}\text{Production}\\\text{in the}\\\text{current period}\end{array} - \begin{array}{c}\text{Amount used to}\\\text{satisfy demand in the}\\\text{current period}\end{array}$$

The average inventory for a period is equal to

$$\frac{\text{Beginning inventory} + \text{Ending inventory}}{2}$$

The cost of a particular plan for a given period can be determined by summing the appropriate costs:

$$\begin{array}{c}\text{Cost for}\\\text{a period}\end{array} = \begin{array}{c}\text{Output cost}\\(\text{Reg} + \text{OT} + \text{Subcontract})\end{array} + \begin{array}{c}\text{Hire/lay off}\\\text{cost}\end{array} + \begin{array}{c}\text{Inventory}\\\text{cost}\end{array} + \begin{array}{c}\text{Back-order}\\\text{cost}\end{array}$$

The appropriate costs are calculated as follows:

Type of Cost	How to Calculate
Output	
Regular	Regular cost per unit × Quantity of regular output
Overtime	Overtime cost per unit × Overtime quantity
Subcontract	Subcontract cost per unit × Subcontract quantity
Hire/lay off	
Hire	Cost per hire × Number hired
Lay off	Cost per layoff × Number laid off
Inventory	Carrying cost per unit × Average inventory
Back order	Back order cost per unit × Number of back-order units

The following examples are only three of many possible options that could be tried. Perhaps some of the others would result in a lower cost. With trial and error, you can never be completely sure you have identified the lowest-cost alternative unless every possible alternative is evaluated. Of course, the purpose of these examples is to illustrate the process of developing and evaluating an aggregate plan rather than to find the lowest-cost plan. Problems at the end of the chapter cover still other alternatives.

In practice, successful achievement of a good plan depends on the resourcefulness and persistence of the planner. A good computer package can eliminate the computational burden of trial-and-error techniques.

Example 1

Planners for a company that makes several models of skateboards are about to prepare the aggregate plan that will cover six periods. They have assembled the following information:

Period	1	2	3	4	5	6	Total
Forecast	200	200	300	400	500	200	1,800

Costs
  Output
    Regular time = $2 per skateboard
    Overtime = $3 per skateboard
    Subcontract = $6 per skateboard
  Inventory = $1 per skateboard per period on average inventory
  Back orders = $5 per skateboard per period

They now want to evaluate a plan that calls for a steady rate of regular-time output, mainly using inventory to absorb the uneven demand but allowing some backlog. They intend to start with zero inventory on hand in the first period. Prepare an aggregate plan and determine its cost using the preceding information. Assume a level output rate of 300 units (skateboards) per period with regular time (i.e., 1,800/6 = 300). Note that the planned ending inventory is zero. There are 15 workers.

Solution

Period	1	2	3	4	5	6	Total
Forecast	200	200	300	400	500	200	1,800
Output							
Regular	300	300	300	300	300	300	1,800
Overtime	—	—	—	—	—	—	
Subcontract	—	—	—	—	—	—	
Output – Forecast	100	100	0	(100)	(200)	100	0
Inventory							
Beginning	0	100	200	200	100	0	
Ending	100	200	200	100	0	0	
Average	50	150	200	150	50	0	600
Backlog	0	0	0	0	100	0	100

Costs

Output							
Regular	$600	600	600	600	600	600	$3,600
Overtime	—	—	—	—	—	—	
Subcontract	—	—	—	—	—	—	
Hire/Lay off	—	—	—	—	—	—	
Inventory	$ 50	150	200	150	50	0	$ 600
Back orders	$ 0	0	0	0	500	0	$ 500
Total	$650	750	800	750	1,150	600	$4,700

Note that the total regular-time output of 1,800 units equals the total expected demand. Ending inventory equals beginning inventory plus or minus the quantity Output – Forecast. If Output – Forecast is negative, inventory is decreased in that period by that amount. If insufficient inventory exists, a backlog equal to the shortage amount appears, as in period 5. This is taken care of using the excess output in period 6.

The costs were computed as follows. Regular cost in each period equals 300 units × $2 per unit or $600. Inventory cost equals average inventory × $1 per unit. Back-order cost is $5 per unit. The total cost for this plan is $4,700.

Note that the first two quantities in each column are givens. The remaining quantities in the upper portion of the table were determined working down each column, beginning with the first column. The costs were then computed based on the quantities in the upper part of the table.

After reviewing the plan developed in the preceding example, planners have decided to develop an alternative plan. They have learned that one person is about to retire from the company. Rather than replace that person, they would like to stay with the smaller workforce and use overtime to make up for the lost output. The reduced regular-time output is 280 units per period. The maximum amount of overtime output per period is 40 units. Develop a plan and compare it to the previous one.

Example 2

Solution

Period	1	2	3	4	5	6	Total
Forecast	200	200	300	400	500	200	1,800
Output							
Regular	280	280	280	280	280	280	1,680
Overtime	0	0	40	40	40	0	120
Subcontract	—	—	—	—	—	—	
Output – Forecast	80	80	20	(80)	(180)	80	0
Inventory							
Beginning	0	80	160	180	100	0	
Ending	80	160	180	100	0	0	
Average	40	120	170	140	50	0	520
Backlog	0	0	0	0	80	0	80
Costs							
Output							
Regular	$560	560	560	560	560	560	$3,360
Overtime	0	0	120	120	120	0	$ 360
Subcontract	—	—	—	—	—	—	
Hire/Lay off	—	—	—	—	—	—	
Inventory	40	120	170	140	50	0	$ 520
Back orders	$ 0	0	0	0	400	0	$ 400
Total	$600	680	850	820	1,130	560	$4,640

The amount of overtime that must be scheduled has to make up for lost output of 20 units per period for six periods, which is 120. This is scheduled toward the center of the planning horizon since that is where the bulk of demand occurs. Scheduling it earlier would increase inventory carrying costs; scheduling it later would increase the backlog cost.

Overall, the total cost for this plan is $4,640, which is $60 less than the previous plan. Regular-time production cost and inventory cost are down, but there is overtime cost. However, this plan achieves savings in back-order cost, making it somewhat less costly overall than the plan in Example 1.

Example 3

A third option is to use temporary workers to fill in during months of high demand. Suppose that it costs an additional $100 to hire and train a temporary worker, and that a temporary worker can produce at the rate of 15 units per period (compared with 20 units per period for regular workers).

Dividing the number of units needed (120) by the output rate of 15 per temporary worker, you find that eight worker-periods are needed (e.g., two workers for four months each, four workers for two months each).

Noting that periods 4 and 5 have the heaviest demand, using four temporary workers for two months each (i.e., periods 4 and 5) seems to be reasonable. The results are summarized in the following plan.

Solution

Period	1	2	3	4	5	6	Total
Forecast	200	200	300	400	500	200	1,800
Output							
Regular	280	280	280	340	340	280	1,800
Overtime	—	—	—	—	—	—	
Subcontract	—	—	—	—	—	—	
Output – Forecast	80	80	(20)	(60)	(160)	80	0
Inventory							
Beginning	0	80	160	140	80	0	
Ending	80	160	140	80	0	0	
Average	40	120	150	110	40	0	460
Backlog	0	0	0	0	80	0	80
Costs							
Output							
Regular	$560	560	560	680	680	560	$3,600
Overtime	—	—	—	—	—	—	
Subcontract	—	—	—	—	—	—	
Hire/Lay off	$ 0	0	0	400	0	0	$ 400
Inventory	$ 40	120	150	110	40	0	$ 460
Back orders	$ 0	0	0	0	400	0	$ 400
Total	$600	680	710	1,190	1,120	560	$4,860

Overall, the total cost for this plan is $4,860, making it the most expensive of the three alternatives examined.

MATHEMATICAL TECHNIQUES

A number of mathematical techniques have been developed to handle aggregate planning. They range from mathematical programming models to heuristic and computer search models. This section briefly describes some of the better-known techniques.

		Period 1	Period 2	Period 3	. . .	Ending inventory period n	Unused capacity	Capacity
	Beginning inventory	0	h	$2h$	. . .	nh	0	I_0
1	Regular time	r	$r+h$	$r+2h$	. . .	$r+nh$	0	R_1
	Overtime	t	$t+h$	$t+2h$	. . .	$t+nh$	0	O_1
	Subcontract	s	$s+h$	$s+2h$	. . .	$s+nh$	0	S_1
2	Regular time	$r+b$	r	$r+h$	. . .	$r+(n-1)h$	0	R_2
	Overtime	$t+b$	t	$t+h$	. . .	$t+(n-1)h$	0	O_2
	Subcontract	$s+b$	s	$s+h$	. . .	$s+(n-1)h$	0	S_2
3	Regular time	$r+2b$	$r+b$	r	. . .	$r+(n-2)h$	0	R_3
	Overtime	$t+2b$	$t+b$	t	. . .	$t+(n-2)h$	0	O_3
	Subcontract	$s+2b$	$s+b$	s	. . .	$s+(n-2)h$	0	S_3
	Demand				. . .			Total

r = Regular production cost per unit
t = Overtime cost per unit
s = Subcontracting cost per unit
h = Holding cost per unit period
b = Backorder cost per unit per perid
n = Number of periods in planning horizon

TABLE 14-4

Transportation notation for aggregate planning

Linear Programming. Linear programming models are methods for obtaining optimal solutions to problems involving the allocation of scarce resources in terms of cost minimization or profit maximization. With aggregate planning, the goal is usually to minimize the sum of costs related to regular labor time, overtime, subcontracting, inventory holding costs, and costs associated with changing the size of the workforce. Constraints involve the capacities of the workforce, inventories, and subcontracting.

The problem can be formulated as a transportation-type programming model (described in detail in the supplement to Chapter 8) as a way to obtain aggregate plans that would match capacities with demand requirements and minimize costs. In order to use this approach, planners must identify capacity (supply) of regular time, overtime, subcontracting, and inventory on a period-by-period basis, as well as related costs of each variable.

Table 14–4 shows the notation and setup of a transportation table. Note the systematic way that costs change as you move across a row from left to right. Regular cost, overtime cost, and subcontracting cost are at their lowest when the output is consumed (i.e., delivered, etc.) in the same period it is produced (at the intersection of period 1 row and column for regular cost, at the intersection of period 2 row and column for regular cost, and so on). If goods are made available in one period but carried over to later periods (i.e., moving across a row), holding costs are incurred at the rate of h per period. Thus, holding goods for two periods results in a unit cost of $2h$, whether or not the goods came from regular production, overtime, or subcontracting. Conversely, with back orders, the unit cost increases as you move across a row from right to left, beginning at the intersection of a row and column for the same period (e.g., period 3). For instance, if some goods are produced in period 3 to satisfy back orders from period 2, a unit back-order cost of b is incurred. And if goods in period 3 are used to satisfy back orders two periods earlier (e.g., from period 1), a unit cost of $2b$ is incurred. Unused capacity is generally given a unit cost of 0, although it is certainly possible to insert an actual cost if that is relevant. Finally, beginning inventory is given a unit cost of 0 if it is used to satisfy demand in period 1. However, if it is held over for use in later periods, a holding cost of h per unit is added for each period. If the inventory is to be held for the entire planning horizon, a total unit cost of h times the number of periods, n, will be incurred.

Example 4 illustrates the setup and final solution of a transportation model of an aggregate planning problem.

Example 4

Given the following information set up the problem in a transportation table and solve for the minimum-cost plan:

	PERIOD		
	1	2	3
Demand	550	700	750
Capacity			
Regular	500	500	500
Overtime	50	50	50
Subcontract	120	120	100
Beginning inventory	100		
Costs			
Regular time		$60 per unit	
Overtime		80 per unit	
Subcontract		90 per unit	
Inventory carrying cost		$1 per unit per month	
Backorder cost		$3 per unit per month	

Solution

The transportation table and solution are shown in Table 14–5. Some of the entries require additional explanation:

a. In this example, inventory carrying costs are $1 per unit per period (costs are shown in the upper right-hand corner of each cell in the table). Hence, units produced in one period and carried over to a later period will incur a holding cost that is a linear function of the length of time held.

b. Linear programming models of this type require that supply (capacity) and demand be equal. A dummy column has been added (unused capacity) to satisfy that requirement. Since it does not "cost" anything extra to not use capacity in this case, cell costs of $0 have been assigned.

c. No backlogs were needed in this example.

d. The quantities (e.g., 100 and 450 in column 1) are the amounts of output or inventory that will be used to meet demand requirements. Thus, the demand of 550 units in period 1 will be met using 100 units from inventory and 450 obtained from regular-time output.

Where backlogs are not permitted, the cell costs for the backlog positions can be made prohibitively high so that no backlogs will appear in the solution.

The main limitations of LP models are the assumptions of linear relationships among variables, the inability to continuously adjust output rates, and the need to specify a single objective (e.g., minimize costs) instead of using multiple objectives (e.g., minimize cost while stabilizing the workforce.)

linear decision rule Optimizing technique that seeks to minimize combined costs, using a set of cost-approximating functions to obtain a single quadratic equation.

Linear Decision Rule. Another optimizing technique, the **linear decision rule**, seeks to minimize the combined costs of regular payroll, hiring and layoffs, overtime, and inventory using a set of cost-approximating functions, three of which are *quadratic* (contain

TABLE 14–5

Transportation solution

Supply from		Demand for Period 1	Demand for Period 2	Demand for Period 3	Unused capacity (dummy)	Total capacity available (supply)
Period	Beginning inventory	0 / 100	1	2	0	100
1	Regular time	60 / 450	61 / 50	62	0	500
	Overtime	80	81 / 50	82	0	50
	Subcontract	90	91 / 30	92	0 / 90	120
2	Regular time	63	60 / 500	61	0	500
	Overtime	83	80 / 50	81	0	50
	Subcontract	93	90 / 20	91 / 100	0	120
3	Regular time	66	63	60 / 500	0	500
	Overtime	86	83	80 / 50	0	50
	Subcontract	96	93	90 / 100	0	100
	Demand	550	700	750	90	2,090

squared terms), to obtain a single quadratic equation. Using calculus, two linear equations (hence, the name *linear decision rule*) can be derived from the quadratic equation. One of these equations can be used to plan the output for each period in the planning horizon, and the other can be used to plan the workforce for each period.

Although the model has found some applications, its chief function seems to be as a benchmark against which proposed techniques can be evaluated. In practice, the model suffers from three limitations: (1) a specific type of cost function is assumed, (2) considerable effort must usually be expended to obtain relevant cost data and develop cost functions for each organization, and (3) the method can produce solutions that are unfeasible or impractical.

Simulation Models. A number of **simulation models** have been developed for aggregate planning. (Simulation is described in detail in the supplement to Chapter 19.) The essence of simulation is the development of computerized models that can be tested under a variety of conditions in an attempt to identify reasonably acceptable (although not always optimal) solutions to problems.

Table 14–6 summarizes these mathematical techniques.

Aggregate planning techniques other than trial and error do not appear to be widely used. Instead, in the majority of organizations, aggregate planning seems to be accomplished more on the basis of experience along with trial-and-error methods. It is difficult to say exactly why some of the mathematical techniques mentioned are not used to any great extent. Perhaps the level of mathematical sophistication discourages greater use; or the

simulation models Computerized models that can be tested under different scenarios to identify acceptable solutions to problems.

TABLE 14-6

Summary of planning techniques

Technique	Solution Approach	Characteristics
Graphical/charting	Trial and error	Intuitively appealing, easy to understand; solution not necessarily optimal
Linear programming	Optimizing	Computerized; linear assumptions not always valid
Linear decision rule	Optimizing	Complex, requires considerable effort to obtain pertinent cost information and to construct model; cost assumptions not always valid
Simulation	Trial and error	Computerized models can be examined under a variety of conditions

assumptions required in certain models appear unrealistic; or the models may be too narrow in scope. Whatever the reasons, none of the techniques to date have captured the attention of aggregate planners on a broad scale. Simulation is one technique that seems to be gaining favor. Research on improved approaches to aggregate planning is continuing.

Aggregate Planning in Services

Aggregate planning for services takes into account projected customer demands, equipment capacities, and labor capabilities. The resulting plan is a time-phased projection of service staff requirements.

Aggregate planning for manufacturing and aggregate planning for services share similarities in some respects, but there are some important differences—related in general to the differences between manufacturing and services:

1. *Services occur when they are rendered.* Unlike manufacturing output, most services can't be inventoried. Services such as financial planning, tax counseling, and oil changes can't be stockpiled. This removes the option of building up inventories during a slow period in anticipation of future demand. On the other hand, service capacity that goes unused is essentially wasted. Consequently, it becomes important to be able to match capacity and demand.

2. *Demand for service can be difficult to predict.* The volume of demand for services is often quite variable. In some situations, customers may *need* prompt service (e.g., police, fire, medical emergency), while in others, they simply *want* prompt service and may be willing to go elsewhere if their wants are not met. These factors place a greater burden on service providers to anticipate demand. Consequently, service providers must pay careful attention to planned capacity levels.

3. *Capacity availability can be difficult to predict.* Processing requirements for services can sometimes be quite variable, similar to the variability of work in a job shop setting. Moreover, the variety of tasks required of servers can be great, again similar to the variety of tasks in a job shop. However, in services, the types of variety are more pervasive than they are in manufacturing. This makes it more difficult to establish simple measures of capacity. For example, what would be the capacity of a person who paints interiors of houses? The number of rooms per day or the number of square feet per hour are possible measures, but rooms come in many different sizes, and because the level of detail (and, thus, the painting implements that can be used) vary tremendously, a suitable measure for planning purposes can be quite difficult to arrive at. Similarly, bank tellers are called upon to handle a wide variety of transactions and requests for information, again making it difficult to establish a suitable measure of their capacity.

4. *Labor flexibility can be an advantage in services.* Labor often comprises a significant portion of service compared to manufacturing. That, coupled with the fact that ser-

vice providers are often able to handle a fairly wide variety of service requirements, means that to some extent, planning is easier than it is in manufacturing. Of course, manufacturers recognize this advantage, and many are cross-training their employees to achieve the same flexibility. Moreover, in both manufacturing and service systems, the use of part-time workers can be an important option.

In self-service systems, the (customer) labor automatically adjusts to changes in demand!

Disaggregating the Aggregate Plan

For the production plan to be translated into meaningful terms for production, it is necessary to *disaggregate* the aggregate plan. This involves breaking down the aggregate plan into specific product requirements in order to determine labor requirements (skills, size of work force), materials, and inventory requirements. This process is described in Chapter 15. At this stage, however, it will be helpful for you to have some understanding of the need for disaggregation and what the term implies.

Working with aggregate units facilitates intermediate planning. However, to put the production plan into operation, one must convert, or decompose, those aggregate units into units of actual products or services that are to be produced or offered. For example, a lawn mower manufacturer may have an aggregate plan that calls for 200 lawn mowers in January, 300 in February, and 400 in March. That company may produce push mowers, self-propelled mowers, and riding mowers. Although all the mowers probably contain some of the same parts and involve some similar or identical operations for fabrication and assembly, there would be some differences in the materials, parts, and operations that each type requires. Hence, the 200, 300, and 400 aggregate lawn mowers that are to be produced during those three months must be translated into specific numbers of mowers of each type prior to actually purchasing the appropriate materials and parts, scheduling operations, and planning inventory requirements.

The result of disaggregating the aggregate plan is a **master schedule** showing the quantity and timing of *specific* end items for a scheduled horizon, which often covers about six to eight weeks ahead. A master schedule shows the planned output for individual products rather than an entire product group, along with the timing of production. The master schedule contains important information for marketing as well as for production. It reveals when orders are scheduled for production and when completed orders are to be shipped.

Once a *tentative* master schedule has been developed a planner can do the **rough-cut capacity planning** to test the feasibility of a proposed master schedule relative to available capacities, to assure that no obvious capacity constraints exist. This means checking capacities of production and warehouse facilities, labor, and vendors to ensure that no gross deficiencies exist that will render the master schedule unworkable. The master schedule then serves as the basis for *short-range* planning. It should be noted that whereas the aggregate plan covers an interval of, say, 12 months, the master schedule covers only a portion of this. In other words, the aggregate plan is disaggregated in stages, or phases, that may cover a few weeks to two or three months. Moreover, the master schedule may be updated monthly, even though it covers two or three months. For instance, the lawn mower master schedule would probably be updated at the end of January to include any revisions in planned output for February and March as well as new information on planned output for April.

Figure 14–4 illustrates the concept of disaggregating the aggregate plan. The illustration makes a simple assumption in order to clearly show the concept of disaggregation: The totals of the aggregate and the disaggregated units are equal. In reality, that is not always true. As a consequence, disaggregating the aggregate plan may require considerable effort.

Figure 14–4 shows the aggregate plan broken down by units. However, it can also be useful to show the breakdown in *percentages* for different products or product families.

master schedule The result of disaggregating an aggregate plan; shows quantity and timing of specific end items for a scheduled horizon.

rough-cut capacity planning Approximate balancing of capacity and demand to test the feasibility of a master schedule.

FIGURE 14–4

Disaggregating the aggregate plan

Aggregate plan	Month Planned output*	Jan.	Feb.	Mar.
		200	300	400

*Aggregate units

Master schedule	Month Planned output*	Jan.	Feb.	Mar.
	Push	100	100	100
	Self-propelled	75	150	200
	Riding	25	50	100
	Total	200	300	400

*Actual units

FIGURE 14–5

The master scheduling process

Inputs

Beginning inventory — Master scheduling → Projected inventory
Forecast → Master production schedule
Customer orders → Uncommitted inventory

Outputs

Master Scheduling

A master schedule indicates the quantity and timing (i.e., delivery times) for a product, or a group of products, but it does not show planned *production*. For instance, a master schedule may call for delivery of 50 cases of cranberry-apple juice to be delivered on May 1. But this may not require any production; there may be 200 cases in inventory. Or it may require *some* production: If there were 40 cases in inventory, an additional 10 cases would be needed to achieve the specified delivery amount. Or it may involve production of 50 or more cases: In some instances, it is more economical to produce large amounts rather than small amounts, with the excess temporarily placed in inventory until needed. Thus, the *production lot size* might be 70 cases, so if additional cases were needed (e.g., 50 cases), a run of 70 cases would be made.

master production schedule (MPS) This schedule indicates the quantity and timing of planned production.

The **master production schedule (MPS)** indicates the quantity and timing of planned production, taking into account desired delivery quantity and timing as well as on-hand inventory. The master production schedule is one of the primary outputs of the master scheduling process, as illustrated in Figure 14–5.

INPUTS

The master schedule has three inputs: the beginning inventory, which is the actual quantity on hand from the preceding period; forecasts for each period of the schedule; and customer orders, which are quantities already *committed* to customers.

OUTPUTS

The master scheduling process uses this information on a period-by-period basis to determine the protected inventory, production requirements, and the resulting uncommitted inventory, which is referred to as **available-to-promise (ATP) inventory.** Knowledge of the uncommitted inventory can enable marketing to make realistic promises to customers about deliveries of new orders.

available-to-promise inventory (ATP) Uncommitted inventory.

The master scheduling process begins with a preliminary calculation of projected on-hand inventory. This reveals when additional inventory (i.e., production) will be needed. Consider this example. A company that makes industrial pumps wants to prepare a mas-

FIGURE 14-6

Weekly forecast requirements for industrial pumps.

	June				July			
	1	**2**	**3**	**4**	**5**	**6**	**7**	**8**
Forecast	30	30	30	30	40	40	40	40

FIGURE 14-7

Eight-week schedule showing forecasts, customer orders, and beginning inventory

Beginning inventory: 64

	June				July			
	1	**2**	**3**	**4**	**5**	**6**	**7**	**8**
Forecast	30	30	30	30	40	40	40	40
Customer orders (committed)	33	20	10	4	2			

ter production schedule for June and July. Marketing has forecasted demand of 120 pumps for June and 160 pumps for July. These have been evenly distributed over the four weeks in each month: 30 per week in June and 40 per week in July, as illustrated in Figure 14–6.

Now, suppose that there are currently 64 pumps in inventory (i.e., beginning inventory is 64 pumps), and that there are customer orders that have been committed (booked) and must be filled (see Figure 14–7).

Figure 14–7 contains the three primary inputs to the master scheduling process: the beginning inventory, the forecast, and the customer orders that have been booked or committed. This information is necessary to determine three quantities: the projected on-hand inventory, the master production schedule, and the uncommitted (ATP) inventory. The first step is to calculate the projected on-hand inventory, one week at a time, until it falls below a specified limit. In this example, the specified limit will be zero. Hence, we will continue until the projected on-hand inventory becomes negative.

The projected on-hand inventory is calculated as follows:

$$\text{Projected on-hand inventory} = \text{Inventory from previous week} - \text{Current week's requirements} \qquad (14\text{–}1)$$

where the current week's requirements is the *larger* of forecast and customer orders (committed).

For the first week, projected on-hand inventory equals beginning inventory minus the larger of forecast and customer orders. Because customer orders (33) is larger than the forecast (30), the customer orders amount is used. Thus, for the first week, we obtain:

Projected on-hand inventory = 64 − 33 = 31

Projected on-hand inventories are shown in Figure 14–8 for the first three weeks (i.e., until the projected on-hand amount becomes negative).

When the projected on-hand inventory becomes negative, this is a signal that production will be needed to replenish inventory. Hence, a negative projected on-hand inventory will require planned production. Suppose that a production lot size of 70 pumps is used, so that whenever production is called for, 70 pumps will be produced. (The determination of lot size was described in Chapter 13.) Hence, the negative projected on-hand inventory

Projected on-hand inventory is computed week by week until it becomes negative

Determining the MPS and projected on-hand inventory

Week	Inventory from Previous Week	Require- ments*	Net Inventory before MPS		(70) MPS		Projected Inventory
1	64	33	31				31
2	31	30	1				1
3	1	30	−29	+	70	=	41
4	41	30	11				11
5	11	40	−29	+	70	=	41
6	41	40	1				1
7	1	40	−39	+	70	=	31
8	31	40	−9	+	70	=	61

*Requirements equals the larger of forecast and customer orders in each week.

in the third week will require production of 70 pumps, which will meet the projected shortfall of 29 pumps and leave 41 (i.e., $70 - 29 = 41$) pumps for future demand.

These calculations continue for the entire schedule. Every time projected inventory becomes negative, another production lot of 70 pumps is added to the schedule. Figure 14–9 illustrates the calculations. The result is the master schedule and projected on-hand inventory for each week of the schedule. These can now be added to the master schedule (see Figure 14–10).

It is now possible to determine the amount of inventory that is uncommitted, and hence, available to promise. Several methods are used in practice. The one we shall employ involves a "look-ahead" procedure: Sum booked customer orders week by week until (but not including) a week in which there is an MPS amount. For example, in the first week, this procedure results in summing customer orders of 33 (week 1) and 20 (week 2) to obtain 53. In the first week, this amount is subtracted from the beginning inventory of 64 pumps plus the MPS (zero in this example) to obtain the amount that is available to promise. Thus,

$$64 + 0 - (33 + 20) = 11$$

64	June				July			
	1	**2**	**3**	**4**	**5**	**6**	**7**	**8**
Forecast	30	30	30	30	40	40	40	40
Customer orders (committed)	33	20	10	4	2			
Projected on-hand inventory	31	1	41	11	41	1	31	61
MPS			70		70		70	70

FIGURE 14–10

Projected on-hand inventory and MPS are added to the master schedule

64	June				July			
	1	**2**	**3**	**4**	**5**	**6**	**7**	**8**
Forecast	30	30	30	30	40	40	40	40
Customer orders (committed)	33	20	10	4	2			
Projected on-hand inventory	31	1	41	11	41	1	31	61
MPS			70		70		70	70
Available-to-promise inventory (uncommitted)	11		56		68		70	70

FIGURE 14–11

The available-to-promise inventory quantities have been added to the master schedule

This inventory is uncommitted, and it can be delivered in either week 1 or 2, or part can be delivered in week 1 and part in week 2. (Note that the ATP quantity is only calculated for the first week and for other weeks in which there is an MPS quantity. Hence, it is calculated for weeks 1, 3, 5, 7, 8.) See Figure 14–11.

For weeks other than the first week, the beginning inventory drops out of the computation, and ATP is the look-ahead quantity subtracted from the MPS quantity.

Thus, for week 3, the promised amounts are 10 + 4 = 14, and the ATP is 70 − 14 = 56.

For week 5, customer orders are 2 (future orders have not yet been booked). The ATP is 70 − 2 = 68.

For weeks 7 and 8, there are no customer orders, so for the present, all of the MPS amount is available to promise.

As additional orders are booked, these would be entered in the schedule, and the ATP amounts would be updated to reflect those orders. Marketing can use the ATP amounts to provide realistic delivery dates to customers.

STABILIZING THE MASTER SCHEDULE

Changes to a master schedule can be disruptive, particularly changes to the early, or near, portions of the schedule. Typically, the further out in the future a change is, the less the tendency to cause problems.

FIGURE 14–12

Time fences in the MPS

The schedule is

time fences Points in time that separate stages of a master schedule.

Master production schedules are often divided into four stages, or phases. The dividing lines between phases are sometimes referred to as **time fences.** In the first phase, usually the first few periods of the schedule, changes can be quite disruptive. Consequently, once established, that portion of the schedule is generally *frozen,* which implies that all but the most critical changes cannot be made without permission from the highest levels in an organization. The purpose, of course, is to achieve a high degree of *stability* in the production system. In the next stage, perhaps the next two or three periods, changes are still disruptive, but not to the extent that they are in the first phase of the schedule. Management views the schedule as *firm,* and only exceptional changes are made. In the third stage, management views the schedule as *full,* meaning that all available capacity has been allocated. Although changes do impact the schedule, their effect is less dramatic, and they are usually made if there is a good reason for doing so. In the final phase, management views the schedule as *open,* meaning that not all capacity has been allocated. This is where new orders are usually entered in the schedule.

Figure 14–12 illustrates time fences.

Summary

Aggregate planning establishes general levels of employment, output, and inventories for periods of 2 to 12 months. In the spectrum of planning, it falls between the broad decisions of long-range planning and the very specific and detailed short-range planning decisions. It begins with an overall forecast for the planning horizon and ends with preparations for applying the plans to specific products and services.

The essence of aggregate planning is the aggregation of products or services into one "product" or "service." This permits planners to consider overall levels of employment and inventories without having to become involved with specific details that are better left to short-range planning. Planners often use informal graphic and charting techniques to develop plans, although various mathematical techniques have been suggested. It appears that the complexity and the restrictive assumptions of these techniques limit their widespread use in practice.

After the aggregate plan has been developed, it is disaggregated or broken down into specific product requirements. This leads to a master schedule, which indicates the planned quantities and timing of specific outputs. Inputs to the master schedule are on-hand inventory amounts, forecasts of demand, and customer orders. The outputs are projected production and inventory requirements, and the projected uncommitted inventory, which is referred to as available-to-promise (ATP) inventory.

The aggregate planning process is summarized in Table 14–7.

Key Terms

aggregate planning, 604
available-to-promise (ATP) inventory, 624
chase demand strategy, 611
level capacity strategy, 611
linear decision rule, 620

master production schedule, (MPS), 624
master schedule, 623
rough-cut capacity planning, 623
simulation models, 621
time fences, 628

TABLE 14–7

Summary of aggregate planning

Purpose

Decide on the combination of:

    Output rates

    Employment levels

    On-hand inventory levels

Objectives

    Minimize cost

    Others, may include

        Maintain a desirable level of customer service

        Minimize workforce fluctuations

Possible Strategies

A. Supply Management

    Level Production

    Allow inventory to absorb variations in demand

    Use back ordering during periods of high demand

    Chase Production

    Vary output by varying the number of workers by hiring or layoffs to track demand

    Vary output throughout the use of overtime or idle time

    Vary output using part-time workers

    Use subcontracting to supplement output

    Mixed Strategy

    Use a combination of level and chase approaches

B. Demand Management

    Influence demand through promotion, pricing, etc.

    Produce goods or services that have complementary demand patterns

Managerial Importance of Aggregate Planning

    Has an effect on:

      Costs

      Equipment utilization

      Customer satisfaction

      Employment levels

      Helps to synchronize flow throughout the supply chain

Solved Problems

Problem 1

A manager is attempting to put together an aggregate plan for the coming nine months. She has obtained a forecast of expected demand for the planning horizon. The plan must deal with highly seasonal demand; demand is relatively high in periods 3 and 4 and again in period 8, as can be seen from the following forecasts:

Period	1	2	3	4	5	6	7	8	9	Total
Forecast	190	230	260	280	210	170	160	260	180	1,940

The department now has 20 full-time employees, each of whom can produce 10 units of output per period at a cost of $6 per unit. Inventory carrying cost is $5 per unit per period, and backlog cost is $10 per unit per period. The manager is considering a plan that would involve hiring two people to start working in period 1, one on a temporary basis who would work only through period 5. This would cost $500 in addition to unit production costs.

a. What is the rationale for this plan?

b. Determine the total cost of the plan, including production, inventory, and back order costs.

Solution

a. With the current workforce of 20 people each producing 10 units per period, regular capacity is 1,800 units. That is 140 units less than expected demand. Adding one worker would increase regular capacity to $1,800 + 90 = 1,890$ units. That would still be 50 units short, or just the amount one temporary worker could produce in five periods. Since one of the two seasonal peaks is quite early, it would make sense to start the temporary worker right away to avoid some of the back-order cost.

b. The production plan for this strategy is as follows:

Period	1	2	3	4	5	6	7	8	9	Total
Forecast	190	230	260	280	210	170	160	260	180	1,940
Output										
Regular	220	220	220	220	220	210	210	210	210	1,940
Overtime	—	—	—	—	—	—	—	—	—	—
Subcontract	—	—	—	—	—	—	—	—	—	—
Output – Forecast	30	(10)	(40)	(60)	10	40	50	(50)	30	0
Inventory										
Beginning	0	30	20	0	0	0	0	20	0	
Ending	30	20	0	0	0	0	20	0	0	
Average	15	25	10	0	0	0	10	10	0	70
Backlog	0	0	20	80	70	30	0	30	0	230
Costs										
Output										
Regular @ $6	$1,320	1,320	1,320	1,320	1,320	1,260	1,260	1,260	1,260	$11,640
Overtime										
Subcontract										
Inventory @ $5	$75	125	50	0	0	0	50	50	0	$350
Backorder @ $10	0	0	200	800	700	300	0	300	0	$2,300
Total	$1,395	1,445	1,570	2,120	2,020	1,560	1,310	1,610	1,260	$14,290

The total cost for this plan is $14,290, plus the $500 cost for hiring and for the layoff, giving a total of $14,790. This plan may or may not be good. The manager would need information on other costs and options before settling on one plan.

Although the calculations are relatively straightforward, the backlogs can sometimes seem difficult to obtain. Consider these rules for computing the backlog:

1. Start with the Output – Forecast value. If this is positive and there was a backlog in the preceding period, reduce the backlog by this amount. If the amount exceeds the backlog, the difference becomes the ending inventory for the period. If they are exactly equal, the backlog and the ending inventory will both be equal to zero.

2. If Output – Forecast is negative, subtract it from the beginning inventory. If this produces a negative value, that value becomes the backlog for that period.

You can also use the appropriate Excel template to obtain the solution:

Prepare a schedule like that shown in Figure 14–10 for the following situation. The forecast for each period is 70 units. The starting inventory is zero. The MPS rule is to schedule production if the projected inventory on hand is negative. The production lot size is 100 units. The following table shows committed orders.

Problem 2

Period	Customer Orders
1	80
2	50
3	30
4	10

Solution

Period	(A) Inventory from Previous Period	(B) Requirements*	(C = B − A) Net Inventory before MPS	MPS	(MPS + C) Projected Inventory
1	0	80	(80)	100	20
2	20	70	(50)	100	50
3	50	70	(20)	100	80
4	80	70	10	0	10

*Requirements equals the larger of forecast and customer orders in each period.

Starting Inv. = 0	1	2	3	4
Forecast	70	70	70	70
Customer orders	80	50	30	10
Projected on-hand inventory	20	50	80	10
MPS	100	100	100	0
ATP	20	50	60	0

1. What three levels of planning involve operations managers? What kinds of decisions are made at the various levels?
2. What are the three phases of intermediate planning?
3. What is aggregate planning? What is its purpose?
4. Why is there a need for aggregate planning?
5. What are the most common decision variables for aggregate planning in a manufacturing setting? In a service setting?
6. What aggregate planning difficulty that might confront an organization offering a variety of products and/or services would not confront an organization offering one or a few similar products or services?
7. Briefly discuss the advantages and disadvantages of each of these planning strategies:
   a. Maintain a level rate of output and let inventories absorb fluctuations in demand.
   b. Vary the size of the workforce to correspond to predicted changes in demand requirements.
   c. Maintain a constant workforce size, but vary hours worked to correspond to predicted demand requirements.
8. What are the primary advantages and limitations of informal graphic and charting techniques for aggregate planning?
9. Briefly describe the planning techniques listed below, and give an advantage and disadvantage for each:
   a. Linear programming
   b. Linear decision rule
   c. Simulation
10. What are the inputs to master scheduling? What are the outputs?
11. Explain the managerial significance of aggregate planning.

Memo Writing Exercises

1. J. B. Ronks is a marketing manager at your company. He is teaching an introductory marketing course at a local college one evening a week and needs a concise explanation of the "what and why of aggregate planning." Because of your knowledge of operations management, he has sent you a memo asking for your help. Write a brief memo providing the explanation Ronks needs.

2. Your immediate supervisor, Rhonda Waters, has raised the possibility of switching from a chase demand strategy to a level-capacity strategy for aggregate planning and wants your opinion on the merits of one versus the other. Write her a one-page memo on this matter.

Problems

1. Refer to Example 1. The president of the firm has decided to shut down the plant for vacation and installation of new equipment in period 4. After installation, the cost per unit will remain the same, but the output rate for regular time will be 450. Regular output is the same as in Example 1 for periods 1, 2, and 3; 0 for period 4; and 450 for each of the remaining periods. Note, though, that the forecast of 400 units in period 4 must be dealt with. Prepare the aggregate plan, and compute its total cost.

2. Refer to Example 1. Suppose that the regular output rate will drop to 290 units per period due to an expected change in production requirements. Costs will not change. Prepare an aggregate plan and compute its total cost for each of these alternatives:

   a. Use overtime at a fixed rate of 20 units per period as needed. Plan for an ending inventory of zero for period 6. Backlogs cannot exceed 90 units per period.

   b. Use subcontracting at a maximum rate of 50 units per period; the usage need not be the same in every period. Have an ending inventory of zero in the last period. Again backlogs cannot exceed 90 units in any period. Compare these two plans.

3. Refer to Example 2. Suppose you can use a combination of overtime and subcontracting, but you cannot use subcontracting in more than two periods. Up to 50 units of subcontracting and either 0 or 40 units of overtime are allowed per period. Subcontracting is $6 per unit, and overtime is $3 per unit. (Hint: Use subcontracting only when overtime units are not sufficient to decrease backlogs to 80 units or less.) Plan for an ending inventory balance of 0 for period 6. Prepare a plan that will minimize total cost.

4. Refer to Example 2. Determine whether a plan to use subcontracting at a maximum rate of 50 units per period as needed with no overtime would achieve a lower total cost than the plan shown in Example 2. Again, plan for a zero inventory balance at the end of period 6.

5. Manager T. C. Downs of Plum Engines, a producer of lawn mowers and leaf blowers, must develop an aggregate plan given the forecast for engine demand shown in the table. The department has a normal capacity of 130 engines per month. Normal output has a cost of $60 per engine. The beginning inventory is zero engines. Overtime has a cost of $90 per engine.

   a. Develop a chase plan that matches the forecast and compute the total cost of your plan.

   b. Compare the costs to a level plan that uses inventory to absorb fluctuations. Inventory carrying cost is $2 per engine per month. Backlog cost is $90 per engine per month.

Month	1	2	3	4	5	6	7	8	Total
Forecast	120	135	140	120	125	125	140	135	1,040

6. Manager Chris Channing of Fabric Mills, Inc., has developed the forecast shown in the table for bolts of cloth. The figures are in hundreds of bolts. The department has a normal capacity of 275(00) bolts per month, except for the seventh month, when capacity will be 250(00) bolts. Normal output has a cost of $40 per hundred bolts. Workers can be assigned to other jobs if production is less than normal. The beginning inventory is zero bolts.

   a. Develop a chase plan that matches the forecast and compute the total cost of your plan. Overtime is $60 per hundred bolts.

   b. Would the total cost be less with regular production with no overtime, but using a subcontractor to handle the excess above normal capacity at a cost of $50 per hundred bolts? Backlogs are not allowed. The inventory carrying cost is $2 per hundred bolts.

Month	1	2	3	4	5	6	7	Total
Forecast	250	300	250	300	280	275	270	1,925

7. SummerFun, Inc., produces a variety of recreation and leisure products. The production manager has developed an aggregate forecast:

Month	Mar	Apr	May	Jun	Jul	Aug	Sep	Total
Forecast	50	44	55	60	50	40	51	350

Use the following information to develop aggregate plans.

Regular production cost	$80 per unit
Overtime production cost	$120 per unit
Regular capacity	40 units per month
Overtime capacity	8 units per month
Subcontracting cost	$140 per unit
Subcontracting capacity	12 units per month
Holding cost	$10
Back-order cost	$20 per unit
Beginning inventory	0 units

Develop an aggregate plan using each of the following guidelines and compute the total cost for each plan. Which plan has the lowest total cost?

a. Use regular production. Supplement using inventory, overtime, and subcontracting as needed. No backlogs allowed.

b. Use a level strategy. Use a combination of backlogs, subcontracting, and inventory to handle variations in demand.

8. Nowjuice, Inc., produces bottled pickle juice. A planner has developed an aggregate forecast for demand (in cases) for the next six months.

Month	May	Jun	Jul	Aug	Sep	Oct
Forecast	4,000	4,800	5,600	7,200	6,400	5,000

Use the following information to develop aggregate plans.

Regular production cost	$10 per case
Regular production capacity	5,000 cases
Overtime production cost	$16 per case
Subcontracting cost	$20 per case
Holding cost	$1
Back-ordering cost	$10 per month per case
Beginning inventory	0

Develop an aggregate plan using each of the following guidelines and compute the total cost for each plan. Which plan has the lowest total cost?

a. Use level production. Supplement using overtime as needed.

b. Use a combination of overtime (500 cases per period maximum), inventory, and subcontracting (500 cases per period maximum) to handle variations in demand.

c. Use overtime up to 750 cases per period and inventory to handle variations in demand.

9. Wormwood, Ltd., produces a variety of furniture products. The planning committee wants to prepare an aggregate plan for the next six months using the following information:

	MONTH					
	1	2	3	4	5	6
Demand	160	150	160	180	170	140
Capacity						
Regular	150	150	150	150	160	160
Overtime	10	10	0	10	10	10

Cost Per Unit	
Regular time	$50
Overtime	$75
Subcontract	$80
Inventory, per period	$ 4

Subcontracting can handle a maximum of 10 units per month. Beginning inventory is zero. Develop a plan that minimizes total cost. No back orders allowed.

10. Refer to Solved Problem 1. Prepare two additional aggregate plans. Call the one in the solved problem plan A. For plan B, hire one more worker at a cost of $200 in that period. Make up any shortfall using subcontracting at $8 per unit, with a maximum of 20 units per period (i.e., use subcontracting to reduce back orders when the forecast exceeds regular output). Note that the ending inventory in period 9 should be zero. Therefore, Total forecast − Total output = Quantity subcontracted. An additional constraint is that back orders cannot exceed 80 units in any period. For plan C, assume no workers are hired (so regular output is 200 units per period instead of 210 as in plan B). Use subcontracting as needed, but no more than 20 units per period. Compute the total cost of each plan. Which plan has the lowest cost?

11. Refer to Solved Problem 1. Suppose another option is to use part-time workers to assist during seasonal peaks. The cost per unit, including hiring and training, is $11. The output rate is 10 units per worker per period for all workers. A maximum of 10 part-time workers can be used, and the same number of part-time workers must be used in all periods that have part-time workers. The ending inventory in period 9 should be 10 units. The limit on backlogs is 20 units per period. Try to make up backlogs as soon as possible. Compute the total cost for this plan, and compare it to the cost of the plan used in the solved problem.

12. Refer to Solved Problem 1. Prepare an aggregate plan that uses overtime ($9 per unit, maximum output 25 units per period) and inventory variation. Try to minimize backlogs. The ending inventory in period 9 should be zero, and the limit on backlogs is 60 units per period. Note that Total output = Total regular output + Overtime quantity. Compute the total cost of your plan, and compare it to the total cost of the plan used in the solved problem.

13. Refer to Solved Problem 1. Prepare an aggregate plan that uses some combination of laying off ($100 per worker), subcontracting ($8 per unit, maximum of 20 units per period, must use for three consecutive periods), and overtime ($9 per unit, maximum of 25 per period, maximum of 60 for the planning horizon). Compute the total cost, and compare it with any of the other plans you have developed. Which plan has the lowest total cost? Assume you start with 21 workers.

14. Verify the transportation solution shown in Example 4.

15. Refer to Example 4. Suppose that an increase in warehousing costs and other costs brings inventory carrying costs to $2 per unit per month. All other costs and quantities remain the same. Determine a revised solution to this transportation problem.

16. Refer to Example 4. Suppose that regular-time capacity will be reduced to 440 units in period 3 to accommodate a companywide safety inspection of equipment. What will the additional cost of the optimal plan be as compared to the one shown in Example 4? Assume all costs and quantities are the same as given in Example 4 except for the regular-time output in period 3.

17. Solve Problem 16 using an inventory carrying cost of $2 per unit per period.

18. Dundas Bike Components Inc. of Wheelville, Illinois, manufactures bicycle wheels in two different sizes for the Big Bike Co. assembly plant located across town. David Dundas, the firm's owner-manager, has just received Big Bike's order for the next six months.

	20-inch Wheels	**24-inch Wheels**
Nov.	1,000 units	500 units
Dec.	900	500
Jan.	600	300
Feb.	700	500
Mar.	1,100	400
Apr.	1,100	600

    a. Under what circumstances will it be possible for David to develop just one aggregate plan rather than two (one for each size wheel)? Explain in two to three sentences without calculations.

    b. Currently Dundas employs 28 full-time, highly skilled employees, each of whom can produce 50 wheels per month. Because skilled labor is in short supply in the Wheelville area, David would like to develop a pure level-output plan. There is no inventory of finished wheels on hand at present, but David would like to have 300 on hand at the end of April. Big Bike will tolerate back orders of up to 200 units per month. Show your level plan in tabular form.

c. Calculate the total annual cost of your plan using these costs:

Regular	$5.00	Hiring	$300
Overtime	$7.50	Layoff	$400
Part-time	NA	Inventory	$1.00
Subcontract	NA	Backorder	$6.00

19. Prepare a master production schedule for industrial pumps in the manner of Figure 14–10 in the chapter. Use the same inputs as the example, but change the MPS rule from "schedule production when the projected on-hand inventory would be negative without production" to "schedule production when the projected on-hand inventory would be less than 10 without production."

20. Update the master schedule shown in Figure 14–10 given these updated inputs: It is now the end of week 1; customer orders are 25 for week 2, 16 for week 3, 11 for week 4, 8 for week 5, and 3 for week 6. Use the MPS rule of ordering production when projected on-hand inventory would be negative without production.

21. Prepare a master schedule like that shown in Figure 14–10 given this information: The forecast for each week of an eight-week schedule is 50 units. The MPS rule is to schedule production if the projected on-hand inventory would be negative without it. Customer orders (committed) are:

Week	Customer Orders
1	52
2	35
3	20
4	12

Use a production lot size of 75 units and no beginning inventory.

22. Determine the available-to-promise (ATP) quantities for each period for Solved Problem 2.

23. Prepare a schedule like that shown in Figure 14–11 for the following situation: The forecast is 80 units for each of the first two periods and 60 units for each of the next three periods. The starting inventory is 20 units. The company uses a chase strategy for determining the production lot size, except there is an upper limit on the lot size of 70 units. Also, the desired safety stock is 10 units. Note: The ATP quantities are based on maximum allowable production, and do not include safety stock. Committed orders are:

Period	Customer Orders
1	82
2	80
3	60
4	40
5	20

CASE

Eight Glasses a Day

The EGAD Bottling Company has recently expanded its bottled spring water operations to include several new flavors. Marketing manager Georgianna Mercer is predicting an upturn in demand based on the new offerings and the in-creased public awareness of the health benefits of drinking more water. She has prepared aggregate forecasts for the next six months, as shown in the following table (quantities are in tankloads):

Month	May	Jun	Jul	Aug	Sept	Oct	Total
Forecast	50	60	70	90	80	70	420

Production manager Mark Mercer (no relation to Georgianna) has developed the following information. (Note that one unit equals 100 bottles, and there are 10,000 bottles per tankload.)

Regular production cost	$10 per unit
Regular production capacity	60 units
Overtime production cost	$16 per unit
Subcontracting cost	$18 per unit
Holding cost	$2
Back-ordering cost	$50 per month per unit
Beginning inventory	0 units

Among the strategies being considered are:

1. Level production supplemented by up to 10 tankloads a month from overtime.

2. A combination of overtime, inventory, and subcontracting.

3. Using overtime for up to 15 tankloads a month, along with inventory to handle variations.

The objective is to choose the plan that has the lowest cost. Which plan would you recommend?

Selected Bibliography and Further Reading

Brandimarte, P., and A. Villa (Eds). *Modeling Manufacturing Systems: From Aggregate Planning to Real-Time Control.* New York: Springer, 1999.

Buxey, G. "Production Planning for Seasonal Demand." *International Journal of Operations and Production Management* 13, no. 7 (July 1993), pp. 4–21.

Fogarty, Donald W., John H. Blackstone Jr., and Thomas R. Hoffmann. *Production and Inventory Management.* Cincinnati: South-Western Publishing, 1991.

Hopp, Wallace J., and Mark L. Spearman. *Factory Physics.* 2nd ed. New York: Irwin/McGraw-Hill, 2001.

Silver, E. A., D. F. Pyke, and R. Peterson. *Inventory Management and Production Planning and Scheduling.* New York: Wiley, 1998.

Sipper, Daniel, and Robert Bulfin Jr. *Production: Planning, Control, and Integration.* New York: McGraw-Hill, 1997.

Vollmann, Thomas E., William L. Berry, and D. Clay Whybark. *Manufacturing Planning and Control Systems.* 4th ed. Burr Ridge, IL: Richard D. Irwin, 1997.

Ware, Norman, and Donald Fogarty. "Master Schedule/Master Production Schedule: The Same or Different?" *Production and Inventory Management Journal,* First Quarter, 1990, pp. 34–37.

File Select View Filter Options Tools Color MDA-Tools Window   Help

ASSEMBL   Palettes:

MANAGE   DRAFTING
STRUC   POINT
VISUALTN   LINE
UPDATE   GRAPHIC
RELOAD   CURVE2
UTILITY   AUXVIEW2
               DETAIL
               OUTLINE
FILE   DIMENS2
READ   ANALYSIS
WRITE   DRAFT
CREATE   SPC->DRW
RENAME   DRWSTD
DELETE   ERASE
MOVE   IDENTIFY
COPY   PLOTEX
QUERY   LAYER
               LIMIT1
               AUXVIEW
               MARKUP
               STANDARD
               PATTERN
               ASSEMBL
               PLOT
               MERGE
               SETS
               TEXTD2
               UTILITY
               TRANSFOR
               FILE

ID = ASSEMBLY SET = *SET1   WSP AXD VU DR 3D EXIT   BR   ZM SC WI NP NS ST   — L =000   RT SK   YES NO INT
ENTER SIZE:X.Y // INS 1ST POINT   YES : CATIA MAIN WINDOW   DRAFT = SHEET   1
                                                                               AXS=ASSEMBLY   VU=OUTLINE

CHAPTER FIFTEEN

MRP and ERP

CHAPTER OUTLINE

MRP, 640
Dependent versus Independent
Demand, 640

An Overview of MRP, 640

MRP Inputs, 642
The Master Schedule, 642
The Bill of Materials, 643
The Inventory Records, 646

MRP Processing, 646
Updating the System, 652

MRP Outputs, 654

Other Considerations, 654
Safety Stock, 654
Lot Sizing, 655

Capacity Requirements
Planning, 657

MRP in Services, 660

Benefits and Requirements of
MRP, 660

MRP II, 661

Newsclip: SAP R/3 Leads Pack of
Enterprise Resource Planning
Software Packages, 663

ERP, 664

Reading: The ABCs of ERP, 664

Reading: Wireless ERP, 668

Summary, 669

Key Terms, 669

Solved Problems, 669

Discussion and Review
Questions, 672

Memo Writing Exercises, 673

Problems, 673

Case: DMD Enterprises, 678

Operations Tour: Stickley
Furniture, 679

Selected Bibliography and Further
Reading, 681

LEARNING OBJECTIVES

*After completing this chapter, you
should be able to:*

1 Describe the conditions under
which MRP is most appropriate.

2 Describe the inputs, outputs, and
nature of MRP processing.

3 Explain how requirements in a
master production schedule are
translated into material
requirements for lower-level
items.

4 Discuss the benefits and
requirements of MRP.

5 Explain how an MRP system is
useful in capacity requirements
planning.

6 Outline the potential benefits and
some of the difficulties users have
encountered with MRP.

7 Describe MRP II and how it
relates to MRP.

8 Describe ERP.

This chapter describes MRP (material requirements planning) and ERP (enterprise resource planning). MRP is a planning and scheduling technique used for batch production of assembled items. The first portion of the chapter is devoted to MRP. The remainder of the chapter is devoted to ERP, which involves the use of extensive software to integrate record keeping and information sharing throughout an organization.

MRP

The raw materials, purchased parts, and other components of assembled items are subject to what is called *dependent demand,* which requires an approach different from the inventory management techniques described in the chapter on inventory management.

DEPENDENT VERSUS INDEPENDENT DEMAND

A major distinction in the way inventories are managed results from the nature of demand for those items. When demand for items is derived from plans to make certain products, as it is with raw materials, parts, and assemblies used in producing a finished product, those items are said to have **dependent demand.** The parts and materials that go into the production of an automobile are examples of dependent demand because the total amount of parts and raw materials needed during any time period is a function of the number of cars that will be produced. Conversely, demand for the *finished* cars is independent—a car is not a component of another item.

dependent demand Demand for items that are subassemblies or component parts to be used in the production of finished goods.

Independent demand is fairly stable once allowances are made for seasonal variations, but dependent demand tends to be sporadic or "lumpy"; large quantities are used at specific points in time with little or no usage at other times. For example, a firm that produces lawn and garden equipment might make a variety of items, such as trimmers, lawn mowers, and small tractors. Suppose that the various products are produced periodically—in one month, push mowers; in the next month, mulching mowers; and in the third month, tractors. Some components may be used in most of the items (e.g., nuts and bolts, screws). It makes sense to have a continual inventory of these parts because they are always needed. On the other hand, some parts might be used for only one item. Consequently, demand for those parts occurs only when that item is being produced, which might be once every eight or nine weeks; the rest of the time, demand is zero. Thus, demand is "lumpy." Because of these tendencies, independent-demand items must be carried on a continual basis, but dependent-demand items need only be stocked just prior to the time they will be needed in the production process. Moreover, the predictability of usage of dependent-demand items means that there is little or no need for safety stock. Figure 15–1 illustrates key differences in independent- and dependent-demand inventories.

An Overview of MRP

material requirements planning Computer-based information system for ordering and scheduling of dependent-demand inventories.

Material requirements planning (MRP) is a computer-based information system designed to handle ordering and scheduling of dependent-demand inventories (e.g., raw materials, component parts, and subassemblies). A production plan for a specified number of finished products is translated into requirements for component parts and raw materials working backward from the due date, using lead times and other information to determine when and how much to order. Hence, requirements for end items generate requirements for lower-level components, which are broken down by planning periods (e.g., weeks) so that ordering, fabrication, and assembly can be scheduled for timely completion of end items while inventory levels are kept reasonably low.

Material requirements planning is as much a philosophy as it is a technique, and as much an approach to scheduling as it is to inventory control.

Historically, ordering and scheduling of assembled products suffered from two difficulties. One was the enormous task of setting up schedules, keeping track of large numbers of parts and components, and coping with schedule and order changes. The other was

FIGURE 15–1

Comparison of independent and dependent demand

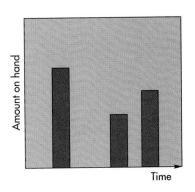

a lack of differentiation between independent demand and dependent demand. All too often, techniques designed for independent-demand items were used to handle assembled items, which resulted in excessive inventories. Consequently, inventory planning and scheduling presented major problems for manufacturers.

In the 1970s, manufacturers began to recognize the importance of the distinction between independent- and dependent-demand items and to approach these two categories in different ways. Much of the burden of record keeping and determining material requirements in many firms has now been transferred to computers, using techniques such as MRP. A great deal of the credit for publicizing MRP and educating potential users about MRP goes to Joseph Orlicky,[1] George Plossl, Oliver Wight, and APICS. APICS offers certification information and exams.

MRP begins with a schedule for finished goods that is converted into a schedule of requirements for the subassemblies, component parts, and raw materials needed to produce the finished items in the specified time frame. Thus, MRP is designed to answer three questions: *what* is needed? *how much* is needed? and *when* is it needed?

The primary inputs of MRP are a bill of materials, which tells the composition of a finished product; a master schedule, which tells how much finished product is desired and when; and an inventory records file, which tells how much inventory is on hand or on order. The planner processes this information to determine the *net* requirements for each period of the planning horizon.

Outputs from the process include planned-order schedules, order releases, changes, performance-control reports, planning reports, and exception reports. These topics are discussed in more detail in subsequent sections. Figure 15–2 provides an overview of an MRP system.

---

[1]Orlicky is the author of *Material Requirements Planning* (New York: McGraw-Hill, 1975).

FIGURE 15–2

Overview of MRP

FIGURE 15–3

A master schedule for end item X

Item: X	1	2	3	4	5	6	7	8
Quanity				100				150

Week number

MRP Inputs

An MRP system has three major sources of information: a master schedule, a bill-of-materials file, and an inventory records file (see Figure 15–2). Let's consider each of these inputs.

THE MASTER SCHEDULE

master schedule One of three primary inputs in MRP; states which end items are to be produced, when these are needed, and in what quantities.

The **master schedule,** also referred to as the *master production schedule,* states which end items are to be produced, when they are needed, and in what quantities. Figure 15–3 illustrates a portion of a master schedule that shows planned output for end item X for the planning horizon. The schedule indicates that 100 units of X will be needed (e.g., for shipments to customers) at the *start* of week 4 and that another 150 units will be needed at the *start* of week 8.

The quantities in a master schedule come from a number of different sources, including customer orders, forecasts, orders from warehouses to build up seasonal inventories, and external demand.

The master schedule separates the planning horizon into a series of time periods or time *buckets,* which are often expressed in weeks. However, the time buckets need not be

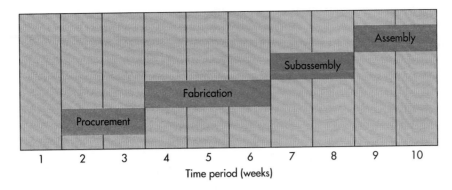

FIGURE 15-4

The planning horizon must cover the cumulative lead time

of equal length. In fact, the near-term portion of a master schedule may be in weeks, but later portions may be in months or quarters. Usually, plans for those more distant time periods are more tentative than near-term requirements.

Although a master production schedule has no set time period that it must cover, most managers like to plan far enough into the future so they have some general idea of probable upcoming demands for the near term. It is important, though, that the master schedule cover the *stacked* or **cumulative lead time** necessary to produce the end items. This amounts to the sum of the lead times that sequential phases of the production or assembly process require, as illustrated in Figure 15–4, where a total of nine weeks of lead time is needed from ordering parts and raw materials until final assembly is completed.

cumulative lead time The sum of the lead times that sequential phases of a process require, from ordering of parts or raw materials to completion of final assembly.

THE BILL OF MATERIALS

A **bill of materials (BOM)** contains a listing of all of the assemblies, subassemblies, parts, and raw materials that are needed to produce *one* unit of a finished product. Thus, each finished product has its own bill of materials.

The listing in the bill of materials is hierarchical; it shows the quantity of each item needed to complete one unit of the following level of assembly. The nature of this aspect of a bill of materials is clear when you consider a **product structure tree,** which provides a visual depiction of the subassemblies and components needed to assemble a product. Figure 15–5 shows an assembly diagram for a chair and a product structure tree for the chair. This chart is a simple product structure tree for a chair. The end item (in this case, the chair, the finished product) is shown at the top of the tree. Just beneath it are the subassemblies, or major components, that must be put together to make up the end item. Beneath each major component are the necessary lesser components. At each stage moving down the tree are the components (parts, materials) needed to make one unit of the next higher item in the tree.

A product structure tree is useful in illustrating how the bill of materials is used to determine the quantities of each of the ingredients (requirements) needed to obtain a desired number of end items.

Let's consider the product structure tree shown in Figure 15–6. End item X is composed of two Bs and one C. Moreover, each B requires three Ds and one E, and each D requires four Es. Similarly, each C is made up of two Es and two Fs. These *requirements* are listed by *level,* beginning with level 0 for the end item, then level 1 for the next level, and so on. The items at each level are *components* of the next level up and, as in a family tree, are *parents* of their respective components. Note that the quantities of each item in the product structure tree refer only to the amounts needed to complete the assembly at the next higher level.

bill of materials (BOM) One of the three primary inputs of MRP; a listing of all of the raw materials, parts, subassemblies, and assemblies needed to produce one unit of a product.

product structure tree Visual depiction of the requirements in a bill of materials, where all components are listed by levels.

Use the information presented in Figure 15–6 to do the following:

Example 1

a. Determine the quantities of B, C, D, E, and F needed to assemble one X.

FIGURE 15-5

Assembly diagram and product structure tree for chair assembly

Assembly diagram

Product structure tree

FIGURE 15-6

A product structure tree for end item X

b. Determine the quantities of these components that will be required to assemble 10 Xs, taking into account the quantities on hand (i.e., in inventory) of various components:

Component	On Hand
B	4
C	10
D	8
E	60

a.

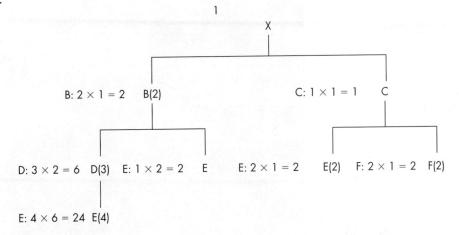

Thus, one X will require:

B: 2

C: 1

D: 6

E: 28 (Note that E occurs in three places, with requirements of $24 + 2 + 2 = 28$)

F: 2

b.

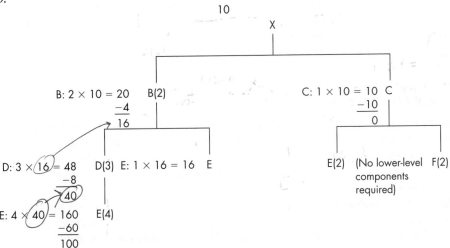

Thus, given the amounts of on-hand inventory, 10 Xs will require:

B: 16

C: 0

D: 40

E: 116

F: 0

Determining total requirements is usually more complicated than Example 1 might suggest. For one thing, many products have considerably more components. For another, the issue of *timing* is essential (i.e., when must the components be ordered or made) and must be included in the analysis. Finally, for a variety of reasons, some of the components/

IBM CAD–CAM software can be used to help prepare a bill of materials. This diagram shows a bill of materials for a pump, along with several different views of the complete product with the subassemblies.

subassemblies may be on hand (i.e., currently in inventory). Consequently, in determining total requirements, the amounts on hand must be *netted out* (i.e., subtracted from the apparent requirements) to determine the true requirements.

Comment. It is extremely important that the bill of materials accurately reflect the composition of a product, particularly since errors at one level become magnified by the multiplication process used to determine quantity requirements. As obvious as this might seem, many companies find themselves with incorrect bills-of-material records. These make it impossible to effectively determine material requirements; moreover, the task of correcting these records can be complex and time-consuming. Accurate records are a prerequisite for effective MRP.

THE INVENTORY RECORDS

inventory records One of the three primary inputs in MRP; includes information on the status of each item by time period.

Inventory records refer to stored information on the status of each item by time period. This includes gross requirements, scheduled receipts, and expected amount on hand. It also includes other details for each item, such as supplier, lead time, and lot size. Changes due to stock receipts and withdrawals, canceled orders, and similar events also are recorded in this file.

Like the bill of materials, inventory records must be accurate. Erroneous information on requirements or lead times can have a detrimental impact on MRP and create turmoil when incorrect quantities are on hand or expected delivery times are not met.

MRP Processing

MRP processing takes the end item requirements specified by the master schedule and "explodes" them into *time-phased* requirements for assemblies, parts, and raw materials using the bill of materials offset by lead times. You can see the time-phasing of requirements in the assembly time chart in Figure 15–7. For example, raw materials D, F, and I must be ordered at the start of week 2, part C at the start of week 4, and part H at the start of week 5 in order to be available for delivery as planned.

The quantities that are generated by exploding the bill of materials are *gross requirements*; they do not take into account any inventory that is currently on hand or due to be received. The materials that a firm must actually acquire to meet the demand generated by the master schedule are the *net material requirements*.

The determination of the net requirements (*netting*) is the core of MRP processing. One accomplishes it by subtracting from gross requirements the sum of inventory on hand and any scheduled receipts, and then adding in safety stock requirements, if applicable:

FIGURE 15-7

Assembly time chart showing material order points needed to meet scheduled availability of the end item

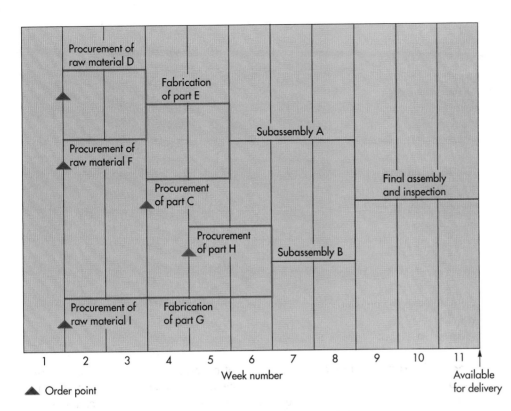

$$
\begin{array}{c}
\text{Net} \\
\text{requirements} \\
\text{in period } t
\end{array}
=
\begin{array}{c}
\text{Gross} \\
\text{requirements} \\
\text{in period } t
\end{array}
-
\begin{array}{c}
\text{Projected} \\
\text{inventory} \\
\text{in period } t
\end{array}
+
\begin{array}{c}
\text{Safety} \\
\text{stock}
\end{array}
\qquad (15\text{–}1)
$$

For simplicity, we will omit safety stock from computations in examples and most problems. Net requirements are sometimes adjusted to include an allowance for waste; but for simplicity, this, too, we will not include in examples or most problems.

The timing and sizes of orders (i.e., materials ordered from suppliers or work started within the firm) are determined by *planned-order releases.* The timing of the receipts of these quantities is indicated by *planned-order receipts.* Depending on ordering policy, the planned-order releases may be multiples of a specified quantity (e.g., 50 units), or they may be equal to the quantity needed at that time. Although there are other possibilities, these two seem to be the most widely used. Example 2 illustrates the difference between these two ordering policies as well as the general concepts of time-phasing material requirements in MRP. As you work through the example, you may find the following list of terms helpful.

Gross requirements: The total expected demand for an item or raw material *during* each time period without regard to the amount on hand. For end items, these quantities are shown in the master schedule; for components, these quantities are derived from the planned-order releases of their immediate "parents."

Scheduled receipts: Open orders scheduled to arrive from vendors or elsewhere in the pipeline by the *beginning* of a period.

Projected on hand: The expected amount of inventory that will be on hand at the *beginning* of each time period: scheduled receipts plus available inventory from last period.

Net requirements: The actual amount needed in each time period.

Planned-order receipts: The quantity expected to be received by the *beginning* of the period in which it is shown. Under lot-for-lot ordering, this quantity will equal net requirements. Under lot-size ordering, this quantity may exceed net requirements. Any

gross requirements Total expected demand for an item or raw material in a time period.

scheduled receipts Open orders scheduled to arrive from vendors or elsewhere in the pipeline.

projected on hand Expected amount of inventory that will be on hand at the beginning of each time period.

net requirements The actual amount needed in each time period.

planned-order receipts Quantity expected to be received by the beginning of the period in which it is shown.

Computer-based MRP procedures at Kirby Refrigeration integrate the manufacturing, financial, and sales systems—enabling optimum business control. Kirby, a manufacturer and wholesaler of air conditioning and refrigeration components, is an Australian company with facilities in Australia and New Zealand.

www.kirby.com

excess is added to available inventory in the *next* time period for simplicity, although in reality, it would be available in that period.

planned-order releases

Planned amount to order in each time period; planned-order receipts offset by lead time.

Planned-order releases: Indicates a *planned* amount to order in each time period; equals planned-order receipts offset by lead time. This amount generates gross requirements at the next level in the assembly or production chain. When an order is executed, it is removed from "planned-order releases" and entered under "scheduled receipts."

These quantities are used in a time-phased plan in the following format. The column for week 0 is used to show beginning inventory.

Week number:	0	1	2	3	4	5	6	7	8
Item:									
Gross requirements									
Scheduled receipts									
Projected on hand									
Net requirements									
Planned-order receipts									
Planned-order releases									

Example 2

A firm that produces wood shutters and bookcases has received two orders for shutters: one for 100 shutters and one for 150 shutters. The 100-unit order is due for delivery at the start of week 4 of the current schedule, and the 150-unit order is due for delivery at the start of week 8. Each shutter consists of two frames and four slatted wood sections. The wood sections are made by the firm, and fabrication takes one week. The frames are ordered, and lead time is two weeks. Assembly of the shutters requires one week. There is a scheduled receipt of 70 wood sections in (i.e., at the beginning of) week 1. Determine the size and timing of planned-order releases necessary to meet delivery requirements under each of these conditions:

only order what you need. No inventory.

1. Lot-for-lot ordering (i.e., order size equal to net requirements).
2. Lot-size ordering with a lot size of 320 units for frames and 70 units for wood sections.

a. Develop a master schedule:

Solution

Week number:	1	2	3	4	5	6	6	8
Quantity:				100				150

b. Develop a product structure tree:

c. Using the master schedule, determine gross requirements for shutters. Next, compute net requirements. Using *lot-for-lot ordering,* determine planned-order receipt quantities and the planned-order release timing to satisfy the master schedule (see Figure 15–8).

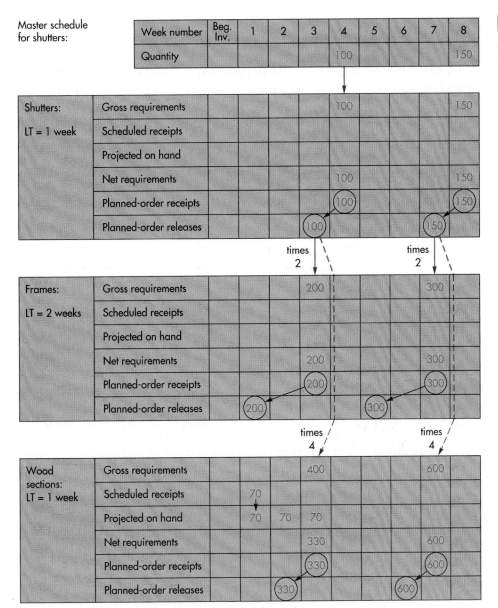

FIGURE 15-8

MRP schedule with lot-for-lot ordering

The master schedule calls for 100 shutters to be ready for delivery, and no shutters are projected to be on hand at the start of week 4, so the net requirements are also 100 shutters. Therefore, planned receipts for week 4 equal 100 shutters. Because shutter assembly requires one week, this means a planned-order release at the start of week 3. Using the same logic, 150 shutters must be assembled during week 7 in order to be available for delivery at the start of week 8.

The planned-order release of 100 shutters at the start of week 3 means that 200 frames (gross requirements) must be available at that time. Because none are expected to be on hand, this generates net requirements of 200 frames and necessitates planned receipts of 200 frames by the start of week 3. With a two-week lead time, this means that the firm must order 200 frames at the start of week 1. Similarly, the planned-order release of 150 shutters at week 7 generates gross and net requirements of 300 frames for week 7 as well as planned receipts for that time. The two-week lead time means the firm must order frames at the start of week 5.

The planned-order release of 100 shutters at the start of week 3 also generates gross requirements of 400 wood sections at that time. However, because 70 wood sections are expected to be on hand, net requirements are $400 - 70 = 330$. This means a planned receipt of 330 by the start of week 3. Since fabrication time is one week, the fabrication must start (planned-order release) at the beginning of week 2.

Similarly, the planned-order release of 150 shutters in week 7 generates gross requirements of 600 wood sections at that point. Because no on-hand inventory of wood sections is projected, net requirements are also 600, and planned-order receipt is 600 units. Again, the one-week lead time means 600 sections are scheduled for fabrication at the start of week 6.

d. Under lot-size ordering, the only difference is the possibility that planned receipts will exceed net requirements. The excess is recorded as projected inventory in the following period. For example, in Figure 15–9, the order size for frames is 320 units, Net requirements for week 3 are 200; thus, there is an excess of $320 - 200 = 120$ units, which become projected inventory in the next week. Similarly, net frame requirements of 180 units are 140 less than the 320 order size; again, the excess becomes projected inventory in week 8. The same thing happens with wood sections; an excess of planned receipts in weeks 3 and 7 is added to projected inventory in weeks 4 and 8. Note that the order size must be in *multiples* of the lot size; for week 3 it is 5 times 70, and for week 7 it is 9 times 70.

MRP provides plans for the end item and each of its subassemblies and components. Conceptually, this amounts to what is depicted in Figure 15–10. Practically speaking, however, the number of components in even a relatively simple product would make the width of the resulting spreadsheet far too wide to handle. Consequently, the plans for the individual components are stacked, as illustrated in the preceding example. Because of this, it is important to refer to the product tree in order to track relationships between components.

Example 2 is useful for describing some of the main features of MRP processing, but it understates the enormity of the task of keeping track of material requirements, especially in situations where the same subassemblies, parts, or raw materials are used in a number of different products. Differences in timing of demands and quantities needed, revisions caused by late deliveries, high scrap rates, and canceled orders all have an impact on processing.

Consider the two product structure trees shown in Figure 15–11. Note that both products have D as a component. Suppose we want to develop a material requirements plan for D given this additional information: There is a beginning inventory of 110 units of D on hand, and all items have lead times of one week. The plan is shown in Figure 15–12. Note that requirements for B and F are not shown because they are not related to (i.e., neither a "parent" nor a "child" of) D.

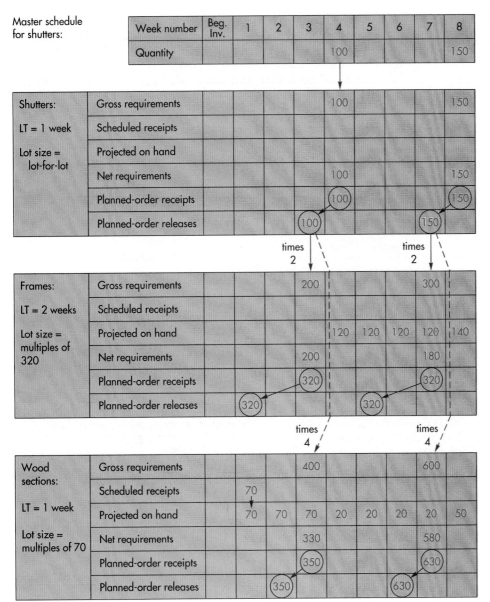

Master schedule for shutters:

Week number	Beg. Inv.	1	2	3	4	5	6	7	8
Quantity					100				150

Shutters:
LT = 1 week
Lot size = lot-for-lot

					4				8
Gross requirements					100				150
Scheduled receipts									
Projected on hand									
Net requirements					100				150
Planned-order receipts					(100)				(150)
Planned-order releases				(100)				(150)	

times 2   times 2

Frames:
LT = 2 weeks
Lot size = multiples of 320

Gross requirements					200				300
Scheduled receipts									
Projected on hand					120	120	120	120	140
Net requirements					200				180
Planned-order receipts					(320)				(320)
Planned-order releases		(320)					(320)		

times 4   times 4

Wood sections:
LT = 1 week
Lot size = multiples of 70

Gross requirements					400				600
Scheduled receipts		70							
Projected on hand		70	70	70	20	20	20	20	50
Net requirements					330				580
Planned-order receipts					(350)				(630)
Planned-order releases				(350)				(630)	

FIGURE 15-9

MRP schedule with lot sizes for components

The term **pegging** denotes working this process in reverse; that is, identifying the parent items that have generated a given set of material requirements for some item such as D. Although the process may appear simple enough given the product trees and schedules shown in this chapter, when multiple products are involved, the process is more complex. Pegging enables managers to determine which product(s) will be affected if orders are late due to late deliveries, quality problems, or other problems.

The importance of the computer becomes evident when you consider that a typical firm would have not one but many end items for which it needs to develop material requirements plans, each with its own set of components. Inventories on hand and on order, schedules, order releases, and so on, must all be updated as changes and rescheduling occur. Without the aid of a computer, the task would be almost hopeless; with the computer, planners can accomplish all of these things with much less difficulty.

pegging The process of identifying the parent items that have generated a given set of material requirements for an item.

Master schedule
for shutters:

Week number	Beg. Inv.	1	2	3	4	5	6	7	8
Quantity									

Item: Shutters									
Gross requirements									
Scheduled receipts									
Projected on hand									
Net requirements									
Planned-order receipts									
Planned-order releases									

Item: Frames							
Gross requirements							
Scheduled receipts							
Projected on hand							
Net requirements							
Planned-order receipts							
Planned-order releases							

Item: Wood sections							
Gross requirements							
Scheduled receipts							
Projected on hand							
Net requirements							
Planned-order receipts							
Planned-order releases							

FIGURE 15–10

Net requirements at each level determine gross requirements at the next

FIGURE 15–11

Two different products have D as a component

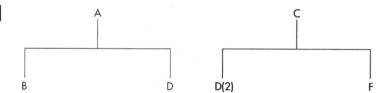

UPDATING THE SYSTEM

A material requirements plan is not a static document. As time passes, some orders will have been completed, other orders will be nearing completion, and new orders will have been entered. In addition, there may have been changes to orders, such as changes in quantity, delays, missed deliveries of parts or raw materials, and so on. Hence, a material requirements plan is a "living" document, one that changes over time. And what we refer to as "Period 1" (i.e., the current period) is continually moving ahead; so what is now Period 2 will soon be Period 1. In a sense, schedules such as these have a *rolling horizon,* which means that plans are updated and revised so that they reflect the next set number of periods.

Master schedule

Week number		1	2	3	4	5	6
Quantity					80	50	

FIGURE 15-12

Material requirements plan for component D

A LT = 1	Beg. Inv.	1	2	3	4	5	6
Gross requirements					80		
Scheduled receipts							
Projected on hand							
Net requirements					80		
Planned-order receipts					80		
Planned-order releases				(80)			

times 1

C LT = 1	Beg. Inv.	1	2	3	4	5	6
Gross requirements					50		
Scheduled receipts							
Projected on hand							
Net requirements					50		
Planned-order receipts					50		
Planned-order releases				(50)			

times 2

D LT = 1	Beg. Inv.	1	2	3	4	5	6
Gross requirements				80	100		
Scheduled receipts							
Projected on hand	110	110	110	110	30		
Net requirements					70		
Planned-order receipts					70		
Planned-order releases				70			

The two basic systems used to update MRP records are *regenerative* and *net change*. A **regenerative system** is updated periodically; a **net-change system** is continuously updated.

A regenerative system is essentially a batch-type system, which compiles all changes (e.g., new orders, receipts) that occur within the time interval (e.g., week) and periodically updates the system. Using that information, a revised production plan is developed in the same way that the original plan was developed (e.g., exploding the bill of materials, level by level).

In a net-change system, the production plan is modified to reflect changes as they occur. If some defective purchased parts had to be returned to a vendor, the manager can enter this information into the system as soon as it becomes known. Only the *changes* are exploded through the system, level by level; the entire plan would not be regenerated.

regenerative system Approach that updates MRP records periodically.

net-change system Approach that updates MRP records continuously.

The regenerative system is best suited to fairly stable systems, whereas the net-change system is best suited to systems that have frequent changes. The obvious disadvantage of a regenerative system is the potential amount of lag between the time information becomes available and the time it can be incorporated into the material requirements plan. On the other hand, processing costs are typically less using regenerative systems; changes that occur in a given time period could ultimately cancel each other, thereby avoiding the need to modify and then remodify the plan. The disadvantages of the net-change system relate to the computer processing costs involved in continuously updating the system and the constant state of flux in a system caused by many small changes. One way around this is to enter minor changes periodically and major changes immediately. The primary advantage of the net-change system is that management can have up-to-date information for planning and control purposes.

MRP Outputs

planned orders Schedule indicating the amount and timing of future orders.

MRP systems have the ability to provide management with a fairly broad range of outputs. These are often classified as *primary reports,* which are the main reports, and *secondary reports,* which are optional outputs.

order releases Authorization for the execution of planned orders.

Primary Reports. Production and inventory planning and control are part of primary reports. These reports normally include the following:

1. **Planned orders,** a schedule indicating the amount and timing of future orders.
2. **Order releases,** authorizing the execution of planned orders.

changes Revisions of due dates or order quantities, or cancellations of orders.

3. **Changes** to planned orders, including revisions of due dates or order quantities and cancellations of orders.

Secondary Reports. Performance control, planning, and exceptions belong to secondary reports.

performance-control reports Evaluation of system operation, including deviations from plans and cost information.

1. **Performance-control reports** evaluate system operation. They aid managers by measuring deviations from plans, including missed deliveries and stockouts, and by providing information that can be used to assess cost performance.
2. **Planning reports** are useful in forecasting future inventory requirements. They include purchase commitments and other data that can be used to assess future material requirements.

planning reports Data useful for assessing future material requirements.

3. **Exception reports** call attention to major discrepancies such as late and overdue orders, excessive scrap rates, reporting errors, and requirements for nonexistent parts.

exception reports Data on any major discrepancies encountered.

The wide range of outputs generally permits users to tailor MRP to their particular needs.

Other Considerations

Aside from the main details of inputs, outputs, and processing, managers must be knowledgeable about a number of other aspects of MRP. These include the holding of safety stock, lot-sizing choices, and the possible use of MRP for unfinished products.

SAFETY STOCK

Theoretically, inventory systems with dependent demand should not require safety stock below the end item level. This is one of the main advantages of an MRP approach. Supposedly, safety stock is not needed because the manager can project usage quantities once the master schedule has been established. Practically, however, there may be exceptions. For example, a bottleneck process or one with varying scrap rates can cause shortages in downstream operations. Furthermore, shortages may occur if orders are late or fabrication or assembly times are longer than expected. On the surface, these conditions lend themselves to the use of safety stock to maintain smooth operations; but the problem becomes more complicated when dealing with multiechelon items (i.e., multiple-level arenas such as assembled products) because a shortage of *any* component will prevent manufacture of the final assembly. However, a major advantage of MRP is lost by holding safety stock for all lower-level items.

MRP systems deal with these problems in several ways. The manager's first step is to identify activities or operations that are subject to variability and to determine the extent of that variability. When lead times are variable, the concept of safety *time* instead of safety *stock* is often used. This results in scheduling orders for arrival or completion sufficiently ahead of the time they are needed in order to eliminate or substantially reduce the element of chance in waiting for those items. When quantities tend to vary, some safety stock may be called for, but the manager must carefully weigh the need and cost of carrying extra stock. Frequently, managers elect to carry safety stock for end items, which are subject to random demand, and for selected lower-level operations when safety time is not feasible.

It is important in general to make sure that lead times are accurate, particularly when the objective is to have incoming shipments of parts and materials arrive shortly before they are needed. Early arrivals increase on-hand inventory and carrying costs, but late arrivals can raise havoc, possibly delaying all following operations. Knowing this, managers may inflate lead times (i.e., use safety time) and cause early arrivals, defeating the objective of matching the arrival of orders with production schedules.

If safety stock is needed, planned order release amounts can be increased by the safety stock quantities for the designated components.

LOT SIZING

Determining a lot size to order or to produce is an important issue in inventory management for both independent- and dependent-demand items. This is called **lot sizing.** For independent-demand items, managers often use economic order sizes and economic production quantities. For dependent-demand systems, however, a much wider variety of plans is used to determine lot sizes, mainly because no single plan has a clear advantage over the others. Some of the most popular plans for lot sizing are described in this section.

A primary goal of inventory management for both independent- and dependent-demand systems is to minimize the sum of ordering cost (or setup cost) and holding cost. With independent demand, that demand is frequently distributed uniformly throughout the planning horizon (e.g., six months, year). Demand tends to be much more lumpy for dependent demand, and the planning horizon shorter (e.g., three months), so that economic lot sizes are usually much more difficult to identify. Consider the situation depicted in Figure 15–13. Period demands vary from 1 to 80 units, and no demand size repeats over the horizon shown.

Managers can realize economies by grouping orders. This would be the case if the additional cost incurred by holding the extra units until they were used led to a savings in setup or ordering cost. This determination can be very complex at times, for several reasons. First, combining period demands into a single order, particularly for middle-level or end items, has a cascading effect down through the product tree; that is, in order to achieve this grouping, you must also group items at lower levels in the tree and incorporate their setup and holding costs into the decision. Second, the uneven period demand

lot sizing Choosing a lot size for ordering or production.

	Period				
	1	2	3	4	5
Demand	70	50	1	80	4
Cumulative demand	70	120	121	201	205

FIGURE 15-13

Demand for part K

and the relatively short planning horizon require a continual recalculation and updating of lot sizes. Not surprisingly, the methods used to handle lot sizing range from the complex, which attempt to include all relevant costs, to the very simple, which are easy to use and understand. In certain cases, the simple models seem to approach cost minimization although generalizations are difficult. Let's consider some of these models.

Lot-for-Lot Ordering. Perhaps the simplest of all the methods is lot-for-lot ordering. The order or run size for each period is set equal to demand for that period. Example 2 demonstrated this method. Not only is the order size obvious, it also virtually eliminates holding costs for parts carried over to other periods. Hence, lot-for-lot ordering minimizes investment in inventory. Its two chief drawbacks are that it usually involves many different order sizes and thus cannot take advantage of the economies of fixed order size (e.g., standard containers and other standardized procedures), and it requires a new setup for each production run. If setup costs can be significantly reduced, this method may approximate a minimum-cost lot size.

Economic Order Quantity Model. Sometimes economic order quantity models (EOQ) are used. They can lead to minimum costs if usage is fairly uniform. This is sometimes the case for lower-level items that are common to different parents and for raw materials. However, the more lumpy demand is, the less appropriate such an approach is. Since demand tends to be most lumpy at the end item level, EOQ models tend to be less useful for end items than for items and materials at the lowest levels.

Fixed-Period Ordering. This type of ordering provides coverage for some predetermined number of periods (e.g., two or three). In some instances, the span is simply arbitrary; in other cases, a review of historical demand patterns may lead to a more rational designation of a fixed period length. A simple rule is: Order to cover a two-period interval. The rule can be modified when common sense suggests a better way. For example, take a look at the demands shown in Figure 15–13. Using a two-period rule, an order size of 120 units would cover the first two periods. The next two periods would be covered by an order size of 81 units. However, the demands in periods 3 and 5 are so small, it would make sense to combine them both with the 80 units and order 85 units.

Part-Period Model. The part-period model represents another attempt to balance setup and holding costs. The term *part period* refers to holding a part or parts over a number of periods. For instance, if 10 parts were held for two periods, this would be $10 \times 2 = 20$ part periods. The economic part period (EPP) can be computed as the ratio of setup costs to the cost to hold a unit for one period. Thus, the formula for computing the EPP is:

$$\text{EPP} = \frac{\text{Setup cost}}{\text{Unit holding cost per period}} \qquad (15\text{–}2)$$

To determine an order size that is consistent with the EPP, various order sizes are examined for a planning horizon, and each one's number of part periods is determined. The one that comes closest to the EPP is selected as the best lot size. The order sizes that are examined are based on cumulative demand. Example 3 illustrates this approach.

The choice of a lot-sizing technique must take into account the nature of demand (degree of uniformity), the relative importance of carrying costs versus ordering costs, and any other considerations that affect ordering. It appears that no single method is suited to all conditions.

Regardless of the lot-sizing method in use, there is always the possibility of adjustments in order sizes due to allowance for shrinkage or scrap, minimum and maximum order quantities established by management (e.g., do not order more than five months' supply), operating or shipping constraints (e.g., 200 pieces per run or 12 dozen per shipment) that require rounding of order sizes (usually up) to these amounts, and similar factors.

Use the part-period method to determine order sizes for this demand schedule:

Example 3

	Period							
	1	**2**	**3**	**4**	**5**	**6**	**7**	**8**
Demand	60	40	20	2	30	—	70	50
Cumulative demand	60	100	120	122	152	152	222	272

Setup cost is $80 per run for this item, and unit holding cost is $.95 per period.

Solution

1. First compute the EPP: EPP = $80/$.95 = 84.21, which rounds to 84 part periods. This is the target quantity.

2. Next, try the cumulative lot sizes, beginning with 60, until the part periods approximate the EPP. Continue this process for the planning horizon. This leads to the following:

on test #2

Period When Order Is Placed	Lot Size	Extra Inventory Carried	× Periods Carried	= Part Periods	Cumulative Part Periods
1	60	0	0	0	0
	100	40	1	40	40
	120	20	2	40	80
	122	2	3	6	86*
5	30	0	0	0	0
	100	70	2	140	140*
8	50	0	0	0	0

*Closest to 84

The computations of part periods indicate that 122 units should be ordered to be available at period 1, and 100 units should be ordered to be available at period 5. The next lot will be ordered for period 8, but there is insufficient information now to determine its size.

The lot sizes considered for period 1 correspond to cumulative demand. Once the best lot size has been identified, the cumulative demand is set equal to zero and then summed beginning with the next period. In this case, the lot size of 122 covers the first four periods, so cumulative demand is started next for period 5. The next lot size covers through period 7, and the count begins again at period 8. Hence, that lot size will be at least 50 units.

The process works well for the first lot size because the cumulative number of part periods is close to the EPP, but the effect of lumpy demand is apparent for the second lot size of 100 (140 part periods is not very close to 84 part periods).

Capacity Requirements Planning

One of the most important features of MRP is its ability to aid managers in capacity planning.

Capacity requirements planning is the process of determining short-range capacity requirements. The necessary inputs include planned-order releases for MRP, the current shop load, routing information, and job times. Key outputs include load reports for each work center. When variances (underloads or overloads) are projected, managers might consider remedies such as alternative routings, changing or eliminating lot sizing or safety stock requirements, and lot splitting. Moving production forward or backward can

capacity requirements planning The process of determining short-range capacity requirements.

be extremely challenging because of precedence requirements and the availability of components.

A firm usually generates a master schedule initially in terms of what is needed and not what is possible. The initial schedule may or may not be feasible given the limits of the production system and availability of materials when end items are translated into requirements for procurement, fabrication, and assembly. Unfortunately, the MRP system cannot distinguish between a feasible master schedule and a nonfeasible one. Consequently, it is often necessary to run a proposed master schedule through MRP processing in order to obtain a clearer picture of actual requirements, which can then be compared to available capacity and materials. If it turns out that the current master schedule is not feasible, management may make a decision to increase capacity (e.g., through overtime or subcontracting) or to revise the master schedule. In the latter case, this may entail several revisions, each of which is run through the system until a feasible plan is obtained. At that point, the master schedule is *frozen,* at least for the near term, thus establishing a firm schedule from which to plan requirements.

Stability in short-term production plans is very important; without it, changes in order quantity and/or timing can render material requirements plans almost useless. The term *system nervousness* describes the way a system might react to changes. The reaction can sometimes be greater than the original change. For example, a small change near the top of a product tree can reverberate throughout much of the lower parts of the tree, causing major changes to order quantities and production schedules of many components. That, in turn, might cause queues to form at various portions of the system, leading to late orders, increased work in process, and added carrying costs.

To minimize such problems, many firms establish a series of time intervals, called **time fences,** during which changes can be made to orders. For example, a firm might specify time fences of 4, 8, and 12 weeks, with the nearest fence being the most restrictive and the farthest fence being the least restrictive. Beyond 12 weeks, changes are expected; from 8 to 12 weeks, substitutions of one end item for another may be permitted as long as the components are available and the production plan is not compromised; from 4 to 8 weeks, the plan is fixed, but small changes may be allowed; and the plan is frozen out to the four-week fence.

Some companies use two fences: one is a near-term *demand* fence, and the other is a long-term *planning* fence. For example, the demand fence might be four weeks from the present time while the planning fence might be 10 weeks away. In the near term, customer orders receive precedence over the forecast. The time beyond the planning fence is available for inserting new orders into the master schedule. Between the demand fence and the planning fence, management must make trade-offs when changes are introduced unless excess capacity is expected to be available.

In establishing time fences, a manager must weigh the benefits of stability in the production plan against the possible negative impact on the competitive advantage of being able to quickly respond to new orders.

Figure 15–14 presents an overview of the capacity planning process. The process begins with a proposed or tentative master production schedule that must be tested for feasibility and possibly adjusted before it becomes permanent. The proposed schedule is processed using MRP to ascertain the material requirements the schedule would generate. These are then translated into resource (i.e., capacity) requirements, often in the form of a series of **load reports** for each department or work center, which compares known and expected future capacity requirements with projected capacity availability. Figure 15–15 illustrates the nature of a load report. It shows expected resource requirements (i.e., usage) for jobs currently being worked on, planned orders, and expected orders for the planning horizon. Given this sort of information, the manager can more easily determine whether capacity is sufficient to satisfy these requirements. If there is enough capacity, he or she can freeze the portion of the master production schedule that generates these requirements. In the load report illustrated in Figure 15–15, planned-order releases in time period 4 will cause an overload. However, it appears possible to accommodate demand by

---

time fences Series of time intervals during which order changes are allowed or restricted; the nearest fence is most restrictive to change, the farthest is least restrictive.

load reports Department or work center reports that compare known and expected future capacity requirements with projected capacity availability.

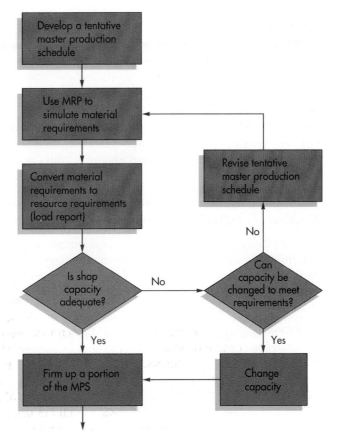

FIGURE 15-14

Using MRP to assist in planning capacity requirements
Source: Stephen Love, *Inventory Control* (New York: McGraw-Hill, 1979), p. 164. Reprinted by permission.

FIGURE 15-15

A hypothetical department load report

slightly shifting some orders to adjacent periods. Similarly, an overload appears likely in period 11, but that too can be handled by shifting some jobs to adjacent time periods. In cases where capacity is insufficient, a manager may be able to increase capacity (by scheduling overtime, transferring personnel from other areas, or subcontracting some of the work) if this is possible and economical, or else revise the master production schedule and repeat the process until an acceptable production schedule is obtained.

If the master production schedule must be revised, this generally means that the manager must assign priorities to orders, if some orders will be finished later than originally planned.

One note of caution is in order concerning capacity load reports. Often, the load reports are only approximations, and they may not give a true picture because the loading does not take into account scheduling and queuing delays. Consequently, it is possible to experience system backups even though a load report implies sufficient capacity to handle projected loads.

An important aspect of capacity requirements planning is the conversion of quantity requirements into labor and machine requirements. One accomplishes this by multiplying each period's quantity requirements by standard labor and/or machine requirements per unit. For instance, if 100 units of product A are scheduled in the fabrication department, and each unit has a labor standard time of 2 hours and a machine standard time of 1.5 hours, then 100 units of A convert into these capacity requirements:

Labor: 100 units $\times$ 2 hours/unit   = 200 labor hours

Machine: 100 units $\times$ 1.5 hours/unit = 150 machine hours

One can then compare these capacity requirements with available department capacity to determine the extent to which this product utilizes capacity. For example, if the department has 200 labor hours and 200 machine hours available, labor utilization will be 100 percent because all of the labor capacity will be required by this product. However, machine capacity will be underutilized.

$$\frac{\text{Required}}{\text{Available}} \times 100 = \frac{150 \text{ hours}}{200 \text{ hours}} \times 100 = 75 \text{ percent}$$

Underutilization may mean that unused capacity can be used for other jobs; overutilization indicates that available capacity is insufficient to handle requirements. To compensate, production may have to be rescheduled or overtime may be needed.

MRP in Services

MRP has applications in services as well as in manufacturing. These applications may involve material goods that form a part of the product–service package, or they may involve mainly service components.

An example of a product–service package is a food catering service, particularly in instances that require preparing and serving meals for large numbers of people. To estimate quantities and costs of an order, the food manager would have to determine the quantities of the ingredients for each recipe on the menu (i.e., a bill of materials), which would then be combined with the number of each meal to be prepared to obtain a material requirements plan for the event.

Similar examples occur for large-scale renovations, such as a sports stadium or a major hotel, where there are multiple repetitions of activities and related materials that must be "exploded" into their components for purposes of cost estimation and scheduling.

Benefits and Requirements of MRP

Benefits. MRP offers a number of benefits for the typical manufacturing or assembly type of operation, including:

1. Low levels of in-process inventories.
2. The ability to keep track of material requirements.
3. The ability to evaluate capacity requirements generated by a given master schedule.
4. A means of allocating production time.

A range of people in a typical manufacturing company are important users of the information provided by an MRP system. Production planners are obvious users of MRP.

Production managers, who must balance workloads across departments and make decisions about scheduling work, and plant foremen, who are responsible for issuing work orders and maintaining production schedules, also rely heavily on MRP output. Other users include customer service representatives, who must be able to supply customers with projected delivery dates, purchasing managers, and inventory managers. The benefits of MRP depend in large measure on the use of a computer to maintain up-to-date information on material requirements.

Requirements. In order to implement and operate an effective MRP system, it is necessary to have:

1. A computer and the necessary software programs to handle computations and maintain records.
2. Accurate and up-to-date
   a. Master schedules
   b. Bills of materials
   c. Inventory records
3. Integrity of file data.

Accuracy is absolutely essential for a successful MRP system. Inaccuracies in inventory record files or bills-of-material files can lead to unpleasant surprises, ranging from missing parts, ordering too many of some items and too few of others, and failure to stay on schedule, all of which contribute to inefficient use of resources, missed delivery dates, and poor customer service. Moreover, implementing MRP can be arduous and costly. Consequently, it is important for companies considering an MRP system to be aware of this and to carefully weigh these factors against the benefits of MRP.

Unfortunately, some firms that have attempted to install an MRP system have seriously underestimated the importance of these items. In many cases, bills of materials are outdated because design changes were not incorporated into the records, leading to parts lists that did not correspond to actual requirements for assembly of the finished product. It is not unusual for a firm to discover that the same part is carried under different part numbers, making it difficult to develop meaningful records. Moreover, some firms have encountered resistance from foremen and others, who argue, "We've managed for 30 years without the stuff, so why bother with it now?"

These obstacles can cause the implementation of an MRP system to take a year or more, taking into account employee education, training, and *convincing,* and correction of record-keeping deficiencies.

On the whole, the introduction of MRP has led to major improvements in scheduling and inventory management, but it has not proved to be the cure-all that many hoped it would be. Consequently, manufacturers are now taking a much broader approach to resource planning. One such approach is referred to as MRP II.

MRP II

In the early 1980s, material requirements planning was expanded into a much broader approach for planning and scheduling the resources of manufacturing firms. This expanded approach has been dubbed **MRP II,** which refers to **manufacturing resources planning.** It has not replaced MRP, nor is it an improved version of it. Rather, it represents an effort to expand the scope of production resource planning and to involve other functional areas of the firm in the planning process. Marketing and finance are the two most notable areas that are affected by and have an impact on the manufacturing plan.

In too many instances, production, marketing, and finance operate without complete knowledge or apparent regard for what other areas of the firm are doing. To be most

manufacturing resources planning (MRP II) Expanded approach to production resource planning, involving other areas of a firm in the planning process, such as marketing and finance.

FIGURE 15-16

An overview of MRP II

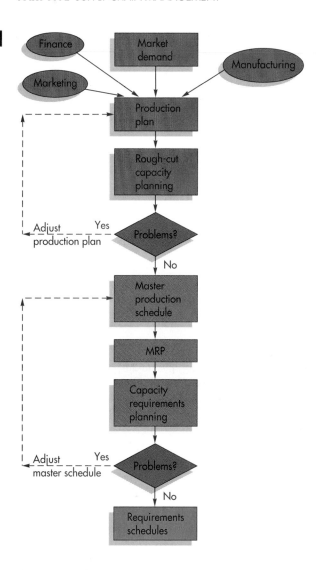

effective, all areas of the firm need to focus on a common set of goals. A major purpose of MRP II is to integrate primary functions and other functions such as personnel, engineering, and purchasing in the planning process.

Material requirements planning is at the heart of the process (see Figure 15–16). The process begins with an aggregation of demand from all sources (e.g., firm orders, forecasts, safety stock requirements). Production, marketing, and finance personnel work toward developing a master production schedule. Although manufacturing people will have a major input in determining that schedule and a major responsibility for making it work, marketing and finance will also have important inputs and responsibilities. The rationale for having these functional areas work together is the increased likelihood of developing a plan that works and with which everyone can live. Moreover, because each of these functional areas has been involved in formulating the plan, they will have reasonably good knowledge of the plan and more reason to work toward achieving it.

In addition to the obvious manufacturing resources needed to support the plan, financing resources will be needed and must be planned for, both in amount and timing. Similarly, marketing resources will also be needed in varying degrees throughout the process. In order for the plan to work, the firm must have all of the necessary resources available as needed. Often, an initial plan must be revised based on an assessment of the availability of various resources. Once these have been decided, the master production schedule can be firmed up.

At this point, material requirements planning comes into play, generating material and schedule requirements. Next, management must make more detailed capacity requirements, planning to determine whether these more specific capacity requirements can be met. Again, some adjustments in the master production schedule may be required.

As the schedule unfolds and actual work begins, a variety of reports help managers to monitor the process and to make any necessary adjustments to keep operations on track.

In effect, this is a continuing process, where the master production schedule is updated and revised as necessary to achieve corporate goals. The business plan that governs the entire process usually undergoes changes too, although these tend to be less frequent than the changes made at lower levels (i.e., the master production schedule).

Most MRP II systems have the capability of performing simulation, enabling managers to answer a variety of "what if" questions so they can gain a better appreciation of available options and their consequences.

Software is an essential component of MRP II systems. There is a wide range of software available, with differing features and capabilities. One of the leading products is Caliach MRP, offered by Manufacturing and Computer Systems. Caliach MRP has an installed user base of over 70,000 users, with an average price of $20,000, according to a survey of manufacturing resource planning software done by APICS. The survey is available at *http://lionhrtub.com/apics/surveys/MRPII97/*ordered-by-install.html.

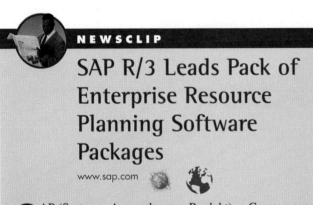

NEWSCLIP

SAP R/3 Leads Pack of Enterprise Resource Planning Software Packages

www.sap.com

SAP (Systeme, Anwendungen, Produkt), a German company, distributes software designed to fully link all functional areas within a company, from financial accounting to sales and human resource planning including many of the manufacturing and planning and control functions.

According to SAP information, the Production Planning and Control module can draw expected demand data directly from the SOP (sales and operations planning) module, which can then be used to create master schedules. Most any kind of production is "covered" within the production planning and control program, from flow/process type systems down to repetitive manufacturing and a kanban specific support system which actually links to a barcode reader. The MRP system within R/3 will calculate quantities and procurement dates down to the raw material level.

The ERP idea is also reflected in the Product Data Management part of R/3, which is basically a database system containing a "material master record" for parts and/or products. This record would typically include part number or component data, design information—possibly including CAD specs. This data object is "central to the R/3 system."

Source: SAP Company press releases.

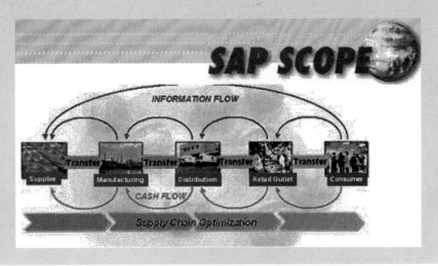

ERP

MRP II combines inputs from other areas of the organization, such as marketing, finance, and accounting, with input from manufacturing for production and capacity planning. MRP II is an effort to integrate the various areas of an organization for planning purposes.

enterprise resource planning (ERP) Integration of financial, manufacturing, and human resources on a single computer system.

ERP (enterprise resource planning) represents an expanded effort to integrate *standardized* record-keeping that will permit *information sharing* among different areas of an organization in order to manage the system more effectively. The following reading does an excellent job of describing ERP.

READING

The ABCs of ERP

Compiled from Reports by Christopher Koch, Derek Slater, and E. Baatz

What is ERP?

How long will an ERP project take?

What will ERP fix in my business?

Will ERP fit the way I do business?

What does ERP really cost?

When will I get payback from ERP—and how much will it be?

What are the unforeseen costs of ERP?

How do you configure ERP software?

How do companies organize their ERP projects?

How does ERP fit with electronic commerce?

What Is ERP?

Enterprise resource planning software, or ERP, doesn't live up to its acronym. Forget about planning—it doesn't do that— and forget about resource, a throwaway term. But remember the enterprise part. This is ERP's true ambition. It attempts to integrate all departments and functions across a company onto a single computer system that can serve all those different departments' particular needs.

That is a tall order, building a single software program that serves the needs of people in finance as well as it does the people in human resources and in the warehouse. Each of those departments typically has its own computer system, each optimized for the particular ways that the department does its work. But ERP combines them all together into a single, integrated software program that runs off a single database so that the various departments can more easily share information and communicate with each other.

That integrated approach can have a tremendous payback if companies install the software correctly. Take a customer order, for example. Typically, when a customer places an order, that order begins a mostly paper-based journey from in-basket to in-basket around the company, often being keyed and rekeyed into different departments' computer systems along the way. All that lounging around in in-baskets causes delays and lost orders, and all the keying into different computer systems invites errors. Meanwhile, no one in the company truly knows what the status of the order is at any given point because there is no way for the finance department, for example, to get into the warehouse's computer system to see whether the item has been shipped. "You'll have to call the warehouse," is the familiar refrain heard by frustrated customers.

How Can ERP Improve a Company's Business Performance?

ERP automates the tasks involved in performing a business process—such as order fulfillment, which involves taking an order from a customer, shipping it and billing for it. With ERP, when a customer service representative takes an order from a customer, he or she has all the information necessary to complete the order (the customer's credit rating and order history, the company's inventory levels and the shipping dock's trucking schedule). Everyone else in the company sees the same computer screen and has access to the single database that holds the customer's new order. When one department finishes with the order it is automatically routed via the ERP system to the next department. To find out where the order is at any point, one need only log into the ERP system and track it down. With luck, the order process moves like a bolt of lightning through the organization, and customers get their orders faster and with fewer mistakes than before. ERP can apply that same magic to the other major business processes, such as employee benefits or financial reporting.

That, at least, is the dream of ERP. The reality is much harsher.

Let's go back to those inboxes for a minute. That process may not have been efficient, but it was simple. Finance did its job, the warehouse did its job, and if anything went wrong outside of the department's walls, it was somebody else's problem. Not anymore. With ERP, the customer service representatives are no longer just typists entering someone's name into a computer and hitting the return key. The ERP screen makes them business people. It flickers with the customer's credit rating from the finance department and the product inventory levels from the warehouse. Will the customer pay on time? Will we be able to ship the order on time? These are decisions that customer service representatives have never had to make before and which affect the customer and every other department in the company. But it's not just the customer service representatives who have to wake up. People in the warehouse who used to keep inventory in their heads or on scraps of paper now need to put that information online. If they don't, customer service will see low inventory levels on their screens and tell customers that their requested item is not in stock. Accountability, responsibility and communication have never been tested like this before.

How Long Will an ERP Project Take?

Companies that install ERP do not have an easy time of it. Don't be fooled when ERP vendors tell you about a three or six month average implementation time. Those short (that's right, six months is short) implementations all have a catch of one kind or another: the company was small, or the implementation was limited to a small area of the company, or the company only used the financial pieces of the ERP system (in which case the ERP system is nothing more than a very expensive accounting system). To do ERP right, the ways you do business will need to change and the ways people do their jobs will need to change too. And that kind of change doesn't come without pain. Unless, of course, your ways of doing business are working extremely well (orders all shipped on time, productivity higher than all your competitors, customers completely satisfied), in which case there is no reason to even consider ERP.

The important thing is not to focus on how long it will take—real transformational ERP efforts usually run between one to three years, on average—but rather to understand why you need it and how you will use it to improve your business.

What Will ERP Fix in My Business?

There are three major reasons why companies undertake ERP:

To integrate financial data—As the CEO tries to understand the company's overall performance, he or she may find many different versions of the truth. Finance has its own set of revenue numbers, sales has another version, and the different business units may each have their own versions of how much they contributed to revenues. ERP creates a single version of the truth that cannot be questioned because everyone is using the same system.

To standardize manufacturing processes—Manufacturing companies—especially those with an appetite for mergers and acquisitions—often find that multiple business units across the company make the same widget using different methods and computer systems. Standardizing those processes and using a single, integrated computer system can save time, increase productivity and reduce headcount.

To standardize HR information—Especially in companies with multiple business units, HR may not have a unified, simple method for tracking employee time and communicating with them about benefits and services. ERP can fix that.

In the race to fix these problems, companies often lose sight of the fact that ERP packages are nothing more than generic representations of the ways a typical company does business. While most packages are exhaustively comprehensive, each industry has its quirks that make it unique. Most ERP systems were designed to be used by discreet manufacturing companies (who make physical things that can be counted), which immediately left all the process manufacturers (oil, chemical and utility companies that measure their products by flow rather than individual units) out in the cold. Each of these industries has struggled with the different ERP vendors to modify core ERP programs to their needs.

Will ERP Fit the Ways I Do Business?

It's critical for companies to figure out if their ways of doing business will fit within a standard ERP package before the checks are signed and the implementation begins. The most common reason that companies walk away from multimillion dollar ERP projects is that they discover that the software does not support one of their important business processes. At that point there are two things they can do: They can change the business process to accommodate the software, which will mean deep changes in long-established ways of doing business (that often provide competitive advantage) and shake up important peoples' roles and responsibilities (something that few companies have the stomach for). Or they can modify the software to fit the process, which will slow down the project, introduce dangerous bugs into the system and make upgrading the software to the ERP vendor's next release excruciatingly difficult, because the customizations will need to be torn apart and rewritten to fit with the new version.

Needless to say, the move to ERP is a project of breathtaking scope, and the price tags on the front end are enough to make the most placid CFO a little twitchy. In addition to budgeting for software costs, financial executives should plan to write checks to cover consulting, process rework, integration testing and a long laundry list of other expenses before the benefits of ERP start to manifest themselves. Underestimating the price of teaching users their new job processes can lead to a rude shock down the line. So can failure to consider data warehouse integration requirements and the cost of extra software to duplicate the old report formats. A few oversights in the budgeting and planning stage can send ERP costs spiraling out of control faster than oversights in planning almost any other information system undertaking.

What Does ERP *Really* Cost?

Meta Group recently did a study looking at the Total Cost of Ownership (TCO) of ERP, including hardware, software, professional services, and internal staff costs. The TCO numbers include getting the software installed and the two years afterward, which is when the real costs of maintaining, upgrading and optimizing the system for your business are felt. Among the 63 companies surveyed—including small, medium and large companies in a range of industries—the average TCO was $15 million (the highest was $300 million and lowest was $400,000). While it's hard to draw a solid number from that kind of a range of companies and ERP efforts, Meta came up with one statistic that proves that ERP is expensive no matter what kind of company is using it. The TCO for a "heads-down" user over that period was a staggering $53,320.

When Will I Get Payback from ERP—And How Much Will It Be?

Don't expect to revolutionize your business with ERP. It is a navel gazing exercise that focuses on optimizing the way things are done internally rather than with customers, suppliers or partners. Yet the navel gazing has a pretty good payback if you're willing to wait for it—a Meta Group study of 63 companies found that it took eight months after the new system was in (31 months total) to see any benefits. But the median annual savings from the new ERP system was $1.6 million per year.

The Hidden Costs of ERP

Although different companies will find different land mines in the budgeting process, those who have implemented ERP packages agree that certain costs are more commonly overlooked or underestimated than others. Armed with insights from across the business, ERP pros vote the following areas as most likely to result in budget overrun.

1. *Training.* Training is the near-unanimous choice of experienced ERP implementers as the most elusive budget item. It's not so much that this cost is completely overlooked as it is consistently underestimated. Training expenses are high because workers almost invariably have to learn a new set of processes, not just a new software interface.

2. *Integration and testing.* Testing the links between ERP packages and other corporate software links that have to be built on a case-by-case basis is another often underestimated cost. A typical manufacturing company may have add-on applications for logistics, tax, production planning and bar coding. If this laundry list also includes customization of the core ERP package, expect the cost of integrating, testing and maintaining the system to skyrocket.

   As with training, testing ERP integration has to be done from a process-oriented perspective. Instead of plugging in dummy data and moving it from one application to the next, veterans recommend running a real purchase order through the system, from order entry through shipping and receipt of payment—the whole order-to-

cash banana—preferably with the participation of the employees who will eventually do those jobs.

3. *Data conversion.* It costs money to move corporate information, such as customer and supplier records, product design data and the like, from old systems to new ERP homes. Although few CIOs will admit it, most data in most legacy systems is of little use. Companies often deny their data is dirty until they actually have to move it to the new client/server setups that popular ERP packages require. Consequently, those companies are more likely to underestimate the cost of the move. But even clean data may demand some overhaul to match process modifications necessitated—or inspired—by the ERP implementation.

4. *Data analysis.* Often, the data from the ERP system must be combined with data from external systems for analysis purposes. Users with heavy analysis needs should include the cost of a data warehouse in the ERP budget—and they should expect to do quite a bit of work to make it run smoothly. Users are in a pickle here: Refreshing all the ERP data in a big corporate data warehouse daily is difficult, and ERP systems do a poor job of indicating which information has changed from day to day, making selective warehouse updates tough. One expensive solution is custom programming. The upshot is that the wise will check all their data analysis needs before signing off on the budget.

5. *Consultants ad infinitum.* When users fail to plan for disengagement, consulting fees run wild. To avoid this, companies should identify objectives for which [their] consulting partners must aim when training internal staff. Include metrics in the consultants' contract; for example, a specific number of the user company's staff should be able to pass a project-management leadership test—similar to what Big Five consultants have to pass to lead an ERP engagement.

6. *Replacing your best and brightest.* ERP success depends on staffing the project with the best and brightest from the business and IS. The software is too complex and the business changes too dramatic to trust the project to just anyone. The bad news is, a company must be prepared to replace many of those people when the project is over. Though the ERP market is not as hot as it once was, consulting firms and other companies that have lost their best people will be hounding yours with higher salaries and bonus offers than you can afford—or that your HR policies permit. Huddle with HR early on to develop a retention bonus program and to create new salary strata for ERP veterans. If you let them go, you'll wind up hiring them—or someone like them—back as consultants for twice what you paid them in salaries.

7. *Implementation teams can never stop.* Most companies intend to treat their ERP implementations as they would any

other software project. Once the software is installed, they figure, the team will be scuttled and everyone will go back to his or her day job. But after ERP, you can't go home again. You're too valuable. Because they have worked intimately with ERP, they know more about the sales process than the salespeople do and more about the manufacturing process than the manufacturing people do. Companies can't afford to send their project people back into the business because there's so much to do after the ERP software is installed. Just writing reports to pull information out of the new ERP system will keep the project team busy for a year at least. And it is in analysis—and, one hopes, insight—that companies make their money back on an ERP implementation. Unfortunately, few IS departments plan for the frenzy of post-ERP installation activity, and fewer still build it into their budgets when they start their ERP projects. Many are forced to beg for more money and staff immediately after the go-live date, long before the ERP project has demonstrated any benefit.

8. *Waiting for ROI.* One of the most misleading legacies of traditional software project management is that the company expects to gain value from the application as soon as it is installed; the project team expects a break, and maybe a pat on the back. Neither expectation applies to ERP. Most don't reveal their value until after companies have had them running for some time and can concentrate on making improvements in the business processes that are affected by the system. And the project team is not going to be rewarded until their efforts pay off.

9. *Post-ERP depression.* ERP systems often wreak havoc in the companies that install them. In a recent Deloitte Consulting survey of 64 Fortune 500 companies, one in four admitted that they suffered a drop in performance when their ERP systems went live. The true percentage is undoubtedly much higher. The most common reason for the performance problems is that everything looks and works differently from the way it did before. When people can't do their jobs in the familiar way and haven't yet mastered the new way, they panic, and the business goes into spasms.

How Do You Configure ERP Software?

Even if a company installs ERP software for the so-called right reasons and everyone can agree on the optimal definition of a customer, the inherent difficulties of implementing something as complex as ERP is like, well, teaching an elephant to do the hootchy-kootchy. The packages are built from database tables, thousands of them, that IS programmers and end users must set to match their business processes; each table has a decision "switch" that leads the software down one decision path or another. By presenting only one way for the company to do each task—say, run the payroll or close the books—a company's individual operating units and far-flung divisions

are integrated under one system. But figuring out precisely how to set all the switches in the tables requires a deep understanding of the existing processes being used to operate the business. As the table settings are decided, these business processes are reengineered, ERP's way. Most ERP systems are not shipped as a shell system in which customers must determine at the minutia level how all the functional procedures should be set, making thousands of decisions that affect how their system behaves in line with their own business activities. Most ERP systems are preconfigured, allowing just hundreds—rather than thousands—of procedural settings to be made by the customer.

How Do Companies Organize Their ERP Projects?

Based on our observations, there are three commonly used ways of installing ERP.

The big bang—In this, the most ambitious and difficult of approaches to ERP implementation, companies cast off all their legacy systems at once and implement a single ERP system across the entire company.

Though this method dominated early ERP implementations, few companies dare to attempt it anymore because it calls for the entire company to mobilize and change at once. Most of the ERP implementation horror stories from the late '90s warn us about companies that used this strategy. Getting everyone to cooperate and accept a new software system at the same time is a tremendous effort, largely because the new system will not have any advocates. No one within the company has any experience using it, so no one is sure whether it will work. Also, ERP inevitably involves compromises. Many departments have computer systems that have been honed to match the ways they work. In most cases, ERP offers neither the range of functionality, nor the comfort of familiarity that a custom legacy system can offer. In many cases, the speed of the new system may suffer because it is serving the entire company rather than a single department. ERP implementation requires a direct mandate from the CEO.

Franchising strategy—This approach suits large or diverse companies that do not share many common processes across business units. Independent ERP systems are installed in each unit, while linking common processes, such as financial bookkeeping, across the enterprise.

This has emerged as the most common way of implementing ERP. In most cases, the business units each have their own "instances" of ERP—that is, a separate system and database. The systems link together only to share the information necessary for the corporation to get a performance big picture across all the business units (business unit revenues, for example), or for processes that don't vary much from business unit to business unit (perhaps HR benefits). Usually, these implementations begin with a demonstration or "pilot" installation in a particularly open-minded and patient business unit where the core business of the corporation will not be disrupted if something goes wrong. Once the project team gets the system up and running and works out all the bugs, the team begins selling other units on ERP, using the first implementation as a kind of in-house customer reference. Plan for this strategy to take a long time.

Slam-dunk—ERP dictates the process design in this method, where the focus is on just a few key processes, such as those contained in an ERP system's financials module. The slam-dunk is generally for smaller companies expecting to grow into ERP.

The goal here is to get ERP up and running quickly and to ditch the fancy reengineering in favor of the ERP system's "canned" processes. Few companies that have approached ERP this way can claim much payback from the new system. Most use it as an infrastructure to support more diligent installation efforts down the road. Yet many discover that a slammed-in ERP system is little better than a legacy system, because it doesn't force employees to change any of their old habits. In fact, doing the hard work of process reengineering after the system is in can be more challenging than if there had been no system at all, because at that point few people in the company will have felt much benefit.

How Does ERP Fit with Electronic Commerce?

After all of that work inventing, perfecting and selling ERP to the world, the major ERP vendors are having a hard time shifting gears from making the applications that streamline business practices inside a company to those that face outward to the rest of the world. These days, the hottest areas for outward-looking (that is, Internet) post-ERP work are electronic commerce, planning and managing your supply chain, and tracking and serving customers. Most ERP vendors have been slow to develop offerings for these areas, and they face stiff competition from niche vendors. ERP vendors have the advantage of a huge installed base of customers and a virtual stranglehold on the "back office" functions—such as order fulfillment. Recently ERP vendors have begun to shrink their ambitions and focus on being the back-office engine that powers electronic commerce, rather than trying to own all the software niches that are necessary for a good electronic commerce Website. Indeed, as the niche vendors make their software easier to hook into electronic commerce Websites, and as middleware vendors make it easier for IS departments to hook together applications from different vendors, many people wonder how much longer ERP vendors can claim to be the primary platform for the Fortune 500.

Questions

1. What is ERP?
2. How can ERP help a business organization?
3. What are some obstacles to implementing ERP?
4. How does ERP fit with e-commerce and supply chain management?

Source: "The ABCs of ERP," *CIO.com,* December 22, 1999.

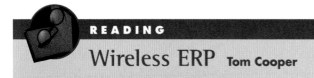

READING

Wireless ERP Tom Cooper

A *wireless, real-time data system is critical to an ERP implementation and proves the key to successful customer relations.*

Imagine investing huge amounts of time and resources implementing an ERP (enterprise resource planning) system in your company. Then imagine you're still batch processing data from your factory floor. That is exactly what one company found itself doing at the cost of $10 million a day in misshipped items, resulting in thousands of hours of rework and hundreds of dissatisfied customers. This was the situation Kimble Glass wanted to avoid when it installed a new SAP system and a new wireless data management system at the same time.

ERP systems have been hailed as the saviors of companies in this fast-moving, Internet-speed, global economy. What isn't always addressed is the need for every part of the organization to supply information to the system in real time. As decisions are made on a minute-by-minute basis, any delays in information increase the chances of the wrong decision being made. As companies have implemented ERP systems, they have frequently forgotten to upgrade their data management systems as well.

This is even more critical as companies recognize the need to manage their goods along the entire supply chain. To provide just-in-time goods to their customers, companies must have real-time data on where those goods are every second of the day. Managing products along the entire supply chain— from the parts coming in the door to sell-through—is not just business theory, it's a fact of life.

Source: Excerpted from an article/case study at *IDSYSTEMS Online,* 2000. Copyright © 1998, 1999, 2000 Helmers Publishing, Inc.

Summary

Material requirements planning (MRP) is an information system used to handle ordering of dependent-demand items (i.e., components of assembled products). The planning process begins with customer orders, which are used along with any back orders to develop a master schedule that indicates the timing and quantity of finished items. The end items are exploded using the bill of materials, and material requirements plans are developed that show quantity and timing for ordering or producing components.

The main features of MRP are the time-phasing of requirements, calculating component requirements, and planned-order releases. To be successful, MRP requires a computer program and accurate master production schedules, bills of materials, and inventory data. Firms without reasonably accurate records or schedules have experienced major difficulties in trying to implement MRP.

MRP II is a second-generation approach to planning that adds a broader scope to manufacturing resource planning because it links business planning, production planning, and the master production schedule.

ERP systems are being implemented which build even further on these linkages by integrating financial, manufacturing, and human resource systems.

Key Terms

bill of materials (BOM), 643
capacity requirements planning, 657
changes, 654
cumulative lead time, 643
dependent demand, 640
enterprise resource planning (ERP), 664
exception reports, 654
gross requirements, 647
inventory records, 646
load reports, 658
lot sizing, 655
manufacturing resources planning
  (MRP II), 661
master schedule, 642
material requirements planning (MRP), 640

net-change system, 653
net requirements, 647
order releases, 654
pegging, 651
performance-control reports, 654
planned-order receipts, 647
planned-order releases, 648
planned orders, 654
planning reports, 654
product structure tree, 643
projected on hand, 647
regenerative system, 653
scheduled receipts, 647
time fences, 658

Solved Problems

The following product structure tree indicates the components needed to assemble one unit of product W. Determine the quantities of each component needed to assemble 100 units of W.

Problem 1

An easy way to compute and keep track of component requirements is to do it right on the tree, as shown in the following figure.

Solution

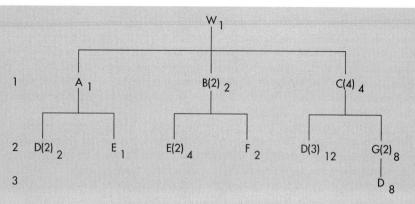

Summary:

Level	Item	(1 W) Quantity	(100 W) Quantity
0	W	1	100
1	A	1	100
	B	2	200
	C	4	400
2	E	5	500
	F	2	200
	G	8	800
3	D	22	2,200

Problem 2

The product structure tree for end item E follows. The manager wants to know the material requirements for ordered part R that will be needed to complete 120 units of E by the start of week 5. Lead times for items are one week for level 0 items, one week for level 1 items, and two weeks for level 2 items. There is a scheduled receipt of 60 units of M at the *end* of week 1 and 100 units of R at the *start* of week 1. Lot-for-lot ordering is used.

Solution

A partial assembly-time chart that includes R and leads to completion of E by the start of week 5 looks like this:

The table entries are arrived at as follows:

Master schedule: 120 units of E to be available at the start of week 5.

Item E: Gross requirements equal the quantity specified in the master production schedule. Since there is no on-hand inventory, net requirements also equal 120 units. Using lot-for-lot ordering, 120 units must be scheduled to be available at the start of week 5. Because there is a one-week lead time for assembly of Es, an order will need to be released (i.e., work started) at the beginning of week 4.

Item M: The *gross* requirements for M are three times the *net* requirements for E, because each E requires three Ms. These must be available at the start of week 4. The net requirements are 60 units less due to the 60 units expected to be on hand at that time. Hence, 300 additional units of M must be available at the start of week 4. With the one-week lead time, there must be an order release at the start of week 3.

Item R: Because each M requires two units of R, 600 Rs will be needed to assemble 300 units of M. However, 100 units will be on hand, so only 500 need to be ordered. Because there is a lead time of two weeks, the 500 Rs must be ordered at the start of week 1.

The master schedule for E and requirements plans for E, M, and R follow.

Master schedule for E

Week number	Beg. Inv.	1	2	3	4	5
Quantity						120

Item: E LT = 1 week		1	2	3	4	5
Gross requirements						120
Scheduled receipts						
Projected on hand						
Net requirements						120
Planned-order receipts						120
Planned-order releases					120	

Multiplied by 3
(see product tree)

Item: M LT = 1 week		1	2	3	4	5
Gross requirements					360	
Scheduled receipts		60				
Projected on hand		60	60	60		
Net requirements					300	
Planned-order receipts					300	
Planned-order releases				300		

Multiplied by 2
(see product tree)

Item: R LT = 2 weeks		1	2	3	4	5
Gross requirements				600		
Scheduled receipts		100				
Projected on hand		100	100	100		
Net requirements				500		
Planned-order receipts				500		
Planned-order releases		500				

Problem 3

Capacity requirements planning. Given the following production schedule in units and the production standards for labor and machine time for this product, determine the labor and machine capacity requirements for each week. Then compute the percent utilization of labor and machines in each week if labor capacity is 200 hours per week and machine capacity is 250 hours per week.

Production Schedule:

Week	1	2	3	4
Quantity	200	300	100	150

Standard Times:

Labor	.5 hour/unit
Machine	1.0 hour/unit

Solution

Convert the quantity requirements into labor and machine requirements by multiplying the quantity requirements by the respective standard times (i.e., multiply each quantity by .5 to obtain the labor hours and multiply each quantity by 1.0 to obtain the machine hours):

Week	1	2	3	4
Quantity	200	300	100	150
Labor hours	100	150	50	75
Machine hours	200	300	100	150

To compute utilization, divide the capacity requirements by the available capacity (200 hours per week for labor and 250 hours per week for machine) and multiply by 100. The results are:

Week	1	2	3	4
Labor	50%	75%	25%	37.5%
Machine	80%	120%	40%	60%

Note that machine capacity in week 2 is overutilized (i.e., capacity is insufficient) because the utilization exceeds 100 percent.

Discussion and Review Questions

1. Contrast independent and dependent demand.
2. When is MRP appropriate?
3. Briefly define or explain each of these terms.
   a. Master schedule
   b. Bill of materials
   c. Inventory records
   d. Gross requirements
   e. Net requirements
   f. Time-phased plan
   g. Low-level coding
4. How is safety stock included in a material requirements plan?
5. What factors can create safety stock requirements in an MRP system?
6. What is meant by the term *safety time*?
7. Contrast *net-change* systems and *regenerative* systems for MRP.
8. Briefly discuss the requirements for effective MRP.
9. What are some of the main advantages and limitations of MRP?
10. How can the use of MRP contribute to productivity?
11. Briefly describe MRP II and indicate how it relates to MRP.
12. What is lot sizing, what is its goal, and why is it an issue with lumpy demand?
13. Contrast planned-order receipts and scheduled receipts.
14. If seasonal variations are present, is their incorporation into MRP fairly simple or fairly difficult? Explain briefly.

15. How does the purpose of ERP differ from the purpose of MRP II?

16. What are some unforeseen costs of ERP?

1. Your manager, Felix Young, wants to know why your estimate of the time it will take to get an MRP system up and running is so long. Young noted that you included an allowance for "potentially inaccurate bill of materials and inventory records," and he wants to know how the company could have operated as well as it has "if the records weren't pretty accurate right now." Write a memo in response to Young's concerns.

2. Suppose you work for a furniture manufacturer, one of whose products is the chair depicted in Figure 15–5. Finished goods inventory is held in a central warehouse in anticipation of customer orders. Finished goods are controlled using EOQ/ROP methods. The warehouse manager, Juan Villa, has suggested using the same methods for controlling component inventory. Write him a brief memo outlining your opinion on doing that.

1. Given the following diagram for a product, determine the quantity of each component required to assemble one unit of the finished product.

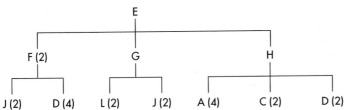

2. The following table lists the components needed to assemble an end item, lead times, and quantities on hand.

Item	End	B	C	D	E	F	G	H
LT (wk)	1	2	3	3	1	2	1	2
Amount on hand	0	10	10	25	12	30	5	0

   a. If 20 units of the end item are to be assembled, how many additional units of E are needed? (*Hint:* You don't need to develop an MRP plan to determine this.)

   b. An order for the end item is scheduled to be shipped at the start of week 11. What is the latest week that the order can be started and still be ready to ship on time? (*Hint:* You don't need to develop an MRP plan for this part either.)

3. The following table lists the components needed to assemble an end item, lead times (in weeks), and quantities on hand.

Item	Lead Time	Amount on Hand	Direct Components
End	1	—	L(2), C(1), K(3)
L	2	10	B(2), J(3)
C	3	15	G(2), B(2)
K	3	20	H(4), B(2)
B	2	30	
J	3	30	
G	3	5	
H	2	—	

a. If 40 units of the end item are to be assembled, how many additional units of B are needed? (*Hint:* You don't need to develop an MRP plan.)

b. An order for the end item is scheduled to be shipped at the start of week 8. What is the latest week that the order can be started and still be ready to ship on time? (*Hint:* You don't need to develop an MRP plan.)

4. Eighty units of end item E are needed at the beginning of week 6. Three cases (30 units per case) of J have been ordered and one case is scheduled to arrive in week 3, one in week 4, and one in week 5. Note: *J must be ordered by the case,* and B must be produced in multiples of 120 units. There are 60 units of B and 20 units of J now on hand. Lead times are two weeks each for E and B, and one week for J.

a. Prepare a material requirements plan for component J.

b. Suppose that in week 4 the quantity of E needed is changed from 80 to 70. The planned order releases through week 3 have all been executed. How many more Bs and Js will be on hand in week 6?

5. End item P is composed of three subassemblies: K, L, and W. K is assembled using 3 Gs and 4 Hs; L is made of 2 Ms and 2 Ns; and W is made of 3 Zs. On-hand inventories are 20 Ls, 40 Gs, and 200 Hs. Scheduled receipts are 10 Ks at the start of week 3, 30 Ks at the start of week 6, and 200 Ws at the start of week 3.

One hundred Ps will be shipped at the start of week 6, and another 100 at the start of week 7. Lead times are two weeks for subassemblies and one week for components G, H, and M. Final assembly of P requires one week. Include an extra 10 percent scrap allowance in each planned order of G. The minimum order size for H is 200 units. Develop each of the following:

a. A product structure tree.

b. An assembly time chart.

c. A master schedule for P.

d. A material requirements plan for K, G, and H using lot-for-lot ordering.

6. A table is assembled using three components, as shown in the accompanying product structure tree. The company that makes the table wants to ship 100 units at the beginning of day 4, 150 units at the beginning of day 5, and 200 units at the beginning of day 7. Receipts of 100 wood sections are scheduled at the beginning of day 2. There are 120 legs on hand. An additional 10 percent of the order size on legs is added for safety stock. There are 60 braces on hand with no safety stock requirement for braces. Lead times (in days) for all items are shown in the following table. Prepare a material requirements plan using lot-for-lot ordering.

Quantity	Lead Time
1–200	1
201–550	2
551–999	3

Table

Wood sections (2)   Braces (3)   Legs (4)

7. Eighty units of end item X are needed at the beginning of week 6, and another 30 units are needed at the beginning of week 8. Prepare a material requirements plan for component D. D can only be ordered in whole cases (50 units per case). One case of D is automatically received every other week, beginning in week 1 (i.e., week 1, 3, 5, 7). Also, there are 30 units of B and 20 units of D now on hand. Lead times for all items are a function of quantity: one week for up to 100 units, two weeks for 101 to 200 units, three weeks for 201 to 300 units, and four weeks for 301 or more units.

8. Oh No!, Inc., sells three models of radar detector units. It buys the three basic models (E, F, and G) from a Japanese manufacturer and adds one, two, or four lights (component D) to further differentiate the models. D is bought from a domestic producer.

Lead times are one week for all items except C, which is two weeks. There are ample supplies of the basic units (E, F, and G) on hand. There are also 10 units of B, 10 units of C, and 25 units of D on hand. Lot sizing rules are lot-for-lot ordering for all items except D, which must be ordered in multiples of 100 units. There is a scheduled receipt of 100 units of D in week 1.

The master schedule calls for 40 units of A to be produced in week 4, 60 units of B in week 5, and 30 units of C in week 6. Prepare a material requirements plan for D and its parents.

9. Assume that you are the manager of a shop that assembles power tools. You have just received an order for 50 chain saws, which are to be shipped at the start of week 8. Pertinent information on the saws is:

Item	Lead Time (weeks)	On Hand	Components
Saw	2	15	A(2), B(1), C(3)
A	1	10	E(3), D(1)
B	2	5	D(2), F(3)
C	2	30	E(2), D(2)
D	1	20	
E	1	10	
F	2	30	

a. Develop a product structure tree, an assembly time chart, and a master schedule.

b. Develop the material requirements plan for component E using lot-for-lot ordering.

c. Suppose now that capacity to produce part E is limited to a maximum of 100 units per period. Revise the planned-order releases for periods 1–4 so that the maximum is not exceeded in any period, keeping in mind an objective of minimizing carrying costs. The quantities need not be equal in every period. Note that the gross requirements for E will remain the same. However, quantities in some of the other rows will change. Determine the new cell values for those rows.

10. Assume that you are the manager of Assembly, Inc. You have just received an order for 40 units of an industrial robot, which is to be delivered at the start of week 7 of your schedule. Using the following information, determine how many units of subassembly G to order and the timing of those orders, given that subassembly G must be ordered in multiples of 80 units and all other components are ordered lot-for-lot. Assume that the components are used only for this particular robot.

Item	Lead Time (weeks)	On Hand	Components
Robot	2	10	B, G, C(3)
B	1	5	E, F
C	1	20	G(2), H
E	2	4	—
F	3	8	—
G	2	15	—
H	1	10	—

11. Determine material requirements plans for parts N and V and subassembly I as described in Solved Problem 2 for each of the following:

a. Assume that there are currently 100 Ns on hand and scheduled receipts of 40 Is and 10 Vs at the beginning of week 3. No Es are on hand; 120 Es are needed at the start of week 5.

b. Assume on-hand and scheduled receipts as in part *a*. Now suppose that 100 Es are needed at the start of week 5 and 50 at the start of week 7. Also, use multiples of these order sizes: N, 800; V, 200. Use lot-for-lot ordering for I.

c. Using your answer to part *b*, update the MRP for V, using the following additional information for each of these cases: (1) one week has elapsed (making it the start of week 2), and (2) three weeks have elapsed (making it the start of week 4). *Note:* Start your revised plans so that the updated time in each case is designated as week 1.

The updated master schedule now has an order for 100 units of E in week 8 of case 1 (i.e., week 9 under the former master schedule). Assume all orders are released and received as planned.

12. A firm that produces electric golf carts has just received an order for 200 carts, which must be ready for delivery at the start of week 8. Information concerning the product structure, lead times, and quantities on hand is shown in the following table. Use this information to do each of the following:

a. Construct a product tree.

b. Construct an assembly time chart.

c. Develop a material requirements plan that will provide 200 golf carts by week 8 assuming lot-for-lot ordering.

Parts List for Electric Golf Cart	Lead Time	Quantity on Hand
Electric golf cart	1	0
Top	1	40
Base	1	20
Top		
Supports (4)	1	200
Cover	1	0
Base		
Motor	2	300
Body	3	50
Seats (2)	2	120
Body		
Frame	1	35
Controls	1	0
Wheel assemblies (4) . . .	1	240

13. Refer to Problem 12. Assume that unusually mild weather has caused a change in the quantity and timing of orders for golf carts. The revised plan calls for 100 golf carts at the start of week 6, 100 at the start of week 8, and 100 at the start of week 9.

a. Develop a master schedule for this revised plan.

b. Determine the timing and quantities for orders for tops and bases.

c. Assume that equipment problems reduce the firm's capacity for assembling bases to 50 units per week. Revise your material plan for bases to reflect this, but still meet delivery dates.

14. A manufacturing firm buys a certain part in varying quantities throughout the year. Ordering cost is $11 per order, and carrying cost is $0.14 per piece per month. Given the following demand schedule for the part for the next eight months,

a. What order sizes would be indicated using an economic part period approach? When should each order be received?

b. What order sizes and times would be used for EOQ sizing? Assume lead time is zero.

c. Compare the total cost of fixed internal ordering with a two-month interval, the EPP approach, and the EOQ approach.

Month	Demand
1	—
2	80
3	10
4	30
5	—
6	30
7	—
8	30

15. A firm periodically produces a part that is a basic component of an assembled product it makes. Each time the part is run, a fixed cost of $125 is incurred. The cost to carry one unit for a week is estimated to be $1.65. For the demand schedule shown, determine the quantity and timing of runs that would be consistent with an economic part period approach. Assume a one-week lead time for each run.

Week	Demand
1	40
2	20
3	100
4	20
5	—
6	20
7	80

16. A company that manufactures paving material for driveways and parking lots expects the following demand for its product for the next four weeks:

Week number	1	2	3	4
Material (tons)	40	80	60	70

The company's labor and machine standards and available capacities are:

	Labor	Machine
Production standard (hours per ton)	4	3
Weekly production capacity (hours)	300	200

   a. Determine the capacity utilization for labor and machine for each of the four weeks.

   b. In which weeks do you foresee a problem? What options would you suggest to resolve any problems? What costs are relevant in making a decision on choosing an option?

17. A company produces two very similar products that go through a three-step sequence of fabrication, assembly, and packaging. Each step requires one day for a lot to be completely processed and moved to the next department. Processing requirements for the departments (hours per unit) are:

	FABRICATION		ASSEMBLY		PACKAGING	
Product	Labor	Machine	Labor	Machine	Labor	Machine
A	2	1	1.5	1	1	.5
B	1	1	1	1	1.5	.5

Department capacities are all 700 hours of labor and 500 hours of machine time, except Friday, when capacities are 200 hours for both labor and machine time. The following production schedule is for next week:

Day	Mon	Tues	Wed	Thurs	Fri
A	200	400	100	300	100
B	300	200	200	200	200

a. Develop a production schedule for each department that shows the capacity requirements for each product and the total load for each day. Ignore changeover time.

b. Evaluate the projected loading for the first three days of the week. Is the schedule feasible? What do you suggest for balancing the load?

18. The MRP Department has a problem. Its computer "died" just as it spit out the following information: Planned order release for item J27 = 640 units in week 2. The firm has been able to reconstruct all the information they lost except the Master Schedule for end item 565. The firm is fortunate because J27 is used only in 565s. Given the following product structure tree and associated inventory status record information, determine what master schedule entry for 565 was exploded into the material requirements plan that killed the computer.

Part Number	On Hand	Lot Size	Lead Time
565	0	Lot-for-lot	1 week
X43	60	120	1 week
N78	0	Lot-for-lot	2 weeks
Y36	200	Lot-for-lot	1 week
J27	0	Lot-for-lot	2 weeks

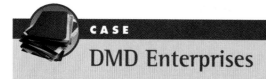

DMD Enterprises

After the "dot com" he tried to start folded, David "Marty" Dawkins decided to pursue his boyhood dream of owning a bike factory. After several false starts, he finally got the small company up and running. The company currently assembles two models Marty designed: the Arrow and the Dart. The company hasn't turned a profit yet, but Marty feels that once he resolves some of the problems he's having with inventory and scheduling, he can increase productivity and reduce costs.

At first, he ordered enough bike parts and subassemblies for four months' worth of production. Parts were stacked all over the place, seriously reducing work space and hampering movement of workers and materials. And no one knew exactly where anything was. In Marty's words, "It was a solid mess!"

He and his two partners eventually managed to work off most of the inventory. They hope to avoid similar problems in the future by using a more orderly approach. Marty's first priority is to develop an MRP plan for upcoming periods. He wants to assemble 15 Arrows and 10 Darts each week, for weeks 4 through 8. The product structure trees for the two bikes follow.

One of Marty's partners, Ann, has organized information on lead times, inventory on hand, and lot-sizing rules (established by suppliers):

Item	Lead Time (weeks)	On Hand	Lot-Sizing Rule
Arrow	2	5	Lot-for-lot
Dart	2	2	Lot-for-lot
X	1	5	Q = 25
W	2*	2	Multiples of 12
F	1	10	Q = 30
K	1	3	Lot-for-lot
Q	1	15	Q = 30
M	1	0	Lot-for-lot

*LT = 3 weeks for orders of 36 or more units on this item.

Scheduled receipts are:

Period 1:   20 Arrows: 18 Ws

Period 2:   20 Darts: 15 Fs

As the third partner, it is your job to develop the material requirements plan.

OPERATIONS TOUR

Stickley Furniture

Introduction

L.&J.G. Stickley was founded in 1900 by brothers Leopold and George Stickley. Located just outside of Syracuse, New York, the company is a producer of fine cherry, white oak, and mahogany furniture. In the late 1980s, the company reintroduced the company's original line of mission oak furniture, which now accounts for over 50 percent of the company's sales.

Over the years, the company experienced both good and bad times, and at one point, it employed over 200 people. But by the early 1970s, the business was in disarray; there were only about 20 full-time employees, and the company was on the brink of bankruptcy. The present owners bought the ailing firm in 1974, and under their leadership, the company has prospered and grown, and now has 900 employees. Stickley has five retail showrooms in New York State, and its furniture is sold nationally by some 100 dealers. In 1994, sales were about $65 million.

Production

The production facility is a large, rectangular building with a 30 foot ceiling. Furniture making is labor intensive, although saws, sanders, and other equipment are very much a part of the process. In fact, electric costs average $40,000 to $50,000 a month. The company has its own tool room where cutting tools are sharpened, and replacement parts are produced as needed.

Worker skills range from low-skilled material handlers to highly skilled craftsmen. For example, three master cabinet makers handle customized orders.

The process (see figure on pg. 680) begins with various sawing operations where large boards received from the lumber mills are cut into smaller sizes. The company recently purchased a computer-controlled "optimizer" saw that greatly improves sawing productivity, and eliminates some waste. Workers inspect and mark knot locations and other defects they find on each piece of lumber before feeding it into the saw. The computer then determines the optimal set of cuttings, given the location of knots and other defects, and standard lengths needed for subsequent operations. Approximately 29,000 board feet are cut each day. Subsequent sawing operations provide additional cuts for specific jobs.

Workers then glue some of the pieces together; they will end up as tops of tables, desks, dressers, or a similar item. Large presses hold 20 to 30 glued sections at a time. Other pieces that will become table or chair legs, chair backs or other items go through various shaping operations. Next comes a series of sanding operations, which remove excess glue from the glued sections, and smooth the surface of both glued pieces and other pieces.

Some of the pieces may require drilling or mortising, an operation in which rectangular holes and other shapes are cut into the wood. The company has a CNC (numerically controlled) router that can be programmed to make grooves and other specialty cuts. Some items require carving, which involves highly skilled workers.

Next, workers assemble the various components, either into subassemblies, or sometimes directly to other components to obtain completed pieces. Each item is stamped with the date of production, and components such as dresser drawers, cabinet doors, and expansion leaves of tables also are stamped to identify their location (e.g., top drawer, left door). Careful records are kept so that if a piece of furniture is ever returned for repairs, complete instructions are available (type of wood, finish, etc.) to enable repair people to closely match the original piece.

The furniture items then usually move to the "white inventory" (unfinished) section, and eventually to the finishing department where workers apply linseed oil or another finish before the items are moved to the finished goods inventory to await shipment to stores or customers.

Aggregate Planning

The company uses a level production plan (maintain steady output and steady labor force). Demand is seasonal; it is highest in the first and third quarters. During the second and fourth quarters, excess output goes into inventory; during the first and third quarters, excess demand is met using inventory. The

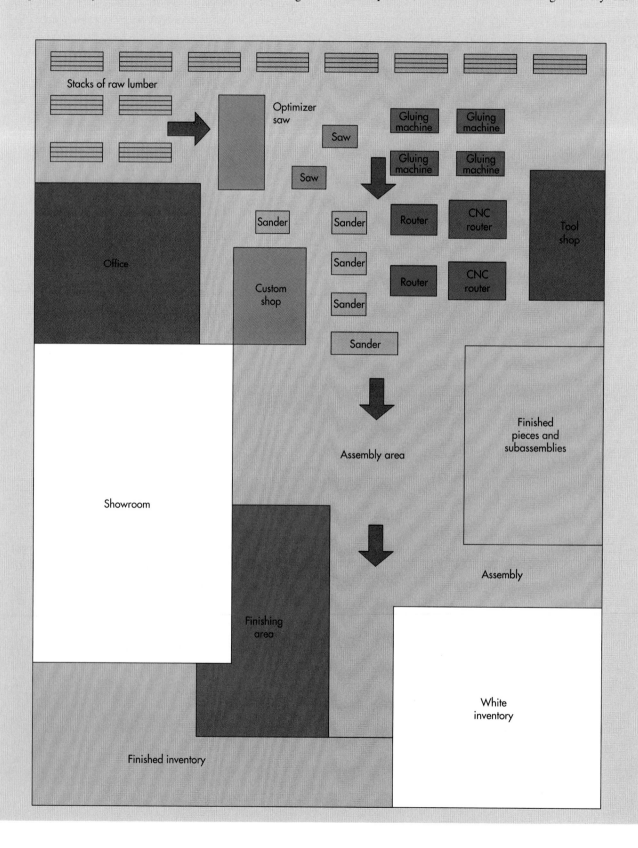

production scheduler uses a schedule that is set for the next 8 to 10 weeks.

Production Control

Job sequence is determined by the amount of remaining inventory (days supply on hand), and processing time. Lot sizes are determined by factoring in demand, setup costs, and carrying costs. Typical lot sizes are 25 to 60 pieces. There are many jobs being done concurrently. Each job is accompanied by a set of bar codes that identify the job and the operation. As each operation is completed, the operator removes a bar code sticker and delivers it to the scheduling office where it is scanned into the computer, thereby enabling production control to keep track of progress on a job, and to know its location in the shop.

The company's policy of level output coupled with seasonal demand patterns means that prior to peak demand periods, excess output is used to build up inventories, which is then drawn down when demand exceeds production capacity during periods of peak production.

Inventory

In addition to the "white" inventory and a small finished goods inventory, the company maintains an inventory of furniture pieces (e.g., table and chair legs) and partially assembled items. This inventory serves two important functions. One is to reduce the amount of time needed to respond to customer orders rather than having to go through the entire production process to obtain needed items, and the other is that it helps to smooth production and utilize idle machinery/workers. Because of unequal job times on successive operations, some workstations invariably have slack time while others work at capacity. This is used to build an inventory of commonly used pieces and subassemblies. Moreover, because pieces are being made for inventory, there is flexibility in sequencing. This permits jobs that have similar setups to be produced in sequence, thereby reducing setup time and cost.

Quality

Each worker is responsible for checking his or her quality, as well as the quality of materials received from preceding operations, and to report any deficiencies. In addition, on several difficult operations quality control people handle inspections, and work with operators to correct any deficiencies. The company is considering a TQM approach, but has not yet made a decision on whether to go in that direction.

Questions

1. Which type of production processing—job shop, batch, repetitive, or continuous—is the primary mode of operation at Stickley Furniture? Why? What other type of processing is used to a lesser extent? Explain.

2. How does management keep track of job status and location during production?

3. Suppose the company has just received an order for 40 mission oak dining room sets. Briefly list the kinds of information the company will need to plan, schedule, and process this job.

4. What benefits, and what problems, would you expect, given the company's level production policy?

5. Can you suggest any changes that might be beneficial to the company? What are they?

Bennett, Wayne D. "The Big Risk for Small Fry." *CIO Magazine,* May 15, 2000.

Davenport, Tom. "Living with ERP." *CIO Magazine,* December 1, 1998.

Davenport, Tom. "Long Live ERP." *CIO Magazine,* March 1, 2000.

Davenport, Tom. *Mission Critical: Realizing the Promise of Enterprise Systems.* Boston: Harvard Business School Press, 2000.

Hopp, Wallace, and Mark L. Spearman. *Factory Physics.* 2nd ed. New York: Irwin/McGraw-Hill, 2001.

Jacobs, Robert F., and D. Clay Whybark. *Why ERP? A Primer on SAP Implementation.* New York: Irwin/McGraw-Hill, 2000.

Jeffery, Bill, and Jim Morrison. "ERP, One Step at a Time." *CIO Magazine,* September 1, 2000.

Kapp, Karl M., Bill Latham, and Hester-Ford Latham. *Integrated Learning for ERP Success.* Boca Raton, FL: St. Lucie Press, 2001.

Orlicky, Joseph. *Material Requirements Planning.* New York: McGraw-Hill, 1975.

Paul, Lauren Gibbons. "The Biggest Gamble Yet" *CIO Magazine,* April 15, 2000.

Pender, Lee. "The Missing Link." *CIO Magazine,* June 15, 2000.

Ptak, Carol A., and Eli Schragenheim. *ERP: Tools, Techniques, and Applications for Integrating the Supply Chain.* Boca Raton, FL: St. Lucie Press, 1999.

Slater, Derek. "An ERP Package for You. . . and You. . . and You. . . and Even You." *CIO Magazine,* February 15, 1999.

Slater, Derek. "The Hidden Costs of Enterprise Software." *CIO Enterprise,* January 15, 1998.

Slater, Derek. "The Vision." *CIO Magazine,* May 15, 2000.

Slater, Derek. "Wanted: ERP People Skills." *CIO Magazine,* March 1, 1999.

Vollmann, Thomas E., William L. Berry, and D. Clay Whybark. *Manufacturing, Planning and Control Systems.* 4th ed. Burr Ridge, IL: Richard D. Irwin, 1997.

Wheatley, Malcolm. "ERP Training Stinks." *CIO Magazine,* June 1, 2000.

Wight, Oliver W. *The Executive's Guide to Successful MRP II.* Williston, VT: Oliver Wight Limited Publications, 1982.

Selected Bibliography and Further Reading

CHAPTER SIXTEEN
Just-In-Time Systems

CHAPTER OUTLINE

Introduction, 684

Reading: The Nuts and Bolts of Japan's Factories, 685

Reading: Romantic JIT and Pragmatic JIT, 687

JIT Goals, 687

Building Blocks, 688
Product Design, 688
Process Design, 689

Reading: Pedal Pushers, 694
Personnel/Organizational Elements, 695

Newsclip: "People" Firms Boost Profits, Study Shows, 696
Manufacturing Planning and Control, 697

Reading: Developing the JIT Philosophy, 702

Converting to a JIT System, 705
Planning a Successful Conversion, 706
Obstacles to Conversion, 707

Reading: JIT and Quality: A Perfect Fit, 708

JIT in Services, 709

Reading: Box Maker Keeps Lid on Lead Times, 709

JIT Purchasing, 711

JIT II, 711

Operations Strategy, 711

Reading: JIT II, 711

Summary, 712

Key Terms, 713

Solved Problems, 713

Discussion and Review Questions, 713

Memo Writing Exercises, 714

Problems, 714

Case: Level Operations, 716

Operations Tour: Boeing, 716

Selected Bibliography and Further Reading, 718

Supplement: Maintenance, 719

LEARNING OBJECTIVES

After completing this chapter, you should be able to:

1 Explain what is meant by the term *just-in-time (JIT) production system.*

2 List each of the goals of JIT and explain its importance.

3 List and briefly describe the building blocks of JIT.

4 List the benefits of the JIT system.

5 Outline the considerations important in converting a traditional mode of production to a JIT system.

6 List some of the obstacles that might be encountered when converting to a JIT system.

Many companies, especially those in manufacturing, are attempting to streamline operations and reduce their investment in inventory by adopting a just-in-time approach to their operations. In a JIT environment, companies strive to operate with minimal inventory rather than stockpiling inventory. This requires designing a system that can operate in this manner and working closely with suppliers so that parts and materials arrive just as they are needed (i.e., just-in-time).

The goal of a JIT system is to achieve a continuous workflow using minimal resources, producing only what is needed, when it is needed. Anything over that amount is viewed as waste.

One obvious benefit of a JIT system is a substantial reduction in both work-in-process and finished goods inventories, which leads to a substantial reduction in the amount of working capital devoted to inventories. Other benefits include balanced production, reduced waste, and high quality.

just-in-time (JIT) Repetitive production system in which processing and movement of materials and goods occur just as they are needed, usually in small batches.

The term **just-in-time (JIT)** is used to refer to a production system in which both the movement of goods during production and deliveries from suppliers are carefully timed so that at each step of the process the next (usually small) batch arrives for processing just as the preceding batch is completed—thus the name, *just-in-time*. The result is a system with no idle items waiting to be processed, and no idle workers or equipment waiting for items to process.

The just-in-time phenomenon is characteristic of *lean production systems,* which operate with very little "fat" (e.g., excess inventory, extra workers, wasted space). JIT pertains to the timing of the flow of parts and material through the system and the timing of services. Companies that employ the JIT/lean production approach typically enjoy a competitive advantage over companies that use a more traditional approach: They have lower processing costs, fewer defects, greater flexibility, and are able to bring new or improved products to the market more quickly.

One aspect of JIT involves production planning and control, which makes JIT one of the two basic approaches to manufacturing planning and control; the other is material requirements planning. JIT is sometimes viewed as a system for repetitive production operations, while MRP is considered a system for batch production. However, they are sometimes applied to similar situations, but the two systems function somewhat differently. MRP systems are fairly complex, requiring extensive and detailed shop floor controls. JIT systems are much simpler, involving only minimal shop floor controls. Moreover, MRP relies on a computer-based component-*scheduling* system to trigger production and deliveries, whereas JIT relies on visual or audible signals to trigger production and deliveries. The two approaches are compared in more detail later in the chapter.

This chapter describes the JIT/lean production approach, including the basic elements of these systems and what it takes to make them work effectively. It also points out the benefits of these systems and the potential obstacles that companies may encounter when they attempt to convert from a traditional system to a JIT/lean production system.

Introduction

www.toyota.com

The JIT approach was developed at the Toyota Motor Company of Japan by Taiichi Ohno (who eventually became vice president of manufacturing) and several of his colleagues. The development of JIT in Japan was probably influenced by Japan being a crowded country with few natural resources. Not surprisingly, the Japanese are very sensitive to waste and inefficiency. They regard scrap and rework as waste, and excess inventory as an evil because it takes up space and ties up resources.

"The Nuts and Bolts of Japan's Factories" by Urban Lehner provides a number of important insights on the just-in-time approach to manufacturing, and some reasons for the successes Japanese manufacturers have achieved.

READING

The Nuts and Bolts of Japan's Factories
Urban C. Lehner

" *If American automobile king Henry Ford I were alive today, I am positive he would have done what we did with our Toyota production system.*"

—Taiichi Ohno

TOYOTA CITY, Japan—Groping to explain "how Japan does it," experts have made much of the close ties between business and government and of the loyalty of Japan's highly skilled workers to their employers. They've noted the fierce competitiveness of Japanese companies in their home market, the nation's high savings rate, even the relative scarcity of lawyers.

Doubtless these are among the pieces needed to solve the puzzle. But some management consultants who've studied how Japan makes such high-quality, competitively priced products say there's another piece often overlooked. The Japanese, they say, have proved themselves increasingly adroit at organizing and running manufacturing operations. Japanese managers may lack the MBAs or the ability to plot big-picture business strategy of their American counterparts. But they know how to run factories.

"There's a growing acceptance that Japanese success is based at least in part on the development of manufacturing techniques that often tend to outrun our own," says management consultant Rex Reid, head of A.T. Kearney's Toyota office.

One of the most interesting examples of Japanese production management skills is a concern quite familiar to Americans: Toyota Motor Co., the largest-selling foreign automaker in the U.S.

Believe in Their System

Toyota officials resist claiming that their way of building autos is better than anyone else's. They're somewhat embarrassed by the exuberant projections of Henry Ford's behavior essayed by their former chief production executive, Taiichi Ohno, in his 1978 book. But Toyota men clearly remain believers in what Mr. Ohno called "the Toyota production system."

For a first-hand look at the system, take a walk through the Tsutsumi plant here in Toyota City, a town of 280,000 in central Japan that's the site of 8 of Toyota's 10 factories. Over here, Muneo Nakahara, 26 years old and an 8-year Toyota veteran, is doing his job. With the help of an overhead crane that Mr. Nakahara controls from a hand-held device, he hoists auto engines onto a conveyor belt that will take them to be matched up with auto bodies.

Mr. Nakahara is lifting the engines onto the conveyor from a small flat-bed truck that has brought them from the engine plant. Only two trucks carrying just 12 engines apiece park at

Mr. Nakahara's post at any given time, so every few minutes an empty truck drives back to the engine plant and a new one takes its place.

That's the first feature of the Toyota system: no inventories. Toyota's factories keep on hand only that amount of parts needed for immediate production, from a few minutes' worth up to a few hours' worth, depending on the part. When fresh parts are needed—and only when they're needed—they're delivered from other Toyota plants or from outside suppliers directly to the production line.

Outsiders who've seen Toyota in action often call this the "kanban system," *kanban* being the Japanese word for the piece of paper enclosed in clear plastic that accompanies each bin of parts. (When a worker on the line begins drawing from a new bin, he removes the kanban and routes it back to the supplier, for whom it serves as an order for a new bin of parts.) But Toyota officials say the pieces of paper are just tools. They call this inventory control aspects of their broader system the "just-in-time" system.

The same philosophy guides the meshing of operations within each plant. An assembly line that is building subcomponents makes just that number of subcomponents immediately needed at the next stage of production. When it's made enough, it's changed over to build some other kind of subcomponent for a while. Likewise, the final assembly line first builds one kind of car, then another, in small lots—only as much as called for in actual orders from Toyota's sales unit. Toyota engineers "average" and "level" production among the lines to coordinate output without building inventories. They compare auto assembly to rowing a boat: Everybody has to be pulling on the oars at the same rate.

"They concentrate very heavily on avoiding end-item and intermediate-item storage," says a Ford official in Detroit who's seen the system at work. "They throw out the whole concept of mass production."

The benefits are substantial. Toyota doesn't need space for inventory, people to handle and control inventory, or borrowed money to finance inventory. "It cuts costs in a lot of ways," says an official of Nissan Motor Co., Japan's second-largest automaker, which has adopted an inventory control system similar to its rival's in some plants.

Then there are the side benefits. Because Toyota is constantly changing over its machines to make new things, its workers have become fast at repair and changeover. In his book, Mr. Ohno cites a mold on a press that took two to three hours to change in the 1940s. Today "it takes only three minutes to change the mold," Mr. Ohno says.

Aside from its emphasis on holding down inventories, Toyota's system stresses quality controls. Throughout the Tsutsumi plant are boards with electric lights to indicate conditions on each assembly line. A red light means a line has been stopped because of a problem. Every worker has a button or cord with which he can stop the line, and he's told to use it whenever he thinks something's wrong with the operation of the line or when he spots defects in the product.

"We lose production temporarily this way," concedes Fujio Cho, manager of the production control department at Toyota's headquarters. "But in our experience stopping lines helps us detect problems early and avoid bad practices."

Another feature that becomes clear is the company's penchant for training workers to do more than one job. The man who runs one machine switches off every few moments to run another. The man who feeds rear windows to a robot also "tags" car shells with instructions telling workers farther down the line what to install in them. This versatility allows Toyota to realign its work force more efficiently when business is bad.

Indeed, "recession" thinking underlies a big part of Toyota's system. Much of the system originated in the late 1940s and early 1950s, when Toyota was producing exclusively for a domestic market that wasn't very strong. The company has been operating on the conventional assumption that it's most efficient to produce in large lots, "but that kind of thinking has pushed us close to bankruptcy, because the large lots we were producing couldn't be sold," says Mr. Cho. Toyota couldn't lay off workers—Japan's a "life-time" employment system— so Toyota executives hit upon the simple yet radical idea that still pervades its operations: Overproduction is waste.

Source: Reprinted by permission of *The Wall Street Journal*, © 1981 by Dow Jones & Company, Inc. All Rights Reserved Worldwide.

In some respects, the just-in-time concept was operational over a half century ago at Henry Ford's great industrial complex in River Rouge, Michigan:

> Nothing in the period that followed was too good for the Rouge; it had the best blast furnaces, the best machine tools, the best metal labs, the best electrical systems, the most efficient efficiency experts. At its maturity in the mid-twenties, the Rouge dwarfed all other industrial complexes. It was a mile and a half long and three quarters of a mile wide. Its eleven hundred acres contained ninety-three buildings, twenty-three of them major. There were ninety-three miles of railroad track on it and twenty-seven miles of conveyor belts. Some seventy-five thousand men worked there, five thousand of them doing nothing but keeping it clean, using eighty-six tons of soap and wearing out five thousand mops each month. By the standards of the day the Rouge was, in fact, clean and quiet. Little was wasted. A British historian of the time, J. A. Spender, wrote of its systems: "If absolute completeness and perfect adaptation of means to end justify the word, they are in their own way works of art." Dissatisfied with the supply and quality of the steel he was getting from the steel companies, Ford asked how much it would cost to build a steel plant within the Rouge. About $35 million, Sorensen told him. "What are you waiting for?" said Ford. Equally dissatisfied with both the availability and the quality of glass, he built a glass factory at the Rouge as well. The price of glass had been roughly 30 cents a square foot early in the life of the T; soon it had soared to $1.50 a foot. With the glass plant at the Rouge, the price of glass came down to 20 cents a foot. Barges carrying iron ore would steam into the inland docks, and even as they were tying up, huge cranes would be swinging out to start the unloading. The process was revolutionary. On Monday morning a barge bearing ore would arrive in a slip, and the ore would go to the blast furnace. By Tuesday it would be poured into a foundry mold and later that day would become an engine. John DeVenter, a business historian, wrote in awe: "Here is the conversion of raw material to cash in approximately thirty-three hours." Some sixty years later Toyota would be credited for its just-in-time theory of manufacturing, in which parts arrived from suppliers just in time to be part of the final assembly. But in any real sense that process began at the Rouge. Toasting Philip Caldwell, the head of Ford who in 1982 was visiting Japan, Eiji Toyoda, of the Toyota company, said, "There is no secret to how we learned to do what we do, Mr. Caldwell. We learned it at the Rouge."[1]

Toyota learned a great deal from studying Ford's operations and based its JIT approach on what it saw. However, Toyota was able to accomplish something that Ford couldn't: A system that could handle variety.

A widely held view of JIT is that it is simply a system for scheduling production that results in low levels of work-in-process and inventory. But in its truest sense, JIT represents a *philosophy* that encompasses every aspect of the process, from design to after the

---

[1]Reprinted with permission of Rawson Associates/Scribner, a division of Simon & Schuster, Inc., from *The Machine That Changed the World*, by James P. Womack, Daniel T. Jones, and Daniel Roos. © 1990 by James P. Womack, Daniel T. Jones, Daniel Roos, and Donna Sammons Carpenter.

sale of a product. The philosophy is to pursue a system that functions well with minimal levels of inventories, minimal waste, minimal space, and minimal transactions. It must be a system that is not prone to disruptions and is flexible in terms of the product variety and range of volume that it can handle.

READING

Romantic JIT and Pragmatic JIT

There are two views of JIT presented in the literature. Paul Zipkin refers to these views as *romantic* JIT and *pragmatic* JIT. Romantic JIT consists of various slogans and idealistic goals such as lot sizes of one, zero inventories, and zero defects. JIT is seen as a "revolution" for manufacturing, one that is relatively simple to install and maintain, and one that can lead to dramatic reductions in work-in-process (WIP) inventory and competitive advantage. Pragmatic JIT, on the other hand, consists of a collection of techniques, some fairly technical, that relate to machine changeovers, layout design, product simplification, quality training, equipment maintenance, and so on.

One problem with romantic JIT is that it is apt to appeal to senior managers, who are not much involved in the day-to-day operations on the shop floor level. They are attracted by the promise of inventory reductions and higher quality. They envision JIT as a quick fix to their problems, and look forward to lower WIP levels and increased inventory turnovers, which will lead to decreased inventory investment and improved cash flow. Thinking that JIT is a relatively simple concept, they expect that lower-level managers and workers will quickly and easily convert to this new way of thinking and soon achieve results, not comprehending the complexity that is involved, or the time they will need to achieve meaningful results. For example, it took Toyota over 20 years to perfect its JIT system!

Adopting the romantic view of JIT can lead to much frustration and disappointment as people on the shop floor struggle to achieve what senior management perceives to be relatively easy. Moreover, cutting back WIP inventories without dealing with the reasons for WIP can quickly lead to chaos on the shop floor, with delays and missed deliveries.

Source: Paul Zipkin, "Does Manufacturing Need a JIT Revolution?" *Harvard Business Review*, January–February 1991, pp. 40–50.

In JIT systems, quality is ingrained in both the product and the process. Companies that use JIT have achieved a level of quality that enables them to function with small batch sizes and tight schedules. JIT systems have high reliability; major sources of inefficiency and disruption have been eliminated, and workers have been trained not only to function in the system but also to continuously improve it.

JIT Goals

The ultimate goal of JIT is a *balanced* system, that is, one that achieves a smooth, rapid flow of materials through the system. The idea is to make the process time as short as possible by using resources in the best possible way. The degree to which the overall goal is achieved depends on how well certain supporting goals are achieved. Those goals are:

1. Eliminate disruptions.
2. Make the system flexible by reducing setup times and lead times.
3. Eliminate waste, especially excess inventory.

Disruptions have a negative influence on the system by upsetting the smooth flow of products through the system, and they should be eliminated. Disruptions are caused by a variety of factors, such as poor quality, equipment breakdowns, changes to the schedule, and late deliveries. All these should be eliminated as much as possible. This will reduce the uncertainty that the system must deal with.

A *flexible system* is one that is robust enough to handle a mix of products, often on a daily basis, and to handle changes in the level of output while still maintaining balance and throughput speed. This enables the system to deal with some uncertainty. *Setup times* and *delivery lead times* prolong a process without adding any value to the product. Moreover, long setup times and long lead times negatively impact the flexibility of the system. Hence, reduction of setup and lead times is very important in a JIT system.

Waste represents unproductive resources; eliminating waste can free up resources and enhance production. *Inventory* is an idle resource, taking up space and adding cost to the system. It should be minimized as much as possible. In the JIT philosophy, other wastes include

a. *Overproduction*—involves excessive use of manufacturing resources.

b. *Waiting time*—requires space, adds no value.

c. *Unnecessary transporting*—increases handling, increases work-in-process inventory.

d. *Processing waste*—makes unnecessary production steps, scrap.

e. *Inefficient work methods*—indicates poor layout and material movement patterns, increases work-in-process inventory.

f. *Product defects*—requires rework costs and possible sales loss due to customer dissatisfaction.

The existence of these wastes is an indication that improvement is possible. The list of wastes can also identify potential targets for continuous improvement efforts.

Sometimes the terms *big JIT* and *little JIT* are used to differentiate attempts to eliminate waste across the board in production activities. Big JIT focuses on vendor relationships, human relations, technology management, and materials and inventory management. Little JIT is more narrowly focused on scheduling materials and services for production.

Building Blocks

The design and operation of a JIT system provide the foundation for accomplishing the aforementioned goals. The foundation is made up of four building blocks:

1. Product design

2. Process design

3. Personnel/organizational elements

4. Manufacturing planning and control

Speed and simplicity are two common threads that run through these building blocks.

PRODUCT DESIGN

Three elements of product design are important for JIT:

1. Standard parts

2. Modular design

3. Highly capable production systems

The first two elements relate to speed and simplicity.

The use of *standard parts* means that workers have fewer parts to deal with, and training times and costs are reduced. Purchasing, handling, and checking quality are more routine and lend themselves to continual improvement. Another important benefit is the ability to use standard processing.

Modular design is an extension of standard parts. Modules are clusters of parts treated as a single unit. This greatly reduces the number of parts to deal with, simplifying assembly, purchasing, handling, training, and so on. Standardization has the added benefit of reducing the number of different parts contained in the bill of materials for various products, thereby simplifying the bill of materials.

JIT requires highly capable production systems. Quality is the *sine qua non* ("without which not") of JIT. It is crucial to JIT systems because poor quality can create major disruptions. Quality must be embedded in goods and processes. The systems are geared to a smooth flow of work; the occurrence of problems due to poor quality creates disruption

Civic and Odyssey CD Player...$349.00 SUGG. RETAIL. *Faceplate subject to change.*

CD PLAYER

Allows you to drive to crisp, distortion-free digital sounds. This sculpted unit is specifically designed to work in conjunction with any Honda audio system equipped with ⊂▭⊃ Compact Disc Controller™ technology so you can operate it through the same buttons that control your stereo, eliminating dashboard clutter and simplifying operation.

Passport CD Player...$349.00 SUGG. RETAIL.

Accord CD Player...$349.00 SUGG. RETAIL.

CASSETTE PLAYER

is specifically designed to work in conjunction with the Accord, CR-V, Prelude or Civic's audio system. You can operate it through the stereo controls, eliminating dashboard clutter and simplifying operation.

Cassette Player offers the features you'd expect. Powered tape loading and eject for smooth operation. Auto reverse that allows uninterrupted listening to both sides of the tape. Single tracks can be repeated if desired. Dolby® B noise reduction can be selected to reduce tape hiss. Music search allows the listener to skip forward or reverse to find a preferred track. The pinch roller releases to protect against damage to the tape and the cassette transport mechanism when the power is shut off. The tape head is made of a hard permalloy head for long term durability. Even the tape door is illuminated so it is easy to load a tape at night.

CONSOLE ASHTRAY with LIGHTER

Convenience and style punctuate this duo. The ashtray with cigarette lighter is a replacement for the factory installed center instrument cover. Color coordinated to vehicle interior.

HONDA ACCESSORIES

Accord Cassette Player...$199.00 SUGG. RETAIL.

Civic Cassette Player...$199.00 SUGG. RETAIL.
Ashtray with Cigarette Lighter...TBD SUGG. RETAIL.

Honda designs product options into its vehicles. Various radio/CD/cassette options are modular and interchangeable among vehicle models.

in this flow. Because of small lot sizes and the absence of buffer stock, production must cease when problems occur, and it cannot resume until the problems have been resolved. Obviously, shutting down an entire process is costly and cuts into planned output levels, so it becomes imperative to try to avoid shutdowns, and to quickly resolve problems when they do appear.

www.honda.com

JIT systems use a three-part approach to quality. One part is to design quality into the product and the production process. High quality levels can occur because JIT systems produce standardized products that lead to standardized job methods, employ workers who are very familiar with their jobs, and use standardized equipment. Moreover, the cost of product design quality (i.e., building quality in at the *design* stage) can be spread over many units, yielding a low cost per unit. It is also important to choose appropriate quality levels in terms of the final customer and of manufacturing capability. Thus, product design and process design must go hand in hand.

PROCESS DESIGN

Seven aspects of process design are particularly important for JIT systems:

1. Small lot sizes
2. Setup time reduction
3. Manufacturing cells
4. Limited work in process
5. Quality improvement
6. Production flexibility
7. Little inventory storage

Small Lot Sizes. In the JIT philosophy, the ideal lot size is one unit, a quantity that may not always be realistic owing to practical considerations requiring minimum lot sizes (e.g., machines that process multiple items simultaneously, heat-treating equipment that processes multiple items simultaneously, and machines with very long setup times). Nevertheless, the goal is still to reduce the lot size as much as possible. Small lot sizes in both the production process and deliveries from suppliers yield a number of benefits that enable JIT systems to operate effectively. First, with small lots moving through the system, in-process inventory is considerably less than it is with large lots. This reduces carrying costs, space requirements, and clutter in the workplace. Second, inspection and rework costs are less when problems with quality occur, because there are fewer items in a lot to inspect and rework.

Small lots also permit greater flexibility in scheduling. Repetitive systems typically produce a small variety of products. In traditional systems, this usually means long production runs of each product, one after the other. Although this spreads the setup cost for a run over many items, it also results in long cycles over the entire range of products. For instance, suppose a firm has three product versions, A, B, and C. In a traditional system, there would be a long run of version A (e.g., covering two or three days or more), then a long run of version B, followed by a long run of version C before the sequence would repeat. In contrast, a JIT system, using small lots, would frequently shift from producing A to producing B and C. This flexibility enables JIT systems to respond more quickly to changing customer demands for output: JIT systems can produce just what is needed, when it is needed. The contrast between small and large lot sizes is illustrated in Figure 16–1. A summary of the benefits of small lot sizes is presented in Table 16–1.

FIGURE 16–1

JIT versus large-lot run sizes

A = units of product A
B = units of product B
C = units of product C

JIT approach

AAA   BBBBBBB   CC   AAA   BBBBBBB   CC   AAA   BBBBBBB   CC   AAA   BBBBBBB   CC

Time ⟶

Large-lot approach

AAAAAAAAAAAA   BBBBBBBBBBBBBBBBBBBBBBBBBBBB   CCCCCCCCC   AAAAAAAAAAAA

Time ⟶

TABLE 16–1

Benefits of small lot sizes

Reduces inventory, lowers carrying costs
Less space required to store inventory
Less rework if defects occur
Less inventory to "work off" before implementing product improvements
Problems are more apparent
Increases production flexibility
Easier to balance operations

It is important to note that the use of small lot sizes is not in conflict with the EOQ approach. The fact is that two aspects of the JIT philosophy support small lot sizes. One is that inventory holding cost is deemed to be high, but because this cost is based on the average inventory, inventory costs can be lowered by reducing the lot size, which reduces average inventory. Second, there is emphasis on reducing the setup cost. Thus, both higher holding costs and lower setup costs act to reduce the optimal lot size.

Setup Time Reduction. Small lots and changing product mixes require frequent setups. Unless these are quick and relatively inexpensive, the time and cost to accomplish them can be prohibitive. In JIT systems, workers are often trained to do their own setups. Moreover, programs to reduce setup time and cost are used to achieve the desired results; a deliberate effort is required, and workers are usually a valuable part of the process.

Setup tools and equipment and setup procedures must be simple and standardized. Multipurpose equipment or attachments can help to reduce setup time. For instance, a machine with multiple spindles that can easily be rotated into place for different job requirements can drastically reduce job changeover time. Moreover, *group technology* may be used to reduce setup cost and time by capitalizing on similarities in recurring operations. For instance, parts that are similar in shape, materials, and so on, may require very similar setups. Processing them in sequence on the same equipment can reduce the need to completely change a setup; only minor adjustment may be necessary.

www.ford.com

More than sixty years have passed since the introduction of Henry Ford's Model A with its all-steel body. Yet, across the world, nearly all motor-vehicle bodies are still produced by welding together about 300 metal parts stamped from sheet steel.

Auto makers have produced these "stampings" by employing one of two different methods. A few tiny craft producers, such as Aston Martin, cut sheets of metal—usually aluminum—to a gross shape, then beat these blanks by hand on a die to their final shape. (A die is simply a hard piece of metal in the precise shape the sheet metal should assume under pounding.)

Any producer making more than a few hundred cars a year—a category that includes auto makers ranging from Porsche to General Motors—starts with a large roll of sheet steel. They run this sheet through an automated "blanking" press to produce a stack of flat blanks slightly larger than the final part they want. They then insert the blanks in massive stamping presses containing matched upper and lower dies. When these dies are pushed together under thousands of pounds of pressure, the two-dimensional blank takes the three-dimensional shape of a car fender or a truck door as it moves through a series of presses.

The problem with this second method, from Ohno's perspective, was the minimum scale required for economical operation. The massive and expensive Western press lines were designed to operate at about twelve strokes per minute, three shifts a day, to make a million or more of a given part in a year. Yet, in the early days, Toyota's entire production was a few thousand vehicles a year.

The dies could be changed so that the same press line could make many parts, but doing so presented major difficulties. The dies weighed many tons each, and workers had to align them in the press with absolute precision. A slight misalignment produced wrinkled parts. A more serious misalignment could produce a nightmare in which the sheet metal melted in the die, necessitating extremely expensive and time-consuming repairs.

To avoid these problems, [Western manufacturers] assigned die changes to specialists. Die changes were undertaken methodically and typically required a full day to go from the last part with the old dies to the first acceptable part from the new dies. As volume in the Western industry soared after World War II, the industry found an even better solution to the die-change problem. Manufacturers found they often could "dedicate" a set of presses to a specific part and stamp these parts for months, or even years, without changing dies.

To Ohno, however, this solution was no solution at all. The dominant Western practice required hundreds of stamping presses to make all the parts in car and truck bodies, while Ohno's capital budget dictated that practically the entire car be stamped from a few press lines.

His idea was to develop simple die-change techniques and to change dies frequently—every two to three hours versus two to three months—using rollers to move dies in and out of position and simple adjustment mechanisms. Because the new techniques were easy to master and production workers were idle during the die changes, Ohno hit upon the idea of letting the production workers perform the die changes as well.

By purchasing a few used American presses and endlessly experimenting from the late 1940s onward, Ohno eventually perfected his technique for quick changes. By the late 1950s, he had reduced the time required to change dies from a day to an astonishing three minutes and eliminated the need for die-change specialists. In the process, he made an unexpected discovery—it actually cost less per part to make small batches of stampings than to run off enormous lots.

There were two reasons for this phenomenon. Making small batches eliminated the carrying cost of the huge inventories of finished parts that mass-production systems required. Even more important, making only a few parts before assembling them into a car caused stamping mistakes to show up almost instantly.

The consequences of this latter discovery were enormous. It made those in the stamping shop much more concerned about quality, and it eliminated the waste of large numbers of defective parts—which had to be repaired at great expense, or even discarded—that were discovered only long after manufacture. But to make this system work at all—a system that ideally produced two hours or less of inventory—Ohno needed both an extremely skilled and a highly motivated work force.

If workers failed to anticipate problems before they occurred and didn't take the initiative to devise solutions, the work of the whole factory could easily come to a halt. Holding back knowledge and effort—repeatedly noted by industrial sociologists as a salient feature of all mass-production systems—would swiftly lead to disaster in Ohno's factory.[2]

Manufacturing Cells. One characteristic of many JIT systems is multiple *manufacturing cells.* The cells contain the machines and tools needed to process families of parts having similar processing requirements. In essence, the cells are highly specialized and efficient production centers. Among the important benefits of manufacturing cells are reduced changeover times, high utilization of equipment, and ease of cross-training operators. The combination of high cell efficiency and small lot sizes results in very *little work-in-process inventory.*

Quality Improvement. The occurrence of quality defects during the process can disrupt the orderly flow of work. Consequently, problem solving is important when defects occur. Moreover, there is a never-ending quest for *quality improvement,* which often focuses on finding and eliminating the causes of problems so they do not continually crop up.

JIT systems sometimes minimize defects through the use of **autonomation** (note the extra syllable *on* in the middle of the word). Also referred to as **jidoka,** it involves the automatic detection of defects during production. It can be used with machines or manual operations. It consists of two mechanisms: one for detecting defects when they occur and another for stopping production to correct the cause of the defects. Thus, the halting of production forces immediate attention to the problem, after which an investigation of the problem is conducted, and corrective action is taken to resolve the problem.

autonomation Automatic detection of defects during production.

jidoka Japanese term for autonomation.

Production Flexibility. The overall goal of a JIT system is to achieve the ability to process a mix of products in a smooth flow. One potential obstacle to this goal is bottlenecks that occur when portions of the system become overloaded. The existence of bottlenecks reflects inflexibilities in a system. Process design can increase *production flexibility* and reduce bottlenecks in a variety of ways. Table 16–2 lists some of the techniques used for this purpose.

---

[2]Reprinted with permission of Rawson Associates/Scribner, a division of Simon & Schuster, Inc., from *The Machine That Changed the World,* by James P. Womack, Daniel T. Jones, and Daniel Roos. © 1990 by James P. Womack, Daniel T. Jones, Daniel Roos, and Donna Sammons Carpenter, pp. 51–53.

TABLE 16-2

Guidelines for increasing production flexibility

1. Reduce downtime due to changeovers by reducing changeover time.
2. Use preventive maintenance on key equipment to reduce breakdowns and downtime.
3. Cross-train workers so they can help when bottlenecks occur or other workers are absent. Train workers to handle equipment adjustments and minor repairs.
4. Use many small units of capacity; many small cells make it easier to shift capacity temporarily and to add or subtract capacity than a few units of large capacity.
5. Use off-line buffers. Store infrequently used safety stock away from the production area to decrease congestion and to avoid continually turning it over.
6. Reserve capacity for important customers.

Source: Adapted from Edward M. Knod Jr. and Richard J. Schonberger. *Operations Management: Meeting Customers' Demands,* 7th ed. (New York: McGraw-Hill, 2001).

A   B   C

FIGURE 16-2

Large rocks (problems) are hidden by a high water level (inventory) in A. Lower water level (B) reveals rocks. Once the large rocks are removed, the water level (inventory) can be lowered (C).

Inventory Storage. JIT systems are designed to *minimize* inventory storage. Recall that in the JIT philosophy, inventory storage is a waste. Inventories are buffers that tend to cover up recurring problems that are never resolved, partly because they aren't obvious and partly because the presence of inventory makes them seem less serious. When a machine breaks down, it won't disrupt the system if there is a sufficient inventory of the machine's output to feed into the next workstation. The use of inventory as the "solution" can lead to increasing amounts of inventory if breakdowns increase. A better solution is to investigate the *causes* of machine breakdowns and focus on eliminating them. Similar problems with quality, unreliable vendors, and scheduling can also be solved by having ample inventories to fall back on. However, carrying all that extra inventory creates a tremendous burden in cost and space and allows problems to go unresolved.

The JIT approach is to pare down inventories gradually in order to uncover the problems. Once they are uncovered and solved, the system removes more inventory, finds and solves additional problems, and so on. A useful analogy is a boat on a pond that has large, hidden rocks. (See Figure 16–2.) The rocks represent problems that can hinder production (the boat). The water in the pond that covers the rocks is the inventory in the system. As the water level is slowly lowered, the largest rocks are the first to appear (those problems are the first to be identified). At that point, efforts are undertaken to remove these rocks from the water (resolve these problems). Once that has been accomplished, additional water is removed from the pond, revealing the next layer of rocks, which are then worked on. As more rocks are removed, the need for water to cover them diminishes. Likewise, as more of the major production problems are solved, there is less need to rely on inventory.

Low inventories are the result of a *process* of successful problem solving, one that has occurred over time. Furthermore, because it is unlikely that all problems will be found and resolved, it is necessary to be able to deal quickly with problems when they do occur. Hence, there is a continuing need to identify and solve problems within a short time span to prevent new problems from disrupting the smooth flow of work through the system.

One way to minimize inventory storage in a JIT system is to have deliveries from suppliers go directly to the production floor, which completely eliminates the need to store incoming parts and materials. At the other end of the process, completed units are shipped out as soon as they are ready, which minimizes storage of finished goods. Coupled with low work-in-process inventory, these features result in systems that operate with very little inventory.

Among the advantages of lower inventory are less carrying cost, less space needed, less tendency to rely on buffers, less rework if defects occur, and less need to "work off" current inventory before implementing design improvements. But carrying less inventory also has some risks: The primary one is that if problems arise, there is no safety net. Another is missed opportunities if the system is unable to respond quickly to them.

READING

Pedal Pushers Tim Stevens

G *reen Gear Cycling adopts big-company, lean-manufacturing principles to produce custom bikes*

Across the street from the Fred Meyer store, behind a NAPA Auto Parts outlet in Eugene, Oregon, lies one of those gems you'd surely miss if you weren't looking for it. It's Green Gear Cycling Inc., manufacturer of Bike Friday, the largest-selling custom-made folding bike in the world. The bike fits into a car trunk, a tight storage space, or an optional suitcase to travel on a plane like regular baggage. (The suitcase even can be converted into a trailer to haul gear.) "Like Robinson Crusoe's man Friday, the Bike Friday is always there when you need it," says Alan Scholz, CEO.

Green Gear's operations are as distinctive as its product. A relatively small company ($3 million in sales, 30 employees, 17,000 sq. ft. of production space), Green Gear uses advanced manufacturing principles—adopted from Toyota Motor Corp. and others normally associated with considerably larger facilities. Management is split between Alan Scholz, who handles the business side, and his younger brother Hanz, product design and development manager.

Because of the uniqueness of its products, the company is able to command a premium price for them, and customers pay in advance. "It's not unusual for someone to call us with plane ticket in hand and say they are going on a trip, [and] can we have a bike ready for them in so many days," says Alan Scholz. "We can accommodate those kinds of requests, from decision-to-buy to riding in three days. Most bike manufacturers have terrible margins and huge leadtimes. They have no levers. We give people what they want, when they want it. If you do that, people are willing to pay you for it."

This year the company will build about 2,000 bikes to customer weight, measurements, and equipment specifications, at an average selling price of $1,700 including the optional case. Twenty-five percent of sales are to overseas customers, primarily in Japan, the UK, Australia, and Europe. On the list of Bike Friday riders are a nuclear weapons inspector who ordered a cycle specifically for his assignment in Iraq; David

Robinson, the center for the NBA's San Antonio Spurs; comedian Dick Smothers; Tour de France winner Greg LeMond; and a woman who is only 52 in. tall, demonstrating the range of vehicles produced. Bike Friday can be offered about 2.5 million different ways depending on size, components, and color. Folding, custom-made recumbent and tandem bikes also are available.

Build-to-Order Basics

Built individually, each Green Gear cycle begins its life as a bundle of tubes, components, and other structures. These are processed through a build-to-order, flow-manufacturing configuration that is organized in a series of cells, a production system the company deployed from the very start. "If you are a batch manufacturer, it's like pulling teeth to get lean and build in production cells," says Scholz. "If you start off that way, the people you hire just think that's the way it's done."

In the first cell, a U-shaped configuration, an operator works multiple pieces of dedicated equipment, all set to run automatically so that he can multitask. Here tubing is cut and shaped into frame members before moving to a welding cell. The cells are designed so that any one cell can do some of the work of the previous or next cell if production runs behind or ahead.

"It works like a track relay with a transition area," says Hanz Scholz. "We've set up everything with single-process–specific tools so there is no process changeover time, which is part of the Toyota Production System (TPS)." The flow motto is "touch it once, do it now." Once work on a bike has begun, it flows through the process without hesitation at any point.

Takt time, the time between completion of bikes at the end of the process, is adjusted based on how sales are going—another TPS concept based on producing to demand, not projection. "We look at sales velocity and set the takt time to deliver units at that rate," says Hanz Scholz. In May of this year the rate averaged one bike every 1.5 hours across the mix of different models (it takes about nine hours to build one bike). When a 50-bike order came in from a Japanese distributor, however, takt time was slashed to 27 minutes. Task-time reductions typically are accomplished with personnel from sales, service, and management departments supplemented with temps brought in to assist production.

Operating in a one-at-a-time flow system rather than in batches maximizes the chances for continuous improvement, according to Alan Scholz, who applies kaizen principles of continuous improvement to each bike. "For us, every bike is a batch, so we have 150 to 200 chances per month to make process improvements. A small manufacturer operating in a large-batch mode can be put out of business if he ruins just one. If you can make improvements as you find them, you can survive as a small manufacturer." When a quality problem is discovered, the operator switches on a red light and all procedures stop until the production cell is adjusted to eliminate the problem.

Stocking parts to cover the many variations of the bicycle would be far too costly for the company so, in lean-manufacturing style, inventory is handled kanban fashion, with parts reordered as they are used and minimum buffer stocks maintained based on vendor response time. Parts are pulled one bike at a time, three days before the ship date established by the customer, "just like Dell," says Scholz. "In fact the only difference between us and Dell is that you can't design a Bike Friday on the Internet … yet." (Michael Dell's wife Susan is a Bike Friday owner.)

"What's unique is that a company our size is handling inventory this way," says Scholz. "Many small companies feel it is too risky to operate like this, but we are proof that it can be successful." The kanban system replenishes inventory a little more often, "but it's a system that doesn't just order parts, it orders the right parts." Replenishing often so the company can operate at low inventory levels is an integral part of the cash-flow management expertise that helps make the company a success.

The company is in the process of moving to a "perpetual inventory" system that is expected to save thousands of dollars more in inventory. Parts will be reordered based on bikes sold, much as Kmart reorders based on sales rung at the cash register. "It's based on an MRP-type system, but without a lot of the things MRP requires," says Scholz. "Again, small companies tend not to have MRP because it costs too much." Green Gear's IS person is creating a system, based on a Microsoft Access database, to allow sales to "talk" to production. "The way it talks to production is through inventory. We'll be replacing inventory with information," Scholz notes.

Customers for Life

Lessons from Green Gear's success with lean manufacturing are applied to customer service and sales as well. Each sales consultant sits at a highly customized computer workstation, but with no desk. "That way it can't get cluttered up," says Hanz Scholz, "and for whatever they are doing, it encourages the 'touch it once, do it now' philosophy." Formerly housed in walled offices, the sales force now works in an open-office area. "If you have walls, you have barriers to the learning process," he adds. "Since we made the move, a lot of the fluctuations disappeared. Now all are selling in a similar way." And, since the change in September, sales are up 50%.

Green Gear practices a "Customers for Life" strategy it adopted from a luxury car dealer in Dallas. The dealer figured a customer that bought exclusively from him would spend in the neighborhood of $300,000 over his or her lifetime. "So," says Alan Scholz, "why nit-pick a $10 part?" A study of Bike Friday customers who have owned their bikes for more than three years shows there were repeat buys for other family members, adding a mountain bike or recumbent to the original "road" purchase, or upgrading to new technology. The company predicts a value of $10,000 to $25,000 for a lifetime customer. Therefore, it provides extra service at no cost when a bike comes in for repairs, or replaces a tire for free.

Source: Excerpted from Tim Stevens, "Pedal Pushers," *Industry Week*, July 17, 2000.

PERSONNEL/ORGANIZATIONAL ELEMENTS

There are five elements of personnel and organization that are particularly important for JIT systems:

1. Workers as assets
2. Cross-trained workers
3. Continuous improvement
4. Cost accounting
5. Leadership/project management

Workers as Assets. A fundamental tenet of the JIT philosophy is that *workers are assets*. Well-trained and motivated workers are the heart of a JIT system. They are given more authority to make decisions than their counterparts in more traditional systems, but they are also expected to do more.

"People" Firms Boost Profits, Study Shows

Companies that treat employees as valuable assets, invest in training programs and use innovative workplace practices are more profitable than those that don't, a study found.

The two-year look at the workplace strategies of American companies was conducted by the management consulting firm Ernst & Young LLP for the Labor Department.

"This is a path-breaking study that shows the surest way to profits and productivity is to treat employees as assets to be developed rather than costs to be cut," Labor Secretary Robert Reich said at a press conference.

For the study, researchers at Harvard and Wharton business schools in partnership with the Ernst & Young Center for Business Innovation, reviewed over 100 papers examining business practices of thousands of U.S. companies.

The report focused on the economic benefits to companies of such Japanese-inspired concepts of labor-management cooperation as Just-In-Time inventory, which moves components to factories only as they are needed.

Among the findings:

- Economic benefits to companies were greatest when they successfully integrated innovations in management and technology with the appropriate employee training and "empowerment" programs.

- Companies investing in employee development enjoy significantly higher market values on average than their industry peers.

- Companies that were first among their competitors in implementing new management practices reaped the largest rewards.

According to the study, Motorola, Inc. estimates it earns $30 for every $1 invested in employee training, while Xerox Corp. found that in cooperation with its employee union it has reduced manufacturing costs by 30 percent and halved the time needed to develop new products.

Cross-Trained Workers. Workers are *cross-trained* to perform several parts of a process and operate a variety of machines. This adds to system flexibility because workers are able to help one another when bottlenecks occur or when a co-worker is absent. It also helps line balancing.

Continuous Improvement. Workers in a JIT system have greater responsibility for quality than workers in traditional systems, and they are expected to be involved in problem solving and *continuous improvement*. JIT workers receive extensive training in statistical process control, quality improvement, and problem solving.

Problem solving is a cornerstone of any JIT system. Of interest are problems that interrupt, or have the potential to interrupt, the smooth flow of work through the system. When such problems surface, it becomes important to resolve them quickly. This may entail increasing inventory levels *temporarily* while the problem is investigated, but the intent of problem solving is to eliminate the problem, or at least greatly reduce the chances of it recurring.

andon System of lights used at each workstation to signal problems or slowdowns.

Problems that occur during production must be dealt with quickly. Some companies use a light system to signal problems; in Japan, such a system is called **andon.** Each workstation is equipped with a set of three lights. A green light means no problems, an amber light means a worker is falling a little bit behind, and a red light indicates a serious problem. The purpose of the light system is to keep others in the system informed and to enable workers and supervisors to immediately see when and where problems are occurring.

Japanese companies have been very successful in forming teams composed of workers and managers who routinely work on problems. Moreover, workers are encouraged to report problems and potential problems to the teams.

It is important that all levels of management actively support and become involved in problem solving. This includes a willingness to provide financial support and to recognize achievements. It is desirable to formulate goals with the help of workers, publicize the goals, and carefully document accomplishments. Goals give workers something tangible to strive for; recognition can help maintain worker interest and morale.

A central theme of a true just-in-time approach is to work toward continual improvement of the system—reducing inventories, reducing setup cost and time, improving quality, increasing the output rate, and generally cutting waste and inefficiency. Toward that end, problem solving becomes a way of life—a "culture" that must be assimilated into the thinking of management and workers alike. It becomes a never-ending quest for improving operations as all members of the organization strive to improve the system.

Workers in JIT systems have more stress than their counterparts in more traditional systems. Stress comes not only from their added authority and responsibility but also from the high-paced system they work in, where there is little slack and a continual push to improve.

Cost Accounting. Another feature of some JIT systems is the method of allocating overhead. Traditional accounting methods sometimes distort overhead allocation because they allocate it on the basis of direct labor hours. However, that approach does not always accurately reflect the consumption of overhead by different jobs. In addition, the number of direct labor hours in some industries has declined significantly over the years and now frequently accounts for a relatively small portion of the total cost. Conversely, other costs now represent a major portion of the total cost. Therefore, labor-intensive jobs (i.e., those that use relatively large proportions of direct labor) may be assigned a disproportionate share of overhead, one that does not truly reflect actual costs. That in turn can cause managers to make poor decisions. Furthermore, the need to track direct labor hours can itself involve considerable effort.

One alternative method of allocating overhead is **activity-based costing.** This method is designed to more closely reflect the actual amount of overhead consumed by a particular job or activity. Activity-based costing first identifies traceable costs and then assigns those costs to various types of activities such as machine setups, inspection, machine hours, direct labor hours, and movement of materials. Specific jobs are then assigned overhead based on the percentage of activities they consume.

activity-based costing Allocation of overhead to specific jobs based on their percentage of activities.

Leadership/Project Management. Another feature of JIT relates to *leadership.* Managers are expected to be leaders and facilitators, not order givers. JIT encourages two-way communication between workers and managers.

Project managers often have full authority over *all* phases of a project; they remain with the project from beginning to end. In the more traditional forms of project management, the project manager often has to rely on the cooperation of other managers to accomplish project goals.

MANUFACTURING PLANNING AND CONTROL

Six elements of manufacturing planning and control are particularly important for JIT systems:

1. Level loading
2. Pull systems
3. Visual systems
4. Close vendor relationships
5. Reduced transaction processing
6. Preventive maintenance and housekeeping

Level Loading. JIT systems place a strong emphasis on achieving stable, level daily mix schedules. Toward that end, the master production schedule is developed to provide *level capacity loading.* That may entail a rate-based production schedule instead of the more familiar quantity-based schedule. Moreover, once established, production schedules are relatively fixed over a short time horizon, and this provides certainty to the system. Even so, some adjustments may be needed in day-to-day schedules to achieve level capacity requirements. Suppliers like level loading because it means smooth demand for them.

A level production schedule requires smooth production. When a company produces different products or product models, it is desirable to produce in small lots (to minimize work-in-process inventory and to maintain flexibility) and to spread the production of the different products throughout the day to achieve smooth production. The extreme case would be to produce one unit of one product, then one of another, then one of another, and so on. While this approach would allow for maximum smoothness, it would generally not be practical because it would generate excessive setup costs.

Mixed-model sequencing begins with daily production requirements of each product or model. For instance, suppose a department produces three models, A, B, and C, with these daily requirements:

Model	Daily Quantity
A	10
B	15
C	5

There are three issues that need to be resolved. One is which sequence to use (C-B-A, A-C-B, etc.), another is how many times (i.e., cycles) the sequence should be repeated daily, and the third is how many units of each model to produce in each cycle.

The choice of sequence can depend on several factors, but the key one is usually the setup time or cost, which may vary depending on the sequence used. For instance, if two of the models, say A and C, are quite similar, the sequences A-C and C-A may involve only minimal setup changes, whereas the setup for model B may be more extensive. Choosing a sequence that has A-C or C-A will result in about 20 percent fewer setups over time than having B produced between A and C on every cycle.

The number of cycles per day depends on the daily production quantities. If every model is to be produced in every cycle, which is often the goal, determining the smallest integer that can be evenly divided into each model's daily quantity will indicate the number of cycles. This will be the fewest number of cycles that will contain one unit of the model with the lowest quantity requirements. For models A, B, and C shown in the preceding table, there should be five cycles (5 can be evenly divided into each quantity). High setup costs may cause a manager to use fewer cycles, trading off savings in setup costs and level production. If dividing by the smallest daily quantity does not yield an integer value for each model, a manager may opt for using the smallest production quantity to select a number of cycles, but then produce more of some items in some cycles to make up the difference.

Sometimes a manager determines the number of units of each model in each cycle by dividing each model's daily production quantity by the number of cycles. Using five cycles per day would yield the following:

Model	Daily Quantity	Units per Cycle
A	10	10/5 = 2
B	15	15/5 = 3
C	5	5/5 = 1

These quantities may be unworkable due to restrictions on lot sizes. For example, Model B may be packed four to a carton, so producing three units per cycle would mean that at times finished units (inventory) would have to wait until sufficient quantities were available to fill a crate. Similarly, there may be standard production lot sizes for some operations. A heat-treating process might involve a furnace that can handle six units at a time. If the different models require different furnace temperatures, they could not be grouped. What would be necessary here is an analysis of the trade-off between furnace lot size and the advantages of level production.

Example 1

Determine a production plan for these three models using the sequence A-B-C:

Model	Daily Quantity
A	7
B	16
C	5

Solution

The smallest daily quantity is 5, but dividing the other two quantities by 5 does not yield integers. The manager might still decide to use five cycles. Producing one unit of Models A and C and three units of Model B in each of the five cycles would leave the manager short two units of Model A and one unit of Model B. The manager might decide to intersperse those units like this to achieve nearly level production:

Cycle	1	2	3	4	5
Pattern	A B(3) C	A(2) B(3) C	A B(4) C	A(2) B(3) C	A B(3) C
Extra unit(s)		A	B	A	

If the requirement for Model A had been 8 units a day instead of 7, the manager might decide to use the following pattern:

Cycle	1	2	3	4	5
Pattern	A(2) B(3) C	A B(3) C	A(2) B(4) C	A B(3) C	A(2) B(3) C
Extra unit(s)	A		A B		A

Pull Systems. The terms *push* and *pull* are used to describe two different systems for moving work through a production process. In traditional production environments, a **push system** is used: When work is finished at a workstation, the output is *pushed* to the next station; or, in the case of the final operation, it is pushed on to final inventory. Conversely, in a **pull system,** control of moving the work rests with the following operation; each workstation *pulls* the output from the preceding station as it is needed; output of the final operation is pulled by customer demand or the master schedule. Thus, in a pull system, work moves on in response to demand from the next stage in the process, whereas in

push system Work is pushed to the next station as it is completed.

pull system A workstation pulls output from the preceding station as it is needed.

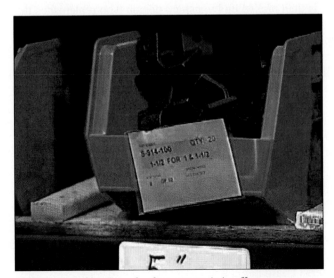

At TriState Industries, a kanban system is in effect to move work through the production system. Shown here, a kanban card provides the authorization to move or work on parts.

Special carts were designed that, when filled, act as a visual signal that they are ready to be moved to the next work cell. An empty cart indicates that it is time to produce, in order to refill the cart.

a push system, work moves on as it is completed, without regard to the next station's readiness for the work. Consequently, work may pile up at workstations that fall behind schedule because of equipment failure or the detection of a problem with quality.

JIT system communication moves backward through the system from station to station. Each workstation (i.e., customer) communicates its need for more work to the preceding workstation (i.e., supplier), thereby assuring that supply equals demand. Work moves "just in time" for the next operation; the flow of work is thereby coordinated, and the accumulation of excessive inventories between operations is avoided. Of course, some inventory is usually present because operations are not instantaneous. If a workstation waited until it received a request from the next workstation before starting its work, the next station would have to wait for the preceding station to perform its work. Therefore, by design, each workstation produces just enough output to meet the (anticipated) demand of the next station. This can be accomplished by having the succeeding workstation communicate its need for input sufficiently ahead of time to allow the preceding station to do the work. Or there can be a small buffer of stock between stations; when the buffer decreases to a certain level, this signals the preceding station to produce enough output to replenish the buffer supply. The size of the buffer supply depends on the cycle time at the preceding workstation. If the cycle time is short, the station will need little or no buffer; if the cycle time is long, it will need a considerable amount of buffer. However, production occurs only in response to *usage* of the succeeding station; work is *pulled* by the demand generated by the next operation.

Visual Systems. In a pull system work flow is dictated by "next-step demand." A system can communicate such demand in a variety of ways, including a shout or a wave, but by far the most commonly used device is the **kanban** card. *Kanban* is a Japanese word meaning "signal" or "visible record." When a worker needs materials or work from the preceding station, he or she uses a kanban card. In effect, the kanban card is the *authorization* to move or work on parts. In kanban systems, no part or lot can be moved or worked on without one of these cards.

The system works this way: A kanban card is affixed to each container. When a workstation needs to replenish its supply of parts, a worker goes to the area where these parts are stored and withdraws one container of parts. Each container holds a predetermined quantity. The worker removes the kanban card from the container and posts it in a designated spot where it will be clearly visible, and the worker moves the container to the workstation. The posted kanban is then picked up by a stock person who replenishes the stock with another container, and so on down the line. Demand for parts triggers a replenishment, and parts are supplied as usage dictates. Similar withdrawals and replenishments—all controlled by kanbans—occur all the way up and down the line from vendors to finished-goods inventories. If supervisors decide the system is too loose because inventories are building up, they may decide to tighten the system and withdraw some kanbans. Conversely, if the system seems too tight, they may introduce additional kanbans to bring the system into balance. Vendors can also influence the number of containers. Moreover, trip times can affect the number: Longer trip times may lead to fewer but larger containers, while shorter trip times may involve a greater number of small containers.

It is apparent that the number of kanban cards in use is an important variable. One can compute the ideal number of kanban cards using this formula:

$$N = \frac{DT(1 + X)}{C} \qquad (16–1)$$

where

N = Total number of containers (1 card per container)

D = Planned usage rate of using work center

T = Average waiting time for replenishment of parts plus average production time for a container of parts

kanban Card or other device that communicates demand for work or materials from the preceding station.

  X = Policy variable set by management that reflects possible inefficiency in the system (the closer to 0, the more efficient the system)

  C = Capacity of a standard container (should be no more than 10 percent of daily usage of the part)

Note that D and T must use the same units (e.g., minutes, days).

Usage at a work center is 300 parts per day, and a standard container holds 25 parts. It takes an average of .12 day for a container to complete a circuit from the time a kanban card is received until the container is returned empty. Compute the number of kanban cards (containers) needed if $X = .20$.

Example 2

$N = ?$

$D = 300$ parts per day

$T = .12$ day

$C = 25$ parts per container

$X = .20$

$$N = \frac{300(.12)(1 + .20)}{25} = 1.728 \text{ (round to two containers)}$$

Solution

Note: Rounding up will cause the system to be looser, and rounding down will cause it to be tighter. Usually, rounding up is used.

  Although the goals of MRP and kanban are essentially the same (i.e., to improve customer service, reduce inventories, and increase productivity), their approaches are different. Neither MRP nor kanban is a stand-alone system—each exists within a larger framework. MRP is basically a computerized system; kanban is a manual system.

  Kanban systems usually have very small lot sizes, short lead times, and high-quality output, and they exemplify teamwork. Kanban is essentially a two-bin type of inventory: Supplies are replenished semiautomatically when they reach a predetermined level. MRP is more concerned with projecting requirements and with planning and leveling capacity by means of the computer.

  A major benefit of the kanban system is its simplicity; a major benefit of MRP is its ability to handle complex planning and scheduling quickly and efficiently. It also handles changes fairly easily. In addition, MRP enables management to answer "what if" questions for capacity planning.

  The philosophies that underlie JIT systems are quite different from those traditionally held by manufacturers. Nonetheless, both approaches have their merits, so it probably would not make sense in most instances to switch from one method of operation to the other. Moreover, to do so would require a tremendous effort. It is noteworthy that at the same time that Western manufacturers are studying kanban systems, some Japanese manufacturers are studying MRP systems. This suggests the possibility that either system could be improved by incorporating selected elements of the other. That would take careful analysis to determine which elements to incorporate as well as carefully implementing selected elements, and close monitoring to assure that intended results were achieved.

  Whether manufacturers should adopt the kanban method is debatable. Some form of it may be useful, but kanban is merely an information system; by itself it offers little in terms of helping manufacturers become more competitive or productive. By the same token, MRP alone will not achieve those results either. Instead, it is the overall approach to manufacturing that is crucial; it is the commitment and support of top management and the continuing efforts of all levels of management to find new ways to improve their manufacturing planning and control techniques, and to adapt those techniques to fit their particular circumstances, that will determine the degree of success.

Comment. The use of either JIT or MRP does not preclude the use of the other. In fact, it is not unusual to find the two systems used in the same production facility. Some Japanese manufacturers, for example, are turning to MRP systems to help them plan production. Both approaches have their advantages and limitations. MRP systems provide the capability to explode the bill of materials to project timing and material requirements that can then be used to plan production. But the MRP assumption of fixed lead times and infinite capacity can often result in significant problems. At the shop floor level, the discipline of a JIT system, with materials pull, can be very effective. But JIT works best when there is a uniform flow through the shop; a variable flow requires buffers and this reduces the advantage of a pull system.

In effect, some situations are more conducive to a JIT approach, others to an MRP approach. Still others can benefit from a hybrid of the two.

READING

Developing the JIT Philosophy

uccessful implementation of JIT requires involvement from all levels of management in all disciplines

"Our improvement in just-in-time has to be credited to the involvement of higher management and management across many disciplines," says Tom Jensch, Avon's director of materials management.

Every two weeks, at Avon's headquarters in New York City, senior management holds an inventory meeting to discuss progress in JIT. Included in that meeting are top-level managers from finance, marketing, merchandising, purchasing and strategic planning.

"It's a working meeting," says Jensch. "You don't just go in and listen to how the inventory numbers came in at the end of the month. We talk about specific marketing plans for items. How risky are they from an inventory standpoint? What can we do to minimize the risk? We can end up affecting designs of new products by getting away from unique containers and using stock containers if that's important to reduce the inventory risks. We talk about marketing flow and what we are going to do if a product oversells or undersells."

Management involvement doesn't begin and end with that one meeting. "We hold a monthly meeting with lower levels of management and nonmanagement people where we process ideas that have come out of the senior management meeting," says Jensch. "We are working to come up with new ideas. In this meeting are the appropriate people from marketing, finance, purchasing and materials control who are actually the hands-on inventory people. They are much closer to the front lines. It's a communication meeting, to share information and then follow up on various inventory projects we have initiated."

In addition, management from New York meets with inventory control people from Avon's three manufacturing facilities every six weeks. "The purpose of these meetings is to review inventory progress with the manufacturing facilities, to bring to them some of the new ideas that have been stimulated here in New York, to hear from them the new ideas and opportunities that they've identified and to see how we can work together to best process those ideas," says Jensch.

One of the ideas that went through this process and was implemented was the Vendor Proximity Program—the development of suppliers closer to Avon's manufacturing facilities. "Personnel at Avon's manufacturing plant in Suffern, N.Y., were having great success with JIT and we realized that all of the plant's suppliers were within a one-day transit time," says Jensch. After discussing this at inventory meetings, the company decided to seek vendors closer to its other two manufacturing sites in Morton Grove, Ill., and Springdale, Ohio.

Source: Reprinted with permission of *Purchasing,* September 1990. © 1990 by Cahners Publishing Company.

Close Vendor Relationships. JIT systems typically have *close relationships with vendors,* who are expected to provide frequent small deliveries of high-quality goods. Traditionally, buyers have assumed the role of monitoring the quality of purchased goods, inspecting shipments for quality and quantity, and returning poor-quality goods to the vendor for rework. JIT systems have little slack, so poor-quality goods cause a disruption in the smooth flow of work. Moreover, the inspection of incoming goods is viewed as inefficient because it does not add value to the product. For these reasons, the burden of ensuring quality shifts to the vendor. Buyers work with vendors to help them achieve the desired quality levels and to impress upon them the importance of consistent, high-quality goods. The ultimate goal of the buyer is to be able to *certify* a vendor as a producer of high-quality goods. The implication of certification is that a vendor can be relied on to deliver high-quality goods without the need for buyer inspection.

Suppliers must also be willing and able to ship in small lots on a regular basis. Ideally, suppliers themselves will be operating under JIT systems. Buyers can often help suppliers convert to JIT production based on their own experiences. In effect, the supplier becomes part of an extended JIT system that integrates the facilities of buyer and supplier. Integration is easier when a supplier is dedicated to only one or a few buyers. In practice, a supplier is likely to have many different buyers, some using traditional systems and others using JIT. Consequently, compromises may have to be made by both buyers and suppliers.

Traditionally, a spirit of cooperation between buyer and seller has not been present; buyers and vendors have had a somewhat adversarial relationship. Buyers have generally regarded price as a major determinant in sourcing, and they have typically used *multiple-source* purchasing, which means having a list of potential vendors and buying from several to avoid getting locked into a sole source. In this way, buyers play vendors off against each other to get better pricing arrangements or other concessions. The downside is that vendors cannot rely on a long-term relationship with a buyer, and they feel no loyalty to a particular buyer. Furthermore, vendors have often sought to protect themselves from losing a buyer by increasing the number of buyers they supply.

Under JIT purchasing, good vendor relationships are very important. Buyers take measures to reduce their lists of suppliers, concentrating on maintaining close working relationships with a few good ones. Because of the need for frequent, small deliveries, many buyers attempt to find local vendors to shorten the lead time for deliveries and to reduce lead time variability. An added advantage of having vendors nearby is quick response when problems arise.

JIT purchasing is enhanced by long-term relationships between buyers and vendors. Vendors are more willing to commit resources to the job of shipping according to a buyer's JIT system given a long-term relationship. Moreover, price often becomes secondary to other aspects of the relationship (e.g., consistent high quality, flexibility, frequent small deliveries, and quick response to problems).

Suppliers. A key feature of many lean production systems is the relatively small number of suppliers used. In traditional production, companies often deal with hundreds or even thousands of suppliers in a highly centralized arrangement not unlike a giant wheel with many spokes. The company is at the hub of the wheel, and the spokes radiate out to suppliers, each of whom must deal directly with the company. In traditional systems, a supplier does not know the other suppliers or what they are doing. Each supplier works to specifications provided by the buyer. Suppliers have very little basis (or motivation) for suggesting improvements. Moreover, as companies play one supplier off against others, the sharing of information is more risky than rewarding. In contrast, lean production companies may employ a tiered approach for suppliers: They use relatively few first-tier suppliers who work directly with the company or who supply major subassemblies. The first-tier suppliers are responsible for dealing with second-tier suppliers who provide components for the subassemblies, thereby relieving the final buyer from dealing with large numbers of suppliers.

The automotive industry provides a good example of this situation. Suppose a certain car model has an electric seat. The seat and motor together might entail 250 separate parts. A traditional producer might use more than 50 suppliers for the electric seat, but a lean producer might use a single (first-tier) supplier who has the responsibility for the entire seat unit. The company would provide specifications for the overall unit, but leave to the supplier the details of the motor, springs, and so on. The first-tier supplier, in turn, might subcontract the motor to a second-tier supplier, the track to another second-tier supplier, and the cushions and fabric to still another. The second-tier suppliers might subcontract some of their work to third-tier suppliers, and so on. Each tier has only to deal with those just above it or just below it. Suppliers on each level are encouraged to work with each other, and they are motivated to do so because that increases the probability that the resulting item (the seat) will meet or exceed the final buyer's expectations. In this "team of suppliers" approach, all suppliers benefit from a successful product, and each supplier bears full responsibility for the quality of its portion of the product. Figure 16–3 illustrates the difference between the traditional approach and the tiered approach.

FIGURE 16–3

Traditional supplier network compared to supplier tiers

a. **Traditional**

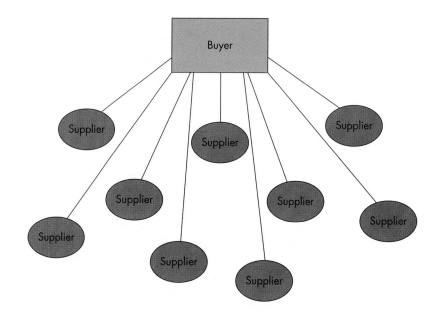

b. **Tiered**

First tier supplier

Second tier suppliers

Third tier suppliers

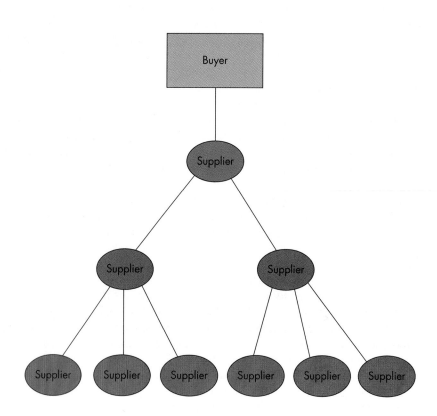

Reduced Transaction Processing. Traditional manufacturing systems often have many built-in transactions that do not add value. In their well-known article, "The Hidden Factory,"[3] Jeffrey G. Miller and Thomas Vollmann identify a laundry list of transaction processing that comprises a "hidden factory" in traditional manufacturing planning and control systems, and point out the tremendous cost burden that results. The transactions can be classified as logistical, balancing, quality, or change transactions.

Logistical transactions include ordering, execution, and confirmation of materials transported from one location to another. Related costs cover shipping and receiving personnel, expediting orders, data entry, and data processing.

Balancing transactions include forecasting, production planning, production control, procurement, scheduling, and order processing. Associated costs relate to the personnel involved in these and supporting activities.

Quality transactions include determining and communicating specifications, monitoring, recording, and followup activities. Costs relate to appraisal, prevention, internal failures (e.g., scrap, rework, retesting, delays, administration activities) and external failures (e.g., warranty costs, product liability, returns, potential loss of future business).

Change transactions primarily involve engineering changes and the ensuing changes generated in specifications, bills of material, scheduling, processing instructions, and so on. Engineering changes are among the most costly of all transactions.

JIT systems cut transaction costs by reducing the number and frequency of transactions. For example, suppliers deliver goods directly to the production floor, bypassing the storeroom entirely, thereby avoiding the transactions related to receiving the shipment into inventory storage and later moving the materials to the production floor. In addition, vendors are certified for quality, eliminating the need to inspect incoming shipments for quality. The unending quest for quality improvement that pervades JIT systems eliminates many of the above-mentioned quality transactions and their related costs. The use of bar coding (not exclusive to JIT systems) can reduce data entry transactions and increase data accuracy.

Preventive Maintenance and Housekeeping. Because JIT systems have very little in-process inventory, equipment breakdowns can be extremely disruptive. To minimize breakdowns, companies use **preventive maintenance** programs, which emphasize maintaining equipment in good operating condition and replacing parts that have a tendency to fail before they fail. Workers are often responsible for maintaining their own equipment.

preventive maintenance Maintaining equipment in good operating condition and replacing parts which have a tendency to fail before they actually do fail.

Even with preventive maintenance, occasional equipment failures will occur. Companies must be prepared for this, so they can quickly return equipment to working order. This may mean maintaining supplies of critical spare parts and making other provisions for emergency situations, perhaps maintaining a small force of repair people or training workers to do certain repairs themselves. Note that when breakdowns do occur, they indicate potential opportunities to be exploited in a JIT environment.

Housekeeping involves keeping the workplace clean as well as keeping it free of any materials that are not needed for production, because those materials take up space and may cause disruptions to the work flow.

housekeeping Maintaining a workplace that is clean and free of unnecessary materials.

The goals and building blocks of JIT are summarized in Figure 16–4.

JIT systems have been described and compared with traditional manufacturing systems in the preceding pages. Table 16–3 on pg. 707 provides a brief overview of those comparisons.

Converting to a JIT System

The success of JIT systems in Japan has attracted keen interest among U.S. manufacturers. A number of well-known firms have converted a portion of their operations to JIT systems.

---

[3]Jeffrey G. Miller and Thomas Vollmann, "The Hidden Factory," *Harvard Business Review,* September–October 1985, pp. 141–50.

FIGURE 16-4

Summary of JIT goals and building blocks
Source: Adapted from Thomas E. Vollmann, William L. Berry, and D. Clay Whybark, *Manufacturing Planning and Control Systems,* 3rd ed. (Burr Ridge, IL: Richard D. Irwin, 1992), p. 76.

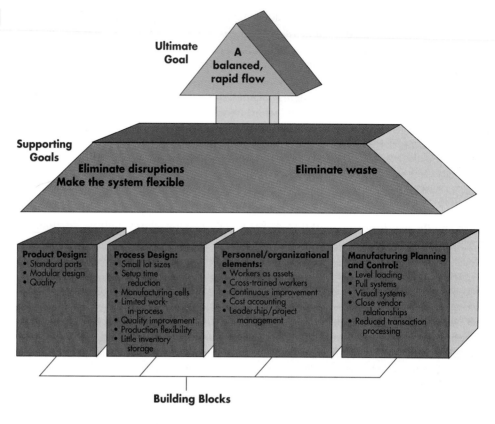

PLANNING A SUCCESSFUL CONVERSION

To increase the probability of successful conversion, companies should adopt a carefully planned approach that includes the following elements:

1. Make sure top management is committed to the conversion and that they know what will be required. Make sure that management is involved in the process and knows what it will cost, how long it will take to complete the conversion, and what results can be expected.

2. Study the operations carefully; decide which parts will need the most effort to convert.

3. Obtain the support and cooperation of workers. Prepare training programs that include sessions in setups, maintenance of equipment, cross-training for multiple tasks, cooperation, and problem solving. Make sure workers are fully informed about what JIT is and why it is desirable. Reassure workers that their jobs are secure.

4. Begin by trying to reduce setup times while maintaining the current system. Enlist the aid of workers in identifying and eliminating existing problems (e.g., bottlenecks, poor quality).

5. Gradually convert operations, beginning at the *end* of the process and working *backward.* At each stage, make sure the conversion has been relatively successful before moving on. Do not begin to reduce inventories until major problems have been resolved.

6. As one of the last steps, convert suppliers to JIT and be prepared to work closely with them. Start by narrowing the list of vendors, identifying those who are willing to embrace the JIT philosophy. Give preference to vendors who have long-term track records of reliability. Use vendors located nearby if quick response time is important. Establish long-term commitments with vendors. Insist on high standards of quality and adherence to strict delivery schedules.

7. Be prepared to encounter obstacles to conversion, which are discussed next.

Factors	JIT	Traditional Philosophy
Inventory	A liability. Every effort must be expended to do away with it.	An asset. It protects against forecast errors, machine problems, late vendor deliveries. More inventory is "safer."
Lot size	Immediate needs only. A minimum replenishment quantity is desired for both manufactured and purchased parts.	Formulas.
Setups	Make them insignificant. This requires either extremely rapid changeover to minimize the impact on production or the availability of extra machines already set up. Fast changeover makes small lot sizes practical and allows the frequent manufacture of a wide variety of parts.	Low priority issue. Maximum output is the usual goal. Rarely does similar thought and effort go into achieving quick changeover.
Queues	Eliminate them. When problems occur, identify the causes and correct them. The correction process is aided when queues are small.	Necessary investment. Queues permit following operations to continue in the event of a problem with the feeding operation. By providing a selection of jobs, factory management has a greater opportunity to match varying operator skills and machine capabilities, combine setups, and contribute to the efficiency of the operation.
Vendors	Coworkers; part of the team. Multiple deliveries for all active items are expected daily. The vendor takes care of the needs of the customer, and the customer treats the vendor as an extension of the factory.	Adversaries. Multiple sources are the rule, and it's typical to play them off against each other.
Quality	Zero defects. If quality is not 100 percent, production is in jeopardy.	Tolerate some scrap.
Equipment maintenance	Constant and effective. Machine breakdowns must be minimal.	As required. Not critical because of queues.
Lead times	Keep them short. This simplifies the jobs of marketing, purchasing, and manufacturing, as it reduces the need for expediting.	The longer the better. Most foremen and purchasing agents want more lead time, not less.
Workers	Management by consensus. Changes are not made until consensus is reached, with or without a bit of arm twisting. The vital ingredient of "ownership" is achieved.	Management by edict. New systems are installed in spite of the workers, not thanks to the workers. Then measurements are used to determine whether or not they're doing their jobs.

Source: Reprinted with permission of *Modern Materials Handling*, June 1982. © 1982 by Cahners Publishing Company.

TABLE 16-3

Comparison of JIT and traditional manufacturing philosophies

OBSTACLES TO CONVERSION

Converting from a traditional system to a JIT system may not be smooth. For example, *cultures* vary from organization to organization. Some cultures relate better to the JIT philosophy than others. If a culture doesn't relate, it can be difficult for an organization to change its culture within a short time. Also, manufacturers that operate with large amounts of inventory to handle varying customer demand may have difficulty acclimating themselves to less inventory.

Some other obstacles include the following:

1. Management may not be totally committed or may be unwilling to devote the necessary resources to conversion. This is perhaps the most serious impediment because the conversion is probably doomed without serious commitment.

2. Workers and/or management may not display a cooperative spirit. The system is predicated on cooperation. Managers may resist because JIT shifts some of the responsibility from management to workers and gives workers more control over the work. Workers may resist because of the increased responsibility and stress.

3. Suppliers may resist for several reasons:

   a. Buyers may not be willing to commit the resources necessary to help them adapt to the JIT systems.

b. They may be uneasy about long-term commitments to a buyer.

c. Frequent, small deliveries may be difficult, especially if the supplier has other buyers who use traditional systems.

d. The burden of quality control will shift to the supplier.

e. Frequent engineering changes may result from continuing JIT improvements by the buyer.

Comment. JIT systems require a cooperative spirit among workers, management, and vendors. Unless that is present, it is doubtful that a truly effective JIT system can be achieved. The Japanese have been very successful in this regard, partly because respect and cooperation are ingrained in the Japanese culture. In Western cultures, workers, managers, and vendors have historically been strongly at odds with each other. Consequently, a major consideration in converting to a JIT system is whether a spirit of mutual respect and cooperation can be achieved. This requires an appreciation of the importance of cooperation and a tenacious effort by management to instill and maintain that spirit.

The Downside of Conversion. Despite the many advantages of JIT production systems, an organization must take into account a number of other considerations when planning a conversion.

The key considerations are the time and cost requirements for successful conversion, which can be substantial. But it is absolutely essential to eliminate the major sources of disruption in the system. Management must be prepared to commit the resources necessary to achieve a high level of quality and to function on a tight schedule. That means attention to even the smallest of details during the design phase and substantial efforts to debug the system to the point where it runs smoothly. Beyond that, management must be capable of responding quickly when problems arise, and both management and workers must be committed to the continuous improvement of the system. Although each case is different, a general estimate of the time required for conversion is one to three years.

Another consideration pertains to small lot sizes. While small lot sizes allow flexibility in changing the product mix and reduced carrying costs and space requirements, they typically result in (1) increased transportation costs and (2) traffic congestion due to frequent deliveries.

Also, converting to a JIT system can sometimes be a formidable undertaking, as illustrated by the following reading. Hence, firms must decide whether a JIT approach will be advantageous.

READING

JIT and Quality: A Perfect Fit

A company that plans to implement just-in-time manufacturing must have an established quality program to use as a foundation, according to several quality leaders in the chemical industry.

"Just-in-time is an integral part of the quality process," says Theodore C. Kuchler, quality manager, Chemicals and Pigments Dept., Du Pont Co. "It is a tool that can be used to accomplish continuous improvement."

From New York to Japan the words "continuous improvement" can be found in corporate literature describing quality programs. But where does just-in-time, or JIT, come into play, particularly in the chemical process industry?

Loosely defined, JIT is a manufacturing concept which eliminates anything that does not add value to the product. Successful quality programs revolve around strong supplier relationships—with purchasing playing a critical role—and top management commitment. And JIT is no different.

"There is a misconception of what just-in-time truly is," says Thomas Cummins, manager, total quality, Monsanto Chemical Co. "The heart of just-in-time is process capability, and the very first need is a stable, capable and predictable process effort."

In order to achieve a capable and predictable process, most companies feel an emphasis on quality is necessary. "Quality and just-in-time are interrelated," says David E. Winkler, vice president, manufacturing convenience meals, Campbell Soup Co.

"Companies can say they have just-in-time, but if they don't have a reliable system in place that is compatible with the just-in-time concept, then they are not going to be very successful," he says.

JIT and quality work well together because both strive to improve the way companies operate. JIT, unlike the quality process, cannot stand alone over the long haul. It is considered by many to be part of the quality process, rather than vice versa.

"Just-in-time without quality?" asks Neal Kane, quality manager, specialty chemicals, Du Pont Co. "It may be possible, but it is very risky. There would be limits as to how far a company could proceed without a quality process."

"You could say you have just-in-time without the quality process," says Gary Childers, manager of quality, planning and administration, Union Carbide Corp. "But eventually the system would break down because you would be placing too much of a demand on it. You need to have the quality process."

Source: Excerpt from "JIT and Quality: A Perfect Fit." Reprinted with permission of *CPI Purchasing,* September 1990. © 1990 by Cahners Publishing Company.

JIT in Services

The discussion of just-in-time has focused on manufacturing simply because that is where it was developed, and where it has been used most often. Nonetheless, services can and do benefit from many JIT concepts. When just-in-time is used in the context of services, the focus is often on the time needed to perform a service—because speed is often an important order winner for services. Some services do have inventories of some sort, so inventory reduction is another aspect of JIT that can apply to services. Examples of speedy delivery ("available when requested") are Domino's Pizza, Federal Express and Express Mail, fast-food restaurants, and emergency services through 911. The following reading describes another example of JIT delivery. Other examples include just-in-time publishing and work cells at fast-food restaurants.

www.dominos.com
www.fedex.com

READING

Box Maker Keeps the Lid on Lead Times

Al Johnson of Davidson Exterior Trim in Americus, Ga., thinks Georgia Box is the best in the business.

"It's our number-one supplier as far as JIT delivery is concerned; it's never early or late," says Johnson. "Moreover, its lead time on any size box is three or four days; other box makers want at least two weeks. And in a pinch we can call in the morning and get boxes by the afternoon."

Davidson (a division of Textron) makes bumpers and fascias for GM and Chrysler—as many as 14,000 bumpers a day when auto business is going strong. That means Davidson needs a lot of boxes, in different sizes but mostly big boxes. A two-week supply could easily fill 50,000 square feet of warehouse space. But thanks to JIT delivery from Georgia Box, only half that space is utilized today, even though the daily production rate is twice what it used to be. In a good year, Davidson would spend as much as $2 million on corrugated boxes.

How is Georgia Box able to offer shorter lead times than other box makers? Short setup times. According to Georgia Box's president, Stanley Walker, setup times can vary from 30 seconds to 15 minutes tops. The industry norm is anywhere from a half-hour to an hour.

Setups are all computerized, says Walker. "For repeat orders, all one has to do is punch in three numbers; for new orders, box dimensions need to be keyed into the computer. With a traditional manual system, you had to go in with wrenches, adjust the scoring, and set ink registrations.

"Very few sheet plants have this type of computerized equipment," adds Walker. "We can produce 50 million square feet of box board per month on one shift." Even the big-time corrugators would be impressed.

Sheet plants, corrugators—that's how the box business is divided up. The latter group comprises the large integrated paper mills that make their own linerboard as well as corrugated boxes, while the much smaller sheet plants buy their board from the corrugators. Sheet plants handle low-volume orders, while the corrugators prefer big production runs.

With short setup times, Georgia Box is able to handle both types of businesses. Since putting in the computerized equipment three years ago, its sales have doubled, from $18 million to $36 million.

Source: Reprinted with permission of *Purchasing,* September 1990. © 1990 by Cahners Publishing Company.

Process improvement and problem solving can contribute to streamlining a system, resulting in increased customer satisfaction and higher productivity. Some of the ways JIT benefits can be achieved in services are:

- Eliminate disruptions. For example, try to avoid having workers who are servicing customers also answer telephones.

- Make the system flexible. This can cause problems unless approached carefully. Often, it is desirable to standardize work because that can yield high productivity. On the other hand, being able to deal with variety in task requirements can be a competitive advantage. One approach might be to train workers so that they can handle more variety. Another might be to assign work according to specialties, with certain workers handling different types of work according to their specialty.

- Reduce setup times and processing times. Have frequently used tools and spare parts readily available. Additionally, for service calls, try to estimate what parts and supplies might be needed so they will be on hand, and avoid carrying huge inventories.

- Eliminate waste. This includes errors and duplicate work. Keep the emphasis on quality and uniform service.

- Minimize work-in-process. Examples include orders waiting to be processed, calls waiting to be answered, packages waiting to be delivered, trucks waiting to be unloaded or loaded, applications waiting to be processed.

- Simplify the process, especially when customers are part of the system (self-service systems including retail operations, ATM and vending machines, service stations, etc.).

JIT service can be a major competitive advantage for companies that can achieve it. An important key to JIT service is the ability to provide service when it is needed. That requires flexibility on the part of the provider, which generally means short setup times, and it requires clear communication on the part of the requester. If a requester can determine when it will need a particular service, a JIT server can schedule deliveries to correspond

At Duke University Medical Center, the supplies for a bypass operation arrive from Baxter International packaged in the order in which they will be used during surgery. Baxter provides this computer-based service along with the supplies, giving it a competitive advantage in the hospital supply industry.

www.baxter.com

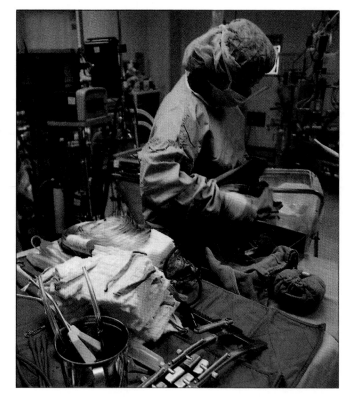

to those needs, eliminating the need for continual requests, and reducing the need for provider flexibility—and therefore probably reducing the cost of the JIT service.

JIT Purchasing

The use of just-in-time manufacturing techniques has created new challenges for purchasing. At the same time, it has made some aspects of purchasing easier. Having fewer supplies to deal with and being able to develop long-term relationships with suppliers are among the easier parts. Having to change from traditional thinking and practices and having to ensure that suppliers make frequent, on-time delivery of small quantities of the needed quality are among the challenges.

JIT II

JIT II is a term that has been applied to the practice of allowing vendors to manage some aspects of buying their products or services for the buyer, as described in the reading below.

Operations Strategy

The JIT philosophy of production offers new perspectives on manufacturing that must be given serious consideration by managers in repetitive manufacturing who wish to be competitive.

Potential adopters should carefully study the requirements and benefits of lean production systems, as well as the difficulties and strengths of their current systems, before making a decision on whether to convert to JIT. Careful estimates of time and cost to convert, and an assessment of how likely workers, managers, and suppliers are to cooperate in such an approach, are essential.

The decision to convert can be sequential, giving management an opportunity to gain firsthand experience with portions of JIT without wholly committing themselves. For instance, improving vendor relations, reducing setup times, improving quality, and reducing waste and inefficiency are desirable goals in themselves. Moreover, a level production schedule is a necessary element of a JIT system, and achieving that will also be useful under a traditional system of operation.

Supply chain management is critical to a JIT operation. There must be close coordination between suppliers and their customers throughout the supply chain. Generally, suppliers are located nearby to facilitate delivery on a daily or even hourly basis. Moreover, suppliers at every stage must gauge the ability of their production facilities to meet demand requirements that are subject to change.

READING

JIT II

JIT II is a philosophy that involves empowering suppliers to assume some of the responsibilities ordinarily done by a company's own buyers. Those responsibilities might include planning, transaction processing, and dealing with quality and delivery on problems that relate to a supplier's products. In some instances, that means having supplier personnel on-site while in others those responsibilities are managed through electronic links from the supplier's site.

Bose Corporation, a producer of premium audio products, began empowering suppliers in the mid-1980s. Lance Dixon, director of purchasing and logistics, dubbed it JIT II. To him, JIT II was a natural extension of the philosophies of agile manufacturing, namely JIT, partnering, and concurrent engineering. Under JIT II, suppliers have access to design engineers; sometimes, support personnel are even permitted to pursue their own engineering change orders.

Bose Corporation has worked to shorten and improve its supply chain both by empowering suppliers and by using direct marketing, including significant focus on the design and quality of the product, to distribute directly to the customer.

The advantages of empowering suppliers include enhanced communications, elimination of redundant steps, improved planning and fulfillment of materials requirements, early supplier involvement in new product planning and design, less inventory, and cost reductions for both supplier and customer. Some of the risks include possible exposure of proprietary technology, reliance on the supplier's personnel to fill gaps in technical knowledge, and supplier complacency.

The list of companies that have embraced this philosophy in at least some portion of their operations is impressive. In addition to Bose, it includes IBM, Honeywell, Intel, and Ingersoll-Rand.

Source: Based on "JIT II Comes of Age," pp. 41–46. Reprinted with permission of *Purchasing,* October 1994. © 1994 by Cahners Publishing Company.

Summary

Just-in-time (JIT) is a system of lean production used mainly in repetitive manufacturing, in which goods move through the system and tasks are completed just in time to maintain the schedule. JIT systems require very little inventory because successive operations are closely coordinated.

The ultimate goal of a JIT system is to achieve a balanced, smooth flow of production. Supporting goals include eliminating disruptions to the system, making the system flexible, reducing setup and lead times, eliminating waste, and minimizing inventories. The building blocks of a JIT system are product design, process design, personnel and organization, and manufacturing planning and control.

Lean systems require the elimination of sources of potential disruption to the even flow of work. High quality is essential because problems with quality can disrupt the process. Quick, low-cost setups, special layouts, allowing work to be pulled through the system rather than pushed through, and a spirit of cooperation are important features of lean systems. So, too, are problem solving aimed at reducing disruptions and making the system more efficient, and an attitude of working toward continual improvement.

Key benefits of JIT/lean systems are reduced inventory levels, high quality, flexibility, reduced lead times, increased productivity and equipment utilization, reduced amounts of scrap and rework, and reduced space requirements. The risks stem from the absence of buffers, such as extra personnel and inventory stockpiles to fall back on if something goes wrong. The possible results of risks include lost sales and lost customers.

Careful planning and much effort is needed to achieve a smoothly functioning system in which all resources needed for production come together at precisely the right time throughout the process. Raw materials and purchased parts must arrive when needed, fabricated parts and subassemblies must be ready when needed for final assembly, and finished goods must be delivered to customers when needed. Special attention must be given to reducing the risk of disruptions to the system as well as rapid response to resolving any disruptions that do occur. Usually, a firm must redesign its facilities and rework labor contracts to implement JIT. Teamwork and cooperation are important at all levels, as are problem-solving abilities of workers and an attitude of continuous improvement. This method views production and management processes in a very different way.

Table 16–4 provides an overview of JIT.

TABLE 16–4

Overview of JIT

JIT originally referred to the timing of movement of materials in a production system to meet customer demand, whether the "customer" was the final consumer or another operation in the production process. It became known for having minimal inventories. It has now come to mean operating a balanced system with minimum waste. In the JIT philosophy, there are seven types of waste:

Waste from overproduction.
Waste of waiting time.
Transportation waste.
Processing waste.
Inventory waste.
Waste of motion.

Elements of JIT include:

Smooth flow of work (the ultimate goal).
Elimination of waste.
Continuous improvement.
Eliminating anything that does not add value.
Simple systems that are easy to manage.
Use of product layouts that minimize time spent moving materials and parts.
Quality at the source: each worker is responsible for the quality of his or her output.
Poka-yoke: fail–safe tools and methods to prevent mistakes.
Preventive maintenance to reduce the risk of equipment breakdown.
Good housekeeping: an orderly and clean workplace.
Set-up time reduction.
Cross-trained workers.
A pull system.

Key Terms

activity-based costing, 697
andon, 696
autonomation, 692
housekeeping, 705
jikoda, 692
just-in-time (JIT), 684

kanban, 700
poka-yoke, 713
preventive maintenance, 705
pull system, 699
push system, 699

Solved Problems

Problem 1

Solution

Determine the number of containers needed for a workstation that uses 100 parts per hour if the time for a container to complete a cycle (move, wait, empty, return, fill) is 90 minutes and a standard container holds 84 parts. An efficiency factor of .10 is currently being used.

$N = ?$
$D = 100$ parts per hour
$T = 90$ minutes (1.5 hours)
$C = 84$ parts
$X = .10$

$$N = \frac{D(T)(1 + X)}{C} = \frac{100(1.5)(1 + .10)}{84} = 1.96 \text{ (round to 2) containers}$$

Problem 2

Determine the number of cycles per day and the production quantity per cycle for this set of products. The department operates five days a week. Assume the sequence A-B-C-D will be used.

Product	Weekly Quantity
A	20
B	40
C	30
D	15

Solution

Convert weekly quantities to daily quantities, and you find that the smallest *daily* quantity is 3 units.

Product	Daily Quantity = Weekly Quantity ÷ 5	Units Short Using 3 Cycles
A	20 ÷ 5 = 4	1
B	40 ÷ 5 = 8	2
C	30 ÷ 5 = 6	–
D	15 ÷ 5 = 3	–

Use three cycles, producing all four products in every cycle. Produce units that are short by adding units to some cycles. Disperse the additional units as evenly as possible. There are several possibilities. One is

Cycle	1	2	3
Pattern	A B(3) C(2) D	A B(3) C(2) D	A(2) B(2) C(2) D
Extra unit(s)	B	B	A

Discussion and Review Questions

1. Some key elements of production systems are listed in Table 16–3. Explain briefly how JIT systems differ from traditional production systems for each of those elements.

2. What is the ultimate goal of a JIT system? What are the supporting goals? What are the building blocks?

3. Describe the philosophy that underlies JIT (i.e., what is JIT intended to accomplish?).

4. What are some of the main obstacles that must be overcome in converting from a traditional system to JIT?

5. Briefly discuss vendor relations in JIT systems in terms of the following issues:
   a. Why are they important?
   b. How do they tend to differ from the more adversarial relations of the past?
   c. Why might suppliers be hesitant about JIT purchasing?

6. Certain Japanese have claimed that Henry Ford's assembly line provided some of the rationale for JIT. What features of assembly lines are common to JIT systems?

7. What is the kanban aspect of a JIT system?

8. Contrast push and pull methods of moving goods and materials through production systems.

9. What are the main benefits of a JIT system?

10. What is the hidden factory, and how does JIT eliminate most of it?

11. What are the benefits of small lot sizes?

Memo Writing Exercises

1. Write a memo to your instructor on the benefits of activity-based costing. Use the Internet if you need more information.

2. The manager of production planning and control, Daryll Jones, wants an explanation of the term *hidden factory*. Write a memo to Jones in which you provide some potential benefits from examining the hidden factors at your company.

Problems

1. A manager wants to determine the number of containers to use for a kanban system to be installed next month. The process will have a usage rate of 80 pieces per hour. Because the process is new, the manager has assigned an efficiency factor of .35. Each container holds 45 pieces and takes an average of 75 minutes to complete a cycle. How many containers should be used? As the system improves, will more or fewer containers be required? Why?

2. A JIT system uses kanban cards to authorize production and movement of materials. In one portion of the system, a work center uses an average of 100 pieces per hour while running. The manager has assigned an efficiency factor of .20 to the center. Standard containers are designed to hold six dozen parts each. The cycle time for parts containers is about 105 minutes. How many containers are needed?

3. A machine cell uses 200 pounds of a certain material each day. Material is transported in vats that hold 120 pounds each. Cycle time for the vats is about two hours. The manager has assigned an efficiency factor of .08 to the cell. The plant operates on an eight-hour day. How many vats will be used?

4. Determine the number of cycles per day and the production quantity per cycle for this set of products:

Product	Daily Quantity
A	21
B	12
C	3
D	15

Use the sequence A-B-C-D.

5. Determine the number of cycles per day and a production quantity per cycle for this set of products that achieves fairly level production:

Product	Daily Quantity
A	22
B	12
C	4
D	15
E	9

Assume the production sequence will be A-B-C-D-E.

6. Determine the number of cycles per day and a production quantity per cycle for this set of products that achieves fairly level production:

Product	Daily Quantity
F	9
G	8
H	5
K	6

Assume the production sequence will be F-G-H-K.

CASE

Level Operations

Level Operations is a small company located in eastern Pennsylvania. It produces a variety of security devices and safes. The safes come in several different designs. Recently, a number of new customers have placed orders, and the production facility has been enlarged to accommodate increased demand for safes. Production manager Stephanie Coles is currently working on a production plan for the safes. She needs a plan for each day of the week. She has obtained the following information from the marketing department on projected demand for the next five weeks:

Model	Weekly Quantity
S1	120
S2	102
S7	48
S8	90
S9	25

The department operates five days a week. One complexity is that partially completed safes are not permitted; each cycle must turn out finished units.

After discussions with engineering, Stephanie determined that the best production sequence for each cycle is S7-S8-S9-S01-S02.

Question

1. What might Stephanie determine as the best production quantity per cycle for each day of the week?

OPERATIONS TOUR

Boeing

www.boeing.com

The Boeing Company, headquartered in Everett, Washington, is one of the two major producers of aircraft in the global market. The other major producer is European Airbus.

Boeing produces three models of aircraft in Everett, 747s, 767s, and 777s. The planes are all produced in the same building. At any one time, there may be as many as six planes in various stages of production. Obviously the building has to be fairly large to accommodate such a huge undertaking. In fact, the building is so large that it covers over 98 acres and it is four stories high, making it the largest building by volume in the world. It is so large that all of Disneyland would fit inside, and still leave about 15 acres for indoor parking! The windowless building has six huge doors along one side, each about 100 yards wide and 40 yards high (the size of a football

field)—large enough to allow a completed airplane to pass through.

Boeing sells airplanes to airlines and countries around the globe. There isn't a set price for the planes; the actual price depends on what features the customer wants. Once the details have been settled and an order submitted, the customer requirements are sent to the design department.

Design

Designers formerly had to construct a mockup to determine the exact dimensions of the plane and to identify any assembly problems that might occur. That required time, materials, labor, time and space. Now they use computers (CAD) to design airplanes, avoiding the cost of the mockups and shortening the development time.

The Production Process

Once designs have been completed and approved by the customer, production of the plane is scheduled, and parts and materials are ordered. Parts come to the plant by rail, airplane, and truck, and are delivered to the major assembly area of the plane they will be used for. The parts are scheduled so they arrive at the plant just prior to when they will be used in assembly, and immediately moved to storage areas close to where they will be used. Time phasing shipments to arrive as parts are needed helps to keep inventory investment low and avoids having to devote space to store parts that won't be used immediately. There is a tradeoff, though, because if any parts are missing or damaged and have to be re-ordered, that could cause production delays. When missing or defective parts are discovered, they are assigned priorities according to how critical the part is in terms of disruption of the flow of work. The parts with the highest priorities are assigned to expediters who determine the best way to replace the part. The expediters keep track of the progress of the parts and deliver them to the appropriate location as soon as they arrive. In the meantime, a portion of the work remains unfinished, awaiting the replacement parts, and workers complete other portions of the assembly. If the supplier is unable to replace the part in a time frame that will not seriously delay assembly, as a last resort, Boeing has a machine shop that can make the necessary part.

Wing and a portion of the fuselage being lowered into plane.

The partially assembled portions of the plane, and in later stages, the plane itself, move from station to station as the work progresses, staying about five days at each station. Giant overhead cranes are used to move large sections from one station to the next, although once the wheel assemblies have been installed, the plane is towed to the remaining stations.

Finished planes are painted in one of two separate buildings. Painting usually adds 400 to 600 pounds to the weight of a plane. The painting process involves giving the airplane a negative charge and the paint a positive charge so that the paint will be attracted to the airplane.

Testing and Quality Control

Boeing has extensive quality control measures in place throughout the entire design and production process. Not only are there quality inspectors, individual employees inspect their own work and the work previously done by others on the plane. Buyers' inspectors also check on the quality of the work.

There are 60 test pilots who fly the planes. Formerly planes were tested to evaluate their flight worthiness in a wind tunnel, which required expensive testing and added considerably to product development time. Now new designs are tested using a computerized wind tunnel before production even begins, greatly reducing both time and cost. And in case you're wondering, the wings are fairly flexible; a typical wing can flap by as much as 22 feet before it will fracture.

Re-engineering

Boeing is re-engineering its business systems. A top priority is to upgrade its computer systems. This will provide better links to suppliers, provide more up-to-date information for materials management, and enable company representatives who are at customer sites to create a customized aircraft design on their laptop computer.

Another aspect of the re-engineering involves a shift to lean production. Key goals are to reduce production time and reduce inventory.

Boeing wants to reduce the time that a plane spends at each work station from 5 days to 3 days, a reduction of 40%. Not only will that mean that customers can get their planes much sooner, it will also reduce labor costs, inventory costs, and improve cash flow. One part of this will be accomplished by moving toward late stage customization, or delayed differentiation. That would mean standardizing the assembly of planes as long as possible before adding custom features. This, and other time saving steps will speed up production considerably, giving it a major competitive advantage. It also wants to reduce the tremendous amount of inventory it carries (a 747 jumbo jet has about 6 million parts, including 3 million rivets). One part of the plan is to have suppliers do more predelivery work by assembling the parts into kits that are delivered directly to the staging area where they will be installed on the aircraft instead of delivering separate parts to inventory. That would cut down on inventory carrying costs and save time.

Boeing is also hoping to reduce the number of suppliers it has, and to establish better links and cooperation from suppliers. Currently Boeing has about 3,500 suppliers. Compare that with GM's roughly 2,500 suppliers, and you get an idea of how large this number is.

Benton, W. C., and Hojung Shin. "Manufacturing Planning and Control: The Evaluation of MRP and JIT Integration." *European Journal of Operational Research* 110 (1998), pp. 411–40.

Blackburn, Joseph D. *Time-Based Competition.* Burr Ridge, IL: Business One Irwin, 1991.

Hopp, Wallace J., and Mark Spearman. *Factory Physics: Foundations of Manufacturing Management.* 2nd ed. New York: Irwin/McGraw-Hill, 2001.

"JIT Manufacturing Is Working Overtime." *Business Week,* November 8, 1999.

Monden, Yasuhiro. "What Makes the Toyota Production System Really Tick?" *Industrial Engineering* 13, no. 1 (January 1981), pp. 38–46.

Spencer, Michael S., and V. Daniel Guide. "An Exploration of the Components of JIT." *International Journal of Operations and Production Management* 15, no. 5 (1995), pp. 72–83.

Sriparavastu, Loknath, and Tarun Gupta. "An Empirical Study of JIT and Total Quality Management Principles Implementation in Manufacturing Firms in the USA." *International Journal of Operations and Production Management* 17, no. 12 (1997), pp. 1215–32.

Swanson, Christine A., and William M. Lankford. "JIT Manufacturing." *Business Process Management Journal* 4, no. 4 (1998), pp. 333–41.

White, Richard E., and John N. Pearson. "JIT Manufacturing: A Survey of Implementations in Small and Large U.S. Manufacturers." *Management Science* 45, no. 1 (January 1999), pp. 1–15.

Vollman, Thomas E., William L. Berry, and D. Clay Whybark. Manufacturing Planning and Control Systems. 4th ed. New York: Irwin/McGraw-Hill, 1997.

Zipkin, Paul H. *Foundations of Inventory Management.* New York: Irwin/McGraw-Hill, 2000.

SUPPLEMENT TO CHAPTER SIXTEEN
Maintenance

SUPPLEMENT OUTLINE

Introduction, 720

Preventive Maintenance, 721

Breakdown Programs, 723

Replacement, 724

Summary, 724

Key Terms, 724

Discussion and Review
    Questions, 724

Problems, 725

Selected Bibliography and Further
    Reading, 725

LEARNING OBJECTIVES

*After completing this supplement,
you should be able to:*

1 Explain the importance of
   maintenance in production
   systems.

2 Describe the range of
   maintenance activities.

3 Discuss preventive maintenance
   and the key issues associated with
   it.

4 Discuss breakdown maintenance
   and the key issues associated with
   it.

5 State how the Pareto phenomenon
   pertains to maintenance decisions.

maintenance All activities that maintain facilities and equipment in good working order so that a system can perform as intended.

Maintaining the production capability of an organization is an important function in any production system. **Maintenance** encompasses all those activities that relate to keeping facilities and equipment in good working order and making necessary repairs when breakdowns occur, so that the system can perform as intended.

Maintenance activities are often organized into two categories: (1) buildings and grounds, and (2) equipment maintenance. Buildings and grounds is responsible for the appearance and functioning of buildings, parking lots, lawns, fences, and the like. Equipment maintenance is responsible for maintaining machinery and equipment in good working condition and making all necessary repairs.

Introduction

The goal of maintenance is to keep the production system in good working order at minimal cost. There are several reasons for wanting to keep equipment and machines in good operating condition, such as to:

1. avoid production disruptions
2. not add to production costs
3. maintain high quality
4. avoid missed delivery dates

When breakdowns occur, there are a number of adverse consequences:

1. Production capacity is reduced, and orders are delayed.
2. There is no production, but overhead continues, increasing the cost per unit.
3. There are quality issues; product may be damaged.
4. There are safety issues; employees or customers may be injured.

Decision makers have two basic options with respect to maintenance. One option is *reactive:* it is to deal with breakdowns or other problems when they occur. This is referred to as **breakdown maintenance.** The other option is *proactive:* it is to reduce breakdowns through a program of lubrication, adjustment, cleaning, inspection, and replacement of worn parts. This is referred to as **preventive maintenance.**

breakdown maintenance Reactive approach; dealing with breakdowns or problems when they occur.

preventive maintenance Proactive approach; reducing breakdowns through a program of lubrication, adjustment, cleaning, inspection, and replacement of worn parts.

Decision makers try to make a trade-off between these two basic options that will minimize their combined cost. With no preventive maintenance, breakdown and repair costs would be tremendous. Furthermore, hidden costs, such as lost production and the cost of wages while equipment is not in service, must be factored in. So must the cost of injuries or damage to other equipment and facilities or to other units in production. However, beyond a certain point, the cost of preventive maintenance activities exceeds the benefit.

As an example, if a person never had the oil changed in his or her car, never had it lubricated, and never had the brakes or tires inspected, but simply had repairs done when absolutely necessary, preventive costs would be negligible but repair costs would be quite high, considering the wide range of parts (engine, steering, transmission, tires, brakes, etc.) that could fail. In addition, property damage and injury costs might be incurred, plus there would be the uncertainty of when failure might occur (e.g., on the expressway during rush hour, or late at night). On the other hand, having the oil changed and the car lubricated every morning would obviously be excessive because automobiles are designed to perform for much longer periods without oil changes and lubrications. The best approach is to seek a balance between preventive maintenance and breakdown maintenance. The same concept applies to maintaining production systems: Strike a balance between prevention costs and breakdown costs. This concept is illustrated in Figure 16S–1.

The age and condition of facilities and equipment, the degree of technology involved, the type of production process, and similar factors enter into the decision of how much preventive maintenance is desirable. Thus, in the example of a new automobile, little preventive maintenance may be needed since there is slight risk of breakdowns. As the car

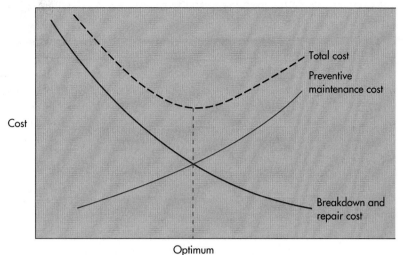

FIGURE 16S-1

Total maintenance cost as a function of preventive maintenance effort

ages and becomes worn through use, the desirability of preventive maintenance increases because the risk of breakdown increases. Thus, when tires and brakes begin to show signs of wear, they should be replaced before they fail; dents and scratches should be periodically taken care of before they begin to rust; and the car should be lubricated and have its oil changed after exposure to high levels of dust and dirt. Also, inspection and replacement of critical parts that tend to fail suddenly should be performed before a road trip to avoid disruption of the trip and costly emergency repair bills.

Preventive Maintenance

The goal of preventive maintenance is to reduce the incidence of breakdowns or failures in the plant or equipment to avoid the associated costs. Those costs can include loss of output; idle workers; schedule disruptions; injuries; damage to other equipment, products, or facilities; and repairs, which may involve maintaining inventories of spare parts, repair tools and equipment, and repair specialists.

Preventive maintenance is *periodic*. It can be scheduled according to the availability of maintenance personnel and to avoid interference with operating schedules. Managers usually schedule preventive maintenance using some combination of the following:

1. The result of planned inspections that reveal a need for maintenance.
2. According to the calendar (passage of time).
3. After a predetermined number of operating hours.

An important issue in preventive maintenance is the frequency of preventive maintenance. As the time between periodic maintenance increases, the cost of preventive maintenance decreases while the risk (and cost) of breakdowns increase. The goal is to strike a balance between the two costs (i.e., to minimize total cost).

Determining the amount of preventive maintenance to use is a function of the expected frequency of breakdown, the cost of a breakdown (including actual repair costs as well as potential damage or injury, lost production, and so on). The following two examples illustrate this.

The frequency of breakdown of a machine per month is shown in the table. The cost of a breakdown is $1,000 and the cost of preventive maintenance is $1,250 per month. If preventive maintenance is performed, the probability of a machine breakdown is negligible.

Example S-1

Should the manager use preventive maintenance, or would it be cheaper to repair the machine when it breaks down?

Number of breakdowns	0	1	2	3
Frequency of occurrence	.20	.30	.40	.10

Solution

The expected number of breakdowns without preventive maintenance is 1.40:

Number of Breakdowns	Frequency of Occurrence	Expected Number of Breakdowns
0	.20	0
1	.30	.30
2	.40	.80
3	.10	.30
	1.00	1.40

Expected cost using repair policy is: 1.40 breakdowns/month $\times$ \$1,000/breakdown = \$1,400. Preventive maintenance would cost \$1,250.

Therefore, preventive maintenance would yield a savings of \$150/month.

Example S-2

Another approach that might be used relates to the time before a breakdown occurs. Suppose that the average time before breakdown is normally distributed and has a mean of 3 weeks and a standard deviation of .60 week. If breakdown cost averages \$1,000 and preventive maintenance costs \$250, what is the optimal maintenance interval?

Solution

Begin by computing the ratio of preventive cost to the sum of preventive and breakdown cost:

$$\frac{\text{Preventive cost}}{\text{Preventive cost} + \text{Breakdown cost}} = \frac{\$250}{\$250 + \$1,000} = .20$$

Find the number of standard deviations from the mean represented by an area under the normal curve of .20 using Appendix B, Table B. It is -0.84. Use this value of z to compute the maintenance interval:

Mean + z standard deviations = $3 - .84(.60) = 2.496$ (round to 2½ weeks)

---

predictive maintenance An attempt to determine when best to perform preventive maintenance activities.

Ideally, preventive maintenance will be performed just prior to a breakdown or failure because this will result in the longest possible use of facilities or equipment without a breakdown. **Predictive maintenance** is an attempt to determine when to perform preventive maintenance activities. It is based on historical records and analysis of technical data to predict when a piece of equipment or part is about to fail. The better the predictions of failures are, the more effective preventive maintenance will be. A good preventive maintenance effort relies on complete records for each piece of equipment. Records must include information such as date of installation, operating hours, dates and types of insurance, and dates and types of repairs.

total productive maintenance JIT approach where workers perform preventive maintenance on the machines they operate.

Some Japanese companies have workers perform preventive maintenance on the machines they operate, rather than use separate maintenance personnel for that task. Called **total productive maintenance,** this approach is consistent with JIT systems and lean production, where employees are given greater responsibility for quality, productivity, and the general functioning of the system.

In the broadest sense, preventive maintenance extends back to the design and selection stage of equipment and facilities. Maintenance problems are sometimes *designed into* a system. For example, equipment may be designed in such a way that it needs frequent maintenance, or maintenance may be difficult to perform (e.g., the equipment has to be partially dismantled in order to perform routine maintenance). An extreme example of this was a certain car model that required the engine block to be lifted slightly in order to change the spark plugs! In such cases, it is very likely that maintenance will be performed less often than if its performance was less demanding. In other instances, poor design can cause equipment to wear out at an early age or experience a much higher than expected breakdown rate. *Consumer Reports,* for example, publishes annual breakdown data on automobiles. The data indicate that some models tend to break down with a much higher frequency than other models.

www.consumerreports.org

One possible reason for maintenance problems being designed into a product is that designers have accorded other aspects of design greater importance. Cost is one such aspect. Another is appearance; an attractive design may be chosen over a less attractive one even though it will be more demanding to maintain. Customers may contribute to this situation; the buying public probably has a greater tendency to select an attractive design over one that offers ease of maintenance.

Obviously, durability and ease of maintenance can have long-term implications for preventive maintenance programs. Training of employees in proper operating procedures and in how to keep equipment in good operating order—and providing the incentive to do so—are also important. More and more, U.S. organizations are taking a cue from the Japanese and transferring routine maintenance (e.g., cleaning, adjusting, inspecting) to the users of equipment, in an effort to give them a sense of responsibility and awareness of the equipment they use and to cut down on abuse and misuse of the equipment.

Breakdown Programs

The risk of a breakdown can be greatly reduced by an effective preventive maintenance program. Nonetheless, occasional breakdowns still occur. Even firms with good preventive practices have some need for breakdown programs. Of course, organizations that rely less on preventive maintenance have an even greater need for effective ways of dealing with breakdowns.

Unlike preventive maintenance, management cannot schedule breakdowns but must deal with them on an irregular basis (i.e., as they occur). Among the major approaches used to deal with breakdowns are the following:

1. *Standby or backup equipment* that can be quickly pressed into service.
2. *Inventories of spare parts* that can be installed as needed, thereby avoiding lead times involved in ordering parts, and *buffer inventories,* so that other equipment will be less likely to be affected by short-term downtime of a particular piece of equipment.
3. *Operators* who are able to perform at least minor repairs on their equipment.
4. *Repair people* who are well trained and readily available to diagnose and correct problems with equipment.

The degree to which an organization pursues any or all of these approaches depends on how important a particular piece of equipment is to the overall production system. At one extreme is equipment that is the focal point of a system (e.g., printing presses for a newspaper, or vital operating parts of a car, such as brakes, steering, transmission, ignition, and engine). At the other extreme is equipment that is seldom used because it does not perform an important function in the system, and equipment for which substitutes are readily available.

The implication is clear: Breakdown programs are most effective when they take into account the degree of importance a piece of equipment has in the production system, and the ability of the system to do without it for a period of time. The Pareto phenomenon exists in such situations: A relatively few pieces of equipment will be extremely important to the functioning of the system, thereby justifying considerable effort and/or expense; some will require moderate effort or expense; and many will justify little effort or expense.

Replacement

When breakdowns become frequent and/or costly, the manager is faced with a trade-off decision in which costs are an important consideration: What is the cost of replacement compared with the cost of continued maintenance? This question is sometimes difficult to resolve, especially if future breakdowns cannot be readily predicted. Historical records may help to project future experience. Another factor is technological change; newer equipment may have features that favor replacement over either preventive or breakdown maintenance. On the other hand, the removal of old equipment and the installation of new equipment may cause disruptions to the system, perhaps greater than the disruptions caused by breakdowns. Also, employees may have to be trained to operate the new equipment. Finally, forecasts of future demand for the use of the present or new equipment must be taken into account. The demand for the replacement equipment might differ because of the different features it has. For instance, demand for output of the current equipment might be two years, while demand for output of the replacement equipment might be much longer.

These decisions can be fairly complex, involving a number of different factors. Nevertheless, most of us are faced with a similar decision with our personal automobiles: When is it time for a replacement?

Summary

Maintaining the productive capability of an organization is an important function. Maintenance includes all of the activities related to keeping facilities and equipment in good operating order and maintaining the appearance of buildings and grounds.

The goal of maintenance is to minimize the total cost of keeping the facilities and equipment in good working order. Maintenance decisions typically reflect a trade-off between preventive maintenance, which seeks to reduce the incidence of breakdowns and failures, and breakdown maintenance, which seeks to reduce the impact of breakdowns when they do occur.

Key Terms

breakdown maintenance, 720
maintenance, 720
predictive maintenance, 722

preventive maintenance, 720
total productive maintenance, 722

Discussion and Review Questions

1. What is the goal of a maintenance program?
2. List the costs associated with equipment breakdown.
3. What are three different ways preventive maintenance is scheduled?
4. Explain the term *predictive maintenance* and the importance of good records.
5. List the major approaches organizations use to deal with breakdowns.
6. Explain how the Pareto phenomenon applies to:
   a. Preventive maintenance.
   b. Breakdown maintenance.
7. Discuss the key points of this supplement as they relate to maintenance of an automobile.
8. What advantages does preventive maintenance have over breakdown maintenance?
9. Explain why having a good preventive maintenance program in place is necessary prior to implementing a JIT system.
10. Discuss the relationship between preventive maintenance and quality.

Problems

1. The probability that equipment used in a hospital lab will need recalibration is given in the following table. A service firm is willing to provide maintenance and provide any necessary calibrations for free for a fee of $650 per month. Recalibration costs $500 per time. Which approach would be most cost effective, recalibration as needed or the service contract?

Number of recalibrations	0	1	2	3	4
Probability of occurrence	.15	.25	.30	.20	.10

2. The frequency of breakdown of a machine that issues lottery tickets is given in the following table. Repairs cost an average of $240. A service firm is willing to provide preventive maintenance under either of two options. #1 is $500 and covers all necessary repairs, and #2 is $350 and covers any repairs after the first one. Which option would have the lowest expected cost, pay for all repairs, service option #1, or service option #2?

Number of breakdowns/month	0	1	2	3	4
Frequency of occurrence	.10	.30	.30	.20	.10

3. Determine the optimum preventive maintenance frequency for each of the pieces of equipment if breakdown time is normally distributed:

Equipment	Average Time (days) between Breakdowns	Standard Deviation
A201	20	2
B400	30	3
C850	40	4

Equipment	Preventive Maintenance Cost	Breakdown Cost
A201	$300	$2,300
B400	$200	$3,500
C850	$530	$4,800

Hall, Robert W. "Total Productive Maintenance—Essential to Maintain Progress." *Target* 3, no. 3 (Fall 1987), pp. 4–11.

Hora, Michael E. "The Unglamorous Game of Managing Maintenance." *Business Horizons* 30, no. 3 (May–June 1987), pp. 67–75.

Mann, Lawrence, Jr. *Maintenance Management.* Rev. ed. Lexington, MA: Lexington Books, 1983.

Nolden, Carol. "Predictive Maintenance: Route to Zero Unplanned Downtime." *Plant Engineering* 41, no. 4 (February 1987), pp. 38–43.

Wireman, Terry. *Preventive Maintenance.* Reston, VA: Reston Publishing, 1984.

Selected Bibliography and Further Reading

CHAPTER SEVENTEEN

Scheduling

CHAPTER OUTLINE

Scheduling Operations, 728
  Scheduling in High-Volume
    Systems, 728
  Scheduling in Intermediate-Volume
    Systems, 730

Scheduling in Low-Volume
  Systems, 731
  Loading, 731
  Sequencing, 738
  Sequencing Jobs through Two Work
    Centers, 745
  Sequencing Jobs When Setup Times
    Are Sequence-Dependent, 747
  Why Scheduling Can Be
    Difficult, 748
  Things a Manager Can Do to
    Achieve Good Scheduling
    Results, 748
  The Theory of Constraints, 748

Additional Service
  Considerations, 749
  Appointment Systems, 749
  Reservation Systems, 750
  Scheduling the Workforce, 750
  Scheduling Multiple Resources, 750

Reading: Servicing Passenger
  Planes, 751

Operations Strategy, 752

Summary, 752

Key Terms, 752

Solved Problems, 752

Discussion and Review
  Questions, 757

Memo Writing Exercises, 757

Problems, 757

Selected Bibliography and Further
  Reading, 762

LEARNING OBJECTIVES

After completing this chapter, you should be able to:

1 Explain what scheduling involves and the importance of good scheduling.

2 Discuss scheduling needs in high-volume and intermediate-volume systems.

3 Discuss scheduling needs in job shops.

4 Use and interpret Gantt charts, and use the assignment method for loading.

5 Discuss and give examples of commonly used priority rules.

6 Describe some of the unique problems encountered in service systems, and describe some of the approaches used for scheduling service systems.

scheduling Establishing the timing of the use of equipment, facilities, and human activities in an organization.

Within an organization, **scheduling** pertains to establishing the timing of the use of specific resources of that organization. It relates to the use of equipment, facilities, and human activities. Scheduling occurs in every organization, regardless of the nature of its activities. For example, manufacturers must schedule production, which means developing schedules for workers, equipment, purchases, maintenance, and so on. Hospitals must schedule admissions, surgery, nursing assignments, and support services such as meal preparation, security, maintenance, and cleaning. Educational institutions must schedule classrooms, instruction, and students. And lawyers, doctors, dentists, hairdressers, and auto repair shops must schedule appointments.

In the decision-making hierarchy, scheduling decisions are the final step in the transformation process before actual output occurs. Many decisions about system design and operation have to be made long before scheduling decisions. They include the capacity of the system, equipment selection, selection and training of workers, and design of products and services. Consequently, scheduling decisions must be made within the constraints established by many other decisions, making them fairly narrow in scope and latitude.

Generally, the objectives of scheduling are to achieve tradeoffs among conflicting goals, which include efficient utilization of staff, equipment, and facilities, and minimization of customer waiting time, inventories, and process times.

This chapter covers scheduling in both manufacturing and service environments. Although the two environments have many similarities, some basic differences are important. We begin with manufacturing environments.

Scheduling Operations

Scheduling tasks are largely a function of the volume of system output. High-volume systems require approaches substantially different from those required by job shops, and project scheduling requires still different approaches. In this chapter, we will consider scheduling for high-volume systems, intermediate-volume systems, and low-volume (job shop) scheduling. Project scheduling is discussed in Chapter 18.

SCHEDULING IN HIGH-VOLUME SYSTEMS

flow system High-volume system with standardized equipment and activities.

flow-shop scheduling Scheduling for flow systems.

Scheduling encompasses allocating workloads to specific work centers and determining the sequence in which operations are to be performed. High-volume systems are characterized by standardized equipment and activities that provide identical or highly similar operations on customers or products as they pass through the system. The goal is to obtain a smooth rate of flow of goods or customers through the system in order to get a high utilization of labor and equipment. High-volume systems are often referred to as **flow systems;** scheduling in these systems is referred to as **flow-shop scheduling,** although flow-shop scheduling can also be used in medium-volume systems. Examples of high-volume products include autos, personal computers, radios and televisions, stereo equipment, toys, and appliances. In process industries, examples include petroleum refining, sugar refining, mining, waste treatment, and the manufacturing of fertilizers. Examples of services include cafeteria lines, news broadcasts, and mass inoculations. Because of the highly repetitive nature of these systems, many of the loading and sequence decisions are determined during the design of the system. The use of highly specialized tools and equipment, the arrangement of equipment, the use of specialized material-handling equipment, and the division of labor are all designed to enhance the flow of work through the system, since all items follow virtually the same sequence of operations.

A major aspect in the design of flow systems is *line balancing,* which concerns allocating the required tasks to workstations so that they satisfy technical (sequencing) constraints and are balanced with respect to equal work times among stations. Highly balanced systems result in the maximum utilization of equipment and personnel as well as the highest possible rate of output. Line balancing is discussed in Chapter 6.

In setting up flow systems, designers must consider the potential discontent of workers in connection with the specialization of job tasks in these systems; high work rates are often achieved by dividing the work into a series of relatively simple tasks assigned to different workers. The resulting jobs tend to be boring and monotonous and may give rise to fatigue, absenteeism, turnover, and other problems, all of which tend to reduce productivity and disrupt the smooth flow of work. These problems and potential solutions are elaborated on in Chapter 7, which deals with the design of work systems.

In spite of the built-in attributes of flow systems related to scheduling, a number of scheduling problems remain. One stems from the fact that few flow systems are *completely* devoted to a single product or service; most must handle a variety of sizes and models. Thus, an automobile manufacturer will assemble many different combinations of cars—two-door and four-door models, some with air-conditioning and some not, some with deluxe trim and others with standard trim, some with CD players, some with tinted glass, and so on. The same can be said for producers of appliances, electronic equipment, and toys. Each change involves slightly different inputs of parts, materials, and processing requirements that must be scheduled into the line. If the line is to operate smoothly, a supervisor must coordinate the flow of materials and the work. This requires scheduling the inputs, the processing, and the outputs, as well as scheduling purchases. In addition to achieving a smooth flow, it is important to avoid excessive buildup of inventories. Again, each variation in size or model will tend to have somewhat different inventory requirements, so that additional scheduling efforts will be needed.

One source of scheduling concern is possible disruptions in the system that result in less than the desired output. These can be caused by equipment failures, material shortages, accidents, and absences. In practice, it is usually impossible to increase the rate of output to compensate for these factors, mainly because flow systems are designed to operate at a given rate. Instead, strategies involving subcontracting or overtime are often required, although subcontracting on short notice is not always feasible. Sometimes work that is partly completed can be made up off the line.

The reverse situation can also impose scheduling problems although these are less severe. This happens when the desired output is less than the usual rate. However, instead of slowing the ensuing rate of output, it is usually necessary to operate the system at the usual rate, but for fewer hours. For instance, a production line might operate temporarily for seven hours a day instead of eight.

High-volume systems usually require automated or specialized equipment for processing and handling. Moreover, they perform best with a high, uniform output. Consequently, the following factors often determine the success of such a system:

1. *Process and product design.* Here, cost and manufacturability are important, as is achieving a smooth flow through the system.

2. *Preventive maintenance.* Keeping equipment in good operating order can minimize breakdowns that would disrupt the flow of work.

3. *Rapid repair when breakdowns occur.* This can require specialists as well as stocks of critical spare parts.

4. *Optimal product mixes.* Techniques such as linear programming can be used to determine optimal blends of inputs to achieve desired outputs at minimal costs. This is particularly true in the manufacture of fertilizers, animal feeds, and diet foods.

5. *Minimization of quality problems.* Quality problems can be extremely disruptive, requiring shutdowns while problems are resolved. Moreover, when output fails to meet quality standards, not only is there the loss of output but also a waste of the labor, material, time, and other resources that went into it.

6. *Reliability and timing of supplies.* Shortages of supplies is an obvious source of disruption and must be avoided. On the other hand, if the solution is to stockpile supplies, that can lead to high carrying costs. Shortening supply lead times, developing reliable supply schedules, and carefully projecting needs are all useful.

SCHEDULING IN INTERMEDIATE-VOLUME SYSTEMS

Intermediate-volume system outputs fall between the standardized type of output of the high-volume systems and made-to-order output of job shops. Like the high-volume systems, intermediate-volume systems typically produce standard outputs. If manufacturing is involved, the products may be for stock rather than for special order. However, the volume of output in such cases is not large enough to justify continuous production. Instead, it is more economical to process these items *intermittently*. Thus, intermediate-volume work centers periodically shift from one job to another. In contrast to a job shop, the run sizes are relatively large. Examples of products made in these systems include canned foods, baked goods, paint, and cosmetics.

The three basic issues in these systems are the *run size* of jobs, the *timing* of jobs, and the *sequence* in which jobs should be processed.

Sometimes, the issue of run size can be determined by using a model such as the economic run size model discussed in Chapter 13 on inventory management. The runsize that would minimize setup and inventory costs is

$$Q_0 = \sqrt{\frac{2DS}{H}} \sqrt{\frac{p}{p-u}} \tag{17–1}$$

Setup cost may be an important consideration. For one thing, setup costs may depend on the order in which jobs are processed; similar jobs may require less setup change between them. For example, jobs in a print shop may be sequenced by ink color to reduce the number of setups needed. This opens up the possibility of reducing setup cost and time by taking processing sequence into account. It also makes sequencing more complex, and it requires estimating job setup costs for every sequence combination.

In another vein, companies are working to reduce setup times and, hence, experience less downtime for equipment changeover. Tactics include off-line setups, snap-on parts, modular setups, and flexible equipment designed to handle a variety of processing requirements.

Another difficulty arises because usage is not always as smooth as assumed in the model. Some products will tend to be used up faster than expected and have to be replenished sooner. Also, because multiple products are to be processed, it is not always possible to schedule production to correspond with optimum run intervals.

Solectron Corporation, a provider of customized electronics manufacturing services and winner of the 1997 Baldrige Award, provides printed circuit assembly for its customers. Because it customizes assemblies, its products are made to order, yet produced in high volume for its large customers.

www.solectron.com

Another approach frequently used is to base production on a master schedule developed from customer orders and forecasts of demand. Companies engaged in assembly operations would then use an MRP approach (described in Chapter 15) to determine the quantity and projected timing of jobs for components. The manager would then compare projected requirements with projected capacity and develop a feasible schedule from that information. Companies engaged in producing processed rather than assembled goods (e.g., food products, such as canned goods and beverages; publishing, such as magazines; paints and cleaning supplies) would use a somewhat different approach; the *time-phasing* information provided by MRP would not be an important factor.

Scheduling in Low-Volume Systems

The characteristics of low-volume systems (job shops) are considerably different from those of high- and intermediate-volume systems. Products are made to order, and orders usually differ considerably in terms of processing requirements, materials needed, processing time, and processing sequence and setups. Because of these circumstances, **job-shop scheduling** is usually fairly complex. This is compounded by the impossibility of establishing firm schedules prior to receiving the actual job orders.

Job-shop processing gives rise to two basic issues for schedulers: how to distribute the workload among work centers and what job processing sequence to use.

job-shop scheduling Scheduling for low-volume systems with many variations in requirements.

LOADING

Loading refers to the assignment of jobs to processing (work) centers. Loading decisions involve assigning specific jobs to work centers and to various machines in the work centers. In cases where a job can be processed only by a specific center, loading presents little difficulty. However, problems arise when two or more jobs are to be processed and there are a number of work centers capable of performing the required work. In such cases, the operations manager needs some way of assigning jobs to the centers.

When making assignments, managers often seek an arrangement that will minimize processing and setup costs, minimize idle time among work centers, or minimize job completion time, depending on the situation.

loading The assignment of jobs to processing centers.

Gantt Charts. Visual aids called **Gantt charts** are used for a variety of purposes related to loading and scheduling. They derive their name from Henry Gantt, who pioneered the use of charts for industrial scheduling in the early 1900s. Gantt charts can be used in a number of different ways, two of which are illustrated in Figure 17–1, which shows scheduling classrooms for a university and scheduling hospital operating rooms for a day.

The purpose of Gantt charts is to organize and clarify the actual or intended use of resources in a *time framework*. In most cases, a time scale is represented horizontally, and resources to be scheduled are listed vertically. The use of the resources is reflected in the body of the chart.

Managers may use the charts for trial-and-error schedule development to get an idea of what different arrangements would involve. Thus, a tentative surgery schedule might reveal insufficient allowance for surgery that takes longer than expected and can be revised accordingly. Use of the chart for classroom scheduling would help avoid assigning two different classes to the same room at the same time.

There are a number of different types of Gantt charts. Two of the most commonly used are the *load chart* and the *schedule chart*.

A **load chart** depicts the loading and idle times for a group of machines or a list of departments. Figure 17–2 on pg. 733 illustrates a typical load chart. This chart indicates that work center 3 is completely loaded for the entire week, center 4 will be available after noon on Tuesday, and the other two centers have idle time scattered throughout the week. This information can help a manager rework loading assignments to better utilize the centers. For instance, if all centers perform the same kind of work, the manager might want

Gantt chart Chart used as visual aid for loading and scheduling purposes.

load chart A Gantt chart that shows the loading and idle times for a group of machines or list of departments.

FIGURE 17–1

Examples of charts used for scheduling

Classroom schedule: Fall   Friday

Room	8	9	10	11	12	1	2	3	4	5
A100	Stat 1	Econ 101	Econ 102	Fin 201	Mar 210	Acct 212			Mar 410	
A105	Stat 2	Math 2a	Math 2b			Acct 210	CCE ———	—	—	—
A110	Acct 340	Mgmt 250	Math 3		Mar 220					
A115	Mar 440		Mgmt 230			Fin 310	Acct 360			

City hospital, surgery schedule   Date: 5/8

Operating room	7	8	Hour 9	10	11	12
A		Peters		Anderson		
B	Henderson					
C	Dun			Smith		

- Scheduled
- Idle
- Cleaning and reading

to free one center for a long job or a rush order. The chart also shows when certain jobs are scheduled to start and finish, and where to expect idle time.

Two different approaches are used to load work centers, *infinite* loading and *finite* loading. **Infinite loading** assigns jobs to work centers without regard to the capacity of the work center. The priority sequencing rules described in this chapter use infinite loading. One possible result of infinite loading is the formation of queues in some (or all) work centers. **Finite loading** projects actual job starting and stopping times at each work center, taking into account the capacities of each work center and the processing times of jobs, so that capacity is not exceeded. One output of finite loading is a detailed projection of hours each work center will operate. Schedules based on finite loading may have to be updated often, perhaps daily, due to processing delays at work centers and the addition of new jobs or cancellation of current jobs. The following diagram illustrates these two approaches.

infinite loading Jobs are assigned to work centers without regard to the capacity of the work center.

finite loading Jobs are assigned to work centers taking into account the work center capacity and job processing times.

Infinite loading

Finite loading

vertical loading Loading jobs at a work center, job by job, usually according to some priority criterion, using infinite loading.

horizontal loading Loading each job on all work centers it will require, one at a time, according to some priority, using finite loading.

Loading can be done in various ways. **Vertical loading** refers to loading jobs at a work center job by job, usually according to some priority criterion. Vertical loading does not consider the work center's capacity (i.e., infinite loading). In contrast, **horizontal loading** involves loading the job that has the highest priority on all work centers it will

Work center	Mon.	Tues.	Wed.	Thurs.	Fri.
1	Job 3			Job 4	
2		Job 3	Job 7		✕
3	Job 1	✕		Job 6	Job 7
4	Job 10				

▨ Processing

✕ Center not available (e.g., maintenance)

© Feldman and Pinedo.

FIGURE 17-2

A Gantt load chart

The same Gantt chart using the Lekin software, included on your CD. This software, developed at NYU, includes multiple scheduling routines along with graphics such as this interactive Gantt chart for scheduling a wide variety of manufacturing systems.

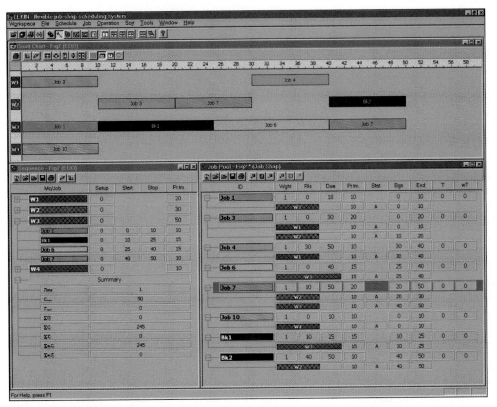

require, then the job with the next highest priority, and so on. Horizontal loading is based on finite loading. One possible result of horizontal loading is keeping jobs waiting at a work center even though that center is idle, so the center will be ready to process a higher priority job that is expected to arrive shortly. That would not happen with vertical loading; the work center would be fully loaded, although a higher priority job would have to wait if it arrived while the work center was busy. So horizontal loading takes a more *global* approach to scheduling, while vertical loading uses a *local* approach. Which approach is better? That depends on various factors: the relative costs of keeping higher priority jobs waiting, the cost of having work centers idle, the number of jobs, the number of work centers, the potential for processing disruptions, the potential for new jobs and job cancellations, and so on. As you can see, the circumstances can be quite complex.

With infinite loading, a manager may need to make some response to overloaded work centers. Among the possible responses are shifting work to other periods or other centers, working overtime, or contracting out a portion of the work. Note that the last two options in effect increase capacity to meet the work load.

FIGURE 17-3

Progress chart for landscaping job

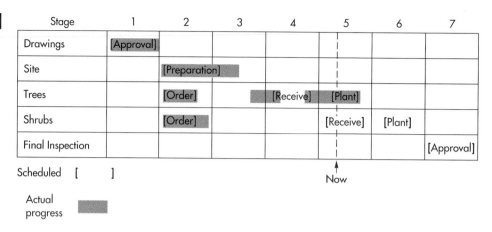

Finite loading may reflect a fixed upper limit on capacity. For example, a bus line will have only so many buses. Hence, the decision to place into service a particular number of buses fixes capacity. Similarly, a manufacturer might have one specialized machine that it operates around the clock. Thus, it is operated at the upper limit of its capacity, so finite loading would be called for.

There are two general approaches to scheduling: forward scheduling and backward scheduling. **Forward scheduling** means scheduling ahead from a point in time; **backward scheduling** means scheduling backward from a due date. Forward scheduling is used if the issue is "How long will it take to complete this job?" Backward scheduling would be used if the issue is "When is the latest the job can be started and still be completed by the due date?"

A manager often uses a **schedule chart** to monitor the progress of jobs. The vertical axis on this type of Gantt chart shows the orders or jobs in progress, and the horizontal axis shows time. The chart indicates which jobs are on schedule and which are behind or ahead.

A typical schedule chart is illustrated in Figure 17–3. It shows the current status of a landscaping job with planned and actual starting and finishing times for the five stages of the job. The chart indicates that approval and the ordering of trees and shrubs was on schedule. The site preparation was a bit behind schedule. The trees were received earlier than expected, and planting is ahead of schedule. However, the shrubs have not yet been received. The chart indicates some slack between scheduled receipt of shrubs and shrub planting, so if the shrubs arrive by the end of the week, it appears the schedule can still be met.

Despite the obvious benefits of Gantt charts, they possess certain limitations, the chief one being the need to repeatedly update a chart to keep it current. In addition, a chart does not directly reveal costs associated with alternative loadings. Finally, a job's processing time may vary depending on the work center; certain stations or work centers may be capable of processing some jobs faster than other stations. Again, that situation would increase the complexity of evaluating alternative schedules. Nonetheless, Gantt charts are the most widely used scheduling tools.

Input/Output Control. **Input/output (I/O) control** refers to monitoring the work flow and queue lengths at work centers. The purpose of I/O control is to manage work flow so that queues and waiting times are kept under control. Without I/O control, demand may exceed processing capacity, causing an overload at the center. Conversely, work may arrive slower than the rate a work center can handle, leaving the work center underutilized. Ideally, a balance can be struck between the input and output rates, thereby achieving effective use of work center capacities without experiencing excessive queues at the work

forward scheduling Scheduling ahead, from some point in time.

backward scheduling Scheduling by working backwards from the due date(s).

schedule chart A Gantt chart that shows the orders or jobs in progress and whether they are on schedule.

input/output (I/O) control Managing work flow and queues at work centers.

	Period					
	1	2	3	4	5	6
Planned	100	100	90	90	90	90
Actual	120	95	80	88	93	94
Deviation	+20	−5	−10	−2	+3	+4
Cum. dev.	+20	+15	+5	+3	+6	+10

Input

Planned	110	110	100	100	100	95
Actual	110	105	95	101	103	96
Deviation	0	−5	−5	+1	+3	+1
Cum. dev.	0	−5	−10	−9	−6	−5

Output

Backlog	40	50	40	25	12	2	0

Note: Figures represent standard hours of processing time.

FIGURE 17–4

A sample input/output report for a work center

	MACHINE			
	A	**B**	**C**	**D**
1	8	6	2	4
2	6	7	11	10
Job 3	3	5	7	6
4	5	10	12	9

TABLE 17–1

A typical assignment problem

centers. A simple example of I/O control is the use of stoplights on some expressway on-ramps. These regulate the flow of entering traffic according to the current volume of expressway traffic.

Figure 17–4 illustrates an input/output report for a work center. A key portion of the report is the backlog of work waiting to be processed. The report reveals deviations-from-planned for both inputs and outputs, thereby enabling a manager to determine possible sources of problems.

The deviations in each period are determined by subtracting "planned" from "actual." For example, in the first period, subtracting the planned input of 100 hours from the actual input of 120 hours produces a deviation of +20 hours. Similarly, in the first period, the planned and actual outputs are equal, producing a deviation of 0 hours.

The backlog for each period is determined by subtracting the "actual output" from the "actual input" and adjusting the backlog from the previous period by that amount. For example, in the second period actual output exceeds actual input by 10 hours. Hence, the previous backlog of 50 hours is reduced by 10 hours to 40 hours.

Assignment Method of Linear Programming. The **assignment model** is a special-purpose linear programming model that is useful in situations that call for assigning tasks or other work requirements to resources. Typical examples include assigning jobs to machines or workers, territories to salespeople, and repair jobs to repair crews. The idea is to obtain an optimum *matching* of tasks and resources. Commonly used criteria include costs, profits, efficiency, and performance.

Table 17–1 illustrates a typical problem, where four jobs are to be assigned to four machines. The problem is arranged in a format that facilitates evaluation of assignments. The

assignment model A linear programming model for optimal assignment of tasks and resources.

Hungarian method Method of assigning jobs by a one-for-one matching to identify the lowest-cost solution.

numbers in the body of the table represent the value or cost associated with each job–machine combination. In this case, the numbers represent costs. Thus, it would cost $8 to do job 1 on machine A, $6 to do job 1 on machine B, and so on. If the problem involved minimizing the cost for job 1 alone, it would clearly be assigned to machine C, since that combination has the lowest cost. However, that assignment does not take into account the other jobs and their costs, which is important since the lowest-cost assignment for any one job may not be consistent with a minimum-cost assignment when all jobs are considered.

If there are to be *n* matches, there are *n*! different possibilities. In this case, there are 4! = 24 different matches. One approach is to investigate each match and select the one with the lowest cost. However, if there are twelve jobs, there would be 479 million different matches! A much simpler approach is to use a procedure called the **Hungarian method** to identify the lowest-cost solution.

To be able to use the Hungarian method, a one-for-one matching is required. Each job, for example, must be assigned to only one machine. It is also assumed that every machine is capable of handling every job, and that the costs or values associated with each assignment combination are known and fixed (i.e., not subject to variation). The number of rows and columns must be the same. Solved Problem 1 at the end of the chapter shows what to do if they aren't the same.

Once the relevant cost information has been acquired and arranged in tabular form, the basic procedure of the Hungarian method is:

1. Subtract the smallest number in each row from every number in the row. This is called a *row reduction.* Enter the results in a new table.

2. Subtract the smallest number in each column of the new table from every number in the column. This is called a *column reduction.* Enter the results in another table.

3. Test whether an optimum assignment can be made. You do this by determining the *minimum* number of lines (horizontal or vertical) needed to cross out all zeros. If the number of lines equals the number of rows, an optimum assignment is possible. In that case, go to step 6. Otherwise go on to step 4.

4. If the number of lines is less than the number of rows, modify the table in this way:

   a. Subtract the smallest uncovered number from every uncovered number in the table.

   b. Add the smallest uncovered number to the numbers at *intersections* of cross-out lines.

   c. Numbers crossed out but not at intersections of cross-out lines carry over unchanged to the next table.

5. Repeat steps 3 and 4 until an optimal table is obtained.

6. Make the assignments. Begin with rows or columns with only one zero. Match items that have zeros, using only one match for each row and each column. Eliminate both the row and the column after the match.

Example 1

Determine the optimum assignment of jobs to machines for the following data (from Table 17–1).

	MACHINE				
	A	**B**	**C**	**D**	**Row Minimum**
1	8	6	2	4	2
Job 2	6	7	11	10	6
3	3	5	7	6	3
4	5	10	12	9	5

a. Subtract the smallest number in each row from every number in the row, and enter the   *Solution*
results in a new table. The result of this row reduction is

	MACHINE			
	A	**B**	**C**	**D**
1	6	4	0	2
Job 2	0	1	5	4
3	0	2	4	3
4	0	5	7	4
Column Minimum	0	1	0	2

b. Subtract the smallest number in each column from every number in the column, and
enter the results in a new table. The result of this column reduction is

	MACHINE			
	A	**B**	**C**	**D**
1	6	3	0	0
Job 2	0	0	5	2
3	0	1	4	1
4	0	4	7	2

c. Determine the *minimum* number of lines needed to cross out all zeros. (Try to cross out
as many zeros as possible when drawing lines.)

d. Since only three lines are needed to cross out all zeros and the table has four rows, this
is not the optimum.

e. Subtract the smallest value that hasn't been crossed out (in this case, 1) from every
number that hasn't been crossed out, and add it to numbers that are at the intersections
of covering lines. The results are

	MACHINE			
	A	**B**	**C**	**D**
1	7	3	0	0
Job 2	1	0	5	2
3	0	0	3	0
4	0	3	6	1

f. Determine the minimum number of lines needed to cross out all zeros (four). Since
this equals the number of rows, you can make the optimum assignment.

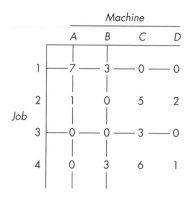

g. Make assignments: Start with rows and columns with only one zero. Match jobs with machines that have a zero cost.

	Machine			
	A	B	C	D
Job 1	7	3	[0]	0
Job 2	1	[0]	5	2
Job 3	0	0	3	[0]
Job 4	[0]	3	6	1

Assignment	Cost
1–C	$ 2
2–B	7
3–D	6
4–A	5
	$20

As you can see, the progress is relatively simple. The simplicity of the Hungarian method belies its usefulness when the assumptions are met. Not only does it provide a rational method for making assignments, it guarantees an optimal solution, often without the use of a computer, which is necessary only for fairly large problems. When profits instead of costs are involved, the profits can be converted to *relative costs* by subtracting every number in the table from the largest number and then proceeding as in a minimization problem.

It is worth knowing that one extension of this technique can be used to prevent undesirable assignments. For example, union rules may prohibit one person's assignment to a particular job, or a manager might wish to avoid assigning an unqualified person to a job. Whatever the reason, specific combinations can be avoided by assigning a relatively high cost to that combination. In the previous example, if we wish to avoid combination 1–A, assigning a cost of $50 to that combination will achieve the desired effect, because $50 is much greater than the other costs.

SEQUENCING

sequencing Determining the order in which jobs at a work center will be processed.

workstation An area where one person works, usually with special equipment, on a specialized job.

Although loading decisions determine the machines or work centers that will be used to process specific jobs, they do not indicate the *order* in which the jobs waiting at a given work center are to be processed. **Sequencing** is concerned with determining job processing order. Sequencing decisions determine both the order in which jobs are processed at various work centers and the order in which jobs are processed at individual **workstations** *within* the work centers.

If work centers are lightly loaded and if jobs all require the same amount of processing time, sequencing presents no particular difficulties. However, for heavily loaded work

FCFS (first come, first served): Jobs are processed in the order in which they arrive at a machine or work center.

SPT (shortest processing time): Jobs are processed according to processing time at a machine or work center, shortest job first.

EDD (earliest due date): Jobs are processed according to due date, earliest due date first.

CR (critical ratio): Jobs are processed according to smallest ratio of time remaining until due date to processing time remaining.

S/O (slack per operation): Jobs are processed according to average slack time (time until due date minus remaining time to process). Compute by dividing slack time by number of remaining operations, including the current one.

Rush: Emergency or preferred customers first.

TABLE 17–2

Possible priority rules

The set of jobs is known; no new jobs arrive after processing begins; and no jobs are canceled.

Setup time is independent of processing sequence.

Setup time is deterministic.

Processing times are deterministic rather than variable.

There will be no interruptions in processing such as machine breakdowns, accidents, or worker illness.

TABLE 17–3

Assumptions of priority rules

centers, especially in situations where relatively lengthy jobs are involved, the order of processing can be very important in terms of costs associated with jobs waiting for processing and in terms of idle time at the work centers. In this section, we will examine some of the ways in which jobs are sequenced.

Typically, a number of jobs will be waiting for processing. **Priority rules** are simple heuristics used to select the order in which the jobs will be processed. Some of the most common are listed in Table 17–2. The rules generally rest on the assumption that job setup cost and time are *independent* of processing sequence. In using these rules, job processing times and due dates are important pieces of information. **Job time** usually includes setup and processing times. Jobs that require similar setups can lead to reduced setup times if the sequencing rule takes this into account (the rules described here do not). Due dates may be the result of delivery times promised to customers, MRP processing, or managerial decisions. They are subject to revision and must be kept current to give meaning to sequencing choices. Also, it should be noted that due dates associated with all rules except S/O and CR are for the operation about to be performed; due dates for S/O and CR are typically final due dates for orders rather than intermediate, departmental deadlines.

The priority rules can be classified as either *local* or *global*. Local rules take into account information pertaining only to a single workstation; global rules take into account information pertaining to multiple workstations. FCFS, SPT, and EDD are local rules; CR and S/O are global rules. Rush can be either local or global. As you might imagine, global rules require more effort than local rules. A major complication in global sequencing is that not all jobs require the same processing or even the same order of processing. As a result, the set of jobs is different for different workstations. Local rules are particularly useful for bottleneck operations, but they are not limited to those situations.

A number of assumptions apply when using the priority rules; Table 17–3 lists them. In effect, the priority rules pertain to *static* sequencing: For simplicity, it is assumed that there is no variability in either setup or processing times, or in the set of jobs. The assumptions make the scheduling problem manageable. In practice, jobs may be delayed or canceled, and new jobs may arrive, requiring schedule revisions.

The effectiveness of any given sequence is frequently judged in terms of one or more *performance measures*. The most frequently used performance measures are:

priority rules Simple heuristics used to select the order in which jobs will be processed.

job time Time needed for setup and processing of a job.

Job flow time. This is the length of time a job is at a particular workstation or work center. It includes not only actual processing time but also any time waiting to be processed, transportation time between operations, and any waiting time related to equipment breakdowns, unavailable parts, quality problems, and so on. Job flow time is the length of time that begins when a job arrives at the shop, workstation, or work center, and ends when it leaves the shop, workstation, or work center. The average flow time for a group of jobs is equal to the total flow time for the jobs divided by the number of jobs.

Job lateness. This is the length of time the job completion date is expected to exceed the date the job was due or promised to a customer. It is the difference between the actual completion time and the due date. If we only record differences for jobs with completion times that exceed due dates, and assign zeros to jobs that are early, the term we use to refer to that is job *tardiness.*

makespan Total time needed to complete a group of jobs from the beginning of the first job to the completion of the last job.

Makespan. **Makespan** is the total time needed to complete a *group* of jobs. It is the length of time between the start of the first job in the group and the completion of the last job in the group.

Average number of jobs. Jobs that are in a shop are considered to be work-in-process inventory. The average work-in-process for a group of jobs can be computed using the following formula:

Average number of jobs = Total flow time/Makespan

If the jobs represent equal amounts of inventory, the average number of jobs will also reflect the average work-in-process inventory.

Of these rules, rush scheduling is quite simple and needs no explanation. The other rules and performance measures are illustrated in the following two examples.

Example 2

Processing times (including setup times) and due dates for six jobs waiting to be processed at a work center are given in the following table. Determine the sequence of jobs, the average flow time, average days late, and average number of jobs at the work center, for each of these rules:

a. FCFS

b. SPT

c. EDD

d. CR

Job	Processing Time (days)	Due Date (days)
A	2	7
B	8	16
C	4	4
D	10	17
E	5	15
F	12	18

Assume jobs arrived in the order shown.

Solution

a. The FCFS sequence is simple A-B-C-D-E-F. The measures of effectiveness are (see table):

(1) *Average flow time:* 120/6 = 20 days.

(2) *Average tardiness:* 54/6 = 9 days.

(3) The *makespan* is 41 days. *Average number of jobs at the work center:* 120/41 = 2.93.

Job Sequence	(1) Processing Time	(2) Flow Time	(3) Due Date	(2) − (3) Days Late [0 if negative]
A	2	2	7	0
B	8	10	16	0
C	4	14	4	10
D	10	24	17	7
E	5	29	15	14
F	12	41	18	23
	41	120		54

The flow time column indicates *cumulative* processing time, so summing these times and dividing by the total number of jobs processed indicates the average time each job spends at the work center. Similarly, find the average number of jobs at the center by summing the flow times and dividing by the total processing time.

b. Using the SPT rule, the job sequence is A-C-E-B-D-F (see the following table). The resulting values for the three measures of effectiveness are

(1) *Average flow time:* 108/6 = 18 days.

(2) *Average tardiness:* 40/6 = 6.67 days.

(3) *Average number of jobs at the work center:* 108/41 = 2.63.

Job Sequence	(1) Processing Time	(2) Flow Time	(3) Due Date	(2) − (3) Days Late [0 if negative]
A	2	2	7	0
C	4	6	4	2
E	5	11	15	0
B	8	19	16	3
D	10	29	17	12
F	12	41	18	23
	41	108		40

c. Using earliest due date as the selection criterion, the job sequence is C-A-E-B-D-F. The measures of effectiveness are (see table):

(1) *Average flow time:* 110/6 = 18.33 days.

(2) *Average tardiness:* 38/6 = 6.33 days.

(3) *Average number of jobs at the work center:* 110/41 = 2.68.

Job Sequence	(1) Processing Time	(2) Flow Time	(3) Due Date	(2) − (3) Days Late [0 if negative]
C	4	4	4	0
A	2	6	7	0
E	5	11	15	0
B	8	19	16	3
D	10	29	17	12
F	12	41	18	23
	41	110		38

d. Using the critical ratio we find:

Job Sequence	Processing Time	Due Date	Critical Ratio Calculation
A	2	7	(7 − 0)/ 2 = 3.5
B	8	16	(16 − 0)/ 8 = 2.0
C	4	4	(4 − 0)/ 4 = 1.0 (lowest)
D	10	17	(17 − 0)/10 = 1.7
E	5	15	(15 − 0)/ 5 = 3.0
F	12	18	(18 − 0)/12 = 1.5

At day 4 [C completed], the critical ratios are:

Job Sequence	Processing Time	Due Date	Critical Ratio Calculation
A	2	7	(7 − 4)/ 2 = 1.5
B	8	16	(16 − 4)/ 8 = 1.5
C	—	—	—
D	10	17	(17 − 4)/10 = 1.3
E	5	15	(15 − 4)/ 5 = 2.2
F	12	18	(18 − 4)/12 = 1.17 (lowest)

At day 16 [C and F completed], the critical ratios are:

Job Sequence	Processing Time	Due Date	Critical Ratio Calculation
A	2	7	(7 − 16)/ 2 = −4.5 (lowest)
B	8	16	(16 − 16)/ 8 = 0.0
C	—	—	—
D	10	17	(17 − 16)/10 = 0.1
E	5	15	(15 − 16)/ 5 = −0.2
F	12	18	—

At day 18 [C, F, and A completed], the critical ratios are:

Job Sequence	Processing Time	Due Date	Critical Ratio Calculation
A	—	—	—
B	8	16	(16 − 18)/ 8 = −0.25
C	—	—	—
D	10	17	(17 − 18)/10 = −0.10
E	5	15	(15 − 18)/ 5 = −0.60 (lowest)
F	—	—	—

At day 23 [C, F, A, and E completed], the critical ratios are:

Job Sequence	Processing Time	Due Date	Critical Ratio Calculation
A	—	—	—
B	8	16	(16 − 23)/ 8 = −0.875 (lowest)
C	—	—	—
D	10	17	(17 − 23)/10 = −0.60
E	—	—	—
F	—	—	—

The job sequence is C-F-A-E-B-D, and the resulting values for the measures of effectiveness are:

(1) *Average flow time:* 133/6 = 22.17 days.

Rule	Average Flow Time (days)	Average Tardiness (days)	Average Number of Jobs at the Work Center
FCFS	20.00	9.00	2.93
SPT	18.00	6.67	2.63
EDD	18.33	6.33	2.68
CR	22.17	9.67	3.24

TABLE 17–4

Comparison of the four rules for Example 2

(2) *Average tardiness:* 58/6 = 9.67 days.

(3) *Average number of jobs at the work center:* 133/41 = 3.24.

Sequence	(1) Processing Time	(2) Flow Time	(3) Due Date	(2) – (3) Days Late
C	4	4	4	0
F	12	16	18	0
A	2	18	7	11
E	5	23	15	8
B	8	31	16	15
D	10	41	17	24
	41	160		58

The results of these four rules are summarized in Table 17–4.

In this example, the SPT rule was the best according to two of the measures of effectiveness and a little worse than the EDD rule on average tardiness. The CR rule was the worst in every case. For a different set of numbers, the EDD rule (or perhaps another rule not mentioned here) might prove superior to SPT in terms of average job tardiness or some other measure of effectiveness. However, SPT is always superior in terms of minimizing flow time and, hence, in terms of minimizing the average number of jobs at the work center and completion time. It is best for each shop or organization to consider carefully its own circumstances and the measures of effectiveness it feels are important, when selecting a rule to use.

Generally speaking, the FCFS rule and the CR rule turn out to be the least effective of the rules.

The primary limitation of the FCFS rule is that long jobs will tend to delay other jobs. If a process consists of work on a number of machines, machine idle time for downstream workstations will increase. However, for service systems in which customers are directly involved, the FCFS rule is by far the dominant priority rule, mainly because of the inherent fairness but also because of the inability to obtain realistic estimates of processing time for individual jobs. The FCFS rule also has the advantage of simplicity. If other measures are important when there is high customer contact, companies may adopt the strategy of moving processing to the "backroom" so they don't necessarily have to follow FCFS.

Because the SPT rule always results in the lowest (i.e., optimal) average completion (flow) time, it can result in lower in-process inventories. And because it often provides the lowest (optimal) average tardiness, it can result in better customer service levels. Finally, since it always involves a lower average number of jobs at the work center, there tends to be less congestion in the work area. SPT also minimizes downstream idle time. However, due dates are often uppermost in managers' minds, so they may not use SPT because it doesn't incorporate due dates.

The major disadvantage of the SPT rule is that it tends to make long jobs wait, perhaps for rather long times (especially if new, shorter jobs are continually added to the system). Various modifications may be used in an effort to avoid this. For example, after waiting for a given time period, any remaining jobs are automatically moved to the head of the line. This is known as the *truncated* SPT rule.

The EDD rule directly addresses due dates and usually minimizes lateness. Although it has intuitive appeal, its main limitation is that it does not take processing time into account. One possible consequence is that it can result in some jobs waiting a long time, which adds to both in-process inventories and shop congestion.

The CR rule is easy to use and has intuitive appeal. Although it had the poorest showing in Example 2 for all three measures, it usually does quite well in terms of minimizing job tardiness. Therefore, if job tardiness is important, the CR rule might be the best choice among the rules.

Let's take a look now at the S/O (slack per operation) rule.

Example 3	Use the S/O rule to schedule the following jobs. Note that processing time includes the time remaining for the current and subsequent operations. In addition, you will need to know the number of operations remaining, including the current one.

Job	Remaining Processing Time	Due Date	Remaining Number of Operations
A	4	14	3
B	16	32	6
C	8	8	5
D	20	34	2
E	10	30	4
F	18	30	2

Solution

Determine the difference between the due date and the processing time for each operation. Divide the amount by the number of remaining operations, and rank them from low to high. This yields the sequence of jobs:

Job	(1) Remaining Processing Time	(2) Due Date	(3) (2) − (1) Slack	(4) Remaining Number of Operations	(5) (3) ÷ (4) Ratio	(6) Rank
A	4	14	10	3	3.33	3
B	16	32	16	6	2.67	2
C	8	8	0	5	0	1
D	20	34	14	2	7.00	6
E	10	30	20	4	5.00	4
F	18	30	12	2	6.00	5

The indicated sequence (see column 6) is C-B-A-E-F-D.

Using the S/O rule, the designated job sequence may change after any given operation, so it is important to reevaluate the sequence after each operation. Note that any of the previously mentioned priority rules could be used on a station-by-station basis for this situation; the only difference is that the S/O approach incorporates downstream information in arriving at a job sequence.

In reality, many priority rules are available to sequence jobs, and some other rule might provide superior results for a given set of circumstances. The purpose in examining these few rules is to provide insight into the nature of sequencing rules. The following section describes a special-purpose algorithm that can be used to sequence a set of jobs that must all be processed at the same two machines or work centers.

SEQUENCING JOBS THROUGH TWO WORK CENTERS[1]

Johnson's rule is a technique that managers can use to minimize the makespan for a group of jobs to be processed on two machines or at two successive work centers (sometimes referred to as a two-machine flow shop).[2] It also minimizes the total idle time at the work centers. For the technique to work, several conditions must be satisfied:

Johnson's rule Technique for minimizing makespan for a group of jobs to be processed on two machines or at two work centers.

1. Job time (including setup and processing) must be known and constant for each job at each work center.
2. Job times must be independent of the job sequence.
3. All jobs must follow the same two-step work sequence.
4. Job priorities cannot be used.
5. All units in a job must be completed at the first work center before the job moves on to the second work center.

Determination of the optimum sequence involves these steps:

1. List the jobs and their times at each work center.
2. Select the job with the shortest time. If the shortest time is at the first work center, schedule that job first; if the time is at the second work center, schedule the job last. Break ties arbitrarily.
3. Eliminate the job and its time from further consideration.
4. Repeat steps 2 and 3, working toward the center of the sequence, until all jobs have been scheduled.

When significant idle time at the second work center occurs, job splitting at the first center just prior to the occurrence of idle time may alleviate some of it and also shorten throughput time. In Example 4, this was not a concern. The last solved problem at the end of this chapter illustrates the use of job splitting.

A group of six jobs is to be processed through a two-machine flow shop. The first operation involves cleaning and the second involves painting. Determine a sequence that will minimize the total completion time for this group of jobs. Processing times are as follows:

Example 4

| Job | PROCESSING TIME (HOURS) | |
	Work Center 1	Work Center 2
A	5	5
B	4	3
C	8	9
D	2	7
E	6	8
F	12	15

a. Select the job with the shortest processing time. It is job D, with a time of two hours.

Solution

[1]For a description of a heuristic that can be used for the case where a set of jobs is to be processed through more than two work centers, see Thomas Vollmann et al., *Manufacturing Planning and Control Systems,* 4th ed. (Burr Ridge, IL: Richard D. Irwin, 1997), p. 532.

[2]S. M. Johnson, "Optimal Two- and Three-Stage Production with Setup Times Included," *Naval Research Quarterly* 1 (March 1954), pp. 61–68.

b. Since the time is at the first center, schedule job D first. Eliminate job D from further consideration.

c. Job B has the next shortest time. Since it is at the second work center, schedule it last and eliminate job B from further consideration. We now have

1st	2nd	3rd	4th	5th	6th
D					B

d. The remaining jobs and their times are

Job	1	2
A	5	5
C	8	9
E	6	8
F	12	15

Note that there is a tie for the shortest remaining time: job A has the same time at each work center. It makes no difference, then, whether we place it toward the beginning or the end of the sequence. Suppose it is placed arbitrarily toward the end. We now have

1st	2nd	3rd	4th	5th	6th
D				A	B

e. The shortest remaining time is six hours for job E at work center 1. Thus, schedule that job toward the beginning of the sequence (after job D). Thus,

1st	2nd	3rd	4th	5th	6th
D	E			A	B

f. Job C has the shortest time of the remaining two jobs. Since it is for the first work center, place it third in the sequence. Finally, assign the remaining job (F) to the fourth position and the result is

1st	2nd	3rd	4th	5th	6th
D	E	C	F	A	B

g. One way to determine the throughput time and idle times at the work centers is to construct a chart:

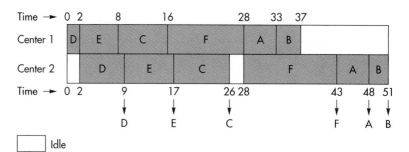

Thus, the group of jobs will take 51 hours to complete. The second work center will wait two hours for its first job and also wait two hours after finishing job C. Center 1 will be finished in 37 hours. Of course, idle periods at the beginning or end of the sequence could be used to do other jobs or for maintenance or setup/teardown activities.

Using the Lekin software on your CD would produce this output:

©*Feldman and Pinedo.*

SEQUENCING JOBS WHEN SETUP TIMES ARE SEQUENCE-DEPENDENT

The preceding discussion and examples assumed that machine setup times are independent of processing order, but in many instances that assumption is not true. Consequently, a manager may want to schedule jobs at a workstation taking those dependencies into account. The goal is to minimize total setup time.

Consider the following table, which shows workstation machine setup times based on job processing order. For example, if job A is followed by job B, the setup time for B will be 6 hours. Furthermore, if job A is completed first, followed by job B, job C will then follow job B, and have a setup time of 4 hours. If a job is done first, its setup time will be the amount shown in the setup time column to the right of the job. Thus, if job A is done first, its setup time will be 3 hours.

		Setup time (hrs.)	Resulting following job setup time (hrs.) is		
			A	**B**	**C**
If the	**A**	**3**	–	6	2
preceding	**B**	**2**	1	–	4
job is	**C**	**2**	5	3	–

The simplest way to determine which sequence will result in the lowest total setup time is to list each possible sequence and determine its total setup time. In general, the number of different alternatives is equal to $n!$, where n is the number of jobs. Here, n is 3, so $n! = 3 \times 2 \times 1 = 6$. The six alternatives and their total setup times are:

Sequence	Setup Times	Total
A-B-C	3 + 6 + 4 =	13
A-C-B	3 + 2 + 3 =	8
B-A-C	2 + 1 + 2 =	5 (best)
B-C-A	2 + 4 + 5 =	11
C-A-B	2 + 5 + 6 =	13
C-B-A	2 + 3 + 1 =	6

Hence, to minimize total setup time, the manager would select sequence B-A-C.

This procedure is relatively simple to do manually when the number of jobs is two or three. However, as the number of jobs increases, the list of alternatives quickly becomes larger. For example, six jobs would have 720 alternatives. In such instances, a manager would employ a computer to generate the list and identify the best alternative(s). (Note that more than one alternative may be tied for the lowest setup time.)

WHY SCHEDULING CAN BE DIFFICULT

Scheduling can be difficult for a number of reasons. One is that in reality, an operation must deal with variability in setup times, processing times, interruptions, and changes in the set of jobs. Another major reason is that except for very small problems, there is no method for identifying the optimal schedule, and it would be virtually impossible to sort through the vast number of possible alternatives to obtain the best schedule. As a result, scheduling is far from an exact science and, in many instances, is an ongoing task for a manager.

Computer technology reduces the burden of scheduling and makes real-time scheduling possible.

THINGS A MANAGER CAN DO TO ACHIEVE GOOD SCHEDULING RESULTS

There are a number of actions that managers can consider to minimize scheduling problems, such as:

- Setting realistic due dates.
- Focusing on bottleneck operations: First, try to increase the capacity of the operations. If that is not possible or feasible, schedule the bottleneck operations first, and then schedule the nonbottleneck operations around the bottleneck operations.
- Considering lot splitting for large jobs. This probably works best when there are relatively large differences in job times.

THE THEORY OF CONSTRAINTS

Another approach to scheduling was developed and promoted by Eli Goldratt.[3] He avoided much of the complexity often associated with scheduling problems by simply focusing on *bottleneck* operations (i.e., those for which there was insufficient capacity—in effect, a work center with zero idle time). He reasoned the output of the system was limited by the output of the bottleneck operation(s); therefore, it was essential to schedule the nonbottleneck operations in a way that minimized the idle time of the bottleneck operation(s). Thus, idle time of nonbottleneck operations was not a factor in overall productivity of the system, as long as the bottleneck operations were used effectively. The result was a technique for scheduling intermittent production systems that was simpler and less time-consuming to use.

The technique uses a *drum-buffer-rope* conceptualization to manage the system. The "drum" is the schedule; it sets the pace of production. The goal is to schedule to make maximum use of bottleneck resources. The "buffer" refers to potentially constraining re-

---

[3]Eli Goldratt, *The General Theory of Constraints* (New Haven, CT: Avraham Y. Institute, 1989).

sources outside of the bottleneck. The role of the buffer is to keep inventory from piling up on either side of the bottleneck operation. The "rope" represents the synchronizing of the sequence of operations to insure effective use of the bottleneck operations. The goal is to avoid costly and time-consuming multiple setups, particularly of capacity constrained resources, so they do not become bottlenecks too.

Goldratt also developed a system of varying batch sizes to achieve the greatest output of bottleneck operations. He used the term *process batch* to denote the basic lot size for a job and the term *transfer batch* to denote a portion of the basic lot that could be used during production to facilitate utilization of bottleneck operations. In effect, a lot could be split into two or more parts. Splitting a large lot at one or more operations preceding a bottleneck operation would reduce the waiting time of the bottleneck operation.

Additional Service Considerations

Scheduling service systems presents certain problems not generally encountered in manufacturing systems. This is due primarily to (1) the inability to store or inventory services, and (2) the random nature of customer requests for service. In some situations, the second difficulty can be moderated by using appointment or reservation systems, but the inability to store services in most cases is a fact of life that managers must contend with.

An important goal in service systems is to match the flow of customers and service capabilities. An ideal situation is one that has a smooth flow of customers through the system. This would occur if each new customer arrives at the precise instant that the preceding customer's service is completed, as in a physician's office, or in air travel where the demand just equals the number of available seats. In each of these situations customer waiting time is minimized, and the service system staff and equipment would be fully utilized. Unfortunately, the random nature of customer requests for service that generally prevails in service systems makes it nearly impossible to provide service capability that matches demand. Moreover, if service times are subject to variability—say, because of differing processing requirements—the inefficiency of the system is compounded. The inefficiencies can be reduced if arrivals can be scheduled (e.g., appointments), as in the case of doctors and dentists. However, in many situations appointments are not possible (supermarkets, gas stations, theaters, hospital emergency rooms, repair of equipment breakdowns). Chapter 19, on waiting lines, focuses on those kinds of situations. There, the emphasis is on intermediate-term decisions related to service capacity. In this section, we will concern ourselves with short-term *scheduling,* in which much of the capacity of a system is essentially fixed, and the goal is to achieve a certain degree of customer service by efficient utilization of that capacity.

Customers waiting to be served. In many situations, appointments are not possible, and waiting lines are inevitable.

Scheduling in service systems may involve scheduling (1) customers, (2) the workforce, and (3) equipment. Scheduling customers often takes the form of appointment systems or reservation systems.

APPOINTMENT SYSTEMS

Appointment systems are intended to control the timing of customer arrivals in order to minimize customer waiting while achieving a high degree of capacity utilization. A doctor can use an appointment system to schedule patients' office visits during the afternoon, leaving the mornings free for hospital duties. Similarly, an attorney can schedule client meetings around court appearances. Even with appointments, however, problems can still arise due to lack of punctuality on the part of patients or clients, no-shows, and the inability to completely control the length of contact time (e.g., a dentist might run into complications in filling a tooth and have to spend additional time with a patient, thus backing up later appointments). Some of this can be avoided by trying to match the time reserved for a patient or client with the specific needs of that case rather than setting appointments at regular intervals. Even with the problems of late arrivals and no-shows, the appointment system is a tremendous improvement over random arrivals.

RESERVATION SYSTEMS

Reservation systems are designed to enable service systems to formulate a fairly accurate estimate of the demand on the system for a given time period and to minimize customer disappointment generated by excessive waiting or inability to obtain service. Reservation systems are widely used by resorts, hotels and motels, restaurants, and some modes of transportation (e.g., airlines, car rentals). In the case of restaurants, reservations enable management to spread out or group customers so that demand matches service capabilities. Late arrivals and no-shows can disrupt the system. One approach to the no-show problem is to use decision theory (described in the supplement to Chapter 5). The problem can also be viewed as a single-period inventory problem, as described in Chapter 13.

SCHEDULING THE WORKFORCE

Scheduling customers is demand management. Scheduling the workforce is capacity management. This approach works best when demand can be predicted with reasonable accuracy. This is often true for restaurants, theaters, rush-hour traffic, and similar instances that have repeating patterns of intensity of customer arrivals. Scheduling hospital personnel, police, and telephone operators for catalog sales, credit card companies, and mutual fund companies also comes under this heading. An additional consideration is the extent to which variations in customer demands can be met with workforce flexibility. Thus, capacity can be adjusted by having cross-trained workers who can be temporarily assigned to help out on bottleneck operations during periods of peak demand.

Various constraints can affect workforce scheduling flexibility, including legal, behavioral, technical—such as workers' qualifications to perform certain operations—and budget constraints. Union contracts may provide still more constraints.

SCHEDULING MULTIPLE RESOURCES

In some situations, it is necessary to coordinate the use of more than one resource. For example, hospitals must schedule surgeons, operating room staffs, recovery room staffs, admissions, special equipment, nursing staffs, and so on. Educational institutions must schedule faculty, classrooms, audiovisual equipment, and students. As you might guess, the greater the number of resources to be scheduled, the greater the complexity of the problem and the less likely that an optimum schedule can be achieved. The problem is further complicated by the variable nature of such systems. For example, educational institutions frequently change their course offerings, student enrollments change, and students exhibit different course-selection patterns.

Some schools and hospitals are using computer programs to assist them in devising acceptable schedules, although many appear to be using intuitive approaches with varying degrees of success.

Airlines are another example of service systems that require the scheduling of multiple resources. Flight crews, aircraft, baggage handling equipment, ticket counters, gate personnel, boarding ramps, and maintenance personnel all have to be coordinated. Furthermore, government regulations on the number of hours a pilot can spend flying place an additional restriction on the system. Another interesting variable is that, unlike most systems, the flight crews and the equipment do not remain in one location. Moreover, the crew and the equipment are not usually scheduled as a single unit. Flight crews are often scheduled so that they return to their base city every two days or more often, and rest breaks must be considered. On the other hand, the aircraft may be in almost continuous use except for periodic maintenance and repairs. Consequently, flight crews commonly follow different trip patterns than that of the aircraft.

There are also other activities that must be scheduled, some of which are described by American Airlines Chairman Robert L. Crandall in the following reading.

Service systems are prone to slowdowns when variability in demand for services causes bottlenecks. Part of the difficulty lies in predicting which operations will become bottlenecks. Moreover, bottlenecks may shift with the passage of time, so that different operations become bottleneck operations—further complicating the problem.

Servicing Passenger Planes   Robert L. Crandall

www.americanair.com

Before takeoff and after landing, you've probably noticed lots of people and various types of vehicles and equipment busily moving around on the ground outside with no apparent game plan, particularly at larger airports. Actually, all that activity is carefully orchestrated, and because the people involved are an important part of our team, I'd like to tell you what the hustle and bustle is all about.

When a flight lands and approaches the terminal, ramp personnel guide the aircraft to its parking position and after it comes to a stop, put chocks under its wheels. As soon as that's been done, other workers hook up ground-based power and air conditioning. Electric power comes from what looks like a large, industrial-strength extension cord plugged into the lower portion of the nose section. Heated or cooled air goes into the cabin via the big yellow hoses that run from the airplane either to the terminal, in cities where we have central air-handling facilities or, in others, to mobile air-handling units.

On the airplane, meanwhile, flight attendants open the door and as passengers begin deplaning, a mechanic squeezes past them to get a debriefing from the cockpit and check to see if any maintenance work must be done.

Once all deplaning passengers are off, the cabin cleaners go into high gear on most flights, cleaning our seatback pockets, tidying up the cabin, cleaning the lavatories, doing a light vacuuming, repositioning safety belts for each seat's next occupant, and so forth. (A more thorough cleaning is done each night.)

Simultaneously, out on the ramp, our people are unloading baggage, freight, and mail from the airplane's belly compartments and beginning the process of sorting by various categories and destinations. In addition to the bags and cargo that have reached their destination, which must be delivered promptly to passengers and shippers, some must be transferred to other American or American Eagle flights, and still others must be transferred to other carriers. Complicating matters further, baggage, freight, and mail are often handled in different facilities on the airport property.

If a meal has been served or is planned for the outbound flight, catering trucks pull up to service the First Class and main cabin galleys. Another special truck services the lavatory holding tanks, and in the midst of all this, mechanics are dealing with any problems reported by the crew and doing their own walk-around inspections.

Once all that is complete, customers start to board the aircraft for its next flight and everything happens in reverse. Ground workers start loading baggage in the forward belly and freight and mail in the rear. Fuel trucks pull up to refuel most flights. The airplanes must be "watered" as well; fresh water is pumped aboard from either a water truck or servicing equipment built into the gate itself. During cold-weather months, deicing trucks add another element of ramp activity as they spray fluid on the airplane's wings and fuselage.

Most of the work on the ramp is done by our own people, principally fleet-service personnel, but there are also various services, like catering, which are performed by contractors.

All this simultaneous activity can create conflicts. Baggage carts unloading the forward hold can encroach on the ground space needed by the trucks catering the First Class cabin, for example, and fuelers perform their function in the space needed by those unloading freight and mail. The ramp crew chiefs are the conductors, orchestrating the entire production, overseeing the detail, and seeing to it that all gets done without mishap—and on time.

It's a delicate balancing act, and although our customers rarely come in contact with the folks working on the ramp, they are an important part of a team that aims to serve every customer well and keep our operation running safely and on time.

Source: *American Way,* March 15, 1995.

A meal supply truck arrives to load supplies onto an American Airlines plane before its scheduled departure.

Scheduling can either help or hinder operations strategy. If a manager does scheduling well, products or services can be made or delivered in a timely manner. Resources can be used to best advantage and customers will be satisfied. Scheduling not performed well will result in inefficient use of resources and possibly dissatisfied customers.

The implication is clear: Management should not overlook the important role that scheduling plays in the success of an organization and the supply chain, giving a competitive advantage if handled well or disadvantage if done poorly. Time-based competition depends on good scheduling. Coordination of materials, equipment use, and employee time is an important function of operations management. It is not enough to have good design, superior quality, and the other elements of a well-run organization if scheduling is done poorly—just as it is not enough to own a well-designed and well-made car, with all the latest features for comfort and safety, if the owner doesn't know how to drive it!

Summary

Scheduling involves the timing and coordination of operations. Such activities are fundamental to virtually every organization. Scheduling problems differ according to whether a system is designed for high volume, intermediate volume, or low volume. Scheduling problems are particularly complex for job shops (low volume) because of the variety of jobs these systems are required to process.

The two major problems in job-shop scheduling are assigning jobs to machines or work centers, and designating the sequence of job processing at a given machine or work center. Gantt load charts are frequently employed to help managers visualize workloads, and they are useful for describing and analyzing sequencing alternatives. In addition, both heuristic and optimizing methods are used to develop loading and sequencing plans. For the most part, the optimization techniques can be used only if certain assumptions can be made.

Customer requirements in service systems generally present very different circumstances than those encountered in manufacturing systems. Some services can use appointments and reservations for scheduling purposes, although not all systems are amenable to this. When multiple resources are involved, the task of balancing the system can be fairly complex.

Key Terms

assignment model, 735	job time, 739
backward scheduling, 734	Johnson's rule, 745
finite loading, 732	load chart, 731
flow-shop scheduling, 728	loading, 731
flow system, 728	makespan, 740
forward scheduling, 734	priority rules, 739
Gantt chart, 731	schedule chart, 734
horizontal loading, 732	scheduling, 728
Hungarian method, 736	sequencing, 738
infinite loading, 732	vertical loading, 732
input/output (I/O) control, 734	workstation, 738
job-shop scheduling, 731	

Solved Problems

Problem 1

The assignment method. The following table contains information on the cost to run three jobs on four available machines. Determine an assignment plan that will minimize costs.

	MACHINE			
	A	**B**	**C**	**D**
1	12	16	14	10
Job 2	9	8	13	7
3	15	12	9	11

In order for us to be able to use the assignment method, the numbers of jobs and machines must be equal. To remedy this situation, add a *dummy* job with costs of 0, and then solve as usual.

Solution

	MACHINE			
	A	**B**	**C**	**D**
1	12	16	14	10
2	9	8	13	7
Job 3	15	12	9	11
(dummy) 4	0	0	0	0

a. Subtract the smallest number from each row. The results are

	MACHINE			
	A	**B**	**C**	**D**
1	2	6	4	0
2	2	1	6	0
Job 3	6	3	0	2
4	0	0	0	0

b. Subtract the smallest number in each column. (Because of the dummy zeros in each column, the resulting table will be unchanged.)

c. Determine the minimum number of lines needed to cross out the zeros. One possible way is

d. Because the number of lines is less than the number of rows, modify the numbers.

(1) Subtract the smallest uncovered number (1) from each uncovered number.

(2) Add the smallest uncovered number to numbers at line intersections.

The result is

	MACHINE			
	A	**B**	**C**	**D**
1	1	5	4	0
2	1	0	6	0
Job 3	5	2	0	2
4	0	0	1	1

e. Test for optimality:

Machine

	A	B	C	D
1	1	5	4	0
2	1	0	6	0
3	5	2	0	2
4	0	0	1	1

Job

Because the minimum number of lines equals the number of rows, an optimum assignment can be made.

f. Assign jobs to machines. Start with rows 1 and 3, since they each have one zero, and columns A and C, also with one zero each. After each assignment, cross out all the numbers in that row *and* column. The result is

Machine

		A	B	C	D
	1	1	5	4	0
	2	1	0	6	0
Job	3	5	2	0	2
	4	0	0	1	1

Notice that there is only one assignment in each row, and only one assignment in each column.

g. Compute total costs, referring to the original table:

```
1-D  . . . $10
2-B  . . . . 8
3-C  . . .  9
4-A  . . .  0
           ────
          $27
```

h. The implication of assignment 4-A is that machine A will not be assigned a job. It may remain idle or be used for another job.

Problem 2

Priority rules. Job times (including processing and setup) are shown in the following table for five jobs waiting to be processed at a work center:

Job	Job Time (hours)	Due Date (hours)
a	12	15
b	6	24
c	14	20
d	3	8
e	7	6

Determine the processing sequence that would result from each of these priority rules:

a. SPT

b. EDD

Solution

Assume job times are independent of processing sequence.

Note: CR = Hour due ÷ Job time

	a. SPT		**b. EDD**	
Job	**Job Time**	**Processing Order**	**Hour Due**	**Processing CR**
a	12	4	15	3
b	6	2	24	5
c	14	5	20	4
d	3	1	8	2
e	7	3	6	1

Priority rules. Using the job times and due dates from Solved Problem 2, determine each of the following performance measures for first-come, first-served processing order: **Problem 3**

a. Makespan
b. Average flow time
c. Average tardiness
d. Average number of jobs at the workstation.

Solution

Job	**Job Time**	**Flow Time**	**Hour Due**	**Hours Late**
a	12	12	15	0
b	6	18	24	0
c	14	32	20	12
d	3	35	8	27
e	7	42	6	36
Total		139		75

a. Makespan $= 42$ hours

b. Average flow time $= \dfrac{\text{Total flow time}}{\text{Number of jobs}} = \dfrac{139}{5} = 27.80$ hours

c. Average tardiness $= \dfrac{\text{Total hours late}}{\text{Number of jobs}} = \dfrac{75}{5} = 15$ hours

d. Average number of jobs at workstation $= \dfrac{\text{Total flow time}}{\text{Makespan}} = \dfrac{139}{42} = 3.31$

S/O rule. Using the following information, determine an order processing sequence using the S/O priority rule. **Problem 4**

Order	**Processing Time Remaining (days)**	**Due Date (days)**	**Number of Operations Remaining**
A 20		30	2
B 11		18	5
C 10		6	2
D 16		23	4

Assume times are independent of processing sequence. **Solution**

Order	(1) Remaining Processing Time	(2) Due Date	(3) (2) − (1) Slack	(4) Number of Operations	(5) Ratio	(6) Rank (sequence)
A 20		30	10	2	5.00	4
B 11		18	7	5	1.40	2
C 10		6	−4	2	−2.00	1
D 16		23	7	4	1.75	3

(Note that one ratio is negative. When negatives occur, assign the *lowest* rank to the *most negative* number.)

Problem 5

Sequencing jobs through two work centers. Use Johnson's rule to obtain the optimum sequence for processing the jobs shown through work centers A and B.

	JOB TIMES (HOURS)	
Job	Work Center A	Work Center B
a 2.50		4.20
b 3.80		1.50
c 2.20		3.00
d 5.80		4.00
e 4.50		2.00

Solution

a. Identify the smallest time: job b (1.50 hours at work center B). Because the time is for B, schedule this job last.

b. The next smallest time is job e (2.00 hours at B). Schedule job e next to last.

c. Identify the smallest remaining job time: job c (2.20 hours at center A). Since the time is in the A column, schedule job c first. At this point, we have:

c, _____, _____, e, b

d. The smallest time for remaining jobs is 2.50 hours for job a at center A. Schedule this job after job c. The one remaining job (job d) fills the remaining slot. Thus, we have:

c-a-d-e-b

Problem 6

For Solved Problem 5, determine what effect splitting jobs c, d, e, and b in work center A would have on the idle time of work center B and on the throughput time. Assume that each job can be split into two equal parts.

Solution

We assume that the processing sequence remains unchanged and proceed on that basis. The solution from the previous problem is shown in the following chart. The next chart shows reduced idle time at center B when splitting is used.

An inspection of these two figures reveals that throughput time has decreased from 20.30 hours to 19.55 hours. In addition, the original idle time was 5.6 hours. After splitting certain jobs, it was reduced to 4.85 hours, so some improvement was achieved. Note that processing times at B are generally less than at A for jobs toward the end of the sequence. As a result, jobs such as e and b at B were scheduled so that they were *centered* around the finishing times of e and b, respectively, at A, to avoid having to break the jobs due to waiting for the remainder of the split job from A. Thus, the greatest advantage from job splitting generally comes from splitting earlier jobs when Johnson's rule is used for sequencing.

Discussion and Review Questions

1. Why is scheduling fairly simple for repetitive systems but fairly complex for job shops?
2. What are the main decision areas of job-shop scheduling?
3. What are Gantt charts? How are they used in scheduling? What are the advantages of using Gantt charts?
4. What are the basic assumptions of the assignment method of linear programming?
5. Briefly describe each of these priority rules:
   a. FCFS   *b.* SPT   *c.* EDD   *d.* S/O   *e.* Rush
6. Why are priority rules needed?
7. What problems not generally found in manufacturing systems do service systems present in terms of scheduling the use of resources?
8. Doctors' and dentists' offices frequently schedule patient visits at regularly spaced intervals. What problems can this create? Can you suggest an alternative approach to reduce these problems? Under what circumstances would regularly spaced appointments constitute a reasonable approach to patient scheduling?
9. How are scheduling and productivity related?
10. What factors would you take into account in deciding whether or not to split a job?
11. Explain the term *makespan*.

Memo Writing Exercises

1. The manufacturing company you work for is about to open a call-in service line that will allow customers to ask technical questions of manufacturing people about their orders. Your manager, Veronica Jones, will be responsible for setting up a schedule for staffing the center. She has asked for your opinion on whether that scheduling would be any different from the job-shop scheduling in current use. Write a one-page memo to her on these scheduling differences.
2. Write a short memo to your new employee, Chuck West, contrasting local and global priority rules. Provide him with the names of a few rules of each type.

Problems

1. Use the assignment method to determine the best way to assign workers to jobs, given the following cost information. Compute the total cost for your assignment plan.

		JOB	
	A	**B**	**C**
1	5	8	6
Worker 2	6	7	9
3	4	5	3

2. Rework problem 1 treating the numbers in the table as profits instead of costs. Compute the total profit.
3. Assign trucks to delivery routes so that total costs are minimized, given the cost data shown. What is the total cost?

ROUTE

	A	B	C	D	E
1	4	5	9	8	7
2	6	4	8	3	5
Truck 3	7	3	10	4	6
4	5	2	5	5	8
5	6	5	3	4	9

4. Develop an assignment plan that will minimize processing costs, given the information shown, and interpret your answer.

MACHINE

	A	B	C
1	12	8	11
2	13	10	8
Job 3	14	9	14
4	10	7	12

5. Use the assignment method to obtain a plan that will minimize the processing costs in the following table under these conditions:

   a. The combination 2-D is undesirable.

   b. The combinations 1-A and 2-D are undesirable.

MACHINE

	A	B	C	D	E
1	14	18	20	17	18
2	14	15	19	16	17
Job 3	12	16	15	14	17
4	11	13	14	12	14
5	10	16	15	14	13

6. The following table contains information concerning four jobs that are awaiting processing at a work center.

Job	Job Time (days)	Due Date (days)
A	14	20
B	10	16
C	7	15
D	6	17

   a. Sequence the jobs using (1) FCFS, (2) SPT, (3) EDD, and (4) CR. Assume the list is by order of arrival.

   b. For each of the methods in part *a*, determine (1) the average job flow time, (2) the average lateness, and (3) the average number of jobs at the work center.

   c. Is one method superior to the others? Explain.

7. Using the information presented in the following table, identify the processing sequence that would result using (1) FCFS, (2) SPT, (3) EDD, and (4) CR. For each method, determine (1) average job flow time, (2) average job lateness, and (3) average number of jobs in the system. Jobs are listed in order of arrival. (*Hint:* First determine the total job time for each job by computing the total processing time for the job and then adding in the setup time. All times and due dates are in hours.)

Job	Processing Time per Unit	Units per Job	Setup Time	Due Date
a	0.14	45	0.7	4
b	0.25	14	0.5	10
c	0.10	18	0.2	12
d	0.25	40	1.0	20
e	0.10	75	0.5	15

8. The following table shows orders to be processed at a machine shop as of 8 A.M. Monday. The jobs have different operations they must go through. Processing times are in days. Jobs are listed in order of arrival.

   a. Determine the processing sequence at the first work center using each of these rules: (1) FCFS, (2) S/O.

   b. Compute the effectiveness of each rule using each of these measures: (1) average completion time, (2) average number of jobs at the work center.

Job	Processing Time (days)	Due Date (days)	Remaining Number of Operations
A	8	20	2
B	10	18	4
C	5	25	5
D	11	17	3
E	9	35	4

9. A wholesale grocery distribution center uses a two-step process to fill orders. Tomorrow's work will consist of filling the seven orders shown. Determine a job sequence that will minimize the time required to fill the orders.

TIME (HOURS)

Order	Step 1	Step 2
A	1.20	1.40
B	0.90	1.30
C	2.00	0.80
D	1.70	1.50
E	1.60	1.80
F	2.20	1.75
G	1.30	1.40

10. The times required to complete each of eight jobs in a two-machine flow shop are shown in the table that follows. Each job must follow the same sequence, beginning with machine A and moving to machine B.

    a. Determine a sequence that will minimize makespan time.

    b. Construct a chart of the resulting sequence, and find machine B's idle time.

    c. For the sequence determined in part a, how much would machine B's idle time be reduced by splitting the last two jobs in half?

TIME (HOURS)

Job	Machine A	Machine B
a	16	5
b	3	13
c	9	6
d	8	7
e	2	14
f	12	4
g	18	14
h	20	11

11. Given the operation times provided:
    a. Develop a job sequence that minimizes idle time at the two work centers.
    b. Construct a chart of the activities at the two centers, and determine each one's idle time, assuming no other activities are involved.

JOB TIMES (MINUTES)

	A	B	C	D	E	F
Center 1	20	16	43	60	35	42
Center 2	27	30	51	12	28	24

12. A shoe repair operation uses a two-step sequence that all jobs in a certain category follow. For the group of jobs listed,
    a. Find the sequence that will minimize total completion time.
    b. Determine the amount of idle time for workstation B.
    c. What jobs are candidates for splitting? Why? If they were split, how much would idle time and makespan time be reduced?

JOB TIMES (MINUTES)

	a	b	c	d	e
Workstation A	27	18	70	26	15
Workstation B	45	33	30	24	10

13. The following schedule was prepared by the production manager of Marymount Metal Shop.

Job	CUTTING Start	CUTTING Finish	POLISHING Start	POLISHING Finish
A	0	2	2	5
B	2	6	6	9
C	6	11	11	13
D	11	15	15	20
E	15	17	20	23
F	17	20	23	24
G	20	21	24	28

Determine a schedule that will result in earlier completion of all jobs on this list.

14. The production manager must determine the processing sequence for seven jobs through the grinding and deburring departments. The same sequence will be followed in both departments. The manager's goal is to move the jobs through the two departments as quickly as possible. The foreman of the deburring department wants the SPT rule to be used to minimize the work-in-process inventory in his department.

PROCESSING TIME (HOURS)

Job	Grinding	Deburring
A	3	6
B	2	4
C	1	5
D	4	3
E	9	4
F	8	7
G	6	2

a. Prepare a schedule using SPT for the grinding department.
b. What is the flow time in the grinding department for the SPT sequence? What is the total time needed to process the seven jobs in both the grinding and deburring departments?
c. Determine a sequence that will minimize the total time needed to process the jobs in both departments. What flow time will result for the grinding departments?

d. Discuss the trade-offs between the two alternative sequencing arrangements. At what point would the production manager be indifferent concerning the choice of sequences?

15. A foreman has determined processing times at a work center for a set of jobs and now wants to sequence them. Given the information shown, do the following:

a. Determine the processing sequence using (1) FCFS, (2) SPT, (3) EDD, and (4) CR. For each sequence, compute the average job tardiness, the average flow time, and the average number of jobs at the work center. The list is in FCFS order.

b. Using the results of your calculations in part a, show that the average flow time and the average number of jobs measures are equivalent for all four sequencing rules.

c. Determine the processing sequence that would result using the S/O rule.

Job	Job Time (days)	Due Date	Operations Remaining
a	4.5	10	3
b	6.0	17	4
c	5.2	12	3
d	1.6	27	5
e	2.8	18	3
f	3.3	19	1

16. Given the information in the following table, determine the processing sequence that would result using the S/O rule.

Job	Remaining Processing Time (days)	Due Date	Remaining Number of Operations
a	5	8	2
b	6	5	4
c	9	10	4
d	7	12	3
e	8	10	2

17. Given the following information on job times and due dates, determine the optimal processing sequence using (1) FCFS, (2) SPT, (3) EDD, and (4) CR. For each method, find the average job flow time and the average job tardiness.

Job	Job Time (hours)	Due Date (hours)
a	3.5	7
b	2.0	6
c	4.5	18
d	5.0	22
e	2.5	4
f	6.0	20

18. The Budd Gear Co. specializes in heat-treating gears for many automobile companies. At 8 A.M., when Budd's shop opened today, five orders (listed in order of arrival) were waiting to be processed.

Order	Order Size (units)	Per Unit Time in Heat Treatment (minutes/unit)	Due Date (min. from now)
A	16	4	160
B	6	12	200
C	10	3	180
D	8	10	190
E	4	1	220

    a. If the due date rule is used, what sequence should be used?

    b. What will be the average job tardiness?

    c. What will be the average number of jobs in the system?

    d. Would the SPT rule produce better results in terms of lateness?

19. The following table contains order-dependent setup times for three jobs. Which processing sequence will minimize the total setup time?

		Setup time (hrs.)	Following job's setup time (hrs.) A	B	C
Preceding Job	**A**	2	–	3	5
	B	3	8	–	2
	C	2	4	3	–

20. The following table contains order-dependent setup times for three jobs. Which processing sequence will minimize the total setup time?

		Setup time (hrs.)	Following job's setup time (hrs.) A	B	C
Preceding Job	**A**	2.4	–	1.8	2.2
	B	3.2	0.8	–	1.4
	C	2.0	2.6	1.3	–

21. The following table contains order-dependent setup times for four jobs. For safety reasons, job C cannot follow job A, nor can job A follow job C. Determine the processing sequence that will minimize the total setup time. (*Hint:* There are 12 alternatives.)

		Setup time (hrs.)	Following job's setup time (hrs.) A	B	C	D
Preceding Job	**A**	2	–	5	x	4
	B	1	7	–	3	2
	C	3	x	2	–	2
	D	2	4	3	6	–

22. Given this information on planned and actual inputs and outputs for a service center, determine the work backlog for each period. The beginning backlog is 12 hours of work. The figures shown are standard hours of work.

		Period 1	2	3	4	5
Input	Planned	24	24	24	24	20
	Actual	25	27	20	22	24
Output	Planned	24	24	24	24	23
	Actual	24	22	23	24	24

Goldratt, Eli, and Jeff Cox. *The Goal: A Process of Ongoing Improvement.* Great Barrington, MA: North River Press, 1992.

Hopp, Wallace J., and Mark L. Spearman. *Factory Physics.* 2nd ed. New York: Irwin/McGraw-Hill, 2001.

Metters, Richard, and Vicente Vargus. "A Comparison of Production Scheduling Policies on Costs, Service Levels, and Scheduling Changes." *Production and Operations Management* 17, no. 8 (1999), pp. 76–91.

Pinedo, M., and X. Chao. *Operations Scheduling with Applications in Manufacturing and Services.* New York: McGraw-Hill/Irwin, 1999.

Silver, E. A., D. F. Pyke, and R. Peterson. *Inventory Management and Production Planning and Scheduling.* New York: Wiley, 1998.

Vollman, Thomas E., William L. Berry, and D. Clay Whybark. *Manufacturing Planning and Control Systems.* 4th ed. Burr Ridge, IL: Irwin, 1997.

PART SIX

Project Management

The chapter in this section covers
various topics related to successfully
managing projects.

CHAPTER EIGHTEEN
Project Management

CHAPTER OUTLINE

Reading: The International Space
  Station Project (ISS), 766

Introduction, 767

Behavioral Aspects of Project
  Management, 768
  The Nature of Projects, 768
  Key Decisions in Project
    Management, 768
  The Project Manager, 769
  Project Champions, 770

Reading: Project Managers Have
  Never Been More Critical, 770

Reading: Five Ways to Pump Up
  Your Champion, 771
  The Pros and Cons of Working on
    Projects, 771

Project Life Cycle, 772

Risk Management, 773

Work Breakdown Structure, 774

Planning and Scheduling with Gantt
  Charts, 774

PERT and CPM, 775
  The Network Diagram, 776
  Network Conventions, 777

Deterministic Time Estimates, 778

A Computing Algorithm, 780

Activity-on-Arrow, 780
Activity-on-Node, 785
Computing Slack Times, 786

Probabilistic Time Estimates, 786

Determining Path Probabilities, 789

Technology, 792

Simulation, 793

Time–Cost Trade-Offs:
  Crashing, 793

Advantages of Using PERT and
  Potential Sources of Error, 797

Strategy, 797

Summary, 798

Key Terms, 798

Solved Problems, 798

Discussion and Review
  Questions, 805

Memo Writing Exercises, 806

Problems, 806

Cases: The Case of the Mexican
  Crazy Quilt, 812
  Time, Please, 813

Reading: Managing Projects with a
  New View, 813

Selected Bibliography and Further
  Reading, 814

LEARNING OBJECTIVES

*After completing this chapter, you
should be able to:*

1 Discuss the behavioral aspects of
  projects in terms of project
  personnel and the project
  manager.

2 Discuss the nature and
  importance of a work breakdown
  structure in project management.

3 Give a general description of
  PERT/CPM techniques.

4 Construct simple network
  diagrams.

5 List the kinds of information that
  a PERT or CPM analysis can
  provide.

6 Analyze networks with
  deterministic times.

7 Analyze networks with
  probabilistic times.

8 Describe activity "crashing" and
  solve typical problems.

The International Space Station Project (ISS)

www.nasa.com

Hopefully, by 2006 the space station assembly will be complete and functional 220 miles above the earth at a cost of more than $40 billion. The station will cover an area of approximately two football fields and have a housing unit the size of a jumbo jet. This space station will conduct research concerning human life and production of products in space. The complexity of the space station and the coordination required among 16 partner nations is daunting.

Russia launched the first piece of the space station on November 20, 1998. This module provides power for future assembly operations. On December 3 of the same year, the United States launched the first space component hub, which serves as the connector for other pieces of the station. This hub also serves as housing for up to seven astronauts. In total it is planned that 34 space deliveries will transport more than 900,000 pounds of materials needed to assemble the completed station. It is estimated that 144 to 160 two-person space walks and 1,800 hours of construction will be needed to assemble the station.

The project has had a bumpy ride to date, and more problems are expected before the project is complete. The project is billions of dollars over budget; the total cost could reach $96 billion. The collapse of the Russian economy has caused delays on their development of a major module of the station. Financial support has been needed to get the Russian effort back on track. Redesign has been continual because of the multiple needs of the partners of the 16 nations; these changes have resulted in costly delays. Some of the risks have been underestimated, and reassessment has suggested failures along the way are inevitable—delivery vehicles blowing up, docking problems, even someone killed during construction. There have been calls to "pull the plug" on the project. Nevertheless, the project moves forward.

The ESA (European Space Agency) is coordinating several ISS projects linked to the development of an ATV (automatic transfer vehicle—not related to all-terrain vehicles), which will supply nine tons of cargo and fuel to the space station. These projects, which include countries and companies from France, Germany, Russian, Italy, will take place in their respective countries under the guidance of ESA. Daimler-Chrysler will produce the estimated 15 ATVs scheduled for delivery between 2003 and 2013. Standard penalty clauses for late delivery are in place. Incentive provisions for continuous improvement of mission success and payload mass are included in the multination endeavor.

Problems are deemed surmountable, and plans to complete the assembly by 2006 are in place. It is expected that the world-class laboratory will lead to discoveries that will touch the lives of everyone in the world. Perhaps the lessons learned will be as valuable as the discoveries.

Source: Clifford F. Gray, and Erik W. Larson, *Project Management: the Managerial Process* (New York: McGraw-Hill, 2000), pp. 466–67.

www.microsoft.com

Consider each of the following examples. See if you can guess what they have in common. The Olympic Games—summer games, winter games, you name it—involve much more than the festivities, the excitement, national pride, and competition among athletes. They all involve a tremendous amount of planning, preparation, and coordinating work that needs to get done before and during the games. Athletes' living quarters and training facilities must be provided, competition schedules must be developed, arrangements for televising events must be made, equipment and crews must be coordinated, transportation and hotel accommodations must be made, and many other activities that go on behind the scenes must be planned and managed so that everything goes off smoothly.

The Microsoft Corporation periodically releases new or updated software. Each release is the result of many people working countless hours writing code, testing programs, and revising code. Design, production, and marketing efforts also have to be coordinated. The reputation and profits of the company are closely related to successful software development.

A few years ago major portions of the Santa Ana freeway in California were destroyed by an earthquake and had to be rebuilt. Thousands of activities had to be planned and coordinated. Thousands of pieces of construction equipment and tons of material had to be coordinated. The rebuilding was successful, and actually completed 70 days ahead of schedule.

The movie *Titanic*, released in late 1997, was the leading box office money maker of all time. And a good thing too, because over $250 million was spent on making the

The formation at the opening ceremony at the 2000 Summer Olympics in Sydney, Australia. Planning and managing the execution of the Olympic Games is a large project that includes long-term construction and improvement of sites as well as precisely timed activities such as the opening ceremony.

movie, also a record. Imagine the immense job of planning and coordinating the script writers, set designers, set builders, camera crews, directors, actors, makeup, costumes, advertising, and more that went into making that movie.

So, what do all of these examples have in common? They were all *projects*. In fact, there are projects going on all around us, every day. Some are large, some are small. Projects are an important way that certain kinds of work get done.

Introduction

Managers typically oversee a variety of operations. Some of these involve routine, repetitive activities, but others involve nonroutine activities. Under the latter heading are **projects:** unique, one-time operations designed to accomplish a set of objectives in a limited time frame. Other examples of projects include constructing a shopping complex, launching a space shuttle, reengineering a business process, merging two companies, putting on a play, and designing and running a political campaign. Examples of projects within business organizations include designing new products or services, designing advertising campaigns, designing information systems, designing databases, software development, and designing web pages.

projects Unique, one-time operations designed to accomplish a specific set of objectives in a limited time frame.

Projects may involve considerable cost. Some have a long time horizon, and some involve a large number of activities that must be carefully planned and coordinated. Most are expected to be completed within time, cost, and performance guidelines. To accomplish this, goals must be established and priorities set. Tasks must be identified and time estimates made. Resource requirements also must be projected and budgets prepared. Once under way, progress must be monitored to assure that project goals and objectives will be achieved.

The project approach enables an organization to focus attention and concentrate efforts on accomplishing a narrow set of objectives within a limited time and budget framework. This can produce significant benefits compared with other approaches that might be considered. Even so, projects present managers with a host of problems that differ in many respects from those encountered with more routine activities. The problems of planning and coordinating project activities can be formidable for large projects, which typically have hundreds or even thousands of activities that must be carefully planned and monitored if the project is to proceed according to schedule and at a reasonable cost.

The chapter introduces the basic concepts of project management. It begins with a brief discussion of some behavioral aspects of project management, along with some of the difficulties project managers are apt to encounter. The main portion of the chapter is devoted to a description of graphical and computational methods that are used for planning and scheduling projects.

Behavioral Aspects of Project Management

Project management differs from management of more traditional activities mainly because of its limited time framework and the unique set of activities involved, which gives rise to a host of unique problems. This section describes more fully the nature of projects and their behavioral implications. Special attention is given to the role of the project manager.

THE NATURE OF PROJECTS

Projects go through a series of stages—a life cycle—which include project definition planning, execution of major activities, and project phaseout. During this life cycle, a variety of skill requirements are involved. The circumstances are analogous to constructing a house. Initially an idea is presented and its feasibility is assessed, then plans must be drawn up and approved by the owner and possibly a town building commission or other regulatory agency. Then a succession of activities occurs, each with its own skill requirements, starting with the site preparation, then laying the foundation, erecting the frame, roofing, constructing exterior walls, wiring and plumbing, installing kitchen and bathroom fixtures and appliances, interior finishing work, and painting and carpeting work. Similar sequences occur on large construction projects, in R&D work, in the aerospace industry, and in virtually every other instance where projects are being carried out.

Projects typically bring together people with diverse knowledge and skills, most of whom remain associated with the project for less than its full life. Some people go from project to project as their contributions become needed, and others are "on loan," either on a full-time or part-time basis, from their regular jobs. The latter is usually the case when a special project exists within the framework of a more traditional organization. Certain kinds of organizations are involved with projects on a regular basis; examples include consulting firms, architects, writers and publishers, and construction firms. In those organizations, it is not uncommon for some individuals to spend virtually all of their time on projects.

Some organizations use a *matrix organization* that allows them to integrate the activities of a variety of specialists within a functional framework. For instance, they have certain people who prepare proposals, others who concentrate exclusively on engineering, others who devote their efforts to marketing, and so on.

KEY DECISIONS IN PROJECT MANAGEMENT

Much of the success of projects depends on certain key managerial decisions, such as:

- Deciding which projects to implement.
- Selecting the project manager.
- Selecting the project team.
- Planning and designing the project.
- Managing and controlling project resources.
- Deciding if and when a project should be terminated.

Deciding Which Projects to Implement. This involves determining the criteria that will be used to decide which projects to pursue. Typical factors include budget, availability of appropriate knowledge and skill personnel, and cost−benefit considerations. Of course, other factors may override these criteria, factors such as availability of funds, safety issues, government-mandated actions, and so on.

Selecting the Project Manager. The project manager is the central person in the project. The following section on project managers discusses this topic.

Selecting the Project Team. The team can greatly influence the ultimate success or failure of a project. Important considerations include not only a person's knowledge and skill base, but also how well the person works with others (particularly those who have already been chosen for the project), enthusiasm for the project, other projects the person is involved in, and how likely those other projects might be to interfere with work on this project.

Planning and Designing the Project. Project planning and design require decisions on project performance goals, a timetable for project completion, the scope of the project, what work needs to be done, how it will be done, if some portions will be outsourced, what resources will be needed, a budget, and when and how long resources will be needed.

Managing and Controlling Project Resources. This involves managing personnel, equipment, and the budget, establishing appropriate metrics for evaluating the project, monitoring progress, and taking corrective action when needed. Also necessary is designing an information system and deciding what project documents should be generated, their contents and format, when and by whom they will be needed, and how often they should be updated.

Deciding If and When a Project Should Be Terminated. Sometimes it is better to terminate a project than to invest any more resources. Important considerations here are the likelihood of success, termination costs, and whether resources could be better used elsewhere.

THE PROJECT MANAGER

The project manager bears the ultimate responsibility for the success or failure of the project. He or she must be capable of working through others to accomplish the objectives of the project. The project manager is responsible for effectively managing each of the following:

1. The *work,* so that all of the necessary activities are accomplished in the desired sequence, and performance goals are met.
2. The *human resources,* so that those working on the project have direction and motivation.
3. *Communications,* so that everybody has the information they need to do their work.
4. *Quality,* so that performance objectives are realized.
5. *Time,* so that the project is completed on schedule.
6. *Costs,* so that the project is completed within budget.

To effectively manage a project, a project manager must employ a certain set of skills. The skills include the ability to motivate and direct team members; make trade-off decisions; expedite the work when necessary; put out fires; and monitor time, budget, and technical details. For projects that involve fairly well-defined work, those skills will often suffice. However, for projects that are less well defined, and thus have a higher degree of uncertainty, the project manager must also employ strong leadership skills. These include the ability to adapt to changing circumstances that may involve changes to project goals, technical requirements, and project team composition. As a leader, the project manager must not only be able to deal with these issues; he or she must also recognize the need for change, decide what changes are necessary, and work to accomplish them.

The job of project manager can be both difficult and rewarding. The manager must coordinate and motivate people who sometimes owe their allegiance to other managers in their functional areas. In addition, the people who work on a project frequently possess specialized knowledge and skills that the project manager lacks. Nevertheless, the manager is expected to guide and evaluate their efforts. Project managers must often function in an environment that is beset with uncertainties. Even so, budgets and time constraints are usually imposed, which can create additional pressures on project personnel. Finally, the project manager may not have the authority needed to accomplish all the objectives of the project. Instead, the manager must sometimes rely on persuasion and the cooperation of others to realize project goals.

Ethical issues often arise in connection with projects. Examples include the temptation to understate costs or to withhold information in order to get a project approved, pressure to alter or make misleading statements on status reports, falsifying records, compromising workers' safety, and approving substandard work. It is the responsibility of managers at all levels to maintain and enforce ethical standards. Moreover, employees often take their cue from managers' behavior, so it is doubly important for managers to model ethical behavior. The Project Management Institute (PMI) has a website (www.pmi.org) that includes a code of ethics for project managers, in addition to other useful information about project management.

The position of project manager has high visibility. The rewards of the job of project manager come from the creative challenges of the job, the benefits of being associated with a successful project (including promotion and monetary compensation), and the personal satisfaction of seeing it through to its conclusion.

PROJECT CHAMPIONS

project champion A person who promotes and supports a project.

Some companies make use of **project champions.** These are people, usually within the company, who promote and support the project. They can be instrumental in facilitating the work of the project manager by "talking up" the project to other managers who might be asked to share resources with the project team as well as employees who might be asked to work on parts of the project. The work that a project champion does can be critical to the success of a project, so it is important for team members to encourage and communicate with the project champion.

READING

Project Managers Have Never Been More Critical Bob Weinstein

Not many people can eloquently describe the changing role of project managers as well as Jonathan Gispan, who teaches the skill to managers at the Lockheed Martin Corporation division in King of Prussia, PA. Gispan spent 38 years of his career working at GE Aerospace as a project manager.

Project mangers have never been more critical, according to this veteran techie. The function's core responsibilities haven't changed, but the players and playing field are very different than they were five years ago.

Gispan views the project manager as the focal point of a complex relationship matrix that includes customers, workers, vendors and bosses. "Project managers make things happen," he says. "Not only do they manage a project from start to finish, they also manage the people who make it happen."

The job requires a jack-of-all-trades who can both understand a problem and solve it. "Project managers must successfully manage the total lifecycle of a project," says Gispan.

"The job requires a super-organized person who knows how to get a project completed quickly and inexpensively and boasts the advanced communication skills necessary to work closely with vendors, project teams and senior management."

Project managers have always had to deal with changing relationships. The big change, according to Gispan, is the speed of change, which has made the project manager's job more difficult. "The changes taking place now are faster and more dramatic than in the past," he says. "Customers are less inclined to give you money for development work, for example. They'd rather save money by using off-the-shelf capabilities. Budgets that used to be reasonably substantial and healthy are now tight."

Gispan adds that corporate mergers and consolidations have complicated the picture. Project managers must deal with complex, often labyrinthine decision-making structures. Getting quick decisions requires work and persistence.

Further complicating the situation is a high worker attrition rate. "A decade ago, the attrition rate was about 3 percent; today it has jumped to almost 10 percent," Gispan explains. "It means project managers have to constantly put together new teams."

Through it all, the project manager must be clear-headed and keep tight rein on projects. It sounds intimidating, yet Gispan sees it as a positive. "The current marketplace keeps you on your toes," he says. "Even though everything is changing at what seems like an overwhelming pace, it is best to view change as a motivator that allows you to keep pace with technology and get better at your job. The idea is not merely to cope with change but to thrive in it. It is more of an attitude than anything else."

What does it take to be a project manager? "You need a good technical base," says Karen Nichols, project manager at EWP Engineering, Inc., a consulting engineering company in Salt Lake City, UT. "That translates to at least five to seven years in the trenches."

That's for starters. "But you also need to know how the business side of the equation works," says Nichols. "This is tough for some technical people because it requires the ability to understand how the two different sides of the business mesh. Project managers must also be familiar with accounting methods as well as sales and marketing strategies. In short, they must know how to manage a project so it makes a profit."

If you're not sure if you're up to the job, Nichols suggests testing the waters by watching other project managers at work.

"You're more likely to get this opportunity at a mid-size to large company," she says.

If you think you have what it takes, ask to work with a project manager. "It won't take you long to find out whether you have an aptitude and natural feel for the work," says Nichols. "Not everyone is happy—or capable of—juggling many balls in the air at once."

Once you get your feet wet, you can move up quickly, adds Gispan. "After you've proven to management that you're organized and can manage several tasks, it won't be long before you are managing everything associated with a program. Get good at it and you'll move up the ranks from project manager to general manager where you are running several company businesses."

And, don't be confused by job titles. Each company has its own unique title for the project manger role. Whatever the title, a project manager is easy to spot. "It's the person who negotiates with all the key players and makes things happen," says Gispan. "Technology companies would perish without them."

Source: Reprinted with permission from the *Rochester Democrat and Chronicle,* February 18. 1999.

READING

Five Ways to PUMP UP Your Champion

- Maintain open, honest dialogue. Schedule meetings and send memos to keep your champion informed, even when things aren't going according to plan. But keep the conversations short.

- Keep your champion engaged. Asking for ongoing input sends a clear signal that he or she plays a crucial role. And don't be afraid to ask for help.

- Create visibility. Throw a party, hang banners or go after an award. Create excitement that will keep your project on the champion's radar screen.

- Instill confidence. Communicate your strategy for success and let your champion know as you attain each milestone.

- Do your part to get end users' support. Clearly define how the project will benefit them and how you and your champion can maintain or boost their support.

Source: Excerpted from Julekha Dash, "Cheering on the Champions," *Computerworld,* November 2, 1998.

THE PROS AND CONS OF WORKING ON PROJECTS

People are selected to work on special projects because the knowledge or abilities they possess are needed. In some instances, however, their supervisors may be reluctant to allow them to interrupt their regular jobs, even on a part-time basis, because it may require training a new person to do a job that will be temporary. Moreover, managers don't want to lose the output of good workers. The workers themselves are not always eager to participate in projects because it may mean working for two bosses who impose differing demands, it may disrupt friendships and daily routines, and it presents the risk of being replaced on the current job. Furthermore, there may be fear of being associated with an unsuccessful project because of the adverse effect it might have on career advancement. In too many instances, when a major project is phased out and the project team disbanded, team members tend to drift away from the organization for lack of a new project and the difficulty of returning to former jobs. This tendency is more pronounced after lengthy projects and is less likely to occur when a team member works on a part-time basis.

In spite of the potential risks, people are attracted by the potential rewards of being involved in a project. One is the dynamic environment that surrounds a project, often a marked contrast to the staid environment of a routine in which some may feel trapped. Some individuals seem to thrive in more dynamic environments; they welcome the challenge of working under pressure and solving new problems. Then, too, projects may present opportunities to meet new people and to increase future job opportunities, especially if the project is successful. In addition, association with a project can be a source of status among fellow workers. Finally, working on projects frequently inspires a team spirit, increasing morale and motivation to achieve successful completion of project goals.

Project Life Cycle

The size, length, and scope of projects varies widely according to the nature and purpose of the project. Nevertheless, all projects have something in common: They go through a life cycle, which typically consists of four phases.

1. *Definition.* This has two parts. (*a*) *Concept,* at which point the organization recognizes the need for a project or responds to a request for a proposal from a potential customer or client. (*b*) *Feasibility analysis,* which examines the expected costs, benefits, and risks of undertaking the project.

2. *Planning,* which spells out the details of the work and provides estimates of the necessary human resources, time, and cost.

3. *Execution,* during which the project itself is done. This phase often accounts for the majority of time and resources consumed by a project.

4. *Termination,* during which closure is achieved. Termination can involve reassigning personnel and dealing with any leftover materials, equipment (e.g., selling or transferring equipment), and any other resources associated with the project.

It should be noted that the phases can overlap, so that one phase may not be fully complete before the next phase begins. This can reduce the time necessary to move through the life cycle, perhaps generating some competitive advantage and cost saving. Although subsequent decisions in an earlier phase may result in waste for some portion of the activity in a following phase, careful coordination of activities can minimize that risk.

Figure 18–1 illustrates the phases in a project life cycle.

FIGURE 18-1

Project life cycle
Source: Adapted from Clifford F. Gray
and Erik W. Larson, *Project Management: The Managerial Process* (New
York: McGraw-Hill, 2000), p. 6.

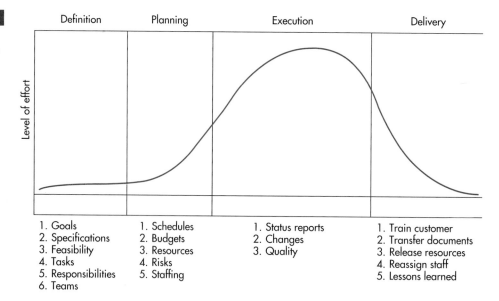

Risk Management

Risks are inherent in projects. They relate to the occurrence of events that can have undesirable consequences, such as delays, increased costs, and an inability to meet technical specifications. In some instances, there is the risk that events will occur that will cause a project to be terminated. Although careful planning can reduce risks, no amount of planning can eliminate chance events due to unforeseen, or uncontrollable, circumstances.

The probability of occurrence of risk events is highest near the beginning of a project and the lowest near the end. However, the cost associated with risk events tends to be lowest near the beginning of a project and highest near the end. (See Figure 18–2.)

Good risk management entails identifying as many potential risks as possible, analyzing and assessing those risks, working to minimize the probability of their occurrence, and establishing contingency plans (and funds) for dealing with any that do occur. Much of this takes place before the start of a project, although it is not unusual for this process to be repeated during the project as experience grows and new information becomes available.

The first step is to identify the risks. Typically, there are numerous sources of risks, although the more experience an organization has with a particular type of work, the fewer and more identifiable the risks. Everyone associated with the project should have responsibility for the task of identifying risks. Brainstorming sessions and questionnaires can be useful in this regard.

Once risks have been identified, each risk must be evaluated to determine its probability of occurrence and the potential consequences if it does occur. Both quantitative and qualitative approaches have merit. Managers and workers can contribute to this effort, and experts might be called on. Experience with previous projects can be useful. Many tools might be applied, including scenario analysis, simulation, and PERT (described later in the chapter.)

Risk reduction can take a number of forms. Much depends on the nature and scope of a project. "Redundant" (backup) systems can sometimes be used to reduce the risk of failure. For example, an emergency generator could supply power in the event of an electrical failure. Another approach is frequent monitoring of critical project dimensions with the goal of catching and eliminating problems in their early stages, before they cause extensive damage. Risks can sometimes be transferred, say by outsourcing a particular component of a project. Risk-sharing is another possibility. This might involve partnering, which can spread risks among partners; this approach may also reduce risk by enlarging the sphere of sources of ideas for reducing the risk.

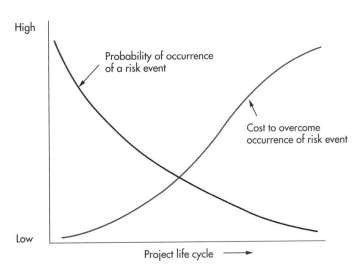

FIGURE 18-2

Risk event probability and cost
Source: Adapted from Clifford Gray and Erik W. Larson, *Project Management: The Managerial Process* (New York: McGraw-Hill, 2000), p. 140.

FIGURE 18-3

Schematic of a work break-down structure

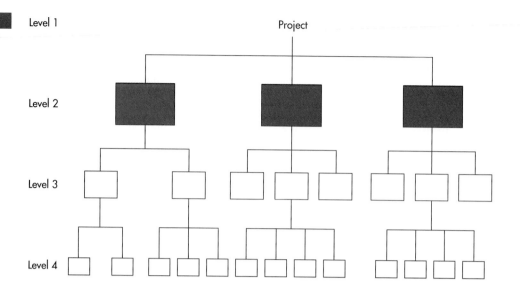

Work Breakdown Structure

work breakdown structure (WBS) A hierarchical listing of what must be done during a project.

Because large projects usually involve a very large number of activities, planners need some way to determine exactly what will need to be done so that they can realistically estimate how long it will take to complete the various elements of the project and how much it will cost. They often accomplish this by developing a **work breakdown structure (WBS),** which is a hierarchical listing of what must be done during the project. This methodology establishes a logical framework for identifying the required activities for the project (see Figure 18–3). The first step in developing the work breakdown structure is to identify the major elements of the project. These are the Level 2 boxes in Figure 18–3. The next step is to identify the major supporting activities for each of the major elements—the Level 3 boxes. Then, each major supporting activity is broken down into a list of the activities that will be needed to accomplish it—the Level 4 boxes. (For purposes of illustration, only a portion of the Level 4 boxes are shown.) Usually there are many activities in the Level 4 lists. Some large projects may involve additional levels, but Figure 18–3 gives you some idea of the concept of the work breakdown structure.

Developing a good work breakdown structure can require substantial time and effort due to the uncertainties associated with a project and/or the size of the project. Typically the portion of time spent on developing the work breakdown structure greatly exceeds the time spent on actually developing a project schedule. The importance of a work breakdown structure is underscored by the fact that it serves as the focal point for planning and doing the project.

Planning and Scheduling with Gantt Charts

The Gantt chart is a popular tool for planning and scheduling *simple* projects. It enables a manager to initially schedule project activities and then to monitor progress over time by comparing planned progress to actual progress. Figure 18–4 illustrates a Gantt chart for a bank's plan to establish a new direct marketing department. To prepare the chart, the vice president in charge of the project had to first identify the major activities that would be required. Next, time estimates for each activity were made, and the sequence of activities was determined. Once completed, the chart indicated which activities were to occur, their planned duration, and when they were to occur. Then, as the project progressed, the manager was able to see which activities were ahead of schedule and which were delaying the project. This enabled the manager to direct attention where it was needed most to speed up the project in order to finish on schedule.

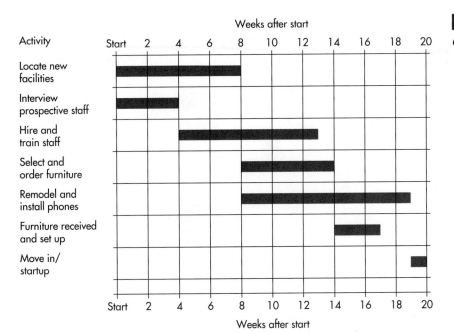

FIGURE 18-4

Gantt chart for bank example

Aside from being a visual tool, an advantage of a Gantt chart is its simplicity. However, Gantt charts fail to reveal certain relationships among activities that can be crucial to effective project management. For instance, if one of the early activities in a project suffers a delay, it would be important for the manager to be able to easily determine which later activities would result in a delay. Conversely, some activities may safely be delayed without affecting the overall project schedule. The Gantt chart does not directly reveal this. On more complex projects, it is often used in conjunction with a *network diagram,* the subject of the following section, for scheduling purposes.

PERT and CPM

PERT (program evaluation and review technique) and **CPM** (critical path method) are two of the most widely used techniques for planning and coordinating large-scale projects. By using PERT or CPM, managers are able to obtain:

1. A graphical display of project activities.

2. An estimate of how long the project will take.

3. An indication of which activities are the most critical to timely project completion.

4. An indication of how long any activity can be delayed without delaying the project.

PERT and CPM were developed independently during the late 1950s. PERT evolved through the joint efforts of Lockheed Aircraft, the U.S. Navy Special Projects Office, and the consulting firm of Booz, Allen & Hamilton in an effort to speed up the Polaris missile project. At the time, the U.S. government was concerned that the Soviet Union might be gaining nuclear superiority over the United States, and it gave top priority for the early completion of the project by the Department of Defense. The project was a huge one, with more than 3,000 contractors and thousands of activities. PERT was quite successful and was generally credited with shaving two years off the length of the project. Partly for that reason, PERT or some similar technique is now required on all large government projects.

CPM was developed by J. E. Kelly of the Remington Rand Corporation and M. R. Walker of DuPont to plan and coordinate maintenance projects in chemical plants.

Although PERT and CPM were developed independently, they have a great deal in common. Moreover, many of the initial differences between them have disappeared as

PERT Program evaluation and review technique, for planning and coordinating large projects.

CPM Critical path method, for planning and coordinating large projects.

www.dupont.com

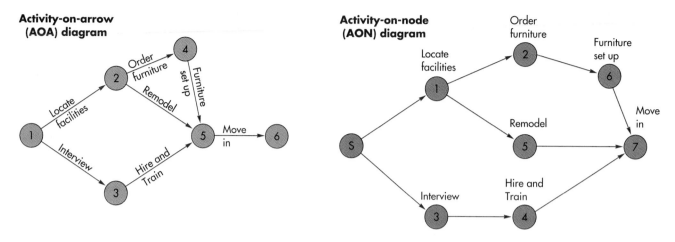

Activity-on-arrow (AOA) diagram

Activity-on-node (AON) diagram

A simple project network diagram

users borrowed certain features from one technique for use with the other. For example, PERT originally stressed probabilistic activity time estimates, because the environment in which it developed was typified by high uncertainty. In contrast, the tasks for which CPM was developed were much less uncertain, so CPM originally made no provision for variable time estimates. At present, either technique can be used with deterministic or probabilistic times. Other initial differences concerned the mechanical aspects of developing project networks. However, from a conceptual standpoint, most of these differences were relatively minor. To avoid confusion, we will not delve into the differences. For practical purposes, the two techniques are the same; the comments and procedures described will apply to CPM analysis as well as to PERT analysis of projects.

THE NETWORK DIAGRAM

network (precedence) diagram Diagram of project activities that shows sequential relationships by use of arrows and nodes.

One of the main features of PERT and related techniques is their use of a **network** or **precedence diagram** to depict major project activities and their sequential relationships. There are two slightly different conventions for constructing these network diagrams. Under one convention, the *arrows* designate activities; under the other convention, the *nodes* designate activities. These conventions are referred to as **activity-on-arrow (AOA)** and **activity-on-node (AON). Activities** consume resources and/or *time*. The nodes in the AOA approach represent the activities' starting and finishing points, which are called **events.** Events are points in time. Unlike activities, they consume neither resources nor time. The nodes in an AON diagram represent activities.

activity-on-arrow (AOA) Network diagram convention in which arrows designate activities.

activity-on-node (AON) Network diagram convention in which nodes designate activities.

Both conventions are illustrated in Figure 18–5, using the bank example that was depicted in the Gantt chart in Figure 18–4. Compare the two. In the AOA diagram, the arrows represent activities and they show the sequence in which certain activities must be performed (e.g., Interview precedes Hire and Train); in the AON diagram, the arrows show only the sequence in which certain activities must be performed while the nodes represent the activities. Activities in AOA networks can be referred to in either of two ways. One is by their endpoints (e.g., activity 2-4) and the other is by a letter assigned to an arrow (e.g., activity *c*). Both methods are illustrated in this chapter. Activities in AON networks are referred to by a letter (or number) assigned to a node. Although these two approaches are slightly different, they both show sequential relationships—something Gantt charts don't.

activities Project steps that consume resources and/or time.

events The starting and finishing of activities, designated by nodes in the AOA convention.

Note that the AON diagram has a starting node, S, which is actually not an activity but is added in order to have a single starting node. Despite these differences, the two conventions are remarkably similar, so you should not encounter much difficulty in understanding either one. In fact, there are convincing arguments for having some familiarity with *both* approaches. Perhaps the most compelling is that both approaches are widely used. However, any particular organization would typically use only one approach, and employees would have to work with that approach. Moreover, a contractor doing work for the organization may be using the other approach, so employees of the organization who deal with the contractor on project matters would benefit from knowledge of the other approach.

Of particular interest to managers are the *paths* in a network diagram. A **path** is a sequence of activities that leads from the starting node to the ending node. For example, in the AOA diagram, the sequence 1-2-4-5-6 is a path. In the AON diagram, S-1-2-6-7 is a path. Note that in both diagrams there are three paths. One reason for the importance of paths is that they reveal *sequential relationships*. The importance of sequential relationships cannot be overstated: If one activity in a sequence is delayed (i.e., late) or done incorrectly, the start of all following activities on that path will be delayed.

Another important aspect of paths is the length of a path: How long will a particular sequence of activities take to complete? The length (of time) of any path can be determined by summing the expected times of the activities on that path. The path with the longest time is of particular interest because it governs project completion time. In other words, expected project duration equals the expected time of the longest path. Moreover, if there are any delays along the longest path, there will be corresponding delays in project completion time. Attempts to shorten project completion must focus on the longest sequence of activities. Because of its influence on project completion time, the longest path is referred to as the **critical path,** and its activities are referred to as **critical activities.**

Paths that are shorter than the critical path can experience some delays and still not affect the overall project completion time as long as the ultimate path time does not exceed the length of the critical path. The allowable slippage for any path is called **slack,** and it reflects the difference between the length of a given path and the length of the critical path. The critical path, then, has zero slack time.

path A sequence of activities that leads from the starting node to the finishing node.

critical path The longest path; determines expected project duration.

critical activities Activities on the critical path.

slack Allowable slippage for a path; the difference between the length of a path and the length of the critical path.

NETWORK CONVENTIONS

Developing and interpreting network diagrams requires some familiarity with networking conventions. Table 18–1 illustrates some of the most basic and most common features of network diagrams. This will provide sufficient background for understanding the basic concepts associated with precedence diagrams and allow you to solve typical problems.

In order to recognize the need to use a dummy activity using the AOA approach when presented with a list of activities and the activities each precedes, examine the "Precedes Activity" list. Look for instances where multiple activities are listed, such as *c,d* in the following list. If *c* or *d* appears separately in the list (as *c* does here), a dummy will be needed to clarify the relationship (see the last diagram in Table 18–1.)

Activity	Precedes Activity
a	c
b	c,d

Here are two more AOA conventions:

For reference purposes, nodes are numbered typically from left to right:

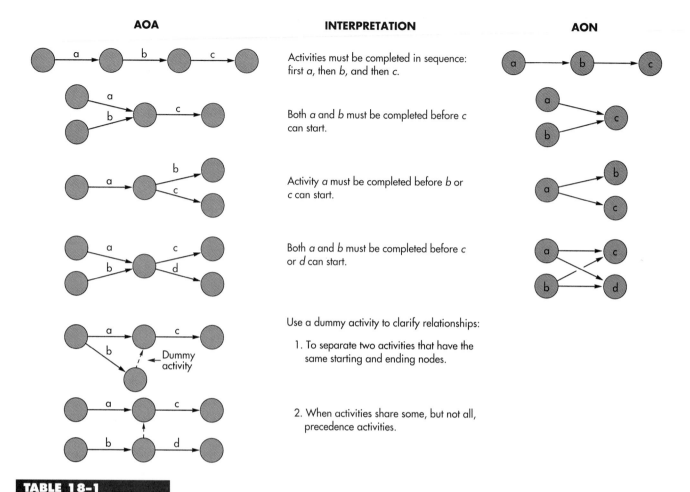

AOA	INTERPRETATION	AON

TABLE 18-1

Network conventions

Starting and ending arrows are sometimes used during development of a network for increased clarity:

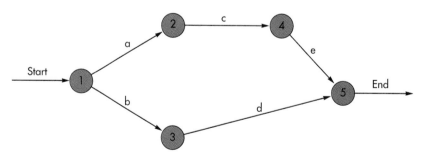

Deterministic Time Estimates

The main determinant of the way PERT and CPM networks are analyzed and interpreted is whether activity time estimates are *probabilistic* or *deterministic*. If time estimates can be made with a high degree of confidence that actual times are fairly certain, we say the estimates are **deterministic.** If actual times are subject to variation, we say the estimates are **probabilistic.** Probabilistic time estimates must include an indication of the extent of probable variation.

This section describes analysis of networks with deterministic time estimates. A later section deals with probabilistic times.

deterministic Time estimates that are fairly certain.

probabilistic Estimates of times that allow for variation.

One of the best ways to gain an understanding of the nature of network analysis is to consider a simple example.

Given the following information:

Example 1

FIGURE 18–6A

AOA diagram

FIGURE 18–6B

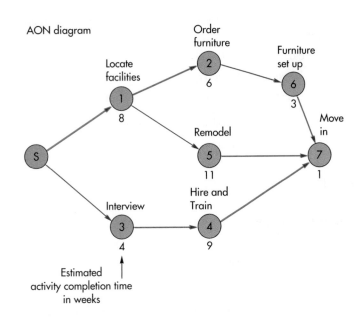

AON diagram

Estimated activity completion time in weeks

Determine:

a. The length of each path.

b. The critical path.

c. The expected length of the project.

d. Amount of slack time for each path.

a. As shown in the following table, the path lengths are 18 weeks, 20 weeks, and 14 weeks.   *Solution*

b. The longest path (20 weeks) is 1-2-5-6, so it is the critical path.

c. The expected length of the project is equal to the length of the critical path (i.e., 20 weeks).

d. We find the slack for each path by subtracting its length from the length of the critical path, as shown in the last column of the table. (*Note:* It is sometimes desirable to know the slack time associated with activities. The next section describes a method for obtaining those slack times.)

Path	Length (weeks)	Slack
1-2-4-5-6	8 + 6 + 3 + 1 = 18	20 − 18 = 2
1-2-5-6	8 + 11 + 1 = 20*	20 − 20 = 0
1-3-5-6	4 + 9 + 1 = 14	20 − 14 = 6

*Critical path length.

A Computing Algorithm

Many real-life project networks are much larger than the simple network illustrated in the preceding example; they often contain hundreds or even thousands of activities. Because the necessary computations can become exceedingly complex and time-consuming, large networks are generally analyzed by computer programs instead of manually. Planners use an algorithm to develop four pieces of information about the network activities:

ES, the earliest time activity can start, assuming all preceding activities start as early as possible.

EF, the earliest time the activity can finish.

LS, the latest time the activity can start and not delay the project.

LF, the latest time the activity can finish and not delay the project.

Once these values have been determined, they can be used to find:

1. Expected project duration.
2. Slack time.
3. The critical path.

ACTIVITY-ON-ARROW

The three examples that follow illustrate how to compute those values using the precedence diagram of Example 1.

Example 2

Compute the earliest starting time and earliest finishing time for each activity in the diagram shown in Figure 18–6a.

Solution

Begin by placing brackets at the two ends of each starting activity:

We determine and place in the brackets for each activity, the earliest starting time, ES, and the earliest finishing time, EF, as follows:

Do this for all activities, beginning at the left side of the precedence diagram and moving to the right side.

Once ES has been determined for each activity, EF can be found by adding the activity time, t, to ES: ES + t = EF.

Use an ES of 0 for all starting activities. Thus, activities 1-2 and 1-3 are assigned ES values of 0. This permits computation of the EF for each of these activities:

$$EF_{1-2} = 0 + 8 = 8 \quad \text{and} \quad EF_{1-3} = 0 + 4 = 4$$

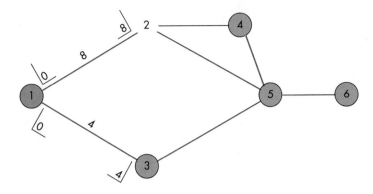

The EF time for an activity becomes the ES time for the next activity to follow it in the diagram. Hence, because activity 1-2 has an EF time of 8, both activities 2-4 and 2-5 have ES times of 8. Similarly, activity 3-5 has an ES time of 4.

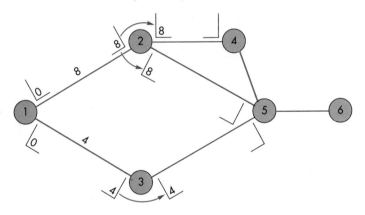

This permits calculation of the EF times for these activities: $EF_{2-4} = 8 + 6 = 14$; $EF_{2-5} = 8 + 11 = 19$; and $EF_{3-5} = 4 + 9 = 13$.

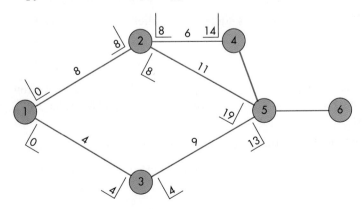

The ES for activity 4-5 is the EF time of activity 2-4, which is 14. Using this value, we find the EF for activity 4-5 is 17; $EF_{4-5} = 14 + 3 = 17$.

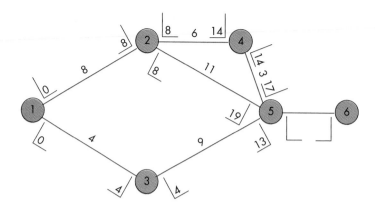

In order to determine the ES for activity 5-6, we must realize that activity 5-6 cannot start until *every* activity that precedes it is finished. Therefore, the *largest* of the EF times for the three activities that precede activity 5-6 determines ES_{5-6}. Hence, the ES for activity 5-6 is 19.

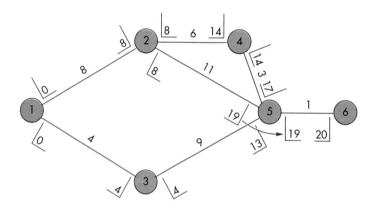

Then the EF for the last activity, 5-6, is 20; $EF_{5-6} = 19 + 1 = 20$. Note that the latest EF is the project duration. Thus, the expected length of the project is 20 weeks.

Computation of earliest starting and finishing times is aided by two simple rules:

1. The earliest finish time for any activity is equal to its earliest start time plus its expected duration, *t*:

$$EF = ES + t \tag{18-1}$$

2. ES for activities at nodes with one entering arrow is equal to EF of the entering arrow. ES for activities leaving nodes with multiple entering arrows is equal to the largest EF of the entering arrow.

Computation of the latest starting and finishing times is aided by the use of two rules:

1. The latest starting time for each activity is equal to its latest finishing time minus its expected duration:

$$LS = LF - t \tag{18-2}$$

2. For nodes with one leaving arrow, LF for arrows entering that node equals the LS of the leaving arrow. For nodes with multiple leaving arrows, LF for arrows entering that node equals the smallest LS of leaving arrows.

Finding ES and EF times involves a *forward pass* through the network; finding LS and LF times involves a *backward pass* through the network. Hence, we must begin with the EF of the last activity and use that time as the LF for the last activity. Then we obtain the LS for the last activity by subtracting its expected duration from its LF.

Example 3

Compute the latest finishing and starting times for the precedence diagram developed in Example 2.

Solution

We must add the LS and LF times to the brackets on the diagram.

Begin by setting the LF time of the last activity equal to the EF of that activity. Thus,

$$LF_{5\text{-}6} = EF_{5\text{-}6} = 20 \text{ weeks}$$

Obtain the LS time for activity 5-6 by subtracting the activity time, t, from the LF time:

$$LS_{5\text{-}6} = LF_{5\text{-}6} - t = 20 - 1 = 19.$$

Mark these values on the diagram:

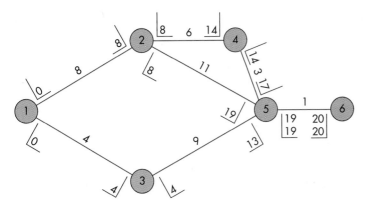

The LS time of 19 for activity 5-6 now becomes the LF time for each of the activities that precede activity 5-6. This permits determination of the LS times for each of those activities: Subtract the activity time from the LF to obtain the LS time for the activity. The LS time for activity 3-5 is $19 - 9 = 10$.

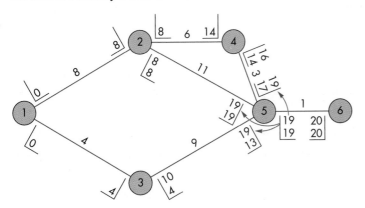

Next, the LS for activity 4-5, which is 16, becomes the LF for activity 2-4, and the LS for activity 3-5, which is 10, becomes the LF for activity 1-3. Using these values, you find the LS for each of these activities by subtracting the activity time from the LF time.

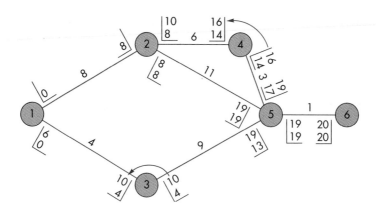

The LF for activity 1-2 is the *smaller* of the two LS times of the activities that 1-2 precedes. Hence, the LF time for activity 1-2 is 8. The reason you use the smaller time is that activity 1-2 must finish at a time that permits all following activities to start no later than their LS times.

Once you have determined the LF time of activity 1-2, find its LS time by subtracting the activity time of 8 from the LF time of 8. Hence, the LS time is 0.

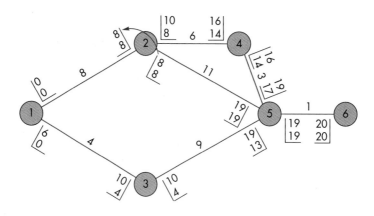

Rules for the Computing Algorithm

(*Note*: In an AON diagram, ignore the start node and/or the finish node, if these are present.)

Forward Pass

For each path, start at the left side of the diagram and work toward the right side.

For each beginning activity: ES = 0.

For each activity: ES + Activity time = EF.

For the following activity: ES = EF of preceding activity. *Note:* If an activity has multiple immediate preceding activities, set its ES equal to the largest EF of its immediate predecessors.

Backward Pass

For each path, start at the right side of the diagram and work toward the left side.

Use the largest EF as the LF for all ending activities.

For each activity: LS = LF − Activity time.

For the preceding activity: LF = LS of following activity. *Note:* If an activity has multiple immediately following activities, set the activity's LS equal to the smallest LS of the following activities.

ACTIVITY-ON-NODE

The computing algorithm is performed in essentially the same manner in the AON approach. The results are shown in Figure 18–7.

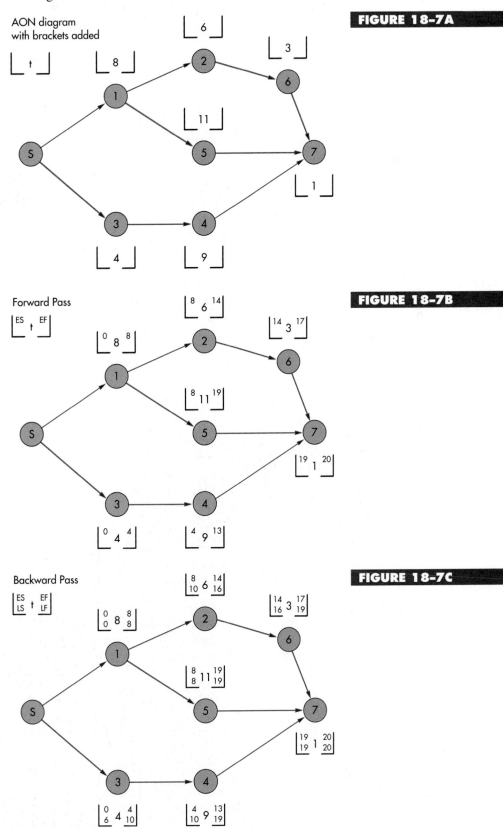

FIGURE 18-7A

AON diagram
with brackets added

FIGURE 18-7B

Forward Pass

FIGURE 18-7C

Backward Pass

COMPUTING SLACK TIMES

The slack time can be computed in either of two ways:

$$\text{Slack} = \text{LS} - \text{ES} \quad \text{or} \quad \text{LF} - \text{EF} \tag{18–3}$$

The critical path using this computing algorithm is denoted by activities with zero slack time. Thus, the table in Example 4 indicates that activities 1-2, 2-5, and 5-6 are all critical activities, which agrees with the results of the intuitive approach demonstrated in Example 1.

Knowledge of slack times provides managers with information for planning allocation of scarce resources and for directing control efforts toward those activities that might be most susceptible to delaying the project. In this regard, it is important to recognize that the activity slack times are based on the assumption that all of the activities on the same path will be started as early as possible and not exceed their expected times. Furthermore, if two activities are both on the same path (e.g., activities 2-4 and 4-5 in the preceding example) and have the same slack (e.g., two weeks), this will be the *total* slack available to both. In essence, the activities have *shared slack*. Hence, if the first activity uses all the slack, there will be zero slack for all following activities on that same path.

Example 4

Solution

Compute slack times for the preceding example.

Either the starting times or the finishing times can be used. Suppose we choose the starting times. Using ES times computed in Example 2 and LS times computed in Example 3, slack times are:

Activity	LS	ES	(LS − ES) Slack
1-2	0	0	0
1-3	6	0	6
2-4	10	8	2
2-5	8	8	0
3-5	10	4	6
4-5	16	14	2
5-6	19	19	0

As noted earlier, this algorithm lends itself to computerization. A computer printout for this problem would appear something like the one shown in Table 18–2.

Probabilistic Time Estimates

The preceding discussion assumed that activity times were known and not subject to variation. While that assumption is appropriate in some situations, there are many others where it is not. Consequently, those situations require a probabilistic approach.

The probabilistic approach involves *three* time estimates for each activity instead of one:

optimistic time The length of time required under optimal conditions.

1. **Optimistic time:** The length of time required under optimum conditions; represented by t_o.

pessimistic time The length of time required under the worst conditions.

2. **Pessimistic time:** The length of time required under the worst conditions; represented by t_p.

most likely time The most probable length of time that will be required.

3. **Most likely time:** The most probable amount of time required; represented by t_m.

Managers or others with knowledge about the project can make these time estimates.

beta distribution Used to describe the inherent variability in activity time estimates.

The **beta distribution** is generally used to describe the inherent variability in time estimates (see Figure 18–8). Although there is no real theoretical justification for using the

TABLE 18-2

Computer printout

		SCHEDULE				
		EARLY		LATE		
ACTIVITY	TIME	ES	EF	LS	LF	SLACK
1-2	8.00	0.00	8.00	0.00	8.00	0.00
1-3	4.00	0.00	4.00	6.00	10.00	6.00
2-4	6.00	8.00	14.00	10.00	16.00	2.00
2-5	11.00	8.00	19.00	8.00	19.00	0.00
3-5	9.00	4.00	13.00	10.00	19.00	6.00
4-5	3.00	14.00	17.00	16.00	19.00	2.00
5-6	1.00	19.00	20.00	19.00	20.00	0.00

THE CRITICAL PATH SEQUENCE IS:

SNODE	FNODE	TIME
1	2	8.00
2	5	11.00
5	6	1.00
		20.00

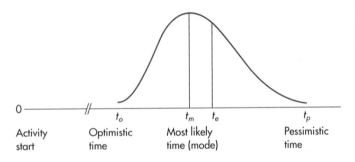

FIGURE 18-8

A beta distribution is used to describe probabilistic time estimates

beta distribution, it has certain features that make it attractive in practice: The distribution can be symmetrical or skewed to either the right or the left according to the nature of a particular activity; the mean and variance of the distribution can be readily obtained from the three time estimates listed above; and the distribution is unimodal with a high concentration of probability surrounding the most likely time estimate.

Of special interest in network analysis are the average or expected time for each activity t_e, and the variance of each activity time, σ_i^2. The expected time of an activity, t_e, is a weighted average of the three time estimates:

$$t_e = \frac{t_o + 4t_m + t_p}{6} \tag{18–4}$$

The expected duration of a path (i.e., the path mean) is equal to the sum of the expected times of the activities on that path:

Path mean = Σ of expected times of activities on the path. $\tag{18–5}$

The standard deviation of each activity's time is estimated as one-sixth of the difference between the pessimistic and optimistic time estimates. (Analogously, essentially all of the area under a normal distribution lies within three standard deviations of the mean, which is a range of six standard deviations.) We find the variance by squaring the standard deviation. Thus,

$$\sigma^2 = \left[\frac{(t_p - t_o)}{6}\right]^2 \quad \text{or} \quad \frac{(t_p - t_o)^2}{36} \tag{18–6}$$

The size of the variance reflects the degree of uncertainty associated with an activity's time: The larger the variance, the greater the uncertainty.

It is also desirable to compute the standard deviation of the expected time for *each path*. We can do this by summing the variances of the activities on a path and then taking the square root of that number; that is,

$$\sigma_{path} = \sqrt{\Sigma(\text{variances of activities on path})} \qquad (18\text{--}7)$$

The expected time of a path is found by summing the expected times of the activities that are on the path.

Example 5 illustrates these computations.

Example 5

The network diagram for a project is shown in the accompanying figure, with three time estimates for each activity. Activity times are in weeks. Do the following:

a. Compute the expected time for each activity and the expected duration for each path.
b. Identify the critical path.
c. Compute the variance of each activity and the variance of each path.

AOA diagram

AON diagram

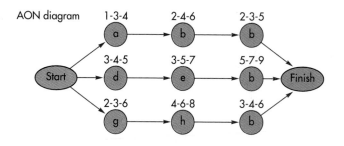

Solution

a.

Path	Activity	t_o	t_m	t_p	$t_e = \dfrac{t_o + 4t_m + t_p}{6}$	Path Total
	a	1	3	4	2.83	
a-b-c	b	2	4	6	4.00	10.00
	c	2	3	5	3.17	
	d	3	4	5	4.00	
d-e-f	e	3	5	7	5.00	16.00
	f	5	7	9	7.00	

	g	2	3	6	3.33 ⎫	
g-h-i	h	4	6	8	6.00 ⎬ 13.50	
	i	3	4	6	4.17 ⎭	

b. The path that has the longest expected duration is the critical path. Because path d-e-f has the largest path total, it is the critical path.

c.

TIMES

Path	Activity	t_o	t_m	t_p	$\sigma^2_{act} = \dfrac{(t_p - t_o)^2}{36}$	σ^2_{path}	σ_{path}
a-b-c	a	1	3	4	$(4 - 1)^2/36 = 9/36$ ⎫		
	b	2	4	6	$(6 - 2)^2/36 = 16/36$ ⎬	$34/36 = 0.944$	0.97
	c	2	3	5	$(5 - 2)^2/36 = 9/36$ ⎭		
d-e-f	d	3	4	5	$(5 - 3)^2/36 = 4/36$ ⎫		
	e	3	5	7	$(7 - 3)^2/36 = 16/36$ ⎬	$36/36 = 1.00$	1.00
	f	5	7	9	$(9 - 5)^2/36 = 16/36$ ⎭		
g-h-i	g	2	3	6	$(6 - 2)^2/36 = 16/36$ ⎫		
	h	4	6	8	$(8 - 4)^2/36 = 16/36$ ⎬	$41/36 = 1.139$	1.07
	i	3	4	6	$(6 - 3)^2/36 = 9/36$ ⎭		

Knowledge of the expected path times and their standard deviations enables a manager to compute probabilistic estimates of the project completion time, such as these:

The probability that the project will be completed by a specified time.

The probability that the project will take longer than its scheduled completion time.

These estimates can be derived from the probability that various paths will be completed by the specified time. This involves the use of the normal distribution. Although activity times are represented by a beta distribution, the path distribution is represented by a normal distribution. The summing of activity times (random variables) results in a normal distribution. This is illustrated in Figure 18–9.

DETERMINING PATH PROBABILITIES

The probability that a given path will be completed in a specified length of time can be determined using the following formula:

$$z = \frac{\text{Specified time} - \text{Path mean}}{\text{Path standard deviation}} \tag{18–8}$$

The resulting value of z indicates how many standard deviations of the path distribution the specified time is beyond the expected path duration. (A negative value of z indicates that the specified time is *earlier* than the expected path duration.) Once the value of z has been determined, it can be used to obtain the probability that the path will be completed by the specified time from Appendix B, Table B. Note that the probability is equal to the area under the normal curve to the left of z, as illustrated in Figure 18–10.

FIGURE 18-9

Activity distributions and the path distribution

Activity

Beta

$+$

Activity

Beta

$+$

Activity

Beta

$=$

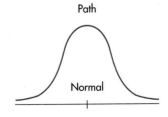
Path

Normal

FIGURE 18-10

The path probability is the area under a normal curve to the left of z

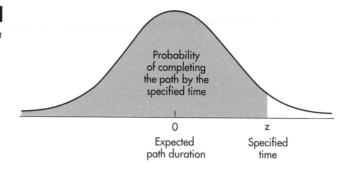

Probability
of completing
the path by the
specified time

0
Expected
path duration

z
Specified
time

If the value of z is $+2.50$ or more, the path probability is close to 100 percent (for $z = +2.50$ it is .9938). Hence, it is very likely the activities that make up the path will be completed by the specified time. For that reason, a useful rule of thumb is to treat the path probability as being equal to 100 percent if the value of z is $+2.50$ or more.

> Rule of thumb: If the value of z is $+2.50$ or more, treat the probability of path completion by the specified time as 100 percent.

The rationale for using a normal distribution is that sums of random variables (activity times) will tend to be normally distributed, regardless of the distributions of the variables. The normal tendency improves as the number of random variables increases. However, even when the number of items being summed is fairly small, the normal approximation provides a reasonable approximation to the actual distribution.

A project is not completed until *all* of its activities have been completed, not only those on the critical path. It sometimes happens that another path ends up taking more time to complete than the critical path, in which case the project runs longer than expected. Hence, it can be risky to focus exclusively on the critical path. Instead, one must consider the possibility that at least one other path will delay timely project completion. This requires determining the probability that *all* paths will finish by a specified time. To do that, find the probability that each path will finish by the specified time, and then multiply those probabilities. The result is the probability that the *project* will be completed by the specified time.

independence Assumption that path duration times are independent of each other; requiring that activity times be independent, and that each activity is on only one path.

It is important to note the assumption of **independence.** It is assumed that path duration times are independent of each other. In essence, this requires two things: Activity times are independent of each other, and each activity is only on one path. For activity times to be independent, the time for one must not be a function of the time of another; if two activities were always early or late together, they would not be considered independent. The assumption of independent *paths* is usually considered to be met if only a *few* activities in a large project are on multiple paths. Even then, common sense should govern the decision of whether the independence assumption is justified.

Example 6

Using the information from Example 5, answer the following questions:

a. Can the paths be considered independent? Why?

b. What is the probability that the project can be completed within 17 weeks of its start?

c. What is the probability that the project will be completed within 15 weeks of its start?

d. What is the probability that the project will *not* be completed within 15 weeks of its start?

Solution

a. Yes, the paths can be considered independent, since no activity is on more than one path and you have no information suggesting that any activity times are interrelated.

b. To answer questions of this nature, you must take into account the degree to which the path distributions "overlap" the specified completion time. This overlap concept is illustrated in the accompanying figure, which shows the three path distributions, each centered on that path's expected duration, and the specified completion time of 17 weeks.

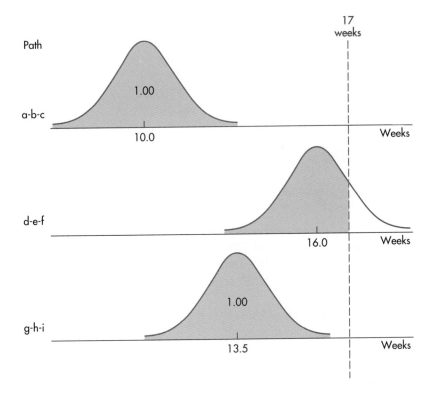

The shaded portion of each distribution corresponds to the probability that the part will be completed within the specified time. Observe that paths a-b-c and g-h-i are well enough to the left of the specified time, so that it is highly likely that both will be finished by week 17, but the critical path overlaps the specified completion time. In such cases, you need consider only the distribution of path d-e-f in assessing the probability of completion by week 17. To do so, you must first compute the value of z using Formula 18–8 for each path. For example, for path d-e-f, we have:

$$z = \frac{17 - 16}{1.00} = +1.00$$

Turning to Appendix B, Table B with $z = +1.00$, you will find that the area under the curve to the left of z is .8413. The computations are summarized in the following table. Note: If the value of z exceeds $+2.50$, treat the probability of completion as being equal to 1.000.

Path	$z = \dfrac{17 - \textbf{Expected path duration}}{\textbf{Path standard deviation}}$	Probability of Completion in 17 Weeks
a-b-c	$\dfrac{17 - 10}{0.97} = +7.22$	1.00
d-e-f	$\dfrac{17 - 16}{1.00} = +1.00$	.8413
g-h-i	$\dfrac{17 - 13.5}{1.07} = +3.27$	1.00

z-values

P(finish by week 17) = P(path a-b-c finish) × P(path d-e-f finish) × P(path g-h-i finish)

= 1.00 × .8413 × 1.00 = .8413

c. For a specified time of 15 weeks, the z values are:

Path	$z = \dfrac{15 - \text{Expected path duration}}{\text{Path standard deviation}}$	Probability of Completion in 15 Weeks
a-b-c	$\dfrac{15 - 10.00}{0.97} = +5.15$	1.0000
d-e-f	$\dfrac{15 - 16.00}{1.00} = +1.00$	.1587
g-h-i	$\dfrac{15 - 13.50}{1.07} = +1.40$	.9192

Paths d-e-f and g-h-i have z values that are less than $+2.50$.

From Appendix B, Table B, the area to the *left* of $z = -1.00$ is .1587, and the area to the *left* of $z = +1.40$ is .9192. The path distributions are illustrated in the figure. The joint probability of all finishing before week 15 is the product of their probabilities: $1.00(.1587)(.9192) = .1459$.

d. The probability of not finishing before week 15 is the complement of the probability obtained in part *c*: $1 - .1459 = .8541$.

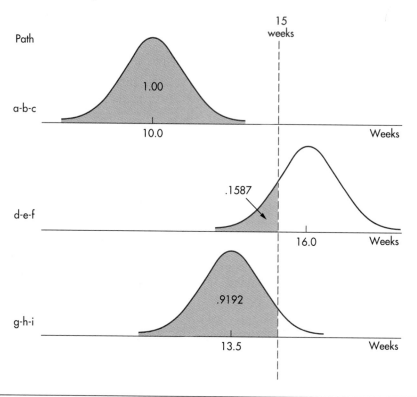

Technology

Technology has had a number of benefits for project management. Among those benefits are the use of computer-assisted design (CAD) to produce updated prototypes on construction and product-development projects, software such as Lotus Notes to keep team members who are in separate locations in close contact, the ability for remote viewing of projects, allowing those in different locations a firsthand view of progress and problems, and computer software.

Project management software is often used to facilitate project management. Here are a few of the many project management software packages that are available: CA-Super Project, Harvard Total Project Manager, Microsoft Project for Windows, and Time Line. The particular version, e.g., 4.0, is not included because new versions are released frequently.

There are many advantages to using a project management software package. Among them are the following:

- It imposes a methodology and a common project management terminology.
- It provides a logical planning structure.
- It can enhance communication among team members.
- It can flag the occurrence of constraint violations.
- It automatically formats reports.
- It can generate multiple levels of summary reports and detailed reports.
- It enables "what-if" scenarios.
- It can generate various chart types, including basic Gantt charts.

Certain requirements are associated with using project management software. One is the need to keep the system current by entering changes as soon as possible. Also, as with any software, as new versions are released, the vendor may drop support for older versions, requiring users to move to the latest version, and that can mean learning to use that version.

One thing to keep in mind is that project management is more than choosing the right software. There is much that a project manager must do. Recall the key decisions that were discussed early in the chapter.

Simulation

We have examined a method for computing the probability that a project would be completed in a specified length of time. That discussion assumed that the paths of the project were *independent*; that is, the same activities are not on more than one path. If an activity were on more than one path and it happened that the completion time for that activity far exceeded its expected time, all paths that included that activity would be affected and, hence, their times would not be independent. Where activities are on multiple paths, one must consider if the preceding approach can be used. For instance, if only a few activities are on multiple paths, particularly if the paths are *much* shorter than the critical path, that approach may still be reasonable. Moreover, for purposes of illustration, as in the text problems and examples, we treat the paths as being independent when, in fact, they may not be.

In practice, when *dependent* cases occur, project planners often use *simulation*. It amounts to a form of repeated sampling wherein many passes are made through the project network. In each pass, a randomly selected value for each activity time is made based on the characteristics of the activity's probability distribution (e.g., its mean, standard deviation, and distribution type). After each pass, the expected project duration is determined by adding the times along each path and designating the time of the longest path as the project duration. After a large number of such passes (e.g., several hundred), there is enough information to prepare a frequency distribution of the project duration times. Planners can use this distribution to make a probabilistic assessment of the actual project duration, allowing for some activities that are on more than one path. Problem 19 in the supplement to Chapter 19 illustrates this.

Time–Cost Trade-Offs: Crashing

Estimates of activity times for projects usually are made for some given level of resources. In many situations, it is possible to reduce the length of a project by injecting additional

Large projects such as bridge construction involve large budgets, many suppliers and employees, and backup plans. Materials, people, processes, and uncontrollable circumstances, such as weather, can cause delays and additional costs.

resources. The impetus to shorten projects may reflect efforts to avoid late penalties, to take advantage of monetary incentives for timely or early competition of a project, or to free resources for use on other projects. In new product development, shortening may lead to a strategic benefit: beating the competition to the market. In some cases, however, the desire to shorten the length of a project merely reflects an attempt to reduce the indirect costs associated with running the project, such as facilities and equipment costs, supervision, and labor and personnel costs. Managers often have certain options at their disposal that will allow them to shorten, or **crash,** certain activities. Among the most obvious options are the use of additional funds to support additional personnel or more efficient equipment, and the relaxing of some work specifications. Hence, a project manager may be able to shorten a project by increasing *direct* expenses to speed up the project, thereby realizing savings on indirect project costs. The goal in evaluating time−cost trade-offs is to identify activities that will reduce the sum of the indirect and direct project costs.

crash Shortening activity durations.

In order to make a rational decision on which activities, if any, to crash and on the extent of crashing desirable, a manager needs certain information:

1. Regular time and crash time estimates for each activity.
2. Regular cost and crash cost estimates for each activity.
3. A list of activities that are on the critical path.

Activities on the critical path are potential candidates for crashing, because shortening noncritical activities would not have an impact on total project duration. From an economic standpoint, activities should be crashed according to crashing costs: Crash those with the lowest crash costs first. Moreover, crashing should continue as long as the cost to crash is less than the benefits derived from crashing. These benefits might take the form of incentive payments for early project completion as part of a government contract, or they might reflect savings in the indirect project costs, or both. Figure 18–11 illustrates the basic relationship between indirect, direct, and total project costs due to crashing.

The general procedure for crashing is:

1. Obtain estimates of regular and crash times and costs for each activity.
2. Determine the lengths of all paths and path slack times.
3. Determine which are the critical activities.

FIGURE 18-11

Crashing activities*

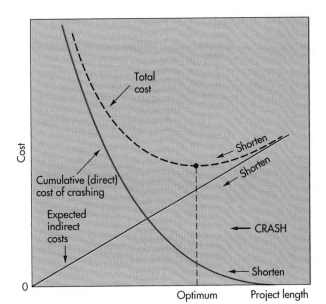

★ Crashing activities reduce indirect project costs and increase direct costs; the optimum amount of crashing results in minimizing the sum of these two types of costs.

4. Crash critical activities, in order of increasing costs, as long as crashing costs do not exceed benefits. Note that two or more paths may become critical as the original critical path becomes shorter, so that subsequent improvements will require simultaneous shortening of two or more paths. In some cases, it will be more economical to shorten an activity that is on two (or more) of the critical paths. This is true whenever the crashing cost of a joint activity is less than the sum of costs of crashing one activity on each separate path.

Using the following information, develop the optimal time–cost solution. Indirect project costs are $1,000 per day.

Example 7

Activity	Normal Time	Crash Time	Cost per Day to Crash
a	6	6	—
b	10	8	$500
c	5	4	300
d	4	1	700
e	9	7	600
f	2	1	800

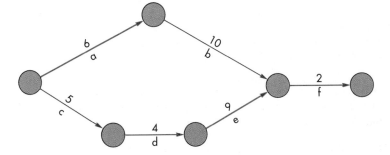

a. Determine which activities are on the critical path, its length, and the length of the other path:

Solution

Path	Length
a-b-f	18
c-d-e-f	20 (critical path)

b. Rank the critical path activities in order of lowest crashing cost, and determine the number of days each can be crashed.

Activity	Cost per Day to Crash	Available Days
c	$300	1
e	600	2
d	700	3
f	800	1

c. Begin shortening the project, one day at a time, and check after each reduction to see which path is critical. (After a certain point, another path may equal the length of the shortened critical path.) Thus:

(1) Shorten activity c one day at a cost of $300. The length of the critical path now becomes 19 days.

(2) Activity c cannot be shortened any more. Shorten activity e one day at a cost of $600. The length of path c-d-e-f now becomes 18 days, which is the same as the length of path a-b-f.

(3) The paths are now both critical; further improvements will necessitate shortening both paths.

The remaining activities for crashing and their costs are:

Path	Activity	Crash Cost (per day)
a-b-f	a	No reduction possible
	b	$500
	f	800
c-d-e-f	c	No further reduction possible
	d	$700
	e	600
	f	800

At first glance, it would seem that crashing f would not be advantageous, because it has the highest crashing cost. However, f is on both paths, so shortening f by one day would shorten *both* paths (and hence, the project) by one day for a cost of $800. The option of shortening the least expensive activity on each path would cost $500 for b and $600 for e, or $1,100. Thus shorten f by one day. The project duration is now 17 days.

(4) At this point, no additional improvement is feasible. The cost to crash b is $500 and the cost to crash e is $600, for a total of $1,100, and that would exceed the indirect project costs of $1,000 per day.

(5) The crashing sequence is summarized below:

Path	LENGTH AFTER CRASHING *n* DAYS: n = 0	1	2	3
a-b-f	18	18	18	17
c-d-e-f	20	19	18	17
Activity crashed		c	e	f
Cost		$300	$600	$800

Advantages of Using PERT and Potential Sources of Error

PERT and similar project scheduling techniques can provide important services for the project manager. Among the most useful features are these:

1. Use of these techniques forces the manager to organize and quantify available information and to recognize where additional information is needed.

2. The techniques provide a graphic display of the project and its major activities.

3. They identify (*a*) activities that should be closely watched because of the potential for delaying the project and (*b*) other activities that have slack time and so can be delayed without affecting project completion time. This raises the possibility of reallocating resources to shorten the project.

No analytical technique is without potential errors. Among the more important sources of errors are:

1. When developing the project network, managers may unwittingly omit one or more important activities.

2. Precedence relationships may not all be correct as shown.

3. Time estimates may include a fudge factor; managers may feel uncomfortable about making time estimates because they appear to commit themselves to completion within a certain time period.

4. There may be a tendency to focus solely on activities that are on the critical path. As the project progresses, other paths may become critical. Furthermore, major risk events may not be on the critical path.

Strategy

Projects can present both strategic opportunities and strategic risks, so it is critical for management to devote adequate attention and resources to projects.

Projects often occur in situations that have some degree of uncertainty, which can result in delays, budget overruns, and failure to meet technical requirements. To minimize the impact of these possibilities, management must ensure that careful planning, wise selection of project managers and team members, and monitoring of the project occurs.

Computer software and tools such as PERT can greatly assist project management. However, care must be taken to avoid focusing exclusively on the critical path. The obvious reason is that as the project progresses, other paths may become critical. But another, less obvious, reason is that key risk events may not be on the critical path. Even so, if they occur, they can have a major impact on the project.

Some projects can benefit from *managing slack*. Activities are monitored according to the percentage complete, so that if activities finish early, following activities can be started early. This may permit the project to finish early, or at least conserve slack to offset problems that might arise later in the project.

Another approach to managing slack is suggested by Goldratt in his book on the *critical chain*.[1] He asserts that people have a tendency to build in extra time in estimated times, and, by insisting that estimates be more realistic, managers can get a more realistic idea of the overall estimated time for a project. Goldratt recognizes that time buffers can be useful in certain instances, so he recommends carefully analyzing the project to identify problem areas, and inserting time buffers for those activities.

---

[1]Eliyahu M. Goldratt, Critical Chain (Great Barrington, MA: North River Press, 1997).

Summary

Projects are composed of a unique set of activities established to realize a given set of objectives in a limited time span. Projects go through a life cycle that involves definition, planning, execution, and delivery/termination. The nonroutine nature of project activities places a set of demands on the project manager that are different in many respects from those the manager of more routine operations activities experiences, both in planning and coordinating the work and in the human problems encountered. Ethical conduct and risk management are among the key issues a project managers must deal with.

PERT and CPM are two commonly used techniques for developing and monitoring projects. Although each technique was developed independently and for expressly different purposes, time and practice have erased most of the original differences, so that now there is little distinction between the two. Either provides the manager with a rational approach to project planning and a graphical display of project activities. Both depict the sequential relationships that exist among activities and reveal to managers which activities must be completed on time to achieve timely project completion. Managers can use that information to direct their attention toward the most critical activities.

Two slightly different conventions can be used for constructing a network diagram. One designates the arrows as activities; the other designates the nodes as activities.

The task of developing and updating project networks quickly becomes complex for projects of even moderate size, so computer software is important. Among the advantages of using project management software are the provision for a logical planning structure, enhanced communication, and automatically formatted charts and reports.

In some instances, it may be possible to shorten, or crash, the length of a project by shortening one or more of the project activities. Typically, such gains are achieved by the use of additional resources, although in some cases, it may be possible to transfer resources among project activities. Generally, projects are shortened to the point where the cost of additional reduction would exceed the benefit of additional reduction, or to a specified time.

Key Terms

activities, 776
activity-on-arrow (AOA), 776
activity-on-node (AON), 776
beta distribution, 786
CPM, 775
crash, 794
critical activities, 777
critical path, 777
deterministic, 778
events, 776
independence, 790
most likely time, 786

network (precedence) diagram, 776
optimistic time, 786
path, 777
PERT, 775
pessimistic time, 786
precedence diagram, 776
probabilistic, 778
project champion, 770
projects, 767
slack, 777
work breakdown structure (WBS), 774

Solved Problems

Problem 1

The following table contains information related to the major activities of a research project. Use the information to do the following:

a. Draw a precedence diagram using AOA.
b. Find the critical path.
c. Determine the expected length of the project.

Activity	Precedes	Expected Time (days)
a	c, b	5
c	d	8
d	i	2
b	i	7
e	f	3

f	m	6
i	m	10
m	End	8
g	h	1
h	k	2
k	End	17

a. In constructing networks, these observations can be useful.

Solution

(1) Activities with no predecessors are at the beginning (left side) of the network.

(2) Activities with multiple predecessors are located at path intersections.

Complete the diagram in sections. Go down the activity list in order to avoid overlooking any activities.

AOA diagram

AON diagram

Here are some additional hints for constructing a precedence diagram.

(1) Use pencil.
(2) Start and end with a single node.
(3) Avoid having paths cross each other.
(4) Have activities go from left to right.
(5) Use only one arrow between any pair of nodes.

Yes   No

b. and *c.*

Path	Length (days)
a-c-d-i-m*	5 + 8 + 2 + 10 + 8 = 33†
a-b-i-m	5 + 7 + 10 + 8 = 30
e-f-m	3 + 6 + 8 = 17
g-h-k	1 + 2 + 17 = 20

*Critical path.
†Expected project duration.

Problem 2

Using the computing algorithm, determine the slack times for the following AOA diagram. Identify the activities that are on the critical path.

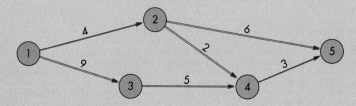

Solution

The task of determining ES, EF, LS, and LF times can be greatly simplified by setting up two brackets for each activity, as illustrated:

The bracket at the left of each activity will eventually be filled in with the earliest and latest *starting* times, and the bracket at the right end of each activity will be filled in with the earliest and latest *finishing* times:

This is accomplished in a two-step process. First, determine the earliest starting times and earliest finishing times, working from left to right, as shown in the following diagram.

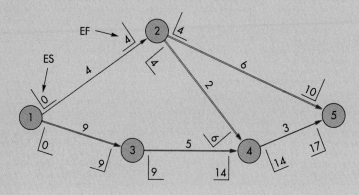

Thus, activity 1-2 can start at 0. With a time 4, it can finish at $0 + 4 = 4$. This establishes the earliest start for all activities that begin at node 2. Hence, 2-5 and 2-4 can start no earlier than time 4. Activity 2-5 has an early finish of $4 + 6 = 10$, and activity 2-4 has an early finish of $4 + 2 = 6$. At this point, it is impossible to say what the earliest start is for 4-5; that will depend on which activity, 3-4 or 2-4, has the latest EF. Consequently, it is necessary to compute ES and EF along the lower path. Assuming an ES of 0 for activity 1-3, its EF will be 9, so activity 3-4 will have an ES of 9 and an EF of $9 + 5 = 14$.

Considering that the two activities entering node 4 have EF times of 6 and 14, the earliest that activity 4-5 can start is the *larger* of these, which is 14. Hence, activity 4-5 has an ES of 14 and an EF of $14 + 3 = 17$.

Now compare the EFs of the activities entering the final node. The larger of these, 17, is the expected project duration.

The LF and LS times for each activity can now be determined by working backward through the network (from right to left). The LF for the two activities entering node 5 is 17—the project duration. In other words, to finish the project in 17 weeks, these last two activities must both finish by that time.

In the case of activity 4-5, the LS necessary for an LF of 17 is $17 - 3 = 14$. This means that both activities 2-4 and 3-4 must finish no later than 14. Hence, their LF times are 14. Activity 3 has an LS time of $14 - 5 = 9$, making the LF of activity 1-3 equal to 9, and its LS equal to $9 - 9 = 0$.

Activity 2-4, with an LF time of 14, has an LS time of $14 - 2 = 12$. Activity 2-5 has an LF of 17 and therefore an LS of $17 - 6 = 11$. Thus, the latest activity 2-5 can start is 11, and the latest 2-4 can start is 12 in order to finish by week 17. Since activity 1-2 precedes *both* of these activities, it can finish no later than the *smaller* of these, which is 11. Hence, activity 1-2 has an LF of 11 and an LS of $11 - 4 = 7$.

The ES, EF, LF, and LS times are shown on the following network.

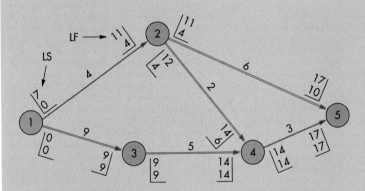

The slack time for any activity is the difference between *either* LF and EF *or* LS and ES. Thus,

Activity	LS	ES	Slack	or	LF	EF	Slack
1-2	7	0	7		11	4	7
2-5	11	4	7		17	10	7
2-4	12	4	8		14	6	8
1-3	0	0	0		9	9	0
3-4	9	9	0		14	14	0
4-5	14	14	0		17	17	0

The activities with zero slack times indicate the critical path. In this case the critical path is 1-3-4-5.

When working problems of this nature, keep in mind the following:

a. The ES time for leaving activities of nodes with multiple entering activities is the largest EF of the entering activities.

b. The LF for an entering activity for nodes with multiple leaving activities is the smallest LS of the leaving activities.

Problem 3

Expected times and variances for the major activities of an R&D project are depicted in the following PERT chart. Determine the probability that project completion time will be

a. Less than 50 weeks.

b. More than 50 weeks.

Solution

a. Compute the mean and standard deviation for each path:

Path	Expected Time (weeks)	Standard Deviation (weeks)
1-2-5-8	$16 + 11 + 24 = 51$	$\sqrt{.69 + .69 + .11} = 1.22$
1-3-6-8	$5 + 18 + 26 = 49$	$\sqrt{.00 + .25 + .11} = 0.60$
1-3-4-7-8	$5 + 10 + 14 + 12 = 41$	$\sqrt{.00 + .25 + .36 + .11} = 0.85$

b. Compute the z for each path for the length specified. For any path that has a z of $+2.50$ or more, treat its probability of completion before the specified time as 1.00. Use

$$z = \frac{50 - t_{path}}{\sigma_{path}}$$

The probability that each path will be completed in 50 weeks or less is shown in the corresponding diagram. (Probabilities are from Appendix B, Table B.) The probability that the project will be completed in 50 weeks or less depends on all three paths being completed in that time. Because z for path 1-3-4-7-8 is greater than $+2.50$, it is treated as having a probability of completion in 50 weeks of 100 percent. It is less certain that the other two paths will be completed in that time. The probability that *both* will not exceed 50 is the *product* of their individual probabilities of completion. Thus, $.2061(.9525) = .1963$.

The probability that the project *will* exceed 50 weeks is the complement of this number, which is $1.000 - .1963 = .8037$. (Note that it is *not* the product of the path probabilities.)

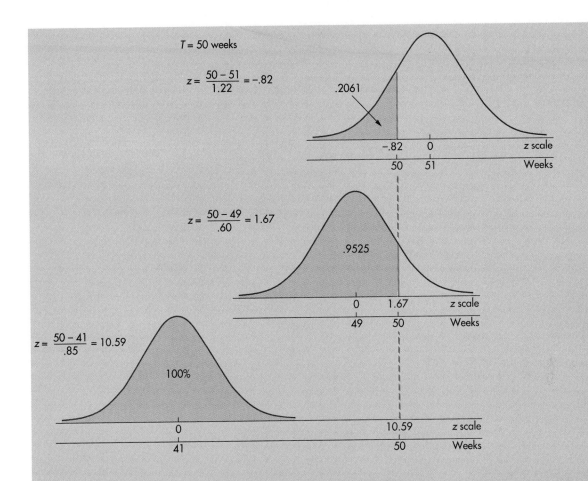

$$T = 50 \text{ weeks}$$

$$z = \frac{50 - 51}{1.22} = -.82$$

.2061

$$z = \frac{50 - 49}{.60} = 1.67$$

.9525

$$z = \frac{50 - 41}{.85} = 10.59$$

100%

Indirect costs for a project are $12,000 per week for as long as the project lasts. The project manager has supplied the cost and time information shown. Use the information to: **Problem 4**

a. Determine an optimum crashing plan.

b. Graph the total costs for the plan.

Activity	Crashing Potential (weeks)	Cost per Week to Crash
a	3	$11,000
b	3	3,000 first week, $4,000 others
c	2	6,000
d	1	1,000
e	3	6,000
f	1	2,000

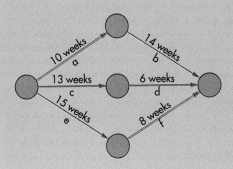

Solution
a. (1) Compute path lengths and identify the critical path:

Path	Duration (weeks)
a-b	24 (critical path)
c-d	19
e-f	23

(2) Rank critical activities according to crash costs:

Activity	Cost per Week to Crash
b	$ 3,000
a	11,000

Activity b should be shortened one week since it has the lower crashing cost. This would reduce indirect costs by $12,000 at a cost of $3,000, for a net savings of $9,000. At this point, paths a-b and e-f would both have a length of 23 weeks, so both would be critical.

(3) Rank activities by crashing costs on the two critical paths:

Path	Activity	Cost per Week to Crash
a-b	b	$ 4,000
	a	11,000
e-f	e	6,000
	f	2,000

Choose one activity (the least costly) on each path to crash: b on a-b and f on e-f, for a total cost of $4,000 + $2,000 = $6,000 and a net savings of $12,000 − $6,000 = $6,000.

(4) Check to see which path(s) might be critical: a-b and e-f would be 22 weeks in length, and c-d would still be 19 weeks.

(5) Rank activities on the critical paths:

Path	Activity	Cost per Week to Crash
a-b	b	$..4,000
	a	11,000
e-f	e	6,000
	f	(no further crashing possible)

Crash b on path a-b and e on e-f for a cost of $4,000 + $6,000 = $10,000, for a net savings of $12,000 − $10,000 = $2,000.

(6) At this point, no further improvement is possible: paths a-b and e-f would be 21 weeks in length, and one activity from each path would have to be shortened. This would mean activity a at $11,000 and e at $6,000 for a total of $17,000, which exceeds the $12,000 potential savings in indirect costs.

b. The following table summarizes the results, showing the length of the project after crashing n weeks:

Path	n = 0	1	2	3
a-b	24	23	22	21
c-d	19	19	19	19
e-f	23	23	22	21
Activity crashed		b	b,f	b,e
Crashing costs ($000)		3	6	10

A summary of costs for the preceding schedule would look like this:

Project Length	Cumulative Weeks Shortened	Cumulative Crashing Costs ($000)	Indirect Costs ($000)	Total Costs ($000)
24	0	0	24(12) = 288	288
23	1	3	23(12) = 276	279
22	2	3 + 6 = 9	22(12) = 264	273
21	3	9 + 10 = 19	21(12) = 252	271
20	4	19 + 17 = 36	20(12) = 240	276

The graph of total costs is as follows.

1. A project manager may need two skill sets—those of a manager and those of a leader. Explain.
2. Explain the term *project champion* and list some ways to keep a champion involved with the project.
3. List the steps in risk management.
4. Give some examples of ethical issues that may arise on projects. What can a project manager do to minimize such issues?
5. What are the key advantages of using project management software?
6. What is a work breakdown structure, and how is it useful for project planning?
7. Identify the term being described for each of the following:
   a. A sequence of activities in a project.
   b. The longest time sequence of activities in a project.
   c. Used when two activities have the same starting and finishing points.
   d. The difference in time length of any path and the critical path.
   e. The statistical distribution used to describe variability of an activity time.
   f. The statistical distribution used to describe project variability.
   g. Shortening an activity by allocating additional resources.
8. List the main advantages of PERT. List the main limitations.
9. Why might a probabilistic estimate of a project's completion time based solely on the variance of the *critical path* be misleading? Under what circumstances would it be acceptable?
10. Define each of these terms, and indicate how each is determined.
    a. Expected activity time.
    b. Variance of an activity time.
    c. Standard deviation of a path's time.
11. Why might a person wish to be involved with a critical path activity? What are some of the reasons one might have for not wanting this association?

Discussion and Review Questions

12. What are some of the potential benefits of working on a special project in one's firm? What are some of the risks?

13. What are some aspects of the project manager's job that make it more demanding than the job of a manager working in a more routine organizational framework?

14. What is the main benefit of a project organization over more traditional forms of operations management for project work?

1. Write a memo to your new employee, June Farber, in which you briefly describe the nature and importance of a work breakdown structure for project planning.

2. You have been assigned to work on a special project outside your department for the next two years. It has not been determined whether this assignment will be full-time or part-time. Write a memo to your supervisor, Henry Armbruster, outlining your reservations about each type of assignment.

3. Write a memo on the impact of technology on project management. Address the memo to your instructor.

Problems

1. For each of the following network diagrams, determine both the critical path and the expected project duration. The numbers on the arrows represent expected activity times.

   a. AOA diagram

   b. AON diagram

c. AOA diagram

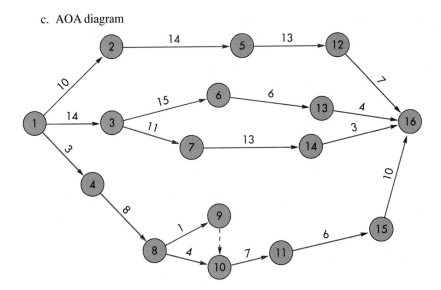

2. Chris received new word processing software for her birthday. She also received a check, with which she intends to purchase a new computer. Chris's college instructor assigned a paper due next week. Chris decided that she will prepare the paper on the new computer. She made a list of the activities she will need to do and their estimated times.

   a. Arrange the activities into two logical sequences.

   b. (1) Construct an AOA network diagram.

        (2) Construct an AON diagram.

   c. Determine the critical path and the expected duration time.

   d. What are some possible reasons for the project to take longer than the expected duration?

Estimated Time (hrs.)	Activity (abbreviation)
0.8	Install software (Inst)
0.4	Outline the paper (Out)
0.2	Submit paper to instructor (Sub)
0.6	Choose a topic (Ch)
0.5	Use grammar-checking routine and make corrections (Ck)
3.0	Write the paper using the word-processing software (Write)
2.0	Shop for a new computer (Sh)
1.0	Select and purchase computer (Sel)
2.0	Library research on chosen topic (Lib)

3. The information in the table pertains to a project that is about to commence. As the project manager, which activities would you be concerned with in terms of timely project completion? Explain.

Activity	Precedes	Estimated Time (days)
A	B	15
B	C, D	12
C	E	6
D	End	5
E	End	3
F	G, H	8
G	I	8
H	J	9
I	End	7
J	K	14
K	End	6

4. *a.* Construct an activity-on-arrow precedence diagram for each of the following cases. Note that each case requires the use of a dummy activity.

   b. Construct an AON diagram for each case.

(1) Activity	Precedes Activity	(2) Activity	Precedes Activity
A	D	J	L, N
B	E, F	K	R
C	G	L	M
D	K	M	End
E	K	N	P
F	H, I	P	End
G	I	Q	S, T
H	End	R	V
I	End	S	V
K	End	V	End
		T	V, W
		W	End

5. For each of the problems listed, determine the following quantities for each activity: the earliest start time, latest start time, earliest finish time, latest finish time, and slack. List the critical activities, and determine the expected duration of the project.

   a. Problem 1*a*.

   b. Problem 1*b*.

   c. Problem 3.

6. Reconsider the network diagram of Problem 1a. Suppose that after 12 weeks, activities 1-2, 1-3, and 2-4 have been finished; activity 2-5 is 75 percent finished; and activity 3-6 is half finished. How many weeks after the original start time should the project be finished?

7. Three recent college graduates have formed a partnership and have opened an advertising firm. Their first project consists of activities listed in the following table.

   a. Draw the precedence diagram.

   b. What is the probability that the project can be completed in 24 days or less? In 21 days or less?

   c. Suppose it is now the end of the seventh day and that activities a and b have been completed while activity d is 50 percent completed. Time estimates for the completion of activity d are 5, 6, and 7. Activities c and h are ready to begin. Determine the probability of finishing the project by day 24 and the probability of finishing by day 21.

		TIME IN DAYS		
Activity	Precedes	Optimistic	Most Likely	Pessimistic
a c		5	6	7
b . . . . h		8	8	11
c . . . . e		6	8	11
d . . . . f		9	12	15
e . . . . End		5	6	9
f . . . . g		5	6	7
g . . . . End		2	3	7
h i		4	4	5
i . . . . End		5	7	8

8. The new director of special events at a large university has decided to completely revamp graduation ceremonies. Toward that end, a PERT chart of the major activities has been developed. The chart has five paths with expected completion times and variances as shown in the table. Graduation day is 16 weeks from now. Assuming the project begins now, what is the probability that the project will be completed before:

   a. Graduation time?

   b. The end of week 15?

c. The end of week 13?

Path	Expected Duration (weeks)	Variance
A	10	1.21
B	8	2.00
C	12	1.00
D	15	2.89
E	14	1.44

9. What is the probability that the following project will take more than 10 weeks to complete if the activity means and standard deviations are as shown below?

Activity	Mean	Standard Deviation
1-2	5	1.3
2-3	4	1.0
1-3	8	1.6

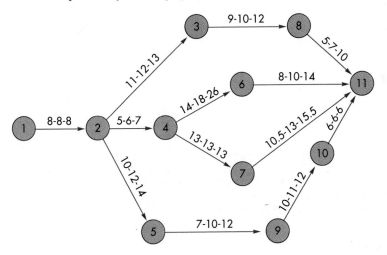

10. The project described in the following table has just begun. It is scheduled to be completed in 11 weeks.

   a. If you were the manager of this project, would you be concerned? Explain.

   b. If there is a penalty of $5,000 a week for each week the project is late, what is the probability of incurring a penalty of at least $5,000?

Activity	Estimated Time (weeks)	Standard Deviation (wks.)
1-2	4	0.70
2-4	6	0.90
1-3	3	0.62
3-4	9	1.90

11. The following precedence diagram reflects three time estimates for each activity. Determine:

   a. The expected completion time for each path and its variance.

   b. The probability that the project will require more than 49 weeks.

   c. The probability that the project can be completed in 46 weeks or less.

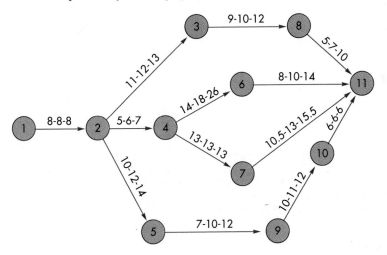

12. A project manager has compiled a list of major activities that will be required to install a computer information system in her firm. The list includes estimated completion times for activities and precedence relationships.

Activity	Precedes	Estimated Times (weeks)
a	d, f	2-4-6
d	e	6-8-10
e	h	7-9-12
h	End	2-3-5
f	g	3-4-8
g	End	5-7-9
b	i	2-2-3
i	j	2-3-6
j	k	3-4-5
k	End	4-5-8
c	m	5-8-12
m	n	1-1-1
n	o	6-7-11
o	End	8-9-13

If the project is finished within 26 weeks of its start, the project manager will receive a bonus of $1,000; and if the project is finished within 27 weeks of its start, the bonus will be $500. Find the probability of each bonus.

13. *a.* Construct an activity-on-node diagram for the set of activities listed in Problem 3.

   b. Construct an activity-on-node diagram for the set of activities listed in Problem 12.

14. The project manager of a task force planning the construction of a domed stadium had hoped to be able to complete construction prior to the start of the next college football season. After reviewing construction time estimates, it now appears that a certain amount of crashing will be needed to ensure project completion before the season opener. Given the following time and cost estimates, determine a minimum-cost crashing schedule that will shave five weeks off the project length.

		Normal Time (weeks)	CRASHING COSTS	
Activity	Precedes		First Week	Second Week
A	B	12	$15,000	$20,000
B	K	14	10,000	10,000
C	D, E, F	10	5,000	5,000
D	G	17	20,000	21,000
E	H	18	16,000	18,000
F	I	12	12,000	15,000
G	M	15	24,000	24,000
H	N, P	8	—	—
I	J	7	30,000	—
J	P	12	25,000	25,000
K	End	9	10,000	10,000
M	End	3	—	—
N	End	11	40,000	—
P	End	8	20,000	20,000

15. A construction project has indirect costs totaling $40,000 per week. Major activities in the project and their expected times are shown in this precedence diagram:

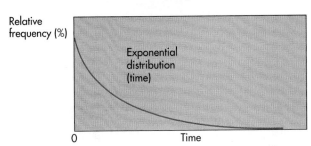

FIGURE 19-4

Poisson and negative exponential distributions

The negative exponential distribution often provides a reasonably good description of customer service times (e.g., first aid care for accident victims). Figure 19–5B illustrates how exponential service times might appear for the customers whose arrivals are illustrated in Figure 19–5A. Note that most service times are very short—some are close to zero—but a few require a relatively long service time. That is typical of a negative exponential distribution.

Waiting lines are most likely to occur when arrivals are bunched or when service times are particularly lengthy, and they are very likely to occur when both factors are present. For instance, note the long service time of customer 7 on day 1, in Figure 19–5B. In Figure 19–5A, the seventh customer arrived just after 10 o'clock and the next two customers arrived shortly after that, making it very likely that a waiting line formed. A similar situation occurred on day 3 with the last three customers: The relatively long service time for customer 13 (Figure 19–5B), and the short time before the next two arrivals (Figure 19–5A, day 3) would create (or increase the length of) a waiting line.

It is interesting to note that the Poisson and negative exponential distributions are alternate ways of presenting the same basic information. That is, if service time is exponential, then the service rate is Poisson. Similarly, if the customer arrival rate is Poisson, then the interarrival time (i.e., the time between arrivals) is exponential. For example, if a service facility can process 12 customers per hour (rate), average service time is five minutes. And if the arrival rate is 10 per hour, then the average time between arrivals is six minutes.

The models described here generally require that arrival and service rates lend themselves to description using a Poisson distribution or, equivalently, that interarrival and service times lend themselves to description using a negative exponential distribution. In practice, it is necessary to verify that these assumptions are met. Sometimes this is done by collecting data and plotting them, although the preferred approach is to use a chi-square goodness-of-fit test for that purpose. A discussion of the chi-square test is beyond the scope of this text, but most basic statistics textbooks cover the topic.

Research has shown that these assumptions are often appropriate for customer arrivals but less likely to be appropriate for service. In situations where the assumptions are not

FIGURE 19-5

Poisson arrivals and exponential service times

A. Customer Arrivals

B. Service Times

reasonably satisfied, the alternatives would be to (1) develop a more suitable model, (2) search for a better (and usually more complex) existing model, or (3) resort to computer simulation. Each of these alternatives requires more effort or cost than the ones presented here.

QUEUE DISCIPLINE

queue discipline The order in which customers are processed.

Queue discipline refers to the order in which customers are processed. All but one of the models to be described shortly assume that service is provided on a *first-come, first-served* basis. This is perhaps the most commonly encountered rule. There is first-come service at banks, stores, theaters, restaurants, four-way stop signs, registration lines, and so on. Examples of systems that do not serve on a first-come basis include hospital emergency rooms, rush orders in a factory, and main frame computer processing of jobs. In these and similar situations, customers do not all represent the same waiting costs; those

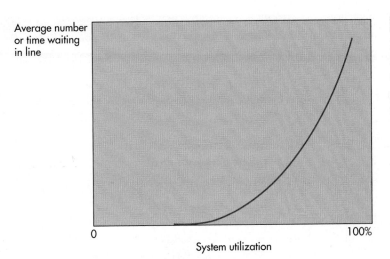

FIGURE 19-6

The average number waiting in line and the average time customers wait in line increase exponentially as the system utilization increases

with the highest costs (e.g., the most seriously ill) are processed first, even though other customers may have arrived earlier.

Measures of System Performance

The operations manager typically looks at five measures when evaluating existing or proposed service systems. Those measures are:

1. The average number of customers waiting, either in line or in the system.
2. The average time customers wait, either in line or in the system.
3. System utilization, which refers to the percentage of capacity utilized.
4. The implied cost of a given level of capacity and its related waiting line.
5. The probability that an arrival will have to wait for service.

Of these measures, system utilization bears some elaboration. It reflects the extent to which the servers are busy rather than idle. On the surface, it might seem that the operations manager would want to seek 100 percent utilization. However, as Figure 19–6 illustrates, increases in system utilization are achieved at the expense of increases in both the length of the waiting line and the average waiting time. In fact, these values become exceedingly large as utilization approaches 100 percent. The implication is that under normal circumstances, 100 percent utilization is not a realistic goal. Even if it were, 100 percent utilization of service personnel is not good; they need some slack time. Thus, instead, the operations manager should try to achieve a system that minimizes the sum of waiting costs and capacity costs.

Queuing Models: Infinite-Source

Many queuing models are available for a manager or analyst to choose from. The discussion here includes four of the most basic and most widely used models. The purpose is to provide an exposure to a range of models rather than an extensive coverage of the field. All assume a Poisson arrival rate. Moreover, the models pertain to a system operating under *steady state* conditions; that is, they assume the average arrival and service rates are stable. The four models described are:

1. Single channel, exponential service time.
2. Single channel, constant service time.
3. Multiple channel, exponential service time.
4. Multiple priority service, exponential service time.

TABLE 19-1

Infinite-source symbols

Symbol	Represents
λ	Customer arrival rate
μ	Service rate
L_q	The average number of customers waiting for service
L_s	The average number of customers in the system (waiting and/or being served)
ρ	The system utilization
W_q	The average time customers wait in line
W_s	The average time customers spend in the system (waiting in line and service time)
$1/\mu$	Service time
P_0	The probability of zero units in the system
P_n	The probability of n units in the system
M	The number of servers (channels)
L_{max}	The maximum expected number waiting in line

To facilitate your use of queuing models, Table 19–1 provides a list of the symbols used for the infinite-source models.

BASIC RELATIONSHIPS

There are certain basic relationships that hold for all infinite-source models. Knowledge of these can be very helpful in deriving desired performance measures, given a few key values. Here are the basic relationships:

> Note: The arrival and service rates, represented by λ and μ, must be in the same units (e.g., customers per hour, customers per minute).

System utilization: This reflects the ratio of demand (as measured by the arrival rate) to supply or capacity (as measured by the product of the number of servers, *M*, and the service rate, μ).

$$\rho = \frac{\lambda}{M\mu} \tag{19–1}$$

The average number of customers being served:

$$r = \frac{\lambda}{\mu} \tag{19–2}$$

The average *number* of customers:

waiting in line for service: L_q [Model dependent. Obtain using a table or formula.]

in the system (line plus being served): $L_s = L_q + r$ (19–3)

The average *time* customers are:

waiting in line: $W_q = \dfrac{L_q}{\lambda}$ (19–4)

in the system: $W_s = W_q + \dfrac{1}{\mu}$ (19–5)

All infinite-source models require that system utilization be less than 1.0; the models apply only to underloaded systems.

The average number waiting in line, L_q, is a key value because it is a determinant of some of the other measures of system performance, such as the average number in the system, the average time in line, and the average time in the system. Hence, L_q will usually be one of the first values you will want to determine in problem solving.

Example 1

Customers arrive at a bakery at an average rate of 18 per hour on weekday mornings. The arrival distribution can be described by a Poisson distribution with a mean of 18. Each clerk can serve a customer in an average of four minutes; this time can be described by an exponential distribution with a mean of 4.0 minutes.

a. What are the arrival and service *rates*?

b. Compute the average number of customers being served at any time.

c. Suppose it has been determined that the average number of customers waiting in line is 3.6. Compute the average number of customers in the system (i.e., waiting in line or being served), the average time customers wait in line, and the average time in the system.

d. Determine the system utilization for $M = 2$, 3, and 4 servers.

a. The arrival rate is given in the problem: $\lambda = 18$ customers per hour. Change the service time to a comparable *hourly* rate by first restating the time in hours and then taking its reciprocal. Thus, (4 minutes per customer)/(60 minutes per hour) = $1/15 = 1/\mu$. Its reciprocal is $\mu = 15$ customers per hour.

b. $r = \dfrac{\lambda}{\mu} = \dfrac{18}{15} = 1.2$ customers.

c. Given: $L_q = 3.6$ customers.

$L_s = L_q + r = 3.6 + 1.2 = 4.8$ customers

$W_q = \dfrac{L_q}{\lambda} = \dfrac{3.6}{18} = .20$ hours per customer, or .20 hours $\times$ 60 minutes/hour = 12 minutes

W_s = Waiting in line plus service

$ = W_q + \dfrac{1}{\mu} = .20 + \dfrac{1}{15} = .267$ hour, or approximately 16 minutes

d. System utilization is $\rho = \dfrac{\lambda}{M\mu}$.

For $M = 2$, $\rho = \dfrac{18}{2(15)} = .60$

For $M = 3$, $\rho = \dfrac{18}{3(15)} = .40$

For $M = 4$, $\rho = \dfrac{18}{4(15)} = .30$

Hence, as the system capacity as measured by $M\mu$ increases, the system utilization for a given arrival rate decreases.

MODEL 1: SINGLE CHANNEL, EXPONENTIAL SERVICE TIME

The simplest model involves a system that has one server (or a single crew). The queue discipline is first-come, first-served, and it is assumed that the customer arrival rate can be approximated by a Poisson distribution and service time by a negative exponential distribution. There is no limit on length of queue.

Table 19–2 lists the formulas for the single-channel model, which should be used in conjunction with formulas 19–1 through 19–5.

TABLE 19-2

Formulas for basic single-server model

Performance Measure	Equation	
Average number in line	$L_q = \dfrac{\lambda^2}{\mu(\mu - \lambda)}$	(19–6)
Probability of zero units in the system	$P_0 = 1 - \left(\dfrac{\lambda}{\mu}\right)$	(19–7)
Probability of n units in the system	$P_n = P_0 \left(\dfrac{\lambda}{\mu}\right)^n$	(19–8a)
Probability of less than n units in the system	$P_{<n} = 1 - \left(\dfrac{\lambda}{\mu}\right)^n$	(19–8b)

to find greater than do this) then subtract by 1

Example 2

An airline is planning to open a satellite ticket desk in a new shopping plaza, staffed by one ticket agent. It is estimated that requests for tickets and information will average 15 per hour, and requests will have a Poisson distribution. Service time is assumed to be exponentially distributed. Previous experience with similar satellite operations suggests that mean service time should average about three minutes per request. Determine each of the following:

a. System utilization.

b. Percentage of time the server (agent) will be idle.

c. The expected number of customers waiting to be served.

d. The average time customers will spend in the system.

e. The probability of zero customers in the system and the probability of four customers in the system.

Solution

$\lambda = 15$ per hour

$\mu = \dfrac{1}{\text{Service Time}} = \dfrac{1 \text{ customer}}{3 \text{ minutes}} \times 60 \text{ minutes per hour}$

$= 20 \text{ customers per hour}$

a. $\rho = \dfrac{\lambda}{M\mu} = \dfrac{15}{1(20)} = .75$

b. Percentage idle time $= 1 - \rho = 1 - .75 = .25$, or 25 percent

c. $L_q = \dfrac{\lambda^2}{\mu(\mu - \lambda)} = \dfrac{15^2}{20(20 - 15)} = 2.25$ customers

d. $W_s = \dfrac{L_q}{\lambda} + \dfrac{1}{\mu} = \dfrac{2.25}{15} + \dfrac{1}{20} = .20$ hour, or 12 minutes

e. $P_0 = 1 - \dfrac{\lambda}{\mu} = 1 - \dfrac{15}{20} = .25$ and $P_4 = P_0 \left(\dfrac{\lambda}{\mu}\right)^4 = .25 \left(\dfrac{15}{20}\right)^4 = .079$

MODEL 2: SINGLE CHANNEL, CONSTANT SERVICE TIME

As noted previously, waiting lines are a consequence of random, highly variable arrival and service rates. If a system can reduce or eliminate the variability of either or both, it can shorten waiting lines noticeably. A case in point is a system with constant service time. The effect of a constant service time is to cut in half the average number of customers waiting in line:

TABLE 19-3

Multiple-channel queuing formulas

Performance Measure	Equation	
Average number in line	$L_q = \dfrac{\lambda\mu\left(\dfrac{\lambda}{\mu}\right)^M}{(M-1)!(M\mu-\lambda)^2}\,P_o$	(19–10)
Probability of zero units in the system	$P_0 = \left[\displaystyle\sum_{n=0}^{M-1}\dfrac{\left(\dfrac{\lambda}{\mu}\right)^n}{n!} + \dfrac{\left(\dfrac{\lambda}{\mu}\right)^M}{M!\left(1-\dfrac{\lambda}{M\mu}\right)}\right]^{-1}$	(19–11)
Average waiting time for an arrival not immediately served	$W_a = \dfrac{1}{M\mu-\lambda}$	(19–12)
Probability that an arrival will have to wait for service	$P_w = \dfrac{W_q}{W_a}$	(19–13)

} for model 3

$$\rightarrow L_q = \frac{\lambda^2}{2\mu(\mu-\lambda)} \quad \text{for model 2} \tag{19–9}$$

The average time customers spend waiting in line is also cut in half. Similar improvements can be realized by smoothing arrival times (e.g., by use of appointments).

Example 3

Wanda's Car Wash & Dry is an automatic, five-minute operation with a single bay. On a typical Saturday morning, cars arrive at a mean rate of eight per hour, with arrivals tending to follow a Poisson distribution. Find:

a. The average number of cars in line.

b. The average time cars spend in line and service.

$\lambda = 8$ cars per hour

$\mu = 1$ per 5 minutes, or 12 per hour

Solution

a. $L_q = \dfrac{\lambda^2}{2\mu(\mu-\lambda)} = \dfrac{8^2}{2(12)(12-8)} = .667$ car

b. $W_s = \dfrac{L_q}{\lambda} + \dfrac{1}{\mu} = \dfrac{.667}{8} + \dfrac{1}{12} = .167$ hour, or 10 minutes

MODEL 3: MULTIPLE CHANNEL

A multiple-channel system exists whenever there are two or more servers working *independently* to provide service to customer arrivals. Use of the model involves the following assumptions:

1. A Poisson arrival rate and exponential service time.

2. Servers all work at the same average rate.

3. Customers form a single waiting line (in order to maintain first-come, first-served processing).

Formulas for the multiple-channel model are listed in Table 19–3. Obviously, the multiple-channel formulas are more complex than the single-channel formulas, especially the formulas for L_q and P_0. These formulas are shown primarily for completeness; you can actually determine their values using Table 19–4, which gives values of L_q and P_0 for selected values of λ/μ and M.

TABLE 19-4

Infinite-source values for L_q and P_0 given λ/μ and M

λ/μ	M	L_q	P_0
0.15	1	0.026	.850
	2	0.001	.860
0.20	1	0.050	.800
	2	0.002	.818
0.25	1	0.083	.750
	2	0.004	.778
0.30	1	0.129	.700
	2	0.007	.739
0.35	1	0.188	.650
	2	0.011	.702
0.40	1	0.267	.600
	2	0.017	.667
0.45	1	0.368	.550
	2	0.024	.633
	3	0.002	.637
0.50	1	0.500	.500
	2	0.033	.600
	3	0.003	.606
0.55	1	0.672	.450
	2	0.045	.569
	3	0.004	.576
0.60	1	0.900	.400
	2	0.059	.538
	3	0.006	.548
0.65	1	1.207	.350
	2	0.077	.509
	3	0.008	.521
0.70	1	1.633	.300
	2	0.098	.481
	3	0.011	.495
0.75	1	2.250	.250
	2	0.123	.455
	3	0.015	.471
0.80	1	3.200	.200
	2	0.152	.429
	3	0.019	.447
0.85	1	4.817	.150
	2	0.187	.404
	3	0.024	.425
	4	0.003	.427
0.90	1	8.100	.100
	2	0.229	.379
	3	0.030	.403
	4	0.004	.406
0.95	1	18.050	.050
	2	0.277	.356
	3	0.037	.383
	4	0.005	.386
1.0	2	0.333	.333
	3	0.045	.364
	4	0.007	.367
1.1	2	0.477	.290
	3	0.066	.327
	4	0.011	.367
1.2	2	0.675	.250
	3	0.094	.294
	4	0.016	.300
	5	0.003	.301

λ/μ	M	L_q	P_0
1.3	2	0.951	.212
	3	0.130	.264
	4	0.023	.271
	5	0.004	.272
1.4	2	1.345	.176
	3	0.177	.236
	4	0.032	.245
	5	0.006	.246
1.5	2	1.929	.143
	3	0.237	.211
	4	0.045	.221
	5	0.009	.223
1.6	2	2.844	.111
	3	0.313	.187
	4	0.060	.199
	5	0.012	.201
1.7	2	4.426	.081
	3	0.409	.166
	4	0.080	.180
	5	0.017	.182
1.8	2	7.674	.053
	3	0.532	.146
	4	0.105	.162
	5	0.023	.165
1.9	2	17.587	.026
	3	0.688	.128
	4	0.136	.145
	5	0.030	.149
	6	0.007	.149
2.0	3	0.889	.111
	4	0.174	.130
	5	0.040	.134
	6	0.009	.135
2.1	3	1.149	.096
	4	0.220	.117
	5	0.052	.121
	6	0.012	.122
2.2	3	1.491	.081
	4	0.277	.105
	5	0.066	.109
	6	0.016	.111
2.3	3	1.951	.068
	4	0.346	.093
	5	0.084	.099
	6	0.021	.100
2.4	3	2.589	.056
	4	0.431	.083
	5	0.105	.089
	6	0.027	.090
	7	0.007	.091
2.5	3	3.511	.045
	4	0.533	.074
	5	0.130	.080
	6	0.034	.082
	7	0.009	.082
2.6	3	4.933	.035
	4	0.658	.065
	5	0.161	.072

λ/μ	M	L_q	P_0
2.6	6	0.043	.074
	7	0.011	.074
2.7	3	7.354	.025
	4	0.811	.057
	5	0.198	.065
	6	0.053	.067
	7	0.014	.067
2.8	3	12.273	.016
	4	1.000	.050
	5	0.241	.058
	6	0.066	.060
	7	0.018	.061
2.9	3	27.193	.008
	4	1.234	.044
	5	0.293	.052
	6	0.081	.054
	7	0.023	.055
3.0	4	1.528	.038
	5	0.354	.047
	6	0.099	.049
	7	0.028	.050
	8	0.008	.050
3.1	4	1.902	.032
	5	0.427	.042
	6	0.120	.044
	7	0.035	.045
	8	0.010	.045
3.2	4	2.386	.027
	5	0.513	.037
	6	0.145	.040
	7	0.043	.040
	8	0.012	.041
3.3	4	3.027	.023
	5	0.615	.033
	6	0.174	.036
	7	0.052	.037
	8	0.015	.037
3.4	4	3.906	.019
	5	0.737	.029
	6	0.209	.032
	7	0.063	.033
	8	0.019	.033
3.5	4	5.165	.015
	5	0.882	.026
	6	0.248	.029
	7	0.076	.030
	8	0.023	.030
	9	0.007	.030
3.6	4	7.090	.011
	5	1.055	.023
	6	0.295	.026
	7	0.019	.027
	8	0.028	.027
	9	0.008	.027
3.7	4	10.347	.008
	5	1.265	.020
	6	0.349	.023
	7	0.109	.024
	8	0.034	.025
	9	0.010	.025

TABLE 19-4

(Concluded)

λ/μ	M	L_q	P_0	λ/μ	M	L_q	P_0	λ/μ	M	L_q	P_0
3.8	4	16.937	.005	4.6	5	9.289	.004	5.3	8	0.422	.005
	5	1.519	.017		6	1.487	.008		9	0.155	.005
	6	0.412	.021		7	0.453	.009		10	0.057	.005
	7	0.129	.022		8	0.156	.010		11	0.021	.005
	8	0.041	.022		9	0.054	.010		12	0.007	.005
	9	0.013	.022		10	0.018	.010	5.4	6	6.661	.002
3.9	4	36.859	.002	4.7	5	13.382	.003		7	1.444	.004
	5	1.830	.015		6	1.752	.007		8	0.483	.004
	6	0.485	.019		7	0.525	.008		9	0.178	.004
	7	0.153	.020		8	0.181	.008		10	0.066	.004
	8	0.050	.020		9	0.064	.009		11	0.024	.005
	9	0.016	.020		10	0.022	.009		12	0.009	.005
4.0	5	2.216	.013	4.8	5	21.641	.002	5.5	6	8.590	.002
	6	0.570	.017		6	2.071	.006		7	1.674	.003
	7	0.180	.018		7	0.607	.008		8	0.553	.004
	8	0.059	.018		8	0.209	.008		9	0.204	.004
	9	0.019	.018		9	0.074	.008		10	0.077	.004
4.1	5	2.703	.011		10	0.026	.008		11	0.028	.004
	6	0.668	.015	4.9	5	46.566	.001		12	0.010	.004
	7	0.212	.016		6	2.459	.005	5.6	6	11.519	.001
	8	0.070	.016		7	0.702	.007		7	1.944	.003
	9	0.023	.017		8	0.242	.007		8	0.631	.003
4.2	5	3.327	.009		9	0.087	.007		9	0.233	.004
	6	0.784	.013		10	0.031	.007		10	0.088	.004
	7	0.248	.014		11	0.011	.077		11	0.033	.004
	8	0.083	.015	5.0	6	2.938	.005		12	0.012	.004
	9	0.027	.015		7	0.810	.006	5.7	6	16.446	.001
	10	0.009	.015		8	0.279	.006		7	2.264	.002
4.3	5	4.149	.008		9	0.101	.007		8	0.721	.003
	6	0.919	.012		10	0.036	.007		9	0.266	.003
	7	0.289	.130		11	0.013	.007		10	0.102	.003
	8	0.097	.013	5.1	6	3.536	.004		11	0.038	.003
	9	0.033	.014		7	0.936	.005		12	0.014	.003
	10	0.011	.014		8	0.321	.006	5.8	6	26.373	.001
4.4	5	5.268	.006		9	0.117	.006		7	2.648	.002
	6	1.078	.010		10	0.042	.006		8	0.823	.003
	7	0.337	.012		11	0.015	.006		9	0.303	.003
	8	0.114	.012	5.2	6	4.301	.003		10	0.116	.003
	9	0.039	.012		7	1.081	.005		11	0.044	.003
	10	0.013	.012		8	0.368	.005		12	0.017	.003
4.5	5	6.862	.005		9	0.135	.005	5.9	6	56.300	.000
	6	1.265	.009		10	0.049	.005		7	3.113	.002
	7	0.391	.010		11	0.017	.006		8	0.939	.002
	8	0.133	.011	5.3	6	5.303	.003		9	0.345	.003
	9	0.046	.011		7	1.249	.004		10	0.133	.003
	10	0.015	.011								

To use Table 19–4, compute the value of λ/μ and round according to the number of decimal places given for that ratio in the table. Then simply read the values of L_q and P_0 for the appropriate number of channels, M. For instance, if $\lambda/\mu = 0.50$ and $M = 2$, the table provides a value of 0.033 for L_q and a value of .600 for P_0. These values can then be used to compute other measures of system performance. Note that the formulas in Table 19–3 and the values in Table 19–4 yield *average* amounts (i.e., expected values). Note also that Table 19–4 can also be used for some single-channel problems (i.e., $M = 1$).

Example 4

Alpha Taxi and Hauling Company has seven cabs stationed at the airport. The company has determined that during the late-evening hours on weeknights, customers request cabs at a rate that follows the Poisson distribution with a mean of 6.6 per hour. Service time is exponential with a mean of 50 minutes per customer. Assume that there is one customer per cab. Find each of the performance measures listed in Table 19–3, and the system utilization.

Solution

$$\lambda = 6.6 \text{ per hour} \qquad M = 7 \text{ cabs (servers)}$$

$$\mu = \frac{1 \text{ customer per trip}}{50 \text{ minutes per trip} \div 60 \text{ minutes per hour}}$$

$$= 1.2 \text{ customers per hour per cab}$$

$\lambda/\mu = 5.5$. From Table 19–4, with $M = 7$; $L_q = 1.674$ and $P_0 = .003$

a. $L_q = 1.674$ customers

b. $P_0 = .003$

c. $W_a = \dfrac{1}{M\mu - \lambda} = \dfrac{1}{7(1.2) - 6.6} = .556$ hour, or 33.36 minutes

d. $W_q = \dfrac{L_q}{\lambda} = \dfrac{1.674}{6.6} = .2536$ hour, or 15.22 minutes

$$P_W = \frac{W_q}{W_a} = \frac{.2536}{.556} = .456$$

e. $\rho = \dfrac{\lambda}{M\mu} = \dfrac{6.6}{7(1.2)} = .786$

The Excel template can also be used to solve Example 4. After entering $\lambda = 6.6$ and $\mu = 1.2$ at the top of the template, the queuing statistics for 7 servers are shown in the second column of the table in the template. The template also provides queuing statistics for 6 through 11 servers for comparison, although these are not required for this example. In addition, the template can be used to increment λ, μ, or the number of servers to further investigate the queuing system.

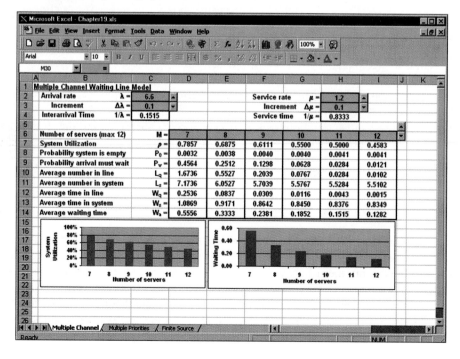

The process can also be worked in reverse; that is, an analyst can determine the capacity needed to achieve specified levels of various performance measures. This approach is illustrated in the following example.

Example 5

Alpha Tax and Hauling also plans to have cabs at a new rail station. The expected arrival rate is 4.8 customers per hour, and the service rate (including return time to the rail station) is expected to be 1.5 per hour. How many cabs will be needed to achieve an average time in line of 20 minutes or less?

λ = 4.8 customers per hour

μ = 1.5 customers per hour

M = ?

$r = \dfrac{\lambda}{\mu} = \dfrac{4.8}{1.5} = 3.2$

W_q(desired) = 20 minutes, or .333 hour

Using $L_q = \lambda \times W_q$, you can solve for L_q: 4.8/hour (.333 hour) = 1.6 units. Thus, the average number waiting should not exceed 1.6 customers. Referring to Table 19–4, with r = 3.2, L_q = 2.386 for M = 4 and 0.513 for M = 5. Hence, five cabs will be needed.

Stop Here

COST ANALYSIS

The design of a service system often reflects the desire of management to balance the cost of capacity with the expected cost of customers waiting in the system. (Note that customer waiting cost refers to the costs incurred by the organization due to customer waiting.) For example, in designing loading docks for a warehouse, the cost of docks plus loading crews must be balanced against the cost of trucks and drivers that will be in the system, both while waiting to be unloaded and while actually being unloaded. Similarly, the cost of having a mechanic wait for tools at a tool crib must be balanced against the cost of servers at the crib. In cases where the customers are not employees (e.g., retail sales), the costs can include lost sales when customers refuse to wait, the cost of providing waiting space, and the cost of added congestion (lost business, shoplifting).

The optimal capacity (usually in terms of number of channels) is one that minimizes the sum of customer waiting costs and capacity or server costs. Thus, the goal is

$$\text{Minimize} \quad \frac{\text{Total}}{\text{cost}} = \frac{\text{Customer}}{\text{waiting cost}} + \frac{\text{Capacity}}{\text{cost}}$$

The simplest approach to a cost analysis involves computing *system* costs, that is, computing the costs for customers in the system and total capacity cost.

An iterative process is used to identify the capacity size that will minimize total costs. Capacity is incremented one unit at a time (e.g., increase the number of channels by one) and the total cost is computed at each increment. Because the total cost curve is U-shaped, usually the total cost will initially decrease as capacity is increased and then it will eventually begin to increase. Once it begins to increase, additional increases in capacity will cause it to continue to increase. Hence, once that occurs, the optimal capacity size can be readily identified.

The computation of customer waiting costs is based on the average *number* of customers in the *system*. This is perhaps not intuitively obvious; instead, it might seem that customer waiting *time* in the system would be more appropriate. However, that approach would pertain to only *one* customer—it would not convey information concerning *how many* customers would wait that long. Obviously, an average of five customers waiting would involve a lower waiting cost than an average of nine. Therefore, it is necessary to focus on the *number* waiting. Moreover, if an average of two customers are in the system, this is equivalent to having *exactly* two customers in the system at all times, even though in reality there will be times when zero, one, two, three, or more customers are in the system.

Example 6

Trucks arrive at a warehouse at a rate of 15 per hour during business hours. Crews can unload the trucks at a rate of five per hour. The high unloading rate is due to cargo being containerized. Recent changes in wage rates have caused the warehouse manager to re-examine the question of how many crews to use. The new rates are: crew and dock cost is $100 per hour; truck and driver cost is $120 per hour.

Solution

(L_q values are from Table 19–4 using $\dfrac{\lambda}{\mu} = \dfrac{15}{5} = 3.0$.)

Crew Size	Crew/Dock Cost	$\left[L_s = L_q + \dfrac{\lambda}{\mu}\right]$ Average Number in System	$[L_s \times \$120]$ Driver/Truck Cost	Total Cost
4	$400	1.528 + 3.0 = 4.528	$543.36	$ 943.36
5	500	.354 + 3.0 = 3.354	402.48	902.48 (minimum)
6	600	.099 + 3.0 = 3.099	371.88	971.88
7	700	.028 + 3.0 = 3.028	363.36	1,063.36

Five crews will minimize the total cost. Because the total cost will continue to increase once the minimum is reached, it is not really necessary to compute total costs for crew sizes larger than six, because total cost increased as the crew size was increased from five to six, indicating that a crew of five is optimal.

One additional point should be made concerning cost analysis. Because both customer waiting costs and capacity costs often reflect estimated amounts, the apparent optimal solution may not represent the true optimum. One ramification of this is that when computations are shown to the nearest penny, or even the nearest dollar, the total cost figures may seem to imply a higher degree of precision than is really justified by the cost estimates. This is compounded by the fact that arrival and service rates either may be approximations or not be exactly represented by the Poisson/exponential distributions. Another ramification is that if cost estimates can be obtained as *ranges* (e.g., customer waiting cost is estimated to range between $40 and $50 per hour), total costs should be computed using both ends of the range to see whether the optimal solution is affected. If it is, management must decide whether to expend additional effort to obtain more precise cost estimates or choose one of the two indicated optimal solutions. Management would most likely choose to employ the latter strategy if there were little disparity between total costs of various capacity levels close to the indicated optimal solutions.

MAXIMUM LINE LENGTH

Another question that often comes up in capacity planning is the amount of space to allocate for waiting lines. Theoretically, with an infinite population source, the waiting line can become infinitely long. This implies that no matter how much space is allocated for a waiting line, one can never be completely sure that the space requirements won't exceed that amount. Nonetheless, as a practical matter, one can determine a line length that will not be exceeded a specified proportion of the time. For instance, an analyst may wish to know the length of line that will probably not be exceeded 98 percent of the time, or perhaps 99 percent of the time, and use that number as a planning value.

The approximate line length that will satisfy a specified percentage can be determined by solving the following equation for *n*:

$$n = \frac{\log K}{\log \rho} \quad \text{or} \quad \frac{\ln K}{\ln \rho} \qquad \text{where } K = \frac{1 - \dfrac{\text{Specified}}{\text{percentage}}}{L_q(1 - \rho)} \qquad (19\text{--}14)$$

The resulting value of *n* will not usually be an integer. Generally, round *up* to the next integer and treat the value as *n*. However, as a practical matter, if the computed value of *n* is less than 0.10 above the next lower integer, round down. Thus, 15.2 would be rounded to 16, but 15.06 would be rounded to 15.

Determine the maximum length of a waiting line for specified probabilities of 95 percent and 98 percent, for a system in which $M = 2$, $\lambda = 8$ per hour, and $\mu = 5$ per hour.

Example 7

Solution

$$r = \frac{8}{5} = 1.6 \quad \text{and} \quad \rho = \frac{8}{2(5)} = .80$$

From Table 19–4, $L_q = 2.844$ customers. For 95 percent, using Formula 19–14.

$$K = \frac{1 - .95}{2.844(1 - .80)} = .088$$

$$n = \frac{\ln .088}{\ln .80} = \frac{-2.4304}{-.2231} = 10.89, \text{ which rounds to } 11$$

For 98 percent

$$K = \frac{1 - .98}{2.844(1 - .80)} = .035$$

$$n = \frac{\ln .035}{\ln .80} = \frac{-3.352}{-.2231} = 15.02, \text{ which rounds to } 15$$

MODEL 4: MULTIPLE PRIORITIES

In many queuing systems, processing occurs on a first-come, first-served basis. However, there are situations in which that rule is inappropriate. The reason is that the waiting cost or penalty incurred is not the same for all customers. In a hospital emergency waiting room, a wide variety of injuries and illnesses need treatment. Some may be minor (e.g., sliver in finger) and others may be much more serious, even life-threatening. It is more reasonable to treat the most serious cases first, letting the nonserious cases wait until all serious cases have been treated. Similarly, computer processing of jobs often follows rules other than first-come, first-served (e.g., shortest job first). In such cases, a **multiple-priority model** is useful for describing customer waiting times.

In these systems, arriving customers are assigned to one of several *priority classes,* or categories, according to a predetermined assignment method (e.g., in a hospital emergency room, heart attacks, serious injuries, and unconscious persons are assigned to the highest priority class; sprains, minor cuts, bruises, and rashes are assigned to the lowest class; and other problems are assigned to one or more intermediate classes). Customers are then processed by class, highest class first. Within each class, processing is first-come, first-served. Thus, all customers in the highest class would be processed before those in the next lower class, then processing would move to that class, and then to the next lower

multiple-priority model
Customers are processed according to some measure of importance.

TABLE 19–5

Multiple-channel priority service model

Performance Measure	Formula	Formula Number
System utilization	$\rho = \dfrac{\lambda}{M\mu}$	(19–15)
Intermediate values (L_q from Table 19–4)	$A = \dfrac{\lambda}{(1-\rho)L_q}$	(19–16)
	$B_k = 1 - \displaystyle\sum_{c=1}^{k}\dfrac{\lambda_c}{M\mu}$	(19–17)
	($B_0 = 1$)	
Average waiting time in line for units in *k*th priority class	$W_k = \dfrac{1}{A \cdot B_{k-1} \cdot B_k}$	(19–18)
Average time in the system for units in the *k*th priority class	$W = W_k + \dfrac{1}{\mu}$	(19–19)
Average number waiting in line for units in the *k*th priority class	$L_k = \lambda_k \times W_k$	(19–20)

class. Exceptions would occur only if a higher-priority customer arrived; that customer would be processed *after* the customer currently being processed (i.e., service would not be *preemptive*).

This model incorporates all of the assumptions of the basic multiple-server model except that it uses priority serving instead of first-come, first-served. Arrivals to the system are assigned a priority as they arrive (e.g., highest priority = 1, next priority class = 2, next priority class = 3, and so on). An existing queue might look something like this:

Within each class, waiting units are processed in the order they arrived (i.e., first-come, first-served). Thus, in this sequence, the first 1 would be processed as soon as a server was available. The second 1 would be processed when that server or another one became available. If, in the interim, another 1 arrived, it would be next in line *ahead of the first 2*. If there were no new arrivals, the only 2 would be processed by the next available server. At that point, if a new 1 or 2 arrived, it would be processed ahead of the 3s and the 4. Conversely, if a new 4 arrived, it would take its place at the end of the line.

Obviously, a unit with a low priority could conceivably wait a rather long time for processing. In some cases, units that have waited more than some specified time are reassigned a higher priority.

Table 19–5 gives the appropriate formulas for this multiple-channel priority service model.

Example 8

A machine shop handles tool repairs in a large company. As each job arrives in the shop, it is assigned a priority based on urgency of the need for that tool. Requests for repair can be described by a Poisson distribution. Arrival rates are: $\lambda_1 = 2$ per hour, $\lambda_2 = 2$ per hour, and $\lambda_3 = 1$ per hour. The service rate is one tool per hour for each server, and there are six servers in the shop. Determine the following information.

a. The system utilization.

b. The average time a tool in each of the priority classes will wait for service.

c. The average time a tool spends in the system for each priority class.

d. The average number of tools waiting for repair in each class.

$\lambda = \Sigma\lambda_k = 2 + 2 + 1 = 5$ per hour

$M = 6$ servers

$\mu = 1$ customer per hour

a. $\rho = \dfrac{\lambda}{M\mu} = \dfrac{5}{6(1)} = .833$

b. Intermediate values. For $\lambda/\mu = 5/1 = 5$; from Table 19–4, $L_q = 2.938$

$$A = \frac{5}{(1 - .833)2.938} = 10.19$$

$$B_0 = 1$$

$$B_1 = 1 - \frac{2}{6(1)} = \frac{2}{3} = .667$$

$$B_2 = 1 - \frac{2 + 2}{6(1)} = \frac{1}{3} = .333$$

$$B_3 = 1 - \frac{2 + 2 + 1}{6(1)} = \frac{1}{6} = .167$$

$$W_1 = \frac{1}{A \cdot B_0 \cdot B_1} = \frac{1}{10.19(1)(.667)} = .147 \text{ hour}$$

$$W_2 = \frac{1}{A \cdot B_1 \cdot B_2} = \frac{1}{10.19(1)(.667)((.333)} = .442 \text{ hour}$$

$$W_3 = \frac{1}{A \cdot B_2 \cdot B_3} = \frac{1}{10.19(.333)(.167)} = 1.765 \text{ hours}$$

c. Average time in system $= W_k + 1/\mu$. In this case, $1/\mu = 1/1 = 1$. Thus:

Class	$W_k + 1 = W$ Hours
1	0.147 + 1 = 1.147
2	0.442 + 1 = 1.442
3	1.765 + 1 = 2.765

d. The average number of units waiting in each class is $L_k = \lambda_k \cdot W_k$. Thus:

Class	$\lambda_k \cdot W_k = L_k$ Units
1	2(0.147) = 0.294
2	2(0.442) = 0.884
3	1(1.765) = 1.765

Using the Excel template, the solution to Example 8 would appear as follows.

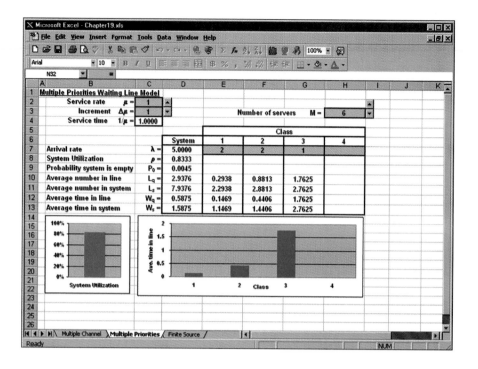

Revising Priorities. If any of the waiting times computed in Example 8 are deemed too long by management (e.g., a waiting time of .147 hour for tools in the first class might be too long), there are several options. One is to increase the number of servers. Another is to attempt to increase the service rate, say, by introducing new methods. If such options are not feasible, another approach is to reexamine the membership of each of the priority classifications because, if some repair requests in the first priority class, for example, can be reassigned to the second priority class, this will tend to decrease the average waiting times for repair jobs in the highest priority classification, simply because the arrival rate of those items will be lower.

Example 9

The manager of the repair shop, after consulting with the managers of the departments that use the shop's services, has revised the list of tools that are given the highest priorities. This is reflected by revised arrival rates. Suppose that the revised rates are: $\lambda_1 = 1.5$, $\lambda_2 = 2.5$, and λ_3 remains unchanged at 1.0. Determine the following information:

a. The system utilization.

b. The average waiting time for units in each priority class.

Solution

$$\lambda = \Sigma\lambda_k = 1.5 + 2.5 + 1.0 = 5.0$$
$$M = 6$$
$$\mu = 1$$

Note that these values are the same as in the previous example.

a. $\rho = 5.0/6(1) = .833$, the same as in the previous example.

b. The value of A, since it is a function of M, μ, and λ, is the same as in the preceding example because these values are the same. Therefore, $A = 10.19$ and

$$B_0 = 1 \text{ (always)}$$

$$B_1 = 1 - \frac{1.5}{6(1)} = .75$$

$$B_2 = 1 - \frac{1.5 + 2.5}{6(1)} = .333$$

$$B_3 = 1 - \frac{1.5 + 2.5 + 1.0}{6(1)} = .167$$

Then

$$W_1 = \frac{1}{10.19(1)(.75)} = .131 \text{ hour}$$

$$W_2 = \frac{1}{10.19(.75)(.333)} = .393 \text{ hour}$$

$$W_3 = \frac{1}{10.19(.333)(.167)} = 1.765 \text{ hours}$$

Example 9 offers several interesting results. One is that through reduction of the arrival rate of the highest priority class, the average waiting time for units in that class has decreased. In other words, removing some members of the highest class and placing them into the next lower class reduced the average waiting time for units that remained in the highest class. Note that the average waiting time for the second priority class also was reduced, even though units were added to that class. Although this may appear counterintuitive, it is necessary to recognize that the *total* waiting time (when all arrivals are taken into account) will remain unchanged. We can see this by noticing that the average *number* waiting (see Example 8, part *d*) is .294 + .884 + 1.765 = 2.943. In Example 9, using the average waiting times just computed, the average number waiting in all three classes is

$$\sum_{k=1}^{3} \lambda_k W_k = 1.5(.131) + 2.5(.393) + 1.0(1.765) = 2.944$$

Aside from a slight difference due to rounding, the totals are the same.

Another interesting observation is that the average waiting time for customers in the third priority class did not change from the preceding example. The reason for this is that the *total* arrival rate for the two higher-priority classes did not change, and the average arrival rate for this class did not change. Hence, units assigned to the lowest class must still contend with a combined arrival rate of 4 for the two higher-priority classes.

Queuing Model: Finite-Source

The finite-source model is appropriate for cases in which the calling population is limited to a relatively small number of potential calls. For instance, one person may be responsible for handling breakdowns on 15 machines; thus, the size of the calling population is 15. However, there may be more than one server or channel; for example, due to a backlog of machines awaiting repairs, the manager might authorize an additional person to work on repairs.

As in the infinite-source models, arrival rates are required to be Poisson and service times exponential. A major difference between the finite- and infinite-source models is that the arrival rate of customers in a finite situation is *affected by* the length of the waiting line; the arrival rate decreases as the length of the line increases simply because there is a decreasing proportion of the population left to generate calls for service. The limit occurs when *all* of the population are waiting in line; at that point the arrival rate is zero since no additional units can arrive.

Because the mathematics of the finite-source model can be complex, analysts often use finite-queuing tables in conjunction with simple formulas to analyze these systems. Table 19–6 contains a list of the key formulas and definitions. You will find it helpful to study the diagram of a cycle that is presented in the table.

Finite-source queuing formulas and notation

	Formulas		Notation†
Service factor	$X = \dfrac{T}{T + U}$	(19–21)	D = Probability that a customer will have to wait in line
Average number waiting	$L = N(1 - F)$	(19–22)	F = Efficiency factor: 1 − percentage waiting in line
Average waiting time	$W = \dfrac{L(T + U)}{N - L} = \dfrac{T(1 - F)}{XF}$	(19–23)	H = Average number of customers being served
Average number running	$J = NF(1 - X)$	(19–24)	J = Average number of customers not in line or in service
Average number being served	$H = FNX$	(19–25)	L = Average number of customers waiting for service
Number in population	$N = J + L + H$	(19–26)	M = Number of service channels
			N = Number of potential customers
			T = Average service time
			U = Average time between customer service requirements per customer
			W = Average time customers wait in line
			X = Service factor

Cycle

Not waiting or being served	Waiting	Being served

Average number:	J	L	H
Average time:	U	W	T

$$F = \frac{J + H}{J + L + H} \quad *$$

*The purpose of this formula is to provide an understanding of F. Because the value of F is needed to compute J, L, and H, the formulas cannot be used to actually compute F. The finite queuing tables must be used for that purpose.

†Adapted from L. G. Peck and R. N. Hazelwood, *Finite Queuing Tables* (New York: John Wiley & Sons, 1958). Reprinted by permission.

Table 19–7 is an abbreviated finite-queuing table used to obtain values of D and F. (Most of the formulas require a value for F.) In order to use the finite-queuing table, follow this procedure:

1. Identify the values for
   a. N, population size.
   b. M, number of servers/channels.
   c. T, average service time.
   d. U, average time between calls for service per customer.
2. Compute the service factor, $X = T/(T + U)$.
3. Locate the section of the finite-queuing tables for N.
4. Using the value of X as the point of entry, find the values of D and F that correspond to M.
5. Use the values of N, M, X, D, and F as needed to determine the values of the desired measures of system performance.

TABLE 19-7

Finite-queuing tables

X	M	D	F	X	M	D	F	X	M	D	F	X	M	D	F
Population 5				.145	3	.011	.999	.310	4	.009	.999	.560	2	.831	.689
.012	1	.048	.999		2	.109	.991		3	.094	.989		1	.993	.357
.019	1	.076	.998		1	.537	.892		2	.402	.919	.580	4	.113	.984
.025	1	.100	.997	.150	3	.012	.999		1	.881	.613		3	.461	.895
.030	1	.120	.996		2	.115	.990	.320	4	.010	.999		2	.854	.670
.034	1	.135	.995		1	.553	.885		3	.103	.988		1	.994	.345
.036	1	.143	.994	.155	3	.013	.999		2	.422	.912	.600	4	.130	.981
.040	1	.159	.993		2	.123	.989		1	.892	.597		3	.497	.883
.042	1	.167	.992		1	.568	.877	.330	4	.012	.999		2	.875	.652
.044	1	.175	.991	.160	3	.015	.999		3	.112	.986		1	.996	.333
.046	1	.183	.990		2	.130	.988		2	.442	.904	.650	4	.179	.972
.050	1	.198	.989		1	.582	.869		1	.902	.583		3	.588	.850
.052	1	.206	.988	.165	3	.016	.999	.340	4	.013	.999		2	.918	.608
.054	1	.214	.987		2	.137	.987		3	.121	.985		1	.998	.308
.056	2	.018	.999		1	.597	.861		2	.462	.896	.700	4	.240	.960
	1	.222	.985	.170	3	.017	.999		1	.911	.569		3	.678	.815
.058	2	.019	.999		2	.145	.985	.360	4	.017	.998		2	.950	.568
	1	.229	.984		1	.611	.853		3	.141	.981		1	.999	.286
.060	2	.020	.999	.180	3	.021	.999		2	.501	.880	.750	4	.316	.944
	1	.237	.983		2	.161	.983		1	.927	.542		3	.763	.777
.062	2	.022	.999		1	.683	.836	.380	4	.021	.998		2	.972	.532
	1	.245	.982	.190	3	.024	.998		3	.163	.976	.800	4	.410	.924
.064	2	.023	.999		2	.177	.980		2	.540	.863		3	.841	.739
	1	.253	.981		1	.665	.819		1	.941	.516		2	.987	.500
.066	2	.024	.999	.200	3	.028	.998	.400	4	.026	.997	.850	4	.522	.900
	1	.260	.979		2	.194	.976		3	.186	.972		3	.907	.702
.068	2	.026	.999		1	.689	.801		2	.579	.845		2	.995	.470
	1	.268	.978	.210	3	.032	.998		1	.952	.493	.900	4	.656	.871
.070	2	.027	.999		2	.211	.973	.420	4	.031	.997		3	.957	.666
	1	.275	.977		1	.713	.783		3	.211	.966		2	.998	.444
.075	2	.031	.999	.220	3	.036	.997		2	.616	.826	.950	4	.815	.838
	1	.294	.973		2	.229	.969		1	.961	.471		3	.989	.631
.080	2	.035	.998		1	.735	.765	.440	4	.037	.996	**Population 10**			
	1	.313	.969	.230	3	.041	.997		3	.238	.960	.016	1	.144	.997
.085	2	.040	.998		2	.247	.965		2	.652	.807	.019	1	.170	.996
	1	.332	.965		1	.756	.747		1	.969	.451	.021	1	.188	.995
.090	2	.044	.998	.240	3	.046	.996	.460	4	.045	.995	.023	1	.206	.994
	1	.350	.960		2	.265	.960		3	.266	.953	.025	1	.224	.993
.095	2	.049	.997		1	.775	.730		2	.686	.787	.026	1	.232	.992
	1	.368	.955	.250	3	.052	.995		1	.975	.432	.028	1	.250	.991
.100	2	.054	.997		2	.284	.955	.480	4	.053	.994	.030	1	.268	.990
	1	.386	.950		1	.794	.712		3	.296	.945	.032	2	.033	.999
.105	2	.059	.997	.260	3	.058	.994		2	.719	.767		1	.285	.988
	1	.404	.945		2	.303	.950		1	.980	.415	.034	2	.037	.999
.110	2	.065	.996		1	.811	.695	.500	4	.063	.992		1	.301	.986
	1	.421	.939	.270	3	.064	.994		3	.327	.936	.036	2	.041	.999
.115	2	.071	.995		2	.323	.944		2	.750	.748		1	.320	.984
	1	.439	.933		1	.827	.677		1	.985	.399	.038	2	.046	.999
.120	2	.076	.995	.280	3	.071	.993	.520	4	.073	.991		1	.337	.982
	1	.456	.927		2	.342	.938		3	.359	.927	.040	2	.050	.999
.125	2	.082	.994		1	.842	.661		2	.779	.728		1	.354	.980
	1	.473	.920	.290	4	.007	.999		1	.988	.384	.042	2	.055	.999
.130	2	.089	.933		3	.079	.992	.540	4	.085	.989		1	.371	.978
	1	.489	.914		2	.362	.932		3	.392	.917	.044	2	.060	.998
.135	2	.095	.933		1	.856	.644		2	.806	.708		1	.388	.975
	1	.505	.907	.300	4	.008	.999		1	.991	.370	.046	2	.065	.998
.140	2	.102	.992		3	.086	.990	.560	4	.098	.986		1	.404	.973
	1	.521	.900		2	.382	.926		3	.426	.906	.048	2	.071	.998
					1	.869	.628						1	.421	.970

TABLE 19-7

(Continued)

X	M	D	F
.050	2	.076	.998
	1	.437	.967
.052	2	.082	.997
	1	.454	.963
.054	2	.088	.997
	1	.470	.960
.056	2	.094	.997
	1	.486	.956
.058	2	.100	.996
	1	.501	.953
.060	2	.106	.996
	1	.517	.949
.062	2	.113	.996
	1	.532	.945
.064	2	.119	.995
	1	.547	.940
.066	2	.126	.995
	1	.562	.936
.068	3	.020	.999
	2	.133	.994
	1	.577	.931
.070	3	.022	.999
	2	.140	.994
	1	.591	.926
.075	3	.026	.999
	2	.158	.992
	1	.627	.913
.080	3	.031	.999
	2	.177	.990
	1	.660	.899
.085	3	.037	.999
	2	.196	.988
	1	.692	.883
.090	3	.043	.998
	2	.216	.986
	1	.722	.867
.095	3	.049	.998
	2	.237	.984
	1	.750	.850
.100	3	.056	.998
	2	.258	.981
	1	.776	.832
.105	3	.064	.997
	2	.279	.978
	1	.800	.814
.110	3	.072	.997
	2	.301	.974
	1	.822	.795
.115	3	.081	.996
	2	.324	.971
	1	.843	.776
.120	4	.016	.999
	3	.090	.995
	2	.346	.967
	1	.861	.756
.125	4	.019	.999
	3	.100	.994
	2	.369	.962
	1	.878	.737
.130	4	.022	.999
	3	.110	.994
	2	.392	.958
	1	.893	.718
.135	4	.025	.999
	3	.121	.993
	2	.415	.952
	1	.907	.699
.140	4	.028	.999
	3	.132	.991
	2	.437	.947
	1	.919	.680
.145	4	.032	.999
	3	.144	.990
	2	.460	.941
	1	.929	.662
.150	4	.036	.998
	3	.156	.989
	2	.483	.935
	1	.939	.644
.155	4	.040	.998
	3	.169	.987
	2	.505	.928
	1	.947	.627
.160	4	.044	.998
	3	.182	.986
	2	.528	.921
	1	.954	.610
.165	4	.049	.997
	3	.195	.984
	2	.550	.914
	1	.961	.594
.170	4	.054	.997
	3	.209	.982
	2	.571	.906
	1	.966	.579
.180	5	.013	.999
	4	.066	.996
	3	.238	.978
	2	.614	.890
	1	.975	.890
.190	5	.016	.999
	4	.078	.995
	3	.269	.973
	2	.654	.873
	1	.982	.522
.200	5	.020	.999
	4	.092	.994
	3	.300	.968
	2	.692	.854
	1	.987	.497
.210	5	.025	.999
	4	.108	.992
	3	.333	.961
	2	.728	.835
	1	.990	.474
.220	5	.030	.998
	4	.124	.990
	3	.366	.954
	2	.761	.815
	1	.993	.453
.230	5	.037	.998
	4	.142	.988
	3	.400	.947
	2	.791	.794
	1	.995	.434
.240	5	.044	.997
	4	.162	.986
	3	.434	.938
	2	.819	.774
	1	.996	.416
.250	6	.010	.999
	5	.052	.997
	4	.183	.983
	3	.469	.929
	2	.844	.753
	1	.997	.400
.260	6	.013	.999
	5	.060	.996
	4	.205	.980
	3	.503	.919
	2	.866	.732
	1	.998	.384
.270	6	.015	.999
	5	.070	.995
	4	.228	.976
	3	.537	.908
	2	.886	.712
	1	.999	.370
.280	6	.018	.999
	5	.081	.994
	4	.252	.972
	3	.571	.896
	2	.903	.692
	1	.999	.357
.290	6	.022	.999
	5	.093	.993
	4	.278	.968
	3	.603	.884
	2	.918	.672
	1	.999	.345
.300	6	.026	.998
	5	.106	.991
	4	.304	.963
	3	.635	.872
	2	.932	.653
	1	.999	.333
.310	6	.031	.998
	5	.120	.990
	4	.331	.957
	3	.666	.858
	2	.943	.635
.320	6	.036	.998
	5	.135	.988
	4	.359	.952
	3	.695	.845
	2	.952	.617
.330	6	.042	.997
	5	.151	.986
	4	.387	.945
	3	.723	.831
	2	.961	.600
.340	7	.010	.999
	6	.049	.997
	5	.168	.983
	4	.416	.938
	3	.750	.816
	2	.968	.584
.360	7	.014	.999
	6	.064	.995
	5	.205	.978
	4	.474	.923
	3	.798	.787
	2	.978	.553
.380	7	.019	.999
	6	.083	.993
	5	.247	.971
	4	.533	.906
	3	.840	.758
	2	.986	.525
.400	7	.026	.998
	6	.105	.991
	5	.292	.963
	4	.591	.887
	3	.875	.728
	2	.991	.499
.420	7	.034	.993
	6	.130	.987
	5	.341	.954
	4	.646	.866
	3	.905	.700
	2	.994	.476
.440	7	.045	.997
	6	.160	.984
	5	.392	.943
	4	.698	.845
	3	.928	.672
	2	.996	.454
.460	8	.011	.999
	7	.058	.995
	6	.193	.979
	5	.445	.930
	4	.747	.822
	3	.947	.646
	2	.998	.435
.480	8	.015	.999
	7	.074	.994
	6	.230	.973
	5	.499	.916
	4	.791	.799
	3	.961	.621
	2	.998	.417
.500	8	.020	.999
	7	.093	.992
	6	.271	.966
	5	.553	.901

TABLE 19-7

(Concluded)

X	M	D	F	X	M	D	F	X	M	D	F	X	M	D	F
.500	4	.830	.775	.560	5	.707	.848	.650	6	.651	.878	.800	6	.939	.747
	3	.972	.598		4	.917	.706		5	.882	.759		5	.991	.625
	2	.999	.400		3	.991	.535		4	.980	.614		4	.999	.500
.520	8	.026	.998	.580	8	.057	.995		3	.999	.461	.850	9	.232	.979
	7	.115	.989		7	.204	.977	.700	9	.040	.997		8	.611	.916
	6	.316	.958		6	.465	.927		8	.200	.979		7	.879	.818
	5	.606	.884		5	.753	.829		7	.484	.929		6	.978	.705
	4	.864	.752		4	.937	.684		6	.772	.836		5	.998	.588
	3	.980	.575		3	.994	.517		5	.940	.711	.900	9	.387	.963
	2	.999	.385	.600	9	.010	.999		4	.992	.571		8	.785	.881
.540	8	.034	.997		8	.072	.994	.750	9	.075	.994		7	.957	.777
	7	.141	.986		7	.242	.972		8	.307	.965		6	.995	.667
	6	.363	.949		6	.518	.915		7	.626	.897	.950	9	.630	.938
	5	.658	.867		5	.795	.809		6	.870	.792		8	.934	.841
	4	.893	.729		4	.953	.663		5	.975	.666		7	.994	.737
	3	.986	.555		3	.996	.500		4	.998	.533				
.560	8	.044	.996	.650	9	.021	.999	.800	9	.134	.988				
	7	.171	.982		8	.123	.988		8	.446	.944				
	6	.413	.939		7	.353	.954		7	.763	.859				

Source: L. G. Peck and R. N. Hazelwood, *Finite Queuing Tables* (New York: John Wiley & Sons, 1958). Reprinted by permission.

One operator loads and unloads a group of five machines. Service time is exponentially distributed with a mean of 10 minutes per cycle. Machines run for an average of 70 minutes between loading and unloading, and this time is also exponential. Find:

Example 10

a. The average number of machines waiting for the operator.

b. The expected number of machines running.

c. Average downtime.

d. The probability that a machine will not have to wait for service.

Solution

$N = 5$

$T = 10$ minutes

$M = 1$

$U = 70$ minutes

$$X = \frac{T}{T + U} = \frac{10}{10 + 70} = .125$$

From Table 19–7, with $N = 5$, $M = 1$, and $X = .125$, $D = .473$ and $F = .920$.

a. Average number waiting, $L = N(1 - F) = 5(1 - .920) = .40$ machine.

b. Expected number running, $J = NF(1 - X) = 5(.92)(1 - .125) = 4.025$ machines.

c. Downtime = Waiting time + Service time:

Waiting time, $W = \dfrac{L(T + U)}{N - L} = \dfrac{.40(10 + 70)}{5 - .40} = 6.957$ minutes

Downtime = 6.957 minutes + 10 minutes = 16.957 minutes

d. Probability of not waiting   = 1 − Probability of waiting

$$= 1 - D$$

$$= 1 - .473 = .527$$

Using the Excel template, the solution to Example 10 would appear as follows:

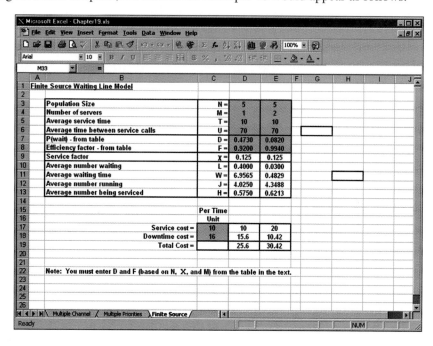

Suppose that in Example 10, operators are paid $10 per hour, and machine downtime costs $16 per hour. Should the department add another operator if the goal is cost optimization?

Example 11

Compare the total cost of the present system with the expected total cost of the proposed system:

Solution

M	Average Number Down, N − J	Average Down Cost (per hour), (N − J) $16	Operator Cost (per hour)	Total Cost (per hour)
1	.975	$15.60	$10	$25.60
2	.651	10.42	20	30.42

Hence, the present system is superior because its total cost is less than the expected total cost using two operators.

NEWSCLIP

Hotels Exploring Easier Customer Check-ins

Salina Kahn

Travelers can avoid line by registering in shuttles or at the airport in some places.

The hotel front desk is no longer the only place where travelers check in and get their room keys.

More hotels are shortening front desk lines by doing that outside their front door—on airport shuttle buses and even at airports.

Hotels have long allowed guests to register via the phone or the Internet and then pick up a key at a special counter or kiosk in the lobby. Now hotels are accelerating express check-in by using wireless technology to program electronic card keys outside the hotel.

The improvements should be popular: 81 percent of business travelers say express check-in and checkout services are very desirable, according to the 1999 Business Travel Monitor by Yesawich, Pepperdine & Brown and Yankelovich Partners.

Hilton plans to use the technology to provide curbside check-in at hotels in Honolulu, New York and Anaheim, Calif., early next year, says John Luke, Hilton vice president.

Starwood Hotels and Resorts will test curbside check-in at the Boston Park Plaza within 60 days.

Other hotels where guests check in before they reach the lobby:

- The Fairmont Vancouver Airport Hotel accepts reservations, checks bags and hands out keys from two "satellite lobbies" in the airport.

- Park Place Entertainment plans to open a check-in counter at McCarran International Airport in Las Vegas early next year.

- Hilton Boston Logan Airport began in September to allow guests to register on the shuttle bus ride from the airport to the hotel.

- The Loews Portofino Bay Hotel in Orlando, Fla., provides curbside check-in.

Source: Reprinted with permission of the *Rochester Democrat and Chronicle*, Rochester, NY. November 7, 1999, p. 1E.

Other Approaches

The discussion in this chapter has focused on designing service systems that achieve a balance between service capacity and customer waiting time. The implication is that decision makers can determine an appropriate level of service capacity. In certain instances, such an approach may not be practical for a variety of reasons. One is that the system may be currently in operation and indicated design changes may be too costly, or space restrictions may prevent changes from being made reasonably. One alternative that is particularly suited for queuing systems in which the customers are people rather than inanimate objects is to provide some form of diversion so that the waiting time becomes more tolerable. This involves taking into account, and taking steps to reduce, the *perceived waiting time*, as opposed to the *actual waiting time*. For example, magazines and newspapers can be placed in waiting rooms, as is usually the case in doctors' and dentists' offices. Auto repair shops sometimes use radio or television, and airlines may provide in-flight movies to help occupy the time. Airlines also serve meals and snacks, which help to make the time spent waiting (flying) more pleasant. Some other measures include placing mirrors where people wait for elevators, and asking people to fill out forms, which makes waiting somewhat constructive.

To carry this concept one step further, it is sometimes possible to derive some benefit from customer waiting. For instance, supermarkets position impulse items near checkout counters and gain additional sales, banks advertise current rates and place brochures describing bank services within easy reach of waiting customers, and restaurants have bars where customers can relax and spend money while waiting for their tables.

The implication in these ideas is that imagination and creativity can often play an important role in system design and that mathematical approaches are not the only ones worth considering.

Summary

Analysis of waiting lines can be an important aspect of the design of service systems. Waiting lines have a tendency to form in such systems even though, in a macro sense, the system is underloaded. The arrival of customers at random times and variability of service times combine to create temporary overloads. When this happens, waiting lines appear. By the same token, at other times the servers are idle.

A major consideration in the analysis of queuing systems is whether the number of potential customers is limited (finite source) or whether entry to the system is unrestricted (infinite source). Five basic queuing models are described, four dealing with infinite-source populations and one dealing with finite-source populations. In general, the models assume that customer arrival rates can be described by a Poisson distribution and that service time can be described by a negative exponential distribution.

Key Terms

channel, 822
finite source, 821
infinite source, 821

multiple-priority model, 835
queue discipline, 824
queuing theory, 818

Solved Problems

Problem 1

Infinite source. One of the features of a new machine shop will be a well-stocked tool crib. The manager of the shop must decide on the number of attendants needed to staff the crib. Attendants will receive $9 per hour in salary and fringe benefits. Mechanics' time will be worth $30 per hour, which includes salary and fringe benefits plus lost work time caused by waiting for parts. Based on previous experience, the manager estimates requests for parts will average 18 per hour with a service capacity of 20 requests per hour per attendant. How many attendants should be on duty if the manager is willing to assume that arrival and service rates will be Poisson-distributed? (Assume the number of mechanics is very large, so an infinite-source model is appropriate.)

Solution

$\lambda = 18$ per hour
$\mu = 20$ per hour

The solution requires a trial-and-error approach that reveals the total cost of feasible alternatives (i.e., a utilization less than 100 percent) and selection of the lowest-cost alternative. Note that the total-cost curve will always be U-shaped; increase the number of servers until the total cost shows an increase over the previous value. The optimum will be the number of servers that produced the previous total cost value. Thus,

Number of Servers, M	L_q^*	$L_q + \dfrac{\lambda}{\mu} = L$	$9M:$ Server Cost (per hour)	$30L_s:$ Mechanic Cost (per hour)	Total Cost (per hour)
1	8.1	$8.1 + 0.9 = 9.0$	$ 9	$270	$279
2	0.229	$0.229 + 0.9 = 1.129$	$18	$ 33.87	$ 52†
3	0.03	$0.03 + 0.9 = 0.93$	$27	$ 27.9	$ 55†

$^*L_q$ from Table 19–4, with $r = \lambda/\mu = 18/20 = 0.9$.
†Rounded.

Hence, two servers will produce the lowest total cost.

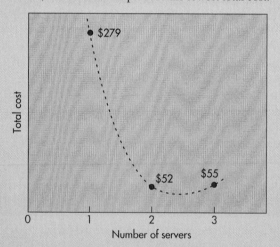

Problem 2

Infinite source. The following is a list of service times for three different operations:

Operation	Service Time
A	8 minutes
B	1.2 hours
C	2 days

a. Determine the service rate for each operation.

b. Would the calculated rates be different if these were interarrival times rather than service times?

Solution

a. The service rate is the reciprocal of service time. Thus, the rates are:

A: 1/8 per minute = .125 per minute, or .125/min. × 60 min./hr. = 7.5 per hour

B: 1/1.2 per hour = .833 per hour

C: 1/2 per day = .50 per day

b. No. In either case, the rate is simply the reciprocal of the time.

Finite source. A group of 10 machines is loaded and unloaded by one of three servers. The machines run for an average of six minutes per cycle, and average time to unload and reload is nine minutes. Each time can be described by an exponential distribution. While running, the machines produce at a rate that would yield 16 units per hour if they did not have to pause to wait for a server and be loaded and unloaded. What is the average hourly output of each machine when waiting and serving are taken into account?

Problem 3

$T = 9$ minutes

Solution

$U = 6$ minutes; $\chi = \dfrac{T}{T+U} = \dfrac{9}{9+6} = .60$

$M = 3$ servers; from Table 19–7, $F = .500$

$N = 10$ machines

a. Compute the average number of machines running:

$J = NF(1 - X) = 10(.500)(.40) = 2$

b. Determine the percentage of machines running, and multiply by output while running:

$\dfrac{J}{N} \times (16 \text{ per hour}) = \dfrac{2}{10} \times (16 \text{ per hour}) = 3.2 \text{ per hour}$

Discussion and Review Questions

1. In what kinds of situations is queuing analysis most appropriate?
2. Why do waiting lines form even though a service system is underloaded?
3. What are the most common measures of system performance in a queuing analysis?
4. What effect would decreasing arrival and service variability have on the effective capacity of a system?
5. What approaches do supermarkets use to offset variations in customer traffic intensity?
6. Contrast *finite* and *infinite* population sources.
7. Will doubling the service rate of a single-channel system reduce the average waiting time in line by a factor of one half? Explain briefly.
8. In a multiple-channel system, what is the rationale for having customers wait in a single line, as is now being done in many banks and post offices, rather than multiple lines? (*Hint:* The average waiting time is unaffected.)
9. What happens to the length of a waiting line in a highly variable (queuing) setting if a manager attempts to achieve a high percentage of capacity utilization?

Memo Writing Exercises

1. Write a half-page memo to your manager, Betty Davis-Brown, comparing the costs and benefits of two options being considered for the placement of a tool crib in your plant, which is fairly large. One option is to have a single, centralized tool crib where employees can check out tools they need, and the other is to have two cribs, one at each end of the plant.
2. Write a short memo to your manager, Tom Peters, explaining why you believe that the multiple priority queuing model should be used for customer complaints.

1. Repair calls are handled by one repairman at a photocopy shop. Repair time, including travel time, is exponentially distributed, with a mean of two hours per call. Requests for copier repairs come in at a mean rate of three per eight-hour day (assume Poisson). Determine:

   a. The average number of customers awaiting repairs.
   b. System utilization.
   c. The amount of time during an eight-hour day that the repairman is not out on a call.
   d. The probability of two or more customers in the system.

2. A vending machine dispenses hot chocolate or coffee. Service time is 30 seconds per cup and is constant. Customers arrive at a mean rate of 80 per hour, and this rate is Poisson- distributed. Determine:

   a. The average number of customers waiting in line.
   b. The average time customers spend in the system.
   c. The average number in the system.

3. Many of a bank's customers use its automatic teller machine to transact business after normal banking hours. During the early evening hours in the summer months, customers arrive at a certain location at the rate of one every other minute. This can be modeled using a Poisson distribution. Each customer spends an average of 90 seconds completing his or her transactions. Transaction time is exponentially distributed. Determine:

   a. The average time customers spend at the machine, including waiting in line and completing transactions.
   b. The probability that a customer will not have to wait upon arriving at the automatic teller machine.
   c. The average number waiting to use the machine.

4. A small town with one hospital has two ambulances to supply ambulance service. Requests for ambulances during nonholiday weekends average .8 per hour and tend to be Poisson-distributed. Travel and assistance time averages one hour per call and follows an exponential distribution. Find:

   a. System utilization.
   b. The average number of customers waiting.
   c. The average time customers wait for an ambulance.
   d. The probability that *both* ambulances will be busy when a call comes in.

5. The following information pertains to telephone calls to a motel switchboard on a typical Tuesday.

Period	Incoming Rate (calls per minute)	Service Rate (calls per minute per operator)	Number of Operators
Morning	1.8	1.5	2
Afternoon	2.2	1.0	3
Evening	1.4	0.7	3

   a. Determine the average time callers wait to have their calls answered for each period and the probability that a caller will have to wait for each period.
   b. For each case in the previous problem, determine the maximum line length for a probability of 96 percent.

6. Trucks are required to pass through a weighing station so that they can be checked for weight violations. Trucks arrive at the station at the rate of 40 an hour between 7 P.M. and 9 P.M. Currently two inspectors are on duty during those hours, each of whom can inspect 25 trucks an hour.

   a. How many trucks would you expect to see at the weighing station, including those being inspected?
   b. If a truck was just arriving at the station, about how many minutes could the driver expect to be at the station?
   c. What is the probability that both inspectors would be busy at the same time?

    d. How many minutes, on average, would a truck that is not immediately inspected have to wait?

    e. What condition would exist if there was only one inspector?

    f. What is the maximum line length for a probability of .97?

7. The manager of a regional warehouse must decide on the number of loading docks to request for a new facility in order to minimize the sum of dock costs and driver-truck costs. The manager has learned that each driver-truck combination represents a cost of $300 per day and that each dock plus loading crew represents a cost of $1,100 per day.

    a. How many docks should be requested if trucks arrive at the rate of four per day, each dock can handle five trucks per day, and both rates are Poisson?

    b. An employee has proposed adding new equipment that would speed up the loading rate to 5.71 trucks per day. The equipment would cost $100 per day for each dock. Should the manager invest in the new equipment?

8. The parts department of a large automobile dealership has a counter used exclusively for mechanics' requests for parts. The time between requests can be modeled by a negative exponential distribution that has a mean of five minutes. A clerk can handle requests at a rate of 15 per hour, and this can be modeled by a Poisson distribution that has a mean of 15. Suppose there are two clerks at the counter.

    a. On average, how many mechanics would be at the counter, including those being served?

    b. What is the probability that a mechanic would have to wait for service?

    c. If a mechanic has to wait, how long would the average wait be?

    d. What percentage of time are the clerks idle?

    e. If clerks represent a cost of $20 per hour and mechanics a cost of $30 per hour, what number of clerks would be optimal in terms of minimizing total cost?

9. One field representative services five customers for a computer manufacturer. Customers request assistance at an average (Poisson-distributed) rate of once every four working days. The field representative can handle an average (Poisson-distributed) of one call per day. Determine:

    a. The expected number of customers waiting.

    b. The average length of time customers must wait from the initial request for service until the service has been completed.

    c. The percentage of time the service rep will be idle.

    d. By how much would your answer to part *a* be reduced if a second field rep were added?

10. Two operators handle adjustments for a group of 10 machines. Adjustment time is exponentially distributed and has a mean of 14 minutes per machine. The machines operate for an average of 86 minutes between adjustments. While running, each machine can turn out 50 pieces per hour. Find:

    a. The probability that a machine will have to wait for an adjustment.

    b. The average number of machines waiting for adjustment.

    c. The average number of machines being serviced.

    d. The expected hourly output of each machine, taking adjustments into account.

    e. Machine downtime represents a cost of $70 per hour; operator cost (including salary and fringe benefits) is $15 per hour. What is the optimum number of operators?

11. One operator services a bank of five machines. Machine running time and service time are both exponential. Machines run for an average of 90 minutes between service requirements, and service time averages 35 minutes. The operator receives $20 per hour in salary and fringe benefits, and machine downtime costs $70 per hour per machine.

    a. If each machine produces 60 pieces per hour while running, find the average hourly output of each machine, when waiting and service times are taken into account.

    b. Determine the optimum number of operators.

12. A milling department has 10 machines. Each operates an average of eight hours before requiring adjustment, which takes an average of two hours. While running, each machine can produce 40 pieces an hour.

    a. With one adjuster, what is the net average hourly output per machine?

    b. If machine downtime cost is $80 per hour and adjuster cost is $30 per hour, how many adjusters would be optimal?

13. Trucks arrive at the loading dock of a wholesale grocer at the rate of 1.2 per hour. A single crew consisting of two workers can load a truck in about 30 minutes. Crew members receive $10 per hour in wages and fringe benefits, and trucks and drivers reflect an hourly cost of $60. The manager is thinking of adding another member to the crew. The service rate would then be 2.4 trucks per hour. Assume rates are Poisson.

    a. Would the third crew member be economical?

    b. Would a fourth member be justifiable if the resulting service capacity were 2.6 trucks per hour?

14. Customers arriving at a service center are assigned to one of three categories, with category 1 given the highest priority. Records indicate that an average of nine customers arrive per hour and that one-third are assigned to each category. There are two servers, and each can process customers at the rate of five per hour. Arrival and service rates can be described by Poisson distributions.

    a. What is the utilization rate for this system?

    b. Determine the average waiting time for units in each class.

    c. Find the average number of customers in each class that are waiting for service.

15. A manager must determine requirements for waiting space for customers. A priority system is used to process customers, who are assigned to one of two classes when they enter the processing center. The highest-priority class has an arrival rate of four per hour; the other class has an arrival rate of two per hour. Both can be described as Poisson-distributed. There are two servers, and each can process customers in an average of six minutes.

    a. What is the system utilization?

    b. Determine the number of customers of each class that are waiting for service.

    c. Determine the average waiting time for each class.

    d. If the manager could alter the assignment rules so that arrival rates of the two classes were equal, what would be the revised average waiting time for each priority class?

16. A priority waiting system assigns arriving customers to one of four classes. Arrival rates (Poisson) of the classes are shown in the following table:

Class	Arrivals per Hour
1	2
2	4
3	3
4	2

    Five servers process the customers, and each can handle three customers per hour.

    a. What is the system utilization?

    b. What is the average wait for service by customers in the various classes? How many are waiting in each class, on the average?

    c. If the arrival rate of the second priority class could be reduced to three units per hour by shifting some arrivals into the third priority class, how would your answers to part b change?

    d. What observations can you make based on your answers to part c?

17. Referring to Problem 16, suppose that each server could handle four customers per hour. Answer the questions posed in the problem. Explain why the impact of reassigning customers is much less than in Problem 16.

18. During the morning hours at a catalog sales department, telephone calls come in at the rate (Poisson) of 40 per hour. Calls that cannot be answered immediately are put on hold. The system can handle eight callers on hold. If additional calls come in, they receive a busy signal. The three customer service representatives who answer the calls spend an average of three minutes with a customer.

    a. What is the probability that a caller will get a busy signal? (*Hint:* Solve for log K or ln K using trial and error.)

    b. What is the probability that a customer will be put on hold?

Stopped at a Light? Why Not Read This, You May Have Time

Anna Wilde Mathews

As red signals grow longer, northern Virginia tries an experimental speedup

At the corner of Fairfax County Parkway and Fair Lakes Parkway, drivers see red.

More than four minutes of it.

Hanging over this crowded intersection in northern Virginia's booming suburbs is one of the longest stoplights in the country. Washington-bound commuters curse it. Highflying tech executives making their way to appointments feel grounded. Prepared motorists bring breakfast to nibble while they wait. Occasionally, a gaggle of geese waddles across the road to a nearby pond, slowing things even more.

"You come out here sometimes, and it brings tears to your eyes, it's so bad," says Jeris J. White, the state transportation manager and former professional-football player who tackles traffic delays here.

Spread of Red

It's happening everywhere—red lights are getting longer. And longer. Cities and towns are quietly, albeit reluctantly, giving the green light to longer traffic signals. Through the 1970s, the typical wait at a red light was 45 seconds or so. The wait started growing in the 1980s and 1990s. Today, 90-second spans aren't uncommon, and some are inching near the three-minute mark. Many of these long lights are their longest only at rush hour, but that's little solace to impatient travelers.

Law-abiding drivers stuck at the two-minute-36-second red light at the corner of DuPont Parkway and Frenchtown Road south of Wilmington, Del., take coffee breaks, work on crossword puzzles and, now and then, do some automotive hugging.

"You see couples getting a little more amorous than you'd expect at a traffic light," says Paul Rada, manager of the nearby Quality Inn. "You've got to do something." Mr. Rada himself has read the comics and eaten his lunch sitting at the light, he says. The truly desperate will "jump out of cars and hit the pedestrian button," hoping it will trigger a light change, adds Larry Koczak, a local mail carrier.

Reasons for the lengthening lights vary: More traffic. Wider streets. More lanes dedicated to left turns. And disagreement among traffic engineers who feel just as stuck as the drivers who endure these lights. "It's crept up gradually," says Scott Wainwright, a Montgomery County, Md., official who chairs a national engineering committee on traffic signals.

Longer red lights are intended to help keep busy intersections clear of anything approaching gridlock. In part, that's because several seconds go to waste every time traffic has to start again when red turns to green.

Yielding to Temptation

But longer lights can encourage antsy drivers to race through yellow lights and run reds, causing accidents and pileups that, in addition to risking injury and death, clog traffic even more. Each year, more than 1.8 million crashes occur at intersections, killing more than 7,800 people, the Federal Highway Administration says.

The federal government has launched a special "Stop Red Light Running" initiative, and localities are cracking down with hidden cameras that snap automatic pictures of scofflaws. For safety's sake, many cities have built more time into stoplight cycles so, for a few seconds, lights at all sides of a given intersection are red—an "all-red" delay designed to clear stragglers and minimize collisions.

All-reds are a source of controversy among traffic engineers. Peter Parsonson, professor of civil engineering at Georgia Tech in Atlanta, says they add an extra margin of safety. But at Marquette University in Milwaukee, David Kuemmel, who is in the department of civil and environmental engineering, argues that the all-red sequence is being used "indiscriminately."

The way to stop frustrated drivers from going through lights is not to make them wait longer, Mr. Kuemmel says. "That's a pet peeve of mine. It's an incentive for motorists to run the red light." The disagreements are further complicated by the lack of conclusive research on the link between light length and crashes.

Many roads are sprouting more left-turn-only lanes, with their own green-arrow turn indicators to keep vehicles that want to turn from backing up forever. But that stretches the light-cycle length. And with extra lanes making streets wider, pedestrians need more time to cross, requiring longer greens to accommodate them.

Even in Las Vegas

"In the old days, when you had two-lane roads, things were different," says Gerry de Camp, a transportation consultant and former manager of the Las Vegas area computer traffic system. Now, he says, "you can have a three-lane left turn, plus a bus lane, and a 12-foot shoulder, yadda, yadda, yadda." Las Vegas has a red light that stretches to two minutes and 45 seconds, although Mr. DeCamp says he tried to keep it from getting any longer. "I wasn't proud of it," he says. "I preferred not to advertise it."

In Northern Virginia, Mr. White, who played cornerback for nine years for the Washington Redskins and other teams, has gone from stopping opposing teams to trying to get vehicles moving. He looks more like a referee on a recent weekday evening as he stands at the Fairfax County intersection, stopwatch in hand, timing a seemingly endless procession of glowing headlights and taillights.

"This is brutal," he says, peering down a line of vehicles that stretches down Fair Lakes Parkway to the horizon, waiting for the light to change. One white sedan waits four minutes and 41 seconds to make a left turn, Mr. White explains why: Southbound traffic on the seven-lane Fairfax County Parkway hasn't eased enough to trigger a change in the computer-controlled light. The light is set to switch automatically only when traffic thins on that road, which typically carries a heavier load than the intersecting one.

"You see any end in sight?" he asks. There is none, for now.

The crossroads appears deceptively rural, with trees and grass at each corner and the nearby pond. But it rests amid gleaming new condominiums, a shopping mall and an office park, and the roads are lined with signs urging drivers to stop and see the latest housing developments under construction.

Standing on one corner, Mr. White offers running sports-style commentary on the traffic flow, groaning occasionally at a bad move. "The truck is going to run the red!" he shouts. "The truck ran the red!"

A Long Red

He varies the light cycles at different times of the day, and uses the longest cycles only during peak rush-hour traffic. But at those times, he says, he has little choice but to keep the Fair Lakes Parkway red light so as to prevent miles-long backups on the Fairfax County Parkway.

Suddenly, Fair Lakes seems to be clearing up. Cars flow smoothly through the intersection and, by the time the light changes to red, none are left waiting. "This is beautiful!" Mr. White cheers. "We cleared the whole side street out. If it's still that way at 6:30 or so, we can open the champagne."

But Mr. White thinks the light still is too long, and this week, he hopes to do something about it. As part of a computer-plotted plan to smooth traffic flows through 76 local intersections, the longest possible red light here will drop from four minutes and 47 seconds to three minutes and 15 seconds.

It'll still be one of the longest reds anywhere, and Mr. White can't be sure the change will stick. "The goal is to move the traffic," he says. "If it doesn't hold up, we'll change it" back.

Source: Reprinted by permission of Dow Jones & Company, Inc., from "Stopped at a Light? Why Not Read This, You May Have Time" by Anna Wilde Mathews, *Wall Street Journal* June 13, 2000, pp. A1 and A12. Permission conveyed through the copyright Clearance Center, Inc.

Selected Bibliography and Further Reading

Buffa, Elwood. *Operations Management.* 3rd ed. New York: John Wiley & Sons, 1972.

Griffin, W. *Queuing: Basic Theory and Applications.* Columbus, OH: Grid Publishing, 1978.

Hillier, Frederick S., and Gerald J. Lieberman. *Introduction to Operations Research,* 3rd ed. San Francisco: Holden-Day, 1980.

Katz, K. L., B. M. Larson, and R. C. Larson. "Prescriptions for the Waiting-in-Line Blues: Entertain, Enlighten, and Engage." *Sloan Management Review,* 32, no. 2 (Winter 1991), pp. 44–53.

Stevenson, William J. *Introduction to Management Science.* 3rd ed. Burr Ridge, IL: Richard D. Irwin, 1998.

SUPPLEMENT TO CHAPTER NINETEEN
Simulation

SUPPLEMENT OUTLINE

Introduction, 854

Steps in the Simulation Process, 854

Monte Carlo Simulation, 856
  Simulating Theoretical
    Distributions, 861

Computer Simulation, 864

Advantages and Limitation of Using
  Simulations, 865

Key Terms, 866

Solved Problems, 866

Discussion and Review
  Questions, 868

Memo Writing Exercises, 868

Problems, 869

Case: Coquille Refinery
  Corporation, 872

Selected Bibliography and Further
  Reading, 872

LEARNING OBJECTIVES

*After completing this supplement,
you should be able to:*

1 Explain what is meant by the term
   simulation.

2 List some of the reasons for
   simulation's popularity as a tool
   for decision making.

3 Explain how and why random
   numbers are used in simulation.

4 Outline the advantages and
   limitations of simulation.

5 Describe the alternatives that a
   manager would reject before
   choosing simulation as a
   decision-making tool.

6 Solve typical problems that
   require the use of simulation.

simulation A descriptive technique that enables a decision maker to evaluate the behavior of a model under various conditions.

Simulation is a descriptive technique in which a model of a process is developed and then experiments are conducted on the model to evaluate its behavior under various conditions. Unlike many of the other models described in the text, simulation is not an optimizing technique. It does not produce a solution per se. Instead, simulation enables decision makers to test *their* solutions on a model that reasonably duplicates a real process; simulation models enable decision makers to experiment with decision alternatives using a *what if* approach.

The use of simulation as a decision-making tool is fairly widespread, and you are undoubtedly familiar with some of the ways it is used. For instance, space engineers simulate space flight in laboratories to permit future astronauts to become accustomed to working in a weightless environment. Similarly, airline pilots often undergo extensive training with simulated landings and takeoffs before being allowed to try the real thing. Many video games are simulations, and universities use management games as a means of simulating business environments. Tire designers evaluate alternative tread designs using machines that simulate conditions that produce tire wear and handling problems.

Introduction

Simulation has applications across a broad spectrum of operations management problems. In some instances, the simulations are quite modest, while others are rather complex. Their usefulness in all cases depends on the degree to which decision makers are able to successfully answer their *what if* questions.

A list of operations management topics would reveal that most have simulation applications. For instance, simulation is often helpful in product design and testing, facilities layout, line balancing, job design, aggregate planning, testing alternative inventory policies, scheduling, waiting lines, and project management. Actually, the list is quite long. The books and articles in the bibliography indicate the richness and breadth of those applications and offer the interested reader an opportunity to explore this fascinating and useful subject in more detail.

Generally, analysts use the simulation approach either because optimization techniques are unavailable or because the assumptions required by an optimizing technique are not reasonably satisfied in a given situation. Waiting-line problems are a good example of the latter reason. Although waiting-line problems are pervasive, the rather restrictive assumptions of arrival and service distributions in many cases are simply not met. Very often, analysts will then turn to simulation as a reasonable alternative for obtaining descriptive information about the system in question.

Other reasons for the popularity of simulation include:

1. Many situations are too complex to permit development of a mathematical solution; the degree of simplification needed would seriously affect the results. In contrast, simulation models are often able to capture the richness of a situation without sacrificing simplicity, thereby enhancing the decision process.
2. Simulation models are fairly simple to use and understand.
3. Simulation enables the decision maker to conduct experiments on a model that will help in understanding process behavior while avoiding the risks of conducting tests on the model's real-life counterpart.
4. Extensive computer software packages make it easy to use fairly sophisticated models.
5. Simulation can be used for a wide range of situations.
6. There have been numerous successful applications of these techniques.

Steps in the Simulation Process

Regardless of the type of simulation involved, certain basic steps are used for all simulation models:

1. Identify the problem and set objectives.
2. Develop the simulation model.
3. Test the model to be sure that it reflects the system being studied.
4. Develop one or more experiments (conditions under which the model's behavior will be examined).
5. Run the simulation and evaluate the results.
6. Repeat steps 4 and 5 until you are satisfied with the results.

The first step in problem solving of any sort is to clearly declare the problem and set objectives that the solution is intended to achieve; simulation is no exception. A clear statement of the objectives can provide not only guidance for model development but also the basis for evaluation of the success or failure of a simulation. In general, the goal of a simulation study is to determine how a system will behave under certain conditions. The more specific a manager is about what he or she is looking for, the better the chances that the simulation model will be designed to accomplish that. Toward that end, the manager must decide on the *scope* and *level of detail* of the simulation. This indicates the necessary degree of complexity of the model and the information requirements of the study.

The next step is model development. Typically, this involves deciding on the structure of the model and using a computer to carry out the simulations. (For instructional purposes, the examples and problems in this chapter are primarily manual, but in most real-life applications computers are used. This stems from the need for large numbers of runs, the complexity of simulations, and the need for record-keeping of results.) Data gathering is a significant part of model development. The amount and type of data needed are a direct function of the scope and level of detail of the simulation. The data are needed for both model development and evaluation. Naturally, the model must be designed to enable evaluation of key decision alternatives.

The validation phase is closely related to model development. Its main purpose is to determine if the model adequately depicts real system performance. An analyst usually accomplishes this by comparing the results of simulation runs with known performance of the system under the same circumstances. If such a comparison cannot be made because, for example, real-life data are difficult or impossible to obtain, an alternative is to employ a test of reasonableness, in which the judgments and opinions of individuals familiar with the system or similar systems are relied on for confirmation that the results are plausible and acceptable. Still another aspect of validation is careful consideration of the assumptions of the model and the values of parameters used in testing the model. Again, the judgments and opinions of those familiar with the real-life system and those who must use the results are essential. Finally, note that model development and model validation go hand in hand: Model deficiencies uncovered during validation prompt model revisions, which lead to the need for further validation efforts and perhaps further revisions.

The fourth step in simulation is designing experiments. Experiments are the essence of a simulation; they help answer the *what if* questions posed in simulation studies. By going through the process, the manager or analyst learns about system behavior.

The fifth step is to run the simulation model. If a simulation model is deterministic and all parameters are known and constant, only a single run will be needed for each *what if* question. But if the model is probabilistic, with parameters subject to random variability, multiple runs will be needed to obtain a clear picture of the results. In this text, probabilistic simulations are the focal point of the discussion, and the comments are limited to them. Probabilistic simulation is essentially a form of random sampling, with each run representing one observation. Consequently, statistical theory can be used to determine appropriate sample sizes. In effect, the larger the degree of variability inherent in simulation results, the greater the number of simulation runs needed to achieve a reasonable level of confidence in the results as true indicators of model behavior.

The last step in the simulation process is to analyze and interpret the results. Interpretation of the results depends to a large extent on the degree to which the simulation model approximates reality; the closer the approximation, the less need to "adjust" the results. Moreover, the closer the approximation of the model to reality, the less the risk inherent in applying the results.

Monte Carlo Simulation

Monte Carlo method Probabilistic simulation technique used when a process has a random component.

random Chance.

There are many different kinds of simulation techniques. The discussion will focus on probabilistic simulation using the **Monte Carlo method.** The technique gets its name from the famous Mediterranean resort associated with games of chance. The chance element is an important aspect of Monte Carlo simulation, and this approach can be used only when a process has a **random,** or chance, component.

In the Monte Carlo method, a manager identifies a probability distribution that reflects the random component of the system under study. Random samples taken from this probability distribution are analogous to observations made on the system itself. As the number of observations increases, the results of the simulation will more closely approximate the behavior of the real system, provided an appropriate model has been developed. Sampling is accomplished by the use of random numbers.

The basic steps in the process are as follows:

1. Identify a probability distribution for each random component of the system.
2. Work out an assignment so that intervals of random numbers will correspond to the probability distribution.
3. Obtain the random numbers needed for the study.
4. Interpret the results.

The random numbers used in Monte Carlo simulation can come from any source that exhibits the necessary randomness. Typically, they come from one of two sources: Large studies depend on computer-generated random numbers, and small studies commonly make use of numbers from a table of random digits like the one shown in Table 19S–1. The digits are listed in pairs for convenience, but they can be used singly, in pairs, or in whatever grouping a given problem calls for.

Two important features of the sets of random numbers are essential to simulation. One is that the numbers are uniformly distributed. This means that for any size grouping of digits (e.g., two-digit numbers), every possible outcome (e.g., 34, 89, 00) has the same probability of appearing. The second feature is that there are no discernible patterns in sequences of numbers to enable one to predict numbers further in the sequence (thus the name *random* digits). This feature holds for any sequence of numbers; the numbers can be read across rows and up or down columns.

TABLE 19S–1

Random digits

	1	2	3	4	5	6	7	8	9	10	11	12
1	18	20	84	29	91	73	64	33	15	67	54	07
2	25	19	05	64	26	41	20	09	88	40	73	34
3	73	57	80	35	04	52	81	48	57	61	29	35
4	12	48	37	09	17	63	94	08	28	78	51	23
5	54	92	27	61	58	39	25	16	10	46	87	17
6	96	40	65	75	16	49	03	82	38	33	51	20
7	23	55	93	83	02	19	67	89	80	44	99	72
8	31	96	81	65	60	93	75	64	26	90	18	59
9	45	49	70	10	13	79	32	17	98	63	30	05
10	01	78	32	17	24	54	52	44	28	50	27	68
11	41	62	57	31	90	18	24	15	43	85	31	97
12	22	07	38	72	69	66	14	85	36	71	41	58

When using the table, it is important to avoid always starting in the same spot; that would result in the same sequence of numbers each time. Various methods exist for choosing a random starting point. One can use the serial number of a dollar bill to select the row, column, and direction of number selection. Or use rolls of a die. For our purposes, the starting point will be specified in each manual example or problem so that everyone obtains the same results.

The process of simulation will become clearer as we work through some simple problems.

Example S-1

The manager of a machine shop is concerned about machine breakdowns. He has made a decision to simulate breakdowns for a 10-day period. Historical data on breakdowns over the last 100 days are given in the following table:

Number of Breakdowns	Frequency
0	10
1	30
2	25
3	20
4	10
5	5
	100

Simulate breakdowns for a 10-day period. Read two-digit random numbers from Table 19S–1, starting at the top of column 1 and reading down.

Solution

a. Develop cumulative frequencies for breakdowns:

(1) Convert frequencies into relative frequencies by dividing each frequency by the sum of the frequencies. Thus, 10 becomes 10/100 = .10, 30 becomes 30/100 = .30, and so on.

(2) Develop cumulative frequencies by successive summing. The results are shown in the following table:

Number of Breakdowns	Frequency	Relative Frequency	Cumulative Frequency
0	10	.10	.10
1	30	.30	.40
2	25	.25	.65
3	20	.20	.85
4	10	.10	.95
5	5	.05	1.00
	100	1.00	

b. Assign random-number intervals to correspond with the cumulative frequencies for breakdowns. (*Note:* Use two-digit numbers because the frequencies are given to two decimal places.) You want a 10 percent probability of obtaining the event "0 breakdowns" in our simulation. Therefore, you must designate 10 percent of the possible random numbers as corresponding to that event. There are 100 two-digit numbers, so we can assign the 10 numbers 01 to 10 to that event.

Similarly, assign the numbers 11 to 40 to "one breakdown," 41 to 65 to "two breakdowns," 66 to 85 to "three breakdowns," 86 to 95 to "4 breakdowns" and 96 to 00 to five breakdowns.

Number of Breakdowns	Frequency	Probability	Cumulative Probability	Corresponding Random Numbers
0	10	.10	10	01 to 10
1	30	.30	.40	11 to 40
2	25	.25	.65	41 to 65
3	20	.20	.85	66 to 85
4	10	.10	.95	86 to 95
5	5	.05	1.00	96 to 00
	100	1.00		

c. Obtain the random numbers from Table 19S–1, column 1, as specified in the problem:

   18   25   73   12   54   96   23   31   45   01

d. Convert the random numbers into numbers of breakdowns:

   18 falls in the interval 11 to 40 and corresponds, therefore, to one breakdown on day 1.

   25 falls in the interval 11 to 40, which corresponds to one breakdown on day 2.

   73 corresponds to three breakdowns on day 3.

   12 corresponds to one breakdown on day 4.

   54 corresponds to two breakdowns on day 5.

   96 corresponds to five breakdowns on day 6.

   23 corresponds to one breakdown on day 7.

   31 corresponds to one breakdown on day 8.

   45 corresponds to two breakdowns on day 9.

   01 corresponds to no breakdowns on day 10.

   The following table summarizes these results:

Day	Random Number	Simulated Number of Breakdowns
1	18	1
2	25	1
3	73	3
4	12	1
5	54	2
6	96	5
7	23	1
8	31	1
9	45	2
10	01	0
		17

The mean number of breakdowns for this 10-period simulation is $17/10 = 1.7$ breakdowns per day. Compare this to the *expected* number of breakdowns based on the historical data:

$$0(.10) + 1(.30) + 2(.25) + 3(.20) + 4(.10) + 5(.05) = 2.05 \text{ per day}$$

Several points are worth noting:

1. This simple example is intended to illustrate the basic concept of Monte Carlo simulation. If our only goal were to estimate the average number of breakdowns, we would not have to simulate; we could base the estimate on the historical data alone.

2. The simulation should be viewed as a *sample*; it is quite likely that additional runs of 10 numbers would produce different means.

3. Because of the variability inherent in the results of small samples, it would be unwise to attempt to draw any firm conclusions from them; in an actual study, much larger sample sizes would be used.

In some cases, it is helpful to construct a flowchart that describes a simulation, especially if the simulation will involve periodic updating of system values (e.g., amount of inventory on hand), as illustrated in Example S–2.

The Excel spreadsheet formulation for this problem is shown below. Note that the alignment of values in columns B, C, and F must be exactly as shown.

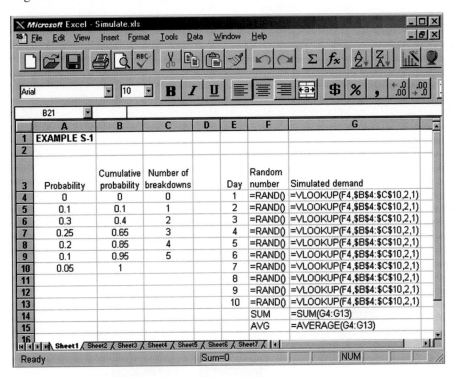

The simulation results are shown in the following screen. Use key F4 to do a simulation or another simulation.

Day	Random number	Simulated demand
1	0.22433	1
2	0.39772	1
3	0.20817	1
4	0.631	2
5	0.28439	1
6	0.16299	1
7	0.9581	5
8	0.66967	3
9	0.07676	0
10	0.06033	0
SUM		15
AVG		1.5

Probability	Cumulative probability	Number of breakdowns
0	0	0
0.1	0.1	1
0.3	0.4	2
0.25	0.65	3
0.2	0.85	4
0.1	0.95	5
0.05	1	

Example S-2

The manager of a small truck dealership wants to acquire some insight into how a proposed policy for reordering trucks might affect order frequency. Under the new policy, two trucks are to be ordered whenever the number of trucks on hand is five or fewer. Due to the nearness of the dealer to the home office, orders can be filled overnight. According to the dealer's records, the probability distribution for daily demand is:

Demand, x	P(x)
0	.50
1	.40
2	.10

a. Construct a flowchart that describes a 10-day simulation.

b. Use two-digit random numbers from Table 19S–1, column 11, reading down. Assume a beginning inventory of seven trucks.

Solution

a.

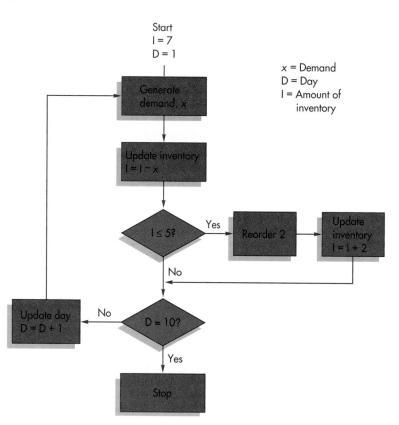

b. (1) Specify random number ranges for demand:

x	P(x)	Cumulative P(x)	Ranges
0	.50	.50	01–50
1	.40	.90	51–90
2	.10	1.00	91–00

(2) Obtain random numbers, convert to demand, update inventory accordingly, and reorder when necessary:

Day	Random Number	Demand, x	Beginning Inventory	Ending Inventory
1 54		1	7	6
2 73		1	6	5 (reorder 2; new beginning inventory = 5 + 2)
3 29		0	7	7
4 51		1	7	6
5 87		1	6	5 (reorder 2; new beginning inventory = 5 + 2)
6 51		1	7	6
7 99		2	6	4 (reorder 2; new beginning inventory = 4 + 2)
8 18		0	6	6
9 30		0	6	6
10 27		0	6	6

SIMULATING THEORETICAL DISTRIBUTIONS

In many instances, a simulation will involve the use of theoretical distributions. Among the most frequently encountered theoretical distributions are the Poisson, normal, and exponential distributions. Being able to simulate these distributions will greatly enhance your knowledge and appreciation of simulation.

Simulation of a Poisson distribution requires the mean of the distribution. Knowledge of the mean enables one to obtain cumulative probabilities for the distribution from Appendix B, Table C; these, in turn, provide the basis for random-number assignments. You can use Table 19S–1 to obtain random numbers; you must read three-digit random numbers from Table 19S–1 to achieve correspondence. Example S–3 illustrates these concepts.

Example S-3

The number of lost-time accidents at a large plant has been determined from historical records to be two per day. Moreover, it has been determined that this accident rate can be well approximated by a Poisson distribution that has a mean of 2.0. Simulate five days of accident experience for the plant. Read random numbers from columns 1 and 2 of Table 19S–1.

TABLE 19S–2

Normally distributed random numbers

	1	2	3	4	5	6	7	8	9	10
1	1.46	−0.09	−0.59	0.19	−0.52	−1.82	0.53	−1.12	1.36	−0.44
2	−1.05	0.56	−0.67	−0.16	1.39	−1.21	0.45	−0.62	−0.95	0.27
3	0.15	−0.02	0.41	−0.09	−0.61	−0.18	−0.63	−1.20	0.27	−0.50
4	0.81	1.87	0.51	0.33	−0.32	1.19	2.18	−2.17	1.10	0.70
5	0.74	−0.44	1.53	−1.76	0.01	0.47	0.07	0.22	−0.59	−1.03
6	−0.39	0.35	−0.37	−0.52	−1.14	0.27	−1.78	0.43	1.15	−0.31
7	0.45	0.23	0.26	−0.31	−0.19	−0.03	−0.92	0.38	−0.04	0.16
8	2.40	0.38	−0.15	−1.04	−0.76	1.12	−0.37	−0.71	−1.11	0.25
9	0.59	−0.70	−0.04	0.12	1.60	0.34	−0.05	−0.26	0.41	0.80
10	−0.06	0.83	−1.60	−0.28	0.28	−0.15	0.73	−0.13	−0.75	−1.49

Solution

First obtain the cumulative distribution from Appendix B, Table C for a mean of 2.0, and make the range assignments:

x	Cumulative Probability	Random Number Ranges
0	.135	001 to 135
1	.406	136 to 406
2	.677	407 to 677
3	.857	678 to 857
4	.947	858 to 947
5	.983	948 to 983
6	.995	984 to 995
7	.999	996 to 999
8	1.000	000

Next obtain three-digit numbers from Table 19S–1. Reading from column 1 and 2 as instructed, you find 182, 251, 735, 124, and 549.

Finally, convert the random numbers into number of lost-time accidents using the established set of ranges. Since 182 falls in the second range, it corresponds to one accident on day 1. The second random number, 251, falls in the same range, indicating one accident on day 2. The number 735 falls between 678 and 857, which corresponds to three accidents on day 3; 124 corresponds to 0 accidents on day 4; and 549 corresponds to two accidents on day 5.

The normal distribution can be important in many problems. There are a number of ways to simulate a normal distribution, but perhaps the simplest is to use a table of normally distributed random numbers, such as Table 19S–2. The basis of the table is a normal distribution with a mean of 0 and a standard deviation of 1.00. Like all such tables, the numbers are arranged randomly, so that when they are read in any sequence they exhibit "randomness." In order to use the table, we must have the parameters of a normal distribution (i.e., its mean and standard deviation) in mind. Numbers obtained from the random number table can then be converted to "actual" values by multiplying the standard deviation by the random number and adding this amount to the mean. That is:

Simulated value = Mean + Random number × Standard deviation   (19S–1)

In effect, the random number equates to a normal z value, which indicates how far a particular value is above or below the distribution mean.

Example S–4

It has been determined that the time required to perform a certain task can be described by a normal distribution that has a mean of 30 minutes and a standard deviation of 4 minutes. Simulate times for three jobs using the first three values in column 1 of Table 19S–2.

Solution

The first three values are: 1.46, −1.05, and 0.15. The simulated values are:

For   1.46:   30 + 1.46(4) = 35.84 minutes.
For −1.05:   30 − 1.05(4) = 25.80 minutes.
For   0.15:   30 + 0.15(4) = 30.60 minutes.

It is important to recognize that Example S–4 involves a continuous variable, whereas the previous examples involved discrete variables. (Remember that discrete variables typically take on only integer values, whereas continuous variables can take on integer and noninteger values.) Whenever possible, a model of a continuous variable should be able to simulate noninteger values as well as integer values.

FIGURE 19S–1

A uniform distribution

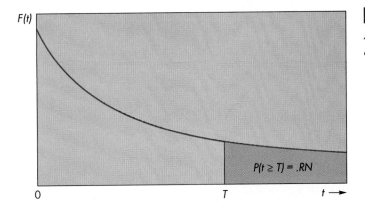

FIGURE 19S–2

A negative exponential distribution

Another continuous type of distribution we can consider is the uniform distribution, in which values may occur anywhere over a continuous range between two extremes, *a* and *b*, as illustrated in Figure 19S–1.

Simulated value = $a + (b - a)$(Random number as a percentage)   (19S–2)

Converting the random number to a percentage simply involves placing a decimal point to the left of the number. For example, 77 becomes .77.

Example S–5 illustrates a simulation involving a uniform distribution.

A third continuous distribution is the exponential distribution. We will concern ourselves with simulating values of negative exponential distributions, as portrayed in Figure 19S–2.

Example S–5

Job times vary uniformly between 10 and 15 minutes. Use Table 19S–1 to simulate job times for four jobs. Read numbers from column 9, going down.

Solution

a = 10 minutes, b = 15 minutes, $b - a$ = 5 minutes

a. Obtain the random numbers: 15, 88, 57, and 28.

b. Convert to simulated values:

Random Number	Computation		Simulated Value (minutes)
15	10 + 5(.15)	=	10.75
88	10 + 5(.88)	=	14.40
57	10 + 5(.57)	=	12.85
28	10 + 5(.28)	=	11.40

With a negative exponential distribution, the probability is fairly high that the random variable will assume a value close to zero. Moreover, the probability decreases as the specified value of the random variable increases. The probability that a random variable will take on a value greater than some specified value T, given that the variable can be described by an exponential distribution with a mean equal to $1/\lambda$, is given by the equation

$$P(t \geq T) = e^{-\lambda t} \tag{19S–3}$$

To simulate exponential values, we obtain a random number, place a decimal point to the left of it, set this equal to the probability $P(T)$, and solve Formula 19S–3 for t. The result is a simulated value from an exponential distribution with a mean of $1/\lambda$.

We can obtain an expression for t by taking the natural logarithm of both sides of the equation. Thus, with $P(T) = .RN$ (for *random number*), we have

$$\ln(.RN) = \ln(e^{-\lambda t})$$

The natural logarithm of a power of e is equal to the power itself, so

$$\ln(.RN) = \ln(e^{-\lambda t}) = -\lambda t$$

Then

$$t = -\frac{1}{\lambda} \ln(.RN) \tag{19S–4}$$

This concept is illustrated in Figure 19S–2.

Values of random numbers can be obtained using Table 19S–1, as demonstrated in the following example.

Example S-6	Times between breakdowns of a certain type of equipment can be described by an exponential distribution with a mean of five hours. Simulate the time between two breakdowns. Read two-digit random numbers from column 3 of Table 19S–1.
Solution	The mean, $1/\lambda$, is 5 hours. The random numbers are 84 and 05. Using Formula 19S–4, the simulated times are:

For 84: $t = -5[\ln(.84)] = -5[-0.1744] = 0.872$ hours.
For 05: $t = -5[\ln(.05)] = -5[-2.9957] = 14.979$ hours.

Note that the smaller the value of the random number, the larger the simulated value of t.

Computer Simulation

Although the emphasis in this supplement has been on manual simulation in order to convey the main concepts, most real-life simulations involve the use of a computer. Computers offer relatively quick and easy means of obtaining results. Many real-life applications involve fairly complex simulation models that have substantial record-keeping requirements for which computers offer a practical solution.

Over the years, programmers have developed a number of simulation languages that make the task of writing simulation programs much simpler. Some of the general-purpose languages are SIMSCRIPT II.5, GPSS/H, GPSS/PC, and RESQ. In addition, a number of other simulation packages are available, some of which have very narrow focuses that relate to queuing or network problems. Most of the simulation packages have certain features in common. For example, they generally provide for random number generation from a variety of statistical distributions, as well as collection and tabulation of simulation results and time keeping.

It should be noted that some managers prefer to write their own simulations or have a member of their staff do so, using spreadsheet software such as MS Excel rather than a simulation language, as illustrated on page 859. In cases where simulation is used infrequently, it can be more practical to use that approach rather than go through the time and effort required to use a specialty language. For simple problems, the slight inefficiency related to the use of a standard language is not usually an important consideration.

Advantages and Limitations of Using Simulations

Among the main advantages of simulation are these:

1. It lends itself to problems that are difficult or impossible to solve mathematically.
2. It permits an analyst to experiment with system behavior while avoiding possible risks inherent in experimenting with the actual system.
3. It compresses time so that managers can quickly discern long-term effects.
4. It can serve as a valuable tool for training decision makers by building up their experience and understanding of system behavior under a wide range of conditions.

Certain limitations are also associated with simulation. Chief among these are:

1. Simulation does not produce an optimum solution; it merely indicates an *approximate* behavior for a given set of inputs. There are two reasons for this:

FIGURE 19S–3

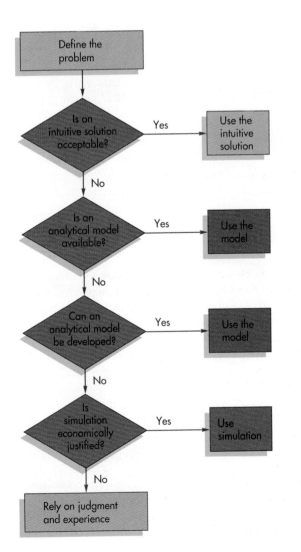

a. By design, there is inherent randomness (i.e., random numbers) in simulation.

b. Simulations are based on models, and models are only approximations of reality.

2. For large-scale simulation, it can require considerable effort to develop a suitable model as well as considerable computer time to obtain simulations.

Because simulation produces an approximate answer rather than an exact solution, and because of the cost of running a simulation study, simulation is not usually the first choice of a decision maker. Instead, depending on the complexity of the situation, intuitive or analytical methods should first be investigated. In simple cases, an intuitive solution very often is acceptable. In more complex cases, an analytical solution is preferable, assuming an appropriate technique is available. If not, it may be possible to develop an analytical model that could be used to generate a solution. If these measures do not suffice, simulation becomes the next logical possibility. Of course, if that is not economically justifiable, the decision maker will have to rely on judgment and experience; in effect, after reevaluating all of the alternatives, the decision maker may revert to an intuitive solution, even though initially that approach did not appear acceptable. Figure 19S–3 outlines this process.

Key Terms

Monte Carlo method, 856
random, 856

simulation, 854

Solved Problems

Problem 1

The number of customers who arrive at a transmission repair shop can be described by a Poisson distribution that has a mean of three per hour. Assuming the distribution holds for an entire eight-hour day, simulate customer arrivals for the first four hours of a day. Read random numbers from Table 19S–1, columns 4 and 5, going down.

Solution

a. Obtain cumulative probabilities of the Poisson distribution from Appendix B, Table C for the mean specified. (Those values are given below for convenience.) Determine the random number ranges.

x	Cumulative Probability
0	.050
1	.199
2	.423
3	.647
4	.815
5	.916
6	.966
7	.988
8	.996
9	.999
10	1.000

b. Obtain the random numbers: 299, 642, 350, and 091 (*Note:* Three-digit numbers are needed because the probabilities are given to three decimal places.)

c. Convert the random numbers to numbers of arrivals. Note where each number falls in the random number range list. For instance, 299 falls between 199 and 423. Interpret this to mean two customers arrive in the first hour. Similarly, 642 is interpreted to mean three customers arrive in the second hour, 350 implies two customers in the third hour, and 091 implies one customer in the fourth hour.

In sum, the number of customers per hour for the four-hour simulation is:

Hour	Number of Arrivals
1	2
2	3
3	2
4	1

Jobs arrive at a workstation at fixed intervals of one hour. Processing time is approximately normal and has a mean of 56 minutes per job and a standard deviation of 4 minutes per job. Using the fifth row of the table of normally distributed random numbers (Table 19S–2), simulate the processing times for four jobs, and determine the amount of operator idle time and job waiting time. Assume the first job arrives at time = 0.

Problem 2

a. Obtain the random numbers from the table: 0.74, −0.44, 1.53, and −1.76.

Solution

b. Convert the random numbers to simulated processing times:

Random Number	Computation	Simulated Time
0.74	56 + 4(0.74) =	58.96
−0.44	56 + 4(−0.44) =	54.24
1.53	56 + 4(1.53) =	62.12
−1.76	56 + 4(−1.76) =	48.96

Note that three of the times are less than the interarrival times for the jobs, meaning the operator may be idle after those three jobs. One time exceeds the one-hour interval, so the next job must wait, and possibly the job following it if the waiting plus processing time exceeds 60 minutes.

c. Compute waiting and idle times:

Job Number	Arrives at	Processing Time, t (minutes)	60 − t Operator Idle (minutes)	t − 60 Next Job Waits (minutes)
1	0	58.96	1.04	—
2	60	54.24	5.76	—
3	120	62.12	—	2.12
4	180	48.96	8.92*	—
			15.72	2.12

*60 − 2.12 − 48.96 = 8.92.

The time between mechanics' requests for tools in a large plant is normally distributed with a mean of 10 minutes and a standard deviation of 1 minute. The time to fill requests is also normal with a mean of 9 minutes per request and a standard deviation of 1 minute. Mechanics' waiting time represents a cost of $2 per minute, and servers represent a cost of $1 per minute. Simulate arrivals for the first nine mechanic requests and their service times, and determine the mechanics' waiting time, assuming one server. Would it be economical to add another server? Explain. Use Table 19S–2, column 8 for requests and column 9 for service.

Problem 3

a. Obtain random numbers and convert to times [see columns (*a*) and (*b*) in the following table for requests and columns (*f*) and (*g*) for service].

Solution

CUSTOMER ARRIVALS					SERVICE		
(a)	**(b)**	**(c)**	**(d)** **(e − c)**	**(e)**	**(f)**	**(g)**	**(h)**
Random→ Number	Time between Arrivals	Cumulative Arrival Time	Customer Waiting Time	Service Begins	Random→ Number	Service Time	**(e + g)** Service Ends
−1.12	8.88	8.88	0.00	8.88	1.36	10.36	19.24
−0.62	9.38	18.26	0.98	19.24	−0.95	8.05	27.29
−1.20	8.80	27.06	0.23	27.29	0.27	9.27	36.56
−2.17	7.83	34.89	1.67	36.56	1.10	10.10	46.66
0.22	10.22	45.11	1.55	46.66	−0.59	8.41	55.07
0.43	10.43	55.54	0.00	55.54	1.15	10.15	65.69
0.38	10.38	65.92	0.00	65.92	−0.04	8.96	74.88
−0.71	9.29	75.21	0.00	75.21	−1.11	7.89	83.10
−0.26	9.74	84.95	0.00	84.95	0.41	9.41	94.36
			4.43				

b. Determine arrival times [column (c)] by successive adding to times between arrivals in column (b).

c. Use arrival times for service start *unless service is still in progress on a previous request.* In that case, determine how long the arrival must wait (e − c). Column (e) values are the sum of starting time and service time [column (g)], which is the time service ends [column (h)]. Thus, service on each new request begins [column (e)] at the same time that service on the previous request ends [column (h)].

d. The simulation and resulting waiting times for the first nine arrivals are shown in the table. Total waiting time is 4.43 minutes.

e. The total cost for the 94.36 minutes (end of service on the ninth request) of the simulation is:

Waiting cost:	4.43 minutes at $2 per minute =	$ 8.86
Server cost:	94.36 minutes at $1 per minutes =	94.36
		$103.22

f. Usually, a second simulation with two servers would be needed (but with the same arrival times so that the results are comparable). However, in this case it is apparent that a second server would increase server cost by about $94 but could not eliminate more than $8.86 of waiting cost. Hence, the second server would not be justified.

Discussion and Review Questions

1. What is a simulation?

2. What are some of the primary reasons for the widespread use of simulation techniques in practice?

3. What are some of the ways managers can use simulation?

4. What role do random numbers play in Monte Carlo simulations?

5. Respond to the following comment: "I ran the simulation several times, and each run gave me a different result. Therefore, the technique does not seem to be useful. I need answers!"

6. List the main advantages of simulation.

7. What are some of the limitations of simulation as a tool for decision making?

Memo Writing Exercises

1. Write a memo to your instructor outlining the advantages and disadvantages of using simulation.

2. Write a memo to your boss, Mae East, on how simulation could (conceptually) be used to improve staffing of customer service telephone lines.

1. The number of jobs received by a small shop is to be simulated for an eight-day period. The shop manager has collected the following data:

Number of Jobs	Frequency
2 or less	0
3	10
4	50
5	80
6	40
7	16
8	4
9 or more	0
	200

   Use the third column of Table 19S–1 and read two-digit numbers, going down. Determine the average number of jobs per day for the eight-day simulation period.

2. Jack M. sells insurance on a part-time basis. His records on the number of policies sold per week over a 50-week period are:

Number Sold	Frequency
0	8
1	15
2	17
3	7
4	3
	50

   Simulate three five-day periods. Use Table 19S–1, column 6 for the first simulation, column 7 for the second, and column 8 for the third. In each case, read two-digit numbers, beginning at the *bottom* of the column and going *up*. For each simulation, determine the percentage of days on which two or more policies are sold.

3. After a careful study of requests for a special tool at a large tool crib, an analyst concluded that demand for the tool can be adequately described by a Poisson distribution with a mean of two requests per day. Simulate demand for a 12-working-day period for this tool using Table 19S–1. Read three-digit numbers from columns 5 and 6 combined, starting at the *top* and reading *down* (e.g., 917, 264, 045).

4. The number of lost-time accidents at a logging firm can be described using a Poisson distribution that has a mean of four accidents per month. Using the last two columns of Table 19S–1 (e.g. 540, 733, 293), simulate accidents for a 12-month period.

5. The time a physician spends with patients can be modeled using a normal distribution that has a mean of 20 minutes and a standard deviation of 2 minutes. Using the table of normally distributed random numbers (Table 19S–2), simulate the times the doctor might spend with the next seven patients. Use column 4 of the table; start at the *bottom* of the column and read *up*.

6. Jobs are delivered to a workstation at random intervals. The time between job arrivals tends to be normally distributed with a mean of 15 minutes and a standard deviation of 1 minute. Job processing time is also normally distributed with a mean of 14 minutes per job and a standard deviation of 2 minutes.

   a. Using Table 19S–2, simulate the arrival and processing of five jobs. Use column 4 of the table for job arrival times and column 3 for processing times. Start each column at row 4. Find the total times jobs wait for processing.

   b. The company is considering the use of new equipment that would result in processing time that is normal with a mean of 13 minutes and a standard deviation of 1 minute. Job waiting represents a cost of $3 per minute, and the new equipment would represent an additional cost of $.50 per minute. Would the equipment be cost justified? (*Note:* Use the same arrival times and the same random numbers for processing times.)

7. Daily usage of sugar in a small bakery can be described by a uniform distribution with endpoints of 30 pounds and 50 pounds. Assuming usage is independent of the day of the week, simulate daily usage for a 10-day period. Read four-digit numbers from Table 19S–1, columns 5 and 6, going *up* from the bottom.

8. Weekly usage of spare parts for a specialized machine can be described by a Poisson distribution with a mean of 2.8 parts per week. Lead time to replenish the supply of spare parts is two weeks (constant). Simulate the total usage of parts during lead time 10 times, and then determine the frequency of lead time demands (i.e., what percentage of times was the demand equal to 2, 3, 4, etc.?). Read four-digit numbers from Table 19S–1, columns 8 and 9, going down.

9. (*Computer exercise.*) Repeat Problem 8 for 100 lead time periods.

10. A repair shop breaks an average of .6 tool per day. The average number of days required to obtain replacements is six. (Parts are delivered by mail once each day.) Both breakages and delivery times can be described by Poisson distributions. Tools are reordered whenever three or more must be replaced.

    a. Draw a flowchart to describe this process.

    b. Simulate breakage and ordering for a 12-day period. Read three-digit numbers from Table 19S–1, columns 5 and 6, going down (e.g., 917, 264), for tool breakage, and columns 7 and 8, going down (e.g., 643, 200), for delivery time. Assume zero tools in inventory to start.

11. (*Computer exercise.*) Repeat Problem 10 for 150 days.

12. Customers arrive randomly at a catalog department of a large store. The time between arrivals varies uniformly between 10 and 20 minutes. Service time is normal with a mean of 15 minutes and a standard deviation of 2 minutes.

    a. Simulate processing and waiting times for nine customers. Read three-digit numbers going down columns 9 and 10 of Table 19S–1 for arrivals (e.g., 156, 884, 576). Use column 8, Table 19S–2, for processing time.

    b. If management can reduce the range of arrival times to between 13 and 17 minutes, what would the impact be on customer waiting times? (Use the same service times and the same random numbers for arrival times from part *a.*) Round arrival times to two decimal places.

12. *a.* <u>**Cust.**</u> <u>**Wait**</u> <u>**Process**</u>

13. Probabilities have been determined for the movements of the ball in a pinball game. These are shown in the accompanying table, along with the points awarded if the ball strikes a given position. Simulate the paths of three balls, and compute the number of points awarded for each ball. Use column 1 of Table 19S–1 for the first ball, column 2 for the second ball, and column 3 for the third ball, reading down the columns.

b. <u>**Cust.**</u> <u>**Wait**</u>

Position	Points
A	400
B	300
C	200
D	100
E	50
F	20

Path	Probability	Path	Probability	Path	Probability
S to A	.30	B to A	.30	D to A	.10
B	.30	B	.20	B	.05
C	.25	C	.20	C	.25
D	.10	D	.15	D	.20
E	.04	E	.10	E	.25
F	.01	F	.05	F	.15
A to A	.25	C to A	.10	E to A	.05
B	.25	B	.15	B	.10
C	.25	C	.20	C	.15
D	.10	D	.15	D	.15
E	.10	E	.25	E	.20
F	.05	F	.15	F	.35

(*Hint:* Construct a cumulative probability distribution for each of the six cases. Each new random number indicates the next position to move to. Each ball must start at S.)

14. Repeat problem 13, using columns 1, 2, and 3 for the next three balls, reading up from the bottom.

15. An analyst found that the length of telephone conversations in an office could be described by an exponential distribution with a mean of four minutes. Reading two-digit random numbers from Table 19S–1, column 6, simulate the length of five calls and compute the simulated average time. Why is the simulated average different from the mean of four minutes?

16. The length of time between calls for service of a certain piece of equipment can be described by an exponential distribution with a mean of 40 minutes. Service time can be described by a normal distribution with a mean of eight minutes and a standard deviation of two minutes. Simulate the time until the first breakdown and the times between three breakdowns, as well as the four service times. For breakdowns, read two-digit numbers from Table 19S–1, column 7; for service times, read numbers from Table 19S–2, column 8.

17. The number of jobs per day that a repair shop gets can be described by a Poisson distribution with a mean of 3.0. Repair time per job can be described by an exponential distribution with a mean of six hours. Simulate the number of jobs received for a four-day period and the repair time for each job. What is the simulated total repair time per day? For number of jobs received, read three-digit numbers from Table 19S–1, row 1; for repair times, read two-digit numbers from row 2.

18. A service operation consists of three steps. The first step can be described by a uniform distribution that ranges between five and nine minutes. The second step can be described by a normal distribution with a mean of seven minutes and a standard deviation of one minute, and the third step can be described by an exponential distribution with a mean of five minutes. Simulate three cycles using two-digit numbers from Table 19S–1, row 4 for step 1; Table 19S–2, row 6 for step 2; and two-digit numbers from column 4 of Table 19S–1 for step 3. Determine the simulated time for each of the three cycles.

19. A project consists of five major activities, as illustrated in the accompanying diagram. Activity times are normally distributed with means and standard deviations as shown in the following table. Note that there are two paths through the project: 1-2-3-5 and 1-2-4-5. Project duration is defined as the largest sum of times along a path. Simulate 12 times for each activity. Use columns 1 and 2 of Table 19S–2 for activity 1-2, columns 3 and 4 for activity 2-3, columns 5 and 6 for activity 2-4, columns 7 and 8 for activity 3-5, and columns 9 and 10 for activity 4-5. Determine the project duration for each of the 12 sets, and prepare a frequency distribution of project duration. Use categories of 25 to less than 30, 30 to less than 35, 35 to less than 40, 40 to less than 45, and 45 or more. Determine the proportion of time that a simulated duration of less than 40 days occurred. How might this information be used?

Activity	Mean (days)	Standard Deviation (days)
1-2	10	2
2-3	12	2
2-4	15	3
3-5	14	2
4-5	8	1

CASE

Coquille Refinery Corporation

The Coquille Refinery Corporation is contemplating building a crude-oil storage and docking facility on the southern coast of France. They plan to import crude oil by ship from the Middle East and distribute this crude oil by pipeline to refineries in the area.

The construction of this facility represents a substantial capital investment. Furthermore, the cost of such a facility is principally determined by its crude-oil storage capacity. You have been asked to study the problem and recommend an appropriate storage capacity; bear in mind that too large a capacity represents an unnecessary expense, but too small a capacity will result in costly later additions to the facility.

A long-term contract has been made with the Middle East supplier to furnish an average daily supply of 300,000 barrels of crude oil. Because its fleet of ships consists of 200,000-barrel tankers, the supplier expects that the arrival of its tankers will follow the distribution below:

Tanker Arrivals per Day	Probability
0	0.1
1	0.5
2	0.2
3	0.2

A review of past production records of refineries in the area suggests the following distribution of crude-oil demand per day:

Barrels per Day	Probability
100,000	0.1
200,000	0.2
300,000	0.3
400,000	0.4

Questions

1. Consider the following issues before you simulate:

   a. What is the expected daily demand for crude oil? Why must this be so?

   b. What assumptions concerning the timing of crude-oil receipts and deliveries would require the greatest oil storage capacity?

   c. What assumption concerning receipts and deliveries would require the least oil storage capacity?

   d. Give a reason based on systems-analysis considerations why back orders should be filled from the next day's receipts rather than considered as lost sales.

2. Develop a Monte Carlo simulation model for Coquille that will generate information useful for resolving the storage capacity problem and simulate 10 days of capacity.

3. Assume a computer program was written to simulate 10,000 days of activity under the assumptions listed in question 1b. From the results of such a simulation the following distribution of oil in storage, after a day's receipts, is determined. (Note: Negative figures represent back orders.)

Oil in Storage, in Thousands	Probability
−300	0.01
−200	0.04
−100	0.06
0	0.07
⋮	⋮
1,000	0.09
1,100	0.08
1,200	0.07
1,300	0.05
1,400	0.03
1,500	0.02
	1.00

   a. What level of crude-oil safety stock should be carried to ensure 95 percent protection against stock-outs (1 stock-out in 20 days)?

   b. If Coquille decides to use the above safety stock, what should be the oil storage capacity to ensure 90 percent protection against overruns (i.e., sufficient capacity to completely accommodate receipts 9 days out of 10)?

4. Note two ways one might determine if the simulation run length of 10,000 days is adequate.

5. Make a list of cost factors that would influence the final selection of oil storage capacity.

Source: James A. Fitzsimmons and Robert S. Sullivan, *Service Operations Management* (New York: McGraw-Hill, 1982), pp. 78–80. Reprinted by permission.

Selected Bibliography and Further Reading

Evans, James R., and David L. Olson. *Introduction to Simulation and Risk Analysis*. Upper Saddle River, NJ: Prentice Hall, 1998.

Harrell, C., and K. Tumay. *Simulation Made Easy: A Manager's Guide*. Norcross, GA: Industrial Engineering and Management Press, 1995.

Hillier, Frederick S., Mark S. Hillier, and Gerald Lieberman. *Introduction to Management Science*. New York: Irwin/McGraw-Hill, 2000.

Law, Averill, and David Kelton. *Simulation Modeling and Analysis*. 3rd ed. New York: McGraw-Hill/Irwin, 2000.

Answers to Selected Problems

CHAPTER 2: COMPETITIVENESS, STRATEGY, AND PRODUCTIVITY

1. Last week: Labor productivity = 37.5 bookcases per worker.
   Week before: Labor productivity = 40 bookcases per worker.

2. A crew size of two had the highest productivity (250 yards installed).

3. Week 1: 5.62.
   Week 2: 5.45.
   Week 3: 5.20.
   Week 4: 5.01.

4. *a.* Before: Labor productivity = 16 carts per worker per hour.
      After: Labor productivity = 21 carts per worker per hour.
   b. Before: Multifactor productivity = .89 carts per dollar.
      After: Multifactor productivity = .93 carts per dollar.

5. 8.33%.

6. 4.3%.

CHAPTER 3: FORECASTING

1. *a.* blueberry = 33, cinnamon = 35, cupcakes = 47.
   b. Demand did not exceed supply.

2. *b.* (1) 20.86, (2) 19, (3) 19.26, (4) 20, (5) 20.4.

3. *a.* 88.16 percent.
   b. 88.54 percent.

4. *a.* 22.   *b.* 20.75.   *c.* 20.72.

5. *a.* Increasing by 15,000 bottles per year.
   b. 275 (i.e., 275,000 bottles).

6. $500 - 20t$.

7. *a.* $Y_t = 208.48 + 19.06t$.   *b.* 588.40   *c.* Week 32.

8. *a.* $Y_t = 195.47 + 7.00t$.   *b.* 307.22.
   $Y_{16} = 307.47$ $Y_{18} = 321.47$
   $Y_{17} = 314.14$ $Y_{19} = 328.47$

11. Q_1: 157.85; Q_2: 175; Q_3: 126.3; Q_4: 325; Q_1 = 322.85.

12. Fri. = 0.79, Sat. = 1.34, Sun. = 0.87.

15.

Day	Relative
1	.902
2	.836
3	.919
4	1.034
5	1.416
6	1.487
7	.427

17. *b.* Jan. 800
       Feb. 810
       Mar. 900
       Apr. 810

20. *b.* $147,000.

21. *b.* $17.90.

22. *b.* −0.985.

23. *b.* $Y = 66.33 + .584x$.   *c.* 90.27.

24. *a.* $r = +.96$.   *b.* $Y = -0.672 + 6.158x$.
    c. About 12 mowers.

27. *a.* $MAD_5 = 5$ *b.* $TS_5 = 1.40$
       $MAD_6 = 5.9$ $TS_6 = -0.17$
       $MAD_7 = 4.73$ $TS_7 = -0.63$
       $MAD_8 = 3.911$ $TS_8 = -0.26$
       $MAD_9 = 4.238$ $TS_9 = -1.42$
          etc.   etc.

28. *a.*

	MSE	MAD
Forecast 1	10.44	2.8
Forecast 2	42.44	3.6
Naive	156	10.7

29. *a.* Initial MAD = 4.727. The tracking signal for month 15 is 4.087, so at that point, the forecast would be suspect.
    b. $\sum$ errors = −1, $\sum$ errors^2 = 345. Control limits: 0 ± 12.38 (in limits). Plot reveals cycles in errors.

CHAPTER 4 SUPPLEMENT: RELIABILITY

1. *a.* .81.   *b.* .9801.   *c.* .9783.
2. .9033.
3. .9726.
4. .93.
5. *a.* .9315.   *b.* .9953.   *c.* .994.
6. *a.* .7876.   *b.* .90 component.
7. *a.* Plan 2 (.9934).
8. *a.* .984.   *b.* .991.
9. .996.
10. .995.
11. .006.
12. *a.* (1) .2725.   *b.* (1) .6671.
       (2) .2019.   (2) .3935.
       (3) .1353.   (3) .1813.
    c. (1) 21 months.   (3) 90 months.
       (2) 57 months.   (4) 138 months.
13. *a.* .6321.   *b.* Three months or 90 days.
14. *a.* .3012.   *b.* .1813.   *c.* .5175.
15. *a.* .2231.   *b.* .8647.
    c. .0878.   *d.* .0302.
16. *a.* .2266.   *b.* .4400.   *c.* .3830.
17. *a.* (1) .9772.   *b.* Approximately zero.
       (2) .5000.
       (3) .0013.
18. *a.* .93.   *b.* .98.
19. .96.

CHAPTER 5: CAPACITY PLANNING

1. *a.* 46,000 units.   *b.* (1) $3,000.
                          (2) $8,200.
    c. 126,000 units.   *d.* 25,556 units.
2. *a.* A: 8,000 units.   *b.* 10,000 units.
       B: 7,500 units.
    c. A: $20,000.
       B: $18,000.
3. *a.* 39,683 units.   *b.* $1.71 (rounded up).
4. *a.* A: $82.
       B: $92.
       C: $100.
    c. A: 0 to less than 178.
       B: Never.
       C: 178+.
5. 1/3 day, 2/3 evening.
6. Vendor best for $Q < 63,333$. For larger quantities, produce in-house at $4 per unit.
7. *a.* Vendor B best for 10,000 and 20,000.
8. 3 cells.
9. Buy 2 Bs.
11. *a.* one: $Q = 80$.   two: $Q = 152$.
12. One line.

CHAPTER 5 SUPPLEMENT: DECISION THEORY

1. *a.* Expand (80).
    b. Do nothing (50).
    c. Indifferent between do nothing and subcontract (55).

    d. Subcontract (10).
2. *a.* Expand (62).
    c. $9 (000).
3. Do nothing: $P(\text{high}) < .50.$
    Subcontract: $.50 < P(\text{high}) < .67.$
    Expand: $P(\text{high}) > .67.$
4. *a.*

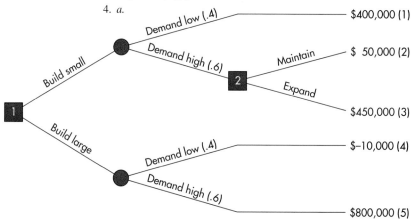

    b. $164,000.
    c. Small 0 to .46.
       Large .46 to 1.00.
5. Subcontract: $1.23.
    Expand: $1.57.
    Build: $1.35.
6. *a.* Relocate.
    b. Renew.
    c. Relocate.
    d. Relocate.
7. *a.* Renew.
    b. EVPI = $1,575,000.
    c. Yes.
9. *b.* Build large: $53.6 million.
       Build small: $42 million.
    c. $12.4.
    d. Build small for $P(\text{high}) < .721.$
       Build large for $P(\text{high}) > .721.$
10. Buy two ($113.5).
11. A: 22.
    B: 25.
13. *a.* New staff.
    b. Redesign.
    c. New staff.
    d. New staff or redesign.
16. *b.* Alternative C.
    c. $P(2) > .625.$
    d. $P(1) < .375.$
17. *b.* Alternative B.
    c. $P(2) < .444.$
    d. $P(1) > .556.$

CHAPTER 6: PROCESS SELECTION AND FACILITY LAYOUT

1. *a.* Minimum is 2.4 minutes, maximum is 18 minutes.
    b. 25 units to 187.5 units.   *c.* Eight.

d. 3.6 minutes.   *e.* (1) 50 units.
(2) 30 units.

2. *a.*

Station	Tasks	Time
1	a	1.4
2	b, e	1.3
3	d, c, f	1.8
4	g, h	1.5

3. *a.*

Station	Tasks	Time
1	f, a	8
2	d, g	13
3	b, c, e	10
4	h, i	14

4. *a.* (3) 11.54%.   (4) 323 units per day.
b. 2.3 minutes.   (3) 182.6 units per day.
(4) 91.3 units per day.

5. *b.* 2 minutes.   *c.* Three stations.

6. *c.* (1) 11.1%.   (2) 11.1%.   (3) 11.1%.

7. *b.* CT = .84 min. or 50.4 sec.
c. N = 3.83 (round to 4) stations.

10.
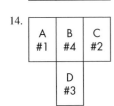

11.

1	5	4
3	8	7
6	2	

13.

3	1	8
9	7	4
5	2	6

14.   TC = $14,150.

A #1	B #4	C #2
	D #3	

16. A: 3; B: 5; C: 1; D: 4; E: 6; F: 2.

17. A: 1; B: 2; C: 5; D: 4; E: 9; F: 8; G: 6; H: 10; I: 7; J: 3.

CHAPTER 6 SUPPLEMENT: LINEAR PROGRAMMING

1. *a.* (1) $x_1 = 2$, $x_2 = 9$, $Z = 35$.
(2) No.
(3) No.

(4) No.
b. (1) $x_1 = 1.5$, $x_2 = 6.25$, $Z = 65.6$.
(2) No.
(3) Yes, S has surplus of 15.
(4) No.
c. (1) $A = 24$, $B = 20$, $Z = \$204$.
(2) Yes. Labor, 420 hr.
(3) No.
(4) No.

2. *a.* $S = 8$, $T = 20$, $Z = \$58.40$.
b. (1) $x_1 = 4.2$, $x_2 = 1.6$, $Z = 13.2$.
(2) Yes. $E = 4.6$.
(3) No.
(4) No.

3. $H = 132$ units, $W = 36$ units, Profit = $6,360.

4. Deluxe = 90 bags, Standard = 60 bags, Profit = $243.

5. $x = 327.27$, $y = 163.64$, $Z = \$1,636.36$.

6. 500 apple, 200 grape, Revenue = $990. Fifty cups of sugar will be unused.

7. *a.* $x_1 = 4$, $x_2 = 0$, $x_3 = 18$.
$s_1 = 3$, $s_2 = 0$, $s_3 = 0$.
$Z = 106$.
b. $x_1 = 15$, $x_2 = 10$, $x_3 = 0$.
$s_1 = 0$, $s_2 = 0$, $s_3 = 5$.
$Z = 210$.

9. $A = 0$, $B = 80$, $C = 50$.
$Z = 350$.
C_A (insignificance): $0 to $3.04.
C_B (optimality): $1.95 to $3.75.
C_C (optimality): $2.00 to $5.00.

11. *a.* board = 0, holder = 50.
b. Cutting = 16 minutes, gluing = 0 minutes, finishing = 210 minutes.

12. *a.* Ham = 37.14, deli = 18, cost = $165.42.
b. Ham = 20, deli = 84, profit = $376.

14. $Z = \$433$.

15. *a.* Machine and materials are binding.
b. No change.
c. No change.
d. Only s_2 would change. It would be 46.
e. None.
f. Yes; $844.

16. *a.* $1.50; range is 510 to 750.
b. $1.50/pound.
c. $0; range 375 to infinity.
d. None.
e. 150 pounds of pine bark.
f. Optimal quantities would not change; Z would increase by $75.
g. Yes, $1,155.
h. Yes, $1,110.

CHAPTER 7: DESIGN OF WORK SYSTEMS

1. 15.08 minutes.

2. *a.* 1.2 minutes.
b. 1.14 minutes.
c. 1.27 minutes.

3.

Element	OT	NT	ST
1	0.46	0.414	0.476
2	1.505	1.280	1.472
3	0.83	0.913	1.050
4	1.16	1.160	1.334

4.

Element	Average
1	4.1
2	1.5
3	3.3
4	2.7

7. 5.85 minutes.

8. 7.125 minutes.

10. 57 observations.

11. 37 cycles.

12. *a.* 12%.   *b.* 163 observations.

13. 377 observations.

CHAPTER 7 SUPPLEMENT: LEARNING CURVES

1. *a.* 178.8 hours.
   b. 1,121.4 hours.
   c. 2,914.8 hours.

2. *a.* 41.47 hours.
   b. 60.55 hours.
   c. 72.20 hours.

3. *a.* 56.928 days.
   b. 42.288 days.
   c. 37.512 days.

5. *a.* $P = 85$ percent.
   b. 26.21 minutes.

6. 87.9 minutes.

7. 201.26 hours.

8. *a.* 11.35 hours.
   b. 13.05 hours.
   c. 13.12 hours.

9. *a.* $80.31.
   b. 10 units.

10. B and C.

12. 30.82 hours.

13. No.

14. 18.76 hours.

15. Art: 20; Sherry: 4; Dave: 10.

16. 7 repetitions.

17. Beverly: 9; Max: 22; Antonio: 5.

CHAPTER 8: LOCATION PLANNING AND ANALYSIS

1. Kansas City: $256,000.

2. *a.* A: 16,854; B: 17,416; C: 17,753.
   b. C: $14,670.

3. *a.* 120 units.   *b.* A: 0 to 119; B: 121+.

4. *a.* B: 0 to 33; C: 34 to 400; A: 400+.

5. C($270,000).

6. Biloxi ($160,000).

7. *a.* (1) outside; (2) city.   *b.* 230 cars.

9. A.

10. *a.* B = C > A.
    b. B > C > A.

11. (5,4) is optimal.

12. (6,7).

13. (6,6).

14. (3,2.21).

CHAPTER 8 SUPPLEMENT: THE TRANSPORTATION MODEL

1. $X_{12} = 15$ $X_{13} = 75$
   $X_{21} = 105$
   $X_{31} = 45$ $X_{32} = 60$
   TC = $1,050

2.

	A	B	C	Dummy
1		500		
2	400			
N1		100	350	50

	A	B	C	Dummy
1		500		
2	400			
N2		100	350	50

3.

	A	B	C
1			210
2	140		
3	80	60	10
Tol.		160	

	A	B	C
1			210
2	60	80	
3		140	10
Cin.	160		

CHAPTER 10: QUALITY CONTROL

1. *a.* .0124.   *b.* 24.40 ounces and 24.60 ounces.

2. *a.* LCL: 0.996 liters.   *b.* Not in control.
   UCL: 1.004 liters.

3. *a.* Mean: LCL is 3.019, UCL is 3.181.
   Range: LCL is 0.1845, UCL is 0.7155.
   b. Yes.

4. Mean: LCL is 78.88 cm.
   UCL is 81.04 cm.
   Range: LCL is 0 cm.
   UCL is 3.95 cm.
   Process in control.

5. *a.*

1	2	3	4
.020	.010	.025	.045

   b. 2.5 percent.
   c. Mean = .025, standard deviation = .011.
   d. LCL = .0011, UCL = .0489.
   e. .0456.
   f. Yes.
   g. Mean = .02, standard deviation = .01.
   h. LCL = 0, UCL = .04.

6. LCL: 0.
   UCL: .0234.
   Revised limits based on 12 samples:
   LCL: 0.
   UCL: .0197.

7. Yes, UCL = 16.266, LCL = 0.

8. Yes, UCL = 5.17, LCL = 0.

9. No, UCL = .079, LCL = .001. No.

10. 35 pieces.

11. One in 30 is "out." Tolerances seem to be met. Approximately 97% will be acceptable.

12. *a.* LCL: 3.73.
    UCL: 3.97.
    Out of control.
    b. Random variations.

13. **NUMBER OF RUNS**

Test	Observed	Expected	Standard Deviation	z	Conclude
a. Med . . .	18	14	2.50	1.6	Okay
U/D . . .	17	17	2.07	0	Okay
b. Med . . .	8	14	2.50	−2.40	Nonrandom
U/D . . .	22	17	2.07	2.41	Nonrandom

14. *a.* Med: $z = -0.52$.
    U/D: $z = -1.47$.
    b. Med: $z = -1.11$.
    U/D: $z = -1.36$.

15. Med: $z = -2.34$.
    U/D: $z = -1.45$.

16. 440 pieces.

18. *a.* 566 units.
    b. 62 units.
    c. $1,160.

19. Med: $z = +0.9177$.
    U/D: $z = +0.5561$.

20. *b.* 4.5, .192.
    c. 4.5, .086.
    d. 4.242 to 4.758.
    f. None.

21. *a.* 1.11.   *b.* Yes.

22. Machines 004 and 005 are capable.

24. C_{pk}: $H = .94$, $k = 1.00$, $T = 1.07$.

26. Melissa.

CHAPTER 10 SUPPLEMENT: ACCEPTANCE SAMPLING

1. *a.* (1) Yes. (2) Yes.   *b.* .0067.

2. *b.* .0390.

3. *c.* .0024.

5. *a.* 0.16.
   b. 2.
   c. (1) Accept.
      (2) .0362.
      (3) .9638.
      (4) p(Type I) = .0362.
          p(Type II) = 0.

CHAPTER 11: TQM AND QUALITY TOOLS

2.

	Res.	Com.
Noisy	10	3
Failed	7	2
Odor	5	7
Warm	3	4

CHAPTER 12: SUPPLY CHAIN MANAGEMENT

1. Use 2-day freight.

2. Use 6-day.

3. Ship 2-day using A.

CHAPTER 13: INVENTORY MANAGEMENT

1.

Item	Category
4021	A
9402	C
4066	B
6500	C
9280	C
4050	C
6850	B
3010	C
4400	B

2. *a.*

Item	Category
K34	C
K35	A
K36	B
M10	C
M20	C
Z45	A
F14	B
F95	A
F99	C
D45	B
D48	C
D52	C
D57	B
N08	C
P05	B
P09	C

3. *a.* 36 bags.

   b. 18 bags.

   c. 135.

   d. $1,080.

   e. Increase by $127.48.

4. *a.* 204 packages.

   b. $611.74.

   c. Yes.

   d. No; TC = $612; only save $.26.

5. *a.* $105.

6. $364.

7. *a.* 1–6: 75 units; 7–12: 91 units.

   b. EOQ requirement.

   c. 1–6: 50 units; 7–12: 100 units.

8. *a.* $1.32.

   b. $24.30.

9. *a.* 4,812.

   b. 15.59 (approx. 16).

   c. .96.

10. *a.* 10,328 bags.

   b. 3,098 bags.

   c. 10.33 days.

   d. 7.75 (approx. 8).

   e. $774.50.

11. *a.* 1,414 units.

   b. 7.07 days.

   c. 120 units.

   d. No.

12. *a.* 37.5 batches.

   b. 1,000 units.

   c. 625 units.

   d. No.

13. *a.* 10,000 boxes.

   b. 1.8 orders.

14. *a.* 600 stones.

   b. 600 stones.

   c. 150 stones on hand.

15. Indifferent between 495 and 1,000 pulleys.

16. A, 500 units.

18. 6,600 feet.

19. *a.* 370 units.

   b. 70 units.

   c. Both smaller.

20. *a.* 91 pounds.

   b. ROP = 691 pounds.

21. *a.* 8.39 gallons.

   b. 34 gallons.

   c. .1423.

22. 70.14 gallons.

23. .1093.

24. ROP = 70.14.

25. *a.* 400 gallons.

   b. 45.02 gallons.

26. *a.* 72 boxes.

   b. .0023.

   c. .0228.

27. *a.* 749 pounds.   *b.* 4.078 pounds.

28. *a.* 134 rolls.

   b. 36 rolls.

   c. .055 per cycle $[\sigma_{dLT} = \sqrt{LT}\sigma_d]$.

   d. .9996.

29. ROP = 77 cases.

30. *a.* −0.40 gal.

   b. −1.98 gal.

31. KO33: 581.

   K144: 458.

   L700: 0.

32. *a.* P34: ROP = 131.1 units.

     P 35: Every 4 weeks.

   b. 306 units.

   c. 334 units.

34. 25 dozen.

35. *a.* Nine spares.   *b.* $C_s \leq \$10.47$.

36. 78.9 pounds.

37. $4.89 per quart.

38. Five cakes.

39. 421.5 pounds.

40. *a.* $0.53 to $1.76.

   c. $56.67 to $190.00.

41. 3 spares.

42. 2 cakes.

CHAPTER 14: AGGREGATE PLANNING

1. *b.* $6,350.

2. *a.* $4,670.

   b. $4,800.

3. *b.* $4,640.

4. $4,970.

7. *a.* $31,250.

   b. $31,520.

8. *a.* 500 cases.

   b. 500 cases.

   c. 750 cases.

10. B: $14,340.

   C: $14,370.

11. $13,475.

12. $13,885.

13. $12,930.

15. $124,960.

16. $126,650; additional cost: $230.

CHAPTER 15: MRP AND ERP

1. F = 2, G = 1, H = 1, J = 6, D = 10, L = 2, A = 4, C = 2.

2. *a.* E = 138.

   b. Week 5.

3. *a.* 360.

   b. Day 1 (now).

4. *a.*

Master Schedule	Week	Beg. Inv.	1	2	3	4	5	6
	Quantity							80

E　　　　LT = 2	Beg. Inv.	1	2	3	4	5	6
Gross requirements							80
Scheduled receipts							
Projected on hand							
Net requirements							80
Planned-order receipts							80
Planned-order releases					80		

B(2)　　　　LT = 1	Beg. Inv.	1	2	3	4	5	6
Gross requirements					160		
Scheduled receipts							
Projected on hand	60	60	60	60	60	20	20
Net requirements					100		
Planned-order receipts					120		
Planned-order releases				120			

J(4) and J(3)　　LT = 1	Beg. Inv.	1	2	3	4	5	6
Gross requirements			480		240		
Scheduled receipts				30	30	30	
Projected on hand	20	20	20	50	80	50	50
Net requirements			460		160		
Planned-order receipts			480		180		
Planned-order releases		480		180			

b. Master
Schedule

Week	Beg. Inv.	1	2	3	4	5	6
Quantity							70

E LT = 2	Beg. Inv.	1	2	3	4	5	6
Gross requirements							70
Scheduled receipts							
Projected on hand							
Net requirements							70
Planned-order receipts							70
Planned-order releases					70		

B(2) LT = 1	Beg. Inv.	1	2	3	4	5	6
Gross requirements					140		
Scheduled receipts							
Projected on hand	60	60	60	60	60	40	40
Net requirements					80		
Planned-order receipts					120		
Planned-order releases			120				

J(4) and J(3) LT = 1	Beg. Inv.	1	2	3	4	5	6
Gross requirements			480		210		
Scheduled receipts				30	30	30	
Projected on hand	20	20	20	50	80	80	80
Net requirements			460		130		
Planned-order receipts			480		180		
Planned-order releases		480		180			

There will be an additional 20 units of B and 30 units of J.

5. *c.*

Master Schedule	Weeks	Beg. Inv.	1	2	3	4	5	6	7
	Quantity							100	100

d.

P LT = 1 wk.	Beg. Inv.	1	2	3	4	5	6	7
Gross requirements							100	100
Scheduled receipts								
Projected on hand								
Net requirements							100	100
Planned-order receipts							100	100
Planned-order releases						100	100	

K LT = 2 wk.	Beg. Inv.	1	2	3	4	5	6	7
Gross requirements						100	100	
Scheduled receipts				10			30	
Projected on hand				10	10	10		
Net requirements						90	70	
Planned-order receipts						90	70	
Planned-order releases				90	70			

G (3) LT = 1 wk.	Beg. Inv.	1	2	3	4	5	6	7
Gross requirements				270	210			
Scheduled receipts								
Projected on hand	40	40	40	40				
Net requirements				230	210			
Planned-order receipts				253	231			
Planned-order releases			253	231				

H (4) LT = 1 wk.	Beg. Inv.	1	2	3	4	5	6	7
Gross requirements				360	280			
Scheduled receipts								
Projected on hand	200	200	200	200	40			
Net requirements				160	240			
Planned-order receipts				200	240			
Planned-order releases			200	240				

6. Master Schedule

Day	Beg. Inv.	1	2	3	4	5	6	7
Quantity					100	150		200

Table	Beg. Inv.	1	2	3	4	5	6	7
Gross requirements					100	150		200
Scheduled receipts								
Projected on hand								
Net requirements					100	150		200
Planned-order receipts					100		150	200
Planned-order releases				100	150		200	

Wood Sections (2)	Beg. Inv.	1	2	3	4	5	6	7
Gross requirements				200	300		400	
Scheduled receipts			100					
Projected on hand			100	100				
Net requirements				100	300		400	
Planned-order receipts				100	300		400	
Planned-order releases			400		400			

Braces (3)	Beg. Inv.	1	2	3	4	5	6	7
Gross requirements				300	450		600	
Scheduled receipts								
Projected on hand	60	60	60	60				
Net requirements				240	450		600	
Planned-order receipts				240	450			
Planned-order releases		240	450	600				

Legs (4)	Beg. Inv.	1	2	3	4	5	6	7
Gross requirements				400	600		800	
Scheduled receipts								
Projected on hand	120	120	120	120				
Net requirements				280	600		800	
Planned-order receipts				308	660		880	
Planned-order releases		968		880				

10. Order 160 units in week 2.

11. *a.* Master Schedule for E.

Week number	1	2	3	4	5	6	7	8
Quantity					120			

Item: E LT = 1 week								
Gross requirements					120			
Scheduled receipts								
Projected on hand								
Net requirements					120			
Planned-order receipts					120			
Planned-order releases				120				

Item: I (2) LT = 1 week	1	2	3	4	5	6	7	8
Gross requirements				240				
Scheduled receipts			40					
Projected on hand			40	40				
Net requirements				200				
Planned-order receipts				200				
Planned-order releases			200					

Item: N (4) LT = 2 weeks	1	2	3	4	5	6	7	8
Gross requirements			800					
Scheduled receipts								
Projected on hand	100	100	100					
Net requirements			700					
Planned-order receipts			700					
Planned-order releases	700							

Item: V LT = 2 weeks	1	2	3	4	5	6	7	8
Gross requirements			200					
Scheduled receipts			10					
Projected on hand								
Net requirements			190					
Planned-order receipts			190					
Planned-order releases	190							

13. *c.* Master Schedule for golf carts.

Week number		1	2	3	4	5	6	7	8	9
Quantity							100		100	100

Item: Golf cart LT = 1 week										
Gross requirements							100		100	100
Scheduled receipts										
Projected on hand										
Net requirements							100		100	100
Planned-order receipts							100		100	100
Planned-order releases						100		100	100	

Item: Bases LT = 1 week										
Gross requirements						100		100	100	
Scheduled receipts										
Projected on hand	20	20	20	20	50	100	50	100	50	
Net requirements						0		0	50	
Planned-order receipts				30	50	50	50	50	50	
Planned-order releases			30	50	50	50	50	50		

14. *a.* EPP = 78.57. Order 120 units in period 2 and 60 units in period 6.

15. EPP = 75.76.

CHAPTER 16: JUST-IN-TIME SYSTEMS

1. 3.
2. 3.
4. 3 cycles.
5. 4 cycles.

CHAPTER 16 SUPPLEMENT: MAINTENANCE

1. Expected recalibration cost = $925 a month.
   Use the service contract.
2. Expected repair cost = $456 a month.
   Option #1: $500.
   Option #2: $422.
3.

Equipment	Ratio	Interval (days)
A201	.115	17.60
B400	.054	25.17
C850	.099	34.88

CHAPTER 17: SCHEDULING

1. 1-A, 2-B, 3-C, TC = 15.
2. 1-B, 2-C, 3-A, TC = 21.
3. 1-A, 2-E, 3-D, 4-B, 5-C; or 1-A, 2-D, 3-E, 4-B, 5-C.
4. 1-B, 2-C, 4-A, TC = 18.
5. *a.* 1-A, 2-B, 3-C, 4-D, 5-E.
   b. 1-E, 2-B, 3-C, 4-D, 5-A.
6. *b.*

	FCFS	SPT	EDD	CR
Av. flow time	26.5	19.75	21	25.75
Av. job tardiness	11	6	6	8.20
Av. no. of jobs	2.86	2.14	2.27	2.78

7. FCFS: a-b-c-d-e.
   SPT: c-b-a-e-d.
   EDD: a-b-c-e-d.
   CR: a-b-c-e-d.

	FCFS	SPT	EDD	CR
Av. flow time	17.40	14.80	16.80	17.10
Av. job tardiness	5.20	5.40	4.60	4.90
Av. no. of jobs	2.72	2.31	2.63	2.63

9. B-A-G-E-F-D-C.
10. *a.* e-b-g-h-d-c-a-f.
    c. 2 hours.
11. *a.* B-A-C-E-F-D.
12. *a.* b-a-c-d-e.
    b. 37 minutes.
    c. 15 minutes.

13. G-A-E-D-B-C-F.

14. *a., b.* Grinding flow time is 93 hours. Total time is 37 hours.

    c. Grinding flow time is 107 hours. Total time is 35 hours.

15. *a.*

	FCFS	SPT	EDD	CR
Av. flow time	15.25	11.12	15.60	15.60
Av. job tardiness. . .	1.7	2.33	0.55	1.15
Av. no. of jobs	3.91	2.85	4.00	4.00

15. *c.* a-c-b-e-d-f

16. b-c-e-a-d.

19. A-B-C.

20. C-B-A.

21. B-C-D-A.

CHAPTER 18: PROJECT MANAGEMENT

1. *a.* 1-3-6-9-11-12: 31.

    b. 1-2-4-6-8-9: 32.

    c. 1-2-5-12-16: 44.

3. Concerned about critical path activities F, H, and J, but also about A, B, C and E.

5. *a.* Summary:

Activity	ES	EF	LF	LS	Slack
1- 2 . . .	0	4	11	7	7
2- 4 . . .	4	13	21	12	8
4- 7 . . .	13	18	26	21	8
7-10 . . .	18	20	28	26	8
10-12 . . .	21	24	31	28	7
2- 5 . . .	4	12	19	11	7
5- 8 . . .	12	19	26	19	7
8-10 . . .	19	21	28	26	7
1- 3 . . .	0	10	10	0	0
3- 6 . . .	10	16	16	10	0
6- 9 . . .	16	20	20	16	0
9-11 . . .	20	25	25	20	0
11-12 . . .	25	31	31	25	0

    b. Summary:

Activity	ES	EF	LF	LS	Slack
1-2	0	5	5	0	0
2-4	5	23	23	5	0
4-6	23	26	26	23	0
6-8	26	35	35	26	0
8-9	35	37	37	35	0
2-5	5	15	17	7	2
5-6	15	19	26	22	7
5-7	15	26	28	17	2
7-8	26	33	35	28	2
1-3	0	8	15	7	7
3-7	8	21	28	15	7

6. 30 weeks.

7. *b.* 24 days: .9686; 21 days: .2350.

8. *a.* .6881.

    b. .3984.

    c. .0204.

9. .3479.

10. *b.* .52.

11. *b.* .0262.

    c. .2085.

12.

Path	Mean	Standard Deviation
a-d-e-h	24.34	1.354
a-f-g	15.50	1.258
b-i-j-k	14.83	1.014
c-m-n-o	26.17	1.658

    27 weeks: .6742; 26 weeks: .4099.

14. Crash schedule (1 week each): C, C, F, F, E, P.

15. *a.* Crash four weeks:

        (1) 7-11, (2) 1-2, (3) 7-11 and 6-10, (4) 11-13 and 4-6.

CHAPTER 19: WAITING LINES

1. *a.* 2.25 customers.

    b. 75 percent.

    c. Two hours.

    d. .5625.

2. *a.* 0.67 customer.

    b. One minute.

    c. 1.33 customers.

3. *a.* 6 minutes.

    b. 0.25.

    c. 2.25 customers.

4. *a.* 40 percent.

    b. 0.1523.

    c. 0.19 hour.

    d. .2288.

5. *a.* Morning: 0.375 minute; .45.

        Afternoon: 0.677 minute; .54.

        Evening: 0.635 minute; .44.

    b. M: 4; A: 8; E: 5.

6. *a.* 4.444 trucks.

    b. 6.67 minutes.

    c. .7104.

    d. 6 minutes.

    e. The system would be overloaded.

    f. 13.186.

7. *a.* One dock.

    b. One dock.

8. *a.* 0.952 mechanic.

    b. 0.229.

    c. 0.056 hr.

    d. 0.60.

    e. Two.

9. *a.* 0.995 customer.

    b. 2.24 days.

    c. 31.1 percent.

    d. 0.875 customer.

10. *a.* .437

    b. 0.53 machine.

    c. 1.33 machines.

    d. 40.72 pieces.

    e. Three.

11. *a.* 28.56 pieces.

    b. Two.

12. *a.* 15.9 pieces.

    b. Three.

13. Three.
14. *a.* .90.
    b. $W_1 = .12$ hour.
        $W_2 = .3045$ hour.
        $W_3 = 2.13$ hours.
    c. $L_1 = .36$.
        $L_2 = .91$.
        $L_3 = 6.39$.
15. *a.* 30.
    b. $L_1 = .034$.
        $L_2 = .025$.
18. *a.* approx. 0.011.
    b. approx. 0.444.

CHAPTER 19 SUPPLEMENT: SIMULATION

1. 5.25 jobs.
2. 1: 80 percent, 2: 40 percent, 3: 40 percent.
5.

Patient	Time
1	19.44
2	20.24
3	17.92
4	19.38
5	18.96
6	16.48
7	20.66

7.

Day	Usage
1 . . .	43.932
2 . . .	48.036
3 . . .	34.908
4 . . .	32.758
5 . . .	42.186
6 . . .	30.438
7 . . .	33.298
8 . . .	41.678
9 . . .	33.526
10 . . .	30.904

8.

Period	Usage

1	2
2	1
3	3
4	1
5	1
6	4
7	5
8	3
9	1
10	2

10. *b.*

Day	Order Size
1	—
2	—
3	—
4	—
5	3
6	—
7	—
8	1
9	—
10	—
11	3
12	—

13. Ball 1: 1,520 points; ball 2: 1,120 points; ball 3: 1,170 points.
14. Ball 1: 2,120 points; ball 2: 720 points; ball 3: 770 points.

Tables

A. Areas under the normal curve, 0 to z,   887
B. Areas under the standardized normal curve
   1. From −∞ to −z,   888
   2. From −∞ to +z,   889
C. Cumulative Poisson probabilities,   890
D. Cumulative binomial probabilities,   892

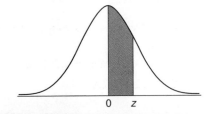

TABLE A	*Areas under the normal curve, 0 to z*								

z	.00	.01	.02	.03	.04	.05	.06	.07	.08	.09
0.0......	.0000	.0040	.0080	.0120	.0160	.0199	.0239	.0279	.0319	.0359
0.1......	.0398	.0438	.0478	.0517	.0557	.0596	.0636	.0675	.0714	.0753
0.2......	.0793	.0832	.0871	.0910	.0948	.0987	.1026	.1064	.1103	.1141
0.3......	.1179	.1217	.1255	.1293	.1331	.1368	.1406	.1443	.1480	.1517
0.4......	.1554	.1591	.1628	.1664	.1700	.1736	.1772	.1808	.1844	.1879
0.5......	.1915	.1950	.1985	.2019	.2054	.2088	.2123	.2157	.2190	.2224
0.6......	.2257	.2291	.2324	.2357	.2389	.2422	.2454	.2486	.2517	.2549
0.7......	.2580	.2611	.2642	.2673	.2703	.2734	.2764	.2794	.2823	.2852
0.8......	.2881	.2910	.2939	.2967	.2995	.3023	.3051	.3078	.3106	.3133
0.9......	.3159	.3186	.3212	.3238	.3264	.3289	.3315	.3340	.3365	.3389
1.0......	.3413	.3438	.3461	.3485	.3508	.3531	.3554	.3577	.3599	.3621
1.1......	.3643	.3665	.3686	.3708	.3729	.3749	.3770	.3790	.3810	.3830
1.2......	.3849	.3869	.3888	.3907	.3925	.3944	.3962	.3980	.3997	.4015
1.3......	.4032	.4049	.4066	.4082	.4099	.4115	.4131	.4147	.4162	.4177
1.4......	.4192	.4207	.4222	.4236	.4251	.4265	.4279	.4292	.4306	.4319
1.5......	.4332	.4345	.4357	.4370	.4382	.4394	.4406	.4418	.4429	.4441
1.6......	.4452	.4463	.4474	.4484	.4495	.4505	.4515	.4525	.4535	.4545
1.7......	.4554	.4564	.4573	.4582	.4591	.4599	.4608	.4616	.4625	.4633
1.8......	.4641	.4649	.4656	.4664	.4671	.4678	.4686	.4693	.4699	.4706
1.9......	.4713	.4719	.4726	.4732	.4738	.4744	.4750	.4756	.4761	.4767
2.0......	.4772	.4778	.4783	.4788	.4793	.4798	.4803	.4808	.4812	.4817
2.1......	.4821	.4826	.4830	.4834	.4838	.4842	.4846	.4850	.4854	.4857
2.2......	.4861	.4864	.4868	.4871	.4875	.4878	.4881	.4884	.4887	.4890
2.3......	.4893	.4896	.4898	.4901	.4904	.4906	.4909	.4911	.4913	.4916
2.4......	.4918	.4920	.4922	.4925	.4927	.4929	.4931	.4932	.4934	.4936
2.5......	.4938	.4940	.4941	.4943	.4945	.4946	.4948	.4949	.4951	.4952
2.6......	.4953	.4955	.4956	.4957	.4959	.4960	.4961	.4962	.4963	.4964
2.7......	.4965	.4966	.4967	.4968	.4969	.4970	.4971	.4972	.4973	.4974
2.8......	.4974	.4975	.4976	.4977	.4977	.4978	.4979	.4979	.4980	.4981
2.9......	.4981	.4982	.4982	.4983	.4984	.4984	.4985	.4985	.4986	.4986
3.0......	.4987	.4987	.4987	.4988	.4988	.4989	.4989	.4989	.4990	.4990

TABLE B

1. *Areas under the standardized normal curve, from $-\infty$ to $-z$*

.09	.08	.07	.06	.05	.04	.03	.02	.01	.00	z
.0002	.0003	.0003	.0003	.0003	.0003	.0003	.0003	.0003	.0003	−3.4
.0003	.0004	.0004	.0004	.0004	.0004	.0004	.0005	.0005	.0005	−3.3
.0005	.0005	.0005	.0006	.0006	.0006	.0006	.0006	.0007	.0007	−3.2
.0007	.0007	.0008	.0008	.0008	.0008	.0009	.0009	.0009	.0010	−3.1
.0010	.0010	.0011	.0011	.0011	.0012	.0012	.0013	.0013	.0013	−3.0
.0014	.0014	.0015	.0015	.0016	.0016	.0017	.0018	.0018	.0019	−2.9
.0019	.0020	.0021	.0021	.0022	.0023	.0023	.0024	.0025	.0026	−2.8
.0026	.0027	.0028	.0029	.0030	.0031	.0032	.0033	.0034	.0035	−2.7
.0036	.0037	.0038	.0039	.0040	.0041	.0043	.0044	.0045	.0047	−2.6
.0048	.0049	.0051	.0052	.0054	.0055	.0057	.0059	.0060	.0062	−2.5
.0064	.0066	.0068	.0069	.0071	.0073	.0075	.0078	.0080	.0082	−2.4
.0084	.0087	.0089	.0091	.0094	.0096	.0099	.0102	.0104	.0107	−2.3
.0110	.0113	.0116	.0119	.0122	.0125	.0129	.0132	.0136	.0139	−2.2
.0143	.0146	.0150	.0154	.0158	.0162	.0166	.0170	.0174	.0179	−2.1
.0183	.0188	.0192	.0197	.0202	.0207	.0212	.0217	.0222	.0228	−2.0
.0233	.0239	.0244	.0250	.0256	.0262	.0268	.0274	.0281	.0287	−1.9
.0294	.0301	.0307	.0314	.0322	.0329	.0336	.0344	.0351	.0359	−1.8
.0367	.0375	.0384	.0392	.0401	.0409	.0418	.0427	.0436	.0446	−1.7
.0455	.0465	.0475	.0485	.0495	.0505	.0516	.0526	.0537	.0548	−1.6
.0559	.0571	.0582	.0594	.0606	.0618	.0630	.0643	.0655	.0668	−1.5
.0681	.0694	.0708	.0721	.0735	.0749	.0764	.0778	.0793	.0808	−1.4
.0823	.0838	.0853	.0869	.0885	.0901	.0918	.0934	.0951	.0968	−1.3
.0985	.1003	.1020	.1038	.1056	.1075	.1093	.1112	.1131	.1151	−1.2
.1170	.1190	.1210	.1230	.1251	.1271	.1292	.1314	.1335	.1357	−1.1
.1379	.1401	.1423	.1446	.1469	.1492	.1515	.1539	.1562	.1587	−1.0
.1611	.1635	.1660	.1685	.1711	.1736	.1762	.1788	.1814	.1841	−0.9
.1867	.1894	.1922	.1949	.1977	.2005	.2033	.2061	.2090	.2119	−0.8
.2148	.2177	.2206	.2236	.2266	.2296	.2327	.2358	.2389	.2420	−0.7
.2451	.2483	.2514	.2546	.2578	.2611	.2643	.2676	.2709	.2743	−0.6
.2776	.2810	.2843	.2877	.2912	.2946	.2981	.3015	.3050	.3085	−0.5
.3121	.3156	.3192	.3228	.3264	.3300	.3336	.3372	.3409	.3446	−0.4
.3483	.3520	.3557	.3594	.3632	.3669	.3707	.3745	.3783	.3821	−0.3
.3859	.3897	.3936	.3974	.4013	.4052	.4090	.4129	.4168	.4207	−0.2
.4247	.4286	.4325	.4364	.4404	.4443	.4483	.4522	.4562	.4602	−0.1
.4641	.4681	.4721	.4761	.4801	.4840	.4880	.4920	.4960	.5000	−0.0

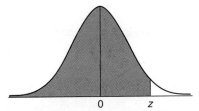

TABLE B
(concluded)
2. Areas under the
standardized normal
curve, from $-\infty$ to
$+z$

z	.00	.01	.02	.03	.04	.05	.06	.07	.08	.09
.0	.5000	.5040	.5080	.5120	.5160	.5199	.5239	.5279	.5319	.5359
.1	.5398	.5438	.5478	.5517	.5557	.5596	.5636	.5675	.5714	.5753
.2	.5793	.5832	.5871	.5910	.5948	.5987	.6026	.6064	.6103	.6141
.3	.6179	.6217	.6255	.6293	.6331	.6368	.6406	.6443	.6480	.6517
.4	.6554	.6591	.6628	.6664	.6700	.6736	.6772	.6808	.6844	.6879
.5	.6915	.6950	.6985	.7019	.7054	.7088	.7123	.7157	.7190	.7224
.6	.7257	.7291	.7324	.7357	.7389	.7422	.7454	.7486	.7517	.7549
.7	.7580	.7611	.7642	.7673	.7703	.7734	.7764	.7794	.7823	.7852
.8	.7881	.7910	.7939	.7967	.7995	.8023	.8051	.8078	.8106	.8133
.9	.8159	.8186	.8212	.8238	.8264	.8289	.8315	.8340	.8365	.8389
1.0	.8413	.8438	.8461	.8485	.8508	.8531	.8554	.8577	.8599	.8621
1.1	.8643	.8665	.8686	.8708	.8729	.8749	.8770	.8790	.8810	.8830
1.2	.8849	.8869	.8888	.8907	.8925	.8944	.8962	.8980	.8997	.9015
1.3	.9032	.9049	.9066	.9082	.9099	.9115	.9131	.9147	.9162	.9177
1.4	.9192	.9207	.9222	.9236	.9251	.9265	.9279	.9292	.9306	.9319
1.5	.9332	.9345	.9357	.9370	.9382	.9394	.9406	.9418	.9429	.9441
1.6	.9452	.9463	.9474	.9484	.9495	.9505	.9515	.9525	.9535	.9545
1.7	.9554	.9564	.9573	.9582	.9591	.9599	.9608	.9616	.9625	.9633
1.8	.9641	.9649	.9656	.9664	.9671	.9678	.9686	.9693	.9699	.9706
1.9	.9713	.9719	.9726	.9732	.9738	.9744	.9750	.9756	.9761	.9767
2.0	.9772	.9778	.9783	.9788	.9793	.9798	.9803	.9808	.9812	.9817
2.1	.9821	.9826	.9830	.9834	.9838	.9842	.9846	.9850	.9854	.9857
2.2	.9861	.9864	.9868	.9871	.9875	.9878	.9881	.9884	.9887	.9890
2.3	.9893	.9896	.9898	.9901	.9904	.9906	.9909	.9911	.9913	.9916
2.4	.9918	.9920	.9922	.9925	.9927	.9929	.9931	.9932	.9934	.9936
2.5	.9938	.9940	.9941	.9943	.9945	.9946	.9948	.9949	.9951	.9952
2.6	.9953	.9955	.9956	.9957	.9959	.9960	.9961	.9962	.9963	.9964
2.7	.9965	.9966	.9967	.9968	.9969	.9970	.9971	.9972	.9973	.9974
2.8	.9974	.9975	.9976	.9977	.9977	.9978	.9979	.9979	.9980	.9981
2.9	.9981	.9982	.9982	.9983	.9984	.9984	.9985	.9985	.9986	.9986
3.0	.9987	.9987	.9987	.9988	.9988	.9989	.9989	.9989	.9990	.9990
3.1	.9990	.9991	.9991	.9991	.9991	.9992	.9992	.9992	.9993	.9993
3.2	.9993	.9993	.9994	.9994	.9994	.9994	.9994	.9995	.9995	.9995
3.3	.9995	.9995	.9995	.9996	.9996	.9996	.9996	.9996	.9996	.9997
3.4	.9997	.9997	.9997	.9997	.9997	.9997	.9997	.9997	.9997	.9998

TABLE C

TABLE C

*Cumulative Poisson
probabilities*

$$P(x \le c) = \sum_{x=0}^{x=c} \frac{\mu^x \cdot e^{-\mu}}{x!}$$

$\mu \backslash x$	0	1	2	3	4	5	6	7	8	9
0.05	.951	.999	1.000							
0.10	.905	.995	1.000							
0.15	.861	.990	.999	1.000						
0.20	.819	.982	.999	1.000						
0.25	.779	.974	.998	1.000						
0.30	.741	.963	.996	1.000						
0.35	.705	.951	.994	1.000						
0.40	.670	.938	.992	.999	1.000					
0.45	.638	.925	.989	.999	1.000					
0.50	.607	.910	.986	.998	1.000					
0.55	.577	.894	.982	.998	1.000					
0.60	.549	.878	.977	.997	1.000					
0.65	.522	.861	.972	.996	.999	1.000				
0.70	.497	.844	.966	.994	.999	1.000				
0.75	.472	.827	.960	.993	.999	1.000				
0.80	.449	.809	.953	.991	.999	1.000				
0.85	.427	.791	.945	.989	.998	1.000				
0.90	.407	.772	.937	.987	.998	1.000				
0.95	.387	.754	.929	.984	.997	1.000				
1.0	.368	.736	.920	.981	.996	.999	1.000			
1.1	.333	.699	.900	.974	.995	.999	1.000			
1.2	.301	.663	.880	.966	.992	.998	1.000			
1.3	.273	.627	.857	.957	.989	.998	1.000			
1.4	.247	.592	.833	.946	.986	.997	.999	1.000		
1.5	.223	.558	.809	.934	.981	.996	.999	1.000		
1.6	.202	.525	.783	.921	.976	.994	.999	1.000		
1.7	.183	.493	.757	.907	.970	.992	.998	1.000		
1.8	.165	.463	.731	.891	.964	.990	.997	.999	1.000	
1.9	.150	.434	.704	.875	.956	.987	.997	.999	1.000	
2.0	.135	.406	.677	.857	.947	.983	.995	.999	1.000	
2.2	.111	.355	.623	.819	.928	.975	.993	.998	1.000	
2.4	.091	.308	.570	.779	.904	.964	.988	.997	.999	1.000
2.6	.074	.267	.518	.736	.877	.951	.983	.995	.999	1.000
2.8	.061	.231	.470	.692	.848	.935	.976	.992	.998	.999

TABLE C (concluded)

μ\x	0	1	2	3	4	5	6	7	8	9	10	11	12	13	14	15	16	17	18	19	20
3.0	.050	.199	.423	.647	.815	.916	.966	.988	.996	.999	1.000										
3.2	.041	.171	.380	.603	.781	.895	.955	.983	.994	.998	1.000										
3.4	.033	.147	.340	.558	.744	.871	.942	.977	.992	.997	.999	1.000									
3.6	.027	.126	.303	.515	.706	.844	.927	.969	.988	.996	.999	1.000									
3.8	.022	.107	.269	.474	.668	.816	.909	.960	.984	.994	.998	.999	1.000								
4.0	.018	.092	.238	.433	.629	.785	.889	.949	.979	.992	.997	.999	1.000								
4.2	.015	.078	.210	.395	.590	.753	.868	.936	.972	.989	.996	.999	1.000								
4.4	.012	.066	.185	.359	.551	.720	.844	.921	.964	.985	.994	.998	.999	1.000							
4.6	.010	.056	.163	.326	.513	.686	.818	.905	.955	.980	.992	.997	.999	1.000							
4.8	.008	.048	.143	.294	.476	.651	.791	.887	.944	.975	.990	.996	.999	1.000							
5.0	.007	.040	.125	.265	.441	.616	.762	.867	.932	.968	.986	.995	.998	.999	1.000						
5.2	.006	.034	.109	.238	.406	.581	.732	.845	.918	.960	.982	.993	.997	.999	1.000						
5.4	.005	.029	.095	.213	.373	.546	.702	.822	.903	.951	.978	.990	.996	.999	1.000						
5.6	.004	.024	.082	.191	.342	.512	.670	.797	.886	.941	.972	.988	.995	.998	.999	1.000					
5.8	.003	.021	.072	.170	.313	.478	.638	.771	.867	.929	.965	.984	.993	.997	.999	1.000					
6.0	.002	.017	.062	.151	.285	.446	.606	.744	.847	.916	.957	.980	.991	.996	.999	.999	1.000				
6.2	.002	.015	.054	.134	.259	.414	.574	.716	.826	.902	.949	.975	.989	.995	.998	.999	1.000				
6.4	.002	.012	.046	.119	.235	.384	.542	.687	.803	.886	.939	.969	.986	.994	.997	.999	1.000				
6.6	.001	.010	.040	.105	.213	.355	.511	.658	.780	.869	.927	.963	.982	.992	.997	.999	.999	1.000			
6.8	.001	.009	.034	.093	.192	.327	.480	.628	.755	.850	.915	.955	.978	.990	.995	.998	.999	1.000			
7.0	.001	.007	.030	.082	.173	.301	.450	.599	.729	.830	.901	.947	.973	.987	.994	.998	.999	1.000			
7.2	.001	.006	.025	.072	.156	.276	.420	.569	.703	.810	.887	.937	.967	.984	.993	.997	.999	.999	1.000		
7.4	.001	.005	.022	.063	.140	.253	.392	.539	.676	.788	.871	.926	.961	.980	.991	.996	.998	.999	1.000		
7.6	.001	.004	.019	.055	.125	.231	.365	.510	.648	.765	.854	.915	.954	.976	.989	.995	.998	.999	1.000		
7.8	.000	.004	.016	.048	.112	.210	.338	.481	.620	.741	.835	.902	.945	.971	.986	.993	.997	.999	1.000		
8.0	.000	.003	.014	.042	.100	.191	.313	.453	.593	.717	.816	.888	.936	.966	.983	.992	.996	.998	.999	1.000	
8.2	.000	.003	.012	.037	.089	.174	.290	.425	.566	.692	.796	.873	.926	.960	.979	.990	.995	.998	.999	1.000	
8.4	.000	.002	.010	.032	.079	.157	.267	.400	.537	.666	.774	.857	.915	.952	.975	.987	.994	.997	.999	1.000	
8.6	.000	.002	.009	.030	.074	.150	.256	.386	.523	.653	.763	.849	.909	.949	.973	.986	.993	.997	.999	.999	1.000
8.8	.000	.002	.007	.024	.062	.128	.226	.348	.482	.614	.729	.822	.889	.935	.964	.981	.990	.995	.998	.999	1.000
9.0	.000	.001	.006	.021	.055	.116	.207	.324	.456	.587	.706	.803	.876	.926	.959	.978	.989	.995	.998	.999	1.000
9.5	.000	.001	.004	.015	.040	.089	.165	.269	.392	.522	.645	.752	.836	.898	.940	.967	.982	.991	.996	.998	.999

TABLE D — Cumulative binomial probabilities

$$P(x \le c) = \sum_{x=0}^{c} \binom{n}{x} p^x (1-p)^{n-x}$$

n	x	.05	.10	.15	.20	.25	.30	.35	.40	.45	.50	.55	.60	.65	.70	.75	.80	.85	.90
1	0	.9500	.9000	.8500	.8000	.7500	.7000	.6500	.6000	.5500	.5000	.4500	.4000	.3500	.3000	.2500	.2000	.1500	.1000
	1	1.0000	1.0000	1.0000	1.0000	1.0000	1.0000	1.0000	1.0000	1.0000	1.0000	1.0000	1.0000	1.0000	1.0000	1.0000	1.0000	1.0000	1.0000
2	0	.9025	.8100	.7225	.6400	.5625	.4900	.4225	.3600	.3025	.2500	.2025	.1600	.1225	.0900	.0625	.0400	.0225	.0100
	1	.9975	.9900	.9775	.9600	.9375	.9100	.8775	.8400	.7975	.7500	.6975	.6400	.5775	.5100	.4375	.3600	.2775	.1900
	2	1.0000	1.0000	1.0000	1.0000	1.0000	1.0000	1.0000	1.0000	1.0000	1.0000	1.0000	1.0000	1.0000	1.0000	1.0000	1.0000	1.0000	1.0000
3	0	.8574	.7290	.6141	.5120	.4219	.3430	.2746	.2160	.1664	.1250	.0911	.0640	.0429	.0270	.0156	.0080	.0034	.0010
	1	.9928	.9720	.9393	.8960	.8438	.7840	.7183	.6480	.5748	.5000	.4253	.3520	.2818	.2160	.1563	.1040	.0608	.0280
	2	.9999	.9990	.9966	.9920	.9844	.9730	.9571	.9360	.9089	.8750	.8336	.7840	.7254	.6570	.5781	.4880	.3859	.2710
	3	1.0000	1.0000	1.0000	1.0000	1.0000	1.0000	1.0000	1.0000	1.0000	1.0000	1.0000	1.0000	1.0000	1.0000	1.0000	1.0000	1.0000	1.0000
4	0	.8145	.6561	.5220	.4096	.3164	.2401	.1785	.1296	.0915	.0625	.0410	.0256	.0150	.0081	.0039	.0016	.0005	.0001
	1	.9860	.9477	.8905	.8192	.7383	.6517	.5630	.4752	.3910	.3125	.2415	.1792	.1265	.0837	.0508	.0272	.0120	.0037
	2	.9995	.9963	.9880	.9728	.9492	.9163	.8735	.8208	.7585	.6875	.6090	.5248	.4370	.3483	.2617	.1808	.1095	.0523
	3	1.0000	.9999	.9995	.9984	.9961	.9919	.9850	.9744	.9590	.9375	.9085	.8704	.8215	.7599	.6836	.5904	.4780	.3439
	4	1.0000	1.0000	1.0000	1.0000	1.0000	1.0000	1.0000	1.0000	1.0000	1.0000	1.0000	1.0000	1.0000	1.0000	1.0000	1.0000	1.0000	1.0000
5	0	.7738	.5905	.4437	.3277	.2373	.1681	.1160	.0778	.0503	.0313	.0185	.0102	.0053	.0024	.0010	.0003	.0001	.0000
	1	.9974	.9185	.8352	.7373	.6328	.5282	.4284	.3370	.2562	.1875	.1312	.0870	.0540	.0308	.0156	.0067	.0022	.0005
	2	.9988	.9914	.9734	.9421	.8965	.8369	.7648	.6826	.5931	.5000	.4069	.3174	.2352	.1631	.1035	.0579	.0266	.0086
	3	1.0000	.9995	.9978	.9933	.9844	.9692	.9460	.9130	.8688	.8125	.7438	.6630	.5716	.4718	.3672	.2627	.1648	.0815
	4	1.0000	1.0000	.9999	.9997	.9990	.9976	.9947	.9898	.9815	.9688	.9497	.9222	.8840	.8319	.7627	.6723	.5563	.4095
	5	1.0000	1.0000	1.0000	1.0000	1.0000	1.0000	1.0000	1.0000	1.0000	1.0000	1.0000	1.0000	1.0000	1.0000	1.0000	1.0000	1.0000	1.0000
6	0	.7351	.5314	.3771	.2621	.1780	.1176	.0754	.0467	.0277	.0156	.0083	.0041	.0018	.0007	.0002	.0001	.0000	.0000
	1	.9672	.8857	.7765	.6554	.5339	.4202	.3191	.2333	.1636	.1094	.0692	.0410	.0223	.0109	.0046	.0016	.0004	.0001
	2	.9978	.9842	.9527	.9011	.8306	.7443	.6471	.5443	.4415	.3438	.2553	.1792	.1174	.0705	.0376	.0170	.0059	.0013
	3	.9999	.9987	.9941	.9830	.9624	.9295	.8826	.8208	.7447	.6563	.5585	.4557	.3529	.2557	.1694	.0989	.0473	.0159
	4	1.0000	.9999	.9996	.9984	.9954	.9891	.9777	.9590	.9308	.8906	.8364	.7667	.6809	.5798	.4661	.3446	.2235	.1143
	5	1.0000	1.0000	1.0000	.9999	.9998	.9993	.9982	.9959	.9917	.9844	.9723	.9533	.9246	.8824	.8220	.7379	.6229	.4686
	6	1.0000	1.0000	1.0000	1.0000	1.0000	1.0000	1.0000	1.0000	1.0000	1.0000	1.0000	1.0000	1.0000	1.0000	1.0000	1.0000	1.0000	1.0000

n	x	.05	.10	.15	.20	.25	.30	.35	.40	.45	P .50	.55	.60	.65	.70	.75	.80	.85	.90
7	0	.6983	.4783	.3206	.2097	.1335	.0824	.0490	.0280	.0152	.0078	.0037	.0016	.0006	.0002	.0001	.0000	.0000	.0000
	1	.9556	.8503	.7166	.5767	.4449	.3294	.2338	.1586	.1024	.0625	.0357	.0188	.0090	.0038	.0013	.0004	.0001	.0000
	2	.9962	.9743	.9262	.8520	.7564	.6471	.5323	.4199	.3164	.2266	.1529	.0963	.0556	.0288	.0129	.0047	.0012	.0002
	3	.9998	.9973	.9879	.9667	.9294	.8740	.8002	.7102	.6083	.5000	.3917	.2898	.1998	.1260	.0706	.0333	.0121	.0027
	4	1.0000	.9998	.9988	.9953	.9871	.9712	.9444	.9037	.8471	.7734	.6836	.5801	.4677	.3529	.2436	.1480	.0738	.0257
	5	1.0000	1.0000	.9999	.9996	.9987	.9962	.9910	.9812	.9643	.9375	.8976	.8414	.7662	.6706	.5551	.4233	.2834	.1497
	6	1.0000	1.0000	1.0000	1.0000	.9999	.9998	.9994	.9984	.9963	.9922	.9848	.9720	.9510	.9176	.8665	.7903	.6794	.5217
	7	1.0000	1.0000	1.0000	1.0000	1.0000	1.0000	1.0000	1.0000	1.0000	1.0000	1.0000	1.0000	1.0000	1.0000	1.0000	1.0000	1.0000	1.0000
8	0	.6634	.4305	.2725	.1678	.1001	.0576	.0319	.0168	.0084	.0039	.0017	.0007	.0002	.0001	.0000	.0000	.0000	.0000
	1	.9428	.8131	.6572	.5033	.3671	.2553	.1691	.1064	.0632	.0352	.0181	.0085	.0036	.0013	.0004	.0001	.0000	.0000
	2	.9942	.9619	.8948	.7969	.6785	.5518	.4278	.3154	.2201	.1445	.0885	.0498	.0253	.0113	.0042	.0012	.0002	.0000
	3	.9996	.9950	.9786	.9437	.8862	.8059	.7064	.5941	.4770	.3633	.2604	.1737	.1061	.0580	.0273	.0104	.0029	.0004
	4	1.0000	.9996	.9971	.9896	.9727	.9420	.8939	.8263	.7396	.6367	.5230	.4059	.2936	.1941	.1138	.0563	.0214	.0050
	5	1.0000	1.0000	.9998	.9988	.9958	.9887	.9747	.9502	.9115	.8555	.7799	.6846	.5722	.4482	.3215	.2031	.1052	.0381
	6	1.0000	1.0000	1.0000	.9999	.9996	.9987	.9964	.9915	.9819	.9648	.9368	.8936	.8309	.7447	.6329	.4967	.3428	.1869
	7	1.0000	1.0000	1.0000	1.0000	1.0000	.9999	.9998	.9993	.9983	.9961	.9916	.9832	.9681	.9424	.8999	.8322	.7275	.5695
	8	1.0000	1.0000	1.0000	1.0000	1.0000	1.0000	1.0000	1.0000	1.0000	1.0000	1.0000	1.0000	1.0000	1.0000	1.0000	1.0000	1.0000	1.0000
9	0	.6302	.3874	.2316	.1342	.0751	.0404	.0207	.0101	.0046	.0020	.0008	.0003	.0001	.0000	.0000	.0000	.0000	.0000
	1	.9288	.7748	.5995	.4362	.3003	.1960	.1211	.0705	.0385	.0195	.0091	.0038	.0014	.0004	.0001	.0000	.0000	.0000
	2	.9916	.9470	.8591	.7382	.6007	.4628	.3373	.2318	.1495	.0898	.0498	.0250	.0112	.0043	.0013	.0003	.0000	.0000
	3	.9994	.9917	.9661	.9144	.8343	.7297	.6089	.4826	.3614	.2539	.1658	.0994	.0536	.0253	.0100	.0031	.0006	.0001
	4	1.0000	.9991	.9944	.9804	.9511	.9012	.8283	.7334	.6214	.5000	.3786	.2666	.1717	.0988	.0489	.0196	.0056	.0009
	5	1.0000	.9999	.9994	.9969	.9900	.9747	.9496	.9006	.8342	.7461	.6386	.5174	.3911	.2703	.1657	.0856	.0339	.0083
	6	1.0000	1.0000	1.0000	.9997	.9987	.9957	.9888	.9750	.9502	.9102	.8505	.7682	.6627	.5372	.3993	.2618	.1409	.0530
	7	1.0000	1.0000	1.0000	1.0000	.9999	.9996	.9986	.9962	.9909	.9805	.9615	.9295	.8789	.8040	.6997	.5638	.4005	.2252
	8	1.0000	1.0000	1.0000	1.0000	1.0000	1.0000	.9999	.9997	.9992	.9980	.9954	.9899	.9793	.9596	.9249	.8658	.7684	.6126
	9	1.0000	1.0000	1.0000	1.0000	1.0000	1.0000	1.0000	1.0000	1.0000	1.0000	1.0000	1.0000	1.0000	1.0000	1.0000	1.0000	1.0000	1.0000
10	0	.5987	.3487	.1969	.1074	.0563	.0282	.0135	.0060	.0025	.0010	.0003	.0001	.0000	.0000	.0000	.0000	.0000	.0000
	1	.9139	.7361	.5443	.3758	.2440	.1493	.0860	.0464	.0233	.0107	.0045	.0017	.0005	.0001	.0000	.0000	.0000	.0000
	2	.9885	.9298	.8202	.6778	.5256	.3828	.2616	.1673	.0996	.0547	.0274	.0123	.0048	.0016	.0004	.0001	.0000	.0000
	3	.9990	.9872	.9500	.8791	.7759	.6496	.5138	.3823	.2660	.1719	.1020	.0548	.0260	.0106	.0035	.0009	.0001	.0000
	4	.9999	.9984	.9901	.9672	.9219	.8497	.7515	.6331	.5044	.3770	.2616	.1662	.0949	.0473	.0197	.0064	.0014	.0001
	5	1.0000	.9999	.9986	.9936	.9803	.9527	.9051	.8338	.7384	.6230	.4956	.3669	.2485	.1503	.0781	.0328	.0099	.0016
	6	1.0000	1.0000	.9999	.9991	.9965	.9894	.9740	.9452	.8980	.8281	.7340	.6177	.4862	.3504	.2241	.1209	.0500	.0128
	7	1.0000	1.0000	1.0000	.9999	.9996	.9984	.9952	.9877	.9726	.9453	.9004	.8327	.7384	.6172	.4744	.3222	.1798	.0702
	8	1.0000	1.0000	1.0000	1.0000	1.0000	.9999	.9995	.9983	.9955	.9893	.9767	.9536	.9140	.8507	.7560	.6242	.4557	.2639
	9	1.0000	1.0000	1.0000	1.0000	1.0000	1.0000	1.0000	.9999	.9997	.9990	.9975	.9940	.9865	.9718	.9437	.8926	.8031	.6513
	10	1.0000	1.0000	1.0000	1.0000	1.0000	1.0000	1.0000	1.0000	1.0000	1.0000	1.0000	1.0000	1.0000	1.0000	1.0000	1.0000	1.0000	1.0000

TABLE D (concluded)

n	x	.05	.10	.15	.20	.25	.30	.35	.40	.45	.50	.55	.60	.65	.70	.75	.80	.85	.90
15	0	.4633	.2059	.0874	.0352	.0134	.0047	.0016	.0005	.0001	.0000	.0000	.0000	.0000	.0000	.0000	.0000	.0000	.0000
	1	.8290	.5490	.3186	.1671	.0802	.0353	.0142	.0052	.0017	.0005	.0001	.0000	.0000	.0000	.0000	.0000	.0000	.0000
	2	.9638	.8159	.6042	.3980	.2361	.1268	.0617	.0271	.0107	.0037	.0011	.0003	.0001	.0000	.0000	.0000	.0000	.0000
	3	.9945	.9444	.8227	.6482	.4613	.2969	.1727	.0905	.0424	.0176	.0063	.0019	.0005	.0001	.0000	.0000	.0000	.0000
	4	.9994	.9873	.9383	.8358	.6865	.5155	.3519	.2173	.1204	.0592	.0255	.0093	.0028	.0007	.0001	.0000	.0000	.0000
	5	.9999	.9978	.9832	.9389	.8516	.7216	.5643	.4032	.2608	.1509	.0769	.0338	.0124	.0037	.0008	.0001	.0000	.0000
	6	1.0000	.9997	.9964	.9819	.9434	.8689	.7548	.6098	.4522	.3036	.1818	.0950	.0422	.0152	.0042	.0008	.0001	.0000
	7	1.0000	1.0000	.9994	.9958	.9827	.9500	.8868	.7869	.6535	.5000	.3465	.2131	.1132	.0500	.0173	.0042	.0006	.0000
	8	1.0000	1.0000	.9999	.9992	.9958	.9848	.9578	.9050	.8182	.6964	.5478	.3902	.2452	.1311	.0566	.0181	.0036	.0003
	9	1.0000	1.0000	1.0000	.9999	.9992	.9963	.9876	.9662	.9231	.8491	.7392	.5968	.4357	.2784	.1484	.0611	.0168	.0022
	10	1.0000	1.0000	1.0000	1.0000	.9999	.9993	.9972	.9907	.9745	.9408	.8796	.7827	.6481	.4845	.3135	.1642	.0617	.0127
	11	1.0000	1.0000	1.0000	1.0000	1.0000	.9999	.9995	.9981	.9937	.9824	.9576	.9095	.8273	.7031	.5387	.3518	.1773	.0556
	12	1.0000	1.0000	1.0000	1.0000	1.0000	1.0000	.9999	.9997	.9989	.9963	.9893	.9729	.9383	.8732	.7639	.6020	.3958	.1841
	13	1.0000	1.0000	1.0000	1.0000	1.0000	1.0000	1.0000	1.0000	.9999	.9995	.9983	.9948	.9858	.9647	.9198	.8329	.6814	.4510
	14	1.0000	1.0000	1.0000	1.0000	1.0000	1.0000	1.0000	1.0000	1.0000	1.0000	.9999	.9995	.9984	.9953	.9866	.9648	.9126	.7941
	15	1.0000	1.0000	1.0000	1.0000	1.0000	1.0000	1.0000	1.0000	1.0000	1.0000	1.0000	1.0000	1.0000	1.0000	1.0000	1.0000	1.0000	1.0000
20	0	.3585	.1216	.0388	.0115	.0032	.0008	.0002	.0000	.0000	.0000	.0000	.0000	.0000	.0000	.0000	.0000	.0000	.0000
	1	.7358	.3917	.1756	.0692	.0243	.0076	.0021	.0005	.0001	.0000	.0000	.0000	.0000	.0000	.0000	.0000	.0000	.0000
	2	.9245	.6769	.4049	.2061	.0913	.0355	.0121	.0036	.0009	.0002	.0000	.0000	.0000	.0000	.0000	.0000	.0000	.0000
	3	.9841	.8670	.6477	.4114	.2252	.1071	.0444	.0160	.0049	.0013	.0003	.0000	.0000	.0000	.0000	.0000	.0000	.0000
	4	.9974	.9568	.8298	.6296	.4148	.2375	.1182	.0510	.0189	.0059	.0015	.0003	.0000	.0000	.0000	.0000	.0000	.0000
	5	.9997	.9887	.9327	.8042	.6172	.4164	.2454	.1256	.0553	.0207	.0064	.0016	.0003	.0000	.0000	.0000	.0000	.0000
	6	1.0000	.9976	.9781	.9133	.7858	.6080	.4166	.2500	.1299	.0577	.0214	.0065	.0015	.0003	.0000	.0000	.0000	.0000
	7	1.0000	.9996	.9941	.9679	.8982	.7723	.6010	.4159	.2520	.1316	.0580	.0210	.0060	.0013	.0002	.0000	.0000	.0000
	8	1.0000	.9999	.9987	.9900	.9591	.8867	.7624	.5956	.4143	.2517	.1308	.0565	.0196	.0051	.0009	.0001	.0000	.0000
	9	1.0000	1.0000	.9998	.9974	.9861	.9520	.8782	.7553	.5914	.4119	.2493	.1275	.0532	.0171	.0039	.0006	.0000	.0000
	10	1.0000	1.0000	1.0000	.9994	.9961	.9829	.9468	.8725	.7507	.5881	.4086	.2447	.1218	.0480	.0139	.0026	.0002	.0000
	11	1.0000	1.0000	1.0000	.9999	.9991	.9949	.9804	.9435	.8692	.7483	.5857	.4044	.2376	.1133	.0409	.0100	.0013	.0001
	12	1.0000	1.0000	1.0000	1.0000	.9998	.9987	.9940	.9790	.9420	.8684	.7480	.5841	.3990	.2277	.1018	.0321	.0059	.0004
	13	1.0000	1.0000	1.0000	1.0000	1.0000	.9997	.9985	.9935	.9786	.9423	.8701	.7500	.5834	.3920	.2142	.0867	.0219	.0024
	14	1.0000	1.0000	1.0000	1.0000	1.0000	1.0000	.9997	.9984	.9936	.9793	.9447	.8744	.7546	.5836	.3828	.1958	.0673	.0113
	15	1.0000	1.0000	1.0000	1.0000	1.0000	1.0000	1.0000	.9997	.9985	.9941	.9811	.9490	.8818	.7625	.5852	.3704	.1702	.0432
	16	1.0000	1.0000	1.0000	1.0000	1.0000	1.0000	1.0000	1.0000	.9997	.9987	.9951	.9840	.9556	.8929	.7748	.5886	.3523	.1330
	17	1.0000	1.0000	1.0000	1.0000	1.0000	1.0000	1.0000	1.0000	1.0000	.9998	.9991	.9964	.9879	.9645	.9087	.7939	.5951	.3231
	18	1.0000	1.0000	1.0000	1.0000	1.0000	1.0000	1.0000	1.0000	1.0000	1.0000	.9999	.9995	.9979	.9924	.9757	.9308	.8244	.6083
	19	1.0000	1.0000	1.0000	1.0000	1.0000	1.0000	1.0000	1.0000	1.0000	1.0000	1.0000	1.0000	.9998	.9992	.9968	.9885	.9612	.8784
	20	1.0000	1.0000	1.0000	1.0000	1.0000	1.0000	1.0000	1.0000	1.0000	1.0000	1.0000	1.0000	1.0000	1.0000	1.0000	1.0000	1.0000	1.0000

Photo Credits

Chapter 1
Page 2: Walter Hodges/Tony Stone Images; **Page 5:** De Lapiere/Liaison Agency; **Page 26:** Charles Gupton/Stock Boston; **Page 32:** Courtesy of Wegmans Food Markets, Inc.; **Page 32:** Courtesy of Wegmans Food Markets, Inc.; **Page 33:** Courtesy of Wegmans Food Markets, Inc.; **Page 33:** Courtesy of Wegmans Food Markets, Inc.

Chapter 2
Page 36: Spencer Grant/PhotoEdit; **Page 39:** Mitch Wojnarowica/The Image Works; **Page 39:** Courtesy of the Hertz Corporation; **Page 45:** Courtesy of Lexus; **Page 45:** Tony Stone Images; **Page 45:** Bonnie Kamin/PhotoEdit; **Page 48:** Courtesy of Federal Express; **Page 52:** © Granata Press/The Image Works

Chapter 3
Page 68: Bill Lai/The Image Works; **Page 87:** Courtesy of Toro; **Page 87:** Courtesy of Toro

Chapter 4
Page 126: Frederic Pitchal/Corbis Sygma; **Page 131:** Kevin Horan/Tony Stone Images; **Page 131:** Courtesy of Chrysler Corporation; **Page 133:** Courtesy of Vlasic; **Page 136:** Bart Ginn; **Page 136:** Paper shredder Bart Ginn; **Page 136:** Steelcase Photo Services; **Page 142:** Chris Jones/The Stock Market; **Page 144:** Art reprinted from October 25, 1991, Issue of *Business Week* by special permission. Copyright 1991 by McGraw Hill, Inc.; **Page 145:** Courtesy of Eastman Kodak; **Page 146:** Courtesy of Eastman Kodak; **Page 148:** Courtesy Toyota Motor Sales, U.S.A., Inc.; **Page 152:** Caroline Parsons

Chapter 5
Page 172: John Garrett/Tony Stone Images; **Page 177:** Alan Levin/Tony Stone Images; **Page 177:** Patrick Ward/Stock Boston; **Page 183:** Rob Crandall/Stock Boston; **Page 183:** Bill Aron/Photo Edit; **Page 189:** Jon Feingersh/Stock Market; **Page 194:** Courtesy High Acres Landfill and Recycling Center

Chapter 6
Page 216: Bill Bachmann/Stock Boston; **Page 220:** David Joel/Tony Stone Images; **Page 220:** Courtesy of Ben and Jerry's Homemade; **Page 220:** Courtesy

of Saturn Corporation; **Page 225:** Spencer Grant/PhotoEdit; **Page 228:** Michael Rosenfeld/Tony Stone Images; **Page 234:** Steve Weinrebe/Stock Boston; **Page 234:** Mercedes Benz **Page 237:** Courtesy of Electric Boat Corporation; **Page 252:** Tom and Dee Ann McCarthy/The Stock Market; **Page 252:** Tom and Dee Ann McCarthy/The Stock Market

Chapter 7
Page 306: David Sams/Stock Boston; **Page 309:** Charles Gupton/Stock Boston; **Page 312:** Michael H. Dunn/The Stock Market; **Page 318:** Greg Girard/The Stock Market; **Page 322:** David Lassman/The Image Works

Chapter 8
Page 354: Michael Stravatu/SYGMA; **Page 360:** Courtesy of Tropicana Products; **Page 366:** Myrleen Ferguson/PhotoEdit; **Page 369:** Courtesy of Mall of America; **Page 369:** Courtesy of Mall of America

Chapter 9
Page 392: Courtesy of Andersen Windows; **Page 397:** Courtesy of Mitutoyo Asia Pacific Pte Ltd.; **Page 399:** Peter Menzel/Stock Boston; **Page 404:** AP/Wide World Photos; **Page 404:** Courtesy of Philip B. Crosby; **Page 404:** Courtesy of Joseph Juran

Chapter 10
Page 416: Charles Thatcher/Tony Stone Images; **Page 421:** Paul Chesley/Tony Stone Images; **Page 423:** Jose Azel /Aurora; **Page 434:** Michael L. Abramson; **Page 455:** Rick Hein-Chicago Sun Times

Chapter 11
Page 468: Courtesy of Trek Corporation; **Page 470:** AP Photo/Charles Bennett; **Page 475:** Courtesy of LL Bean Inc.; **Page 488:** Courtesy of Motorola Corporation; **Page 490:** The Image Works

Chapter 12
Page 502: Courtesy of American President Line; **Page 510:** © JB Pictures, Ltd.; **Page 510:** © JB Pictures, Ltd.; **Page 510:** © JB Pictures, Ltd.; **Page 510:** © JB Pictures, Ltd.; **Page 510:** © JB Pictures, Ltd.; **Page 510:** © JB Pictures, Ltd.; **Page 513:** Dennis Paillard; **Page 517:** Jim Hansen

Chapter 13
Page 540: Linc Cornell/Stock Boston; **Page 545:** John Coletti/Stock Boston; **Page 549:** Elena Roolraid/PhotoEdit; **Page 551:** John Edwards/Tony Stone Images; **Page 551:** David Joe/Tony Stone Images

Chapter 14
Page 602: Kaluzny Thatcher/Tony Stone Images; **Page 606:** Courtesy of Rubbermaid Corporation; **Page 610:** Alan Schien/The Stock Market; **Page 613:** Courtesy of International Business Machines Corporation

Chapter 15
Page 638: Courtesy of International Business Machines Corporation; **Page 638:** Courtesy of International Business Machines Corporation; **Page 648:** Courtesy of Kirby U.S.A. Inc.; **Page 679:** Courtesy of Stickley Furniture

Chapter 16
Page 682: Courtesy of Ford Motor Company; **Page 689:** Courtesy of Honda Automotive; **Page 699:** Tri State Industries, footage courtesy of Mac Lean Media, Inc.; **Page 699:** Tri State Industries, footage courtesy of Mac Lean Media, Inc.; **Page 710:** Ron Havis/SABA; **Page 712:** © 1994 Cahners Publishing Co.; **Page 717:** Courtesy of the Boeing Company

Chapter 17
Page 726: Thatcher Poulides/Tony Stone Images; **Page 730:** Courtesy of Solectron; **Page 733:** © Feldman and Pinedo; **Page 747:** © Feldman and Pinedo; **Page 749:** Vincent De Witt/Stock Boston; **Page 751:** Tony Freeman/PhotoEdit

Chapter 18
Page 764: Courtesy of NASA; **Page 767:** Corbis/SYGMA; **Page 794:** Bill Pogue/Tony Stone Images

Chapter 19
Page 816: Mark Wagner/Tony Stone Images; **Page 820:** Jeff Greenberg/PhotoEdit

Company Index

A.T. Kearney, 685
Allen-Bradley, 228, 594
Amazon.com, 516
American Airlines, 750–751
American Express, 489
Apple Computer Inc., 358
Arthur D. Little & Co., 133
Aston Martin, 691
AT&T, 359, 489, 497
Atlas Door, 50–51
Avon, 702

Bain & Co., 363
Baxter International, 710
Bell Atlantic Corp., 25, 359
Bell Telephone Labs, 23, 394
Ben and Jerry's, 220
Birmingham Steel Corp., 367
Bloomingdales, 369
BMW, 362
Boeing Co., 4, 716–717
Booz, Allen & Hamilton, 775
Bose Corp., 711–712
Boston Consulting Group, 504
Boston Markets, 48
Bruegger's Bagel Bakery, 597
Burger King, 57, 606
Burgmaster Corp., 60–61

CalComp, 474–475
Campbell Soup Co., 506, 709
Canon, 489
Carnegie Group Inc., 367
Caterpillar Inc., 145
Chrysler Corp., 131, 144, 225–227, 594, 709
Coca-Cola, 46
Compaq Computer, 105, 511
Con Agra Inc., 270
CPC International, 364
Crucible Steel, 322
Cummins Engine, 489

Davidson Exterior Trim, 709

Dell Computer, 47, 105, 520
Delta Airlines, 594
Digital Equipment Corp., 358
Domino's Pizza, 709
Dow Chemical Co., 490
DuPont Co., 545, 708, 775

Eastman Kodak Co., 25, 46, 131,
    145–147, 489
EWP Engineering, Inc., 771
Express Mail, 709

Federal Express Corp., 48, 497, 515–516, 709
Federated Department Stores, 516
Fingerhut, 516–517
Firestone Tire, 31, 135
Fisher-Price Toy Co., 362
Florida Power and Light, 489
Ford Motor Co., 22, 27, 31, 46, 130–131, 135,
    144, 223–224, 242, 406, 470, 548, 594
Fuji Photo Film Co., 146

General Electric, 471, 498
General Motors Corp., 46, 129, 135, 137,
    144, 223, 226, 229, 364, 372, 510, 594,
    691, 709
Georgia Box, 709
Global Metallurgical, 41
Green Gear Cycling Inc., 694–695

Harvey Industries, 594
Hearst Magazines, 132
Hershey Foods, 489
Hertz, 39
Hewlett-Packard, 474, 489, 498, 506
Hoechst, A.G., 362
Honda, 394, 689
Honeywell, 712
Houdaille Industries Inc., 60–61

IBM, 41, 46, 137, 538–539, 613, 646, 712
Ingersoll-Rand, 712
Ingram Micro Inc., 105

Insight Inc., 363
Intel, 498, 712
IPSCO, Inc., 363
ITT, 405

Jays Foods, 454–455
JCPenney, 4

Keebler, 133
Kellogg Co., 26
Kirby Refrigeration, 648
Kmart, 4, 364, 695
Kohlberg Kravis Roberts & Co., 60–61
Konica Corp., 146
KPMG, 105
Kurt Salmon Associates, 514

L.L. Bean, 471, 475, 489
Lew-Mark Baking Co., 61
Lincoln Electric Co., 335
Lockheed, 474, 770, 775

McCormick, 128
McDonald's, 48, 434, 606
McMillan Consulting, 105
Macy's, 610
Magnetic Technologies Corp., 147
Manufacturing and Computer Systems, 663
Martin Co., 395
Martin Marietta, 404
MCI Communications Corp., 358–359
Mercedes-Benz, 234, 367
Mercer Management Consulting, 363, 511
Mexx, 363–365
Microsoft Corp., 252, 766
Mitsubishi Electric, 50, 318
Mitutoyo, 397
Monsanto Chemical Co., 708
Morton International, 271–273
Motorola, 470–471, 488, 498

NAPA Auto Parts, 694
National Bicycle, 506

NationsBank Corp., 497
Nissan Motor Co., 394, 685
Nucor Steel, 223

Outsource Enterprises of Rochester, 147

Pepperidge Farms, 224
PepsiCo, 46, 220
Photikon Corp., 146–147
Pier One, 517
Pipian Bike, 5
Procter & Gamble, 489

Quigley Corp., 175

Rand Corp., 74
Remington Rand Corporation, 775
Richard Change Associates, 499
Rubbermaid Inc., 606
Ryder, 508

SAP, 663
Sears, 4, 423
Shell Oil Co., 594
Sherwin-Williams, 423
Siemens, A.G., 362
Skynet Worldwide Courier, 41
Solectron Corp., 730
Sony Corp., 132, 366–367
Spartan Stores, 514
Sport Obermeyer, 506
Stickley Furniture, 679–681
Stryker Howmedica, 49

Textron, 709
Thompson Factory, 142
Toyota Motor Co., 45, 49, 148, 251, 394, 489, 684–686
Toys "R" Us, 515
TriState Industries, 699
Tropicana, 360

Union Carbide, 25, 41
United Parcel Service, 146, 514–516, 594–595
United States Postal Service, 65
University Games Corp., 362

Van Waters & Rogers, 504
Varian Associates Inc., 496–497
Vlasic Foods International, 133–134

Wallace Co., 497
Wal-Mart, 4, 423, 507, 513, 516–517, 522
Webvan Group, 516
Wegmans Food Markets, 31–34
Wendy's, 606
Western Electric, 23
Whirlpool, 60

Xerox Corp., 145–147, 471, 474, 489

Zac Precision, 474

Subject Index

ABC approach, **548**–550
Abernathy, W.J., 352
Acceptable quality level (AQL), 460–461
Acceptance sampling, 458–467; *See also*
   Quality control
   acceptable quality level, 460–461
   average quality of inspected lots,
      463–464
   defined, 458
   inspection, 418–422
   operating characteristic (OC) curve,
      459–463
   sampling plans, 458–459
Accidents, causes of, 321–322
Accounting
   cost, 697
   forecasting and, 70
   function of, 11, 529
Accuracy, in forecasting, 96–98
Activities, 776
Activity-based costing, 697
Activity-on-arrow (AOA), 776–777,
   780–784
Activity-on-node (AON), 776–777, 785
Additive model, 87–88
Advertising and promotion, 608
Aggregate planning, 604–636; *See also*
   Capacity planning
   capacity options, 608–610
   choosing a strategy, 612–613
   concept of aggregation, 605–606
   defined, 604
   demand, 608, 610–612
   disaggregating the plan, 623–624
   informal techniques, 613–618
   inputs, 607
   linear programming, 619–621
   master scheduling, 605, 623–628
   mathematical techniques, 618–622
   overview of, 606–607
   planning levels, 604–605
   services, 622–623
   simulation models, 621–622

Aggregate planning—*Cont.*
   strategies for meeting uneven demand,
      610–612
Akao, Yoji, 152
Alampi, James, 504
Alber, Karen, 526
Algorithms, use in PERT, 780–786
Allen, Robert E., 497
Alliances, strategic, 509
Allison-Koerber, Deborah, 103
Allowance factor, in time studies, 326–328
American National Standards Institute
   (ANSI), 409
American Production and Inventory Control
   Society (APICS), 6, 550, 641
American Society for Quality (ASQ), 6
American Society for Quality Control
   (ASQC), 394–395
Anders, George, 525
Andon, 696
Angus, Robert B., 814
Ansari, Shahid, 413
AOQ, 463–464
AOQL, 464
Applied research, 131
Appointment systems, 749
Appraisal costs, 402
Apte, Uday M., 157, 195, 224, 242, 273
AQL, 460–461
Argote, Linda, 352
Arrival and service patterns, 822–824
Assembly line; *See also* **Line balancing**
   balancing of, 242–251
   defined, 5, **233**–234
Assignable variation, 423
Assignment model, 735
Association for Systems Management, 6
Associative forecasting techniques, 91–96
Associative model, 73, 91–96
Attributes, 426, 430–433
Audits, of suppliers, 535
Automatic identification and data capture
   (AIDC), 547

Automation, 222–230
   computer-aided manufacturing
      (CAM), 223
   computer-integrated manufacturing
      (CIM), 228
   fixed, 223
   flexible, 224
   flexible manufacturing system (FMS),
      227–228, 240
   numerically controlled machines (N/C), 223
   programmable, 223
   robots, 223–225
Autonomation, 692
Availability, 165
Available-to-promise inventory (ATP), 624
Average, moving, 77–79, 103, 107
Average outgoing quality (AOQ), 463–464
Average outgoing quality limit (AOQL), 464
Average quality of inspected lots, 463–464
Averaging techniques, 76–81, 107
Avery, Rod, 359
Awad, Elias M., 316
Awards, for quality, 406–409
Ayres, R.U., 242

Baatz, E., 664
Back orders, 608
Backward scheduling, 734
Baker, Stephen, 366–367
Balance delay, 246
Balance sheet approach to problem solving,
   488
Balancing transactions, 705
Baldrige Award, 406–408
Baldwin, Carliss C., 157
Ballou, Ronald H., 384, 525
Banham, Russ, 362
Bar coding, 546–547
Barnes, Ralph M., 341
Bartlett, Christopher A., 48n, 66
Basic research, 131
Batch processing, 219–222
Behavioral approach, to job design, 309–311

Belkauoi, Ahmed, 352
Bell, Janice, 413
Benchmarking, 471, 488–489
Bender, Paul S., 525
Bennett, Wayne D., 681
Benton, W.C., 718
Bernstein, Aaron, 66
Berry, William L., 601, 636, 681, 706, 718, 762
Besterfield, Dale H., 413, 456, 500
Besterfield, Glen, 413, 456, 500
Besterfield-Micha, Carol, 413, 456, 500
Besterfield-Sacre, Mary, 413, 456, 500
Beta distribution, 786
Bhatnagar, Rohit, 525
Bias, 98
Bidding, competitive, 532, 535
Bierman, Harold, 215, 304, 390
Bill of materials (BOM), 643
Billington, C., 521n, 526
Binding constraints, 290
Blackburn, Joseph D., 66, 718
Blackstone, John H., 601, 636
Blackwell, Kristina, 525
Blackwell, Roger D., 525
Block, M.R., 413
Blueprinting, 230
Blumenstein, Rebecca, 229, 372
Bolwijn, P.T., 195, 273
BOM, 643
Bonini, Charles P., 215, 304, 390
Bottleneck operations, 56, 189, 748
Bounded rationality, 198
Bounds, Gregory, 34
Bovet, David, 525
Brainstorming, 487
Brandimarte, P., 636
Brassard, Michael, 500
Break-even point (BEP), 185–187
Breakdown maintenance, 720
Bridger, R.S., 341
Brooks, Roger B., 601
B2B, 517–518
Budgeting, 10
Buffa, Elwood, 852
Bulfin, Robert, Jr., 636
Bull-whip effect, 521–522
Business organizations, functions within, 6–12
Business plan, 604–605
Business-to-business (B2B) commerce, 517–518
Butman, J. Juran, 413
Buxley, G., 636

c-chart, 432–433
CAD, 142–143
CAM, 223
Campy, James, 34
Capability analysis, 438–440
Capacity, 174, 607–610
Capacity planning, 174–195; *See also*
    Aggregate planning
    defining and measuring, 175–177
    determining requirements, 178–180
    developing alternatives, 180–183
    evaluating alternatives, 184–189
    factors affecting, 177–179

Capacity planning—*Cont.*
    importance of, 174–175
    planning service capacity, 183–184
    rough-cut, 623
Capacity requirements planning, 657–660
Capezio, Peter, 405, 413
Cappels, Thomas, 500
Carlisle, Brian, 341
Carpenter, Donna Sammons, 692n
Carrying costs, 547–548, 551–556
Cartin, Thomas J., 470n
Cartwright, Edmund, 21
Carvajal, Doreen, 370
Carville, Richard O., 146
Cases
    An American Tragedy: How a Good
        Company Died, 60–61
    The Case of the Mexican Crazy Quilt,
        812–813
    Chick-n-Gravy Dinner Line, 494
    Coquille Refinery Corporation, 872
    Dewey Stapler Company, 595–596
    DMD Enterprises, 678
    Eight Glasses a Day, 635–636
    Harvey Industries, 594–595
    Hazel, 30–31
    Hazel Revisited, 63
    Home-Style Cookies, 61–63
    Level Operations, 716
    M&L Manufacturing, 123–124
    Product Recall, 353
    Son, Ltd., 304
    Tiger Tools, 453–454
    Time, Please, 813
    Tip Top Markets, 494–496
    Total Recall, 31
    Toys, Inc., 453
    UPD Manufacturing, 593
Cash flow, 188
Cause-and-effect diagrams, 406, 479, 481,
    483–484
Cellular layouts, 238–240; *See also* Facilities
    layout
Cellular manufacturing, 238–240
Center of gravity method, 376–379
Centered moving average, 89–90
Central limit theorem, 424
Centralized inspection, 421
Centralized purchasing, 533
Certainty, 198–199
Certification
    quality, 409
    supplier, 535, 702–703
Chakrapani, C., 413
Chang, Richard, 499–500
Change transactions, 705
Changeover time, 49
Changes, 654
Channel, 822
Chao, X., 762
Chapman, Chris, 814
Chase demand strategy, 611–612
Check sheets, 478–481
Chopra, Sunil, 525
CIM, 228
Clark, Andrew, 484

Clark, Kim B., 157
Clark, Timothy, 484
Classification system, for inventory, 548–550
Cleland, David I., 814
Clements, James P., 814
Climate, impact on location decisions, 361
Closeness ratings, 255–256
Cohen, Morris A., 157, 195, 224, 242, 273
Cole, R.E., 413
Colvin, Geoffrey, 34, 66
Common variability, 423
Community factors in location decisions,
    365, 368
Compensation, 333–336
Competencies, distinctive, 44–45
Competitive bidding, 532, 535
Competitive edge, 44
Competitiveness, 38–40; *See also* **Strategies**
Computer-aided design (CAD), 142–143
Computer-aided manufacturing
    (CAM), 223
Computer applications
    CIM, 228
    computer-aided design, 142–143
    e-business, 24
    e-commerce, 506, 515–517
    e-procurement, 538–539
    EDI, 513–514, 538
    ERP, 664–669
    geographical information system (GIS),
        361, 366
    linear programming, 291–293, 735–736
    MRP; *See* **Material requirements**
        planning (MRP)
Computer-integrated manufacturing
    (CIM), 228
Computerized numerical control (CNC), 223
Concurrent engineering, 141–142
Condit, Donald F., 595
Condon, James D., 146–147
Conlin, William, 474
Constraints
    binding, 290
    defined, **276**
    plotting of, 280–283
    redundant, 287
Consumer surveys, used to forecast, 74
Consumer's risk, 461
Continual system, 545
Continuous improvement, 471, 696–697
Continuous processing, 221–222
Continuous stocking levels, 574–576
Contracts, with suppliers, 535
Control, 8
Control charts, 424–438
    attributes, 426, 430–433
    defined, 99, 424, 481
    errors, 425–426
    examples of, 479, 482, 487
    forecasting and, 99–102
    mean, 427–430
    range, 428–430
    run tests, 435–438
    variables, 426–430
    when to use, 434–435
Control limits, 425

Conversion process, 8–9
CONWHIP (constant work in process), 522
Cooper, Tom, 668
Copacino, William C., 525
Core function, of an organization, 12
Corner points, 287–288
Corporate downsizing, 26
Correlation, 94
Cost accounting, 697
Cost analysis, 833–834
Cost-profit-volume analysis, 373–375
Cost-volume analysis, 185–188
Costs
    activity based, 697
    appraisal, 402
    carrying, 547–548, 551–556
    distribution, 376
    ERP, 665–666
    excess, 574
    failure, 401
    fixed, 185–187
    holding, 512, 547–548
    maintenance, 720–721
    ordering, 548, 551–556
    prevention, 402
    quality, 401–402
    shortage, 548, 574
    step, 186–187
    total cost, 665–666
    transportation, 253–255, 359–360, 375
    variable, 185–187
Counting systems, for inventory, 550
Cox, Jeff, 762
C$_{pk}$, 440–441
CPM (critical path method), 18, 775; *See also* **PERT (Program evaluation and review technique)**
CR (critical ratio), 739–744
Craft production, 21, 28
Crainer, Stuart, 34
Crandall, Robert L., 750–751
Crash, 794–796
Critical activities, 777
Critical path, 777
Critical path method (CPM), 18, 775; *See also* **PERT (Program evaluation and review technique)**
Critical ratio, 739–744
Crosby, Philip, 395, 404–405
Cross, K.F., 500
Cross-docking, 522
Cross training, 251, 696
CRP, 657–660
Cullinane, Thomas P., 814
Cummins, Thomas, 708
Cumulative lead time, 643
Cumulative trauma disorders, 322–323
Cunningham, J. Barton, 341
Curvilinear regression analysis, 96
Customer needs, 44
Customer research, 132–133
Customer satisfaction, 25
Customer service, 39, 44
Customization, mass, 138–139
Customized output, 13
Cycle counting, 550

Cycle time, 243–247
Cycles, 75–76, 90–91

Dale, Barrie G., 413
Dalla-Vicenza, Mario, 363
Danner, David L., 341
Darnell, Michele, 133
Dash, Julekha, 771
Davenport, Tom, 681
Davis, Stanley B., 413, 456
Day, Susan, 144
Decentralized purchasing, 533
Decision making
    capacity planning; *See* Capacity planning
    under certainty, 198–199
    decision trees, 201–203
    environments, 198
    establishing priorities, 19–20
    ethics and, 20
    expected monetary value (EMV) criterion, 200–201
    expected value of perfect information, 203–204
    models, 17–18, 23
    poor decision making, causes of, 197–198
    quantitative methods, 18–19
    under risk, 200–201
    sensitivity analysis, 204–206
    systems approach, 19
    trade-offs, 19
    under uncertainty, 199–200
Decision Sciences Institute, 6
Decision theory; *See* Decision making
Decision trees, 201–203
Decision variables, 275
Delayed differentiation, 138–139, **522**
Delivery time, 49
Dell, Michael, 47
Delphi method, 74, 103
Delurgio, Stephen, 124
Demand
    aggregate planning and, 607–608
    dependent, 640–641
    independent, 640–641
    lumpy, 640
    meeting uneven, 610–612
    prediction of; *See* **Forecasting**
Demand chain, 504
Demand forecasts, 547
Deming, W. Edwards, 395, 402–403, 409, 474, 497
Deming Prize, 402, 409
Deming wheel, 475
Dependent demand, 640–641
Depth skills, 335
Derman, C., 456
Design, of products and services
    availability, 165
    capacity and, 178
    component commonality, 147
    computer-aided design (CAD), 142–143
    concurrent engineering, 141–142
    customer research and, 132–133
    design time, 49
    environmental issues, 134–135, 143–144
    ethical issues, 134–135

Design, of products and services—*Cont.*
    forecasting, 70
    ideas for new/redesigned, 130–134
    JIT, 688–689
    legal issues, 134–135
    life cycles, 136–137, 221
    manufacturing and, 141–147
    mass customization and, 138–139
    objectives of, 130
    production requirements, 143
    quality and, 397–398
    quality function deployment (QFD), 130, 150–154
    reasons for, 128–129
    recycling, 143–144
    reliability and, 139–140, 159–164
    remanufacturing, 144–147
    research and development, 131–132
    reverse engineering, 130
    robust design, 140–141
    services, 147–150
    standardization, 137–138
    systems, 12
Design for assembly (DFA), 143
Design for disassembly (DFD), 145
Design for manufacturing (DFM), 143
Design for operations, 130
Design for recycling (DFR), 143
Design for response, 133
Deterministic time estimates, 778–780
Detroit-type automation, 223
DeWeaver, Mary Feeherry, 814
Differentiation
    delayed, 138–139, 522
    product or service, 38
Dimensions of quality, 395–**396**
Direct numerical control (DNC), 223
Disaggregation, 623–624
Discounts, quantity, 558–563
Discrete stocking levels, 576–577
Disintermediation, 522
Distinctive competencies, 44–45
Distribution costs, 376
Distribution function, 12
Distribution requirements planning (DRP), 514
Division of labor, 22
Dixon, Lance, 711
Dobbins, H., 34
Dodge, H.F., 23, 394
Dornier, Phillippe-Pierre, 525
Double sampling plan, 458–459
Double smoothing, 85
Downsizing, 26
DRP, 514
Drum-buffer-rope, 748
Due date, rule for sequencing, 739–740, 743–744
Duncan, A.J., 467
Duray, Rebecca, 157
Dynamic line balancing, 251

e-business, 24
e-commerce, 506, 515–517
Earliest due date (EDD), 739–740, 743–744
Eberle, Ted, 341

Ebersole, Phil, 145, 147
Economic lot sizes, 544
Economic order quantity (EOQ), 551–577
  basic model, 551–556
  defined, 551
  economic production quantity, 556–558
  fixed-order-interval model, 571–574
  MRP and, 656
  quantity discounts, 558–563
  reorder points, 564–571
  single period model, 574–577
Economic production quantity (EPQ),
  556–558
Economies of scale, 21
EDD (earliest due date), 739–740, 743–744
EDI, 513–514, 538
Efficiency, 56
Efficiency school, 309
Efficient consumer response (ECR),
  513–**514**
Ehrsam, Fred, 363
80–20 rule, 480
Electronic data interchange (EDI),
  513–514, 538
Emerson, Harrington, 22
Empowerment, 471, 488
Engineering, interface with purchasing, 529
Englund, Randall L., 814
Enrick, Norbert L., 467
Enterprise resource planning (ERP),
  664–669; *See also* **Material requirements**
  planning (MRP)
Environment
  environmentally responsible
    manufacturing, 25–26
  ISO 14000, 412
  product design issues, 134–135
  recycling, 143–144, 174
  trends, 25–26
Environmental Protection Agency (EPA), 135
Environmental scanning, 46
Environmentally responsible manufacturing,
  25–26
EOQ; *See* **Economic order quantity (EOQ)**
Eppen, G.D., 215
Eppinger, Steven D., 157
Epple, Dennis, 352
Equivalent current value, 188
Equivalent interest rate, 188
Ergonomics, 309
Erlang, A.K., 818
Ernst, Ricardo, 525
ERP, 664–669
Errors, 96–102, 425–426
Esayian, Harry, 474
Esseling, Erik K.C., 413
Ethics
  design issues and, 134–135
  operations management, 40
  project management, 770
  purchasing, 533–534
  quality issues, 402
Ettlie, John, 195, 273
Evans, James R., 456, 872
Evans, P., 66
Events, 776

Exception reports, 654
Excess cost, 574
Executive opinions, used to forecast,
  73–74, 103
Expected monetary value (EMV) criterion,
  200–**201**
Expected value of perfect information
  (EVPI), 203–204
Exponential smoothing, 80–81, 85–87,
  103, 107
External failures, 401

Fabrication, 5
Fabrycky, W.J., 352
Facilities, location of; *See* Location planning
Facilities layout; *See also* Location planning;
    Process selection and design
  capacity planning; *See* Capacity planning
  cellular layouts, 238–240
  combination layouts, 238
  fixed-position, 237–238
  line balancing, 242–251
    cycle time, 243–247
    guidelines for, 247–249
    parallel workstations, 250–251
    precedence diagrams, 245, 248–249
    procedures, 245–246
  process layouts, 235–237, 251–258
  product layouts, 232–235, 242–251, 258
  service layouts, 240–241
Factor-rating, 375–376
Fail-safing, 471
Failure, 139
Failure costs, 401
Failure rates, 161–163
Fazel, Farzaneh, 473n, 500
FCFS (first come, first served), 739–743
Fearon, Harold E., 539
Feasibility, range of, 296
Feasible solution space, 276, 278, 283
Feedback, 8
Feigenbaum, Armand, 395, 404–405
Feitzinger, Edward, 157
Fender, Michel, 525
Finance function, 9–10, 70
Financial analysis, 188–189
Finite loading, 732, 734
Finite source
  defined, **821**
  queuing models, 839–844
Finucane, James, 359
First come, first served rule, 739–743
Fishbone diagram, 406, 481, 483
Fisher, Marshall, 506n, 525
Fitzgerald, Kevin R., 528, 539
Fitzsimmons, James A., 872
5W2H approach, 489
Fixed automation, 223
Fixed costs, 185–187
Fixed-order-interval (FOI) model, 571–574
Fixed-period ordering, 656
Fixed-position layout, 237–238; *See also*
    Facilities layout
Flattening, of the organization, 26
Flexibility, 38, 44, 180, 692–693
Flexible automation, 224

Flexible factories strategy, 46
Flexible manufacturing system (FMS),
  227–228, 240
Florida, Richard L., 367
Flow process chart, 314, 316
Flow-shop scheduling, 728
Flow system, 728–729
Flowcharts, 230–231, **478**–480
Flynn, Mike, 229
FMS, 227–228, 240
Focused factories strategy, 46
Fogarty, Donald W., 239, 601, 636
Foolproofing, 471
Foote, David, 813
Ford, Henry, 684, 686
Forecasting, 70–124
  accuracy, 96–98
  approaches to, 73
  associative techniques
    curvilinear and multiple regression, 96
    simple linear regression, 91–96, 107
  based on judgment and opinion, 73–75,
    103
  based on time series data
    averaging, 76–81, 103, 107
    cycles, 75–76, 90–91
    naive methods, 75–76, 107
    seasonality, 75–76, 87–90, 179–180
    trend adjusted exponential smoothing,
      85–87, 103, 107
    trends, 75–76, 81–85, 107
  choosing a technique, 103–104
  common features, 71–72
  computers and, 104
  control of, 107
  defined, 70
  demand, 547
  elements of a good, 72
  formulas used in, 107
  naive approach, 75–76, 107
  steps in the process, 72–73
  uses of data, 70–71
Foreign locations, 361–362, 370–373
Forward scheduling, 734
Foster, Thomas A., 413
Fowler, Oscar S., 34
Francis, Richard L., 273, 384
Freivalds, Andris, 341
Fulfillment, of orders, 515–516
Functional strategies, 42
Furrer, Matt, 105

Gantt, Henry, 22
Gantt charts, 22, **731**–733, 774–775
Garvin, David A., 396n, 413
Gass, S.I., 304
General Agreement on Tariffs and Trade
  (GATT), 25, 371
Geographical information system (GIS),
  361, 366
Georgoff, D.M., 124
Ghare, P.M., 352
Ghattas, R.G., 814
Ghoshal, Sumantra, 48n, 66
Gido, Jack, 814
Giffith, Gary K., 500

Gilbreth, Frank, 22–23, 315–316, 318
Gilbreth, Lillian, 23, 318
Gillespie, Lori Ciprian, 814
Gilmore, James, 157
Gispan, Jonathan, 770
Gitlow, Howard, 456, 500
Glaxner, Wayne, 229
Global locations, 361–362, 370–373
Global supply chain, 515
Globalization, 25
Goals, 41–42
Goetsch, David L., 413, 456
Goldratt, Eliyahu M., 748–749, 762, 797n, 814
Goods-service continuum, 8, 10
Goods versus services operations, 14–16
Gorman, Michael E., 157
Gould, F.J., 215
Graham, Robert J., 814
Grant, Eugene L., 429, 456
Graphical linear programming, 278–290
    defined, 278
    feasible solution space, 283
    minimization, 288–290
    objective function line, 283–287
    plotting constraints, 280–283
    procedures, 278–280
    redundant constraints, 287
    slack and surplus, 290
    solutions/corner points, 287–288
Gravity method, center of, 376–379
Gray, Clifford F., 766, 772–773, 814
Greenspan, Alan, 63–64
Griffin, W., 852
Griffith, Gary K., 456
Grimshaw, David J., 384
Gronski, Linda, 474
Groover, Mikell P., 157, 239, 250n, 273
Gross requirements, 647
Group incentive plans, 335
Group technology, 238–240, 691
Grover, Varun, 44n
Growth strategies, 48
Gryna, Derek S., 413
Gryna, Frank M., 413, 456, 467
Guide, V. Daniel, 718
Gundersen, Norman A., 814
Gupta, Tarun, 718

Hachman, Mark, 66
Hall, Robert W., 725
Hammer, Michael, 34
Handfield, Robert B., 526
Hargreave, James, 21
Harrell, C., 872
Harrington, H. James, 413
Harris, F.W., 23
Harry, Mikel, 500
Hausman, Warren H., 215, 304, 390
Hazelwood, R.N., 840, 843
Hendrick, Thomas E., 195
Hendricks, Kevin B., 500
Hertzberg, Frederick, 23
Heskett, James L., 157
Heuristic rule, 256
Hill, Terry, 44, 66, 195, 273, 526, 539

Hillier, Frederick S., 304, 852, 872
Hillier, Mark S., 304, 872
Hinckley, John, 226
Histograms, 478–479, 481
Hoffmann, Thomas R., 239, 601, 636
Holding costs, 512, **547**–548
Holland, Max, 60–61
Holstein, William J., 66
Holusha, John, 27
Hopp, Wallace J., 124, 601, 636, 681, 718, 762
Hopp, William, Jr., 34
Hora, Michael E., 725
Horizontal loading, 310, **732**–733
Horizontal skills, 335
House of quality, 150–151
Housekeeping, 705
Hout, Thomas, 46n
Howe, Tom, 454
Howley, Lauraine, 49
Human relations movement, 22–23
Human resources, 11, 70
Hungarian method, 736
Huse, Edgar F., 340

Illumination, working conditions and, 320
Implied warranties, 135
Incentives, 333–336
Independence, 790
Independent contractors, 609
Independent demand, 640–641
Independent events, 159–160
Indexes, 88, 94
Industrial engineering function, 12
Industrial Revolution, 21
Infinite loading, 732–733
Infinite source, 821
Information technology, 25
Information velocity, 519
Input/output (I/O) control, 734–735
Inputs, 8–9, 607, 642–646
Inspection, 418–422; See also **Acceptance sampling**
Institute for Operations Research and the Management Sciences (INFORMS), 6
Institute of Industrial Engineers, 6
Interchangeable parts, 22, 137
Intermittent processing, 235
Internal failures, 401
Internal rate of return (IR), 188
International Organization for Standardization (ISO), 409–410
Internet
    business-to-business (B2B) commerce, 517–518
    e-business, 24
    e-commerce, 506, 515–517
    e-procurement, 538–539
Interviewing, 488
Inventory, 542
Inventory management, 541–601; See also **Aggregate planning; Material requirements planning (MRP)**
    ABC approach, 548–550
    bar coding, 546–547
    bull-whip effect, 521–522
    carrying costs, 547–548, 551–556

Inventory management—Cont.
    classification system, 548–550
    costs, 547–548, 551–556
    counting system, 545–547
    cycle counting, 550
    cycles, 552
    demand forecasts, 547
    DRP, 514
    economic order quantity (EOQ)
        basic model, 551–556
        defined, 551
        economic production quantity, 556–558
        fixed-order-interval model, 571–574
        quantity discounts, 558–563
        reorder points, 564–571
        single period model, 574–577
    functions of, 543–544
    JIT, 693–694
    lead time information, 547
    objectives of, 544
    ordering costs, 548, 551–556
    records, 646
    requirements for effective, 545–550
    safety stock, 564–565, 654–655
    service level, 565, 568–571
    shortages, 568–571
    stocking levels, 574–577
    turnover of, 544
    velocity, 519–520
Inventory models, 18
Inventory records, 646
Inventory turnover, 544
Inventory velocity, 519–520
Ireland, Samuel,, 414
Irregular variation, 75–76
Ishikawa, Kaoru, 406
Ishikawa diagram, 483
ISO 9000, 409–410
ISO 14000, 412

Jacobs, Robert F., 681
Jacques, March Laree, 414
Japan Prize, 409
Japanese manufacturers, influence of, 23, 44
Jeffery, Bill, 681
Jensch, Tom, 702
Jidoka, 692
JIT; See **Just-in-time (JIT)**
JIT II, 711–712
Job design, 308–323; See also **Work measurement**
    behavioral approaches, 310–311
    methods analysis, 313–315
    motion study, 315–318
    motivation, 311
    specialization, 309–310
    teams, 312–313
    working conditions, 318–323
Job enlargement, 310
Job enrichment, 310–311
Job rotation, 310
Job-shop scheduling, 731
Job shops, 219–222
Job splitting, 745
Job time, 739–740
Johnson, Al, 709

Johnson, S.M., 745n
Johnson's rule, 745
Jones, Daniel T., 34, 686n, 692n
Jorgensen, Karen, 341
Judgmental forecasts, 73–75
Juran, Joseph M., 395, 403–405, 414, 456, 467, 497, 500
Just-in-time (JIT), 684–718
    converting to, 705–708
    defined, 694
    deliveries, 514–515
    goals of, 687–688
    history of, 684–686
    inventory control, 693–694
    JIT II, 711–712
    kanban, 700–701
    level loading, 697–699
    lot sizes, 690
    manufacturing planning and control, 697–705
    personnel organizational elements, 695–697
    process design, 689–694
    product design, 688–689
    production flexibility, 692–693
    pull systems, 699–700
    purchasing, 711
    services, 709–711
    setup time reduction, 691–692
    supplier relationships, 702–704
    visual systems, 700–701

Kahn, Salina, 844
Kaiser plan, 335
Kaizen, 471
Kalian, Arianna, 229
Kaminsky, Philip, 516, 526
Kanabar, Vijaay, 814
Kanban, 700–701
Kano model, 153–154
Kapp, Karl M., 681
Katz, K.L., 852
Keating, Barry, 124
Kelly, J.E., 775
Kelton, David, 872
Kerzner, Harold, 814
Kilbridge, M.D., 273
Kinni, Theodore B., 499
Klammer, Thomas, 413
Knod, Edward M., Jr., 693
Knowledge-based pay, 335
Koch, Christopher, 664
Kodak plan, 335
Kolarik, William J., 456
Koopman, John, 363–365
Kouvelis, Panos, 525
Kuchler, Theodore C., 708
Kumpe, T., 195, 273

La Lopa, Joseph M., 414
Labor factors, impact on location decisions, 361
Lankford, William M., 718
Laplace, 199–200
Larson, B.M., 852
Larson, Erik W., 766, 772–773, 814
Larson, Melissa, 814

Larson, R.C., 852
Latamore, G. Berton, 521
Latham, Bill, 681
Latham, Hester-Ford, 681
Law, Avrill, 872
Lawrence, Carol, 413
Layout of facilities; *See* Facilities layout
Lead time, 11, 523, 547, 643
Leadership, 697
Lean production, 26–28, 251, 684; *See also*
    Just-in-time (JIT)
Learning curves
    applications, 347–349
    concept of, 343–347
    limitations, 349–350
Least squares line, 91–92
Leavenworth, Richard, 429, 456
Lee, Hau L., 157, 521n, 526
Leenders, Michiel R., 539
Legal issues
    design of products/services, 134–135
    liability, 135, 399
    UCC, 135
    warranties, 135
Lehner, Urban, 684–685
Level capacity strategy, 611–612
Level loading, 697–699
Levy, Richard M., 497
Liability, 135, 399
Lieberman, Gerald J., 304, 852, 872
Liebhaber, Richard, 358–359
Lientz, Bennet P., 500, 814
Life cycle, 136–137, 221, 772
Lincoln plan, 335
Lindsay, W.M., 456
Line balancing
    aggregate planning, 619–621
    cycle time, 243–247
    defined, **243**
    guidelines for, 247–249
    parallel workstations, 250–251
    precedence diagrams, 245, 248–249
    procedures, 245–246
Linear decision rule, 620–621
Linear programming, 274–304
    aggregate planning, 619–621
    computer solutions, 291–293
    graphical programming, 278–290
        feasible solution space, 283
        minimization, 288–290
        objective function line, 283–287
        plotting constraints, 280–283
        procedures, 278–280
        redundant constraints, 287
        slack and surplus, 290
        solutions and corner points, 287–288
    models, 275–278, 735–736
    sensitivity analysis, 293–297
    simplex method, 290
Linear regression analysis, 91–96, 107
Linear trend equation, 81–84
List reduction approach to problem solving, 488
Load chart, 731–733
Load reports, 658–660
Loading, 731

Location planning, 355–390
    evaluating alternatives, 373–379
        center of gravity method, 376–379
        cost-profit-volume analysis, 373–375
        factor rating, 375–376
        transportation model, 375, 385–390
    factors affecting, 358–370
        community, 365, 368
        regional factors, 359–362, 368
        site-related factors, 366–368
    global locations, 361–362, 370–373
    importance of, 356
    location options, 357
    multiple plant manufacturing strategies, 367–369
    objectives of, 357
    procedures, 357–358
    service and retail locations, 369–371
Locational cost-profit-volume analysis, 373–375
Logistical transactions, 705
Logistics, 510–515; *See also* Supply chain management
Long-term capacity needs, 179
Loper, Marvin, 813
Lot-for-lot ordering, 649–650, 656
Lot sizes, 655–657, 690–691
Lot tolerance percent defective (LTPD), 461
Love, Stephen, 659
Lovelock, Christopher H., 157
Low cost labor strategy, 44
Lumpy demand, 640
Lund, Robert T., 145
Lynch, R.L., 500
Lyne, Jack, 384

McCaslin, John, 420
McGinnis, Leon F., Jr., 273, 384
McGregor, Douglas, 23
Machine productivity, 52
Machine shop, 236
McKee, Sandra L., 814
McNeil, Gordon H., 147
McNulty, Steven, 134
McPherson, K., 273
MAD, 97–101, 107
Maintenance
    breakdown, 720, 723
    costs, 720–721
    defined, **720**
    predictive, 722
    preventative, 233, 705, 720–722
    replacement, 724
    responsibility of, 12
    total productive, 722
Make or buy
    defined, 219
    factors to consider, 219, 509, 531–532
Makespan, 740
Malhotra, Manoj K., 44n
Management compensation, 335–336
Management information systems (MIS), 11, 70
Management science techniques, 23
Mann, Lawrence, Jr., 725
Mantel, Samuel, 814

Manufacturability, 11, **130**
Manufacturing cells, 224, 692
Manufacturing planning and control, 697–705
Manufacturing resources planning (MRP II), 661–663; *See also* **Material requirements planning (MRP)**
Manufacturing systems
    automation systems, 222–230
    cellular, 238–240
    computer-integrated manufacturing (CIM), 228
    designing for, 141–147
    flexible manufacturing, 46, 227–228, 240
    JIT; *See* **Just-in-time (JIT)**
Marecki, Richard F., 414
Margretta, Joan, 66, 526
Markels, Alex, 358
Market area plant strategy, 368
Marketing
    customer research, 132–133
    financial strategy, 43
    forecasting and, 70
    function of, 10–11
    order qualifiers and winners, 44
Markets, location decisions and, 360–361
Martin, Judith, 818
Martin, Justin, 526
Martin, Tony, 359
Maslow, Abraham, 23
Mass customization, 138–139
Mass production, 22, 28
Masson, Bernard, 474
Master production schedule (MPS), 624, 642–643
Master schedule, 605, **623**–628, 642–643
Masters, Robert, 473n
Material handling, 224
Material requirements planning (MRP), 640–664; *See also* Inventory management
    benefits and requirements, 660–661
    bill of materials, 643–646
    capacity requirements planning, 657–660
    defined, 640
    dependent versus independent demand, 640–641
    ERP, 664–669
    inputs, 642–646
    inventory records, 646
    JIT, 684
    lot sizing, 655–657
    master schedule, 642–643
    MRP II, 661–663
    outputs, 654
    overview of, 640–642
    processing, 646–654
    safety stock, 654–655
    services, 660
    updating records, 652–654
Mathematical models, 17
Mathews, Anna Wilde, 851
Maximax, 199–200
Maximin, 199
Maximum line length, 834–835
Maynard, Micheline, 548
Mayo, Elton, 23

Mean absolute deviation (MAD), 97–101, 107
Mean control chart, 427–430
Mean squared error (MSE), 97–101, 107
Mean time between failures (MTBF), 161–163
Mears, P., 500
Meczkowski, Frank, 133–134
Meindl, Peter, 525
Meredith, Jack R., 215, 814
Methods analysis, 313–315
Methods-time measurement (MTM), 329–330
Metters, Richard, 762
Metz, Peter J., 526
Meyers, Fred E., 341
Microfactory, 371
Micromotion study, 318
Midgley, Maureen, 229
Milakovich, M.E., 414
Milas, Gene H., 273
Miller, Jeffrey G., 705
Milligan, Glenn W., 157
Minimax regret, 199–200
Minimization, 288–290
MIS, 11, 70
Mission, 40–41
Mission statement, 40–41
Mitra, Amitava, 456, 500
Mixed model line, 251
Models
    additive, 87–88
    assignment, 735–736
    associative, 73
    decision making, 17–18, 23
    defined, **17**
    EOQ
        basic, 551–556
        fixed-order-interval, 571–574
        single period, 574–577
    finite source, 839–844
    infinite source, 825–839
    inventory, 18
    Kano, 153–154
    linear programming, 275–278
    mathematical, 17
    multiple channels, 829–833
    multiple priority, 835–839
    multiplicative, 87–88
    part period, 656
    physical, 17
    project, 18
    quantitative, 23
    schematic, 17
    simulation, 621–622
    single channel, 827–829
    statistical, 18
    transportation, 375, 385–390
Modular design, 139, 688
Monden, Yasubiro, 718
Monroe, Joseph, 195, 273
Monte Carlo method, 856–857
Montgomery, Douglas C., 456
Moog, Bob, 362–363
Moore, Franklin, 195
Moore, Jeffrey H., 215
Moran, Linda, 341

Morehouse, Debra, 405, 413
Morgan, Jim, 536n
Morrison, Jim, 681
Most likely time, 786
Motion study, 22, 315–318
Motivation, 311
Motivational theories, 23
Moving assembly line, 22
Moving average, 77–79, 103, 107
MPS, 624
MRP; *See* **Material requirements planning (MRP)**
MRP II, 661–663
MSE, 97–101, 107
MTBF, 161–163
Multiple channel systems, 829–833
Multiple plant manufacturing strategies, 367–369
Multiple-priority model, 835–839
Multiple regression analysis, 96
Multiple-sampling plan, 459
Multiplicative model, 87–88
Mundel, Marvin E., 341
Murdick, R.G., 124
Musslewhite, Ed, 341
Muther, Richard, 255n, 273
Muther grid, 255

NAFTA, 362
Naive forecast, 75–76, 107
National Association of Purchasing Management (NAPM), 6, 533
National Institute of Standards, 400
National Institute of Standards and Technology, 406
Negative exponential distribution, 822–823
Negotiation, 532–533
Net-change system, 654–655
Net requirements, 647
Netting, 646
Network conventions, 777–778
Network (precedence) diagram, 776–777
Neubauer, Dean, 456
Newsbite, A QFD Snapshot, 152–153
Newsboy problem, 574
Newsclips
    $$$, 542
    Desperately Seeking e-Fulfillment, 516–517
    Efficient Consumer Response, 514
    Ford Triples Its Billion-Dollar Cost-Cutting Goal, 548
    High Forecasts Can Be Bad News, 97
    Hotels Exploring Easier Customer Check-Ins, 844–845
    Innovative MCI Unit Finds Culture Shock in Colorado Springs, 358–359
    Less Trash Leaves Landfills in a Bind, 174
    Medical Mistakes Kill Almost 98,000 a Year, 400
    More Cars Come with a Shade of Green - Recycled Materials, 144
    Oops!, 420
    "People" Firms Boost Profits, Study Shows, 696

Newsclips—*Cont.*
  Productivity Gains Curb Inflation, 57
  SAP R/3 Leads Pack of Enterprise
    Resource Planning Software
    Packages, 663
  A Strategy for Continuous Improvement, 49
  A Strong Channel Hub, 105
  Supply Chain Optimization at Internet
    Speed, 521
  Time-Based Innovation, 49–51
  Toyota Mixes and Matches, 251
  Vying for Patients, Hospitals Think
    Location, Location, 370
Nichols, Ernest L., Jr., 526
Nichols, Karen, 771
Niebel, Benjamin W., 315, 317, 319–321,
  328, 341
Noise and vibration, working conditions
  and, 320
Nolden, Carol, 725
Nonlinear trend, 81–82
Normal operating conditions, 139
Normal time, in work measurement, 325–327
North American Free Trade Agreement, 362
Numerically controlled machines (N/C), 223

Objective function, 275
Objective function line, 283–287
Objectives
  of location decisions, 357
  of product and service design, 130
Observed time, in work measurement,
  325–327
OC curve, 459–463
Occupational Health and Safety
  Administration (OSHA), 135
Occupational Safety and Health Act, 322
Office layouts, 241
Ohno, Taiichi, 684–685, 691–692
Ohsone, Kozo, 132
Olson, David L., 872
On-site inspection, 421
Ono, Yumiko, 270
Operating characteristic (OC) curve,
  459–463
Operations management
  careers in, 6
  decision making, 17–20
  defined, 4–5
  evolution of, 21–24
  forecasting; *See* **Forecasting**
  functions of, 7–9
  goods versus services operations, 14–16
  Japanese influence on, 23
  role of managers, 12, 16
  scope of, 12–13
  service operations, 14–16
  standardization, 13
  strategy; *See* **Strategies**
  transformation process, 8–10
  trends, 24–28
Operations plan, 605
Operations strategy, 43–44
Operations Tour
  Boeing, 716–717
  Bruegger's Bagel Bakery, 597

Operations Tour—*Cont.*
  In the Chips at Jays, 454–455
  High Acres Landfill, 194
  Morton Salt, 271–273
  PSC, Inc., 598–600
  Stickley Furniture, 679–681
  US Postal Service, 65–66
  Wegmans Food Markets Inc., 31–34
Opinions, forecasts based on, 73–74
Oppenheim, Alan, 456, 500
Oppenheim, Bohdan W., 500
Oppenheim, Rosa, 456, 500
Opportunity losses, 200
Optimistic time, 786
Order cycles, 544
Order fulfillment, 515–516
Order qualifiers, 44
Order release, 654
Order winners, 44
Ordering costs, 548, 551–556
Organizations
  accounting function, 11
  competitiveness and, 38–40
  finance function, 9–10
  flattening of, 26
  functions within, 6–12
  human resources function, 11
  marketing function, 10–11
  missions, 40–41
  operations function, 7–9
  reasons for failure, 40
  strategy, 40–43
Orlicky, Joseph, 641, 681
Osborn, Jack D., 341
OSHA, 322
Oswald, Lawrence J., 229
Ott, Ellis, 456
Ouchi, William, 23
Output, 8–9, 13–14, 654
Output-based system, 333–334
Outsourcing, 47, **218,** 506, 531–532
Owens, James, 34

p-Chart, **431**–432
Padmanaghan, V., 526
Paired comparisons approach to problem
  solving, 488
Parallel workstations, 250–251
Parameter design, 140–141
Parameters, 276
Pareto, Vilfredo, 480
Pareto analysis, 479–482, 487
Pareto phenomenon, 20
Part-period model, 656
Partnerships, 519, 536–537
Patel, Keyur, 105
Path, 777
Paul, Lauren Gibbons, 681
Pay systems, 333–336
Payback, 188
Payoff table, 197
PDSA, 475–477, 484
Pearson, John N., 718
Peck, L.G., 840, 843
Pegging, 651
Pender, Lee, 681

Performance-control reports, 654
Performance measurement
  sequencing, 739–740
  supply chain, 509–510
Periodic system, 545
Perpetual inventory system, 545–546
Personnel, 11, 695–696
PERT (Program evaluation and review
  technique)
  activity-on-arrow, 776–777, 780–784
  activity-on-node, 776, 785
  advantages of using, 797
  algorithms, use of, 780–786
  defined, **775**
  deterministic time estimates, 778–780
  network conventions, 777–778
  network diagram, 776–777
  probabilistic time estimates, 786–792
  slack time, computing of, 786
Pessimistic time, 786
Peterson, R., 601, 636, 762
Pfeiffer, Raymond S., 34
Physical models, 17
Pine, B. Joseph, III, 157
Pinedo, M., 762
Pingho, LeRoy, 359
Pipeline inventories, 544
Plan-do-study-act (PDSA) cycle,
  475–477, 484
Planned-order receipts, 647–648
Planned-order release, 648–650
Planned orders, 654
Planning reports, 654
Planning time, 49
Plant layout; *See* Facilities layout
Plant location; *See* Location planning
Plossl, George, 641
Plotting constraints, in graphical linear
  programming, 280–283
Point-of-sale (POS) system, 513, 547
Poisson distribution, 822–823
Pokayoke, 471
Pooler, David J., 539
Pooler, Victor H., 539
Population source, 821
Powers, Richard, 363
Prasad, Biren, 157
Precedence diagram, 245, 248–249, 776–777
Predetermined prices, 532
Predetermined time standards, 329–330
Predictive maintenance, 722
Predictor variables, 91
Present value (PV), 188
Preventative maintenance, 233, 705, 720–722
Prevention costs, 402
Pricing
  competitiveness and, 38, 44
  demand options and, 608
  determination of, 532–533
Priorities, establishment of, 19–20
Priority rules, 739–745
Probabilistic time estimates, 778, 786–792
Probability, 159
Problem solving, 18–19, 475–477; *See also*
  Decision making
Process batch, 749

Process capability, **438**–442
Process charts, 314–315
Process control, 418
Process design, 689–694
Process improvement, 25, **477**–478
Process layouts, 235–237, 252–258; *See also* Facilities layout
Process plant strategy, 368–369
Process selection and design, 218–232; *See also* Facilities layout
   automation, 222–230
   defined, 218
   make or buy decisions, 218–219
   process systems, 219–222
   service process design, 230–231
Process systems, 219–222
Process variability, 424, **438**
Processing time, 49
Producer's risk, 461
Product design; *See* Design, of products and services
Product differentiation, 38
Product layout, 232–235, 242–251, 258; *See also* Facilities layout
Product liability, 135, 399
Product plant strategy, 368
Product safety, 135
Product structure tree, 643–645
Production and Operations Management Society (POMS), 6
Production control, 511–512
Production flexibility, 692–693
Production line, 233, 235
Production plan, 605
Production systems
   craft, 21, 28
   lean, 26–28, 251
   maintenance of, 720–725
   mass, 22, 28
Productivity, 15, **51**–57
Program evaluation and review technique; *See* **PERT (Program evaluation and review technique)**
Programmable automation, 223
Project, 222
Project champion, 770
Project management, 767–814; *See also* **Scheduling**
   behavioral aspects, 768–772
   CPM, 775
   crashing, 793–796
   ethics 770
   Gantt charts, 731, 774–775
   key decisions in, 768–769
   life cycle, 772
   PERT
      activity-on-arrow, 776–777, 780–784
      activity-on-node, 776, 785
      advantages of using, 797
      algorithms, use of, 780–786
      defined, 775
      deterministic time estimates, 778–780
      network conventions, 777–778
      network diagram, 776–777
      probabilistic time estimates, 786–792
      slack time, computing of, 786

Project management—*Cont.*
   project manager, role of, 697, 769–770
   risk management, 773
   simulation, 793
   technology, 792–793
   work breakdown structure, 774
Project Management Institute (PMI), 6, 770
Project models, 18
Projected on hand, 647
Projects, 767
Promotion, 608
Przasnyski, Zbigniew H., 500
Ptak, Carol A., 526, 681
Public relations function, 12
Pull system, 699–700
Pulliam, Susan, 97
Purchasing, 528–539; *See also* Supply chain management
   centralized versus decentralized, 533
   certification of suppliers, 535
   cycle of, 530
   determining prices, 532–533
   e-procurement, 538–539
   EDI, 513–514, 538
   ethics, 533–534
   interfaces, 528–529
   JIT, 74
   make or buy, 218–219, 509, 531–532
   negotiation, 532–533
   outsourcing, 47, 218, 506, 531–532
   partnerships, 519, 536–537
   relationship with suppliers, 535–536, 702–704
   responsibility of, 11, 507
   selecting suppliers, 533–535
   strategic alliances, 509
   supplier management, 533–537
   value analysis, 530–531
Purchasing cycle, 530
Push system, 699
Pyke, D.F., 636, 762
Pyzdek, Thomas, 414

QFD, 130, 150–154
Quality, 393–414; *See also* Quality control; **Total quality management (TQM)**
   awards for, 406–409
   Baldrige Award, 406–408
   benefits of good, 400
   certification of, 409
   consequences of poor, 398–400
   continuous improvement, 471, 696–697
   costs of, 401–402
   defined, **394**
   determinants of, 396–398
   dimensions of, 395–396
   ethics and, 402
   evolution of, 394–395
   gurus, 402–406
   importance of, 25
   ISO 9000, 409–410
   ISO 14000, 412
   kaizen, 471
   responsibility for, 400–401
   strategies based on, 48

Quality—*Cont.*
   TQM; *See* **Total quality management (TQM)**
Quality at the source, 472
Quality-based strategy, 48
Quality circles, 406, **487**–488
Quality control, 417–467; *See also* **Quality**
   acceptance sampling
      acceptable quality level, 460–461
      average quality of inspected lots, 463–464
      defined, 458
      operating characteristic curve, 459–463
      sampling plans, 458–459
   control charts; *See* **Control charts**
   defined, 418
   inspection, 418–422
   JIT, 692
   process capability, 438–442
   process control, 418
   quality function deployment (QFD), 130, 150–154
   service sector, 15
   six-sigma, 471, 488
   statistical process control; *See* **Statistical process control (SPC)**
   total quality management (TQM); *See* **Total quality management (TQM)**
Quality function deployment (QFD), 130, **150**–154
Quality of conformance, 398, 421
Quality of design, 397–398
Quality transactions, 705
Quantitative approach to problem solving, 18–19
Quantitative models, 23
Quantity discounts, 558–563
Queue discipline, 824–825
Queuing models, infinite source, 825–839
Queuing techniques, 18
Queuing theory, 818
Quick response, 513

Radford, G.S., 394
Radio frequency identification (RFID), 547
Ragsdale, Cliff T., 304
Rajan, Murli, 490
Random, 856
Random variations, 75–76, **423**
Range control chart, 428–430
Range of feasibility, 296
Range of optimality, 294
Raw materials, location decisions and, 359–360
Rea, Kathryn P., 500, 814
Readings
   The ABCs of ERP, 664–668
   Aesop on Quality Systems, 410–412
   Agile Manufacturing, 27
   Baldrige Core Values and Concepts, 407–408
   Benchmarking Corporate Websites of Fortune 500 Companies, 490
   Box Maker Keeps the Lid on Lead Times, 709

Readings—*Cont.*
  CalComp: Disaster Becomes Success, 474–475
  Continuous Improvement on the Free-Throw Line, 484–485
  Delivering the Goods, 510–511
  Designing Supermarkets, 241
  Developing the JIT Philosophy, 702
  E-Procurement at IBM, 538–539
  Economic Vitality, 63–64
  Electric Car Drives Factory Innovations, 229–230
  Five Ways to PUMP UP Your Champion, 771
  Global Strategy: GM is Building Plants in Developing Nations to Woo New Markets, 372
  The International Space Station Project (ISS), 766
  JIT and Quality: A Perfect Fit, 708–709
  JIT II, 711–712
  Making Hotplates, 340–341
  Making It (Almost) New Again, 145–147
  Making Quality Pay: Return on Quality, 496–498
  Manager's Journal: When Customer Research Is a Lousy Idea, 132–133
  Managing Projects With a New View, 813–814
  New U.S. Factory Jobs Aren't in the Factory, 366–367
  Not-So-Clear Choices: Should You Export, or Manufacture Overseas?, 362–365
  The Nuts and Bolts of Japan's Factories, 685–686
  Pedal Pushers, 694–695
  Productivity Gains at Whirlpool, 60
  Project Managers Have Never Been More Critical, 770–771
  Quality Programs Don't Guarantee Results, 498–499
  RFID, 547
  Romantic JIT and Pragmatic JIT, 687
  Servicing Passenger Planes, 751
  Stopped at a Light? Why Not Read This, You May Have Time, 851–852
  Swimming Upstream, 499–500
  Tour de Force, 225–227
  Using Information to Speed Execution, 520
  Vlasic on a Roll with Huge Pickle Slices, 133–134
  Waiting - A New Popular Pastime: Miss Manners, 818
  What Works to Cut CTD Risk, Improve Job Productivity?, 322–323
  Wireless ERP, 668
  Workplace Upheavals Seem to be Eroding Employees' Trust, 311–312
  Would You Like That Rare, Medium or Vacuum-Packed?, 270–271
Receiving, 529
Recycling, 143–144, 174
Redesign of products and services; *See* Design, of products and services
Reduced transaction processing, 705

Redundancy, 159
Redundant constraints, 287
Reed, Michael E., 497
Reeser, Clayton, 813
Regenerative system, 654–655
Regional factors, location decisions and, 359–362, 368
Regression, 91–96
Regret, 200
Reimann, Curt W., 498
Reina, Dennis, 312
Reina, Michelle, 312
Reliability, 139–140, 159–164
Remanufacturing, 144–147
Reorder point (ROP), 564–571
Repetitive processing, 220–222
Replacement, of equipment or parts, 724
Research and development, 131–132
Reservation systems, 750
Response time for complaints, 49
Retail sector
  layout, 240–241
  location planning, 369–371
  superstores, 32
Return on investment (ROI), 543
Reverse engineering, 130
Risk, 198, 200–201
Risk management, 773
Ritter, Diane, 500
Roach, Stephen, 66
Robinson, Alan, 489
Robitaille, Denise E., 410
Robot, 223–225
Robust design, 140–141
Rolling horizon, 607, 652
Romig, H.G., 23, 394
Roos, Daniel, 34, 686n, 692n
Rosenthal, Stephen R., 157
Ross, D.F., 66, 526
Ross, Joel E., 414
Ross, S.M., 456
Rough-cut capacity planning, 623
Rowe, G., 124
Run, 435
Run charts, 484, 486
Run tests, 435–438
Rush, 739

S/O (slack per operation), 739, 744–745
Sabath, Robert, 510
Sabolik, Jerome, 359
Safety, 321
Safety stock, 564–565, 654–655
Salegna, Gary, 473n, 500
Salesforce opinions, 74
Sampling
  distribution, 424
  plans, 458–459
  work, 331–333, 336
Sasser, W. Earl, Jr., 157
Scale-based strategy, 44
Scanlan, Phillip M., 498
Scanlon plan, 335
Scanning, environmental, **46**
Scatter diagrams, 479, 481–482
Schardt, David, 241

Schedule chart, 734
Scheduled receipts, 647
Scheduling, 728–762; *See also* Project management
  appointment system, 749
  assignment model, 735
  backward, 734
  defined, 728
  forward, 734
  Gantt charts, 731, 774–775
  high-volume systems, 728–729
  Hungarian method, 736
  intermediate-volume systems, 730–731
  job-shop/low-volume systems, 731
  loading, 731–738
  multiple resources, 750
  problems with, 748
  reservation system, 750
  sequencing
    Johnson's rule, 745
    makespan, 740
    priority rules, 739–745
    sequence dependent setup times, 747–748
  service system, 749–751
  theory of constraints, 748–749
  workforce, 750
Schematic models, 17
Scherkenbach, W.W., 414
Schiller, Zachary, 60
Schilling, Edward G., 456
Schlesinger, Leonard A., 157
Schmidt, C.P., 215
Schonberger, Richard J., 474, 693
Schorr, John E., 539
Schragenheim, Eli, 526, 681
Schroeder, Richard, 500
Scientific management, 21–22
SCOR (Supply Chain Operations Reference Model), 509
Scott, Gerald, 225
Seasonal indexes, 88
Seasonal relative, 88–89
Seasonal variations, 87–90, 179–180
Seasonality, 75–76, 87–90
Sebastianelli, Rose, 473n, 490
Self-directed teams, 312–313
Sensitivity analysis, 204–206, **293**–297
Sequencing, 738–748
  Johnson's rule, 745
  makespan, 740
  priority rules, 739–745
  sequence dependent setup times, 747–748
Service blueprint, 230
Service design, 147–150; *See also* Design, of products and services
Service level, 565, 568–571
Service-oriented organizations, 7
Service sector
  aggregate planning and, 622–623
  capacity planning, 183–184
  designing for, 147–150
  differentiation, 38
  facilities layout, 240–241
  versus goods, 14–16
  location planning, 369–371

Service sector—*Cont.*
  MRP, 660
  operations, 14–16
  process design, 230–231
  productivity, 55
  scheduling, 749–751
Setrakian, Scott, 363–364
Setup time reduction, 522, 691–692
Shadow price, 295
Shafer, Scott M., 814
Shaw, John C., 157
Sheffi, Yossi, 525
Shellenbarger, Sue, 311
Shewhart, Walter, 23, 394, 484
Shewhart cycle, 475
Shin, Hojung, 718
Short-term capacity needs, 179
Shortage costs, 548, 574
Shortages, 568–571
Shulman, L.E., 66
Shunk, Dan L., 273
Silver, E.A., 601, 636, 762
Silverstein, Judith, 517, 526
Simchi-Levi, David, 516, 526
Simchi-Levi, Edith, 516, 526
Simo chart, 318–319
Simple linear regression, 91–96, 107
Simplex, 290
Simulation, 854–872
  advantages and disadvantages of using,
    865–866
  computer simulation, 864–865
  defined, 854
  Monte Carlo method, 856–857
  project management and, 793
  steps in the process, 854–856
  theoretical distribution, 861–864
Simulation models, 621–622
Simultaneous chart, 318–319
Simultaneous development, 141
Singhal, Vinod R., 500
Single channel, 827–829
Single-period model, 574–577
Single-sampling plan, 458
Sipper, Daniel, 636
Sirkin, Harold, 504
Site-related factors, location planning and,
  366–368
Six-sigma, 471, 488
Slack, 290, 777, 786
Slack per operation (S/O), 739, 744–745
Slater, Derek, 664, 681
Smith, Adam, 22
Smith, Gerald, 456, 500
Smith-Daniels, Dwight, 814
Smoothing, 80–81, 85–87, 107
Snook, David M., 146
SPC; *See* **Statistical process
  control (SPC)**
Spearman, Mark L., 34, 124, 601, 636, 681,
  718, 762
Special variation, 423
Specialization, 309–310
Specifications, 438–439
Spence, Randy, 134
Spencer, Michael S., 718

SPT (shortest processing time),
  739–744
Sriparavastu, Loknath, 718
Stalk, George, Jr., 46n, 49, 51, 66
Stamatis, D.H., 414
Standard elemental times, 329
Standard parts, 688
Standard time, 323
Standardization, 13, 22, **137**–138, 688
Statistical models, 18
Statistical process control (SPC), 421–438;
    See also Quality control
  control charts
    attributes, 426, 430–433
    defined, 424
    errors, 425–426
    mean, 427–430
    range, 428–430
    run tests, 435–438
    variables, 426–430
    when to use, 434–435
  control process, 422–423
  variations and control, 423–424
Stauffer, Robert, 273
Steele, Daniel C., 44n
Steeples, Marion M., 414
Steinberg, Neil, 454
Step costs, 186–187
Stevens, Tim, 694–695
Stevenson, William J., 215, 304, 387n, 390,
  500, 814, 852
Stocking levels, 574–577
Stockouts, 544
Stoll, Henry, 195, 273
Stopwatch time study, 324–329
Storage layout, 240
Straight piecework, 334
Straker, D., 500
Strategic alliances, 509
Strategic partnering, 519, 536–537
Strategic planning, 25
Strategies, 40–51
  defined, **40**
  external facts affecting, 46
  flexible factories, 46
  focused factories, 46
  formulation of, 44–48
  functional, 42
  goals, 41–42
  growth, 48
  internal factors affecting, 46–47
  low cost labor, 44
  missions, 40–41
  operations, 43–44
  organizational, 40–43
  quality based, 48
  scale-based, 44
  tactics, 41–42
  time-based, 48–51
Stum, David, 311
Subcontracting, 610
Suboptimization, 198
Substitutability, of parts, 147
Sullivan, Robert S., 872
Summers, Donna, 414, 456, 476, 500
Superstores, 32

Suppliers
  audit, 535
  certification of, 535, 702–703
  JIT systems, 702–704
  management of, 533–537
  partnering with, 519, 536–537
  quality and, 472
  selection of, 533–535
  strategic alliances, 509
Supply chain, 24–25, 504–505
Supply chain management, 504–526; *See also*
    Purchasing
  benefits of effective, 506–507
  challenges, 520–523
  defined, 504–505
  distribution requirements planning, 514
  e-commerce, 506, 515–517
  electronic data interchange, 513–514, 538
  elements of, 507–509
  global supply chains, 515
  JIT, 514–515
  keys to effective, 517–518
  logistics and, 510–515
  managing the chain, 507–510
  need for, 506
  performance measures, 509–510
  steps in creating effective, 519
  strategic, tactical, operating issues,
    509–510
Supply chain optimization (SCO), 521
Surplus, 290
Surveys, consumer, 74
Sutton, Margaret, 814
Swanson, Christine A., 718
SWOT analysis, 44
System, 19
System design, 12; *See also* Process selection
  and design
System operation, 12
Systems approach, to decision making, 19

Tactics, 41–42
Taguchi, Genichi, 140–141, 406
Tamimi, Nabil, 473n, 490
Tangible output, 14
Taxes, impact on location decisions, 361
Taylor, Bernard W., 215, 304
Taylor, Frederick Winslow, 21–22, 309, 394
Teams
  decision making, 488
  incentive plans for, 335
  problem solving, 471
  self-managed, 312–313
Technology
  impact on operations, 25
  management of, 230–232
Temperature and humidity, 319–320
Teplitz, Charles J., 352
Ternicko, John, 157
Terry, David, 475
Tersine, Richard J., 532n, 601
Theory of constraints, 748–749
Theory X, Y, Z, 23
Therbligs, 316–318
Third party logistics, 515
Third-party maintainers (TPMs), 520

Three-sigma, 429
Time, 38–39, 44
Time based competition, 605
Time-based strategy, 48–51
Time-based system, 333–334
Time buckets, 642–643
Time estimates
   deterministic, 778–780
   probabilistic, 786–792
Time fences, 628, 658
Time reduction, 25
Time series, 75
Time series data, forecasting methods using
   averaging, 76–81, 107
   cycles, 75–76, 90–91
   naive method, 75–76, 107
   seasonality, 75–76, 87–90
   trend, 75–76, 81–85, 107
   trend adjusted exponential smoothing,
     85–87, 103, 107
Time studies, 324–329
Time value of money, 188
Tippett, L.H.C., 23
Tolerances, 438
Torgersen, P.E., 352
Total cost of ownership (TCO), 665–666
Total productive maintenance, 722
Total quality management (TQM), 470–500
   approach to, 470–471
   continuous improvement, 471, 696–697
   criticisms of, 473
   defined, 470
   elements of, 471–472
   obstacles to implementing, 473
   problem solving process, 475–477
   process improvement, 477–478
   tools
     benchmarking, 471, 488–489
     brainstorming, 487
     cause and effect diagrams, 479, 481,
       483–484
     check sheets, 478–481
     control charts, 479, 481–482, 487
     5W2H approach, 489
     flowcharts, 478–480
     histograms, 478–479, 481
     interviewing, 488
     Pareto analysis, 479–482
     quality circles, 406, 487–488
     run charts, 484, 486
     scatter diagrams, 479, 481–482
Toyota Production System (TPS), 694
TQM; *See* **Total quality management
   (TQM)**
Tracking signal, 98, 107
Trade-off decisions, 19
Traffic management, 512
Training, 251, 696
Transfer batch, 749
Transformation processes, 8–10
Transportation
   costs, 253–255, 359–360, 375
   model, 375, 385–390
   traffic management, 512

Treece, James B., 366–367
Trend
   analysis of, 81–85, 107
   defined, **75**–76
**Trend-adjusted exponential smoothing,
   85**–87
Trend equation, 81–84
Tumay, K., 872
Turban, Efraim, 215
Turnover, of inventory, 544
Two-bin system, 546
Type I error, 425–426
Type II errors, 426

U-shaped layouts, 235
UCC, 135
Ulrich, Karl T., 157
Uncertainty, 198–200
Uniform Commercial Code (UCC), 135
**Universal Product Code (UPC), 513,
   546**–547
Upton, David, 195, 273

Value-added, 8–9
Value analysis, 530–531
Value chains, 504–505
Van Nimwegen, Harm, 413
Vargus, Vicente, 762
Variable costs, 185–187
Variables, 426–430
Variations and control, in SPC, 423–424
Velocity, 519–520
Vendor analysis, 535
Vendors; *See* Suppliers
Ventilation, 320
Vertical loading, 310–311, **732**
Vertical skills, 335
Villa, A., 636
Visual JIT systems, 700–701
Viswanathan, S., 525
Vollmann, Thomas E., 601, 636, 681,
   705–706, 718, 745n, 762
Vranizan, Michelle, 474

Wagar, Keith, 514
Wages, 333–336
Waiting lines, 818–852
   analysis of, 189
   arrival and service patterns, 822–824
   cost analysis, 833–834
   finite source models, 839–844
   goals of analysis for, 819–821
   infinite source model, 825–839
     basic relationship, 826–827
     multiple channel, 829–833
     multiple priorities, 835–839
     single channel, 827–829
   managerial implications of, 819
   maximum line length, 834–835
   multiple priorities, 835–839
   number of servers/channels, 822
   performance measures, 825
   population source, 821
   queue discipline, 824–825

Waiting lines—*Cont.*
   queuing theory, 818
   reasons for, 819
   system characteristics, 821–825
Walker, M.R., 775
Walker, Stanley, 709
Walker, William T., 526
Ward, Stephen, 814
Ware, Norman, 636
Warehousing
   cross-docking, 522
   DRP, 514
   layout, 240
Warranties, 135
Wartzman, Rick, 60
Watt, James, 21
Weatherford, Larry R., 215
Weighted average, 78–80
Weinstein, Bob, 770
Werner, Helmet, 367
Wester, L., 273
Whang, Seunjin, 526
Wheatley, Malcolm, 681
Wheeler, John, 255n
White, Daryl, 511
White, John A., 273, 384
White, Richard E., 718
Whitney, Eli, 22
Whybark, D. Clay, 601, 636, 681, 706, 718,
   762
Wiesenborn, Gary, 359
Wight, Oliver W., 596, 641, 681
Wilkerson, Ella Mae, 134
Wilson, J. Holton, 103, 124
Wilson, Larry W., 601
Winkler, David E., 708
Wireman, Terry, 725
Womack, James P., 34, 686n, 692n
Woolsey, Gene, 542
Work breakdown structure, 774
Work breaks, 320–321
Work measurement, 323–333; *See also* **Job
   design**
   predetermined time standards, 329–330
   standard elemental times, 329
   stopwatch time study, 324–329
   work sampling, 331–333, 336
Work system design; *See* **Job design**
Worker-machine chart, 314, 317
Workers as assets, 695
Workforce, scheduling of, 750
Working conditions, 318–323
Workstation, 243, 250–251, **738**
Wright, G., 124

Yablonsky, Dennis, 367

Zangwill, Willard I., 132–133
Zenger, John, 341
Zero defects, 395
Zipkin, Paul H., 687, 718
Zucco, James, 359
Zuckerman, A., 414

Areas under the standardized normal curve, from − ∞ to + z

z	.00	.01	.02	.03	.04	.05	.06	.07	.08	.09
.0	.5000	.5040	.5080	.5120	.5160	.5199	.5239	.5279	.5319	.5359
.1	.5398	.5438	.5478	.5517	.5557	.5596	.5636	.5675	.5714	.5753
.2	.5793	.5832	.5871	.5910	.5948	.5987	.6026	.6064	.6103	.6141
.3	.6179	.6217	.6255	.6293	.6331	.6368	.6406	.6443	.6480	.6517
.4	.6554	.6591	.6628	.6664	.6700	.6736	.6772	.6808	.6844	.6879
.5	.6915	.6950	.6985	.7019	.7054	.7088	.7123	.7157	.7190	.7224
.6	.7257	.7291	.7324	.7357	.7389	.7422	.7454	.7486	.7517	.7549
.7	.7580	.7611	.7642	.7673	.7703	.7734	.7764	.7794	.7823	.7852
.8	.7881	.7910	.7939	.7967	.7995	.8023	.8051	.8078	.8106	.8133
.9	.8159	.8186	.8212	.8238	.8264	.8289	.8315	.8340	.8365	.8389
1.0	.8413	.8438	.8461	.8485	.8508	.8531	.8554	.8577	.8599	.8621
1.1	.8643	.8665	.8686	.8708	.8729	.8749	.8770	.8790	.8810	.8830
1.2	.8849	.8869	.8888	.8907	.8925	.8944	.8962	.8980	.8997	.9015
1.3	.9032	.9049	.9066	.9082	.9099	.9115	.9131	.9147	.9162	.9177
1.4	.9192	.9207	.9222	.9236	.9251	.9265	.9279	.9292	.9306	.9319
1.5	.9332	.9345	.9357	.9370	.9382	.9394	.9406	.9418	.9429	.9441
1.6	.9452	.9463	.9474	.9484	.9495	.9505	.9515	.9525	.9535	.9545
1.7	.9554	.9564	.9573	.9582	.9591	.9599	.9608	.9616	.9625	.9633
1.8	.9641	.9649	.9656	.9664	.9671	.9678	.9686	.9693	.9699	.9706
1.9	.9713	.9719	.9726	.9732	.9738	.9744	.9750	.9756	.9761	.9767
2.0	.9772	.9778	.9783	.9788	.9793	.9798	.9803	.9808	.9812	.9817
2.1	.9821	.9826	.9830	.9834	.9838	.9842	.9846	.9850	.9854	.9857
2.2	.9861	.9864	.9868	.9871	.9875	.9878	.9881	.9884	.9887	.9890
2.3	.9893	.9896	.9898	.9901	.9904	.9906	.9909	.9911	.9913	.9916
2.4	.9918	.9920	.9922	.9925	.9927	.9929	.9931	.9932	.9934	.9936
2.5	.9938	.9940	.9941	.9943	.9945	.9946	.9948	.9949	.9951	.9952
2.6	.9953	.9955	.9956	.9957	.9959	.9960	.9961	.9962	.9963	.9964
2.7	.9965	.9966	.9967	.9968	.9969	.9970	.9971	.9972	.9973	.9974
2.8	.9974	.9975	.9976	.9977	.9977	.9978	.9979	.9979	.9980	.9981
2.9	.9981	.9982	.9982	.9983	.9984	.9984	.9985	.9985	.9986	.9986
3.0	.9987	.9987	.9987	.9988	.9988	.9989	.9989	.9989	.9990	.9990
3.1	.9990	.9991	.9991	.9991	.9991	.9992	.9992	.9992	.9993	.9993
3.2	.9993	.9993	.9994	.9994	.9994	.9994	.9994	.9995	.9995	.9995
3.3	.9995	.9995	.9995	.9996	.9996	.9996	.9996	.9996	.9996	.9997
3.	.9997	.9997	.9997	.9997	.9997	.9997	.9997	.9997	.9997	.9998